Companion to Baroque Music

Companion to Baroque Music

Compiled and edited
by Julie Anne Sadie

Foreword by
Christopher Hogwood

UNIVERSITY OF CALIFORNIA PRESS
Berkeley and Los Angeles

University of California Press
Berkeley and Los Angeles, California

Published by arrangement with Macmillan Publishing, a Division of Simon & Schuster Inc.

Printed in the United States of America

printing number
1   2   3   4   5   6   7   8   9   10

Library of Congress Cataloging-in-Publication Data

Companion to baroque music / compiled and edited by Julie Anne Sadie ;
    foreword by Christopher Hogwood.
        p.   cm.
    Originally published: New York : Schirmer Books, 1991.
    Includes bibliographical references (p.   ) and index.
    ISBN 0-520-21414-5 (alk. paper)
    1. Music—17th century—History and criticism.   2. Music—18th
century—History and criticism.   I. Sadie, Julie Anne.
ML193.C56   1998
780'.9'032—dc21   97-37695
                                                                             CIP
                                                                             MN

The paper used in this publication meets the minimum requirements of American
National Standard for Information Sciences—Permanence of Paper for Printed Library
Materials, ANSI Z39.48-1984. ⊚

Contents

Illustrations

Plates

Maps

(Town maps reproduced by courtesy of the British Library. Other maps drawn by John Gilkes.)

Music Examples

Abbreviations

anon.	anonymous
apptd	appointed
attrib.	attributed to
b	born
bk	book
BWV	Bach-Werke-Verzeichnis
c.	century
c	*circa*

    (NB *c*1620–85 = both dates approximate
            *c*1620–1685 = 1st date approximate; 2nd date firm)

chap(s).	chapter(s)
comp.	composed
d	died
ded.	dedicated to
ed.	editor, edited by
edn	edition
Eng.	English
estab.	established
fl	*floruit* (flourished)
Fr.	French
It.	Italian
MS(S)	manuscript(s)
nr	near
orig.	original, originally
perf(s).	performed, performance(s)
posth.	posthumous, posthumously
pub.	publish, publishing
pubd	published
r.	reigned, ruled
repr.	reprinted
rev.	revised
RV	Ryom-Verzeichnis [Vivaldi]
suppl(s).	supplement(s)
trans.	translation, translated by
vol(s).	volume(s)

Letters indicating pitch

C′ — B′   C — B   c — b   c′ — b′   c″ — b″   c‴ — b‴

Foreword

'The past is a foreign country', L. P. Hartley reminds us at the beginning of *The Go-Between*; 'they do things differently there'. In the arts we spend more of our time in this territory than in our own land, savouring its confusing yet comforting ways, enjoying its artistic legacy while often forgetting its political and social shell in our enthusiasm to get at the cultural pearl. Until recently, almost instinctively, its differences were absorbed into a technological assessment of music's progress. We assumed the superiority of the later over the earlier ('the seed sown by Stamitz developed into the full Classical symphony of late Mozart'), the modern over the old ('our Steinway, so much more resonant that Mozart's slight *fortepiano*'), the public over the private (the opera aria over devotional hymn), the composer over the patron, the studied phrase over the impromptu gesture. But it was not always so, and a delight in the music of the 17th and 18th centuries is soon tempered by some puzzlement as we realize that, in the Age of Patronage, they did things differently.

The lure of the Baroque, at least in the broad view, began at much the same time as the arrival of the LP. It had been preceded by another important 20th-century invention, the concept of 'chamber orchestra'. These two, with the connivance of Vivaldi, ensured that every cultured household soon had daily access to a handful of well-seasoned *concerti*; everyone was indelibly convinced that the 'Albinoni Adagio' was actually by Albinoni. As a consultative, sometimes almost archival, attitude to records developed, so the number of light anthologies declined, and the greatest omissions from the standard concert repertory were repaired; we began to appreciate the clavichord and the counter-tenor, the Bach cantata and the Handel *opera seria*, though still in ignorance of their appropriate visual and social setting.

At the same time an attitude to the Baroque developed which can only be described as 'best buy', and with it that unfortunate corollary of the Ur-text, the 'Ur-performance'. 'Wie es eigentlich gewesen' ('As it really was'), the catch-phrase of Leopold von Ranke in the 1830s, became again the watch-word, and a surfeit of Olde Musicke made life in the recreative arts begin to look like one endless historical romance. The death of the past and its resurrection as history can produce as much nostalgia as archaeology; the challenge in all recreative arts is to combine the science of discovering expression in texts with the art of communicating it.

Some commentators still hold that we are busy historicizing ourselves, that musical ventures into past contexts and countries are a form of creative anachronism, as misleading and laughable as Inigo Jones's certainty that Stonehenge was a Roman monument. The opposing school would counter Ezra Pound's exhortation to 'Make it New' with a demand that all works be recreated 'brand old', taking advantage of historical information to try and reconcile the demands of 'then' and 'now', blending archaeology and passion. Over the last 20 years, it has been the Baroque period in particular that has focused our attention on the inherited obligation to temper instinct with information. A dizzying increase in available repertory and styles of performance, constant debate on the value of Telemann as a composer, or the

Baroque oboe as an instrument, leaves most music-lovers gasping for digestible information and a sense of context.

Cult phrases, fashionable adjectives and buzz-words confuse, but also galvanize the forum. Once it was 'terrace dynamics', followed by 'hemiola', then 'non-vibrato'; tempo and metronome markings seem to be the present kiwi-fruit of *nouvelle musicologie*, but may soon be as dated as *Asphalt-Lyrik*. The over-examined term 'authentic' is gradually being allowed to slink back to its old position (Lionel Trilling), and in its place Andrew Porter has suggested HIP – the Historically Informed Performance. This concept, well-designed to rebuild bridges and demolish ghettos, in its turn requires HAL – the Historically Aware Listener. This sensible musician seeks to strike the happy mean, and develop 'informed instinct', the heart endorsed by the head.

Such a form of accommodation is, I feel, one of the most elusive aspects of any debate on performance, simply because there are so few norms. Some artists would, by instinct, like to see themselves as rebels against all information, arguing that information is old, and that therefore tradition is stultifying. Others would so manipulate their instincts that, like some bonsai creation, they become totally constrained by external information and devoid of natural independence. (This is the attitude that Stravinsky is so often, and wrongly, said to have asked of his interpreters.)

Part of the problem is the need for us to ignore the surface; since our first reactions may often be lopsided or imperfectly informed, one must pass to that state where the information is allowed free passage, even when the instinct rebels. I, for instance, have an instinctive dislike of the ornamented form of capital Q in the type-face known as Bookman; but this instinctive recoil is balanced by the ability we all have to look through the actual forms of letters and comprehend words. The instinct is subordinated to the information, and I do not feel any personal animosity towards either Queen Elizabeth, Quantz or the Salomon Quartet.

Bertrand Russell prescribed 'immunity to eloquence' as a condition of intelligent appraisal of writing, and the same also goes for musical interpretation that needs must begin with a cool appraisal of the printed note. *Of course* one is moved, *of course* one's heart responds and one hopes to be the medium whereby an audience's collective heart resonates in consonance with this feeling. But it is very easy, in these days of 'one size fits all', to over-react, to milk the passing moment for more than it asks or more than the structure can bear; 'tasteful' is out, 'dramatic' is in, the composer's expectations are superseded by those of the marketeers – 'Does it sell?', 'Do they applaud?' – and an interpretative school based on the 'Look at Me!' principle.

Such display of over-indulgence in personal vanity on a podium (or even from the harpsichord), the 'Moi!' school, is very similar to the type of Shakespearian acting on which I was brought up; every line was spoken in *italics*, with sudden underlining and shocking CAPITALIZATION to add yet more emphasis. When Pelion was finally in place on Ossa, I was left wondering what had happened to the poetry – sometimes even to the story.

We have conditioned ourselves to extremes of stimulation incompatible with the code of intention of the creator. We have asked, as it were, for the Rembrandt to be relegated to the gallery store-room and a 12-times enlargement with 'colour enhancement' to be hung in its place. A silly analogy, you may say; but if a painting were to dissolve into small pots of its component colours at the end of every day as the gallery doors closed, imagine how scrupulously you would ask the staff to follow the artist's prescription when the paint was reapplied to the canvas the following morning. In the concert-hall, where there is less credit for similar scruples, the cavalier approach to 'enhanced' interpretation can lead to a total destruction of the composer's code of intentions and system of rhetoric, a crime surely worse than the employment of an incorrect accidental, a tasteless ornament or a less than authentic instrument.

Like the new and (we hope) passing enthusiasm for devising ever more coloured versions of old black and white movies, it amounts to laying on more paint rather than cleaning the picture. I have to confess to an old-fashioned preference for Handel the colour he started off. You may rightly ask how can one be so presumptuous as to 'know' what that was, but I would rather make some progress along such a line of thought, even with difficulty and experiment, than sell out to the school of obligatory italics and car-chases which presupposes that whatever colour he was, it wasn't good enough. The historical approach is far from limiting; it actually offers a greater freedom of choice, a multiple choice of 'correct' readings. But it will inhibit most musicians from following the uninhibited creed of Wanda Landowska who declared that, however others played his music, she played Bach *his* way.

The new and undogmatic spirit will, I believe, eventually lead towards a co-ordination where instinct and information begin to mesh, that delicious moment when it suddenly sounds and feels 'inevitable'. Maybe it is not 'as it really was'; who knows? We will surely continue on the path of 'knit your own Baroque', but at least with a healthy spirit of agnosticism it will be with more regard to the prescribed pattern and purpose and less for the perverse pleasure of hearing the needles clash.

Christopher Hogwood
Cambridge

A Short Explication

By acquiring this book, you have gained the materials for exploring anew the Baroque era of music. The *Companion to Baroque Music* is designed to be accessible to enthusiasts while at the same time being a useful tool for specialists. Those seeking a potted history, listening notes for the best-loved works or neatly-columned worklists will be disappointed; but these are to be found in the classic work by Manfred Bukofzer,[1] the more recent surveys of Claude Palisca[2] and Lorenzo Bianconi[3] and *The New Grove Dictionary of Music and Musicians*.[4] By its very nature, a companion repays the time one spends with it. And as with a friend, the *Companion* cannot be all things to all people, although it is hoped that with familiarity will come greater pleasure and fresh insights into a much-loved repertory.

I have attempted to present music and musicians in terms of their social, temporal and topographical contexts. The traditional biographical dictionary of composers, performers, writers on music, instrument makers, music publishers and the like is here parcelled out geographically by country and in some cases by region or city. Each smaller 'dictionary' is augmented by a mine of cross-references to secondary places of work (though not necessarily of study or apprenticeship), which may alert the browser to the varied foreign influences at work in a given place, besides explaining the absence of an entry from that particular dictionary.[5] The separation of musicians by locality also points up the phenomenon of 'centres of excellence' – violin making in Cremona, brass instrument making in Nuremberg, organ building in North Germany, publishing in Amsterdam and London, singing in Ferrara, Florence and Mantua, string playing in Bologna, Milan and Paris, and opera in Venice, Naples, Dresden and Hamburg.

The index coordinates the various regional dictionaries in addition to providing references to the overviews written by specialists and to the essays under the headings 'Baroque Forces and Forms' and 'Performing Practice Issues', as well as to the Chronology. The maps may provoke new thoughts about the proximity of musicians and institutions and their roles in the dissemination of styles and taste.

The *Companion to Baroque Music* subscribes to the boundaries traditionally set for this period of music, namely the years 1600–1750, which embody – though not exclusively – the age of the *basso continuo*, symbolized by the birth of opera in Florence at the outset and the death of J. S. Bach at the close. But nothing is ever quite that tidy in the history of man, not to say of music. The last decade of the 16th century witnessed the deaths of Zarlino (1590), Palestrina (1594) and Lassus (1594), all of whom greatly affected 17th-century composers; indeed, Giovanni Gabrieli lived only a few years into the century but exerted a profound influence upon several generations of composers. Just beyond the other end of our arbitrary spectrum are the 'Querelle des Bouffons' (1752), the publications of Quantz,[6] J. J. Rousseau,[7] C. P. E. Bach[8] and L. Mozart[9] which report earlier 18th-century instrumental practices, and the death of Handel (1759).

The biographical coverage of the *Companion* is of course selective. Great effort has been made to balance it. The reader may, however, become aware of 'national styles' within the dictionaries, although all the entries are the work of a single author;

this impression would seem largely to be the result of the character of the source materials, but it is also a reflection of the apparently inextinguishable *esprit du temps* or *Zeitgeist*. By isolating traditions of music-making – composers and their protégés – within a geographical hierarchy, we can make a fresh set of comparisons. The presence of entries and cross-references to resident foreign musicians (as, for example the Germans in Poland) adds further colour and perspective to our impressions of the musical life in these places and, in the course of the period, reveals interesting changes in the patterns of the migration of musicians, which is in general from south to north.

As to who qualifies for inclusion, it is those composers and musicians who flourished during the period 1600–1750. Those born in the late 16th century who – though perhaps better known as exponents of Renaissance music – nevertheless flourished for a significant time in the 17th century and contributed works or performances in the *seconda prattica* (such as monody) appear; those born after 1715, with certain exceptions,[10] do not. Characteristic of composers of the early 17th century is the versatility of their compositional techniques, which enabled them – by necessity – to produce works in both *prima* and *seconda prattica*, depending upon the commission. By contrast, the modes of expression employed by most early 18th-century composers tended to evolve from their own particular inherited late-Baroque national style to a single (derivative though some were), often lighter-weight and more cosmopolitan *galant* or pre-Classical style.

The somewhat unorthodox format of the *Companion* is intended to help the reader re-examine assumptions and confront fallacies. The essays on places address the social conditions under which musicians worked and which determined the evolution of art music. In this sense, the essays provide a counterbalance for the dictionaries, in which I have sought to present the human face. The intimate scale of the individual dictionaries should, for example, enable the reader to gain an impression of what it was like to be a musician in a given place: the spectrum of employment opportunities[11] and the 'pecking order' within different generations of musicians, as well as their relative openness to outside influences.

As with 'Places and People', the annotated Chronology is meant to be consulted in a variety of ways. To be sure, most of the details contained within it appear elsewhere in the book, but by its format the Chronology reveals the synchrony of events and presents a wide-ranging if cryptic musical history of the era as a whole. Whether one surveys a year or a decade, follows the events of a controversy – of which there were many – or consults it like a musical *Guinness Book of Records*, a greater sense of connections between musicians will inevitably emerge.

The format of the Chronology reflects the geographic ordering of the 'Places and People' section and presents both significant details of the lives of musicians and events relating to institutions and music. Consequently, the relative import of the events, however selectively chosen for inclusion, may not always be self-evident. This provides a useful example of how the dictionaries, index and chronology can be used complementarily: references to important performances – such as Monteverdi's *L'Orfeo* (1607), Luigi Rossi's *Orfeo* (1647), Cesti's *Il pomo d'oro* (1668), Lully's *Cadmus et Hermione* (1673), Fux's *Costanza e Fortezza* (1723), Gay's *Beggar's Opera* (1728), Rameau's *Hippolyte et Aricie* (1733) and the Dublin *Messiah* (1742) – or the effect of the death of a composer such as Lully (1687), or the influence of a publication such as Corelli's op. 5 violin sonatas occur in many entries. Also included in the Chronology are those works familiar to most Baroque music lovers, such as Purcell's *Dido and Aeneas* (1689), Handel's *Rinaldo* (1711), Bach's *Brandenburg Concertos* and the B minor Mass, which made little or no impact on the course of music history. The reader may therefore distinguish between the forces of musical evolution and music appreciation.

What, then, about the music and, in particular, how it should be performed? These topics are properly the domain of the essays on forces and forms, in which the qualities of the voices, the state-of-the-art instruments and the predominant forms and genres are surveyed. In each of these realms the aesthetic elements of national styles and 'good taste' are factors, and the commonly held assumptions of their day – along with a discussion of what is meant by 'authenticity', how and why it is so zealously pursued in our day, and what the listener should look for in a live or recorded performance – form the subjects of the essays in the section entitled 'Performing Practice Issues'.

Make of it what you will.

Julie Anne Sadie
London

Notes

1 *Music in the Baroque Era* (New York, 1947); chaps. 1 ('Renaissance *versus* Baroque Music'); 12 ('Sociology of Baroque Music').

2 *Baroque Music* (Englewood Cliffs, 2/1981).

3 *Music in the Seventeenth Century* (Cambridge, 1987).

4 S. Sadie, ed. (London, 1980), 20 vols.

5 Those musicians of no fixed abode who toured throughout their careers are gathered together in the sections labelled *Itinerant Musicians*.

6 *Versuch einer Anweisung die Flöte traversiere zu spielen* (Berlin, 1752; Eng. trans. and ed. E. R. Reilly, 1966).

7 *Lettre sur la musique française* (Paris, 1753; excerpts chosen by O. Strunk, Eng. trans. and ed, in *Source Readings in Music History*, New York, 1950).

8 *Versuch über die wahre Art das Clavier zu spielen* (Berlin, 1753, 1762; Eng. trans. and ed. W. J. Mitchell, 1949), 2 pts.

9 *Versuch einer gründlichen Violinschule* (Augsburg, 1756; Eng. trans. and ed. E. Knocker, 2/1951).

10 Some will protest that entries on Boyce, Burney, Hawkins, La Borde, C. P. E. Bach and even Domenico Scarlatti do not belong in a dictionary of Baroque-era musicians, but in each case the subject either composed in the late Baroque style or wrote about it, its traditions and exponents.

11 One has only to contrast the frustrations suffered by Monteverdi, Schütz and J. S. Bach on account of their employers with the freedom to travel enjoyed by Froberger, Handel and Hasse (not to mention the castratos and the prima donnas).

Acknowledgments

I should like to express my gratitude to the Dent editors Julia Kellerman and Malcolm Gerratt for their support and enthusiasm throughout the long and evolutionary gestation of this handbook; Nigel Fortune and Tim Carter for their extremely useful comments on the manuscript; the text editors, Judy Nagley and Ingrid Grimes, for their meticulous understanding of the inner workings of the text, and in particular to Judy for her unstinting help with the index; Elisabeth Agate, for her sensitive and imaginative selection of works of art to underscore and enhance the text; John Gilkes, for his intrepid pursuit of historical cartography; Tabitha Collingbourne, for her careful rendering of the music examples; my fellow writers who rose so magnificently to the task; and, most of all, to my dear husband Stanley, whose contribution extends far beyond his essay to every corner of the book and without whose example I could never have summoned the necessary perseverance.

J.A.S.

I Places and People

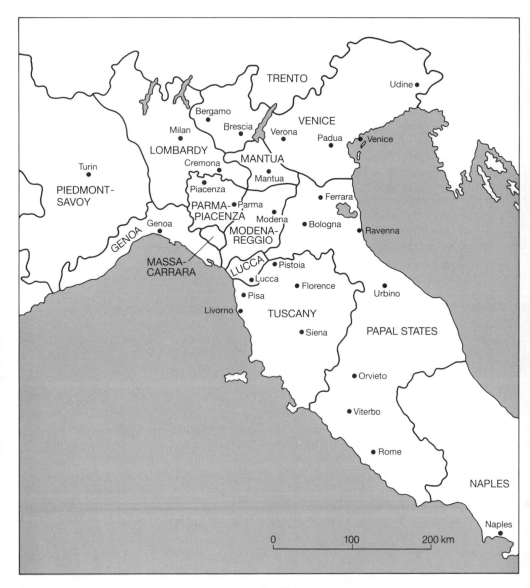

Italy in the 17th and 18th centuries (principal political boundaries)

Italy

An Italian Overview

Prince Metternich's notorious dismissal of Italy as 'a geographical expression' did not lack a grain of truth at the time of writing (1849). As late as the 19th century it was still possible to argue that cultural and linguistic unity, of which Italy had for centuries enjoyed a fuller measure than many of her European neighbours, was irrelevant to political allegiance, a factor more dependent on dynastic fortunes, diplomatic adjustments and military successes. A complex history of foreign invasion, inter-city rivalry and the ruthless pursuit of personal ambition – all of these complicated by the presence on Italian soil of the papacy – lay behind the periodically shifting political mosaic that the peninsula presented at the beginning of the modern era.

Not too much should be made of the distinction between native-ruled and foreign-ruled territories, since the latter drew most of their officialdom, including their governors or viceroys, from the local élites and, until the Age of Reform, interfered little with traditional laws and customs. Nevertheless, the foreign dimension in Italian politics aided the spread of Italian culture outwards, leading to a curious 'domination' in reverse through which Italian, not German, became the language of polite conversation and of letters at the imperial court in Vienna; between Spain and Italy, however, the cultural exchange was less one-sided (though in music Italy dominated).

During the period of the musical Baroque in Italy, roughly from 1600 to 1750, three large territories remained constantly under either imperial or Spanish rule. The duchy of Milan (Lombardy) and the kingdoms of Naples and Sicily all belonged to Spain until by the Peace of Utrecht (1713), concluding the War of the Spanish Succession, Milan and Naples were transferred to Austria (Sicily followed in 1720, exchanged with Savoy for Sardinia). The Treaty of Vienna (1735, ratified 1738), concluding the War of the Polish Succession, returned Naples and Sicily, under a common crown, to Spain, although not as a hereditary possession; its first king was the Infant Don Carlos. Other territories came during our period under the sway of the Habsburgs or the Spanish Bourbons through force of arms or a dynastic void. The duchy of Mantua, ruled by the Gonzagas since 1328, paid the price for supporting France against Austria despite being an imperial fief and became attached to the empire in 1710; the duchy of Parma and Piacenza, alienated from the papacy in 1545 by Pope Paul III, who donated it to his natural son Pierluigi Farnese, passed, through the marriage of Elisabetta Farnese into the Spanish Bourbons, to a cadet branch of the Spanish royal house in 1731; the grand duchy of Tuscany came to the Austrians (though, like Parma and Piacenza, not as a hereditary possession) when Franz Stephan, Duke of Lorraine and later emperor, succeeded Gian Gastone, last of the Medici, in 1737.

Cutting a broad swathe across central Italy, with considerable extensions to the south-west (Rome) and north-east (Bologna, Ferrara), were the 13 provinces making up the Papal States. These provinces, each administered by a high-ranking church-man with a title such as legate, vice-legate or governor, enjoyed a considerable degree of freedom from Rome in secular affairs, often preserving elements of an earlier history as principalities or free communes. Ferrara, indeed, reverted to the church only in 1598, after Alfonso II d'Este, whose family had held the duchy as papal vicars since 1332, died without male issue; the duchy of Urbino, since 1508 held by the Della Rovere family, devolved similarly in 1631. Whereas Lombardy, Sicily, Naples and most of the other territories we shall discuss were highly cen-tralized – reducible, ultimately, to a capital city and its hinterland – the Papal States resembled more an agglomeration of self-contained statelets, each with its historic capital: Rome, Bologna, Ravenna, Ancona and so on.

Of the independent territories other than those whose absorption by Spain or Austria has already been mentioned the most important were the duchy of Savoy (including Piedmont) in the north-west, the republic of Venice in the north-east and the duchy of Modena north of Tuscany. Savoy, which officially became part of the kingdom of Sardinia after 1720, bore strong traces of its continuous involvement over the centuries with France. French was the language of the court at Turin, and the extent of French influence is illustrated by the fact that whereas the rest of the peninsula mostly kept 'Italian' time, in which the 24-hour cycle began at nightfall (the system goes back to medieval times and is related to the canonical hours), Savoy kept 'French' time, beginning the cycle at midnight.

Venice, whose extensive administrative area on the Italian mainland – the so-called 'Terraferma veneta', or 'Veneto' – stretched from Bergamo in the west to Udine in the east and bordered the Po in the south (we will ignore here her possessions along the western seaboard of modern Yugoslavia and Greece and elsewhere in the eastern Mediterranean), was in some respects, geographical and cultural, only peripherally Italian; yet in political terms she represented the concept of 'Italy', past and – many believed – future, better than any other state, having arisen from the debris of the Western Roman Empire and against all odds preserved her independence ever since. Venice's elaborate constitution, which reserved political power for a patrician class comprising between 2.5 and 4% of the population of the city of Venice, and many observances in her public life (such as the wearing of the toga by her nobles and the long prohibition of wigs in the Great Council) emphasized symbolically this historical or – where history failed – mythical succession to republican and imperial Rome. Her proximity to the Ottoman empire in the east and to Austria and Germany in the north (via major Alpine passes, notably the Brenner), made Venice a favoured entrepôt for cultural as well as material products. Even after her manufacturing industry, like that of virtually all Italy, had gone into decline in the 16th and 17th centuries, and her maritime activity was curtailed by increasingly successful competition from English and French fleets in the 18th century, Venice kept afloat through the development of agriculture on the mainland and the growth of tourism – the term is not anachronistic – in the capital; it has been estimated that in the years around 1700 there were in Venice at Carnival time (January and February) around 30,000 foreign visitors, as compared with only 140,000 permanent residents.

Modena and Reggio, which were ruled, together with Ferrara, by the Este family, remained in its possession after the cession of Ferrara to the papacy. The consequent removal of the Este court from Ferrara to Modena ushered in a period of intense cultural activity belying Modena's slight political significance, especially under Francesco II (reigned 1662–94).

For completeness, a group of small independent states adjoining Modena must be mentioned: the republic of Lucca to the south; the duchy of Massa and Carrara to the west; the republic of Genoa further west, curling round the coastline. None of these distinguished itself in music between 1600 and 1750, and we shall hear no more of them.

If the political map of Italy seemed to bear out Metternich's words, two factors tended to weld the fragments together; the Italian language and the Roman Catholic church. Although the people spoke – and still speak – an immense variety of dialects, a common literary language had been forged in the 13th and 14th centuries through the examples of Dante (1265–1321), Petrarch (1304–74) and Boccaccio (1313–75). Despite its label of Tuscan, since it was associated historically with the region of Florence, this literary Italian was soon cultivated by the educated throughout Italy, so that no irony attaches to the fact that the first great codifier of Italian linguistic and literary usage, Pietro Bembo (1470–1547), was a Venetian. It is worth mentioning, however, that Venetian dialect aspired, like lowland Scottish, to an independent literary status; writing in dialect – with some relevance for comic opera – also existed, notably in Bologna and Naples.

At a time – the 17th century – when the literary cultures of some other European nations had hardly begun to acquire their classic works, the Italians could look back on a tradition of lyric and epic poetry, drama and prose spanning four centuries. But it was a conservative tradition that weighed down heavily on the writer, challenging him with precedents at every turn. This tendency to conservatism was reinforced by the unique relationship to Latin that Italian enjoyed. The visible reminders, natural and man-made, of the Roman past; the lexical and grammatical similarities of the two languages; the wide acquaintance with classical authors stimulated by the Renaissance humanists and the development of printing: all these made the work of the writers of Antiquity as relevant as that of the post-Dante Italian school. When one reads the *argomento* before the libretto of an Italian Baroque opera, where the source of the plot, in Ovid or Livy perhaps, is dutifully identified, one realizes that the classical author is as close to the experience of the opera-goer as an Ariosto or Tasso.

The symbiosis of Italian and Latin is strikingly illustrated, albeit unhappily from a literary standpoint, in the Latin texts of Baroque motets, which, if we can believe Grosley, were often penned by sacristans, thus men of only moderate education;[1] here the accidence of Latin is wondrously assimilated to the syntax and fashionable imagery of contemporary Italian to produce a result too smooth and innocent to deserve the epithet 'barbarous'.

Almost without exception the *letterato* was not a professional writer in the modern sense but a member of the leisured élite (the aristocracy and upper citizenry), hence distinctly superior socially to the typical musician, who belonged to the artisan class. For this reason opera librettos give the name of the author of the drama as a matter of course but that of the composer of the music as a mere courtesy, easy to forget. Whereas musicians organized themselves on a local basis in associations like the Venetian Società S Cecilia (founded in 1690) that were concerned primarily with their members' welfare, writers came together on a wider, sometimes national basis, and with purely artistic goals in mind. These literary clubs were commonly known as 'academies' (*accademie*), a term borrowed from the garden near Athens in which Plato and his followers once met and which, confusingly for us today, was used in many other senses in Baroque Italy (for a private concert, for a literary or musical composition performed in public, for an educational institution etc.). The Camerata, which, meeting in Florence between around 1573 and 1587 in the house of Count Giovanni de' Bardi, provided an intellectual basis for the introduction of monody and therefore, indirectly, of opera, was such an academy. Another famous and influential example was the Arcadian Academy (Accademia degli Arcadi) set up formally in Rome in 1690 to honour the memory of the late Queen Christina of Sweden, a leading patron of literature and the other arts. In order to recreate in their imagination the Peloponnesian Arcadia of old the members all adopted 'Arcadian' names proper to shepherds or nymphs and participated in pseudo-classical ceremonies. Their essential business, however, was the classically inspired reform of taste in Italian letters, to be achieved by purging from them the uncouth and unseemly. The prestige of the Arcadians grew so fast that within a few years many existing literary academies in other cities had become affiliated to Arcadia, while others were created as 'colonies'. Arcadia became a nation-wide network of clubs imposing common literary standards that one finds observed equally in the Venetian Apostolo Zeno (1668–1750) and the Roman Pietro Metastasio (1698–1782), the two most eminent writers of *melodrammi* in the first half of the 18th century.

The short–lived Società Albrizziana (1724–45), named after the Venetian printer who founded it, even surpassed the Arcadians in the breadth of its membership, which grew to over 800 both inside and outside Italy and included a pope (Benedict XVI) and 14 cardinals. It demonstrates how truly national in character and homogeneous in outlook the literary environment of Italy was.

The religious environment was almost as homogeneous. What religious minorities there were – notably Waldenses in Piedmont and Jewish communities in several cities – had a low social profile and lived, from the point of view of the majority, on the margins of national life. In the spiritual sphere the papacy was, on one level, supranational, but the recruitment of all popes and most curial officials from the Italian élite and the residence of most cardinals (a disproportionate number of them also Italians) in Rome lent Italian Catholicism a peculiarly indigenous quality.

The demographic, economic and social significance of the Italian clergy can hardly be overstated. It comprised not only parish priests and the hierarchy set above them but also monks and nuns, 'regular clerks' in non-monastic orders such as those of the Jesuits and the Barnabites, and secular priests (*abati*). With no public system of education in existence, the regular clerks – Jesuits, Somaschians and Scolopi (these last pioneers of free schooling in the vernacular for the poor) – dominated the instruction of the young, while the secular clergy formed a vital element of the intelligentsia in a society where the church provided almost the only means of upward mobility for the mass of the population.

The size of the clergy in relation to the total population varied quite considerably from state to state. In Tuscany, where about half the land was in church hands, they numbered 27,000, or around 3% of the population, in 1738. The Veneto and the kingdom of Naples harboured a more typical proportion of around $2-2\frac{1}{2}\%$. In Piedmont, where, significantly, large landed properties were less common, they constituted under $1\frac{1}{2}\%$. The prominence of church buildings in the urban landscape was equally striking; in the late 18th century Bologna could boast 200 churches and chapels, 36 monasteries and 28 convents of nuns.

A penumbra of pious laymen surrounded the clergy; they were grouped in bodies that bore different names (*confraternita, scuola, congregazione, accademia*) but served similar devotional, charitable or propagandistic purposes. Their importance for music lies above all in their cultivation of the oratorio genre, the musical weapon of the Counter-Reformation.

Small wonder, then, that the church was the major employer of musicians and, for the general population, the main point of access to 'art' music. Every large church had its *cappella* or *coro* (these terms embrace singers and players alike) directed by a *maestro di cappella*. Except in convents of nuns, where the singers would naturally all be female, the choirs were made up of men and boys, the latter reinforced and sometimes entirely replaced by adult falsettists and castratos. There would be one or more fixed organs, each with its appointed player, and it was very common for their number to be augmented on special occasions by portative organs. Particularly in more prosperous northern Italy, a church would often employ a complementary band of strings led by a *maestro dei concerti*, normally the principal violinist. In Rome and its area of influence the fashion arose in the last third of the 17th century to have the orchestra headed not by a single player but by a concertino, or 'small ensemble', consisting of the principal and co-principal violinists, a cellist and possibly also a continuo player for the trio. In Corelli's concerti grossi composed from the 1680s onwards and their many imitations this sytem of organization is 'written into' the musical language so perfectly that one is in danger of overlooking its other important aspects relating to the salary structure, management and spatial disposition of the orchestra. Some orchestras also included wind instruments in solo, doubling (*rinforzo*) or continuo roles. Harpsichords and plucked stringed instruments such as the lute and theorbo supported the organ in its continuo function.

The permanent musical establishment of a church was usually of the appropriate size for services of middling importance such as those on Sundays. In services of a more routine nature the instrumentalists other than the organist might perhaps be dispensed with, and the choir might perform succinctly in *a cappella* style (note that in Baroque usage this expression embraces not only performance by unaccompanied voices but also performance with instruments doubling vocal parts strictly) or revert to plainsong, allowing the organ or a handful of strings to provide the element of contrast. On the other hand, for feasts of exceptional importance extra performers were commonly drafted in. Indeed, some churches such as that of the convent of S Lorenzo in Venice had no *coro* of their own, but, as if to compensate, celebrated the feast of the titular saint with an outsize choir and orchestra recruited for the event from far and wide (see Plate 1).

In the early 17th century the singers of a *cappella* tended to outnumber the instrumentalists by something like two to one (at S Marco, Venice, in 1643 the proportion was 35:18). Orchestral performance in the modern sense (that is, with more than one instrument to each string part) took root in the second half of the century, gradually bringing the typical strength of the instrumental section up to parity with the vocal section. The approximately 70 musicians that S Marco employed in the 18th century were exceptionally numerous even for the principal church of a large city; the 28 musicians (16 singers, 12 instrumentalists) at S Petronio, Bologna, in 1663 present a more typical picture. The employment that churches offered was not 'full-time' as we understand the concept today, for there was time and opportunity for the members of a *cappella* to supplement their modest salaries by accepting engagements elsewhere.

Quite apart from the financial strain that a large musical establishment imposed, the positioning of the musicians in churches not originally built with such numbers in mind often proved difficult and led to curious and original solutions. It was often impossible for them all to be contained, as at S Petronio, within the chancel where the canonical stalls were also accommodated, and it became accepted practice to house them in special choir-lofts or even on improvised platforms within the nave itself. The two organs facing one another across the nave of the Venetian church of S Lorenzo, each surrounded by its own *coro*, offer a favourite, characteristically Italian solution. Being divided into two bodies, incidentally, did not mean that the musicians had to be given works specially written to take advantage of the spatial separation; undoubtedly, most of the music performed *in due cori* was written as if for an undivided ensemble.

More radically, the musicians could be situated at the west end of the nave, causing the congregation to turn their seats towards the performers and – to the amused amazement of foreign visitors – their backs to the high altar.

This partial dissociation of music from the rite (which it serves as an accompaniment or commentary rather than as an actual ingredient) was possible in Catholicism, where the validity of the rite depends on the acts of the celebrant and his assistants, not on the participation of the congregation. When a motet or piece of instrumental music (toccata, ricercar, canzona, sonata, sinfonia etc) coincided with the recitation of the liturgy, the latter took place in a low voice, so reconciling liturgical propriety with musical integrity.

The musical centrepiece of a service was, for the Mass, a setting of sections of the Ordinary; for Vespers and Compline, the psalms and canticle. The four great Marian antiphons, each in its appointed season, for the end of the canonical day were also regularly set. Because of the greater average length and complexity of Baroque vocal compositions compared with their 16th-century counterparts – a factor connected with the introduction of instruments and the cultivation of a more florid vocal style – a process of increasing selectivity and rationalization becomes evident after 1600. The *Messa* commonly becomes reduced to the *Kyrie* and *Gloria* (the *Credo*, or part of it, is set as a separate entity; the *Sanctus* and *Agnus Dei* only rarely). In Vespers the antiphons are replaced by motets or instrumental pieces, and in psalm settings preference is given to those psalms belonging to several liturgies rather than few. Although composers often set to music in cyclic fashion all the relevant parts of a given service, we know from contemporary descriptions that in practice the music was more likely to be heard in the form of extracts than as a complete whole. The modern concert audience that can hear Monteverdi's *Vespers* (1610) from start to finish is privileged.

The general uniformity of Divine Service across Italy was tempered by the tolerance of small local peculiarities or liturgical forms cultivated by particular religious orders. Court chapels were a special case, for here two sources of authority, Rome and the secular power, each had to make themselves felt. Venice, which, as a republic, possessed no court in the ordinary sense and was, indeed, notably unostentatious in its use of music in state ceremony, made the ducal church of S Marco into a repository of autonomous cultural expression. Here, and in certain local churches, a special rite believed to have a historical connection with the superseded Aquileian rite was observed, resulting in the musical setting of many texts foreign to the Roman rite. In Rome itself, the pope's own singers, based in the Cappella Sistina but often performing elsewhere, were another institution *sui generis*. They were recruited internationally and subject to a strict corporate discipline that forbade them to occupy outside posts or to marry. As if to emphasize the retrospective, *stile antico* nature of their repertory, they performed entirely without instruments.

Courts themselves, after churches, offered musicians the best opportunities of regular employment. Much of the music in a court, as in a church, was an accompaniment to other activities – banqueting and dancing in particular. The musical genres qualified by the expression 'da camera' (literally, 'for the chamber') are written, ostensibly, for court use, though their cultivation inevitably filtered down to less exalted sections of society. Some musically-inclined rulers held *conversazioni* (*accademie*): private concerts at which the favourite genre was the continuo-accompanied solo cantata (most courts employed operatic singers who were released to sing in the great theatres of Venice, Rome, Bologna or Naples during the season, but returned to court in the off-season and devoted themselves to the chamber repertory). This sheltered milieu was a haven for *dilettanti*, the gentle-born amateurs that Italy produced in such large numbers and whose reluctance to perform before a wider audience stemmed not so much from lack of confidence as from a desire to preserve social distance.

The high points of music-making in court were the musical contributions to the *feste* organized to celebrate birthdays, name-days, births, weddings, state visits and other occasions of rejoicing. Opera was born, in Florence and Mantua, as just another novel form of musical-dramatic entertainment in this festive context. Once entrepreneurially managed public opera came to the fore (the first public opera house, that of S Cassiano in Venice, opened in 1637), the many court theatres where operas had been, and continued to be, given (in Turin, Parma, Modena etc.) quickly adapted their style, practice and repertory to that of the public theatres, so that the rich diversity and lavish ingenuity of the early court operas was lost. This convergence is illustrated by the practice in Naples of transferring the same works between the viceregal palace and the public opera house of S Bartolomeo (opened in 1654).

In the middle of the 17th century there arose a new genre that took its poetic character from the cantata and its dramatic character from the opera. This was the serenata, named after the *sereno*, or clear night sky, under which, with copious illumination from torches and candles, many of its performances took place. In scale (typically lasting between one and two hours), sentiment (lighthearted, often amorous), resources (from two singers upwards, with orchestra, occasionally choir) and, above all, adaptability, the serenata was the ideal musical complement of a *festa*. If theatrical facilities existed or could be improvised, it could be given in theatrical style; if not, the singers could read from their parts and scenery could be limited to a simple background as often employed for oratorio performances. Serenata performances took advantage of the special features of palaces and their grounds; they were given in great halls, courtyards, pavilions, loggias, lakes, rivers, gardens – the possibilities were endless. Although not the exclusive property of courts (they were cultivated also by academies and institutions such as colleges and convents), the serenata encapsulates more fully than any other genre the essence of the 'courtly' in music.

Crudely stated, the music at any court was as good as the purse of its ruler was deep and his commitment high, for musicians would willingly flock to wherever they could enjoy superior pay, conditions and recognition. This made the state of music particularly vulnerable to fluctuating interest and financial investment among successive rulers. The discontinuity shown by Mantua is not untypical. Under Vincenzo I (reigned 1587–1612) music flourished under masters such as Giaches de Wert, Benedetto Pallavicino, Salamone Rossi and Monteverdi; but the caprice or lack of interest of his successor, Francesco II, resulted in Monteverdi's abrupt dismissal and ushered in a period of quiescent mediocrity aggravated by uncertainties of dynastic succession, until the last Gonzaga duke, Ferdinando Carlo (reigned 1665–1708) splendidly – and ruinously – revived musical life, engaging Antonio Caldara as his director. After the Habsburg takeover the first governor, Prince Philip of Hessen-Darmstadt (in office 1714–35), maintained the high standards, enticing Vivaldi from Venice to become his *maestro di cappella da camera* (director of secular music including opera) between 1718 and 1720; he also acted as patron to Locatelli. When Philip was recalled to Vienna the government of Mantua passed for some years to the Milanese authorities, and the lustre of musical activity once more dimmed.

The personal taste of a ruler inevitably determined the emphases in musical life. Under Francesco II of Modena it was not opera but oratorio (100 performed between 1680 and 1691) that dominated vocal music; in instrumental music the *sonata da camera*, in the hands of such excellent resident composers as Giuseppe Colombi, G. B. Vitali and G. M. Bononcini, enjoyed special favour. In addition, Francesco was an assiduous collector of secular vocal music (cantatas, oratorios, operas) that today forms a valuable nucleus of the music in the Biblioteca Estense.

Apart from the courts of rulers there existed a host of petty or subsidiary courts formed by other members of ruling families, the minor nobility, high prelates and ambassadors. In the usage of the time the term 'court' refers to a style of life to which anyone of sufficient rank (and unearned income) could aspire with social approval. In Florence, where Grand Duke Cosimo III (reigned 1670–1721) interested himself more in religion than music, his son Ferdinando (lived 1663–1713; he was sometimes honorifically styled 'Ferdinando III', although he did not live to succeed his father) established around 1690 a brilliant court with a private theatre in the Villa di Pratolino, an associated church (S Felicità) and a regular series of concerts held in the prince's apartments. The composers indebted to Ferdinando for patronage included Antonio Veracini, the two Scarlattis, Albinoni and Handel. A good keyboard player himself, Ferdinando provided the workshop where Bartolomeo Cristofori built, just before 1700, the first piano. In Rome in those years a comparable role was performed by cardinals (Pamphili, Ottoboni) and feudal princes (Caetani, Ruspoli), who between them supported a vast army of rank-and-file musicians giving their services now to one, now to the other patron.

Courts frequently travelled, commuting seasonally between city and country residences and, in slimmer form, accompanying the head of the court on his or her travels abroad. When Vincenzo I went to the Turkish wars in 1595, Monteverdi had to follow him to Hungary. State visits, which entailed the exchange of musical compliments between visitor and visited, provided the musicians of one locality with a rare opportunity to meet those of another and promoted the diffusion of new styles. Visiting Venice in 1716, the electoral prince of Saxony, Friedrich August, brought with him an élite group of musicians who used their stay for two distinct purposes: their first task was to entertain the prince and repay his hosts with music; but they also followed an old German tradition of using Italy as a 'finishing school' to which, in other circumstances, they might have been sent on leave.

The third main source of institutional support for music was the opera. We have no space to deal in detail with its music and dramaturgy, but some broad features of its organization within Italy deserve mention. The opera houses themselves were built and owned by members of the aristocracy, individually or in consortium, but their management was commonly entrusted, season by season, to independent entrepreneurs who paid the lease of the building and all the other costs, hoping eventually to gain a profit. Most of an impresario's takings would not materialize until the time of the performances, when tickets of admittance to the parterre would be sold nightly at the door (and an extra charge made for seats, if required). However, a useful fund of working capital could be secured before the season opened through the leasing out of boxes for its duration to an inner circle of wealthy patrons; the same box was often taken by a member of the same family every season, giving the appearance of an inherited asset.

In Venice and some other important centres the principal – often the only – season was that of 'Carnival', which in Venice ran from Boxing Day to Shrove Tuesday, long enough to take up to three successive operas. Venice also had a shorter 'autumn' season which ought to be regarded as the preliminary part of the Carnival season, since management and singers rarely changed; this began in mid November, when enough of the nobility had returned from their second *villeggiatura* of the year, and ended in mid December. In Naples, however, the corresponding pair of seasons occurred two months earlier. Provincial centres such as Ancona or Ferrara had to be content with brief seasons in the spring or summer organized by touring companies based in one of the metropolitan centres. This arrangement was highly rational since it paralleled the seasonal movement of the nobility between town and country and gave operatic singers the chance to fill an otherwise fallow stretch between winter and autumn.

The most expensive item in the impresario's budget was the cast of singers. In the late Baroque period he would need a set of singers, often four, for the principal roles containing several arias apiece, and two or three further singers for the minor roles with only a token aria, if that. For a season 'star' singers such as Faustina Bordoni or Farinelli could command fees of over 1000 sequins, or about £450 in contemporary British money. In addition, a pair of comic singers for the *intermezzi* or a corps de ballet for danced entr'actes might be needed. Small wonder that impresarios desperately sought to cut costs by reducing or eliminating the chorus and retrenching the stage machinery that in the 17th century had been one of the glories of opera.

The singers were predominantly high voices, the males being castratos or falsettists. It was perfectly normal to sing the part of a character of the opposite sex: what mattered was the voice *per se*. Tenors and basses were not excluded, but tended to sing less prominent roles – except in comic *intermezzi*, where the male singer was always a *basso buffo*.

Once the cast had been engaged, the impresario had to find a 'drama'. This could be specially commissioned from a poet and thus perfectly tailored to requirements, or an old drama could be used, most likely with some adaptation. The civil and ecclesiastical censorship operating all over Italy required texts to be submitted for prior approval, and then printed so that what was sung could be compared with what had been approved. The poet or the impresario would have the libretto printed at his own expense and hope to cover costs by its sale to opera-goers and through the generosity of the patron to whom it was dedicated. Such librettos, as well as being complete 'programmes' in the modern sense, presented the text in an ideal literary form intended to be valued on that account by connoisseurs of literature and bibliophiles, quite irrespective of the composer's contribution.

The music could be commissioned in the same way as the literary text. If, on the other hand, an earlier setting was appropriated, it was likely that alterations would be made, if only because the combination of voices would rarely be the same as in the earlier production. The universal adoption of da capo form in the years before 1700 turned the aria into a fully detachable and readily transferable unit. Since these arias did not deal with the specifics of a plot – significantly, personal names are rarely mentioned in them – but expressed in a conventional, generalized way states of mind such as anger, fortitude and tenderness, they lent themselves easily to new contexts: hence the ready-made *arie di baule*, or 'suitcase arias', with which singers liked to travel, and the *pasticci* cobbled together from texts and musical settings of diverse origins.

Each theatre had its stock of scenery representing palace antechambers, woodland glades, rocky promontories, or whatever; the system of gliding wings on rails attached to a winch concealed underneath the stage, an invention of Giacomo Torelli (1608–78), made rapid scene changes and near-instantaneous transformations part of the general operatic vocabulary. An average of two or three changes of set in each of the three acts was expected. In the terminology of the time the much more numerous changes of 'scene' refer not to the scenery but to an alteration of the characters on stage brought about by an entrance or an exit. Since it was customary for a singer to sweep off the stage to applause after his aria, most arias occur, almost by definition, at the end of a scene, in the so-called 'exit' position.

Baroque opera was a co-operative but not fully integrated endeavour. Its successful marriage of music, words and spectacle was founded on the assumption that each party – librettist, composer, singer, painter, engineer – acted autonomously but anticipated (that is, knew from experience) the style and approach of the others: a perfect recipe for conservatism. The potential reusability of each component, with consequent saving of work and expense, favoured adherence to convention. It is significant that it was not public opera but court opera (see Plate 2), subject to autocratic direction and less inhibited by budgetary considerations, that spearheaded the reform movement in the age of Gluck.

Whatever its artistic limitations, the public opera of Baroque Italy was a truly popular musical-dramatic form such as existed nowhere else at the time in Europe. It was, in effect, the national theatre, since spoken tragedy and comedy had a much more restricted appeal. The obverse of this popularity was the notoriously casual behaviour of Italian audiences, perceptively commented on by Burney in these words: 'I shall have frequent occasion to mention the noise and inattention at the musical exhibitions in Italy; but music there is cheap and common, whereas in England it is a costly exotic, and more highly prized'.[2]

This easy access to music implied the existence of large numbers of professional musicians. Musical skills, like those of any other trade, were most commonly acquired in the family circle, as one can easily see from the membership lists of musicians' guilds and associations. Famous musical dynasties such as the Scarlattis in Naples, the Laurentis in Bologna and the Somis family in Turin were only the most talented and successful representatives of a general pattern. Seminaries also imparted the rudiments of music to their students, and the *Scuole pie* of Bologna contributed much to the unrivalled tradition of singing in that ciy. Some musicians established schools of music in their own homes, though these amounted to little more than a group of private pupils.

For a more institutionalized and systematic mode of music teaching we have to turn to the so-called conservatories of Naples and Venice. The four Neapolitan conservatories – S Maria di Loreto, S Maria della Pietà dei Turchini, Poveri di Gesù Cristo and S Onofrio a Capuana – originally catered only for orphaned boys, though their success later brought in fee-paying male students, some even from abroad. Three were state-supported and one (the Gesù Cristo) was under the archbishop. The aim of the conservatories was to prepare those boys showing talent for a musical career, in which they were notably successful, as one can see from the list of their ex-pupils, which includes the names of Mancini, Sarro, Porpora, Vinci, Leo and Pergolesi. Every effort was made to integrate the boys into the general musical life of the city, and their services were frequently hired out. That their conditions of study were not always ideal is amusingly commemorated in Burney's description of a 'Dutch concert' at S Onofrio, where all manner of sounds from students practising cheek by jowl mingled cacophonously.

The character and aims of the four Venetian conservatories, called *ospitali* (or, in Venetian fashion, *ospedali*), were very different. The Pietà, by far the largest of the four, took in foundlings; the others (the Mendicanti, the Incurabili and the Ospedaletto) catered for orphans and the poor. Boys did not figure prominently at the *ospedali*, since they left at an early age to serve apprenticeships. The girls were divided into commoners, who were trained in ordinary domestic duties, and *figlie di coro*, who were to staff the chapel choir and orchestra of their institution. On reaching adulthood some of the girls were permitted to marry (albeit with difficulty if they were good musicians) and some entered convents, but large numbers stayed on for the rest of their lives. Musical training was provided purely for the benefit of the *ospedali*, whose well-advertised services attracted large congregations and brought in revenue through the hiring out of seats and the generosity of benefactors; it was in fact the custom to insist that *figlie* released into matrimony undertook, in their marriage contract, not to sing in public. As in all female convents, the performers had to be screened off for the sake of their modesty from the congregation, a task accomplished by grilles and gauzes. The element of mystery that this occasioned – would the sight of a particular *figlia* be as angelic as her sound? – caught the fancy of several writers, notably Rousseau.

In each institution the *figlie di coro* were organized in a pyramidal hierarchy serving both musical and disciplinary ends. At the Pietà, for instance, the *coro* was headed by two *maestre di coro*, who had under them a cadre of other *maestre*, followed by the ordinary members of the *coro* and then the beginners and others not yet admitted into the *coro*; 14 *figlie* were 'privileged' that is, they were allowed to give musical instruction to girls from patrician families coming in from outside. For many purposes the *coro* was self-sufficient, supplying from within its ranks all the necessary teaching and performing expertise. All the *ospedali* employed a male musical director (*maestro di coro*), whose most important task was the composition of new works, and a teacher of singing. Teachers of instruments were hired and fired as the need arose; the legendary association of Vivaldi with the Pietà was much less continuous than has popularly been supposed, for he was out of its service in 1710, 1718–34 and after 1738, preserving the relationship, if at all, merely through the sale of compositions.

The Pietà, which had the best reputation for instrumental music among the Venetian conservatories, prided itself on the variety of its instruments; in Vivaldi's period these included, among the strings, the viola d'amore and a full consort of *viole all'inglese* (similar to the former but with more numerous sympathetic strings) and, among the woodwind, the chalumeau and the clarinet. Venice's exceptionally close contact, through trade and travel, with the German-speaking lands made her particularly receptive to several instruments, including the above, that were widely known beyond the Alps but rare in Italy. Strangely, Venice was slower than a number of other Italian centres to take up the oboe and, especially, the transverse flute, which does not seem to have been played in public there before the 1720s.

In Italy, even more than elsewhere, the instruments of the violin family held sway. We know from the reports of André Maugars and Thomas Hill that by the middle of the 17th century the viol family had fallen into disuse there. By 1600 Cremona had already become the leading European centre of violin-making; it remained so until the end of the Baroque, thanks to the Amati, Bergonzi, Guarneri, Rugeri and Stradivari families, though Venice (Bellosio, Gobetti, Goffriller, Montagnana, Serafin) eventually ran it close.

In the 17th century, when ensemble music for strings commonly required two or even three viola parts, violas were manufactured both in small (alto) and large (tenore) sizes corresponding to the register in which their parts were respectively written. Towards the end of the century, when the practice of limiting the violas to a single alto part became general, the manufacture of violas dropped sharply. Indeed, the pendulum swung even further, so that from the 1720s onwards, particularly in Rome and Naples, one finds much orchestral writing that dispenses altogether with the viola, a practice strongly deplored by Algarotti in his *Saggio sopra l'opera in musica* (1755). 'Violone' was the all-purpose name given to the bass instruments, which ranged from an instrument tuned like the cello but of larger dimensions to a true contrabass instrument (violone grosso); the violoncello (or violoncino) proper came into being around the middle of the 17th century, at first as an instrument playing a line distinct from, and often more elaborate than, the continuo part. In the 18th century this smaller instrument replaced the type of violone playing at 'eight-foot' pitch, leaving the 'sixteen-foot' instrument as the sole bearer of that name.

Italian organs and harpsichords were of characteristic design and strongly influenced the style of the music written for them. Unlike contemporary French and German organs, which had an extended pedalboard, and English organs, which usually had none, Italian organs had about an octave of pedal 'pulldowns' good for little more than sustaining the occasional pedal-note rather in the manner of the sostenuto pedal on a Steinway grand piano. Italian organ music of the Baroque period differs technically (as opposed to generically) little from harpsichord music beyond a greater commitment to counterpoint and a more sustained manner. The Italian Baroque harpsichord spurned the complexities of north European instruments; it rarely had more than one manual and emphasized brightness and clarity over power and tonal variety. The simplicity and portability of Italian harpsichords caused them often to be used for accompaniment in multiples, like the portative organs described earlier, hence the frequency of the direction 'senza cembal*i*' (rather than 'senza cembal*o*') in musical scores.

Whereas the countries of north-west Europe began the Baroque period with quite modest music-publishing industries but ended it with flourishing, large-scale ones, the fortunes of the Italian music-publishing industry followed, if anything, the reverse path. These divergent trends clearly have technological, economic, socio-logical and purely musical dimensions, and we still await the studies that would enable us to understand fully their complex relationship. Meanwhile, one can point to at least some of the factors involved.

In Italy the art of engraving music, the result of which is to present the music in a form similar to the handwritten but more regular, never took root; there was no publisher employing this technique to compare with Estienne Roger in Amsterdam, John Walsh in London or Charles-Nicolas Le Clerc in Paris. Instead, Italy remained faithful to the process, perfected in the 16th century, of printing music in a single impression from movable type. Cumbersome and unsightly at best, this form of reproduction posed acute problems to the compositor (for instance, how could symbols in standard lengths such as ties or slurs be matched accurately to the enormous variety of distance between note-heads?), and consequently problems of interpretation to the reader. It could not beam quavers and shorter values together, a fact that both reduced legibility and wasted space. Above all, it was expensive and grew increasingly so. Relatively little music was published by Italian printers at their own expense, thus as a commercial venture stimulated by public demand. Rather, the conditions resembled those of the modern 'private' publication; the composer or his patron paid the printer for the full cost of his work and then made arrangements to place the bulk of the edition on sale through the same printer's bookshop. After use the type was distributed and would need to be reset in the event of a new edition (whereas the plates of an engraved edition could be stored and reused whenever needed, so that a purchaser could quite literally order a 'customized' example of a work). To a limited extent Italian printer-booksellers exchanged their stock in order to put works into wider circulation, but no properly organized national, let alone international, sales network comparable with that of Roger ever developed. Examples of Italian editions of musical works from the 16th to the 18th century abound in north European libraries, but these are rarely 'exported' copies; they were bought at source by visitors to Italy.

Music was published either for reasons of prestige – in which case it represented, so to speak, a long-term investment by the composer – or because it belonged to a popular genre and medium guaranteeing that the volume of sales would bring unit costs down to or below those of handwritten copies. In the early 17th century, when Venice was the dominant centre of music printing in Italy, sacred and secular vocal music in four or five parts formed the core of the repertory; in the late 17th century, when Bologna joined and soon overtook Venice, the focus of attention switched to instrumental music: sonatas and the incipient concerto. In the first decade of the 18th century the spectacular rise of Amsterdam and London, where music printed in Italy could expect to be 'pirated' within a few years and then sold to a far wider (in all senses) music-buying public, caused a very severe contraction in Italian music publishing, from which it did not recover until the next century. We know from the prefaces of works published in Rome during this critical period by the minor but by no means negligible violinist-composer Giuseppe Valentini that having one's music printed could be prohibitively expensive; in fact, Valentini supplies whole lists of works of his awaiting publication if only a Maecenas will provide the necessary subvention. Although we do not yet know the details of composers' contracts with their publishers in Amsterdam and elsewhere beyond the Alps, it is clear that publication entailed no great expense to them – perhaps rather the reverse – since dedications are so often absent. In 1711 Vivaldi, who had previously entrusted his works to first one (Sala) and then another (Bortoli) local printer, sent his third opus, *L'estro armonico*, directly to Roger in Amsterdam, pointedly disparaging the Italian publishers in his foreword; *en masse*, other Italian composers followed his lead, setting in motion a vicious spiral. One unintended consequence of this new direct relationship between Italian composers of instrumental music and transalpine publishers was that the former came, gradually, to shape their style according to the dictates of northern rather than indigenous taste; in contrast, vocal music, which was rarely published at that time, preserved its specifically Italian character. When the ascendancy of German music became confirmed later in the century, Italian instrumental music found itself without a 'home base' to which it could retreat for recuperation, whereas Italian vocal music continued much as before.

Two further, mutually related factors worked against the success of music publishing in late-Baroque Italy: the highly developed music-copying industry and the ephemerality of public taste. Some words of Burney sum up the situation as it had already existed for several decades before 1771: 'The art of engraving music there [Venice] seems to be utterly lost, as I was not able to find a single work printed in the manner we print music in England. [...] Musical compositions are so short-lived in Italy, such is the rage for novelty, that for the few copies wanted, it is not worth while to be at the expence of engraving, and of the rolling-press. Indeed there, as in Turkey, the business of a transcriber furnishes employment for so many people, that it is cruel to wish to rob them of it, especially as that trade seems more brisk and profitable than any other.'[3]

Music copying benefited from the fact that Italy had pioneered the manufacture of music manuscript paper as understood today. In Venice we find, from around 1700 or earlier, special music paper on which, by means of a combination rastrum (Paul Everett's term for a fixed assembly of multi-nibbed instruments (rastra) capable of drawing several staves at a time), 10, 12 or more stave-lines have been ruled four times on each side of an extra-large sheet of thick paper, which, folded twice and cut, yields a quire of four leaves. In Rome and Bologna we find a similar system in use, except that there the staves are ruled after the folding and cutting. The fact that manuscript paper was acquired by composers in ready-made form sometimes influenced the scoring of the music in a way that underlines how heavily conditioned by practical considerations the world of 18th-century music could become. In the popular 10-stave paper, for example, there was an incentive to limit the number of staves used to five so that two systems could be fitted in on every page; hence the high incidence of arias in which the staff occupied by the viola in the instrumental ritornellos is elsewhere taken over by the voice, causing the viola to drop out, or of double concertos for violin in which the second soloist appropriates the staff belonging to the orchestral first violins.

Copyists frequently worked in collectives ('copying shops'), dividing the work of writing out the parts or score of a single composition between several hands. As Burney says, they were well paid, earning about 15 *soldi* (fourpence) per completed quire. They were the indispensable intermediaries between Italian composers and foreign visitors; many an anthology of cantatas or operatic arias taken back to England must owe its choice of works to the recommendation (and privileged access to music) of copyists.

Charles Jennens's description of Italy as 'the Land of Musick' – intentionally ironical, since he was only too aware of its symptoms of decline at the time of writing (1739) – gives one image of Italy in foreign eyes that remained constant during the 150 years from Monteverdi to Galuppi. In a purely quantitative sense it was indisputably true; the social 'investment' in music was higher in Italy than anywhere else, though one must remember that in the second half of the period, through tourism and the emigration of musicians, the 'dividends' were increasingly exported. It has often been suggested that the continued flourishing of Italian music amid conditions of economic decline and political instability was a case of 'far bella figura' in the spirit of an ageing beauty applying an ever greater quantity of cosmetics. In reality, the causes of Italian backwardness were the same as those of its pre-eminence in music: the persistence of feudal social relations. It was the 'done thing' for the nobility to endow churches, patronize the opera and give direct employment to musicians, thus providing the economic sustenance for music's cultivation. In an interesting passage referring to the year 1735 Goldoni comments that dedications (of librettos, but the point must surely be equally valid for music) 'had declined from the good fortune they had enjoyed in former times':[4] fewer persons of quality wished to play Maecenas. So we end the Baroque period in Italy not only at the point where sonata form is introduced or where the hegemony of instrumental music dominated by Germans begins, but also at the point where the old, aristocratic order begins to disintegrate while the new, bourgeois order is still far from consolidation.

Michael Talbot
University of Liverpool

Notes

1 P. J. Grosley: *Nouveaux mémoires ou observations sur l'Italie et sur les Italiens* (Paris and London, 1764), vol. 2, p. 53.
2 C. Burney: *The Present State of Music in France and Italy* (London, 1771), p. 66n.
3 Op. cit., pp. 189–90.
4 C. Goldoni: *Commedie* (Venice, 1761–), vol. 13, p. 10.

Biographical Dictionary: Italy

1 Piedmont-Savoy

Aglié, Count Filippo [Philippe] d' (1604–67). Savoy courtier, diplomat, poet, choreographer and composer. Count Aglié was a gifted aristocrat who served Cardinal Maurizio of Savoy in Turin, then Duke Carlo Emanuele I (1630–7) and finally Duchess Cristina, as her chief counsellor and confidant. He spent four years in Paris at the end of the reign of Louis XIII (1640–3), where he would have attended a variety of French court *spectacles*. For Turin he wrote or devised at least 30 entertainments between 1624 and 1660 – ballets (which he choreographed in the French style), plays with music, water displays and carousels, which he tailored to the tastes, personalities and political climate at the Savoy court.

Astorga, Emanuele d'. See ITALY *9 Sicily*.

Bordoni, Faustina. See ITALY *10 Itinerant Musicians*.

Chiarini, Giuseppe. See FRANCE *1 Paris and Versailles*.

Fiorè. Father and son working at the Turin court. Angelo Maria Fiorè (*c*1660–1723) was a cellist and composer at the Parma court (1688–95) and also played in the church orchestra of Madonna della Steccata (1689–95), before taking up a post at the ducal court in Turin. There his reputation as a virtuoso cellist flowered, and he attracted distinguished pupils. In 1698 he published his *Trattenimenti da camera*, a collection of duets for cello and harpsichord or violin and cello.

Earlier, in 1697, he and his young son Andrea Stefano (1686–1732) were inducted as members of the Accademia Filarmonica in Bologna. Andrea Stefano was a child prodigy who by the age of 13 already held a post as *musico di camera* to the Duke of Savoy and had published a collection of trio sonatas (*Sinfonie da chiesa*). He studied in Rome during the period 1703–7 and composed operas for the Milan Carnivals of 1706 (*Sidonio*; text by Pariati) and 1707 (*La casta Penelope*; text by Pariati), before being appointed *maestro di cappella* of the Turin court in 1707. By then the Teatro Regio was closed and, until it reopened in 1715, Fiorè was free to compose operas for Vienna (1708–10), Barcelona (1711)

and Reggio Emilia (1713); he composed *Il trionfo d'Amore* for the reopening. When Quantz visited Turin in 1726 he was full of praise for Fiorè's orchestra, which was led by G.B. Somis.

Ghignone, Giovanni Pietro. See FRANCE *1 Paris and Versailles* [Guignon, Jean-Pierre].

Granata, Giovanni Battista. See ITALY *7 Papal States: Bologna-Ferrara*.

Hasse, Johann Adolf. See NORTHERN EUROPE *4 Saxony and Thuringia: Dresden*.

India, Sigismondo d'. See ITALY *10 Itinerant Musicians*.

Isabella Leonarda [Calegari, Isabella] (1620–*c*1700). Italian nun from Novara, who became a provincial mother superior in 1693. She was a poet and composer of Masses, motets, sacred concertos and sonatas which she published in 20 collections (1665–1700) in Bologna, Milan and Venice. She set many of her own highly expressive texts, sometimes interrupting arias with recitatives; in the sacred concertos she employed violins. Her first published music appeared in a collection (1640) by Gasparo Casati, *maestro di cappella* of Novara Cathedral.

Juvarra, Filippo. See ITALY *7 Papal States: Rome*.

Lalouette, Jean François. See FRANCE *1 Paris and Versailles*.

Lanzetti, Salvatore (*c*1710–80). Neapolitan cellist and composer who contributed to the changing image of the cello as a solo instrument, independent of continuo functions. After training at the Naples Conservatorio di S Maria di Loreto, Lanzetti worked at the Lucca court chapel, before taking up a permanent appointment at the Turin court of Vittorio Amedeo II in 1727. He spent much of his career on tour in Europe and at least 15 years in London (late 1730s–early 1750s), where he was highly acclaimed. In 1736 he became the first cello soloist to appear in Paris at the Concert Spirituel. His sonatas (his principal collection, op. 1, was published in Amsterdam in 1736) are technically as demanding as the Vivaldi violin concertos, particularly in terms of bowing, and reflect their grander proportions.

La Pierre, Paul de (1612–after 1690). Provençal violinist, dancing-master and composer who spent most of his career at the Turin court. La Pierre is first heard of at Dijon in 1640, performing in a ballet. From 1644 until 1661 he led the Montpellier consulate's violin band, appearing with Molière's troupe in a performance of the *Ballet des incompatibles* (1654). La Pierre first visited Turin in 1660, when a violin band from his native Avignon performed at the wedding celebrations of the Duke of Parma and Princess Margherita. He accepted a post there in 1662 as dancing-master to Carlo Emanuele II, charged with composing dance music for ballets and operas. In 1671 he led the Turin court's equivalent of the Vingt-quatre Violons, which became the foundation of the Piedmont school of violin playing.

Lonati, Carlo Ambrogio. See ITALY *10 Itinerant Musicians.*

Normand, Marco Roggero [Marc-Roger] (1663–1734). French cousin of François Couperin, working from 1688 at the Turin court where he was known as 'Couprin'. Several years later Couperin initially passed off his own italianate sonatas, some of which were later incorporated into *Les nations* (1726), as those of an Italian cousin. In 1690 Normand became attached to the household of the Prince of Carignan as a harpsichord teacher to the children; in 1699 he was appointed organist of the Turin royal chapel by the King of Sardinia, Vittorio Amedeo II.

Porro, Giovanni Giacomo. See CENTRAL EUROPE *1 South Germany: Munich.*

Quantz, Johann Joachim. See NORTHERN EUROPE *1 North Germany: Berlin.*

Reggio, Pietro. See BRITISH ISLES *1 London.*

Royer, Joseph-Nicolas-Pancrace. See FRANCE *1 Paris and Versailles.*

Senesino. See ITALY *10 Itinerant Musicians.*

Somis, Giovanni Battista (1686–1763). Violinist, influential teacher and composer. Generations of the Somis family had held musicians' posts in the ducal chapel at Turin before Giovanni Battista became a violinist there in 1699. He had been taught the violin by his father, Francesco Lorenzo (1663–1736), but in 1703 he was sent to Rome to study with Corelli (he may also have travelled to Venice to study with Vivaldi). When he returned to Turin in 1707 he was made *maestro di violino* and *capo di cappella*, posts he retained to the end of his life. Although he toured very little – in 1733 he went to Paris where he played at the Concert Spirituel and published his opp. 4 and 5 sonatas and trios (and in 1740 the cello sonatas and opp. 7 and 8, conceived for amateurs) – his playing and teaching exerted an influence comparable to that of Tartini. His Italian pupils included Gaetano Pugnani (later Viotti's teacher) and G. P. Ghignone, and among the French who sought him out were J.-M. Leclair *l'aîné* and L.-G. Guillemain. He composed as many as 150 concertos, all but nine of which are lost; those that do survive reveal a style halfway between Vivaldi and Tartini.

Somis is important as a sonata composer for the way in which he smoothed the distinctions between church and chamber sonatas, short-ening the latter to three movements (slow–fast–fast) and leaving off dance titles, except in op. 6. His first *allegro* movements are cast in an incipient Classical sonata form, whereas his slow movements hark back to the *sonata da chiesa*.

Stradella, Alessandro. See ITALY *7 Papal States: Rome.*

2 Lombardy

Aliprandi, Bernardo. See CENTRAL EUROPE *1 South Germany: Munich.*

Amati, Nicola (1596–1684). Important Cremonese violin maker whose students included Andrea Guarneri, Francesco Rugeri, G.B. Rogeri, Giacomo Gennaro and Antonio Stradivari. Nicola Amati was the grandson of Andrea (*d* before 1580), who was responsible for formulating the proportions of the modern violin, viola and cello. The plague which struck in the early 1630s left Nicola virtually the only Italian violin maker of any stature and the sole exponent of the Cremonese tra-dition. To remedy this situation he took on many gifted pupils and, ultimately, was sur-passed not by his own son, Girolamo (1649–1740), but by Antonio Stradivari. Nicola's most prized instruments are those built to his own wider design, the 'Grand Amati', and are elegant in every detail.

Assandra, Caterina (*fl* 1609). Nun at the Convent of S Agata at Lomello (nr Milan) and an early composer of concertato motets. Only her op. 2 *Motetti* (1609, in two and three parts with continuo) survive.

Bononcini, Giovanni. See ITALY *5 Modena-Reggio.*

Bordoni, Faustina. See ITALY *10 Itinerant Musicians.*

Ceruti, Roque. See IBERIAN PENINSULA AND COLONIES *3 New World.*

Cima, Giovanni Paolo (*b c*1570). Milanese organist and *maestro di cappella* who was important as a composer of early trio sonatas.

Of particular interest is his 1606 collection of contrasting *Partito di ricercari, canzoni alla francese* (to which were appended directions for tuning a clavichord so that it could be played in any key) and the 1610 *Concerti ecclesiastici*, which includes the first known violin sonata and a through-composed *sonata a tre* for violin, cornett and continuo (also the first known of the genre).

Donati, Ignazio. See ITALY *10 Itinerant Musicians.*

Fontana, Giovanni Battista. See ITALY *4 Venice.*

Grancino, Giovanni (*fl c*1685–*c*1726). The most important Milanese violin maker before G.B. Guadagnini and the teacher of C.G. Testore. Grancino's instruments, based on Amati patterns, are less pretentious in appearance than those made for wealthier clients in Cremona. Many of his cellos have survived, though most have been cut down in size.

Grandi, Alessandro. See ITALY *4 Venice.*

Guarneri. Three generations of Cremonese violin makers. Andrea (*c*1626–98) was apprenticed to Nicola Amati in 1641. Yet, in spite of this influence, he was one of the first to make smaller cellos. His eldest son, Pietro Giovanni (1655–1720), left Cremona for Mantua where he became a court musician; the few instruments he made reveal the hand of a perfectionist. Andrea's younger son, Giuseppe Giovanni Battista (1666–*c*1739), who became his father's assistant, inherited the business. The cellos he made, dating from the 1690s, are particularly fine. From 1715 he was assisted by his two sons. After learning the craft, Pietro (1695–1762) went to Venice where he was influenced by the work of Matteo Goffriller, Domenico Montagnana and Carlo Tononi; his instruments from the period 1730 to 1750 are much esteemed. Bartolomeo Giuseppe, known as 'del Gesù' (1698–1744), was a highly original maker whose instruments – prized for their responsiveness, strength and extraordinary beauty of tone – rank with those of Antonio Stradivari.

Lampugnani, Giovanni Battista. See ITALY *10 Itinerant Musicians.*

Legrenzi, Giovanni. See ITALY *4 Venice.*

Locatelli, Pietro Antonio. See LOW COUNTRIES *1 United Provinces.*

Lonati, Carlo Ambrogio. See ITALY *10 Itinerant Musicians.*

Marini, Biagio. See ITALY *10 Itinerant Musicians.*

Monteverdi, Claudio. See ITALY *3 Mantua.*

Perroni, Giovanni. See CENTRAL EUROPE *3 Austro-Hungary: Vienna.*

Rognoni Taeggio, Francesco (*d* before 1626). Virtuoso instrumentalist (violin, viol and flute), composer and the author of an important treatise, *Selva de varii passaggi* (1620), in which he differentiated between vocal and instrumental diminutions and described complex bow strokes. Rognoni was the son of Riccardo Rognoni (*d* 1619/20), an instrumentalist and the author of a didactic treatise (1592) in which he addressed the differences between diminutions for string and wind instruments, and also devoted considerable space to the bow stroke.

Francesco's first appointment was at the Polish court of Sigismund III, but he soon returned to Italy, settling in Milan. From 1610 he served the Prince of Masserano and from 1613 until 1624 he was director of music to the governor of Milan. His last appointment was as *maestro di cappella* of S Ambrogio. He was knighted and made a count Palatine.

Rugeri, Francesco ['Il Per'] (1620–*c*1695). The first Cremonese violin maker to make smaller cellos (in advance of Andrea Guarneri and Antonio Stradivari). Rugeri was Nicola Amati's first pupil and appears to have initially exported his own instruments with his teacher's label on them; after 1670 he usually signed them 'Il Per'. His sons Vincenzo and Giacinto (*fl* 1675–1730) worked with him, though neither achieved their father's greatness. From 1685 Francesco lived in Modena.

Sammartini, Giovanni Battista (1700/01–75). Important Milanese composer of sacred vocal and orchestral music. In contrast to his elder brother Giuseppe, Giovanni Battista remained all his life in their native Milan where he served as *maestro di cappella* for as many as 11 churches at any given time. In 1758 he helped to found a Milanese philharmonic society, after nurturing orchestral playing there over many years. His music – sonatas, quartets and quintets, concertos, overtures and *sinfonie* – circulated widely and was published as far afield as London (where Giuseppe resided); other sonatas and symphonies were falsely attributed to him. He composed three operas and several secular cantatas, as well as oratorios and sacred cantatas, most of which are now lost.

Quantz visited him in 1726; Gluck came to Milan to study with him during 1737–41. Later, J.C. Bach, Luigi Boccherini, Leopold Mozart and Charles Burney sought him out. He was active as a judge in competitions and as a conductor at the court in Milan. The changes taking place in mid 18th-century Italian music are reflected in his chamber music and *sinfonie*, particularly in the development of Classical sonata form.

Sammartini, Giuseppe. See BRITISH ISLES *1 London*.

Stradivari, Antonio (1644–1737). Supreme violin maker whose career spanned 70 years and whose instruments remain today the most admired of all. As a pupil of Nicola Amati in Cremona, Stradivari inherited a 100-year-old tradition of instrument making to which he contributed the crowning achievements. His sons Francesco (1671–1743), Omobono (1679–1742) and, much later, Paolo (1708–75) assisted him in his workshop. Approximately 650 instruments survive. His earliest were harps, lutes, mandolines, guitars and tromba marinas (1666–80), as well as bowed instruments. From 1680 onwards his workshop was in the Piazza S Domenico, Cremona, where he concentrated on violins and cellos.

Amati's death in 1684 freed Stradivari to pursue his own innovations, intended to strengthen the tone of his instruments. During the 1690s he experimented with the elegant 'Long Strad' pattern, which produced instruments of a darker, more Brescian tonal quality. Stradivari's finest instruments – broader in shape and bearing his secret varnish (remarkable for both its beauty and acoustical properties) – date from the first two decades of the 18th century and in particular 1715, when the 'Alard' violin, considered the most perfect in existence, was made. The ease of response and richness of tone of these instruments are unrivalled.

From the turn of the century Stradivari experimented with the size of his cellos. His earlier instruments had been made to a large pattern, but, inspired by the success of G.P. Maggini's smaller cellos, he designed a smaller pattern which has in turn influenced all subsequent makers. Like the violins from this period, the 20 cellos that survive (the 'Duport', currently owned by Rostropovich, is considered the finest) are highly responsive and breathtakingly resonant. During his last decade (1727–37) Stradivari produced narrower cellos, similar in proportion to the 'Long Strad' violins.

Testore. Family of Milanese violin makers, known for the speed at which they turned out remarkably resonant, inexpensive instruments: Carlo Giuseppe (*fl* 1690–*c*1720), his sons Carlo Antonio (*fl c*1720–after 1760) and Paolo Antonio (*fl c*1725–60), and Paolo's son Pietro (*fl* 1750–60). Carlo Giuseppe was trained by Giovanni Grancino and was the most gifted of the line. Testore instruments can be distinguished by the diagonal bulge of the scroll's volute; Carlo Antonio's instruments are characterized by a flat-backed pegbox and a double set of lines, without purfling, scratched into the back.

Viadana [Grossi da Viadana], **Lodovico** (*c*1560–1627). Forward-looking friar, *maestro di cappella* and teacher. He was one of the first to compose and publish an indispensable continuo part for a collection of sacred vocal *concerti* (1602) and one of the first to advocate specific *ad libitum* practices. Viadana was *maestro di cappella* at a convent in Cremona when, in 1602, he published the widely acclaimed *Concerti ecclesiastici* for one to four voices. Three further collections of sacred vocal music followed: the 1607 *Missa dominicalis* (for solo voice and continuo), which is the earliest known example of liturgical monody; the ambitious 1612 *Salmi a 4 cori* (disposed as a *coro favorito* of five solo voices and three four-part choirs doubled by strings, cornetts, bassoon and trombones, and accompanied by three organs and chitarrone – but apparently adaptable for two choirs), which he probably composed while employed at Fano Cathedral in the hope of gaining the notice of the Venetian officials at S Marco; and the *Sacri concentus* (1615). In 1610 Viadana published a single volume of *Sinfonie musicali*, for eight instruments and organ continuo, which he named after Italian cities.

Visconti, Gasparo. See BRITISH ISLES *1 London*.

Vitali, Filippo. See ITALY *10 Itinerant Musicians*.

Zani, Andrea (1696–1757). Violinist from Casalmaggiore (nr Cremona) and transitional composer whose music is successively cast in Baroque, *galant* and Classical styles. Around 1730 Zani went to Vienna where he gained a reputation as a virtuoso and teacher but never acquired a court post; by 1738 he was back at home, where he remained for the rest of his life. He published Vivaldian violin sonatas and *sinfonie da camera* in Casalmaggiore in the late 1720s, *concerti a quatro con suoi ripieni*, a collection of *galant* sonatas entitled *Pensieri armonici* in Vienna in 1735 and another in Paris *c*1740; a Classical-style trio was published posthumously (1764) in London.

Zuccari, Carlo. See ITALY *10 Itinerant Musicians*.

3 Mantua

Ariosti, Attilio. See ITALY *10 Itinerant Musicians.*

Baroni, Leonora. See ITALY *10 Itinerant Musicians.*

Buonamente, Giovanni Battista (*d* 1642). Mantuan musician, thought to have been a pupil of Salamone Rossi – a singer, violinist and composer of some of the earliest trio sonatas. Buonamente served as a chamber musician to the Gonzagas (possibly under Monteverdi) and then at the imperial court in Vienna (1626–31). His first three books of violin sonatas are lost, although the subsequent four survive (1626–37); they encompass canzona and variation forms, sinfonias and dances; many are based on popular tunes. About 1631 he became a Franciscan monk, enabling him to accept posts at churches in Parma (1632) and Assisi (1633). Only a few of his sacred vocal works (motets, Offices and Masses) survive.

Corbetta, Francesco. See ITALY *10 Itinerant Musicians.*

Farina, Carlo. See NORTHERN EUROPE *4 Saxony and Thuringia: Dresden.*

Frescobaldi, Girolamo. See ITALY *7 Papal States: Rome.*

Gagliano, Marco da. See ITALY *6 Tuscany.*

Leo da Modena. See ITALY *4 Venice.*

L'Épine, Margherita de. See BRITISH ISLES *1 London.*

Lonati, Carlo Ambrogio. See ITALY *10 Itinerant Musicians.*

Monteverdi, Claudio (Giovanni Antonio) (1567–1643). Important pivotal figure between the Renaissance and Baroque styles. He was a composer of the first rank who was remarkably aware of his place in the mainstream of the contemporary musical continuum and, at the same time, uniquely able gracefully to integrate the innovations of form, text setting, harmony and ornamentation with the traditions he had inherited. He is admired above all for his ability to penetrate the deeper layers of meaning in poetic texts and to bring the characters in his musical dramas to life.

Monteverdi, Cremonese by birth, spent the first part of his career in Mantua in the service of the first Vincenzo Gonzaga, whose musicians were a small but distinguished group. There he remained until shortly after the duke's death in 1612, collecting and publishing (in Venice) most of his madrigals (books 3–5 and the 1607 *Scherzi musicali*),

becoming embroiled in a controversy with the conservative G.M. Artusi, and producing a full-scale French-style ballet (*Il ballo delle ingrate*, 1608; text by Rinuccini), as well as two of the most famous works in the history of opera: *L'Orfeo* (1607; text by Striggio) and *L'Arianna* (1608; text by Rinuccini). In 1599 Monteverdi had married another of the duke's musicians, a singer Claudia de Cattaneis, with whom he had three children; her death in 1607 had a profound and lasting effect on him.

During the 1590s he travelled with the duke to Austria and Hungary (1595), and Flanders (1599). Although he was appointed *maestro di cappella* in 1601, he had expected the post much earlier, and his dissatisfaction with the working conditions in Mantua increased with time. The popularity of his madrigals was fanned by the controversy over the merits of the *seconda prattica* – and, more particularly, those of certain questionable innovations in part-writing which Artusi found in several of Monteverdi's as yet unpublished madrigals – conducted in pamphlets and the prefaces to his fifth book of madrigals (1605) and the 1607 *Scherzi musicali* (written by Monteverdi's younger brother Giulio Cesare). In 1610 he published in Venice the versatile and wide ranging *Sanctissimae virgini missa senis vocibus ad ecclesiarum choros ac Vespere pluribus decantandae* (better known today as the *Vespers*), dedicated to Pope Paul V, in the justifiable hope that he might increase his prestige as a composer of sacred music and attract a better post. Later, in 1620, when invited to return to Mantua, he firmly declined, though he had never stopped composing music for the court (for example, the welcome ballet *Tirsi e Clori*, 1616) and, indeed, continued to do so (working on a coronation opera *La finta pazza Licori*, 1627, which was never performed and is now lost).

Monteverdi took up the post of *maestro di cappella* at S Marco, Venice, in 1613 and quickly set about revitalizing the choir by hiring new virtuoso singers and instrumentalists and augmenting its repertory with works by Lassus and Palestrina as well as his own, which were later published in two large and varied collections: *Selva morale e spirituale* (1641) and *Messa . . . et salmi* for four voices (1650). In order to continue undertaking commissions from religious confraternities, noble patrons and secular academies, Monteverdi relied upon protégés such as Francesco Cavalli, Alessandro Grandi and Giovanni Rovetta for the running of the choir. He composed the *Combattimento di Tancredi e Clo-*

rinda (with its revolutionary *stile concitato*; text by Tasso) for a private performance in Venice (1624), music for *intermedi* to entertain the Farnese court at Parma (1628) and the opera *Proserpina rapita* (text by Strozzi) for a Venetian wedding in 1630, as well as music for Mantua. He also found it possible to produce further madrigal collections in 1614, 1619 (the seventh, *Concerto*, entirely devoted to post-1600 genres), 1638 (*Madrigali guerrieri et amorosi*, which includes *Il ballo delle ingrate*, the *Combattimento* and the *Lamento della ninfa*), and 1632 (*Scherzi musicali*, which includes the vocal chaconne for two tenors and a continuo ground bass 'Zefiro torna'); the final collection appeared posthumously in 1651. Having survived the plague that hit Venice in 1630–1, Monteverdi took holy orders the following year.

The opening of the public opera houses in Venice from 1637 onwards led to a demand for productions of operas from the aging composer (now in his 70s). *Il ritorno d'Ulisse in patria* (which survives in a manuscript score in Vienna; text by Badoaro) and a revival of *L'Arianna* (now lost, except for the famous lament) were performed in 1640, *Le nozze d'Enea con Lavinia* the year after and *L'incoronazione di Poppea* (text by Busenello) in 1643 (which survives in manuscripts in Venice and in Naples, where it was performed by a Venetian troupe possibly including Francesco Manelli and Benedetto Ferrari). Monteverdi died in Venice later that year.

Monteverdi's earliest surviving opera *L'Orfeo*, though grounded in late Renaissance traditions, catapulted monody – by his superior fluency and craftsmanship – beyond the limitations imposed on it by the more self-conscious Florentines. *L'Orfeo* was altogether grander in scale than the works of Peri and Caccini and without parallel in its use of virtuoso instrumentalists (in the opening Toccata, Orfeo's aria 'Possente spirto' – with solos for two violins and two cornettos, etc. – and in the variety of continuo instrumentation throughout). The loss of so many of his dramas, particularly *L'Arianna* which was extremely popular when given, and the uncertainties surrounding the authenticity of *Il ritorno d'Ulisse* and *Poppea* would seriously hamper a proper assessment of Monteverdi as an opera composer were it not for the wealth of dramatic and rhetorical devices woven into his madrigals which corroborate and amplify the techniques employed in the extant operas.

Orlandi, Santi (*d* 1619). Florentine composer who followed his employer (Prince Fer-

dinando Gonzaga) to Rome and then to Mantua, where he succeeded Monteverdi in 1612. During the first decade of the century Orlandi published five volumes of madrigals, of which only fragments of three volumes survive; also lost is the music for his 1617 opera *Gli amori di Aci e Galatea*.

Peri, Jacopo. See ITALY 6 *Tuscany*.

Rasi, Francesco (1574–1621). Important tenor soloist, chitarrone player, composer and poet of noble birth who in the 1590s served Grand Duke Ferdinando I of Tuscany and Carlo Gesualdo, before taking up a permanent post with the Duke of Mantua in 1598. In 1600 he sang in the first performances of Peri's *Euridice* and Caccini's *Il rapimento di Cefalo* in Florence. In 1607 he took the title role in Monteverdi's *L'Orfeo* in Mantua. The following year he sang in Marco da Gagliano's *Dafne* and published the first of two collections of monody, *Vaghezze di musica* (for which he provided many of the texts); his *Madrigali* appeared in 1610. While on tour in Austria in 1612 Rasi dedicated a manuscript of secular and sacred continuo songs to the Prince-Archbishop of Salzburg. Although he composed an opera, *Cibele, ed Ati*, for the 1617 wedding celebrations of his patron Ferdinando Gonzaga and Catarina de' Medici, it was never performed. His last collection of music (1620) contained four 'dialoghi rappresentativi' for three solo singers and continuo. His poetry was issued in Venice, in seven volumes entitled *La cetra di sette corde* (1619).

Rossi, Salamone (1570–*c*1630). Mantuan instrumentalist and composer associated with the Gonzaga court, where he was a contemporary of Monteverdi. Rossi lived and worked all his life in the Jewish ghetto of Mantua. Apart from his sister (Madama Europa) who was a singer, he had no relations among the other 17th-century musicians of that name. He was known as a teacher (Leo da Modena was one of his pupils) and is thought to have belonged to one of the Jewish theatrical troupes flourishing at that time, for although he dedicated his first collections of canzonettas (1589) and five-part madrigals (1600) to Vincenzo Gonzaga and contributed *intermedi* and incidental music to plays given at the ducal court, Rossi never held a regular appointment there (he was classified among the *musici straordinarii*) – mainly because he was ineligible to join the choir. It is assumed that he died when the ghetto was destroyed after the imperial troops sacked Mantua in 1630, which was then besieged by plague.

In addition to five books of madrigals, published during the first quarter of the century, Rossi issued in Venice four instrumental collections of *sinfonie*, sonatas and dances, as well as the *Hashirim asher lish'lomo* (1622–3, containing 33 polyphonic settings of Hebrew songs for use in synagogue services). The madrigal collections – conservative in many ways – are nevertheless important as early examples of the inclusion of an instrumental bass: the first (1600) has tablature for chitarrone, the second (1602) and third (1603) include a *basso continuo* part without figures, and the fourth (1610) and fifth (1622) have figures. The instrumental collections document the transition between the homogeneous canzona and the polarized texture of the emerging Italian trio sonata. As with some of the madrigals, Rossi included an unfigured part for the chitarrone; he also indicated dynamics.

Silvani [Valsini], Francesco (*b c*1660). Prolific librettist, working in Mantua at the Gonzaga court and, after the death of the last duke in 1708, in Venice. G.M. Bononcini, Alessandro Scarlatti, Antonio Caldara, J.A. Hasse, Nicola Porpora and Nicolò Jommelli were among those who set his texts, and Egidio Duni, Handel and Gluck used adaptations.

Striggio, Alessandro (?1573–1630). Mantuan nobleman, the son of the composer of the same name, a diplomat in the service of the Gonzagas, librettist and viol player. Striggio published his father's last three books of madrigals in 1596–7. In the course of his career he was made a count, then a marquis and finally chancellor in 1628. He prepared opera librettos for Monteverdi – *L'Orfeo* (1607) and, in all probability, *Tirsi e Clori* (1616) – and for Marco da Gagliano – *Il trionfo d'onore* and *Il sacrificio d'Ifigenia* (both performed in 1608). He died of the plague in Venice.

4 Venice

Alberti, Domenico. See ITALY *10 Itinerant Musicians.*

Albinoni, Tomaso Giovanni [Zuane] (1671–1751). Prolific Venetian composer of operas, cantatas and instrumental chamber music. Albinoni came from a prosperous background and considered himself a musical *dilettante.* That his talents as a violinist, singer and composer were actively encouraged is evident from the impressive list of southern European nobility to whom his early collections of sonatas and concertos were dedicated. A lifelong resident of Venice, Albinoni married an opera singer, Margherita Raimondi (*d* 1721), and composed as many as 81 operas (by his own count) several of which were performed in northern Europe from the 1720s onwards. In 1722 he travelled to Munich at the invitation of the Elector of Bavaria to supervise performances of *I veri amici* and *Il trionfo d'amore* as part of the wedding celebrations for the Prince-Elector and the daughter of the late Emperor Joseph I.

However, it is as a composer of instrumental music (99 sonatas, 59 concertos and 9 sinfonias) that he is known today. In his lifetime these works were favourably compared with those of Corelli and Vivaldi. His solo cantatas were equally successful, although the insularity of his style – melodically alive but harmonically idiosyncratic – has often been remarked upon. He is credited with being the first Italian to compose oboe concertos (op. 7, 1715) and the first regularly to employ three movements in his concertos (op. 2, 1700).

Alghisi, Paris Francesco (1666–1733). Brescian organist, teacher and composer. Through Orazio Polaroli (with whom he studied at Brescia Cathedral) Alghisi acquired a post at the Polish court (*c*1681–3). Upon returning to Brescia he entered the order of S Filippo Neri and by 1693 was appointed *maestro di cappella* to their Congregazione dell'Oratorio, for whom he composed oratorios (1689–1705). He also served as cathedral organist and belonged to the Brescian Collegio dei Nobili and the Bolognese Accademia Filarmonica. In addition to sacred music, Alghisi composed two operas for the Venetian Teatro SS Giovanni e Paolo (1690, 1691) and published single collections of trio sonatas (1693) and cantatas (by 1694; now lost).

Artusi, Giovanni Maria. See ITALY *7 Papal States: Bologna-Ferrara.*

Bembo, Antonia. See FRANCE *1 Paris and Versailles.*

Bernacchi, Antonio Maria. See ITALY *10 Itinerant Musicians.*

Bernardi, Stefano. See ITALY *10 Itinerant Musicians.*

Bertali, Antonio. See CENTRAL EUROPE *3 Austro-Hungary: Vienna.*

Biffi, Antonio (1666/7–1733). Venetian contralto. In 1702 he succeeded G.D. Partenio as *maestro di cappella* at S Marco and *maestro di coro* of the Conservatorio dei Mendicanti. He composed sacred music and oratorios.

Bononcini, Giovanni Maria. See ITALY *5 Modena-Reggio.*

Bonporti, Francesco Antonio. See ITALY 7 *Papal States: Rome.*

Bontempi, Giovanni Andrea. See NORTHERN EUROPE 4 *Saxony and Thuringia: Dresden.*

Bordoni, Faustina. See ITALY 10 *Itinerant Musicians.*

Boschi, Giuseppe Maria (*fl* 1698–1744). Bass singer, famous for his opera performances in villainous and tyrannical roles. Boschi divided his career between Venice and London, with a three-year spell (1717–20) in Dresden. He met Handel in Venice and with his wife, the contralto Francesca Vanini (*d* 1744), took part in the 1709 performances of *Agrippina.* Together they followed Handel to London and during the 1710–11 season established themselves with the Queen's Theatre Company, taking part in performances of Handel's *Rinaldo.* After his stint in Dresden Boschi joined the Royal Academy company, with whom he regularly took major roles in productions of Handel, Giovanni Bononcini and Ariosti. He and his wife returned in 1728 to Venice, where Boschi continued to sing operatic roles for at least one season, thereafter taking up a place in the choir of S Marco.

Brescianello, Giuseppe Antonio. See CENTRAL EUROPE 1 *South Germany.*

Burnacini, Giovanni and Lodovico. See CENTRAL EUROPE 3 *Austro-Hungary: Vienna.*

Caffarelli. See ITALY 10 *Itinerant Musicians.*

Caldara, Antonio. See CENTRAL EUROPE 3 *Austro-Hungary: Vienna.*

Calegari, Francesco Antonio (1656–1742). Venetian *maestro di cappella*, composer of sacred music, teacher and theorist. Calegari was a Franciscan monk who studied with Antonio Lotti. He was *maestro di cappella* at S Francesco, Bologna (1700), and S Maria Gloriosa dei Frari, Venice (1701–3), before taking up a more permanent post (1703–27) at the Basilica di S Antonio, Padua (where Tartini was *primo violino e capo di concerto*). His last years were spent in Venice, at S Maria Gloriosa dei Frari. According to F.A. Vallotti, his most important pupil, Calegari developed a theory of chord inversions, at much the same time as Rameau, though he never published it. His most important treatise (*Ampla dimostrazione degli armoniali musicali tuoni*, 1732) treats dissonance in figured basses.

Caresana, Cristoforo. See ITALY 8 *Naples.*

Castello, Dario (*fl* early 17th c.). Venetian wind player and composer. His two collections of *Sonate concertate in stil moderno per sonar nel organo overo spineta con diversi instrumenti*, published in 1621 and 1629, represent an important contribution to the development of an instrumental idiom. Presumably his sonatas were composed for the wind ensemble he directed in Venice: they are scored for two to four instruments, in seven to nine sections, and employ many changes of tempo; as in the sonatas of Salamone Rossi and Biagio Marini, the treble parts (playable on the flute, cornett or violin) are the most demanding.

Cavalli, Francesco (1602–76). Highly successful early Venetian opera composer who was associated all of his life with S Marco. Cavalli, born Caletti (he later took the name of his patron, Federico Cavalli), showed such promise as a boy soprano that at the age of 14 he was given a place in the chapel of S Marco. His association there with Monteverdi was to be a major influence on his subsequent career both at S Marco and in the Venetian opera houses. In 1639 he became the second organist at S Marco, and he assumed the duties of principal organist long before he was appointed to that post in 1665. Within hours of his appointment (in 1639) Cavalli's first opera, *Le nozze di Teti e di Peleo*, was premièred at the historic Teatro S Cassiano, which was the scene of further productions during the next decade.

Cavalli is known to have composed almost 30 operas (principally in collaboration with Giovanni Faustini) for the Venetian opera houses – the Teatro S Moisè, S Apollinare, S Salvatore and SS Giovanni e Paolo, as well as S Cassiano – among them the popular *Egisto* (1643), which was performed in Paris as early as 1646, *Ormindo* (1644), *Doriclea* (1645), *Giasone* (libretto by G.A. Cicognini, 1648/9), *Calisto* (1651/2), *Eritrea* (1652), *Xerse* (libretto by N. Minato, 1654/5) and *Erismena* (libretto by A. Aureli, 1655). His operatic style – the recitatives, the strophic and ground-bass arias, the comic and warlike *concitato* elements, and particularly the laments (inspired by Monteverdi's *Arianna*) – was inevitably very much influenced by the music of his mentor. Cavalli also composed for the opera houses of Naples (where he helped to found a tradition of opera during the 1650s), Milan and Florence.

In 1660 Cavalli was prevailed upon by Cardinal Mazarin to travel to Paris, where *Ercole amante* was to be performed in a grand new theatre (replete with machinery) being built by Carlo Vigarani for the wedding celebrations of Louis XIV. In the event, *Xerse* was performed instead, and then in a makeshift theatre in the Louvre; the treble role of Xerse was transposed to suit a baritone, and the acts were interlarded with ballet *entrées* provided by Lully. *Ercole amante*, also encumbered with extensive ballet scenes, was finally performed two years later (on 7 February 1662), by which time the powerful italophile cardinal had died and the Italians were no longer as welcome in Paris. The performance itself was a disaster: the machinery was noisy, which together with the inherently bad acoustics of the new theatre made it impossible to hear the text of the opera; to make matters worse, Lully's ballets (in which the king and queen danced) overwhelmed the opera in splendour and duration. Disillusioned, Cavalli returned to Venice, and in 1668 was appointed *maestro di cappella* at S Marco.

Černohorský, Bohuslav Matěj (1684–1742). Bohemian minorite organist, teacher and composer who worked in Italy – at Assisi (1710–15) and Padua (1715–20 and 1731–41) – for most of his career. In Prague he was attached to a monastery (1720–31), where he nurtured a school of late Baroque Bohemian composers. His pupils included Tartini and Gluck.

Cesti, Antonio. See ITALY *10 Itinerant Musicians*.

Corradi, Giulio Cesare (*d* 1701/2). Venetian librettist whose *opera seria* texts were popular with such composers as Giovanni Legrenzi, Carlo Pallavicino, P.A. Ziani, the Pollarolos, Albinoni and P.F. Alghisi during the last quarter of the 17th century. Almost all of his librettos were based on historical subjects and required machinery and a ballet troupe for the *entr'actes*; two employed choruses and most incorporated comic scenes.

Cuzzoni, Francesca. See ITALY *10 Itinerant Musicians*.

Dall'Abaco, Evaristo Felice. See CENTRAL EUROPE *1 South Germany: Munich*.

Draghi, Antonio. See CENTRAL EUROPE *3 Austro-Hungary: Vienna*.

Durastanti, Margherita. See ITALY *10 Itinerant Musicians*.

Facco, Giacomo. See IBERIAN PENINSULA AND COLONIES *1 Spain*.

Farinel, Jean-Baptiste. See FRANCE *1 Paris and Versailles*.

Faustini. Managers of Venetian public opera theatres during the mid 17th century. Giovanni Faustini (*c*1619–51), director of the Teatro S Aponal, was also a skilful opera librettist who collaborated with Cavalli from 1642 on such works as *Egisto* (1643), *Ormindo* (1644), *Doriclea* (1645), *Calisto* (1651/2) and *Eritrea* (1652) which had their first performances at the Teatro S Cassiano and the Teatro S Apollinare. His brother Marco (*d* after 1675) succeeded him at S Aponal, and

thereafter managed first the Teatro S Cassiano (from 1658) and then the Teatro SS Giovanni e Paolo (1661–7) where he staged productions of Giovanni's dramas. His correspondence reveals much about theatre practices of the day.

Fedeli [Saggione]. Venetian family of musicians and composers. Carlo (*c*1622–85) was a string bass player at S Marco from 1643 and *maestro de concerti* from 1661. His four sons played under him – Alessandro (*b c*1653), Antonio (*fl* 1686–93), Ruggiero (?*c*1655–1722) and Giuseppe [Joseph Saggione] (*fl* 1680–1733) – before going their separate ways. In addition to his duties at S Marco, Carlo played in theatre orchestras, composed several operas

Venice (*Novum totius Italiae Theatrum*, 1705)

and served as *maestro di strumenti* (1662–72) at the Mendicanti. In 1685 he published a set of 12 sonatas, some of which incorporate a concertante cello part.

Ruggiero Fedeli was a viola player, opera singer, and composer of sacred and secular vocal music who held a string of appointments at German courts, notably Berlin and Kassel, but also Bayreuth, Dresden, Hanover, Brunswick (where his opera *Almira* was performed in 1703) and Wolfenbüttel. He served as composer of the Berlin court chapel (1691–4, 1702), composed funeral music for Queen Sophia Charlotte in 1705 and was made court composer and conductor in 1708. Meanwhile, Ruggiero had been *Kapellmeister* at Kassel from 1700 until 1702, a post to which he returned definitively in 1709.

Giuseppe Fedeli played the trombone and double bass. Around the turn of the century he settled in Paris where, with Montéclair, he became the first double bass player in the orchestra of the Académie Royale de Musique (*c*1701). In 1706 his opera *The Temple of Love* was performed in London at the Haymarket Theatre. In Paris he published a collection of violin sonatas in 1715 and three *recueils d'airs français dans le goût italien* (1728), and contributed to popular anthologies.

Ferrandini, Giovanni Battista. See CENTRAL EUROPE *1 South Germany: Munich*.

Ferrari ['dalla Tiorba'], Benedetto (1603/4–81). Theorbist, opera librettist and composer who collaborated with Francesco Manelli on the earliest operas for the public theatres of Venice. Ferrari sang with the choir of the Collegio Germanico in Rome (1617–18), was associated with the Farnese court at Parma (1619–23) and may have worked in Modena before taking up residence in Venice (1633–44). In Venice he published two collections of madrigals and arias (*Musiche varie*, 1633 and 1637; many of the texts were his own) and prepared librettos for Manelli's *L'Andromeda* (1637), which marked the opening of the Teatro S Cassiano, and *La maga fulminata* (1638). For the first season of the Teatro SS Giovanni e Paolo in 1639 he wrote both libretto and music for *L'Armida*. Perhaps his most important work is *Il pastor regio* (1640), for which he again wrote both text and music; although the score is lost, the haunting final ostinato-bass duet 'Pur ti miro, pur ti godo' is preserved as the finale in the surviving manuscripts of Monteverdi's *L'incoronazione di Poppea*.

Ferrari toured as a theorbist with the Venetian company (led by Manelli) in residence at Bologna during the 1640–41 season; after returning to Venice, he departed again in 1644, following the performances of his *Il principe giardiniero*, for Modena where he renewed his connections with the Este court (for whom he wrote and composed ballets). In 1651 he was employed at the Viennese court of Ferdinand III as an instrumentalist and the director of court festivities, but two years later he returned to Modena, where he spent his last years.

Fiocco. See Low COUNTRIES *2 South Netherlands*.

Fontana, Giovanni Battista (*d c*1630). Brescian violinist who worked in Rome, Venice and Padua. He composed duo and trio sonatas for violin, cornetto and continuo (innovative in their inclusion of bass concertante parts for cello or bassoon), which were published posthumously in Venice in 1641. Together with Biagio Marini (a fellow Brescian), Fontana was an important figure in the early development of the Italian solo sonata.

Fontei, Nicolò (*d*1647). Organist and composer associated with Giulio and Barbara Strozzi in Venice. Fontei settled in Venice before 1634, entered the priesthood and undoubtedly attended the meetings of Strozzi's Accademia degli Unisoni (founded in 1637). Little is known of his professional activities, other than that in 1640 he failed, in competition with Cavalli, to gain the post of second organist at S Marco. However he did publish three books of *Bizzarrie poetiche* (1635, 1636, 1639), settings for one to three voices of Giulio Strozzi's poetry, dedicated to Barbara Strozzi: the first book contains the earliest known published examples of the rondo cantata (a structure that particularly occupied him), while the second is taken up with solo arias, and the third contains his finest bel canto arias (in triple time). In 1642 his only known opera, *Sidonio e Dorisbe*, was mounted at the Teatro S Moisè. Some of Fontei's sacred works call for large forces, such as his Masses and psalms (1647) which require as many as eight voices, violins and continuo.

Fonteio, Giovanni. See NORTHERN EUROPE *2 Scandinavia*, Nielsen, Hans.

Förster, Kaspar. See NORTHERN EUROPE *7 Itinerant Musicians*.

Gabrieli, Giovanni (*c*1553/6–1612). Organist at S Marco, composer and important transitional figure. Gabrieli presided over the change from *prima* to *seconda prattica*, and his own music represents one of the stylistic high points of the Renaissance, while incorporating elements of the modern style of Monteverdi. Using a polychoral texture as a starting-point, Gabrieli assigned parts – then whole choruses – to instruments. He made ensembles of instruments contrast with voices and with tutti ensembles, as well as with one another in sectional motets such as *In ecclesiis benedicite Domino* from the *Symphoniae sacrae* (1615). He designated instrumental pieces 'canzonas' and 'sonatas', and in the *Sonata pian e forte* from the *Sacrae symphoniae* (1597) he became the first composer to specify dynamics. In his later works he often gave the organ a continuo role. Gabrieli was one of the most famous and certainly most dedicated teachers of his time; pupils came from all over Europe and Scandinavia. His last and most important pupil was Heinrich Schütz, whose *Psalmen Davids* (1619) and *Cantiones sacrae* (1625) best demonstrate Gabrieli's influence.

Gabrielli, Domenico. See ITALY *7 Papal States: Bologna-Ferrara.*

Galuppi, Baldassare (1706–85). Prolific composer of operas and oratorios which, though composed within the boundaries of the Baroque era, belong to the early Classical period. His importance in this context is as a prominent *opera buffa* composer. Galuppi (known as 'Il Buranello' after the Venetian island where he was born) worked primarily in Venice as a *maestro di cappella* at the Ospedale dei Mendicanti (1740–51), later at S Marco (vice-*maestro* in 1748 and *maestro* from 1762) and then at the Ospedale degli Incurabili. He spent three years from 1765 as *maestro di cappella* to Catherine the Great in St Petersburg; his presence there decisively influenced the course of Russian music. Wherever he worked he imposed strict discipline, thereby considerably raising the standards of performance. For these institutions he composed liturgical music and oratorios.

Galuppi's earliest theatrical success came as a composer of *opera seria*. As early as 1729 *Dorinda* was presented at S Samuele. But he composed his finest works in the 1740s, while in London at the King's Theatre (1741–3) and in Vienna at the Burgtheater (1748–9); he also composed for the Italian opera houses at Milan, Mantua, Modena, Reggio, Rome, Verona, Naples, Padua and Livorno. *Demofoonte* (text by Metastasio) was commissioned in 1749 for the Teatro del Buen Retiro in Madrid. His first, tentative essay in *opera buffa* came in 1745 – *La forza d'amore*, written for S Cassiano, Venice. Like Pergolesi's *La serva padrona*, Galuppi's comic operas were popularized by travelling companies. Among his best-loved works were those with librettos by Goldoni, such as *L'Arcadia in Brenta* (1749) and *Il filosofo di campagna* (1754). Galuppi enjoyed popular acclaim wherever he went, but his popularity was ephemeral and quickly waned after his death. He spent his last years in Venice and died a wealthy man.

Gasparini, Francesco. See ITALY *7 Papal States: Rome.*

Gnocchi, Pietro (1677–1771). Brescian priest, scholar and composer who at the age of 85 was finally appointed *maestro di cappella* at Brescia Cathedral. Gnocchi studied in Venice and travelled in Austria, Bohemia and Saxony. He was a prolific writer and composer, the author of a 25-volume history of ancient Greek colonies, a treatise on Brescian memorial tablets and a 12-volume manuscript collection of *Salmi brevi*. He entitled his six-voice antiphonal *Magnificat* settings 'Il capo di buona Speranza' and 'Il rio de la plata', and his four-voice Masses 'Europe', 'Asia', 'Africa' and 'America'.

Goffriller, Matteo (*c*1659–1742). Venetian maker of string instruments, working from 1690 until 1720. The diversity of pattern and quality among his instruments, together with an almost complete absence of labels, have meant that until recently many were misattributed. His cellos, based on the large Amati pattern and nearly all subsequently cut down, are particularly prized.

Goldoni, Carlo (1707–93). Playwright and *opera buffa* librettist, called the 'father of modern Italian comedy'. Although trained in law, Goldoni aspired to be an *opera seria* poet; but in 1734, to augment the income from his duties as poet of the Teatro S Giovanni Grisostomo, he began writing intermezzos for a Venetian comedy troupe. From 1743 until 1748 he practised law in Tuscany, during which time Neapolitan *opera buffa* was successfully introduced in Venice. This hiatus allowed him to formulate a new vision of both spoken and musical Italian comedy (in terms of form and content) that would ultimately dignify the genre and ensure a wider European audience.

In his *opera buffa* librettos Goldoni simplified the plot (by reducing the proportion of recitative and thus hastening the action), allowed for a greater variety of aria and ensemble forms and called for more elaborate scenery. Each year from 1748 until 1762, he wrote at least six spoken comedies and as many as five *opera buffa* librettos which were set by composers such as G.B. Lampugnani, Niccolò Piccinni, Baldassare Galuppi and Egidio Duni (and later Giovanni Paisiello, F.L. Gassmann and Antonio Salieri), effectively dominating the Venetian stages.

In 1756 he prepared three librettos for the Bourbon court at Parma (where he was made court poet), which were so successful that in 1762 he was invited to Paris by the Comédie-Italienne. For his services as Italian tutor to Princess Adélaïde at Versailles he received a pension which enabled him to retire.

Grandi, Alessandro (?1586–1630). Important north Italian contemporary of Monteverdi and composer of church music in the concertato style. Grandi held appointments at Ferrara (as *maestro di cappella* of the Accademia della Morte, the Accademia dello Spirito Santo and finally at Ferrara Cathedral), before moving to Venice in 1617, where he became a singer at S Marco under Monteverdi. In 1620 he became Monteverdi's deputy, a post he retained until 1627. While there he put aside the polyphonic techniques that had served so well in his motets of the decade 1610–20 (however, his dramatic lament *Plorabo die ac nocte*, from that period, for the Madonna and three onlookers – all of whom have extended solos – is but one example of his early use of monody and dialogue style) and embraced the monodic style, concentrating on composing solo and concerted motets which gave greater scope to his gifts as a melodist and dramatist.

Grandi imbued all his music with remarkable emotional intensity, as in his motet *O quam tu pulchra es* (1625), but it is his use of instruments – effectively grafting the trio sonata on to monody – that characterizes his Venetian period. Moving beyond his popular collections of concertato madrigals (1615, 1622), he is thought to have coined the term 'cantata' by publishing four collections of secular *Cantade et arie* during the 1620s.

Grandi left Venice for Bergamo in 1627, when he was appointed *maestro di cappella* at S Maria Maggiore. In contrast to his earlier works, his music for Bergamo is on a grand scale, calling upon his strengths as a composer for combined solo, instrumental and choral forces. He carried the concertato principle further by juxtaposing groups of soloists and a choir with instrumental doubling in his 1629 collection of eight-part psalms. Grandi died in the 1630 outbreak of plague.

Grillo, Giovanni Battista (*d* 1622). Italian organist and composer who, after apparently studying with Giovanni Gabrieli, spent his early career in the service of Archduke Ferdinand of Austria in Graz. By 1612 he had returned to Venice, where he was elected organist of the Scuola Grande di S Rocco (a religious confraternity); despite a challenge by Giovanni Picchi, he was confirmed in the post in 1613. From 1615 he was organist at Santa Madonna dell'Orto and four years later was appointed first organist at S Marco. His *Sacri concentus ac symphoniae* (1618) owe much to Gabrieli; he also composed motets and, with Monteverdi and others, contributed music for the Requiem Service for Cosimo II of Tuscany in 1621.

Grimani, Maria Margherita. See CENTRAL EUROPE *3 Austro-Hungary: Vienna.*

Grossi, Giovanni Francesco. See ITALY *10 Itinerant Musicians.*

Handel, George Frideric. See BRITISH ISLES *1 London.*

Hasse, Johann Adolf. See NORTHERN EUROPE *4 Saxony and Thuringia: Dresden.*

Il Verso, Antonio. See ITALY *9 Sicily.*

Ivanovich, Cristoforo (1628–89). Dalmatian theatre historian and librettist working in Venice. Ivanovich held posts of *sotto-canone* (1676) and *canone* (1681) at S Marco while working on an index of Venetian opera performances during the period 1637–87, which also contains an important discussion of theatre practices. His own opera librettos were set by P.A. Ziani (*La Circe*, 1665), G.M. Pagliardi, Cavalli (*Il Coriolano*, 1669) and G.D. Partenio.

Kapsberger, Johann Hieronymus. See ITALY *7 Papal States: Rome.*

Lambranzi, Gregorio (*fl* early 18th c.). Ingenious Venetian choreographer and author of a lavishly illustrated (101 engraved plates) book on theatrical dance, published in Nuremberg: *Neue und curieuse theatralische Tanz-Schul* (1716). In it he included dances for two tennis players, fishermen, soldiers and gymnasts.

Laurenti, Antonia Maria Novelli. See ITALY *7 Papal States: Bologna-Ferrara.*

Legrenzi, Giovanni (1626–90). Organist and highly influential composer. Legrenzi worked in a number of north Italian cities: Bergamo, where he served as organist at S Maria Maggiore (1645–56); Ferrara, as *maestro di cappella* of the Accademia dello Spirito Santo (1656–65); and, finally, Venice, where he held a number of appointments in succession, culminating in that of *maestro di cappella* at S Marco (1685 until his death). There were difficult moments, such as in 1654 when he was temporarily dismissed from his post at Bergamo, and the disappointments of not becoming *Kapellmeister* at the Viennese court or *maestro di cappella* at either Milan

Cathedral (1669) or S Petronio, Bologna (1671).

He had to wait nearly ten years – half of them as vice-*maestro* – for the post at S Marco, having been passed over in 1676 when Natale Monferrato was appointed to succeed Cavalli, but during his tenure there as *maestro*, the *cappella* and the *concerto* of strings, cornetts, bassoon and trombones were expanded with the enthusiastic backing of the procurators. Legrenzi's extant sacred music (psalms and motets for a wide spectrum of forces) dates from his years at Bergamo and Ferrara; only a five-part Mass in *stile antico* (1689) survives from his Venetian years.

It was in Ferrara that Legrenzi began composing operas (very much in the style of P.A. Ziani and Cesti) for the Teatro S Stefano. In this he had been encouraged by a newly acquired patron and friend, Hippolito Bentivoglio, who provided him with a number of librettos. Such was the success of *L'Achille in Sciro* (1663) that it was produced in Venice the following year, at the Teatro S Salvatore, thereby establishing Legrenzi as an opera composer with whom to reckon. He wrote at least 14 operas for Venice (1668–84) and one for the Teatro Ducale in Mantua (1682). Several of his operas were revived during his lifetime – in particular, *Zenobia e Radamisto* (1665), *Germanico sul Reno* (1676), *Lisimaco riamato* (1682) and *Giustino* (1683) – at Bologna, Brescia, Macerata, Milan and Modena, and, after his death, at Florence, Genoa, Rome, Verona and Vicenza. He set at least one oratorio text by Bentivoglio, *Oratorio del giudito* (1665), which was performed not at Ferrara but at Vienna (when he was hoping to gain an appointment). During 1676–8 three oratorios were performed at the Accademia della Morte and two at the Chiesa di S Filippo Neri in Ferrara.

Among the most important features of Legrenzi's operas and oratorios were his instrumental sinfonias – comprising sonatas and dances – and aria ritornellos. To his formidable command of the traditions of fugal writing (inherited from Frescobaldi) and the manipulation of large forces (influenced by Gabrieli) Legrenzi brought a modern taste for incisive melodies and clear tonal harmonies. Six large collections of instrumental music – including sonatas for violin and continuo, trio and quartet sonatas, as well as two Venetian polychoral sonatas in six parts – were published in Venice (1655, 1656, 1663, 1673 and two posthumously), which served as an important influence on the sonatas and con-certos of Giuseppe Torelli, Vivaldi and even J.S. Bach.

Leo [Leone] da Modena (?1571–?1648). Jewish writer on music and a founder of the Accademia Musicale Ebraica (1629–39) in Venice. Leo lived in the Jewish ghetto of Mantua where he was a pupil of Salamone Rossi, whose polyphonic settings of Hebrew songs, *Hashirim asher lish'lomo* ('The Songs of Solomon') he edited in 1622; in the preface he presented a defence of the use of polyphonic singing in the synagogue, citing Talmudic and rabbinical sources.

Leoni, Leone (*c*1560–1627). Veronese composer who from 1588 to 1627 was *maestro di cappella* of Vicenza Cathedral and a member of the Accademia Olimpica. He composed madrigals and motets, some of which use instrumental trios in alternation with choral passages (1615), revealing his awareness of the stylistic transformation taking place.

L'Épine, Margharita de. See BRITISH ISLES *1 London*.

Lonati, Carlo Ambrogio. See ITALY *10 Itinerant Musicians*.

Lotti, Antonio (*c*1667–1740). Venetian *maestro di cappella* and teacher, prolific composer in the transitional style of the late Baroque and early Classical periods. Though Lotti was attached to S Marco for much of his career, his father had been *Kappellmeister* at Hanover and he himself worked in Dresden (1717–19). He was taught by Giovanni Legrenzi (whose 1683 opera *Giustino* was for a time attributed to Lotti) and was himself the teacher of such composers as Domenico Alberti, Girolamo Bassani, Baldassare Galuppi, Michelangelo Gasparini and Benedetto Marcello. His operatic career was confined to the period 1692–1719, during which he provided a steady stream of operas for the Venetian theatres of S Angelo, S Cassiano and S Giovanni Grisostomo, as well as for the Redoutensaal and Neues Opernhaus in Dresden (see Plate 8). At S Marco he was employed as an alto, organist and, from 1736, *primo maestro di cappella*; he composed a large quantity of music with organ accompaniment for the choir. His *Miserere* in D (1733) was regularly sung at the basilica on Maundy Thursday during the 18th century. He was a founder member of the musical fraternity of S Cecilia (estab. 1690) and was associated with the Ospedale degli Incurabili, where he exerted an important influence on the style of singing of his pupils, for whom he composed solo motets, choral works and oratorios.

In 1705 he published a collection of *Duetti,*

terzetti e madrigali a più voci, which he dedicated to Emperor Joseph I (presumably in the vain hope of gaining a post at the Habsburg court). His pupil Benedetto Marcello wrote critically of the collection (*c*1711–16) and Giovanni Bononcini later attempted to pass one of the works off as his own at a meeting of the Academy of Ancient Music in London (1731) – the Academy sought testimony from Lotti in Venice and, to the embarrassment of Bononcini and Maurice Greene, published a report the following year supporting Lotti. Lotti also composed a number of solo cantatas (some with strings) and occasional works for the doge's banquets.

Madonis, Luigi (*c*1690–*c*1770). Venetian violinist and composer working abroad. Madonis spent the first half of his career based in Venice (where he very probably was a pupil of Vivaldi) and the second in St Petersburg. From Venice, he toured with the Peruzzi opera troupe to Breslau in 1725 and Brussels in 1727; two years later they were in Paris to perform at the Concert Spirituel. Madonis remained for a while in the service of the Venetian ambassador in Paris, where he published a collection of violin sonatas (1731). Upon his return to Venice he was invited by Empress Anna's envoy to join the Russian court orchestra; accompanied by his brother (a violinist and horn player), he travelled to St Petersburg in 1733. Five years later he published a collection of 12 'symphonies' (actually suites for violin, cello and continuo, dedicated to the empress) which are among the few examples of Baroque music written and printed in Russia. Upon the coronation of the Regent Elizabeth in 1742, Madonis was appointed *Kapellmeister*; he retired in 1767. He was married twice, to an Italian woman and then a Russian.

Maggini, Giovanni Paolo (*c*1581–*c*1632). Highly esteemed violin maker of the Brescian school (a pupil of Gasparo da Salò), whose violas and cellos are thought to be the first on a small model; though compact in size, his violins are valued for their breadth of tone and depth of response and were much copied in their day. Maggini's influence is particularly evident in the instruments of Stradivari and Guarneri; he also made bass viols and Brescian citterns.

Manelli, Francesco [?'Il Fasolo'] (1594–1667). Singer, poet and composer who collaborated with the poet-composer Benedetto Ferrari on the earliest opera productions presented at the new opera houses in Venice during the late 1630s. After an early stint at Tivoli Cathedral, Manelli went to Rome (1624), where he met and married a Roman singer (Maddalena). They pursued their careers separately until 1637, when he joined his wife in Venice and began working with Ferrari. Manelli composed *L'Andromeda* (text by Ferrari) for the opening in 1637 of the Teatro S Cassiano, where their *La maga fulminata* was performed the following season; along with his wife, he took multiple roles in both productions. While holding a post in the choir of S Marco as a bass in 1639, Manelli also found time to collaborate with Giulio Strozzi on *La Delia*, which opened the new Teatro SS Giovanni e Paolo; *L'Adone* (once thought to be by Monteverdi) followed soon after. His last Venetian opera, *L'Alcate*, was performed at the Teatro Novissimo in 1642. In the interim he served as impresario for a tour by a Venetian troupe (which included Ferrari) to Bologna, where his wife (in the role of Venus) and their son Costantino (Cupid) sang in performances of *La Delia* and Monteverdi's *Il ritorno d'Ulisse in patria*. His last years were spent in Parma, where he composed musical dramas for the Farnese court theatre. None of his operas survives.

Marazzoli, Marco. See ITALY 7 *Papal States: Rome.*

Marcello. Two Venetian brothers, *nobili dilettanti*, the elder a composer, the younger a writer on music and a teacher, as well as a composer. Alessandro (1669–1750) sang, played the violin and composed music under his academic pseudonym, 'Eterio Stinfalico'. He and his younger brother were taught to play by their father, a Venetian senator, and took part in the weekly concerts held in their home. Later they were admitted to the Accademia dell'Arcadia in Rome. Although an amateur, Alessandro was well equipped as a composer: he is best known for his oboe concerto in D minor, which Bach transcribed for keyboard (BWV974), but about 1740 he also published at Augsburg a collection of violin solos and wind concertos entitled *La cetra* (for two flutes, oboe, bassoon, strings and continuo), which represent the late Venetian Baroque concerto style.

Benedetto Marcello (1686–1739) was forced by his father to pursue a career in law. After being chosen by lot in 1707 to sit on the Grand Council of the Republic, he held a series of important posts in public service: he was governor of Pola from 1730 until 1737, and chamberlain of Brescia from 1738 until his death; he also worked as an advocate and magistrate. In spite of these responsibilities, he pursued a musical career on several fronts.

In addition to the Roman Accademia dell'Arcadia (where he was known as 'Driante Sacreo'), Benedetto belonged to the Bolognese Accademia Filarmonica. He may have written an opera libretto (*La fede riconosciuta*) and then set it for Vicenza in 1707; certainly Alessandro Scarlatti set it in 1710. In 1709 G.M. Ruggieri set another of his librettos, *Arato in Sparta*.

Marcello published a set of 12 *Concerti a cinque* in 1708, then a collection of recorder sonatas in Amsterdam in 1717. But it was only in 1724 that he really began to achieve wider fame as a composer: his settings in cantata style of the first 50 psalms (paraphrased in Italian), which appeared in eight volumes over a two-year period under the title *Estro-poetico-armonico*, attracted favourable comment from Telemann, Mattheson, Giovanni Bononcini and D.N. Sarro. He composed over 400 cantatas and, in 1725, was commissioned to compose a serenata for Emperor Charles VI's birthday. Among his other works were two collections of cello sonatas (*c*1732 and *c*1734), concertos and sinfonias, and, from the last years of his life, sacred music cast in a conservative style.

His name was most closely associated with satire and criticism. He is thought to have written the *Lettera famigliare d'un accademico filarmonico ed arcade discorsiva sopra un libro di duetti, terzetti e madrigali a più voci* (1705), which castigated a much praised collection by Antonio Lotti. Certainly he was the unrepentant author of the satire on Italian opera – particularly that of Vivaldi and his contemporaries – known as *Il teatro alla moda* (1720), and of a satire on castrato singers entitled *Il flagello dei musici* (1721), containing two madrigals. Nevertheless, his pupils included the opera singer Faustina Bordoni and the composer Baldassare Galuppi; another became his wife in 1728. He died of consumption, leaving unfinished a final literary work, *L'universale redenzione*.

Marini, Biagio. See ITALY *10 Itinerant Musicians*.

Mauro. Venetian family of stage designers and engineers who worked not only in the Venetian theatres but also throughout Italy and at Dresden, Munich and Paris. Gaspare (*fl* 1657–*c*1719) and Pietro Mauro (*fl* 1669–*c*1697) often worked together, sometimes with Domenico Mauro (*fl* 1669–1707), on productions of the operas of Cavalli, Cesti, Antonio Sartorio, Giovanni Legrenzi and P.A. Ziani. To meet the challenge of staging comic operas shorn of myth and allegory new techniques of illusion were required: the Mauros employed split backcloths and devised more natural stage properties; they created sets made up of partly enclosed rooms in buildings of several storeys; and they developed new angled perspectives with more than one vanishing-point. They were also respected designers of Venetian ceremonial barges (*peòtes*) used for theatrical regattas on the canals.

The sons of Gaspare and Domenico followed them in the profession. Domenico's son Alessandro (*fl c*1709–1748) was the most successful and innovative. He worked with Lotti, Leonardo Leo, Nicola Porpora and J.A. Hasse on *opera seria* productions for court performances in which he was able to introduce formal elements of bourgeois realism, which he and his family had developed for the public opera houses of Venice.

Merula, Tarquinio (1594/5–1665). Cremonese violinist, organist and composer. Merula was a gifted musician but of unstable temperament, unable to remain in any post for long – though he did serve five years (1621–6) as organist to Sigismund III at Warsaw. He was lucky merely to be dismissed as *maestro di cappella* at S Maria Maggiore, Bergamo, after committing acts of indecency towards pupils in 1632. But when he returned to Bergamo six years later to take up the joint posts of *maestro di cappella* and organist at the cathedral adjacent to S Maria Maggiore, the authorities there refused to allow their musicians to perform at the cathedral as long as he remained in charge. He was a member of the Bolognese Accademia dei Filomusi and a Knight of the Golden Spur.

Merula was among the first to compose motets with instrumental (string) accompaniment: *Il primo libro de motetti e sonate concertati* (1624) and *Libro secondo de concerti spirituali con alcune sonate* (1628) were published in Venice. He also composed Masses and Vesper psalms (using ostinato basses), concerted madrigals and *canzonette*; he even contributed to a Venetian opera, *La finta savia* (1643). However, his most important legacy is his four collections of violin *canzoni* (1615–51) in which he gradually developed what became known as the *sonata da chiesa* by reducing the texture from four to two or three parts and by sharpening the contrasts between one section and the next.

Minato, Nicolò. See CENTRAL EUROPE *3 Austro-Hungary: Vienna*.

Mingotti, Angelo and **Pietro.** See ITALY *10 Itinerant Musicians*.

Monferrato, Natale (*c*1603–85). Organist,

composer and, ultimately, *maestro di cappella* at S Marco. As a pupil and assistant of Giovanni Rovetta, Monferrato had expected to succeed him at S Marco in 1668, but was passed over for Cavalli who, nearly 30 years earlier, had also been preferred for the post of second organist; Monferrato was finally appointed (to the disappointment of Cavalli's protégé Giovanni Legrenzi) in 1676 and proved himself an excellent *maestro*. He composed motets and psalms for performances at the Mendicanti and Masses in the *stile antico* for S Marco. He owned and operated a publishing firm with Giuseppe Sala.

Montagnana, Domenico (*c*1687–1750). String instrument maker working in Venice. Montagnana first worked with Matteo Goffriller, then started his own business in 1711. He built large cellos renowned for their tone.

Monteverdi, Claudio. See ITALY *3 Mantua.*

Moratelli, Sebastiano. See NORTHERN EUROPE *5 West Germany and the Rhineland.*

Nacchini, Pietro (1694–1765). The pre-eminent Venetian organ builder of his day, who produced about 500 instruments for Venice and the surrounding cities. He invented the *tiratutti*, or stop-knob, which unites all of the ripieno ranks and was the forerunner of composition pedals.

Neri [Negri], Massimiliano (?1615–66). Organist and composer. The son of a musician who had served at the courts of Munich, Neuburg and Düsseldorf, Neri spent most of his life in Venice: from 1644 to 1664 he was first organist at S Marco and simultaneously at the church of SS Giovanni e Paolo; from 1655 he was also *maestro di musica* at the Ospedaletto. That he maintained important connections with the Viennese court is clear from his elevation to the nobility, the gift of Emperor Ferdinand III in 1651. He travelled to Cologne in 1663 and took up posts as organist and *Kapellmeister* there the following year.

Though he was well known during his life for his instrumental music, most is now lost. However his op. 1 sonatas and canzonas for three to four instruments (1644) demonstrate his command of fugal writing, graceful slow movements and virtuoso passage-work; his op. 2 sonatas for three to 12 instruments (1651) are important precursors of the early 18th-century Venetian concertos.

Nicolini. See ITALY *10 Itinerant Musicians.*

Notari, Angelo. See BRITISH ISLES *1 London.*

Pallavicino, Carlo. See ITALY *10 Itinerant Musicians.*

Pallavicino, Stefano Benedetto. See NORTHERN EUROPE *4 Saxony and Thuringia: Dresden.*

Pariati, Pietro (1665–1733). Poet and librettist. Pariati collaborated with Apostolo Zeno, whom he met about 1699 in Venice, soon after his release from prison (where he had served three years); Zeno provided the scenarios and Pariati the lyrical verses for their dramatic texts, which were collected and published in Venice (1744), Paris (1757) and elsewhere in Europe, and were set by such composers as Francesco Gasparini, Giovanni Porta, Nicolò Jommelli, C.F. Pollarolo, G.M. Orlandini and Baldassare Galuppi. In 1714 Pariati was invited to the Viennese court of Charles VI, and Zeno joined him four years later; their collaboration continued until 1729 when Zeno retired and his place at court was assumed by Metastasio. Pariati also wrote opera, oratorio, serenata and cantata librettos on his own which were set by Antonio Lotti, Gasparini, Albinoni, Nicola Porpora, Francesco Feo and F.B. Conti.

Partenio, Gian Domenico (before 1650–1701). Venetian singer, opera composer and *maestro di cappella* at S Marco. Partenio was trained there and served as vice-*maestro di cappella* (from 1685), before succeeding G.B. Volpe in 1692. He was also associated with the Ospedale dei Mendicanti and the Ospedale degli Incurabili, and founded the Società S Cecilia comprising 100 performers and teachers (including Giovanni Legrenzi and Volpe). Partenio's patrons included Prince Eugenio of Savoy, as well as a German duchess and two Italian counts. The earliest of his five operas, *Genserico* (1669; text by Beregan), was for a time attributed to Cesti.

Pederzuoli, Giovanni Battista. See CENTRAL EUROPE *3 Austro-Hungary: Vienna.*

Perti, Giacomo Antonio. See ITALY *7 Papal States: Bologna-Ferrara.*

Pescetti, Giovanni Battista (*c*1704–66). Venetian opera composer who replaced Nicola Porpora as director of the ill-fated Opera of the Nobility in London. Pescetti worked in the Venetian theatres from 1725 until 1732 (sometimes collaborating with Baldassare Galuppi), before making his way to London in 1736. While there he became known as a harpsichordist as well as an opera composer, and in 1739 published a set of keyboard sonatas to which were appended arrangements of the overture and arias from his opera *La conquista del velo d'oro* (given at the King's Theatre the previous year). By 1747 he had returned to Venice and in 1762 was appointed second organist at S Marco. Pescetti also composed oratorios, of which only *Gionata* survives.

Platti, Giovanni Benedetto. See NORTHERN EUROPE *6 Middle Germany*.

Pollarolo. Composers, father and son. Carlo Francesco Pollarolo (*c*1653–1723) was an organist, *maestro di cappella* and prolific opera composer of the late Venetian School; between 1680 and 1722, he composed 85 operas and 13 oratorios. He succeeded his father as organist at Brescia Cathedral in 1676 and from the mid 1680s he was active as an opera and oratorio composer, producing works for Vienna, Venice and Verona as well as Brescia. When in 1690 he took up the post of second organist at S Marco, he was already well known as an opera composer.

Between 1691 and 1707 Pollarolo produced at least one opera a year for the prestigious Teatro S Giovanni Grisostomo and had revivals of other works performed at the theatres of S Angelo, S Cassiano and S Fantino. He was fond of special effects – offstage singers and instrumentalists and echoes (in *Onorio in Roma*, 1692, he employed both a five-part orchestra on stage and three-part *concertino* complement) – and was one of the first Venetian composers to write for the oboe (*La forza della virtù*, 1693). Passages of expressive arioso were superseded by larger-scale accompanied arias, which in turn were interrupted by dramatic accompanied recitative, contrasting long sections of *secco* recitatives. Although choruses are to be found only in his oratorios, he did incorporate short trios, quartets and quintets into his opera finales.

In 1702 he competed unsuccessfully for the post of *primo maestro* at S Marco, losing by only one vote to Antonio Biffi. From 1696 until shortly before his death Pollarolo served as *maestro di cappella* of the Ospedale degli Incurabili, for whom he composed Latin oratorios. His son Antonio (1676–1746) assumed his duties as assistant *maestro di cappella* at S Marco in 1702 and finally rose to *primo maestro*, succeeding Antonio Lotti, in 1740. He composed operas (mostly lost) in the first years of the century, then oratorios for the Venetian *ospedali* (1714–18); in 1716 he composed an *Oratorio per il Ss Natale* for Rome and in 1724 a serenata, *I tre voti*, for the Austrian ambassador to Venice.

Porpora, Nicola. See ITALY *10 Itinerant Musicians*.

Porta, Giovanni (*c*1675–1755). Well-born Venetian composer whose opera *Numitore* (text by Rolli) inaugurated the first season (1720) of the Royal Academy of Music in

London. Porta reportedly worked in Rome between 1706 and 1716 in the household of Cardinal Ottoboni, before returning to Venice to devote himself over the next decade to opera. In 1726 he accepted an appointment as *maestro di coro* at the Ospedale della Pietà; in addition to his teaching and conducting duties he composed a large quantity of motets, continuing – if more slowly – to produce operas. Following an unsuccessful bid to become *maestro di cappella* at S Marco, Porta left Venice for Munich, where he became *Hofkapellmeister* in 1737. He produced several operas, cantatas, and serenatas and a large quantity of church music for the Pietà and the Bavarian court.

Priuli, Giovanni (*c*1575–1629). Venetian organist and composer whose music was indelibly influenced by his teacher Giovanni Gabrieli. Priuli's first post was in the service of the Duchess of Urbino in Venice, and from 1609 until 1612 he was associated with the Scuola di S Rocco; during that time he published three collections of madrigals which demonstrate his skill in both *a cappella* and concertato idioms. He worked for the Habsburgs from about 1615 until 1622, first as *Hofkapellmeister* at the Graz court of Archduke Ferdinand and then, from 1619, when the archduke became Emperor Ferdinand II, at Vienna. He published two volumes of *Sacri concentus* (1618–19) for five to 12 voices, demonstrating a preference for lower voices; separate instrumental music for liturgical use is appended to them. In spite of his period of residence in Austria, all his music (other than single works in anthologies) was published in Venice. Two further collections of madrigals appeared in 1622 and 1625 and two volumes of concerted Masses in 1624.

Rigatti, Giovanni Antonio (1615–49). Priest, singer and composer associated with S Marco, where he worked with Giovanni Rovetta. At the age of 20 Rigatti was appointed *maestro di cappella* at Udine Cathedral, a post he held for only two years. By 1646 he had become *maestro di cappella* to the Patriarch of Venice; he also taught at the Ospedale degli Incurabili.

Rigatti's music inevitably owes much to Monteverdi's. His sacred works include two books of solo motets, three of concertante motets (with parts for violins) and four of psalm settings. In 1640 he dedicated his volume of *Messa e salmi* to the Holy Roman Emperor Ferdinand III, presumably in the hope of gaining a position – which in the event did not materialize – at the Viennese court. Rigatti published two collections of secular music, *Musiche concertate cioe madrigali* (1636) and *Musiche diverse* (1641), which are melodious, varied by changes in dynamics and tempo and coherent in their structure (many, in fact, rely upon popular ground basses).

Ristori, Giovanni Alberto. See NORTHERN EUROPE *4 Saxony and Thuringia: Dresden.*

Rogeri, Giovanni Baptista (*fl c*1670–*c*1705). Bolognese violin maker, admired for the elegant appearance of his instruments, who worked at Brescia from about 1675. He was assisted by his son Pietro Giacomo ['Ruggerius'] (*fl c*1690–1720), a fine craftsman whose instruments are prized for their tone.

Roseingrave, Thomas. See BRITISH ISLES *1 London.*

Rosenmüller, Johann (*c*1619–1684). Organist, teacher and composer, who was forced to leave Leipzig in 1655 and sought refuge for nearly 30 years in Venice, before returning as *Kapellmeister* to the Wolfenbüttel court towards the end of his life. After studies in theology at the University of Leipzig, Rosenmüller taught at the Thomasschule for well over a decade (1642–55), with the expectation of one day becoming *Kantor* of the Thomaskirche; he also served as organist of the Nicolaikirche from 1651 and as *Kapellmeister in absentia* of the Altenburg court in 1654. In connection with his teaching he published two collections of ensemble suites, *Paduanen* (1645) and *Studenten-Music* (1654), as well as sacred concertos (influenced by Schütz's *Symphoniae sacrae*, for which Rosenmüller served as Leipzig distributor) – *Kern-Sprüche* (1648) and its sequel (1652–3). Sadly his reputation was hopelessly tarnished by his conviction for practising homosexuality with schoolboys and his subsequent escape from prison.

By 1658 Rosenmüller had found his way to Venice, where he first worked as a trombonist at S Marco. He took on pupils, among them J.P. Krieger (1673–4), and commissions: his music included solo cantatas, 53 settings of Latin psalms (some for solo voice, violins and continuo, others for double choruses, soloists and instruments). In 1667 he published a collection of five-part *Sonate da camera*. During this time many of his works found their way back to Germany in manuscript copies, a few bearing dedications to prominent people at the Wolfenbüttel court. From 1678 until 1682 he was associated with the Ospedale della Pietà. His past forgotten, Rosenmüller was able to spend his last years in a respected post in his native Germany.

Rovetta, Giovanni (*c*1595–1668). Priest,

singer and composer working in the shadow of Monteverdi, whom he assisted (from 1627) and then succeeded (1644) as *maestro di cappella* at S Marco. Rovetta's first collection of *Salmi concertati* (1626) was actually a *potpourri* of concertato motets, psalms and instrumental pieces; the quality and promise of his work – on a par with that of Alessandro Grandi and Ignazio Donati – is evident in the 'Salve regina' for tenor duet in which declamation, counterpoint and imaginative harmony are wielded with skill and sensitivity to the text. He provided instrumental parts for his ceremonial Masses and psalms (op. 4, 1639), while his four volumes of motets (1635, 1639, 1648, 1650) are scored more intimately, for two to four voices and organ. Likewise, his three volumes of madrigals (1629, 1640, 1645) embrace a compendium of current forms and possible forces, and are greatly indebted to Monteverdi. Rovetta is known to have produced two operas (both lost) in the late 1640s.

Sacrati, Francesco (1605–50). Opera composer active in Venice, where he collaborated with the stage designer Giacomo Torelli during the 1640s, before briefly taking up posts as *maestro di cappella* of the 'Commedia a li musici' (based in Bologna) and Modena Cathedral. His most important opera was *La finta pazza* (libretto by G. Strozzi), which celebrated the opening of the Venetian Teatro Novissimo in 1641; four years later it became one of the first Italian operas to be performed in Paris, undoubtedly at the suggestion of Torelli, who was by then working on the sets and machinery for the French court entertainments devised by Cardinal Mazarin.

Sala, Giuseppe (*fl* 1676–1715). Printer, publisher and bookseller active in Venice between 1685 and 1705. Earlier Sala had been associated in business with the composer Natale Monferrato (*d* 1685), from whose house at S Giovanni Grisostomo they ran their business. Their earliest known print was Monferrato's own *Salmi concertati a 2 voci con violini e senza* (1676). Sala continued the business after Monferrato's death, publishing psalms (by Sartorio and Cazzati), motets (by Legrenzi, Allegri, Bonporti, G.M. Bononcini and Gasparini), cantatas (by Caldara, Gregori and Albinoni) and sonatas (by Vitali, Legrenzi, Corelli, Torelli and Marcello).

Sartorio, Antonio (1630–80). A leading Venetian opera composer during the 1660s and 1670s who also served as *Kapellmeister* of the Catholic Hanover court of the italophile Duke Johann Friedrich (1665–75). Sartorio maintained his connections – indeed, his base of operations – in Venice, where he often spent the winter during his years at Hanover, ostensibly acquiring musicians for the following year's musical productions; in 1672 he spent the entire year in Venice, during which he composed and produced three operas, *L'Adelaide*, *L'Orfeo* and *Massenzio* (which opened early in 1673). He claimed to have composed *Massenzio* (containing 78 arias and duets) in 13 days after Cavalli's opera of the same name was dropped from production. In 1667 his double opera *La prosperità d'Elio Seiano* and *La caduta d'Elio Seiano* was performed during the Venetian Carnival (the librettist, Minato, wished them to be performed on successive nights but Sartorio and the singers objected).

In 1676 he returned definitively to Venice and became vice-*maestro di cappella* at S Marco. That same year his heroic opera *Giulio Cesare in Egitto* was performed at the Teatro S Luca (where most of his operas had been given). Four more operas followed and a fifth, *La Flora*, was completed by Marc' Antonio Ziani and performed at the Teatro S Angelo at the end of 1680. Sartorio was a gifted aria composer, at home in many formats and affects, but best when composing laments on ostinato basses and trumpet arias (he also frequently used trumpets in his sinfonias), and when juxtaposing heroic and comic characters.

Scarlatti, Alessandro. See ITALY *7 Papal States: Rome.*

Senesino. See ITALY *10 Itinerant Musicians.*

Silvani, Francesco. See ITALY *3 Mantua.*

Steffani, Agostino. See NORTHERN EUROPE *1 North Germany.*

Strada del Pò, Anna Maria. See BRITISH ISLES *1 London.*

Stradella, Alessandro. See ITALY *7 Papal States: Rome.*

Strozzi. Father and adopted daughter, the one a prolific poet and librettist who founded the Accademia degli Unisoni, the other a singer and composer of solo arias and cantatas. Giulio Strozzi (1583–1652), a member of the well-known Florentine family, first gained distinction as the librettist of Monteverdi's *La finta pazza Licori* (1627) and *Proserpina rapita* (1630); Monteverdi also set his sonnets *I cinque fratelli* (1628). He was an important force in the development of Venetian opera in the 1630s and 1640s. For the opening of the Teatro SS Giovanni e Paolo in 1639 Francesco Manelli set *La Delia*; for the opening of the Teatro Novissimo two years later Francesco Sacrati set *La finta pazza*, which was also

performed before the French court in 1645. Cavalli set his last libretto, *Veremonda*, given in Naples in 1652.

Strozzi had been trained in law and became an apostolic prothonotary in Rome where he helped to found the literary Accademia degli Ordinati. He lived in Padua and then Urbino before returning to Venice in the early 1620s, where he became a member of the Accademia degli Incogniti. By founding and hosting the Accademia degli Unisoni he was able to provide his adopted daughter Barbara (1619–*c*1664) with a stimulating intellectual and musical circle, which would not otherwise have been open to a woman. His desire to develop and promote her was not merely an expression of filial love: among his unpublished works was a volume of 'Elogii delle donne virtuose del nostro secolo'.

With Barbara presiding at the meetings of the Unisoni, discourses were read (and later published in the *Veglie de' Signori Unisoni*, 1638, dedicated to Barbara) and music performed. Presumably many of her works were composed to be performed on these occasions; at least one other member of the academy, Nicolò Fontei, provided her with volumes of songs (using texts supplied by Giulio Strozzi; 1635, 1636). The unorthodoxy of her participation (possibly as a courtesan) at these meetings was pointedly acknowledged in a manuscript series of eight 'Satire, e altre raccolte per l'Accademia de gli Unisoni' (1637) but later praised by members of the Incogniti (the Unisoni's parent academy) in a collection of eulogies to Giulio (1647).

Barbara Strozzi studied composition with Cavalli, whose influence may be seen in her 1644 collection of madrigals (settings of her father's texts dedicated to the Grand Duchess of Tuscany) for two to five voices and continuo, although in general her style is more lyrical than Cavalli's. Several of her works were included next to Cavalli's in contemporary anthologies. She published eight collections of her music – a significant enough achievement for a woman at that time – but in sheer numbers she published more cantatas than any other 17th-century composer. The cantatas, as well as the arias and duets, which appeared during the 1650s (the 1651 collection was dedicated to Ferdinand II of Austria), are musically original and reflect her literary background (in the sensitive treatment of text) and her training as a singer (in her idiomatic handling of voices). Particularly attractive are the ground-bass lament *Udite, amanti, la Cagione* (1651), the solo cantata *Lagrime mie*

(1659) and the final collection of *Arie a voce sola* (1664).

Taglietti. Two Brescian musicians, probably brothers, who were associated with the Jesuit Collegio dei Nobili. Giulio (*c*1660–1718) and Luigi (1668–1715) were both composers of instrumental music which was published in Bologna, Venice and Amsterdam (by Pierre Mortier). Giulio, a violinist, brought out a collection of four solo violin concertos (op. 8) in about 1709, antedating Vivaldi's (op. 3) by two years; his instrumental collections include the *Arie da sonare* (op. 10, *c*1711) and *Pensieri da camera* (op. 12, *c*1714).

Tartini, Giuseppe (1692–1770). Paduan violinist, composer, teacher and theorist. One of the greatest violinists of the 18th century, Tartini brought the virtuoso sonata and violin concerto to their highest mid-18th-century state (a mixture of *galant* and *empfindsam* styles). Like many gifted people Tartini was unconventional. He rebelled against his parents' intention that he should become a monk, though he did take minor orders; he briefly studied law in 1709 at Padua, but excelled rather more at fencing; he married in 1710, incurring the displeasure of the Bishop of Padua and obliging himself to take up asylum in a monastery at Assisi. But it was there that his study of music began.

Eventually in 1715 he was pardoned and allowed to live with his wife. It was probably in the following year, however, that he heard Veracini play at a private concert in Venice and promptly parted with her in order to devote himself exclusively to the violin. By 1721 he was made *primo violino e capo di concerto* at the Basilica di S Antonio in Padua, with the freedom to travel and play elsewhere. In 1723 (threatened with a paternity suit) he departed with his cellist friend Antonio Vandini for Prague, where he was a soloist at the coronation celebrations of Emperor Charles VI; they remained there, in the service of the Bohemian court chancellor Count Kinsky, until 1726, when they returned to Padua.

In 1727 Tartini founded a violin school (where he also taught harmony and counterpoint) which attracted students from far and wide, among them J.G. Graun, Pietro Nardini, J.G. Naumann, G.A. Paganelli and A.-N. Pagin; he was an excellent correspondent and kept in touch with his students after they left him. Tartini's *Traité des agréments* (published just after his death) must have existed in manuscript, for the use of his pupils, long before Leopold Mozart compiled his *Violinschule* (1756); likewise, his *Trattato di musica*, setting out his controversial theories of acoustics, was widely read in manuscript and discussed before it was published in 1754.

Most of Tartini's surviving music dates from after 1728, much of it for S Antonio; of the many contemporary editions of his music only the sonata prints of 1734 and 1745 and the trios published in London in 1750 were personally supervised. His first collections were published in Amsterdam – the *Sei concerti a 5* in 1728 and the *VI sonate* in 1732 – which greatly enhanced his reputation abroad; further collections of sonatas and concertos (*a 8*) followed in 1734, 1740 and 1743. The sonatas exhibit a three-movement plan, slow introduction–Allegro–contrasting finale, all in the same key and cast in binary structures. The concertos show the progressive influence of Vivaldi in their pattern of fast–slow–fast, with the slow movement in a contrasting key; the outer movements rely upon the alternation of four tutti *ritornelli* with extended solo passages, increasingly characterized by regular four-bar phrases and elaborate cadence formulae. Tartini's music is not as predictable as Vivaldi's and in fact became gradually less technical and more expressive in the mid 1740s.

His international solo career ended in 1740 when he injured an arm at Bergamo. He retreated to Padua and the company of the theorist F.A. Vallotti and the astronomer Gianrinaldo Carli, with whom he could discuss *musica speculativa*, temperament and acoustics. He claimed to have discovered the phenomenon of the 'difference tone' or 'third sound' as early as 1714; he wrote about it in the *Trattato* and later in the *De' principi* (1767), though his arguments are flawed by mathematical inaccuracies.

Tartini was a member of the Accademia dei Ricovrati and the Congregazione dei Musicisti (for whom he and Vandini occasionally played). He habitually appended poetic mottoes (purloined from Metastasio's dramas) to his instrumental music and secret ciphers to manuscripts. Most of his music circulated in manuscript copies, making accurate dating impossible, but several collections of concertos were published in Amsterdam, sonatas and the *L'arte del arco* (containing 38 variations on a Corelli gavotte, 1758) in Paris, and other instrumental works in London, Rome and Padua. He produced a few sacred works – *canzoncine sacre* for one to three voices, motets and a *Stabat mater* for three voices. Tartini retired from S Antonio in 1765, suffered a mild stroke in 1768 and died of gangrene (from an ulcerated foot) two years later.

Tesi, Vittoria. See ITALY *10 Itinerant Musicians.*

Tessarini, Carlo. See ITALY *10 Itinerant Musicians.*

Tononi, Carlo. See ITALY *7 Papal States: Bologna-Ferrara.*

Torelli, Giacomo. See FRANCE *1 Paris and Versailles.*

Torelli, Giuseppe. See ITALY *7 Papal States: Bologna-Ferrara.*

Turini, Francesco (*c*1589–1656). Italian organist and composer, born in Prague. After his appointment as the Prague court organist at the age of 12, Turini studied in Venice and Rome; though he returned to Prague, he was next heard of in Venice, in the service of G.F. Morosini. In 1620 he became organist at Brescia Cathedral, where he remained until his death. Once settled, he began to publish his music: the three collections of madrigals with parts for two violins and continuo which appeared in 1621, 1624 and 1629 may be reckoned among the earliest concertato vocal chamber music. The first book is especially notable for containing one of the earliest separate trio sonatas (for two violins and continuo); the title of the second book uses the term 'cantata' (meaning an extended recitative); and in the third Turini suggests using a chitarrone with keyboard to accompany the violins. He published solo motets in 1629 and 1640 and a collection of Masses in 1643.

Usper, Francesco (before 1570–early 1641). Organist, composer and priest working in Venice. He was devoted to the confraternity of S Giovanni Evangelista, where he was known as 'Sponga'. Along with Monteverdi and G.B. Grillo, Usper contributed music to a Requiem Mass (now lost) honouring the Medici Grand Duke, Cosimo II, which was performed at the church of SS Giovanni e Paolo in 1621. He had hoped to succeed Grillo as organist at S Marco, but although he served as an interim organist (1622–3), he failed to gain a permanent appointment. In addition to Masses, motets and psalms, Usper published one of the earliest collections of Venetian ensemble canzonas, the *Ricercari et arie francesi* (1595). His *Compositioni armoniche* (1619) is a *potpourri* of sacred and distinctly varied instrumental genres (comprising two sinfonias, two canzonas, two capriccios and a sonata).

Valentini, Giovanni. See CENTRAL EUROPE *3 Austro-Hungary: Vienna.*

Vallotti, Francesco Antonio (1697–1780). *Maestro di cappella* at Padua, composer and theorist, known for his system of unequal temperament for tuning keyboard instruments. Vallotti maintained later in life that he and F.A. Calegari had worked out the mathematical relationship between the root position and inversions of chords in 1728 (apparently without knowledge of Rameau's 1722 *Traité de l'harmonie*), although the first volume of his *Della scienza teorica e pratica* was not published until the year of his death and the remaining three (passed on to Padre Martini in 1783) not until 1950. In them he described intervals and chords, and offered practical musical guidance – notably in the form of his tuning system. He prepared other theoretical works and was an energetic correspondent.

Vallotti was elected *maestro di cappella* at the Basilica di S Antonio, Padua, in 1730, after studies with Calegari, his predecessor; in addition to a choir of 16, he inherited a superb orchestra of 16 strings (led by Tartini – with whom he shared a keen interest in mathematics – and including the cellist Antonio Vandini) and several wind players which flourished until 1749. He composed a variety of sacred music in the concerted choral style and, as a devoted contrapuntist, transcribed many of Palestrina's Masses during his tenure.

Vandini, Antonio (*c*1690–*c*1771). Franciscan friar and cellist who from 1721 was first cellist at the Basilica di S Antonio, Padua, where he became a close friend and colleague of Tartini. Vandini had earlier served as *maestro di violoncello* at Bergamo Cathedral and in Venice, replacing Vivaldi (who may have composed concertos for him), at the Ospedale della Pietà. In 1723 he accompanied Tartini to Prague, where they played in the music for the celebrations marking the coronation of Charles VI; afterwards they remained until 1726 in the service of the Bohemian court chancellor Count Kinsky, declining invitations to London and, instead, returning to Padua. For 20 years (from 1728) Vandini and Tartini regularly played together for the Accademia dei Ricovrati and the Congregazione dei Musicisti; Tartini composed two concertos for Vandini. They lived together in their last years (after the death of Tartini's wife in 1769), and Vandini is thought to have compiled the materials for Tartini's biography after the composer's death in 1770.

Veracini, Francesco Maria. See ITALY *6 Tuscany.*

Verocai, Giovanni. See ITALY *10 Itinerant Musicians.*

Vivaldi, Antonio (Lucio) (1678–1741). Virtuoso violinist and important composer of violin sonatas, trio sonatas, concerti grossi and, in particular, solo concertos, which epitomize the Italian violin idiom of the early 18th century. Vivaldi's handling of solo and ripieno forces and materials greatly influenced his contemporaries and the succeeding generation of European composers – among them Tartini, P.A. Locatelli, Bach and Telemann.

Known as 'il prete rosso' because of his red hair, Vivaldi was associated nearly all his life (if off and on) with the Venetian Ospedale della Pietà. He took up his first post there as *maestro di violino* in 1703, and much of his music was composed for his pupils there. The intermittency of his employment at the Pietà was a reflection of the nature of his genius. Though a priest (he was tonsured in 1693), he was a volatile man (who admittedly channelled much of his considerable energy into violin pyrotechnics), ambitious, remarkably vain, penurious and extremely sensitive to criticism (he felt that he was not taken seriously as a composer – particularly of opera – and indeed such respected contemporaries as Goldoni, Benedetto Marcello, C.P.E. Bach and Quantz found his music banal).

He was often absent from Venice for Carnival seasons and when his concertos and operas were performed as far afield as Amsterdam (where his instrumental chamber music was commissioned and published by Roger and Le Cène), Dresden, Vienna and Prague. His integrity as a priest was compromised by innuendos regarding his relationships with the contralto Anna Giraud, formerly his pupil, and her sister Paolina, who travelled in his entourage; in 1738, the Cardinal-Archbishop of Ferrara forbade him to enter the city because he persisted in sinful behaviour and refused to say Mass. Vivaldi suffered from chronic bronchial asthma, exacerbated by the rigours of travel, and when he died in Vienna he was buried in a pauper's grave.

After publishing his first two collections of Corellian trio (1705) and solo sonatas (1709) in Venice, Vivaldi formed with Estienne Roger (the Amsterdam music printer and publisher) an important alliance which greatly expedited the dissemination of his violin music throughout Europe: *L'estro armonico* (concertos for 1, 2 and 4 solo violins; op. 3) appeared in 1711, *La stravaganza* (solo concertos; op. 4) in 1714, duo and trio sonatas (op. 5) in 1716, the two collections of *Concerti a 5 stromenti* (opp. 6 and 7) in 1716–17, *Il cimento dell'armonia e dell'inventione* (containing the 'Four Seasons'

concertos; op. 8) in 1725, *La cetra* (op. 9) in 1727 and string concertos (opp. 11 and 12) in 1729. The first complete set of flute concertos ever to be published appeared in 1728 as op. 10. Vivaldi dedicated op. 9 to Emperor Charles VI and was rewarded with money and a gold medallion and chain.

Vivaldi was a gifted orchestrator. Of approximately 350 solo concertos over 100 were for instruments other than the violin and flute, including the recorder (2), flautino (3), oboe (20), viola d'amore (6), mandoline (1), cello (27) and bassoon (39) – some of which duplicate one another as transcriptions (Vivaldi was a great self-borrower). There are over 40 double concertos for two violins, two trumpets etc., as well as for unusual combinations such as viola d'amore and lute; at least 30 concertos for three or more soloists (like the *Concerto funebre* RV579 for violin, oboe, chalumeau and 3 violas all'inglese); 60 *concerti ripieni* (similar to opera sinfonias); 20 concertos for groups of solo instruments (without a ripieno complement); and a few for double string orchestra and soloists. Many bear descriptive titles, alluding to the original performance and the soloists, other titles are simply programmatic, while still others make reference to a technical feature of the solo part. About 1730 he stopped composing new music for publication in Amsterdam.

During this period Vivaldi was also actively composing vocal music (much with instrumental accompaniment and, occasionally, obbligatos): solo cantatas (for *conversazioni* and the female voices at the Pietà); serenatas; operas (of which 21 survive); a variety of sacred music (well known are the *Gloria* RV589 and the *Magnificat* RV610–11); and oratorios (*Juditha triumphans*, 1716, met with particular acclaim). His earliest opera, *Ottone in villa* (text by Lalli), was performed in 1713, though at Vicenza rather than Venice. However, soon afterwards he became attached as both a composer and entrepreneur to the Venetian Teatro S Angelo, where *Orlando finto pazzo* (text by Braccioli) was performed in 1714; he maintained this association over the years and, fittingly, his last opera, *Feraspe* (text by Silvani) was given there in 1739, although his operas were occasionally produced at the nearby theatres of S Samuele and S Moisè.

Vivaldi also eagerly sought the opera public beyond the lagoon: the Teatro Capranica in Rome and the archducal theatre in Mantua were frequent Carnival venues for his operas, as well as the theatres at Milan, Florence, Reggio, Ferrara and Verona. The Sporck theatre in Prague mounted *Argippo* (text by Lalli) in 1730 and *Alvilda* the following spring; *Didone*, a *pasticcio* with arias by Vivaldi, was performed in London in 1737. His music (many autographs survive) was rationally and comprehensively catalogued by Peter Ryom (1974).

Volpe [**Rovettino**], **Giovanni Battista** (*c*1620–91). Organist at S Marco, who eventually became *maestro di cappella* in 1690, and composer of a volume of eight-part *Vesperi* (1649) and three operas for the Teatro SS Giovanni e Paolo (1659–64).

Wagenseil, Georg Christoph. See CENTRAL EUROPE *3 Austro-Hungary: Vienna.*

Zeno, Apostolo. See CENTRAL EUROPE *3 Austro-Hungary: Vienna.*

Ziani. Two prominent Venetian opera composers, who each spent several years at the Viennese court. Pietro Andrea Ziani (*d*1684) was a contemporary of Cavalli and a leading exponent of burlesque comedy. He later proved himself an oratorio and instrumental composer of some contrapuntal skill. His first opera, *La guerriera spartana*, was performed at the Teatro S Apollinare in 1654. After working in Innsbruck (1662), Vienna (1663–9) and Dresden (1666–7) he returned to Venice, where he succeeded Cavalli as first organist at S Marco in 1669; a decade later he finally settled in Naples, where he was associated with the Conservatorio S Onofrio and had court appointments which enabled him to re-stage many of his Venetian and Viennese operas.

The career of his nephew Marc'Antonio (*c*1653–1715) followed along similar lines. In 1679 his first opera, *Alessandro magno in Sidone*, was performed at the Teatro SS Giovanni e Paolo, followed by a steady stream of operas throughout the 1680s (when he was *maestro di cappella* at S Barbara in Mantua) and the 1690s, when he was regarded as one of the leading opera composers, with a particular flair for musical characterization and instrumental colour. At the turn of the century he too travelled to Vienna, where he composed operas for the Hoftheater and the Teatro Favorita, as well as oratorios (which show his brilliant contrapuntal technique to best advantage) and *sepolcri*. Though hardly any separate instrumental music survives, the operas and oratorios contain much solo writing for strings (violin, cello, viol and lute) and wind (bassoon, trombone and chalumeau), along with substantial ensemble ritornellos juxtaposing string and wind instruments. In 1712 he was made *Kapellmeister* at the imperial court, a post he held at his death.

5 Modena-Reggio

Bassani, Giovanni Battista. See ITALY *7 Papal States: Bologna-Ferrara.*

Bononcini. Modenese family of string players and composers. Giovanni Maria Bononcini (1642–78) studied the violin and composition with Uccellini, whose technique antedated by more than a decade that of the famous violin school of the neighbouring city of Bologna. Bononcini's own trio sonatas – while less tonally defined and technically demanding (with the exception of the fugal movements of the *sonate da chiesa*) – are important precursors of Corelli's opp. 1–4. He published his first collection (*Primi frutti del giardino musicale*) in Venice in 1666; collections of popular French and Italian dances (which were intended to be danced) and others containing *sonate da chiesa* appeared in the years immediately following. His last set of trios (op. 12) appeared in the year of his death. Five years earlier he had published a treatise (*Musico prattico*) which circulated widely and influenced such later writers as J.G. Walther (*Praecepta der musikalische Composition*, 1708) and Mattheson (*Der vollkommene Capellmeister*, 1739). Bononcini also left cantatas and a volume of madrigals (1678); of a *dramma da camera*, dedicated to Emperor Leopold I and performed at the Modena court theatre in 1677, only the libretto survives. When Bononcini died he left three young sons, all of whom became musicians.

Giovanni (1670–1747) was the eldest and most successful son. A cellist, he received his musical training in Bologna from G.P. Colonna. While there he published two collections of trios (1685) and three of *sinfonie* (1685–7); he was a member of the Accademia Filarmonica, a musician at S Petronio (for which he composed two Lenten oratorios, 1687–8) and finally *maestro di cappella* at S Giovanni in Monte until 1689 (his four double-choir Masses, published in 1688 as op. 7, were composed for the services there).

From Bologna he went to Milan to take up a commission from the Duke of Modena, and then to Rome – via Bologna, where he played in Cardinal Pamphili's orchestra. While in the service of Filippo Colonna in Rome, Bononcini collaborated with the poet Silvio Stampiglia on six serenatas, an oratorio and five operas, of which the last, *Il trionfo di Camilla*, was the highlight of the 1696–7 Naples Carnival. By this time his operas were in production throughout Italy, though his reputation had been made as much by his cantatas as by his operas.

Such was the impact of his music that in 1698 he was recruited to the court of Leopold I, in Vienna, where he became a particular favourite of the heir Joseph (reigned 1705–11). Stampiglia, along with Bononcini's younger brother Antonio Maria (1677–1726) – also a cellist in Pamphili's orchestra and an opera composer – soon joined him in Vienna. Though Giovanni produced operas, oratorios and dozens of cantatas while in Vienna, he eagerly seized any opportunity to present his music elsewhere: the restrictions on musical entertainment occasioned by the War of the Spanish Succession allowed the two Bononcinis to visit the Berlin court in 1702, and the year of mourning imposed in 1705–6 after the death of the emperor enabled Giovanni to travel to Italy. Meanwhile, between 1706 and 1709, his opera *Camilla* was given 64 performances in London at the Theatre Royal, Drury Lane, becoming the first Italian opera to gain popularity on the English stage (in part because it was sung in translation by English singers). After the death of Emperor Joseph I in 1711, both brothers left the court for Italy, although Giovanni maintained his connections by returning to Rome in the service of the Viennese ambassador, for whom he composed *Astarto* (text by Rolli) in 1715.

He remained in Rome until 1719 when he was invited to London by the Earl of Burlington to become a composer for the Royal Academy of Music under Handel's direction. He was warmly received in London where *Astarto* opened the second season at the King's Theatre in the Haymarket late in 1720, outshining Handel's own operas. The following year he contributed the second act (the first and third were by fellow cellist Filippo Amadei and Handel) to *Muzio Scevola*; *L'odio e l'amore* (text by Rolli) followed a month later at the Haymarket Theatre. After a promising start, Bononcini miscalculated the implications of accepting a commission from the Jacobite Duchess of Buckingham in 1722 to set the choruses of a play (*Marcus Brutus*) by her late husband. His own Catholicism became an issue, with the result that his Academy contract was not renewed in the autumn of 1722, although the decision was reversed a year later (*Erminia*, 1719, and *Farnace* were produced in 1723). He spent the summer of 1723 in Paris where he was offered a position by the regent's mistress and, indeed, spent the following summer there, along with singers (including Cuzzoni) from London.

Bononcini returned to London, however, and accepted a position as director of the private concerts of the Duchess of Marlborough, a position he held until 1731. In 1727 his opera *Astianatte* (text by Haym) was presented at the Haymarket, amid sensational publicity sought by the rival admirers of Cuzzoni and Faustina. At about that time his involvement in the Academy of Ancient Music came abruptly to an end when Maurice Greene presented a work he assumed to be Bononcini's; certain that the work was by Lotti, Bernard Gates exposed the deception at the performance, deeply embarrassing Bononcini and Greene.

Bononcini maintained his connections in France, visiting again in 1731 and then in 1733, having left London definitively after yet another awkward episode concerning the second edition of his sonatas for violin or flute (1722). In Paris, his music (including the *Laudate pueri* for voices and orchestra) was performed at the Concert Spirituel. 1735 saw him in Lisbon and by the middle of the following year he had arrived in Vienna where he remained until his death a decade later. During that time two of his operas (one on a text by Zeno, the other by Metastasio) and an oratorio were performed; his last known work is a *Te Deum*, commissioned by the empress in 1741.

Giovanni Maria [Angelo] Bononcini (1678–1753), named after his father who died an hour before his birth, remained in Italy all his life, as a cathedral cellist in Modena for 30 years, then in Venice and Rome where he pursued a career as a violinist. He was a member of the Accademia di S Cecilia for over 40 years.

Bordoni, Faustina. See ITALY *10 Itinerant Musicians*.

Castaldi, Bellerofonte. See ITALY *10 Itinerant Musicians*.

Chelleri, Fortunato. See ITALY *10 Itinerant Musicians*.

Corselli, Francesco. See IBERIAN PENINSULA AND COLONIES *1 Spain*.

De Grandis, Vincenzo. See ITALY *10 Itinerant Musicians*.

Ferrari, Benedetto. See ITALY *4 Venice*.

Fiorè, Angelo Maria. See ITALY *1 Piedmont-Savoy*.

Gabrielli, Domenico. See ITALY *7 Papal States: Bologna-Ferrara*.

Goldoni, Carlo. See ITALY *4 Venice*.

Grossi, Giovanni Francesco. See ITALY *10 Itinerant Musicians*.

India, Sigismondo d'. See ITALY *10 Itinerant Musicians*.

Manelli, Francesco. See ITALY *4 Venice.*

Marazzoli, Marco. See ITALY *7 Papal States: Rome.*

Perroni, Giovanni. See CENTRAL EUROPE *3 Austro-Hungary: Vienna.*

Perti, Giacomo Antonio. See ITALY *7 Papal States: Bologna-Ferrara.*

Pistocchi, Francesco Antonio Mamiliano. See ITALY *7 Papal States: Bologna-Ferrara.*

Rugeri, Francesco. See ITALY *2 Lombardy.*

Sportonio, Marc'Antonio. See ITALY *9 Sicily.*

Tesi, Vittoria. See ITALY *10 Itinerant Musicians.*

Uccellini, Marco (*c*1603–80). *Maestro di cappella* and composer of at least seven collections of violin music – sonatas, sinfonias and dances – which represent an important stage in the development of an idiomatic repertory. From the 1640s, Uccellini worked in Modena where he was head of instrumental music at the Este court and later *maestro di cappella* at the cathedral until 1665, when he joined the Farnese court at Parma.

Vigarani, Gaspare and **Carlo.** See FRANCE *1 Paris and Versailles.*

Vitali, Giovanni Battista and **Tomaso Antonio.** See ITALY *7 Papal States: Bologna-Ferrara.*

6 Tuscany

Agazzari, Agostino (1578–*c*1640). Sienese *maestro di cappella*, composer and theorist whose 1607 treatise on continuo playing had an immediate and widespread influence. Like those of many composers of his day, Agazzari's earliest published works were madrigals for three, five and six voices and indeed his first collection of motets, published in Rome in 1602, is also *a cappella.* But from 1603 onwards his sacred works incorporate a separate *basso continuo* part. While in Rome for several years at the turn of the century, Agazzari composed a *dramma pastorale* entitled *Eumelio* for the 1605 Carnival celebrations at the Seminario Romano; it comprised recitatives, strophic arias for solo voice and continuo and choruses, after the style of Cavalieri's *Rappresentatione di Anima et di Corpo* (1600).

Shortly thereafter Agazzari returned to Siena where he took up the post of organist and *maestro di cappella* at the cathedral. He was made a member of the Accademia degli Intronati and took the name 'Armonico Intronato' (which appeared on all of his publications from 1606 onwards). He made his reputation by publishing one of the earliest treatises on how to accompany an ensemble from an unfigured bass, *Del sonare sopra 'l basso con tutti li stromenti e dell'uso loro nel conserto* (1607). A model of concision, Agazzari's treatise divides continuo instruments into two groups, foundation and ornamenting, of which the lute, theorbo and harp belong to both. It was commended by Adriano Banchieri and a version of it incorporated into his *Conclusioni nel suono dell'organo* (1609); Michael Praetorius quoted and paraphrased large tracts of it in the third volume of *Syntagma musicum* (1618).

Archilei [*née* Concarini], **Vittoria** ['La Romanina'] (1550–1620s). Roman soprano and protégée of Cavalieri during the 1680s who became a much respected early exponent of the monodic style. Vittoria Concarini was gifted as a lutenist and dancer as well as a singer; with her husband Antonio Archilei (also a singer and lutenist) she took part in the *intermedi* performed at the Medici court in Florence. Caccini (1600), Peri (1600/01) and d'India (1609) all made reference not only to the quality of her voice but to her musicianship, her command of *passaggi* and the expressive devices of the Florentine style. Marino wrote a poem on 'La morte di Vittoria cantatrice famosa' which was published in 1629.

Babbi, Gregorio. See ITALY *10 Itinerant Musicians.*

Bardi, Giovanni de' (1534–1612). Count of Vernio, Italian military hero; student of Greek and Latin, poet, playwright, composer and creator of Medici court *intermedi* in the 1580s; patron, member of a number of academies and the leader of his own Florentine Camerata (*fl* 1573–87). Bardi's importance to students of Baroque music lies in his role as a muse to the 16th/17th-century composers who formulated what later came to be known as the *seconda prattica.* His home was the gathering place of nobles and musicians where music was played and discussed in terms of its poetry, philosophy and theoretical basis. Though never present at these meetings, Girolamo Mei (1519–94) exerted a profound influence through his correspondence with Bardi and Vincenzo Galilei, in which he encouraged the reform of polyphony through experiments with monody, based on the ideals of ancient Greek music. Galilei and Giulio Caccini were active members of what Caccini referred to in 1600 as 'Bardi's camerata'. Bardi addressed a discourse on ancient music and singing to Caccini; Galilei dedicated his *Dialogo della musica antica et della moderna* (1581) to Bardi. Bardi himself published at least three madrigals in which he sought to follow the teaching of Mei regarding the importance of 'keeping the line intact', 'attending to the expression of the words and the conceit', and 'limiting text repetition to the minimum'.

Bordoni, Faustina. See ITALY *10 Itinerant Musicians.*

Brunelli, Antonio (*c*1575–by 1630). *Maestro di cappella*, organist, composer and writer on music working in Tuscany. Brunelli was trained in the Roman sacred polyphonic tradition by G.M. Nanino. His first post was at the cathedral at San Miniato (near Pisa), whence he issued his first didactic treatise, *Regole utilissime* (1606). In 1607 he became *maestro di cappella* of Prato Cathedral, where he remained until taking up appointments to the Grand Duke of Tuscany and the Cavalieri di S Stefano at Pisa in 1612; by that time his treatise on singing, *Regole et dichiarationi* (1610), and first collections of *scherzi* and *arie* in the Florentine style had appeared. His brother succeeded him at Pisa in 1630.

Caccini. Family of Florentine musicians headed by Giulio Caccini (1551–1618), a celebrated singer and instrumentalist at the Medici court, once a member of Bardi's Florentine Camerata and an early composer of monody. Caccini was best known during his lifetime as a gifted tenor who accompanied himself on the lute, chitarrone, viol and harp. Under the influence of Bardi, Galilei and Mei, Caccini sought to create music that both affected the soul and delighted the senses; the result was *stile recitativo* in which 'one could almost speak in tones' in the mid 1580s, though it was not until the turn of the century that he published any of his monodies. *Il rapimento di Cefalo* was performed as part of the wedding festivities honouring Maria de' Medici and Henri IV of France in October 1600, and although he had composed music for Peri's *Euridice* (also part of the wedding entertainment), he quickly composed and had published his own *Euridice* by December 1600.

Caccini was also well known as a singing-teacher: he trained members of his family, who became known as 'il concerto Caccini', as well as the castrato Giovanni Gualberto Magli. Maria de' Medici invited the family consort to the French court in Paris during the winter and spring of 1604–5. *Le nuove musiche* (1602) was Caccini's most important publication: the solo madrigals and strophic songs in it are both lyrical and declamatory; the ornamentation (*passaggi*) and figured bass are explained in the preface, which is considered a major source of early 17th-century performing practice.

Francesca Caccini ['La Cecchina'] (1587–*c*1640) was Giulio's eldest daughter and musical heir: she sang and accompanied herself on the lute, guitar and harpsichord, wrote poetry, composed and taught. Though she remained all her life in the service of the Medici, she toured widely with her family and later with her husband Giovanni Battista Signorini. For the Medici she composed large-scale entertainments, culminating in an opera, *La liberazione di Ruggiero dall'isola d'Alcina*, which was performed in Florence in 1625; she dedicated her first and only book of songs and duets to Cardinal Carlo de' Medici in 1618. As one would expect from a singer, her music is richly idiomatic and exploits the emotional range of the voice through chromaticism, word-painting and brilliant written-out ornamentation.

Her younger sister Settimia ['La Flora'] (1591–*c*1638) was also a singer and composer of secular monodies. With her sister and father she sang at the French court (1604–5); after her return to Italy she took part in the first performance of Monteverdi's *Arianna* in 1608 at Mantua. The following year she married the composer Alessandro Ghivizzani (*c*1572–*c*1632) and together they worked first at the Medici court in Florence and then for the Gonzagas in Mantua. After her husband's death in 1632 she returned to the Medici court.

Caffarelli. See ITALY *10 Itinerant Musicians.*

Cavalieri, Emilio de' (*c*1550–1602). Roman noble at the Medici court and composer, who was one of the first to set a play in monody; he was also a singing-teacher, dancer and choreographer. As a diplomat he exerted a decisive influence on papal elections during the 1590s. After his successful management of the 1589 *intermedi* for the wedding festivities of Maria de' Medici and Henri IV of France, Cavalieri produced his own pastorals and in October 1600 the *Euridice* of Rinuccini and Peri.

Cavalieri belonged to the circle of poets and musicians gathered around Bardi, with whom he collaborated on lavish entertainments for the Grand Duke of Tuscany. Along with Peri and Caccini he experimented with speech-like recitative and figured bass in his settings of pastoral texts by Bardi, Tasso and Laura Guidiccioni (*Aminta*, 1590), Guarini and others. Many of his works were composed for the court soprano Vittoria Archilei and contained virtuoso passage-work and symbols for ornaments. His most important work is the *Rappresentatione di Anima et di Corpo ... per recitar cantando* which was performed in Rome in February 1600 before the members of the Collegio Sacro. In addition to long tracts of dialogue set in monodic recitative, the *Rappresentatione* contains madrigals and songs in dance metres. It is reckoned as the first dramatic work set entirely to music; the printed score is the earliest one to offer a figured bass.

Cesti, Antonio. See ITALY *10 Itinerant Musicians.*

Chelleri, Fortunato. See ITALY *10 Itinerant Musicians.*

Conti, Francesco Bartolomeo. See CENTRAL EUROPE *3 Austro-Hungary: Vienna.*

Corsi, Jacopo (1561–1602). Florentine noble and minor composer who, after Bardi, became the central figure in the early development of opera at Florence. Tasso, Rinuccini, and Peri regularly met at his palace to discuss dramatic poetry and perform music in the new *stile rappresentativo.* Corsi is remembered in particular for his collaboration with Peri and Rinuccini on *Dafne* (1598) and in the production of *Euridice*, performed at the Pitti Palace in 1600 as part of the wedding celebrations of Maria de' Medici and Henri IV of France.

Cristofori, Bartolomeo (1655–1731). Keyboard instrument maker and the inventor of the pianoforte. From 1690 Cristofori was in the service of Prince Ferdinando de' Medici at the Florentine court, where by 1698 he was engaged in the construction of an 'arpicembalo che fà il piano e il forte'. Only three pianos survive (one from 1720 at the Metropolitan Museum of Art, New York, has a compass of four and a half octaves), one harpsichord (1722) and a double-strung spinet (1693).

Cuzzoni, Francesca. See ITALY *10 Itinerant Musicians.*

Della Ciaia, Azzolino Bernardino (1671–1755). Though not a musician by trade, Della Ciaia is remembered for a collection of keyboard music (*c*1727) and for having commissioned a remarkable organ for Pisa, on behalf of the Cavalieri di S Stefano, to which he belonged. The organ – still considered the best in Tuscany – was provided by a small army of organ builders with more than 60 registers, five manuals (the fifth, controlled by a harpsichord) and five organs (of which three can be played on a single manual); it was modified in 1839. Della Ciaia's surviving

music (including six sonatas for harpsichord, each comprising an idiomatic toccata, a three-part canzona and two binary movements) was composed while at sea with the Cavalieri di S Stefano (1688–1704).

Del Turco, Giovanni (1577–1647). Florentine nobleman and court official who composed modest five-part madrigals. A contemporary of Jacopo Corsi, Del Turco studied composition with Gagliano (who in 1604 dedicated his second collection of madrigals to Del Turco). When Gagliano founded the Accademia degli Elevati in 1607, Del Turco became its secretary; in that same year he was mentioned in Giulio Cesare Monteverdi's preface to his brother Claudio's *Scherzi musicali.* In 1614 he dedicated his second book of madrigals (which contains a lament on the death of Corsi) to Grand Duke Cosimo II and was handsomely rewarded with the post of director of court music, which he held for more than a decade. Del Turco belonged to the Cavalieri di S Stefano, Pisa.

Doni, Giovanni Battista (1595–1647). Florentine classicist, philologist and music theorist of the post-Mei/Galilei generation. Though at heart a Greek scholar, Doni bowed to parental pressure and pursued a career in law. He succeeded almost in spite of himself, gaining a succession of diplomatic appointments at the Vatican that would take him to Paris and Madrid and ultimately the privileged post of secretary of the College of Cardinals (1629).

It was not until the 1630s that Doni turned to music and then it was to the singular task of rediscovering ancient Greek music. Dismayed by the current static quality of monody, he felt that a more complete revival of Greek music might provide fresh impetus to modern music. He wrote a series of treatises describing the ancient Greek system of *tonoi*, classifying types of monody and reforming solmization and staff notation. He had instruments constructed – in particular, the 'amphichordal' lyre or 'lyra Barberina' (named after his papal patron Urban VIII) which could be played in ancient modes – and induced composers such as Frescobaldi and Luigi Rossi to compose for them. His *Compendio del trattato de' generi e de' modi della musica* (1635) and *Annotazioni sopra il Compendio* (1640), both published in Rome, contain criticism of dramatic music.

Fantini, Girolamo (*fl* 1630–8). Chief court trumpeter to Ferdinando II, Grand Duke of Tuscany, and the author of an important treatise on his instrument (*Modo per imparare a sonare di tromba*, published in Frankfurt,

1638), which not only contains the first known trumpet sonatas but also promoted the use of the trumpet outside its traditional realms of military and ceremonial music.

Frescobaldi, Girolamo. See ITALY *7 Papal States: Rome.*

Gagliano, Marco da (1582–1643). Prominent Florentine composer and distinguished cleric, best known for his 1608 opera *Dafne* (text by Rinuccini), although he was a prolific composer of madrigals, monodies and *sacre rappresentazioni* (oratorios). Gagliano was a pupil of Luca Bati and from an early age a member of the Compagnia dell'Arcangelo Raffaello, a lay religious confraternity for boys of the middle and upper classes, where he came to know Cosimo de' Medici, Ottavio Rinuccini, Jacopo Peri, Giovanni del Turco and Giovanni de' Bardi – men with whom he would later be associated. He took up his first post as assistant to the *maestro di cappella* at S Lorenzo in 1602, the same year in which he published the first of six books of madrigals; at the end of 1608 he was elevated to *maestro*. In that same year he was instrumental in the founding of the Florentine Accademia degli Elevati, distinguished by its membership, rules and strict devotion to music; their patron was Cardinal Ferdinando Gonzaga.

Soon after, Gagliano began to write music for the Gonzaga court entertainments at Mantua. *Dafne* was presented there during the Carnival of 1608. The opera was greatly admired and particularly praised by Peri for its successful musical declamation. Less austere than the earlier efforts of Peri and Caccini, *Dafne* has more in common with Monteverdi's *L'Orfeo* (1607) in its mixture of madrigal and recitative styles. Of special interest is Gagliano's preface to the edition in which he makes clear his concern for the production as a whole: how to deploy the instrumentalists and singers, the occasions and circumstances in which ornamentation is to be used, and general stage directions.

In 1609 Gagliano was appointed *maestro di cappella* at the Medici court and at S Maria del Fiore (the Florentine cathedral). In 1615 he was made apostolic prothonotary at S Lorenzo; his collection of chamber monodies (*Musiche*) also appeared in that year. His *Responsoria maioris hebdomadae* (1630/31) served to keep alive his memory until well into the 19th century. His younger brother, Giovanni Battista (1594–1651), was also active as a composer, musician and teacher in Florence.

Galilei, Vincenzo (*d* 1591). Tuscan theorist,

acoustician and composer, lutenist and singer, who led the trend towards the monodic style of the 17th century; he was the father of the scientist Galileo Galilei. As a young man Galilei studied with Zarlino in Venice and in 1570–1 embarked on a compendium of his teacher's *Le istitutioni harmoniche*. The following year he took up residence in Florence, became acquainted with Bardi, and entered into a correspondence with Mei (the eminent authority on Greek music) which formed the basis for his *Dialogo della musica antica et della moderna*, dedicated to Bardi and published in 1581. In it he criticized Zarlino's theories of tuning and demonstrated how the Greek modes differed from the church modes; deeply influenced by Greek theory and philosophy, he advocated the return to music based on a single melodic line accompanied by a lute, limited by the rhythm and affection of the poetry, and he revived the concept of sung tragedies. These ideas were taken up and developed by Cavalieri, Corsi, Rinuccini, Peri and Caccini.

Gatti, Theobaldo di. See FRANCE *1 Paris and Versailles.*

Geminiani, Francesco. See BRITISH ISLES *1 London.*

Giustini, Lodovico (Maria) (1685–1743). Pistoian composer, who served all of his life as organist of the Congregazione dello Spirito Santo (where he succeeded his father). In 1732 he published in Florence the earliest known piano music, *Sonate da cimbalo di piano e forte detto volgarmente di martelletti* (op. 1), which employs dynamic markings and expressive indications.

Goldoni, Carlo. See ITALY *4 Venice.*

Grua, Carlo Luigi Pietro. See NORTHERN EUROPE *5 West Germany and the Rhineland.*

Habermann, Franz. See CENTRAL EUROPE *3 Austro-Hungary.*

Handel, George Frideric. See BRITISH ISLES *1 London.*

Hasse, Johann Adolf. See NORTHERN EUROPE *4 Saxony and Thuringia: Dresden.*

India, Sigismondo d'. See ITALY *10 Itinerant Musicians.*

Lampugnani, Giovanni Battista. See ITALY *10 Itinerant Musicians.*

Lanzetti, Salvatore. See ITALY *1 Piedmont-Savoy.*

Lully, Jean-Baptiste. See FRANCE *1 Paris and Versailles.*

Melani, Jacopo and **Atto.** See ITALY *10 Itinerant Musicians.*

Moniglia, Giovanni Andrea (1624–1700). Physician to Cardinal Gian Carlo de' Medici and comic librettist, whose *La Tancia*, set by Jacopo Melani in 1657, inaugurated the Florentine Teatro della Pergola. Cavalli composed music for *Ipermestra* and Jacopo Melani *Ercole in Tebe* for Florence; the settings of Lorenzo Cattani (a frequent collaborator) do not survive. In the following decade Melani set at least two librettos for Pisa, and Cesti, Legrenzi, Pasquini and P.A. Ziani followed with operas for Venice and Vienna. He published his librettos in three volumes of *Poesie dramatiche* (1689–90).

Orlandi, Santi. See ITALY *3 Mantua.*

Orlandini, Giuseppe Maria (1675–1760). Florentine *maestro di cappella* and prolific opera composer. Orlandini had a varied career in the service of Prince Giovanni Gastone (Grand Duke of Tuscany from 1723), at the cathedral and at S Michele; he composed heroic operas on librettos by Zeno for Bologna (where in 1719 he became a member of the Accademia Filarmonica), Rome, Venice, Naples, Milan, Ferrara, Reggio Emilia and Turin, as well as Florence. However, his importance lies as a composer of the comic *intermezzo Serpilla e Bacocco* (1722); originally called *Il marito giocatore* for a performance in Venice in 1719, it became the most frequently performed musical drama in the 18th century. The arias are short – the text is set syllabically over simple accompaniments – and are characterized by repeated notes and rhythms over often static harmonies. He prepared other *intermezzi* for Rome, Venice, Munich, Copenhagen and St Petersburg (where *Il marito geloso* was performed in 1734).

Pagliardi, Giovanni Maria (1637–1702). Church musician and composer of oratorios and operas. Pagliardi worked primarily in Florence, where he served as *maestro di cappella* (succeeding Cesti) to the Grand Duke of Tuscany, at the church of S Lorenzo and, in his last years, at the cathedral. His oratorio *L'innocenza trionfante* was performed in Genoa at Ss Annunziata in 1660, and several collections of motets were published in Rome during the mid 1670s. But it was not until 1672 that he produced his first (and most popular) opera, *Caligula delirante* (text by Gioberti), at the Teatro SS Giovanni e Paolo in Venice, followed by *Lisimaco* (text by Ivanovich) the next year. He subsequently composed operas for Florence which were performed at the Pitti Palace, the Teatro della Pergola and at Pratolino (the duke's second home).

Peri, Jacopo ['Zazzerino'] (1561–1633). Composer who contributed significantly to the early development of dramatic recitative, and Orphic singer (he accompanied himself at the keyboard or on the chitarrone). Peri came from an aristocratic Florentine family and acquired a post among the musicians at the Medici court. He may have been a member of Bardi's Camerata and during the 1580s collaborated on *intermedi* with his teacher Cristofano Malvezzi and Striggio, among others. He became associated with Jacopo Corsi in the 1590s, and together they collaborated on the music for Rinuccini's tragi-comedy *Dafne*, which was performed during Carnival 1598. His most important work – and the earliest opera to survive in complete form – is *Euridice* (text by Rinuccini); the 1st performance also included music by Giulio Caccini. The drama is entirely conveyed by either solo singers or four- and five-part chorus. By imitating the rhythm and melody of speech – achieved in part through his use of chromaticism and silence – in recitatives, such as the two monologues for Orpheus, he initiated the traditions of opera. *Euridice* was performed at the Palazzo Pitti on 6 October 1600 as part of the wedding celebrations for Henri IV of France and Maria de' Medici.

Although Peri spent his life in Florence, he corresponded with Ferdinando Gonzaga, who commissioned for the Mantuan court songs and two theatre works (which may never have been completed or performed). In 1609 Peri published a collection of songs (*Le varie musiche*) and was for a time closely associated with Francesca Caccini, accompanying her with her husband in the entourage of Carlo de' Medici on a trip to Rome in 1616. In the 1620s he collaborated with Marco da Gagliano on at least three *sacre rappresentazioni* (oratorios) which were performed for the Compagnia dell'Arcangelo Raffaello. They also worked together on two librettos by Salvadori; Peri composed the elaborate music for Chlorys in *La Flora*, which was also given for a Medici wedding, in 1628.

Puliaschi, Giovanni Domenico. See ITALY *7 Papal States: Rome.*

Rinuccini, Ottavio (1562–1621). Florentine nobleman, librettist and poet who wrote the first drama to be sung entirely 'in the manner of the ancients'. As a member of the court Rinuccini was actively involved in the royal entertainments. He also belonged to the Accademia Fiorentina and the Alterati, though not to Bardi's Camerata. However he did collaborate with Bardi on *intermedi* for the 1589 wedding celebrations of Grand Duke Ferdinando I and during the 1590s he worked with Corsi, Peri and Caccini, producing musical dramas sung in recitative style: *Dafne* (1598; performed at Corsi's home) and *Euridice* (1600).

He claimed to have penned the text of *Dafne* 'solely to test the power of music'. In 1608 the Accademia degli Elevati (of which Rinuccini was also a member) commissioned a new setting of *Dafne* from Gagliano; that same year Rinuccini also collaborated with Monteverdi on the *Ballo dell'ingrate*, which was inspired by his encounter with French court ballet while in Paris (1600–4) as one of Maria de' Medici's entourage. He also wrote texts for madrigals, of which Monteverdi's ground-bass settings of 'Zefiro torna' and the 'Lamento della ninfa' are well known.

Rossi, Luigi. See ITALY *7 Papal States: Rome.*

Saracini, Claudio ['Il Palusi'] (1586–1649). Sienese nobleman, singer, lutenist and composer of monodies, considered with Sigismondo d'India to be the finest monodist of his day. His six books of *Musiche* (including 129 solo songs, duets, trios and theorbo pieces) were published during the decade 1614–24 and were dedicated to archbishops and princes; individual songs were dedicated to such people as Monteverdi, who greatly influenced his music. With the exception of a *Stabat mater* he set only Italian texts, particularly favouring the erotic verses of Marino for his madrigals. His command of declamation and word-painting, harmony and dissonance were formidable.

Sbarra, Francesco (1611–68). Luccan poet and librettist, working at the Habsburg courts during the last decade of his life. In Lucca he belonged to the Accademia degli Oscuri and later the Accademia degli Accesi. After the death of his wife (1645) he entered the priesthood, serving as a canon of Lucca Cathedral. He wrote occasional poetry, including tragic and comic *intermedi*, during the 1640s, gaining wider notoriety with the production of Cesti's setting of *Alessandro vincitor di se stesso* at the Teatro SS Giovanni e Paolo in Venice. In 1659 he was appointed court poet and counsellor to Archduke Ferdinand Karl in Innsbruck, in succession to G.F. Apolloni, and in 1665 moved to the Viennese court where, in addition to producing texts for *sepolcri* and ballets, he collaborated again with Cesti on the extravagant *Il pomo d'oro*, for the 1668 wedding celebrations of Leopold I and Margareta Teresa of Spain.

Stuck, Jean-Baptiste. See FRANCE *1 Paris and Versailles.*

Tenaglia, Antonio Francesco. See ITALY *7 Papal States: Rome.*

Tesi, Vittoria. See ITALY *10 Itinerant Musicians.*

Veracini. Florentine violinists and composers, an uncle and his famous nephew. Antonio Veracini (1659–1733) was trained by his father before entering the service of Grand Duchess Vittoria of Tuscany (d 1694) in 1682. With the exception of two trips to Rome to meet Corelli and another to Vienna, he remained in Florence all his life. In 1700 he was elected *maestro di cappella* at the church of S Michele, and eight years later assumed the directorship of his father's music school, where he trained his nephew, Francesco Maria Veracini. He composed oratorios for various religious confraternities (though only the librettos survive).

Francesco Maria (1690–1768) was one of the finest violinists of his day. The son of an undertaker – though otherwise from a family of musicians and artists – he studied first with his uncle and then with G.M. Casini (organist at Florence Cathedral). In 1711 he left Florence for Venice, where he appeared as a guest soloist at the Christmas services at S Marco and at a Mass in honour of the new Holy Roman ambassador at S Maria Gloriosa dei Frari a few months later. After a brief visit to Florence in 1712 for the performance of his oratorio *Il trionfo della innocenza patrocinata da S Niccolò*, he returned to Venice.

In 1714 Veracini travelled to London, where he gave benefit concerts and performed his own concertos between acts of operas at the Queen's Theatre. The following year he was at the electoral court in Düsseldorf for performances of his oratorio *Mosè al mar' rosso*. Hardly had he resettled in Venice before he began soliciting a post in Dresden, by dedicating a set of solo sonatas (1716) to the Prince-Elector Friedrich August I of Saxony. Under pressure from his son, the elector hired Veracini at a salary equal to that of his *Kapellmeister* (J.B. Volumier), which inevitably caused dissension among the other court musicians. He remained in Dresden until 1722 when, in desperation, he jumped from a third-storey window – an action precipitated by a plot against his life by his jealous colleagues, or so he later alleged in his treatise – and was apparently none the worse for it.

After a stop at Prague Veracini travelled home to Florence, where for a while he was content to play in private concerts, while composing oratorios, a Mass and in 1730 a *Te Deum* honouring the election of a Florentine pope, Clement XII; but he was back in

London by 1733 where, according to Burney, 'there was no concert now without a solo on the violin by Veracini'. The Opera of the Nobility presented his *Adriano in Siria* (text by Corri after Metastasio) in 1735, followed by *La Clemenza di Tito* (1737; text by Corri) and *Partenio* (1738; text by Rolli).

He returned to Florence in 1738, his uncle, wife and mother having died in the interim, but by 1741 was in London once again. He performed concertos between the acts of Handel's revised *Acis and Galatea* and at several benefit concerts. In his last opera, *Rosalinda* (text by Rolli), performed in 1744, Veracini resorted to the inclusion of a well-known ballad tune, 'The Lass of Paties Mill', and again in his op. 2 *Sonate accademiche* ('Tweed's Side'). Crossing the Channel in 1745, he was shipwrecked, escaping with his life but not his manuscripts.

From 1750 until his death he lived in Florence, where from 1755 he served as a *maestro di cappella*, continuing to play and conduct until his last years. His crotchety-toned treatise, *Il trionfo della pratica musicale* (op. 3), was written at the very end of his life.

Vitali, Filippo. See ITALY *10 Itinerant Musicians.*

Vittori, Loreto. See ITALY *7 Papal States: Rome.*

Wagenseil, Georg Christoph. See CENTRAL EUROPE *3 Austro-Hungary: Vienna.*

Zipoli, Domenico. See IBERIAN PENINSULA AND COLONIES *3 New World.*

7 Papal States

Bologna-Ferrara

Albergati, Pirro (1663–1735). Bolognese nobleman, patron and composer. Though Albergati never became a member of the Accademia Filarmonica he was a prominent figure in Bologna. He held public offices and presided at civic ceremonies. Between 1686 and 1732 he contributed oratorios to the annual Lenten music; his operas and serenatas are all lost. These and other works – cantatas, concertos and sonatas – could be heard at his palace. He was a friend of Corelli and the patron of G.M. Bononcini and the cellist Giuseppe Jacchini. He dedicated his op. 5 *Pletro armonico* (ten quartet sonatas for two violins, cello obbligato and continuo) to Leopold I.

Alberti, Giuseppe Matteo (1685–1751). Bolognese violinist at S Petronio and composer of sonatas and concertos. Alberti was a member of the Accademia Filarmonica and served as its *principe* at different times from 1721. His concertos, particularly popular in England, were among the first to show the influence of Vivaldi.

Aldrovandini, Giuseppe Antonio Vincenzo (1672/3–1707). Bolognese composer of both comic and serious opera whose dissolute ways led to his early death by drowning in a canal. His talent was widely acknowledged by his peers; in 1695 he became a member of the Accademia Filarmonica and was also associated with the Accademia del Santo Spirito in Ferrara. The success of his comic operas, dating from the last years of the 17th century, was compromised by the disapproval of the Bolognese church authorities: *Gl'inganni amorosi scoperti in villa* – in which all but the leading roles were sung in Bolognese dialect – was at first suspended because of certain *doubles entendres* in the libretto.

Aleotti. Ferrarese sisters and composers. Raffaella Aleotti (*c*1570–after 1646) and her sister Vittoria (*c*1573–after 1620) were the daughters of the Duke of Ferrara's architect, Giovanni Battista Aleotti. They were taught to play the organ and the harpsichord and to compose. Both entered the Augustinian convent of S Vito where they continued to pursue music. In 1593 Raffaella assumed the direction of the 'Concerto grande', an ensemble of about two dozen singers and instrumentalists which during her tenure was much admired by musicians such as Artusi and Gesualdo; Vittoria served as her assistant. In 1598 Pope Clement VIII and the Queen of Spain attended a performance given by the 'Concerto grande'; so impressed was the queen that she invited Raffaella to become her organist, an offer Raffaella nevertheless declined. Raffaella's *Sacrae cantiones* (1593) were among the earliest Italian motets in the concertate style. Vittoria's madrigals appeared in the anthology *Il giardino de musici ferraresi* (1591), and in the same year their father published a book of Vittoria's four-part madrigals entitled *Ghirlanda de madrigali.*

Arresti, Giulio Cesare (1625–*c*1704). Organist at S Petronio (Bologna), composer and one of the founders of the Accademia Filarmonica (1666). In 1659 Arresti mounted a bitter, even vicious campaign against his superior, Maurizio Cazzati, which ended in Cazzati's resignation and Arresti's accession to his post as *maestro di cappella* in 1671. He began by anonymously circulating a *Dialogo fatto tra un maestro ed un discepolo desideroso d'approfittare nel contrappunto*, in manuscript, concerning errors Arresti noted in Cazzati's *Messa primi toni* (1655). He included the *Kyrie*, annotated with corrections, in his own op. 1 *Messa e Vespro della beata virgine* (1663), and a year later scored Cazzati's op. 33 psalms (noting certain infelicities of counterpoint) in his own *Gare musicali*. To these attacks Cazzati replied with dignity and eloquence. Arresti's son Floriano (*c*1660–1719) followed his father as an organist at S Petronio and was a member of the Accademia Filarmonica; he composed oratorios and operas, most of which are lost.

Artusi, Giovanni Maria (*c*1540–1613). Bolognese composer and influential theorist whose well-publicized polemics around the turn of the century were critical of the *seconda prattica*. Artusi was a 16th-century writer whose importance to students of the Baroque era centres on his dispute, during the first decade of the 17th century, with Claudio Monteverdi and his brother Giulio Cesare concerning the propriety of certain of Monteverdi's madrigals.

Artusi had been a pupil of Zarlino in Venice and remained devoted to his writings throughout his life. He published a number of important treatises as well as open letters: his *Seconda parte dell'arte del contraponto* (1589), following three years after the post-Zarlinian *L'arte del contraponto ridotta in tavole* (1586), concentrates on the use of dissonance in counterpoint and in text setting; in *L'arte del contraponto* (1598) he consolidated his views, having taken a secondary role in the exchange between Zarlino and another of his pupils, Vincenzo Galilei, in 1588–90. Shortly thereafter Artusi became embroiled in a dispute with Bottrigari who, in *Il Desiderio* (1594), criticized Artusi's views on the tuning of instrumental ensembles (*concerti*). Two of Artusi's publications relating to this controversy, *L'Artusi* (1600) and the *Seconda parte dell'Artusi* (1603), also criticize the use of dissonance and modes in the madrigals of an unnamed composer, whom everyone knew to be Monteverdi.

Much has been written about the ensuing debate, because out of it sprang the formulation of the ideals of the Florentine innovators, expressed by Monteverdi as the *seconda prattica*. In the preface to his fifth book of madrigals (1605) Monteverdi defended his harmonic licence as being a written reflection of the vocal ornamentation and improvisation currently in use, as well as of accepted instru-

mental practices; his brother continued his defence in the preface ('Dichiaratione') to the *Scherzi musicali* (1607). The following year Artusi published his final reply in Venice, under a pseudonym, entitled *Discorso secondo musicale di Antonio Braccino da Todi per la dichiaratione della lettera posta ne' Scherzi musicali del sig. Claudio Monteverdi*.

Banchieri, Adriano [Tomaso] (1568–1634). Benedictine monk, *seconda prattica* composer and prolific writer whose commentary on early 17th-century music practice remains an important primary source. Banchieri worked as an organist and composer in a succession of Italian monasteries before finally settling in his native Bologna. Most of his music, sacred and secular, was published in Venice, though he seems to have spent only a year there in 1605, the year of his *L'organo suonarino* (op. 13), which in addition to organ masses contains instructions and examples of how to accompany liturgical chant and to realize figured bass. Even in his sacred works the *seconda prattica* prevails: his psalms are in *concertato* style, his *Concerti ecclesiastici* contain early examples of a separate instrumental bass part, and his Masses offer a compendium of early 17th-century styles. Banchieri's instrumental *canzoni alla francese* from the turn of the century employ continuo parts. Of his many *commedia dell'arte* canzonettas and madrigals, only those published in the 1620s (including revisions of earlier works) incorporate violins and continuo.

Banchieri wrote on many non-musical subjects, though always under a pseudonym (either Camillo Scaliggeri dalla Fratta or Attabalippa dal Peru). Of his many works on music, the *Cartella musicale* (1614) is one of the most important theoretical treatises; in it he extended hexachord solmization to include the variable seventh step, *ba* (B flat) and *bi* (B natural), discussed the metrical implications of bar-lines and the use of the tie (*legatura moderna*), and included a brief table of vocal ornaments.

Bartolotti, Angelo Michele. See FRANCE 1 *Paris and Versailles*.

Bassani, Giovanni Battista (*c*1657–1716). *Maestro di cappella*, violinist, organist and composer of trio sonatas. A pupil of Legrenzi and G.B. Vitali, Bassani was employed by the Accademia della Morte in Ferrara from 1667, succeeding Tosi as *maestro di cappella* there in 1683/4, and then at Ferrara Cathedral in 1686. In the meantime he had served as *maestro di cappella* and organist of the Confraternità del Finale at Modena and had been a member of the Accademia Filarmonica at Bologna since 1677.

Although known for his mastery of instrumental idioms, he composed at least 15 oratorios and nine operas (for Bologna, Venice, Ferrara and Verona), as well as concerted Masses and many sacred and secular cantatas. It is significant that the secular cantatas are restricted to voice and continuo, whereas the sacred cantatas employ two violins in an opening sinfonia and concerted arias. Between 1710 and 1712 he composed 78 services (in cycles) for use at Ferrara Cathedral. In 1712 he accepted appointments at Bergamo, as *maestro di cappella* at S Maria Maggiore and teacher at the music school known as the Congregazione di Carità.

Bernacchi, Antonio Maria. See ITALY *10 Itinerant Musicians.*

Bernardi, Bartolomeo. See NORTHERN EUROPE *2 Scandinavia.*

Bononcini, Giovanni. See ITALY *5 Modena-Reggio.*

Brunetti, Domenico (*c*1580–1646). Organist and *maestro di cappella* at Bologna Cathedral, one of the first composers to publish accompanied monodies. *L'Euterpe* (1606) contains monodic madrigals and arias as well as duets and trios that can be performed either *a cappella* or with continuo; in the vocal solos, duos and trios of the *Concentus cum gravi et acuto ad organum* (1609) the instrumental bass part includes a written-out part for the right hand which is sometimes melodic but otherwise harmonically conceived. Brunetti founded the Accademia dei Filaschisi in 1633.

Calegari, Francesco Antonio. See ITALY *4 Venice.*

Cazzati, Maurizio (*c*1620–77). Priest, organist, composer and *maestro di cappella* at S Petronio, who suffered vilification by his subordinates and other members of the Bolognese musical establishment. Cazzati's tenure at Bologna (1657–71) began well enough, with the institution of needed administrative reforms to the *cappella musicale*. But resentment surfaced within a short time when unconventional passages in his op. 17 *Messa primi toni* (1655) were criticized by Lorenzo Petri (later *maestro di cappella* at Bologna Cathedral) and Giulio Cesare Arresti (Cazzati's first organist, and successor at S Petronio). The dissension erupted in 1659 and finally eased in 1667 when Cazzati reissued op. 17 with the errors – passages he once considered pleasing to the ear – corrected. In the meantime his op. 33 *Salmi da capella* (1663) were also subjected to Arresti's harsh scrutiny in *Gare musicali* (1664). Cazzati, who eloquently defended himself throughout, was nevertheless censured – no doubt at Arresti's instigation – by the newly founded Accademia Filarmonica; in response Cazzati organized his own academy which, significantly, was subsidized by the canons of S Petronio.

Cazzati is known today by his instrumental works – Venetian canzonas, collections of dances such as the op. 15 *Correnti e balletti alla francese e all'itagliana* (1654), and sonatas such as those for trumpet and strings (op. 35, 1665) – which found a regular place in the services at S Petronio. Because of the general hostility towards him prevailing in Bologna, he eventually found it necessary to set up his own printing press to produce most of his editions from 1666 onwards. In 1670 he became the first to publish solo violin sonatas there. Cazzati resigned his post in 1671 for that of *maestro di cappella* to Duchess Anna Isabella Gonzaga at Mantua.

Colonna, Giovanni Paolo (1637–95). Bolognese church musician – organist, *maestro di cappella*, and composer at S Petronio – and organ builder, the son of a respected Brescian builder. Colonna went to Rome to study with Abbatini, Benevoli and Carissimi before returning to Bologna in the late 1650s; his own pupils included Giovanni Bononcini. He was an active member of the Accademia Filarmonica, which he helped to found in 1666. In 1685 he contributed to a dispute, conducted by correspondence with G.B. Vitali and others, over the parallel fifths in the Allemande of Corelli's op. 2 no. 3, which served further to separate the Bolognese and Roman schools. Owing to ill health Colonna declined in 1694 the coveted post of *maestro di cappella* at Bologna Cathedral, offered to him by Pope Innocent XII (to whom Colonna had recently dedicated his third book of psalms).

Colonna's importance as a composer is based on his oratorios – though only six survive – poised as they are between those of Carissimi and Handel. While he composed several collections of motets, they too are in the Roman style of Carissimi and Graziani; the *Messe e salmi concertati* (1691) best represent his mature style. Emperor Leopold I was sufficiently impressed with what he had heard of Colonna's sacred music to request copies of his entire output: 83 of his works, preserved at the Nationalbibliothek (Vienna), effectively document the practices at S Petronio, especially the instrumental disposition of the *cappella*, which incorporated trumpets.

Corbetta, Francesco. See ITALY *10 Itinerant Musicians.*

Degli Antoni. Bolognese musicians and composers, important for their instrumental chamber music. Pietro (1648–1720) was an instrumentalist active in the Accademia Filarmonica (which he helped to charter in 1666 and served six times as *principe*) and *maestro di cappella* of three Bolognese churches, for which he composed a variety of vocal music (concerted Masses, motets, oratorios and chamber cantatas). But it is his role in the development of the *sonata da camera* and *sonata da chiesa*, expressed in the opp. 4 (1676) and 5 (1686) for violin and continuo, that is of special interest: in these works he relied upon vocal models to create a dramatic, declamatory instrumental style. His younger brother Giovanni Battista (1660–after 1696), a gifted organist in his day and also a member of the Accademia Filarmonica, is now remembered for his collection of 12 *Ricercate* (1687), the earliest known printed collection for solo cello.

Fabri, Annibale Pio. See ITALY *10 Itinerant Musicians.*

Farinelli. See ITALY *10 Itinerant Musicians.*

Ferrari, Benedetto. See ITALY *4 Venice.*

Franceschini, Petronio (*c*1650–80). Bolognese cellist and composer of operas for the Teatro Formagliari. Franceschini was one of the founding members of the Accademia Filarmonica and took his turn as *principe* in 1673; he served as a cellist at Bologna Cathedral (1675–80) and *maestro di cappella* at the Arciconfraternità di S Maria della Morte. His life was cut short soon after arriving in Venice to compose an opera, *Dionisio*, for the Teatro SS Giovanni e Paolo, which might have inaugurated a new phase of his career. He only composed one act of it; it was completed by G.D. Partenio and performed in 1681. Legrenzi directed his funeral music. In addition to operas, Franceschini composed oratorios, motets, cantatas and sonatas (one *sonata da chiesa* requires two trumpets and trombone in addition to strings and organ).

Gabrielli, Domenico (1651–90). Bolognese cello virtuoso, known as 'Mingàn dal viulunzaal', and composer. Gabrielli divided his career between Bologna, Venice and Modena. In Bologna he was a member of the Accademia Filarmonica and, from 1680 to 1687, first cellist at S Petronio. His canons, solo ricercares and sonatas for cello – among the earliest of their kind – reveal an idiomatic conception and flair for the instrument. He studied composition with Legrenzi in Venice and composed operas for the theatres there, as well as for those in Modena, Turin and Bologna. His cantatas, oratorios and operas were mostly produced in Venice; in them he often gave the cello and trumpet (as well as other instruments) concertante roles as, for example, in *Flavio Cuniberto* (1682) and *San Sigismondo* (1687).

Galli-Bibiena. See CENTRAL EUROPE *3 Austro-Hungary: Vienna.*

Gesualdo, Carlo. See ITALY *8 Naples.*

Giacobbi, Girolamo (1567–1629). Bolognese composer who was one of the first outside Florence to write in the monodic style. Giacobbi was associated throughout his life with S Petronio (rising from choirboy to *maestro di cappella*, 1604–28), where his sacred music – motets (1601) in the style of Palestrina and concerted vesper psalms (1609) in the contemporary Venetian style – was performed. Of more significance were his *intermedi* for pastoral plays, although only his *Dramatodia* (1608), in which the influence of Monteverdi's *L'Orfeo* is evident, remains. Giacobbi was an active member of the Bolognese Accademia de' Floridi (known from 1625 as the Accademia dei Filomusi), which met in his home.

Goretti, Antonio (*c*1570–1649). Ferrarese music patron and composer of madrigals. He amassed a large music library and collection of instruments, and may have been 'L'Ottuso', who defended Monteverdi and the principles of the *seconda prattica* in the controversy with Artusi around 1600. In 1618 and 1627–8 he collaborated with Monteverdi on festival music for the Parma court. In 1612 his brother Alfonso published *Dell'eccellenze, e prerogative della musica* in Ferrara.

Granata, Giovanni Battista (*d* after 1684). Guitarist and prolific composer for his instrument. Born in Turin, Granata was an innovative player, a pupil of Corbetta, and became the finest exponent of the Bolognese school. He published seven collections (1646–84) in Bologna, which included ensemble music for guitar with violins, bass viol and continuo as well as solos. His enthusiasm for the lute and its technique is evident from the virtuoso idiom of his music (the *battute* textures of the early collections are replaced by plucked, lute textures and ensembles of guitar and continuo) and from the inclusion of pieces specifically for the *chitarra tiorbata* (1659). In the preface to his fourth collection (1659) he accused his teacher of plagiarism; Corbetta accused him of the same in his first volume of *La guitarre royale*, published in Paris in 1671.

Grandi, Alessandro. See ITALY *4 Venice.*

Hasse, Johann Adolf. See NORTHERN EUROPE *4 Saxony and Thuringia: Dresden.*

Jacchini, Giuseppe Maria (*c*1663–1727). Bolognese cellist, *maestro di cappella* and composer of trumpet and string sonatas and concertos. He studied with Domenico Gabrielli and Perti, before becoming a member of the Accademia Filarmonica in 1688 and a member of the orchestra at S Petronio the following year. According to Padre Martini, Jacchini was an exceptionally fine cellist and known as a sensitive accompanist who improvised on the bass. Written-out evidence of this practice is found in his op. 4 concertos (1701), six of which contain cello obbligatos.

Laurenti. Bolognese family of instrumentalists, singers and composers. Bartolomeo Girolamo Laurenti (1644–1726) was the leader of the S Petronio orchestra (he shared his desk with G. Torelli) and an early member of the Accademia Filarmonica; he published chamber music. His son Girolamo Nicolò (*d* 1751) took his place in the orchestra when he retired in 1706, advancing to the directorship in 1734. He took work outside Bologna and was praised by Quantz (1726) for his leadership of the opera orchestra at the Venetian Teatro S Giovanni Grisostomo. Another son, Pietro Paolo (*c*1675–1719), played the cello and viola as well as the violin at S Petronio, and composed at least six operas and 11 oratorios, as well as cello sonatas. Both brothers were also members of the Accademia Filarmonica.

Antonia Maria Novelli Laurenti ['La Coralli'] (*fl* 1715–35) was a singer who began her career at the Teatro Formagliari and became well known throughout northern Italy. In 1719 she took up an appointment proffered by F.M. Veracini in Dresden, but by 1721 was in Venice, appearing in operas while a *virtuosa di camera* in the service of Friedrich August I of Saxony.

Legrenzi, Giovanni. See ITALY *4 Venice.*

Leopardi, Venanzio. See ITALY *10 Itinerant Musicians.*

Manelli, Francesco. See ITALY *4 Venice.*

Marazzoli, Marco. See ITALY *7 Papal States: Rome.*

Martini, Padre **Giovanni Battista** (1706–84). Prolific Bolognese writer on music, theorist, composer and teacher of such composers as J.C. Bach, Grétry, Jommelli and Mozart. Martini became a Franciscan monk in the early 1720s and in 1725 took up the post of *maestro di cappella* at S Francesco, Bologna, where he remained until his retirement. Though he suffered from chronic ill health,

Padre Martini was devoted to his work in Bologna, amassing a huge library and portrait collection of his pupils as well as other distinguished musical figures (such as Farinelli, Gluck and Charles Burney), and rarely ventured away (he declined a post at the Vatican); perhaps to compensate, he maintained a vigorous correspondence with a number of musicians, scholars and even monarchs.

In 1758 the Accademia Filarmonica belatedly waived their rule excluding monks and received him into their midst; in 1776 he was made a member of the Arcadi di Roma. Nearly 1500 of his works (not counting nearly 1000 canons), mostly in manuscript, survive: among them are oratorios, Masses, secular arias, sinfonias, concertos, 96 keyboard sonatas (including the *Sonate d'intavolatura per l'organo e'l cembalo*, 1742), as well as a number of treatises and an only partly completed *Storia della musica* (1761); his greatest theoretical work was *Esemplare ossia Saggio fondamentale* (1774).

Melani, Alessandro. See ITALY *10 Itinerant Musicians.*

Nicolini. See ITALY *10 Itinerant Musicians.*

Pellegrini, Domenico (*d* after 1662). Bolognese guitarist and composer of *Armoniosi concerti* (1650), containing nine suites for guitar (including a passacaglia that modulates through 22 keys) and useful remarks on performing practice. Pellegrini also composed cantatas.

Perti, Giacomo Antonio (1661–1756). *Maestro di cappella* at S Petronio for 60 years, a composer of sacred music, opera and oratorio, and a noted teacher of such composers as Giuseppe Torelli and G.B. Martini. Although Perti spent time in Parma, studying counterpoint with Giuseppe Corso, and in Venice, where a number of his operas were performed, Bologna was his home and S Petronio the focus of his ambition. He was a life-long member of the Accademia Filarmonica and several times assumed its highest office (*principe*). He may have entertained hopes of gaining the patronage of Leopold I by dedicating to him his first publication (*Cantate morali e spirituali*) in 1688, but it earned him only a gold chain and medallion – and then only by the intercession of his pupil Torelli. His efforts to gain the post of vice-*maestro di cappella* at S Petronio were decisively prejudiced by his having sided against the *maestro di cappella* G.P. Colonna in a dispute over the function of parallel fifths in Corelli's op. 2 no. 3. Nevertheless Perti succeeded Colonna in 1696, remaining in the post for the rest of his life (Padre Martini claimed that Perti was invited to succeed A. Draghi at the Habsburg court in 1697 but refused).

His sacred music runs the gamut of genres and was highly regarded in its day. He was equally at home in both the contrapuntal *a cappella* style and the concerted style (in which he employed strings, trumpets and obbligato instruments). Under his stewardship the number of musicians regularly employed at S Petronio grew to 36 in 1723, and as many as 153 were employed for special services in 1718 and 1719. His operas, the first dating from 1679, were written primarily for Bologna and Venice, although several were staged at Pratolino by Ferdinando III de' Medici between 1707 and 1710.

Pistocchi, Francesco Antonio Mamiliano (1659–1726). Contralto castrato, who worked in Germany and Austria as well as Italy, gifted teacher (much admired by P.F. Tosi) and composer. Pistocchi was a child prodigy – the son of a musician at S Petronio – whose collection of *Capricci puerili* was published when he was only eight. At the age of 11 he became a singer at S Petronio, but was soon in such demand elsewhere that he and his father were dismissed from service five years later. His engagements took him to Parma (1686–95), Ansbach (where he was the Margrave of Brandenburg's *Kapellmeister*, 1696–9), Berlin (accompanied by his friend Giuseppe Torelli, 1697) and Vienna (again with Torelli, 1699), though he considered Bologna to be his home; from 1687 he was a member of the Accademia Filarmonica there. During his years away Pistocchi corresponded with G.A. Perti in Bologna, who arranged for peripatetic status at S Petronio to be conferred upon Pistocchi and Torelli when they returned in 1700. He was made a *virtuoso di camera e di cappella* by Prince Ferdinando of Tuscany in 1702 and continued to sing in operas until 1705. His pupils included Antonio Bernacchi, Annibale Pio Fabri and G.B. Martini. His association with S Petronio ceased in 1708 and he took holy orders the following year.

Rogeri, Giovanni Baptista. See ITALY *4 Venice.*

Sances, Giovanni Felice. See CENTRAL EUROPE *3 Austro-Hungary: Vienna.*

Sandoni, Pietro Giuseppe (1685–1748). Well-travelled Bolognese keyboard player and composer of operas, oratorios and keyboard sonatas – the first of their kind to be published in England (1726–8). Sandoni began and ended his career in Bologna where he was

a member (and four times *principe*) of the Accademia Filarmonica. He toured as a keyboard improvisor, playing in Vienna, Munich and London, where his skill was inevitably compared with that of Handel. The two became friendly and Sandoni returned to Venice to engage Cuzzoni on Handel's behalf for the Royal Academy of Music; later he became embroiled in conflicts between Handel and Bononcini. Sandoni and Cuzzoni married and returned to Venice via Vienna in 1728, but were back in London in 1734; the following season Sandoni's opera *Issipile* (text by Metastasio) was performed. They criss-crossed Europe again to spend 1737–8 in Florence and by 1740 were in Amsterdam.

Senesino. See ITALY *10 Itinerant Musicians.*

Tononi. Family of Bolognese violin makers. Both Giovanni (*d* 1713) and Carlo (*d* 1730) made instruments from Amati patterns. After moving to Venice Carlo adopted some of the prevailing conventions; he is known for his violas, modelled on an Amati contralto viol (1615).

Torelli, Giuseppe (1658–1709). Veronese virtuoso string player and prolific composer of sonatas and concertos. Torelli's first connections were with Bologna, where during the 1680s he studied composition with G.A. Perti, became a member of the Accademia Filarmonica and S Petronio orchestra and was a close friend of Pistocchi. He played the violin, viola and tenor viol. He composed a large quantity of orchestral music with trumpets (to take advantage of the talented Giovanni Pellegrino Brandi) and published collections of duo sonatas for violin and cello (*Concertino per camera*, 1688), trio sonatas (1686) and *sinfonie* for two to four instruments (1687, 1692), which he dedicated to noble patrons.

In 1696 the S Petronio orchestra was disbanded for a five-year period, during which Torelli toured Germany and Austria with Pistocchi. They took up posts as *Konzertmeister* and *Kapellmeister* at the Ansbach court of the Margrave of Brandenburg in 1696 and the following year were briefly in Berlin, performing for the Electress Sophie Charlotte, to whom Torelli dedicated a collection of *concerti musicali* (1698). From Ansbach they travelled to Vienna in 1699, and while there Torelli composed further chamber music as well as an oratorio (*Adam aus dem irrdischen Paradiess verstossen*, 1700) which was performed in the imperial chapel. Torelli and Pistocchi returned to Bologna in 1700 and resumed their places under Perti at S Petronio.

Torelli's most important contribution was

to the development of the concerto. The unique character of the S Petronio orchestra gave rise to juxtapositions of solo trumpets and oboes with ritornello strings, which Torelli varied by giving solo violins prominence in the slow movements. Passages for a single violin also occur in the 1698 collection. A further collection of *concerti grossi* (op. 8) was published posthumously in 1709.

Tosi, Pier Francesco. See ITALY 10 *Itinerant Musicians*.

Tricarico, Giuseppe. See ITALY 7 *Papal States: Rome*.

Ursino, Gennaro. See ITALY 8 *Naples*.

Vitali. Bolognese father and son, who were string players and influential composers of sonatas. Giovanni Battista Vitali (1632–92) worked in his native Bologna, where he had studied with Cazzati at S Petronio, and later in Modena at the Este court. While in Bologna he sang and played the *violoncino* (which he also referred to as a 'violone da brazzo') at S Petronio from 1658; he took up membership in the Accademia Filarmonica in 1666 and composed at least two oratorios for the SS Accademici Unanimi (1672). He was appointed *maestro di cappella* at S Rosario in 1673. The following year he left Bologna for Modena where he was first made a vice-*maestro di cappella* to Duke Francesco II and then *maestro di cappella* in 1684, though he stepped down two years later. As a member of the Accademia dei Dissonanti in Modena he contributed several cantatas to their gatherings.

Vitali is best known as a composer of *sonate da chiesa* and *da camera*. Opp. 1 (1666), 3 (1679) and 4 (1668) are *sonate da camera* made up of Italian dances, some of which adhere to the regular patterns intended for dancing while others are more irregular and contrapuntal; within individual sonatas Vitali experimented with variation as a unifying principle. Opp. 2 (1667) and 5 (1669) are *sonate da chiesa*; within each sonata there is a fast fugal movement in a duple metre followed by a slow homophonic movement and a fast dance movement in a triple metre. Vitali's later instrumental collections – opp. 8 (1683), 11 (1684), 12 (1685) and 14 (1692) – contain stylized French dances; he was the first to include bourrées and minuets in *sonate da camera*. Perhaps his most remarkable contribution was his 1689 *Artificii musicali* which anticipated J.S. Bach's *Musical Offering* by nearly 60 years: it contains 60 instrumental works which systematically document the art of counterpoint (in canons as well as in rep-resentative contemporary forms) arranged according to difficulty.

His eldest son Tomaso Antonio (1663–1745) accompanied him to Modena and eventually became leader of the court orchestra. In 1692 he published a posthumous collection of his father's trio sonatas and the following year embarked upon the publication of his own (three collections appeared between 1693 and 1695); in his op. 4 *Concerto di sonate* for violin, cello and continuo (1701), which follows close on the heels of Corelli's op. 5, he mixed *chiesa* and *camera* movements. The famous chaconne popularly attributed to him is now known not to be his.

Rome

Abbatini, Antonio Maria (1609/10–1677). Composer and scholar from Città di Castello, the teacher of G.P. Colonna, Domenico dal Pane and probably J.P. Krieger and Cesti. Abbatini studied in Rome and held a succession of short appointments as *maestro di cappella* at the Seminario Romano, S Giovanni in Laterano, the Gesù, S Maria Maggiore and S Luigi dei Francesi. During the 1640s he was involved in the preparation of a new edition of Gregorian hymns and helped Athanasius Kircher to assemble the monumental treatise *Musurgia universalis*, which appeared in 1650.

Abbatini published at least six books of sacred canzonas, as well as a 16-voice Mass and numerous motets; he also composed cantatas and operas. He contributed *secco* recitative and the ensemble finales – among the earliest of their kind – to Acts I and III of Marco Marazzoli's comic opera *Dal male il bene*, which was performed at the Palazzo Barberini in 1653. Thanks to Cesti's influence at the Habsburg court, Abbatini's *Ione* was performed at the Vienna Hoftheater in 1664; *La comica del cielo* was performed at the Palazzo Rospigliosi in Rome four years later.

Agazzari, Agostino. See ITALY 6 *Tuscany*.

Agostini, Paolo (*c*1583–1629). Organist and composer of Roman polychoral music who in 1626 succeeded Vincenzo Ugolini at the Cappella Giulia in the Vatican. Agostini is remembered as a brilliant contrapuntist who could weave several canons into a single Mass movement and manipulate up to eight choirs within a musical texture.

Allegri, Gregorio (1582–1652). Roman singer and composer whose *Miserere* is performed annually during Holy Week by the papal choir. Allegri was himself a papal singer under

Rome (Matthias Seutter: *Veteris et Modernae urbis Romae Ichnographia et Accurata Designatio*, 1720) The Vatican is bottom left, S Maria Maggiore is top centre, with S Giovanni in Laterano further to the right.

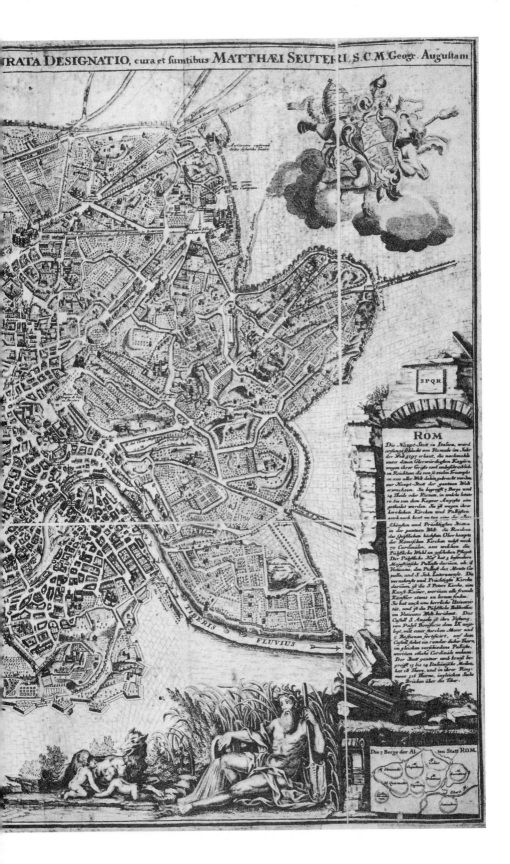

TRATA DESIGNATIO, cura et sumtibus MATTHÆI SEUTERI, S.C.M. Geogr. Augustam

SPQR

ROM

Die Haupt-Statt in Italien, ward
anfangs Schade von Romulo im Jahr
der Welt 3197 erbaut, ste ward...
unter dem Glorwürdigsten Kaysern
wegen ihrer Größe und unaussprechlich-
en Reichtum die von so vielen Triumphe
en aus aller Welt zusammengebracht
zur Haupt-Statt der gantzen Welt
erwachsen. Sie begreifft 7 Berge und
14 Theile oder Rienen, in welche hinte-
re Zeu von dem Kayser Augusto ein-
getheilet worden. Sie ist wegen ihrer
herrlichen Kirchen und Pallästen
auch noch heut zu Tag eine der Ru-...
schönsten und Prächtigsten Statt-
en in der gantzen Welt, die Residenz
des Geistlichen höchsten Ober-haupts
der Römischen Kirchen nebst weit
zu Cardinalen, von welchen die
Päpstliche Wahl zu geschehen pfleget.
Der Päpstliche Hof hat 3 besondere
Mayestätische Pallaste darinen, als J
Vaticano, den Pallast des Monte Cavallo, und S. Job. Laterranende. Die
vornehmste und Prächtigste Kirche
darinen, ist the S. Peters Kirche, eine
Kunst-Kammer, worinen alle fremd-
Künstler etwas zu lernen finden.
Sie hat auch eine herrliche Universi-
tät, wie of the Päpstliche Bibliothec
im Vaticano Welt berühmt. Das
Castell S. Angelo ist ihre Vestung
von Pabst Bonefacio dem II auge-
legt, mit einer durchaus Mauer
z Bastionen Größtert, auf dem
Castell stehet ein runder dicker Thurn,
im gleichen verschiedene Pallaste,
worinen ettliche Cardinale wohnen.
Der Statt gantzer, und kraft begreifft 15 bis 14 Italienische Meilen,
hat 18 Thore, und in ihrer Ring-
maur 316 Thurne, ingleichen Sach-
Brücken über die Thor.

TIBERIS FLUVIUS

Die 7 Berge der Al-...ten Statt ROM.

Urban VIII and many of his works – *a cappella* motets, six- and eight-part Masses, Lamentations and a *Te Deum* – were composed for the papal choir, though he did compose *concertini* (1618, 1619) for two to five voices with continuo for the choirs of other churches. However he is remembered entirely by his *Miserere*, a work in which five-part *falsobordone* chant alternates with ornamented passages in four parts. Although the ornamented sections were kept secret for many years, Mozart copied the *Miserere* out from memory, and, through the offices of Charles Burney, it was published by Novello in London.

Amadei, Filippo (*fl* 1690–1730). Roman cellist and composer. Amadei was associated with Cardinal Ottoboni – for whom he composed operas (*Teodosio il giovane* was performed at the cardinal's palace in 1711, with sets by Juvarra), oratorios (*L'Abele*, 1708) and cantatas – and with the cellists of the Società del Centesimo attached to the Congregazione di S Cecilia. As 'Sigr Pippo' he spent about five years in London playing in the Royal Academy of Music orchestra from 1719; while in London he was also a recitalist with the violinist Giovanni Carbonelli and composed for the theatre (in 1721 he contributed the first act of *Muzio Scevola* to which Giovanni Bononcini and Handel also contributed acts).

Anerio, Giovanni Francesco (*c*1567–1630). Roman priest, *maestro di cappella* and composer whose *Teatro armonico spirituale* (1619) contributed significantly to the rise of the vernacular oratorio. In contrast to his elder brother Felice (*c*1560–1614), who succeeded Palestrina as composer of the papal choir (1594) and with Soriano reformed the Roman Gradual (1611), Anerio composed in both *prima* and *seconda prattica*. He published a collection of spiritual madrigals for one to four voices (*Selva armonica*, 1617) and another (for the Oratorio di S Filippo Neri) including short oratorios, *Teatro armonico spirituale* (1619), in which he incorporated instrumental obbligatos – the first known instance of their use by a Roman composer.

Archilei, Vittoria. See ITALY 6 *Tuscany*.

Astorga, Emanuele d'. See ITALY 9 *Sicily*.

Badia, Carlo Agostino. See CENTRAL EUROPE 3 *Austro-Hungary: Vienna*.

Baroni, Leonora. See ITALY 10 *Itinerant Musicians*.

Benevoli, Orazio (1605–72). Roman composer to whom the 53-part *Missa salisburgensis* has been wrongly attributed. Benevoli began his career as a choirboy at S Luigi dei Francesi

under Vincenzo Ugolini and Lorenzo Ratti. By 1624 he himself was made *maestro di cappella* at one of the Vatican churches, where he served until 1630, thereafter taking up other appointments in Rome. In 1644 he went to Vienna to become *Kapellmeister* to Archduke Leopold Wilhelm, but returned to Rome in 1646 to assume the duties of *maestro di cappella* at S Maria Maggiore; later that year he succeeded Virgilio Mazzocchi at the Cappella Giulia, where he remained for the rest of his life. Little of his music was published until recently; all of it is sacred, in both post-Palestrina and monodic styles. See also CENTRAL EUROPE 2 *Salzburg* Biber, Heinrich Ignaz Franz von; Hofer, Andreas.

Berardi, Angelo (*c*1636–1694). Prolific Italian church composer and *maestro di cappella*, as well as an important writer on 17th-century counterpoint. Berardi held posts as organist and *maestro di cappella* at various places before finally taking up a post at S Maria, Trastevere, Rome. His earliest surviving treatise, *Ragionamenti musicali* (1681), elaborates on his teacher Marco Scacchi's tripartite division of musical styles according to function – church, chamber and theatre. Together, his *Documenti armonici* (1687) and *Miscellanea musicali* (1689) present a comprehensive study of counterpoint and dissonance; the *Documenti* includes a canon for 32 sopranos. His last two treatises are retrospective: the *Arcani musicali* (1690) offers instruction in composing *a cappella* Masses and polychoral music, and *Il perchè musicale* (1693) reviews the *seconda prattica*.

Bergerotti, Anna. See FRANCE 1 *Paris and Versailles*.

Bernabei. See CENTRAL EUROPE 1 *South Germany: Munich*.

Bernardi, Stefano. See ITALY 10 *Itinerant Musicians*.

Bononcini. See ITALY 5 *Modena-Reggio*.

Bonporti, Francesco Antonio (1672–1749). Ambitious priest, who tried in vain to advance in the church, and composer of instrumental music and concerted solo motets (1701). Bonporti was educated in Trent, Innsbruck and Rome where, in addition to his theological studies at the Collegio Germanico, he was a pupil of Corelli. From the relative obscurity of a post at Trent Cathedral (1697), he sought no less a post than that of chaplain to the Holy Roman Emperor; for his efforts he gained only an honorific post as 'aulic familiar' to Charles VI. By 1740 he had only got as far as Padua, from where he unsuccessfully petitioned the Empress Maria Theresa in 1746. Bonporti is known today as the composer of ten *invenzioni da camera* (1712) for violin and continuo, once attributed to J.S. Bach but now known to have been merely copied by him.

Bontempi, Giovanni Andrea. See NORTH-ERN EUROPE *4 Saxony and Thuringia: Dresden*.

Bordoni, Faustina. See ITALY *10 Itinerant Musicians*.

Buti, Francesco. See FRANCE *1 Paris and Versailles*.

Caffarelli. See ITALY *10 Itinerant Musicians*.

Caproli [Caprioli del Violino], **Carlo** (1615/20–1692/5). Roman violinist and organist, one of the leading Italian cantata composers of the mid 17th century. Caproli was well connected, having been an organist under Carissimi at the Collegio Germanico (1643–5) and a violinist under Luigi Rossi at S Luigi dei Francesi (1649–61). From 1653 he was also in the service of Prince Ludovisio Pamphili, who was not particularly pleased when in 1654 Caproli departed for Paris (with the encouragement of his librettist Francesco Buti and Cardinal Barberini), where he had been invited by Cardinal Mazarin to produce a comic opera. *Le nozze di Peleo e di Teti* (lost, except for the text) was performed nine times at the Petit Bourbon; the young Louis XIV danced in the accompanying ballet *entrées* composed by Lully. In recognition of his success, Caproli was made *maître de la musique du cabinet du Roy*. He returned in 1659 to Rome where he took up a post at the Congregazione di S Cecilia. He was a prolific composer of solo and ensemble cantatas, many of which employ instruments, and he produced at least five oratorios, of which only *David' prevaricante e poi pentito* (1683) survives.

Carestini, Giovanni. See ITALY *10 Itinerant Musicians*.

Carissimi, Giacomo (1605–74). The most important Italian composer of oratorios and cantatas of his day, and an influential teacher; his music, largely disseminated in manuscript copies, continued to be performed until the 19th century. Only the barest facts are known of his life. He sang in the choir and later served as organist at Tivoli Cathedral during the mid 1620s, then moved to Assisi. From 1629 until his death he was *maestro di cappella* at the Jesuit Collegio Germanico and at S Apollinare in Rome. He was offered posts at S Marco, Venice, and at the Habsburg court, Vienna, but declined them. He is thought to have provided music for the Roman academies and, during the 1650s, is known to have organized Lenten performances at the Oratorio del Ss Crocifisso. In 1656 the exiled Swedish Queen Christina appointed him her *maestro di cappella del concerto di camera*; many of his secular cantatas were composed for her. A number of important composers are thought to have been his pupils, among them G.P. Colonna, K. Förster, J.K. Kerll, Christoph Bernhard and M.-A. Charpentier.

Most of Carissimi's works cannot be precisely dated because they survive in manuscript copies rather than autographs or editions. Although Pope Clement X attempted to protect the autographs by establishing an archive at S Apollinare, they disappeared in 1773, after the dissolution of the Jesuit order. The *Missa a quinque et a novem* (1665–6) was exceptional in that it was published in Cologne, not Rome; some of the motets were also printed in Cologne, Konstanz and Rome during Carissimi's lifetime.

In three-quarters of the 150 surviving cantatas, which fall crucially between those of Luigi Rossi and those of Alessandro Scarlatti and Stradella, Carissimi experimented with a wide variety of aria forms for soprano and continuo. While ever attentive to the rhythm and message of his texts, Carissimi revelled in the additional freedom to underscore their sensuousness. *Vittoria, mio core* is an important early example of bel canto style; the duo cantata *I filosofi* stands out for its spirited dialogue.

Because of the chamber music proportions and professionalism of the Collegio Germanico *cappella*, Carissimi composed motets and oratorios in the concertato idiom, relying in particular on solo voices (the oratorios additionally employ a *historicus* or narrator). Choruses in the oratorios sharply contrast with the solo voices and contribute moments of high drama, as in *Jonas* and *Judicium extremum*. Conveying the rhetoric of a text was of paramount importance to Carissimi, and accordingly the distinction between recitative and aria is often blurred; Mattheson later wrote (1740) that Carissimi was known throughout Italy as 'the musical orator' during his lifetime. To underscore the emotional content of texts such as those of *Jephte* and *Judicium Salomonis* he repeated key phrases and used changes of mode, dissonant harmonies and leaps, as well as conventional ornamentation; these devices were later codified by his German pupil Christoph Bernhard. Athanasius Kircher, his contemporary in Rome, noted in 1650 that Carissimi 'surpasses all others in moving the minds of the listeners to whatever affection he wishes'.

Castrucci. See BRITISH ISLES *1 London*.

Cavalieri, Emilio de'. See ITALY 6 *Tuscany.*
Cesti, Antonio. See ITALY *10 Itinerant Musicians.*
Christina (1626–89). Queen of Sweden (1644–54), who abdicated her throne and quit her country in order to embrace Catholicism; the far-reaching sacrifices she made for her faith provided the Catholic church with unprecedented Counter-Reformation propaganda. She was a highly intelligent, cultivated woman, if slightly *outrée* in demeanour (for example, she wore men's clothing). She had been groomed for power and, having forsaken her own throne, settled for the ear of the pope: she intervened in the Franco-Spanish War during the 1650s, and plotted unsuccessfully (and disastrously for the equerry who exposed her) with the French first minister, Cardinal Mazarin, to become Queen of Naples (1656–7). She spent most of the rest of her life in Rome, presiding over first one, then two academies, in which music played an important part, and providing important patronage for Rome's finest musicians.

Christina's father, Gustavus II Adolphus, was killed in battle in 1632. During her minority the regent (Axel Oxenstierna) made an alliance with France (1635) which led to the frenchifying of the Swedish court. Attracted by French music and dancing, the young Christina hired a dancing-master (Antoine de Beaulieu) in 1637, then six French violinists (led by Pierre Verdier) a decade later. At first they were kept separate from the German musicians under *Kapellmeister* Andreas Düben, but were later amalgamated after the further acquisition of an Italian troupe under Alessandro Cecconi in 1652. She also took an interest in English music, thanks to the English ambassador Sir Bulstrode Whitelocke, who organized concerts of viol music.

Her interest in the culture of other European countries was not confined to music. She had a flair for languages and was an avid collector of art. She admired the French diplomat Pierre Chanut and even more the philosopher René Descartes – who spent his last months in Stockholm, taking part in an ongoing dialogue with her on philosophy and mathematics and collaborating on a ballet (*La naissance de la paix*) to celebrate her birthday in December 1649. After Descartes' death early in 1650, the philosopher Marcus Meibom was appointed a royal librarian – after dedicating his *Antiquae musicae auctores septem* (1652) to the queen.

Aware that she must pave the way for her abdication, she channelled a deep affection for her cousin into a battle with the nobility over his right to succeed her and, after involving the non-noble Estates (the burghers, clergy and peasants) in the Diet of 1650, she was able to ensure that he became King Charles X Gustavus. When she did abdicate, on 6 June 1654, she moved swiftly (having smuggled her art collection out in advance), taking in her entourage Cecconi and other musicians. Her first stop was the South Netherlands (Antwerp and Brussels), where on Christmas Eve she formally became a Catholic. From there she went to Innsbruck, where she was greeted with great pomp by Archduke Ferdinand who then celebrated her conversion with a week of festivities that included a performance of Cesti's *L'Argia* (text by Apolloni).

She chose to enter Rome incognito and established herself at the Palazzo Farnese. On Christmas Day 1655 she took communion from Pope Alexander VII and a month later (24 January) founded an academy of prominent artists and intellectuals, devoted to the re-establishment of classical ideals. Many musicians were associated with the academy (known as the Accademia dell'Arcadia after her death), including Marco Marazzoli, Marc' Antonio Pasqualini, Giuseppe Melani, Alessandro Scarlatti and Corelli (who dedicated his op. 1 to her in 1681). During her first year in Rome, performances of Marazzoli's *La vita humana* (at the Palazzo Barberini), A.F. Tenaglia's *Il giudizio di Paride* (at the Palazzo Pamphili) and Carissimi's *Historia di Abraham et Isaac* (at the Collegio Germanico) were given in her honour – evidence of her acceptance in Roman aristocratic circles.

From 1659 she lived at the Palazzo Riario, where in 1671 she had the theatre rebuilt: as the Teatro Tordinona it became the first public opera house in Rome. In 1680 she founded a second academy, at which music (a sinfonia and a vocal work) was always performed. Christina spent several years abroad, in Paris (1656–8), Stockholm (1660–2) and Hamburg (1666–8).

Cifra, Antonio (1584–1629). Prolific composer of the Roman school. Cifra, a pupil of G.B. Nanino, held posts in Rome (1605–9) at the Seminario Romano and the Collegio Germanico, during which time he published the first two (of six) books of conventional five-part madrigals, before taking up a permanent post as *maestro di cappella* at the Santa Casa, Loreto. He returned to Rome in 1622 to serve at S Giovanni in Laterano, until 1626. An initial volume of vesper psalms (1601) was followed by eight books of concertato motets for two to four voices and continuo (1609–15) – many of which appeared in contemporary German anthologies – and five of Masses in the post-Palestrina style, as well as further collections of polychoral psalms and motets. His most adventurous music, solo monodies, may be found in the two volumes of *Scherzi sacri* (1616, 1618); their secular counterparts (1613, 1614, 1615, 1617) are characterized by their reliance upon the Romanesca or other bass tunes as a formal device.

Colista, Lelio (1629–80). Roman lutenist, guitarist and composer of trio sonatas. Colista remained all his life in Rome, travelling abroad only once to Paris in the huge entourage of Cardinal Chigi in 1664. During the 1660s he was *maestro di cappella* at S Marcello and much in demand as a performer. He is known to have composed at least two oratorios (1661, 1667) in addition to cantatas and sonatas for the meetings of the Roman academies (he became a member of the Arciconfraternità delle Sacre Stimmate at S Francesco in 1675). His grandson Mattei (*c*1705–1772) was organist at S Giovanni in Laterano when Burney visited Rome in 1770. By their imitative counterpoint, the chains of suspensions and 'walking basses', Colista's trio sonatas anticipate the achievements of Corelli and, although forgotten in Italy in the wake of the younger man's polished chamber music, they were performed elsewhere in Europe well into the 18th century. Purcell's trio sonatas are also said to have been influenced by them.

Colonna, Giovanni Paolo. See ITALY *7 Papal States: Bologna-Ferrara*.

Corelli, Arcangelo (1653–1713). Important Italian composer of sonatas and concertos, the most influential violinist of the Baroque era. Corelli came from a well-to-do provincial family and enjoyed the comfortable patronage in Rome of a succession of distinguished royal and clerical music lovers, as evidenced by the dedications to his six published collections of instrumental music.Little is known of his early history save that he was admitted to the Bolognese Accademia Filarmonica in 1670. By 1675 he had made his way to Rome where, as second violin to Carlo Mannelli, he initially found work in churches and theatres.

Corelli's first real patron was the Swedish Queen Christina, also resident in Rome; the trio *sonate da chiesa* he composed for her first academy appeared in 1681 as op. 1. It was not long before he gained the attention of Cardinal Pamphili: he played in the Sunday academies at the Palazzo al Corso, then organized them,

assisted by his student Matteo Fornari and the Spanish-born cellist Giovanni Lorenzo Lulier – together they must have performed the trio sonatas and concertino parts in Corelli's concertos. In 1685 Corelli dedicated his op. 2 trio *sonate da camera* to the cardinal, who eventually put him in charge of his music in 1689. The op. 3 (1689) trio *sonate da chiesa* were dedicated to the Duke of Modena.

A year later Corelli moved his lodging from one cardinal's palace to that of another: Cardinal Ottoboni became his next important patron. Corelli was charged with organizing the Monday academies and performances of operas at the Cancelleria, and in 1694 he dedicated his op. 4 to his patron. The famous op. 5 sonatas for violin and continuo (first published in 1700 and reprinted 42 times during the 18th century), embodying the perfection of Italian church and chamber sonata idioms, were dedicated to the Electress Sophie Charlotte of Brandenburg. In 1708 he became a member of the distinguished Accademia dell'Arcadia, along with Pasquini and Alessandro Scarlatti. When he died in 1713 his body was interred in the Pantheon. One year later Fornari undertook the publication in Amsterdam of Corelli's op. 6 concertos, which gained immediate popularity.

Corelli had a reputation for perfectionism: his playing was both elegant and learned, his publications contained only the polished gems of a much larger output. His bands were trained like those of Lully to play uniformly and with precision. He had many eager pupils, among them Italians – Carbonelli, Castrucci, Gasparini, Geminiani, Somis – as well as foreigners such as Anet, Herrando and Störl. His sonatas and concertos were the standard-bearers for subsequent Baroque and pre-Classical composers; four movements were established as the norm, and the harmony was firmly tonal (reinforced by progressions of sixth chords, 'walking basses' and the cliché 'Corelli clash' at cadences); his demands on the players were always idiomatic and slow movements perforce skeletal, to allow soloists the opportunity truly to demonstrate their musicianship. Geminiani, Bach, Tartini and Veracini arranged, borrowed and emulated specific works. Corelli is a central figure in two *apothéose* works (1724–5) by Couperin.

Costanzi, Giovanni Battista (1704–78). Roman cellist (known as 'Giovannino del Violoncello'), *maestro di cappella* and prolific composer. Costanzi, very probably a protégé of Lulier, was taken into Cardinal Ottoboni's service in 1721. The cardinal provided

Costanzi with the libretto for *Carlo Magno*, which was performed at the Cancelleria in 1729, and made possible a series of lucrative appointments as *maestro di cappella*. Costanzi stopped composing secular dramas about 1740 and concentrated on sacred genres. However all his oratorios and cantatas are lost. His surviving music inevitably contains virtuoso cello passages; he left a cello concerto and three sonatas, one of which is for two cellos. His most famous pupil was Luigi Boccherini. Costanzi was a member of the Congregazione di S Cecilia and was elected president three times (1740, 1754 and 1769). In 1755 he became *maestro di cappella* of the Cappella Giulia.

Dal Pane, Domenico (*c*1630–94). Roman soprano castrato and composer in the old polyphonic style. Dal Pane trained under Abbatini at S Maria Maggiore before taking up a place in the Viennese imperial court chapel in 1650. While there he published a collection of madrigals, dedicated to Emperor Ferdinand II, in the old polyphonic style. In 1654 he returned definitively to Rome where, as the finest castrato of his day, he simultaneously entered the service of the papal chapel and that of the Pamphili family. He sang that year in the performance of Marco Marazzoli's *La vita humana* honouring Queen Christina of Sweden at the Palazzo Barberini. In 1669 he became *maestro di cappella* of the Cappella Sistina, retiring a decade later; in that capacity he composed *a cappella* parody Masses (based on Palestrina motets). In 1675 he published a collection of more forward-looking sacred concertos for virtuoso singers (which he had composed for the Corpus Christi celebrations in the Borghese chapel at S Maria Maggiore) and a book of motets.

De Grandis, Vincenzo. See ITALY *10 Itinerant Musicians.*

Doni, Giovanni Battista. See ITALY *6 Tuscany.*

Durastanti, Margherita. See ITALY *10 Itinerant Musicians.*

Eberlin, Daniel. See NORTHERN EUROPE *4 Saxony and Thuringia.*

Fabri, Annibale Pio. See ITALY *10 Itinerant Musicians.*

Ferrari, Benedetto. See ITALY *4 Venice.*

Foggia, Francesco (1604–88). Prolific Roman composer of liturgical music. He worked at the Dresden, Munich and Innsbruck courts as a young man, returning to Italy to take up appointments first at Narni Cathedral, then at Montefiascone, before becoming *maestro di cappella* at S Maria Maggiore in Rome (1677).

Foggia studied with Antonio Cifra and Paolo Agostini (even marrying his daughter) and, having mastered counterpoint and polyphony, was the last of the Romans to embrace the style of Palestrina – though he did sometimes use continuo (more often than not as an option).

Fontana, Giovanni Battista. See ITALY *4 Venice.*

Frescobaldi, Girolamo (1583–1643). Renowned Italian keyboard virtuoso and composer. Mersenne remarked that 'all his knowledge is at the ends of his fingertips'. From the beginning Frescobaldi's career as player and composer flourished under the patronage of the wealthiest and best-placed connoisseurs of music in Italy. He himself came from a well-to-do Ferrarese family who cultivated their son's extraordinary gifts as an organist and whose friend, the composer Luzzasco Luzzaschi, took him as a pupil. Gesualdo too was a mentor.

In Rome by 1604 Frescobaldi had attracted the attention of the Bentivoglios. When in 1607 Guido Bentivoglio was appointed papal nuncio to Flanders, he took Frescobaldi with him to Brussels; during Frescobaldi's ten months there he published virtuoso five-part madrigals. Back in Italy in 1608 and under the protection of Enzo Bentivoglio he published his first book of four-part fantasias (having published ensemble canzonas the year before) in Milan, before taking up duties as an organist at S Pietro in Rome. The following year Bentivoglio – hoping to acquire the services of a gifted soprano – sought to arrange a marriage between Frescobaldi and one of Caccini's daughters; however Frescobaldi's reputation was sufficient to merit a counter-offer of a similar nature from Florence, which created a temporary stalemate.

Frescobaldi maintained his association with S Pietro throughout his career, though his patrons changed, occasioning leaves of absence – three months at the Gonzaga court in 1615 and six years in Florence at the court of the Grand Duke of Tuscany (1628–34). He married and had children; later in life he took on pupils, Froberger, Kerll and Tunder among them. From 1612 until 1628 he had as patron the influential Cardinal Pietro Aldobrandini and, upon his return from Florence in 1634, the powerful Barberini family. He was frequently heard at the musical academies of the wealthy Roman clergy and aristocracy and was richly rewarded.

Although Frescobaldi's *Fiori musicali* (1635) for organ is his best-known collection, those from his Aldobrandini period – the harpsichord toccatas, ricercares and *canzoni franzesi* of 1615, the capriccios of 1624, and the harpsichord and organ toccatas and canzonas of 1627 – contain some of his most important work. The early works are intensely virtuoso, influenced by the toccatas of Luzzaschi, Pasquini and Macque. The capriccios combine the vitality, seriousness, experimentation and florid ornamentation of his earlier works with maturity. The subsequent book of toccatas (1637) takes his style – dramatic sectional contrasts, linear counterpoint, bizarre harmony, complex rhythm and thrilling virtuosity – to its limits. Another collection of *Canzoni alla francese* was published posthumously in 1645.

Fux, Johann Joachim. See CENTRAL EUROPE *3 Austro-Hungary: Vienna.*

Galli-Bibiena, Francesco. See CENTRAL EUROPE *3 Austro-Hungary: Vienna.*

Gasparini, Francesco (1661–1727). Prolific opera composer, teacher of Quantz, Platti, Domenico Scarlatti and Benedetto Marcello and author of *L'armonico pratico* (1708). Gasparini had been a pupil of Legrenzi in Venice before settling in 1689 in Rome, where he became associated with Corelli, Alessandro Scarlatti and Pasquini in Cardinal Pamphili's orchestra. His first Roman opera (*Il Roderico*) was performed in 1694, and his first set of cantatas published the following year. The latter were highly esteemed in their day for the technical skill and graceful elegance with which he infused them. He returned to Venice in 1701 as *maestro di cappella* at the Ospedale della Pietà, where he succeeded in expanding the music faculty (Vivaldi was one of his appointees), while devoting most of his energies to composing a steady stream of operas for the Teatro S Cassiano.

During the 1709 Carnival his setting of Zeno's *Atenaide* was performed at the Vienna court, and in 1719 *L'oracolo del fato* was also given at the Hoftheater. Gasparini composed operas for Naples, Bergamo, Florence (1715 Carnival) and Milan, as well as Rome, where he had once again taken up residence in 1713. Ill health forced him to decline the post of *maestro di cappella* at S Giovanni in Laterano in 1725.

Giustiniani, Vincenzo (1564–1637). Noble Roman patron of the arts and amateur music theorist, important for the short *Discorso sopra la musica* of 1628, written in the form of a letter, in which he described the musicians and practices of his day. He amassed a fine art collection at his villa at Bassano, near Rome.

Graziani, Bonifazio (1604/5–64). *Maestro di cappella* at the Seminario Romano (as well as the Gesù church) and composer. A contemporary of Carissimi, Graziani composed at least two oratorios and a quantity of motets, of which six books for solo voice and continuo were repeatedly reprinted (the third book, published in 1658, was his finest). His strengths lay in his dramatic flair, his mastery of vocal declamation and a fluency apparent in his arioso writing and in his treatment of small vocal ensembles. His scores contain numerous tempo and dynamic markings.

Grossi, Giovanni Francesco. See ITALY *10 Itinerant Musicians.*

Handel, George Frideric. See BRITISH ISLES *1 London.*

Hasse, Johann Adolf. See NORTHERN EUROPE *4 Saxony and Thuringia: Dresden.*

Haym, Nicola Francesco. See BRITISH ISLES *1 London.*

India, Sigismondo d'. See ITALY *10 Itinerant Musicians.*

Jovernardi, Bartolomé. See IBERIAN PENINSULA AND COLONIES *1 Spain.*

Juvarra, Filippo (1676–1736). Architect, who renovated the private Roman theatres of Cardinal Ottoboni (1709) and Prince Capranica (1713), and stage designer, who sought by means of complex architectural structures and play of light to create the aesthetic counterpart of the dramatic works on which he collaborated. He was responsible for the exquisite Arcadian sets for Alessandro Scarlatti's *Il circo* (1712). In addition to the cardinal and the prince, Juvarra worked as a set designer for the Queen of Poland, in residence in Rome at the Palazzo Zuccari. In 1714 he was made chief architect to Vittorio Amedeo II of Savoy, with responsibility for building projects in Portugal and Spain as well as Turin, where in 1722 he built a stage in the Palazzo Reale and modernized the Teatro Regio. He died in Madrid.

Kapsberger, Johann Hieronymus [Giovanni Girolamo] (*c*1580–1651). German lute virtuoso and composer, who lived all his life in Venice and Rome, where in 1610 he founded an academy. Kapsberger grew up in Venice, where his father, a German colonel, was stationed. After publishing his first collection of chitarrone pieces in Venice he moved to Rome in 1604–5. He composed both vocal (sacred and secular) and instrumental music (for plucked instruments), gaining the friendship of such men as the poet Giulio Rospigliosi and the polymath Athanasius Kircher, *entrée* to other Roman academies, and the patronage of Pope Urban VIII, whose poems he set in 1624. Two years earlier he was chosen to compose a dramatic work for the celebrations marking the canonization of Ignatius Loyola (*Apotheosis seu Consecratio SS Ignatii et Francisci Xaverii*). His son, Philipp Bonifaz, gained a post in the service of Cardinal Francesco Barberini. Unfortunately a substantial portion of his music and his chitarrone treatise (*Il Kapsberger della musica*) are lost. He published numerous collections of solo lute and chitarrone music (toccatas, partitas and dances) and left manuscripts of *Sinfonie a quattro* for violin, cornett, plucked instrument and harpsichord.

Kircher, Athanasius (1601–80). Formidable German polymath, resident in Rome, whose monumental *Musurgia universalis* (1650) influenced nearly every German music theorist for a century to come. Kircher's array of academic credentials encompassed studies in mathematics, the physical sciences, philosophy, theology and languages. After serving as a professor of mathematics, philosophy and oriental languages at the University of Würzburg in 1629, he escaped to France when invasion by the Swedish army was imminent. For a brief time he taught at the Jesuit college in Avignon but, in 1633, was appointed court mathematician to Emperor Ferdinand II in Vienna – a post he never took up, preferring instead to accept a professorship at the Collegio Romano. Kircher published 30 books and was an indefatigable correspondent, devoted to popularizing (among other things) the study of Egyptian culture and civilization (he was among the first to decode hieroglyphics). He was an energetic collector of antiquities, and the Museum Kircherianum attracted many visitors throughout the 18th century.

Kircher's interest in music grew logically out of his devotion to the Quadrivium, and the *Musurgia universalis* is strongly rooted in Germanic traditions. In addition to long tracts on acoustics and musical instruments, he devoted space to the affective nature of music, quoting extended passages (and providing a unique source for some of the music); he also discoursed on the history of music in ancient cultures and the healing qualities of music. Though evidently not a musician, he is said to have invented a composing machine (*arca musarithmica*).

Landi, Stefano (1586/7–1639). A leading Roman composer of his day. Although Landi worked all his life as a church musician, his most important works were for the theatre.

He served the Barberinis for several years and with their assistance joined the papal choir (as an alto) in 1629. His opera *Il Sant'Alessio* (text by Rospigliosi) – the first to be based on a historical subject and hence to characterize ordinary mortals – was performed at the Palazzo Barberini in 1632. In 1634 he contributed music to a new edition of hymns, commissioned by the pope, and in 1635 set Ottaviano Castelli's *I pregi di primavera* as a cantata for a performance at the pope's summer residence, Castel Gandolfo. Landi had been trained in Rome at the Collegio Germanico and at the Seminario Romano where, in addition to studying rhetoric and philosophy, he worked with the *maestro di cappella*, Agazzari. His first opera, *La morte d'Orfeo*, was commissioned in 1619 by the Borghese family. The dedications to his collections of arias and psalms reveal further princes and cardinals among his patrons.

In *La morte d'Orfeo* Landi showed himself to be at ease blending the *stile antico* of his Masses and five-part madrigals with the *stile moderno* of his concertato Magnificat, Vesper psalms and monodic arias. This integration of practices did not however always go down well: in 1629 members of the papal choir balked at performing his responsories because of their modern idiom. *Il Sant'Alessio* was conceived for a grand occasion, incorporating several choruses and substantial orchestral sinfonias – the first opera overtures – and requiring elaborate sets and machinery in order that Religion be transported in a cloud and the Devil enveloped in flames.

Leoni, Giovanni Antonio (*d* after 1652). Violinist, composer and teacher working in Rome, in the service of Cardinal G.B. Pallotta (who sponsored concerts at the Santa Casa, Loreto). His sonatas and sinfonias circulated widely in manuscript as well as in printed editions.

Leopardi, Venanzio. See ITALY *10 Itinerant Musicians.*

Liberati, Antimo (1617–92). Outspoken composer and theorist of the Roman school responsible for stimulating the Palestrina revival during the second half of the 17th century. Before becoming a musician Liberati was a notary at the Viennese court (1637–43). In 1644 he took orders and became a pupil first of Gregorio Allegri and then of Orazio Benevoli; in 1661 he took up a post as an alto in the Cappella Giulia, where he remained (while undertaking duties as organist and *maestro di cappella* at three Roman churches). Liberati's devotion to Palestrina's music is clearly set forth in his manuscript *Epitome della musica* (1666), dedicated to Pope Alexander VII. His disapproval of the Roman opera and oratorio composers (Landi, Marazzoli, the Mazzocchis and Luigi Rossi) is tacitly expressed in an open letter published in 1685; among post-Palestrinians Liberati admired Allegri, Benevoli, Nanino and Cifra. Elsewhere, in manuscript, he complained about the modern practices being introduced in the Cappella Sistina and the so-called parallel fifths in Corelli's op. 2 no. 3.

Lilius, Wincenty. See NORTHERN EUROPE *3 Poland.*

Lonati, Carlo Ambrogio. See ITALY *10 Itinerant Musicians.*

Lorenzani, Paolo. See FRANCE *1 Paris and Versailles.*

Lulier, Giovanni Lorenzo ['Giovanni del Violone'] (*c*1650–early 18th century). Spanish-born cellist and composer who worked all his life in Rome, where he was considered the finest cellist of his day. Lulier was a member of the *cappella* at S Luigi dei Francesi until at least 1699 and was employed (along with Corelli, Pasquini and Alessandro Scarlatti) by Cardinals Ottoboni and Pamphili (who provided him with cantata and oratorio texts). He also composed oratorios for performances in Modena and Florence, collaborating on two with Scarlatti and other composers during the early years of the 18th century. Although no solo cello music by Lulier survives, vocal works incorporating concertante parts do.

Maccioni, Giovanni Battista. See CENTRAL EUROPE *1 South Germany: Munich.*

Manelli, Francesco. See ITALY *4 Venice.*

Mannelli, Carlo ['Carlo del Violino', 'Carluccio di Pamfilio'] (1640–97). Roman castrato, violinist and composer whose treatise on violin playing (*Studio del violino*) is lost. With the violinist C.A. Lonati, Mannelli represents a link between Caproli and Corelli. Mannelli received his training as a singer and violinist thanks to Prince Camillo Pamphili. In 1657 he sang in P.A. Ziani's opera *Le fortune di Rodope e Damira* at the Teatro S Apollinare, Venice, and in 1660 took up a post as a soprano at S Luigi dei Francesi, Rome: he is also known to have sung in Lenten oratorios presented by the Arciconfraternità del Ss Crocifisso at S Marcello, Rome.

Mannelli became a member of the Congregazione di S Cecilia in 1663 and twice served as *guardiano* of the instrumentalists; he made the Congregazione the sole heir to his estate, which included an endowment for needy members. He published his first col-lection of *sinfonie* for violin and continuo some time before 1666 and in 1668 succeeded Caproli as the leader of Cardinal Pamphili's band; in 1675 he gained the post of first concertino violin at S Giovanni dei Fiorentini (Corelli was among the *ripieno* violinists). His op. 2 trio sonatas (each in five movements) appeared in 1682, and about that time Corelli succeeded him as the leader of Pamphili's musicians; he published a second volume of trio sonatas in 1692. His commanding violin technique is evident from a single surviving work for violin and continuo which employs extensive double-stopping.

Marazzoli, Marco [Marco dell'Arpa] (*c*1602–1662). Priest, singer, virtuoso harpist and a leading Roman composer (along with Luigi Rossi and Carissimi) of cantatas (379 survive) and oratorios; he collaborated with Rospigliosi and Virgilio Mazzocchi on the earliest comic opera, *Chi soffre, speri* (1637). Trained at Parma Cathedral, Marazzoli had become attached to the musical establishment of Cardinal Antonio Barberini in Rome by 1631 – though he did not settle there until 1637, when he gained an appointment in the papal chapel. The innovative *Chi soffre, speri*, to which he contributed at least the *intermedio* to Act II (the rest was by Mazzocchi), was produced that year at the Barberini family theatre. During his first years in Rome he provided Latin oratorios for the Oratorio del Ss Crocifisso.

Marazzoli continued to retain his appointments with the cardinal and the Vatican while travelling during the 1630s and 40s, to Ferrara (where his first important opera, *L'Armida*, was given at the Teatro della Sala Grande in 1641) and to Venice (where his 'festa teatrale' *Gli amori di Giasone e d'Issifile* was presented at the Teatro SS Giovanni e Paolo in 1642). He returned to Rome for the performance of *Le pretensioni del Tebro e del Po* which marked the return of General Taddeo Barberini from his latest military campaign, and early in 1643 Marazzoli's new opera, *Il capriccio*, was performed at the French embassy. An invitation from Cardinal Mazarin to perform in Paris followed: *Il capriccio* was adapted as a *comédie-ballet* for a performance before the French court in 1645. He increased his favour with the queen, Anne of Austria, by composing chamber cantatas for her, and in return he received a pension.

Meanwhile, in 1645, the Barberini family sought exile in France after a dispute with the Pamphili family; it was not until 1653 that they were reconciled and able to return to

Rome. During their absence Marazzoli pursued his duties at the papal chapel as well as at S Maria Maggiore and the Chiesa Nuova, for whom he composed a variety of liturgical music and cantatas. The wedding of Maffeo Barberini to Olimpia Giustiniani in 1653 occasioned the reopening of the Barberini Teatro de' Quattro Fontane, with performances of *Dal male il bene* (text by Rospigliosi and music by Marazzoli and Abbatini). Although he maintained his connection with the papal chapel to the end of his life, Marazzoli seems to have left the Barberini household by 1656, when he dedicated his sacred opera, *La vita humana*, to his new patron, the exiled Queen Christina of Sweden; at the end of his life he was associated with the Chigi family – and in particular with Pope Alexander VII.

Maugars, André. See FRANCE *1 Paris and Versailles.*

Mazarin, Jules. See FRANCE *1 Paris and Versailles.*

Mazzocchi. Two brothers working as composers in Rome. Domenico Mazzocchi (1592–1665) served the powerful Cardinal Ippolito Aldobrandini; thanks to the generous support of the cardinal as well as Popes Urban VIII and Innocent X, Domenico lived a life of luxury. He composed at least one opera (*La catena d'Adone*, 1626), seven Latin oratorios and one Italian one (*Coro di profeti*, 1638), and published settings of Latin poems by Pope Urban VIII (*Poemata*), a collection of *Dialoghi e sonetti* and a book of *Madrigali* in 1638. The *Dialoghi e sonetti* are dramatically conceived (none is more effective than the lament of Mary Magdalene); the *Madrigali*, which may be performed with viol consort, employ a sequence of dynamic indications, including *echo* and *messa di voce*. A varied collection of *Musiche sacre, e morali*, including early cantatas, followed two years later. In 1642 he became embroiled in a controversy over the connection between an ancient Etruscan town and his native Civita Castellana, which put an end to his composing; some of the *Sacrae concertationes* published in 1664 apparently date from the 1630s and 40s.

Virgilio Mazzocchi (1597–1646) rose meteorically through the ranks of Roman *maestri di cappella*: in 1628 he was at S Giovanni in Laterano and, from 1629, at the Cappella Giulia where he was much esteemed as a teacher. His music includes concertato motets (*Sacrae flores*, 1640) and double-choir liturgical music (*Psalmi vespertini*, 1648), as well as madrigals, oratorios and operas: *Chi soffre, speri* (1637), a comic opera on which he col-

laborated with Marazzoli; and *L'innocenza difesa* (1641), a sacred opera performed at the Palazzo Barberini.

Melani. See ITALY *10 Itinerant Musicians.*

Metastasio, Pietro. See CENTRAL EUROPE *3 Austro-Hungary: Vienna.*

Nanino, Giovanni Bernardino (*c*1560–1623). Church musician and influential teacher, younger brother of Giovanni Maria Nanino (1543/4–1607), who had been Palestrina's successor as head of the Roman school. After training as a boy soprano at Vallerano Cathedral, Nanino assumed his brother's post as *maestro di cappella* at S Luigi dei Francesi, Rome, in 1591 and in 1608 took up a similar post at S Lorenzo in Damaso, where his patron was Cardinal Montalto. He left published collections of madrigals and motets.

Orgas, Annibale. See NORTHERN EUROPE *3 Poland.*

Orlandi, Santi. See ITALY *3 Mantua.*

Ottoboni, Pietro (1667–1740). Cardinal, librettist and important music patron in Rome (along with Benedetto Pamphili), who descended from a noble Venetian family. Early in his life Ottoboni took up residence in Rome. His great-uncle supervised his education and, after being elected Pope Alexander VIII in 1689, made him a cardinal. As vice-chancellor of the church, Ottoboni lived in the Palazzo della Cancelleria where he held Accademie Poetico-Musicali and operas and oratorios were performed (see Plate 3). As curator of the Cappella Sistina and the Congregazione di S Cecilia he was acquainted with the best Roman musicians, whom he commissioned to set his verses (among them Attilio Ariosti, Caldara, Corelli, C.F. Pollarolo and Tomaso Vitali) and contracted to perform at the Cancelleria (Corelli, for example, was in his employ from 1690 until 1713).

Pacelli, Asprilio. See NORTHERN EUROPE *3 Poland.*

Pamphili, Benedetto (1653–1730). Roman cardinal, music patron and librettist of noble birth, contemporary with Pietro Ottoboni. Pamphili's great uncle was Pope Innocent X, and his family had been prominent in Roman social and artistic circles. He was well educated in philosophy and theology and became a cardinal in 1681. Except for the time he spent in Bologna as the papal legate (1690–3), he lived in Rome, at the Palazzo Pamphili on the Corso, where his Sunday academies were well attended; in 1684 he commissioned Carlo Fontana to build a theatre there. He wrote librettos, set by composers such as Alessandro Scarlatti, Pasquini, C.F. Cesarini and Handel, for oratorios and cantatas, which formed the centrepieces of his lavish musical entertainments at the Palazzo Pamphili. The Gasparinis and Bononcinis played in his orchestra under the leadership of Corelli.

Pasqualini, Marc'Antonio (1614–91). Roman soprano castrato and composer of cantatas. Pasqualini entered the service of Cardinal Antonio Barberini after training as a chorister at S Luigi dei Francesi under Ugolini. In 1630 he became a singer in the papal chapel, remaining there until 1659. Notwithstanding his post at the Vatican, Pasqualini continued to appear in the cardinal's private theatrical productions such as Luigi Rossi's *Il palazzo incantato di Atalante* (1642) and travelled to Paris in 1646 to sing in Rossi's splendid *Orfeo* (1647) at the Palais Royal.

Pasquini, Bernardo (1637–1710). Tuscan virtuoso keyboard player, important teacher and composer who greatly contributed to the development of Roman opera and oratorio. Pasquini enjoyed a very successful and varied career in Rome where, from 1664, he was organist of S Maria in Aracoeli and was involved in the oratorio productions of the Arciconfraternità del Ss Crocifisso. His patrons included the exiled Queen Christina, the Princes Colonna and Giambattista Borghese (whom he served from *c*1670), and the Cardinals Ottoboni and Pamphili. For them he composed chamber music (including cantatas), oratorios and operas. Corelli was a frequent partner in chamber music and led the opera orchestras for Pasquini's *Dov'è amor è pietà* at the Teatro Capranica (1679) and *L'Accademia per musica* at the palace of Queen Christina (1687). Pasquini and Corelli were *guardiani* of their respective instruments in the Congregazione di S Cecilia and with Alessandro Scarlatti became members of the Accademia dell'Arcadia in 1706. Pasquini visited the courts of Leopold I and Louis XIV; his portrait was painted and, at his death, a medal was struck in his honour.

Pasquini's manuscript music for harpsichord, particularly the toccatas, reveals a player and composer of Frescobaldi's stature, inventive and forward-looking. In the dance suites he established the basic pattern of the keyboard suite as *allemande–corrente–giga* (though any dance could be replaced with another or an aria, *bizzaria*, etc.) and he is notable for the sheer number and variety of his variation and passacaglia pieces. His 28 harpsichord sonatas (half are for two harpsichords) are unique for having been notated only in figured bass.

His oratorios and operas were mainstream works, composed at much the same time (the 1670s and 1680s), but whereas the operas were composed for performances in Rome some of the oratorios (*c*17 are known) were commissioned for Modena (three in 1687), Palermo (1688) and Florence (1693–4). The extant operas include one for the Palazzo Chigi (*La sincerità con la sincerità*, 1672), one for the Teatro Tordinona (*L'amor per vendetta*, 1673), at least two for the Palazzo Colonna (*La donna ancora è fedele*, 1676; *L'Arianna*, 1685; and possibly *La caduta del regno dell'Amazzoni*, 1678). Cardinal Pamphili provided the text for his oratorio *Sant'Agnese* (1677). Pasquini prepared *Saggi di contrappunto* (1695) and a lost *Regole per ben suonare il cembalo o organo* for his pupils, who included Francesco Gasparini, Zipoli, J.P. Krieger and Georg Muffat.

Peranda, Marco Gioseppe. See NORTHERN EUROPE *4 Saxony and Thuringia: Dresden.*

Peri, Jacopo. See ITALY *6 Tuscany.*

Pitoni, Giuseppe Ottavio (1657–1743). Devotee of Palestrina, writer on music theory and history, working in Rome. Pitoni was an extremely capable musician who held numerous church appointments simultaneously; he also served Cardinal Ottoboni from 1692 until 1731. From 1719 he was *maestro* of the Cappella Giulia. He was much admired as a composer for his brilliant counterpoint and polychoral technique, and his writings include an early dictionary of church musicians (*Notitia de contrapuntisti e de compositori di musica, c*1725), as well as treatises on harmony and counterpoint.

Porpora, Nicola. See ITALY *10 Itinerant Musicians.*

Porro, Giovanni Giacomo. See CENTRAL EUROPE *1 South Germany: Munich.*

Porta, Giovanni. See ITALY *4 Venice.*

Puccitelli, Virgilio. See NORTHERN EUROPE *3 Poland.*

Puliaschi, Giovanni Domenico (*fl* early 17th c.). Eminent Roman singer and chitarrone player whose collection of virtuoso monodies, *Musiche varie* (1618), contains an important essay on singing. Puliaschi sang in the papal chapel from 1612 and was renowned for his ability to sing in alto, tenor and bass ranges. Caccini included two 'arie particolari' of wide tessitura in *Nuove musiche e nuova maniera di scriverle* (1614), which may have been composed for Puliaschi. In 1620 he visited the Florentine court and performed with Francesca Caccini and her children.

Quagliati, Paolo (*c*1555–1628). Italian nobleman, organist and composer in Rome. Quagliati was organist at S Maria Maggiore and from 1605 to 1608 served Cardinal Odoardo Farnese. His earliest publications were three-part *canzonette*, and his sacred music ranged from monodies to 12-part works. In 1606 he composed a celebratory work entitled *Il carro di fedeltà d'amore* – made up of short solos, duets and a concluding five-part concerted madrigal – which was performed on a decorated cart in the street. His last patrons were members of the Ludovisi family, of whom Cardinal Alessandro Ludovisi became Pope Gregory XV in 1621; he was accordingly favoured with the posts of apostolic prothonotary and papal chamberlain. When the pope's nephew married Gesualdo's daughter Isabella in 1623, Quagliati marked the occasion with a collection of music entitled *La sfera armoniosa*.

Ravenscroft, John (*d* by 1708). English amateur violinist, residing in Rome, where (along with Sir John Clerk and Lord Edgcumbe) he had lessons with Corelli. He composed two collections of trio sonatas (1695 and 1708 posth.) dedicated to his likely patron, Prince Ferdinando of Tuscany; nine of his op. 1 *sonate da chiesa* were reissued in Amsterdam by Le Cène in *c*1735 as Corelli's op. 7.

Rolli, Paolo Antonio. See BRITISH ISLES *1 London*.

Rospigliosi, Giulio (1600–69). Pope Clement IX; the earliest and most important Roman librettist of both sacred and comic opera. Rospigliosi first gained notoriety while in the service of the Barberini family, at whose Teatro de' Quattro Fontane the earliest settings of his texts were performed – notably Landi's *Il Sant'Alessio* (1632), Virgilio Mazzocchi and Marazzoli's *Chi soffre, speri* (1637) and Luigi Rossi's elaborate machine opera *Il palazzo incantato di Atlante* (1642). From 1644 to 1655 he was the papal nuncio in Spain, during which time Marazzoli collaborated with Abbatini on a setting of *Dal male il bene* (1653) as a comic opera and *La vita humana* (1656) as a sacred opera. In 1657 Rospigliosi was made a cardinal and, ten years later, elected pope, though he reigned only two years.

Rossi, Luigi (*c*1597–1653). One of the leading Roman composers of his day, esteemed in particular as a composer of cantatas; he was also a lutenist and keyboard player, who during the late 1640s served at the French Regency court of Anne of Austria. Luigi Rossi spent his early career in Naples where he had been a pupil of Giovanni de Macque. In 1621 he entered the service of the Borghese family in Rome and six years later married the well-known harpist Costanza de Ponte; in 1633 he assumed the organist's post at S Luigi dei Francesi which he retained until his death. He visited the Florentine court of Ferdinando II de' Medici but remained with the Borgheses until 1641 when he took up a place among the musicians of Cardinal Antonio Barberini, with whom he became closely associated. Rossi's first opera (a seven-hour epic given coherence by its exquisite architectural form), *Il palazzo incantato di Atlante* (text by Rospigliosi), caused much excitement during the Carnival celebrations at the Palazzo Barberini theatre (Quattro Fontane) the following year, as much because of its distinguished cast of singers – among them Pasqualini, Vittori and Savioni – ornate costumes and elaborate machinery as for its music. The musicians in the Barberini household met, in the spirit of an academy, during the summer months of 1644 at Rossi's home.

The Barberinis' decision to live in exile in France from 1645 precipitated Rossi's call to Paris the following year: Cardinal Mazarin was eager that Rossi should repeat his success at the French court. In 1647 his second and more lyrical opera, *Orfeo* (lasting six hours), was performed by Italian singers including Leonora Baroni, imported for the occasion – though only after delays created by the death of Rossi's wife and the necessary enlargement of the Palais Royal theatre. Such was its success that it was performed again in honour of the visiting English queen, Henrietta Maria, and Rossi's fervent wish that his brother-in-law be awarded the benefice of the Vatican's Cappella S Petronilla (in the gift of the French monarch) was immediately granted. Rossi also composed cantatas for the queen's private entertainment and even accompanied the Italian singers on these occasions; during the court's residence at Fontainebleau, Rossi worked with the French musicians, becoming friendly with the singer Pierre de Nyert, whose command of interpretation he much admired. Rossi returned to Rome, only to be recalled to Paris, although this time his fortunes were thwarted by the Fronde; no Italian operas, or other theatrical spectacles, were produced in Paris during 1648–9, when many Italians had cause to fear for their lives. Rossi was allowed to depart without incident and, en route for Rome, was reunited near Lyons with the Barberini entourage in the autumn of 1648.

Rossi, Michelangelo [Michel Angelo del Violino] (1601/2–56). Virtuoso violinist, well travelled in Italy, whose mentor was Frescobaldi and patrons included the Este, Bentivoglio, Sforza and Barberini families; he composed keyboard music and at least two operas. He took part (in the role of a violin-playing Apollo) in the performances of his first opera, *Erminia sul Giordano*, which was lavishly produced (with sets by Bernini) in 1633 at the Palazzo Barberini in Rome; his second, *Andromeda*, was performed at the 1638 wedding festivities of Cornelio Benti-voglio and Costanza Sforza at Ferrara. His collection of *Toccate e correnti* (?1640), for organ or harpsichord, is in effect a pallid reflection of Frescobaldi's second volume (1627). He spent the last part of his life in Rome, where he was acquainted with the Germans Athanasius Kircher and Caspar Schott.

Sances, Giovanni Felice. See CENTRAL EUROPE *3 Austro-Hungary: Vienna.*

Savioni, Mario (1608–85). Roman singer and composer. At only 12 years of age Savioni took a role in Filippo Vitali's *Aretusa* (1620) and, until his voice broke, was a chorister in the Cappella Giulia. In 1642 he sang in Luigi Rossi's lavish *Il palazzo incantato di Atlante*, at the Palazzo Barberini theatre (Quattro Fontane), and again became associated with the Vatican as a singer in the papal choir, serving as its director for almost a decade (1659–68). With the exception of two lost oratorios, Savioni confined his music to small forms – madrigals, sacred concertos, solo motets and cantatas, of which over 150 survive.

Scarlatti, Alessandro (1660–1725). Important and prolific opera composer who brought to a conclusion the 17th-century Italian traditions of dramatic music initiated by Monteverdi and developed by Cavalli, Cesti, Carissimi and Stradella. Scarlatti's career was divided between Rome and Naples. Sicilian-born, he was trained in Rome, and his first large-scale works (an oratorio for the Oratorio del Ss Crocifisso and the popular *Gli equivoci nel sembiante*) were performed there when he was only 19. His patrons from the outset were of the highest rank, among them the exiled Queen Christina of Sweden, the Cardinals Pamphili and Ottoboni and, in Florence, Prince Ferdinando de' Medici. In 1684 Scarlatti moved to Naples, where he took the post of *maestro di cappella* to the viceroy, the Marquis del Carpio; he was accompanied by his burgeoning family – which came to include ten children, two of whom became professional musicians – and his younger brother Francesco (1666–after 1741), who was engaged to lead the violins.

For the next two decades Scarlatti dominated Neapolitan opera, producing over 40 works, which were first performed at the vice-regal Palazzo Reale and then at the public theatre of S Bartolomeo, where Scarlatti was employed as the director along with nine singers, five instrumentalists and a copyist. In contrast to contemporary five-act Venetian operas, which continued to rely upon mythological characters and stage machinery, Scarlatti's shorter three-act 'drammi per musica' centred on the characterization of kings and confidants, lovers and servants. From 1695 they incorporated three-movement sinfonias which soon became standard for all Italian operas. *Il Pirro e Demetrio* (1694) and *La caduta de' Decemviri* (1697) were particularly successful. While resident in Naples Scarlatti occasionally returned to Rome to supervise Carnival performances of new operas, contributions to *pasticci* and cantatas at the Palazzo Doria Pamphili and the Villa Medicea (at nearby Pratolino), as well as oratorios at Ss Crocifisso, the Palazzo Apostolico and the Collegio Clementino. Astonishingly, he also produced at least ten serenatas, nine oratorios and 65 cantatas for Naples.

Scarlatti moved back to Rome at the end of 1703, seeking a quieter life, as assistant *maestro di cappella* at S Maria Maggiore (the public theatres had been closed by papal decree since 1700, so operas were performed only occasionally and in private). In this capacity he was required to compose motets and Masses in both strict (papal) and concertato styles, according to the occasion. To augment his income he renewed his connections with the cardinals and formed new ones with Marquis Ruspoli, concentrating now on oratorios, celebratory serenatas and cantatas. In 1706 he was elected, along with Pasquini and Corelli, to the Accademia dell'Arcadia, where he must have met Handel in 1707. From 1702 until 1708 he sent Prince Ferdinando de' Medici quantities of oratorios and church music and four operas, which the prince had performed at Siena, Livorno and Florence. Scarlatti also composed and directed two five-act tragedies for the 1707 Venetian Carnival: *Il Mitridate Eupatore* and *Il trionfo della libertà* (both performed at the Teatro S Giovanni Grisostomo). Upon his return to Rome he was made *maestro di cappella* at S Maria Maggiore, but the salary was so meagre that he was ultimately forced, in 1709, to return to his posts in Naples.

During the next decade he produced 11 operas employing greater instrumental resources, of which *Il Tigrane* (1715) was his

Neapolitan masterpiece. His 'commedia in musica', *Il trionfo dell'onore* (1718), was also very successful. Inexplicably, Scarlatti turned to new genres, separate orchestral music (of which 12 *Sinfonie di concerto grosso* were published in 1715) and keyboard toccatas which demonstrate his command of fugue and variation techniques. He maintained his connections in Rome, returning there in 1718 to oversee his opera *Telemaco* at the Teatro Capranica, in 1719 for *Marco Attilio Regolo* and finally in 1721 for *La Griselda* (his last opera); he produced a lavish *Messa di S Cecilia* for soloists, chorus and strings, performed there in October 1720. His last years were spent in Naples, teaching (Hasse was his pupil from 1722), composing cantatas (which ultimately numbered over 600, mostly for soprano and continuo), a serenata and a set of sonatas for flute and strings (probably composed for Quantz, who visited him in 1724).

Scarlatti, Domenico. See IBERIAN PENINSULA AND COLONIES *1 Spain.*

Spiridio. See NORTHERN EUROPE *7 Itinerant Musicians.*

Stampiglia, Silvio (1664–1725). Roman librettist who collaborated principally with Giovanni Bononcini and Alessandro Scarlatti. In addition to opera librettos, he produced serenata and oratorio texts for Naples, Rome and Vienna (where he was in residence from 1707 to 1713). One of his most popular operas was Bononcini's setting of *Il trionfo di Camilla*, first performed in Naples in 1696. Stampiglia became a member of the Roman Accademia dell'Arcadia in 1690.

Stradella, Alessandro (1644–82). Versatile Roman composer, whose flamboyant private life as a Don Juan ended violently with his murder. Stradella was evidently a man of independent ways and means, a composer by choice. He lived until 1677 in Rome, where he held posts with Queen Christina and Lorenzo Colonna; he also provided music for churches and confraternities. His first dramatic work (*Accademia d'amore*) was staged at the Palazzo Colonna in 1665, and other commissions for secular cantatas, prologues, *intermezzi*, operettas and oratorios followed. In them he clearly differentiated between aria and recitative – though he employed a variety of forms and degrees of speech rhythm – and juxtaposed voices and instruments in concerto fashion. He composed idiomatic *sonate da chiesa* for one or two violins and continuo, and at least one sonata for trumpet and strings; one *sonata di viole* – actually a concerto grosso with a concertino section of two violins and lute –

antedates the *concerti grossi* of Corelli (whose op. 6 of 1714 remains the earliest published collection).

In 1669 he became involved (with the abbot Antonio Sforza and the violinist C.A. Lonati) in an attempt to embezzle money from the church, and was forced to leave Rome in some haste. He returned the following year when his friends Count d'Alibert and the librettist Filippo Acciaiuoli opened the Tordinona theatre with a new production of Cavalli's *Scipione affricano*, incorporating a prologue and other additional music by Stradella. His remarkably swift rehabilitation is attested to by commissions from the Colonna family for music to honour Pope Clement X and for the 1671 wedding celebrations of Anna Teresa Pamphili Aldobrandini and Prince Giovanni Andrea Doria of Genoa.

When the theatres closed for Holy Year in 1675 Stradella turned to sacred genres, although his oratorio *S Giovanni Battista* (text by Ansaldi), which was presented at S Giovanni dei Fiorentini (Corelli was among those who took part), was more than usually resplendent with passions normally reserved for operas; this was in part because he preferred librettos – apart from that of *S Editta* by Orsini – which offered him scope for developing the characters. He also composed sacred Latin cantatas for a variety of forces.

Two years later, having found it necessary again to absent himself from Rome, Stradella went to Venice, where he became romantically involved with a pupil from the Contarini family; together (and without her family's consent) they travelled to Turin for the opening of Count d'Alibert's Teatro Regio. Close behind was a posse of Contarini men who were only just restrained by the regent from killing Stradella, who quickly departed from Turin alone. He was next heard of in Genoa, where he spent the rest of his short life. His early *opera buffa* – *Il Trespolo tutore* (*c*1677) – was composed for Genoa, and his *opere serie* – *La forza dell'amor paterno* (1678) and *Le gare dell'amor eroico* (1679) – were presented at the Teatro Falcone. Towards the end of his life he composed an oratorio, *Susanna* (1681; text by Giardini), for Modena, where his music continued to be performed for more than a decade after his death; he was murdered by a jealous soldier, following a romantic dispute, in Genoa. In Rome his opera *Il moro per amore* (text by Orsini) was given its first performance at the Teatro Capranica in 1695.

Tecchler, David (*c*1666–after 1747). The

leading cello maker of the early 18th-century Roman school. Tecchler was born in Augsburg but worked in Rome, where he produced a large quantity of very large, very fine Cremonese-inspired cellos; his violins are more Germanic in design.

Teixeira, António. See IBERIAN PENINSULA AND COLONIES *2 Portugal.*

Tenaglia, Antonio Francesco (*c*1610/20–after 1661). Florentine lutenist and keyboard player, composer of music dramas and cantatas. Tenaglia worked mainly in Rome for the Aldobrandini, Pamphili and Barberini musical establishments, though he spent some time (*c*1648) at the Neuburg-Düsseldorf court. In 1653 there was a possibility of succeeding Luigi Rossi at the French court, but a formal invitation was never proffered; he participated in the Roman festivities for Queen Christina in 1656. Tenaglia was best known as a composer of cantatas, which were considered by Berardi (1681) to be the equals of those by Carissimi, Luigi Rossi and the German Christoph Bernhard.

Tessarini, Carlo. See ITALY *10 Itinerant Musicians.*

Tregian, Francis. See BRITISH ISLES *1 London.*

Tricarico, Giuseppe (1623–97). Composer and teacher from Gallipoli, who worked in Rome and Ferrara before serving as *Kapellmeister* to the Viennese Dowager Empress Eleonora (1660–3). Trained in Naples, Tricarico spent the 1640s and early 50s in Rome, where he published church music, such as his *Concentus ecclesiastici* (1649) for two to four voices. While serving as *maestro di cappella* of the Accademia dello Spirito Santo at Ferrara (1654–9), and later in Vienna, Tricarico composed operas and oratorios. In 1663 he returned to Gallipoli, where he spent the rest of his life as a teacher.

Valentine, Robert (*c*1680–*c*1735). English flautist, recorder player and composer of chamber music, from a prominent musical family in Leicester. He chose to spend most of his life in Rome, arriving around the turn of the century, in the entourage of Sir Thomas Samwell (MP for Coventry, 1714–22). To judge by the dedications of his works, his Italian patrons were the Grand Duke of Tuscany and the Duke of the Oratina. He returned to London in 1731.

Valentini, Giuseppe. See ITALY *10 Itinerant Musicians.*

Valentini, Pier Francesco (*c*1570–1654). Noble Roman amateur composer and theorist, who was considered one of the most learned contrapuntists of his day. Valentini studied with G.B. Nanino, the highly influential *maestro di cappella* at S Maria Maggiore. In 1629 he published a collection of canons (the best known was the *Illos tuos*) and, two years later, the remarkable *Canone nel modo Salomonis* for 96 voices, which could be expanded to an apocalyptic 144,000, singing at different speeds and in different metres; Kircher cited these works (with musical examples) in his *Musurgia universalis* (1650). Valentini also published collections of concerted motets, two books of madrigals (1654) and two of *canzonette* (1657). Much of his music – a large number of *canzonette spirituali* and at least two operas – is lost. He published a *Trattato della battuta musicale* (1643) on determining pulse in a performance and also wrote on temperament and tuning, counterpoint and tonality. *Duplitonio* (MS, n.d.) sets out his theory of 24 modes in which the original 12 are augmented by an additional dozen based on arithmetical subdivisions.

Vitali, Filippo. See ITALY *10 Itinerant Musicians.*

Vittori, Loreto (1600–70). One of the earliest operatic castratos (along with Marc'Antonio Pasqualini); also a composer, poet and librettist. Vittori was discovered in the choir of Spoleto Cathedral by Maffeo Barberini (then Bishop of Spoleto, but soon to be Pope Urban VIII), who in 1617 introduced him in Rome. By 1619 he was in Florence, taking part in music dramas (such as Peri's and Gagliano's *Lo sposalizio di Medoro e Angelica*) for Grand Duke Cosimo II. Vittorio returned to Rome two years later (after the death of the duke), secured the patronage of Cardinal Lodovico Ludovisi and joined the papal choir.

The esteem in which he was held was confirmed by his elevation to 'Cavaliere della Milizia de Gesù Cristo' by the pope (*c*1623). In addition to his duties at S Pietro, he took opera roles (such as the sorceress in Domenico Mazzocchi's *La catena d'Adone*, 1626) and travelled freely to sing at Bologna, Florence and Parma (where he probably took part in Monteverdi's *Mercurio e Marte* in 1628). In 1637 he renewed his association with the Barberini family and in 1642 sang with his papal colleague, Pasqualini, in the first performance of Luigi Rossi's *Il palazzo incantato di Atlante*. Erythraeus (G.V. Rossi) described his manner of singing in *Pinacotheca*, published in Amsterdam in 1645.

Vittori's surviving texts and music include a pastoral opera *La Galatea* (1639), another secular drama *La fiera di Palestrina*, *La Santa Irene* (1644), *La pellegrina costante* (1647) and

a collection of monodies (1649). He wrote about his life in verse: *La Troja rapita* (1662).
Weiss, Silvius Leopold. See NORTHERN EUROPE *7 Itinerant Musicians*.

8 Naples

Alborea, Francesco. See CENTRAL EUROPE *3 Austro-Hungary: Vienna*.
Babbi, Gregorio. See ITALY *10 Itinerant Musicians*.
Bordoni, Faustina. See ITALY *10 Itinerant Musicians*.
Caffarelli. See ITALY *10 Itinerant Musicians*.
Caresana, Cristoforo (*c*1640–1709). Organist, tenor and composer, working at Naples from 1658. Caresana is thought to have studied in Venice with P.A. Ziani before joining the musicians of the Neapolitan royal chapel. In 1659 he gained a post as tenor and, eight years later, that of organist; he retired in 1704. Caresana was a member of the Congregazione dell'Oratorio (1659–1706), where he was known as 'Il Veneziano', *maestro di cappella* at the Conservatorio di S Onofrio (1688–90) and from 1699 *maestro* of the Tesoro di S Gennaro at Naples Cathedral. He composed vocal exercises (1681), some of which were reprinted for use at the Paris Conservatoire in 1819, and a tutor with music for two voices (1693), revealing by its expressiveness and rhythmic vitality a precedent for the music of Pergolesi.
Cerone, Pietro. See IBERIAN PENINSULA AND COLONIES *1 Spain*.
Corradini, Francesco. See IBERIAN PENINSULA AND COLONIES *1 Spain*.
Cuzzoni, Francesca. See ITALY *10 Itinerant Musicians*.
Durante, Francesco (1684–1755). Neapolitan composer, known abroad for his church music, and distinguished teacher who numbered Pergolesi, Paisiello, Sacchini and Piccinni among his pupils. Details of Durante's travels within and without Italy are not known with certainty. He was thrice married and affiliated with three of Naples' conservatories. His extant music encompasses a wide spectrum of liturgical and devotional music, secular duets, instrumental concertos and keyboard works. Durante possessed a fluent technique and was adept at composing in a strict style as well as a mixed one, replete with highly expressive chromaticism and coloratura. Of particular significance is his eight-voice *Messa dei morti*

(1746) and his chamber duets based on recitatives from the solo cantatas of Alessandro Scarlatti. Durante's wider popularity is attested to by Rousseau and Burney.
Faggioli, Michelangelo (1666–1733). Neapolitan lawyer, practising in both canon and civil courts, and amateur composer, who in 1706 composed the music for the earliest known comic opera in Neapolitan dialect, *La Cilla* (text by Tullio). It was performed on several occasions before and after the new year (1707) at the palace of Fabrizio Carafa, Prince of Chiusiano, and remarked upon in contemporary Neapolitan journals. *La Cilla* was a romantic village farce which relied upon mistaken identity as its principal comic device; there were 66 short arias, duets and trios, all sung in Neapolitan dialect. In 1709 Faggioli composed an oratorio (title and occasion unknown) and a cantata *Didone abbandonata da Enea*, which shows him equal to the expressive demands of a serious and pathetic text.
Fago. Neapolitan father and son who were composers and teachers. Francesco Nicola Fago (1677–1745), known as 'Il Tarantino', studied with Provenzale at the Neapolitan Conservatorio S Maria della Pietà dei Turchini, where he himself taught for 35 years. He married the sister (Caterina Speranza Grimaldi) of the soprano virtuoso Nicolini and, of their many children, Lorenzo (1704–93) followed in his father's footsteps.

Francesco Nicola's first post was as *primo maestro* of the Conservatorio di S Onofrio (1704–8), but from 1705 he was based at the Turchini where his pupils included Falco, Feo, Majo, Leo and Jommelli, as well as his own son Lorenzo. In 1709 he added to his responsibilities by taking on the post of *maestro di cappella* of the Tesoro di S Gennaro at Naples Cathedral, where he succeeded Caresana.

Fago composed several *opere serie* and in 1712 collaborated with Falco on an *opera buffa*, *Lo Masiello*; but he was known primarily as a composer of sacred music. He belonged to the generation of Mancini and Sarro – both of whom devoted themselves to opera – and though he was very much influenced by the music of Scarlatti he preferred to compose in the contrapuntal, polychoral style.

Lorenzo Fago succeeded his father at the Tesoro di S Gennaro in 1731, having already held the post of organist of the *primo coro*, and six years later was made *secondo maestro* at the Turchini, where he assisted his father (until 1740) and then Leo; he succeeded Leo as *primo maestro* in 1744, remaining until 1793. He was more important as a teacher than as a composer and, indeed, devoted himself to promoting his father's music.

Falco [De Falco], Michele (?1688–after 1732). *Maestro di cappella* and one of the first musical collaborators of Neapolitan *opera buffa*. Falco studied with F.N. Fago at the Conservatorio di S Onofrio before becoming a member of the Reale Congregazione e Monte dei Musici in 1712 (whom he served as an elected governor, 1716–31). His first *opera buffa*, *Lo Lollo pisciaportelle* (text by Orilia) was given in 1709 at the home of Baron Achille Paternò; it had only one act and required only five characters. His second comic opera, *Lo Masiello* (text by Orilia), composed in collaboration with his teacher Fago, was more elaborate (in three acts and incorporating vocal ensembles elsewhere in addition to the finales); it was performed before the governor of the Conservatorio di S Onofrio in 1712.

Farinelli. See ITALY *10 Itinerant Musicians.*

Feo, Francesco (1691–1761). Neapolitan teacher, *maestro di cappella* and composer, whom Burney described as 'one of the greatest Neapolitan masters of his time'. Feo studied with F.N. Fago at the Conservatorio S Maria della Pietà dei Turchini, along with his contemporaries Leo and Majo. Unlike Leo and Durante, Feo rejected the *stile antico* – though not counterpoint *per se* – and instead explored the polychoral and concertato techniques he had inherited from Fago. In 1713 he made his début as an opera composer with *L'amor tirannico ossia Zenobia* and the following year produced a *dramma sacro*, *Il martirio di S Caterina*, for the 1714 Neapolitan Carnival. By the time he took up a teaching post at the Conservatorio di S Onofrio in 1723, Feo had composed numerous comic scenes for Neapolitan performances of operas and had written music for Metastasio's 1723 reworking of D. David's *La forza della virtù* – Metastasio's first tentative effort as a librettist.

For the next 20 years Feo composed oratorios, sacred cantatas and liturgical music for the church of the Annunziata, where he became *maestro di cappella* in 1726. He also produced *opere serie* and *intermezzi* for Turin and Rome and accepted commissions from outside Italy (serenatas for Madrid in 1738 and an oratorio for Prague the following year). He resigned from S Onofrio in 1739 to become *primo maestro* of the Conservatorio dei Poveri di Gesù Cristo, but retired in 1743 when the conservatory was converted to a seminary.

Gesualdo, Carlo, Prince of Venosa, Count of Conza (*c*1561–1613). Nobleman and eccentric composer of often bizarrely chromatic late-Renaissance madrigals, who, ironically, enhanced his fame by murdering his wife after confronting her 'in flagrante delicto di fragrante peccato' with the Duke of Andria (1590) and, ultimately, by going mad. Although an accomplished composer from an early age, Gesualdo began publishing his madrigals only after taking up temporary residence in Ferrara and marrying his second wife, Leonora d'Este, in 1594 (he had already published sacred music in the late 1580s). Six books appeared between 1594 and 1611, though the music was little affected by the stylistic changes taking place elsewhere in Italy and represents the endpoint of a particularly idiosyncratic compositional technique.

After living in the isolation of his estate at Gesualdo, the prince was greatly stimulated by the thriving musical life of Ferrara, where he became friendly with Luzzasco Luzzaschi and other virtuosos at the ducal court, who in turn influenced his subsequent music, as did the microtonal arcicembalo (devised by Nicola Vicentino) which was among the Este court instruments. When he returned with his bride to the castle at Gesualdo in 1595, he sought to create a musical establishment of his own, even engaging a palace printer (G.G. Carlino of Naples). But he suffered from melancholia and declined; he ill-treated his wife, whose family eventually began divorce proceedings, and had the added misfortune to lose both of his sons, leaving no heir.

Greco, Gaetano (*c*1657–*c*1728). Neapolitan keyboard composer, *maestro di cappella* of Naples (1704–20) and important teacher at the Conservatorio dei Poveri di Gesù Cristo (1695–1728). Greco, himself a pupil of Ursino, taught Domenico Scarlatti, Porpora, Piccinni, Vinci and possibly Pergolesi. By the vitality of its musical invention, his own keyboard music betrays the influence of Alessandro Scarlatti (with whom he may have studied); none of it was published during his lifetime.

Grossi, Giovanni Francesco. See ITALY *10 Itinerant Musicians.*

Handel, George Frideric. See BRITISH ISLES *1 London.*

Hasse, Johann Adolf. See NORTHERN EUROPE *4 Saxony and Thuringia: Dresden.*

Lanzetti, Salvatore. See ITALY *1 Piedmont-Savoy.*

Leo, Leonardo (Ortensio Salvatore de) (1694–1744). Important Neapolitan composer of oratorios and operas, who was attached to the viceregal court throughout his career. Leo was educated at the Turchini, where his first *dramma sacro, S Chiara, o L'infedeltà abbattuta*, was performed in 1712; such was its reception that it was repeated at the viceroy's palace, thereby paving the way for his appointment there as an organist a year later. In 1714, while simultaneously holding appointments as *maestro di cappella* to the Marchese Stella and of S Maria della Solitaria as well as the one at court, Leo produced his first *opera seria, Il Pisistrato* (text by Lalli). After the subsequent success in 1718 of his second opera, *Sofonisba* (text by Silvani), he began composing theatre music in earnest, producing at least one serious and almost as many comic operas each year from 1720 until his death; to judge by the number of operas he produced, 1735 was the climax of his career.

Though not as gifted as his contemporaries Pergolesi, Vinci and Hasse, Leo was nevertheless a craftsman, able to turn his skills to whatever was required. As early as 1723 Leo experimented with comic opera in dialect (*La 'mpeca scoperta*), contributing *intermezzi* and *commedie musicali* of a higher calibre than most. When there was a lull in the late 1720s in commissions from the Teatro S Bartolomeo for serious operas, he found opportunities to compose theatre music for Rome and Venice. Alessandro Scarlatti's death in 1725 made possible his appointment as first organist of the viceregal chapel, and Vinci's in 1730, along with Hasse's departure for Dresden, enabled him once again to command the most important commissions at S Bartolomeo. During the 1730s he was frequently absent from Naples in order to supervise the performances of his operas and oratorios (*S Elena al Calvario* and *La morte di Abele* – both seem to date from 1732 – were performed in 1734 and 1738 in Bologna).

Somehow he found time to teach at the Turchini (1734–7) and was ultimately appointed *primo maestro* in 1741 (having served in that capacity at the Conservatorio di S Onofrio since 1739). At much this time he came into conflict with his contemporary Francesco Durante over the degree of consonance to be ascribed to the interval of the fourth, so that Neapolitans were for a time divided between the 'Leisti' and 'Durantisti' camps.

Through the viceroy he received commissions from the Spanish court, though he is not known to have visited there. Instead he assumed Mancini's vacated post as court vice-

maestro di cappella in 1737 and soon embarked on a reform of Neapolitan church music, composing *a cappella* works with organ which favoured the use of *cantus firmi* and counterpoint. His most enduring work is the *Miserere* (1739) for double choir and organ. Near the end of his life Leo wrote two treatises, *Instituzioni o regole del contrappunto* and *Lezioni di canto fermo*, of important significance to the development of the Neapolitan school. In the 1742–3 revivals of his 1739 Metastasio operas *Il Ciro riconosciuto* and *Olimpiade* he incorporated a chorus for the first time in Neapolitan opera.

Lonati, Carlo Ambrogio. See ITALY *10 Itinerant Musicians*.

Majo, Giuseppe de (1697–1771). Organist, composer and *maestro* at the Neapolitan court. Majo experimented with *opera buffa* in the late 1720s (his *Lo vecchio avaro* was performed at the Teatro dei Fiorentini in 1727). However, between 1736 and his death he held a series of court appointments, overcoming (with the assistance of Queen Maria Amalia) the challenges by Porpora, Lorenzo Fago and Durante to become *primo maestro* in 1745. Though required to compose sacred music, he also occasionally produced a serenata or an *opera seria* for the Teatro S Carlo.

Mancini, Francesco (1672–1737). Neapolitan organist, *maestro di cappella* and transitional opera composer, working in the shadow of Alessandro Scarlatti. Mancini was trained at the Conservatorio S Maria della Pietà dei Turchini. After the success of his first opera (*Ariovisto*) in 1702 at the theatre of S Bartolomeo, Mancini attempted to succeed Scarlatti (while he was on leave in Florence) as the Neapolitan court *maestro di cappella*. His efforts did not go altogether unrewarded: the following year he was appointed first organist.

But his ambitions hardly ended there: in 1707, during the war of succession between the Spanish and Austrians, Mancini curried favour with the Austrians by composing a *Te Deum* to celebrate their victory. In response he was made *maestro di cappella* by the commander of the imperial forces; however, when the Austrian viceroy arrived Mancini was demoted and Scarlatti (who had been in Rome) promptly reinstated. He became *maestro di cappella* of the Conservatorio S Maria di Loreto (1720–35) and in 1725 (on the death of Scarlatti) secured the long-coveted court post. When the French army reconquered Naples in 1734, Mancini ingratiated himself with the new rulers, who in turn allowed him to continue in his post. He was forced to retire after suffering a stroke in 1735. Mancini composed at least 19 operas, as well as serenatas, cantatas, oratorios and liturgical works for Naples.

Mascitti, Michele. See FRANCE *1 Paris and Versailles.*

Matteis, Nicola (i). See BRITISH ISLES *1 London.*

Mele, Giovanni Battista. See IBERIAN PENINSULA AND COLONIES *1 Spain.*

Nicolini. See ITALY *10 Itinerant Musicians.*

Orefice, Antonio (*fl* 1708–34). Neapolitan composer of the first comic opera in Neapolitan dialect to be performed on a public stage, *Patrò Calienno de la Costa*, performed at the Teatro dei Fiorentini in 1709. In that same year he collaborated with Mancini and Albinoni on an *opera seria*, *Engelberta* (text by Pariati, after Zeno), for the court. He collaborated on other works with Leo and Sarro, both of whom, in addition to Vinci, were greatly influenced by him. Orefice's seven arias from *Le finte zingare* (1717) represent the earliest surviving music from a comic opera in Neapolitan dialect.

Palazzotto e Tagliavia, Giuseppe. See ITALY *9 Sicily.*

Pergolesi, Giovanni Battista (1710–36). Composer from Iesi in Pergola who was instrumental in the rise of *opera buffa*, though his widespread fame came posthumously – the result of frequent reprints of his *Stabat mater* and performances abroad of his comic *intermezzi* by Italian touring companies. The 1752 performances of *La serva padrona* in Paris ignited the 'Querelle des Bouffons'. Though Pergolesi's life was painfully short – indeed, he is thought to have suffered from a physical deformity and tuberculosis – and his composing confined to a six-year period, he produced a remarkable amount of music for diverse Italian patrons. His last weeks were spent at a Franciscan monastery in Pozzuoli, where he composed two of his finest works, the *Stabat mater* (for solo voices and strings), which was composed for a Neapolitan confraternity, and the *Salve regina* in C minor (for soprano and strings).

Pergolesi studied at the Neapolitan Conservatorio dei Poveri di Gesù Cristo with Greco, Vinci and Durante during the 1720s; while there he sang in the choir and, as a violinist, led the string band. His earliest work, a *dramma sacro*, *Li prodigi della divina grazia nella conversione di San Guglielmo Duca d'Aquitania*, was performed at a monastery in 1731 by the conservatory pupils. He tried his hand at *opera seria* with *Alessandro Severo* (revised as *Salustia*; text by Morelli, after Zeno), but it was hastily got up, and the *primo uomo*, Nicolini, fell fatally ill just before the opening in 1732, ensuring that it met with scant success.

In that same year, as *maestro di cappella* to Prince Ferdinando Colonna Stigliano, Pergolesi composed his first *commedia musicale*, for the Teatro dei Fiorentini: *Lo frate 'nnamorato* (text in Neapolitan dialect by Federico) delighted the audiences. It was important as the first and finest completely independent musical comedy. Towards the end of 1732 there was an earthquake in Naples, after which thanksgiving celebrations were organized; Pergolesi contributed a double-chorus Mass and Vesper psalms.

His next and ultimately most important *opera buffa* commission came from the court: *Il prigionier superbo* was performed during the birthday celebrations of the empress in August 1733. In itself *Il prigionier superbo* was not of great importance (it employed a small cast, dispensed with a *primo uomo*, relying instead upon an alto *prima donna*), but the *intermezzo* he composed to accompany it – *La serva padrona* (text by Federico) – has, by its simplicity, vitality and apt characterization, become one of the most important musical dramatic works of the 18th century.

The following year Pergolesi was appointed vice-*maestro di cappella* of Naples under D.N. Sarro, but when the Spanish troops threatened Naples, Prince Ferdinando and his entourage departed for Rome. While Pergolesi was there his *Mass in F* (commissioned by another Neapolitan noble, the Duke of Maddaloni) was performed with acclaim at S Lorenzo in Lucinda. When he returned to Naples later in 1734 it was in the service of the Duke of Maddaloni; he composed sacred music and chamber music (the duke was a cellist) for his household.

Pergolesi spared nothing in preparing his last Neapolitan *opera seria*, *Adriano in Siria* (text by Metastasio) with an *intermezzo*, *La contadina astuta* (text by Mariani). Through the duke, Pergolesi had been invited to compose an opera for the birthday of the dowager queen, which was then performed at the Teatro S Bartolomeo late in 1734. In spite of the virtuoso arias he contrived for Caffarelli (the *primo uomo*), the production failed to find favour.

His next opera, *L'Olimpiade* (1735; text by Metastasio), fared no better, though for quite different reasons. It was commissioned for the

Roman Carnival and performed at the Teatro Tordinona. The preparations were beset with political intrigue as Metastasio and the singers battled for Pergolesi's allegiance; then the Roman theatres were closed for festivals and mourning. When the opera was finally performed Pergolesi is said to have been struck with an orange by a member of the audience. In spite of its inauspicious beginning, *L'Olimpiade* was very popular elsewhere in Italy during the late 1730s and early 1740s; in London a *pasticcio* based on it entitled *Meraspe* was performed in 1742.

Already ravaged by illness, Pergolesi composed his last *opera buffa* during the summer of 1735: *Il Flaminio* (text by Federico) was performed at the Teatro Nuovo, Naples, that autumn. It was an instant success and continued to be performed up to 1750. He began a wedding serenata, *Il tempo felice*, for the Prince of Sansevero (to be performed at Torremaggiore in December 1735) but handed it over to Nicola Sabatini to finish. While Pergolesi died virtually unknown outside Italy, in death he achieved almost instant fame. Such was the demand for his music all over Europe that his name found its way into other composers' works, increasing his supposed *opera omnia* many times over and obscuring his real legacy.

Piani, Giovanni Antonio. See FRANCE *1 Paris and Versailles.*

Porpora, Nicola. See ITALY *10 Itinerant Musicians.*

Porsile, Giuseppe. See CENTRAL EUROPE *3 Austro-Hungary: Vienna.*

Provenzale, Francesco (*c*1626–1704). Neapolitan composer – one of the driving forces behind the establishment of Neapolitan opera – and teacher. Provenzale was particularly active as an opera composer in the 1650s and again in the 1670s, although he may well have collaborated on some of the anonymous operas performed there in the 1660s. His first opera, *Il Ciro* (1653), was performed in 1654 with supplementary music by Cavalli at SS Giovanni e Paolo, Venice. Likewise, *Xerse* (?1655) and *Artemisia* (?1657) seem to have been adaptations of Cavalli's operas of the same names. As a composition instructor at the Neapolitan Conservatorio S Maria di Loreto, Provenzale encouraged his pupils to compose and perform sacred operas, and in 1672 he himself composed two. Only two operas that are entirely his own work survive, *Lo schiavo di sua moglie* (1671) and *La Stellidaura vendicata* (1674); they reveal his skill at composing chromatic laments and

freely alternating forms. His involvement in opera decreased as the works of M.A. Ziani and Alessandro Scarlatti became popular on the Neapolitan stage.

As Naples' *maestro di cappella*, from 1665 he was dedicated to the development and enrichment of the city's musical life. He taught at S Maria di Loreto from 1663 until 1675 and was then director of the Conservatorio S Maria della Pietà dei Turchini until 1701; simultaneously he was *maestro di cappella* to the Tesoro di S Gennaro at Naples Cathedral (1686–99). The only post that eluded him was that of *maestro di cappella* to the viceregal court: P.A. Ziani was appointed in 1680 and Scarlatti four years later; instead Provenzale had to content himself with being their second-in-command (*maestro onorario*).

Riccio, Benedetto (?1678–after 1710). Neapolitan amateur composer who, with Faggioli, Orefice and Mauro, created *opera buffa* in Neapolitan dialect. His *L'alloggiamentare* (text by Gianni) was performed in 1710 at the Teatro dei Fiorentini; it contained 57 short musical items, many of which were ensembles, including an onstage serenata and a dance. Riccio also composed an *opera seria* and two *melodrammi sacri*.

Salvatore, Giovanni (*d* ?1688). Neapolitan priest, organist, composer and *maestro di cappella*. Many years after studying at the Conservatorio S Maria della Pietà dei Turchini, Salvatore returned to teach there (1662–73). He also held posts as organist of S Severino and *maestro di cappella* of S Lorenzo. In the course of his work he composed sacred vocal music and in 1641 published in open score for organ his *Ricercari a 4 voci*, containing ricercares, canzonas, a set of variations and organ Masses. His last appointments were as rector and *maestro di cappella* of the Conservatorio dei Poveri di Gesù Cristo.

Sarro, Domenico Natale (1679–1744). Neapolitan *maestro di cappella* and *opera seria* composer, working in the shadow of Leonardo Vinci. Once a pupil at the Conservatorio di S Onofrio, Sarro competed unsuccessfully for the post of *maestro di cappella* at court in 1703, but within a year was appointed vice-*maestro di cappella*, only to lose the post in 1708 upon the arrival of the Austrian viceroy following the War of Succession. In order to live he composed serenatas to mark visits by foreign dignitaries, weddings and birthdays, as well as sacred operas for the Neapolitan confraternities.

After composing a number of *opere serie* early in his career (before the Austrian occupation), he began again in earnest about 1718. Among his best works were *Alessandro Severo* (1719; text by Zeno), *Ginevra Principessa di Scozia* (1720; text by Salvi) and *Didone abbandonata* (1724), which was the first setting of a major Metastasio libretto and antedates Vinci's by two years. In 1728 Sarro became Greco's successor as *maestro di cappella* to the city of Naples and in 1737 followed Mancini at court. When the Teatro S Carlo opened in 1737, Sarro's *Achille in Sciro* (text by Metastasio) was performed.

Scarlatti, Alessandro. See ITALY *7 Papal States: Rome.*

Scarlatti, Domenico. See IBERIAN PENINSULA AND COLONIES *1 Spain.*

Senesino. See ITALY *10 Itinerant Musicians.*

Strada del Pò, Anna Maria. See BRITISH ISLES *1 London.*

Strozzi, Gregorio (*c*1615–1687). Organist and composer of choral, didactic and keyboard music. Strozzi served as an organist at Ss Annunziata, Naples (1634), and then as a chaplain in Amalfi (1645), eventually becoming a doctor of both canon and civil law. His *Capricci da sonare cembali, et organi* (1687) is a compendium of current keyboard forms and one of the last Italian keyboard sources to be printed in open score.

Trabaci, Giovanni Maria (*c*1575–1647). Neapolitan tenor, organist and composer. Trabaci was appointed organist of the Spanish viceroys' chapel in 1601, succeeding Giovanni de Macque as *maestro di cappella* in 1614. From 1603 until 1611 he was associated with the Capoa di Balzo family and from 1625 to 1630 the Oratorio dei Filippini. He composed a wide variety of music, motets (some Gesualdian in character) – including five volumes dedicated to the Virgin Mary – and other sacred music, madrigals and other secular vocal forms. He also published two collections of keyboard works (1603 and 1615), anticipating the transformational, chromatic style of Frescobaldi; they include ricercares, canzonas, capriccios and versets that – except for two works for the chromatic harpsichord – could equally be played by an instrumental ensemble.

Ursino, Gennaro (1650–1715). Neapolitan *maestro di cappella* and composer. Ursino was trained at the Conservatorio S Maria della Pietà dei Turchini, where in 1675 he was appointed assistant director under Provenzale, whom he succeeded in 1701. Simultaneously, from 1686 he assisted his teacher Giovanni Salvatore – by then director of the Conservatorio dei Poveri di Gesù Cristo – and

then succeeded him in 1688; he resigned this post in 1695 but, after the turn of the century, took on the *maestro di cappella* posts at two churches and at the Jesuit college; he resigned his post at the Turchini in 1705. In these various capacities he composed a variety of polychoral and concertato motets, as well as sacred dramatic works.

Veneziano. Father and son, who worked in Naples as organists, *maestri di cappella* and composers. Gaetano Veneziano (1656–1716) went to study with Provenzale at the Neapolitan Conservatorio S Maria di Loreto in 1666; later, in 1684, he became its *maestro di cappella*. During the Spanish occupation of Naples he served as the court *maestro di cappella* (succeeding Alessandro Scarlatti in 1704), but relinquished his post when the Austrians captured Naples in 1707. Veneziano composed sacred music, much of it in a polychoral style.

His son Giovanni (1683–1742) also profited briefly from the Spanish rule: in 1704 he was made one of three court organists (along with Mancini and Domenico Scarlatti), though they were all dismissed in 1707; 28 years later, he applied to be readmitted to the court chapel (claiming unfair dismissal) and won. He also associated with the Loreto and served as second *maestro* from 1716. Veneziano was one of the earliest Neapolitans to compose comic operas in the local dialect. Two of his works (*Lo mbruoglio de li nomme* and *Patrò Tonno d'Isca*, both with texts by 'Agasippo Mercotellis') were performed at the Teatro dei Fiorentini in 1714 and *Lo Pippo* (text by 'Persio Segisto') the following year.

Vinci, Leonardo (*c*1690–1730). Neapolitan composer who was prominent in the 1720s among the post-Scarlattian generation of *opera seria* composers. Vinci was a pupil of Gaetano Greco at the Conservatorio dei Poveri di Gesù Cristo (where he served as *maestro di cappella* in the last years of his life), before taking up a post as *maestro di cappella* to the Prince of Sansevero. While in his service (1719–24), Vinci became involved with the circle of composers composing comedies in Neapolitan dialect; from 1722 until 1730 he composed at least three *opere serie* each year and travelled between Naples and Venice, Parma and Rome to direct performances.

Vinci's *opere serie* benefited from his apprenticeship in *opera buffa* and were very much a forum for experiments, such as the use of sonata form and driving arpeggiated ritornellos (foreshadowing the Mannheim rocket), as well as *parlando* dialogue recitatives and abrupt harmonic shifts without benefit of modulation. *Didone abbandonata* (1726; text by Metastasio) and *Artaserse* (1729; text by Metastasio), both composed for the Roman Teatro delle Dame, were among his finest operas. *Artaserse* was chosen for performance on a number of important occasions, including a 1738 gala performance at the Teatro S Carlo (which opened in Naples in 1737) and the inauguration of Dresden's first public opera house in 1746.

After the death of Scarlatti in 1725 Vinci became Mancini's vice-*maestro di cappella* at the Neapolitan court, a post he continued to hold until his death (possibly the result of poisoning). Pergolesi studied with him at the very end of his life.

9 Sicily

Astorga, Emanuele (Gioacchino Cesare Rincón) d' (1680–?1757). Sicilian baron of Spanish descent and composer of cantatas. Astorga composed an opera, *La moglie nemica*, which may have had autobiographical overtones (his father had earlier attempted to murder his mother), and performed it privately in 1698 at Palermo for a group of aristocratic amateurs. He spent some time in Rome among those intimate with Spain's papal ambassador and there he composed cantatas on texts by Sebastiano Biancardi. With Biancardi he travelled to Genoa, where he composed another opera (*Dafni*) in 1709, and elsewhere. Later that year he was summoned by Charles III to Barcelona, remaining there until Charles was made Holy Roman Emperor. After spending 1711–14 in Vienna he returned to Palermo, inheriting his title and lands, married and became a senator of Palermo in 1718. In 1721 he and his wife parted amicably and Astorga departed definitively for Lisbon.

Del Buono, Gioanpietro. Mid-17th-century composer (probably a monk) who published in Palermo a collection of *Canoni, oblighi et sonate in varie maniere sopra l'Ave maris stella* (1641), of which the 14 harpsichord sonatas are the earliest examples of the genre. They are self-contained *partite* in the style of Frescobaldi and employ a *cantus firmus* in the lower of two inner parts; the fifth is entitled 'Fuga cromatica' and the seventh 'Stravagante, e per il cimbalo cromatico'.

Il Verso, Antonio (?c1560–1621). Sicilian poet, historian, prolific mannerist composer and teacher of Palazzotto e Tagliavia. Il Verso was a pupil of Pietro Vinci, whose music he published posthumously and parodied slavishly. With the exception of a five-year stay in Venice (1600–5), where he came under the influence of Giovanni Gabrieli, Il Verso worked all his life in Palermo without an official post, supporting himself by teaching and composing. He left motets and *ricercari*, as well as 15 books of madrigals for three, five and six voices.

India, Sigismondo d'. See ITALY *10 Itinerant Musicians.*

Palazzotto e Tagliavia, Giuseppe (?c1587–1633). Noble Sicilian churchman who, along with Sigismondo d'India, was the most important composer active in Sicily during the early part of the 17th century. Palazzotto e Tagliavia was a pupil of Il Verso and remained in Sicily all his life, apart from a year in Naples (1617) in the service of the viceroy. His excellent madrigals show the influence of Gesualdo and Monteverdi, as well as that of his teacher and Claudio Pari (who had published four collections in Palermo by 1619). His sacred music includes motets for one to four voices and continuo (1616), at least three volumes of *Sacre canzoni musicali* (only the third, from 1631, survives) and a collection of *Messe brevi concertate* (1632) for double choir and organ.

Palotta, Matteo. See CENTRAL EUROPE *3 Austro-Hungary: Vienna.*

Sportonio, Marc'Antonio ['Il Bolognese'] (c1631–after 1680). Mezzo-soprano castrato and composer who became a leading figure in the musical life of Palermo. Sportonio, like his friend Venanzio Leopardi, was a pupil of Carissimi at the Collegio Germanico in Rome before taking up a post with the Duke of Modena. He and Leopardi travelled to Paris at the end of 1646 to take part in the performances of Luigi Rossi's *Orfeo* several months later (1647). Sportonio is next heard of in Palermo, where in 1655 he organized the first performance of an opera, Cavalli's *Giasone*, and took a comic role in the production. He composed operas himself, among them *La Flavia imperatrice* (1669), *Caligola* (1675) and *La Fiordispina* (1678), which was repeated at the viceregal court in 1680 and at the Teatro S Bartolomeo, Naples. At the end of his life he helped to found the 'Unione dei musici' in Palermo.

10 Itinerant Musicians

Alberti, Domenico (*c*1710–1746). Singer, who often accompanied himself on the harpsichord, and composer of at least three operas and about 36 harpsichord sonatas which established him as the originator of the 'Alberti bass'. He was trained by Biffi and Lotti in Venice and in 1736 travelled to Spain as a page to the Venetian ambassador, where Farinelli heard and admired his singing. He later took up a post in the Roman household of Marquis Molinari. His operas, dating from the late 1730s, are settings of Metastasian librettos for Venice; his sonatas (only 14 survive) are cast in the *galant* style and testify to his refined craftsmanship.

Albrici. Family of Roman musicians who went as far north as Sweden before settling in Dresden. Domenico Albrici, a singer, and his two sons, Vincenzo (1631–96) and Bartolomeo (*c*1640–87), left Rome in the early 1650s, travelling through Germany to reach the Swedish court of Queen Christina. Vincenzo had been a boy soprano at the Collegio Germanico under Carissimi and since 1646 organist (and *maestro di cappella*) at the Chiesa Nuova, while Bartolomeo had sung in the Cappella Giulia. For three months (1652–3) they performed with 15 other Italian musicians at the Swedish court (Vincenzo later joined Queen Christina in Rome in 1658).

By 1654 the two brothers had established themselves at the Dresden electoral court: Vincenzo was appointed joint vice-*Kapellmeister* with Bontempi under Schütz; Bartolomeo took up the organ post, which he held until 1666. Vincenzo returned to Dresden from Italy in 1662, but stayed only a short time: from 1664 until early 1668 he was in London – where he was joined by his brother in 1666 – at the court of Charles II. Bartolomeo remained in London, performing and teaching, and in 1679 published some harpsichord pieces. Vincenzo went back to Dresden, visited Paris and in 1676 was appointed director of Italian music at Dresden, but when the Italians were dismissed four years later he severed his own long-standing connection there.

By temporarily converting to Protestantism Vincenzo gained the organ post at the Leipzig Thomaskirche in 1681, but within months opted for the directorship of music at Prague's St Augustin. His Latin motets for voices and instruments were preserved in Sweden by Gustav Düben.

Algarotti, Francesco (1712–64). Cosmopolitan poet, librettist and neo-classic reformer, known by his *Saggio sopra l'opera in musica* (1755). After studies in Rome and Bologna, Algarotti sought out the intellectual centres of Europe – London, Paris (where he lived with Voltaire) and Berlin, where Frederick the Great gave him a post (1740) and made him a count. During the 1740s he worked at Dresden as well as Berlin, adapting and versifying Italian opera librettos to suit the kings of Prussia and Poland (August III was also Elector of Saxony). In 1753 he returned to Italy, in poor health, and wrote the *Saggio*.

Algarotti's central point in the *Saggio* is that all aspects of music should be subordinated to a unifying poetic idea. His preference for severity and remoteness reflected his admiration for Greek dramas; to illustrate his assertions he included with the essay a sketch for *Enea in Troia* (after Virgil) and a French libretto for *Iphigénie en Aulide* (after Euripides and Racine), which Gluck set for Paris. His well-known admiration for C. H. Graun's *Montezuma* (1755) was perhaps based partly on the fact that Frederick the Great was personally responsible for the libretto (which Tagliazucchi translated from French into Italian).

Ariosti, Attilio (1666–?1729). Cosmopolitan Italian composer, monk and courtier who performed diplomatic missions. Ariosti was a musician whose gifts as an organist served him in religious circles, and as a harpsichordist, cellist and viola d'amore soloist at various European courts. Known as 'Frate Ottavio' (after his investiture as a monk in 1688), Ariosti composed a controversial oratorio, *La passione* (1693), memorable for its mad scene and programmatic 'sinphonie infernale'. While briefly in the service of the Duke of Mantua (1696–7) he turned his talents to opera and had at least two operas performed in Venice (where the duke regularly spent the Carnival season).

From Mantua Ariosti went by the invitation of the electress to Berlin, where his presence – a Catholic monk at a Protestant court – created a stir. Though he held no official position, he composed several Italian operas, the first of their kind to be performed in Berlin. But he was, by any standards, a controversial character and in 1703 was recalled to Italy by his order; however, en route he paused in Vienna and was invited to stay. He finally returned to Italy as an agent of Joseph I in 1707–8. Ariosti accumulated substantial wealth and had, since his days in Berlin, become accustomed to a life of luxury. When Joseph I died in 1711, the empress-regent expressed her own disapproval of him by dismissing him and recommending to the pope that he be expelled from his order.

By 1716 he is known to have been in London, where he appeared as a viola d'amore soloist between the acts of Handel's *Amadigi*. His six lessons for the viola d'amore (1724), dedicated to George I, remain his best-known music, while his successful London operas of the 1720s, *Coriolano* and *Vespasiano*, have faded into oblivion, though they do contain further examples of atmospheric instrumental music and many attractive cantabile arias. When Ariosti died, in much reduced circumstances, his compatriot Rolli composed a burlesque epitaph which made reference to his undignified habit of begging money from acquaintances.

Babbi, Gregorio (Lorenzo) (1708–68). High tenor who was considered one of the finest exponents of the expressive style; he had a tessitura of two octaves (*c–c''*) which he augmented with falsetto notes. Babbi began his career in the service of the Grand Duke of Tuscany, before taking up a post at the Neapolitan court of Charles III in 1741. Eventually he and his wife, Giovanna Guaetta, became part of the company in residence at the Teatro S Carlo. In 1755 he was invited to Lisbon to sing in a performance of Mazzoni's *Antigono*. He was pensioned in 1759.

Baroni, Leonora (1611–70). Singer who was called 'L'Adrianella' after her mother, Andreana Basile (*c*1580–*c*1640). Basile was an accomplished contralto and instrumentalist who by her musical gifts and social position (acquired through marriage to a Calabrian nobleman, Muzio Baroni) helped to popularize the monodic style. She held an appointment at the Gonzaga court in Mantua (1610–24) and was considered by Monteverdi to be the finest singer of her day. Leonora, named after the late Duchess of Mantua, followed in her mother's footsteps, touring with her so that by the age of 16 her artistry and beautiful voice were already widely acclaimed in the highest circles of Italian society.

In 1633 the Baroni family took up residence in Rome where their salon attracted large and distinguished audiences. André Maugars wrote warmly of Leonora while he was in Rome in 1639. She was regularly invited to sing at the Palazzo Barberini; it was there that she met the secretary to Cardinal Barberini,

Giulio Cesare Castellani (whom she married in 1640), and Cardinal Mazarin, who arranged an invitation from the Queen Regent of France for Leonora and her husband to visit Paris in 1644. Her many accomplishments, musical and literary, inspired contemporary poets to dedicate verses to her, among them the future Pope Clement IX and John Milton, who heard her sing in Rome.

Bernacchi, Antonio Maria (1685–1756). Bolognese alto castrato, famous for his technical and artistic virtuosity, who was much in demand throughout Europe during the first third of the 18th century. Bernacchi was a pupil of Pistocchi at S Petronio, Bologna, before making his début in Genoa in 1703. His first patron was the Austrian emperor's ambassador to Venice, during 1709–10. He subsequently spent much time abroad – at the electoral courts of Düsseldorf and Munich (1720–7), where he studied counterpoint with Bernabei, at Mannheim, at the Viennese imperial court and in London at the King's Theatre (1716–17, 1729) – while fulfilling heavy commitments in Italy (he appeared in at least 22 Venetian operas). Among the operas in which he made his name were Orlandini's *Carlo Rè d'Alemagna* (Parma, 1714), Gasparini's *Il Bajazet* (Milan, 1719), Alessandro Scarlatti's *Griselda* (Rome, 1721) and Handel's *Lotario* (London, 1729).

He was not always popular – especially in London, where in 1729 Senesino commanded more affection – and was later criticized by Algarotti (1755) for relying upon technique to carry the day. A.M. Zanetti drew famous caricatures of him (see Plate 22). He retired to Bologna in 1736 (where since 1722 he had been a member of the Accademia Filarmonica) to found an important singing-school. He counted Metastasio, Farinelli and Padre Martini among his friends.

Bernardi, Stefano (*c*1585–1636). Veronese *maestro di cappella*, theorist and composer. Bernardi worked in Rome, where he published motets (for two to five voices and continuo), and Verona, where he produced a counterpoint treatise (*Porta musicale*, 1615); he was also associated with the Bolognese Accademia Filarmonica, for whom he composed the *Concerti academici* (1616; for three to six singers and players with continuo). He briefly held a post in the service of Archduke Carl Joseph, Bishop of Breslau and Bressanone (*d* 1624), before settling in Salzburg in 1624. Three years later he was made a Doctor of Law and in 1628 provided a *Te Deum* for 12 choirs for the consecration of Salzburg Cathedral.

Among his earliest works were three collections of five-part madrigals, published in Venice (1611, 1616 and 1619), which document his own transition from *prima* to *seconda prattica*. Even after moving to Austria he continued to publish music in Venice – psalms, Masses, motets and sacred concertos. His 1637 collection of *Salmi concertati* is particularly important for the way in which he singled out the soprano soloist in each of the psalms, juxtaposing solos with vibrant four-part ripieno sections.

Bononcini, Giovanni. See ITALY 5 *Modena-Reggio*.

Bordoni [Hasse], **Faustina** (1700–81). Venetian mezzo-soprano, considered one of the finest singers and actresses of her day, who from 1730 was the wife of Johann Adolf Hasse. Patrician by birth, Faustina Bordoni became a wealthy woman in her own right, the beneficiary of lavish awards from dukes and princes and much in demand at the opera houses of Italy, Germany and England. She was a particular favourite of the Empress of Austria, endearing herself by performing duets with Maria Theresa (1725–6).

Once the pupil of Gasparini and the protégée of the Marcellos, she began her career in the service of the Elector Palatine. She made her opera début in Venice in 1716 in a production of C. F. Pollarolo's *Ariodante*, and she was also heard there in operas by Albinoni, Lotti, Gasparini, Vinci and others. In 1723 she sang in Torri's *Griselda* at Munich, where she was enthusiastically received. In Vienna, where she was heard in the operas of Fux and Caldara, she was even more sought after. In 1726 she appeared in London at the King's Theatre, with Cuzzoni (they had already appeared together in 1718) and Senesino, in Handel's *Alessandro*. The following two seasons she appeared in productions by Ariosti and Bononcini, as well as by Handel. The much publicized rivalry between Bordoni and Cuzzoni came to a head during a performance of Bononcini's *Astianatte* (6 June 1727); nevertheless they performed together later that year in a St Cecilia's Day concert.

Bordoni returned to Italy in June 1728 to sing at Florence and, during the next few years, in the opera houses of Venice, Parma, Turin, Milan and Rome. After her marriage to Hasse she devoted herself primarily to promoting his music; within a year they were installed at the Dresden court, where Hasse remained in the post of *Kapellmeister* and she as a *virtuosa da camera* for more than 30 years. In 1750 they visited Paris, where her singing

was still very much admired. In the interim she frequently returned to Italy to sing at Venice, Naples and elsewhere until her retirement in 1751. Tosi, Quantz and Burney praised her range, facility and dramatic flair.

Caffarelli [Majorano, Gaetano] (1710–83). Mezzo-soprano castrato who toured extensively in Italy and to France, England and Spain. Born Majorano, Caffarelli took his patron's name. After studies with Porpora (who admired his voice, if not his manner) at Naples, he went to Rome, where he was heard in opera roles from 1726 onwards. In 1730 he became chamber virtuoso to the Grand Duke of Tuscany and four years later appeared with Farinelli in the Venetian production of Geminiano Giacommelli's *Merope* (text by Zeno). Shortly thereafter he took up a post with the King of Naples, enabling him to sing regularly at the S Bartolomeo and S Carlo theatres. He spent eight months in London during the 1737–8 season, where he took the title roles in Handel's *Faramondo* and *Serse* at the King's Theatre. The following year he sang at a royal wedding in Spain. Invitations from other European royalty followed: he remained at the French court almost a year during 1753, during which time a Concert Spirituel was specially organized for him; his stay at the Portuguese court two years later enabled him to purchase a dukedom. He was considered an unpleasant person, rude and unprofessional, who nevertheless possessed an uncommonly beautiful and well-trained voice, surpassed only by that of Farinelli.

Caldara, Antonio. See CENTRAL EUROPE 3 *Austro-Hungary: Vienna*.

Carestini, Giovanni (*c*1705–60). Best travelled of the Italian castratos, who enjoyed the admiration of fellow musicians and monarchs alike. Carestini made his début in Rome in 1721 when he sang in Alessandro Scarlatti's *Griselda*; two years later he sang in the production of Fux's *Costanza e fortezza* at the coronation of Charles VI at Prague. Two seasons at the Viennese court were followed by three in London (1733–5), where he was much acclaimed in the works of Handel, creating the role of Ruggiero in *Alcina*. He returned to Italy, only to reappear in London four years later. In 1747 he took up a post at the Dresden court, from there went to the Berlin court, and then in 1754 to St Petersburg. Burney pronounced him not only an imaginative musician but also an attractive person of intelligence and refinement.

Castaldi, Bellerofonte (1580/1–1649). Colourful and well-travelled Modenese poet, theorbist and guitarist, composer and engraver. From 1603 he was forced to travel, having been banished from Modena for his part in the killing of his brother's murderer, and was subsequently imprisoned several times because of his writings. He engraved his own collections of music – *Capricci* (1622), for two theorbos, and *Primo mazzetto di fiori musicalmente colti dal giardino bellerofonteo* (1623), for one to three voices, which carry bizarre titles and performance indications.

Cesti, Antonio [Pietro] (1623–69). The outstanding Italian musician of his day whose final years in Vienna crowned his career. He was a Franciscan monk, a composer of operas and cantatas (and apparently little sacred music) and a tenor. Cesti received his musical training in Rome, probably from Abbatini, Luigi Rossi and Carissimi. His first employment was as a singer (1645–8) at the Florentine court of Ferdinando II, Grand Duke of Tuscany, and at the Sienese court of Prince Mattias de' Medici (1647). After failing to gain the post of *maestro di cappella* at Pisa Cathedral, Cesti went to Venice, where at the Teatro SS Apostoli in 1649 his opera *Orontea* was enthusiastically received. *Orontea* (text by Cicognini) signalled the first real challenge to Cavalli's supremacy in Venice. Cesti found time to tour with opera companies while producing further operas (*Alessandro vincitor di se stesso* (text by Sbarra) at the Teatro SS Giovanni e Paolo and *Il Cesare amante* (text by Varotari) at the Teatro Grimano, both in 1651) and to have an affair with the singer Anna Maria Sardelli. None of this was favourably looked upon by his monastery in Arezzo, and Cesti was soundly admonished for his 'dishonourable and irregular life'.

In 1652 Cesti sought refuge in the service of Archduke Ferdinand Karl at Innsbruck, where he remained five years, occasionally returning to Venice. His *La Cleopatra* (a revision of *Il Cesare amante*) inaugurated the archducal Komödienhaus in 1654, and *L'Argia* (text by Apolloni) – replete with stage machinery and four *corps de ballet* – was performed the following year to mark the visit of Queen Christina of Sweden. *La Dori* (text by Apolloni), first performed in 1657 and later as the archduke's contribution to the Florentine wedding celebrations of Grand Duke Cosimo III and Marguerite Louise d'Orléans, was his most successful opera for Innsbruck (during the next 30 years it was produced 20 times).

Cesti returned to Rome in 1658, apparently with the encouragement of Ferdinand Karl, Cosimo III and Leopold I, to seek release from his vows. While there his singing gained the attention of Pope Alexander VII, who insisted he join the papal choir. Under the threat of excommunication he nevertheless returned to Innsbruck at the end of 1661, a secular priest and a Knight of the Order of S Spirito. His *La magnanimità d' Alessandro* (text by Sbarra) was performed for another visit by Queen Christina in 1662, and *La Semirami* (text by Moniglia) in 1665. He maintained his connections with the Venetian theatres – *Il Tito* (text by Beregan) was produced at the Teatro Grimano in 1666 – and with the imperial court in Vienna, where he finally took up a post as 'capelan d'honore und intendenta delle musiche theatrali' in 1666.

The next two years were the most fruitful and gratifying of his career: *Le disgrazie d'Amore* (1667; text by Sbarra) and the magnificent *Il pomo d'oro* (1668; text by Sbarra) are his greatest masterpieces, the former distinguished for its music, the latter for its scale and setting (five acts, 24 stage sets by Burnacini and a large orchestra; see Plates 11 and 12). He also arranged court performances of operas by Abbatini and his nephew Remigio Cesti. Cesti ended his days in Florence, where he had been made *maestro di cappella*.

61 manuscript cantatas survive, though their provenance (for whom, when and where) has yet to be established. Differences in Cesti's operas reflect the theatres for which they were composed: those for Venice require small forces and rely upon recitative for narrative and arias and ariosos for moments of reflection; those for the Florentine, Innsbruck and Viennese courts make use of larger forces (including choruses and dancers) and more complex scenery, employing accompanied recitative for moments of high drama. Such distinctions are not so germane to the cantatas. He employed Monteverdi's *stile concitato* in *L'Argia* but avoided Cavalli's descending chromatic ostinato basses; he used chromaticism to underscore emotive words and scenes. His comic scenes involving servants were particularly adored.

Chelleri [Keller], Fortunato (1686/90–1757). Italian composer who became *Hofkapellmeister* to Prince-Bishop Johann Philipp Franz von Schönborn at Würzburg in 1722 and then to the Landgrave of Hesse at Kassel in 1724. He was brought up by his uncle (a priest and *maestro di cappella* at Piacenza Cathedral) when his father (an amateur musician) emigrated to Germany. He was an established opera composer before he left Italy: his first opera, *La Griselda* (text by

Zeno), was performed at the ducal theatre in Piacenza in 1707, and *Alessandro il grande* (text by Zeno) in Cremona the following year; *Zenobia in Palmira* (text by Zeno and Pariati) was performed in Barcelona in 1709 and Milan in 1710. His own German connection was established in 1715 when he became *maestro della camera* to the Electors Palatine, resident at Florence until 1719.

At Würzburg he composed oratorios, putting opera firmly aside except occasionally to revive his old works, and played in the orchestra of the prince-bishop's brother, Count Rudolf Franz Erwein, at Schloss Wiesentheid. In 1723 he was made a privy councillor, but the next year his patron died and Chelleri sought the post at Kassel, whence he visited London (1726–7) and Stockholm (1732–4), after the landgrave's death and the accession of his son Friedrich (1730), who was also King of Sweden. Chelleri published instrumental music in London, Paris, Amsterdam, The Hague and Kassel.

Corbetta, Francesco (*c*1615–1681). The finest virtuoso guitarist-composer of his day, equally at home at the Austrian, French and English courts. Corbetta taught in Bologna, where he published a collection of *Scherzi armonici* in 1639, and served the Duke of Mantua (*c*1643, at which time he published a collection of *Varii capricii* in Milan), before touring abroad. During the late 1640s, he was in Austria in the service of the archduke (somehow managing to publish a second collection of *Varii scherzi* in Brussels in 1648); during the 1650s he was in Paris at the invitation of Cardinal Mazarin.

At the same time he became a favourite of the exiled Charles II and, as his teacher and private musician, accompanied the king back to England, where the guitar was soon much in vogue after the Restoration. By 1671 Corbetta was back in Paris, where he published a volume of pieces, entitled *La Guitarre royalle* (dedicated to Charles II), for voices, guitar and continuo (along with instructions for realizing continuo parts on the guitar and a belated refutation of charges of plagiarism that had been levelled at him by his pupil G. B. Granata in 1659). He found employment as *maître de guitarre* to the dauphin (publishing a set of duets in 1674 as a second volume of *La Guitarre royalle*, dedicated this time to Louis XIV). He returned to London in 1675 for the performances of Crowne's court masque *Calisto*. Corbetta died in Paris.

Cuzzoni, Francesca (*c*1698–1770). Famous Italian soprano, the rival of Faustina Bordoni.

Cuzzoni made her Venetian début in the company of Faustina Bordoni in C.F. Pollarolo's *Ariodante* (1718); they met again in London, where they sang together in Handel's *Alessandro* in 1726 and Bononcini's *Astianatte*, though the audience attending the 6 June 1727 performance witnessed a scandalous row between the two women. By contrast with Faustina, Cuzzoni was an eccentric and temperamental artist, neither beautiful nor a great actress. Her voice was her gift, and her two-octave compass ($c'–c'''$) exceeded that of her rival. Her intonation, ornamentation and breath control were extraordinary; the sheer expressive power of her voice was praised by Tosi, Quantz, Le Blanc, Mancini and Burney.

In Venice she had been a chamber virtuoso to the Grand Duchess Violante of Tuscany. In London she was a member of Handel's Royal Academy company, taking major roles in all his operas between 1723 and 1728. She travelled to France in 1724, where she was received with approbation. She returned to Italy in 1729 to perform in the opera houses of Naples, Venice, Florence and elsewhere, before reappearing in London for several seasons (1734–6) with the Opera of the Nobility. She continued to travel between northern Europe – to Amsterdam, where she was imprisoned for debt in 1742, and London, where the Prince of Wales arranged a benefit concert in 1750 to meet her expenses – and Italy. In her last years she resorted to button-making to support herself.

De Grandis, Vincenzo (1631–1708). *Maestro di cappella* and composer at a succession of courts, institutions and churches. His first appointment was at Hanover, in the service of Duke Johann Friedrich of Brunswick (1667), where from 1674 until 1680 he served as *maestro di cappella*. Simultaneously he held similar appointments in Rome at the Seminario Romano, the church of the Gesù (1670–1) and with the Pamphili family (1672–4). De Grandis returned to Italy in 1680 and two years later was appointed *maestro di cappella* of the Este court at Modena; one of his cycle of eight oratorios on the life of Moses was performed there each year, beginning in 1682. His last post was at the Santa Casa, Loreto (1685–92). De Grandis's father, 'Il Romano' (1577–1646), with whom he shared his name, was a singer and composer who from 1625 served as *maestro di cappella* of the papal choir.

Donati, Ignazio (*c*1575–1638). *Maestro di cappella* at a succession of provincial cathedrals (culminating in Milan in 1631) and composer who did much to popularize the small-scale concertato motet. Donati published four volumes of motets for two to five voices (1612, 1616, 1618, 1629) and two volumes of solo motets (1634, 1636) which incorporate ornamentation. He combined both conservative and progressive elements in his motets, preferring to set joyous texts; he experimented with contrasting groups of voices and instruments. Donati's single collection of psalms (*Salmi boscarecci*, 1623) offers optional ripieno parts; in an extended preface he suggested practical ways to adapt the works for one to four choirs and to add instruments according to the occasion, and described how to vary the spatial disposition of the musicians.

Durastanti, Margherita (*fl* 1700–34). Dramatic soprano, equally known at home and abroad. Durastanti was in the service of the Marquis Ruspoli (1707–15) in Rome when Handel visited there in 1707–8. Handel composed many of his Italian cantatas for her, and she sang the role of Magdalene in the first of the Easter 1708 performances of his *La Resurrezione* (Pope Clement XI intervened and had her replaced by a castrato on the second night). Between 1709 and 1712 Durastanti divided her time between Rome and Venice, where as *prima donna* at the Teatro S Giovanni Grisostomo she sang in operas by Lotti and C.F. Pollarolo, as well as in the title role of Handel's *Agrippina* (1709).

In 1719 Veracini arranged for her to sing with the Dresden court opera company, and it was at Dresden that Handel heard her in Lotti's *Teofane* and invited her to London for the following season at the Haymarket Theatre. She made her London début in the Royal Academy of Music's production of Porta's *Numitore* and subsequently sang in dramatic works by Bononcini, Alessandro and Domenico Scarlatti and Handel. When her daughter was born in 1721 (she was married to the musician Casimiro Avelloni), George I and the Princess Royal stood as godparents. Soon afterwards she made a trip to Italy via Munich (en route she was robbed of all her jewels), but returned to London for the 1722–3 and 1723–4 seasons to sing in operas by Bononcini, Ariosti and Handel. Handel invited her to London again in 1733 to sing in a series of revivals.

Fabri, Annibale Pio ['Balino'] (1697–1760). Bolognese tenor, who did much to popularize the tenor voice at home and abroad, and composer of oratorios. Like Bernacchi and many others Fabri was a pupil of Pistocchi and the subject of caricatures by A.M. Zanetti. His first appointment was in Rome, in the service of the Marquis Ruspoli (1710–11), though his first public performance was in Bologna (1716). Fabri continued to maintain his connections with Bologna as a member of the Accademia Filarmonica (from 1719). Handel recruited him in 1729 for London, where he appeared at the King's Theatre with Bernacchi in Handel's new opera *Lotario*, and from there he went to Vienna, where he became a virtuoso to Emperor Charles VI. He spent the 1738–9 season in Madrid, where he appeared in seven operas staged at the royal palace and the public theatre. After his retirement from the Italian stage at the end of 1748 he accepted an appointment in the Portuguese royal chapel, where he remained until his death.

Farinelli [Broschi, Carlo; Farinello] (1705–82). Influential Italian soprano castrato who spent half of his active career travelling and the last two decades resident in Madrid; he was knighted in 1750 by Ferdinand VI. Metastasio and Burney, among others, considered him the standard-bearer of the florid vocal style in *opera seria* after 1730. Farinelli was the protégé of Porpora in Naples and through him met Metastasio, who became a lifelong friend. In 1720 Farinelli made his début in Porpora's serenata *Angelica e Medoro* and three years later took the principal role in his *Adelaide*. The following year he embarked on an extended tour that took him to Vienna, Paris and London, where he joined Porpora at the Opera of the Nobility for three seasons (1734–7). He was extremely popular wherever he went, so beautiful was his voice and so superb his technique, though he was criticized for his stage deportment and a tendency to overindulge in spectacular effects.

An engagement at the Spanish court proved so felicitous that he gave up the stage permanently for the private chambers of Philip V (until 1746) and Ferdinand VI (until 1759). Farinelli took charge of the music at the royal chapel and ultimately became director of the royal theatres (see Plate 21). During his tenure the opera house was redesigned, and lavish productions of Italian operas were staged. He also acquired a herd of Hungarian horses and somehow became involved in a project to redirect the River Tagus.

With the accession of Charles III Farinelli returned to Italy, taking with him the extensive collection of paintings, keyboard instruments and manuscripts that he had inherited from Domenico Scarlatti. He retired to Bologna, where he occupied himself by playing the harpsichord and viola d'amore, composing poetry and music, and receiving callers such as Padre Martini, Gluck, Mozart, Casanova, Burney, the Electress of Saxony and Emperor Joseph II.

Fedeli, Ruggiero. See ITALY *4 Venice.*

Ferrari, Benedetto. See ITALY *4 Venice.*

Ferri, Baldassare. See NORTHERN EUROPE *3 Poland.*

Gnocchi, Pietro. See ITALY *4 Venice.*

Grossi, Giovanni Francesco (1653–97). Castrato singer, known as 'Siface' (after the role he took in Cavalli's *Scipione affricano* in Rome in 1671), who was murdered on the road between Ferrara and Bologna by angry kinsmen of the Marchesa Marsili (with whom Grossi had boasted of having an affair). From 1675 Grossi was attached to Francesco II d'Este, Duke of Modena, who allowed him to tour extensively throughout Italy and abroad. In Venice he sang at the opening of the Teatro S Giovanni Grisostomo in 1678; in Rome he gained the attention of Queen Christina of Sweden; in Naples he sang in Alessandro Scarlatti's *Pompeo* (1684). At the invitation of the duke's sister, James II's queen, Grossi travelled to England in 1686; en route through France he stopped in Paris, where he was much acclaimed, though he was not invited to sing at Versailles. In London in 1687 he created a sensation when he sang at the Catholic chapel at Whitehall and again in a private concert at Pepys's house. Purcell marked his departure for Italy with a harpsichord piece entitled 'Sefauchi's Farewell' (published in *Musick's Handmaid*, 1689). Whatever his musical gifts, Grossi was said to have been tactless and self-centred, choosing to sing only when the spirit moved him.

India, Sigismondo d' (*c*1582–1629). Sicilian nobleman, singer and prolific composer of secular monody, second only to Monteverdi as a composer of secular vocal music. As a young man (1600–10) D'India travelled widely throughout Italy. He served the dukes of Savoy and the Este court. In 1608 he was in Florence, where Vittoria Archilei and Caccini performed his monodies; in Rome his music was heard in the palaces of Pope Urban VIII and his cardinals. From 1611 until 1623 he was in Turin, composing and directing chamber music at the court of the Duke of Savoy. While there he produced ten collections of secular music and a *favola pescatoria, Zalizura.* His last years were spent in Modena and Rome. At the Este court in Modena he completed his final volume of madrigals (containing an extended cycle on Guarini's *Il pastor fido*) in 1624, and in 1626 his Requiem Mass was

performed at the funeral of Isabella d'Este. In Rome, where he was attached to Cardinal Maurizio (son of the Duke of Savoy), his *Missa 'Domine, clamavi ad te'* was performed in 1626 at the Cappella Giulia.

D'India was master of old and new – truly a man of his time – who composed and published polyphonic madrigals (from 1606) and monodic songs (from 1609) throughout his life. For him, elaborate counterpoint and expressive declamation were never in contention. Today he is best known for his five collections of monodies entitled *Musiche*, comprehending 84 strophic arias, variations, solo madrigals and laments. The laments, set to his own texts, are among his finest compositions, rich in rhythmic variety as well as unusual and poignant chromaticism; they compare favourably with Monteverdi's.

Lampugnani, Giovanni Battista (1706–86). Milanese harpsichordist and popular north Italian composer of heroic operas such as *Candace* (1732) and *Antigono* (1736). He was the resident composer for the 1743–4 season at the King's Theatre in London, and while there he composed two bravura operas, *Alfonso* and *Alceste* (both 1744), and published trio sonatas in which the first movements are cast in an early sonata form. He was last heard of in Milan when he served as second harpsichordist to the young Mozart in the 1770 performance of *Mitridate.* He may have been related to the oratorio librettist of the same name (*fl* 1690–8), who served the papal nuncio in Warsaw and Vienna and was later a Tuscan court correspondent in London; he wrote texts for *drammi per musica* to celebrate royal weddings.

Leopardi, Venanzio (*d c*1658). Well-travelled singer (contralto and tenor), instrumentalist and composer of solo cantatas. He worked in Bologna as a musician and valet to Cardinal Colonna, in Rome, where he studied under Carissimi at the Collegio Germanico (1646), in Paris, where he sang in Luigi Rossi's *Orfeo* (1647), and in Vienna, serving Empress Eleonora (from 1656).

Lonati, Carlo Ambrogio ['Il Gobbo della Regina'] (*c*1645–*c*1710/15). Milanese tenor, violinist and composer who was closely associated with Alessandro Stradella. Lonati's first appointment was at the Naples court during the mid 1660s, where he took part in a production of Cavalli's *Scipione affricano* (1664). From 1668 until 1677 he was in Rome at the Congregazione di S Cecilia, where he became acquainted with the castrato G.F. Grossi and Stradella. In 1673 the exiled Swedish Queen

Christina made him the leader of her string band, hence his pathetic sobriquet ('the queen's hunchback'); in the same year he also became principal violinist of the prestigious orchestra at S Luigi dei Francesi.

More coveted positions came his way during the next two years – first the job of concertino violinist at the Oratorio delle Stimmate at S Francesco and then at the Oratorio del Ss Crocifisso at S Marcello. The collection of sonatas he dedicated to Leopold I in 1701 no longer exists, but they are said to have employed seventh position, scordatura and extensive double-stopping; unfortunately only a few of his instrumental works survive to document his brilliant violin technique.

In 1677 the public theatres were closed by Pope Innocent XI, prompting Lonati and Stradella to depart first for Venice and Turin, then Genoa, where Lonati immediately mounted two opera productions at the Teatro Falcone – *Amor stravagante* (for which he made a few changes and additions to Pasquini's music of 1673) and his own *Amor per destino*. Soon after the murder of Stradella in 1682 he departed from Genoa.

During the 1680s he was associated with the Mantuan court, though he must have been in Venice during 1684–5 for the production of his opera *Ariberto e Flavio*. In 1686 his opera *I due germani rivali* was given at Modena, as well as his only oratorio *L'innocenza di Davide* (text by Sacrati); it was surely not a coincidence that Stradella's *Il Trespolo tutore* (c1677) was revived there that year. In 1687 he accompanied Grossi to England and by 1690 was back in Genoa for the performance of his new opera *Antioco, principe della Siria*. His operas are characteristic of the late 17th-century Venetian style, relying upon da capo arias, brilliant concertante instrumental accompaniments and *stile concitato* for moments of high drama. His cantatas stand alongside those of Stradella and Alessandro Scarlatti.

Madonis, Luigi. See ITALY *4 Venice.*

Manelli, Francesco. See ITALY *4 Venice.*

Marini, Biagio (c1587–1663). Brescian instrumentalist, who travelled as far afield as Brussels and Düsseldorf, and composer of concerted sacred music and violin sonatas (most of which are now lost). Marini served as a violinist at S Marco, Venice, under Monteverdi (1615) and at the Farnese court at Parma (1621), before becoming *Kapellmeister* at the Wittelsbach court (Neuburg an die Donau).

While still in Venice Marini published his earliest extant collections – two volumes of sinfonias, canzonas, sonatas and dances (for two to three players), which employ tremolo for the first time and indicate when the violinists should add 'affetti'. In Marini's next surviving collection (op. 8) from his period in Germany, sonatas and sinfonias are differentiated in terms of length and degree of complexity; one sonata requires scordatura and the 'Capriccio in modo di un lira' triple-stops. Over 25 years separate op. 8 from op. 22 (1655), which contains highly chromatic ensemble sonatas in clearly defined *da camera* and *da chiesa* forms.

Marini returned to Italy in 1649 as *maestro di cappella* at S Maria della Scala, Milan, but held a number of subsequent posts at Ferrara, Venice and Vicenza during the 1650s. His last years were divided between Brescia and Venice.

Mauro. See ITALY *4 Venice.*

Melani. The name of as many as three musical families in Pistoia during the 17th century, of whom three sons of Domenico di Sante Melani (a bell-ringer at Pistoia Cathedral) achieved prominence: Jacopo, Atto and Alessandro. The rest found employment in religious institutions and at the courts of the Duke of Bavaria, Archduke Sigismund of Austria, Archduke Ferdinand Karl at Innsbruck, the Grand Duke of Tuscany and the exiled Queen Christina of Sweden.

Jacopo Melani (1623–76) became the leading 17th-century composer of comic operas. After travelling to Paris with his brother Atto in 1644, he settled down as organist of Pistoia Cathedral, becoming *maestro di cappella* in 1667. During that time he composed all but one of his operas, mostly for Florence (though the anonymous 1652 opera, *Helena rapita da Theseo*, mounted at SS Giovanni e Paolo, Venice, may also have been his). Jacopo belonged to the Florentine Accademia de' Sorgenti, for whom he composed various *intermedi*; five of his operas (texts by Moniglia) were presented by the Immobili (a Florentine dramaturgical academy) at the Teatro della Pergola (1657–61, 1680). His lavish *festa teatrale*, *Ercole*, performed as part of the 1661 wedding celebrations of Cosimo III de' Medici and Marguerite Louise d'Orléans, is thought to have influenced Cavalli's celebratory *Ercole amante* (1662) and Cesti's even grander *Il pomo d'oro* (1668). In 1667 he moved to Rome, where the following year his operatic satire on absolutism, *Il Girello*, was performed (with a prologue by Stradella) at the Palazzo Colonna: it proved to be extraordinarily popular, signalling a new era of Roman comic opera.

Atto Melani (1626–1714) was an alto castrato, diplomat and composer of solo cantatas whose correspondence chronicling musical events in Paris during 1644–61 remains his most important legacy. Like his brother Jacopo, he benefited from the patronage of the Florentine Prince Mattias de' Medici, who arranged for him first to study in Rome with Luigi Rossi and M.A. Pasqualini and then to travel to Paris, where he took part in Rossi's *Orfeo* (1647). Atto was at first very popular at the French court where, having survived the Fronde, he remained as a naturalized citizen and a *gentilhomme de la chambre* until shortly after the death of his principal patron, Cardinal Mazarin, when his star declined: he was snubbed by Francesco Buti, who refused to include a role for him in the libretto for Cavalli's *Ercole amante*, and then had the added misfortune to become involved in the notorious Fouquet scandal which ultimately forced him to return to Rome. During his time in Paris he had served as a secret diplomatic courier between Mazarin and Mattias de' Medici, to whom his extant correspondence was addressed, and soon after arriving in Rome he became involved in papal politics. He gave his last public performance in 1668. Privately, he took credit for the election of his patron, Cardinal Giulio Rospigliosi, to the papacy in 1667; Clement IX subsequently arranged posts for Melani's brothers and paved the way for Atto's definitive reinstatement in 1679 as politician and diplomat at the French court.

Alessandro Melani (1639–1703), a composer of both sacred and secular music, served as *maestro di cappella* at Orvieto and Ferrara Cathedrals before replacing his brother Jacopo at Pistoia. Thanks partly to Atto's influence with Pope Clement IX, he was made *maestro di cappella* of S Maria Maggiore, Rome, in 1667 and of S Luigi dei Francesi five years later. His Roman patrons included Ferdinando de' Medici and Francesco II d'Este, and he is thought – on the evidence of a 1685 oratorio – to have performed diplomatic as well as musical services for the King of Poland. He published three collections of motets (for eight to ten voices) and left many works in manuscript, among them eight oratorios (destined for Rome, Palermo, Bologna, Modena and Florence), the most popular of which was a *pasticcio*, *Il fratricidio di Caino* (1683), to which Pasquini and Alessandro Scarlatti also contributed music. Alessandro's operas include only one for Rome, *L'empio punito* (1669; text by Acciaiuoli), notable for being the first based on the Don Juan story. It was commissioned by Cardinal Colonna; others were composed for Siena, Florence, Modena and Bologna, reflecting (as with his oratorios) his many aristocratic connections.

Mingotti. Venetian opera impresarios, Angelo (*c*1700–after 1767) and Pietro (*c*1702–59), who managed a travelling opera troupe. The company of eight singers (three men and five women) performed serious and comic operas with local orchestras. From 1736 they were based in Graz. In 1747 they were invited to Dresden to perform under Gluck for a royal wedding; Pietro's wife Regina proved such a sensation at the electoral court (in Gluck's *festa teatrale Le nozze d'Ercole e d'Ebe*) that she was offered and accepted a post. The troupe went on without her to Copenhagen where, with royal patronage, they established themselves. The following year they worked again with Gluck in Copenhagen and Hamburg. Copenhagen remained their base until 1756, when Pietro retired. Angelo continued his association with the troupe, which was based in Bonn during the mid 1760s.

Neri, Massimiliano. See ITALY *4 Venice*.

Nicolini [Grimaldi, Nicolò] (1673–1732). Leading Neapolitan alto castrato, as much praised for his acting as his singing, which was greatly enhanced by formidable breath control and a compass of *a–f''*. Nicolini was of humble but decidedly musical origins. After studies with Provenzale, he made his début at the age of 12 in his teacher's opera *La Stellidaura vendicata* (1685). Much of his career was centred in Naples (where he was attached to the Cappella del Tesoro di S Gennaro at the cathedral and the royal chapel) and Venice (where in 1705 he was knighted). Nicolini mastered a huge repertory, taking roles in the current operas of Alessandro Scarlatti, C. F. Pollarolo, Manzo, Mancini, Lotti, Leo, Porpora and Vinci at the S Bartolomeo theatre and royal palace in Naples, as well as in the Venetian operas of the Pollarolos, Gasparini, Caldara, Albinoni, Orlandini and Hasse. During the rehearsals for Pergolesi's first opera, *Salustia*, Nicolini became mortally ill and had to be replaced.

He spent the years 1708–12 and 1715–17 in London. On the first trip he sang at the Queen's Theatre in Alessandro Scarlatti's *Pyrrhus and Demetrius* (arranged by Haym, partly in English and partly in Italian; see Plate 23); praise from Addison and Steele is remarkable evidence of his distinguished performances. Although he sang (on contract) in every opera staged at the Queen's Theatre during the next three years, Nicolini also became involved in the company administration, advising on repertory and how to remodel the theatre in the current Venetian style. After singing the title role in Handel's *Rinaldo* in 1711 and 1712, he departed for Venice, but returned to sing in *Amadigi* (1715).

Pallavicino, Carlo (*d* 1688). Paduan organist and opera composer who divided his career between Padua (1665–6 and 1673), Venice (where he was *maestro di coro* at the Ospedale degli Incurabili, 1674–85) and Dresden (court vice-*Kapellmeister*, 1667–72; *Kapellmeister*, 1672, 1686–8). While working as organist of S Antonio in Padua, Pallavicino's first operas, *Demetrio* and *Aureliano*, were performed in Venice at the Teatro S Moisè in 1666; *Il tiranno humiliato* was given the following year at SS Giovanni e Paolo. From 1675 to 1685 his operas – *Vespasiano* (1678; text by Corradi) in particular – enjoyed great popularity.

On his first trip to Dresden he joined Vincenzo Albrici, Bontempi and Peranda, working under Schütz; he returned there in 1686 at the request of Elector Johann Georg III to take charge of Italian court opera. He was accompanied on his second journey by his precocious 14-year-old son, Stefano Benedetto, who two years later was appointed court poet (see NORTHERN EUROPE *4 Saxony and Thuringia: Dresden*). Carlo began setting one of his son's librettos (*Antiope*) but died before completing it – a task undertaken by N. A. Strungk.

Pistocchi, Francesco Maria Mamiliano.
See ITALY *7 Papal States: Bologna-Ferrara.*

Porpora, Nicola (Antonio) (1686–1768). Mainstream Italian composer of vocal music and opera, well known all over Europe, and the teacher of Farinelli, Caffarelli and J.A. Hasse. Porpora was born in Naples. He was trained as a musician at the Conservatorio dei Poveri di Gesù Cristo and fulfilled his first important opera commission, *Agrippina* (1708), for the royal palace. His early patrons were the Prince of Hessen-Darmstadt (resident in Naples 1709–13 as an Austrian army general) – who must have been responsible for the 1714 commission of *Arianna e Teseo* (text by Pariati) at the Vienna Hoftheater – and the Portuguese ambassador to Naples.

From 1715 until 1721 Porpora was *maestro di cappella* at the Neapolitan Conservatorio di S Onofrio where he gained a reputation as a singing-teacher. At the same time he was producing serenatas (on Metastasio's earliest texts, among them *Angelica*, 1720) and more operas for the Vienna Hoftheater. His operas also gained popularity in Rome – where he and Domenico Scarlatti collaborated on *Berenice regina d'Egitto* in 1718 at the Teatro Capranica – and in Milan and Reggio Emilia, perhaps because they were very conventional, relying heavily upon the virtuoso display of the singers in the ubiquitous da capo arias. In 1726 he accepted the post of *maestro* of the Venetian Ospedale degli Incurabili, in the hope of one day gaining the coveted post of *maestro di cappella* at S Marco; when he failed, he accepted the invitation proffered in 1733 by the newly formed Opera of the Nobility in London.

The Opera of the Nobility opened in December 1733 with Porpora's *Arianna in Nasso* (text by Rolli), sung by Senesino and others of Handel's singers. The company's avowed purpose was to bring down Handel's Royal Academy of Music, but despite their considerable musical resources they were unsuccessful; by the time they closed in 1737, Porpora had already returned to Venice, having composed five of his finest operas, an oratorio, a serenata and various *pasticci* on their behalf.

A certain restlessness now affected him, so that barely a year later (in 1738) he was back in Naples as *maestro di cappella* at the Conservatorio di S Maria di Loreto; then, in 1742, he was in Venice, first to produce an opera, *Statira* (text by Silvani), at S Giovanni Grisostomo, and later as *maestro di coro* at the Ospedale della Pietà – although he was asked to resign the following year (only to take up a similar post at the Ospedaletto). In addition to his teaching duties he composed sacred operas and oratorios, Masses, motets and other sacred works for these institutions.

A change of scene seemed to bring happier results: from 1747 until 1751 he was employed at the Dresden court as the singing-teacher to the electoral princess. In his first year there his opera *Filandro* (text by Cassani) was performed at the electoral theatre under the direction of his former pupil Hasse. He was made court *Kapellmeister* in 1748 and *Ober-Kapellmeister* the following year. He retired and moved to Vienna during the winter of 1752–3, where he gave singing lessons to aristocratic ladies; it was very probably through Metastasio that he met Haydn, who became his valet, pupil and accompanist at lessons. But his final years were spent in his native Naples, in virtual poverty.

Porta, Giovanni. See ITALY *4 Venice*.
Sandoni, Pietro Giuseppe. See ITALY *7 Papal States: Bologna-Ferrara*.
Sbarra, Francesco. See ITALY *6 Tuscany*.
Senesino [Bernardi, Francesco] (*d* 1759). Sienese alto castrato who derived his name from his birthplace. Though arrogant and difficult to work with, Senesino was a brilliant actor, unsurpassed for his delivery of recitative, and a strong singer. His early operatic career was centred in Italy, with appearances in Venice, Bologna, Naples and Genoa. In 1717 he took up a highly remunerative post at Dresden but was dismissed four years later for his insubordination at rehearsals; in the meantime, Handel had heard him in 1719 singing in Lotti's *Teofane* and was sufficiently impressed to recruit him for the second season of the Royal Academy (1720–1); he appeared in Bononcini's *Astarto* at the King's Theatre in November 1720. He remained with the company until it was disbanded in 1728, then went back to Italy for two seasons before returning to London to sing with the new Royal Academy company. After three seasons under Handel, Senesino joined the Opera of the Nobility in 1734 under Rolli and Porpora. He returned definitively to Italy in 1736, refused an engagement in Madrid (1739) and appeared in public for the last time in 1740.

Steffani, Agostino. See NORTHERN EUROPE *1 North Germany*.

Tesi (Tramontini), Vittoria (1700–75). Florentine contralto, known as 'La Moretta', well known in Germany and Vienna, as well as in Italy. After starting her career in Parma, in the service of Prince Antonio, Tesi went to Dresden in 1719 to sing with Durastanti and Senesino in the operas of Lotti. From 1721 to 1747 she sang in all the major centres of Italian opera; in 1739 she was in Madrid and in 1741 at Frankfurt, where she sang in the coronation music for the emperor. Tesi took the title roles in Gluck's Metastasian *Ipermestra* (Venice, 1744) and *Semiramide riconosciuta* (Vienna, 1748). While in Vienna she also took the title roles in two of Jommelli's Metastasian operas in 1749. She remained in Vienna, where during the 1750s her singing career declined and she devoted more time to teaching. She enjoyed the patronage of Empress Maria Theresa, who made her an honorary *virtuosa della corte imperiale*, and lived a life of luxury at what is now the Palais Auersperg; there she met Casanova in 1753 and the Mozarts in 1762. Her admirers included Quantz, Mancini, Metastasio and Burney.

Tessarini, Carlo (*c*1690–1766). Virtuoso violinist, composer of Vivaldian string music and author of a violin tutor *Gramatica di musica* (1741), published in Rome, which addresses high-position playing. Tessarini began his career in Venice in 1720 as a violinist at S Marco. His first collection of violin sonatas dates from 1729, the year in which he became leader of concerts at the Venetian Conservatorio SS Giovanni e Paolo. From 1731 until 1757 he was associated with Urbino Cathedral, although he was frequently absent (on tour or in residence elsewhere). He served Cardinal Wolfgang Schrattenbach in Brno from 1735 to 1738 and in Rome in 1740 and 1742. Around 1743 he travelled to France and in 1747 to the Netherlands, settling in Amsterdam in 1761. He published sonatas, trios, *sinfonie*, concertos and *ouvertures* in Paris and Amsterdam, as well as in Venice.

Tosi, Pier Francesco (*c*1653–1732). Castrato, composer of chamber cantatas and teacher, remembered today for his important treatise on singing, *Opinioni de' cantori antichi e moderni*, published in Bologna in 1723 (known to English readers in its 1742 translation by J.E. Galliard as *Observations on the Florid Song*). One of the finest singers of his day, praised especially for his expressive style, Tosi was engaged in London (1692), at the Viennese court (1705–11, as composer and diplomat to Count Johann Wilhelm of the Palatinate) and the Dresden court (1719), and at Bologna (1723). In 1730 he took holy orders.

Valentini, Giuseppe (1681–1753). Florentine violinist and composer. If not actually a pupil of Corelli, Valentini was certainly a follower who composed sonatas for one and two violins, violone and continuo; his concertos, however, are more Vivaldian. In all his music he favoured remote keys and the highest reaches of the violin. Only isolated details of his life are known. From about 1708 until 1713 he served the Marquis Ruspoli in Rome. While in the service of the Prince of Caserta at Cisterna, Valentini produced at least two operas, *La finta rapita* (1714) and *La costanza in amore* (1715), as well as several oratorios and cantatas. From 1737 to 1752 he was *maestro* of the Cappella Borghese. Some of his string concertos appeared in anthologies printed in Amsterdam (1716–17); other collections were published separately as opp. 7 (1710) and 9 (1724).

Veracini, Francesco Maria. See ITALY *6 Tuscany*.

Verocai, Giovanni (*c*1700–?1747). Venetian violinist and composer who was appointed leader of the Breslau Stadttheater orchestra in 1727. Two years later he entered the service of Friedrich August I, Prince-Elector of Saxony and King of Poland, thus obligating himself to spend seven months of the year at Dresden and the remaining five at Warsaw. He remained with Friedrich August until 1731, when he and 21 other musicians from the Polish court were invited to Moscow for a ten-month stay at the court of Empress Anna Ivanova; Verocai remained until 1738. His last appointment was as *Kapellmeister* and opera director at the ducal court of Brunswick-Wolfenbüttel, where he annually composed one or two operas on Metastasian texts, with principal roles for his German wife, who was a court singer.

Vitali, Filippo (*c*1590–1653). Singer, priest and composer whose *favola in musica*, *L'Aretusa*, was staged in Rome (1620). Vitali worked in Florence before joining the papal choir as a protégé of the Barberini family in the early 1630s. In 1642 he returned to Florence as *maestro di cappella* at S Lorenzo, but moved to Bergamo in 1648 to take up a similar post at S Maria Maggiore. Vitali left both sacred music (his 1636 *Hymni* are cast in the Roman polyphonic style) and secular, including a number of books of madrigals, solo and ensemble arias and Florentine *intermedi*.

Zuccari, Carlo (1704–92). Much-travelled violinist and composer from Casalmaggiore (nr Cremona). In 1723 Zuccari went to Vienna in the entourage of Count Pertusati and then remained in Olomouc for four years. In 1736 he settled in Milan, where he founded a school and led orchestras under G. B. Sammartini. In 1760 he was in London, where he published six Corellian trio sonatas and a set of 12 adagios (in plain and ornamented versions) entitled *The True Method of Playing an Adagio*. He returned to Italy in 1765.

France

Paris and its Environs

The Baroque era of French music spans the reigns of four Bourbon kings – Henri IV, Louis XIII, Louis XIV and Louis XV – and three regents – Maria de' Medici, Anne of Austria and Philippe of Orléans. Almost all the surviving music was composed to meet the needs of court and aristocratic life, which reached its zenith during the reign of Louis XIV (1661–1715). The royal *spectacles* – entertainments combining poetry or drama, vocal music, dance, processions, costumes and scenic effects created by unseen (if noisy) machinery and dazzling fireworks – encapsulate the extravagance and self-consciousness of the French court and the desire of Louis XIV in particular to impress the world.[1]

The palaces, the manners and the language of the Ancien Régime, so assiduously cultivated at the academy of Jean-Antoine de Baïf at the end of the 16th century and in the salons of the *femmes savantes* (or *précieuses*, as they were also known) in the 17th, were aped by other European courts as far away as Stockholm, Berlin, Dresden and Turin well into the 18th century. But full productions of French operas were rarely mounted outside Paris and the royal châteaux, among which Versailles was pre-eminent. In general, the French kings encouraged their subjects to cultivate a national style, while the regents and their ministers (several of whom were foreign-born) actively sought the invigoration of outside influences, and in particular that of Italian art and music.

During much of the century, this tension was to prove alternately stifling and creative as artistic freedom was first encouraged and then curtailed. The long shadow of Jean-Baptiste Lully, the Italian-born architect of French music at the court of Louis XIV and, by his manipulations, the sole composer and entrepreneur of opera in Paris during most of the 1670s and 80s, continued to hang over the next generation of French composers and almost as many writers on aesthetics. Louis XIV's revocation of the Edict of Nantes in 1685 drove thousands of Protestant merchants and skilled craftsmen into exile, seriously destabilizing the French economy, which was already compromised by war debts and corrupt tax laws. Had it not been for the earlier efforts of Louis XIV's brilliant minister of finance Jean-Baptiste Colbert to centralize in Paris all the agencies of French society, the great flowering of literature, music, architecture and fine arts might never have taken place, nor the emblems of French wealth and culture conveyed to the rest of Europe.

Cardinal Richelieu established the Académie Française in 1635 and the Académie Royale de Peinture et de Sculpture in 1648. Under Colbert, five more were founded: the Académie Royale de Danse (1661), the Académie des Inscriptions, Médailles et Belles-Lettres (1663), the Académie des Sciences (1666), the Académie Royale de Musique (1669) and, finally, the Académie Royale d'Architecture (1671). The charisma of Louis XIV, the splendour of Versailles and the might of the French army eased the task of the corps of French diplomats negotiating alliances, treaties and marriages in what was essentially a protracted struggle for the domination of

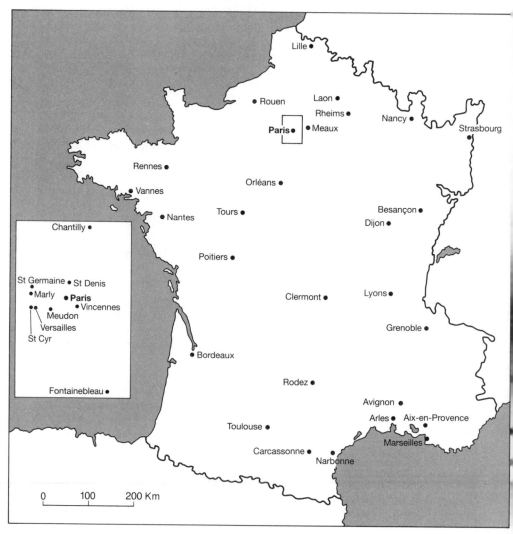

France. The Paris area and main provincial centres

Europe between the Bourbons and their Austrian cousins, the Habsburgs, throughout the 17th century and well into the 18th.

The French fondness for spectacles extended to all segments of the population. Before the first Versailles era (1683–1715) Paris had been the royal showcase for *ballets de cour*, *comédie-ballets* and *tragédies lyriques*. As early as the 1620s Louis XIII had ballets performed at the Hôtel de Ville for the pleasure of ordinary Parisians. But even from the time of Henri IV ballets had served as a useful means of glorifying the monarch, who was represented by mythological and allegorical characters as an enlightened and benevolent peacemaker. By using art as propaganda, the Bourbon kings became legendary in their own time, while their subjects happily basked in the reflected glory.

Ballets de cour[2] – made up of a loose series of solo airs, recited verses, danced *entrées* and a *grand ballet* performed by the king and several dozen nobles – were regularly performed in the huge hall of the Petit Bourbon, the Louvre and the Palais Royal. The three Louis each danced principal roles in their day. In 1617 Louis XIII danced the role of the fire demon in the *Ballet d'Armide*, a work requiring the services of 64 singers, 28 strings and 14 lutes. In anticipation of the 1660 celebrations of the marriage of Louis XIV to the Spanish Infanta, work began on the Salle des Machines in the Tuileries palace; but building delays meant that it was not inaugurated until 1663, when the performances of Cavalli's wedding opera *Ercole amante* (with Louis XIV dancing the role of the sun in Lully's *entrées*) finally took place. As late as 1720 Louis XV appeared there in Lalande's *Les folies de Cardenio*, when the hall reopened following its refurbishment.

Midway through the 1640s the Roman Cardinal Barberini and his entourage sought asylum at the French court. Cardinal Mazarin, the regent's chief minister and an old friend of the Barberinis, eagerly welcomed them, along with their entourage that included musicians such as the soprano Leonora Baroni and the castrato Atto Melani. Barberini's secretary, the librettist Francesco Buti, took charge of the musicians and was responsible for organizing performances of Italian opera and recruiting the designer and machinist Giacomo Torelli, as well as a cast of distinguished singers and the composer Luigi Rossi himself, who in 1647 set Buti's text for the opera *Orfeo*. It was performed at the Palais Royal, in Italian – though with a French prologue and ballets interleaved.

The Princes of the Blood, who greatly resented the powerful Cardinal Mazarin, seized upon the opportunity to ridicule him which was offered by the unprecedented expense of an opera production in a foreign language few understood and sung in freakish tones by castratos. *Mazarinades* (satirical songs about the chief minister) were circulated, and the queen was criticized for her part in the patronage of the Italians. When the princes briefly rose to greater power in 1648, they jailed many Italians who had lacked the foresight to flee; compelled to resort to Frenchmen for his theatrical entertainments, Mazarin cunningly subverted them for the purpose of securing the throne for Louis XIV. With his support, Pierre Corneille collaborated with Charles Dassoucy at the Théâtre du Marais on *Andromède* (1650), a *tragédie avec machines*, in which the Sun was implored in the prologue to halt his progress across the sky in order to pay homage to the King of France.

Meanwhile, the poet Isaac de Benserade was being commissioned to create ballets for the annual Carnival revels; his verses were elegant, topical and predictably monarchist. Lully became his principal collaborator, not merely as the composer but also as a dancer. Louis XIV took six roles, including that of Apollo, the Sun God, in the 1651 *Ballet du Roy des Festes de Bacchus*. The image of the Sun, signalling the dawn of a golden era, was chosen for Louis XIV before his birth. In 1663 the sun was proclaimed his official emblem by the Académie des Inscriptions et Belles-Lettres; later, Versailles and, indeed, all the royal châteaux were made resplendent with golden images of the sun and Apollo. Each of the academies, including the Académie Royale de Musique, contributed in their own way to the royal allegory. Apollo was, after all, also the god of music and thus imbued with the harmony of the cosmos, as well as the ruler of the planets and the sun itself.

When in 1652 Mazarin resumed his governorship of the regency, he immediately reinstated the foreign singers under Buti in his *cabinet italien* and embarked on plans for the production of a new Italian opera, by Carlo Caproli. *Le nozze di Peleo e di Teti* (text by Buti) was performed with a ballet whose *intermèdes* were interleaved between the acts. The king again took six roles; Torelli created machines that sent a chariot across the sky and a mechanical eagle to transport Jupiter. But this particular kind of marriage of French and Italian genres only just survived Mazarin, who died in 1661. The ill-fated *Ercole amante* was his last venture. Here he invoked the collaboration of Cavalli, Lully and the machinist Gaspare Vigarani; when the day came and the theatre was not yet complete, Cavalli's *Xerse* was hurriedly mounted in its place, replete with a French overture, a monarchist prologue and 20 spectacular ballet *entrées* by Lully. When *Ercole amante* was finally presented, the court journalist Loret devoted 200 lines to Lully's ballet and only four to Cavalli's opera, which lasted six hours.

Louis XIV learnt early and well the efficacy of absolutism. At home he exercised control through an elaborate code of etiquette and an extensive bureaucracy which left no one in doubt as to his place. Having been exiled from Paris as a child during the Fronde, he retained little affection for the city, pausing there only during Carnival each year. He much preferred his country châteaux at Fontainebleau, Versailles, Marly, Saint Germain and Chantilly. As a result, several thousand people – nobles, personal servants, musicians, military and maintenance personnel – were obliged to accompany him on an annual circuit. The châteaux were the scene of sumptuous feasts, theatricals and *ballets de cour*, masked balls, indoor and outdoor concerts, fireworks and water displays, each requiring appropriate music. Card playing and gambling, intrigue and romance were counterbalanced by daily attendance at Mass, where, by the king's command, music was sung and played – in contravention of the restrictions on its use in Catholic services laid down by the Council of Trent a century earlier and more recently by the Archbishop of Paris (1662). In 1669, eight years after ascending the throne, Louis XIV decided to convert his father's hunting-lodge at Versailles into a palace of unprecedented magnificence; 13 years later, in 1682, the court finally moved there.

The *musiciens du roi* were only one of many groups of skilled servants at Versailles. They each held one or more positions in the music of the chapel, chamber and stable (Écurie), a system inherited from the reign of Louis XIII and greatly augmented in that of Louis XIV.[3] Positions were bought and sold, though most often they were inherited. *Ordinaires*, as they were known, were recruited from the lower-middle class Parisian families of musicians belonging to the Confrérie de St Julien-des-Ménestriers. Their salaries depended upon rank, tenure and, in some cases, the instrument they played; those attached to the chamber were paid the most. They divided their time according to three-month semesters, commuting between Versailles and Paris, where they performed, composed and taught the daughters of the aristocracy (and, during the course of the period, the rich *bourgeoisie*) – from whom they gained assistance in publishing their music, in part to enhance their positions at court.

The musicians of the chapel included lay and ecclesiastical singers, organists, a string band and a cornettist; for special services their number was augmented by the voices of women (most often wives and daughters of the *ordinaires*) and, notably, Italian castratos, as well as further instruments from the chamber and Écurie. The chamber and large ensemble motets were the backbone of these services, as they were later to be in Paris at the Concert Spirituel. The king preferred Low Mass to the more formal and regulated High Mass so that he could be assured of hearing one *grand* and two *petits motets*, which he favoured over settings of the Ordinary.

The *grand motet*[4] is a peculiarly French music invention – a sacred counterpart of *spectacle* – employing a Latin liturgical text (studded with *double entendres* paralleling the King with God), vocal soloists (the *petit choeur*), a chorus (the *grand choeur*) and an orchestra in a series of contrasting movements; such works were performed to best advantage on special occasions such as the celebrations of military and naval victories (real or idealized), royal births, marriages and deaths. Although Lully contributed many fine examples, such as the *Miserere mei Deus* of 1664, to the *grand motet* repertory and François Couperin to the *petit motet*, it was Michel-Richard de Lalande, in his capacity as the longest-serving *surintendant* of the chapel music at Versailles, who provided most. The beauty of Lalande's *Beati omnes* (1698) is said to have reduced the entire court to tears at the ceremonial departure in 1700 of the Duke of Anjou (Louis XIV's grandson) for Spain, where he was to be crowned king.

At first the musicians of the chamber were limited to lute, viol and harpsichord players; later they included violinists of the Petits Violons, flautists and the like. Among them were such men as Robert de Visée, Marin Marais and François Couperin, Jean-Féry Rebel and Michel de La Barre (see Plate 6); women instrumentalists such as Couperin's harpsichordist daughter Marguerite-Antoinette, and the viol player Marie-Anne Ursule de Caix, were appointed to the chamber only in the 1730s. The chamber musicians were expected to perform at the king's *levée*, at mealtimes, in private entertainments in the king's rooms (and those of Mme de Maintenon, whom he secretly wed in 1683 after the death of the queen), at the *couchée* and on the thrice-weekly *jours d'appartement*, when the king made his rooms available to the court for a buffet supper, a concert, card playing, billiards and dancing. The Vingt-quatre Violons du Roi, attached to the chamber, performed on feast days, for royal ballets and celebrations of state.

The musicians of the Écurie – brass, woodwind and percussionists (among them the great musical dynasties of Hotteterres and Philidors) – performed on occasions associated with military and outdoor pageantry: parades, *fêtes*, hunts and for ceremonies to greet visiting dignitaries, as well as on the battlefields, on barges in the Versailles canal, with the Vingt-quatre Violons at coronations and funerals, and at a measured distance from Louis XIV when he took the air in the château gardens.

Jean-Baptiste Lully occupied a unique position in the affections of the king. His subsequent collaboration with Molière during the 1660s was calculated to please His Majesty greatly, although Molière's trenchant satire often hit rather too close to home. Together 'the two Baptistes' produced comedies with musical *intermèdes* – among them *Le mariage forcé* (1664) and *Monsieur de Pourceaugnac* (1669) – at the Palais Royal theatre and at the royal châteaux. Lully's *intermèdes* were in effect miniature operas and in the course of the collaboration they gradually outgrew the plays. When in February 1670 Louis XIV danced in public for the last time in a performance of the *comédie-ballet Les amants magnifiques*, the time was ripe for Lully to produce a fully-fledged French opera.

The inevitable rupture with Molière came in 1672, when Lully succeeded in buying the bankrupt Pierre Perrin's share of the royal *privilège* for the new Académie Royale de Musique – whose personnel included an orchestra, singers (many of them members of the *musiques de cour*), dancers, conductors and *répétiteurs*, stage designers and machinists, tailors and the like. Having perceived that public opinion was also swinging in favour of sung drama, Lully was determined to capitalize on the modest if promising success of the previous administrators. Molière was ruined by Lully's ambition and, although he entered upon a promising partnership with the out-standingly gifted Marc-Antoine Charpentier, he died soon after, in 1673. *Comédie-ballet*, which had always been controversial, was eclipsed (some would say suffocated) by the new, entirely sung, blatantly panegyric and allegorical dramas which it had nurtured. When Molière died Lully was quick to appropriate the theatre at the Palais Royal for his own productions.

He now chose to collaborate with the librettist Philippe Quinault. Between 1673 and 1686 they produced 12 *tragédies lyriques*, each consisting of a prologue and five acts, of which *Alceste* (1674; see Plate 4), *Atys* (1676) and *Armide* (1686) are the best known. Lully expanded the elements of his *intermèdes* – recitative, airs, duos, choruses and instrumental music (some of which was for dancing) – adding pro-grammatic effects and a *passacaille* near the end. In these operas the art of infusing musical entertainment with royal symbolism and political propaganda reached its apex. The prologues were, in effect, allegorical newsreels in which events of the realm were interpreted favourably, and the heroes of both operas and prologues were always assumed to be refracted images of the king. Lully and Quinault only once miscalculated: the jealous and spiteful Juno of *Isis* (1677) was widely interpreted as an unflattering portrayal of the king's mistress, Mme de Montespan. Quinault, Lully's scapegoat, was obliged to retire for a season, as a popular song of the day made clear.

Lully enjoyed an unusual degree of intimacy with the king (after Lully's death Lalande was similarly marked out). It was a measure of the king's regard that he was able to turn a blind eye to Lully's bisexuality – an exception that he also reluctantly made for his own brother, Monsieur (who was after all the father of the future regent, the Duke of Orléans), sharply at odds with the king's own personal law which he imposed upon his courtiers. Following Lully's acquisition of the Académie Royale de Musique, he was granted further privileges that amounted to a virtual monopoly of musical entertainment in Paris. With his astute investments and business acumen, Lully grew wealthy on the revenues of his posts, the box office proceeds and the royalties arising from his monopoly.

Lully's success was ultimately to the detriment of French music. He brooked no competition, be it French or foreign. Only a few Italian composers, pre-eminent among them Paolo Lorenzani (whom Louis XIV appointed *maître de musique* to the queen and sent back to Italy to recruit castratos for the chapel), attempted to establish themselves in Paris during the Lullian epoch. However, a number of Italians, including Vincenzo Albrici and Agostino Steffani, and Germans – among them Georg Muffat, J. S. Kusser, J. P. Förtsch, R. I. Mayr and J. C. F. Fischer – came to study and experience Lully's music at first hand. Such a French composer as Charpentier, who had studied in Italy, suffered seemingly unjustified discrimination. No one other than Lully was allowed to produce *tragédies lyriques* in public, unless they had been commissioned by the Jesuits as sacred Lenten fare: 'useful exercise and dignified diversion', as was the case with Charpentier's *David et Jonathas* (1688), a work which the *Mercure* nevertheless had no hesitation in describing as an opera. Discouraged by the general lack of opportunity, composers channelled their creativity into sacred and chamber music genres.

Ironically, shortly after the court moved to Versailles in 1683, the reign of the Sun King began its evening. In the 1680s Louis XIV lost both his trusted minister Colbert and his Machiavellian *surintendant de musique*, Lully. The cost of fitting out the château and city of Versailles had in itself been astronomic and would continue for decades to come. Then there was the disastrous series of military defeats, two famines (1693–4 and 1709–10) and the continuing domestic tensions between factions of the Catholic Church (the Roman Jesuits versus the Gallic Jansenists) which the sacrifice of the Huguenots in 1685 failed to stem. The neglect of the nation's agriculture, the shortcomings of the policies of absolutism – and its reliance upon a social hierarchy in which the well born played little or no responsible role – were becoming painfully evident, with no solutions in sight. It was this same state of affairs, a century later, that was to precipitate the Revolution.

For a time the grandiose *spectacles* continued, in part to hide the awful truth from the rest of Europe. Colbert had stressed that it was especially important to cultivate the arts in time of war. So, in the years following Lully's tragic accident in 1687, the Académie (now under his son-in-law's direction) presented regular revivals of his operas, as well as dozens of works by his French assistants – Pascal Collasse, Henry Desmarets, Jean François Lalouette and Marin Marais – and several rising stars, among them André Campra, Michel Pignolet de Montéclair and André-Cardinal Destouches, though none before Jean-Philippe Rameau truly captured the enthusiasm of French audiences.

But as the king grew older and more reliant upon the pious Mme de Maintenon, he gradually stopped bothering to keep up the pace and the pretence. By 1704 he no longer attended public performances, preferring instead the intimacy of the concerts and comedies organized by Mme de Maintenon in her rooms. In 1711 he lost his son, the Grand Dauphin (a keen opera lover and italophile), and in the following year his grandson and eldest great-grandson in the measles epidemic that ravaged Paris and the court. He died on 1 September 1715, having outlived many of the policies undertaken during his 54-year reign.

Meanwhile, in Paris there had always been a core of aristocrats – rich, cosmopolitan and less in awe of the king and his *maître de musique* – who imported foreign music and musicians to perform in the fashionable salons of their *hôtels*. During the first two regencies, Cardinals Richelieu (at the behest of Maria de' Medici) and Mazarin (Anne of Austria's trusted minister) had actively encouraged Italian musicians to come to Paris; Mazarin's fondness for Italian opera led him to be improvident in his importations, something the Frondeurs, a faction of the Princes of the Blood and other members of the aristocracy, particularly resented. Louis

XIV's cousin, the Duchess of Guise (whose family had sided with the Frondeurs and was therefore not welcome at court), was herself an ardent italophile. At her home in the Marais district Charpentier – who had spent three years in the mid 1660s studying in Rome, probably with Carissimi – composed and performed during the 1670s and 80s some of the earliest French oratorios, cantatas and an ensemble sonata in which French and Italian styles are deliberately juxtaposed.

The eager Paris *bourgeoisie*, parodied by Molière with his Monsieur Jourdan (in *Le bourgeois gentilhomme*, 1670), sought to emulate the upper classes by hiring musicians to play and teach in their homes. Clerics, like Claude Nicaise of the Dijon Sainte Chapelle, René Ouvrard of the Paris Sainte Chapelle, Abbé Matthieu of the Paris *quartier* St André-des-Arts and the provincial lexicographer-cleric Sébastien de Brossard, collected, copied and circulated early French essays in the Italian genres as well as manuscripts and prints of Italian music by Cavalli, Carissimi, Legrenzi, Stradella and others. Around the turn of the century, prominent musicians such as the harpsichordists François Couperin, Louis-Nicolas Clérambault and Elisabeth-Claude Jacquet de la Guerre held regular gatherings in their homes to perform the latest French sonatas and cantatas, from manuscript parts.

As the cultural life of the court faded, the musical events in Paris drew many of the younger generation, not least of them the dauphin, his half-sister the Princess of Conti and their cousin the Duke of Orléans – once the pupil of Charpentier and later regent during the minority of his great-nephew Louis XV (1715–21). In July 1714 the Duchess of Maine (who was out of favour at Versailles) inaugurated a series of entertainments for the younger courtiers at her château known as the 'Grandes Nuits de Sceaux'. Her *maître de musique*, Jean-Joseph Mouret, was responsible for the musical portions of the evenings and provided among other things the first French lyric comedy, *Le mariage de Ragonde et de Colin* (1714), which predated Rameau's better known *Platée* by 30 years. Although the last of these *soirées* took place in May 1715, they signalled the beginning of a new, less formal era of music in French society.[5]

During the regency of the Duke of Orléans the Tuileries palace became the official residence of the court and the Palais Royal that of the regent, who preferred to maintain a separate household and his own staff of musicians, under Charles-Hubert Gervais – many of them Italian – in addition to the regular *musiques de cour*. Philippe had never been cultivated by Louis XIV, who distrusted all Princes of the Blood other than his own heirs, and though the duke remained loyal to the boy king (the future Louis XV) he nevertheless used his temporary position of power to loosen many of the absolutist policies of his uncle's long reign. Court decorum was relaxed, and the princes were given a trial voice in government, which they quickly proved unfit to exercise. He had hoped to reform the nation's tax structure through the *dîme royale* and to institute private banking, but failed in both. Where Louis XIV had trod a careful path between the rival Catholic factions, the duke inclined towards Jansenism.

It was at least a period of relative international calm, a balance of European power having finally been achieved with the Treaty of Utrecht (1713–15). The doors were flung open to foreign influences and, in contrast to the grandeur and ostentation of the royal *spectacles* of the previous reign, the Paris town houses of the Princess of Conti, the Prince of Carignan (from 1730 director of the Opéra), the financier Pierre Crozat and, later, the *fermier général* Alexandre-Jean-Joseph le Riche de la

Pouplinière became the venues for intimate concerts of sonatas and cantatas and, eventually, symphonies.

Musical entertainment had already come within the reach of the bourgeois class. Now more than ever before musicians were being employed to teach children to play, sing and compose, bringing about a boom in composition and music publishing. After the many engraved prints produced by the Bonnart *atelier* during the late 17th century, portraying young aristocrats performing music in courtly settings, there came the paintings of Antoine Watteau, which took music-making out of doors.[6] In order to induct Watteau into the Académie Royale de Peinture et de Sculpture, a new subject category, the *fête galante*, had to be formulated; musical analogues soon followed, notably the immensely popular *opéra-ballet* of André Campra, *L'Europe galante* (1697), reflecting in its title – not to say its more cosmopolitan musical style – the decentralization of music that was taking place during the regency. So although the forces of absolutism were to be regrouped under Louis XV, that which had been undone in large part would remain so.

When Louis XV and the court returned to Versailles in 1725, the cultural life of Paris continued undiminished. The king had only the most passing interest in music and the arts, although his wife, the Polish princess Marie Leszczynska, was a music lover and italophile, his daughters were all accomplished musicians and his mistress, Mme de Pompadour, would later skilfully and energetically pursue both music and the decorative arts. The queen only rarely ventured to Paris (the first occasion was in 1728, three years after her marriage) and in 1735 directed her *maître de musique*, Destouches (by that time also musical director of the Académie Royale de Musique), to arrange private 'concerts chez la reine' at Versailles and Marly of programmes recently performed in Paris, in particular at the Concert Spirituel.

The Concert Spirituel[7] was organized in 1725 by Anne Danican Philidor, a son of the royal music librarian, to present regular subscription concerts for the public at the Tuileries palace which were announced in the *Mercure*. The singers and orchestra of the Académie Royale de Musique performed in these concerts during Lent and at other times of year when opera was suspended. Much the most successful series of its day, the Concert Spirituel continued at the Salle des Suisses in the Tuileries palace under Mouret (1728–33), François Rebel (1734–48) and others until 1790. The Concert Italien (1726) and the Concert Français (1727–30) were short-lived. Two Lalande motets and Corelli's Christmas Concerto were performed at the first concert, in March 1725. *Grands motets* (Lalande's especially), virtuoso violin sonatas and concertos were recurring items on the programmes. From the beginning the Concert Spirituel served as a forum for solo violinists such as Jean-Baptiste Anet and the Savoyard Jean-Pierre Guignon. In 1728 the brilliant Italian-trained virtuoso Jean-Marie Leclair *l'aîné* made his début. Many foreign virtuosos such as the Turin violinist (and Leclair's mentor) G. B. Somis (1733) made the Concert Spirituel part of their European tours.

But it should not be assumed that Italian music was favoured by the Parisian public at the expense of their own native art. Taste in music simply grew to accommodate them both, out of which developed what Couperin *le Grand* called 'les goûts-réünis'. In the late 1690s Sébastien de Brossard was already working on a dictionary which would interpret and frenchify Italian musical terms.[8] Early French essays in the trio sonata genre by Jacquet de La Guerre, Jean-Féry Rebel, Couperin and Clérambault largely remained in manuscript, though Rebel and

Couperin did eventually publish theirs. The publication in Paris of violin sonatas by Italian expatriates Michele Mascitti (from 1704) and G. A. Piani (1712), along with those of Corelli's op. 5 (1708), encouraged young composer-violinists such as François Duval, J.-F. Dandrieu, J.-B. Senaillé and Louis Francoeur to bring out their own solo collections. But the relevance of distinguishing between French and Italian styles of playing is evident as late as 1738, when Michel Corrette published *L'école d'Orphée*. French essays in the cantata genre by J.-B. Morin, J.-B. Stuck, Jacquet de La Guerre, Campra, Montéclair and Clérambault followed close behind. Clérambault's *Orphée*, which appeared in his first collection of cantatas (1710), was the most popular of its kind and epitomized the French cantata.

Even before the turn of the century, music engraving and publishing had begun to flower in Paris.[9] Undaunted by the Ballard monopolies on the printing of operas performed by the Académie, *grands motets*, and collections (known as *recueils*) of *airs de cour*, music *ateliers* and shops such as that of Henry Foucault ('à la Règle d'or' from 1692) sprang up, often run by musicians and their wives, selling solo and chamber music in bound volumes or *en blanc* – composers had short runs of their music printed, a page or a group of pages at a time, replenishing the shop stock with amended versions (this accounts for the differences between one surviving copy and another). With the rise in private musical establishments and, during the Regency, two official royal retinues of musicians, a lively competition for patrons and aristocratic pupils was inevitable. Method books for singing and playing the viol, violin and harpsichord proliferated, along with music for amateurs as well as virtuosos. The engraved dates of publication, lists of sellers and dedications on the title pages effectively document this phenomenon, as do the names of the *pièces de caractère* contained within each collection. Composers seeking a wider market had their works published or reprinted by the enterprising Amsterdam firm of Estienne Roger and Michel-Charles Le Cène.

The vitality of Parisian musical life proved a magnet to foreign royalty, ambassadors, artists and musicians. The exiled Elector of Bavaria, who for a time in the 1690s had been the governor of the South Netherlands, maintained close connections with the Paris–Versailles musical establishment, which he drew upon for performances of Lully operas and private entertainments during the years 1704–6, which were in fact subsidized by Louis XIV. G. P. Telemann (1707 and 1738) and J. J. Quantz (1726) – to name but two prominent German musicians of the era – visited Paris and were greatly influenced by their first-hand exposure to the French style.

In 1702 François Raguenet and Jean Laurent Le Cerf de La Viéville (both from Rouen) entered into a famous debate on the strengths and weaknesses of the French and Italian musical styles[10] which in turn initiated a varied series of articles and books on the aesthetic implications. During the regency of Philippe d'Orléans, in 1715, the Opéra-Comique was created in the Foire St Laurent, offering largely satirical entertainment, while both the Nouveau Théâtre Italien at the Palais Royal, with Mouret as their composer (1717–38), and the Comédie-Italienne, at the Hôtel de Bourgogne (after a 20-year absence), opened the following year. The Académie continued its seasons of Lully revivals, *tragédies lyriques* and *opéra-ballets* with mixed success, and was taken over by the City of Paris in 1749.

During the 1690s Theobaldo di Gatti was the only foreign composer to have a musical dramatic work (*Coronis*, 1691) performed by the Académie, and then probably only because of the patronage of the Princess of Conti. New *tragédies lyriques* by French composers hardly fared better, however magnificent their music. Charpentier's magnificent *Médée* (1693; text by Thomas Corneille) and the operas of Desmarets, Jacquet de La Guerre, Marais, Gervais and Louis de la Coste all suffered by their close proximity to the Lullian era.

As *maître de musique* at Notre Dame, André Campra was wary enough to have his *opéra-ballet L'Europe galante* (text by La Motte) presented anonymously in 1697, although he could count upon the powerful backing of the Duke of Orléans. In the event, it created a sensation. His *Le carnaval de Venise* (text by Regnard), with an Italian-texted fourth act and a final ballet, followed in 1699; thus assured of success, he abandoned his post at Notre Dame to devote himself to dramatic music. But when he tried his hand at *tragédies lyriques* they were never as popular as the *opéra-ballets*, with the exception of *Tancrède* (text by Danchet), which he wrote as a vehicle for Mlle Maupin in 1702.

The Académie continued to present both tragedies and lighter comic and balletic forms. J.-F. Salomon's tragedy *Médée et Jason* (text by S.-J. Pellegrin and La Roque) and T.-L. Bourgeois' *opéra-ballet, Les amours déguisés* (text by Fuzelier), both from 1713, and Mouret's *opéra-ballet* cum *comédie lyrique, Les festes ou Le triomphe de Thalie* (1714; text by La Font), stand out. While the works of Campra and Destouches dominated the new productions, many new composers – among them the flautist Michel de La Barre, François Bouvard, J.-B. Stuck and J.-B. Matho – were also getting their works performed. Lalande composed dramatic and balletic works for Fontainebleau, eschewing the Parisian public at the Palais Royal, while Clérambault and Couperin appear to have abstained altogether.[11]

Controversy surrounded the first performances of Montéclair's innovative sacred tragedy, *Jéphté* (text by S.-J. Pellegrin), in 1732. First the temperamental soprano Catherine Nicole Le Maure sang only on the threat of imprisonment – and then so badly that on the opening night the audience hissed her off the stage. Then the Archbishop of Paris, Cardinal de Noailles, temporarily stopped the performances because of the biblical subject. In spite and because of the brouhaha, *Jéphté* was a tremendous success; Montéclair's orchestration and spatial effects were highly original and must have impressed Rameau, with whom Montéclair had carried on a dialogue in the pages of the *Mercure* (1729–30).

It was Rameau's superbly conceived *Hippolyte et Aricie* (1733; text by S.-J. Pellegrin) that ushered in a new era of French dramatic music, distracting many writers – notably Jean-Jacques Rousseau with his highly critical *Dissertation sur la musique moderne* (1743) – from their concerns with national styles to those existing within the French tradition, in particular those of Lully and Rameau. Rameau was 50 years old when he composed *Hippolyte et Aricie*, having perfected his craft in *galant* chamber music genres like the cantata, the *petit motet* and the sonata (though none seems to have survived). Before select audiences in Parisian drawing rooms, Rameau assimilated the da capo aria and *ariette* and the use of concertante instruments in even more idiomatic and colourful ways, so that *Hippolyte et Aricie* embodies the fruits of these experiments: cosmopolitan in style and in keeping with a progressive concept of 'les goûts-réunis'.

The threads of the old 'style classique' and the new Rococo styles were thus spun out and interwoven in a rich musical fabric appropriate to an urbane, lighthearted segment of society (see Plate 5), oblivious to the social injustices already fomenting revolution. There were also those who were observing and taking stock. The creative vitality of the Grand Siècle had passed and was followed by an Alexandrian age of assessment and tributes. The achievements of the period were recorded by Voltaire in his *Siècle de Louis XIV* (1751). Évrard Titon du Tillet[12] proposed a vast monument, a 'French Parnassus', to honour French poets and musicians, and was the first to compile their biographies, while Couperin *le Grand* composed musical apotheoses to Lully (1725) and Corelli (1724), chronicling their hypothetical reception on Mount Parnassus. The literary and musical achievements of the Louis XV era are summarized in the writings of Louis d'Aquin de Château-Lyon.[13]

Julie Anne Sadie
London

Notes

1 Of general interest and easily accessible in paperback are: A. Cobban: *A History of Modern France* (Harmondsworth, 3rd edn, 1984), i (1715–1799); D. Ogg: *Louis XIV* (Oxford, 1967); and G. Parker: *Europe in Crisis (1598–1648)* (London, rev. edn, 1982). With respect to music, see *Bibliography*; the intrepid enthusiast will wish to consult the French periodical '*Recherches*' *sur la musique française classique* and *La musique à la cour de Louis XIV et de Louis XV d'après les mémoires de Sourches et Luynes: 1681–1758*, ed. N. Dufourcq (Paris, 1970).

2 M.F. Christout: *Le ballet de cour de Louis XIV (1643–1672)* (Paris, 1967).

3 For archival details and commentary on the employment of musicians at the court between 1661 and 1733, see M. Benoit's companion volumes, *Musiques de Cour, Chapelle, Chambre, Écurie* and *Versailles et les musiciens du Roi* (Paris, 1971). For the earlier years of the period, see C. Massip: *La vie des musiciens de Paris au temps de Mazarin: 1643–1661* (Paris, 1976).

4 J. R. Mongrédien's *Catalogue thématique des sources du grand motet français (1663–1792)* (Munich, New York, London & Paris, 1984) will provide a useful starting-point.

5 R. Viollier: *Jean-Joseph Mouret. Le musicien des grâces* (Paris, 1950).

6 A. P. de Mirimonde: *L'iconographie musicale sous les rois Bourbons: la musique dans les arts plastiques (xvii–xviii siècles)*, 2 vols. (Paris, 1975, 1977).

7 C. Pierre's *Histoire du Concert Spirituel (1725–1790)* (Paris, 1975) incorporates a diary of all performances.

8 Brossard began by publishing a short glossary with his 1695 collection of *Élevations et motets à voix seule avec la basse continue* and then greatly expanded it in his *Dictionnaire de musique* (1703).

9 A. Devriès and F. Lesure: *Dictionnaire des éditeurs de musique français* (Geneva, 1979).

10 F. Raguenet: *Parallèle des italiens et des françois, en ce qui regarde la musique et les opéras* (Paris, 1702; Eng. trans., 1709); J. L. Le Cerf de La Viéville: *Comparaison de la musique italienne et de la musique française*, 3 vols. (Brussels, 1704–6); and Raguenet: *Défense du Parallèle* (Paris, 1705).

11 In 1716 Clérambault published a separate cantata entitled *La muse de l'Opéra* which includes a continuo part for double bass – an instrument associated exclusively with theatre music. Couperin's eighth *Concert dans le goût théâtral* from *Les goûts-réünis ou Nouveaux concerts* (1724) has been reconstructed by Peter Holman as an orchestral suite from a hypothetical stage work (see 'An orchestral suite by François Couperin?', *Early Music*, xiv.1 (1986), pp.71–6). Holman's version has been recorded by John Eliot Gardiner and the English Baroque Soloists.

12 É. Titon du Tillet: *Le Parnasse François* (Paris, 1732; suppls. 1743, 1755).

13 L. D'Aquin de Château-Lyon: *Siècle littéraire de Louis XV ou Lettres sur les hommes célèbres* (Paris, 1753), pt. 1.

Biographical Dictionary: France

1 Paris and Versailles

Aglié, Filippo d'. See ITALY *1 Piedmont-Savoy*.

Anet, Jean-Jacques-Baptiste ['Baptiste'] (1676–1755). Violinist and composer, the first French violinist to gain a reputation as a soloist in the early 18th century. His playing was described as noble and energetic, impassioned and unfailingly accurate. After studying in Rome with Corelli, who is said to have 'embraced him tenderly and made him a present of his bow', he served the exiled Elector of Bavaria, Louis XV (as a member of the Vingt-quatre Violons), and Louis XV's father-in-law, the former King of Poland. In 1725 Anet represented the French violin school in some of the first programmes of the Concert Spirituel, appearing with the Italian virtuoso J.-P. Guignon.

Antier, Marie (1687–1747). Singer at the Paris Opéra (1711–41), whose beautiful, flexible voice and ability to sing in all styles was remarked upon by Destouches in a letter of 1728. Antier came to Paris from Lyons and was trained as a singer and actress by the distinguished Lully interpreter Marthe Le Rochois. After her début in 1711 she sang in as many as five productions each season, taking leading roles (especially after 1720 when she was appointed *première actrice*) in Lully revivals, as well as in new productions by Rameau (including *Hippolyte et Aricie* and *Castor et Pollux*) and others. In 1721 she was appointed a *musicienne de la chambre du roi*. In addition to her commitments at the Opéra, Antier sang at the Concert Spirituel and the Concert Français, distinguishing herself with performances of French cantatas, as well as at private performances of *opéra-ballets* at the Palais des Tuileries. She was the *maîtresse en titre* to the Prince of Carignan and the wife of a bureaucrat (Jean Duval), whom she married in 1726; however, her affair with the music-loving financier Le Riche de la Pouplinière the following year ended in scandal.

Aubert, Jacques (1689–1753). Dancing-master, violinist and composer from a family of court musicians. Aubert was for many years a member of the Vingt-quatre Violons and the Académie Royale de Musique, in which he served as the orchestra's leader. He frequently performed at the Concert Spirituel, in his own violin concertos, which (along with those of Guignon) were among the first to be composed in Paris. Although his instrumental compositions are mainly in Italian genres, they show the influence of French dance rhythms and ornamentation. Aubert also composed comic operas, ballets and *divertissements* for the fair theatres (*foires*) and the Opéra.

Bacilly, Bénigne de (*c*1625–1690). Composer, teacher and author of an important singing treatise elucidating the performing practices of the *air de cour*: his *Remarques curieuses sur l'art de bien chanter* (1668) is addressed to French poetry, its explication, pronunciation and rhythms, and shows how ornamentation can serve to enhance a text.

Ballard. Family of royal music printers whose beautiful editions won them a virtual monopoly as well as many grace-and-favour appointments. The firm was founded in the mid 16th century by Robert Ballard (*c*1525/30–1588) and a cousin, Adrian Le Roy. Robert's son Pierre (?1575/80–1639), appointed royal music printer by Henri IV, issued collections of *airs de cour*, lute and organ music, and printed the musical examples for Mersenne's *Harmonie Universelle* (1636–7). His son Robert (*c*1610–1673) ran the firm from 1639 and became sole printer to Louis XIV, producing the earliest editions of Lully's music in full score, music treatises and a long-running series of song collections.

Robert was succeeded in 1675 by his son Christophe (1641–1715) who presided over the firm in its greatest prosperity: four presses, nine helpers and two apprentices were employed at the turn of the century. Under his direction the most important editions were produced of Académie operas by Lully, Charpentier, La Guerre, Collasse, Campra, Marais and others, as well as collections of *grands motets* (1684–6). He also inaugurated an extremely successful monthly publication of *airs sérieux et à boire*.

A turn in the family's fortunes was signalled by the advent of printing from engraved plates, a technique developed by the English and the Dutch: the Ballard monopoly covered only prints produced from the older movable type. Christophe's son Jean-Baptiste-Christophe (*c*1663–1750) continued to print

Paris (C. Inselin: *Plan de la Ville, Cité et Université, de Paris, ses Faubourgs et ses Environs*, 1740?)

the scores of Académie operas and issued Rameau's *Traité de l'harmonie* (1722) and *Nouveau système* (1726). The firm declined under his son and successor Christophe-Jean-François (*c*1710–1765).

Barbey, Guillaume (*fl c*1716–42). Parisian string instrument maker known for his beautiful viols which were the pride of players such as Marais and the Forquerays; the elder Forqueray owned two Barbey viols – one for solo music, the other for accompanying. As many as four Barbey bass viols (*c*1720) are known to survive, as well as a later *pardessus de viole*.

Baroni, Leonora. See ITALY *10 Itinerant Musicians*.

Barrière, Jean (*c*1705–1747). Cellist and composer from Bordeaux who took up a place in the Paris Opéra orchestra and published four collections of cello sonatas which chronicle his own assimilation of the Italian style. His first two sets, published before a three-year sojourn in Rome (1736–9), are indebted to the rich traditions of French solo viol playing: they contain passages of multiple stops, arpeggiated chords and passage-work in the highest register; a second, sometimes independent, cello contributes to the accompaniment. His third and fourth sets, published after his return, are very italianate in their virtuosity and require the use of the left-hand thumb, a technique he seems to have introduced into France.

Bartolotti, Angelo Michele (*d* after 1669). Bolognese guitarist, theorbo player and composer working in Paris. René Ouvrard (1666) considered him 'without doubt the most skilful theorbo player in France and Italy'. He published in Florence and Rome (1640 and *c*1655 respectively) two collections for guitar and in Paris a treatise for theorbists on continuo accompaniment which complements those of Fleury (1660) and Delair (1690).

Bataille, Gabriel (*c*1575–1630). Lutenist, poet and composer of *airs de cour*, ballets and *musique mesurée*, who with Antoine de Boësset served Maria de' Medici as music director. He was succeeded by his sons Gabriel (*c*1614–1676) and Pierre. From 1608 until 1615 collections of his airs were published annually by his friend Pierre Ballard; thereafter this series of *Airs de différents autheurs [sic], mis en tablature de luth* was continued by Boësset.

Beauchamp, Pierre de (1636–1705). Dancer and choreographer, an important figure in the development of French ballet. Pierre (not Charles-Louis) Beauchamp served as Louis XIV's personal dancing-master for 22 years. As Lully's collaborator he supervised ballets and later choreographed operas for the Académie Royale de Musique. Beauchamp played a significant role in the Académie Royale de Danse, inventing and giving official acknowledgment to steps (including the five positions of the feet) and step patterns (such as the minuet and bourrée).

Beaujoyeux, Balthasar de [Belgioioso, Baldassare de] (*c*1535–87). Italian ballet master and violinist at the French court whose *Circé* (1581) was the first French dramatic production to unite poetry, music and dance. Beaujoyeux – shrewd in affairs of the French court – became *valet de chambre* to a succession of sovereigns. As 'master of the revels' he organized lavish entertainments, sparing no expense. His greatest triumph was *Circé ou le Balet [sic] comique de la Royne*, performed in 1581 as part of the wedding celebrations of the Duke of Joyeuse and the queen's sister. Thousands were said to have attended the performance, for which d'Aubigny and La Chesnaye contributed the verses, Lambert de Beaulieu and Jacques Salmon the music, Jacques Patin the scenery and Beaujoyeux the dances.

Bédos de Celles, François (1709–79). Organ builder whose *L'art du facteur d'orgues* (1766–78) provides important descriptions, with illustrations, of the construction of French Classical organs, as well as remarks on organ performance practice – ornamentation, articulation and registration. He also contributed reports to the *Mercure de France* on newly installed organs.

Bembo, Antonia (*fl* 1690–1710). Venetian singer and composer working at the French court. Although her name does not appear in the well-known memoirs of the day, the *Mercure galant* or the court records, she left five manuscript volumes of sacred and secular music, dedicated to Louis XIV and preserved in his library. Indeed, all that is known of her life has been gleaned from the title pages and dedications of these volumes: they include a collection of aria and cantata settings of Italian, French and Latin texts (*Produzioni armoniche*); two *Te Deum* settings (one dated 1704); an opera (on the same text by Buti which Cavalli had set for the royal wedding celebrations more than 40 years earlier), *L'Ercole amante*, which was performed before the king in 1707; and *Les sept Pseumes, de David*. As a foreign woman and a composer, Antonia Bembo was exceptional in having gained the attention and respect of the French monarch and should be compared with her contemporary Elisabeth-Claude Jacquet de la Guerre.

Benserade, Isaac de (1613–91). Court poet who elevated *ballet de cour* to a literary form. Benserade's gifts as a writer of panegyrical verse were usefully employed in turn by Richelieu, Mazarin and Louis XIV. His elegant, polished verse was peopled with an eclectic cast of historical, mythological and allegorical characters, who presented everyday occurrences in the king's life and important events of the realm with equal ceremony. He counted among his friends La Fontaine, La Rochefoucauld and Madame de Sévigné; among his foes Molière, Racine and Boileau.

Benserade collaborated with a series of composers – the greatest of whom were Lambert and Lully – and the choreographer Beauchamp to create the literary, musical and visual spectacle of *ballet de cour*. In this he had the full support of the king, who danced the part of the Sun in Benserade's first work, the *Ballet de Cassandre* (1651). In all his 23 ballets Benserade sought to flatter his sovereign, who in turn extracted political advantage from the adulatory celebrations. Lully learnt much from Benserade's example and by the late 1650s had made his influence felt in this genre. Music took precedence altogether in the *Ballet de Flore* (1669). But when the king stopped taking part in the *ballets de cour* (February 1670) he signalled their decline: three years later Lully presented his first *tragédie lyrique*, *Cadmus et Hermione*, to a text by Quinault.

Berain, Jean (1640–1711). Stage designer who rose through the ranks as a stage decorator and costume designer responsible for court *mascarades*, *pompes funèbres* and theatre productions. In 1680 he succeeded Vigarani as set designer and machinist for the Académie productions of Lully's *tragédies lyriques*, and for his first production, *Proserpine* (1680), he created the illusion of Mount Etna erupting, an effect much praised by the *Mercure*. The spectacular scene from *Phaëton* (1683), in which Neptune rises out of the sea and is transformed into a lion, was also highly acclaimed. In all, Berain applied his ingenuity to more than 80 productions.

Bergerotti, Anna (*b* c1630). Roman soprano working at the French court in the Cabinet Italien (1655–64), who returned to Italy in 1669. Bergerotti sang in performances of *ballets de cour*, as well as at receptions such as that for the Duke of Mantua hosted by Mazarin in 1655, and at the 1662 Ténèbres services at the Église aux Feuillants; she usually appeared with other sopranos, including the Frenchwomen Anne de La Barre and Hilaire Dupuy. Her name appears regularly in the journal of Loret, who unfailingly praised her voice and described her as the 'aimable Bergéroty'. She took a principal role in Cavalli's *Xerse*, which was performed as part of the wedding festivities for Louis XIV and the Spanish Infanta Maria Theresa in 1660. She was the only *cantatrice étoile* in the 12-strong Cabinet Italien (which included her brother Carlo Andrea), created by Mazarin and directed by Gian Francesco Tagliavacca, which was eventually suppressed by Lully; their last performance before Louis XIV was in an *entrée* of *Le mariage forcé* in 1664. She continued as a *musicienne de la chambre* until 1669.

Bernier, Nicolas (1665–1734). Composer, thought to have been the earliest French composer to study in Italy (with Caldara in Rome) and then to make his way successfully into the highest echelons of the *musiques de cour*. He very probably mixed with the circle of composers in Paris experimenting with the sonata and cantata forms in the 1690s and was one of the first to publish collections of cantatas after the turn of the century. Bernier was a friend and teacher of Philippe d'Orléans, who in 1704 helped him to succeed Charpentier as *maître de musique* at the Sainte-Chapelle. He married a daughter of Marin Marais and in 1723 became one of three *sous-maîtres* who followed Lalande at the Chapelle Royale. In those posts he produced a wide variety of sacred music and a treatise on two-part counterpoint (*Principes de composition*). His *Miserere* and *Cum invocarem* were among the first works performed at the Concert Spirituel (1725).

Berteau, Martin (1708–71). Founder of the French school of cello playing. Berteau served the exiled King of Poland (Louis XV's father-in-law) and taught at the Collège des Quatre Nations, Paris, where his pupils included J. B. Tillière, François Cupis, J.-B.-A. J. Janson, L.-A.-J. Janson and J.-P. Duport. He composed violin and cello sonatas; six of the latter, first published under the pseudonym 'Sgr. Martino' in 1748, make particular use of thumb technique, chords and harmonics. His characterful playing was warmly praised by La Borde. J.-B. S. Bréval (1804) and J.-L. Duport (1806) included pieces by him in their cello tutors.

Berthod, Blaise (*c*1610–77). The only known French castrato singer (whose sobriquet, 'L'incommodé', reflects the French unease with regard to the practice of castration). Born in Lyons, Berthod served from 1634 as a singer (usually listed among the *dessus muez et* *cornets*) in the Chapelle Royale, where he was succeeded in 1678 by Jean Gaye. He is frequently mentioned in Loret's journal during the 1650s and early 1660s; Loret particularly admired his voice, describing it as like that of an angel or a virgin, sweet and clear, and equally appropriate 'pour cabinet et pour chapelle'. Louis XIV was said to be surprised and delighted by his voice when he first heard Berthod sing at the Louvre in 1661.

Bizey, Charles (*fl* 1716–52). Woodwind instrument maker who was one of the first in France to build a one-keyed flute with alternative upper middle joints of different lengths. He also made two- and three-keyed oboes, bass oboes (doubled back like bassoons), oboes d'amore, alto recorders, bass flutes and bassoons. His instruments are marked with the royal symbols of a *fleur-de-lis* and a sun.

Blainville, Charles Henri (*c*1710–77). Cellist, mediocre composer, controversial theorist who claimed to have discovered the third mode (or *mode mixte*), and author of a treatise on vocal composition and performance (*L'esprit de l'art*, 1754) and a history of music (1767). Several of Blainville's works were performed at the Concert Spirituel, among them a *double quatuor symphonie* (1741), a *symphonie* in the third mode (1751) and several sacred vocal works (during the 1760s). He composed light secular vocal music and an opera, as well as concerti grossi, trio sonatas, and sonatas for treble viol and for two cellos. He was a conservative composer, who took Lully's side against the Ramistes and whose theories brought criticism from Daquin and La Borde.

Blamont, François Colin de (1690–1760). Versailles composer of stage music, knighted by Louis XV in 1750. Blamont, the pupil of Lalande and protégé of the Duchess of Maine (in whose 'Grandes Nuits de Sceaux' he participated), became *surintendant de la musique de chambre* in 1718. In that capacity he composed courtly *pièces d'occasion*, *petits motets* and, with Fuzelier, devised the first *ballet héroïque* (a sub-species which eclipsed *opéra-ballet*), *Les festes grecques et romaines* (1723). He published three books of cantatas in the cosmopolitan style of 'les goûts-réünis' (the first in 1723, the others in 1729), with symphonies, da capo arias and concerto *ritournelles*; *Circé*, of the third book, proved the most popular. His motets were performed at the Concert Spirituel, his cantatas and *divertissements* at the Concert Français. In 1729 he published a posthumous edition of 40 *grands motets* by Lalande and, in 1754, his own *Essai sur les goûts anciens et modernes de la musique*

française (in which he was critical of Jean-Jacques Rousseau).

Blanchet. Important Parisian family of harpsichord makers. François Étienne Blanchet (1695–1761) was the most famous member of the family; his instruments were much prized for their tone and response. Together with his son, of the same name, he 'modernized' Ruckers harpsichords, installing new jacks, slides and keyboards as well as building new double-manual instruments; his daughter married Armand-Louis Couperin. François Couperin is known to have owned a Blanchet and Balbastre a rebuilt Ruckers.

The Fleming Pascal-Joseph Taskin (1723–93) joined the firm, duly married the son's widow and took over the business; his step-son Armand François Nicholas Blanchet (1763–1818), who published a manual on tuning keyboard instruments (*Méthode abrégée pour accorder le clavecin et le forte-piano*, 1797–1800), joined Taskin in the workshop, building pianos as well as harpsichords. To the Blanchet harpsichord, Taskin added a sliding coupler and the ornate – either lacquered or painted – decoration of the case; he also improved the resonance, particularly of the bass.

Blavet, Michel (1700–68). Flautist and composer, popular at the Concert Spirituel. Blavet's flute playing was as admired in Germany as in France: Frederick the Great tried unsuccessfully to attract him to his court; Telemann, Marpurg and Quantz praised his beautiful tone, perfect intonation and virtuoso technique. Blavet preferred to remain in Paris in the service of the Count of Clermont, performing regularly as a soloist at the Concert Spirituel. He composed stage works with italianate *secco* recitatives for performances in his patron's private theatre at Berny, but is best known for his single surviving flute concerto and his collections of flute sonatas. His commitment to teaching is represented by the breathing indications found in his op. 2 and the range of difficulty represented in the pieces of his *recueils*.

Boësset. Antoine de Boësset, Sieur de Villedieu (1586–1643) was the leading composer of *airs de cour*, which were much admired for their natural and refined melodies. Such was Boësset's popularity that he easily acquired a portfolio of court appointments – including *maître des enfants de la chambre du roy* (1613), *maître de la musique de la reine* (1615), *sécretaire de la chambre du roy* (1620), *surintendant de la musique du roy* (1623) and *conseiller et maître d'hotel ordinaire du roy* (1632) – which he passed on to his eldest son Jean-Baptiste de Boësset, Sieur de Dehault (1614–85), at his death. In about 1640 Marin Mersenne devised a contest between Antoine de Boësset and the Dutch Catholic priest Joan Albert Ban, ostensibly to discover who could compose the best air on the text 'Me veux-tu voir mourir'. Boësset put forward the better air, although, in Ban's defence, Mersenne had unfairly weighted the contest to favour Boësset.

J.-B. Boësset is now generally thought to be the composer of three Masses previously ascribed to his father; he also collaborated with Lully on airs for *ballets de cour* (1653–66).

Boismortier, Joseph Bodin de (1689–1755). Prolific composer and popularizer of the flute in France. Boismortier's opus numbers reach 100, offering sonatas and concertos for an array of instruments – recorder, flute, musette, oboe, bassoon, viol, *vielle*, violin and cello – equalled in this period only by Vivaldi. Boismortier was the first in France to publish not only concertos (for five flutes, 1727), but specifically a solo concerto (op. 26, for cello, viol or bassoon, 1729). Most of his chamber music was intended for amateurs, offering a variety of performing options. In addition he composed four stage works, cantatas, airs and sacred works (his 1741 motet *Fugit nox* was popular Christmas fare at the Concert Spirituel for over 20 years). Two treatises on playing the flute and *pardessus* are lost.

Bonnet-Bourdelot. Family of physicians and music historians. Pierre Bourdelot (1610–85), a physician to Louis XIII, actively cultivated a circle of writers, artists and musicians. Together with his nephew, Pierre Bonnet-Bourdelot (1638–1708), who was chief physician to the Duchess of Burgundy, he gathered together the sources for a proposed book on the history of music and dance. The nephew completed a manuscript history of music, the first of its kind in French, though it was his brother Jacques (1644–1724), a parliamentary treasurer, who published it as the *Histoire de la musique et de ses effets depuis son origine jusqu'à présent* in 1715; subsequent Dutch and German editions were appended to Le Cerf de La Viéville's *Comparaison de la musique italienne et de la musique française* (1704–6) as volumes ii–iv without acknowledgment. Jacques Bonnet brought out *Histoire générale de la danse sacrée et profane* in 1723, thereby realizing his uncle's original intentions.

Bononcini, Giovanni. See ITALY 5 *Modena-Reggio*.

Bourgeois, Thomas-Louis (1676–*c*1750). Gifted countertenor who was a rather slender composer of cantatas and *divertissements*. Bourgeois published an early collection of *Pièces en trio* in 1701, before taking the post of *maître de musique* at Strasbourg Cathedral and later Toul. By 1708 he was back in Paris, singing at the Opéra, though he took brief engagements in the Low Countries as well as in provincial France. Also in 1708 he published his first book of cantatas. In 1713 he produced an *opéra-ballet*, *Les amours déguisés*, and the following year contributed *Le Comte de Gabalis* to the 'Grandes Nuits de Sceaux'. Another *opéra-ballet* followed in 1715 (*Les plaisirs de la paix*), and at much that time he was appointed *surintendant de la musique* to the Duke of Burgundy. He continued to produce cantatas – the most popular was *Zéphire et Flore* from his second book (1718) – and in 1721 he collaborated with Aubert on *Diane* for a private performance at Chantilly. He left his post in 1721 for the itinerant life of conducting his *divertissements* in provincial capitals.

Boyvin, Jacques. See FRANCE 2 *Provinces*.

Brossard, Sébastien de. See FRANCE 2 *Provinces*.

Buffardin, Pierre-Gabriel. See NORTHERN EUROPE 4 *Saxony and Thuringia: Dresden*.

Buterne, Jean-Baptiste (*c*1650–1727). Organist from Toulouse who in 1678 became an organist of the Chapelle Royale; he also held posts in Paris churches, sharing that of St Étienne-du-Mont with his brother David from 1685 to 1705. He left 'petites règles pour l'accompagnement' in manuscript; none of his music survives. He retired from the court in 1721 and was succeeded at Versailles by Dandrieu.

Buti, Francesco (*d* 1682). Italian librettist and impresario who, with the support of Cardinal Mazarin, introduced Italian opera at the French court. Educated in law, Buti served as secretary to Cardinal Antonio Barberini in Rome; also in the employ of the cardinal was the composer Luigi Rossi, who set Buti's oratorio text *Giuseppe, figlio di Giacobbe*. In 1645 the Barberinis sought exile in France, and Buti accompanied them to Paris where he quickly caught the eye of Cardinal Mazarin. To Buti, Mazarin delegated authority over the Italian musicians at court. Buti also wrote librettos for court ballets and operas – including Rossi's *Orfeo* (1647), Carlo Caproli's *Le nozze di Peleo e di Teti* (1654) and Cavalli's *Ercole amante* (1662). Mazarin rewarded him with French citizenship and a generous pension.

Caccini. See ITALY 6 *Tuscany*.

Caffarelli. See ITALY 10 *Itinerant Musicians*.

Caix d'Hervelois, Louis de (*d c*1760). Bass viol player and composer. Caix d'Hervelois remains a shadowy figure in the history of viol playing, despite the five collections of *pièces de violes* he published over a 30-year period. He never held a court appointment, unlike the other viol-playing Caix family from Lyons – François-Joseph (*d* after 1751) and his children, who included a daughter Marie-Anne Ursule (1715–51) – and contented himself instead with the patronage of lesser nobles. Nevertheless, Le Blanc (1740) placed him next to Marais and the elder Forqueray in the 'empire de la viole'.

Camargo, La. See FRANCE *1 Paris and Versailles*, Cupis de Camargo, Marie-Anne.

Cambert, Robert (*c*1627–1677). Organist for 22 years at St Honoré, Paris, and composer who collaborated with Pierre Perrin on some of the earliest *pastorales*, or *comédies françoises en musique*. Their *Pastorale d'Issy* (1659) was performed before Louis XIV, the Queen Mother (in whose household Cambert later served) and Mazarin; Cambert contributed an overture, 14 songs and a series of *ritournelles* (now lost). They collaborated on *Ariane* in the same year. A decade later, in 1669, Cambert and Perrin were formally granted a royal privilege to establish 'académies d'opéra'. In spite of the success of *Pomone* (1671), the academy went bankrupt; with Lully's acquisition of the privilege in 1672, Cambert's career as an opera composer was effectively blocked.

He decided to make a new start in London, where he and a former pupil, Louis Grabu, established in 1674 a Royal Academy of Musick at the Theatre Royal, Bridges Street, Covent Garden. *Ariane* was performed, with additional music by Grabu, to celebrate the marriage of the Duke of York. They also adapted *Pomone* for a performance at Windsor before Charles II later that year.

Campra, André (1660–1744). Important figure in Parisian musical life at the turn of the century as a composer of both dramatic and sacred music. Unique among his contemporaries, Campra followed in the footsteps of Charpentier: he was a gifted composer of dramatic music who nevertheless spent much of his career in the service of the church. The times were kinder to him than to Charpentier. After spending his early years in the south of France (at Aix-en-Provence, Arles and Toulouse), he quickly found his feet in Paris where, within six months of his arrival in 1694, he was installed as *maître de musique* at the cathedral of Notre Dame, and as early as 1698 he was composing music for the Latin trag-

edies performed at the Jesuit college in Paris, Louis le Grand.

The italophiles – the dukes of Chartres (later regent) and Sully and the Duchess of La Ferté – soon patronized him for *divertissements*. Their success led him to devise larger-scale *opéra-ballets*, though initially he took the precaution of publishing in his brother Joseph's name. However, Campra had accurately gauged the public's taste for frivolous entertainment, involving ordinary people in comic situations, and such was the popularity of *L'Europe galante* (1697; text by La Motte) that he resigned the prestigious post at Notre Dame in 1700 to concentrate on *tragédie lyrique* and *opéra-ballet*.

He assumed a post as *conducteur* at the Opéra, where all his major dramatic works (texts by Danchet) were subsequently performed. He composed nine tragedies, among them *Hésione* (1700), *Tancrède* (1702) and *Idoménée* (1712), and four *opéra-ballets* which, in addition to *L'Europe galante*, include *Les Muses* (1703), *Les fêtes vénitiennes* (1710) and *Les ages* (1718). Campra took up the incomplete setting of *Iphigénie en Tauride* begun in the mid 1690s by Desmarets (exiled in Spain), composed a prologue and scenes for all five acts, and then arranged for its performance by the Académie in 1704. During this time he also produced three books of cantatas which encapsulate his operatic style – reliance on da capo arias, expressive use of harmony and artful melodies, and a keen sense of instrumental colour (whether with virtuoso soloists or massed to create storms, shipwrecks, earthquakes or slumber) – and contributed music to the Duchess of Maine's 'Grandes Nuits de Sceaux' in 1714 and 1715. In 1722 Campra was appointed *maître de musique* to the Prince of Conti.

After the death of the regent he returned to the church, taking up one of the *sous-maître* positions at Versailles ceded by Lalande in 1723. For the Chapelle he composed *grands motets* which are themselves very operatic in style. He published five books of *petits motets* – veritable cantatas with sacred texts – and two books of psalms; many works remained unpublished, including a *Messe de Requiem* (*c*1722). In 1730 Campra succeeded Destouches as *inspecteur général* of the Académie Royale de Musique in Paris.

Caproli, Carlo. See ITALY *7 Papal States: Rome*.

Carlier, Crespin. See FRANCE *2 Provinces*.

Castel, Louis-Bertrand (1688–1757). Jesuit mathematician, physician and theorist. Castel arrived in Paris from the provinces in 1720 to take up a teaching post at the Jesuit school. As a scientist he was preoccupied with the relationship between sound and colour, and spent 30 years developing an 'ocular harpsichord' inspired by the theories of Athanasius Kircher, Newton, Descartes and Constantijn Huygens. As a journalist he contributed critical reviews of the music and theories of Rameau to the *Mercure de France* and the *Journal de Trévoux*.

Cavalli, Francesco. See ITALY *4 Venice*.

Cercamanan, Anne Fonteaux de (*d c*1719). Soprano who, according to Loret's journal, sang annually at the Église aux Feuillants with La Barre and Hilaire during the late 1650s and early 1660s and took part in the performances of Perrin's *Pastorale d'Issy* at the Louvre in 1659. During the early 1660s she appeared in *ballets de cour* and in 1678 she was appointed *chantre extraordinaire de la musique de la chambre*.

Certain, Marie-Françoise (*d* 1711). Parisian harpsichordist and companion to Lully who presided over a regular music salon at her home near the Palais Royal. Titon du Tillet wrote warmly of the precision of her playing and her command of repertory, and Hubert Le Blanc saw her as a mediator between French and Italian tastes. She left a library of over 100 volumes of music – ballets and operas by Lully, motets, airs and collections of harpsichord *pièces* from D'Anglebert to Jacquet de la Guerre; she owned a variety of instruments which included a recorder, guitar, two treble and two bass viols, an Italian *basse de violon*, two harpsichords and a theorbo.

Chambonnières, Jacques Champion, Sieur de (1601/2–1672). Founder of the French Classical school of harpsichord playing and composer. Chambonnières is usually credited with having adapted the lute idiom to the harpsichord. He composed exclusively for the solo harpsichord but only published two collections (1670). His fluency – indeed delicacy – and command of ornamentation are attested to by Mersenne and Le Gallois. He was the teacher and mentor of the Couperin brothers, Hardel, D'Anglebert (who assumed his court post in 1662 and later composed a moving *tombeau* in his honour), N.-A. Lebègue, Robert Cambert and G. G. Nivers.

In 1641 he inaugurated a series of private concerts (the 'Assemblée des Honnestes Curieux') which took place on Wednesdays and Saturdays at noon. Two years later he took over his father's court post as a *gentilhomme ordinaire* of the king's chamber, and during the

1650s danced alongside Lully and the young Louis XIV in the *Ballet de la nuit* (1653) and in the *intermèdes* of Carlo Caproli's *Le nozze di Peleo e di Teti* (1654). Throughout his life Chambonnières donned aristocratic titles to enhance his reputation yet, according to the viol player Jean Rousseau, he was forced, ultimately, to resign his royal post because he was unwilling to acquire the techniques of figured bass accompaniment, preferring instead to disguise his ignorance by affecting the attitudes of a dilettante.

Charpentier, Marc-Antoine (1643–1704). Versatile and prolific French composer of sacred and theatrical music which rivalled that of Lully. Until recently Charpentier and his music have been little known and appreciated, largely because he never held a court appointment, nor, with the exception of a few airs, *petits motets* and a post-Lullian opera, was his music published. He had a remarkable career, partly in the service of the church and related institutions on the fringes of the court and partly with the Comédie Française, as Molière's troupe became known.

He was one of the first French composers to study in Italy (some time between 1662 and 1667), where he absorbed the polychoral and concertato styles and became acquainted with the sonata, the cantata and oratorio genres. His models were Carissimi (with whom he is thought to have studied), the Mazzocchis, Orazio Benevoli and Francesco Beretta. He introduced their music to italophile gatherings in Paris and at the Marais *hôtel* of the Duchess of Guise, along with his own oratorios and motets, theatrical pieces, the earliest French cantatas and a virtuoso sonata for eight instruments (which predated by nearly a decade the experiments of Couperin, Jean-Féry Rebel and E.-C. Jacquet de la Guerre).

His music, for the most part contained in 28 manuscript volumes of 'Meslanges' (now available in facsimile), is preserved in the Paris Bibliothèque Nationale and is mainly sacred. These are working scores, with names of singers and instrumentalists as well as performing indications written in the margins. Charpentier composed sacred music for the varied resources of churches, private chapels and convents; 11 Masses, 84 psalm settings and 207 motets survive. In the early 1680s he provided music for the Masses of the Dauphin, which Louis XIV attended when in Paris. As composer and *maître de musique* at the principal Jesuit church in Paris, Charpentier composed music for services and for the Latin dramas presented by the Jesuit colleges. Critical of Charpentier's use of opera singers in productions such as *David et Jonathas* (1688), Le Cerf called the church of St Louis in the rue St Antoine 'l'église de l'opéra'.

In 1698 Charpentier was appointed *maître de musique* at the Sainte Chapelle, a post second only to that of the directorship of the Chapelle Royale at Versailles. (Earlier, in 1683, illness had prevented him from competing for one of the four coveted posts of *sous-maître* of the Chapelle Royale; the king did, however, award him a pension in respect of his service to the dauphin.) The music composed for the Sainte Chapelle, such as his Mass 'Assumpta est Maria' (?1699) and his dramatic motet *Judicium Salomonis* (1702), ranks among his finest.

Much of his theatrical music is lost, but that which survives amply demonstrates Charpentier's sensitivity to text in both tragic and comic veins. Again, his experience was wide: *pastorales*, for the courtly entertainments of the Duchess of Guise, the dauphin and later the Duke of Chartres (with whom he graciously collaborated on an opera, *Philomèle*, given at the Palais Royal); overtures, witty *intermèdes* and incidental music for the comedies of Molière and his successors at the Comédie Française; and a single masterpiece of lyric tragedy, *Médée*, presented by the Académie in 1693 which was nevertheless received with the same coldness showered upon all new operas of the immediate post-Lullian era. His colourful use of harmony, praised by his contemporaries, was set against a clear sense of tonality, and his expressively phrased melodies and word painting contributed to the dramatic impact of his music. He adored contrast – of instrumental and vocal forces and timbres, keys (describing them in his *Règles de composition* (?c1692) in terms of different expressive characters) and other compositional techniques – which he counterbalanced with an equal passion for symmetry.

His relationship with Lully is implicit if unstated in contemporary sources. His italophilia was unfashionable in the early years of the reign, and Lully's superior connections at court and ruthless ambition effectively blocked his path. But it was to Charpentier that Molière turned in 1672 when Lully abandoned his comedies for the loftier heights of tragedy. And even when Lully was gone, the repressiveness and prejudice that were his legacy hampered those left behind.

Chédeville. Family of musette players, makers and composers, of whom three bro-thers stand out: Pierre (1694–1725), Esprit Philippe (1696–1762) and Nicolas (1705–82). All three played in the orchestra of the Académie Royale de Musique and acquired court appointments in the Grands Hautbois through their relations, the Hotteterres. Pierre is known only as a player. Esprit Philippe gained a further appointment in 1738 in the Hautbois et Musettes de Poitou, while Nicolas was popular as a musette master to the daughters of Louis XV.

The younger two composed and arranged chamber music for musettes and hurdy-gurdies – suites, sonatas and concertos – in a pseudo-rustic style in keeping with the fashion at court. Nicolas's op. 6 *Amusements de Bellone ou Les plaisirs de Mars* (by 1737) was inspired by his campaign stint with the Prince of Conti, and accordingly the movements make reference to battle; his arrangements include versions of sonatas by Dall'Abaco and concertos by Vivaldi. Esprit Philippe and Nicolas also made musettes. Nicolas enlarged the lower compass and rearranged the keys on the little chanter. Many of Esprit Philippe's musettes were beautifully executed in ivory, silver and gold, with rosewood chanters.

Chiarini, Giuseppe (*d* 1678). Savoyard castrato working at the French court in the Cabinet Italien (1659–64). In Turin Chiarini had served at the Savoy court from 1650 as a member of the Musici Armonici, a select group of castrato singers. In spite of his popularity, he was forced to leave in 1659 because of scandal and went to Paris, where in 1660 he appeared in the lavish nuptial performances of Cavalli's *Xerse*; two years later he sang in Cavalli's *Ercole amante*. Lully employed him in the *Ballet de l'Impatience* (1661). As a member of the Cabinet Italien, Chiarini appeared in one of Lully's *entrées* in Molière's *Le mariage forcé* (threatened by the popularity of the Italian troupe, Lully took steps to curtail their appearances). In 1666 Chiarini wrote to Carlo Emanuele II, Duke of Savoy, begging to be allowed to return home; his petition was granted.

Clérambault, Louis-Nicolas (1676–1749). Parisian harpsichordist, organist and distinguished composer of cantatas. Clérambault belonged to a family who had been in royal service since the 15th century. His father, Dominique (c1644–1704), was a member of the Vingt-quatre Violons (1670–82). Louis-Nicolas divided his career between church organ appointments in Paris and a post at Versailles. In his capacity as organist he composed a variety of sacred works and published a *livre d'orgue* (c1710); at Versailles he supervised the concerts requested by Madame de Maintenon, who had him appointed organist at the Maison Royale de St Cyr.

His reputation as a fine organist was exceeded only by that which he achieved as a composer of secular chamber music. Like his older contemporary François Couperin, Clérambault devoted himself to small forms, which he infused with his own version of 'les goûts-réunis' (although his *pièces de clavecin* of 1704 remain, like Couperin's, in a purely French vein). He published five collections of cantatas (1710–26) which contain some of the finest examples in the repertory. *Orphée* (1710), scored for high voice, flute, violin and continuo, was the most popular French cantata of the 18th century, so exquisite are its melodies and ensemble timbres, so affecting its harmony. Clérambault's son César-François-Nicolas (d 1760) was also an organist and composer of cantatas.

Clicquot. Family of royal organ builders at work during the 17th and 18th centuries. The two most important members of the Clicquot family were Robert (c1645–1719) and his grandson François-Henri (1732–90). Robert, the protégé of his brother-in-law Étienne Énocq (d 1682), gained a foothold at court with the help of Colbert (d 1683), Louis XIV's minister of finance. He was taken into partnership by the celebrated builder Alexandre Thierry, whom he succeeded at the turn of the century as the pre-eminent Parisian maker. Although none of his instruments survives, the case of the organ he built (1710–11, with the assistance of Julien Tribuot) for the chapel at Versailles is still in place. Robert's sons Jean Baptiste (1678–1746) and Louis-Alexandre (c1684–1760), father of François-Henri, became organ builders.

The organs by François-Henri Clicquot represent the final flowering of the French classical tradition. His instruments, which included those at St Roch, Paris, and St Louis, Versailles, were praised by Bédos de Celles (1766–78) and the players Daquin, A.-L. Couperin and Balbastre. He also modernized many of the famous 17th-century Parisian organs such as that of St Gervais.

Colin de Blamont, François. See FRANCE *1 Paris and Versailles*, Blamont, François Colin de.

Collasse, Pascal (1649–1709). Composer who worked at Paris and Versailles. Collasse came to Paris from Rheims. After his training as a choirboy at St Paul he joined the coterie of young musicians assisting Lully with his Aca-

démie productions. From composing inner voices for the large-scale ensemble numbers he rose to become Lully's secretary (after the disgrace of Lalouette) and a *batteur de mesure*. This connection assured him of gaining one of the four posts of *sous-maître* of the Chapelle Royale in 1683. There he joined Nicolas Coupillet, Guillaume Minoret and Lalande; two years later he took on the additional posts of *compositeur de la musique de la chambre* and *maître des pages*.

While composing *grands motets* and a setting of Racine's *Cantiques spirituels* for performances at nearby St Cyr, Collasse maintained his association with the Académie in Paris. In fact he was the only Lully protégé to mount a successful *tragédie lyrique* (albeit only one): *Thétis et Pélée* (1689; text by Fontenelle) remained in the Académie repertory for well over 70 years. His *Ballet des saisons* (1695) was also particularly popular – due in part to the novel 100-bar tempest which later influenced Campra's *Tancrède* (1702) and Marais' *Alcyone* (1706) – and can be seen as an important precursor of Campra's *L'Europe galante* (1697). Like Charpentier, Lalande, Lalouette, Campra, Clérambault, Desmarets and Royer he contributed *intermèdes* to the Jesuits' productions of Latin tragedies during the 1680s.

Having served Lully faithfully, until his death, Collasse had been led to expect a pension and house from the estate. Lully's heirs thought differently and accused him of plagiarism (pointing to resemblances between a chorus in Lully's *Ballet des muses* of 1666 and Collasse's *Ballet des saisons*, in order to discredit his claim). Collasse did possess manuscript works by Lully and admitted to having borrowed from them. In 1696 he went to Lille, armed with a *privilège* to found an opera company, but returned to Paris in 1700 after his theatre was destroyed by fire. It is said that after retiring in 1708 from his court posts, Collasse took up alchemy and died in pathetic circumstances.

Constantin, Louis (c1585–1657). Violin virtuoso and composer who served Louis XIII as one of the Vingt-quatre Violons. He became *roi des joueurs d'instruments* in 1624, a post which gave him the power to levy taxes on instrumentalists formally entering the profession. Only one work, *La pacifique* (1636) for six instruments, survives in a manuscript of the Philidor Collection (Bibliothèque Nationale, Paris).

Corbetta, Francesco. See ITALY *10 Itinerant Musicians*.

Corneille, Pierre (1606–84). Poet and dramatist, who dominated Parisian theatre from 1635 until 1665, and one of the original members of the Académie Française. His plays became the basis for many opera librettos of the 17th and 18th centuries. Corneille used drama as a forum for examining contemporary morals and politics, and such was the force of his ideas that he excited both intense antagonism and admiration from his audiences. Between 1629 and 1674 he produced dramatic works, working in a variety of forms and with equally varied themes; he was particularly fond of interrupting the flow of action with moments of reflection. He saw music as incidental to drama and involved himself in a limited way with opera.

He did collaborate with composers on at least two occasions. The first time was with Charles Dassoucy, who was invited simply to provide incidental music, without *récits*, for *Andromède* (1650). The second occasion was with the infinitely higher-powered Lully, Molière and Quinault on the *tragédie-ballet Psyché* (1671). Lully organized an orchestra of 300 and a corps of 70 dancers, forcing Corneille against his will to defer to musical considerations; afterwards he vowed never again to enter into such a venture.

Corrette, Michel (1709–95). Parisian organist, composer and arranger of popular tunes, and the author of performance practice manuals for such diverse instruments as the organ, *pardessus*, double bass, viola and hurdy-gurdy. His violin treatise, *L'école d'Orphée* (1738), contains advice on how to differentiate between French and Italian styles; in his cello method (1741) he advised viol players on how to become cellists. Corrette reveals himself in his anecdotal writings as a lively musical personality. He was a prolific, if mediocre, composer of music in lighter genres popular with amateur musicians, such as the *vaudeville*, *ariette*, *cantatille* and *sonatille*, as well as of sonatas, suites and concertos.

A trip to England resulted in *contredanses angloises* (1740) for flute duo; his many stage works for the Opéra-Comique and the *foire* theatres inspired several collections of *concertos comiques* for three violins and continuo. He delighted in unusual combinations of instruments, evidenced by his works for bagpipes (*musette*) and hurdy-gurdy (*vielle*) with other instruments; *Le Phénix* (1738), for four cellos (viols or bassoons), and *Les délices de la solitude* (c1739), for cello, viol, bassoon and continuo, illustrate his experimental attitude. In his capacity as a church organist he composed motets, a *Te Deum*, Masses and *Leçons*

des ténèbres. His social connections were such that in 1734 he was made *Grand maître des Chevaliers du Pivois* and in 1750 *Chevalier de l'Ordre de Christ*.

Couperin, François (*le Grand*) (1668–1733). Parisian harpsichordist, organist and composer; the finest keyboard and chamber music exponent of the French classical school and an important mediator between French and Italian styles. Couperin was an only child, a brilliant organist whose uncle, Louis, and father, Charles, had preceded him at St Gervais in Paris. On his 18th birthday he officially inherited his father's position, occupied in the interim by Lalande, for whom François had deputized from the age of ten. Lalande, clearly his mentor, praised the young man's innovative 1690 collection of *pièces d'orgue* as 'dignes d'être données au publique' and no doubt helped to establish him as a court organist in 1693. For his part, Couperin wasted little time: he collected a coat of arms in 1696 and the order of Chevalier de Latran in 1702, although he had to wait patiently (1700–17) to acquire the younger D'Anglebert's post as *ordinaire de la chambre pour le clavecin*; in a departure from tradition, he passed that post on to his daughter, Marguerite-Antoinette, in 1730.

Couperin divided his time between Paris and Versailles. Heavy commitments to teach the harpsichord and organ hampered the publication of the vocal and instrumental chamber music arising from his posts. After the appearance in 1690 of his *Pièces d'orgue* (in manuscript copies with engraved title pages), he contributed no further works for organ. Instead he turned his attention to the import of the Italian sonatas and cantatas being performed in private concerts during the 1690s; his own trio and quartet *sonades* in the Corellian style – some of which were absorbed into his 1726 collection *Les nations* – were initially circulated in manuscripts under an anagram of his name. The discerning collector Sébastien de Brossard acquired copies and later described them in the catalogue of his collection as 'good and most excellent music which requires only a good performance'. Couperin's interest in the Italian style, as represented by Carissimi and distilled by Charpentier, spilled over into his sacred vocal music (from the 1690s to the end of the reign in 1715), particularly his motets, *versets* and *leçons de ténèbres*: the published collections of *versets* (1703–5) include in the margins the names of the first performers, among them his cousin Marguerite-Louise Couperin.

Meanwhile he was amassing a quantity of superlative harpsichord pieces which began appearing in elegantly engraved editions only in 1713, well after those of his colleagues Clérambault, Dandrieu, Jacquet de la Guerre, Le Roux, Marchand and Rameau. Ever the individualist, Couperin chose to group his *pièces* into *ordres* rather than suites, and relied much less on dance movements than his contemporaries, preferring the freer and more evocative *pièces de caractère*. He was also the first to use titles to any great degree, though he asked to be 'forgiven for not explaining them all'. Some paid homage to people, others to natural phenomena and abstractions; some were satirical, others merely flattered. He published four collections (1713, 1716–17, 1722 and 1730), in which the numbering of *ordres* runs consecutively. In his portrait by André Boüys his hand rests on a copy of *Les idées heureuses* from the second *ordre*. Concerned that, in spite of the careful annotations made in the editions, his pieces might not be properly performed, Couperin published *L'art de toucher le clavecin* (1716) to elucidate the fingering, his use of ornaments (whose notation he standardized) and *notes inégales*; he also included eight preludes that could serve as introductions to the eight *ordres* of the first and second books. A manuscript treatise, *Règle pour l'accompagnement*, offers rules for realizing figured bass and the treatment of dissonance.

In his publications of the early 1720s he offered a wide variety of ways in which the French and Italian styles might be united. In 1722 the *Concerts royaux* (for one to three players) were appended to the third book of harpsichord *ordres*. Two years later he issued the brilliantly assimilated *Apothéose de Corelli* within a second collection of *concerts*, aptly entitled *Les goûts-réünis*, in which the French and Italian elements are so subtly blended as to be barely extricable. The *Concert instrumental sous le titre d'Apothéose composé à la mémoire immortelle de l'incomparable Monsieur de Lully* (1725) allegorized the synthesis: Lully and Corelli are received by Apollo on Mount Parnassus, where together they conceive 'La paix du Parnasse' in the form of an integrated *sonade en trio*.

A more direct juxtaposition of French classical and Italian styles occurs in *Les nations* (1726) (which contained, in four partbooks, four extended works, each half-*sonade* and half-*ordre*) and in the exquisitely crafted suites for bass viols (1728), of which the first is a French *ordre* and the second an Italian *sonata*

da chiesa. In his prefaces to these editions he further elaborated on his quest for a united style. Early in the century Le Cerf described Couperin as a 'serviteur passionné de l'Italie'; he also epitomized – by his playing and his *pièces de clavecin*, his deeds and his place in French society – all that was admirable in the French classical tradition.

Brahms and Friedrich Chrysander edited the first complete edition of Couperin's harpsichord pieces (1871–88), and in 1933 L'Oiseau-Lyre (Monaco) issued the complete works, lacking only the *petits motets* and airs that have since been discovered and incorporated into the new collected edition now in progress.

Couperin, Louis (*c*1626–1661). Gifted player of the harpsichord, organ and viol, who is best known for his unmeasured preludes. Louis Couperin, uncle of François Couperin *le Grand*, arrived in Paris from nearby Chaumes by 1651. Two years later he took up the post of organist at St Gervais, which was to remain in the family throughout the 17th and 18th centuries. He became part of the regency *musique de chambre*, not as a keyboard player – although Chambonnières' post had been offered to him – but as a violinist. He is known to have performed in at least four Lully ballets during the late 1650s. On his early death he was succeeded at St Gervais by his brother Charles (1638–79).

He composed *fantaisies*, division basses, cantus firmus *versets* and *carillons* for organ, much of which remain in private hands, as do two pieces for shawm choir (perhaps composed for Louis XIV's wedding), and several five-part string works. Among his 16 preludes one is marked 'à l'imitation de Mr Froberger', whom he had met in his early years in Paris.

Cousser, Jean Sigismond. See NORTHERN EUROPE 7 *Itinerant Musicians*, Kusser, Johann Sigismund.

Coypeu, Charles. See FRANCE 1 *Paris and Versailles*, Dassoucy, Charles.

Cupis de Camargo, Marie-Anne (1710–70). *Première danseuse* at the Paris Opéra (1726–51) who created major roles in Rameau's operas. 'La Camargo', as she was known, was a colourful – sometimes scandalous – person both on and offstage. Her family, originally from Brussels, moved to Paris when her dancing career began to blossom. Like other dancers and actresses of the Louis XV era, she was the mistress of a count and a popular figure in the Parisian salons; she shortened her skirts in order better to display her footwork and was famed for her leaps. Her success kindled the jealousy of her teacher, Françoise Prévost, and her contemporary Marie Sallé. Her brothers, in particular the violinist Jean-Baptiste (1711–88) and the cellist François (1732–1808), were active at the Concert Spirituel.

Cuzzoni, Francesca. See ITALY *10 Itinerant Musicians.*

Dagincour, François. See FRANCE *2 Provinces.*

Dandrieu, Jean-François (*c*1682–1738). Highly esteemed organist and harpsichordist who, in 1705, published some of the earliest French trio sonatas. Dandrieu and his sister Jeanne-Françoise, who was also an accomplished keyboard player, were students of J.-B. Moreau. Afterwards she joined the musicians of the Elector of Bavaria (whose court was in residence in France) while he took up the organ post at St Merry. By 1710 he assumed his uncle Pierre's duties at St Barthélemy, which later passed to Jeanne-Françoise. In 1721 he became an organist of the Chapelle Royale.

During the first two decades of the 18th century Dandrieu published several collections of harpsichord pieces, which he revised and published again, along with old airs and *noëls* by himself and his uncle (though he failed to identify which), modernizing them to suit the current taste for more italianate *galant* music. The second of the new series of harpsichord books (1728) opens with 'La Lully', conceived in the French style, inevitably followed by 'La Corelli', in a mixed style. His last collection (1739) is entitled *Premier livre de pièces d'orgue* and contains transcriptions of earlier harpsichord pieces.

D'Anglebert, Jean-Henri (1635–91). Parisian keyboard player in the service of Gaston, Duke of Orléans, and later Louis XIV; his book of *Pièces de clavecin* (1689) remains a principal source for the French classical style. In it he included monumental fugues for organ, arrangements of overtures, airs and dances from Lully operas, four harpsichord suites containing unmeasured preludes and a short treatise on accompaniment. His table of ornaments remains the most complete of its kind; its signs, many of them new, quickly entered common practice. By his skilful arrangements of lute music (in letter notation), D'Anglebert forged the earliest and most important tangible link between the lute and harpsichord idioms; these arrangements of music by the lutenists René Mesangeau, Pinel and the Gaultiers survive in an autograph manuscript (Bibliothèque Nationale, Paris,

Rés. 89ter). D'Anglebert's son Jean-Baptiste-Henri succeeded him as *ordinaire de la chambre du roy pour le clavecin*, a post François Couperin acquired in 1717.

Daquin, Louis-Claude (1694–1772). Parisian organist, harpsichordist and composer. Daquin was a prodigy who played for the king at the age of six and gained his first organ appointment (at the Petit St Antoine) six years later. Competing against Rameau in 1727, he won the post at St Paul and succeeded his teacher Louis Marchand at the Cordeliers in 1732. His appointment in 1739 as *organiste du roi* confirmed his place as the outstanding French organist of his day. His gifts as a composer were less brilliant (he was known more for his *noëls* than his harpsichord pieces, which appeared in 1735). His son, Pierre-Louis d'Aquin de Château-Lyon (1720–97), recounted his life in the *Lettres sur les hommes célèbres* (1752).

Dassoucy, Charles (1605–77). Lutenist, composer and satirical poet working in Paris during the mid 17th century. Dassoucy, also known as Coypeu, played in the Paris performances of Cavalli's *Egisto* and Luigi Rossi's *Orfeo* in 1646 and 1647. He wrote the text and music for at least two pastorales (now lost) and composed music for Pierre Corneille's tragedy *Andromède*, which Cardinal Mazarin commissioned in 1650 for performance (with machinery by Torelli) at the Petit Bourbon; both works figure prominently in the development of French dramatic music. Dassoucy left Paris for the provinces in 1653 (he met Molière in Lyons and was imprisoned in Montpellier); his travels in Italy about 1660 inspired him to write a book (*Les aventures d'Italie*, 1677). By about 1670 he returned to Paris, hoping to renew his connections with Molière, whose collaboration with Lully was ending, but Charpentier was chosen instead.

Delair, Étienne Denis (*d* after 1727). Parisian theoretician who in 1690 published a *Traité d'accompagnement pour le théorbe et le clavessin*, which contains different methods of accompanying from an unfigured bass.

Demachy, Sieur (*fl* 1685–92). Bass viol player and the first in France to publish solo music for that instrument. Demachy, a pupil of Nicolas Hotman, was a vociferous proponent of the self-sufficient chordal style of playing, inherited from the lute, in contrast to that of Sainte-Colombe and his followers (Marin Marais and Jean Rousseau), who generally favoured the instrument's melodic character. In 1685 Demachy published unaccompanied suites – half in tablature, half in staff notation –

a year before Marais brought out his monumental first volume of *pièces de violes*.

Denis. Family of keyboard and string instrument makers, among whom Jean Denis is remembered for the treatise (2/1650) on tuning the spinet, in which he distinguished between vocal and instrumental pitch.

Descartes, René (1596–1650). Philosopher and mathematician who made his mark on the history of music theory with his *Compendium musicae* (written in 1618, though not published until 1650, in Utrecht). Descartes represents the link between 16th-century humanists and 17th-century scientists: by employing a deductive scientific method, he was able to define the relationship between physical and psychological phenomena in music. He was a friend and correspondent of Marin Mersenne and Constantijn Huygens, and lived for 20 years in the United Provinces (1629–49). He died in Stockholm, having only just taken up a post at Queen Christina's court.

Desmarets, Henry (1661–1741). Talented Parisian composer on the fringe of the court. Desmarets began a promising career as a disciple of Lully: his first opera (*Endymion*, 1682) and motet (*Beati quorum*, 1683) were performed at Versailles, and a *divertissement* (1686) at Fontainebleau. But youth worked against him when in 1683 the four crucial positions at the Chapelle Royale went to others, older and better connected; ironically, one of those who succeeded, Nicolas Coupillet, was later dismissed for passing off one of Desmarets' compositions as his own. He petitioned to go abroad to study the Italian style, but was impeded by Lully, who felt (according to Destouches) that his command of the French style must not be subverted. After Lully's death Desmarets' *tragédie lyrique*, *Didon* (1693; text by Mme Gillot de Sainctonge), was warmly received, though subsequent productions – with the exception of *Vénus et Adonis* (1697; text by J.-B. Rousseau) – failed. But in 1699 he went to Spain, having eloped with a young woman, and as a result his music was not performed at court until 1722. In exile he was appointed *maître de la chambre* (1701), but left Madrid in 1707 to take a post as *surintendant de la musique* to the Duke of Lorraine at Lunéville. Friends in Paris, including J.-B. Matho and Philidor, made efforts to promote his music in his absence: his airs were published in the Ballard *recueils*, his unfinished score of *Iphigénie en Tauride* was completed by Campra and given at the Opéra (1704), while his *grand motet*, *Cum invocarem*, was published by Philidor

(1714). But after failing in 1726 in his bid to succeed Lalande as a *sous-maître* at the Chapelle Royale, he resigned himself to remaining in the provinces.

Desplanes, Jean-Antoine. See FRANCE 1 *Paris and Versailles*, Piani, Giovanni Antonio.

Destouches, André Cardinal (1672–1749). Remarkable figure in French musical life during the first half of the 18th century. Destouches was of aristocratic stock, entitling him to *entrée* in circles usually closed to musicians. As a boy he was educated by the Jesuits and under their protection travelled to Siam (1687–8). Before becoming known as a composer and gaining acclaim as a musical administrator, Destouches served in the king's musketeers. He left the army in 1694 to pursue a career in music, studying for a time with Campra. He collaborated with his cousin, the librettist Antoine Houdar de La Motte, on a series of tragedies, of which the *pastorale-héroïque Issé* (1697) and *Omphale* (1701) were particularly successful. When the directorship of the Académie Royale de Musique became vacant in 1712 Destouches served in the interim, before being appointed *inspecteur général* in 1713. In 1728 he was finally made director.

From 1718 Destouches was in demand at court. He collaborated with Lalande on a ballet, *Les éléments*, in which the young Louis XV danced (appearing as himself in the prologue) at the Tuileries palace in 1721; it was successfully mounted at the Opéra in 1725. In 1726 he and Blamont jointly assumed Lalande's post as *surintendant de musique de la chambre*, and with it responsibility for the queen's concerts. He numbered among his friends the princes of Conti and Monaco; the latter had made possible the performance of *Issé* at Fontainebleau in 1697; such was its reception that the king ordered it to be performed as part of the wedding festivities for the Duke and Duchess of Burgundy two months later. Despite his prolific output of airs, *comédie-ballets* (such as *Le carneval et la folie*, 1703), tragedies and motets, Destouches never overcame the stigma of being an amateur composer.

Dieupart, Charles. See BRITISH ISLES 1 *London*.

Doni, Giovanni Battista. See ITALY 6 *Tuscany*.

Dornel, Louis-Antoine (*c*1680–after 1756). Parisian organist who was among the first French composers to publish solo (1711) and trio (1713) sonatas in the Italian style. In his day his motets were performed at the Concert

Spirituel and the Académie Française, where he was *maître de musique*; his airs appeared in the *Mercure* and the popular anthologies issued by the Ballards.

Dubos, Abbé Jean-Baptiste (1670–1742). Formidable French intellectual and diplomat known to musicians by his *Réflexions critiques sur la poésie, la peinture et la musique* (Paris, 1719; Eng. trans. 1748), in which he asserted the superiority of music and painting over poetry to convey meaning.

Dubuisson (*d* by 1688). Viol player and teacher. A contemporary of Sainte-Colombe, Dubuisson was praised in 1680 as one of the 'grands virtuoses du moment'. His manuscript pieces (in tablature and staff notation, dated 1 September 1666, in the Library of Congress, Washington, DC) represent the earliest extant French source of solo bass viol music.

Du Caurroy, Eustache (1549–1609). Highly esteemed composer of sacred polyphony and fantasies. Du Caurroy served as *surintendant de la musique* at the court of Henri IV, at whose funeral in 1610 his *Missa pro defunctis* (1606; pubd. 1636) was performed. He claimed to have learnt his craft 'by reading good authors [Zarlino] and imitating the ancients [Josquin]'. Possessed of a mathematical mind, he became interested in *musique mesurée* and was a member of the Académie de Poésie et de Musique and the Académie du Palais. Apart from the Mass, which became the official royal Requiem, Du Caurroy's fantasies for three to six instruments (1610) remain his most important works. Nicolas Formé erected a monument to him; Marin Mersenne praised him in words.

Dufaut (*d* by 1686). Lutenist considered by European contemporaries to be one of the finest of the 17th century. As many as 80 lute pieces survive in manuscript and printed sources – German and English, as well as French – giving evidence of the use of new tunings and carefully notated improvisatory effects.

Dumanoir, Guillaume (1615–97). Important mid-century Parisian violinist and author of a treatise on *Le mariage de la musique avec la danse* (1664), written in response to the establishment of the Académie Royale de Danse. Dumanoir was a member of the Confrérie de St Julien, as well as of the Vingt-quatre Violons du Roi, which he often led during the 1650s. From 1657 to 1668 he held the coveted title of *roi et maître des ménestriers*, in succession to Louis Constantin.

Du Mont (de Thier), **Henry** (1610–84). Walloon organist and composer of motets who pursued his career in Paris and at the court of Louis XIV. Du Mont held a succession of important court posts – harpsichordist to the queen (1660), *sous-maître* (1663) and composer (1672) of the Chapelle Royale, and *maître de la musique de la reine* (1673) – before retiring in 1683. All the while he served as organist of St Paul, composing concerted vocal music. His italianate *Cantica sacra* (1652) represents the first printed collection of *petits motets*; they are scored for two and three voices, viols or violins and continuo.

Vocally, Du Mont established a fluent style of dramatic French monody; his symphonies and accompaniments are often independent of the vocal lines. His early experimentation with these and other Italian techniques – dialogue and double chorus – came to fruition in the *grands motets* published posthumously. Du Mont's panegyric *grands motets*, along with those of Pierre Robert and Lully, set the standard for much of the next century. Charpentier and Lalande in particular were much influenced by his control of the multiple forces of instruments, *petit choeur* and *grand choeur*.

Duphly, Jacques (1715–89). Harpsichordist, teacher and composer, ranked with Armand-Louis Couperin, Claude-Bénigne Balbastre and Louis-Alexandre Le Grand. His keyboard pieces are best represented by the haunting *rondeau* (*Troisième livre*, 1758) immortalizing the playing of the flamboyant bass viol player Antoine Forqueray.

Dupuy, Hilaire (*d* 1709). Soprano, *chantre extraordinaire de la musique de la chambre* and sister-in-law of Michel Lambert (and thus able to claim Lully as a relation). Mlle Hilaire, as she was known, had been a pupil of Pierre de Nyert before early success in the Parisian salons led to solo roles in the *ballets de cour* of the late 1650s and 1660s and a post in the royal music. She is frequently characterized in Loret's journal as 'la sage Mlle. Hilaire' and, on one occasion in 1666, as 'la charmante Syreine Hilaire'. In 1661 Loret remarked upon the influence of her brother-in-law (also a protégé of Nyert) in the *Ballet de l'impatience*, when, according to him, she sang 'Lambertiquement'. She usually sang with Anne de La Barre, Anna Bergerotti and Anne Fonteaux de Cercamanan, and together they also took part in the annual Holy Week services (Ténèbres) at the Église aux Feuillants; in 1663 Hilaire, La Barre and Cercamanan appeared there with Lambert, Saint-Christophe (another soprano), Lully, Molière and the lutenist-viol player Nicolas Hotman.

Duval, François (1672/3–1728). Violinist,

known for his performances of Corelli sonatas, and composer who made his way through the ranks of patronage to become a member of the Vingt-quatre Violons in 1714. Duval's 1704 collection of violin sonatas, dedicated to his patron, the Duke of Orléans, was the first to be published in France. A collection of trio sonatas, dedicated to the Duke of Noailles, appeared two years later, and a second collection of violin sonatas, dedicated to the king, in 1707.

Expilly, Gabriel (*c*1630–90). Court bass viol player and composer of sacred music who in 1663 became one of the four *sous-maîtres* of the Chapelle Royale. His post as viol player in the *musique de chambre* was acquired by Antoine Forqueray in 1689.

Farinel. Two violinists and composers from a family of French musicians working in Turin. Michel Farinel (*b* 1649) made several important connections early in his career: he studied with Carissimi in Rome and married the daughter of Robert Cambert in Paris. He travelled to Portugal and England, where his set of variations on 'La folia' for violin and continuo (thenceforth known as 'Farinel's Ground') was published by Playford in *The Division Violin* (1685). Through his father-in-law he became associated with Henry Guichard, whose party of musicians travelling to Madrid to take up posts at court he joined in 1679. Farinel became the superintendent of music and ballets to the Spanish queen (the daughter of the Duke of Orléans), but returned to France and briefly held an appointment at Versailles (1688).

His brother Jean-Baptiste (1655–1726) pursued his career in Germany. In 1680 he was appointed *Konzertmeister* at the Hanover court and spent the years 1691–5 at the Osnabrück court; after returning to Hanover he was ennobled by the elector, who eventually sent him to Venice, where he passed the rest of his life. Farinel left flute concertos and stage music.

Farinelli. See ITALY *10 Itinerant Musicians.*

Fedeli, Giuseppe. See ITALY *4 Venice.*

Fel, Marie (1713–94). Famous soprano of the Académie Royale de Musique. A pupil of Mme Van Loo, she sang at the Concert Spirituel and the Concerts chez la Reine. From 1739 she took leading roles, often opposite Pierre de Jélyotte, in over 100 productions, including Rameau's operas. She retired in 1758. Quentin La Tour's well known pastel portrait of her (1757) hangs in the Louvre.

Feuillet, Raoul-Auger (1659/60–1710). Dancer, choreographer and author of an influential book on dance. Feuillet was much indebted to Pierre de Beauchamp, whose work formed the basis of the track notation for individual steps and floor patterns set out in Feuillet's *Chorégraphie ou l'art de décrire la danse* (1700). This system of notation made possible wider transmission of French court dances throughout Europe. Feuillet published further choreographies of his own and others in a series of annual *recueils* (1700–9). In all, he published over 350 – including 41 of his own – in a wide variety of forms, for court balls as well as virtuoso theatrical performances (giving the names of the dancers for whom the steps were intended). Feuillet's pupil Joseph Dezais (*fl* 1710–22) continued to publish the *recueils* after his death.

Fischer, Johann. See NORTHERN EUROPE *7 Itinerant Musicians.*

Fleury, Nicolas (*c*1630–after 1678). *Haute-contre*, theorbist and composer of airs from Châteaudun who served the Duke of Orléans (1657–78) and in 1660 published a *Méthode pour apprendre facilement à toucher le théorbe sur la basse-continue.*

Formé, Nicolas (1567–1638). Composer and canon of the Sainte Chapelle. Formé served Henri IV (eventually succeeding Eustache Du Caurroy in 1609) and Louis XIII, to whom he dedicated a Mass (now lost) in 1638. Influenced by the Venetian double-choir motet – a form also cultivated by Claude Le Jeune, Du Caurroy and Charles D'Ambleville – Formé was the first French composer to contrast the forces of *petit* and *grand choeurs*, preparing the way for the *grands motets* of the later 17th century. Anecdotes about his unconventional behaviour abound, yet as a musician he was nevertheless held in some esteem.

Forqueray. Bass viol players and composers, father and son. Antoine Forqueray (1671/2–1745) gained Louis XIV's attention when as a child he played the *basse de violon* at the king's supper. In view of his exceptional talent, the viol was deemed a more suitable instrument for him, and his playing soon rivalled that of his elder court contemporary Marin Marais. But unlike Marais, Forqueray often chose to perform Italian repertory and in particular violin sonatas. His flamboyant manner was reflected in his playing. He was uncommonly cruel to his wife and son, yet acceptable as a teacher for the regent and the Elector of Bavaria.

Jean-Baptiste-Antoine Forqueray (1699–1782) overcame the stigma of a prison sentence and exile, instigated by his father, to succeed him at court and to publish two heavily edited versions of his father's *pièces*. Along with his second wife, Marie-Rose Dubois, who was a harpsichordist, he was counted among the best Parisian musicians of his day. His pupils included Princess Henriette-Anne (whose portrait by Nattier hangs in her father's state bedroom at Versailles) and Prince Frederick William of Prussia, with whom he carried on a correspondence (1767–9) about viol playing and repertory, which sheds important light on the instrument's late history.

Two years after his father's death Jean-Baptiste brought out a unique collection of *pièces* in his father's name in two versions – one for viol and continuo, the other for harpsichord alone. In the preface he claimed that only three of the 32 are by him, as are all the basses and the fingering (and, presumably, the intricate bowing), although it now seems that they are in fact almost entirely his own work. The pieces are technically demanding – if ingeniously idiomatic and harmonically adventurous – in stark contrast to the few extant manuscripts known to be the work of his father.

Foucault, Henry (*fl* 1690–1720). Parisian music dealer and publisher who in the 1690s challenged the Ballard monopoly with engraved editions. Foucault ran a busy shop and *atelier* in the rue St Honoré, where the engravers Henri de Baussen, Claude Roussel and François du Plessy produced editions of the latest chamber music and treatises, as well as manuscript copies of extracts from Lully's operas and early ballets, which remain today an important source for reconstructing these works. Old editions, particularly of operas, were bought and sold. Though he contravened Christophe Ballard's royal privilege, there was no lasting enmity: Foucault advertised in Ballard's publications, and the two families intermarried. Foucault's widow sold the shop and *atelier* to François Boivin and Michel Pignolet de Montéclair in 1721.

Francoeur, François (*le cadet*) (1698–1787). Violinist and successful composer who collaborated on a variety of theatrical works with the composer François Rebel (*Pyrame et Thisbé*, 1726, was an early success). François was the best known of four Francoeurs who held posts at the Opéra and at court. His elder brother Louis (1692–1745) was also a violinist, who had joined the Opéra in 1704 and the Vingt-quatre Violons in 1710 (becoming their leader in 1717); he published two collections of violin sonatas. Their father, Joseph (*c*1662–*c*1741), joined the Opéra orchestra in 1713, the same year as François.

Early on François became a member of the *musique de chambre* at Versailles, though it was not until 1730 that he gained a place in the Vingt-quatre Violons; in 1744 he became *surintendant de la musique de chambre*, succeeding Blamont. In 1739 he became *maître de musique* at the Opéra and four years later joint *inspecteur*, along with his friend and collaborator of over 45 years François Rebel. Together they managed the Opéra during the 1750s, becoming unwillingly embroiled in the 'Querelle des Bouffons'. In 1764 François was ennobled by Louis XV. His son Louis-Joseph ('Francoeur *neveu*'; 1738–1804) followed in his father's footsteps.

Fuzelier, Louis (1674–1752). Important French librettist and from 1744 the co-editor of the *Mercure de France*. Over a considerable period of time during the early 18th century Fuzelier's dramas dominated the repertory of the Parisian theatres – those of the fairs and the Comédie-Italienne, as well as the Opéra and the Comédie Française. His first librettos were parodies of Lully operas for marionettes; in collaboration with Le Sage and D'Orneval he continued (1716–30) to produce parodies of Lully and of more modern composers such as Campra, Destouches and Marais. His most important works were the librettos for the Opéra: a *tragédie lyrique* (Matho's *Arion*, 1714; *opéra-ballets* (Campra's *Ballet des ages*, 1718); and *ballets héroïques* (such as Blamont's *Les festes grecques et romaines*, 1723, and Rameau's *Les Indes galantes*, 1735). He also contributed six works to the Comédie Française, the most popular of which was the one-act *Momus fabuliste* (1719), and many cantata texts for Bernier, Campra, Courbois and Stuck.

Gallot. Family of lutenists. Jacques Gallot (*d c*1690) published a collection (after 1670) of lute pieces, including titled works and *tombeaux* to his departed royal patrons, Turenne and Condé. Henry François Gallot, Sieur de Franlieu (*d* after 1684), was responsible for compiling a sizeable collection of guitar music, which includes at least 85 pieces by Corbetta (his teacher) and a dozen pieces for the 'guitarre theorbée'.

Garnier, Gabriel (*d c*1730). Organist in Paris and at Versailles, praised by Titon du Tillet and Pierre-Louis Daquin (1752–3), who claimed Garnier performed Couperin's harpsichord pieces better than the composer himself; for his part, Couperin named one of his finest pieces after his colleague. From 1684 until 1702 Garnier was organist at St Louis-des-Invalides; thereafter he held one of the four appointments as a royal organist with

Nivers, Buterne and Couperin. In 1719 he took up a further post as organist of St Roch, Paris. No music has survived.

Gatti, Theobaldo di (*c*1650–1727). Florentine bass viol (*basse de violon* and later double bass) player and composer working in Paris. Naturalized in 1675, 'Téobalde' gained the protection of the Princess of Conti and became a member of the orchestra of the Académie Royale de Musique. He composed *Coronis*, a *pastorale héroïque* (1691), and *Scylla*, a *tragédie lyrique*, which includes a 'concert de basses' for bass voice and three bass instruments; its first performance in 1701 may have occasioned the début of the double bass at the Opéra.

Gaultier. Two related lutenist-composers. Ennemond ('le vieux Gaultier', 1575–1651) served Maria de' Medici at the French court from 1600 until 1631, as *valet de chambre* and personal lute teacher. His skill was such that he was sent to England in 1630 to play for Charles I. Although he was 28 years senior to his cousin Denis ('Gaultier le jeune', 1603–72), they were closely associated until Ennemond's retirement. Their music appears together in manuscripts and prints – *La rhétorique des dieux* (*c*1652), *Pièces de luth* (*c*1670) and *Livre de tablature* (*c*1672) – often with conflicting attributions. In contrast to Ennemond, Denis never held a royal appointment, making his way instead among the private salons of Paris; and it was he, not Ennemond, who arranged for the engraving of their many character pieces and *tombeaux*, genres which they pioneered. The form and adventurous harmonic style of their music influenced Froberger and the 17th-century French school of harpsichordists.

Gautier, Jacques (*d* before 1660). French lutenist known as 'Gautier d'Angleterre'. After a murder scandal in 1617 Gautier fled to England, where he served the Duke of Buckingham and taught Queen Henrietta Maria, to whom he caused offence by making indiscreet remarks. As his playing was his greatest asset, he toured on the continent – to the Netherlands and Spain, where portraits of him were painted by Lievens and Van Dyck. Only a few pieces by him survive in manuscript.

Geoffroy, Jean-Nicolas (*d* 1694). Organist and composer, known only by a mammoth collection of harpsichord pieces (compiled posthumously), containing 19 harpsichord suites, several pieces for both organ and viols, and dialogues for viol and harpsichord. In style they owe something to Lebègue and are characterized by unorthodox harmony, at once inventive and unfocused.

Gervais, Charles-Hubert (1671–1744). Parisian composer who was a lifelong servant to Philippe de Bourbon, nephew of Louis XIV. Gervais rose in rank as his employer became duke first of Chartres, then of Orléans and finally regent during Louis XV's minority: he acquired the royal posts of *maître de musique* (1700), *intendant de la musique* (1712) and *sous-maître* of the Chapelle Royale (1723), where his colleagues were Lalande, Campra and Nicolas Bernier. He left 45 motets, a ballet, cantatas and airs, and three operas which illustrate the transition between Lully and Rameau; *Méduse* (1697) owes much to the former and *Hypermnèstre* (1716), with its varied and imaginative orchestrations, foreshadows the latter.

Gigault, Nicolas (*c*1627–1707). Organist at four Paris churches – first at St Honoré (1646–52), then cumulatively St Nicolas-des-Champs (from 1652), St Martin-des-Champs (from 1673) and the Hôpital du Saint Esprit (from 1685). As a composer he published two collections of organ music containing *noëls* with variations (1683), the earliest of this genre, and *versets* (1685). He may have been Lully's teacher, but certainly in 1706 he was among the jury that awarded Rameau the organ post at Ste. Madeleine-en-la-Cité.

Gillier, Jean-Claude (1667–1737). Parisian composer of comedy theatre music. Gillier was associated with the Comédie Française, first as a *basse de violon* player, then as a composer in collaboration with the playwrights Regnard and Dancourt. He made several trips to London, where he published collections of songs in 1698 and 1723, and was popular in Paris and at court: in 1713 he became associated with the fair theatres, contributing *divertissements* and vaudeville finales to at least 70 productions by Le Sage, Fuzelier, D'Orneval and Favart. He also composed for the Théâtre Italien.

Gobert, Thomas (*d* 1672). Composer and from 1654 *sous-maître* of the Chapelle Royale. Associated throughout his life with the Sainte Chapelle, Gobert, along with Nicolas Formé and Jean Veillot, did much to develop the French double-chorus motet. He is also credited in a letter of 1646 to Constantijn Huygens with having employed a continuo part in his *Antiennes récitatives* (lost), predating the Paris publication in 1647 of Huygens's own *Pathodia sacra*.

Goldoni, Carlo. See ITALY 4 *Venice*.

Gouy, Jacques de (*d* after 1650). Composer

of airs. His collection of four-part settings of Godeau's paraphrases of the psalms (1650) was reprinted in Amsterdam and London, in response to the plight of the Huguenot refugees who had fled the consequences of the revocation of the Edict of Nantes (1685). The preface describes Parisian musical life in the second quarter of the 17th century.

Grabu, Louis. See BRITISH ISLES 1 *London*.

Grandval, Nicolas Racot de (1676–1753). Parisian musician and writer. Although Grandval was a respectable keyboard player – at one time organist at St Eustache – and a composer of harpsichord pieces, numerous airs and cantatas, he is best remembered as a satirist. He wrote *divertissements* for the Comédie Dancourt and the Théâtre Français, and parodies of the most popular Clérambault cantatas, *Orphée* and *Léandre et Héro*.

Grossi, Giovanni Francesco. See ITALY 10 *Itinerant Musicians*.

Guédron, Pierre (*c*1570–*c*1619). Singer and composer of airs and *ballets de cour*. Guédron held a succession of court appointments under Henri IV and Louis XIII so that by 1619 he had attained the position of *surintendant*. He composed the music for no fewer than nine ballets and published five books of airs. His early polyphonic airs bear the stamp of *musique mesurée*; the solo pieces (*récits*) composed after 1608 are declamatory in style, showing the influence of contemporary Italian music. Many of his airs appeared in anthologies and inspired sets of variations for harpsichord and lute by Scheidt, Sweelinck and Giles Farnaby. Doni, Mersenne and Bacilly praised him.

Guichard, Henry, Sieur d'Hérapine (*fl* 1670–early 18th c.). Librettist and architect, the Duke of Orléans's *intendant et ordonnateur des bâtiments* who was passionately involved in the early musical dramatic productions of Sablières and Perrin; he was also the librettist for J.-F. Rebel's *Ulysse* (1703). Guichard was well placed to make an important contribution to French musical drama, had not Lully ruthlessly prevented Sablières and Perrin from producing *pastorales* after 1672. A lawsuit against Lully created scandal, and in 1674 Guichard had to content himself with a *privilège* authorizing him to found an Académie Royale des Spectacles. Discontented, he set off with a company of 40 for Madrid in 1679 with the intention of setting up a music academy with the patronage of the Queen of Spain (daughter of the Duke of Orléans). He remained in Spain for many years and then retired to Grenoble.

Guignon, Jean-Pierre [Ghignone, Giovanni Pietro] (1702–74). Italian virtuoso violinist and composer who took French citizenship in 1741 and whose name is unpleasantly associated with a series of professional rivalries. In 1725 Guignon (a pupil of G.B. Somis at Turin) appeared with Anet at the Concert Spirituel; the occasion was specially contrived to pit the exponents of current Italian and French violin playing against one another. In 1741 Louis XV appointed him *roi et maître des ménestriers*. Guignon toured at different times with Guillemain, J.-B.-A. Forqueray and Mondonville, whom he once dislodged from an appointment to the dauphin; he also succeeded in driving Anet and Leclair from Versailles. Guignon published collections of sonatas and trios and performed at least two concertos at the Concert Spirituel.

Guillemain, Louis-Gabriel (1705–70). Parisian violinist and composer of *galant* chamber music. Guillemain's life began well enough: under the protection of the Count of Rochechouart he was given violin lessons both in France and Italy (he studied in Turin with G.B. Somis). In 1737 he became an *ordinaire* at the French court and was frequently heard at Versailles in private concerts and in the theatre orchestra of Madame de Pompadour; in 1748 his ballet-pantomime *L'opérateur chinois* was performed there. He published a substantial amount of chamber music, including virtuoso violin works, trios, quartets, concertos and pre-Classical italianate trio symphonies. However, his was not a happy life: he was profligate and alcoholic, and eventually committed suicide.

Hardel [Ardel], **Jacques** (*d* before 1680). Minor harpsichordist and composer who belonged to a family of instrument makers and musicians; he was in the service of the Duchess of Orléans. The last of Chambonnières' pupils, Hardel was said to have taken down his teacher's last works by dictation. His own Gavotte in A minor was widely circulated in manuscript collections, even into the 18th century; Louis Couperin composed a *double* for it. Le Gallois mentioned him in 1680 as 'the late Hardel'.

Hotman, Nicolas (*d* 1663). Influential viol player, theorbist and composer of German origin at the French court. Hotman was probably the pupil of André Maugars and the teacher of Sainte-Colombe; his playing was greatly admired by Mersenne, Gantez and Loret. He composed *airs de cour* (Ballard issued a posthumous collection in 1664), as well as solo music for lute, theorbo and viol. He served the Duke of Orléans for six years until 1661, when he took up half of the court post (Sébastien Le Camus assumed the other half) vacated by Louis Couperin.

Hotteterre, Jacques-Martin ['Le Romain'] (1674–1763). The most famous of a multi-talented family of musicians (see Plate 6) whose members served at court in the Haut-bois et Musettes de Poitou and the Grands Hautbois. He was skilled as a musette and transverse flute player, much in demand as a teacher and gifted as a maker of these instruments. His treatise *Principes de la flûte traversière* (1707) was the first of its kind and remains an important source of information on tonguing and ornamentation. He further contributed to the elucidation of French performing practices with the publication of his suites for flute in 1708 – particularly in their revised version of 1715, with further ornaments in the music and a table of ornaments appended – and *L'art de préluder* in 1719, which includes a section devoted to metre and rhythmic alteration. His musette tutor (1737) is considered to be the best of its kind from the 18th century.

Jacquet. Parisian musicians and instrument makers. Jehan (*d* after 1658) and his son Claude (1605–75) made harpsichords that merited praise from Mersenne. The organists Pierre (*c*1666–1729), his brother Nicolas and their remarkable sister Elisabeth-Claude descended from another branch of the family (see below).

Jacquet de La Guerre, Elisabeth-Claude (1666/7–1729). Exceptionally gifted Parisian harpsichordist and composer, rewarded with royal favour and a prominent place on Titon du Tillet's 'Le Parnasse François' after her death. As a young girl Jacquet was acclaimed for her brilliant improvisation and was given royal protection. In 1687 she published a collection of *pièces de clavecin* – the first by a woman. Clearly aware of the artistic freedom afforded by the death of Lully, Jacquet (by then married to the organist Marin de La Guerre) seized the opportunity to produce a *tragédie lyrique* (*Céphale et Procris*, 1694) at the Académie Royale de Musique; she was the only woman to do so. She took an interest in the latest Italian genres and dabbled in trio sonata composition, like Couperin and Rebel. Widowed in 1704, she remained in Paris with her son, giving concerts at her home on the Île St Louis and later in the *quartier* of St Eustache, where she was later buried. In the early years of the 18th century she was among the first to publish collections of italianate violin sonatas and sacred and secular cantatas,

as well as the harpsichord suites (1707) by which she is best known.

Jélyotte, Pierre de (1713–97). Highly esteemed *haute-contre* heard at Versailles and the Paris Opéra during the mid 18th century. Jélyotte made his début in 1733 in a revival of Blamont's *ballet héroïque*, *Les festes grecques et romaines* (1723). After the retirement of Denis-François Tribou, Rameau created all of his principal high tenor roles for Jélyotte, who was frequently paired with the soprano Marie Fel. At court he was a favourite of Madame de Pompadour, in whose private entertainments he sang works of his own composition and played the guitar and cello. In Paris he appeared very occasionally at the Concert Spirituel and retired from the Opéra in 1765.

La Barre, Anne de (1628–88). Court soprano who was the daughter of the organist Pierre de La Barre. During the regency of Anne of Austria La Barre took part in the performances of Luigi Rossi's *Orfeo* (1647), for which she was warmly praised. From late in 1652 until late 1655 she toured northern Europe, visiting Huygens at The Hague and working first at the Swedish court of Queen Christina and then, after the queen went into exile, at the Danish court.

Back in Paris by 1656, La Barre took major roles in court ballets – such as Lully's bilingual *Ballet de la raillerie* (1659), in which the popular Italian soprano Anna Bergerotti and La Barre were required to take opposing sides on behalf of Italian and French music – and Italian operas such as Cavalli's *Ercole amante* in 1662. During Lent she appeared with other popular singers in concerts at the Église des Feuillants in Paris and elsewhere. The court diarist Loret makes many flattering references to her performances during the last years of the regency. In 1661 La Barre was appointed *fille ordinaire de la musique de chambre du roi*, a prestigious post which she retained until 1686.

La Barre, Michel de (*c*1675–1743/4). The first important French flautist and an innovative composer. La Barre popularized the transverse flute in France at the beginning of the 18th century. In 1702 he published the first suites for flute and continuo which were modelled on those for bass viol and continuo by Marin Marais. They are an important early source of articulation and ornamentation, predating Hotteterre's *Principes* by five years.

In 1704 he joined the Hautbois et Musettes de Poitou of the royal Écurie and in the following year became a flautist in Louis XIV's *musique de chambre*. He appears, with four other court musicians (Marais and the Hotteterres), in a group portrait attributed to Robert Tournières (London, National Gallery; see Plate 6). In 1707 La Barre published the earliest trio sonatas specifically for two flutes and continuo and in 1709 suites for two unaccompanied flutes (a genre he invented). He also composed airs and theatre music.

La Borde [Laborde], Jean-Benjamin-François de (1734–94). Librettist, writer on music and composer whose colourful life was ended by the guillotine. La Borde learnt composition from Rameau and the violin from Antoine Dauvergne. He composed many *opéras-comiques* and six collections of chansons, but is principally remembered as the author of the massive four-volume *Essai sur la musique ancienne et moderne* (1780). The scope of the *Essai* was broad enough to include *trouvère* music in original notation; of particular value today are the biographical entries on 17th- and 18th-century musicians.

La Camargo. See FRANCE 1 *Paris and Versailles*, Cupis de Camargo, Marie-Anne.

La Coste, Louis de (*c*1675–mid 1750s). Singer, opera composer and provincial opera administrator. La Coste began his career as a member of the Paris Opéra chorus. In 1697 his own *opéra-ballet*, *Aricie*, was performed by the Académie and was followed by at least seven *tragédies lyriques*, of which *Philomèle* (1705) and *Créüse* (1712) were the most successful. He and his wife secured a three-year *privilège* to produce operas in Lille but returned to Paris when it expired.

L'Affilard, Michel (*c*1656–1708). Singer, composer and the first to indicate tempos by metronome indications for individual movements. L'Affilard, a singer in the Chapelle Royale from 1683, wrote a treatise on sightsinging, the *Principes très-faciles pour bien apprendre la musique* (1694), which contains *airs de mouvement* based on dance rhythms; it evidently found a wide audience, for it reached 11 editions. The most important edition, the fifth (1705), includes metronomic indications based on Joseph Sauveur's pendulum, breath marks, carefully worked out ornamentation and *notes inégales*, making it a valuable microcosm of French Baroque performing practice.

La Fontaine, Jean de (1621–95). Poet, fabulist and dramatist whose musical intimates included Michel Lambert, Lully and Madame de Sévigné. La Fontaine, at home in the sophisticated company of Molière and Racine, Madame de La Fayette and La Rochefoucauld,

entertained hopes of collaboration with Lully. His *Amours de Psyché et de Cupidon* (1659) inspired the *tragédie-ballet Psyché* devised by Molière and Lully in 1671. When Molière died, La Fontaine wrote *Daphné* (a graceful, lyric *pastorale*) for Lully; when it did not suit Lully's rather grander conception, the disappointed La Fontaine vented his displeasure in a satirical verse entitled *Le florentin* (1674).

Three years later he broadened his criticism of Lully to opera in general in a letter to Pierre de Nyert; for La Fontaine (as well as for Boileau, La Bruyère and Saint-Evremond) graceful sentiments were being obscured by inept verses, coarse voices and ridiculous machinery. Nevertheless, he was persuaded to compose the dedicatory verses for the publication of Lully's *Amadis* (1684) and *Roland* (1685).

La Guerre, Elisabeth-Claude Jacquet de. See FRANCE 1 *Paris and Versailles*, Jacquet de la Guerre, Elisabeth-Claude.

Lalande [Delalande], Michel-Richard de (1657–1726). The most prominent court musician of his day and the leading composer of *grands motets*. Lalande was a Parisian organist and harpsichordist, a contemporary of Marin Marais, the mentor and predecessor of François Couperin at St Gervais and, in effect, Lully's successor at court. Blamont, his pupil and assistant, referred to him as the 'Latin Lully'. Lalande accumulated a great deal of power at court, first as one of the four *sous-maîtres* of the Chapelle Royale (1683), gradually acquiring the other three posts by 1714. In the interim he also collected appointments as *surintendant de la musique de la chambre* (1689), *maître de la chambre* (1695), *maître de la chapelle* (1704) and *compositeur de la musique de chambre* (1709).

He was his parents' 15th child, a gifted chorister and a promising violinist whose ambitions were nipped in the bud by Lully, who refused him a place in the Académie orchestra. His first patron, the Duke of Noailles, helped him to acquire his first royal post – that of music master to the Princesses of the Blood. When in 1684 he married for the first time, the king paid for the wedding. His first wife was Anne-Renée Rebel (1663–1722), sister of Jean-Féry Rebel, by whom he had two musically gifted daughters: Marie-Anne (*b* 1686) and Jeanne (*b* 1687) often sang at the king's Mass before their tragic deaths from smallpox during the epidemic in 1711. His second wife was Marie-Louise de Cury (1692–1775), a viol player by whom he had one daughter Marie-Michelle (1724–81). His many emoluments enabled him to acquire three residences and a private coach. After the death of Louis XIV (1715) he gradually relinquished his posts to pupils and relatives.

Titon du Tillet acknowledged Lalande's contribution to French musical life by according him a medallion (along with Marais and Elisabeth-Claude Jacquet de La Guerre) on his projected monument of Mount Parnassus; only Lully ranked higher. Although he was somewhat at odds with Lully, Lalande would not have gained one of the chapel *sous-maître* posts without Lully's tacit approval. Lully could easily have thwarted the performances at Fontainebleau in 1682 of an operatic entertainment, on which Lalande collaborated with Lorenzani, and again in 1686, when Lalande produced his *Ballet de la jeunesse* (an important precursor of *opéra-ballet*) for the court. Nor was Lalande's role in the clandestine performances of Italian music in Paris held against him, nor – for that matter – the clear influence of Charpentier's rich, italianate, harmonic vocabulary on his music.

Lalande was devoted to Louis XIV, and in his various capacities at Versailles faithfully sought to honour his sovereign, particularly by the *grands motets*, the musical genre he brought to greatest perfection. Of the 70 he composed, 64 survive mainly in three collections (two MSS and one posthumous edition) which give testimony to the endless revision and refinement to which they were subjected. Lalande employed a diversity of elements – *galant* concertante airs, homophonic *petits choeurs* and contrapuntal *grands choeurs* – yet achieved organic music, often thematically related from one section to the next. The *Beati omnes* (1698) was performed with great effect when the Duke of Anjou set off from Versailles in 1700 for Spain where he was to become king. His best-known work, the deeply expressive *De profundis*, was popular at the Concert Spirituel throughout the 18th century.

Lalouette, Jean François (1651–1728). Parisian composer, at one time Lully's lieutenant and at the turn of the century *maître de chapelle* at Notre Dame. Lalouette's early association with Lully augured well for his future, but his failure to achieve lasting fame must be attributed in part to the excesses of pride and indolence. As Lully's pupil he had been entrusted with the composition of the inner parts in the scores of his *tragédies lyriques* and was rewarded with the coveted post of Lully's secretary and one of the *batteurs de mesure*; he threw it away by boasting of having composed

the best music in the controversial *Isis* (1677), leaving himself open as a scapegoat when the opera offended Madame de Montespan. He was hived off to the Savoy court at Turin as their resident composer of French music, but he was dismissed within the year for producing so little. He returned to Paris and set about testing Lully's monopoly by mounting an opera of his own in Paris; hardly had it opened when the authorities closed it down. His failure to gain one of the four royal *sous-maître* posts in 1683 reconfirmed his official disgrace.

Although he is thought to have travelled in Italy and lived for a time in Rome (where he may have composed at least one concerto), his next known post was as choirmaster at Rouen Cathedral (1693–5). Reacceptance into the Parisian musical establishment finally came in 1700, when he succeeded Campra at Notre Dame. He left the post in 1716 but returned two years later, when it had become evident that his *grands motets* were not being performed as he wished, and remained until 1727. In 1726 his *Miserere* was performed at the Concert Spirituel.

Lambert, Michel (1610–96). Singer, lute and theorbo player, teacher and composer of *airs de cour*. Lambert was employed as a singer in the household of Cardinal Richelieu. In 1661 he became *maître de musique de la chambre du roi* and a year later further consolidated his position at court with the marriage of his daughter to Lully, hence the unique privilege of being interred in the same tomb with Lully. Lambert's sister-in-law was Hilaire Dupuy ('Mlle Hilaire'), a court soprano of the stature of Anne de La Barre and Anne Fonteaux de Cercamanan.

Lambert was a prolific composer of airs who gave special attention to the proper declamation of texts by the king's poets Benserade and Quinault. Although most of Lambert's music is lost, approximately 300 airs and nine *leçons de Ténèbres* survive, which richly attest to his skill and grace. Bénigne de Bacilly cited Lambert's airs in his singing treatise of 1668. Abbé Perrin addressed a sonnet to him, Boileau immortalized him in a verse of his third satire, and Lainez wrote a cantata text entitled 'Le tombeau de Lambert'.

La Motte, Antoine Houdar de (1672–1731). Important dramatist and librettist of the post-Lullian period. La Motte made his name in 1697 when he successfully collaborated first with Campra on the *opéra-ballet L'Europe galante* and then with Destouches on the *pastorale-héroïque Issé*. The novelty of his texts lay in their fantasy elements and La Motte's strong preference for the natural over mere imitation of nature. Commissions for *tragédies lyriques* from Destouches, Collasse, Dauvergne and Marais, *opéra-ballets*, and *comédie-ballets* from La Barre, Destouches and Dauvergne followed.

In 1710 La Motte was elected to the Académie Française; thereafter he devoted himself to more serious literary and aesthetic pursuits. His versifications of Old Testament stories were set as cantatas by Elisabeth-Claude Jacquet de La Guerre, Clérambault and Destouches.

Langhedul, Matthijs. See LOW COUNTRIES *2 South Netherlands.*

Lanzetti, Salvatore. See ITALY *1 Piedmont-Savoy.*

La Pouplinière, Alexandre-Jean-Joseph Le Riche de (1693–1762). *Fermier général,* patron of music, art and literature. La Pouplinière's Paris home – across from the present Bibliothèque Nationale – and Passy estate were the scenes of many concerts given by his own orchestra, often under his direction, as well as more intimate performances (1731–53) by the Rameaus and Mondonvilles and their circle. Also present on these occasions were Voltaire and Marmontel, the Van Loos and the La Tours.

Lebègue, Nicolas-Antoine (*c*1631–1702). Laonais harpsichordist, organist, composer and teacher of Nicolas de Grigny. Lebègue arrived in Paris about 1660 and became one of the *organistes du roi* in 1678. He was much in demand as an expert on organs and was a popular composer, judging from the numerous reprints of his collections for harpsichord and organ. His elegantly poised harpsichord pieces bear the influence of Chambonnières and Louis Couperin, and compare well with them, though they are more formal and less personalized. The three volumes of organ music offer virtuoso and lesser players a unique compendium of secular and sacred works.

Le Camus, Sébastien (*c*1610–1677). Treble viol and theorbo player and composer of *airs de cour.* Le Camus began in royal service about 1640; during the regency he served Gaston d'Orléans and from 1660 was one of the new queen's *surintendants de la musique;* the following year he took up half the post (shared with Nicolas Hotman) of viol player to Louis XIV. As a result, he became wealthy and lived very comfortably with a mistress in the Grand Arsenal. Though he did not publish any of his music, his son Charles collected a volume of *airs à deux et trois parties* (settings of poems

by Quinault and others), which he brought out with an important preface in 1678.

Le Cerf de La Viéville, Jean Laurent. See FRANCE *2 Provinces.*

Leclair. Family of violinists and composers from Lyons, of whom the two most distinguished members were brothers who shared the same name. Jean-Marie Leclair *l'aîné* (1697–1764) travelled widely as a virtuoso violinist and was well received wherever he went. At the court of Orange he was decorated with the Croix Néerlandaise du Lion. He was renowned for his ability to play double stops perfectly in tune and with equal assurance in the French and Italian styles – mastery of the latter was gained in Turin after studies with G.B. Somis. In Paris he performed his own sonatas and concertos at the Concert Spirituel and at Versailles he was an *ordinaire* (from 1733), although a quarrel with J.-P. Guignon over the directorship of the court orchestra led him to resign his post after only four years.

Whether in Paris, London, The Hague (where from 1738 until 1743 he spent three months each year, serving as *maître de chapelle* to the wealthy commoner François du Liz from 1740) or Kassel (late in 1728 he performed there with Locatelli), he never lacked for royal and wealthy bourgeois patrons, to judge from the dedications in his published music (engraved, with the exception of op. 1, by his second wife Louise Roussel). Leclair's only opera, *Scylla et Glaucus,* was presented at the Opéra in 1746. His last years were spent in the service of a former pupil, the Duke of Gramont, as director of his private theatre at Puteaux, west of Paris. He was murdered late one evening as he returned home.

Leclair's music presents a successful synthesis of French and Italian styles in which French rhythms and ornamentation are grafted onto Corellian sonatas and Vivaldian concertos. The violin parts require a player of his own calibre – fearless in high positions, dextrous enough to execute double trills and left-hand tremolo (his own invention), and in command of a lightning-quick bow.

Jean-Marie Leclair *le cadet* (1703–77) remained all his life in Lyons, where he became the honoured director of the Académie des Beaux-Arts and 'secretary in perpetuity' of the Lyons Concert. He was known as an excellent player and teacher, if a modest composer.

Lemaire, Louis (1693/4–*c*1750). Prolific composer of small-scale vocal music. Lemaire was a chorister at Meaux Cathedral under Sébastien de Brossard. As a young man he began contributing airs to the Ballard *recueils* in 1712, and in 1724 brought out a popular collection of cantatas, *Les quatre saisons*. Lemaire is best known as a composer of at least 66 *cantatilles* – short but elaborate Rococo cantatas, also cultivated by J.-J. Mouret and L.-A. Lefèbvre – which between 1728 and 1736 were regularly performed at the Concert Français and the Concert Spirituel. His motets, which began appearing about 1728, were also sung at the Concert Spirituel during the late 1720s and early 30s. He also composed chamber music for combinations of strings (including hurdy-gurdy), wind (including trumpet and musette) and percussion instruments (1743).

Le Rochois, Marthe (*c*1658–1728). Dramatic soprano and teacher who from 1678 to 1698 was the *première actrice* of the Académie Royale de Musique, appearing in the original productions of Lully's *Proserpine*, *Persée*, *Amadis*, *Roland* and *Armide*. Her remarkable acting and, in particular, her declamation were noted by Le Cerf de La Viéville. Titon du Tillet praised her sense of gesture, her mastery of pantomime and, above all, her good taste. Her performances greatly influenced the next generation of opera singers.

Le Roux, Gaspard (*d* 1705/7). Parisian harpsichordist and composer of a collection of harpsichord pieces (1705), which were published in a format adaptable to performances by a trio, a single melody instrument with keyboard, or two keyboard instruments.

Lorenzani, Paolo (1640–1713). Roman composer, resident for 16 years in Paris, where he was instrumental in popularizing Italian music at a time when Lully reigned supreme. Lorenzani was trained by Orazio Benevoli at the Cappella Giulia in the Vatican, where, at the age of 55, he succeeded Francesco Beretta as *maestro di cappella*. But it is his years in Paris, 1678–94, that are chiefly of interest. In 1678 one of his motets was performed by Louis XIV, who expressed his approval by installing Lorenzani as *surintendant de la musique de la reyne*. However, even with the added support of the *Mercure galant* and the patronage of Madame de Montespan's brother and Mazarin's nephew, Lorenzani never gained sufficient popularity to challenge Lully.

For his part, Lully attempted to block the performance of Lorenzani's Italian pastoral *Nicandro e Fileno* at Fontainebleau in the autumn of 1681 and, in spite of his continuing opposition, a *sérénade en forme d'opéra*, to which Lorenzani contributed Italian music

and Lalande French music, was performed there a year later. Lully's interference may have been a decisive factor in Lorenzani's failure to gain one of the four coveted positions as *sous-maître de la chapelle royale* in 1683. That, together with the death of the queen, signalled his decline in court circles. In Paris he found employment as *maître de chapelle* of the Theatine convent, directing performances of *saluts en musique* attended by italophile aristocrats and musicians alike. His French opera *Orontée*, presented by the Académie Royale de Musique in 1688, a year after Lully's death, attracted little interest; likewise his lavish 1693 edition of motets dedicated to Louis XIV.

Louis XIII (1601–43). King of France (the son of Henri IV and Maria de' Medici), music patron, composer and dancer. Only nine years old when his father was assassinated (1610), Louis XIII did not rule until 1614, and then only with the assistance of powerful ministers such as the Duke of Luynes (1617–21) and Cardinal Richelieu (1624–42). In 1615 he was married to the Spanish Infanta (Anne of Austria), though it was not until 1638 that their son, the future Louis XIV, was born.

Louis XIII inherited his father's music establishment of 30 chapel musicians and the Vingt-quatre Violons du Roi, which were augmented on special occasions such as the carousel of 1612 (requiring 100 trumpets) and his return from Brittany in 1614 (for which Jacques Mauduit organized mass concerts of voices and instruments). Louis XIII loved dance music and solo airs with lute accompaniment (*airs de cour*); and, with the encouragement of Richelieu, both forms of cultural amusement became important parts of daily court life.

Deeply religious, Louis XIII is said to have kept up his spirits during the siege of La Rochelle in 1628 by composing motets. He knew how to set psalms and occasionally conducted his chapel choir. In 1635 he personally took charge of the creation of a court entertainment, composing both text and music and choreographing the *Ballet de la Merlaison* for performances at his château at Chantilly. The following year Mersenne published a royal air ('Tu crois, o beau soleil'), in a keyboard arrangement, in *Harmonie Universelle*.

Louis XIV (1638–1715). King of France (the son of Louis XIII and Anne of Austria), music patron, instrumentalist and dancer. Louis XIV grew up amidst political turmoil, presided over by his mother and Cardinal Jules Mazarin (1643–61). During his minority he was forced to flee Paris three times (when the Princes of the Blood and lesser nobility temporarily gained the upper hand), and made absolutism the cornerstone of his reign (which began officially after the death of Mazarin – 'L'état, c'est moi'), excluding the ambitious aristocracy from high office in his government. In 1660 he married the Spanish Infanta, Maria Teresa (daughter of Philip IV), by whom he had six children of whom only the dauphin survived; in about 1683 he secretly married Madame de Maintenon, the former governess of his bastard children. As king, Louis XIV not only consolidated his power within France, he made France the leading European power during the late 17th century through a series of aggressive wars.

During his reign French culture – music and the arts – became (with that of the Italians) greatly admired and imitated throughout Europe. As a young man, Louis XIV was an excellent dancer and took part in many of the lavish *ballets de cour* performed at his palaces and châteaux between 1650 and 1670; he played the guitar and was particularly fond of performances of keyboard music. He surrounded himself with fine musicians, foreign as well as French, among whom Lully gained his confidence and with it high office and fabulous wealth. Together, the king and his Florentine musician created French opera (*tragédie lyrique*), which served not only as a cultural symbol of France but also as a domestic political tool to distract the aristocracy. The *grand motet*, a genre to which Lully contributed significantly, came to symbolize Louis XIV's religious authority. With the king's support Lully raised the standards of French orchestral playing and those of court music in general. Music accompanied every event in the king's life, from the mundane to the ceremonial, and accordingly he augmented his music establishment to unprecedented proportions, at the same time institutionalizing it by an elaborate hierarchy of posts and privileges. The king established academies in all branches of the arts – including music (1669) and dance (1661) – and greatly encouraged the development of distinctly French styles of performance.

Loulié, Étienne (*c*1655–*c*1707). Parisian *maître de musique*, theorist, and inventor of the *sonomètre* (1699), for tuning keyboard instruments, and the *chronomètre* (1701), a metronomic pendulum. Loulié held no court or church appointments but like M.-A. Charpentier he was a member of the Duchess of Guise's household. He published three theor-

etical treatises and bequeathed a number of manuscript works – including an important treatise on viol playing, with particular reference to bow strokes – to his friend Sébastien de Brossard.

Lully [Lulli], Jean-Baptiste [Giovanni Battista] (1632–87). Phenomenally successful Italian composer, naturalized French, the creator of *tragédie lyrique* and an important contributor to the *grand motet*: the most powerful exponent of the French Baroque style. In 1646 the young Lully accompanied the Chevalier de Guise from Florence to Paris, where he was made a *garçon de chambre* to the chevalier's niece, Mlle de Montpensier. He spent six years in her service at the Tuileries palace, during which time he mastered several instruments, including the violin and harpsichord, and studied composition with Nicolas Métru. As a member of a noble household, he gained entry to *divertissements*, balls and other court *spectacles*, from which he learnt the popular French dances and heard the Vingt-quatre Violons du Roi and the finest singers of the day perform. He heard Racine declaimed and, in 1647, attended Luigi Rossi's *Orfeo*, lavishly produced at the Louvre.

1653 marked the beginning of his rise at court. Already known to the young Louis XIV as a dancer – they danced together in the *Ballet de la nuit* in February of that year – Lully succeeded the Italian violinist Lazzarini as *compositeur de la musique instrumentale du roi*, charged with composing *ballets de cour*. Cardinal Mazarin thrust him into prominence by engaging him to compose ballet *intermèdes* to monarchist texts by Isaac de Benserade for the 1654 production of Caproli's comic opera *Le nozze di Peleo e di Teti*. His ballet music was much admired by Loret, the court journalist, and Racine declared the music of the *Ballet de l'Impatience* (1661) to be 'on the path to the heart'. Lully's *intermèdes* for Cavalli's *Xerse* (1660) and *Ercole amante* (1662) succeeded in overwhelming the Italian operas they were meant to complement.

A gifted comedian, as well as musician and dancer, Lully joined with Molière to produce a series of *comédie-ballets* which were performed at the royal châteaux and in Paris, beginning with *Le mariage forcé* (1664) and ending with *Le bourgeois gentilhomme* (1670). Lully contributed what were ultimately miniature operas, interrelated and interleaved with the acts of Molière's satirical comedies, and just as Lully's ballet *intermèdes* usurped the place of Italian opera, so too, gradually, did his operatic *intermèdes* command the prominence originally accorded to the plays. This was especially the case in the *grands divertissements royaux*, *George Dandin* (1668) and *Les amants magnifiques* (1670). But whereas the sharp satire of Molière's comedies often trod dangerously near royal toes, Lully created an entertainment uniquely suited to the sycophantic taste of the French court (see Plate 4).

When in 1672 Pierre Perrin failed in his efforts to establish financially secure *académies d'opéra*, Lully stepped in with royal backing and bought him out. A series of highly restrictive royal patents enabled him to gain a monopoly on the use of music on the French stage. The king granted him the right to produce for the Parisian public the works first presented before him, the right to charge admission (even to titled persons and royal household officers) and the ownership of his airs (the right to publish them). Lully also persuaded the king to issue an ordinance limiting the number of singers and instrumentalists that could perform with other Parisian theatre troupes. Molière was the first to suffer, and upon his death a year later Lully took over his theatre at the Palais Royal, unceremoniously turning out his troupe (the future Comédie Française).

By that time Lully was already collaborating with Philippe Quinault in producing *tragédies lyriques* on a grand scale, employing the machinist and architect Carlo Vigarani and the *maître de danse* Pierre de Beauchamp. The king provided him with 3,000 *livres* to convert Molière's theatre into the Académie Royale de Musique. From 1673 until his death (excepting only 1679 and 1681) Lully and Quinault produced an opera every year. Le Cerf describes in detail their working methods and the autocratic manner in which Lully governed every aspect of the Académie. Strict discipline meted out to the orchestra was equally applied to the singers and technicians. The Académie was efficiently and profitably run. Lully was the first to benefit and, being a shrewd businessman, he made the most of his wealth, investing it and diversifying. The king granted him letters of nobility, and in 1681 Lully triumphantly acquired one of the coveted offices of *secrétaire du roi*.

Tragédie lyrique grew logically out of *ballet de cour* and *comédie-ballet* (though Lully stopped incorporating comic scenes after his third opera, *Thésée* (1675). Armed with the lessons of these genres, he set out to create a musical counterpart to the great spoken tragedies of his day. He adhered to as many of the unities of French drama as possible. Proper

declamation of text was placed above all musical considerations, recitatives were by necessity multimetrical and choral textures universally homophonic. As in all other performances in which Lully had a hand, precision of instrumental and vocal ensembles was *de rigueur*.

Operas were preceded by prologues, which are in fact allegorical newsreels, interpreting events of the reign, while the operas themselves make contemporary analogies, following the tradition of the *ballets de cour*. Moral attitudes are proffered in dialogues such as that between Love and Glory in *Alceste* (1674); in the prologue to *Proserpine* (1680) Discord is violently plunged into an abyss. While the king was always symbolized by the heroic characters, his mistress Mme de Montespan fared less well: Quinault was given mandatory leave after unflatteringly portraying her as the jealous Juno in *Isis* (1677). Never at a loss, Lully arranged to collaborate with Thomas Corneille and Fontenelle on his very successful *tragédie lyrique*, *Bellérophon* (1679). In due course Lully requested that Quinault be reinstated, and it was as much a mark of the royal favour in which Lully was held as indicative of the declining power of the lady (who was shortly to be permanently displaced by Mme de Maintenon) that Quinault regained his post and dared to satirize Mme de Montespan again in *Proserpine* and *Persée* (1682).

Lully capitalized upon the technical resources of the Académie to create moments of great spectacle: military battles in *Cadmus et Hermione* (1673), *Thésée* (1675), *Bellérophon* and *Amadis* (1684); the funeral cortèges of *Alceste* (1674), *Psyché* (1678) and *Amadis*; the wedding *divertissement* of *Roland* (1685); and magical transformations, such as in *Phaéton* (1683), when Neptune turns into a lion after emerging from the sea, and the apparition of the ghost in *Amadis*. Just as memorable are the powerful monologues of *Atys* (1676) and *Armide* (1686), which depended upon the superlative acting of such singers as Marthe Le Rochois.

Lully's success was deeply resented in many quarters. He was the object of bitter satire (in verse, song and theatrical parody) and embarrassing innuendo about his homosexual activities. Some of his critics were incensed that an Italian should have gained such a powerful position and then been extolled as the father of French music. Others, suffering under his oppressive restrictions, despaired of gaining opportunities to compose and have stage music performed. The *Mercure galant* decried the fact that Parisians were offered but one opera each year. So tight was his grip, so self-serving his outlook that, after his death in 1687 from gangrene, his successors were ill-prepared to assume his mantle. That vacuum in turn created an artistic crisis that would not be fully resolved until Rameau produced *Hippolyte et Aricie* in 1733. In the interim, the flamboyant Italian style Lully had sought to ban from court music gained a foothold in sacred and chamber music genres, while his operas continued to dominate the Académie offerings to the extent that new works, however well tailored to Lully's pattern, were poorly received.

Although never associated with the Chapelle Royale, Lully took pains to become a dominating force there, especially after the king's marriage to the pious Mme de Maintenon in 1683. It was he who proposed the 1683 competition to determine the four *sous-maîtres* of the Chapelle Royale and then very probably influenced the outcome by impeding the candidature of Paolo Lorenzani and Charpentier. Lully's own *grands motets* were included with those of Henry Du Mont and Pierre Robert in a sumptuous folio edition, printed by royal command, 1684–6. The *Miserere mei Deus* (1664) was a particular favourite of the king's. Lully's *petits motets* were composed for a Paris convent. Early in 1687 he fatally injured himself while conducting a *Te Deum* in celebration of the king's recovery from illness.

In all his major works Lully sought to gain royal approbation through flattery on the grandest scale. The predilections of the king were catered for, his views on subjects carefully incorporated, the events of his reign presented in a favourable light, his own person endlessly allegorized, his wisdom and mercy equated with that of God. The precision with which music and dance were executed, the sumptuousness of the productions – the lavish sets, ingenious machinery and exquisite costumes – and the large vocal and orchestral forces (*petits* and *grands choeurs*) employed were unfeasible elsewhere in Europe and thus the envy of every court. The import of the text always took precedence over the music. The tone of the texts, particularly those by Benserade and Quinault, was carefully struck to maximize the panegyric effect of a ballet or an opera. Similarly, the texts of the *grands motets* reinforced the image of French royal absolutism.

No Lully autograph manuscripts have been authenticated, although many manuscripts date from his lifetime and just after. He was the first French musician to be formally eulogized (by Charles Perrault) and was a pivotal figure in Titon du Tillet's 'Le Parnasse Francois' (1727–60). Many French composers wrote *tombeaux* in his memory; in Couperin's programmatic *Concert instrumental sous le titre d'Apothéose composé à la mémoire immortelle de l'incomparable Monsieur de Lully* (1725) listeners follow Lully's ascent to Parnassus and his meeting with Corelli, after which a reconciliation of French and Italian styles is effected.

Madonis, Luigi. See ITALY *4 Venice.*

Marais, Marin (1656–1728). Bass viol player at court, composer and teacher who brought solo viol playing to its most idiomatic and refined state. Marais reached the highest ranks of the *musique de chambre* and was warmly treated by the king. Titon du Tillet compiled his biography, including many intimate and charming anecdotes, and accorded him a medallion on his 'Parnasse François'. As a young man Marais had gained the attention of Lully, under whom he served as an apprentice and conductor of the Académie before producing four of his own *tragédies lyriques. Alcyone* (1706) – because of its effective tempest scene – was particularly influential and merited four revivals in the course of the 18th century.

Marais was an immaculate and expressive player who understood his instrument well. He brought a degree of precision to the notation of his more than 500 *pièces de violes* – replete with fingering, bowing and ornamentation – that set a standard for all viol players. His approach to the instrument is discussed at length in Jean Rousseau's *Traité de la viole* (1687) and in Hubert Le Blanc's polemical *Défense de la basse de viole* (1740). In 1686 he became the first in France to publish *pièces* for viol and continuo and in 1692 the first to publish *pièces en trio*. He published five books of *pièces de violes* in all, including works for two and three viols. In addition to dance movements grouped in suites, they contain *tombeaux* (for his mentors Meliton, Lully and Sainte-Colombe), *plaintes* and a rich variety of *pièces de caractère*: variations on 'La Folia' (1701), an evocation of *La guitare* (1711), an amusing *Suite d'un goût étranger* (1717) and the outlandish *Tableau de l'opération de la taille* (1725). In 1723 he published a collection of three extended chamber works for violin, bass viol and continuo.

His style of playing and composition sharply contrasted with that of his younger contemporary Antoine Forqueray. Le Blanc likened them to an angel and a devil. Both were acknowledged virtuosos: Marais perfected the French style – miniaturist and refined – while Forqueray cultivated a brashly emotional italianate style. Both served Louis XIV and for a time were associated with the Elector of Bavaria while he was governor of the Spanish Netherlands. However, one belonged to the old guard, the other to the *avant-garde*.

Several of Marais' 19 children became accomplished viol players: Roland (*b* 1680) was a member of the Académie orchestra and published two collections of *pièces de violes* (1735, 1738); Vincent succeeded his father at court. In addition to the likeness on the medallion reproduced in Titon du Tillet's *Le Parnasse François* (1732), Marais' portrait was painted and later engraved by André Boüys; he is also among the musicians in the well-known group portrait by Robert Tournières (London, National Gallery; see Plate 6).

Marazzoli, Marco. See ITALY 7 *Papal States: Rome.*

Marchand, Louis (1669–1732). Virtuoso harpsichordist and organist. Marchand took Paris by storm when he arrived from Lyons. His prowess as an organist quickly brought him posts in a succession of churches, where his playing always assured a large crowd. He served briefly as an *organiste du roi*, resigning in 1713 in order to tour abroad. On tour in Germany in 1717 he abruptly quit Dresden to avoid taking part in a competition with J.S. Bach. At home his playing was praised by Rameau, Titon du Tillet and D'Aquin de Château-Lyon. But he was (by several accounts) a difficult person – unreliable, violent and maledictory. Of his small musical legacy (which included a few airs and cantatas), only two harpsichord suites (1702) were published.

Mascitti, Michele (1663/4–1760). Neapolitan violinist and composer who worked in France. Mascitti travelled extensively in Europe before settling in 1704 in Paris, where he quickly established himself as an exponent of the Corellian style and accordingly was offered and accepted a place among the distinguished musicians employed by the italophile Duke of Orléans. He wasted little time in issuing his first collection of chamber music (1704), which he followed at greater leisure with a further eight collections of duo and trio sonatas and concertos (the string concertos of 1727 were the first to be published by a composer in

France); several were reprinted many times in the Low Countries and England. He was a popular figure about Paris and was known by his Christian name. After the duke's death he became associated with the Crozats, a prominent bourgeois Parisian family, and lived at the home of Pierre Crozat, a powerful financier well known as a champion of Italian music. Mascitti was naturalized in 1739 and the following year chose to marry and retire.

Masson, Charles (*fl* 1680–1700). Church musician and the author of the most important treatise on composition before Rameau, the *Nouveau traité* (1694); in it he illustrated major and minor modes, vocal counterpoint and the role of figured bass in accompaniment, with examples from Lully.

Matho, Jean-Baptiste (*c*1660–1746). Singer and *maître de musique* at court, and the only notable Breton composer of the era. Matho held royal posts from 1684 and although he was a skilful composer of ballets and *divertissements* his only opera, *Arion* (1714), failed. In 1734 he and J.-N.-P. Royer were jointly made *maître de musique des enfans de France*.

Mauduit, Jacques (1557–1627). The last surviving member of Baïf's Académie de Poésie et de Musique, a composer of *musique mesurée* and the leading conductor of his day, responsible for introducing the viol consort in France. According to Mersenne, Mauduit was an aristocrat, well educated in languages though self-taught in music, who held a court post as *secrétaire du roi*. During the Siege of Paris in 1589 and 1590 he played a vital role in protecting the interests of the Académie and later organized their concerts and meetings. He published very little of his music, which included four-voice *chansonettes mesurées*, airs, *psaumes mesurés* and instrumental fantasias. He composed an *ode mesurée* to celebrate Louis XIII's return from Brittany in 1614, requiring the services of 135 singers, lutenists and viol players. Three years later he conducted *La délivrance de Renaud*, a ballet with music by Mauduit, Pierre Guédron, his son-in-law Antoine de Boësset and Gabriel Bataille which was performed by 92 singers and 45 instrumentalists.

Maugars, André (*c*1580–*c*1645). Viol player, ecclesiastic and diplomat whose 'Response faite à un curieux sur le sentiment de la musique d'Italie', written from Rome in October 1639, became the first in a long series of written comparisons between performing practices in Italy and France. Earlier in his career Maugars spent four years at the court of James I, where he came into contact with the great viol player Alfonso Ferrabosco the elder. Upon his return to Paris Maugars capitalized on his command of English by taking up a post as interpreter under Cardinal Richelieu and publishing in 1624 a French translation of Francis Bacon's *Advancement of Learning* (1605). He left the French court in 1630 to become prior of St Pierre Eynac, near Puy, where he continued to translate the works of Bacon. In spite of Maugars' absence from Paris, Mersenne praised his viol playing in his *Harmonicorum libri* (which appeared in 1635). By 1638 Maugars was in Rome, where he met and heard the finest Italian musicians of the day.

Maupin (1670–1707). Soprano and *comédienne*, the daughter of Sieur d'Aubigny (secretary to the Count of Armagnac). She sang in the revivals of Lully operas, as well as new productions with music by Collasse, Destouches and Campra, presented in Paris and at Versailles by the Académie Royale de Musique between 1690 and 1705. Maupin's most important roles include Medea in Bouvard's *Médus, Roi des Mèdes* (1702), in which she replaced Mlle Desmatins at short notice, and Clorinda in Campra's *Tancrède* (1702), which he is said to have composed specially for her.

Renowned for her beauty as well as her voice (the Marquis of Dangeau swore she had the most beautiful voice in the world), Maupin led a colourful life as both the mistress of men such as the Elector of Bavaria and a lesbian who was fond of dressing as a man and duelling – a sport which she pursued with skill and nerve, leaving at least three men dead. Following an unsuccessful love affair with the soprano Fanchon Moreau, Maupin attempted suicide; then, after her performances in Michel de La Barre's *La vénitienne* (1705), she apparently retired to Provence with her husband.

Mauro. See ITALY *4 Venice*.

Mazarin, Cardinal **Jules** [Mazzarini, Giulio Raimondo] (1602–61). Italian cardinal who became a naturalized French citizen and the first minister during the regency of Anne of Austria; in that capacity he attempted to establish Italian opera in France. Mazarin arrived in Paris in 1634, carrying the portfolio of papal nuncio, and stayed on to assist Cardinal Richelieu in his capacity as first minister. Mazarin developed a close relationship with the queen, and when Louis XIII died he effectively took over the reins of state.

Wealthy, his power assured, he set about establishing Italian opera in 1643 by importing the most prestigious Italians: first the composer Marco Marazzoli, then the soprano Leonora Baroni and the castrato Atto Melani, the machinist Giacomo Torelli and the composer Luigi Rossi. The glittering 1647 production of Rossi's *Orfeo* gave Mazarin's jealous opponents in Parlement the opening they needed to foment rebellion. In satirical *mazarinades* they insinuated that the excesses of a single opera production contributed to the admittedly poor state of the French economy. Within a year not only were the Italians banished, but the young Louis XIV, the regent and her chief minister were forced to seek exile in the suburbs of Paris. No sooner had Mazarin regained control of the government in 1653 than plans for a production of Caproli's *Le nozze di Peleo et di Teti* (1654) were under way. But, in spite of the French ballets inserted between the opera's acts, Caproli's production failed to change public opinion.

Mazarin's final efforts were lavished on the 1660 wedding celebrations for Louis XIV. From Cavalli, the most famous opera composer of the day, he commissioned *Ercole amante*, though neither the opera nor the *théâtre des machines* was ready on time. Instead, Cavalli's *Xerse* was performed, and *Ercole amante*, replete with ballets by Lully, was given later (1662), though too late for the cardinal's own pleasure.

Melani. See ITALY *10 Itinerant Musicians*.

Ménestrier, Claude-François (1631–1705). Jesuit and author of *Des représentations en musique anciennes et modernes* (1681). In the late 1660s the Lyons-born Ménestrier travelled to Italy, Germany, the Low Countries and England, before settling in Paris. In *Des représentations* and his other writings on ballet and the history of ceremonies and public festivals, he gives detailed descriptions of performances of Italian operas and French ballets, as well as of the use of music at tournaments, carousels and other public spectacles.

Mersenne, Marin (1588–1648). Well-travelled priest, mathematician, music theorist and important French writer. Though not a practical musician, Mersenne applied his skill in mathematics and physics to music. Of his 24 published works six are devoted entirely or mainly to music. *Harmonie Universelle* (1636–7) is best known to musicians for its classification of instruments. He contributed most to the study of acoustics, defining the nature of sound, observing vibrating strings and columns, and formulating theories regarding partial harmonics, echo and resonance. He wrote on the nature of consonance and dissonance, and on tuning and temperament, and voiced opinions on national styles of performance and pedagogical techniques.

Minoret, Guillaume (*c*1650–1717). Parisian *maître de musique* and composer of motets. Minoret served at Orléans Cathedral before taking up a post at St Germain l'Auxerrois in Paris in 1679. In 1683 Minoret was among the four winners of the *sous-maîtres* competition held by Louis XIV. He retired from royal service in 1714, having exerted a much more modest influence than his more forward-looking colleague Lalande.

Molière [Poquelin, Jean-Baptiste] (1622–73). Brilliant actor and playwright who collaborated on *comédie-ballets* with Lully and Charpentier. Lully attached himself to Molière soon after Mazarin's death (1661), aware that such an association with an actor so popular at court could further his own prospects. For Molière's part, the addition of music and ballet – so close to the king's heart – could only enhance his comedies, especially if they could be interrelated. In the beginning, drama took precedence over music and dance, as in *Le mariage forcé* and *La princesse d'Élide*, produced for the outdoor festivities at Versailles in 1664. As time went on the collaboration equalized, foreshadowing the *opéra comique* of a century later. But the ambitious Lully gradually contrived to extend the *intermèdes* until they overpowered the drama, as seen in *Les amants magnifiques* and *Le bourgeois gentilhomme* (1670).

Their last joint production, *Psyché* (1671), a *tragédie-ballet*, became for Lully a draft for the 1678 *tragédie lyrique* of the same name, on which occasion he collaborated with Thomas Corneille and Fontenelle. His own status assured, Lully terminated the collaboration with Molière and, playing upon his greater influence with the king, gradually made it impossible for Molière to carry on as before. Molière turned to Charpentier: together they revised three of the old *comédie-ballets* to conform with the new restrictions and then collaborated on *Le malade imaginaire* (1673), in which Molière played the title role; during the fourth performance he ruptured a blood vessel in a fit of coughing and died.

Mollier [Molière], **Louis de** (*c*1615–1688). Court dancer, poet (contemporary with the dramatist Molière), lutenist, lute teacher and composer. Mollier became attached to the court in 1644 as a lutenist and dancer. He accompanied singers in both the chapel and the chamber and taught Louis XIV; he danced alongside Lully and the young king in almost every *ballet de cour* performed between 1644 and 1665. He wrote texts and music for at least four ballets and the music for two operas (now lost) – *Les amours de Céphale et d'Aurore* (1677) and *Andromède* (1678) – before he (like the other Molière) was squeezed out by Lully's monopoly. The *Mercure galant* (November 1678) carried a review of the performance of *Andromède* (in which the young Elisabeth-Claude Jacquet [de la Guerre] accompanied on the harpsichord), mentioning that places at a series of concerts *chez* Mollier were much in demand. His daughter Marie-Blanche (1644–1733) was a famous court singer and dancer.

Mondonville, Jean-Joseph Cassanéa de (1711–72). Languedoc violinist, composer and conductor. Like Campra before him, Mondonville successfully pursued careers in sacred and secular music, at Versailles and in Paris. From 1734 he was much in demand as a violinist at the Concert Spirituel, where he performed alone and with Michel Blavet, Jean-Pierre Guignon and Marie Fel; in 1739 he delighted audiences with sonatas appropriately entitled *Les sons harmoniques* (1738). He became part of the circle around La Pouplinière where he met his wife, the gifted harpsichordist Anne-Jeanne Boucon (once a pupil of Rameau). At court he quickly rose from posts as violinist of the chapel and chamber to *sous-maître* in 1740 and, four years later, *intendant*.

Simultaneously Mondonville was making his way as a composer and conductor. He published collections for accompanied harpsichord – the *sonates* with violin (1734) and the *Pièces de clavecin avec voix ou violon* (1748) – which are his best-known music today. He led the opera orchestra at the Concert de Lille (from late 1734 until 1737). He composed *grands motets* for the Concert Spirituel and operas for the Académie in Paris and Mme de Pompadour's Théâtre des Petits-Cabinets at Versailles. Among his *grands motets*, the *Jubilate Deo* (1734), *Venite exultemus* and *Nisi Dominus* (both 1743) were performed annually over several decades. Mondonville's most popular theatre pieces for the Opéra were his *ballet-héroïque*, *Le Carnaval du Parnasse* (1749), and opera *Titon et l'Aurore* (1753). The libretto for his opera *Daphnis et Alcimadure* (1754) incorporates Gascon dialect.

Montéclair, Michel Pignolet de (1667–1737). Versatile musician, composer, theorist and teacher. Montéclair belonged to the generation of composers active during the period between Lully and Rameau. In the early 1690s he travelled to Italy, returning to Paris by 1695 when he published the cantata-like *Adieu de Tircis à Climène* in the October issue of Ballard's *Recueil d'airs sérieux et à boire*.

With Giuseppe Fedeli he is credited with the introduction of the double bass into the Académie Royale de Musique (*c*1701). Montéclair held a post as *basse de violon* in the *petit choeur* of the opera orchestra from 1699 to 1737. During that time he produced three books of imaginatively crafted cantatas, an important *opéra-ballet*, *Les festes d'été* (1716), and an opera, *Jephté* (1732), as well as several important treatises. His *Méthode facile pour apprendre à jouer du violon* (1711–12) was the first of its kind to be published in France, and his *Principes de musique* (1736) is one of the most important sources of French vocal ornamentation of the early 18th century. He taught the daughters of Couperin and carried on a debate (1729–30) with Rameau in the pages of the *Mercure de France*. The music shop he founded in Paris with his nephew François Boivin became an important outlet for chamber music.

Moreau, Jean-Baptiste (1656–1733). Composer, author of a lost treatise (*L'art mélodique*) and teacher; he taught composition to Montéclair, Clérambault and Dandrieu and singing to his daughter Marie-Claude, Marguerite-Louise Couperin and the Dandrieu daughters. Moreau came to Paris after holding posts as *maître de musique* at the cathedrals of Langres and Dijon. Eager to become known at court, he composed a *Te Deum* and got it performed in 1687 to celebrate the recovery of the king from illness. He further resorted to just the sort of audacious behaviour (a minor act of impropriety towards a lady of the court) for which Louis XIV used to reward Lully – to the astonishment of the court musicians and members of the court such as Titon du Tillet, who considered him little more than a country bumpkin.

Moreau's prize was a commission to compose, at rather short notice, a *divertissement* entitled *Les bergers de Marly*, in 1687. Racine took a liking to him and collaborated on *Esther* (1689) and *Athalie* (1691) for the girls at St Cyr; Moreau was also one of those who set Racine's *Cantiques spirituelles* (1695). But by the time the *Cantiques* had appeared Moreau was already in disgrace, having incurred the disapproval of Mme de Maintenon by composing a *divertissement*, *Zaïre*, around the licentious verses of Laînez. He was banished to Languedoc as the *surintendant de*

musique, though he soon sold the benefice and returned to Paris a wealthy man. Thereafter he confined himself to teaching at St Sulpice.

Morin, Jean-Baptiste (1677–1754). Composer of cantatas. Morin was one of a group of composers, among them J.-B. Stuck and Campra, in the service of the italophile Duke of Orléans at the turn of the century. In 1706 he became the first to publish a collection of cantatas; he subsequently published two more (1707, 1712), in which he consciously combined French melodies with Italian harmonic and rhythmic vitality to create his own synthesis of the two styles.

Moulinié, Étienne (*c*1600–after 1669). Languedoc composer who in 1628 became the *maître de musique* of Louis XIII's brother, Gaston of Orléans. Moulinié served the duke until his death in 1660, when he returned to Languedoc. During his tenure in Paris he composed motets, *airs de cour* (sometimes using Italian and even Spanish texts), ballet music and *pièces d'occasion*.

Mouret, Jean-Joseph (1682–1738). Provençal singer who became the most popular composer of the regency and known posthumously as the 'musicien des grâces'. Within a short time of arriving in Paris from Avignon in 1707 Mouret showed himself to be not only a gifted composer but also an able administrator. The Duchess of Maine made him *surintendant* of music at Sceaux, where he was responsible for the musical contributions to the 16 élite 'Grandes Nuits' of 1714–15. Mouret's *Le mariage de Ragonde et de Colin* (1714; text by Néricault Destouches) broke new ground as the first true lyric comedy, over 30 years before Rameau's *Platée*.

Also in 1714 he became formally associated with the Académie Royale de Musique as a conductor and composer; his *tragédies lyriques* failed miserably, while his *ballet-héroïques* – including *Les amours des Dieux* (1727; text by Fuzelier), in which La Camargo danced a much acclaimed solo, and *Le triomphe des sens* (1732; text by Roy) – succeeded brilliantly. In 1717 Mouret began a 20-year stint with the Nouveau Théâtre Italien at the Palais Royal as a prolific composer of *divertissements*, which were published in six volumes. He also contributed *divertissements* to the Théâtre Français.

Mouret secured a place at court by acquiring the post of chamber singer in 1720 and, upon the accession of Louis XV in 1722, provided the music for the elaborate entertainment – an idealization of the fair theatres – hosted by the regent at his Château de Villers-

Cotterets. In 1728 Mouret was appointed artistic director of the Concert Spirituel, which provided a venue for the performance of his motets, cantatas, *cantatilles* and *suites de symphonies*. Disappointments in the late 1730s led to his insanity and, in 1738, his death.

Nivers, Guillaume Gabriel (*d* 1714). Important Parisian organist and influential composer and theorist. Nivers served throughout his career as organist at St Sulpice, gradually acquiring a series of court appointments as one of the four organists of the Chapelle Royale (1678), *maître de musique* to the queen (1681) and director of music at St Cyr (1696). He published three collections of organ *versets*, comprehending all the French styles and forms of the day, as well as two collections of motets. Unusual for the time was his keen interest in Gregorian chant; he edited several collections and produced two treatises on the subject. His *Traité de la composition de musique* (1667) was widely circulated.

Normand, Marc-Roger. See ITALY *1* Piedmont-Savoy [Normand, Marco Roggero].

Nyert, Pierre de (*c*1597–1682). Nobleman whose interest in the Italian dramatic vocal style helped to establish it in Paris. A fine singer himself, Nyert travelled in 1633 to Rome, where he was much taken with the operas he heard at the Barberini palace. Returning to Paris as *valet* to the king, he performed in *ballets de cour* and had an influence on Bénigne de Bacilly, the major writer on 17th-century French singing.

Opitz, Martin. See NORTHERN EUROPE *7* Itinerant Musicians.

Ouvrard, René (1624–94). Provincial ecclesiastic, composer and theorist, whose interests ranged widely beyond theology and music to the arts and sciences. He travelled to Italy in 1655 and, in Rome, came into contact with Carissimi, whose music he admired above that of all others. Originally from near Tours, Ouvrard was appointed *maître de musique* at the Sainte Chapelle in 1663 after having held appointments at Bordeaux Cathedral (1657) and St Just Cathedral, Narbonne (1660).

In Paris Ouvrard frequented the music circles where Italian music was performed and amassed a large collection of Italian music, which he freely lent. His pupils at the Sainte Chapelle included the theorist Étienne Loulié; he would have known and admired Charpentier, who had probably studied in Rome with Carissimi in the mid 1660s. Although his own music is lost, his writings have survived. *Secret pour composer en musique* appeared in 1658 under a pseudonym (Du Reneau), and

two further treatises were published in the late 1670s. Between 1663 and 1693 he carried on an important correspondence with a fellow ecclesiastic and italophile, Claude Nicaise (1623–1701), canon of the Sainte Chapelle, Dijon. In 1679 he returned to Tours as canon of St Gatien.

Pasqualini, Marc'Antonio. See BRITISH ISLES *1* London.

Pécour, Louis Guillaume (?1651–1729). Gifted dancer, ballet master and choreographer who succeeded Pierre de Beauchamp as ballet master of the Académie Royale de Musique in 1687. Of his choreographies 114 survive – 46 social dances and 68 theatre dances.

Pellegrin, Simon-Joseph (1663–1745). Monk, who as an almoner sailed twice with the French fleet to the orient; poet, dramatist and librettist to most of the composers of dramatic music during the first half of the 18th century. Thanks to the intervention of Mme de Maintenon, Pellegrin was granted a papal dispensation which made it possible for him to live at the Cluny monastery and work in Paris fulfilling commissions for comedies and tragedies. In gratitude he versified Bible texts, which were sung to the airs of Lully, Lambert and Campra by the girls at the royal convent school at St Cyr. But it was said that he was 'mornings a Catholic, evenings an idolator, the altar paid for his dinner, the theatre for his supper', and ultimately he was excommunicated by the Archbishop of Paris. Although he collaborated with a long list of composers, among them J.-B. Stuck, Campra, Henry Desmarets and F. C. de Blamont, his most important librettos were for Montéclair's *Jephté* (1732) and Rameau's *Hippolyte et Aricie* (1733). He is credited with instigating the famous conflict between the Lullistes and the Ramistes.

Perrin, Pierre (*c*1620–1675). Poet and librettist of early French operas who founded the Académie Royale de Musique. Though a mediocre poet, ridiculed by Boileau and Saint-Evremond, his texts were nevertheless set by such composers as Lully, Michel Lambert, Chambonnières, Étienne Moulinié and J.-B. de Boësset. Until 1660 Perrin held an appointment as *introducteur des ambassadeurs* in the household of Gaston of Orléans, where he made the acquaintance of several Italian cardinals (among them Della Rovere, the ambassador to France) and became interested in Italian opera. He unscrupulously assumed the title of Abbé and set about gaining support for operas in French. He succeeded in gaining the ear of Colbert, Louis XIV's finance minister, who in 1669 made possible the conferment of a 12-year privilege, in the form of *Lettres patentes*, to establish 'académies d'opéra' on Perrin and the composer Robert Cambert. In 1671 they produced *Pomone*, with machines and dancing, which received 146 performances. In spite of the apparent popularity of the *pastorale*, the academy was soon bankrupted because of poor management, landing Perrin in a debtor's prison. In 1672 Lully offered him a pension and enough money to discharge his outstanding debts in return for his share of the privilege. Perrin gratefully accepted.

Pescheur, Pierre (*d* 1637–40). Innovative organ builder credited with perfecting the French classical organ. Praised by Mersenne for his craftsmanship, Pescheur belonged to a family of organ builders; his father, Nicolas (*d* 1616), was well known for his renovations. Of the modifications Pierre Pescheur made in 1628 to the organ of St Gervais in Paris, only a few stops remain. The organ that he built for his own parish church of St Étienne-du-Mont (1631–6) became the model for French organ building throughout the 17th century.

Pezold, Christian. See NORTHERN EUROPE 4 *Saxony and Thuringia: Dresden.*

Philidor. Large French family of instrumentalists and composers prominent in the *musiques de cour*. Of the many members of this family known to have played various combinations of instruments – flute, oboe, crumhorn, bassoon, tromba marina, viol and drums – two made particularly important contributions to French musical life. André Danican Philidor *l'aîné* (*c*1647–1730) was in royal service for 60 years as a member of the *Écurie*, Chapelle and Chamber, and a composer of *opéra-ballets* (performed at Versailles and nearby Marly, 1687–1700). However, he is remembered as the royal music librarian, organizer and principal copyist (1684–1729) of court music. The Philidor Collection, in part lost and divided for many years, now resides in the libraries of Paris and Versailles.

His son Anne Danican (1681–1728) showed early promise as a dramatic composer, having had by the age of 20 two *pastorales* and an opera performed at Marly. His greatest achievement was the foundation in 1725 of the Concert Spirituel at the Salle des Suisses of the Tuileries palace, which until 1790 presented concerts of instrumental and sacred vocal music to the public on days when the Académie Royale de Musique was not performing operas. Anne Danican's half-brother

François-André-Danican Philidor (1726–95) distinguished himself as an important composer of *opéra comique* and as a gifted chess player.

Philippe de Bourbon (1674–1723). Duke of Chartres and Orléans, nephew of Louis XIV, Regent of France (1715–23), amateur musician and italophile. It was from Charpentier that Philippe de Bourbon gained his knowledge of music, not only French but Italian. Together they collaborated on an opera, *Philomèle*, which was performed at the Palais Royal in 1694. Assisted by C.-H. Gervais and other members of his musical staff, the duke composed *Renaud et Armide* (1705) and *Penthée* (1705; rev., 1709). He employed both French and Italian musicians (among them Nicolas Bernier, Campra, François Duval, C.-H. Gervais, Michele Mascitti, J.-B. Morin and J.-B. Stuck) and encouraged the composition and publication of cantatas and violin sonatas in the Italian style, thereby fostering a more cosmopolitan French style known as *les goûts réünis*. During his regency a lighter, gayer music prevailed, echoing the rococo themes of the painter Antoine Watteau.

Piani, Giovanni Antonio [Desplanes, Jean-Antoine] (1678–after 1757). Neapolitan violinist who worked in Paris from 1704. He became principal violinist to the Count of Toulouse in 1712; in that year he produced a collection of sonatas for violin or flute which contain valuable indications of dynamics, fingering and bowing, as well as tempo and ornamentation. In 1721 Piani took up a place at the Viennese imperial court and was placed in charge of instrumental music by 1757.

Quinault. Singers and composers associated with the Comédie Française. Jean-Baptiste Maurice Quinault (1687–1745) possessed a particular gift for comedy and composed at least 24 *divertissements* and *intermèdes* for the Théâtre Français (in whose company he acted until joining the Comédie Française in 1734). He also composed the music for a *ballet-héroïque* performed at the Paris Opéra in 1729. His sister Marie-Anne-Catherine (1695–1791) sang at the Opéra from 1709, moving to the Comédie Française in 1714. Several motets for the Chapelle Royale have been ascribed to her.

Quinault, Philippe (1635–88). Parisian poet and dramatist who collaborated with Lully on the creation of the *tragédies lyriques* of the 1670s and 1680s. Quinault's gifts as a writer were nurtured in the *salons précieux*, and by the time he joined Lully in 1671 he had already assumed a place in the Académie Française.

Though independently wealthy, Quinault welcomed the royal patronage, assured by the success of Lully's production of *Psyché*, the lavish ballet mounted at the Tuileries early in 1671. Thereafter (except for 1677, when he made an extremely unflattering allusion to Mme de Montespan in *Isis*, which cost him two years in the provinces), a new Quinault libretto was set nearly every year by Lully to inaugurate the Carnival season. *Armide* (1686) was their most popular creation.

11 of his librettos were *tragédies lyriques*, based on classical myths and legends and overlaid with symbolism designed to flatter the king. By means of allegory, Quinault incorporated in the prologues official interpretations of recent political events. Like Lully and Louis XIV he believed that lavish spectacles intimidated foreign enemies and usefully distracted the French nobility.

Racine, Jean (1639–99). Powerful and influential poet and dramatist, deeply influenced by Jansenism and classical Greek tragedy, who, jointly with Nicolas Boileau-Despréaux, became Louis XIV's royal historiographer in 1677. Racine and Boileau belonged to a clique of writers that included the fabulist Jean La Fontaine and the comedian Molière, which exerted considerable pressure on other writers and, in particular, on the composer Lully. Racine greatly admired Lully's music and wrote of the *Ballet de l'impatience* (1660) that 'it is on the path of the heart'.

His first tragedy, *La Thébaïde*, was staged in 1664; his last, *Phèdre*, was first seen by the king at J.-B. Colbert's home in Sceaux in 1677. *Iphigénie* was performed with musical interludes at Saint-Germain at the beginning of 1680. In the early 1670s Lully parted company with Molière and took up with Philippe Quinault, with whom he created the immensely successful *tragédie lyrique*. Racine must have felt a mixture of jealousy of Lully and contempt for Quinault (whose verse he found demeaning to the traditions of Greek tragedy).

Strengthened by his appointments to the Académie Française in 1673 and to the Académie des Inscriptions in 1683, he was able to voice criticism of Quinault's *tragédie lyrique* librettos in advance of their performance. Both he and Boileau took every opportunity to trivialize Quinault's verse, yet when in 1682 they were given the opportunity to supersede Quinault by collaborating with Lully on *La chute de Phaëton*, they balked, finding the task altogether odious (in Boileau's prologue, Poetry reproaches Music for her

pretensions). Nevertheless, Racine did collaborate with Lully three years later on *L'Idylle de la paix*, which was performed in a temporary theatre constructed in the orangery of the Sceaux château of the Marquis de Seignelay.

After Lully's death and the eclipse of Quinault, Racine was invited by Mme de Maintenon to provide religiously edifying theatre works with music for the young women of the Maison Royale St Louis at St Cyr. Accordingly he collaborated with J.-B. Moreau on *Esther* (1689) and *Athalie* (1691). Settings of Racine's *Cantiques spirituelles* by Moreau, Lalande and Collasse and Jean-Noël Marchand (1666–1710) were published in 1695.

Racquet, Charles (1597–1664). Distinguished member of a family of organists and composers. Racquet became organist of Notre Dame at the age of 21. While still a young man he toured Germany with acclaim. Mersenne praised his counterpoint and included what were to be his only published works in *Harmonie Universelle* (1636–7); upon his death Denis Gaultier composed a *tombeau* in his honour.

Rameau, Jean-Philippe (1683–1764). Pre-eminent French musician of the 18th century, particularly remembered for his operas and his innovative treatises on harmonic theory; in recognition of his genius Louis XV conferred nobility upon him shortly before his death. But Rameau spent the first 40 years of his life in the relative obscurity of the provinces. He made a short but important trip to Milan, and was for a time a violinist in the Lyons Opéra. He held organ posts in Avignon, Clermont and Dijon (where he was born) and visited Paris from 1706 until 1709 (during which time he held two organ posts, was offered a third, and published his first book of harpsichord *pièces*). About 1713 he moved to Lyons, where he contributed *grands motets* to the Lyons Concert (1714). While at Clermont (1715–22) he formulated his theories of harmony, which were mathematically derived and indebted to Zarlino and Descartes.

In 1722 he settled permanently in Paris. With the publication that year of his *Traité de l'harmonie* he gained the immediate attention and respect of Parisian musicians. But while his music – harpsichord pieces, cantatas and music for the fair theatres – was also much admired, he was unable to win an organ post in Paris. He took on pupils, among them the talented Marie-Louise Mangeot, who became his wife in 1726. Following the appearance of his third book of harpsichord pieces, which like his second (1724) was largely devoted to *pièces de caractère*, he published his *Observations sur la méthode d'accompagnement pour le clavecin* in the *Mercure de France* (February 1730), drawing upon his own brilliant technique of improvising on a figured bass. In 1727 he competed unsuccessfully with Daquin for the organ post at St Paul, bringing to a close his career as a church organist. By then he had published his second and more controversial harmony treatise, *Nouveau système de musique théorique* (1726), which led to polemical exchanges with Montéclair in the pages of the *Mercure de France* (1729–30).

Rameau was to be embroiled for the rest of his life in controversies concerning his music and writings. His early operas, of which the first was produced in his 50th year, provoked a lengthy dispute between the old guard Lullistes and the forward-looking Ramistes. *Hippolyte et Aricie* (1733) was a stunning success, exciting strong passions because of the emphasis placed on music. Voltaire quoted Rameau as saying: 'Lully needs actors but I need singers' (and, over the years, fine singers he had, among them the *haute-contre* Pierre de Jélyotte and the sopranos Marie Antier, Sophie Arnould and Marie Fel). Of *Hippolyte et Aricie* Campra is said to have remarked that there was enough music in this opera to make ten operas by any other composer and, prophetically, that 'this man will eclipse us all'. Although *Hippolyte* is a *tragédie lyrique* and owes much to the Lullian tradition, it is a work of its time, more cosmopolitan (that is to say more Italian), richer melodically and harmonically, more imaginatively orchestrated, and, by the regular insertion of *divertissements* in each act, less concerned with dramatic continuity than Lullian operas. His librettists were the finest of their day: Pellegrin, Voltaire, Fuzelier, Bernard and Cahusac. In addition to *tragédies lyriques* – *Hippolyte et Aricie*, *Castor et Pollux* (*c*1737), *Dardanus* (*c*1739), *Zoroastre* (*c*1749) and *Les Boréades* (1763) and several lost or abandoned works – Rameau composed musical dramas in a variety of other genres. *Platée* (1745), Rameau's most successful *comédie lyrique*, pokes fun at gods; however, the central theme, that of Platée's ugliness, borders on tragedy.

The French love of the exotic is exploited in the *opéra-ballets*, such as *Les Indes galantes* (1735) and *Les fêtes d'Hébé* (*c*1739), where each of the acts has its own setting and plot. *Pygmalion* (*c*1748) demonstrates Rameau's skill in encapsulating a wide range of emotions within the confines of a single act. The *pastorales héroïques* – *Zaïs* (*c*1748), *Naïs* (1749) and *Acante et Céphise* (*c*1751) – offer gods and supernatural effects in rustic, out-of-doors settings, in keeping with Rococo taste.

During this period Rameau found a pleasant haven *chez* La Pouplinière (the financier), whom he served as *maître de musique* (from about 1735 until 1753. Rameau and his family lodged at his various residences and belonged to the stimulating circle of writers, artists and musicians gathered around La Pouplinière. The rich musical resources – singers, players and dancers – of Paris were augmented by virtuoso clarinettists and horn players brought in from Germany and Bohemia, providing Rameau with a private forum. It was for this circle that the virtuoso *Pièces de clavecin en concerts* (1741) were composed.

But the idyll was disturbed by the occasional tempest: within a couple of years, Rameau became involved in a second, rather unpleasant dispute with a former pupil over the degree to which he had acknowledged the sources of his *Génération harmonique* (1737), which investigated, among other things, the relationships between reciprocal tones and the overtone series, and between thoroughbass and fundamental bass. Louis-Bertrand Castel's open letter appeared in the *Journal de Trévoux*, and Rameau's rebuttal in *Le pour et contre* (1738). At much the same time Rameau was also required to defend his theories of temperament against the criticism of Louis Bollioud-Mermet of the Lyons Académie des Beaux-Arts.

Rameau gained an important foothold at court during the 1740s. He became *compositeur de la musique de la chambre du roy* in 1745 and composed a *comédie-ballet*, *La princesse de Navarre* (with Voltaire), and *Platée* for the celebrations of the dauphin's wedding. In 1748 Rameau and Voltaire produced *Les surprises de l'amour* for the Théâtre des Petits-Cabinets of Mme de Pompadour. His place at Versailles secure, his works well received in Paris and in the provinces, his theories acclaimed by learned societies, Rameau was at the height of his career.

From 1752 until his death in 1764 Rameau composed less and wrote more, feeling there was yet much he could elucidate. In 1750 he had published *Démonstration du principe de l'harmonie*, on which he had collaborated with a pupil, the *philosophe* Diderot; it was widely considered his finest thinking on the subject of harmony. Another pupil and *encyclopédiste*, D'Alembert, thought to popularize Rameau's theories by publishing a volume of *Éléments de musique théorique et pratique suivant les principes de M. Rameau* (1752); so successful was it that Marpurg translated it into German (1757). Still to come were Rameau's *Observations sur notre instinct pour la musique* (1754), the *Code de musique pratique* (1760), the *Origine des sciences* (1762) and the *Vérités également ignorées et intéressantes tirées du sein de la nature* (*c*1764), in which he sought to associate musical proportions with those of a universal cosmic principle. He corresponded with Mattheson and Martini and strongly influenced Tartini, Marpurg and Helmholtz. His theories of harmony still form the basis of the modern study of tonal harmony.

Rameau was, by all accounts, a difficult and eccentric person who often found it hard to get on with people. He fell out with the management of the Opéra during the 1740s, taxed the patience of Voltaire and incurred the hatred of Jean-Jacques Rousseau, whose *Les muses galantes* (1745), an *opéra-ballet* inspired by *Les Indes galantes*, was roughly dismissed by Rameau. A decade later Rousseau wrote articles for the *Encyclopédie* which Rameau, having himself declined to write, criticized in a series of pamphlets; D'Alembert and Diderot were forced to defend Rousseau in the preface to volume vi (which appeared in 1756). Rameau's estrangement from the *philosophes* was Rousseau's revenge.

Nevertheless 1500 people attended Rameau's memorial service in Paris, held at the Pères de l'Oratoire; 180 musicians from the Opéra performed the *musiques de cour* operatic contrafacta. A number of other services were held in Paris and in the provinces. The *éloge* (1765) compiled by the secretary of the Dijon Académie, Dr Hugues Maret, remains an important biographical source. With the tercentenary celebrations of 1983 came renewed interest in Rameau. His major writings have been issued in facsimile.

Rameau, Pierre (*fl* early 18th century). French dancing-master to the Queen of Spain and authority on French court dances. Rameau is remembered by two important treatises published in 1725: *Le maître à danser*, a beautifully illustrated essay on the French style of dancing, describes correct posture and the steps and patterns of various social dances (particularly the minuet), as well as offering a valuable guide to etiquette at court balls; the *Abrégé de la nouvelle méthode* presents important advances on R.-A. Feuillet's notation, evident in 12 of Louis Pécour's choreographies which had already been published by Feuillet.

Rebel. Family of court musicians. Jean Rebel (*d* 1692) was a tenor who held a post in the court chapel and took major roles in Lully's *Le bourgeois gentilhomme*, *Cadmus et Hermione* and *Alceste*. At the age of ten Rebel's eldest child, Anne-Renée (1663–1722), took her place as a singer at court, where she became a favourite of Louis XIV. In due course the king provided her dowry and wedding when she married Lalande in 1684. Her brother was the versatile musician Jean-Féry Rebel *le père* (1666–1747).

As early as the age of eight Jean-Féry's playing was known to the king and Lully, assuring him of future posts in the Académie Royale de Musique and the Vingt-quatre Violons. In the 1690s he was among those remarked upon by Le Cerf who composed violin sonatas in the Italian style. Rebel was appointed principal violin of the Académie in 1699 and a year later he journeyed to Spain in the entourage of the Duke of Anjou, returning in 1705 to Académie and court duties as a player and administrator in charge of the music for spectacles and ceremonies. In spite of Lully's encouragement of his early operatic efforts, *Ulysse* (1703) proved a disappointment. In 1712–13 he finally published his duo and trio sonatas. At much the same time he began composing choreographed *symphonies* for the dancers of the Académie; *Les caractères de la danse* (1715) was created for Françoise Prévost. He is best known for his programmatic *symphonie*, *Les élémens* (1737).

His son François (1701–75), known as Rebel *le fils*, inherited his father's musical and administrative gifts. At 13 he joined the Académie orchestra and at 16 was assured of succeeding his father in the Vingt-quatre Violons. He became involved in the Concert Spirituel as both violinist and conductor, and in 1726 he and François Francoeur performed violin duets there. Their collaboration extended to composition – together they produced a succession of theatre works, beginning with *Pirame et Thisbé* (1726) – and, ultimately, to the administration of the Académie. In the course of his tenure at court (1727–55), Rebel *le fils* rose to the post of *surintendant*; in addition, he took charge of the orchestra of Mme de Pompadour's Théâtre des Petits-Cabinets. In 1760 he was ennobled by Louis XV and made a Chevalier de l'Ordre de St Michel.

Rinuccini, Ottavio. See ITALY 6 *Tuscany*.

Roberday, François (1624–80). Organist (who trained as a royal goldsmith) and composer. In 1659 Roberday became *valet de* *chambre* to the regent, Anne of Austria, and the following year published his only surviving work, *Fugues, et caprices, à quatre parties,* which reflects the influence of Frescobaldi and Froberger, as well as of Titelouze.

Robert, Pierre (*c*1618–1699). *Maître de musique* and royal *sous-maître* and composer of motets. Robert served at the cathedrals of Senlis, Chartres and Notre Dame before being appointed one of four *sous-maîtres* (with Henry Du Mont, Gabriel Expilly and Thomas Gobert) at the Chapelle Royale in 1663. He worked primarily with Du Mont, sharing the *sous-maître* posts with him from 1669; so effective was their professional rapport that three years later they were jointly made *compositeurs de la musique de la chapelle et de la chambre*. They retired in 1683, and at the king's request Ballard printed their *grands motets* (24 by Robert), together with several by Lully, in a folio edition the following year. Robert's *grands motets* may be distinguished from those of his contemporaries by his individual deployment of the *petit choeur*. André Danican Philidor copied ten of his *petits motets* into a manuscript dated 1688.

Rossi, Luigi. See ITALY *7 Papal States: Rome.*

Rousseau, Jean (1644–*c*1700). Viol player, composer and the author of *Traité de la viole* (1687), which chronicles the history of the viol and usefully describes the different manners of playing, ornamentation and transposition. A student of Sainte-Colombe and an ardent admirer of Marin Marais, Rousseau particularly championed what he called 'jeu de mélodie', in opposition to Demachy, who promoted the art of 'jeu de s'accompagner'. Rousseau also published a popular singing treatise (1678).

Rousseau, Jean-Baptiste (1671–1741). Poet, best known to musicians for his contribution to the development of the French cantata as a minor poetic form (three *récits* alternating with three *airs de mouvement*). In his collection of texts Bachelier (1726) claimed that Rousseau's cantatas were not only the earliest, but also the finest. J.-B. Morin, Nicolas Bernier, Montéclair, F. C. de Blamont and C.-H. Gervais were among those who set his texts. His *tragédie lyrique* librettos were set by Pascal Collasse (*Jason,* 1696) and Henry Desmarets (*Vénus et Adonis,* 1697), although neither opera had any success. He was banished from Paris in 1712 for dabbling in satirical verse.

Rousseau, Jean-Jacques (1712–78). Influential Swiss writer, who contributed many articles on music to Diderot and D'Alembert's *Encyclopédie* (1751–65), and philosopher,

whose ideas were influential in pre-Revolutionary politics: his most important non-musical treatises were *Le contrat social* and *Émile,* both published in 1762. He was also a composer. Rousseau went to Paris in 1742, hoping to gain acknowledgment as a composer as well as a writer. This he achieved, but with many qualifications, for he was a miserable, self-absorbed and accordingly socially inept person, vulnerable to bouts of hypochondria and paranoia. He risked and suffered great disappointments and mis-understanding in literary as well as musical circles by entertaining an unrealistic opinion of himself and never admitting he might be mistaken or inconsistent; in his *Confessions* he admitted wishing to demonstrate his superiority over one circle by being accepted in the other.

He rightly admired Rameau, whose treatise on harmony had been his tutor and whose articles he had undertaken for the *Encyclopédie*; Rousseau looked to him for approval when his system of musical shorthand was rejected by the Académie des Sciences. But his esteem was not reciprocated: Rameau brusquely dismissed his system as inadequate for all but the simplest accompanied melodies. Deeply wounded, Rousseau published a defence in his *Dissertation sur la musique* (1743).

A sojourn in Venice (1743–4) as the secretary to the French ambassador interrupted Rousseau's work on an *opéra-ballet* based on Rameau's *Les Indes galantes.* He completed *Les muses galantes* in 1745 and was at first blocked in his attempts to present it before Rameau (who by this time must have considered him to be a pest), but he finally persuaded La Pouplinière to have it performed. Rameau was reluctant to attend, and, when in the event he did, he was severe in his verdict: the best of it must have been plagiarized, the rest composed by a musical ignoramus. From that moment Rameau and Rousseau were acknowledged foes. Rousseau naïvely mounted a parody of Rameau's *La princesse de Navarre* (1745), presented shortly after it, also at Versailles. Rousseau and Rameau later clashed in 1753–4 over Lully's setting of Armide's monologues and, in particular, the dramatic role of the orchestra.

Rousseau's greatest musical success came in 1752 at Fontainebleau with *Le devin du village,* an *intermède* composed of simple melodies and italianate instrumental music which heralded the advent of *opéra comique.* It was performed throughout the second half of the 18th century and inspired Charles Burney's English adaptation, *The Cunning-Man* (1766). In 1753 Rousseau weighed in to the 'Querelle des Bouffons' with his *Lettre sur la musique française*, in which he concluded that opera in the French language – lacking marked accentuation and being more expressive of ideas than sentiments – could not succeed, though Gluck later proved him wrong. Instead, he saw spoken drama with instrumental interjections (later known as melodrama) as a viable alternative: his *Pygmalion* was presented at Lyons in 1770. Two years earlier, he published a *Dictionnaire de musique*.

Royer, Joseph-Nicolas-Pancrace (*c*1705–1755). Savoyard keyboard player, composer and a director of the Concert Spirituel. Royer was born a gentleman at the court of Savoy in Turin, where he took up music as a hobby, studying the harpsichord and organ with François Couperin's cousin Marc-Roger Normand, court organist and *controllore della cappella*. On his father's death he was left penniless and in 1725 turned to music as a career.

His first step was to move to Paris and become a naturalized French citizen. At first he lived on the meagre earnings from teaching singing and the harpsichord. He had ambitions to compose theatre music and had already been involved in *opéra comique* when his first *tragédie lyrique*, *Pyrrhus* (1730), was performed at the Opéra. A post at the Opéra as a *maître de musique* soon materialized and was followed in 1734 with a court appointment, held jointly with J.-B. Matho until his death in 1746, as a *maître de musique des enfans de France*. His most important theatre piece was *Zaïde* (1739), an *opéra-ballet* which enjoyed many revivals during the following three decades.

In 1748 Royer and the violinist Gabriel Capperan took over the direction of the Concert Spirituel, which had been under the auspices of the Académie Royale de Musique and, within months, would come under the control of the City of Paris. In 1753 Royer acquired the post of *maître de musique de la chambre du roi*.

Sainte-Colombe. Family of viol players, of whom Sieur de Sainte-Colombe (*fl* second half of the 17th century) is a prominent figure in the development of the French school of viol playing. By his title, Sainte-Colombe belonged to the minor nobility, though he appears to have had no court connections and was thus a gifted amateur. He learned the viol from Nicolas Hotman and was himself the teacher of Meliton, Danoville, Jean Rousseau and Marin Marais, as well as his own children (two daughters and a son), with whom he gave concerts in his home. According to Titon du Tillet, Sainte-Colombe practised the viol in a tree house. Le Gallois mentioned him with Dubuisson and Marais in his famous letter of 1680, and Danoville acknowledged Sainte-Colombe's teaching in his treatise of 1687, calling him 'the Orpheus of his time'. Jean Rousseau dedicated his *Traité de la viole* (1687) to him, attributing to him the introduction of a bottom, seventh string and strings overspun with silver wire. In 1691 Abraham du Pradel included his name among the finest viol teachers of the day, and in 1701 Marais published a *tombeau* in his memory. Sainte-Colombe composed a large collection of *concerts* for two equal bass viols, incorporating passages of free rhythm (often merely written-out trills), which were never published (67 survive).

Sainte-Colombe *le fils* is known to have been in Edinburgh for at least six months in 1707, where he gave lessons (leaving behind copies of some of his father's *concerts*), and in London in 1713, when he gave a benefit concert at Hickford's Rooms.

Saint-Evremond, Charles de Saint-Denis. See BRITISH ISLES 1 *London*.

Saint-Lambert, ?Michel de (*fl c*1700). Harpsichordist and author of two important treatises on playing. Though little is known of his life he was evidently an experienced teacher and a friend of Louis Marchand. His *Principes de clavecin* (1702) offers useful chapters on keyboard ornamentation with examples taken from contemporary collections. His *Nouveau traité de l'accompagnement* (1707) elucidates current harmonic theory and suggests two logical notational reforms in relation to clefs and signatures for minor keys.

Sallé, Marie (1707–56). Dancer at the Paris Opéra, a pupil of the virtuoso Françoise Prévost and a rival of La Camargo, with whom she appeared regularly, despite their divergent styles. Unlike most of her contemporaries, Marie Sallé divided her career between France and England. She was first seen at the Foire St Laurent, then at the Opéra in a 1721 revival of Campra's *Les fêtes vénitiennes*, although her début as a soloist did not take place until 1727 (in J.-J. Mouret's *Les amours des Dieux*). Meanwhile, at the invitation of John Rich, Sallé and her brother spent the 1725 season at the Lincoln's Inn Fields Theatre. She returned to London regularly, appearing at the Drury Lane Theatre and Covent Garden, where she danced the role of Terpsichore in the prologue of Handel's *Il pastor fido* (1734).

She was a daring innovator, abandoning a formal costume and mask in a 1729 performance of J.-F. Rebel's *Les caractères de la danse*; in 1734 she danced with her hair down, wearing only a simple muslin robe, in *Pygmalion* at Drury Lane. She was gifted at mime and the portrayal of attitudes and emotions. She outraged an audience at a 1735 performance of Handel's *Alcina* by appearing dressed as a man. In Paris she gained acclaim for her performances in Rameau's *Les Indes galantes* (1735), *Castor et Pollux* (1737) and *Les fêtes d'Hébé* (1739). Hers was a style of dancing known less for its virtuosity than for its delicacy, finesse and unaffected expression.

Salomon, Joseph-François (1649–1732). Provençal court instrumentalist and composer. Salomon arrived in Paris in about 1679 and soon gained an appointment as harpsichordist and organist to the queen, and later as viol player in the *musique de chambre*. However, in 1683 he competed unsuccessfully in the trials for the *sous-maître* posts. He was noted for his sensitive accompaniment of vocal soloists and choirs. His best-known work was a *tragédie lyrique*, *Médée et Jason* (text by S.-J. Pellegrin and La Roque), which was performed by the Académie in 1713.

Sauveur, Joseph (1653–1716). Acoustician who coined such terms as 'acoustics', 'node' and 'loop'. Sauveur published a *Principes d'acoustique et de musique* (1701), in which he correctly interpreted beats, despite being said to have no ear for music. His papers were published in the *Mémoires de l'Académie Royale des Sciences* (1704–16).

Senaillé, Jean-Baptiste (c1688–1730). Parisian violinist and composer, praised by Titon du Tillet for the precision and delicacy of his playing. A pupil of G.A. Piani, Senaillé published two of the earliest French collections of violin sonatas in the Italian style (1710 and 1712), before taking up his father's place in the Vingt-quatre Violons in 1713. He published three further collections (1716, 1721 and 1727), travelled in Italy (1717–19) and was a soloist at the Concert Spirituel (1728–30).

Sicard, Jean (*fl* late 17th–early 18th century). Bass singer and composer who, while working in Paris, published 17 books of *airs sérieux et à boire* (1666–83); his airs (many of them very elaborate) include some for two violins and bass voice, as well as dialogues and laments. He dedicated his fourth book (1669) to the court singer Pierre de Nyert and his 12th

(1677) to his daughter (who contributed an air to this collection and five more to later books), expressing in the dedication his hope that she too might become known as a composer. In 1710 he became director of the Académie Royale de Musique en Provence.

Silbermann, Andreas. See CENTRAL EUROPE *1 South Germany.*

Somis, Giovanni Battista. See ITALY *1 Piedmont-Savoy.*

Sportonio, Marc'Antonio. See ITALY *9 Sicily.*

Stuck, Jean-Baptiste [Batistin] (1680–1755). Italian cellist of German descent, much admired for his French cantatas. Stuck was the first important cellist to work in Paris. He arrived there in about 1705 and found employment first with the Prince of Carignan and then with the Duke of Orléans, who made him an *ordinaire du roi* during the regency. In his four books of cantatas, which appeared between 1706 and 1714, he mixed and juxtaposed Italian and French styles. His French operas were less successful, though his *divertissement L'union de la musique italienne et françoise* (1722) proved very popular. Stuck appeared as a soloist with the Académie Royale de Musique and at the Concert Spirituel.

Tessarini, Carlo. See ITALY *10 Itinerant Musicians.*

Thierry. Family of organ builders. Pierre Thierry (1604–65), a pupil of Crespin Carlier, altered the organ at St Gervais to Louis Couperin's specifications. Elsewhere in Paris he built the organs at St Paul (1644–6), Les Mathurins – which incorporated the first combined wind-chest for the *Grand orgue* and *Récit* – and St Germain-des-Prés (1661). His son Alexandre (1646/7–99) built the organ for Mme de Maintenon's school at St Cyr in 1685. His finest work was for the Paris churches of St Séverin (1675) and St Eustache (1681–9). Pierre's grandson François (1677–1749) incorporated the first *Bombarde* manual into the organ at Notre Dame (1730–3).

Thomelin, Jacques-Denis (c1640–1693). The most distinguished member of a long line of organists who in 1678 became one of four royal organists, along with N.-A. Lebègue, G.G. Nivers and J.-B. Buterne. Simultaneously he held posts in Paris at St Germain-des-Prés (from 1667) and St Jacques-la-Boucherie (from 1669), where large crowds gathered to hear him play on feast days. He was the guardian and mentor of François Couperin, who succeeded him at court.

Titon du Tillet, Évrard (1677–1762). French aristocrat and man of letters who devoted his life to the erection of a colossal monument glorifying the departed poets and musicians of the Louis XIV era; today he is remembered by the anecdotes he published in the monumental *Le Parnasse François* (1732) and its supplements, concerning the lives of the poets and musicians he honoured.

Titon du Tillet was the son of the wealthy director-general in charge of royal armaments. He forsook military and legal careers to make his way at court as the *maître d'hôtel* to the ill-fated Duchess of Burgundy (d 1712). After her death he sought to gain the favour of Louis XIV (d 1715), then Louis XV, by drawing up plans to erect a 60-foot 'Parnasse François' in Paris (where the Arc de Triomphe now stands). On his Mount Parnassus, statues and medallions of the most distinguished French poets and musicians of the era were to be stationed; the names of lesser lights would be inscribed with scrolls. While the project never got beyond a bronze model, sculpted by Louis Garnier with additional figures by Augustin Pajou (Musée de Versailles), it nevertheless remains the first French representation of genius in true-life form.

To publicize the project Titon du Tillet published a *Description du Parnasse François* (1727), containing biographies of departed poets and musicians, among them Louis Couperin, Lambert, Lully, Collasse and Charpentier. Apart from the *éloges* published after the death of Lully, they are the earliest published accounts of the lives of musicians. A much enlarged version appeared in 1732, with supplements in 1743 and 1755; many of the entries were based on personal acquaintance with the subjects.

Torelli, Giacomo (1608–78). Italian architect, stage designer and machinist who made his name by designing the Teatro Novissimo, Venice (1641), with innovative stage machinery, enabling an entire scene to be changed in a single operation. He was soon invited by Mazarin to Paris to install similar machinery in the theatres of the Hôtel du Petit Bourbon (1645) and the Palais Royal (1647). He remained there until the early 1660s, designing the sets for the productions of the Italian opera troupe, *ballets de cour* and French plays – notably Corneille's *Andromède* (1650). Torelli's set designs, like those of his Venetian contemporaries (particularly the elder Burnacini), created areas of action through series of transverse and longitudinal lines within the scenery.

Valentini, Giuseppe. See ITALY *10 Itinerant Musicians*.

Veillot, Jean (d 1662). Priest and important musical figure in Parisian religious life who was among the first to compose in the *grand motet* style. Veillot served as choirmaster at Notre Dame and the Benedictine abbey of Montmartre; he was a canon of the Sainte Chapelle and abbot of Bois-Aubry. In 1643 he became a *sous-maître* of the royal chapel along with Thomas Gobert. Of his music only three double-choir motets survive. To say the least, they betray Nicolas Formé's influence which, according to the historian Sauval, Veillot gained by malefaction: after Formé's death Veillot apparently stole his music from a cupboard kept locked by Louis XIII.

Verdier, Pierre. See NORTHERN EUROPE *2 Scandinavia*.

Vigarani. Italian theatre architects, scenery designers and machinists. Gaspare Vigarani (1586/8–c1663) was summoned from his post at the Modena court to France by Cardinal Mazarin in 1659 to supervise the spectacles in honour of the marriage of Louis XIV. He had a Salle des Machines specially constructed in the Tuileries palace for his production of Cavalli's *Ercole amante* (1662) – though it took much longer than expected to complete and was never altogether satisfactory, owing to its vastness and the noisiness of the machinery.

His son Carlo (1623–before 1713) joined forces with Lully and Molière to produce three lavish *divertissements* at Versailles (1664, 1668, 1674). Carlo took French citizenship in 1673 and was associated with Lully at the founding of the Académie Royale de Musique. He designed the Salle Jeu de Paume and supervised the renovation of the Théâtre du Palais Royal. His collaboration with Lully ended in 1680, when he was succeeded by a Frenchman, Jean Berain.

Visée, Robert de (late 17th–early 18th century). Highly regarded court musician who excelled on the guitar and theorbo, as well as on the viol and as a singer. Robert de Visée joined the king's *musique de chambre* in 1680 and published his first collection of suites for the five-course guitar two years later. He was a regular performer with such musicians as R.-P. Descoteaux, Philibert and Antoine Forqueray in the private concerts given *chez* Mme de Maintenon until Louis XIV's death. In 1719 he was appointed guitar teacher to the young Louis XV and was succeeded in his posts by his son François a year later. In addition to the two collections of guitar pieces (the second appeared in 1686), Visée published in 1716 works for lute and theorbo in score – many of them duplicate the earlier guitar selections – which include arrangements of music by Lully, Forqueray and François Couperin.

Westhoff, Johann Paul von. See NORTHERN EUROPE *4 Saxony and Thuringia*.

Zenti, Girolamo. See BRITISH ISLES *1 London*.

2 The Provinces

Antier, Marie. See FRANCE *1 Paris and Versailles*.

Besard, Jean-Baptiste (*c*1567–after 1617). Doctor of Law and Medicine from Besançon, lutenist, anthologist and early writer on the performance practice of the lute. Besard was a man of letters who lived abroad, pursuing his various professions. In Rome he learned to play the lute. In Cologne he published the monumental *Thesaurus harmonicus* (1603), a ten-volume anthology of lute music notated in French tablature, containing solo pieces in all the principal forms of the day, lute songs and pieces for lute ensemble by at least 21 composers (among them Lorenzini, Dowland, Vincenzo Galilei, the elder Alfonso Ferrabosco, Valentin Bakfark and Besard himself). Appended to the music is an important treatise, *De modo in testudine libellus*, dealing in particular with the subtleties of left-hand technique; Besard revised it while in Augsburg as *Ad artem testudinis*, enlarging upon right-hand technique, and published it with his second anthology of lute music, *Novus partus* (1617). The treatise was translated and published in Germany and England – evidence that it was well known and admired.

Böddecker, Philipp Friedrich. See CENTRAL EUROPE *1 South Germany*.

Bourgeois, Thomas-Louis. See FRANCE *1 Paris and Versailles*.

Bouzignac, Guillaume (before 1592–after 1641). Important southern French composer of Latin sacred music and chansons. Bouzignac has been slow to receive the attention he deserves as a major figure of the first half of the 17th century because his music rests entirely in manuscript and much of it has only recently been attributed to him. His life was spent in the service of the church at Narbonne, Grenoble, Carcassonne, Rodez and Tours, and yet he was well enough known for Mersenne and Annibal Gantez to write of his distinction as a composer; Brossard owned copies of six of his works. Bouzignac's music reveals a training in the classical counterpoint of the Franco-Netherlands school and yet is up to date in its treatment of text. Of special note is his use of recurring melodic, rhythmic and harmonic formulae to express emotions and natural phenomena, especially in his narrative motets.

Boyvin, Jacques (*c*1649–1706). Organist at Notre Dame Cathedral, Rouen, and composer of two books of organ suites (1689/90 and 1700); a *Traité abrégé de l'accompagnement* served as a preface to the second book and then was published separately in 1705. Boyvin took up his first post in 1663 at the Hôpital des Quinze-Vingts (an institution for the blind) in Paris, serving until 1674, when he was appointed to the post at Rouen. He remained in Rouen for the rest of his life, supervising the building of a new organ (1686–9) by Robert Clicquot, with four manuals plus pedal couplers and more than 40 ranks. He was succeeded at Notre Dame by his pupil François Dagincour.

Brossard, Sébastien de (1655–1730). Ecclesiastic, the author of the first French dictionary of music, theorist, composer and bibliophile. Brossard was a passionate advocate of Italian music: during the 1680s he spent time in Paris (serving as a canon at Notre Dame from 1684) and was among the first in France to compose sonatas and sacred cantatas, and the only one to interpret Italian terminology for French musicians. He became a close friend of the theorist Étienne Loulié and frequented the concerts at the *hôtel* of the Duchess of Guise organized by Charpentier.

He left Paris for Strasbourg in 1687, shortly after the death of Lully. While *maître de chapelle* at Strasbourg Cathedral (1687–98) he founded an Académie de Musique in Strasbourg, where he conducted his own works and arrangements of the music of others, and became an avid collector of music and treatises. In 1695 he spent several months in Paris, where he made contact with the circle of musicians experimenting with the Italian style, among them François Couperin, E.-C. Jacquet de la Guerre, Clérambault and J.-F. Rebel. He returned there again in 1698, hoping to win the post of *maître de musique* at the Sainte Chapelle, but it went to Charpentier.

His final post was at the Cathedral of St Étienne at Meaux, where he remained for the rest of his life, composing and writing. His library, which he eventually sold to Louis XV in return for a pension, contains many unique works in manuscript as well as rare printed editions; he prepared a catalogue (1724), annotating it with valuable and characterful remarks which afford an interesting perspective on the dissemination of music at the turn of the century. Brossard is known today by his terminological *Dictionnaire de musique* (1701), which survives only in the 1703 edition.

Campra, André. See FRANCE *1 Paris and Versailles*.

Carlier, Crespin (*d* before 1640). Organ builder whose early career in the South Netherlands influenced his work in France. Carlier built organs for several cathedrals, among them Poitiers, Tours, Chartres and that of his native Laon. In 1600 Titelouze commissioned him to improve the organ at Rouen Cathedral, which thereafter was considered the finest French organ of its day. Working in Paris from 1631, Carlier collaborated with the Langheduls (the Flemish organ builder and his son) on an innovative instrument for St Jacques-la-Boucherie. His work was continued by his pupil Pierre Thierry.

Castel, Louis-Bertrand. See FRANCE *1 Paris and Versailles*.

Collasse, Pascal. See FRANCE *1 Paris and Versailles*.

Dagincour, François (1684–1758). Organist, harpsichordist and composer from Rouen who worked in Paris (as a pupil of Lebègue and as organist of Ste Madeleine-en-la-Cité), before taking up the post of his first teacher, Jacques Boyvin, at Notre Dame Cathedral, Rouen, in 1706. He retained this post for the next 52 years, although from 1714 until 1730 he served a semester each year as one of the organists of the Chapelle Royale at Versailles. In 1733 he published a collection of harpsichord pieces which were very much influenced by Couperin in character and format; a second volume was announced but never appeared. For organ, only a single manuscript collection of *versets* survives.

Danielis, Daniel (1635–96). Walloon composer who, after 20 years' service as *Kapellmeister* at Güstrow, competed unsuccessfully in 1683 for one of the posts as *sous-maître* of the French Chapelle Royale. The following year he became *maître de chapelle* at St Pierre, Vannes; his motets for one to four voices (of which 72 survive, 13 in a Philidor anthology compiled in 1688) were sung throughout the 18th century.

Dassoucy, Charles. See FRANCE *1 Paris and Versailles*.

Desmarets, Henry. See FRANCE *1 Paris and Versailles*.

Galli-Bibiena, Francesco. See CENTRAL EUROPE *3 Austro-Hungary: Vienna*.

Gantez, Annibal (*c*1600–68). Composer and writer on music. Gantez was a much-travelled ecclesiastical musician who served as *maître de chapelle* or *maître des enfants* at innumerable institutions throughout France, particularly in the south. In the course of his career he composed at least two Masses (1642), a *Te Deum* (1661), and collections of airs and *chansons à boire*. His observations on French musical life were published in *L'entretien des musiciens* (1643).

Gautier, Pierre (*c*1642–1696). Musician and entrepreneur. Based in Marseilles, Gautier was instrumental in bringing the musical standards and tastes of Paris to Provence. At first a player and teacher of organ and harpsichord, he became an opera-house director, conductor and composer of some regional standing. In 1684 Lully granted him permission to establish an opera house at Marseilles – the first in the provinces; six months later it opened with a performance of *Le triomphe de la paix* (libretto and music by Gautier). Using performers hired from Paris, he mounted productions of Lully's *tragédies lyriques*, among them *Armide*, and in 1687 another of his own operas, *Le jugement du soleil*, had a gala performance in celebration of Louis XIV's recovery from an operation. Gautier's operatic style is less dependent upon Lully and more individual than that of many of his Parisian contemporaries. He was lost at sea in 1696.

Gilles, Jean (1668–1705). Provençal composer of sacred music. Gilles spent most of his life in Aix (where he was a student of Guillaume Poitevin) and Toulouse. Despite his isolation from the mainstream of French musical life, his *Messe des morts* became one of the best-known works of the 18th century (Mattheson remarked upon its beauty). It was posthumously published, and performed at Rameau's funeral in 1764; a decade later it was performed at the death of Louis XV. In the meantime it was frequently heard at the Concert Spirituel, performed with large forces and a carillon part for the ending provided by Michel Corrette.

Grigny, Nicolas de (1672–1703). Organist and composer, one of a family of organists in Rheims. Like many of his contemporaries he duly produced a single volume of organ music (1699). It stands out, together with that of François Couperin (1692), because of the manner in which formidable contrapuntal and ornamentation techniques are subjugated to musical expression.

Habermann, Franz. See CENTRAL EUROPE *3 Austro-Hungary*.

Harris, Thomas. See BRITISH ISLES *1 London*.

Isnard, Jean-Esprit (1707–81). Gifted organ builder whose beautiful instrument at the Basilique St Maximin-en-Var (1773) survives intact as the sole unaltered exemplar of a French classical organ. He also built organs for the cathedrals at Tarascon, Marseilles and Aix-en-Provence.

Jélyotte, Pierre de. See FRANCE *1 Paris and Versailles*.

Kircher, Athanasius. See ITALY *7 Papal States: Rome*.

La Coste, Louis de. See FRANCE *1 Paris and Versailles*.

Lalouette, Jean François. See FRANCE *1 Paris and Versailles*.

La Pierre, Paul de. See ITALY *1 Piedmont-Savoy*.

Lebègue, Nicolas-Antoine. See FRANCE *1 Paris and Versailles*.

Le Cerf de La Viéville, Jean Laurent, Seigneur de Freneuse (1674–1707). Poet and champion of French music, born in Rouen. Le Cerf is known by his three-volume *Comparaison de la musique italienne et de la musique française*, published in Brussels (1704–6), and written in refutation of François Raguenet's *Parallèle* of 1702. In it Le Cerf set out to define, by means of anecdotes, dialogues, letters and discourses, the musical aesthetics of the Lullian era and to demonstrate their absence in contemporary Italian music.

Leclair, Jean-Marie. See FRANCE *1 Paris and Versailles*.

Lemaire, Louis. See FRANCE *1 Paris and Versailles*.

Marchand, Louis. See FRANCE *1 Paris and Versailles*.

Matho, Jean-Baptiste. See FRANCE *1 Paris and Versailles*.

Maugars, André. See FRANCE *1 Paris and Versailles*.

Maupin. See FRANCE *1 Paris and Versailles*.

Maximilian II Emanuel. See CENTRAL EUROPE *1 South Germany: Munich*.

Molière. See FRANCE *1 Paris and Versailles*.

Mondonville, Jean-Joseph Cassanéa de. See FRANCE *1 Paris and Versailles*.

Moreau, Jean-Baptiste. See FRANCE *1 Paris and Versailles*.

Motteux, Peter Anthony. See BRITISH ISLES *1 London*.

Moulinié, Étienne. See FRANCE *1 Paris and Versailles*.

Mouret, Jean-Joseph. See FRANCE *1 Paris and Versailles*.

Ouvrard, René. See FRANCE *1 Paris and Versailles*.

Poitevin, Guillaume (1646–1706). Provincial cleric, composer and teacher of Jean Gilles and Campra, active in Aix-en-Provence.

Raguenet, François (*c*1660–1722). Born in Rouen, he was a priest and author of the controversial *Parallèle des Italiens et des François, en ce qui regarde la musique et les opéras* (1702; Eng. trans., 1709). Raguenet came to know and love Italian music while visiting Rome in 1698. Upon his return to France he set about examining the relative virtues of Italian and French music. His ultimate espousal of Italian music in the *Parallèle* elicited a lengthy response from his fellow Rouenais Le Cerf de La Viéville in the form of the *Comparaison*, which appeared in 1704–6. Raguenet reinforced his position in a *Défense du Parallèle* (1705). The exchange between Raguenet and Le Cerf provoked an artistic *crise* that had been brewing since the death of Lully and would occupy French composers and aesthetes in the coming decades.

Rameau, Jean-Philippe. See FRANCE *1 Paris and Versailles*.

Robert, Pierre. See FRANCE *1 Paris and Versailles*.

Rossi, Luigi. See ITALY *7 Papal States: Rome*.

Salomon, Joseph-François. See FRANCE *1 Paris and Versailles*.

Sicard, Jean. See FRANCE *1 Paris and Versailles*.

Silbermann, Andreas. See CENTRAL EUROPE *1 South Germany*.

Smith, John Christopher. See BRITISH ISLES *1 London*.

Titelouze, Jehan (1562/3–1633). The first of the early French organists to compose substantial works for his instrument. Titelouze settled permanently in Rouen (having entered the priesthood in 1585), where he became organist of the cathedral. Although he quickly became much sought after as a consultant on organ installation and renovation, Titelouze was also a writer who won prizes for his poetry. He made frequent trips to Paris and corresponded with Mersenne about unusual musical phenomena. His organ music is indebted to liturgical vocal traditions and strictly adheres to the eight church modes. Much of it is in the form of *versets* or variations based on plainsong. *Le Magnificat* (1626) contains eight ingeniously crafted cycles of *versets*.

Trichet, Pierre (1586/7–?1644). Provincial collector of musical instruments and the author of the incomplete *Traité des instruments de musique*. Trichet was a remarkable man, a

lawyer in the Parliament of Bordeaux, the
author of tragedies, epigrams and poetry, and
an authority on witchcraft. While his *Traité* is
less useful than the treatises on instruments
published by Praetorius and Mersenne (with
whom Trichet corresponded), it makes reference to a wealth of literary sources, ancient
and modern, from outside the usual musical
sphere, and hence is of great interest to
present-day scholars.

Northern Europe

German Courts and Cities

During the 17th and 18th centuries, the geographical area which comprised the German-speaking lands was extensive and disparate. Towns and cities on the Baltic coast which are now in the Soviet Union were once part of Protestant Germany (for example Kaliningrad, formerly Königsberg), as were cities as far south as Nuremberg and Stuttgart. Moreover, the influence of the German-speaking lands was of considerable importance in the Scandinavian countries, where German Lutheranism was firmly established. At the end of the Middle Ages, the German-speaking lands were a group of autonomous states, each with its own ruler, with no single focus of political or cultural activity. However, the states were still loosely bound together by the Holy Roman Empire. Originally founded by Charlemagne to defend the cause of Christianity in the West, the empire had lost much of its relevance by the end of the Middle Ages, owing to the reduced threat from the Moors and the Turks. One important and distinctive feature of the empire which did remain was the presence throughout the German-speaking lands of imperial cities – cities which were governed not by the local nobility but by the Holy Roman Emperor. However, since by the 17th century the emperor wielded negligible authority, these cities were effectively self-governed, a fact that added to the political complexity of Germany at this time. Unaffected by the prohibitive taxation inflicted by the nobility upon most towns and cities, trade in the imperial cities was able to flourish. Fortune-hunters appeared from all over Europe, and some of the wealthier tradesmen were even in a position to lend money to the nobility. Life in Hamburg, for example, was dominated by financial matters to such an extent that one 17th-century prayerbook carried details of the stock exchange, and showed a picture of stockbrokers on its title page. The organist who was appointed to the Jakobikirche in 1720 was described by one contemporary journalist as being able to improvise more successfully with his money than with his fingers. However, despite their freedom from the nobility, the imperial towns were neither havens of democracy nor of capitalism; authority lay with a council of town officials whose presence was determined either by hereditary status or by wealth, and trade was restricted by the continuing strength of the medieval trade guilds.

At the beginning of the 17th century, the German-speaking lands constituted one of the most prosperous regions of Europe. In the 16th century trade had been based on the metal industries, concentrated on the main imperial towns of the south-west such as Frankfurt and Nuremberg, but by the turn of the 17th century trading interests were moving towards agriculture and the linen industry, bringing about a significant increase in the prosperity of the eastern lands. Important links emerged between the Baltic ports (such as Danzig – now the Polish city Gdańsk – Rostock, Lübeck and Hamburg) and the major ports of southern Europe, particularly Venice, the northerners exchanging their grain and linen for the exotic products of the south, such as fruit and spices. The main trading route across land between north and south gravitated from Frankfurt and the Rhineland to the newly flourishing area of Leipzig and the river Elbe, with Hamburg at its mouth. Such trading connections form an important background to the close stylistic links between the music of Hamburg and Venice in the early 17th century: for example, between the polychoral style of composers such as Andrea and Giovanni Gabrieli and that of Michael Praetorius.

In 1618, however, an uprising in Bohemia precipitated the Thirty Years War, a bitter conflict which threatened the trading activity of all the German-speaking lands. Many historians have attempted to piece together an accurate picture of the extent of the devastation caused by the war, some estimating that it took over a hundred years for the population to restore itself to its pre-war level, but even the most optimistic accounts indicate much hardship from sieges, massacres and plagues. During the course of the war the fate of the German lands fell increasingly into the hands of foreign powers. Denmark, Sweden and France each in turn proclaimed themselves the defenders of the north German Protestant lands against the advancing armies of the Catholic south, although the presence of foreign troops was treated with only guarded acceptance by the German people. At the conclusion of the conflict, France ensured the maintenance of the disunity of the German-speaking lands so that they would remain susceptible to French influence and even invasion. The Rhineland was thus a highly vulnerable region (one of the major factors in its decline as an important trading route), and it was only the collaboration of the other major European powers that prevented France from realizing her expansionist desires. The hardship endured by the German people during the Thirty Years War affected every aspect of German life, including music. The writings of the Dresden *Kapellmeister* Heinrich Schütz make frequent reference to the difficulties faced by musicians at this time. One notable musical feature of this period was the prominence of sacred works for a few voices and continuo, a reflection of the generally sparse forces available for music-making during the war.

With a fortunate outcome at the Peace of Westphalia in 1648, and the demise of Sweden's influence south of the Baltic, the north-eastern state of Brandenburg became increasingly powerful during the second half of the century, aided by its expanding economy. On the acquisition of Prussia, the Elector of Brandenburg became the first King of Brandenburg-Prussia, and Berlin emerged as an important political and cultural centre. The third king, Frederick the Great, was not only the pivotal character behind what were arguably the two most significant developments in the history of 18th-century Germany – the rise to a major European power of Brandenburg-Prussia, and the impact of the Enlightenment – but was also one of Europe's most zealous and fascinating patrons of music.

The German musician was faced with the possibility of employment in two very different environments – a court, as an employee of the ruling nobleman, or a town or city, as an employee of the town council or the church.

By comparison with other European courts, the German courts were exceptional in their cosmopolitan nature, being dominated by Italian and French culture. To the aspiring German noblemen Italy represented all that was enviable in terms of art, whilst the French court at Versailles provided the model for the style and manners of their courtly society. Foreign musicians had been welcomed at the German courts long before the 17th century, but with the improving fortunes of

Italian music in the 16th century and the acknowledged supremacy of Italy in other forms of art, Italian musicians became the most popular. If Germans tended to fill the ranks of the instrumentalists at the courts, the Italians were in demand chiefly as singers, but they also held many of the top *Kapellmeister* posts. The principal reason for this was the fashion for opera, the genre that offered rulers the most complete artistic expression of their own power and influence. Since the duties of the *Kapellmeister* usually included responsibility for the music of the Italian operas performed at court, Italians were extremely eligible for such posts. Vast sums of money were spent on all aspects of operatic production, and rival rulers vied with each other to attract the best Italian musicians by offering large salaries. Antonio Sartorio, the Italian *Kapellmeister* at the court of Hanover, received a salary of 600 thalers in 1667, whilst his two German assistants received in the same year only 300 and 220 thalers. Even the Italian scribe at the Dresden court in 1680 received a higher income than the German organist. By the early 18th century, the situation had become ludicrous. The top salary awarded to a German musician at the Dresden court in 1717 was 1200 thalers, whereas the leading seven Italian musicians collected a combined total of 32,000 thalers, averaging over 4500 thalers each. At some places Italians were also employed as instrumentalists – usually violinists. One such example is the violinist Giuseppe Torelli who worked at the court of Ansbach. Many courts experienced difficult relations between the Italian and German musicians. Dresden witnessed several disputes: in 1666 Christian Dedekind formed a group at the court specifically for German musicians, known as the *Kleine deutsche Musik*, but he eventually resigned; and Johann Heinichen's quarrel with some Italian singers led to an opera's being temporarily disbanded. The writer and musician Johann Mattheson complained that Italian musicians made all the money and then returned to Italy, and published in his Hamburg journal an anonymous letter from Berlin which deplored the customary blind adulation of foreigners at the expense of indigenous talent.

The increasing importance of all aspects of French court life at the German courts from the middle of the 17th century was in part due to the outcome of the Thirty Years War, in which France had acted as the chief guarantor of the safety of the independent German states. It became common for young German noblemen to be sent to the French court in order to acquire its manners, dress and language, and some naturally gained a taste for its music. The Count of Promitz, having experienced such visits himself, commissioned Georg Philipp Telemann to compose overtures in the French style, and Duke Ernst Ludwig, resident at Darmstadt, himself composed a set of *Douze suites et symphonies*. Frenchmen were employed at the German courts mainly for comedy acting and dancing, but French musicians also found work there, often as part of an acting or dancing troupe, such as that engaged by the Dresden court in 1708, which comprised seven men and six women who mainly sang and danced, and four violinists. Probably the most successful Frenchman in Germany was the violinist Jean Baptiste Volumier, who was *Konzertmeister* in charge of dance music at the Berlin court in the 1690s and subsequently director of the court orchestra at Dresden. Whereas most German musicians who travelled abroad to study during the 17th century went to Italy (of whom the most famous was Heinrich Schütz), for some, France became an increasingly attractive alternative. Johann Kusser, who worked at the Ansbach court and later at the Hamburg opera in the late 17th century, had formerly studied for six years with Jean-Baptiste Lully in Paris, calling himself Jean Cousser. Both Volumier and Kusser became particularly famous for introducing to Germany the high standard of orchestral playing at the French court.

With the Italian dominance of opera and the vogue for things French, German musicians often faced considerable competition for their livelihood at the courts. However, all musicians were subject to the whims of their court employer, who could increase or cut back expenditure on music without a moment's notice. Music was just another aspect of court finance, although it was naturally of more importance to some patrons than others. Frederick the Great provides many examples of both the advantages and disadvantages of the system of courtly patronage. On the one hand, he avidly continued the work of Friedrich Wilhelm I in establishing Berlin as a major musical centre, to the point where it rivalled the longstanding supremacy of the Dresden court in musical excellence. He was also exceptional in his enthusiastic promotion of German composers, offering them unprecedented levels of pay. But against these positive features must be placed the disadvantage of the restricted nature of his musical outlook. The musical life of the Berlin court effectively stood still during the course of his reign, since he tolerated the music of only a handful of composers, in particular Carl Heinrich Graun, Johann Adolf Hasse and Johann Joachim Quantz. When Charles Burney visited the court in the 1770s he was astonished to find a musical style which was over 30 years out of date. Frederick considered French music worthless, and Italian music meaningless beyond its role as a harmless vehicle for the prowess of Italian singers. With regard to German singers he is credited with the remark that he would as soon expect to receive pleasure from the neighing of his horse. In this climate a musician seeking originality, such as C. P. E. Bach, had little future. By contrast with the enormous salaries offered to Graun and Quantz, Bach's income remained meagre throughout his time at the court, and he suffered the humiliation of seeing a deputy harpsichordist appointed on twice his salary. The frustration of Franz Benda's years at the Berlin court can be inferred from the comment in his autobiography that he had accompanied the flautist–monarch in concertos at least ten thousand times.

The principal benefits to be derived from court employment were the wide range of musical opportunities, from church music to opera, the possibility of a handsome wage, and, perhaps most important for a creative musician, contact with many other musicians, both German and foreign. The prestige offered by court employment is evident from the way that musicians in town or church employment who held honorary court titles tended to sign themselves first with their honorary titles and only second with that of their actual employment. Examples include Johann Mattheson, who was able to sign himself as *Kapellmeister* to the Duke of Schleswig-Holstein, and J. S. Bach, who during his time at Leipzig gathered the titles of *Kapellmeister* to the Prince of Saxe-Weissenfels and the Prince of Anhalt-Cöthen, and Royal Polish and Electoral Saxon Court Composer.

The German musician who found work in a town or city, away from the affectations and rarefied atmosphere of court life, lived amongst ordinary German people who had no particular predilection for foreign matters beyond possibilities for trade, and was subject to the generally more stable authority of a town council. Since the Middle Ages most prosperous German towns and cities could boast a permanent band of musicians, financed by the town council. During the 17th century such bands usually numbered about seven players, although their ranks were often increased for special occasions by the addition of apprentice musicians and amateurs. All kinds of instruments were employed by the town musicians, from flutes and violins to horns and trumpets, but the musical scope of the groups was inevitably limited by the fact that their main function was the provision of dance music and fanfares. However, in certain places the leadership of able musicians, such as Johann Schop in Hamburg or Johann Christoph Pezel in Leipzig, brought a considerable reputation to their groups, and did much to improve the generally poor impression of town musicians held by the church and court musicians. Quantz provides a fairly isolated example of a famous musician who began his career in a town band, in his case that of Merseburg.

Apart from domestic music-making, chamber and ensemble music in the towns centred on groups of amateurs and interested professionals who met together, usually under the title of a collegium musicum. Such groups sprang up all over Germany during the 17th century, and were often based in the popular town coffee houses. The collegium musicum founded in Hamburg in 1660 by the organist of the Jacobikirche, Matthias Weckmann, had up to 50 members. It performed the latest music from all over Europe, including much Italian music. In some places a wealthy private citizen played host to a concert series, such as that organized by the Imperial Ambassador in Hamburg on Sundays in 1700. University students were another source of music-making, which often went beyond their traditional diet of drinking songs. As a law student in Leipzig, Georg Philipp Telemann formed a particularly lively collegium musicum from amongst his fellow students. Besides giving regular concerts, this group of up to 40 singers and instrumentalists also took part in performances at the opera house and services at the university church.

The chief musical post on offer in the towns and cities was that of *Stadtkantor*. Each place developed its own set of duties for the holder of this post, and a variety of titles was used, but the *Stadtkantor* usually held responsibility for the music at all the main churches, taught at the central school, and directed the music at all the major civic and ecclesiastical occasions. The problems associated with the holding of such a post usually resulted from the extent and nature of the *Stadtkantor's* authority. He had to maintain good relations principally with the town council, but also with his assistants at the various churches, the organists, the town and church instrumentalists, and the *Rektor* (headmaster) of the school. In this last case, problems appear to have been particularly common. J. S. Bach held a lengthy dispute with the *Rektor* of the Thomasschule in Leipzig about authority over the choristers, and Samuel Scheidt had experienced difficulties a century earlier in nearby Halle. In Frankfurt and Nuremberg the school duties fell to a separate *Kantor*, and the chief musician was known as the town *Kapellmeister*. This situation may well have appeared attractive to musicians elsewhere in Germany. At the time when Bach applied for the post of *director chori musici* in Leipzig and *Kantor* of the Thomasschule in 1722, a number of applicants for the post objected to the requirement that they should teach Latin at the school. Bach surmounted the problem by offering to pay a deputy for this duty. But even in Frankfurt there could be occasion for dispute between the *Kapellmeister* and the *Rektor*, as, for example, when *Kapellmeister* Johann Herbst argued with the *Rektor* over whether the school *Kantor* should be allowed to direct some of the music in church.

Opera achieved only limited success as a commercial venture in a few of the more prosperous cities, and the authorities generally considered it unsuitable for the

Stadtkantor to be involved with such enterprises. It was the Dresden court *Kapellmeister* Nicolaus Strungk who was given authority to direct the opera house in Leipzig when it opened in 1693. A notable exception was Georg Philipp Telemann, who in 1722 became both *Stadtkantor* and director of the opera in Hamburg despite having initially been banned from operatic involvement.

The differing environments and opportunities afforded by court and town employment led many musicians to move from one form of employment to the other. Bach moved from court posts at Weimar and Cöthen to the chief town post at Leipzig, but subsequently entertained thoughts of returning to a court position, particularly during his recurrent disputes with the town council. In a letter to an old school friend working in Danzig, Bach tells of his arrival in Leipzig, where prospects seemed good:

But since (1) I find that the post is by no means so lucrative as it had been described to me; (2) I have failed to obtain many of the fees pertaining to the office; (3) the place is very expensive; and (4) the authorities are odd and little interested in music, so that I must live amid almost continual vexation, envy, and persecution; accordingly I shall be forced, with God's help, to seek my fortune elsewhere.[1]

Bach was particularly envious of the musical life of the Dresden court (see Plate 8), where he eventually at least held an honorary title. In a note to the Leipzig town council Bach again mentions the problem of poor wages:

... one need only go to Dresden and see how the musicians there are paid by His Royal Majesty; it cannot fail, since the musicians are relieved of all concern for their living, free from *chagrin*, and obliged each to master only a single instrument: it must be something choice and excellent to hear.[2]

Bach touches on another difficulty here: the fact that most town musicians were expected to be fluent on a number of instruments. Johann Quantz, during his apprenticeship at Merseburg, studied no fewer than eleven instruments, although he specialized in just three: violin, oboe and trumpet. Quantz himself was made aware of the shortcomings of the system when he, like Bach, had the good fortune to travel to the Dresden court. Although Quantz went on to become one of the richest German court musicians of his day, he was not insensitive to the problems of town musicians. Whilst commenting on what he saw as a decline in the standard of organ playing in Germany at this time, Quantz points out that 'the much too small wages at most places provide a poor inducement for application to the science of organ playing'.[3] Bach was probably delighted when his son Carl Philipp Emanuel secured a post at the newly prestigious Berlin court, but on account of his poor treatment there C. P. E. Bach eventually sought a town post; in 1755 he failed to obtain the post formerly held by his father at Leipzig, but in 1768 he followed his godfather Telemann as *Stadtkantor* in Hamburg.

A significant factor for organists was that the most famous organs in Germany were generally to be found in the spacious surroundings of the large town churches, rather than in the court chapels. Some churches even had two large instruments. During Dieterich Buxtehude's tenure of the post of organist at the Marienkirche in Lübeck, even the smaller of the two organs was equipped with three manuals, pedals and 38 stops. On at least two occasions J. S. Bach was tempted to leave court employment for such a post, one at the Liebfrauenkirche in Halle, where plans were afoot for a major rebuild of the organ, and the other at the Jakobikirche in Hamburg, which housed one of Germany's most celebrated instruments.

In the 17th century, German society was dominated at all levels by religion. Well over a hundred years after the Reformation, German intellectual life continued to be centred on traditional theological matters at a time when the new doctrines of the Age of Reason were gaining much ground elsewhere in Europe. One of the main reasons why music flourished above almost all other forms of artistic activity in Germany during the 17th century was that Martin Luther had held strong views on the importance of music. He considered music the greatest treasure in the world next to the Word of God, and repeatedly laid stress on the immense value of music as an integral part of divine worship. The central position of music in the Lutheran liturgy meant that music was less susceptible to the destructive effects of the Thirty Years War than some forms of art. The strength of Lutheranism also supported the production of religious poetry in this period, and religious music and poetry came together in some forms of church music and also in songs for domestic use. Books of religious songs enjoyed an enormous popularity in Germany during the 17th century, and accounted for a large proportion of music publishing.

In the latter half of the 17th century Lutheranism found itself increasingly under attack from Calvinism. The Calvinists had gained a firm foothold in the German-speaking lands when they were granted equal rights with the Lutheran majority at the end of the Thirty Years War. They objected to the elaborate church music of the Lutherans, whether the lengthy motets or the frequent chorale improvisations from the organists, as they were afraid that the music might become an end in itself rather than a means of praising God. The same objection was also raised within the Lutheran church by the Pietist movement. Many prominent Lutheran musicians became involved with this movement and composed sacred songs, often in direct collaboration with a Lutheran poet, as in the case of the organist Nikolaus Hasse and Pastor Heinrich Müller in Rostock.

While religious songbooks for domestic use were obviously not a matter for religious dispute, opera certainly was. It was considered by many to be a corrupting influence on account of its customary adoption of secular subject matter, in particular Greek mythology. The opera house in Berlin was condemned as 'the Devil's Chapel', and denounced for its use of effeminate foreigners in depraved music and wild French dance. The Calvinists rejected all aspects of opera, including its music. By contrast, many Lutherans welcomed opera to Germany, and hoped that composers of church music would take advantage of the new musical styles that it brought. Just as some Catholic motets were sung in Lutheran churches with revised texts, so favourite operatic arias came to be performed with religious texts substituted. The Leipzig theologian G. E. Scheibel saw no reason why a church congregation should not be moved to tears with powerful music in the same way as the audience at an opera house; one of the leading figures in the establishment of the opera house at Hamburg was the Pastor of the Catharinenkirche, H. E. Elmenhorst. Even so, commercial opera houses were always founded in the face of considerable religious opposition.

The chequered history of opera in Germany reveals much about German culture and society in this period. In France, composers were able to draw upon a rich tradition of indigenous secular literature, but German composers had no equivalent tradition from which to build a German form of opera. The operas performed in

Germany were mostly sung to Italian librettos, either in Italian or in complete or partial translation, but the tales of classical mythology held little interest for most of German society. At the commercial German opera houses, such as that in Hamburg (founded 1678), Italian opera initially delighted with its novelty and spectacle, but then failed to sustain the public's interest, causing a number of opera houses to close. Some attempt was made to found a German form of opera based on religious themes, but this was overshadowed and eventually eclipsed by the growing popularity of the oratorio and cantata. It is perhaps significant that the two most successful German operatic composers of the early and mid 18th century – Johann Adolf Hasse and George Frideric Handel – found their fame mostly outside Germany, Hasse in Italy and Handel in England. The union of national music and literature found in the operatic masterpieces of Lully or Alessandro Scarlatti is paralleled in Germany not by any operatic achievement, but by the Passions of J. S. Bach.

By the beginning of the 18th century, German opinion was becoming subject to the spirit of rationalism. Many devout Lutherans welcomed the fresh attitudes fostered by the philosophers. The musical writings of Mattheson, for example, breathe the spirit of the new age. He argued for a fundamentally new approach to music in German society, and saw the key to its acceptance as being a change in the traditional view of musical education which held as its main aim the provision of able singers for the chorales on Sundays. He wished for a new openness towards music in all its aspects, which would keep up with the latest developments in music and not be obsessed with the past. Mattheson bemoaned the fact that music could not be studied as an independent science at the universities, and expressed a desire to establish an endowment for a professorial chair in music at Leipzig. However, he also commented that if a suitable teacher could be found for the school of his home town (thus at a more fundamental level in society), he would like that ten times more. In Hamburg, Mattheson found himself at odds with a less progressively minded *Stadtkantor*, but he managed to find a refuge for his views at the cathedral, because this was an imperial institution and therefore outside the jurisdiction of the *Stadtkantor*. Here Mattheson was able to adopt all the latest developments in musical style, and also to employ singers from the opera, pioneering the use of women in church music. Mattheson's radical opinions brought him into confrontation not only with members of the Hamburg establishment but also with traditionalists all over North Germany. A pamphlet appeared from the theology faculty at the University of Göttingen which condemned Mattheson's acceptance of the new '*theatralisches Kirchenmusic*', and a major criticism of his views written by the town organist at Erfurt challenged Mattheson's questioning of traditional music theory. Mattheson did much work as a translator, of both political and musical documents, and his interest in philology helped to establish a thorough German vocabulary for musical criticism. In his *Critica musica*, the first German music periodical, Mattheson reproduced the famous articles of Raguenet and Le Cerf de La Viéville on the relative merits of French and Italian music in both the original French, and, in columns opposite, German translation.

The writings of Mattheson and others like him may be viewed as a significant branch of the revival of literature in 18th-century Germany. In addition to periodicals, major dictionaries and biographical works appeared during the course of the century, as well as treatises on performance, and these placed Germany in the forefront of European musical literature. Initially the leading free towns of Hamburg and Leipzig were the centres for the new publications, but with the accession to the Prussian throne of Frederick the Great in 1740, Berlin became increasingly important.

In his youth, Frederick the Great had revelled in the cosmopolitan atmosphere of the Berlin court, and in particular the access this had given him to foreign music, literature and philosophy (see Plate 9). Although his uncultured and militaristic father Friedrich Wilhelm I had suppressed these elements at court to some extent, they had far from disappeared altogether, and the young Frederick's interests were treated with great sympathy by his French tutor and governess. Friedrich Wilhelm was quite unable to stifle his son's interests, although his attempts to do so were both frequent and harsh. Denounced by his father as a 'flautist and poet' – a description that was intended to be wholly derogatory – Frederick boldly signed himself '*Frédéric le philosophe*' at the age of 16, and soon counted the likes of Voltaire amongst his friends and correspondents. On his accession to the throne, Frederick began to transform life in Berlin, both at court and in the city, changing everything that he had so disliked about his father's rule. A new opera house was immediately commissioned for the court, and new freedoms were granted to the ordinary citizens of Berlin. The radical philosopher Christian Wolff was reinstated as a professor at the University of Halle, having been expelled by Friedrich Wilhelm I, and the court *Kapellmeister* Carl Heinrich Graun was sent off to Italy to recruit new singers. Frederick's liberal religious views turned Berlin into a home for religious refugees from far beyond the borders of Brandenburg-Prussia. The new intellectual and philosophical environment which Frederick the Great created in Berlin formed the background to Berlin's new role as the chief centre of musical theory and criticism. The performance treatises of Johann Quantz and C. P. E. Bach are perhaps the two most famous musical products of Frederick's Berlin, but other notable contributions include Friedrich Wilhelm Marpurg's *Der critische Musicus an der Spree*, the first journal devoted to reviews of musical compositions. Frederick's narrow musical opinions may seem inconsistent with his liberalism in other matters, but there were a number of contradictory features in his character. The youth who, under the pretence of hunting, would hide in the woods playing flute duets, and who began his military training by wounding himself when he fell off his horse onto his own sword in full view of the army generals, went on to become one of Europe's most powerful and respected men. He far excelled the military exploits of his father, despite his insistence on taking his flute and a clavichord with him on his conquests.

The political disunity of the 17th-century German-speaking lands caused music, like all other forms of art, to be particularly susceptible to foreign influence. Our understanding of German music of this period is constantly illuminated by the examination of its foreign elements, not least the music of J. S. Bach, where different national styles are sometimes treated separately and at other times skilfully combined. In France, François Couperin and others had attempted to marry the French and Italian styles to create a higher form of musical art (seen, for example, in works such as Couperin's *Les goûts réunis*), but Johann Quantz claimed for the Germans a pre-eminent role in the ideal of the union of national styles:

If one has the necessary discernment to choose the best from the styles of different countries, a *mixed style* (ein *vermischter Geschmack*) results that, without overstepping the bounds of modesty, could well be called *the German style*, not only because the Germans came upon it first, but because it has already been established at different places in Germany for many years, flourishes still, and displeases in neither Italy, nor France, nor in other lands.[4]

Geoffrey Webber
Gonville and Caius College, Cambridge

Notes

1 H. T. David and A. Mendel: *The Bach Reader: A Life of Johann Sebastian Bach in Letters and Documents* (New York, 1945; rev. 2nd edn, 1966), 125.
2 Ibid., p. 123.
3 J. J. Quantz: *Versuch einer Anweisung die Flöte traversiere zu spielen* (Berlin, 1752); Eng. trans. and ed. E. R. Reilly: *On Playing the Flute* (London, 1966), 339.
4 Ibid., p. 341.

Biographical Dictionary
Northern Europe

1 North Germany

Abel. Father and son instrumentalists and composers. Clamor Heinrich (1634–96) served as a viol player and organist at the Celle (1662–4) and Hanover (1664–85) courts, and later as a town musician at Bremen (1694–6). In 1674 he published a collection of suites entitled *Erstlinge musikalischer Blumen*. His son, Christian Ferdinand (*c*1683–1737), was a viol player and violinist who, after serving in the army, took up a post in 1715 at the court of Prince Leopold of Anhalt-Cöthen where, two years later, J. S. Bach was appointed *Kapellmeister*. Most probably, Bach composed his sonatas for harpsichord and bass viol to play with Abel. Christian Ferdinand was the father of the distinguished viol player and colleague of J. C. Bach, Carl Friedrich Abel (1723–87).

Albert, Heinrich (1604–51). Cousin of Heinrich Schütz, he was an organist at Königsberg Cathedral and composer of eight volumes of popular sacred and secular *Arien* (1638–50). As a young man he assisted his cousin at Dresden before reading law at the University of Leipzig, where he was in contact with Schein. He spent a year as a prisoner of the Swedish army and, once back in Königsberg, put his experience to use by serving two years as an authority on the science of fortification. However, from late 1630 he worked exclusively as a musician.

Albert's *Arien* were originally composed as occasional works and are annotated in the printed volumes with dedicatees, dates and occasions; most are short, strophic and syllabically set, though others – such as that for Martin Opitz's visit to Königsberg in 1638 – are more ambitious. He used foreign melodies as well as his own, and as many as 25 of his became chorales. Of particular interest are his prefaces, containing valuable information on performing practice, including nine rules of continuo playing; according to Johann Mattheson (who knew these prefaces), Albert was adamant that continuo playing should not sound 'like hacking cabbage'.

Baltzar, Thomas. See BRITISH ISLES *1 London*.

Böhm, Georg (1661–1733). Organist at the Lüneburg Johanniskirche and composer of chorale *partite*. Böhm studied with pupils of the Bach family at Ohrdruf, Goldbach and Gotha, then at the University of Jena (1684). In 1693 he was in Hamburg where he came into contact with J. S. Kusser, J. A. Reincken and Buxtehude (who was nearby at Lübeck and greatly influenced Böhm's keyboard style). Five years later he succeeded Christian Flor at Lüneburg, where the young J. S. Bach studied from 1700 until 1703.

Böhm's chorale *partite* were conceived for domestic use, for the harpsichord rather than the organ. He particularly favoured variation form (chorales over ground basses). For the organ he composed at least one chorale fantasia, preludes and fugues (in the manner of Buxtehude); for voices he composed songs, Passions and sacred cantatas.

Bokemeyer, Heinrich (1679–1751). *Kantor*, composer, theorist and collector whose extensive library of books and music is now part of the Deutsche Staatsbibliothek collection. He studied composition with Georg Österreich at Brunswick where in 1704 he was appointed *Kantor*, a post he also held at Schleswig (1712–17) – where he learned to sing 'alla siciliana' from the Italian *Kapellmeister* Bartolomeo Bernardi – and Wolfenbüttel (from 1717 until his death).

He regularly corresponded with J. G. Walther and, in 1739, joined Mizler's corresponding society. Bokemeyer contributed to Johann Mattheson's *Critica musica*, providing Mattheson with the impetus to develop his doctrine of melody, thereby exposing the transition from Baroque to Classical styles. See also NORTHERN EUROPE *1 North Germany*, Österreich, Georg.

Brade, William (1560–1630). English viol and violin player, known as a fine practitioner of divisions, and composer of dances, who worked in Germany and Denmark. Brade's first post was at the Brandenburg court *c*1590, whence he moved to the court of King Christian IV in Copenhagen four years later, subsequently dividing his time between the two courts until 1606. Thereafter, he spent little more than two years at any court – Bückeburg, Copenhagen, Halle, Güstrow,

Berlin – or city: he served as a city musician in Hamburg (1608–10 and 1613–15), where he published three of his five collections of dances. His last appointment was as *Hofkapellmeister* to Duke Friedrich III of Schleswig-Holstein (1622–5), after which he returned to Hamburg.

Bressand, Friedrich Christian (*c*1670–1699). Poet and librettist and stage director who spent his short career working at the Brunswick-Wolfenbüttel court. Born to servants in the household of the Margrave of Baden-Durlach, Bressand possessed literary gifts that were quickly recognized and nurtured. He gained an appointment as secretary to Duke Anton Ulrich of Brunswick and from 1690 until 1699 he was actively involved in court opera productions, providing J. S. Kusser, Reinhard Keiser, J. P. Krieger, G. C. Schürmann, P. H. Erlebach and Georg Bronner with librettos – some of which were translations or adaptations of plays by Corneille and Racine. Many of these productions were subsequently mounted by the Hamburg Opera.

Bruhns, Nicolaus. See NORTHERN EUROPE 2 *Scandinavia*.

Burmeister, Joachim (1564–1629). A leading theorist who developed the doctrine of musical–rhetorical figures and explored the interrelationship of *musica practica, musica poetica* and *musica theorica* in a series of treatises at the turn of the century, of which *Musica autoschediastikē* (1601) is the most important. Burmeister served as *Kantor* of the Nikolaikirche and Marienkirche at Rostock from 1589 until 1593, when he gained a master's degree from the university and became a *collega classicus*.

Buxtehude, Dieterich (1637–1707). Scandinavian-born organist, and the leading German composer between Schütz and Bach. From 1668 he served at the Marienkirche, Lübeck, where he continued and expanded the annual series of public concerts between Martinstide and Christmas known as Abendmusiken which had been inaugurated by his predecessor Franz Tunder. In addition to his organ duties, Buxtehude also served as *Werkmeister* at the prestigious Marienkirche, charged with its management. Of his life, little more is known except that he married Tunder's daughter, by whom he had seven daughters.

Buxtehude had connections the circle around J. A. Reincken in Hamburg which included Bernhard, Weckmann and Theile – he is depicted with Reincken in a group portrait, painted by Johannes Voorhout in 1674, entitled 'Domestic Music Scene' – and was sought out by Johann Mattheson, Handel and Bach near the end of his life. Pachelbel dedicated his *Hexachordum Apollinis* (1699) to him. His most successful pupils were Nicolaus Bruhns, and his successor and son-in-law J. C. Schieferdecker. He travelled very little, yet he had an impressive command of classical, Scandinavian and modern European languages (French and Italian as well as German).

Because so little of it was published, much of his music – sacred vocal and keyboard works – has not survived and is impossible to date; of the 99 works preserved in the Düben collection (Uppsala), many are autographs; and 20 vocal works survive in the Deutsche Staatsbibliothek (Berlin). Though they probably never met, Gustav Düben, Swedish court *Kapellmeister*, was an avid collector of Buxtehude's music; Buxtehude in turn dedicated his 1680 cycle of seven cantatas, on the parts of Christ's body, *Membra Jesu nostri*, to Düben.

Buxtehude's most important vocal works were his German cantatas, incorporating instrumental sonatas, polychoral concerto movements and strophic arias – genres to which he also separately contributed. His chorale settings were most often cantional with instrumental accompaniment and interludes. His most ambitiously scored work was a *Benedicam Dominum* for two vocal and four instrumental choirs. Only three oratorio texts survive as testimony to the music he composed over the years for the Abendmusiken. In addition to music for the Marienkirche, he also composed occasional music, of which eight wedding pieces survive.

During his lifetime Buxtehude's keyboard music was widely known through manuscript copies (no autographs have survived). The Marienkirche and its organ were destroyed in World War II, but the latter is known to have been a three-manual instrument with 52 stops – 15 for the pedals, which figure prominently in his music. Though strongly associated with chorale settings, Buxtehude composed a large number of free works, incorporating improvisatory sections of great virtuosity and highly accomplished fugues, as well as ostinato pieces beloved of Bach, and later, Brahms. His chorale settings include preludes used to introduce congregational singing, fantasias and sets of variations (much indebted to Sweelinck and Scheidt). Buxtehude also composed a dance suite based on a chorale melody (*Auf meinen lieben Gott*) for harpsichord; five other sets of variations and

19 French-influenced suites also survive (although those depicting the nature of the seven known planets do not).

Among Buxtehude's extant music are 20 published sonatas for one or two violins, viol and continuo, which appeared in 1694 and 1696, although he is known to have composed for larger ensembles. The trios, in a free style, make considerable technical demands upon the violinist and viol player, and provide evidence of the calibre of players he had at his disposal.

De Grandis, Vincenzo. See ITALY *10 Itinerant Musicians.*

Farinel, Jean-Baptiste. See FRANCE *1 Paris and Versailles.*

Fischer, Johann. See NORTHERN EUROPE *7 Itinerant Musicians.*

Flor, Christian (1626–97). Organist at the Johanniskirche in Lüneburg, teacher, organ adviser and song composer. His strophic songs on texts by Johann Rist are eccentric in their use of remote keys and experimental metres, and his *St Matthew Passion* (1668) is an early example of the genre. Flor was associated with the Johanniskirche from as early as 1658 (when he played the harpsichord in Passion performances); he became deputy organist in 1668 and principal in 1676. He had hoped to succeed his colleague Michael Jacobi as *Kantor* in 1663, but the post went to Friedrich Funcke.

Förster, Kaspar. See NORTHERN EUROPE *7 Itinerant Musicians.*

Friderici, Daniel (1584–1638). Rostock composer and highly respected writer on music whose treatise, *Musica figuralis* (1618), was well known throughout Germany. He studied in a number of North German cities, lastly at Rostock University (1612), before accepting a post with Count Anton Günther of Oldenburg in 1614. However, in 1618 he returned to Rostock as *Kantor* of the Marienkirche, published his treatise and organized the music for the 200th anniversary of the founding of Rostock University (which awarded him a master's degree in recognition the following year). He was eventually appointed *Kapellmeister* of all the Rostock churches and became a leading figure there for the rest of his life. As a composer, he eschewed chorales and continuo parts (until his 1633 collection of secular songs), for simple, homophonic, text-orientated settings.

Funcke, Friedrich (1642–99). *Kantor* of the Johanniskirche in Lüneburg for 30 years, composer of occasional music (such as his *Danck- und Denck-Mahl*, a concerto com-memorating a devastating storm in 1666), and a *St Matthew* (attributed) and a *St Luke Passion* (1683). Funcke studied theology at Wittenberg (1660–61) and served as *Kantor* at Perlesberg before succeeding Michael Jacobi at Lüneburg (1663), where he tried to upgrade the conditions for church musicians and to have German, rather than Latin, congregational hymns.

Handel, George Frideric. See BRITISH ISLES *1 London.*

Harms, Johann Oswald. See NORTHERN EUROPE *4 Saxony and Thuringia: Dresden.*

Hertel, Johann Christian. See NORTHERN EUROPE *4 Saxony and Thuringia.*

Jacobi, Michael (1618–63). Well-travelled *Kantor* at the Lüneburg Johanniskirche. Jacobi studied law at the University of Strasbourg (1641) and travelled extensively in Europe before taking up posts as *Kantor* at Kiel in 1648 and Lüneburg three years later. He provided strong leadership at Lüneburg, raising standards, lobbying the city fathers for money to create choral scholarships, to hire instrumentalists, and to purchase music and instruments. Under his supervision the first Passions were performed at Lüneburg. Even before he went to Kiel he was actively collaborating with the poet Johann Rist, who insisted on simple settings that would have universal appeal and rejected the stylish technique Jacobi had acquired in the course of his study abroad.

Kunzen, Johann Paul (1696–1757). Saxon singer, instrumentalist, composer and administrator, whose most important posts were as director of the Hamburg Opera (1723–5) and organist and overseer of the Marienkirche in Lübeck (1732). He studied with Johann Kuhnau and Telemann at Leipzig (1716–18) before taking up the post of *Kapellmeister* at Zerbst. Kunzen had been a child prodigy on the organ as well as a singer and violinist, and undertook concert tours during the early 1720s.

While director of the Hamburg Opera he produced a Passion and several operas; when his contract ended he stayed in Hamburg, earning a living as a private music teacher. During 1728–9 he and his son Adolph Carl (1720–81) travelled to England where he met Handel and Pepusch. At Lübeck from 1732, Kunzen was occupied with composing occasional music and reorganizing the traditional Advent Abendmusiken as a successful subscription series. In 1747 he became a member of Mizler's corresponding society.

Meder, Johann Valentin (1649–1719).

Singer and organist who, after a number of posts in North Germany and Denmark, became *Kapellmeister* of the Marienkirche in Danzig. Meder was also a composer, whose sacred works were much influenced by his contact with Buxtehude. He also composed at least four operas, of which *Die beständige Argenia* (1680) was dedicated to the King and Queen of Sweden, and *Nero* became the first German opera to be performed in Danzig. However, the members of Danzig city council were not content for one of their prominent churchmen to be involved in the theatre, and Meder lost his post after the 1698 performances of *Die widerverehligte Coelia*.

Österreich, Georg (1664–1735). Singer, composer, music collector and copyist who initiated the 'Bokemeyer' collection (the principal manuscript source for German Protestant music of the second half of the 17th century and the repository of unique copies of Italian and German cantatas). Österreich studied at Magdeburg, Leipzig (with Johann Schelle at the Thomasschule) and Hamburg (at the Johanneum).

He served as a tenor under Johann Theile at the Brunswick-Wolfenbüttel court (1686–9) before becoming *Kapellmeister* of the Schleswig-Holstein court at Gottorf, where he remained until 1702, except for a two-year hiatus as *Kapellmeister* in Coburg. He returned to Gottorf when the new Duke Friedrich IV (who had dismissed the musicians in 1694) agreed to hire more musicians. In 1702 (on the death of Friedrich IV) he moved back to Brunswick, enjoyed the comfort made possible by the revenue from a brewery he had inherited, and renewed his court connections as singer, acting *Kapellmeister* and, ultimately, court *Kantor*.

He composed sacred concertos, cantatas and occasional pieces while copying hundreds of sacred and secular works as well as treatises on the practices of Carissimi and Schütz by Bernhard. Eventually he sold his collection to a friend and former pupil, Heinrich Bokemeyer; roughly half the collection survives.

Pape, Heinrich (1609–63). Organist and prolific songwriter married to the sister of the poet Johann Rist. Pape studied at Hamburg with Jacob Praetorius before taking a long-term post at nearby Altona (1630–62); at the end of his life he was appointed organist at St Jacobi in Stockholm (1662).

Pepusch, Johann Christoph. See BRITISH ISLES 1 *London*.

Pfleger, Augustin (*c*1635–1686). Bohemian-born *Kapellmeister* and composer of Latin sacred concertos and German Pietist cantatas. Pfleger began and ended his career as *Kapellmeister* to the Duke of Saxe-Lauenburg at Schlackenwerth (Bohemia). In 1662 he accepted a lesser rank (as vice-*Kapellmeister*) to Duke Gustav Adolph of Mecklenburg at Güstrow, where he was occupied with the composition of sacred concertos (89 of which were composed in 1664). Three years later he was appointed *Kapellmeister* of the Schleswig-Holstein court at Gottorf; he was succeeded by Johann Theile in 1673. He returned to Schlackenwerth only in his last year.

Praetorius, Michael (?1571–1621). Organist, versatile and prolific composer of Lutheran church music and theorist. Among over a thousand works he produced a solitary collection of instrumental French dances (*Terpsichore*, 1612); his *Syntagma musicum*, an important (if incomplete) treatise addressing sacred music, instruments and musical forms, appeared in three parts between 1614 and 1618.

After three years as organist at the Frankfurt Marienkirche, Praetorius gained a post at the Brunswick-Wolfenbüttel court of Duke Heinrich Julius in 1595 and remained until 1613, with long stays at the Kassel court of Landgrave Moritz of Hesse in 1605 and 1609. While in Wolfenbüttel he published most of his music – most importantly, his systematically arranged nine-part *Musae Sioniae* (1607–10) – assembling vast numbers of hymn texts and melodies. Other collections were devoted to Latin motets (1607) and madrigal parodies (1611). Between 1606 and 1612 Praetorius collaborated with the distinguished organ builder Esaias Compenius.

After the death of Duke Heinrich Julius in 1613 Praetorius joined the Dresden court, ostensibly during the mourning period at the Wolfenbüttel court. While serving as *Kapellmeister* Rogier Michael's assistant at Dresden he also developed connections with Magdeburg (from 1614) and Halle (1616) and composed music for Sondershausen and Kassel as well. At Dresden he became acquainted with Heinrich Schütz – with whom he was invited, along with Scheidt, to ceremonies marking the reorganization of music at Magdeburg Cathedral in 1618; together the three also visited Leipzig, Nuremberg and Bayreuth the following year.

Meanwhile, Praetorius's frequent absence from the Wolfenbüttel court contributed to the decline of its music, and in 1620 he was not reappointed. A wealthy man, he endowed a foundation for the poor in his will.

Reusner, Esaias (1636–79). Silesian lutenist and composer. Esaias Reusner, son of a lutenist–composer of the same name, was a child prodigy who held a succession of appointments in Poland and North Germany. While still a child he became a page (1648) to the Swedish general Count Wittenberg, resident in Breslau, then an employee of the royal war commissioner (1649) and finally a valet at the Polish court of Princess Radziwiłł, before returning to Breslau in 1654. From 1655 until 1672, he served as lutenist to Georg III, Duke of Silesia, afterwards moving to Leipzig where he first taught at the university for a year before becoming a chamber musician at the Berlin court of Elector Friedrich Wilhelm of Brandenburg. He published two collections of lute music (*Delitiae testudinis*, 1667, and *Neue Lauten-Früchte*, 1676) in the French lute style; these contain 28 suites unified by key.

Rist, Johann (1607–67). Poet (whose texts were set by a whole generation of North German composers including Heinrich Schütz, Andreas Hammerschmidt, Heinrich Pape, the elder Johann Schop and Thomas Selle), lifelong pastor at Wedel (nr Hamburg) and modest composer. Rist wrote straightforward, strophic poems, reflecting Martin Opitz's reforms, on both sacred and secular themes. He was made poet laureate in 1644, became a member of the Fruchtbringende Gesellschaft in 1647, was ennobled in 1653 and founded his own literary academy in 1660.

Rosenmüller, Johann. See ITALY *4 Venice*.

Sartorio, Antonio. See ITALY *4 Venice*.

Scheibel, Gottfried Ephraim (1696–1759). Forward-looking Breslau theologian who wrote an important treatise on the value of music (to influence the emotions of the congregation) in the Protestant church service: *Zufällige Gedancken von der Kirchenmusic* (1721). Towards that end he advocated the use of the theatrical style and parody technique (substituting sacred texts in opera arias). He was also one of the first to assert that women should be allowed to sing in church choirs to alleviate the shortage of good boy sopranos. He was in close contact with Johann Mattheson and they exchanged dedications in publications of 1726–7. A second treatise, a history of church music, appeared in 1738.

Schieferdecker, Johann Christian (1679–1732). Organist and composer who in 1707 succeeded Buxtehude at the Marienkirche, Lübeck. Schieferdecker belonged to a family of ministers and church musicians working at Weissenfels and Zeitz. He was sent to the Thomasschule (1692–7) at Leipzig and stayed on at university, during which time his first two operas were performed. In 1702 he went to Hamburg where, while serving as an accompanist at the Hamburg Opera, he produced three more operas. With his appointment at Lübeck (made on condition that he wed Buxtehude's daughter), he seems to have severed his connections with the Hamburg Opera, and invested his creative energies in the service of the church and community: he continued the prestigious Advent Abendmusiken, provided a panegyric or supplicative cantata annually for civic observances and in 1715 published a collection of chamber suites and sonatas.

Schildt, Melchior (1592/3–1667). Organist from a family who, for over a century and a quarter, filled organ posts at the three oldest churches in Hanover, and (with Scheidemann) one of the founders of the North German organ school. After lessons with his father Antonius and Andreas Crappius, Schildt studied with Sweelinck in Amsterdam (1609–12). Before taking up his father's place at the Marktkirche in 1629, he served at the Hauptkirche in Wolfenbüttel (1623–6) and at the Danish court of Christian IV (1626–9). With the exception of one chorale concerto (*Ach mein herzliebes Jesulein*), Schildt apparently composed only keyboard music – variations, such as those on Dowland's *Lachrymae*, and chorale-based organ works.

Schnitger, Arp (1648–1719). Prolific organ builder, working in North Germany and the Netherlands and assisted by his two sons Johann Georg [Jürgen] (1690–after 1733) and Franz Caspar (1693–1729). Schnitger acquired a number of privileges which assured him of a near monopoly in the trade. With his sons and his assistants he built 150 instruments of all types, admired for their flexibility on all manuals and pedals, and enlarged or rebuilt many others. The organ of the Nicolaikirche in Hamburg (1682–7) is considered to be his finest extant instrument. His sons settled in the Netherlands after his death.

Schop. See NORTHERN EUROPE *1 North Germany: Hamburg*.

Schürmann, Georg Caspar (1672/3–1751). Opera singer, composer and opera conductor at the Brunswick-Wolfenbüttel court. Schürmann began his career as an alto in the Hamburg Opera, with whom he first appeared at the Brunswick court (1697); he was engaged on the spot by Duke Anton Ulrich. He remained at the court for the rest of his life, but for absences to Venice (1701–2), Meiningen (where he served as visiting *Kapellmeister* until about 1706) and Naumburg (for the 1706 summer Petri-Paul fair).

In addition to composing more than 40 operas (only three survive intact), conducting and producing, Schürmann translated and arranged many Italian operas for the pleasure of the court. His own operas were a reflection of his experiences at Hamburg and Venice and as a singer – emphasizing lyrical da capos with written-out coloratura ornamentation, and declamatory recitatives. But though he continued to conduct opera, after 1739 he restricted his composing to sacred and occasional genres.

Schütz, Heinrich. See NORTHERN EUROPE 4 *Saxony and Thuringia: Dresden.*

Siefert, Paul. See NORTHERN EUROPE 3 *Poland.*

Simpson, Thomas (1582–after 1630). English viol player, composer and music editor who worked on the Continent until the late 1620s where, with William Brade, he popularized the English style of viol playing. By 1608 he was at the court of the Elector Palatine at Heidelberg, from where he published his collection of paired dances (*Opusculum*) in 1610, and from 1615 until 1621 at that of Count Ernst III of Holstein-Schaumburg at Bückeburg. The following year he took up a place at the Danish court of Christian IV. In 1621 he brought out an anthology (*Taffel-Consort*) of 50 works for four instruments and continuo; he left three collections of consort music in manuscript.

Sophie Elisabeth (1613–76). Duchess of Brunswick-Lüneburg, librettist and composer of occasional music and sacred songs who was a patroness, pupil and friend of Heinrich Schütz. The daughter of the music-loving Duke Johann Albrecht of Mecklenburg-Güstrow, Sophie Elisabeth received a thorough musical education at Güstrow and Kassel (where the court took refuge during the Thirty Years War).

As the wife of Duke August the Younger of Brunswick-Lüneburg, Sophie Elisabeth took responsibility for the musical life of his court. An orchestra was formed in 1638, and Schütz came frequently to Brunswick and then to their ancestral castle at Wolfenbüttel to advise and collaborate with the duchess on works such as the 1644 *Theatralische neue Vorstellung von der Maria Magdalena.* From 1655 Schütz served as an absentee *Kapellmeister* to the duke and duchess; their frequent exchange of letters provides precious details of their relationship. Sophie Elisabeth composed special family entertainments (see Plate 7) – Singspiels, such

as *Friedens-Sieg* (1648), festive cantatas like the *Glückwünschende Freudensdarstellung* (1652), ballets and incidental theatre music – to honour her husband on his birthday each year until 1656. She continued to compose even after his death, and published two collections of devotional songs (1651, 1667).

Steffani, Agostino (1654–1728). Influential Italian musician – organist, *Kapellmeister* and composer of operas, sacred music and chamber duets – who in later life exercised considerable power as a churchman and diplomat. Steffani came from a Venetian/Paduan family. By the age of 13 he had a post as a singer at the Munich court of Elector Ferdinand Maria of Bavaria, and received organ lessons from J. K. Kerll, the court *Kapellmeister*. In 1672 he was given leave to study in Rome with Ercole Bernabei, then *maestro di cappella* at S Pietro, and when, in 1674, Bernabei succeeded Kerll at the Bavarian court, Steffani returned in his party. Steffani became court organist and, during 1678–9, visited the Paris and Turin courts.

In 1680 he was ordained as a priest and appointed to the specially created post of director of chamber music by the new elector, Maximilian II Emanuel, though it was as an opera composer that he was most active. He balanced musical and clerical appointments so skilfully that a diplomatic career followed closely: he was entrusted with negotiations for the elector's marriage to Princess Sophie Charlotte of Hanover which failed, but led to his appointment as *Kapellmeister* to the Hanover court of Duke Ernst August in 1688.

At Hanover an Italian opera company had just been established in the new theatre. Eight of the ten works performed there between 1689 and the death of the duke in 1698 were by Steffani (with texts by Mauro); he accommodated the prevailing francophilia by writing French overtures and accompanied arias, and incorporating dance-rhythms into his arias. The duke, recognizing Steffani's gifts as a negotiator, sent Steffani to Vienna to press the case for elevating Hanover to the status of an electoral court; in 1693, as envoy extraordinary to the Bavarian court in Brussels, he tried in vain to influence the elector to side with the emperor rather than Louis XIV.

In 1703 Steffani took up non-musical duties as a privy councillor and president of the Spiritual Council for the Palatinate at the Düsseldorf court; he also served as president of the Palatine Government and as the first *rector magnificus* of Heidelberg University (1703–5). He was appointed Grand Almoner to Elector

Johann Wilhelm in 1706, and in 1709, after six months in Rome successfully mediating in a dispute between the pope and the emperor, Steffani was made Apostolic Vicar in North Germany. Working from Hanover, he became involved in the foundation and maintenance of missions and churches in Brunswick, the Palatinate and Prussia. Although he retired to Padua in 1722, he was recalled to Hanover in 1725. Such was his stature abroad that in 1727 the recently founded Academy of Vocal Music in London made him their president; while he remained *in absentia*, he did send the academy copies of his music.

Until 1702 Steffani steadily composed the duets for which he was well known: elegantly crafted (from 1702 he occupied his spare moments with their revision), they contain as many as six movements (solos and duets) in a variety of forms. What little music he composed during his later years passed as that of his copyist Gregorio Piva.

Stobaeus, Johann (1580–1646). A leading exponent of the chorale-based Königsberg School. Stobaeus spent his life in Königsberg: he was educated at the university under Johannes Eccard (1600), appointed to the Königsberg Kapelle as a bass (1602), then *Kantor* of the cathedral church and school (1603–26), and finally court *Kapellmeister*. He composed hymns, motets, a collection of *Cantiones sacrae* (1624) and quantities of occasional music on texts by Königsberg poets. In 1647 Marco Scacchi published a collection in his memory.

Strungk, Nicolaus Adam. See NORTHERN EUROPE 7 *Itinerant Musicians*.

Theile, Johann (1646–1724). *Kapellmeister*, teacher, composer of dramatic and concerted sacred music, and the author of six treatises on counterpoint, of which the *Musikalisches Kunst-Buch* (n.d.) was the most influential. Theile's first publication was a collection of *Weltliche Arien* (1667), which were probably intended for the Leipzig collegium musicum, of which he was a member during his days as a law student. He subsequently had lessons with Schütz in Dresden and became acquainted (at the very least) with Buxtehude in 1673, the year in which he published his *St Matthew Passion* in Lübeck and was appointed *Kapellmeister* at the ducal court of Gottorf. The next two years were spent composing dramatic entertainments for Duke Christian Albrecht, before the Kapelle was disbanded in 1675.

Theile took up residence in Hamburg where his first opera, *Adam und Eva*, inaugurated the new Theater am Gänsemarkt in 1678. He held two further *Kapellmeister* posts, at Wolfenbüttel (1685–91) and Merseburg (1691–4) and seems to have worked at the Berlin court where, according to the preface to his unpublished *Andächtige Kirchen-Music*, he served as Friedrich III's oboe instructor. His *Musikalisches Kunst-Buch* may have inspired Bach's *Die Kunst der Fuge*; certainly Theile was one of the first to compose large-scale vocal choral fugues.

Torri, Pietro. See CENTRAL EUROPE 1 *South Germany: Munich*.

Tunder, Franz (1614–67). Organist of the Marienkirche in Lübeck from 1641 and composer who played an important role in the development of the Lutheran cantata. Tunder had been a child prodigy and appears to have travelled to Florence where he would have met Frescobaldi. At Lübeck he gradually acquired other appointments at the Marienkirche; he organized evening concerts, known as Abendmusiken, at which solo motets, sacred arias, chorale cantatas, instrumental ensemble music and organ pieces were performed in the organ gallery. Only a few of his works survive, most of them for organ (preludes and chorale fantasias). Tunder was succeeded by his son-in-law, Dieterich Buxtehude.

Venturini, Francesco (*c*1675–1745). French (or possibly Walloon) musician at the Hanover court. Despite his Italian name Venturini was considered as one of the French musicians under J.-B. Farinel who were required to perform orchestral music in the French style. In 1713 he was appointed *Konzertmeister* and the following year published 12 orchestra suites in Amsterdam, dedicated to Elector Maximilian II Emanuel; he eventually became *Kapellmeister*.

Weber, Georg (*c*1616–after 1653). Clergyman and songwriter who worked in Stockholm and Danzig before taking up the posts of vicar and succentor at Magdeburg Cathedral. His accompanied songs were Italian in their vocal elaboration but German in their use of viol ritornellos; the texts – passionate and Pietist – were more often than not his own.

Berlin

Algarotti, Francesco. See ITALY 10 *Itinerant Musicians*.

Ariosto, Attilio. See ITALY 10 *Itinerant Musicians*.

Bach, Carl Philipp Emanuel (1714–88). Famous keyboard player and teacher, the author of a renowned treatise on keyboard playing (*Versuch über die wahre Art das Clavier zu spielen*, 1753–62) and second son of J. S. Bach. Emanuel Bach spent the first 30 years of his career at the court of Frederick the Great (1738–68) and the last 20 as the *Kantor* at Hamburg. Well educated and independent-minded, thanks to his father's encouragement and support, Emanuel found himself infinitely more at home in the company of the Hamburg intellectuals (among them the *Sturm and Drang* poets) than he had been with the Prussian courtiers. Although a true exponent of the pre-Classical style, Emanuel composed many works for Berlin – chamber works and virtuoso harpsichord concertos – in the late German Baroque style. He was, perhaps, the greatest exponent of the clavichord – the instrument he most favoured because of its unmatched expressive capacities, ideal for the intense sensibility of his music (the so-called *empfindsamer Stil*); he was also pre-eminent as a harpsichordist and pianist, though he chafed at the limitations of these instruments.

Carl Philipp Emanuel Bach was born in Weimar, the son of Johann Sebastian and his first wife, Maria Barbara; Telemann was his godfather. His musical education took place at home: sessions with his father were augmented by evenings of chamber music with their relatives and his father's colleagues and pupils as well as by the encounters with musicians from afar who came to meet his father. Emanuel's general education was acquired at the Lutheran seminary at Cöthen and the Thomasschule at Leipzig; afterwards he pursued studies in law at the University of Leipzig (1731) and the University of Frankfurt an der Oder (1734–8). During his last Leipzig years, he began composing harpsichord concertos and chamber music while serving as his father's part-time assistant.

It had been their plan that he should travel after completing his studies; J. S. Bach's patron, Count von Keyserlingk, the Russian ambassador to Dresden, wished Emanuel to accompany his son on a tour of Europe, but Prince Frederick of Prussia pre-empted this arrangement with an invitation to his musical establishment at Ruppin (which already boasted the services of the Bendas and the Grauns). His duties included accompanying (and sometimes composing the music for) Frederick's thrice-weekly evenings of *galant* chamber music, which continued at Berlin and Potsdam (at the Sanssouci palace) after

Frederick became king in 1740; he was assisted on these occasions by Christoph Nichelmann, later by K. F. C. Fasch.

In 1743 he produced his famous, turbulent Prussian Sonatas (a heady mixture of *Empfindsamkeit* and Classical sonata form which may have put off Frederick, their royal dedicatee), and the Württemberg Sonatas (dedicated to his pupil, Duke Carl Eugen) the following year, as well as numerous sinfonias, concertos and harpsichord 'sonatinas', ensemble sonatas and songs. In 1749 he provided a *Magnificat* for the Christmas Vespers. The Berlin Opera was dominated by the works of J. A. Hasse and C. H. Graun, and offered no opportunity for Bach to develop that side of his composing technique, although his interest and natural flair for it is hinted at by the expressive recitative style he pursued in his keyboard works.

His father visited him twice, in 1741 and 1747; between these visits, Emanuel married and fathered two of his three children. After his father's death in 1750, Emanuel's young half-brother Johann Christian came to live in his household and became one of his pupils. Emanuel inherited the collection of family manuscripts (known as the 'Alt-Bachisches Archiv') as well as approximately one third of his father's music (the rest being divided between Friedemann and his stepmother, Anna Magdalena).

The publication in 1753 of the first part of his systematically conceived keyboard treatise greatly enhanced Emanuel's already formidable reputation as a teacher. Restless, and weary of the court routines and lowly pay, he began the search for a new post. In 1753 he applied for the post of *Kantor* at Zittau and two years later for his father's old post at Leipzig, but was unsuccessful on each occasion. With the outbreak of the Seven Years War (1756–63) the number of performances at Sanssouci declined, and salaries were not paid (forcing Emanuel to sell some of his father's music and, in particular, the copper plates for *Die Kunst der Fuge*. Prospects of employment elsewhere seemed even more remote.

The death of his godfather in 1767 provided the way forward, although for a time Frederick was reluctant to release him. In 1767, at the age of 53, Emanuel left Berlin, carrying with him the honorific post of *Kapellmeister von Haus aus* to the king's sister, Princess Amalia, to succeed Telemann as *Kantor* and *director musices* at Hamburg. The recognition and opportunities he had sought for so long were finally within his grasp. Like his father's at Leipzig, his duties included teaching at the church school, attending to administrative details and directing the music at Hamburg's five main churches (amounting to 200 performances a year), as well as faithfully providing the annual Passion music (usually containing – of necessity – borrowed music) and other occasional music for civic ceremonies. In the year following his appointment he produced his Handelian oratorio *Die Israeliten in der Wüste* (1768–9).

After the relative inactivity of his years at court, Emanuel responded to these demands with skill and enthusiasm. He organized a concert series in which choral and dramatic works by his father and Handel as well as Telemann, Graun, Hasse, Gluck and Haydn were performed for the public; in 1772, Michael Arne conducted the first German performance of *Messiah*. A circle of poets, university professors and local intellectuals gathered around him; his house became a magnet for travellers such as Charles Burney, who, in the *Present State of Music in Germany ...* (1773), described an evening spent with Emanuel, who improvised at the clavichord for him: ' ... he grew so animated and possessed, that he not only played, but looked like one inspired'. Emanuel also provided him with an autobiographical sketch.

Since he had already moved beyond most of the contrapuntal technique inherited from his father, it remained for him to shake off the shallower affectations of the Berlin court. Thus unburdened, he turned his talents to composing with modular Classical themes that could be broken down into motifs and then varied in clear, homophonic textures; his compositional process had, in turn, an important influence on Ludwig van Beethoven. Emanuel cast his six three-movement *sinfonien* for Gottfried van Swieten (1773) with energetic outer movements and deeply expressive and intimately textured slow movements. After years of writing flute-orientated chamber music (albeit sometimes with obbligato keyboard parts), he turned to forms in which the keyboard emerged as the dominant force. With van Swieten's patronage, he also published six important collections of solo keyboard sonatas '*für Kenner und Liebhaber*' (1779–87) – 'for connoisseurs and amateurs' – which underscore his determination to appeal to a wide spectrum of the public. He also left some 50 keyboard concertos and 250 songs.

Bach, Wilhelm Friedemann. See NORTHERN EUROPE *4 Saxony and Thuringia: Dresden*.

Baron, Ernst Gottlieb. See NORTHERN EUROPE *4 Saxony and Thuringia*.

Benda, Franz (1709–86). Bohemian violinist, teacher and composer who worked for 53 years at the court of Frederick the Great. Much that is known of Benda has been gleaned from his colourful autobiography (1763). The son of a town musician, he became a chorister at the Nicolaikirche in Prague (1718), where he began his studies on the violin. Two years later (when still only 11 years old) he ran away to Dresden, where he sang and played in the Hofkapelle. He returned to Prague in time for the coronation celebrations of Charles VI in 1723, taking part in the performances of J. J. Fux's *Costanza e Fortezza* and J. D. Zelenka's Latin comedy *Melodrama de Sancto Wenceslao*. For the next three years he devoted himself to the violin, after which he secured a minor post at Vienna (1726–9); but in 1729 he and the violinist Georg Czarth removed to Warsaw where they eventually found employment in the court orchestra.

With the death of the Polish King August II in 1733, Benda went to Dresden, whence he was recruited by Prince Frederick of Prussia, who was assembling an ensemble of instrumentalists at Ruppin. It was the beginning of a long and close relationship: Frederick rescued Benda's family from religious persecution in Bohemia by arranging for them to emigrate to Prussia, and as several (including four of Benda's own children) were musicians, places were found for them in the burgeoning royal music.

While serving the prince as *Konzertmeister*, Benda continued his musical studies with the Grauns and although he never became a first-rank composer (he produced sonatas, concertos, *sinfonie* and capriccios), he became famous in his day as a distinctive violinist – the master of a rich cantabile tone – and the founder of the Berlin school of violin playing. The existence of both simple and ornamented versions (presumably written down for or by students) of 33 violin sonatas bestows greater import upon them than they might otherwise have merited. Like J. J. Quantz, Benda published little of his music.

Brade, William. See NORTHERN EUROPE *1 North Germany*.

Carestini, Giovanni. See ITALY *10 Itinerant Musicians*.

Crüger, Johannes (1598–1662). *Kantor* of the Nicolaikirche in Berlin from 1622, theorist and composer, who compiled several important collections of chorales. Crüger was a close friend and colleague of the chorale poet Paul

Gerhardt (deacon of the Nicolaikirche from 1657). In 1647 he published his *Praxis pietatis melica* which was repeatedly reprinted, first with continuo accompaniment, later with optional instrumental parts. A further collection, *Psalmodia sacra*, appeared in 1657. Crüger was succeeded as *Kantor* by J. G. Ebeling.

Ebeling, Johann Georg (1637–76). Composer, writer and educator, who from 1662 served as *Kantor* of the Nicolaikirche, Berlin. Ebeling received his musical training from Michael Jacobi at Lüneburg and studied theology at the University of Helmstedt. After two years in Hamburg, where he was associated with Weckmann's collegium musicum, Ebeling succeeded Johannes Crüger in Berlin. He published settings (with independent instrumental parts) of Paul Gerhardt's hymns (1666/7) and a history of music, *Archaiologia Orphicae* (1675).

Fedeli, Ruggiero. See ITALY *4 Venice*.

Frederick II [Frederick the Great] (1712–86). King of Prussia, patron of the arts, flautist and composer. As the eldest son of Friedrich Wilhelm I [the Barracks King], Frederick II was the object of great expectations. His father insisted on a military training, but Frederick preferred the pen and the flute to the sword, and French clothes and manners to Prussian military regalia (see Plate 9).

As a child he had been allowed to study thoroughbass. At the age of 16, while visiting Dresden, he heard J. J. Quantz play the flute and also attended his first opera, J. A. Hasse's *Cleofide*. He invited Quantz to visit him in Berlin for lessons, which were interrupted in 1730 by the king. Rebellious, the 18-year-old prince tried to run away to England; to bring him to heel, the king had one of Frederick's accomplices beheaded in his presence. To appease his father, he married (1733) – though the union was apparently never consummated – and took up the command of a regiment.

To please himself, he took up residence at Ruppin and then at Rheinsberg (1735–40), gradually assembling a group of instrumentalists who included the Grauns, the Bendas, Christoph Schaffrath and J. G. Janitsch. Quantz resumed his visits and only officially joined the court after Frederick had succeeded to the throne in 1740; C. P. E. Bach took up his appointment in 1740. The following year the court moved to Sanssouci, the royal palace near Potsdam, where the intellectual élite – among them Voltaire – regularly gathered. J. S. Bach visited his son at Potsdam in 1741 and 1747, when he transformed a

theme by Frederick into the monumental *Musikalisches Opfer*. At the zenith of his power (1754), Frederick had more than 50 musicians in his employ, of whom about 40 were instrumentalists.

Frederick II made C. H. Graun his *Kapellmeister*; as the court opera composer, Graun was immediately sent to Italy to procure the finest singers. Their showcase was a new royal opera house (which opened in Berlin in 1742) where, until the start of the Seven Years War (1756), two Carnival operas were produced annually. Frederick took an active role in the production of these operas – predominantly by Graun and Hasse – and assisted in the writing and selection of the librettos to be set (he was responsible for the text of Graun's *Montezuma*, 1755).

He made Quantz his chamber composer and director of instrumental *soirées*, at which concertos and chamber music with flute predominated. As a lifelong pupil of Quantz, he allowed the flautist the exceptional privilege of commenting on his playing. With the assistance of Graun and Quantz, he composed dramatic and chamber music, some of which, though intended solely for court performances, was published posthumously. Frederick published his opinions on music in *Lettres au public* (1753).

Galli-Bibiena, Giuseppe. See CENTRAL EUROPE *3 Austro-Hungary: Vienna*.

Gerhardt, Paul (1607–76). Lutheran theologian, poet and composer of chorale tunes. After studies in Wittenberg, Gerhardt appears to have spent most of his life in Berlin, where in 1657 he became a deacon at the Nicolaikirche, though he was dismissed in 1669 for refusing to sign a declaration of tolerance towards the reigning Calvinists.

His texts stimulated an outpouring of settings by his colleagues Johannes Crüger and J. G. Ebeling, as well as Nikolaus Hasse, Jacob Hintze, J. C. Graupner and J. F. Doles. The librettist Erdmann Neumeister incorporated individual stanzas into a cantata cycle, B. H. Brockes used his lines in the *St John Passion* which Handel, Johann Mattheson and Telemann set; and so too Picander in the *St Matthew Passion* text he prepared for Bach. His own tunes (134 survive) were composed for private devotions.

Graun. Two brothers of a family of musicians who served Frederick the Great. Johann Gottlieb (1702/3–1771) was a violinist and prolific composer of trio sonatas, concertos and symphonies. Before joining Crown Prince Frederick's Ruppin establishment in 1732, he was

Konzertmeister at Merseburg where in 1726 he met J. S. Bach and took on the young W. F. Bach as a pupil. With the accession of Frederick in 1740, Johann became leader of the new Berlin Opera orchestra. None of his music – often superior to that of his brother – was published during his lifetime and indeed his achievements were always overshadowed by the glittering operatic successes of Carl Heinrich (1703/4–1759).

Carl Heinrich was a musician of many parts: tenor, cellist and composer. Like Johann, Carl was devoted to serving Frederick the Great: from 1740 until his death, he was *Kapellmeister* of the Prussian court and chief composer of the Berlin Opera. Earlier, he had been attached to the Brunswick court, during which time he had composed six operas (five to German texts). He produced a further 26 operas for Berlin – many on well-known *opera seria* librettos by Zeno and Metastasio, others adapted from French models. Frederick the Great provided Graun with the libretto for *Montezuma* (1755).

Composer and king were friends – a privileged relationship maintained at great price, for Graun was thus doubly obliged to please Frederick. The king's wishes always overrode personal artistic considerations: when in 1745 Frederick ordered Italian sinfonias instead of French overtures, and cavatinas instead of da capo arias, he got them; when in 1746 Frederick was not satisfied with an aria in *Demofoonte*, Graun was forced to incorporate another by his rival J. A. Hasse. One of Graun's most enduring works, his *Te Deum*, commemorated Frederick's victory at Prague in 1756. News of a Prussian defeat at Züllichau three years later is said to have precipitated Graun's death. Although Graun's operas represent a last flowering of Baroque opera, his finest music is to be found in his *galant* Passion *Der Tod Jesu* (1755), in which he felt himself freer to pursue his own muse.

Hesse, Ludwig Christian. See NORTHERN EUROPE 5 *West Germany and the Rhineland.*

Janitsch, Johann Gottlieb (1708–c1763). Silesian composer and bass viol player at the court of Frederick the Great. Janitsch was one of the original, 17-strong orchestra – also including the Grauns and the Bendas – that moved from Ruppin to Rheinsberg in 1736. In addition to providing music for masquerade balls at Sanssouci, he composed a variety of chamber music, of which his *galant* quartets (occasionally employing the violino piccolo, viola pomposa, oboe d'amore or the violetta) are of particular interest.

Jarzębski, Adam. See NORTHERN EUROPE 3 *Poland.*

Linike. Three musicians of undocumented relationship, working at the Prussian court until its dissolution in 1713. Ephraim (1665–1726) was a violinist at the court from 1690. Christian Bernhard (1673–1751) was a cellist and court musician at Berlin until 1716, when he was appointed to the chapel of Margrave Christian at Cöthen, where he was a colleague of J. S. Bach and C. F. Abel. Johann Georg (c1680–after 1737) was a violinist and composer of instrumental music who served after 1713 as director of music at Weissenfels; he was in London from 1721 until about 1725 when he became leader of the Hamburg Opera orchestra under Reinhard Keiser.

Pistocchi, Francesco Antonio Mamiliano. See ITALY 7 *Papal States: Bologna-Ferrara.*

Praetorius, Bartholomaeus (c1590–1623). Court cornettist and composer. Praetorius served Elector Johann Sigismund of Brandenburg (1613–20), during which time he published a collection of dances (1616) inspired by William Brade's *Newe ausserlesene Paduanen und Galliarden* (1614). For the last three years of his life he worked at the Swedish royal chapel.

Quantz, Johann Joachim (1697–1773). The greatest exponent of German 18th-century flute playing, flute maker, composer, teacher and author, whose writings include *Versuch einer Anweisung die Flöte traversiere zu spielen* (1752, an invaluable source of performing practices of the late Baroque era), and an autobiography (published by Marpurg in 1754). Although his name is usually linked with that of his well-known pupil and patron, Frederick the Great, Quantz had a full and varied career prior to taking up a post at the Prussian court in 1741.

The son of a village blacksmith and nephew of a Merseburg town musician, Quantz was apprenticed to a musician, J. A. Fleischhack, under whom he learned to play the violin, oboe, string bass and harpsichord. In 1716 he became a member of the Dresden town band, but by the next year had travelled south to Vienna where he studied counterpoint with J. J. Fux and J. D. Zelenka. He divided his time during the next six years (1719–25) between Dresden and the Polish court chapel in Warsaw, where he served as an oboist. Only when it became evident that there was little future for him as an oboist did he turn to the flute (after studies with P. G. Buffardin).

He travelled to Prague in order to take part in the performances of Fux's *Costanza e Fortezza* (mounted for the coronation of Charles VI), and to Italy with the Polish ambassador. In Rome he became friendly with J. A. Hasse and studied with Francesco Gasparini. He spent several months in Paris (1726–7), where he made many friends – among them Michel Blavet, Antoine Forqueray and J. P. Guignon – and had alterations (another closed key and an additional hole next to E flat) made to his flute. During a ten-week spell in London (1727), he met Handel, before returning to Dresden and an appointment in the Hof kapelle.

Quantz began teaching the young Prussian prince to play the flute in 1728, while on a state visit to Berlin with August II, returning twice yearly until at last, in 1741, he accepted unprecedentedly well-paid appointments as court flautist, director and composer of chamber music. In the meantime, he married (1737), composed quantities of mixed-style sonatas and Vivaldian concertos, and began making innovative flutes (by increasing the bore to enhance the low registers and devising a sliding head to enable the player to tune his instrument a semitone in either direction), much prized by Frederick.

Once installed at Sanssouci, Quantz occupied himself with organizing musical *soirées* in which the king performed. In this capacity he composed exclusively for the king and, accordingly, in a simpler style than he might otherwise have affected: the king's penchant for passages of triplet thirds caused Kirnberger to remark on the resemblance of Quantz's music to rows of sugar loaves. A devoted pupil to the end, Frederick is said to have composed the last movement for a sonata left incomplete at Quantz's death.

Quantz is known today less as a composer than as an important writer. His memoirs contain important insights into the musical life of the places he visited. His wide-ranging treatise offers much more than instructions to flute players: he discusses performance on other instruments, the duties of the accompanist and the leader and, perhaps most importantly, makes clear comparisons between the Italian, French and German styles of the late Baroque era (1725–50) – their forms and genres – and provides a perspective from which his readers may evaluate music of the period.

Reusner. See NORTHERN EUROPE *1 North Germany.*

Rowe, Walter (*d* ?1647). English viol player and composer at the Berlin Hof kapelle. Thought to have been a pupil of Alfonso Ferrabosco the younger, Rowe took up his appointment in Berlin in 1614, visiting William Brade at Hamburg *en route* from England. Highly esteemed as a player and teacher, his pupils included S. T. Staden and the Brandenburg princesses, for one of whom he compiled a songbook. His son, of the same name (*d* 1671), was also a viol player to the Elector of Brandenburg.

Sebastiani, Johann (1622–83). Conservative composer of sacred and occasional music, best known for his large-scale *St Matthew Passion* (by 1663), who served as *Kantor* of Königsberg (1661) and then *Kapellmeister* to the Elector of Brandenburg (1663–79).

Stricker, Augustin Reinhard (*d* after 1720). Tenor and violinist who preceded J. S. Bach as *Kapellmeister* at Cöthen (1712–17). Before taking up that post, he served in the court orchestra in Berlin (from 1702), where he produced two German operas (one in collaboration with J. B. Volumier and Gottfried Finger). At Cöthen, Stricker published a collection of Italian cantatas (1715). His last appointment was at the court at Neuburg, in the service of the Elector Palatine Carl Philipp. Johann Mattheson dedicated *Das beschützte Orchestre* (1717) to him.

Torelli, Giuseppe. See ITALY *7 Papal States: Bologna-Ferrara.*

Volumier, Jean Baptiste. See NORTHERN EUROPE *4 Saxony and Thuringia: Dresden.*

Hamburg

Bach, Carl Philipp Emanuel. See NORTHERN EUROPE *1 North Germany: Berlin.*

Becker, Dietrich (1623–79). Violinist (whose first post in Holstein was as an organist in 1645), and composer of chamber music. Becker turned to the violin in the early 1650s, gaining a post at the Celle court chapel in 1658. He returned to Hamburg as a municipal violinist in 1662, succeeding Johann Schop the elder as the director of the Ratsmusik five years later. In 1668 he published *Musicalische Frühlings-Früchte*, a collection of sonatas and suites for three to five instruments, followed by two further collections of trios in 1674 and 1679. In 1674 Becker was appointed director of music at Hamburg Cathedral and four years later published *Traur- und Begrabnüss-Musik* for voices and instruments.

Bernhard, Christoph. See NORTHERN EUROPE *4 Saxony and Thuringia: Dresden.*

Brade, William. See NORTHERN EUROPE 1 *North Germany.*

Brockes, Barthold Heinrich (1680–1747). Poet and founder of the Teutschübenden Gesellschaft (1715), whose Passion oratorio libretto (1712), poetically paraphrased from all four gospels, was set by most of the prominent Lutheran composers of the day – including Reinhard Keiser, Telemann, Handel and Johann Mattheson – and used in part by Bach for his *St John Passion*. Brockes was a pupil at the Johanneum and the Gymnasium before studying law at Halle (1700–02), where he held weekly concerts in his quarters.

At Hamburg he became a member of the senate in 1720 and remained involved in civic affairs throughout his life. A European tour following the completion of his studies left him with a taste for art and antiquities as well as botany. His 1712 collection of devotional poetry was reprinted more than 30 times in the decade that followed.

Bronner, Georg (1667–1720). Organist and composer who was associated as both administrator and composer at the Hamburg Opera. Almost from the beginning, Bronner divided his time between his duties as the organist of the Heilig Geist hospital (where he succeeded his father, Christoph, in 1689), and the theatre. From 1693 until 1702 he composed operas, collaborating on some of them with Johann Mattheson and J. C. Schieferdecker. In 1696, the year in which he took on additional duties as deputy organist at the Nicolaikirche, Bronner published six sacred concertos which demonstrate his command of text-setting, harmony and vocal ornamentation. Like his operas, his two oratorios are lost. In 1715 he published a book of chorales, notable for its versatile settings (solo versions with figured and unfigured basses as well as vocal trios).

Bruhns, Nicolaus. See NORTHERN EUROPE 2 *Scandinavia.*

Conradi, Johann Georg (d 1699). *Kapellmeister* who, during the 1690s, served as music director of the Hamburg Opera. In that capacity he composed at least nine operas, of which *Die schöne und getreue Ariadne* (1691) is the earliest surviving opera composed especially for Hamburg. Conradi originated in Middle Germany, where he was director of music at the court of Oettingen-Oettingen from 1671 until 1682, then *Kapellmeister* at the Ansbach court of the cultured Margrave Johann Friedrich, for whom he composed sacred music (now lost). With the death of the margrave, Conradi sought a similar post and

in 1687 obtained one at Römhild, where he assembled a fine orchestra.

Conradi must surely have composed operas prior to his appointment at Hamburg, for his Hamburg operas reveal a well-developed and cosmopolitan technique which effectively combined French overtures and dances with both highly charged recitatives and da capo arias.

Feind, Barthold (1678–1721). Lawyer by profession, librettist and aesthetician by persuasion. Feind wrote texts – notable for their development of character and emotional intensity, and frequently incorporating scenes of violence – for Reinhard Keiser and Christoph Graupner between 1705 and 1719, in spite of periods of exile and imprisonment. Well educated (at the universities of Halle and Wittenberg) and well travelled (in France and Italy), Feind became actively involved in Hamburg politics; for his opinions, he was hung in effigy (1707), and a performance of Graupner's *L'amore ammalato* on a text by Feind was stopped by demonstrators (1708), impelling him to leave Hamburg, though he was quickly absolved of guilt and permitted to return. However, in the interim he served as a tutor to the son of a Swedish baron, a connection which later (1717) led to his arrest and imprisonment by the Danish during the Swedish–Danish war. His *Deutsche Gedichte ... sammt einer Vorrede ... und Gedanken von der Opera* (1708) remains an important source of North German opera aesthetics.

Förtsch, Johann Philipp (1652–1732). Royal physician and diplomat whose early career was spent as a singer and composer. Förtsch studied music at Frankfurt, then medicine, philosophy and law at the universities of Jena and Erfurt; he travelled for several years, then settled in Hamburg where he sang with the Ratschor and the Opera. Though he was later to become the resident composer at the Hamburg Opera, producing two operas a year from 1684 until 1690, Förtsch was away from Hamburg during the early 1680s, directing the Hofkapelle at Gottorf and completing his doctorate in medicine at the University of Kiel.

After a very successful period in Hamburg he put aside musical ambitions and became court physician first to his Gottorf patron, Christian Albrecht of Schleswig-Holstein, then to the Bishop of Lübeck, for whom he also undertook political and diplomatic missions. In addition to operas, he composed church cantatas for Gottorf and wrote two treatises on music.

Franck, Johann Wolfgang (1644–1710). Franconian composer, who worked in his native Ansbach and Hamburg before settling in London in 1690. His first appointment was as tutor to the daughters of the Ansbach royal household in 1666, although by 1668 he had been granted leave to study in Italy. He returned with new ideas and standards with which he set about transforming the Ansbach Hofkapelle. As *Director der Comoedie*, he imposed a Lullian discipline on the orchestra and composed at least one ballet and two Venetian-style operas. He also provided sacred music and in 1677 became chaplain.

His progress there came to an abrupt end in 1679 when he was accused of assassinating another court musician. He secured legal asylum in Hamburg where he was immediately named director of the Theater am Gänsemarkt. He had produced 17 operas by the time he left Hamburg in 1687, including *Aeneas* (1680), which incorporates the earliest known aria with trumpet obbligato, and *Cara Mustapha* (1686), an opera about the Turkish siege of Vienna, in which he blended French, German and Italian traits. From 1682 until 1686 he also served as director of music at the Lutheran cathedral. In London he published songs and collaborated on concerts with Robert King.

Graupner, (Johann) Christoph. See NORTHERN EUROPE 5 *West Germany and the Rhineland*.

Grünewald, Gottfried. See NORTHERN EUROPE 7 *Itinerant Musicians*.

Harms, Johann Oswald. See NORTHERN EUROPE 4 *Saxony and Thuringia: Dresden*.

Hunold, Christian Friedrich ['Menantes'] (1681–1721). Saxon novelist, aesthetician and librettist who worked in Hamburg (1700–06). Hunold was educated in Arnstadt, Weissenfels and Jena. He settled in Hamburg where he gained a reputation as a critic and writer. Reinhard Keiser recognized his gifts and commissioned an adaptation of *Salomon* in 1703, then collaborated on an opera (*Der gestürzte und wieder erhöhte Nebucadnezar*, 1704) and an oratorio (*Der blutige und sterbende Jesus*, 1705). However, he made life quite impossible for himself by publishing a frank account of the scandalous affairs of singers and others associated with the Hamburg Opera entitled *Satyrischer Roman*; threatened with lawsuits and assassination, he returned to Saxony. He immediately published an important survey of the conventions pertaining to opera, oratorio and cantata texts (*Theatralische, galante und geistliche Gedichte*, 1706) and, in 1708, took up the relatively innocuous post as lecturer in poetry and rhetoric at the University of Halle, studying law after gaining a doctorate in 1714. A year later he published a useful introduction to German literary and rhetorical terminology (*Einleitung zur teutschen Oratorie*).

Keiser, Reinhard (1674–1739). *Kapellmeister*, public opera house administrator and an important and original composer of German opera, working mainly in Hamburg. His start in life was not auspicious: his father Gottfried (*d c*1712) abandoned his family in the year of Reinhard's birth. Fortunately, Reinhard was able to gain a place at the Thomasschule in Leipzig, where from 1685 he would have learnt from Johann Schelle and Johann Kuhnau.

Keiser held a varied succession of minor court posts – among them, *Cammer-Componist* at the Brunswick court (early 1690s), *Kapellmeister* to the Duke of Mecklenburg at Schwerin (1700) and *Kapellmeister* (not *Hofkapellmeister* as he had hoped) at Copenhagen (1721–2) – and was a guest at others (including the Stuttgart court of the Duke of Württemberg); but it was at Hamburg that he made his mark, as a director–composer of the Theater am Gänsemarkt. When Keiser arrived in Hamburg, he had already proved his abilities as the composer of three theatre pieces for the Brunswick court.

Keiser worked quickly, producing as many as eight new operas in 1698–9 and 26 between 1709 and 1718. He favoured the texts of Postel, Hinsch and Feind and, during his trouble-ridden tenure as director at the Theater am Gänsemarkt (1702–7), he worked closely with the text adapter Drüsicke, producing 17 operas of his own as well as new operas by Johann Mattheson, Handel and Gottfried Grünewald. Many of his operas were in fact Singspiels composed to mark special occasions – royal birthdays, weddings, and coronations as far afield as London and Vienna. His use of Lower Saxon dialect (*Plattdeutsch*) in the arias and comic scenes of *Der Carneval von Venedig* (1707) created a sensation (macaronic texts in Italian and German were not uncommon); like a number of his other later operas, *Carneval* incorporates arias by Christoph Graupner. More importantly, Keiser's imaginative use of instruments and formidable powers of characterization ensured the popularity both of his operas and his oratorios.

However, the competition to have works performed in Hamburg was lively and whenever Keiser was absent (1707–8, 1718–23) his music was neglected in favour of that of Handel and Graupner. When he returned to Hamburg briefly in 1721, he had to mount the production of *Der siegende David* at the Drillhaus. But it was Telemann who – both as *Kantor* of the Johanneum with responsibilities to the five principal Hamburg churches, and as director of the Hamburg Opera from 1722 – ultimately blocked his advancement there. Keiser's rapport with Mattheson was more fruitful. They enjoyed a close, stimulating friendship, regularly performing one another's music, and Keiser contributed to Mattheson's *Das neu-eröffnete Orchestre* (1713). Both Telemann and Mattheson provided obituaries on Keiser's death.

After a final spate of operas, composed between 1723 and 1730, Keiser spent his last years as a *Canonicus minor*, composing only sacred music. Over the years he had gained wide recognition for his oratorios, including an early setting of Brockes's *Passion* (1712), and in 1736 composed a *Te Deum*. His *St Mark Passion* (?1717) influenced Bach's *St Matthew Passion* a decade later.

Kremberg, Jakob. See NORTHERN EUROPE 7 *Itinerant Musicians*.

Kusser, Johann Sigismund. See NORTHERN EUROPE 7 *Itinerant Musicians*.

Lorentz, Johann. See NORTHERN EUROPE 2 *Scandinavia*.

Lustig, Jacob Wilhelm. See LOW COUNTRIES 1 *United Provinces*.

Mattheson, Johann (1681–1764). Hamburg composer and important writer who chronicled the transition from German Baroque to pre-Classical styles in his books, his periodical *Critica musica* – the first German music periodical – and his theoretical treatises. As the son of a tax collector, Mattheson benefited from family wealth and ambition: as a child he was instructed in foreign languages, fencing, riding, dancing and drawing as well as on musical instruments (organ, viol, violin, flute, oboe and lute); later he studied law and education at the Johanneum.

During the 1690s he served for a time as a page at the court of the Count von Güldenlöw and began singing in the chorus and taking minor roles in Hamburg Opera productions. He made his début with the company as a soprano soloist in 1696, but within a year his voice had changed and so from 1697 until 1705 he sang tenor roles. In all, he took part in about 65 new operas, also conducting (under J. G. Conradi, J. S. Kusser – from whom he acquired knowledge of the Italian style – and Reinhard Keiser) and composing his own

operas, of which *Die Plejades* (1699) was the first.

He befriended the young Handel (four years his junior) on the latter's arrival in Hamburg in 1703, guided him in his first efforts to compose dramatic music and secured a place for him among the second violins and as a deputy harpsichordist in the opera orchestra. In late summer that first year they travelled together to nearby Lübeck to meet Buxtehude (and his daughter), who was retiring from his organ post at the Marienkirche. However, their friendship was severely tested by an incident which took place during a performance of Mattheson's *Cleopatra* in 1704: a disagreement erupted when Mattheson, who was singing the role of Antonius, attempted to unseat Handel at the harpsichord after Antonius's suicide in the middle of the third act; when Handel refused to retire Mattheson challenged him to a duel. Handel's life was said to have been saved by a well-placed coat button. That Mattheson took the leading role in Handel's *Almira* in 1705 is evidence that, having spent their passions, they were able to repair their friendship.

Although an accomplished – indeed, it is said, virtuoso – organist, Mattheson never took up any of the posts, available or proffered, such as that at Lübeck or as Reincken's successor at the Catharinenkirche. Instead, he became tutor to the son of Sir John Wich, the English ambassador, and then long-serving secretary to Wich himself in 1706. Because of his background, Mattheson rose with ease to the demands of his new post. He was entrusted with diplomatic missions abroad as the ambassador's official representative, becoming an excellent English speaker, well versed in English law, politics and economics. In 1709 he married an English woman. Far from abandoning his career in music, Mattheson took on additional responsibilities as music director of the cathedral (1715–28) and as *Kapellmeister* to the Duke of Holstein (1719), all the while remaining in the service of Sir John.

During the next quarter of a century, Mattheson was extremely prolific as a composer and writer, producing many translations of English books, pamphlets and articles. Among the music he composed were cantatas, serenades, a *Magnificat* and an oratorio, *Das Lied des Lammes*. Increasing deafness forced his retirement from the cathedral as early as 1728, although he continued to compose until as late as 1760, when he produced his own funeral oratorio, *Das fröhliche Sterbelied*, which Telemann conducted four years later.

His first (and most far-reaching) book on music was *Das neu-eröffnete Orchestre* (1713). In it he attempted to sweep away the traditional attitudes on music theory (such as the validity of solmization and the church modes for contemporary music) and aesthetics, and to encourage their re-examination and reformulation. To his ear the interval of a fourth could be considered either consonant or dissonant, according to the context; major and minor scales could be shown to have different affective connotations. He also made a plea for native German composers to assert themselves more decisively instead of acquiescing to the resident Italians. Inevitably, it stimulated a conservative response which Mattheson quashed with well-placed satire. The criticism came from the theorist J. H. Buttstett, writing in *Ut, mi, sol, re, fa, la, tota musica et harmonia aeterna* (1716), which Mattheson parried with *Das beschützte Orchestre* (1717), to which Buttstett obdurately replied with *Der wider das Beschützte Orchestre ergangenen öffentlichen Erklärung* (2/1718). *Das neu-eröffnete Orchestre* became a rallying point for Enlightenment musical intellectuals and was the subject of some of the first lectures on music for more than a century at a German university, given by C. G. Schröter at the University of Jena in 1724.

In 1722 he inaugurated his innovative journal *Critica musica*, which survived until 1725, during which time he produced 24 issues. Intent upon presenting a wide range of views, he published in the first issue his own annotated translation of Raguenet's controversial *Parallèle des italiens et des françois* (1702), along with Le Cerf de La Viéville's reply, the *Comparaison de la musique italienne et de la musique française* (1704–6). Recent musical events are chronicled and new books reviewed; excerpts from his correspondence with Handel, J. J. Fux, Telemann, Johann Kuhnau, J. D. Heinichen, J. P. Krieger and Johann Theile are included in the subsequent issues. Mattheson sought, in *Der musicalischer Patriot* (1728), to justify the use of the theatrical style in Lutheran church music. Digressing, he wrote of his experiences at the Hamburg Opera, providing an inventory of the works performed there, and attributing the collapse of the Opera to the decline in the taste of the public. A devout Lutheran later, he donated most of his wealth to the rebuilding of the great organ (which had been destroyed by fire) at the Michaeliskirche.

There followed two treatises on keyboard playing, the *Grosse General-Bass-Schule* (1731),

with instructions to the soloist on how to improvise from a bass, and the *Kleine General-Bass-Schule* (1735), aimed at the accompanist wishing to realize a figured bass. Drawing upon his experiences as a court and cathedral music director, he published *Der vollkommene Capellmeister* in 1739, in which he provided the would-be *Kapellmeister* with all the necessary training and guidance needed – whether in the service of a church, city or court. Its importance lies in his systematic presentation of musical rhetoric, the 'Doctrine of the Affections', which he believed was conveyed by melody. His last and most valuable work was the *Grundlage einer Ehren-Pforte* (1740), a lexicon based on reminiscences, excerpts from correspondence and autobiographies contributed by 149 German musicians; notably absent from the list is Bach, who declined to supply Mattheson with the details of his life.

Mingotti. See ITALY *10 Itinerant Musicians.*

Neumeister, Erdmann (1671–1756). Poet and pastor of the Jacobikirche in Hamburg from 1715 until 1755, he wrote nine cycles of cantata texts for the entire church year. J. P. Krieger composed music for at least 79 of his texts (many before they met in Weissenfels in 1704). Neumeister's two cycles for the Eisenach court (1711 and 1714) were set by Telemann while many other composers, including Bach, set individual texts.

Niedt, Friedrich Erhard. See NORTHERN EUROPE *4 Saxony and Thuringia.*

Postel, Christian Heinrich (1658–1705). Poet and prolific opera librettist originally from Freiburg, working in Hamburg. After studies at the Hamburg Johanneum, and at Leipzig and Rostock universities (where he read law), Postel spent five years travelling to the Low Countries, England and France before embarking on his law career in 1688. Soon afterwards, through his friend Gerhard Schott (one of the founding administrators), he became involved in the Hamburg Opera, contributing librettos – strong on character development within stereotyped plots – which were set by J. G. Conradi, J. P. Förtsch and J. S. Kusser.

Praetorius, Jacob (1586–1651). Organist, teacher and composer who served from 1603 as organist of the Petrikirche. Praetorius studied with Sweelinck (who, in turn, composed a motet for Praetorius's wedding in 1608) and was himself the teacher of Matthias Weckmann and Berendt Petri, among others. In 1635 his daughter married a Danish pupil, Johann Lorentz. While Petri was a pupil

1 A Venetian noblewoman takes the veil in S Lorenzo; painting (c 1740s) by Gabriele Bella. At least 50 musicians, positioned on both sides of the church, can be seen taking part in the ceremony.

2 Opera performed in the private theatre of the Turin royal palace as part of the celebrations marking the arrival of the Princess of Piedmont in 1722; engraving by A. Aveline after Filippo Juvarra.

3 Staged performance of G.B. Costanzi's oratorio *Componimento sacro* given at the Palazzo della Cancelleria, Rome, in 1727 for members of the Accademia dell'Arcadia.

4 Outdoor performance of J.-B. Lully's *tragédie lyrique Alceste* in the Cour de Marbre at Versailles on 4 July 1674; engraving (1676) by J. Le Pautre.

5 *Le temps de la soirée*, one of a series of engravings (*Les heures du jour*, 1738) by F.A. Aveline depicting aristocratic life in the Rococo era; after Mondon *le fils*.

6 Michel de La Barre and other musicians (thought to be the viol player Marin Marais and the wind players Louis and Nicolas Hotteterre); painting (*c* 1710) attributed to Robert de La Tournières [Levrac]. The music is copied from La Barre's *Troisième livre de trios, pour les violons, flutes et hautbois* (1707).

7 Viol consort at the Brunswick court of Duke August the Younger; painting (1645) by Albert Freyse.

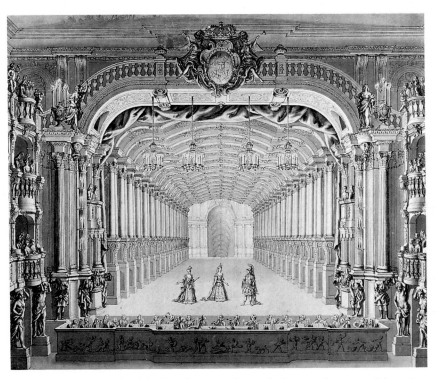

8 Stage and orchestra pit of the Dresden court theatre during a performance of Antonio Lotti's *Teofane* in 1719; pen-and-ink drawing by Heinrich Christoph Fehling.

9 Concert at Sanssouci, Potsdam, with Frederick the Great as flute soloist; engraving (after 1740) by P. Haas.

10 Interior of Augsburg Cathedral; detail of a painting (1616) by Tobias Maurer. In the gallery at the west end of the cathedral musicians seem to be taking part in the service; the organist may be Christian Erbach.

11 The imperial theatre, Vienna, during the performance of Antonio Cesti's *Il pomo d'oro* (composed for the marriage of Leopold I and Margareta Teresa of Spain) in 1668; engraving by F. Geffels.

12 Cesti's *Il pomo d'oro*; engraving by M. Küssel after Lodovico Burnacini's design for Act IV, scene 14 (Fortezza di Marte) which conveys something of the scale of the occasion.

13 Performance of J.J. Fux's *Costanza e Fortezza* given in the arena of Prague castle as part of the celebrations for the coronation of Emperor Charles VI as King of Bohemia in 1723; engraving by Birckart after Giuseppe Galli-Bibiena.

14 Concert in the Guild of Shoemakers, Zurich, 1753; photographic reproduction (of a lost original) from the *Zürcher Taschenbuch* (1911).

(1609–11), he compiled a manuscript (the *Visby Tablature*) of organ music (some of it requiring three manuals plus pedals) by Praetorius and his father. Praetorius also composed four-part chorale settings and motets.

Reincken, Johann Adam (1623–1722). Organist, teacher and composer of either Netherlands or Alsatian background. After studies with Heinrich Scheidemann at Hamburg (1654–7), Reincken briefly took up the organ post at the Berghkercke in Deventer, only to return to Hamburg in 1658 as Scheidemann's assistant at the Catharinenkirche. Five years later he succeeded him.

Reincken was a close friend of Johann Theile, with whom he founded the Hamburg Opera in 1678, and Dieterich Buxtehude, who visited him from Lübeck. The young Bach went to hear him play sometime between 1700 and 1702, taking away copies of Reincken sonatas to transcribe. Reincken composed chamber music for Johann Theile's collegium musicum, though only his *Hortus musicus* (1687) survives. He wrote manuscript virtuoso organ music to show off the power of his technique and that of the four-manual organ at his disposal; this is best summed up in his extended fantasia, *An den Wasserflüssen Babylon*.

Rowe, Walter. See NORTHERN EUROPE *1 North Germany: Berlin*.

Scheibe, Johann Adolph. See NORTHERN EUROPE *2 Scandinavia*.

Scheidemann, Heinrich (*c*1595–1663). A leading organist, teacher (a founder of the North German organ school) and composer of chorale-based music. His studies with Sweelinck (1611–14) proved stimulating, and Scheidemann was able to take Sweelinck's keyboard style a step further, refining the organ idiom in particular. Scheidemann was inspired by Scheidt's chorale ricercares (1624), and his own chorale compositions include transcriptions for organ of vocal monodies and virtuoso chorale fantasias, requiring two manuals plus pedals; these in turn influenced the next generation of organ composers. Scheidemann also composed works without a *cantus firmus*, notably works labelled 'Praeambulum', which foreshadowed the paired prelude and fugue; his *Magnificat* settings were the most highly esteemed of all. His music circulated widely in manuscript.

In 1629 he succeeded his father as organist of the Catharinenkirche in Hamburg, where he remained, assisted in his last years by his pupil and successor, J. A. Reincken. Scheidemann was a friend of Thomas Selle, Jacob

Praetorius, Johann Schop the elder and Matthias Weckmann, and the collaborator of the poet Johann Rist.

Schickhardt, Johann Christian. See LOW COUNTRIES *1 United Provinces*.

Schop. Family of instrumentalists and composers, of whom Johann the elder (*d* 1667) was most prominent. After a probationary post in the Wolfenbüttel Hofkapelle, Johann Schop – a violinist who also played the viol, lute, cornett and trombone – spent time at the Danish court (from 1615) where he was much influenced by the English and Italian string players. His stay was cut short by a plague epidemic in 1619 which forced him hastily to return to Germany. By 1621 he was the leading municipal viol player and director of the Ratsmusik (the council musicians' collective) in Hamburg, although it was as one of the earliest German violinists that he made the greatest impact. In 1634 he accompanied Heinrich Schütz and Heinrich Albert to Copenhagen for a royal wedding; during the celebrations, he won a contest with the French violinist Jacques Foucart. He returned to Hamburg in spite of Christian IV's efforts to keep him. Schop composed sacred concertos and solo songs.

His son, Johann Schop the younger (1626–after 1670), was also a viol player and song composer; as a member of the Schwerin court, he accompanied Duke Christian Ludwig to Paris several times, evidently taking part in performances of operas, and is thought to have visited England. Albert Schop (1632–after 1667), an organist and song composer, studied with Heinrich Scheidemann before taking up a court post at Güstrow in 1655.

Schütz. See NORTHERN EUROPE *6 Middle Germany*.

Selle, Thomas (1599–1663). *Kantor* at the Hamburg Johanneum and prolific (if mediocre) composer of vocal music. Though more at ease in lighter forms, Selle wrote a *St John Passion* (1641) that ranks as one of the most important of the period. He studied at Leipzig and served as *Kantor* at several northwest German cities before taking the Hamburg post in 1641. In addition to his academic duties he took on the responsibilities (maintenance of standards) of the civic director of church music in Hamburg. In these capacities he composed sacred concertos and occasional works. His settings of texts by Rist mark him out as one of the Hamburg school of songwriters.

Steffkin, Theodore. See BRITISH ISLES *1 London*.

Strungk, Nicolaus Adam. See NORTHERN
EUROPE 7 *Itinerant Musicians.*

Telemann, Georg Philipp (1681–1767).
Acknowledged as the leading German composer of his day, prolific and independent of
mind, Telemann helped in many ways to
bridge the gap between Baroque and Classical
eras. He served as *Kapellmeister* at various
Saxon courts and later as *Kantor* of the
Hamburg Johanneum (from 1721); his entre-
preneurial skills in publishing, advertising and
distributing his music, much of which was
intended for accomplished amateurs, established his international reputation; he was also
an avid correspondent whose contacts
included J. S. Bach, C. P. E. Bach (his
godson), J. C. Bach and Handel. Largely self-
taught, he was an inspiration to many younger
musicians such as J. F. Fasch, G. H. Stölzel,
Christoph Graupner, J. G. Pisendel and J. D.
Heinichen. As a theorist, Telemann exerted
an important influence upon Johann Mattheson, J. G. Walther, J. A. Scheibe, J. J. Quantz,
J. F. Agricola and F. W. Marpurg. He became
the sixth member of Mizler's corresponding
society. His life is documented in three autobiographies, written at the request of Mattheson (1718 and 1739) and Walther (1729).
Because of his important contribution to the
development of the amateur side of music-
making, his significance both as a composer
and a musical force were, until relatively
recently, grossly underrated.

Telemann showed himself to be deeply
gifted in music at an early age, mastering the
violin, flute, zither and keyboard by the age of
ten and composing an opera (*Sigismundus*, on
a text by Postel) two years later – to the consternation of his family (particularly his
mother's side), who disapproved of music.
However, such resistance served only to
reinforce his determination to persevere in his
studies through transcription and modelling
his works upon those of such composers as
Agostino Steffani, Johann Rosenmüller,
Corelli and Antonio Caldara. After pre-
paratory studies at the Hildesheim Gymnasium, he matriculated in law (at his
mother's insistence) at Leipzig University in
1701. That he had little intention of putting
aside his interest in music is evident from his
stop at Halle, *en route* to Leipzig, in order to
make the acquaintance of the young Handel.

Indeed, away from his mother's eye, Telemann turned most of his attention to music-
making. Early on at Leipzig, his setting of a
psalm was performed at the Thomaskirche
and was so well received that the mayor

rewarded him with a commission to compose
a cantata for every other Sunday – to the
outrage of the newly appointed *Kantor*,
Johann Kuhnau, who exerted all his influence
to curtail Telemann's activities at Leipzig.
Within a year of his arrival, Telemann had
founded a student collegium musicum, which
presented regular public concerts, and had
been appointed music director of the Leipzig
Opera, for which he composed operas, sang
and recruited students as singers and members
of the orchestra instead of importing them
from abroad. In 1704 Telemann stepped down
from the directorship – also undertaking not
to appear on stage – to take up the organ
post at the Neukirche, though he continued to
compose operas.

No doubt bored with the rantings of
Kuhnau and impatient to make something
more of his life, Telemann did not stay long
in Leipzig. In 1705 he accepted an appointment as *Kapellmeister* to the cosmopolitan
court of Count Erdmann II of Promnitz at
Sorau (now Żary), where the vogue for the
French and Italian styles provided him with a
new challenge. His association with the Sorau
Kantor and theorist Wolfgang Caspar Printz
and the reformist poet Erdmann Neumeister
as well as the proximity to Berlin and contact
with Polish folk music all proved stimulating.
But Telemann's tenure was cut short by the
imminent prospect of invasion by the Swedish
army, causing the court to be hurriedly disbanded. He visited Paris in 1707.

His next appointment was as the Eisenach
court *Konzertmeister* in charge of singers, with
Pantaleon Hebenstreit as leader of the orchestra. His appointment there (some time
between 1706 and 1708) just overlapped with
the presence of Bach, who left in 1708 to take
up posts at the Weimar court. Telemann had
every reason to assume that this would be
a period of relative stability and accordingly
plunged into composing church cantatas,
occasional pieces, orchestral and instrumental
chamber music. He married and soon his wife
was with child, a state of affairs that ended
tragically with her death in 1711.

A change of scene became necessary and so
he went to the free imperial city of Frankfurt
am Main to take up duties as director of
municipal music and *Kapellmeister* of the Barfüsserkirche. Together with his activities as
director of the Frauenstein Society and the
collegium musicum, which presented weekly
concerts, Telemann's new posts suited his
talents very well. He composed occasional
music for civic ceremonies, five year-long

cycles of church cantatas, oratorios, orchestral music and a wealth of chamber music, much of which was published; only the opportunity to produce opera was lacking, though he continued to supply works to the Leipzig Opera. He married again (gaining citizenship through marriage) and became a family man.

While on a visit to Eisenach in 1716, he was honoured with an appointment as a visiting *Kapellmeister* (he continued to send new works until 1729); he also served the court as a diplomatic correspondent. Further acknowledgment of his increasing stature came the following year when Duke Ernst of Gotha invited him to become *Kapellmeister* of all his various courts. This in turn forced improvements in his situation at Frankfurt. A trip to Dresden in 1719 for the festivities in honour of the newly married Prince Elector Friedrich August II and Archduchess Maria Josepha of Austria made possible a reunion with Handel, the opportunity to hear operas by Lotti and the dedication of a collection of violin concertos to the *Konzertmeister* Pisendel.

Then in 1721, the coveted post of *Kantor* of the Hamburg Johanneum – a post that traditionally carried with it teaching responsibilities and the directorship of Hamburg's five principal churches – became vacant, and Telemann was invited to succeed Joachim Gerstenbüttel. Here, at last, was a prestigious post that would provide him with seemingly unlimited opportunities to compose and perform. As *Kantor*, he would be stretched as never before: he was required to compose two cantatas a week, annually to produce a new Passion, and to provide occasional works for church and civil ceremonies. And such was his vitality and creative impetus that, in spite of heavy responsibilities, he apparently eagerly sought and fulfilled additional commissions from home and abroad.

The prospect of being actively involved in the Hamburg Opera – his opera *Der geduldige Socrates* (text by König, after Minato) had already been performed there earlier that year – was perhaps over-optimistic, for there was (at least initially) strong opposition among the city fathers to his participation. Telemann reacted characteristically by threatening to resign: he applied for the post of *Kantor* of the Leipzig Thomaskirche and in 1722 was chosen over Bach, Graupner and three other candidates; while the city council refused to grant his release, they were obliged to improve his salary and withdraw their objections to his association with the Hamburg Opera.

Telemann thereupon redoubled his activi-

ties at Hamburg, increasing the number of public concerts given at the churches, the Drill-Hall and at a tavern known as the 'Lower Tree-House', at which a wide variety of sacred and secular music was performed. They were patronized by prominent Hamburgers and supported by paid admission. More to the point, he was made music director of the Hamburg Opera, remaining in that capacity until its closure in 1738; in addition to his own operas and those of Reinhard Keiser, Handel's London operas were performed there during his tenure. He produced both serious and comic works (notable among them his 1725 *intermezzo Pimpinone*), many of which have been lost, or survive only as excerpts published in *Der getreue Music-Meister*.

Telemann was also active as a publisher, issuing 43 collections under his own imprint (from pewter plates he himself engraved) between 1725 and 1740, including a cycle of 72 sacred cantatas, *Der getreue Music-Meister* (which was issued weekly during 1728–9 and was the first German publication of its kind), the three-part *Musique de Table* (1733) and the *Nouveaux Quatuors* (published in Paris, 1738), which he underwrote with subscriptions from Germany and abroad. The popular appeal of his music lay in its *galant* character – especially in his keyboard (*Fugues légères et petits jeux*, 1738–9) and chamber music – and technical approachability. He produced editions of works with reduced scoring, and suggested alternatives for instrumentation in order to make the music more accessible. But his greatest contribution was to popularize the French overture, a genre he had mastered at Sorau, transforming it with programmatic elements and transporting it from the court salon to the concert hall.

Telemann's second trip to Paris in 1737 was occasioned by the need to prevent the pirating of his chamber music. By 1734 the French publisher Boivin had issued an unauthorized collection of his trio sonatas and, just before Telemann's arrival, Le Clerc acquired a privilege to reprint five of his collections (again without permission). Once in Paris, Telemann wasted no time in acquiring his own privilege and immediately issued two new editions. However, what he lost in revenues he made up in popular acclaim. His music was well received at court and at the Concert Spirituel and further pirated editions appeared during the 1740s.

Around 1740, Telemann felt the need to alter his pace. Though he continued to compose Passions and occasional works, he produced relatively little music. Even more to the point, he sold the plates of all his editions. His intention was to devote himself to writing. Having had to struggle to acquire his musical training, Telemann felt passionately about making music more accessible to amateurs. He was highly regarded as a teacher and felt a compulsion to write treatises which, in the event, he was unable fully to realize. He included an essay on performing recitative in the cycle of sacred cantatas known as *Harmonischer Gottes-Dienst* (1725–6) and instructions on ornamentation in his amateur chamber music editions, but only his amateurs' tutor, *Singe-, Spiel- und Generalbass-Übungen* (1733), appeared separately.

Many other theoretical works were announced in the press but never appeared – a treatise on instruments, another on recitative, still another on composition as well as a translation of J. J. Fux's *Gradus ad Parnassum*; the essay on the integration of the theatrical style into church music promised in the preface to the cantata cycle *Musicalisches Lob Gottes* (published in Nuremberg, 1744) is a notable loss. Inspired by the oratorios of Handel, he returned to composition with new determination during the last dozen years of his life.

Tielke, Joachim (1641–1719). Master string instrument maker working in Hamburg from about 1666. Such was the excellence of his instruments and the lavishness of his decoration – ebony and ivory predominating – that many of his instruments were commissioned by royalty and nobility; as a result, a large proportion of his instruments have survived, among them viols, violins, lutes, guitars and citterns.

Weckmann, Matthias (1619–74). Organist and composer whose music represents an important link between that of Schütz and Bach. Weckmann greatly benefited from the cosmopolitan training he received from Schütz as a chorister at Dresden and, on Schütz's recommendation, from Jacob Praetorius at Hamburg. In 1637 he returned to Dresden to serve as organist of the electoral chapel, although he interrupted his tenure there in 1642 to spend five years as organist of the Danish court under Schütz. A contest between Weckmann and Froberger, which ended in friendship, was said by Mattheson to have taken place in Dresden. In 1655 he was appointed *Kantor* of the Jacobikirche in Hamburg where, in 1660, he founded and composed for the collegium musicum which, with the assistance of the leading Hamburg

musicians, gave weekly concerts at the cathedral.

A composer of some originality and flexibility, Weckmann wrote choral and vocal chamber music that reveals a sensitivity to text and a predilection for concertante instruments. The instrumental music – trio sonatas and organ preludes, toccatas and fugues – is characterized by an excellent mastery of counterpoint. About half of the keyboard music once attributed to Weckmann is now known to be the work of others.

2 Scandinavia

Agrell, Johann Joachim. See NORTHERN EUROPE *6 Middle Germany*.

Albrici. See ITALY *10 Itinerant Musicians*.

Baltzar, Thomas. See BRITISH ISLES *1 London*.

Berlin, Johan Daniel (1714–87). German-born Norwegian organist, composer, inventor of a 'cembalo da gamba verticale' [a keyboard viol] and author of the first Danish–Norwegian music textbook (*Musikalske elementer*, 1744). After studies with his father Heinrich, Berlin went to Copenhagen for further study. He served from 1737 until 1767 as a civic musician in Trondheim and from 1740 as organist of the cathedral. He composed chamber and orchestral music and arranged concerts in Trondheim, yet still found time to serve as inspector of the city's waterworks and fire chief. He amassed a large library of music and instruments. In the course of building keyboard instruments he devised a mechanism that would allow him to vary the dynamics (in 1751 he built a piano with a pedal). He was a founder member of the royal Norwegian Scientific Association (1760).

Bernardi, Bartolomeo (*c*1660–1732). Bolognese violinist and composer working from 1703 at the Danish court, where, in 1710, he was appointed director of music. Only the duo and trio sonatas he published in Bologna (where he was a member of the Accademia Filarmonica) and Amsterdam at the turn of the century survive.

Bertouch, Georg von (1668–1743). German-born Norwegian military officer, violinist and composer who corresponded with Mattheson and Bach. He studied with Daniel Eberlin at Eisenach, then at Jena and Kiel universities. In the company of Johann Nicolaus Bach (with whom he had studied the organ at Jena) he travelled to Italy, where he met some Danes who persuaded him to return with them to Denmark.

He joined the Danish army and in 1719 was promoted to commandant of Christiania (Oslo), where he put much energy into enriching the city's musical life. He sent copies of his compositions to Mattheson, who addressed Bertouch in the dedication of *Das beschützte Orchestre* (1717), and published in Hamburg – perhaps with Mattheson's assistance – accounts of supernatural musical phenomena he had experienced near Bergen (*Etwas Neues unter der Sonnen!* also contains the earliest published Norwegian folkdance). Having reached the rank of lieutenant-general, he retired in 1740.

Borchgrevinck, Melchior (?*c*1570–1632), Netherlands-born Danish organist, composer and anthologist who was the first to publish major collections of music in Denmark. When his father, Bonaventura Borchgrevinck, was appointed director of music to King Christian IV in 1587, the boy became a treble in the chapel; but by 1593 it was Melchior who ranked as the best-paid musician at court. He made trips to Danzig (1596) and London (1597) to hire musicians and to purchase instruments, and to Venice – leading a party of Danish musicians including Mogens Pedersøn and Hans Nielsen – to study with Giovanni Gabrieli. Upon his return he was made chief court organist and canon of Roskilde Cathedral. Such was his prestige that the following year he was again allowed to travel to Venice, remaining until 1602. He was subsequently made principal instrumentalist (1603) and principal director (1618) at the Danish court. He contributed one madrigal to each of the two volumes of five-part madrigals (*Giardino novo bellissimo di varii fiori musicali scieltissimi*) that he compiled in 1605–6.

Brade, William. See NORTHERN EUROPE *1 North Germany*.

Bruhns, Nicolaus (1665–97). German-born organist, violinist, viol player and composer who studied with Buxtehude in Lübeck during the early 1680s before settling in Denmark, where he sought contact with the Italian musicians who were there. In 1689 he was appointed organist at the Stadtkirche, Husum. A virtuoso violinist, Bruhns was renowned for taking his violin up to the organ loft and playing chordal music while accompanying himself on the organ pedals during services. The influence of Buxtehude is evident in his virtuoso solo cantatas, organ preludes, fugues and toccatas.

Chelleri, Fortunato. See ITALY *10 Itinerant Musicians*.

Christina. See ITALY *7 Papal States: Rome*.

Descartes, René. See FRANCE *1 Paris and Versailles*.

Dowland, John. See BRITISH ISLES *1 London*.

Düben. Three generations of a family of musicians of German origins who played important roles in the musical life of Stockholm and at the Swedish court. Andreas Düben (*c*1597–1662), a pupil of Sweelinck, was appointed second organist at the Stockholm court in 1620. His brother Martin (also an organist) joined him there in 1625, at much the same time as Andreas took on duties at the German Church. Andreas rose to become court conductor in 1640. His son Gustav (*c*1628–1690) studied in Germany (1645–7) before taking up duties at court in 1648. At his father's death, Gustaf inherited his post at the German Church.

Gustaf is the best known of the Dübens for his collection of autograph manuscripts and printed editions of some 1500 vocal and 300 instrumental works – some of them unique – by contemporary German, French and Italian composers, now conserved at the University of Uppsala. His sons, Gustaf (1660–1726) and Anders von Düben (1673–1738), were – as the addition of 'von' to their name suggests – ennobled. Gustaf succeeded his father in 1690 as conductor of the court orchestra, but relinquished the post to Anders in 1698 in order to take a non-musical role in court affairs; Anders held it until 1713, journeying abroad at some point to study in Paris. Both became barons and Masters of the Royal Household.

Fischer, Johann. See NORTHERN EUROPE *7 Itinerant Musicians*.

Förster, Kaspar. See NORTHERN EUROPE *7 Itinerant Musicians*.

Freithoff, Johan Henrik (1713–67). Norwegian violinist and composer of virtuoso music. Freithoff travelled during the 1730s to Smyrna and Constantinople before deciding to petition the King of Denmark for a post in the Danish civil service. He arrived in Copenhagen, where his violin playing was much admired, and was immediately appointed violinist extraordinary (1744), but had to wait several months before being made a secretary in the Danish chancellery.

Galli-Bibiena, Carlo. See CENTRAL EUROPE *3 Austro-Hungary: Vienna*.

Geist, Christian (*c*1640–1711). North German bass singer, organist and composer working in Scandinavia. Geist worked at both the Danish and Swedish courts during the

1670s. He served as a singer in Copenhagen and as an organist in Stockholm (during which time he composed sacred chamber concertos for voices and strings). He returned to Copenhagen and in 1685 married the widow of the organist J. M. Radeck, inheriting his posts at Helligaandskirken and the Trinitatis Kirke. In 1689 he also succeeded Lorentz at the Holmens Kirke. He and his family perished in the plague epidemic of 1711.

Hintz, Ewald. See NORTHERN EUROPE 3 *Poland*.

Hurlebusch, Conrad Friedrich. See NORTHERN EUROPE 7 *Itinerant Musicians*.

Keiser, Reinhard. See NORTHERN EUROPE 1 *North Germany: Hamburg*.

Kremberg, Jakob. See NORTHERN EUROPE 7 *Itinerant Musicians*.

La Barre, Anne de. See FRANCE 1 *Paris and Versailles*.

Lorentz, Johann (*c*1610–1689). Danish organist based in Copenhagen, who nevertheless spent time in Hamburg. Lorentz was already the organist of the Vor Frue Kirke when the Danish King Christian IV granted him leave to study in Germany and Italy (1631–3); he married the daughter of Jacob Praetorius in 1635 and succeeded his father-in-law as organist of the Petrikirche in 1651 – though he chose instead to return to a post at St Nikolaj (where his father, also called Johann, had built the organ) in Copenhagen, where he initiated weekday concerts. Lorentz was also organist of the Holmens Kirke. He and his family, along with the family of P. C. Schindler, died tragically in a fire that destroyed the new royal opera house in 1689.

Meder, Johann Valentin. See NORTHERN EUROPE 1 *North Germany*.

Mingotti. See ITALY 10 *Itinerant Musicians*.

Niedt, Friedrich Erhard. See NORTHERN EUROPE 4 *Saxony and Thuringia*.

Nielsen, Hans (*c*1580–1626). Danish court lutenist and composer who published a volume of five-part madrigals in Venice under the Italian pseudonym Giovanni Fonteio. Nielsen studied composition with Giovanni Gabrieli (1599 and 1602–4) in Venice and the lute with Gregory Huet (*d c*1616) at Wolfenbüttel (1606–8). When war caused the Danish royal chapel personnel to be trimmed, Nielsen went abroad to Heidelberg. However, in 1623 he returned to succeed Mogens Pedersøn as assistant director of the royal chapel.

Pape, Heinrich. See NORTHERN EUROPE 1 *North Germany*.

Pedersøn, Mogens (*c*1583–1623). The first native Danish instrumentalist and composer to be appointed assistant director of the royal chapel (under his teacher Melchior Borchgrevinck). He accompanied Borchgrevinck to Italy in 1599 to study with Giovanni Gabrieli and went there again in 1605, remaining four years. While in Venice, he published his first collection of five-part madrigals (1608), dedicated to Christian IV. In 1611 he travelled to England to serve the Danish-born Queen Anne (James I's consort), for whom he composed viol consort music. He also published a second volume of Italian madrigals and left behind further manuscripts that Francis Tregian copied while in prison. His collection of five-part settings of Danish texts, *Pratum spirituale* (1620), was the first of its kind by a Danish composer.

Praetorius, Bartholomaeus. See NORTHERN EUROPE 1 *North Germany: Berlin*.

Price, John. See CENTRAL EUROPE 1 *South Germany*.

Ravn, Hans Mikkelsen (*c*1610–63). Danish priest, educationist and music theorist who was the first to address the subject of Danish art music in *Heptachordum danicum seu Nova solsisatio* (1646).

Reggio, Pietro. See BRITISH ISLES 1 *London*.

Ritter, Christian (1645/50–after 1717). German organist and composer working alternately in Germany and Sweden. From the mid-1660s he was at the Halle court where he was eventually appointed organist. In 1681 he took up a similar post at the Stockholm court, quickly rising to vice-*Kapellmeister* before returning to Germany to serve in a dual capacity at Dresden. Ritter returned to Stockholm as *Kapellmeister* in 1688, remaining at least until 1699.

Roman, Johan Helmich (1694–1758). The first important native Swedish composer. Roman followed his father in royal service in 1711 as a player of the violin and oboe. In recognition of his talent, he was given leave to study in England (1715–21) where, as a pupil of J. C. Pepusch, he became acquainted with Attilio Ariosti, Giovanni Bononcini, Francesco Geminiani and Handel. When he returned to Sweden, he was appointed vice-*Kapellmeister*, then *Kapellmeister* in 1727. In 1731 he inaugurated the first public benefit concerts in Stockholm, in which amateur and royal chapel musicians joined. During the mid-1730s he travelled extensively throughout Europe, collecting music for the chapel. He was elected to the Swedish Royal Academy of Science in 1740.

Roman was particularly influenced by

Handel and acquired many of his works for the Swedish court; dubbed 'the Swedish Handel', he adopted Handel's choral style in his *Jubilate* and *Te Deum*, while his instrumental music (suites, sinfonias, overtures, solo concertos and sonatas) reflects his contact with the music of Lully and Tartini. His best-known work is an orchestral suite entitled *Drottningholms-musiquen*, composed for a royal wedding in 1744. He also composed cantatas and sacred songs for one or two voices, obbligato instruments and continuo. The number of surviving works is made problematic by Roman's reluctance to sign his works, though around 400 are attributed to him. After his retirement to south-east Sweden he occupied himself with the translation of theoretical treatises into Swedish.

Rudbeck, Olof (1630–1702). Gifted Swedish polymath knowledgeable in medicine (he discovered the lymph glands about 1652), botany, architecture, engineering and surveying, fine arts and music. He lectured and served as *Rektor* (from 1661) at the University of Uppsala, where he played an active role in the musical activities. Rudbeck had an excellent bass voice and was proficient on several instruments. He acquired instruments for the university and ensured the continuity of its musical life by providing eight scholarships for musicians. When a new university organ was installed by Hans Heinrich Cahman in 1698, Rudbeck personally built the case. With his pupil Harald Vallerius, Rudbeck prepared a new Swedish hymnbook (1697), commissioned by the king.

Schacht, Matthias Henriksen (1660–1700). Danish musician, composer and writer on music. Schacht was an intrepid intellectual who pursued serious investigations on a broad range of topics. He was educated at the University of Copenhagen and in Germany before taking up the relatively humble posts of town musician and teacher in his native Visby (on the Swedish island of Gotland, under Danish occupation). He wrote numerous scholarly papers (some of which he published), including one on music which contains a biographical dictionary of musicians (completed on 1 January 1687); E. L. Gerber consulted it in the preparation of his *Lexikon* (1790–92).

Scheibe, Johann Adolph (1708–76). *Kapellmeister*, composer, theorist and controversial writer on music who published the fortnightly, later weekly, *Critischer Musikus* (1737–40). The son of a Leipzig organ builder, Scheibe was blinded in one eye (at the age of six) while playing in his father's workshop. A

reverse in the Scheibe family finances meant he had to abandon his law studies at the university. He tried, initially without success, to gain an organ appointment, but he was impeded by having been largely self-taught.

With the encouragement of Telemann, Scheibe moved to Hamburg in 1736 as a writer on music and composer of both vocal and instrumental music (solo flute and violin concertos). Within a few years, acknowledgment of his musicianship came: in 1739 Margrave Friedrich Ernst, the Governor of Holstein, appointed him his *Kapellmeister*, and the following year he went to the Danish court of Christian VI (*d* 1747), where he was soon made *Kapellmeister*. With the death of the Danish king Scheibe was dismissed; almost 20 years later he returned to the court from the island of Als where, in the interim, he had occupied himself with setting up a proper music school for children, translating Danish classics, writing a biography of Holberg and composing.

Whereas most of his writings survive, little of his music does. His infamous criticisms of Bach (which appeared early in the pages of his journal in 1737 and were parried by Birnbaum, Mizler and Schröter) undermined his credibility, causing all his writings to be considered sceptically, if at all. As an Enlightenment figure, Scheibe sought Rationalism and identification with nature. A propos music, his main assertion was that German music need not be so closely based on Italian models. Among his contemporaries he admired Telemann, J. A. Hasse and C. H. Graun.

Schickhardt, Johann Christian. See LOW COUNTRIES 1 *United Provinces*.

Schildt, Melchior. See NORTHERN EUROPE 1 *North Germany*.

Schindler, Poul Christian (1648–1740). Danish court viol player (from 1674) who had studied in Dresden during the 1670s, and composed the first Danish opera, *Der vereinigte Götterstreit* (1689; German text by P. A. Burchardt). A disastrous fire at its second performance destroyed the new opera house, killing most of the audience (including his wife and daughter and the organist Johann Lorentz and his family). Although Schindler was in line to become court composer when Frederik IV succeeded Christian V in 1703, his music was not sufficiently italianate to suit the king, and the Bolognese composer Bartolomeo Bernardi was appointed instead.

Schop, Johann. See NORTHERN EUROPE 1 *North Germany: Hamburg*.

Schröder, Lorentz (*d* before 1647). German-born Danish organist, keyboard instrument maker and a writer on contemporary Danish musical life. Schröder held the organ post at the Helligaandskirken in Copenhagen and, from 1632, a royal privilege to build keyboard instruments. In 1639 he published *Ein nützliches Tractätlein vom Lobe Gottes*, in which he argued for the inclusion of music as one of the seven liberal arts.

Schütz, Heinrich. See NORTHERN EUROPE *4 Saxony and Thuringia: Dresden*.

Simpson, Thomas. See NORTHERN EUROPE *1 North Germany*.

Vallerius, Harald (1646–1716). Swedish mathematician and music theorist as well as director of music, lecturer and organist at the University of Uppsala. Vallerius was a pupil of Olof Rudbeck in the 1660s before taking his place on the faculty. He produced three theoretical works – *Disputatio physico-musica de sono* (1674), *Disputatio physico-musica de modis* (1686) and *Disputatio de tactu musico* (1698) – which set an important precedent at the university for writing music dissertations. In 1697 he and his teacher edited a Swedish royal hymnal, though it is believed that Vallerius was the major collaborator.

Verdier, Pierre (1627–1707). French violinist and composer associated with the Swedish court from about 1647. Verdier (with five other French violinists) was originally contracted by Count Magnus Gabriel de La Gardie for the royal chapel of Queen Christina and remained at the court until his death. Of his music, only a motet and a lament survive.

Weber, Georg. See NORTHERN EUROPE *1 North Germany*.

Weckmann, Matthias. See NORTHERN EUROPE *1 North Germany: Hamburg*.

Zenti, Girolamo. See BRITISH ISLES *1 London*.

3 Poland

Alghisi, Paris Francesco. See ITALY *4 Venice*.

Anerio, Giovanni Francesco. See ITALY *7 Papal States: Rome*.

Benda, Franz. See NORTHERN EUROPE *1 North Germany: Berlin*.

Erben, (Johann) Balthasar (1626–86). Energetic *Kapellmeister* of the Marienkirche at Danzig (from 1658) and composer of sacred concertos. Erben first applied for the Marienkirche post in 1653 but was awarded a travel stipend instead; he went first to Regensburg, where he met Froberger, and then to Rome.

During his tenure at Danzig, he was responsible for improving the standard of church music.

Farina, Carlo. See NORTHERN EUROPE *4 Saxony and Thuringia: Dresden*.

Ferri, Baldassare (1610–80). Italian castrato singer, trained in Rome by Ugolini, who from 1625 served the future King Władysław IV at the Warsaw court for the next 30 years and then Emperor Ferdinand III and, later, Leopold I at the Vienna court. His travels took him to Stockholm (1654) and London (1669–70s); he retired to Italy. G. A. Bontempi (1695) eulogized him, praising his range, breath control and command of the trill.

Fierszewicz, Daniel (*d* after 1707). Tenor at the Wawel Cathedral Chapel in Kraków, (where he succeeded Bartłomiej Pękiel during the winter of 1670/71), and later a singer at the Warsaw chapel. When the Dresden and Warsaw court chapels were amalgamated in 1697 he moved to Dresden.

Fischer, Johann. See NORTHERN EUROPE *7 Itinerant Musicians*.

Förster, Kaspar. See NORTHERN EUROPE *7 Itinerant Musicians*.

Freisslich. Half-brothers who were composers who served in succession as *Kapellmeister* of the Marienkirche in Danzig. Maximilian Dietrich (1673–1731) sang in the choir and studied with his predecessor, J. V. Meder, before assuming his post in 1699. Johann Balthasar Christian (1687–1764) was music director of the Sondershausen Hofkapelle for a decade before taking up his brother's post at his death. He proved to be a vigorous *Kapellmeister* and fluent composer, ready to provide occasional cantatas for civic and Polish royal events in addition to the sacred music required for the Marienkirche services.

Gebel, Georg. See NORTHERN EUROPE *4 Saxony and Thuringia*.

Gorczycki, Grzegorz Gerwazy (*c*1667–1734). Director of music at Wawel Cathedral Chapel in Kraków and the composer of concertato liturgical music. Gorczycki was a priest who studied in Vienna and Prague before his ordination. After a brief spell in Pomerania as *Rektor* of a missionary academy he returned to Kraków where he joined the Wawel Cathedral Chapel in 1694, becoming its director four years later. He died (of complications, following a cold) shortly after conducting the chapel at the coronation ceremonies for King August III (Elector Friedrich August II of Saxony), which took place at Kraków.

Hakenberger, Andreas (*c*1574–1627). German lutenist and composer who worked in the Warsaw court chapel (1602–7) before becoming *Kapellmeister* of the Marienkirche in Danzig (in spite of being Catholic, a factor that caused initial objection to his appointment) in 1708. Although his first publication was a collection of German songs (1610), he favoured the Counter-Reformation style (Latin texts and large forces) over that of other North German composers. In 1716 he published a collection of polychoral motets with continuo (*Harmonia sacra*).

Heinichen, Johann David. See NORTHERN EUROPE *4 Saxony and Thuringia: Dresden.*

Hintz, Ewaldt (*d* after *c*1666). Danzig-born organist and composer, who studied with Froberger before being appointed organist of the Danish court (1656–60). In 1660 he returned to Danzig where he succeeded Paul Siefert at the Marienkirche.

Jarzębski, Adam (*d* 1648/9). Violinist, composer, who was an important figure in the development of east European chamber music, and the author of a verse description of Warsaw (1643). Jarzębski served as a violinist in the chapel of the Elector of Brandenburg in Berlin (1612–15) and spent a year studying in Italy, before taking up a post at the Warsaw court in the winter of 1616–17. At some point, he transcribed vocal works of Palestrina, Lassus, Claudio Merulo and Giovanni Gabrieli for two instruments, adding ornamentation and a harmonic bass. His own music is known through a manuscript copy of his published edition of *Canzoni e concerti* (1627) for two to four instruments and continuo. His duties in Warsaw included tutoring senators' children and advising on the building of the royal palace at Ujazdów.

Kremberg, Jakob. See NORTHERN EUROPE *7 Itinerant Musicians.*

Lampugnani, Giovanni Battista. See ITALY *10 Itinerant Musicians.*

Lilius [Gigli]. Family of musicians, Italian in origin, working in Poland. Wincenty (*b c*1640) was born in Rome and served as a composer at the Graz court during the 1590s before taking up a post in King Sigismund III's chapel in Kraków and Warsaw around 1600. He was the composer of polychoral motets. Szymon (*d* after 1652) was an organist and organ builder with connections at court. Franciszek (*d* 1657) was the most prominent family member, serving as a musician and composer at court and, from 1630, as music director at Kraków Cathedral (succeeding Annibale Orgas). He also toured, performing in Danzig and Lüneburg as well as Breslau. As a composer, Franciszek was proficient in the *prima prattica* and the *seconda prattica*.

Merula, Tarquinio. See ITALY *4 Venice.*

Mielczewski, Marcin (*d* 1651). Composer at the Warsaw royal chapel (by 1638) and director of music to the Bishop of Płock (brother of the Polish king) for the last six years of his life. Mielczewski composed a variety of music in both the *prima prattica* and the *seconda prattica*. In his instrumental canzonas, as well as in popular religious songs, he quoted Polish folktunes and dance rhythms (he was the first to incorporate the mazurka). He contributed a double canon *a 4* to Marco Scacchi's controversial *Cribrum musicum* (1643).

Mizler von Kolof, Lorenz Christoph. See NORTHERN EUROPE *4 Saxony and Thuringia.*

Niżankowski, Andrzej (1591/2–1655). Dominican friar and virtuoso organist who was taught by Frescobaldi. Niżankowski served as organist of S Maria sopra Minerva in Rome (1633–4) before returning to Kraków as the organist of a Dominican abbey.

Opitz, Martin. See NORTHERN EUROPE *7 Itinerant Musicians.*

Orgas, Annibale (*c*1585–1629). Italian musician who spent the last ten years of his life in Kraków. From 1594 until about 1607, Orgas was a soprano at the Collegio Germanico in Rome, whither he returned in 1610 as deacon (after studying at the Seminario Romano) and again in 1613 as *maestro di cappella* (after a posting at Avellino). Before departing for Poland in 1619 (he may have been recruited by Asprilio Pacelli, his former colleague at the Collegio Germanico), Orgas published a collection of motets for four to eight voices (*Sacrarum cantionum ... liber primus*) in Venice. At Kraków, Orgas was appointed cathedral choirmaster, although as a foreigner he had to contend with attempts to restrict his policies.

Pacelli, Asprilio (1570–1623). Italian musician active in Rome before 1603 when he became an influential *Kapellmeister* at the court of King Sigismund III in Warsaw. Trained in the Counter-Reformation Roman style, Pacelli transmitted it to the Polish court; he also brought high standards of performance which enabled the chapel to earn a high reputation. In Rome he had served as *maestro di cappella* of the Collegio Germanico (1595–1601) and, briefly, of S Pietro; he visited Warsaw in 1601, paving the way for his appointment two years later. He composed madrigals as well as sacred polychoral works, of which the *Sacre cantiones* (1609) and his posthumously published Masses were particularly popular in Warsaw and elsewhere in Germany.

Pękiel, Bartłomiej (*d c*1670). Organist and leading Polish composer of his era who worked at the Warsaw court chapel – first as Marco Scacchi's assistant, then as his successor (1653) – and, from 1658, in Kraków as director of music at the Wawel Cathedral Chapel, where he succeeded Franciszek Lilius. Working in Warsaw, Pękiel composed concertato polychoral Masses and organ music; for Kraków, he composed *a cappella* Masses and motets. His four-voice *Missa pulcherrima ad instar Praenestini* (based on a mixture of Gregorian chant, Polish carols and his own melodies) is considered to be his finest work, though it is not known why its title refers to Palestrina.

Puccitelli, Virgilio (1599–1654). Roman priest and librettist. From about 1630, while in the service of Prince Władysław Sigismund (from 1634, King Władysław IV), he was instrumental in the organization of music at the Polish court. He also served as a secretary to the king, undertaking diplomatic missions to Italy (1638–9) and France (1640). Puccitelli wrote librettos for nine tragic operas (Marco Scacchi set several of his texts) and a number of ballets in which the heroic characters were identified with the king. Pensioned in 1649, he returned to Italy.

Quantz, Johann Joachim. See NORTHERN EUROPE *1 North Germany: Berlin.*

Reusner, Esaias. See NORTHERN EUROPE *1 North Germany.*

Ristori, Giovanni Alberto. See NORTHERN EUROPE *4 Saxony and Thuringia: Dresden.*

Rognoni Taeggio, Francesco. See ITALY *2 Lombardy.*

Różycki, Jacek (*d* in or after 1697). Aristocratic director of music to four Polish kings before the unification of the Warsaw and Dresden chapels in 1697 when he was made joint *Kapellmeister* with J. C. Schmidt. Różycki composed four-part hymns, similar to Protestant chorales, as well as motets and sacred concertos which he infused with Polish folksongs.

Scacchi, Marco (*c*1600–1681/7). Italian composer and writer, born near Viterbo, who classified modern musical styles in terms of function – church, chamber and theatre – and strongly urged they be considered exclusive of one another (*Epistola* to Christoph Werner, *c*1648). From 1628 until 1649 Scacchi was in Warsaw, serving as choirmaster to the Polish court under three kings (Sigismund III, Władysław IV and John Casimir II).

He composed freely in all styles, including the *stile antico*, though never in a mixed style, an issue he felt so strongly about that during the 1640s (while Kaspar Förster the younger was his pupil) he became embroiled in a feud between Kaspar Förster the elder, *Kapellmeister* at the Marienkirche, Danzig, and the church's organist Paul Siefert, who slandered remarks made by Scacchi on the Italian style. Scacchi made the mistake of taking Siefert's *Psalmen Davids, nach francösischer Melodey* (1640) to task in a Latin treatise, *Cribrum musicum ad triticum Syferticum* ('Musical Sieve for the Syfert Wheat'), published in Venice in 1643: Siefert replied that as a former pupil of Sweelinck he followed the 'Belgian' school rather than the Italian, and that Scacchi had failed to take into account the impact of national styles on period practices. In 1649 Scacchi published in Warsaw a *Breve discorso sopra la musica moderna*, in which he urged the recognition of distinct styles as opposed to a single, integrated style. He retired to his native Gallese, near Viterbo, in 1649.

Schmidt, Johann Christoph. See BRITISH ISLES *1 London*, Smith.

Siefert, Paul (1586–1666). German organist and composer. A pupil of Sweelinck (1607–9), Siefert served at Danzig's Marienkirche for most of his career, though he also spent time in Königsberg (1611–16) and at the Warsaw court (1616–1623). As a composer, Siefert – like other prominent North German composers (Scheidt and Heinrich Scheidemann among them) – refused to be tied by tradition or contemporary Italian models.

In Danzig he became involved in a bitter feud with Kaspar Förster, choirmaster at the Marienkirche, which resulted in two dozen petitions to the city council. Marco Scacchi wrote in support of Förster (*Cribrum musicum*, 1643), attempting to discredit Siefert (who had preceded Scacchi at the Warsaw court) as a composer; however, in applying criteria based on an Italian sacred style to North German chorale motets (Siefert's *Psalmen Davids, nach francösischer Melodey*, 1640) Scacchi vitiated his own argument.

Strungk, Nicolaus Adam. See NORTHERN EUROPE *7 Itinerant Musicians.*

Strutz, Thomas (*c*1621–1678). Organist and composer in Danzig where he served first at St Trinitatis (from 1642) and then at the Marienkirche, as Paul Siefert's successor. In 1656 he published a collection of simple, folklike four- and five-part songs (in lieu of motets) for Sundays and religious festivals in *Lobsingende Hertzens-Andacht*; for his texts, he used those of J. Maukisch, a Danzig educational reformer. Instead of a biblical text for his Passion oratorio, *Zweyfache Christliche Auffmunterung* (1664), Strutz relied upon a lyrical paraphrase, interleaved with well-known chorales to be sung by the congregation.

Valentini, Giovanni. See CENTRAL EUROPE *3 Austro-Hungary: Vienna.*

Verocai, Giovanni. See ITALY *10 Itinerant Musicians.*

Weber, Georg. See NORTHERN EUROPE *1 North Germany.*

Zangius, Nikolaus. See NORTHERN EUROPE *7 Itinerant Musicians.*

Zieleński, Mikolaj (*fl* 1611). Polish organist, director of music to the Archbishop of Gniezno (the Polish primate) and important transitional composer whose extant music – two liturgical cycles of motets and sacred symphonies published in 1611 – presents a compendium of Renaissance and early Baroque styles. The *Communione* contains 66 works of which 53 are antiphons (among them, the earliest known Polish monodies), concertato works (for three to six voices with parts for optional string, wind and plucked instruments) and purely instrumental music (2 fantasias for three instruments and one for four). By contrast, the two-volume *Offertoria* contains 56 polychoral works (mostly for eight voices, instruments and continuo), including 44 Offertories and a 12-part *Magnificat*.

4 Saxony and Thuringia

Abel, Christian Ferdinand. See NORTHERN EUROPE *1 North Germany.*

Adlung, Jakob (1699–1762). Erfurt organist of the Predigerkirche (succeeding J. H. Buttstett), keyboard instrument maker and scholar of music theory and aesthetics. Adlung was a friend of J. G. Walther and an intellectual peer of Johann Mattheson and L. C. Mizler. After studying at the University of Jena (1723–6) he took up the organ post at Erfurt, also teaching the organ and languages at the local Gymnasium. Of his publications, his *Anleitung zu der musikalischen Gelahrtheit* (1758) is a vast compendium of theoretical and practical information for both scholars and amateurs, just as the *Musica mechanica organoedi* (posth., 1768) is an encyclopedic reference book for

organ builders, which includes specifications of more than 80 instruments.

Ahle, Johann Rudolf (1625–73). Thuringian civil servant, organist of the Blasius Kirche, Mühlhausen (from 1654), and prolific composer–poet of sacred concertos and *Arien*. Ahle was a prominent citizen in Mühlhausen who was elected mayor in the year of his death and, at the same time, well known throughout Thuringia as an organist. He composed the text and music for many sacred songs of a popular nature for one to four voices, instruments and continuo; his only surviving instrumental music is a collection of dances (1650).

Bach, Johann Christoph (1642–1703). Thuringian organist and composer considered the most significant Bach family member before Johann Sebastian. After serving two years as organist of the Arnstadt Kapelle, J. C. Bach was appointed town and court organist at Eisenach, where he remained until his death. He composed keyboard music, and chorale and aria motets with instruments.

Bach, Johann Nicolaus (1669–1753). Son of Johann Christoph, he studied at Jena with J. N. Knüpfer, whom he succeeded as town organist in 1694 and leader of the Kollegienkirche collegium musicum in 1719; however, his efforts to succeed his father at Eisenach were in vain. Although he was a talented composer, little of his music has survived, and what there is gives no hint of his travels in Italy. Johann Nicolaus also built harpsichords and organs.

Bach, Johann Sebastian. See NORTHERN EUROPE *4 Saxony and Thuringia: Leipzig.*

Bach, Wilhelm Friedemann. See NORTHERN EUROPE *4 Saxony and Thuringia: Dresden.*

Baron, Ernst Gottlieb (1696–1760). Itinerant Saxon lutenist, composer and writer on music who published in Nuremberg an important source on the history and practice of lute playing: *Historisch-theoretisch und practische Untersuchung des Instruments der Lauten* (1727). Baron composed solo music for the lute, trios and *galant* concertos. He studied in his native Breslau and Leipzig (philosophy and law); between 1719 and 1728 he travelled between the Saxon courts before taking up a four-year post at Gotha in 1728. His last post (from 1737) was with Crown Prince Frederick of Prussia (king after 1740)

Beer, Johann (1655–1700). Musician, theorist and novelist. Beer was educated at Regensburg where he was a contemporary of Pachelbel at the Gymnasium Poeticum. After briefly studying theology at the University of Leipzig, he took up a post as a singer in the Halle

Hofkapelle of Duke August of Saxe-Weissenfels. He moved with the court to Weissenfels in 1680 (under Duke Johann Adolf I) and was made *Konzertmeister* in 1685. While a favourite of the duke and frequently required as a travelling companion, Beer also undertook performing engagements and was in demand as a teacher and composer (he had three operas to his credit). In the course of his career he declined court posts at Coburg and Copenhagen. He wrote satirical novels and several books on music, including the punningly titled *Ursus murmurat* (1697), in which he criticized the education of church musicians. Beer died in a shooting accident.

Bernardi, Stefano. See ITALY *10 Itinerant Musicians.*

Bertouch, Georg von. See NORTHERN EUROPE *2 Scandinavia.*

Birkenstock, Johann Adam. See NORTHERN EUROPE *5 West Germany and the Rhineland.*

Brade, William. See NORTHERN EUROPE *1 North Germany.*

Briegel, Wolfgang Carl. See NORTHERN EUROPE *5 West Germany and the Rhineland.*

Buttstett, Johann Heinrich (1666–1727). Organist of the Predigerkirche at Erfurt (from 1691), where he had been a pupil of Pachelbel in 1678, *Ratsorganist* (1693) and composer. He took exception, in his *Ut, mi, sol, re, fa, la, tota musica et harmonia aeterna* (1716), to Johann Mattheson's progressive views as expressed in *Das neu-eröffnete Orchestre* (1713), pronouncing them a prescription for chaos. Mattheson countered with satire in *Das beschützte Orchestre* (1717) and Buttstett concluded the public dispute with *Der wider das Beschützte Orchestre ergangenen öffentlichen Erklärung* (2nd edn, 1718).

Deinl, Nikolaus. See NORTHERN EUROPE *6 Middle Germany.*

Drese, Adam (*c*1620–1701). Thuringian *Kapellmeister*, viol player, teacher and composer. Drese served as a cathedral musician in Merseburg during the 1640s, during which time he travelled to Warsaw to study with Marco Scacchi. While holding the post of director of music (from *c*1650) to Duke Wilhelm IV of Saxe-Weimar, Drese took the opportunity to visit Dresden (where he studied with Schütz in 1652 and again in 1656) and Regensburg (1653), which enabled him to introduce the Italian style at the Weimar court. Following the death of the duke in 1662, many of his musicians were absorbed into the Jena court where Drese became *Kapellmeister* and private secretary to Duke Bernhard. After the duke's death, Drese was appointed *Kapellmeister* at Arnstadt, to the Count of Schwarzburg, who required him to put aside secular composition and devote himself instead to Pietist music.

Eberlin, Daniel (1647–*c*1715). Temperamental administrator, violinist and composer, admired by Johann Mattheson and Telemann. After serving as a treble in the Gotha Hofkapelle (1661), Eberlin studied at Jena with Adam Drese (1663–5). He spent most of his career at the Eisenach court in a variety of posts – musician, registrar, private secretary, *Kapellmeister*, secretary and master of the mint – although he also spent time in Rome (1668–71), Nuremberg (1673–5) and Kassel (1678–85 and 1705 onwards). Though a gifted administrator, he nevertheless fell out with the musicians at Eisenach and Kassel, so that from 1685 he held only non-musical posts. He was dismissed as master of the Eisenach mint after an audit in 1692; from 1705 he served as a captain of the Kassel militia. Eberlin published a set of trio sonatas in Nuremberg (1675) and left a number of cantatas in manuscript.

Erlebach, Philipp Heinrich (1657–1714). *Kapellmeister* at the court of Count Albert Anton of Schwarzburg-Rudolstadt from 1681 and a versatile composer. Erlebach was trained at the East Friesian court before becoming a musician and valet at the Rudolstadt court in 1678. Although he composed comic operas, ballets and pastorales, he was most active as a composer of cantatas. Erlebach produced six cantata cycles (those from the period 1706 to 1710 were known in Rudolstadt as 'oratorio cantatas'), incorporating a variety of forms and textures. He also composed French and Italian-style chamber music, publishing in Nuremberg in 1693 a set of French overtures and, the following year, a collection of trio sonatas for one or two violins, bass viol and continuo.

Falckenhagen, Adam. See NORTHERN EUROPE *6 Middle Germany.*

Fasch, Johann Friedrich (1688–1758). *Kapellmeister*, violinist, organist and innovative composer. Although none of Fasch's music was ever published, Telemann performed a cycle of his church cantatas at Hamburg in 1733, J. G. Pisendel performed his concertos at the Dresden court and Bach transcribed his overtures for the Leipzig collegium musicum. Fasch came from a family of Lutheran *Kantors*, trained under Johann Kuhnau at the Thomasschule (where he was a contemporary of Telemann), and then studied at the University of Leipzig, founding his own collegium musicum in rivalry with that of Telemann. Afterwards, he travelled widely, pausing at Darmstadt to study composition with Christoph Graupner and Gottfried Grünewald.

He held a varied succession of posts as a violinist at Bayreuth (1714), organist at Greiz (until 1721) and *Kapellmeister* at Lukaveč, before taking up a permanent appointment as *Kapellmeister* at Zerbst in 1722. Most of his vocal music (including 12 complete cantata cycles, 16 Masses and four operas) is lost, although his instrumental music (61 concertos, 90 orchestral suites and a lesser number of symphonies and sonatas) survive. He had a particular penchant for wind instruments and used them in pairs in his concertos.

Fleming, Paul (1609–40). Much admired lyric poet whose reform verse, influenced by Opitz and Schein, was set by Andreas Hammerschmidt, C. C. Dedekind, David Pohle and, later, Bach. Fleming had been a pupil of J. H. Schein (who taught him Latin and German poetry) at the Leipzig Thomasschule from 1621 before entering the university to study medicine. After acquiring a PhD and MA, Fleming joined the entourage of Duke Friedrich of Schleswig-Holstein on a trip to Moscow and Persia in 1633; he returned then in 1636 and stayed three years. In spite of his success as a poet, he renewed his study of medicine at the University of Leiden, but his early death cut short a life of considerable promise.

Förster, Christoph (Heinrich) (1693–1745). *Kapellmeister*, violinist and composer. After lessons in composition with J. D. Heinichen at Weissenfels, Förster took up an appointment as a violinist in the Merseburg court orchestra (1717–42). In that capacity he composed French overtures and orchestral suites, Italian sinfonias and *galant* chamber music; a set of symphonies was subsequently published in Nuremberg (1747), and Telemann engraved his set of *Duetti oder Trii* (for two violins and optional continuo) for publication in Paris (n.d.). After establishing connections with the court of Prince Friedrich Anton of Schwarzburg-Rudolstadt, Förster was appointed vice-*Kapellmeister* in 1743, succeeding Johann Graf as *Kapellmeister* two years later. He composed Masses and sacred cantatas for the Rudolstadt court.

Franck, Melchior (*c*1579–1639). Important composer of German Protestant music during the first half of the 17th century: Franck published in excess of 40 collections of motets between 1601 and 1636, as well as 30 settings of the *Magnificat*. He was much indebted to H. L. Hassler, from whom he learnt both the Netherlands and Venetian polychoral styles. In the winter of 1602–3 Franck gained an appointment as *Kapellmeister* to the music-loving Prince Johann Casimir of Coburg, which provided him with an excellent environment in which to compose and publish until the 1630s, when the exigencies of the Thirty Years War impinged upon the cultural life of the court. In addition to more than 600 sacred works, Franck composed secular vocal music for his pupils (witty, eclectic quodlibets and songs) and homophonic dance collections for four to six instruments (his *Deliciae convivales* of 1627).

Franck, Salomo (1659–1725). Court administrator at Arnstadt (1689), Jena (1697) and Weimar (from 1701), and poet who provided Bach with cantata texts for Weimar and Leipzig.

Freisslich, Johann Balthasar Christian. See NORTHERN EUROPE *3 Poland.*

Freylinghausen, Johann Anastasius (1670–1739). Theologian and editor of the highly influential Pietist songbook, the *Geistreiches Gesang-Buch* (1704, 1714). Freylinghausen was educated at the universities of Jena and Halle, where he assisted the leading Pietist A. H. Francke (whose daughter Freylinghausen later married). In 1715 he took a post at the Ulrichskirche, Halle.

Gebel. Breslau father and son composer-organists. Georg Gebel (1685–*c*1750) was an organist and composer whose precocious eldest son Georg (1709–55) was composing serenades and a German opera at the age of 16. The younger Georg left Breslau in 1735, resigning an organ post at a church there, and that of *Kapellmeister* at the court of Oels, to become court composer and harpsichordist to Count Brühl in Warsaw, where he learnt to play the pantaleon. In 1750 he accepted the post of *Kapellmeister* at the Rudolstadt court.

Graf. Family of German musicians. Born in Nuremberg, Johann (1684–1750) served in an army regiment in Hungary as an oboe master before training in Vienna as a violinist and composer. His next posts were in the court bands of the Elector of Mainz and the Prince Archbishop of Bamberg. In 1722 he was appointed *Konzertmeister* at the Rudolstadt court, and later (1739) promoted to *Kapellmeister*. Johann composed and published several collections of violin sonatas and one of string quartets (*Sechs kleine Partien*, 1739). Six of his sons also pursued musical careers.

Hammerschmidt, Andreas (1611/12–1675). Bohemian-born Protestant organist and composer working at Zittau. Hammerschmidt's family left Bohemia during the Thirty Years War (1626) to escape religious persecution. After short-term posts at Weesenstein and Freiberg, Hammerschmidt succeeded Christoph Schreiber in 1639 as organist of the Johanniskirche at Zittau, where the three organs made it possible to exploit concerto effects. There he collaborated with the *Kantor*, Simon Crusius, to improve the standards of the church choir and local Gymnasium, both much depleted following the war. For the choir he composed 14 collections of concertato sacred music; and for the school, instrumental music and secular songs (*Weltliche Oden*). No organ music survives.

Hertel, Johann Christian (1699–1754). String player – one of the best viol players of his day – and prolific composer of instrumental music. The son of the *Kapellmeister* at Oettingen (Jakob Christian, *fl c*1667–*c*1726), Hertel became *Kapellmeister* and director of music at Eisenach (1733–41). After studies in theology at Halle, he went to Darmstadt to study the bass viol with E. C. Hesse in 1717. The following year he was appointed viol player at the Eisenach court of Duke Johann Wilhelm, who allowed Hertel to tour throughout Germany and Holland; in 1726 he visited Bach in Leipzig. After the Eisenach Hofkapelle was disbanded in 1741, Hertel held a similar post at the Mecklenburg-Strelitz court until 1753. His son Johann Wilhelm (1727–89) was a violinist, keyboard player and composer.

Handel, George Frideric. See BRITISH ISLES *1 London*.

Hunold, Christian Friedrich. See NORTHERN EUROPE *1 North Germany: Hamburg*.

Johann Ernst (1696–1715). Prince of Weimar, violinist and composer whose life was tragically cut short. He learnt the violin from a court musician, G. C. Eilenstein, and the keyboard from the town organist, J. G. Walther, who presented the prince with a treatise (*Praecepta der musikalischen Composition*) on his 12th birthday. He must have been greatly stimulated by the arrival of Bach as court organist in 1708. Walther later prepared a catalogue of his works, Telemann – who had dedicated his own first published work (*Six Sonates à violon seul*, 1715) to the prince – engraved and published his op. 1 violin concertos in 1718, and Mattheson included him in his *Ehren-Pforte* (1740).

Kauffmann, Georg Friedrich (1679–1735). Thuringian organist and composer who inherited from his teacher, J. F. Alberti (1710), the dual post of organist of the Merseburg court and cathedral; he seems later to have been appointed court director of church music and then *Kapellmeister*. In 1722–3, Kauffmann was a finalist in the competition for the Leipzig cantorship which went to Bach. He composed an oratorio and cantatas, as well as organ chorale preludes, planned as a cycle but never completed, which were nevertheless published in his *Harmonische Seelenlust* (1733–6).

Keiser, Reinhard. See NORTHERN EUROPE *1 North Germany: Hamburg*.

Kerll, Johann Kaspar. See CENTRAL EUROPE *3 Austro-Hungary: Vienna*.

Kirchhoff, Gottfried (1684–1746). *Kapellmeister*, organist and composer from a family of *Stadtpfeifer*. A contemporary of Handel at Halle, Kirchhoff was also a pupil of F.W. Zachow. He was appointed *Kapellmeister* to the Duke of Holstein-Glücksburg (1709), and then organist in Quedlinburg two years later. In 1714 he settled finally in Halle to accept the dual post of organist and *director musices* at the Liebfrauenkirche, which Bach had already declined. Kirchhoff composed occasional music, including a work for the bicentenary of the Reformation in Halle (1741), cantatas, chorale preludes and violin sonatas.

Kobelius, Johann Augustin (1674–1731). Weissenfels organist of the Jacobikirche, Sangerhausen, and court composer of operas (1715–29). Kobelius was appointed to the municipal organ post in 1702 by the intervention of the Duke of Weissenfels after Bach had won the competition.

Krebs, Johann Ludwig (1713–80). Saxon organist–composer. His father Johann Tobias Krebs (1690–1762) studied in Weimar, later commuting from his post at Buttelstedt to study first with J. G. Walther and later Bach. Johann Ludwig received his musical training from 1726 onwards at the Leipzig Thomasschule under Bach (serving as a cantata copyist, 1729–31), and later, while a student at the university (1735–7), he played the harpsichord in Bach's collegium musicum. He applied unsuccessfully for Bach's post in 1750. Meanwhile, he held organ posts at the Marienkirche, Zwickau (1737–43), and at the Zeitz court (from 1744); in 1755 he was appointed organist of the Altenburg court of Prince Friedrich.

J. L. Krebs seems to have composed exclusively instrumental music, most of it unmistakably influenced by Bach: a three-part

Clavier Übung containing settings of German chorales, organ preludes and fugues, brilliant double concertos for two harpsichords, duo and trio sonatas, and fantasias for a single wind instrument (oboe, trumpet, oboe d'amore or flute) and organ. His organ music was particularly admired by J. N. Forkel.

Krieger, Johann (1652–1735). Singer, organist, composer and *director chori musici* for 53 years at Zittau. Like his brother, Johann Philipp Krieger, he was trained in Nuremberg, where he worked with Heinrich Schwemmer and G. C. Wecker while singing in the choir at the Sebald Kirche. He obtained his posts through his brother, following him to Bayreuth in 1672 and taking over the organist's duties when Johann Philipp was named *Kapellmeister* five years later. Johann briefly held posts as *Kapellmeister* at Greiz and Eisenberg (where he composed at least one opera) before settling in Zittau (first as organist of the Johanniskirche, then as *director chori musici*) in 1682.

In his early years at Zittau he composed songs (publishing a large collection in 1684) and Singspiels. However, his fame rests on two published collections of keyboard music: *Sechs musicalische Partien* (comprising allemande, courante, sarabande and gigue, with optional dances inserted before the gigue) appeared in 1697, and the *Anmuthige Clavier-Übung* (containing preludes, ricercares, fugues, fantasias, toccatas and a chaconne) – of which Handel owned a copy – in 1698.

Krieger, Johann Philipp (1649–1725). Keyboard player, composer of over 2000 church cantatas (only 74 survive) and elder brother of Johann Krieger. Born in Nuremberg, Johann Philipp was a pupil of Gabriel Schütz before going to Copenhagen to study the organ with Johannes Schröder and composition with Kaspar Förster. Though subsequently offered a post in Norway (at Christiania), he preferred to return home. He acquired the post of *Kapellmeister* at Bayreuth and in 1673 was granted permission by Margrave Christian Ernst to study in Venice and Rome. On his way back north in 1675 he paused in Vienna, where he was rewarded for his playing with ennoblement. He terminated his connections with Bayreuth and spent time in Frankfurt am Main and Kassel, where in each instance he was offered employment; he accepted the organ post at the Halle court in 1677. With the death of the duke three years later, the court moved to Weissenfels, and Krieger was made *Kapellmeister* by the new Duke Johann Adolph I.

Krieger was an extremely prolific composer of Latin and German texted italianate cantatas; he also produced 18 operas on German librettos and a variety of instrumental music. He published two sets of trio sonatas – one for two violins and continuo (1688) and the other for violin, bass viol and continuo (1693) – and a collection of *Lustige Feld-Music* (1704) for four wind instruments.

Kühnel, August. See NORTHERN EUROPE 7 *Itinerant Musicians.*

Lampe, John Frederick. See BRITISH ISLES *1 London.*

Leopold (1694–1728). Prince of Anhalt-Cöthen, music patron of Bach, bass singer and instrumentalist (violin, bass viol and harpsichord). The eldest son of Prince Johann Georg who died in 1704, Leopold was educated at the Ritterakademie in Berlin (1708–10), then embarked on a grand tour (1710–13), during which time he studied in Rome with J. D. Heinichen. When he returned to Cöthen, he took advantage of the recent dissolution of the Berlin *Kapelle* and hired A. R. Stricker as his *Kapellmeister*, along with six other musicians (including Stricker's wife who was a soprano and lutenist).

Upon his majority in 1716, the prince enlarged his *Kapelle* to include three violins, two flutes, two trumpets, three ripienists and single players of the bass viol, cello, oboe, bassoon, timpani and organ, and the following year he engaged Bach as his new *Kapellmeister*. Bach's tenure came to an end in 1722, though he retained the title of *Kapellmeister* until the prince's death.

Linike. See NORTHERN EUROPE *1 North Germany: Berlin.*

Madonis, Luigi. See ITALY *4 Venice.*

Mizler von Kolof, Lorenz Christoph (1711–78). Franconian physician, mathematician, lecturer, amateur musician and writer on music who in 1738 founded the Korrespondierenden Sozietät der Musicalischen Wissenschaften, to which Handel and Bach belonged. Although a polymath, Mizler devoted much of his energy to music. He acquired his practical knowledge of music at Ansbach. In 1731 he began studies at Leipzig University, where he was greatly influenced by the philosopher and literary critic J. C. Gottsched. But he dedicated his theology thesis (*Quod musica ars sit pars eruditionis philosophicae, c*1734) to Johann Mattheson, whose *Neu-eröffnete Orchestre* (1713) he so much admired. After further studies in medicine and law at Wittenberg, Mizler returned to Leipzig in 1737 as a university lecturer in music. Convinced that music should be treated as a science, Mizler chose Mattheson's book as the subject of his lectures.

At much the same time he started a publishing business which produced a monthly magazine entitled *Neu eröffnete musikalische Bibliothek*, through which the corresponding society communicated (1738–54). It contained criticism and commentary of new books and music; members contributed theoretical papers on which discussion was encouraged. Mizler devoted 200 pages to a not uncritical review of Mattheson's *Vollkommene Capellmeister* (1739).

Mizler spent the second half of his life in the service of the Polish Count Malachowski of Konskie, as his secretary, librarian, tutor and court mathematician. He continued to pursue his formal studies in medicine at the University of Erfurt (1747) and gained a formidable command of the Polish language, its history and literature. In 1747 he settled in Warsaw, serving as court physician from 1752, but still found time to publish and sustain the corresponding society (which grew to 20 members). In 1757 he was made a member of the Erfurt Academy of Sciences; ten years before his death, he was ennobled.

Molter, Johann Melchior. See CENTRAL EUROPE *1 South Germany*.

Motz, Georg (1653–1733). Court organist, *Kantor* and outspoken South German writer on the impact of secular musical styles on German Protestant music. Although a Protestant, Motz worked at the Catholic court of Prince Johann Seyfried of Eggenberg (nr Graz) during the 1670s. Briefly at the beginning of the 1680s (after a four-month journey to Italy), he served the prince's brother Duke Johann Christian of Krumau (Bohemia); but ill at ease with court life, Motz left to become *Kantor* at Tilsit, where he remained after 1682. As a riposte to the Pietist Christian Gerber's diatribe against the use of music in Protestant services (*Unerkandte Sünden der Welt*, 1690), Motz published *Die vertheidigten Kirchen-Music* (1703) and *Abgenötigte Fortsetzung der vertheidigten Kirchen-Music*, citing Renaissance and Baroque theorists, Luther and the Bible in support.

Neumark, Georg (1621–81). Well-travelled writer, song composer and viol player. Neumark spent much of his life in the service of Duke Johann Ernst of Weimar as chancellor, librarian and court poet. He wrote novels as well as sacred and secular poetry, setting the latter to music. His *Fortgepflanzter musikalisch-poetischer Lustwald* (1652), a collection

of continuo songs, incorporated independent instrumental parts for violin and bass viol. In 1653 he became a member of the Fruchtbringende Gesellschaft and, later, the Order of the Pegnitzschäfer.

Niedt, Friedrich Erhard (1674–1708). Composer and writer on performance practice. All that is known of his life is that he studied with J. N. Bach at Jena, published the first two parts of his well-known *Musicalische Handleitung* (1700, 1706) in Hamburg (Mattheson published the third part in 1717, and a much-expanded second edition of Part 2 appeared in 1721), and that he died in Copenhagen. The treatise addresses thoroughbass, counterpoint, improvisation, canon, chorale and recitative style. None of his music survives.

Österreich, Georg. See NORTHERN EUROPE *1 North Germany*.

Pachelbel, Johann. See NORTHERN EUROPE *6 Middle Germany*.

Pezel, Johann Christoph. See NORTHERN EUROPE *4 Saxony and Thuringia: Leipzig*.

Pfeiffer, Johann. See NORTHERN EUROPE *6 Middle Germany*.

Pohle, David (1624–95). Composer and instrumentalist. A pupil of Heinrich Schütz, Pohle held a number of posts before becoming *Konzertmeister* (1660) and soon afterwards *Kapellmeister* (1661) at Halle. From 1674 he gained additional court appointments at Weissenfels and Zeitz; when in 1678 he was appointed *Kapellmeister* at Zeitz, he relinquished his place at Halle to his deputy, J. P. Krieger. Four years later he moved to a similar post at the Merseburg court. None of his music – Latin and German sacred works, Singspiels and sonatas – was published during his lifetime.

Printz, Wolfgang Caspar (1641–1717). Composer, theorist, historian and (from 1664) music director at the Sorau court, who greatly influenced Johann Mattheson and J. G. Walther. An early intention to become a Lutheran minister proved impractical in the Catholic Upper Palatinate region where Printz had grown up, so he turned to music, briefly taking up a post as a tenor at the Heidelberg court chapel in 1661, then departing for Italy in the entourage of a Dutch nobleman. While in Rome he met Athanasius Kircher and began collecting the music and treatises that would enable him to write his own tracts. In 1664 he took a permanent post at Sorau with Count Leopold of Promnitz. He lost his library in a fire in 1684, but survived an attempt to poison him in 1688.

Printz played string and keyboard instruments and composed a large number of concertos and seven-part *canzonette* (lost), but is remembered for having written 22 treatises on music history and theory, of which only six survive. Of particular significance are the well documented *Historische Beschreibung der edelen Sing- und Kling-Kunst* (1690) – considered the first major German history of music – and the three-volume *Phrynis Mitilenaeus oder Satyrischer Componist* (1696).

Profe, Ambrosius (1589–1661). Musician, teacher, theorist, editor and merchant in Breslau. The suppression of Lutheranism in Silesia in 1629 meant that Profe turned to commerce when he was no longer able to work as a *Kantor* and schoolmaster. When he gained the organ post of the Elisabethkirche in 1633 he prudently continued in business; in 1649 his career as a musician ended abruptly when part of the church collapsed, destroying the organ.

During the 1640s Profe was active as an anthologist, composer and textbook writer: in 1641 he published his *Compendium musicum*, in which he rejected the old method of hexachord solmization; over a five-year period (1641–6) he published the four-volume *Geistliche Concerten und Harmonien*, in 1646 a collection of Christmas lullabies (to be sung in the *Magnificat*) and in 1649 a *Corollarium* containing 27 works by Giovanni Rovetta and three unique works by Schütz, among others.

Römhild, Johann Theodor (1684–1756). Organist and composer who succeeded G. F. Kauffmann as both *Kapellmeister* to the Duke of Saxe-Merseburg and organist of Merseburg Cathedral in 1735. From 1690 Römhild had been a pupil – along with J. C. Graupner, J. F. Fasch and J. D. Heinichen – at the Leipzig Thomasschule, under Johann Schelle and Johann Kuhnau, and then at the university. In 1708 he became *Kantor* of a school in Spremberg (Lusatia); other posts in the area followed and in 1726 he was appointed *Kapellmeister* to Duke Heinrich of Spremberg, who was shortly to become the next Duke of Saxe-Merseburg. At Merseburg he composed more than 200 sacred cantatas and a *St Matthew Passion*.

Scheidt, Samuel (1587–1654). Distinguished organist, teacher and composer who lived and worked all of his life in Halle, serving as *Kapellmeister* at the ducal court from 1619. He was a pupil of Sweelinck in Amsterdam and a respected contemporary of Michael Praetorius, J. H. Schein and Heinrich Schütz. His first important post came in 1609 when

he was appointed court organist to Margrave Christian Wilhelm of Brandenburg. Scheidt was invited, along with Praetorius and Schütz, to help with the reorganization of the music at Magdeburg Cathedral. Together with Johann Staden they also took part in the dedication of the new organ at the Bayreuth Stadtkirche the following year.

In his new post as *Kapellmeister* at Halle, Scheidt worked tirelessly to provide the court with new music, which he then published. In 1620 he published a collection of polychoral motets, *Cantiones sacrae* (for eight voices, paralleling Schein's 1615 *Cymbalum Sionium*), in which he combined the influences of Sweelinck and the Italian concerto style with German chorales. He then revised two of the motets and included them among 12 sacred concertos – notable for the absence of chorales and adorned with sinfonias, virtuoso obbligato instrumental parts and continuo – in *Pars prima concertuum sacrorum* (1622). His three-volume *Tabulatura nova* (1624) was the first German keyboard collection to be published in open score and contains sets of both chorale and dance variations. Between 1621 and 1627 he also produced four volumes of dance music (for four or five instruments and *basso seguente*) comparable to Schein's 1617 *Banchetto musicale*, under the title *Ludi musici*.

Political events caused the court to disband in 1625, though Scheidt retained his title without salary, forcing him to rely on teaching (his best-known pupil was Adam Krieger) and commissions from abroad in order to support his family over the next few years. From 1628 until 1630, he served as *director musices* at the Marktkirche, though disputes with the organist and the *Rektor* of the Gymnasium ended with his resignation. He continued to publish music during the 1630s, issuing four volumes of *Geistliche Concerte* (1631–40) and one of *Liebliche Krafft-Blümlein* (1635) for the smaller forces appropriate to the more austere times.

By the time Scheidt had been reinstated as court *Kapellmeister* in 1738, he had lost four of his children in the plague of 1636, but despite this personal tragedy, he continued to compose and publish. In 1642 he presented his patron, Duke August, with a set of more than 100 sacred madrigals for five voices (now lost) and a collection of instrumental sinfonias (which were printed in 1644). In 1650 he published 100 four-part chorale settings for organ (*Tabulatur-Buch*) which attest to his skilful devotion throughout his life to the chorale variation technique.

Schickhardt, Johann Christian. See Low
COUNTRIES *1 United Provinces.*

Schröter, Christoph Gottlieb (1699–1782).
Saxon organist, composer, inventor and music
theorist whose home in Nordhausen was ran-
sacked and library destroyed by the French
army in 1761. Schröter was trained at the
Dresden royal chapel before studying theology
at Leipzig. He later worked as a music copyist
to Antonio Lotti at Dresden and then as secretary and a musician to a baron, in whose
entourage he travelled to the Netherlands and
England as well as within Germany. In 1724
he settled in Jena where he lectured on the
significance of Johann Mattheson's *Neu-
eröffnete Orchestre* (1713) and the mathematical basis of music theory; he also founded
a collegium musicum there. But eight years
later he was appointed organist at Nordhausen, a post he held for 50 years.

In 1737 Schröter joined in the outcry
against J. A. Scheibe's criticisms of J. S. Bach,
published in the *Critischer Musikus*. Two years
later he became one of the first members of
Mizler's corresponding society, which allowed
him a forum for his often critical views of
people and their theories. Although he
erroneously believed that he had invented the
piano (as he claimed in Marpurg's *Kritische
Briefe*, 1760–64), he seems to have been the
first German to repeat Cristofori's achievements. Schröter also invented a mechanism
for organists which would allow changes of
dynamics on both the manuals and the pedals
without changing registration. His most
influential treatise, *Deutliche Anweisung zum
General-Bass*, dates from the early 1750s, but
was not published until 1772.

Sorge, Georg Andreas (1703–78). Thuringian organist, composer of keyboard music,
expert on organ building and prolific writer of
treatises. Notable among these are his *Anleitung zur Fantasie* (1767), which is a guide
to extemporization at the keyboard, and the
Vorgemach der musicalischen Composition
(1745–7), which presents a cogent synthesis of
contemporary theoretical thought. From the
age of 19, Sorge served in the relative obscurity of Lobenstern as court and civic organist,
publishing his treatises at his own expense and
eschewing other appointments. In 1747 he
became a member of Mizler's corresponding
society.

Stölzel, Gottfried Heinrich (1690–1749).
Saxon *Kapellmeister*, composer and theorist.
After studies at the University of Leipzig,
where he was involved in opera and the collegium musicum, and casual work as a singing

and harpsichord teacher in Breslau, Stölzel
travelled widely in Italy (1713–15). At Venice
he met Francesco Gasparini, Alessandro Marcello, C. F. Pollarolo and Vivaldi; at Florence,
he declined a post because of his Protestant
convictions. He spent three years in Prague, a
year in Bayreuth (where he contributed music
to the bicentenary celebrations of the Reformation) and then two years as *Kapellmeister*
at Gera, before taking up a permanent post at
the court of Saxe-Gotha in 1720.

For each of these courts he composed
theatre pieces, usually pastorales; for Prague
and Gotha, he composed oratorios. J. S. Bach
included his partita in G minor in the *Clavier-
Büchlein* for W. F. Bach (1720). Stölzel composed 12 annual cantata cycles, an *Enhar-
monische Sonata* for harpsichord and a
concerto grosso for four orchestras. His only
printed work, a treatise on canon, appeared in
1725. In 1739 he became a member of Mizler's
corresponding society.

Strattner, Georg Christoph (*c*1644–1704).
Hungarian-born German *Kapellmeister* and
composer of a Passion cantata, *Sehet doch, ihr
Menschenkinder* (1692), for voices and instruments, which was an important precursor of
the Passion oratorio. Strattner was a protégé
of S. F. Capricornus at Pressburg and
Stuttgart. He was appointed *Kapellmeister* at
the court of Baden-Durlach (1666–82), then
of the Barfüsserkirche at Frankfurt am Main
(1682–92), where he was required to compose
simple Pietist music. Convicted of adultery
and banished from Frankfurt, Strattner
sought a new life in Weimar where, in 1695,
he became court vice-*Kapellmeister* under
J. S. Drese and, two years later, director of
the opera house.

Stricker, Augustin Reinhard. See NORTH-
ERN EUROPE *1 North Germany: Berlin.*

Telemann, Georg Philipp. See NORTHERN
EUROPE *1 North Germany: Hamburg.*

Vogler, Johann Caspar (1696–1763). Keyboard player and composer who, during the
late 1730s, served as deputy mayor, then
mayor of Weimar. Vogler studied with Bach
(who considered him among his best pupils)
at Arnstadt (1706) and Weimar (1710–14), as
well as with P. H. Erlebach and A. N. Vetter
at Rudolstadt. After an initial organ post at
Stadtilm (1715), he was appointed court
organist (subsequently acquiring additional
teaching and harpsichord duties) at Weimar
in 1721. His *Vermischte musikalische Choral-
Gedanken* for organ appeared in 1737.

Walther, Johann Gottfried (1684–1748).
Organist, composer, teacher, theorist and lexi-

cographer. Walther's importance lies as much in his place in German musical life as in his contributions to it. He was a skilled organist, with a secure post at the Weimar court from 1707 onwards, and composed vocal music and chorale preludes, of which the latter may be favourably compared with those of his cousin, J. S. Bach.

Walther and Bach became close friends during Bach's tenure at Weimar. Walther was also acquainted with Andreas Werckmeister, from whom he received encouragement and gifts of treatises and music. He came to know many others through correspondence undertaken in the production of his *Musicalisches Lexicon* (1732), the first German musical dictionary and the first in any language to include both biographies and terms, ancient and modern; his manuscript revisions found their way into E. L. Gerber's 1790–92 *Lexicon der Tonkünstler*. His autobiography appears in Mattheson's *Grundlage einer Ehren-Pforte* (1740), and further illuminates the nature of his friendships and professional acquaintanceships.

Walther was appointed as music teacher of Prince Johann Ernst (nephew of the Duke of Weimar), to whom he dedicated a manuscript treatise containing a summary of 17th-century theoretical sources, a discussion of mid Baroque compositional techniques – particularly those dealing with text setting – and an explanation of German musical rhetorical figures. In 1721 he was appointed *Hofmusicus* at Weimar.

Wender, Johann Friedrich (1655–1729). Saxon organ builder whose instrument at the Neukirche at Arnstadt (1701–3) was tested by Bach. Impressed with his work, Bach subsequently commissioned him to enlarge the organ at Mühlhausen (1708–9), to Bach's own specifications. Wender's instruments were also highly regarded by Johann Kuhnau and Johann Mattheson.

Werckmeister, Andreas (1645–1706). Important central German theorist, composer and respected organ expert who held a succession of organ posts in Thuringia. Though not university-trained, Werckmeister was well read and possessed of a wide-ranging intellect. He knew the treatises of Glarean, Zarlino and Michael Praetorius; he corresponded with J. G. Walther and exerted an important influence on Walther's *Praecepta der musicalischen Composition* (1708).

Werckmeister published six major treatises of his own. The *Orgel-Probe* (1681) describes ways of testing both new and renovated

instruments. His writings on tuning and temperament – in particular, *Musicalische Temperatur* (1st edn lost; 2nd edn 1691) – are equally relevant to modern readers: his system of tempering four intervals of a fifth (C–G, G–D, D–A, B–F sharp) and tuning the remaining eight perfect, known today as 'Werckmeister III', enables keyboard players to perform satisfactorily in all keys without retuning. Werckmeister's thoroughbass manual *Die nothwendigsten Anmerckungen und Regeln*, 1698), with its emphasis on harmony rather than counterpoint, is as much for composers as accompanists. The themes of religion and mathematics pervade all of his writings, coming together (as they did for Bach) in a belief in the mystic significance of number in music.

Westhoff, Johann Paul von (1656–1705). Violinist virtuoso, composer of idiomatic unaccompanied partitas (1696) and linguist at the Weimar court. Westhoff must have travelled in Italy as well as France in order to acquire the fluency necessary to serve as the royal tutor of French and Italian. In 1682, while Westhoff was in Paris, he played for Louis XIV; that same year, the *Mercure galant* advertised a sonata for violin and continuo by Westhoff in December and, the following month, an unaccompanied suite (which appears to be the earliest known multi-movement work for unaccompanied violin).

Witt, Christian Friedrich (c1660–1716). *Kapellmeister*, keyboard player (the son of Johann Ernst Witt, Altenburg court organist), composer, teacher and compiler of one of the most important hymnals (*Psalmodia sacra*, 1715) of the early 18th century. Witt was a lifelong servant to Friedrich I, Duke of Saxe-Gotha, who sent him to Vienna and Salzburg, and to Nuremberg, where he studied composition with G. C. Wecker (1685–6). He served as chamber organist at the Gotha court from 1686, then vice-*Kapellmeister* (1694) and finally *Kapellmeister* from 1713. In addition to the hundred-odd tunes he contributed to the *Psalmodia sacra*, Witt composed rather old-fashioned church cantatas (including the 'Rentweinsdorf' cycle), French ensemble suites, Italian sonatas and harpsichord pieces.

Zachow, Friedrich Wilhelm (1663–1712). Organist at the Marienkirche, Halle, composer and teacher of Gottfried Kirchhoff, J. G. Ziegler and Handel. Zachow came from a family of Leipzig *Stadtpfeifer*, very likely attended the Thomasschule, and held a post in Eilenburg (1676) before taking up his duties at Halle in 1684. As well as organ preludes and fugues based on chorale tunes, Zachow composed Masses and cantatas encompassing all the current forms and textures, in fugal and concerted styles. The cantatas incorporate extended and richly scored instrumental movements and obbligato instruments in the recitatives as well as the arias. Because of the quality and character of this music, he is considered a worthy precursor of Bach.

Ziegler, Johann Gotthilf (1688–1747). Saxon organist and composer (who had been a child prodigy), teacher and the author of three unpublished treatises. The first half of Ziegler's career was spent in short spells of study with such musicians as Christian Pezold at the Dresden Sophienkirche, F. W. Zachow at the Halle Marienkirche, Bach at the Weimar court and Johann Theile at Naumburg; and a longer period at the University of Halle in pursuit of degrees in law and theology, during which time he came under the influence of the eminent Pietist theologian A. H. Francke. He travelled in Germany, playing with court and church orchestras as well as civic collegiums.

In 1716 he took up the post of assistant organist at the Ulrichskirche in Halle where, after 1718, he remained as *director musices* and organist for the rest of his life. Like Zachow and Gottfried Kirchhoff, he taught and contributed greatly to the musical life of Halle. Although little of his music survives, he is known to have composed at least three cycles of cantatas and the funeral music for Friedrich Wilhelm I in Berlin in 1740, as well as other commissions for occasional music from outside Halle.

Dresden

Albert, Heinrich. See NORTHERN EUROPE *1 North Germany*.

Albrici. See ITALY *10 Itinerant Musicians*.

Algarotti, Francesco. See ITALY *10 Itinerant Musicians*.

Bach, Wilhelm Friedemann (1710–84). Organ virtuoso, scholar and composer known as 'the Halle Bach', the eldest and much-loved son of Johann Sebastian Bach. Though unquestionably gifted, Friedemann was also deeply flawed, and not sufficiently disciplined or visionary to realize fully his innate abilities. Educated at the Lateinschule in Cöthen, the Thomasschule and the university in Leipzig, Friedemann showed himself to be very intellectual, excelling at mathematics, philosophy and law. His musical training came from his father, who compiled the *Clavier-Büchlein* for him in 1720 (the year of his mother's death); when he was 12 his father presented him with the first volume of *Das wohltemperirte Clavier*.

Like his father, he never ventured further afield than Berlin. In 1729, armed with an invitation for Handel to visit the Bach family in Leipzig (which was never taken up), Friedemann met Handel at Halle. Two years later he accompanied his father to Dresden (where in 1733 Friedemann was appointed organist at the Sophienkirche).

Though not connected with the Dresden court, Friedemann gained the admiration and friendship of such musicians as Pantaleon Hebenstreit (vice-*Kapellmeister*), P. G. Buffardin, J. A. Hasse, Faustina Bordoni and Silvius Weiss. Because the Sophienkirche post was only part-time, Friedemann took on pupils – among them the harpsichordist J. G. Goldberg – and composed flute duets and harpsichord concertos. But he was ill-at-ease in Dresden and so ultimately sought more congenial surroundings in Halle, where in 1746 he was appointed organist at the Liebfrauenkirche (a post for which his father had once competed), with responsibility for the music at the two other principal churches there.

In the event, Halle too had its drawbacks: Friedemann had exchanged the frivolity and intellectual freedom of Dresden for Pietist sobriety. The limitations of his new environment were all the more evident to him after visiting his younger brother Carl Philipp Emanuel at the Berlin court with his father in 1747 and his half-brother Johann Christian in 1750. The death of his father in 1750 seems to have been devastating to Friedemann; marriage the following year could not fill the void. And although he continued to compose instrumental music and cantatas, he relied upon his father's example or simply borrowed from his own earlier works, rather than developing a new and more integrated style as Emanuel was able to do.

When the opportunity to quit Halle came in 1762, in the form of a *Kapellmeister* post at Darmstadt, Friedemann mismanaged the negotiations and found himself with a title but no salary. Apparently demoralized and unmindful of the consequences (perhaps already suffering from the mental instability that later afflicted him), he left his organ post at the Liebfrauenkirche in 1764 without notice or prospects of employment elsewhere. He and his family remained in Halle for several years – living off the proceeds of the sale of his wife's property – before moving first to Brunswick in 1770, where he gave recitals and sold his father's manuscripts (of which he was chief custodian) to meet their expenses, and then to Berlin four years later. Through his brother he gained the patronage of Princess Anna Amalia and pupils; but by this time his deteriorating mental health had become marked. He repaid the friendship of the court composer J. P. Kirnberger with groundless slander in a ludicrous attempt to discredit and unseat him from his post, and presumed to pass off his father's music as his own. During 1778–9 he attempted to compose an opera, *Lausus und Lydie* (now lost). However, there were those who took pity on his dependents and, a few months after his death, mounted a benefit performance for them of Handel's *Messiah* in Berlin.

Bernhard, Christoph (1628–92). Pomeranian singer, composer and important theorist at Dresden who defined three styles of composition according to the interrelationship of words and music in his *Tractatus compositionis augmentatus*. Along with Heinrich Albert, Johann Klemm, Johann Theile and Matthias Weckmann, Bernhard was one of Heinrich Schütz's principal disciples, training and serving under him from 1649. In 1655 he was appointed vice-*Kapellmeister* and two years later travelled to Italy to study in Rome with Carissimi and to recruit musicians for the court of the elector, Johann Georg. However, rivalries between German and Italian musicians made life at court unsupportable, and in 1663 Bernhard left to join Weckmann at Hamburg. Within a year he succeeded Thomas Selle as *Kantor* of the Johanneum, charged additionally with the direction of church music in the four main Hamburg churches. He became involved in Weckmann's collegium musicum and published a collection of 20 sacred concertos for one to four voices (*Geistliche Harmonien*) which he dedicated to the city fathers. Schütz commissioned a five-voice funeral motet in the style of Palestrina – even providing Bernhard with the text – two years before he died (1672): an indication of the esteem in which he continued to hold his pupil and colleague. In 1674 Bernhard returned to the Dresden court as vice-*Kapellmeister* and, under Elector Johann Georg III, was promoted to *Kapellmeister* in 1681.

Bernhard's writings are undated and circulated in manuscript, but it seems likely that he wrote *Von der Singe-Kunst* for the choirboys in his charge during the early years at Dresden, and the *Tractatus* and the *Ausführlicher Bericht vom Gebrauche der Con- und Dissonantien* later. The three styles explicated in the *Tractatus* are the *stylus gravis* (or *prima prattica*) and *stylus luxurians*, which is divided into *communis* and *teatralis*, according to where music in these styles was performed, and the types of acceptable dissonance conveyed therein. Bernhard's music manuscripts are preserved in the collection of Gustaf Düben.

Bontempi, Giovanni Andrea [Angelini] (*c*1624–1705). Italian castrato singer, composer of the first Italian opera to be staged in northern Germany, theorist and author of the first music history in Italian. As a young singer, Bontempi was entrusted to Cardinal Francesco Barberini in Rome. Having perfected his singing under Virgilio Mazzocchi, he took up a post in 1643 at S Marco, Venice, where he worked with Monteverdi, Giovanni Rovetta and Cavalli. In 1650 he travelled north to Dresden to enter the service of the Elector Johann Georg I. There he was associated with Schütz, to whom he dedicated his important treatise on counterpoint, the *Nova ... methodus* (1660). Bontempi became involved in theatrical productions and in 1664 added the posts of stage designer and master of the machines to his portfolio.

Two years earlier his opera *Il Paride* was performed as part of the marriage celebrations of the Margrave of Brandenburg and the Princess of Saxony. It incorporated much splendour and a variety of musical–dramatic genres including the comic *intermezzo*; Bontempi himself described the work as an 'erotopegnio musicale'. It was in fact the first Italian opera to be staged in northern Germany. Bontempi returned briefly to Italy (1666–70), and when he returned to Dresden his only other surviving opera was staged: *Dafne* (1671), on which he collaborated with Peranda, represents an early attempt to integrate Italian and German styles.

When the elector died in 1680, Bontempi retired to his native Perugia. There, in 1695, he published his *Historia musica* – which, though important as the first of its kind in Italian, dwelt mainly on his theories of Greek music, and only briefly discussed the music of his day (Burney and Hawkins were highly critical of it).

Bordoni, Faustina. See ITALY *10 Itinerant Musicians.*

Boschi, Giuseppe Maria. See ITALY *10 Itinerant Musicians.*

Buffardin, Pierre-Gabriel (*c*1690–1768). Provençal-born flautist and teacher, working at the Dresden court (1715–50). Little is known of his early life or training, beyond the fact that, as a young man, Buffardin accompanied the French ambassador to Constantinople. However, his pupils included Johann Jacob Bach (the younger brother of J. S. Bach), J. J. Quantz, F. J. Götzel and P. G. Florio. According to the Dutch flautist Antoine Mahaut, Buffardin invented a divided foot-piece with a tuning slide for his flute. He visited Paris at least twice – in 1726 and 1737 he appeared at the Concert Spirituel – before retiring there in 1750.

Dedekind, Constantin Christian (1628–1715). Bass singer, violinist, song composer and poet, whose primary post at the Dresden court was as a tax collector (though he also held musical appointments). Dedekind received his initial training at the renowned Quedlinburg abbey, under the direction of the Landgravine of Hesse, before seeking out Christoph Bernhard at Dresden (1646). In 1654 he gained an appointment as a chapel singer, and in 1666 he became leader of the court orchestra. Ultimately, tensions between the Italian and German musicians at Dresden forced him to resign in 1675.

He published two large collections of solo and duo songs with continuo: the *Aelbianische Musen-Lust* (1657), containing 146 sacred and secular strophic solo songs, with instrumental ritornellos and obbligato parts; and the *Musicalischer Jahrgang und Vesper-Gesang* (1673–4), containing 120 sacred concertos with recitatives, ariosos and da capo arias for two voices and continuo (he also provided parts for an optional bass voice and two violins). Dedekind's efforts to become a music publisher failed, and he turned to poetry (abandoning music altogether during the last half of his life), signing his song, oratorio and *intermedi* texts with his pseudonym 'Con Cor D'.

Durastanti, Margherita. See ITALY *10 Itinerant Musicians*.

Farina, Carlo (*c*1600–1640). Italian violinist who advanced the art of violin playing in Germany, and an early composer of trio sonatas; in particular, he greatly influenced the German violinists David Cramer, the elder Johann Schop and Johann Vierdanck. Farina was a contemporary of Salamone Rossi and G. B. Buonamente at Mantua before departing for Dresden, where in 1625 he was made *Kapellmeister*. Between 1626 and 1628 he published programmatic trio sonatas, whose special effects included imitations of other instruments and even animals, through use

of idiomatic devices such as col legno, sul ponticello, glissandos, scordatura and chords; here and there, Polish and Hungarian rhythms are evident, perhaps reflecting his travels.

Fierszewicz, Daniel. See NORTHERN EUROPE *3 Poland*.

Gerber, Christian (1660–1731). Pietist clergyman and writer who denounced the place of music in Protestant worship. Gerber published *Unerkandte Sünden der Welt* in Dresden in 1690; in it he marshalled quotations from the Scriptures and Luther's writing to support his contention. His somewhat shaky arguments were ably countered (with citations from the same venerable sources) by Georg Motz, writing from Tilsit in 1703 and again in 1708. Gerber responded in *Unerkannte Wohlthaten Gottes* (1711).

Harms, Johann Oswald (1643–1708). Important North German stage designer and painter at the Dresden court (from 1766), who was influenced by the Venetian (Mauro, Santurini and Mazzarini) and Viennese (Burnacini) sets and machines he saw during his travels between 1669 and 1672. While he emphasized architectonic formalism in his sets, his experience as a muralist (of urban and rural settings) raised the artistic quality of his work above that of his contemporaries. He created the sets for about 50 productions of operas by J. S. Kusser, Agostino Steffani, J. P. Krieger, Reinhard Keiser and the young Handel, produced in Saxony (Dresden, Eisenberg and Weissenfels) and northern Germany (Hanover, Wolfenbüttel, Brunswick and Hamburg).

Hasse, Johann Adolf (1699–1783). Unique example of a German composer who gained wide popularity in Italy. *Kapellmeister* at the Dresden court for most of his life, Hasse won international acclaim for his bel canto settings of Metastasio *opere serie*. He divided his time between Dresden and Venice, though he developed strong connections in Naples, Vienna and Berlin. Intertwined with his career was that of his wife, the famous soprano Faustina Bordoni, who served as his prima donna while undertaking independent engagements.

The migratory patterns of Hasse's life were set early in life. After stints as a tenor at the Hamburg Opera (1718) and the Wolfenbüttel court (where in 1721 he took the title role in his own first opera, *Antioco*, in which German recitatives alternated with Italian arias and choruses), Hasse embarked in 1722 on a tour of Italy. He settled in Naples, where he embraced the Catholic faith and gained the patronage of Marquis Vargas Maccina. He probably had composition lessons with Nicola

Porpora, then Alessandro Scarlatti, and in 1725, after the success of his serenata *Antonio e Cleopatra* – sung by Farinelli and Vittoria Tesi before an audience that included J. J. Quantz – important commissions began coming his way. Between 1726 and 1729 he produced seven operas for the Teatro S Bartolomeo, which included *Astarto* (1726; text by Zeno, rev. by Pariati), *Attalo* (1728; text by Aureli) in which Carestini sang, and the *opera buffa La sorella amante* (1729), as well as eight *buffo intermezzi* for the Neapolitan court. *Artaserse* (his first setting of a text by Metastasio) was commissioned for the Venetian Carnival and performed at the Teatro S Giovanni Grisostomo. While in Venice, he met Faustina Bordoni and was invited to Dresden.

Aware of the honours that awaited him there, Hasse characteristically took his time in taking them up – pausing at Parma, Milan and Naples to oversee the productions of three new operas and at Vienna for a court performance of his oratorio *Daniello* (1731). Later in 1731, he married Faustina Bordoni (shortly to be appointed prima donna at the electoral court) and was confirmed as *Kapellmeister* (in preference to the resident candidates, G. A. Ristori, J. B. Volumier and J. D. Zelenka) at Dresden. His tenure was inaugurated with the opera *Cleofide* (1731; a revision of Metastasio's *Alessandro nell'Indie*) at the Zwinger palace; of such import was the occasion that Bach, accompanied by his son Wilhelm Friedemann, travelled specially to Dresden to attend.

But after a matter of months, the Hasses were off to Italy for performances of new operas at Turin (*Catone in Utica*, text by Metastasio) at the end of 1731, and Rome (*Cajo Fabricio*, text after Zeno), Venice (*Demetrio*, text by Metastasio; and *Euristo*, text by Lalli, in which Cuzzoni, not the indisposed Bordoni, sang) and Naples (*Issipile*, text by Metastasio, which was composed to celebrate the birthday of Charles VI) in 1732. The following year was spent in Venice, Bologna – where *Siroe* (text by Metastasio) was given a gala première at the Teatro Malvezzi – and Vienna. Hasse was invited to London as director of the Opera of the Nobility but declined, perhaps partly out of deference to Handel, whom he had met in 1729; for his part, Handel purloined arias from Hasse's operas in his *pasticci*.

Most of 1734 was spent in Dresden, where he supervised revivals of his Italian operas and composed an oratorio (*Serpentes ignei in deserto*); the Hasses might have stayed longer had the elector (who was also King of Poland) not taken the court to Warsaw at the end of the year. As they were not required to follow, he and Faustina headed for Venice where they remained two years. Hasse took on the duties of *maestro di cappella* at the Ospedale degli Incurabili, for which he composed a *Salve regina* (1736) while also producing new operas: *Tito Vespasiano* (1735, text by Metastasio) was performed at the Teatro Pubblico, Pesaro – Faustina and Carestini taking the leading roles – and *Alessandro nell'Indie* (1736, text by Metastasio) at S Giovanni Grisostomo, Venice.

Hasse's next stay in Dresden was more productive: in 1737 and 1738 he produced five operas on texts by the Italian court poet S. B. Pallavicino. When, inevitably, the Saxon court moved to Warsaw in 1738, the Hasses were immediately off to Venice. They returned to Dresden in 1740 and stayed four years, during which time he composed one or two Carnival operas and a birthday opera for the king each October, while revising old ones such as *Demetrio*, which was performed with Pergolesi's *La serva padrona* interleaved between the acts. In 1742 Frederick the Great and his army conquered Silesia; the peace treaty was signed in Dresden, and there the king attended a performance of Hasse's *Lucio Papirio* (1742, text by Zeno) which led to performances of Hasse's operas in Berlin and Potsdam. Around this time he composed his famous oratorio *I pellegrini*.

Such was Hasse's growing prestige that in 1743 he was invited to compose the first settings of two new Metastasio texts: *Antigono* (1743) for Hubertusburg, and *Ipermestra* (1744) for a Habsburg wedding in Vienna. Having previously set only revised versions of Metastasio librettos, he embarked on a long-term project of revising them in the light of the original versions; such was Metastasio's satisfaction with his music that during the 1760s Hasse was to compose all the original *opera seria* and *festa teatrale* settings of his texts.

The years 1744–5 were spent in Venice and Vienna, where he was the favourite of Empress Maria Theresa. When the Hasses returned to Dresden in 1745 it was to prepare for a state visit by Frederick the Great. During the nine-day visit, Hasse's *Te Deum* and his opera *Arminio* (on a text by G. C. Pasquini, the new court poet) were performed; the Hasses themselves were required to present chamber music concerts. At the end of 1745 the Dresden Opera House closed and though a temporary theatre was erected in the courtyard of the Zwinger palace for Mingotti's troupe, the incentive to compose operas for Dresden declined.

In 1746 the Hasses left for Italy, stopping *en route* in Munich, where he was commissioned to compose an opera, *La Spartana generosa* (text by Pasquini). The occasion was the double wedding of Elector Maximilian III Joseph to the Saxon Princess Maria Anna and his sister Maria Antonia to Crown Prince Friedrich Christian – unions that would forge the strongest of links between Dresden and Munich. The Hasses were deeply offended by Maria Antonia's choice of Porpora as her music tutor and Regina Mingotti as the new prima donna at Dresden. These indignities were offset by Hasse's effective retirement to the post of *Oberkapellmeister* when Porpora was appointed *Kapellmeister* at Dresden in 1748.

After a spell in Venice, the Hasses returned to Dresden in 1749 for the production of *Il natal di Giove* (text by Metastasio, who wrote detailed instructions to Hasse on how to treat it) at Hubertusburg. But when the court went again to Warsaw, they took up an invitation to the French court, where Maria Josepha of Saxony was *dauphine*. During their stay, Hasse composed harpsichord sonatas, a cantata on a French text and a *Te Deum* in D, and revised *Didone abbandonata* (1742) for the second time, along with his *intermezzo Pimpinella e Marcantonio* for performances at Versailles. His arias and the *Te Deum* were subsequently performed at the Concert Spirituel.

The Hasses were back in Dresden for the start of the 1751–2 Carnival, at which *Leucippo* (1747, text by Pasquini, twice revised) and *Ciro riconosciuto* (1751, text by Metastasio) were performed with Faustina and the castrato Felice Salimbeni, who had been recently won away from the Berlin court. They were to be Faustina's final operatic roles; she last sang in public in a performance of *I pellegrini* the following Easter.

During the 1750s the Hasses continued to divide their time between Venice and Dresden, where they had opportunities to entertain Frederick the Great, whose court they in turn occasionally graced (in 1753, Hasse was presented with a snuff box and a ring by the king) despite the political estrangement between him and the Saxon elector. Hasse continued to revise his old Metastasio operas. *L'Olimpiade* (1756, text by Metastasio) was Hasse's last opera for Dresden, and thereafter his new productions were given at Warsaw (where the Dresden court was in exile

during the Third Silesian War), Naples and Vienna.

From 1757 until 1760 the Hasses lived in Venice and then spent two years in Vienna before returning to Dresden in 1762 at the end of the war. Their home, the opera house and the court library of sacred music had been destroyed by Frederick the Great's army. The death of Elector Friedrich August II further demoralized the court; with the new reign, musical entertainment was severely curtailed. The great flowering of music at Dresden was at an end. The Hasses were unceremoniously released from service without pensions.

They found a congenial haven in Vienna, where he was commissioned to compose a *festa teatrale*, *Egeria* (text by Metastasio), for the coronation of Joseph II in 1764 and *Romolo ed Ersilia* (text by Metastasio) for the wedding of Archduke Leopold to the Spanish Bourbon princess Maria Luisa in 1765. They met the Mozarts on their visit to Vienna in 1769 and again in Milan in 1771. In 1773 they retired to Venice where, in virtual oblivion, they succumbed to bankruptcy. Faustina died in 1781 and Hasse little more than a year later.

Although his music continued to be performed in Dresden and Berlin, it had slipped too far out of fashion to be revived in Italy. J. A. Hiller – who composed a lament in Hasse's honour, published editions of his arias (with written-out ornamentation) and *I pellegrini* (in German), and extolled him in his writings – served as his sole advocate. See also ITALY *10 Itinerant Musicians*, Bordoni, Faustina.

Hebenstreit, Pantaleon (1667–1750). Inventor and chief exponent of the pantaleon; violinist, teacher and composer working in North Germany and Saxony. While serving as a tutor to the children of a village pastor, Hebenstreit and the pastor (himself a skilled craftsman) developed a dulcimer instrument on which to accompany village dances. By 1697 their instrument had become an altogether much grander creation, spanning five octaves, doubly strung (185 gut and metal strings) and measuring nine feet in length. To popularize the invention Hebenstreit took it on tour to Berlin, Dresden, Leipzig and Weissenfels, where in 1698 he was appointed dancing-master to Duke Johann Georg. Until Pantaleon's visit to the French court in 1705, the instrument had no name; Louis XIV remedied this deficiency by calling it after its maker-practitioner. Two decades later, Abbé de Châteauneuf reminisced in his *Dialogue sur la musique des anciens* (1725) about a performance he had heard Hebenstreit give in a Paris salon.

Imbued with enthusiasm for French music, Hebenstreit returned to Saxony as dancing-master at the Eisenach court; but when in 1709 he was passed over in favour of Telemann – an admirer of Hebenstreit's artistry and command of the French style – for the post of *Kapellmeister*, Hebenstreit decided to tour. After playing for the emperor at Vienna he was rewarded with a gold chain but no post. He fared better at the Dresden court, where in 1714 he was appointed as a chamber musician and pantaleonist (with added compensation to cover the cost of strings). From 1729 Hebenstreit was charged with sacred music-making at the palace, and officially appointed court director of Protestant church music five years later; in 1740 he was elevated to privy councillor.

Hebenstreit took on pantaleon pupils, including J. C. Richter, C. S. Binder, Georg Gebel and Georg Noëlli (who performed in England in 1767). In 1717 Gottfried Grünewald (vice-*Kapellmeister* at Darmstadt) gave a recital on the pantaleon. No music seems to have been published for this instrument, and it is likely that Hebenstreit and his disciples improvised or performed transcriptions. However, the instrument's popularity ebbed in the late 1720s with the development of the fortepiano. Hebenstreit jealously guarded his instrument, to its detriment: when in 1727 Gottfried Silbermann (who hitherto had been building pantaleons exclusively for Hebenstreit and his pupils) began mass-producing them in Freiberg, Hebenstreit obtained a royal writ against the firm.

Heinichen, Johann David (1683–1729). *Kapellmeister* at Dresden, keyboard player, versatile composer and the author of an important thoroughbass treatise (1711; completely rewritten and much augmented as *Der General-Bass in der Composition*, 1728). Heinichen was educated at the Leipzig Thomasschule, where he studied with Johann Kuhnau and then served as his assistant, and at the university, where he read law. He spent three years in Weissenfels, practising as an advocate and composing operas for Leipzig; but not until 1709 did he decide to devote himself to music, with the blessing of Duke Johann Georg of Weissenfels and his *Kapellmeister*, J. P. Krieger.

Heinichen worked briefly at Leipzig as director of the collegium musicum, and then as court composer at Zeitz and Naumburg, during which time he produced the initial version of his treatise. But he decided to investigate Italian music at first hand, and so in

1710 he departed, making Venice his base until 1716. While in Rome in 1712 he tutored the young Prince Leopold of Anhalt-Cöthen, and at least two of his operas – *Mario* and *Le passioni per troppo amore* (both 1713) – were performed at the Teatro S Angelo, Venice.

In 1717 he was appointed *Kapellmeister* at Dresden, sharing responsibilities for the court music there and in Poland (August the Strong was both Elector of Saxony and King of Poland) with J. C. Schmidt (the *Oberkapellmeister*). In this capacity he composed a quantity of cantatas, serenades and instrumental music in a cosmopolitan, *galant* style, as well as sacred music, but only one opera (*Flavio Crispo*, 1720) which, in the event, was never performed. Towards the end of his life he devoted himself to an ambitious revision of his thoroughbass treatise.

Kittel, Caspar (1603–39). Theorbist, composer and lifelong servant of the Dresden Hofkapelle, who was associated with Heinrich Schütz as both pupil and colleague. He was sent to Italy in 1624, where he was joined by Schütz; they travelled back together in 1629. He was appointed instrumental inspector in 1632, and the following year deputized for Schütz while he was in Denmark. With the publication of his *Arien und Cantaten* (texts by Opitz), Kittel became the first German composer to use the Italian term 'cantata', by which he meant strophic variations. His son Christoph (*fl* 1641–80) was appointed Hofkapelle organist in 1660 and was succeeded in turn by his son, Johann Heinrich (1652–82).

Klemm, Johann (*c*1595–after 1651). Dresden court organist (1625), composer of fugues (*Partitura seu Tabulatura italica*, 1631) and publisher – not only of his own music, but of at least two collections by Heinrich Schütz (the second *Symphoniae sacrae*, 1647; and the *Geistliche Chormusik*, 1648). From the age of ten, Klemm sang in the Dresden court chapel. In 1613 the elector sent him to study with Christian Erbach in Augsburg, where he remained for two years. At Dresden he took charge of the music education of the choristers under Schütz, serving also as his amanuensis.

Kremberg, Jakob. See NORTHERN EUROPE 7 *Itinerant Musicians.*

Krieger, Adam (1634–66). Dresden court organist and composer of secular strophic *Arien*. Krieger studied at Halle and Leipzig before succeeding Johann Rosenmüller as organist of the Nicolaikirche in Leipzig. In 1657 he founded a collegium musicum the same year he was among the musicians recruited for the court of the new Dresden

Elector Johann Georg II. His songs (contained in two collections, one of which was published posthumously) were highly regarded for their expressiveness, and some of them entered the chorale repertory.

Laurenti, Antonio Maria Novelli. See ITALY *7 Papal States: Bologna-Ferrara.*

Lotti, Antonio. See ITALY *4 Venice.*

Mauro. See ITALY *4 Venice.*

Mingotti. See ITALY *10 Itinerant Musicians.*

Pallavicino, Carlo. See ITALY *10 Itinerant Musicians.*

Pallavicino, Stefano Benedetto (1672–1742). Italian-born Dresden and Düsseldorf court poet who was a leading reformer of the opera libretto and son of the composer Carlo Pallavicino. After being educated at Salò, the young Pallavicino accompanied his father to Dresden in 1686, and within two years was appointed court poet. With the exception of the period 1695–1716, when he was at Düsseldorf (serving as private secretary to the Elector Palatine as well as court poet), Pallavicino spent nearly all of his life at the Dresden court. He was a prolific writer of opera, oratorio and cantata texts for J. A. Hasse, Antonio Lotti, Agostino Steffani and J. H. von Wilderer, and published a much-respected translation of Horace. In 1744 a four-volume edition of his works was published posthumously.

Peranda, Marco Gioseppe (*c*1625–75). Italian alto and composer who succeeded Heinrich Schütz as *Hofkapellmeister* at Dresden in 1672. From Rome he was recruited by Christoph Bernhard for the new Hofkapelle inaugurated in 1656 at Dresden. Peranda allied himself not with the Italians (G. A. Bontempi and Bartolomeo Albrici), but with Schütz, and thus advanced steadily at court (vice-*Kapellmeister* in 1661, *Kapellmeister* two years later), and was able to exert an important influence on contemporary Saxon and North German composers. His music includes Masses (he remained a Catholic) and oratorios (including a *St Mark Passion* long attributed to Schütz), as well as portions of two operas, *Dafne* (1671) and *Jupiter und Io* (1673), on which he collaborated with Bontempi.

Pezold, Christian (1677–1733). Organist at the Dresden court (from 1697) and Sophienkirche (1703), teacher and composer of virtuoso keyboard music and chamber music. Pezold visited Paris in 1714 and Venice two years later. He was highly praised by Johann Mattheson, and his pupils included C. H. Graun.

Pisendel, Johann Georg (1687–1755). Saxon violin virtuoso and composer of sonatas and concertos who succeeded J. B. Volumier as *Kapellmeister* at Dresden in 1728. Pisendel was trained at the Ansbach court chapel, where he studied with F. A. M. Pistocchi and Giuseppe Torelli. In 1709 he left the court orchestra to travel, visiting Weimar (where he met Bach), Leipzig (to study with J. D. Heinichen) and Darmstadt, before joining the renowned Dresden court orchestra in 1712. His travels were furthered by regular tours undertaken by the prince–elector to France (1714), Berlin (1715), Italy (1716–17), Vienna (1718), Berlin (1728 and 1744) and Warsaw (1734). In this way he gained the friendship and respect of such contemporaries as Vivaldi, Tomaso Albinoni, Telemann, J. A. Hasse and J. J. Quantz. His pupils included J. G. Graun and Franz Benda.

Porpora, Nicola. See ITALY *10 Itinerant Musicians.*

Praetorius, Michael. See NORTHERN EUROPE *1 North Germany.*

Price, John. See CENTRAL EUROPE *1 South Germany.*

Quantz, Johann Joachim. See NORTHERN EUROPE *1 North Germany: Berlin.*

Richter, Johann Christoph (1700–85). Dresden court organist, pantaleonist and composer of operas and instrumental music. Richter served as court organist for 50 years. By electoral command he learnt the pantaleon from Hebenstreit, after whose departure in 1734 Richter became the official court practitioner of that instrument (he was also required to perform on Hebenstreit's porcelain glockenspiel). After 1750 Richter was responsible for the music performed in the Protestant court services, and in 1760 was appointed *Kapellmeister*.

Ristori, Giovanni Alberto (1692–1753). Italian composer at the Dresden court from 1717 until his death. Ristori was the son of Tommaso Ristori, director of an Italian comedy troupe which toured northern Europe. He gained a modest reputation as an opera composer in Italy – *Orlando furioso* (1713, text by Braccioli) and *Euristeo* (1714) were produced in Venice – before joining his wife and parents on tour in 1715 to Dresden. Two years later he was appointed director of the *cappella polacca* (which counted among its dozen members the young J. J. Quantz and Franz Benda) at the Warsaw court.

Because he did not hold an appointment as an opera composer, his opportunities to compose operas were limited. Nevertheless,

Ristori became the first in Germany to produce an *opera buffa*, *Calandro* (text by S. B. Pallavicino), in 1726. Frederick the Great attended a performance during the 1728 Carnival and was sufficiently taken with it to ask for a copy of the score. But the appointment of Hasse as *Kapellmeister* in 1730 meant an end to Ristori's prospects at Dresden.

He spent much of the next two years on tour with his father's troupe, first in Russia during the winter of 1731–2 – where *Calandro* became the first Italian opera to be performed in Moscow – and then in Poland. He returned briefly to Dresden for the Easter performance of his oratorio *La deposizione della croce di Nostro Signore.*

Until 1744 he remained mainly in Warsaw, providing sacred and occasional music when the court was in residence, although in 1737 he travelled to Naples in the entourage of Princess Maria Amalia, who married the King of the Two Sicilies; while he was there, several of his works were performed at the Teatro S Carlo. Also in 1737, Ristori's *pasticcio Didone abbandonata* (text by Metastasio) was performed in London at Covent Garden (there is no evidence to suggest that he was present for the performances). He spent his last years in Dresden and was rewarded for his long years of service in 1750 with an appointment as Hasse's vice-*Kapellmeister.*

Ritter, Christian. See NORTHERN EUROPE 2 *Scandinavia.*

Schmidt, Johann Christoph (1664–1728). *Kapellmeister*, organist, teacher and minor composer at the Dresden court. Schmidt began as a chorister under Christoph Bernhard in 1676, eventually himself becoming master of the choristers in 1687 and second organist in 1692. With the accession of August the Strong as elector in 1694, Schmidt was sent to Italy to study, returning two years later as vice-*Kapellmeister* and chamber organist under N. A. Strungk, whom he succeeded in 1698.

As August the Strong was also King of Poland, Schmidt was charged with organizing the music for the Catholic services at Kraków and Warsaw as well as for the Protestant services at the Dresden court. During his tenure he assembled a highly acclaimed orchestra which included P. G. Buffardin, Pantaleon Hebenstreit, Christian Pezold, J. G. Pisendel, J. C. Richter, F. M. Veracini, J. B. Volumier and J. D. Zelenka. From 1717, at the time of his promotion to *Oberkapellmeister*, Schmidt was assisted by his eventual successor, J. D. Heinichen. Schmidt's pupils included

C. H. Graun, Melchior Hofmann and C. G. Schröter.

Schütz, Heinrich (1585–1672). *Kapellmeister* of the Dresden court for nearly half a century, distinguished teacher and composer without peer in 17th-century Germany. His command of both German and Italian compositional techniques – in form, style and texture – and the extraordinary expressive power of his text settings were much prized by his patrons, and drew such pupils as Heinrich Albert, Christoph Bernhard, Johann Theile and Matthias Weckmann. Much of his music remained in manuscript and has been lost, though, miraculously, 500 works survive, almost all of them for the Lutheran church (and without recourse to chorales). In spite of his post, Schütz could afford to have only a few of his works printed, although those he did see through the press were printed on paper with a watermark combining his family crest and personal monogram. Never content with what he had achieved, he was continually revising even his published works. It seems entirely appropriate that in 1647 the admiring members of the Dresden Hofkapelle called this visionary figure, who showed German musicians the way forward, 'the Orpheus of our time'.

Schütz was fortunate to come from a prosperous Saxon family who, from 1590, owned an inn at Weissenfels. In 1598 his musical talent so impressed an overnight guest, Landgrave Moritz of Hessen-Kassel (himself an amateur composer), that a year later, the young Schütz was taken to Kassel, made a choirboy and sent to a school for the children of the Hesse court. He studied counterpoint with the court *Kapellmeister*, Georg Otto, and although he began studies in law at the University of Marburg in 1608, the landgrave sent him to Venice the following year to continue his musical training with Giovanni Gabrieli.

Recognizing Schütz's potential, and wishing to work with him further, Gabrieli had the Margrave of Brandenburg (who was visiting Venice) intercede with Landgrave Moritz late in 1610 to secure an additional year's scholarship. During his third year in Venice, Schütz produced a collection of Gabrielian madrigals (1611) which he dedicated to Moritz and served as Gabrieli's deputy at S Marco, where he would have remained longer had not Gabrieli died. He returned to Hesse in 1613 with a ring, a token of Gabrieli's admiration and affection for the young Saxon.

Hardly had Schütz resumed his duties at

Hesse than he was invited by the Elector of Saxony, Johann Georg I, to play for him at Dresden. The electoral chapel was, at that time, in a state of transition: the *Kapellmeister* Rogier Michael was eager to retire and Michael Praetorius, *Kapellmeister* at Wolfenbüttel, was serving as visiting musical director. The elector was clearly set on Schütz as his new *Kapellmeister*, though he was mindful of the esteem in which he was held by Moritz – and of the need to proceed gently if he were to pluck him from the bosom of the Hesse court. Hence, Schütz stayed only a few months, and then, with the reluctant assent of the landgrave, returned to Dresden to direct the chapel music in 1615, ostensibly for two years. Once ensconced, Schütz was charged with the formidable task of organizing and providing music for the gamut of religious and political ceremonies – which in the first year included the centenary of the Reformation and a state visit by Emperor Matthias; meanwhile the landgrave sought in vain to reclaim his *Kapellmeister* from the determined elector. For his pàrt Schütz retained a lasting loyalty to Moritz and his court, and over the next 30 years regularly sent music and also trained musicians for the chapel.

In addition to providing the masterful italianate concerted psalms (in German translations, which were published in 1619 as the *Psalmen Davids*) for the centenary, and a ballet (only the libretto survives) for the emperor's visit, Schütz was invited, along with Praetorius and Scheidt, to assist in the reorganization of the music at Magdeburg Cathedral in 1618; the following year they met in Bayreuth where they were joined by Johann Staden for the inauguration of the Stadtkirche organ, on which all four musicians performed. In 1623 he published the *Historia der ... Aufferstehung ... Jesu Christi* (in which the Evangelist's part, notated as plainsong, is accompanied by four viols, whose players are instructed to improvise on long notes) and the Latin *Cantiones sacrae* two years later – the year in which his family life ended with the death of his wife and the entrusting of his two young daughters to the care of their grandmother.

After the rigours of producing the first German opera, *Dafne* (lost; text by Opitz after Rinuccini), for the 1627 wedding festivities for the elector's daughter and Landgrave Georg II of Hessen-Darmstadt at Torgau, Schütz won permission to revisit Italy. In Venice he met Monteverdi and eagerly absorbed the recitative style. While there he

sent quantities of music and instruments to Dresden, engaged at least one musician (the violinist Francesco Castelli) and published his *Symphoniae sacrae* (1629), for three to six parts and continuo. Upon his return to Dresden he plunged into the arrangements and composition of music for the centenary of the Augsburg Confession (1630). When, in 1630, Schein died, Schütz honoured his Leipzig colleague's last wish by composing a memorial motet, *Das ist je gewisslich wahr*.

During the 1630s and 40s, the vicissitudes of the Thirty Years War spelled the decline of the Dresden musical establishment, and Schütz took the opportunity to spend time at the temporarily more prosperous Danish court. Not surprisingly, the elector was reluctant to release him. The immediate pretext was an invitation from Crown Prince Christian to take charge of the music for his wedding to one of the elector's daughters. When he finally arrived in Copenhagen late in 1633 – having stopped in Hamburg to collect Matthias Weckmann and Daniel Hämmerlein – Schütz was immediately appointed *Kapellmeister* to King Christian IV. He went back to Dresden in 1635, undoubtedly with the intention of returning to Copenhagen, and published both the *Musicalische Exequien* – a German Requiem for Prince Heinrich Posthumus of Reuss (in three sections and scored for six soloists and continuo) – and the *Erster Theil kleiner geistlichen Concerten* (small-scale sacred concertos, without instruments, which reflect the austerity of the times) in 1636. After the publication of the second part in 1639, Schütz was given permission to spend 18 months as *Kapellmeister* at Hildesheim; such was the disarray at the Dresden court and the debt in back wages owed to him that Schütz had little trouble securing permission for another two years' leave of absence in Denmark, beginning in 1642.

He returned to Dresden in 1645 via the Wolfenbüttel court, by which time he was 60 years old and ready to retire. However, the elector insisted on a compromise: Schütz would continue to work six months a year for the next ten years, composing occasional music and taking charge of the music at major court events. He also published the second part of the *Symphoniae sacrae* (1647), which he dedicated to Prince Christian of Denmark, and the *Geistliche Chor-Music* (1648), an outstanding collection of 29 German motets in five to seven parts with continuo, dedicated to the Leipzig city council. The latter followed his intervention in the theoretical dispute between Paul Siefert and Marco Scacchi (1646), with whom he sided, and demonstrated his own command both of counterpoint and the modern Italian style. In 1650 he published his third and last collection of *Symphoniae sacrae*, for three to six voices and

The pre-war standards at the Dresden court were slow to return after the Peace of Westphalia in 1648; although more singers and instrumentalists had been hired, there was no money to pay them. Over a two-and-a-half year period, Schütz received no pay; his requests to be released from service and suggestions for a successor were ignored. In an attempt to mollify him, Elector Johann Georg I appointed G. A. Bontempi to share the duties of the *Kapellmeister* (Schütz and Bontempi each took half the Kapelle and responsibility for the performances in alternate weeks). Schütz was outraged and pressed his case for retirement more strongly but had still made no progress when the elector died in 1656.

Under the new elector Schütz was made *Ober-Kapellmeister* and the day-to-day running of the Kapelle was left to Bontempi and Vincenzo Albrici. Schütz spent less and less time in Dresden, returning there on business and for special court events. During the 1660s he planned and oversaw the formation of a new Kapelle for the elector's brother, the Duke of Saxe-Zeitz, and composed some of his most powerful music: the Christmas *Historia* (1660; only the Evangelist's part was published, in 1664), *Die sieben Wortte [The Seven Last Words ... of Jesus Christ]* (n.d.) and the first versions of his unaccompanied *St John* (1665), *St Matthew* and *St Luke* Passions (both 1666). In 1664 he prepared a catalogue of his works which he entrusted to Duke August of Brunswick-Lüneburg.

As Germany's economy began to recover from the Thirty Years War, salaries improved (Schütz's pension eventually amounted to twice his previous full-time salary); at the age of 84, he was belatedly honoured by the elector with the gift of a gold cup. Hard of hearing and increasingly frail, Schütz commissioned his own eulogy in a strict five-voice setting of Psalm CXIX.54 – a text that he used for his own last work, for eight voices and instruments – from his pupil Christoph Bernhard. Death followed an attack of apoplexy, and he was buried with much ceremony in the portico of the Frauenkirche.

Senesino. See ITALY *10 Itinerant Musicians.*

Strungk, Nicolaus Adam. See NORTHERN EUROPE *7 Itinerant Musicians.*

Tesi, Vittoria. See ITALY *10 Itinerant Musicians.*

Tosi, Pier Francesco. See ITALY *10 Itinerant Musicians.*

Veracini, Francesco Maria. See ITALY *6 Tuscany.*

Volumier [Woulmyer], **Jean Baptiste** (*c*1670–1728). Excellent Flemish violinist and composer who trained in Paris and made his career in Berlin and Dresden where he introduced the French style. At Berlin he served in the Elector of Brandenburg's chapel as *Konzertmeister*, in charge of ballet music. When he was dismissed, in 1708, he took up the same post at the Dresden court where under his influence a lively school of violin playing developed; F. W. Marpurg particularly praised Volumier's orchestra. He was a friend of Bach and in 1717 planned the ill-fated competition at Dresden between Bach and Louis Marchand.

Walther, Johann Jakob (*c*1650–1717). Virtuoso violinist and composer who served at the electoral courts of Dresden (as 'primo violinista da camera' from 1674) and Mainz (as a clerk and 'Italian secretary' from 1681). Walther's only peer was H. I. F. von Biber in Salzburg: both were renowned for their technical bravura, which relied upon *bariolage*, multiple stops and dramatically wide tessitura. Although Walther eschewed the practice of scordatura (retuning the violin), he chose to follow Biagio Marini and Carlo Farina by indulging in imitations of birds and musical instruments. He published two collections of programmatic violin music, *Scherzi da violino solo* (1676) and *Hortulus chelicus* (1688).

Weckmann, Matthias. See NORTHERN EUROPE *1 North Germany: Hamburg.*

Weiss, Silvius Leopold. See NORTHERN EUROPE *7 Itinerant Musicians.*

Zelenka, Jan Dismas (1679–1745). Bohemian double bass player and composer of undoubted originality who worked all his life at the Dresden court in the shadow of J. A. Hasse. Though considered a church composer during his lifetime, Zelenka is known today by his instrumental music. A devout Catholic, he studied at the Clementinum in Prague and played in the orchestra of Count Hartig, who in 1710 recommended him for the post at Dresden, where he remained for the rest of his life. His tenure at Dresden was interrupted by studies with J. J. Fux in Vienna and Antonio Lotti in Venice in 1715; upon his return to Vienna in 1717, he reputedly taught Quantz. In 1723 Zelenka travelled to Prague with a contingent of Dresden musicians for the coronation of Charles VI, at which his *Melodrama de Sancto Wenceslao* was performed. He was appointed vice-*Kapellmeister* in 1721 but was forced to concede the *Kapellmeister* post to Hasse in 1731.

Zelenka produced three oratorios, at least 20 Masses, three dozen cantatas and 18 *a cappella* motets as well as psalms, Offertories, Vespers, antiphons and arias; most of his church music was lost in 1945, when the unique manuscripts in which it survived were destroyed. His instrumental works – six virtuoso trio sonatas for two oboes, bassoon and continuo (1715–16) and nine orchestral concertos (1733) fashionably inscribed with chronograms – fared better because they had been published during his lifetime and survived in multiple copies.

Zelenka's music is idiosyncratic and in its way quite powerful, much as Gesualdo's was in his day. Zelenka's counterpoint studies with Fux bore exotic fruits: his harmony is coloured by third-relationships, modal interchange, chains of suspensions, 9th chords and unsettling (if deeply expressive) accidentals. Both Bach and Telemann are known to have admired his music.

Ziani, Pietro Andrea. See ITALY *4 Venice*.

Leipzig

Bach, Carl Philipp Emanuel. See NORTHERN EUROPE *1 North Germany: Berlin*.

Bach, Johann Sebastian (1685–1750). Supreme genius of the late Baroque era, who, like Handel, composed masterpieces in virtually all the musical genres of the day. Unlike Handel, Bach spent his entire working life in Saxony and Thuringia, composing primarily for the Lutheran liturgy and publishing relatively little. Such international reputation as he did enjoy was based upon his formidable skill as a performer and composer of keyboard music. Bach behaved, by all accounts, with great modesty in the company of his peers and yet, because of his clear sense of destiny, had little patience with some of his intransigent employers, whose appraisal was limited to a consideration of his usefulness to them. Each of the five principal posts he held – at Arnstadt, Mühlhausen, Weimar, Cöthen and Leipzig – enabled him to exercise different sides of his creative powers which, nevertheless, evolved irrespective of the demands placed upon him from outside, for his was a creative odyssey bounded only by time. Pos-

sessed of great technical skill and originality, he composed prodigiously throughout his life, with astonishing command of detail and overall conception.

Born into a tradition of professional music-making, Johann Sebastian Bach was the last child of the Eisenach *Stadtpfeifer* Johann Ambrosius Bach and Maria Elisabeth Lämmerhirt. His early education at Eisenach (with the *Kantor*, A. C. Dedekind, at the Georgenkirche) was interrupted by the deaths of his parents in 1694 and 1695. He and his brother Jacob found a home with their elder brother Johann Christoph, organist at Ohrdruf, who also instructed them in music and organ building. While attending the Lyceum at Ohrdruf, Johann Sebastian spent his free time copying the music of Froberger, Pachelbel and J. K. Kerll.

When he was 15, Bach was sent to the Michaelisschule at Lüneburg where he sang in the Mettenchor until his voice broke. His studies included genealogy and heraldry – in addition to history, mathematics, science, poetry and Lutheranism, and he must have spent countless hours playing and copying scores from the excellent music library there. He was befriended by Georg Böhm, the Johanniskirche organist, and J. A. Reincken, organist at the Catharinenkirche in nearby Hamburg. He also had many opportunities to hear the French orchestra of the Celle court, through the agencies of Thomas de La Selle (who was the dancing-master at the Ritterakademie in Lüneburg and a member of the Celle orchestra).

Precociously, at the age of 17, he applied for the organist's post at the Jakobikirche in Sangerhausen, won it, and would have taken it up had not the Duke of Weissenfels exercised his right to appoint an older candidate. After several months as a violinist and lackey in the service of Duke Johann Ernst at Weimar, Johann Sebastian went to Arnstadt in 1703 to examine a newly installed organ at the Neukirche; his playing so impressed the church fathers that, in spite of having promised the organ post to Andreas Börner, they appointed Bach in his stead. Too young and intolerant to be an effective teacher, Bach soon clashed with the authorities over the scope of his job. Although his playing duties were not heavy, he antagonized his congregation with needlessly complicated hymn accompaniments and bold embellishments at final fermatas; he balked at working with the choristers and audaciously demanded that a *Kapellmeister* be appointed to train them. His relations with his employers further deteriorated after his absence for an extended period in 1705 to visit Buxtehude at Lübeck (a journey he undertook on foot).

A vacancy in Mühlhausen at the Blasiuskirche provided the desired opportunity to leave Arnstadt, he resigned his post and took up the new one in 1707; money inherited from his great-uncle enabled him to marry his cousin, Maria Barbara Bach (*b* 1684). He had only just settled into his job – composing organ music and conservatively styled cantatas, which included *Aus der Tiefen rufe ich, Herr, zu dir* (BWV131) and *Gottes Zeit ist die allerbeste Zeit* (BWV106, a funeral cantata known as the *Actus tragicus*), and planning the renovation of the organ – when the Duke of Weimar offered him the post of *Hoforganist*, together with that of *Kammermusicus*, for which he was expected to play violin and viola in the court orchestra. He was released from his contract at Mühlhausen, on condition that he continue to supervise the renovation. In fact, many in the congregation were relieved to see him go, having found it difficult to adjust to his music and feeling uneasy at his early demand for a larger salary which had accompanied the news of an expected addition to his family.

Bach's return to Weimar marked the beginning of a particularly productive and fulfilling period in his life. He composed most of his organ music, including the preludes and fugues, toccatas and fugues (notably the C major, BWV564), arrangements of some of Vivaldi's concertos (which in turn exerted a powerful influence on Bach's own music), the *Orgel-Büchlein* (*c*1713–16), chorale settings and other organ works (pre-eminently the Passacaglia in C minor, BWV582). He also produced harpsichord music, which reveals his assimilation of the Italian and French styles, and enough sacred chamber cantatas – such as *Christ lag in Todesbanden* (BWV4) and the settings of Salomo Franck texts, *Komm, du süsse Todesstunde* (BWV161) and *Der Himmel lacht!* (BWV31) – to establish a characteristic personal style that would prevail in his larger-scale Leipzig cantatas.

Besides music for the Weimar court, Bach undertook commissions such as one for a panegyric hunting cantata – *Was mir behagt* (BWV208) – to celebrate the birthday of Duke Christian of Weissenfels in 1713. A fair copy of the Brandenburg Concertos was presented in 1721 to the Margrave of Brandenburg (who neither acknowledged the gift, nor bothered to have them performed). In these, Bach

pursued a series of important experiments with mixed solo and concerto grosso formats, innovative combinations of instruments, and the first use of transverse flute and harpsichord as concertino soloists. He must also have composed instrumental chamber music, though none survives. During this time, Bach accumulated a large number of students and fathered six children, among them Wilhelm Friedemann (1710) and Carl Philipp Emanuel (1714). His closest colleagues included Telemann (nearby at Eisenach until 1712) and J. G. Walther (organist of the Weimar Stadtkirche and his cousin).

From the beginning, Bach took a keen interest in new and recently renovated organs. As his reputation grew, he was increasingly summoned to examine them, whereupon he would often be invited to apply for the organist's post. While in Halle to purchase music in 1713, he played the Liebfrauenkirche organ, which was undergoing enlargement. He so impressed the authorities that he was offered the post on the spot, which had been vacant since the death of Handel's teacher, F. W. Zachow, in 1712. This offer (which he probably never seriously intended to take up) in turn facilitated his promotion to *Konzertmeister* (1714) at Weimar. Whatever temporary offence Bach may have given to the Liebfrauenkirche authorities, it had been overcome by 1716 when he was invited, along with Johann Kuhnau and C. F. Rolle, to examine the organ (which entailed meeting the builders, writing a report, performing on the instrument and attending a banquet). While Bach's fame as an organist, particularly as an improviser, was confirmed by Mattheson in *Das beschützte Orchestre* (1717), he was accumulating drafts of harpsichord music – and even polished examples, such as the English Suites (BWV806–11) – which further enhanced his reputation as a formidable exponent of keyboard playing.

Late in 1716 Bach learnt – perhaps from Telemann himself (who had served as Carl Philipp Emanuel's godfather in 1714) – that the Duke of Weimar was negotiating to hire Telemann as his *Kapellmeister*, a post Bach must have coveted. His pride and ambition evidently stirred, Bach quietly began seeking an appointment as *Kapellmeister* elsewhere. He did not have far to look: an alliance by marriage between the Weimar and Cöthen courts in 1716 would seem to have paved the way for Bach's move to Cöthen the following year, but it was deliberately delayed for a time by Duke Wilhelm Ernst, who was much dis-

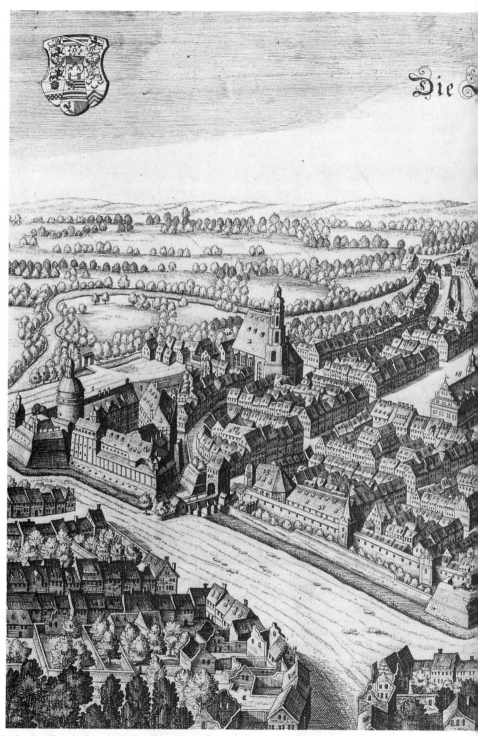

Leipzig (Frederick de Wit: *Theatrum Praecipuarum totius Europe Urbium,*
1689–95)

Leÿpßig.

2 Thomaskirche
13 Paulinerkirche
15 Petrikirche
18 Rathaus
22 Nicolaikirche
26 Thomasschule

gruntled by the apparent opportunism of his new relation, Prince Leopold of Anhalt-Cöthen.

The duke prevaricated: Bach was allowed to visit Dresden, where he was invited to take part, with the French organist Louis Marchand, in a contest of extemporization (Marchand fled, apparently in terror of being shown up) and to take part in the Weimar celebrations in 1717 of the bicentenary of the Reformation. Then, in a fit of pique, sparked off by Bach's incessant demands to be released from service, the duke imprisoned him for almost a month before finally dismissing him just before the new year. Instead of earning honours and emoluments, Bach and his family departed in virtual disgrace.

At least in Prince Leopold, Bach had finally gained an understanding patron, musically literate and intent upon possessing a Kapelle of renowned excellence. Bach was paid twice as much as his predecessor (A. R. Stricker), sent to Berlin (1719) to order a new harpsichord, and included in the prince's entourage on his holidays at Karlsbad – though it was while he was there in 1720 that Bach's wife died. During a visit to Hamburg shortly afterwards, Bach conducted his cantata *Ich hatte viel Bekümmernis* (BWV21), met the aged J. A. Reincken, and declined the organist's post at the Jacobikirche.

Bach married again late in 1721: Anna Magdalena Wilcke, 16 years his junior, was one of the court singers and a chamber musician. But a week later, Prince Leopold also married; his wife (a cousin), the Princess of Anhalt-Bernburg, was not a music-lover and resented her husband's preoccupation. The rapport between the prince and his *Kapellmeister* was inevitably affected – a state of affairs that contributed to his determination to apply for the dual post in Leipzig of *Kantor* of the Thomasschule and civic *director musicus* when it became vacant (on the death of Johann Kuhnau) in 1722.

During his short, six-year tenure at Cöthen, Bach composed and polished many of his most enduring monuments of instrumental music: pre-eminent among them, the *Clavier-Büchlein* (1720), which he dedicated to his son Friedemann, the six French Suites (BWV812–17), the monumental *Wohltemperirtes Clavier* (Well-Tempered Clavier, 1722), containing 24 preludes and fugues in all keys, the two- and three-part Inventions (BWV772–801); the solo violin suites and partitas (BWV1001–6); and the solo cello suites (BWV1007–12). Other works, such as the harpsichord and viola da gamba sonatas (BWV1027–9) and the harp-

sichord concertos (BWV1052–6, 1058), were begun at Cöthen and completed in Leipzig.

While each of the solo works, for violin, cello and harpsichord, is acknowledged as a sublime essay in its genre, the sets as a whole demonstrate the scientific character of his genius, which enabled him systematically to explore all the ramifications of the musical elements within an idiom, and to superimpose and synthesize them as no one had done before or since. Even when he parodied or transcribed someone else's music he was able to create a truly new work. Because of irresponsible stewardship of many of the autographs after Bach's death (some of which were inevitably unique sources), much of his chamber music is lost, though some works have survived in copies and others have been tentatively reconstructed from later harpsichord concerto arrangements.

Six musicians, among them Telemann and Christoph Graupner, applied for the Leipzig appointment. Telemann – who as a student at Leipzig University had founded the collegium musicum and served both as organist of the Neukirche and as an unconventional director of the Leipzig Opera – was the obvious choice; but his employers, the Hamburg city council, refused to release him from his contract. Similarly, Graupner – who had been a pupil at the Thomasschule – was offered the posts; he too was forced to decline, lacking the necessary permission from his employer, the Landgrave of Hessen-Darmstadt, to leave his post as court *Kapellmeister*. One can only speculate on Bach's feelings as he accepted the posts, but as the young wife of the Cöthen prince had in the meantime died, the pressure to leave would no longer have been a factor in his decision. As a mark of affection and respect, Bach was allowed to retain his title until the death of the prince in 1728 and he and his wife returned to Cöthen on several occasions to perform. It would appear that, in the interval of almost a year during which the negotiations took place, Bach had shifted his sights and was eagerly looking forward to the challenges of working in a large and important city.

The Bach family moved to Leipzig in the spring of 1723 and within a week his first cantata for Leipzig (BWV75) was performed at the Nicolaikirche (the town church), where many of his finest choral works – including half his cantatas, the *St John Passion* (1724, his first large-scale work for Leipzig) and the *Christmas Oratorio* (1734–5) – would later be heard. Having secured a deputy to assume his obligations to teach non-musical subjects (specifically Latin) at the Thomasschule, Bach divided his time between teaching daily lessons in practical musicianship, composing vocal music (cantatas in particular) and administering church music throughout Leipzig. The school provided him with upwards of 60 boys (including his own sons) to disperse between the four principal churches, though Bach himself directed only choral music (usually his own cantatas) at the Nicolaikirche or the Thomaskirche (on alternate Sundays), calling upon instrumentalists from the university collegium musicum when necessary. As *director musices* he composed and arranged performances of music for civic occasions.

Considered the greatest German keyboard improviser of his day, Bach continued to the end of his life to maintain his profile as an organist by travelling, largely within Saxony, to advise and inaugurate new organs such as the ones at Störmthal (nr Leipzig) in 1723, Gera in 1724, Dresden in 1725 and 1736, Kassel in 1732 (when he is thought to have performed the virtuoso Toccata and Fugue in D minor (BWV538) and Naumburg in 1746 – opportunities that enabled him to perform with local musicians and to popularize his music (particularly the cantatas) more widely. He also gave organ recitals at the Altenburg Schlosskirche in 1739 and at Potsdam before Frederick the Great in 1747. Experience had taught him never to assume that his present situation was secure or necessarily ideal, and indeed, his relationships with colleagues and the Leipzig council were often strained.

At several points, Bach seems to have contemplated leaving Leipzig. He visited and provided occasional music for the court of Duke Christian of Saxe-Weissenfels (as he continued to do for Prince Leopold at Cöthen); in 1729, only months after his honorific appointment at Cöthen had expired, he acquired a similar post at the Weissenfels court (which he retained until 1736). In 1730 he wrote to an old school friend, Georg Erdmann, (who was working in Danzig as a diplomatic representative and legal adviser to the Russian court), pouring out his dissatisfaction with his present circumstances and making clear his readiness to consider new alternatives, though nothing appears to have come of it.

He undoubtedly harboured an expectation – which came to a head with the death of Elector Friedrich August I in 1733 – of gaining a post at Dresden, where he would have found scope to develop himself as a com-

poser of dramatic music. To demonstrate his facility in Catholic genres (and thus his fitness for a court appointment), Bach presented the *Kyrie* and *Gloria* of the then incomplete B minor Mass (BWV232) to the new Elector Friedrich August II in 1733, and it was surely no coincidence that the Leipzig collegium musicum presented a series of secular cantatas to celebrate the elector's name day that year.

Bach had embarked upon his work in Leipzig with vigour and determination, setting the standards for singers and instrumentalists alike in the cantatas that make up the first of the annual cycles he wrote there (1723–4). But within a few months, he found himself at odds with Johann Gottlieb Görner, organist at the Nicolaikirche (who had earlier served at the university Paulinerkirche) and director of J. F. Fasch's old collegium musicum at Leipzig University. In the interim between Kuhnau's death and his replacement by Bach, Görner had usurped the prerogative of the *director musices* to conduct the Sunday and feast day services as well as those for special feast days and academic ceremonies at the Paulinerkirche, but even petitions to the Elector of Saxony failed to reverse the situation. For Bach it meant a reduction in his expected income at a time when his family was growing annually by one child (his 20th and last was born in 1742). So when it came to the 1727 memorial service for the Electress Christiane Eberhardine at the Paulinerkirche, Bach did not hesitate to exercise his right to organize the music, which included his setting of a cantata text – the *Trauer Ode* (BWV198) – by the Leipzig University professor of poetry, Johann Christoph Gottsched.

By 1727 Bach had assembled at least three cycles of sacred cantatas, at the rate of at least one cantata per week since his arrival in Leipzig. The principal Sunday service began at 7 a.m. and a cantata, with a text relevant to a designated New Testament reading, was performed before the sermon began at 8 a.m.; the cantata therefore was required to last about 20 minutes. In contrast to his earlier chamber cantatas for Weimar, the Leipzig cycles – of which Bach's obituary states there were five – were conceived for up to 12 singers and 18 instrumentalists. The first cycle was assembled under great pressure, which meant that he occasionally resorted to borrowing from earlier works. Simultaneously, he produced the *Magnificat* in E flat (later revised in D) for the Christmas 1723 Vespers service, the first of his Passions, the *St John*, for the 1724 Good Friday service at the Nicolaikirche, and, for the following Christmas, a *Sanctus* that was later to have a place in the B minor Mass.

By the time he embarked on the second cycle of cantatas, in mid 1724, he had got into his stride. The *St John Passion* contained all the components of a cantata – dramatic recitatives, arias with instrumental obbligatos conveying deeply personal responses to the events of the story, devotional chorales and massive chorale fantasias for voices and instruments, plus the narration of the Gospel text by an 'Evangelist' – but on a profound and grand scale hitherto unknown in Protestant Germany. The *St Matthew Passion*, first given on Good Friday 1727 or 1729 at the Thomaskirche and revived in 1736, was to exceed even *St John* in its proportions and dramatic force. Among the many cantatas produced during the next year were *Jesu, der du meine Seele* (BWV78), in which the opening movement is, characteristically, at once a chorale fantasy and a passacaglia; the well-known setting of Franck's *Ein feste Burg* (BWV80), which incorporates Martin Luther's hymn; and perhaps his most beautiful cantata of all – *Wie schön leuchtet der Morgenstern* (BWV1), which concluded the cycle on the Feast of the Annunciation. The *Easter Oratorio* (BWV249) was performed on 1 April 1725.

In the second cycle Bach settled on the format most commonly associated with the sacred cantata: a symmetrical series of recitatives and arias (some with obbligato instruments), framed by chorale movements (usually a large, orchestrated chorale fantasy at the beginning and a simple four-part setting at the end). He drew his texts from a number of librettists, among them the Leipzig poetess Marianne von Ziegler. Rather than beginning a third cycle immediately, Bach decided to wait until Christmas, making do with other composers' cantatas (including those of his distant cousin, Johann Ludwig Bach) in addition to revivals and parodies of his own works in the interim.

The third cycle begins with *Unser Mund sei voll Lachens* (BWV110) which, graced with a French overture employing trumpets and drums, adapted from the fourth of the orchestral suites, was performed on Christmas Day 1725. Bach made use of orchestral movements composed at Weimar or Cöthen in other cantatas; eager to make the most of his opportunities to play outside Leipzig, he incorporated virtuoso organ parts in some of the cantatas. Instruments play a programmatic role in *Ich will den Kreuzstab gerne tragen* (BWV56), in which life is likened to a stormy voyage and God's pity is the anchor. In *Ich habe genug* (BWV82) of 1727, for solo bass, music and text are perfectly matched in the aria 'Schlummert ein' ('Fall asleep'). In *Ich geh und suche mit Verlangen* (BWV49) of 1726 – and again in the popular *Wachet auf, ruft uns die Stimme* (BWV140) of 1731 – Bach used a dialogue text, in which a bridegroom and bride represent Christ and the Soul. Of his fourth cycle (1727–8), largely based on texts by Picander (the pen-name of C. F. Henrici, who also provided the texts for the monumental *St Matthew* and the lost *St Mark* (1731) Passions, as well as for the cantata *Wachet auf*), only seven settings survive. The fifth cycle disappeared in its entirety, though a number of later sacred cantatas do survive, including *Jauchzet Gott in allen Landen* (BWV51) of 1730 for solo soprano, with its stirring finale.

From the beginning, Bach gained greater satisfaction from his duties as *director musices* than from those as *Kantor* of the Thomasschule, a post he actually found quite demeaning after having served as a court *Kapellmeister*. When, in 1728, he was required to forfeit to the sub-deacon of the Nicolaikirche the right to choose the Vesper hymns, he adopted an altogether more determined stance with regard to his professional dominion. Bach assumed control over the collegium musicum in 1729, remaining its director until 1741 (with a brief break, 1737–9); this must have put him in a position to simplify the rehearsal schedules for the weekly services and to augment his salary, as well as providing a welcome forum for his instrumental music. During this period, he probably composed the second and third orchestral suites, as well as the violin concertos (BWV1041–2), the double violin concerto (BWV1043) and the triple concerto (BWV1044), published the first two parts of the *Clavier-Übung* (1726–31 and 1735) and began arranging earlier concertos for two to four harpsichords.

In addition to his collegium commitments, a great deal of music-making took place at his home, where students, his private pupils (numbering about 80 over the years), colleagues and friends joined the Bach family in private performances of his and other people's music; in consequence, a great deal of music copying also went on under his roof by trusted pupils in order to supply scores and parts to the collegium and for sale. But as early as 1730, complaints, conveyed by the council, were made about his frequent absence from daily singing lessons; in reply, Bach penned a memorandum entitled a 'Short but much-needed outline for a well-regulated church music, together with some impromptu thoughts on the decline of the same'. The *Kantor* and the council were plainly at odds.

At the Thomasschule, things briefly improved under the new rectorship (1729–34) of Johann Matthias Gesner, Bach's old Weimar colleague, a music-lover and a great admirer of the composer. Gesner instituted a desperately needed programme of renovation of the buildings and set in train educational reforms which were not fully established when he resigned his post to take up a professorship at the University of Göttingen. He was succeeded by Johann August Ernesti, who felt that despite the school's long and distinguished tradition of music education, too much emphasis was being placed on music in the curriculum, and he accordingly made rigorous efforts to curb it.

Bach cast an eye towards Dresden. Although Hasse had just been appointed *Kapellmeister*, Bach must have felt there was still a place for his expertise. He visited Dresden in 1731 with his eldest son, Friedemann, played at court and at the Sophienkirche (where two years later Friedemann was appointed organist), and attended a performance of Hasse's first opera for Dresden, *Cleofide*. In 1733 he submitted a petition – along with copies of the *Kyrie* and *Gloria* of the unfinished B minor Mass – to the new Elector Friedrich August II, regarding his possible appointment to the largely honorific post of *Hofkomponist*. Though unsuccessful, Bach was unbowed. He continued to provide the court with new music and mounted collegium concerts at Leipzig in the elector's honour. A second petition succeeded (albeit with the intervention of his Dresden patron Count von Keyserlingk) and thereafter Bach signed himself as Dresden *Hofcompositeur*. By way of acknowledging this honorary appointment, Bach presented a two-hour recital on the new Silbermann organ at the Frauenkirche.

The evidence of his output during the 1730s – more chamber music and fewer sacred cantatas – speaks for itself. Relations with the *Rektor* steadily deteriorated and so it is hardly surprising that Bach should have thrown most of his creative energies into the collegium. Collegium concerts normally took place at the Zimmermannische Kaffee-Haus on Fridays in winter and Wednesdays in summer (when the concerts were held in the garden); during the weeks of trade fairs in Leipzig they performed on Tuesdays as well. Although Bach's music (including *Der Streit zwischen Phoebus und Pan* (BWV201), the *Coffee Cantata* (BWV 211), and keyboard music published in the *Clavier-Übung* (1735, 1739, 1741–2) and the second volume of *The Well-Tempered Clavier*) formed the core of the collegium repertory, they also performed works by Telemann, Handel, P. A. Locatelli and N. A. Porpora, and attracted guest performances by J. A. Hasse, Faustina Bordoni, Franz Benda and J. D. Zelenka from nearby Dresden, J. G. Graun from Merseburg and, in 1739, by the virtuoso lutenist S. L. Weiss.

In 1737 Bach was the victim of an anonymous attack on his music, published by the 'progressive' writer Johann Adolf Scheibe in the sixth issue of *Der critische Musikus*. While careful to acknowledge Bach's skill as a performer and a composer *per se*, Scheibe found his musical textures turgid and overworked: 'one admires their onerous labour and exceptional care, which nevertheless counts for nothing since it conflicts with Nature'. The following year, Bach's Leipzig colleague, Johann Abraham Birnbaum (a university lecturer in rhetoric) responded on his behalf, point by point, in an anonymous pamphlet. In the course of the ensuing exchange of polemics (1739, 1745), Mizler's corresponding society became involved, even though Bach had not yet become a member. Instead of demoralizing him, this aesthetic confrontation with the next generation seems to have fired Bach's determination all the more to explore the ultimate ramifications of his compositional technique through the Goldberg Variations, the *Musikalisches Opfer* ('Musical Offering'), the remaining sections of the B minor Mass and *Die Kunst der Fuge* ('The Art of Fugue') and, at the same time, must have spurred him on to compose an up-to-date work like the burlesque Peasant Cantata (BWV212) in 1742.

With the death in 1741 of Gottfried Zimmermann (proprietor of the Leipzig coffee house), who had not only provided the venue for the collegium concerts but also had a hand in their organization, Bach ended his own association with the ensemble (which continued to give concerts until superseded by the less professional Grosse Concert in 1743). At 56, Bach could hardly have savoured his 'retirement' from the collegium, especially in the knowledge that his wife, Anna Magdalena, was expecting his 20th child. Accordingly, he paid a visit to Berlin and the court at Potsdam, where his son Emanuel was already serving as harpsichordist to Frederick the Great, and then returned home via Dresden in order to see Count von Keyserlingk, whom he presented with a set of keyboard variations (on a 32-bar sarabande found in the second volume of the *Clavier-Büchlein*); known today as the Goldberg Variations (after the count's harpsichordist, Johann Gottlieb Goldberg, whose duty it was to amuse his insomniac employer far into the night), they were published soon afterwards in Nuremberg.

In the course of the 1740s, Bach was gradually blinded by cataracts – an affliction he shared with Handel. With the assistance of his wife and son, Johann Christoph Friedrich (*b* 1732, later referred to as the 'Bückeburg Bach'), Bach divided his energies between composing (*The Art of Fugue* was begun about 1740 and published incomplete and posthumously by his sons in 1751) and putting his older works – chorales, cantatas and the Passions – in order. In 1747 he finally became a member of Mizler's corresponding society, contributing the *Canon triplex*. Later, in 1754, the society's journal, *Musikalische Bibliothek*, was to include an important obituary of Bach, containing the earliest catalogue of his works, co-authored by his son Emanuel and J. F. Agricola.

Partly at the instigation of Count von Keyserlingk and partly in order to visit his son and family, Bach made one final trip to Potsdam in 1747. Although Frederick the Great was not a particular fan of Bach's music, he seized upon the opportunity to exploit his knowledge of organs. Upon his arrival, Bach was invited to take part in the evening chamber music at Sanssouci. Frederick provided Bach with a theme on which to improvise a fugue on the new pianoforte; this Bach gracefully did, having taken the precaution to familiarize himself with the instruments of Silbermann (to whom he suggested a refinement of the mechanism), after which he was commanded to improvise a six-part fugue on a theme of his choice. According to J. N. Forkel (Bach's first biographer, 1802), whose source was Friedemann, the king ignored Bach's infirmities and insisted that he demonstrate his skill on each of the organs in Potsdam (probably an exaggeration) the following day. Before returning to Leipzig, Bach took the opportunity to examine the new Berlin opera house. At home again, Bach immediately set about augmenting the original improvisation on the king's theme with other contrapuntal settings (canons, two keyboard ricercares and a trio sonata with a part for flute). Within two months, an engraved and bound copy of the first part of the *Musical Offering* had been dispatched to the king. As in the case of the Brandenburg Concertos, the precious gift of homage was never acknowledged.

By 1749 Bach's health no longer permitted him to continue work on the didactic *Art of Fugue*. The following spring he underwent surgery at the hands of Handel's English oculist, John Taylor, and briefly regained his sight; but a second operation proved unsuccessful. Bach died on 28 July 1750 of complications following a stroke. Despite having earned a good living all his life, he was able to leave little for his widow and youngest children (15-year-old Johann Christian was almost immediately sent to live with Emanuel). Bach's extensive music library and instruments (eight harpsichords, two lute-harpsichords, a spinet, lute and ten further string instruments) were divided up between Anna Magdalena and his nine surviving children. There was also a portrait by E. G. Haussmann.

Funck, David. See NORTHERN EUROPE 7 *Itinerant Musicians.*

Görner, Johann Gottlieb (1697–1778). Leipzig organist whose appointment as music director of the Paulinerkirche (after Johann Kuhnau) offended Bach at the beginning of the latter's tenure as *Kantor*, though Görner had belonged to the Leipzig musical establishment long before Bach's appointment there. A native Leipziger, educated at the Thomasschule and the university, he held organ posts at the university (from 1716) and the Nicolaikirche (from 1721). Nevertheless, he and Bach worked together for the next 27 years, during which time Görner took charge of the second collegium musicum (founded by J. F. Fasch in 1708) and was appointed organist at the Thomaskirche in 1729. In contrast to his distinguished colleague, Görner had few claims to be taken seriously as a composer.

Gottsched, Johann Christoph (1700–66). Poet, dramatist, philosopher and literary critic whose controversial views on opera libretto (and hence opera) stimulated much discussion among contemporary German writers on music. From 1725 Gottsched lectured at the University of Leipzig; in 1727 he served as leader of the Leipzig Deutschübenden-poetischen Gesellschaft, through which he vainly attempted to create a single German national language; and that same year he became dramatist for a theatre troupe led by Johann and Caroline Neubers. He married a musician–composer, Adelgunda Victoria Kulmus, and many of his university students – including J. A. Scheibe, L. C. Mizler, J. A. Hiller and A. G. Baumgarten – were musicians. Scheibe composed incidental music for the plays he wrote for the troupe. Gottsched founded two periodicals and secured his fame with his *Versuch einer critischen Dichtkunst* (1730). J. S. Bach, his contemporary in Leipzig, set two of his cantata texts and the *Trauer-Ode* (1727).

His literary publications only touch upon music (ode, cantata and opera) in terms of poetic forms. Although his vast library included about 660 opera librettos, he had little opportunity to attend performances, so his criticism of opera focuses on its weakness as a form. Gottsched believed that as there was no precedent for opera among ancient poetic forms and because it failed to conform either to the rules of tragedy or those of comedy, it was a bastard form. He considered it unnatural and indecent. His pupils, Mizler and Scheibe, challenged him on these points in their periodicals, *Musikalische Bibliothek* and *Critischer Musikus*. As a literary reformer with musical connections, he prepared the ground for the musical reforms of Gluck.

Graupner, (Johann) Christoph. See NORTHERN EUROPE *5 West Germany and the Rhineland*.

Grünewald, Gottfried. See NORTHERN EUROPE *7 Itinerant Musicians*.

Henrici, Christian Friedrich (1700–64). Saxon poet, dramatist and the librettist for many of Bach's cantatas, the *St Matthew* and *St Mark* Passions, who wrote under the pseudonym 'Picander'. Henrici earned his living as a postal administrator. He moved from Dresden to Leipzig in 1720 where he produced collections of devotional poems (1724–5, 1728), which served for Bach's cantatas, and three plays (1726). He also penned erotic verse, satires and secular cantata texts, including that for the *Coffee Cantata* (BWV211). His successful collaboration with Bach spanned two decades.

Hoffmann, Melchior (*c*1685–1715). Composer and conductor working in Leipzig. Hoffmann was trained in the Dresden royal chapel before undertaking studies at the University of Leipzig in 1702. With the departure of Telemann in 1704, Hoffmann took over the direction of the Leipzig collegium musicum, increasing its membership to 40 musicians. He also held posts at the Neukirche and the opera, imposing high standards upon all who worked under him. He visited London in 1710.

Horn, Johann Caspar (*c*1630–85). South German physician and composer, who pursued his medical career at Leipzig. There he belonged to a circle of amateurs (1663–72)

led by the Thomaskirche *Kantor*, Sebastian Knüpfer. During the 1660s and 1670s, Horn published six collections of dances (one in the Italian style and five in the Lullian style). He also composed secular and sacred vocal music, which appeared in the *Musicalischer Tugend- und Jugendgedichte* (1678) and *Geistliche Harmonien* (1680–81).

Knüpfer, Sebastian (1633–76). Bavarian-born *Kantor* of the Leipzig Thomaskirche, director of civic music and a composer of concerted sacred music. After finishing his studies at the Regensburg Gymnasium Poeticum, Knüpfer arrived in Leipzig without a job; not until 1657 was he appointed *Thomaskantor*. Following in the musical and intellectual traditions of Sethus Calvisius and J. H. Schein, Knüpfer was responsible for revitalizing the musical traditions at Leipzig after the Thirty Years War. His music is much indebted to Schütz.

Kuhnau, Johann (1660–1722). Bohemian polymath, musically accomplished – as a keyboard player, theorist and the composer of the first Passion oratorio to be performed in Leipzig – as well as a mathematician and linguist. In addition to translations, he produced a satirical novel (*Der musicalische Quack-Salber*, 1700) which is important for its remarks on the social status of musicians. Kuhnau pursued careers as a lawyer and *Kantor* of the Thomaskirche, and was succeeded in the latter by Bach.

Kuhnau (or Kuhn, as his family was known in Bohemia before they fled the Counter-Reformation regime there) studied in Dresden and Italy and then in Zittau, where he served as interim *Kantor* and organist of the Johanniskirche (1681–2). While a law student at the University of Leipzig, he actively performed and composed; after applying twice for the organ post at the Thomaskirche, he was appointed in 1684. And although he was practising law from 1688, he nevertheless found time to direct a collegium musicum and publish four sets of keyboard music: two volumes of suites (*Neuer Clavier-Übung*, 1689, 1692), and two of sonatas (*Frische Clavier Früchte*, 1696, and the *Biblische Historien*, 1700).

As *Thomaskantor*, from 1701, Kuhnau had also to accept responsibility for both university music (at the Paulinerkirche) and civic music, and was expected to take charge – to varying degrees – of music at the other main Leipzig churches (the Thomaskirche, Nicolaikirche, Petrikirche and Johanniskirche). He composed cantatas for their services although, as with those of Bach, they were never published and, as a result, many were lost. During this period musical standards were falling at the Thomasschule, in part because the best pupils were recruited for the local opera and Telemann's collegium musicum. Nevertheless, his own pupils included J. F. Fasch (who established another collegium in 1708), Christoph Graupner and J. D. Heinichen. Dogged by ill health in his last years, Kuhnau was dealt a further humiliating blow when Telemann gained the mayor's permission to compose for the Thomaskirche. The 1721 performance of Kuhnau's *St Mark Passion* can be seen as the crowning achievement of his career.

Pezel, Johann Christoph (1639–94). Silesian town bandsman (*Ratsmusiker*) and composer of *Ratsmusik*. Pezel must have travelled in Italy, for he was known for his command of the language. He was made a Leipzig *Stadtpfeifer* in 1670, the year in which he published a collection of 40 one-movement sonatas for five-part band (*Hora decima musicorum*), which were performed twice daily from the Rathaus tower. He aspired to the position of *Kantor* at the Thomaskirche but lacked the necessary qualifications. Pezel moved eastwards to Bautzen when the plague threatened Leipzig in 1681 and published a second collection of *Fünff-stimmigte blasende Music* in Frankfurt four years later.

Reiche, Gottfried (1667–1734). Leipzig *Stadtpfeifer* for whom Bach composed his first trumpet parts. Originally from Weissenfels, Reiche learnt his trade in Leipzig, where he rose to *Kunstgeiger* (1700), *Stadtpfeifer* (1706) and finally senior *Stadtpfeifer* (1719). Reiche's services were so highly valued that as early as 1694 his salary was augmented as an incentive to remain in Leipzig, and on the occasion of his 60th birthday, the city council arranged for his portrait to be painted by E. G. Haussmann (who painted that of Bach); it was later engraved by C. F. Rosbach.

Rosenmüller, Johann. See ITALY *4 Venice*.

Scheibe, Johann Adolph. See NORTHERN EUROPE *2 Scandinavia*.

Schein, Johann Hermann (1586–1630). Leipzig *Thomaskantor*, poet, teacher and composer. Schein was an important contemporary of Schütz, though his creative output was cut short by illness and a relatively early death.

He acquired his musical training at the Dresden Hofkapelle and later spent four years (1608–12) studying law at the University of Leipzig – though the publication of the *Venus Kräntzlein* in 1609 (and probably the ribald drinking songs contained in the *Studenten-*

Schmauss, not published until 1626) is evidence of his active participation in university musical life. Upon finishing his studies he took a post as music director and tutor at the residence of a wealthy school friend who, two years later (1615), helped to make possible his appointment as *Kapellmeister* at the count of Duke Johann at Weimar. At much the same time, he published his first collection of motets (five- to 12-part settings of Latin and German biblical texts), *Cymbalum Sionium* (1615).

A year later he was appointed *Kantor* of the Leipzig Thomaskirche, a post which also carried with it the direction of choral music at the Nicolaikirche and teaching duties (singing, Latin grammar and syntax) at the Thomasschule. During the next dozen years, Schein composed and published his remaining music while nurturing pupils such as the poet Paul Fleming and the composer Heinrich Albert. The variation suites for viols (containing pavanes, galliards, courantes, allemandes and tripla) he had composed for Weissenfels and Weimar appeared in 1617 under the title *Banchetto musicale*; thereafter all his music incorporated continuo parts.

To signal his intention of working in the new Italian idiom, Schein called his next publication *Opella nova* (1618); it contains sacred concertos based on Lutheran chorales in the style of Viadana's *Cento concerti ecclesiastici* (1602). A second volume appeared in 1626: it was more expressive, less dependent upon the chorale and incorporated obbligato instruments. Plagued by a startling array of ailments – tuberculosis, gout, scurvy and kidney stones – Schein still managed to publish half a dozen collections of sacred and secular music (some of them bearing double titles in Italian and German), and to provide other occasional music for wedding and funerals, in accordance with his position, during his remaining years. In 1723 he produced the *Fontana d'Israel* or *Israelis Brünlein*, containing choral settings (five voices and *basso seguente*) of Old Testament texts conceived in the Italian madrigal style. His final sacred collection was of hymns: the *Cantional* of 1627 was tailored to the tastes and liturgical needs of the Leipzig churches. It was the first of its kind to incorporate figured bass. Over 40 were entirely by Schein, though he edited and reharmonized many others. The *Cantional* was enlarged (2nd edn, 1645) by the next *Thomaskantor*, Tobias Michael.

Schein's secular music included the popular and oft-reprinted *Musica boscareccia* or *Wald-Liederlein* in three parts (1621, 1626 and 1628), and scored for two sopranos and bass (which was provided with both text and figures, offering a variety of possible realizations). In 1624 Schein published the *Diletti pastorali* or *Hirten Lust*, considered to be the first published collection of German continuo madrigals.

Schelle, Johann (1648–1701). Thuringian *Kantor* of the Leipzig Thomaskirche and composer of sacred cantatas. Schelle received his early training under Schütz at the Dresden chapel, though he was soon sent to augment the musical forces at the Wolfenbüttel court (where Schütz was *Kapellmeister in absentia*). After his voice broke he was placed in the care of Sebastian Knüpfer at the Thomasschule in Leipzig.

In 1677 he succeeded Knüpfer as *Kantor* – a post which, in addition to duties at the Thomaskirche and Thomasschule (teaching Latin and catechism) required his services as *director chori musici* at two other Leipzig churches. Never a popular choice, Schelle added to the tensions between orthodox Lutherans and Pietists by instituting reforms such as the introduction of chorale cantatas into the (Protestant) liturgy and the study of German music in place of Italian settings of Latin texts. Schelle excelled as a composer of chorale cantatas (though few were published or survived, which he cast in an alternation of choral, solo and instrumental movements, and scored for five-part choir, strings, bassoons and continuo. He was succeeded by his cousin, Johann Kuhnau.

Schieferdecker, Johann Christian. See NORTHERN EUROPE *1 North Germany.*

Selle, Thomas. See NORTHERN EUROPE *1 North Germany: Hamburg.*

Strungk, Nicolaus Adam. See NORTHERN EUROPE *7 Itinerant Musicians.*

Telemann, Georg Philipp. See NORTHERN EUROPE *7 Itinerant Musicians.*

Theile, Johann. See NORTHERN EUROPE *1 North Germany.*

5 West Germany and the Rhineland

Agrell, Johan Joachim. See NORTHERN EUROPE *6 Middle Germany.*

Baptiste, Ludwig Albert Friedrich (1700–*c*1764). Violinist, dancing-master and composer of *galant* sonatas and other instrumental chamber music. He travelled widely before taking up an appointment at Kassel in 1726. Many works have been wrongly attributed to him. Baptiste's father, Johann, was a French dancing-master employed from 1703 at the Darmstadt court.

Baudrexel, Philipp Jakob (1627–1691). Swabian priest, *Kapellmeister* and composer of sacred music. Baudrexel studied at the Roman Collegio Germanico with Carissimi during the 1640s and became a priest in 1651. He held a variety of clerical and musical posts: parish priest, canon and choir director at Augsburg Cathedral (1654), court chaplain at Fulda to Margrave Bernhard Gustav of Baden-Durlach (1672–9) and *Kapellmeister* at Mainz to both court and cathedral.

Bernacchi, Antonio Maria. See ITALY *10 Itinerant Musicians.*

Birkenstock, Johann Adam (1687–1733). A leading violinist of his day and composer of instrumental chamber music. Birkenstock acquired an international training by studying first in Kassel with Ruggiero Fedeli, then in Berlin with J. B. Volumier, in Bayreuth with Carlo Fiorelli and finally in Paris with François Duval. In 1709 he took up his place in the Kassel court orchestra. During a stint in Amsterdam in 1722 Birkenstock published his first collection of sonatas. He declined an appointment offered by the King of Portugal (who was also visiting Holland) and accepted instead the post of *Kapellmeister* at Kassel (1725). On the death of the landgrave, Birkenstock left Kassel for Eisenach where he served as *Hofkapellmeister* until his death.

Böddecker, Philipp Friedrich. See CENTRAL EUROPE *1 South Germany.*

Briegel, Wolfgang Carl (1626–1712). Organist, composer and *Kapellmeister* at Darmstadt. Briegel was a treble at the Frauenkirche, Nuremberg, where he was trained by J. A. Herbst and came into contact with S. T. Staden, J. E. Kindermann and J. M. Dilherr, and their music. He took up his first court post in 1650, when he was appointed first *Kantor* at Gotha and music tutor to the family of Duke Ernst the Pious, and later, *Kapellmeister*. When the duke's daughter married Landgrave Ludwig VI of Hessen-Darmstadt, Briegel became their *Kapellmeister* (1771), a post he retained until his death, with the assistance of Christoph Graupner and E. C. Hesse. He published volumes of dialogue cantatas, motets and *Geistliche Arien*, as well as instrumental music. His *Musikalisches Tafelkonfekt*, for four voices, violins and continuo, appeared in 1672. He also composed a number of operas, ballets and Singspiels for Darmstadt.

Chelleri, Fortunato. See ITALY *10 Itinerant Musicians.*

Dall'Abaco, Joseph-Marie Clément. See CENTRAL EUROPE *1 South Germany: Munich.*

Diessener, Gerhard. See BRITISH ISLES *1 London.*

Eberlin, Daniel. See NORTHERN EUROPE *4 Saxony and Thuringia.*

Farina, Carlo. See NORTHERN EUROPE *4 Saxony and Thuringia: Dresden.*

Fedeli, Ruggiero. See ITALY *4 Venice.*

Foggia, Francesco. See ITALY *7 Papal States: Rome.*

Graf, Johann. See NORTHERN EUROPE *4 Saxony and Thuringia.*

Graupner, (Johann) Christoph (1683–1760). Saxon keyboard player and prolific composer who from 1712 served as *Kapellmeister* at the Darmstadt court. Among his friends he counted Telemann, whom he had known since his days as a member of the Leipzig collegium musicum, and among his students, J. F. Fasch. Graupner's place in German musical life makes him of special interest. He was the pupil, copyist and amanuensis of Johann Schelle and Johann Kuhnau at the Thomasschule in Leipzig, where he was later (1722–3) to compete with Telemann and Bach for the cantorship. (Upon Telemann's withdrawal, Graupner had intended to accept the post, but was prevented by the Landgrave of Hessen-Darmstadt, who refused to release him from his contract.)

From 1706 until 1709 Graupner lived in Hamburg. From 1707, he was associated with the Theater am Gänsemarkt as the harpsichordist; he also composed five operas and collaborated with Keiser on a further three. Graupner went to Darmstadt as the vice-*Kapellmeister* under Wolfgang Carl Briegel, whom he succeeded in 1712. In addition to operas, he composed an astounding 1418 church cantatas (in contrast to a mere 24 secular cantatas), 113 symphonies (mostly in three movements), about 50 Vivaldian concertos, over 80 overtures, 36 sonatas and assorted keyboard music.

Grua, Carlo Luigi Pietro (*b c*1665). Florentine singer and composer working at the Catholic German courts. Grua's first post was in the Hofkapelle of the Elector of Saxony in Dresden (1691). Although he was appointed vice-*Kapellmeister* in 1693 and his opera *Camillo generoso* was performed during Carnival, he left the following year to take up a similar post under J. H. Wilderer at the Pala-

tine court in Düsseldorf. He remained until 1720, moving to Heidelberg when the Düsseldorf and Innsbruck musical establishments were amalgamated, but resigned when the court moved again to Mannheim. He composed subsequent operas for the court and for Venice, and at one point took on the job of recruiting musicians for Agostino Steffani at Würzburg.

Grünewald, Gottfried. See NORTHERN EUROPE *7 Itinerant Musicians.*

Hayne, Gilles. See LOW COUNTRIES *2 South Netherlands.*

Herbst, Johann Andreas (1588–1666). Nuremberg violinist, more significant as a theorist than as a composer. He served as *Kapellmeister* to the court of Philipp V of Butzbach (1614–18; and then in the service of the landgrave's brother in Darmstadt) and to the city of Frankfurt am Main (1623–36), where he eventually returned – in the capacity of a church musician – in 1644, after a period in Nuremberg as *Kapellmeister*.

His two treatises form his most important legacy: *Musica practica* (1642), meant as a pedagogical approach to singing and vocal ornamentation, and *Musica poetica* (1643), which gives practical advice to composers on the use of musical–rhetorical figures; the latter was the first of its kind to be published in German rather than Latin.

Hertel, Johann Christian. See NORTHERN EUROPE *4 Saxony and Thuringia.*

Hesse, Ernst Christian (1676–1762). Virtuoso Thuringian viol player who toured widely, composer and war secretary at the Darmstadt court. He was appointed in 1692 as a viol player, but in the next two years he studied law and then took up a post in the government chancellery while studying composition and continuing to play in the court orchestra.

In 1698 he studied in Paris simultaneously with Antoine Forqueray and Marin Marais, rivals who (according to E. L. Gerber) discovered they shared a pupil only when he gave a concert devoting half to the music and playing style of each. He returned in 1701 a polished player and also served as Secretary for War. In 1705 he toured as a viol virtuoso to Hamburg (where he met Handel, Johann Mattheson and Reinhard Keiser), the Netherlands and London (where he performed with Thomas Clayton and J. E. Galliard for Queen Anne). Soon after his appointment as *Kapelldirektor* at Darmstadt, he embarked on a tour of Italy and he was probably the solo viol player in the 1708 Easter performances of

Handel's *Resurrezione* in Rome. During 1709 and 1710 he was in Dresden and Vienna, where he played at court with Pantaleon Hebenstreit.

About 1712 he composed an opera, *La fedeltà coronata*, in which the soprano Johanna Elisabeth Döbricht (1692–1786) probably sang; they married in 1713 and subsequently toured. But in 1714 Hesse resigned his musical posts after a confrontation between sopranos that involved his wife, though he retained his cabinet posts. In addition to his opera, only a divertimento, a flute sonata and a duo for viol and continuo survive.

Their third son, Ludwig Christian (1716–72), followed in his father's footsteps, training first as a viol player, studying law and becoming a Darmstadt government lawyer and court chamber musician. In 1741 he was appointed to similar posts in Berlin under Frederick the Great. His viol music is lost.

Jeep, Johannes. See NORTHERN EUROPE 6 *Middle Germany*.

Kraft, Georg Andreas (*c*1660–1726). Composer at the Düsseldorf court of Elector Palatine Johann Wilhelm, who sent him to Rome to study with Corelli. Upon his return Kraft worked – with positive results – to achieve the same kind of precision in the electoral court orchestra that he had observed in Rome. In this he was encouraged by both J. H. von Wilderer and Sebastiano Moratelli. Kraft took part in the chapel's contribution to the coronation ceremonies of the emperor at Frankfurt am Main in 1711 and, having handed over his posts to his son Sebastian Johannes, he retired in 1716 rather than following the court to Heidelberg and Mannheim.

Krieger, Johann Philipp. See NORTHERN EUROPE 4 *Saxony and Thuringia*.

Kühnel, August. See NORTHERN EUROPE 7 *Itinerant Musicians*.

Lehms, Georg Christian (1684–1717). Poet and librarian to the court of Darmstadt (from 1710) who compiled a dictionary of German poetesses (1715). Lehms wrote five cycles of sacred cantata texts (1711–16) for Christoph Graupner and Gottfried Grünewald; the 1711 collection (*Gottgefälliges Kirchen-Opffer*) was known to Bach, who set two texts while in Weimar and eight more in Leipzig.

Marini, Biagio. See ITALY 10 *Itinerant Musicians*.

Mingotti, Angelo. See ITALY 10 *Itinerant Musicians*.

Moratelli, Sebastiano (1640–1706). Italian instrumentalist, composer and spiritual adviser who worked as a chamber musician at the Viennese court of the dowager empress before being transferred to the court of Elector Palatine Johann Wilhelm at Düsseldorf (*c*1680). He remained there for the rest of his life (though he returned to Vienna twice in the 1680s in the electoral retinue), and was succeeded by J. H. von Wilderer. By 1687 he had been appointed *Kapellmeister* and was charged with composing operas and serenades, though none survives; in 1688 he became honorary chaplain to the electress and, a few years later, spiritual counsellor to the elector himself.

Moritz (1572–1632). Landgrave of Hessen-Kassel, known as 'Moritz der Gelehrte', who was Heinrich Schütz's first employer and life-long mentor as well as a composer of *stile antico* music. Moritz succeeded his father in 1592, ruling until 1627 when he was succeeded by his son. His reign saw the flowering of music and drama – under his patronage the earliest German court theatre, the Ottoneum (named after his *Kapellmeister* Georg Otto), was opened in 1605. Quickly perceiving the promise of the young Schütz, Moritz sent him to study in Italy in 1609 and, reluctantly, relinquished him to the Dresden elector in 1615.

Neri, Massimiliano. See ITALY 4 *Venice*.

Pallavicino, Stefano Benedetto. See NORTHERN EUROPE 4 *Saxony and Thuringia: Dresden*.

Pez, Johann Christoph. See CENTRAL EUROPE 1 *South Germany: Munich*.

Praetorius, Michael. See NORTHERN EUROPE 1 *North Germany*.

Rosier, Carl (1640–1725). Flemish violinist and composer working in Cologne, where he eventually became *Kapellmeister* of both the court and the cathedral. Prior to 1675, he was a violinist (and at some point vice-*Kapellmeister*) at the Bonn court of Elector Maximilian Heinrich. He also spent 1683–99 in the United Provinces where he was associated with Carolus Hacquart. He composed Masses and motets for both Bonn and Cologne, and published collections of motets, trio sonatas (for brass and wind as well as strings) and French overtures. Rosier's daughter, Maria Anna, married the Netherlands composer Willem de Fesch.

Schenck, Johannes. See LOW COUNTRIES 1 *United Provinces*.

Schickhardt, Johann Christian. See LOW COUNTRIES 1 *United Provinces*.

Sophie Elisabeth. See NORTHERN EUROPE 1 *North Germany*.

Steffani, Agostino. See NORTHERN EUROPE 1 *North Germany*.

Strattner, Georg Christoph. See NORTHERN EUROPE *4 Saxony and Thuringia.*

Telemann, Georg Philipp. See NORTHERN EUROPE *1 North Germany: Hamburg.*

Tenaglia, Antonio Francesco. See ITALY *7 Papal States: Rome.*

Tesi, Vittoria. See ITALY *10 Itinerant Musicians.*

Uffenbach, Johann Friedrich Armand von (1687–1769). Well-travelled civil servant and amateur musician at Frankfurt am Main, who organized concerts and founded a private learned society similar to that of Mizler in Leipzig. Uffenbach kept diaries – in which he recorded the music he heard – of his travels in Germany, England, Switzerland, Italy and France. He studied law in Strasbourg (completing his degree in 1714) and lute with 'Gallot *le jeune*' in Paris (1715). He endowed the University of Göttingen with his library, which included his journals and correspondence with important musicians of the day as well as his extensive collection of music.

Veracini, Francesco Maria. See ITALY *6 Tuscany.*

Walther, Johann Jacob. See NORTHERN EUROPE *4 Saxony and Thuringia: Dresden.*

Weiss, Johann Jacob. See CENTRAL EUROPE *1 South Germany.*

Weiss, Silvius Leopold. See NORTHERN EUROPE *7 Itinerant Musicians.*

Wilderer, Johann Hugo von (1670/1–1724). Bavarian-born composer at the Düsseldorf court (from 1696) and later at Mannheim. In 1696 Wilderer became vice-*Kapellmeister* and then in 1703 *Kapellmeister* at Düsseldorf. During his tenure, Agostino Steffani was in residence at the court (1703–9) and Handel visited it (1710). Wilderer composed operas, oratorios, motets and cantatas; a *Kyrie* and *Gloria* by him were copied by Bach, whose own B minor *Kyrie* bears some resemblance to Wilderer's. When the Elector Palatine Johann Wilhelm was succeeded by his brother Carl Philipp of Innsbruck in 1716, the Düsseldorf and Innsbruck courts were amalgamated and moved first to Neuburg, then Heidelberg and finally to Mannheim in 1720. In 1723 he became joint *Kapellmeister* with Jakob Greber and together they founded the famous Mannheim orchestra. His sacred opera *Esther* was performed in 1723 as an oratorio at Heidelberg and as an opera, less than three months before his death, at Mannheim.

6 Middle Germany

Agrell, Johan Joachim (1701–65). Swedish violinist, harpsichordist and composer who resided in Nuremberg. After studies at Uppsala University, Agrell took up a post as a court violinist at Kassel. Like his teacher, J. H. Roman, he travelled widely, to England, France and Italy, before being appointed *Kapellmeister* and *director musices* at Nuremberg in 1746. His extant music is instrumental – sonatas, harpsichord concertos and symphonies – and owes much to Roman and Fortunato Chelleri (whom he would have encountered in Sweden).

Arnold, Georg (*d* 1676). South German organist and composer who, at the end of the Thirty Years War (1649), took up an appointment as court organist at Bamberg, where he provided new music for the cathedral and assisted Spiridio and Matthias Tretzscher in the reconstruction of damaged organs. He published his music – polychoral and concertato – in Nuremberg, Innsbruck and Bamberg.

Bassani, Giovanni Battista. See ITALY *7 Papal States: Bologna-Ferrara.*

Briegel, Wolfgang Carl. See NORTHERN EUROPE *5 West Germany and the Rhineland.*

Carestini, Giovanni. See ITALY *10 Itinerant Musicians.*

Chelleri, Fortunato. See ITALY *10 Itinerant Musicians.*

Conradi, Johann Georg. See NORTHERN EUROPE *1 North Germany: Hamburg.*

Deinl, Nikolaus (1665–1725). Nuremberg organist and composer. Deinl was a pupil of Heinrich Schwemmer and G. C. Wecker, whom he assisted at the Egidienkirche. After studies with J. P. Krieger at Weissenfels, Deinl returned to Nuremberg as the organist of a succession of churches. At the Spitalkirche he was ultimately named *Kantor* and *director musices* in 1701. He was much admired as a musician and teacher.

Denner. Nuremberg family of woodwind instrument makers. Johann Christoph Denner (1655–1707), a player as well as a skilled craftsman, has been credited with having developed the clarinet. He experimented with tuning joints, the shape of the bore and the placement of note holes on his instruments (oboes, clarinets, bassoons, recorders, rackets and chalumeaux). His instruments were renowned for their superior playing properties. His sons continued his work, adding the transverse flute to their inventory.

Dilherr, Johann Michael (1604–69). Popular poet and theologian. Dilherr lived and worked in Saxony until 1642 when he left a professorship at Jena University to take up the post of headmaster at the Nuremberg Egidien Gymnasium; within four years he had also become a senior figure in the hierarchy of the Sebaldkirche. He was a member of the Pegnesische Blumenorden (a society of poets and scholars), and wrote poetry for S. T. Staden and J. E. Kindermann. The dialogues, on which he collaborated with Kindermann – *Mosis Plag* (1642) was the first – for the services at the Sebaldkirche, are important in the evolution of the German oratorio. Dilherr delivered a public oration, *De ortu et progressu, usu, et abusu musicae*, in 1643 and produced at least one musical composition of his own (*Heilige Chorwoche*, 1653).

Eberlin, Daniel. See NORTHERN EUROPE *4 Saxony and Thuringia.*

Ehe. Nuremberg family of brass instrument makers contemporary with the Haas and Hainlein families. Isaak (1586–1632) and Georg Ehe (1595–1668) founded the firm, though they quarrelled and one sued the other. They made trumpets, horns and trombones of the highest standard, often intricately decorated. Another family member, Friedrich Ehe (1669–1743), was one of the first to make higher-pitched, doubly-wound trumpets (one instrument from 1741 survives) which were played in late 18th- and early 19th-century orchestras.

Falckenhagen, Adam (1697–1761). Lutenist who, after a long apprenticeship at Weissenfels, Dresden (where he studied with S. L. Weiss), Jena and Weimar, was appointed a 'Virtuosissimo' of the Bayreuth court by Margrave Friedrich in 1736. In Nuremberg during the 1740s, he was one of the last important lutenists to publish collections of solo and chamber music for his instrument.

Fischer, Johann. See NORTHERN EUROPE *7 Itinerant Musicians.*

Franck, Johann Wolfgang. See NORTHERN EUROPE *1 North Germany: Hamburg.*

Franck, Melchior. See NORTHERN EUROPE *4 Saxony and Thuringia.*

Graf, Johann. See NORTHERN EUROPE *4 Saxony and Thuringia.*

Haas. Most famous of the Nuremberg families of brass instrument makers. Johann Wilhelm Haas (1649–1723) learnt the trade from Hans Hainlein. His sons, Wolf Wilhelm (1681–1760) and Ernst Johann Conrad (1723–92), signed their father's name to their instruments, which, for three generations, were much sought after throughout Europe. Twelve solid-silver state trumpets, made by Wolf Wilhelm Haas in 1744 for the Elector Palatine Carl Theodor, survive.

Haiden, Hans (1536–1613). Copper merchant, musical instrument inventor and maker, organist and writer who served as a Nuremberg senator. He invented the *Geigenwerk*, a keyboard instrument which depended on parchment-covered wheels (instead of jacks) to produce a bowed string effect with vibrato and dynamic shading as well as sustaining power. He publicized it in a pamphlet, published in Latin (1605) and German (*Geigenwerk, musicale instrumentum reformatum*, 1610); when describing the *Geigenwerk*, Praetorius quoted from this pamphlet in his *Syntagma musicum* (ii, 1618). In 1606 Haiden's son Hans Christoph (1572–1617) gave a performance on it in Kassel before Moritz, Landgrave of Hesse.

Hainlein. Nuremberg family of brass instrument makers (previously coppersmiths). The first members of the family to make instruments were Sebastian the elder (*d* 1631), and his brother Sebastian the younger (1594–1655), a trombonist and aspiring *Stadtpfeifer* (a status he never attained) whose son Paul (1626–86) not only made trumpets and trombones but also held organ posts in Nuremberg and composed modest songs and instrumental music. Paul was sent to Munich (1646–7) and Italy (1647–8) to study and, in 1655, succeeded J. E. Kindermann as organist of the Egidienkirche; three years later he gained the prestigious post of organist at the Sebaldkirche. Paul's son Michael (1659–1725) was also a maker who devised a new bell shape, later popularized by makers of the Haas family.

Haussmann, Valentin (1565/70–1614). Well-travelled poet, editor and composer, who published most of his songs and dance music in Nuremberg. Haussmann was educated in Regensburg and held posts at a succession of courts, cities and bourgeois households. At some point he must have spent time in Poland, because he included Polish dances in his first publication of instrumental music (1598). He translated Italian texts into German and reset existing melodies. In 1604 he issued three further collections – a potpourri of songs and dances and two collections of dances for five or six viols and (for the first time in Germany) an occasional violin. He also tried his hand at a monothematic *fuga*.

Herbst, Johann Andreas. See NORTHERN EUROPE *5 West Germany and the Rhineland.*

Hurlebusch, Conrad Friedrich. See NORTH-
ERN EUROPE 7 *Itinerant Musicians.*
Jeep, Johannes (1581/2–1644). Organist and
composer whose tenure (1613–25) at the Wei-
kersheim court as *Kapellmeister*, organist and
diplomat was interrupted by the Thirty Years
War. Jeep received his training at Celle and
then spent time in Nuremberg where he came
in contact with H. L. Hassler, Valentin
Haussmann (who in 1607 composed a song
entitled 'Jep, Dillentent') and J. A. Herbst,
who influenced his popular *Studentengärtleins
erster Theil* (1605). He also travelled to Paris
and Venice. In 1607 he published his first
collection of four-part hymns and psalm settings, which won praise from Praetorius; after
the dissolution of the Hohenlohe court at Wei-
kersheim, Jeep devoted his energies to completing a Hohenlohe hymnbook, which
appeared in 1629. His last years were spent in
Frankfurt am Main, as organist of the
cathedral and civic *Kapellmeister.*
Kindermann, Johann Erasmus (1616–55).
The most original composer of the Nuremberg
School. A pupil of Johann Staden, Kindermann benefited from study in Venice and
Rome (1635), which gave him a fluency in all
the genres current in his day. Having begun
as a bass singer and violinist at the Frauenkirche, he became second organist there in
1636; after serving a few months as organist
at Schwäbisch-Hall, he took up the organ post
at the Egidienkirche in Nuremberg. His pupils
included Heinrich Schwemmer, G. C. Wecker, Johann Agricola and Augustin Pfleger.

Although Kindermann composed primarily
vocal music (motets, dialogues and cantatas)
in both the *prima prattica* and the *seconda
prattica*, he published two important instrumental collections. The *Harmonia organica*
(1645) – the last German collection to be
notated in tablature and one of the first to be
engraved – is idiomatically particular to the
organ, exploiting its technical and acoustical
possibilities in 25 contrapuntal pieces. The
Canzoni, sonatae (1653) contains 41 works for
one to three violins, cello and continuo, and
provides one of the first instances of scordatura.
Kircher, Athanasius. See ITALY 7 *Papal
States: Rome.*
Krieger, Johann. See NORTHERN EUROPE 4
Saxony and Thuringia.
Krieger, Johann Philipp. See NORTHERN
EUROPE 4 *Saxony and Thuringia.*
Kusser, Johann Sigismund. See NORTHERN
EUROPE 7 *Itinerant Musicians.*
Löhner, Johann (1645–1705). Nuremberg

tenor, organist at St Lorenz (from 1694) and
composer of more than 300 devotional songs
and three known operas. Löhner acquired his
musical training from his uncle, G. C. Wecker,
who adopted him in 1660. He worked in Bayreuth and travelled to Vienna, Salzburg and
Leipzig before settling in Nuremberg in 1672.
Pachelbel, Johann (1653–1706). Remarkable
organist, teacher and composer known today
mainly through his three-part Canon in D
over an ostinato bass. Though he is usually
associated with Nuremberg, it was only in the
last decade of his life that Pachelbel served as
organist of the Sebaldkirche. A gifted intellectual, he was awarded a scholarship to study
at the Regensburg Gymnasium Poeticum
(1670) and although a Lutheran, in 1673 he
accepted the post of deputy organist at the
Stephansdom, Vienna, where he undoubtedly
encountered German and Italian Catholic
music. He served as Eisenach court organist
under the *Kapellmeister* Daniel Eberlin for a
year before taking up the organ post at the
Erfurt Predigerkirche in 1678.

He remained 12 years at Erfurt, marrying
and establishing a close friendship with the
Bach family. In accordance with his duties at
the Predigerkirche – and being restrained
from improvising within the service – Pachelbel composed a wealth of chorale preludes
which embrace all of the textures and techniques of the day, as well as organic and seamless toccatas, polythematic ricercares (in white
notation), modal fantasias in a variety of styles,
and chaconnes and fugues of great vitality
and artistry. After the plague of 1683, during
which he lost his first wife and baby, he published the *Musicalische Sterbens-Gedancken*
(which contains four sets of chorale
variations). He also composed at least 21 harpsichord suites, which not only reveal the
cosmopolitan influence of Froberger but also
his own fascination with tempered tuning –
that is to say, little-used keys – and enharmonic notes.

In 1690 Pachelbel took up residence in
Stuttgart, at the Württemberg court, where he
enjoyed the patronage of Duchess Magdalena
Sibylla. But his stay was cut short by the threat
of French invasion in 1692. In the interim,
before succeeding G. C. Wecker at Nuremberg, Pachelbel served as the town organist at
Gotha. During this final and distinguished
phase of his career, he produced motets, sacred
concertos (which draw upon combinations of
biblical, chorale and other poetic texts), and
11 settings of the *Magnificat* (employing five-
part chorus and double choruses, wind, brass

and strings), as well as 95 *Magnificat* fugues for organ, which represent a synthesis of Lutheran and Catholic sacred styles. In the late 1690s he published a collection of six suites for two violins and continuo (*Musicalische Ergötzung*), conceived for amateur music making, and the *Hexachordum Apollinis* (1699) for organ or harpsichord.

Three of his four children followed him into musical careers: Wilhelm Hieronymus (1686–1764), much his father's most promising pupil, became organist at the Sebaldkirche (after J.C. Richter) and a composer of keyboard music; Carl Theodor (1690–1750), also an organist and composer, emigrated to North America when he was about 40 years of age, and worked on the east coast in Boston, Newport, New York and Charleston; Johann Michael (*b* 1692) was an instrument maker.

Pfeiffer, Johann (1697–1761). Violinist and composer of instrumental music at the Weimar and Bayreuth courts. Pfeiffer studied at the universities of Halle and Leipzig before taking up an appointment as a violinist at the Weimar court in 1720. He remained there until 1733, serving as *Kapellmeister* from 1726 and travelling in the Low Countries and France with Duke Ernst August during 1729–30. From 1734 he served Margravine Wilhelmine at Bayreuth and was honoured with the title of *Hofrat* in 1753. Pfeiffer composed sonatas for one instrument (viola d'amore, viol, oboe d'amore, violino piccolo and lute) – some accompanied by harpsichord obbligato – as well as overtures, symphonies and concertos.

Pistocchi, Francisco Antonio Mamiliano. See ITALY 7 *Papal States: Bologna-Ferrara.*

Platti, Giovanni Benedetto (*c*1700–1763). Venetian composer who in 1722 took up a post at the court of the Bishop of Würzburg (along with his compatriots G. B. Bassani and Fortunato Chelleri). When the bishop died in 1724, most of the musicians dispersed, although Platti stayed on as a singing teacher and *virtuoso di camera* – for he was also proficient on the flute, oboe, violin, cello and harpsichord. Not surprisingly, his early sonatas are cast in the Italian Baroque style and the later ones in the German *galant* style.

Schmid, Balthasar (1705–49). Distinguished Nuremberg music engraver and printer, whose work can be seen in the first editions of J. S. Bach's *Clavier-Übung* and the Goldberg Variations, C. P. E. Bach's Prussian Sonatas and Telemann's portrait and autobiography. Schmid was also a composer of chamber music for amateurs.

Schütz. Nuremberg instrumentalists and composers, father and sons. Gabriel Schütz (1633–1710) learnt the viol from Nicolaus Bleyer while studying in Lübeck. After a year in Hamburg he settled in Nuremberg in 1656 where ten years later, after touring in South Germany as a viol and cornett soloist, he was formally appointed a town musician. Firm in his Protestantism, Schütz remained at Nuremberg, despite offers of posts at the Catholic courts of Stuttgart and Vienna. Only trio sonatas and partitas for flute, violin, viol and continuo survive. He taught J. P. Krieger and Konrad Höffler as well as his sons, Johann Jacob and Jacob Balthasar (1661–1700; a singer, violinist and composer of chamber music). Both sons were associated with the Ansbach court. Jacob Balthasar Schütz married the daughter of Paul Hainlein.

Schwemmer, Heinrich (*d* 1696). Nuremberg singing teacher, composer of sacred vocal music and joint civic *director chori musici* (producing music for weddings and funerals) with Paul Hainlein. Schwemmer worked with G. C. Wecker (a fellow pupil of J. E. Kindermann) in training the next generation of Nuremberg musicians.

Spiridio. See NORTHERN EUROPE 7 *Itinerant Musicians.*

Staden, Johann (1581–1634). Nuremberg organist and versatile composer who founded the Nuremberg School. Staden was a prodigy who had gained a reputation as a celebrated organist by the age of 18. After serving as court organist at Bayreuth (from about 1604 until 1611), Staden returned to Nuremberg where he held a series of church posts, crowned by that at the Sebaldkirche. He was invited back to Bayreuth by Margrave Christian in 1618 – along with Michael Praetorius, Scheidt and Schütz – to test the new organ there. His most important pupils were his son Sigmund Theophil Staden and J. C. Kindermann.

Staden popularized the use of *basso continuo*, advocated independent instrumental accompaniments and introduced the solo concerto to Nuremberg audiences. After publishing German polyphonic songs (1606–10) and Latin motets (*Harmoniae sacrae*, 1616), with and without continuo, Staden published the first major sacred music (for solo voices, choruses and mixed vocal and instrumental ensembles) with German texts: *Kirchen-Music* (1615–16). Like Schein and Melchior Franck he composed motet dialogues (two are included in *Hauss-Music*, 1628); his *Hertzentrosts-Musica* became, in 1630, the first collection of monodies to be published in Nuremberg.

Staden, Sigmund Theophil (1607–55). Leading Nuremberg instrumentalist, composer and theorist who composed the first extant Singspiel. He was the son of Johann Staden, from whom he learnt the violin, organ and composition.

At the age of 13 he was given a grant by the Nuremberg city council to study in Augsburg with Jakob Paumann (once the protégé of Lassus at Munich); during his three years with Paumann, Staden mastered a variety of keyboard and wind instruments (cornett, trombone and bassoon) and the viola, while pursuing a course of lessons in composition. Apart from six months' leave to study the viol and viola bastarda in Berlin with Walter Rowe the elder during 1627, Staden passed his career fruitfully in Nuremberg as a city instrumentalist (from 1627) and organist of St Lorenz (from 1634).

In 1643 he directed a large-scale concert of music by himself, Lassus, Hans Leo Hassler (whom he had met while in Augsburg) and Giovanni Gabrieli, which required the services of all the musicians of Nuremberg. The following year he produced *Seelewig*, a Singspiel, 'in the Italian manner'. He published it, along with eight other theatre pieces (made up of strophic songs, spoken dialogue and instrumental interludes) in the journal *Frauenzimmer Gesprächspiele* during the 1640s. In 1644 and 1645 Staden collaborated with Johann Klaj on sacred plays not unlike Singspiels – containing solos, choruses and instrumental interludes in alternation with spoken text – which were performed on Sunday evenings at the Sebaldkirche. He also organized the music for the banquet held in 1649 at which Nurembergers celebrated the end of the Thirty Years War.

Though hardly the products of a profound or forward-looking composer, Staden's strophic songs, which appeared in two collections (*Seelen-Music*, 1644–8, and *Musicalischer Friedens-Gesänger*, 1651), were locally acclaimed. His *Rudimentum musicum* (3rd edn, 1648) served the Nuremberg schools as a useful elementary theoretical text.

Torelli, Giuseppe. See ITALY *7 Papal States: Bologna-Ferrara.*

Torri, Pietro. See CENTRAL EUROPE *1 South Germany: Munich.*

Wecker, Georg Caspar (1632–95). Nuremberg organist and minor composer. With Heinrich Schwemmer (who taught singing and rudiments of music), he was the influential keyboard and composition teacher of Nikolaus Deinl, J. B. Schütz, Max Zeidler, Johann Krieger and Pachelbel. Wecker himself had studied with Kindermann and, after a succession of posts at Nuremberg churches, was appointed organist at the Sebaldkirche in 1686.

Weigel. Nuremberg family of engravers, publishers and art dealers. Christoph ('der Ältere') (1654–1725) founded the family firm, specializing in art, music and books on music. His brother Johann Christoph (1661–1725) published some of Pachelbel's music and a series of plates entitled *Musicalisches theatrum* (*c*1722) depicting instrumentalists being led by a conductor (see Plates 28 and 29). Christoph ('der Jüngere') (1703–77) printed the second volume of Bach's *Clavier-Übung* in 1735.

7 Itinerant Musicians

Baron, Ernst Gottlieb. See NORTHERN EUROPE *4 Saxony and Thuringia.*

Fischer, Johann (1646–1716/17). Violinist and composer who, after studies with S. F. Capricornus in Stuttgart, travelled extensively throughout his life. Of particular significance were the five years (1665–70) spent in Paris working as one of Lully's copyists. After spending the 1670s and 80s in South and central Germany (at Stuttgart, Augsburg and Ansbach), he took a post in the Latvian court of Duke Friedrich Casimir of Kurland (1690–7). During the first decade of the new century he worked mainly in the north – in Poland, Lüneburg, Schwerin and Copenhagen – as well as in Bayreuth. His final years were spent in Brandenburg, as *Kapellmeister* to Margrave Philipp Wilhelm at Schwedt.

Förster, Kaspar (1616–73). Bass singer known for his three-octave range, composer and *Kapellmeister*. A native North German, he studied in Rome with Carissimi (1633–6) – also spending time in Venice in the 1650s – and then brought the Italian style northwards to Danzig and the Danish court. Förster also studied with Marco Scacchi while serving as a singer and choral conductor at the Warsaw court (*c*1638–43), during which time Scacchi became involved in the dispute between Förster's father (of the same name) and Paul Siefert at the Danzig Marienkirche. From

1652 until 1655, and again from 1661 until his retirement in 1667, Förster worked at the Danish court. In between, he returned first to Danzig where he undertook his father's *Kapellmeister* duties (1655–7) then to Venice, where he served as an army captain, fighting in the fifth Turkish war (after which he was made a Knight of the Order of St Mark).

He composed sacred vocal music, which incorporated very low bass parts (presumably to suit himself), and instrumental works, some of which became part of the repertory of the Hamburg collegium musicum (Förster visited Hamburg on his retirement and became friendly with Christoph Bernhard). Johann Mattheson praised his voice in the *Grundlage einer Ehren-Pforte* (1740) and mentioned a sonata (now lost) in which each of the players was directed to improvise for eight bars in a free style.

Franck, Johann Wolfgang. See NORTHERN EUROPE *1 North Germany: Hamburg.*

Funck, David (*c*1630–after 1690). Bohemian-born instrumentalist (proficient on the violin, clavichord and guitar), composer, poet and writer on music who, despite his obvious talents, was unable to apply them. His life appears to have been characterized by physical and emotional instability and, as a result, he managed to publish only one collection of dance music (*Stricturae viola di gambicae, ex sonatis, ariis, intradis, allemandis*), for four equal viols, which appeared in Leipzig, Jena and Rudolstadt in 1677. Although well known in its day, his *Drama passionale* (for which he wrote both text and music) does not survive.

Grünewald, Gottfried (1675–1739). Singer, pantaleonist and composer. Grünewald worked as a bass in the Hamburg Opera in 1703, while composing operas (lost) for Leipzig; in 1704 he sang the title role in his *Germanicus* at Leipzig, Hamburg and Naumburg. It was probably while at Weissenfels (1709–11), serving as court vice-*Kapellmeister* and chamber singer under J. P. Krieger, that he learnt to play the pantaleon (its inventor and chief exponent, Pantaleon Hebenstreit, had been at the Weissenfels court 1698–1706). In 1713 he took a permanent appointment as vice-*Kapellmeister* at Darmstadt under his Hamburg colleague Christoph Graupner. Graupner composed opera roles especially for Grünewald, and together they provided cantata cycles for the royal chapel over a 20-year period (1719–39).

Haussmann, Valentin. See NORTHERN EUROPE *6 Middle Germany.*

Hebenstreit, Pantaleon. See NORTHERN EUROPE *4 Saxony and Thuringia: Dresden.*

Hesse, Ernst Christian. See NORTHERN EUROPE *5 West Germany and the Rhineland.*

Hurlebusch, Conrad Friedrich (*c*1696–1765). Much-travelled harpsichord virtuoso, organist and composer who used his native Brunswick as a base. From there, he first went to Hamburg and Vienna, where he spent two years, before travelling on to Italy. In 1721 he returned to Brunswick via the Bavarian court where he declined a post because of his Protestant faith. In Brunswick he composed his first opera, *L'innocenza difesa*, for the court but instead of taking a permanent post, he accepted the post of *Kapellmeister* of the Swedish court (1721–5). After resigning, he travelled in northern Germany. He became acquainted with Telemann and Johann Mattheson at Hamburg and attempted, in vain, to secure an invitation to the English court from Hanover. Before returning to Brunswick he visited Kassel, Eisenach, Gotha and Bayreuth, where in 1726 he composed Carnival music and declined a court post. The following year he completed *Flavio Cuniberto* (never performed) and a theoretical treatise. Although he hoped to secure a post at Hamburg or St Petersburg, none materialized. His last appointment was as organist of the Oude Kerk in Amsterdam (1743). As in Hamburg, where he had once been the subject of an anonymous pamphlet, Hurlebusch attracted continued criticism in Amsterdam.

Kremberg, Jakob (*c*1650–*c*1718). Polish-born instrumentalist, composer and poet who served as a chamber musician to a Brandenburg court official at Halle (1677), the Swedish court at Stockholm (1678) and the Elector of Saxony at Dresden (1691). By 1689 he was in Dresden where he published his *Musicalische Gemüths-Ergötzung*, a collection of accompanied secular songs to which he appended instructions on ornamentation and playing bowed and plucked instruments. He worked for two seasons at the Hamburg Opera (1693–5) with J. S. Kusser and by 1697 he had settled in London. He made himself known there first as a freelance instrumentalist (Kremberg was among the first to give concerts at Hickford's Dancing School) and by 1706 held a court appointment; two years later he joined the Twenty-four Violins.

Krieger, Johann Philipp. See NORTHERN EUROPE *4 Saxony and Thuringia.*

Kühnel, August (1645–*c*1700). Well-travelled viol player and composer; his son Johann Michael was also an instrumentalist, proficient on the viol, violin and lute. While serving at the Zeitz court (1661–5) Kühnel went to Paris to refine his viol playing. Still in the employ of the Zeitz court, he toured in Germany, performing in Dresden, Frankfurt am Main (1669) and Munich (1680–81), where he refused a post for reasons of religion. In 1682 and 1685 he visited London where, according to the *London Gazette* (1685), he performed 'upon the Barritone'. In 1686 he exchanged his Zeitz post for one at Darmstadt, serving the Landgravine Elisabeth Dorothea as her viol player and instrumental director (under W. C. Briegel) for the next two years, after which he was appointed to a similar post at Weimar. His last appointment was as *Kapellmeister* at Kassel (1695–9), during which time he published a set of 14 *Sonate ô partite* (1698) for one and two viols with continuo.

Kusser, Johann Sigismund (1660–1727). Contentious Hungarian violinist and composer who travelled in Germany, England and Ireland after six years' study with Lully in Paris (where he was known as Cousser). His training in the French orchestral style made him much sought after. In 1682 he published a collection of orchestral overtures and airs, *Composition de musique suivant la méthode française*, and quickly gained an appointment at the Ansbach court to train the orchestra.

In 1690 he became opera *Kapellmeister* at the court of Brunswick-Wolfenbüttel, but left abruptly for Hamburg after disputes with both court poet and the opera manager. He fared little better at Hamburg: he quarrelled with the opera manager, Jakob Kremberg, who refused to let Kusser use the theatre for his opera *Porus* (1693); to Kremberg's consternation, Kusser produced it elsewhere with great success. Two years later, Kremberg left and Kusser assumed his duties at the Hamburg Opera, raising the standards and broadening the repertory with the works of Carlo Pallavicino and Agostino Steffani. However, he soon became more interested in organizing a touring company, which he accompanied south to Nuremberg, Augsburg, Stuttgart and Munich (1697–8). He returned to Stuttgart in 1700 as *Oberkapellmeister* and published two more collections of orchestral suites; the following year he went to Italy to recruit musicians. Eventually he fell out with his colleagues and, in 1704, resigned to seek new opportunities in Britain, where he spent the next 22 years – first as a private tutor in London and then as the Chapelmaster of Trinity College, Dublin (1711), and the king's 'Master of the Musick' in Ireland (1717). Rela-

tively little is known of his years in England and Ireland.

Löhner, Johann. See NORTHERN EUROPE 6 *Middle Germany*.

Opitz, Martin (1597–1639). Influential Silesian Protestant poet whose verses were set by the leading 17th-century German composers, literary theorist who led the way to important reforms, and librettist. Opitz travelled widely through necessity during the Thirty Years War; in 1630 he was in Paris, awaiting the defeat of the Catholics in Silesia, but when the Protestants were suppressed in 1635, Opitz took refuge in Poland. Nevertheless, most of his patrons were Catholic – Emperor Ferdinand II, who made him his court poet in 1625 and later ennobled him (Opitz became 'von Boberfeld'), a Silesian count whom Opitz accompanied on a political mission to Poland, and King Władysław IV.

Opitz inaugurated the modern era of German poetry by writing in High German, avoiding false rhymes and regularizing metres and strophic forms. Heinrich Albert, Andreas Hammerschmidt, C. C. Dedekind, Jacob Hintze, Caspar Kittel, J. E. Kindermann and Schütz set his texts. Opitz the librettist adapted Rinuccini's *Dafne* for Schütz, whose lost opera (1627), is considered to have been the first German opera.

Rosenmüller, Johann. See ITALY 4 *Venice*.
Schickhardt, Johann Christian. See LOW COUNTRIES 1 *United Provinces*.
Spiridio (1615–85). Carmelite organist and composer who published at least three volumes of *Nova instructio pro pulsandis organis, spinettis, manuchordis* (1669–75), containing valuable evidence about performing practices. Spiridio travelled widely in Germany and held posts in Rome (at the Collegio Germanico in 1643), the South Netherlands, Prague (1660) and Bamberg (1664).
Strungk, Nicolaus Adam (1640–1700). Violinist, organist and composer who worked in his native North Germany, Saxony and Vienna. The son of Delphin Strungk (1600/01–1694), organist of the Marienkirche in Brunswick, Nicolaus Adam assisted his father from an early age. His earliest appointments were as a violinist at the courts of Wolfenbüttel and Celle (1660). He spent the years 1661–5 at the Viennese court, returning to Celle only to find that the court orchestra had been disbanded, so he took a post at the Hanover court of Elector Johann Friedrich, interrupting his tenure at Hanover to serve as cathedral and municipal *Kapellmeister* of Hamburg (1678–82). While in Hamburg he

composed his most successful operas, *Esther* (1680) and *Semiramis* (1681). He returned to Hanover as court composer and organist (1682–6), though he spent the last two years in Rome (where in 1685 he met Corelli) and Vienna.

In 1688 Strungk was appointed vice-*Kapellmeister* and chamber organist at the Dresden court under Christoph Bernhard, whom he succeeded at *Kapellmeister* four years later. At much the same time he acquired the necessary permission to found an opera house in Leipzig, inaugurating it in 1693 with his *Alceste*. Encouraged by the initial success of the opera house and eager to escape the tensions between German and Italian musicians at Dresden, Strungk resigned his post and moved to Leipzig in 1696.

Weiss, Silvius Leopold (1686–1750). Virtuoso lutenist and composer of nearly 600 pieces. Originally from Düsseldorf, Weiss belonged to a family of court lutenists working in south-west Germany. Silvius was the most gifted of the family and sought the rewards available to a virtuoso. In 1706 he gained an appointment at the Breslau court of Count Carl Philipp and composed his earliest surviving partita. He soon gained the attention of the Polish Prince Alexander Sobieski, who took him to Rome, where he mixed with the Scarlattis and other musicians at the residence of the prince's mother, Queen Maria Casimira.

After six years in Rome, Weiss returned to Germany – to Kassel and home to Düsseldorf, before accepting a very highly paid post in the Dresden Hof kapelle (ultimately becoming the highest paid instrumentalist there). Under the terms of his employment he was allowed to tour, so over the next decade he made trips to Prague (1717, 1723 – to play in the music for the coronation festivities of Charles VI), London (1718), Vienna (1718–19), Munich (1722) and Berlin (1728), where he became friendly with J. J. Quantz and the lute-playing sister of Frederick the Great, Wilhelmine. He is known to have visited Bach and performed with the collegium musicum at Leipzig in 1739.

Weiss's music is polished and idiomatic. His suites (notated in tablature and called 'Suonaten' and 'Partien') begin with unmeasured preludes that make use of his highly developed fingering systems and idiomatic legato style. Unlike the suites, his concertos for lute with other instruments have not survived. See also CENTRAL EUROPE *1 South Germany*, Weiss.

Zangius, Nikolaus (*c*1570–*c*1618). *Kapellmeister* and composer of sacred and secular *Gesellschaftslieder*. Zangius worked in North Germany, Poland and Bohemia: he was appointed *Kapellmeister* to the Prince-Bishop Philipp Sigismund of Brunswick-Wolfenbüttel at Iburg, then at Danzig (1599), where his tenure was interrupted by plague. He took refuge at the imperial court in Prague, and ended up at Berlin (1612), where he was followed by other musicians from Prague.

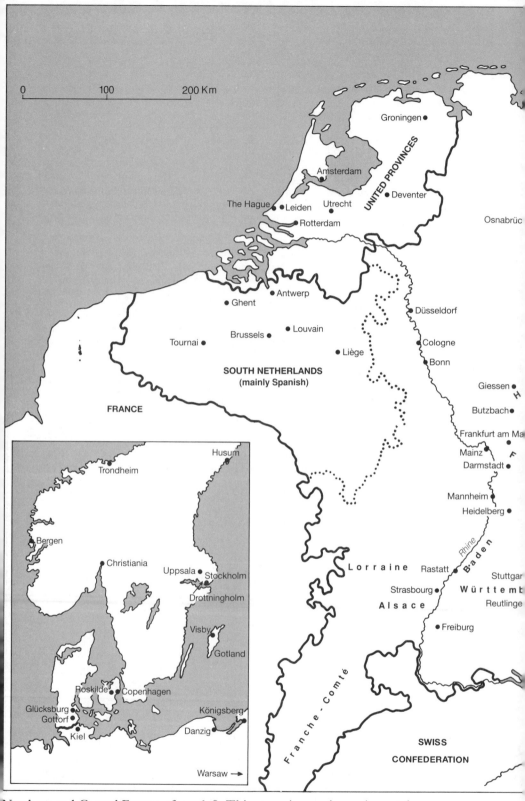

Northern and Central Europe after 1648. This map gives major regions and boundaries after the Thirty Years War, but does not attempt to show complex political divisions.

Main borders: ....
Holy Roman Empire borders: _____

Central Europe

The Austro-German Courts

The history of music 1600–1750 in the Habsburg lands of Austro-Bohemia and in the southern German region of Bavaria centres on the relationship between indigenous talents and traditions, and outside influences.

Among the historical events and developments that primarily affected the shaping of this musical culture were the religious tensions and changes that erupted most markedly in the first half of the 17th century, and the rise of the Habsburg dynasty. While the dynastic faith of the Habsburgs was firmly established as Catholic, before 1600 the Protestant Reformation had been allowed to encroach into the territories of central Europe, where it took diverse forms (including a strong Calvinist following in Bohemia); thus in the period 1550–1600 there was religious and educational diversity, and an impression of tolerance (as one Catholic observer noted: 'In affairs of religion everyone does as he pleases'),[1] with the Catholic establishment in central Europe surviving alongside the varied manifestations of Protestantism. A decisive change in attitudes came about after 1600. The strength of the Counter-Reformation, growing slowly from the 1550s on, increased to a point where the intellectual zeal of the Jesuit movement (expressed for example in the founding of educational institutions such as the Clementinum (1556) in Prague) was now matched by the political ambitions of the Habsburgs. Although these developments unfolded in a much more complex and less consistent way than can be suggested by a brief summary, nevertheless by 1620, with the Battle of the White Mountain (near Prague), the Counter-Reformation in central Europe entered an aggressive phase marked by policies that were designed to enforce the essential Catholic religious unity regarded as an expression of loyalty to the house of Habsburg. Wars, rebellions, purges, persecution and enforced exile replaced the relatively peaceful situation obtaining previously. In Bohemia after 1620 Protestant leaders were dealt with severely and the Protestant community at large was subject to punitive measures. The Thirty Years War (1618–48), here as elsewhere, caused devastation to the indigenous populace and to the stability of its culture. From this period of political and religious unrest emerged the crucial status of the Habsburg territories as centres of the Counter-Reformation. With the Peace of Westphalia in 1648 the house of Habsburg, traditionally holders of the title Holy Roman Emperor and (from the 16th century onwards) Kings of Bohemia and Hungary, now gained decisive sovereignty over its inherited lands of Austria and over Bohemia. The Habsburg emperors were secured in their leadership of German Catholicism.

Among the Habsburg Emperor Ferdinand II's supporters at the Battle of the White Mountain were Count Tilly's efficient Bavarian troops. Bavaria too was an important scene of Counter-Reformation activity, from the intellectual and educational strides of the 16th century to the more military political activism of the 17th century. The Catholic university of Ingolstadt in Bavaria (founded 1476) nurtured generations of Jesuit Counter-Reformers: Emperor Ferdinand II, whose mother Maria was descended from the Bavarian ruling family, was himself educated at Ingolstadt University. These Jesuit centres – Ingolstadt, the Prague Clementinum, the Michaeliskirche (inaugurated, with much musical pomp, in 1597) and Collegium Gregorianum (founded 1574) both in Munich, among other colleges and churches – also formed leading centres of musical activity. The Jesuit dramas performed with music, cultivated in southern Germany, Austria and Bohemia, have been seen as preparing the ground for the enthusiastic adoption of Italian opera. (The Benedictine institutions in Austria – among them Salzburg University – were similarly centres of music and drama). Their educative aims were directed not only at the student performers (through Latin texts) but also at the audiences: biblical and allegorical subjects were conveyed vividly through the combination of dramatic action, spectacular scenes and costumes, fine rhetoric and music. From the mid 16th century, Jesuit dramas became required entertainment at court festivities, as opera was to become later: celebrated occasions such as the wedding of Wilhelm, heir apparent to the dukedom of Bavaria, and Renata of Lorraine in 1568, when the splendid Munich court musical events were under the direction of Lassus, included performances of Jesuit dramas – in this particular case a *Tragedy of Samson the Strong*, with incidental music by Lassus. Biblical subjects might include those with musical implications such as the drama of King David (*David . . . prudens*) performed at the Clementinum in 1673. There is evidence that the music of the Jesuit dramas (much of which has not survived) was designed to match characters and *Affekte* rather than simply to decorate the action.

It could be said that court music itself was designed not only to decorate court life, but also to convey and consolidate fundamental religious and political ideals. The maintenance of a Hofkapelle (often founded on illustrious precedents such as the grandiose Kantorei directed at Munich by Lassus as *Hofkapellmeister*, 1563–94) was inspired at the Baroque courts by a network of interlocking motives, personal, cultural, political and religious. The organization and location of a Hofkapelle might suffer changes imposed by political events. Munich court musicians moved in the early 18th century with their elector (Maximilian II Emanuel) first to Brussels and then in exile to France (the court becoming increasingly francophile in taste) before returning to Munich in 1715. Meanwhile, performances of Italian opera ceased temporarily at Munich. It cannot be assumed however that the fortunes of a court necessarily affected the long-term continuity of its musical life. While Vienna was catastrophically disrupted by the great plague of 1679–80 and by the Turkish threat culminating in the siege of the city in 1683, the overall impression is of a continuing concern for (and vast expenditure on) music at court, even in difficult times. Clearly musical patronage depended on factors besides the purely political or economic. Personal piety was one important factor, given public expression through music and ceremonial. The celebration of *Gottesdienst* (Divine Service) with the emperor and his entourage regularly in attendance at various churches and chapels in Vienna was a spectacular event. It served to emphasize the identification of Habsburg rule with the Catholic faith. Ferdinand II practised devoutly, and daily, the observances pertaining to his religion. Under Ferdinand and his successors, members of the central Habsburg Hofkapelle in Vienna kept up the composition and performance of liturgical music (in learned *stile antico* as well as in modern concertato style), intricately linked with the court and church calendars. Court composers were not limited to practising an ephemeral art of little wider significance. Although much court music was naturally of an occasional kind, its style was not therefore necessarily trivial. The tradition of *stile antico* in Vienna found its apogee in Fux, who regarded it as his vocation to preserve the old style with its deeply learned associations, and whose teachings continued to influence profoundly the study of counterpoint well beyond his own time.

Personal taste and patronage formed another crucial element in court music. Among some remarkable individuals responsible for musical patronage was the gifted Henriette Adelaide of Savoy, who (apparently homesick at the Munich court, where she came in the 1650s as the young bride of the Elector Ferdinand Maria) gathered around her for her own distraction and cultural satisfaction a coterie of Italian artists. She herself wrote poetry (there is a court reference to her as 'nostra illustre poetessa'),[2] sang, danced in ballets, and played lute and harp: there are records of family music-making with Henriette Adelaide as singer, Ferdinand Maria playing cembalo, and his brother Maximilian Philipp performing on the recorder. A particular favourite was Giovanni Battista (Giambattista) Maccioni, Munich court chaplain, poet and musician, and outstandingly talented as a harpist. Maccioni taught Henriette Adelaide harp, and collaborated with her on the texts of various musico–dramatic works. In his dedication of the libretto of his *dramma musicale L'Ardelia* (1660) to Henriette Adelaide he refers to the 'darkness' of his soul, which could not have found illumination without the 'bright rays' of the illustrious Adelaide's lofty intellect.[3] Besides the required adulation there seems to be real admiration here for Henriette Adelaide as patroness and connoisseur.

A succession of equally notable musical patrons occupied the powerful post of prince-archbishop at the court of Salzburg. The widely cultured Archbishop Wolf Dietrich (r. 1587–1612) had studied at the Catholic Collegio Germanico in Rome and envisaged, as well as a redesigned Salzburg, a re-creation of his Italian life on Austrian soil: his first *Hofkapellmeister* was the Cremonese Tiburtio Massaino. Significantly, Wolf Dietrich's last *Kapellmeister*, Peter Guetfreund, italianized his name to become Pietro Bonamico. Wolf Dietrich's successor, also an alumnus of the Roman Collegio Germanico, Archbishop Marcus Sitticus von Hohenems (r. 1612–19; brother of another important patron of the arts, Count Kaspar von Hohenems), was even more deeply interested in Italian culture: through his Italian mother and her connections, as well as his own inclinations, he was inspired to maintain a link with Italy during his Salzburg reign. In Rome he built the Palazzo Altemps; among its accoutrements was an integral theatre (restored and still in use this century for theatrical performances). At his Salzburg residence the italianate court theatre (inaugurated 1614) was described by the chronicler Matthias Weiss (first *Rektor* of Salzburg University, founded 1622 with its own theatres) as very fine and artistically arranged with changeable scenery ('versabilibus machinis').[4] And at the nearby palace of Hellbrunn (built 1615 as the Archbishop's summer residence) he instigated seemingly the first 'natural' theatre of the time and the first such on Austro-German ground, the Steintheater, created out of a rocky grotto that lent itself to transformation into an outdoor stage with generous accommodation for audience, and was obviously particularly well suited to the performance of pastorals. In pioneering Italian Baroque theatre design at Salzburg, Marcus Sitticus also pioneered the introduction of opera from Italy: from 1614 onwards his court and guests witnessed performances of a series of Italian operas including an *Orfeo* (1614, repeated 1617–19 for various state visits) and an *Andromeda* (1616, repeated 1617–

18) at the Residenz-Theater to celebrate the marriage of his nephew Jakob Hannibal II von Hohenems to Anna Sidonia, and probably identical with an *opera in musica*, *Il Perseo*, put on in 1619 for the visit of the Archduke Leopold (librettists and composers are not known). The cultivation of Italian opera continued during the reign of another italophile archbishop, Paris Lodron (r. 1619–53), and subsequently: when the Elector Ferdinand Maria of Bavaria and his wife Henriette Adelaide came on a visit to Hellbrunn in 1670 an opera was put on at the Steintheater to mark the occasion.

Vienna – administrative centre of the Habsburg Empire – was also an important centre of Italian Baroque theatre and music drama. Here, too, a distinguished line of gifted and generous patrons in the Habsburg emperors ensured the continuing importance of the city musically throughout the Baroque period, and here, too, there were strong links with Italy; both Ferdinand II and Ferdinand III married members of the Gonzaga family. Ferdinand III, Leopold I, Joseph I and Charles VI were themselves composers of opera, oratorio, church and chamber music, and not merely in occasional dilettante fashion: Leopold I composed and collected music (mainly by contemporary Italians: Carissimi, Pasquini, Stradella) with an assiduousness more to be expected of a professional musician.[5] The emperors, and members of their families (such as Leopold's second wife Claudia Felicitas of Tyrol), played and sang in musical performances; Charles VI liked to direct operas from the harpsichord. As knowledgeable composers and performers, and discerning listeners, these imperial patrons were in a position to attract excellent personnel and to extract the best from the court musicians in their employ. Their courts also attracted some of the finest Italian architects and stage designers – the Burnacinis in the reign of Ferdinand III and Leopold I (see Plate 12), the Galli-Bibienas in the reign of Charles VI (see Plate 13) – and librettists such as Minato, Zeno and Metastasio. Appreciation of music was part of a general and informed interest in the arts. (The Habsburgs founded and patronized various Italian-style *accademie* in Vienna). Emperor Leopold wrote poetry in Italian (the language cultivated by aristocratic Austrian society at the time). Charles VI was fluent in several languages and a keen collector of *objets d'art*. Contemporary commentators perceived such cultural and intellectual interests as affording, when time permitted, a welcome relief to the administrative cares of high imperial office. For the Habsburgs, music was perhaps the most congenial of all those interests.

The ramifications of such enlightened patronage were multifarious and far-reaching. One aspect concerns the practice of dedicating compositions to aristocratic and church leaders. Symptomatic of the Austro-German sympathy for the new Italian Baroque style is the frequency with which Italian composers in the early 17th century – among them Claudio Monteverdi – dedicated madrigals, sacred concertato works and instrumental sonatas to various Austro-German rulers and their families. Dedications might also imply the hope of (perhaps further) patronage, or convey gratitude for favours already granted. The court composer, later *Hofkapellmeister*, Fux, in dedicating his *Missa Ss Trinitatis* to Emperor Leopold, expressed appreciation of his faith in Fux's abilities; it has been suggested that this Mass was dedicated to the emperor specifically in thanks for Fux's appointment to the recently-established post of *Hofkomponist*. The emperor had made this appointment in 1698 'proprio motu' (that is, by the unusual procedure of deciding on his own initiative without formally consulting the court musical administration).

He may have had some earlier opportunity of hearing Fux's compositions and determined then to secure his services for the Hofkapelle. (Such talent-scouting was common, and extended to the practice of enticing students to abandon their courses: the *Rektor* of Graz University complained that the *alumni musici* from the Jesuit college, the Ferdinandeum, were encouraged by the Styrian nobility and clergy to run away in order to enter their service). Fux's subsequent career shows how support of the court musicians encompassed the granting of subsidies which enabled their works to be published, thus reflecting glory on the court and portraying their achievements more lastingly among a wider public. A number of Fux's works in different genres, including his opera *Elisa* (1719), his *Concentus musico-instrumentalis* (1701) – dedicated to Emperor Leopold's son, later Emperor Joseph I – and the celebrated *Gradus ad Parnassum* (1725), dedicated to the Emperor Charles VI, were all printed at the expense of his imperial patrons. (Vienna, though established as a 'musical capital' – 'eine Hochburg der Musik'[6] – was not at that time as flourishing a centre of music printing as it was to become later in the 18th century. Viennese Baroque music tended to be published outside Austria; for example at Augsburg, Nuremberg and Amsterdam.) The imperial patron might also be honoured in the title of a court composition, as with the *Aria Augustissimi … Imperatoris Ferdinandi III* by the court organist Wolfgang Ebner, published at Prague in 1648. (There are examples of the musician almost as court chronicler, referring to contemporary events: Poglietti's suite *Ribellione di Ungheria* and the pieces in Fux's *Concentus* entitled 'Die Freude der treuen Untertanen' and 'Die in Verwirrung gestürzten Feinde' commemorated imperial victories.)

The Viennese Imperial Library (K. K. Hofbibliothek, now absorbed into the Österreichische Nationalbibliothek) contained some splendid presentation volumes of music in manuscript. Among them were some landmarks in Baroque keyboard music, most notably the collected (though not complete) works of Froberger in a set of codices dedicated to the Viennese emperors and displaying the beautiful calligraphy, lavish gold-tooled leather covers and elaborate decorative designs (incorporating imperial motifs) characteristic of the special care taken in preparing such presentation copies. The variety of forms represented here (toccatas, fantasias, ricercars, capriccios, canzonas, variations and dances) may have been intended to demonstrate to his employers the range of the composer's capabilities. Froberger's keyboard works furnish further examples of pieces in which imperial personages appeared by name: the Lamentations he composed (analogous to the French *tombeau*) included two intensely expressive memorials to Ferdinand III and Ferdinand IV. Another aspect of imperial patronage illustrated by Froberger's career was the readiness with which the emperors granted study leave and the necessary financial support, in particular for journeys to Italy so that their court musicians might learn the much-favoured Italian style at source, under the guidance of such outstanding composers as Carissimi, Frescobaldi and Pasquini. Among court documents for 1637 is a reference to Froberger's grant from the emperor for a journey to Rome ('Davon ist dem Röm. Kays. May. und Cammer Musico Johann Jacobus Froberger auf vorhabende raiss nachn Rom 100 fl. allergn. verwilligt worden …').[7] These study visits had varied and important implications for the cultivation of Italian music in Vienna and elsewhere.

Besides the inevitable connections with Rome (Salzburg exemplifies these, and was indeed labelled 'the northern Rome', just as Munich was dubbed 'the German

Rome'), the Catholic lands of Austro-Germany preserved important links with Venice. The grandeur of the Venetian polychoral style, the more intimate attractions of the few-voiced concertato style, the richly developed musical and scenic effects of Venetian opera, found a ready reception on South German and Austrian soil. The manifestations and implications of this Venetian influence were wide-ranging. Andrea and Giovanni Gabrieli worked at the Munich Hof kapelle of Duke Albrecht V (r. 1550–79), to whom the elder Gabrieli later dedicated sacred vocal works. The fashion in Munich for Venetian polychoralism lasted into the 17th century and beyond: the new chapel (1603) in Duke Maximilian's residence was equipped with two organs; and during a special centenary celebration at the Augustinerkirche in 1724 a festive Mass was performed 'unter einer gedoppelten Musique auf beiden Chören'.[8] Much polychoral music in the Venetian style was published at Munich by Nikolaus Henricus (son-in-law of the Munich printer Adam Berg); among such publications was the *Circus symphonicus* (1608) by Lassus's second son Rudolph, *Hoforganist* at Munich from 1589 and *Hof komponist* from 1609. During the golden age of Italian opera in Munich, from the 1650s to the 1680s, Venice was a vital source of influence. (The Austro-German courts later became centres of the Neapolitan style in opera, oratorio and liturgical music.) Some leading contributors to the Munich court operas of the earlier period, such as Kerll's librettist, the court poet Domenico Gisberti, and the court musical director Agostino Steffani, were themselves of Venetian origin. The talented designer Santurini came from Venice to Munich (returning to Venice to run his own theatre) and astounded the court with a remarkable repertoire of scenes, machines and costumes, mixing the courtly Baroque and the fantastic, and displaying the technical sophistication characteristic of mid-17th-century Venetian opera. Not only composers were sent by their aristocratic patrons to Italy to further their education. The local designer Caspar Amort travelled to Italy to study at electoral expense, entering the court service in the 1640s soon after his return to Munich. Patronage of Italian opera might entail performances of works from outside, such as Cavalli's *Egisto* (1643) and his *Giasone* (1650), both at Vienna; or of works by Italians in residence at Austro-German courts, as with Cesti's *Il pomo d'oro* (1668; see Plates 11 and 12), also at Vienna, or the collaboration between the librettist Ferrari and the Viennese (Veronese-born) court composer Antonio Bertali, whose typically Venetian operatic comedy of disguise, *L'inganno d'amore*, was produced by the Vienna Hof kapelle during the Imperial Diet at Regensburg, 1653. Although Italians inevitably dominated the composition (both textual and musical) and the stage performance of opera, as indeed they dominated the Hof kapellen altogether, nevertheless German and Austrian composers were by no means excluded. Kerll at Munich, Biber at Salzburg and Fux at Vienna furnish examples of excellent composers encouraged by their employers to rival their Italian colleagues in the pre-eminently Italian genre of opera.

In opera and allied forms, as in instrumental music, the presence of a noble patron was frequently acknowledged: the patron or patroness might take part personally. By convention, prologues and epilogues referred directly or allegorically, and in laudatory fashion, to the court rulers and their families, or to visiting dignitaries. The splendour and colour of these festive operas can hardly be over-estimated (nor that of the court theatres: if none of the great rooms of the official residence was deemed adequate for a particular occasion then a new theatre might be built lavishly to house performers and spectators; such were the origins of the Salvatortheater constructed by Santurini at Munich). The most celebrated festal operas – Cesti's *Il pomo d'oro* for the marriage of the Emperor Leopold I to Margareta Teresa, daughter of the King of Spain; Fux's *Costanza e Fortezza* (incorporating the imperial motto) for the coronation of the Emperor Charles VI as King of Bohemia at Prague in 1723 – gave a notable impetus to the fashion for Italian opera in Austro-Germany and Bohemia (see Plate 13), but they were simply the peaks of a constant round of operatic and other entertainments put on at great expense to mark the enormous number of occasional and recurrent celebrations arising at court. For coronation anniversaries, name-days, birthdays, the birth of an heir, betrothals, weddings and state visits, a whole series of events might be arranged, together forming a kind of gigantic 'Gesamtkunstwerk' with music taking an important role. Typical ingredients of such court festivities included hunts, dramatic tournaments, ballets – the Viennese equestrian ballets were especially famous, though ballets on foot were also popular – and operas, firework displays, masked balls, feasts with *Tafelmusik*, all fulfilling the dual function of providing enjoyment for members of the court and exhibiting its glories to the guests. Considerable ingenuity was exercised in devising ways of honouring the celebrants. For the wedding of Ferdinand III and Maria of Spain in 1631, a *Balletto a cavallo* (equestrian ballet) was designed to form the names Ferdinand and Maria. Much reinforcing of the ruler's authority was exerted amid the splendours of these performances. A vast gathering assembled to honour the Emperor Leopold I on a visit to Munich in 1658 saw, among other spectacles, the young Elector Ferdinand Maria appearing as the sun god in a gold chariot, with Prince Maximilian Philipp as the moon god in a silver chariot, in G. B. Maccioni and J. K. Kerll's *Applausi festivi*. The scope of the entertainment might be on a cosmic scale: in the *Applausi festivi*, apart from representations of the sun, moon, stars, rainbow and so on, there were the chorus representing various nations (including the more exotic – Africans and Americans) paying homage, and Mounts Vesuvius and Etna sending their fires up to heaven. For the music of these entertainments (much of it lost, though librettos and scenic designs often survived) the composers must have matched the constant visual stimulus with appropriate musical magnificence. In a *Turnierspiel* (tournament play) such as the *Applausi festivi* the wind instruments would naturally play a central part. Court trumpeters and drummers were trained to a high standard. Performances of tournament plays took place in purpose-built halls (the enormous Turnierhaus at the Munich court, for example) or outdoors. Outdoor performances of opera (also exploiting the wind instruments to splendid effect) might require specially designed stages, as with the open-air theatre built by the celebrated Vienna court architect Giuseppe Galli-Bibiena at the Hradschin (royal castle) in Prague for Fux's *Costanza e Fortezza*. There was usually a canopy to protect the emperor and empress and their immediate entourage, but other spectators were less comfortably accommodated: in a letter of 1716 to Alexander Pope, the English traveller Lady Mary Wortley Montagu evoked the contrast between the magical qualities of the open-air scenery in a performance of Fux's *Angelica vincitrice di Alcina* at the summer palace Favorita in Vienna (complete with fleets of ships on the water), and the effect of a sudden shower of rain ('the ladies all sitting in the open air, exposes them to great inconveniences ... the opera was broken off, and the company crowded away ...'). Lady Mary Wortley Montagu commented that 'Nothing of that kind ever was more magnificent; and I can easily believe what I was told, that the decorations and habits cost the emperor thirty thousand pounds sterling'.[9] In all, a complete set of festivities for a special celebration, involving hundreds of performers and thousands of spectators and lasting days or even weeks, might cost some 50–70,000 florins (Gulden).

As *Hofkapellmeister* (1715–40) Fux earned a yearly salary of 3100 florins; as vice-*Hofkapellmeister* (1711–15) he had earned 1600 florins, and this was the amount paid to Caldara as vice-*Hofkapellmeister* under Fux. A 1729 list of the imperial musicians has, besides Fux as *Kapellmeister* and Caldara as vice-*Kapellmeister*, various administrators, court composers, organists, a cembalist, theorbists, violinists, a viol player, cellists, trombonists, cornettists, oboists, bassoonists, horn players, trumpeters and drummers. In general, numbers increased over the Baroque period (with some reduction during the Thirty Years War and in the 1740s under Maria Theresa). In Fux's time the orchestral forces at the Vienna Hofkapelle numbered in all some 50 players, excluding the court trumpeters and drummers. The colourful scoring of Fux's church music in the grand concertato style, and the virtuosic solo instrumental parts, reflect the variety and quality of the ensemble at his disposal. In his 'Latest Reports' of the imperial court (*Allerneueste Nachrichten vom Röm. Kais. Hofe*, Hanover, 1732), J. B. Küchelbecker stressed the emperor's generosity and suggested that the excellent conditions of service led to his Imperial Majesty's having 'the best virtuosi in all the world' ('die vortrefflichsten Virtuosen in aller Welt').[10] While the regular court reports in the press give an impression of the public pomp and ceremony attached to the membership of the Imperial Hofkapelle, the court archives afford a more personal insight into the lives of these musicians. Understandably, money matters figure prominently. In 1656 it was recorded that the *Hofkapellmeister* Antonio Bertali, after a total of 25 years' service 'with great diligence and effort' ('mit grossen vleiss, und mühe') wished to draw attention to his relatively low salary, and in particular would like to be able 'to help his son graduate'.[11] There are frequent references to journeys of the Hofkapelle to other courts for ceremonial visits and performances. Again there are human glimpses beneath the official protocol: also in 1656 the vice-*Kapellmeister* Sances requested gracious permission to be excused from a projected journey to Prague, on account of his wife's illness, as he could not leave her with their nine young children.[12] Extra payments might be made to the musicians for performances outside Vienna. In addition to the basic salary there were many such opportunities to earn occasional payments. Court musicians might hold several related posts concurrently; in the early decades of the 18th century when Fux was vice-*Hofkapellmeister* he was also *Domkapellmeister* at St Stephan's, and directed the Kapelle of Joseph I's widow, Wilhelmine Amalia. Apart from salaries, miscellaneous expenses connected with the Hofkapelle included payments for teaching (as well as teaching within the Hofkapelle, court musicians taught members of the ruling family), purchase of instruments, clothing (naturally most often for the choristers), wedding presents, pensions paid to musicians and their families: the total expended on the Hofkapelle was, as Küchelbecker remarked, substantial in the extreme.

One important item of expenditure was the recruitment of musicians for the Hofkapelle, often effected by agents and contacts in Italy. (This was the general practice at the Austrian and South German courts. After his return to Italy in the early 1660s, Maccioni was active in recommending Italian singers and composers for the Munich court.) Naturally the singers appearing at these courts were predominantly Italians (including both castratos and female sopranos), among them such famous names as Faustina Bordoni and Farinelli, at Munich and Vienna. In the earlier Baroque period an interesting reflection of the change from Netherlands domination to Italian leadership in music comes in the records of personnel at the Austrian and South German courts. By the late Baroque the courts were overrun with Italian musicians. At Vienna the two most powerful posts of *Hofkapellmeister* and vice-*Hofkapellmeister* were regularly occupied by Italians during the period 1660–1740: Sances, Draghi, Pancotti, Ziani and Caldara. In this period the only non-Italians to hold these posts were J. H. Schmelzer and Fux. Native talent flourished particularly in the sphere of keyboard music where, with a few distinguished exceptions, Italians after the mid 17th century contributed comparatively little. While Italians took over so many of the court posts, Austrians and Germans remained the most prominent in the lists of court and church organists. Georg Muffat at Salzburg, Kerll at Munich and Vienna, Ebner, Froberger, Murschhauser (organist of Unsere Liebe Frau, Munich), Gottlieb Muffat (Vienna) and Pachelbel (organist at the Stephansdom, Vienna, in the 1670s) made significant contributions to an Austro-German keyboard tradition founded on a strong sense of heritage and on fruitful teacher–pupil relationships. In Bohemia, town organists' posts were often passed down through several generations of one family, and many leading Bohemian musicians in the 18th century came from local organists' families (including Franz and Georg Benda, Černohorský, Johann Stamitz, Franz Tůma and Johann Dismas Zelenka). Traditionally the Bohemian *Kantoren* (the title was applied to schoolmasters, but its musical implications were not accidental) were entrusted with musical duties in church, and applicants for schoolmasters' posts were expected to be well qualified in singing and organ-playing; surviving documents show that musical ability together with the obligatory fidelity to Catholic beliefs was placed before general pedagogical considerations.

On the one hand there are extant records of aristocratic patronage confirming the impression that a significant amount of Italian musical culture was imported into Austria, southern Germany and Bohemia. In the early 18th century Count Franz Anton Sporck employed an Italian opera troupe, led by Denzio, to perform Venetian operas at the theatre in his Prague residence and at his country seat. Through Denzio's connections with Vivaldi, several Vivaldi operas appeared in the Prague repertory. (Comments such as 'Estata molto applaudita' were entered by Count J. J. von Wrtba (*d* 1734) in the librettos of some operas by Vivaldi that were performed at Sporck's theatre.)[13] On the other hand musical education bound up with the church, and popular music-making, relatively immune to sophisticated foreign influences, continued to be embedded in Bohemian life. One interesting aspect of this concerns the Jewish musical community in Prague. Their oppressed state, and their concentration in the ghetto area, ensured the continuity of a traditional and individual style of performance. In the mid 17th century there was a Jewish guild of some 20 string- and wind-players. At a festive procession in the ghetto to mark Archduke Leopold's birthday in 1716 some 40 or 50 instrumentalists accompanied the singers. Other town music guilds complained that the Jewish musicians lowered the standing of the art; but these guilds were generally uneasy about possible rivals ranging from court *Kapellisten* to Jesuit students (the students might be willing to play at feasts and balls for less money than the official guilds). In Prague, in addition to imported musicians and musical events, there were local traditions featuring music for special occasions. To commemorate St John of Nepomuk there was an annual procession in boats up the river Vltava, with water-music to accompany the traditional pilgrimage to the saint's statue at the Charles Bridge. Local composers such as František Brixi and his brother Šimon contributed to the music written for this ceremony. The combination of music, spectacle and ceremonial was as endemic in folk religious culture as it was in court society. At Salzburg music featured in a rich communal cult of theatrical folk processions and pageants associated with secular and sacred feast days. The archbishops themselves took an interest, and indeed appeared personally, in such processions: it may have been thought wise to draw them in to some extent under the archbishop's control. (One aspect of music not directly centred on the courts was the production of instruments: Austria, Bohemia and Bavaria were richly endowed with instrument makers, again often working in a family tradition.)

In a variety of ways, both fruitful and detrimental, court, peasant and 'bürgerlich' cultures impinged on one another. There were significant attempts to absorb folk culture into the artistic recreations of the aristocracy. A favourite entertainment at the imperial court in Vienna was the *Wirtschaft*, in which the emperor and empress dressed up as a country innkeeper and his wife, offering hospitality to their guests. A 'peasant wedding' (*Bauern-Hochzeit*) of this kind for Shrove Tuesday in February 1731 featured, besides 'Host: his majesty the Emperor' and 'Hostess: her majesty the Empress' (*Wirt* and *Wirtin*), a colourful collection of village characters (including a village Jew and Jewess, bride and bridegroom and their parents), and peasant couples in different national costumes (Spanish, English, French, Italian, Bohemian, Austrian, Swabian, Tyrolean and Moravian), these roles all being taken by members of the nobility. This event could almost serve as an allegory of Viennese court music, where folk elements – especially in instrumental dance-suites such as those of Schmelzer and Fux – jostled with the fashionable Italian and French styles. Often collected together under Latin titles, these works expressed the typical mélange of different cultures, learned and popular elements, which made up the Austro-German Baroque style.

Susan Wollenberg
University of Oxford

Notes

1 Quoted in R. Evans: *The Making of the Habsburg Monarchy* (Oxford, 1979), 13.
2 Quoted in R. Münster and H. Schmid, eds.: *Musik in Bayern* (Tutzing, 1972), 180.
3 Quoted in H. Bolongaro-Crevenna: *L'Arpa festante: die Münchner Oper 1651–1825* (Munich, 1963), 30.
4 Quoted in A. Kutscher: *Das Salzburger Barocktheater* (Vienna, Leipzig and Munich, 1924), 32.
5 Correspondence shows much evidence of his critical appreciation of performances, e.g. of operas, and of his musical enthusiasm (Z. Kalista, ed.: *Korespondence císaře Leopolda I. s Humprechtem Janem Černínem z Chudenic*, Prague, 1936).
6 See A. Liess: *Fux* (Vienna, 1948), 27.
7 See P. Nettl: 'Zur Geschichte der kaiserlichen Hofmusik-Kapelle von 1636 bis 1680', *Studien zur Musikwissenschaft*, xvi (1929), 71.

8 Quoted in Münster and Schmid, op. cit., p. 162

9 See Lady Mary Wortley Montagu: *Letters*, ed. Lord Wharncliffe, rev. W. Moy Thomas, 2 vols. (London, 1893), i.238.

10 Quoted in A. Liess: *Fuxiana* (Vienna, 1958), 24.

11 See H. Knaus: 'Die Musiker im Archivbestand des kaiserlichen Obersthofmeisteramtes 1637–1705', Österreichische Akademie der Wissenschaften, *Sitzungsberichte*, no. 254 (Vienna, 1967), 52

12 See Nettl, op. cit., *Studien zur Musikwissenschaft*, xviii (1931), 28.

13 See T. Volek and M. Skalická: 'Vivaldis Beziehungen zu den böhmischen Ländern', *Acta musicologica*, xxxix (1967), 72.

I am grateful to the late Denis Arnold, and to Robert Evans and F. W. Sternfeld, for their advice on various points in this essay.

S.W.

Biographical Dictionary
Central Europe
1 South Germany

Amalia Catharina, Countess of Erbach (1640–97). Pietist poet and composer; the daughter of the Count of Waldeck and, from 1664, the wife of Count Georg Ludwig of Erbach. The countess published the collection *Andächtige Sing-Lust* (1692); it contained devotional poems for domestic use, some of which she provided with melodies and figured bass.

Baudrexel, Philipp Jakob. See NORTHERN EUROPE *5 West Germany and the Rhineland.*

Beer, Johann. See NORTHERN EUROPE *4 Saxony and Thuringia.*

Bernacchi, Antonio Maria. See ITALY *10 Itinerant Musicians.*

Böddecker, Philipp Friedrich (1607–3). Organist, bassoonist and composer who held a number of posts in South Germany before settling in 1652 at Stuttgart as organist of the collegiate church there. Böddecker, who was from a large family of musicians, held posts as an instrumentalist at the Darmstadt and Durlach (nr Karlsruhe) courts. He moved to Frankfurt am Main in 1638 as organist of the Barfüsserkirche, then to Strasbourg in 1642 as cathedral organist, where, in 1650, he published his *Melos irenicum* (a richly scored setting of the *Te Deum*). He also composed eight sácred concertos for soprano and continuo (*Sacra partitura*, n.d.), considered to be some of the earliest idiomatic violin sonatas, and a bassoon sonata (a passacaglia 'sopra la monica').

Brescianello, Giuseppe Antonio (*c*1690–1758). Venetian violinist and composer who became *Kapellmeister* of the Württemberg court at Stuttgart. Brescianello was originally recruited northwards in 1715 by the Elector of Bavaria, who had recently returned to Munich from exile, but within the year Brescianello succeeded J. C. Pez as *Kapellmeister* and *maître des concerts de la chambre* at the court at Stuttgart.

His ambitions as an opera composer were thwarted by lost opportunity; *La Tisbe*, 1717–18, his pastoral opera dedicated to Archduke Eberhard Ludwig, failed to be produced by the Stuttgart Opera, and for two years (1719–21) Reinhard Keiser vainly attempted to unseat Brescianello from his court post. In 1731 Brescianello was promoted to *Rath und Oberkapellmeister*, only to be dismissed in 1737 when the court was declared insolvent. To earn money he published *12 concerti e sinphonie* [*sic*], the following year in Amsterdam. But in 1744, with the regency of Duke Carl Eugen, Brescianello was reappointed *Oberkapellmeister*.

Capricornus, Samuel Friedrich (1628–65). Bohemian-born *Kapellmeister* of the Württemberg court at Stuttgart (from 1657), composer and teacher. From a family of Hungarian refugees, Capricornus was well educated in theology, languages and philosophy; he taught at Reutlingen and Pressburg, where from 1651 until 1657 he also served as municipal *Kapellmeister*. At Stuttgart he clashed with P. F. Böddecker (organist of the collegiate church), who had coveted the *Kapellmeister* post; Capricornus was further beleaguered by illness and a failed marriage. His music circulated widely in manuscript and prints, though most of his secular music (chamber music, ballets and operas) is lost. An admirer of Carissimi (to whom he sent copies of his music in 1653), Capricornus composed a variety of up-to-date sacred music, some of it with independent instrumental parts.

Erbach, Christian (1568/73–1635). Augsburg organist, widely respected teacher and composer in the service of Marcus Fugger during the 1590s. From 1602, when he succeeded his colleague Hans Leo Hassler as organist of St Moritz, his municipal posts included those of city organist and leader of the Stadtpfeifer. Between 1604 and 1606 he published three volumes of *Modi sacri tripertiti*. Erbach was appointed assistant organist at Augsburg Cathedral in 1614, becoming principal organist in 1625 (see Plate 10). Unusually, he counted both Protestants and Catholics among his pupils.

Finger, Gottfried. See BRITISH ISLES *1 London.*

Fischer, Johann. See NORTHERN EUROPE *7 Itinerant Musicians.*

Fischer, Johann Caspar Ferdinand (*c*1670–1746). *Hofkapellmeister* to Margrave Ludwig Wilhelm of Baden and composer who popularized French-style music at court. It is not known whether Fischer visited Paris (details of his life before 1692 are unknown), but it seems likely that he did. His first publications – *Le journal du printems* (1695) and *Les pièces de clavessin* (1696) – proclaim his francophilia. *Le journal du printems* contains orchestral suites (each with an overture, set of dances and concluding chaconne or *passecaille*) for two trumpets and five-part strings. Together with those of J. S. Kusser (1682) and Georg Muffat (1695, 1698), these suites rank as outstanding early examples of German essays in French genres. The harpsichord suites were reissued in 1698 as *Musicalisches Blumen-Büschlein* and in 1702 Fischer published 20 organ preludes and fugues for organ, entitled *Ariadne musica*.

With the death of the margrave in 1716 the court moved from Schlackenwerth to Rastatt where the 11-year regency preceding the accession of Margrave Ludwig Georg (1727) stimulated a new flowering of musical entertainment, such as the three-act Singspiel Fischer composed for the wedding of Ludwig Georg in 1721. Fischer's last publication was his *Musicalischer Parnassus* (1738), a collection of keyboard suites, each named after a muse.

Froberger, Johann Jacob. See CENTRAL EUROPE *3 Austro-Hungary: Vienna.*

Galli-Bibiena. See CENTRAL EUROPE *3 Austro-Hungary: Vienna.*

Greber, Jakob. See CENTRAL EUROPE *3 Austro-Hungary.*

Grua, Carlo (Alisio) Pietro (*c*1700–1773). *Kapellmeister* and composer at the Mannheim court from 1734 until his death, probably the son of the Florentine composer Carlo Luigi Pietro Grua. In 1742 his *Meride* (text by Pasquini) inaugurated the new court opera; his *La clemenza di Tito* celebrated the elector's wife's birthday in 1748. During the 1740s he produced five oratorios, but with the arrival of Ignaz Holzbauer in 1753, Grua turned his energies exclusively to sacred music.

Hochbrucker. Instrument makers and harpists, of whom Jakob (*b c*1673) is credited with having invented the pedal harp. The son of a violin maker in Augsburg, Jakob moved to Donauwörth where he also built lutes and violas. His son Simon (1699–*c*1750) was primarily a harpist, responsible for introducing his father's invention throughout Germany and abroad. He undertook tours with his harp, playing in Vienna (1729), Leipzig and Brussels (1739), North Germany (1750) and Paris where, in the late 18th century, harp playing flourished – largely because of Marie Antoinette's patronage and the energetic efforts of Madame de Genlis.

Horn, Johann Caspar. See NORTHERN EUROPE *4 Saxony and Thuringia: Leipzig.*

Keiser, Reinhard. See NORTHERN EUROPE *1 North Germany: Hamburg.*

Knüpfer, Sebastian. See NORTHERN EUROPE *4 Saxony and Thuringia: Leipzig.*

Kraft, Sebastian Johannes. See NORTHERN EUROPE *5 West Germany and the Rhineland.*

Kusser, Johann Sigismund. See NORTHERN EUROPE *7 Itinerant Musicians.*

Marini, Biagio. See ITALY *10 Itinerant Musicians.*

Molter, Johann Melchior (1696–1765). Versatile composer who travelled widely in Italy (1719–22, 1737–8) and held *Kapellmeister* posts in Karlsruhe (1722–33, 1742–65) and his native Eisenach (1734–41). Molter's career at the Baden-Durlach (Karlsruhe) court was interrupted by the War of Polish Succession and that at the Eisenach chapel ended with the death of his patron, Duke Wilhelm Heinrich. His trips to Italy, financed by his patrons, brought him into contact with Tomaso Albinoni, the Marcellos, Alessandro Scarlatti, Vivaldi, Leonardo Leo, Pergolesi, Sammartini and others; their influence is evident in his numerous concertos (for one solo instrument and orchestra) and wind chamber music (he wrote for unusual hybrid instruments such as the flauto cornetto and the flauto d'amore as well as for clarinet and harp). He also composed cantatas and oratorios, but no operas.

Muffat, Georg. See CENTRAL EUROPE *2 Salzburg.*

Muffat, Gottlieb. See CENTRAL EUROPE *3 Austro-Hungary: Vienna.*

Neri, Massimiliano. See ITALY *4 Venice.*

Nielsen, Hans. See NORTHERN EUROPE *2 Scandinavia.*

Pachelbel, Johann. See NORTHERN EUROPE *6 Middle Germany.*

Price, John (*d* 1641). Versatile English instrumentalist working on the Continent. Price served 20 years (1605–25) at the Württemberg court in Stuttgart, then at the Dresden court (1629–33) and the Danish court (1634) before settling in Vienna in 1637. Mersenne would appear to have heard him play on the three-hole flute; in 1611 he was handsomely paid for playing the cornett and viola bastarda. Schütz had little respect for him, though while at Dresden, he amazed many listeners with his simultaneous performances on the viol and English 'pfeifflin'.

Printz, Wolfgang Caspar. See NORTHERN EUROPE *4 Saxony and Thuringia.*

Silbermann. Family of organ builders and instrument makers, working to the highest standards, and based in Strasbourg and Freiberg. Andreas Silbermann (1678–1734) learnt his craft in Strasbourg and Alsace before going to Paris in 1704 to work with François Thierry; while there he became closely acquainted with the virtuoso organist Louis Marchand. The instruments he built after his return to Strasbourg were a synthesis of the best of the French and German schools. His son Johann Andreas (1712–83) followed him in the business, building 54 organs in Alsace, Lorraine, Baden and Switzerland; in addition he served in the Strasbourg Senate.

Gottfried Silbermann (1683–1753) was trained by his brother and managed the firm in Andreas's absence, but in 1711 he moved to Freiberg, where he built an organ for the cathedral (completed in 1714). Gottfried was also much sought after as a clavichord maker – C. P. E. Bach owned one for 50 years – although his innovative *cembal d'amour* never caught on. Until 1727 he built pantaleons for Hebenstreit; in the mid 1730s he began building grand pianos modelled on those of Cristofori; he took J. S. Bach's criticisms to heart and ultimately won his praise. Frederick the Great commissioned two of his pianos. Death came as he was working on the organ for the Catholic Hofkirche in Dresden, which his pupil Zacharias Hildebrandt completed.

Simpson, Thomas. See NORTHERN EUROPE *1 North Germany.*

Stainer, Jacob (?1617–83). Tyrolean violin maker who learnt the trade in Italy (albeit from a German maker); he was denounced as a suspected heretic in 1669. Stainer lived in Absam but travelled a great deal, visiting monasteries, churches and courts, selling and repairing instruments. When not suffering from manic depression, he built instruments rivalling those of Stradivari in varnish and tone

Strattner, Georg Christoph. See NORTHERN EUROPE *4 Saxony and Thuringia.*

Tecchler, David. See ITALY *7 Papal States: Rome.*

Techelmann, Franz Matthias. See CENTRAL EUROPE *3 Austro-Hungary: Vienna.*

Tůma, František Ignác Antonín. See CENTRAL EUROPE *3 Austro-Hungary: Vienna.*

Weiss. Family of lutenists, of whom Silvius Leopold achieved international fame (see NORTHERN EUROPE *5 West Germany and the Rhineland*). His father, Johann Jacob Weiss (*c*1662–1754), was the court lutenist at Düsseldorf and moved with the court first to Heidelberg in 1718 and then to Mannheim two

years later. Another son, Johann Sigismund (after 1690–1737), joined his father at the Palatine chapel and stayed on, becoming director of instrumental music in 1732 and *Konzertmeister* two years later. He composed chamber music and concertos.

Wilderer, Johann Hugo von. See NORTHERN EUROPE *5 West Germany and the Rhineland.*

Zindelin, Philipp (*c*1550–1622). Instrumentalist (cornett and organ), teacher and progressive composer who worked for most of his life in Augsburg under the patronage of the influential Fugger family. For a time, Zindelin was also in the service of Cardinal Andreas at Konstanz and had connections at the Munich and Innsbruck courts. He composed exclusively music for chapel and cathedral use. Though Latin in conception, some of his music makes use of chorales (a sign of the religious climate in Augsburg). His 1615 collection of *Magnificat* settings and antiphons with continuo is one of the earliest German publications in the *seconda prattica* style.

Munich

Albinoni, Tomaso Giovanni. See ITALY *4 Venice.*

Aliprandi, Bernardo (*c*1710–*c*1792). Milanese(?) cellist and composer working at the Bavarian court from at least 1731; his son of the same name (1747–1801) was also a court cellist. Aliprandi was appointed composer of chamber music in 1737, succeeding G. B. Ferrandini, and *Konzertmeister* in 1744. He composed at least two operas and a *Stabat mater* (1749) for soprano, alto and chamber orchestra as well as music for the Jesuit college in Munich. He retired to Frankfurt am Main in 1778.

Bernabei. Roman family of musicians working in Munich. Ercole Bernabei (1622–87) held two important posts in Rome as organist and *maestro di cappella*, succeeding Luigi Rossi at S Luigi dei Francesi (1653–65, 1667–72), and serving in the interim at S Giovanni in Laterano (1665–7), before following Orazio Benevoli at the Cappella Giulia in 1672. He was adept at composing in both the *stile antico* and the *stile moderno*; well known among his works in the latter are 15 three-voice pieces entitled *Concerto madrigalesco* (1669). In 1674, he was appointed *Kapellmeister* to Prince Ferdinand Maria of Bavaria; Agostino Steffani accompanied him as his general *factotum* to Munich. In this post, Bernabei was required to compose operas, of which only two librettos survive.

His elder son, Giuseppe Antonio (?1649–1732), was a priest; he was *maestro di cappella* at S Luigi dei Francesi and oratorio organist at S Marcello (just as his father had been) before joining Ercole in 1677 at Munich as his vice-*Kapellmeister*, and succeeding him as *Kapellmeister* ten years later. Although Pietro Torri was the official court opera composer, Giuseppe Antonio composed operas, sinfonias, serenades and sacred music for the Bavarian court. His younger brother Vincenzo (1660–1732/6) was a gifted keyboard player, for a time very active in Roman opera circles, but irresponsible about money. In order to keep an eye on him, his father arranged an organ post at Munich from 1684.

Bernacchi, Antonio Maria. See ITALY *10 Itinerant Musicians*.

Bernardi, Stefano. See ITALY *10 Itinerant Musicians*.

Bordoni, Faustina. See ITALY *10 Itinerant Musicians*.

Brescianello, Giuseppe Antonio. See CENTRAL EUROPE *1 South Germany*.

Dall'Abaco. Italian string players and composers, father and son, working in Germany and the Netherlands. Evaristo Felice (1675–1742) was a Veronese composer–cellist and violinist in the service of Maximilian II Emanuel of Bavaria, whom Dall'Abaco accompanied to exile in the Low Countries and France before returning to Munich in 1715 as *Konzertmeister* (and, two years later, an elector councillor). While in the Netherlands, he married, and his son, Joseph-Marie-Clément, was born. Predictably, the later sonatas and concertos (especially from op. 4 onwards) of Evaristo Felice betray his exposure to French music during his northern sojourn. Although he published only six collections they give every sign of being carefully compiled. Back in Munich, he held 'academies' in his home.

Joseph-Marie Clément Dall'Abaco (*c*1710–1805) studied in Venice before taking up a post as chamber music cellist (*Hofmusikus mit dem Violoncell*) of the electoral chapel at Bonn. In 1740 he was in London and 1749 in Vienna, where his music for five cellos was performed. In 1766 he was made a baron at the Munich court.

Durastanti, Margherita. See ITALY *10 Itinerant Musicians*.

Ferrandini, Giovanni Battista (*c*1710–1791). Venetian oboist and composer, who spent most of his life at the Munich court.

Trained at the Conservatorio dei Mendicanti by Antonio Biffi, Ferrandini first served at the court of Duke Ferdinand in 1722, then that of the elector in 1723, though only in 1737 was he appointed director of chamber music. Ferrandini composed cantatas and trio sonatas as well as operas. Among his pupils he counted the Elector Maximilian III Joseph and his sister, Maria Antonia Walpurgis. In 1753 his opera *Catone in Utica* (text by Metastasio) inaugurated the Cuvilliéstheater. Owing to ill health he spent some time in Padua, where he continued to compose for the Bavarian court; the Mozarts visited him there in 1771. He returned to Munich shortly before his death.

Foggia, Francesco. See ITALY *7 Papal States: Rome*.

Hasse, Johann Adolf. See NORTHERN EUROPE *4 Saxony and Thuringia: Dresden*.

Henricus, Nikolaus (*c*1575–1654). Munich court printer who printed the posthumous collection of the works of Orlande de Lassus, compiled by his sons, in 1604. Henricus learned his trade from the court printer Adam Berg, whose daughter he married in 1597 and whom he succeeded on his death. Like Berg, he had to become a citizen of Munich and to convert to Catholicism before gaining ducal permission to found a printing firm of his own.

Kerll, Johann Kaspar. See CENTRAL EUROPE *3 Austro-Hungary: Vienna*.

Kühnel, August. See NORTHERN EUROPE *7 Itinerant Musicians*.

Lassus. Descendants of Orlande de Lassus, working at the Bavarian court chapel. Ferdinand de Lassus (*c*1560–1609), a court singer and composer from 1584, was appointed *Kapellmeister* at Munich in 1602; his son of the same name (1592–1630) studied in Rome before also becoming *Kapellmeister* at Munich (1616–29). The elder Ferdinand's brother Rudolph (*c*1563–1625) was an organist and prolific composer in both the *prima prattica* and the *seconda prattica*; he joined the chapel in 1585 and served as court organist from 1589. Together, Ferdinand and Rudolph compiled an anthology of their father's music and published it as his *Magnum opus musicum* in 1604.

Maccioni, Giovanni Battista (*d c*1678). Italian harpist, composer, librettist and chaplain (possibly from Orvieto). He worked at the Munich court (1651–61) and then at the papal court, as a special envoy charged with the recruitment of castratos. At Munich, Maccioni was a favourite of the new electress, Henriette Adelaide of Savoy, whom he taught to play the harp. She commissioned a number of musical dramatic works for which he composed the librettos and sometimes the music. His appropriately titled *L'arpa festante* (1653) was the first Italian operatic work (an extended scene with five soloists, recitatives, arias, duets and a finale) to be performed at the Munich court. Maccioni may have provided J. K. Kerll with the libretto for the tournament music, *Applausi festivi* (1658).

Mauro. See ITALY *4 Venice*.

Maximilian II Emanuel (*d* 1726). Elector of Bavaria who served as Governor of the Spanish Netherlands (1692–9, returning there in exile, 1704–6). His prowess as a bass viol player and taste for French music greatly benefited from his contact with the French court, whose king deemed it mutually beneficial to subsidize the elector's final years of exile in France at Compiègne (1709–15).

Even in exile, Maximilian II Emanuel maintained a large staff of Italian musicians, including Pietro Torri, P. A. Fiocco and E. F. Dall'Abaco as well as Germans such as J. C. Pez and R. I. Mayr. He also employed French musicians such as J.-J.-B. Anet, Hilaire Verloge and Jeanne-Françoise Dandrieu (a singer and sister to Jean-François Dandrieu); Antoine Forqueray tutored him on the viol, Marin Marais composed trios (lost) for his court and Elisabeth-Claude Jacquet de la Guerre dedicated her third book of cantatas (n.d.) to him. While Governor of the Spanish Netherlands Maximilian II Emanuel was able to enjoy performances of Lully operas (under Fiocco's direction).

His idyll was disturbed by the War of the Spanish Succession: having sided with France, his forces were defeated by the English at Höchstädt in 1704, which in turn led to his temporary exile in the south Netherlands and France. However, in 1715 he returned with his musicians (who now included Jacques Loeillet) to Munich, where they enlivened the court wth lavish theatre productions.

Mayr, Rupert Ignaz (1646–1712). *Kapellmeister*, violinist who studied with Lully (*c*1683–5), and composer. His sacred music was more influenced by Carissimi and J. K. Kerll than by Lully. Mayr held posts at Freising, Eichstätt, Regensburg and Passau during the 1670s and early 1680s, before accepting a permanent appointment at the Munich court of Elector Maximilian II Emanuel in 1683; when the musical life at court was suspended owing to the War of the Spanish Succession, Mayr returned to the prince-bishopric of Freising as *Kapellmeister*.

Murschhauser, Franz Xaver (1663–1738). Music director at Unsere Liebe Frau, Munich, organist–composer and theorist. Murschhauser, a pupil of Siegmund Auer and J. K. Kerll, published two volumes of organ fantasies and fugues (1696, 1703–7) based on plainsong melodies, and a backward-looking treatise (*Academia musico-poetica bipartita*, 1721), brutally satirized in the first volume of Johann Mattheson's *Critica musica* (1722).

Neri, Massimiliano. See ITALY *4 Venice*.

Pez, Johann Christoph (1664–1716). *Kapellmeister*, singer, instrumentalist and composer who worked at the court in his native Munich, as well as at those of Bonn and Stuttgart. Pez came from a family of musicians associated with the Petrikirche, the Munich parish church known for its thriving music school. A tenor, and viol and lute player, he attended the Jesuit school (where only plainsong and *a cappella* singing were allowed), and was eventually appointed choirmaster (1687). Soon after his appointment to a chamber music post at the electoral court, Pez was sent to Rome to study. His music was always to be greatly influenced by the five years he spent there (his italianate works include cantatas and occasional theatre music), though he was also much indebted to J. K. Kerll.

He returned to Munich in 1692, but left for Bonn almost immediately, since Elector Maximilian II Emanuel was in residence in Brussels. At Bonn he was initially charged with improving the Kapelle of the Archbishop-Elector of Cologne, and was then confirmed as *Kapellmeister* in 1696. He returned to Munich in 1701 and was appointed *Kapellmeister* of the Württemberg court at Stuttgart. Pez published instrumental collections in London and Amsterdam as well as Augsburg (where he also issued his sacred music).

Porro, Giovanni Giacomo (*c*1590–1656). Italian organist and composer, working as *Kapellmeister* in Munich from about 1633. Porro served as organist to the Duke of Savoy in Turin (from 1681) before taking up a post in Rome as *maestro di cappella* of S Lorenzo in Damaso in 1723. However, his career as an organist was not yet behind him: from 1626 he was a deputy organist at S Pietro and, four years later, took over Frescobaldi's duties while the latter was in Florence.

In 1633 he sought work at the electoral court in Munich but was not rewarded with a post until two years later, when he was appointed vice-*Kapellmeister* – and *Kapellmeister* soon after – to Elector Maximilian I.

Porro composed sacred music, including 187 psalms and 208 antiphons, as well as around 200 madrigals. From 1651, with the accession of Elector Ferdinand Maria, Porro was encouraged to produce Italian opera in Munich. He was succeeded by J. K. Kerll.

Porta, Giovanni. See ITALY *4 Venice.*

Sandoni, Pietro Giuseppe. See ITALY *7 Papal States: Bologna-Ferrara.*

Steffani, Agostino. See NORTHERN EUROPE *1 North Germany.*

Torri, Pietro (*c*1650–1737). North Italian organist, *Kapellmeister* and composer working at the Bavarian court in Munich and the Spanish Netherlands. Torri's first appointment was as *Kapellmeister* to the Margrave of Bayreuth in 1672, but after 12 years' service he left to travel in Italy. Five years later (1689) he was appointed organist at the Bavarian court of Maximilian II Emanuel, though he also composed secular music: in 1690 his serenata *Gli oracoli di Pallade e di Nemesi* was performed before Emperor Leopold I and further serenatas and operas followed.

In 1692 he accompanied the elector (as *maître de chapelle*) to the Spanish Netherlands, interrupting his stay there to deputize as *Kapellmeister* at the Hanover court in 1696. During this period he composed operas, oratorios and instrumental chamber music, all of which were equally indebted to French and Italian traditions. When he returned to Munich in 1701 he was obliged to accept the lesser post of director of chamber music (as Ercole Bernabei was already the Munich court *Kapellmeister*). However, when the elector was exiled to Brussels in 1704, Torri accompanied him and took on additional duties as *maître de chapelle* at Ste Gudule. Two years later the English laid siege to Brussels, and the elector fled to French territory (Mons and Namur) with Torri and the other court musicians in tow. Despite the fact that P. A. Fiocco succeeded Torri as *maître de chapelle* at this time (1706), Torri remained in the elector's retinue and returned to Munich as *Hofkapell-Director* in 1715. In that capacity he composed occasional cantatas and operas (at the rate of one per year) for the Hoftheater. On the death of Bernabei in 1732, Torri was at last appointed *Hofkapellmeister.*

2 Salzburg

Bernardi, Stefano. See ITALY *10 Itinerant Musicians.*

Biber, Heinrich Ignaz Franz von (1644–1704). Bohemian-born *Kapellmeister* at the Salzburg court (from 1670/1), composer and violin virtuoso – the finest practitioner of the art of scordatura – whose only peer in all of Europe was J. J. Walther. Biber worked at Kroměříž (central Moravia) during the 1660s, at the court of the prince-bishop (an ardent music-lover and amateur violin, viola and bass player) Count Liechtenstein-Kastelkorn of Olomouc, in whose library most of the extant Biber autographs are preserved. He must have known that the count would not wish to release him from service, because in 1670 he departed without making formal petitions; this breach was forgiven and the Kroměříž court continued to be the regular recipient of new music from Biber.

By the end of 1670 Biber had arrived in Salzburg where he immediately gained an appointment in the archbishop's Kapelle. There he remained for the rest of his life, composing operas (only *Chi la dura la vince*, 1687, survives) and school dramas, *a cappella* Masses, large-scale concerted works (the anonymous 53-part *Missa salisburgensis* of 1682 has been attributed to either Biber or Hofer), as well as instrumental music for the court. His only colleague of comparable stature was the court organist, Georg Muffat. In spite of his fabulous, polyphonic violin technique, Biber apparently never toured and was known only through his published editions of solo and ensemble music which began to appear about 1676. An excellent choir trainer, he was duly appointed vice-*Kapellmeister* in 1679 and *Kapellmeister* five years later. Having earlier come to the attention of Leopold I, Biber was ennobled in 1690.

The remarkable scordatura Mystery (Rosary) Sonatas for violin and continuo published that year were composed as postludes for the special October services devoted to the Rosary Mysteries, at Salzburg Cathedral. The occasional nature of the music was underscored by the inclusion in the edition of engraved depictions of the 15 mysteries plus another of a guardian angel with a child (preceding a single, unaccompanied passacaglia). A collection of ensemble music for strings and trumpets also appeared in 1676, which he followed with two further collections of string music for one or two violins, two violas and bass (1680, 1683).

That as a soloist Biber was not exclusively wedded to the scordatura idiom is reflected in the violin *Sonatae* he published in Nuremberg in 1681 (which include sets of virtuoso variations ascending to 6th and 7th positions), only two of which employ this technique. But it was a measure of the popularity of his richly polyphonic music that, eight years after his death, a collection of previously unpublished scordatura trio sonatas (*Harmonia artificiosa-ariosa*) was issued.

Biechteler von Greiffenthal, Matthias Sigismund (*c*1670–*c*1744). *Kapellmeister* to the Prince-Archbishop of Salzburg (1690–1712) and prolific composer of concerted sacred music. Biechteler was educated at the Jesuit University at Graz and served as a singing teacher to the cathedral choristers at Salzburg, before taking up the post of *Kapellmeister*. He was ennobled for his services in 1724.

Bonamico, Pietro. See below.

Guetfreund, Peter (*c*1570–1625). *Kapellmeister* to the Prince-Archbishop of Salzburg, known by the italianization of his name (Pietro Bonamico); alto singer and composer of sacred music. Guetfreund was attached to the Baden-Württemberg court chapel under Ferdinand de Lassus (from 1588), before taking up a post under Johann Stadlmayr at Salzburg. In 1608 he succeeded Stadlmayr as *Kapellmeister*, though he was briefly displaced by Francesco Turco in 1613, during the transition from one prince-archbishop to the next.

Hofer, Andreas (1629–84). *Kapellmeister*, both at Salzburg Cathedral (from 1666) and to the Prince-Archbishop of Salzburg (from 1679), organist and composer of large-scale works which very likely include the 53-part *Missa salisburgensis* (1682) once ascribed to Orazio Benevoli and still sometimes attributed to Biber. Hofer was educated at Salzburg's Benedictine university and held a post as organist at a Styrian monastery in the early 1650s. In 1654 he returned to Salzburg and was appointed vice-*Kapellmeister* to the prince-archbishop.

Muffat, Georg (1653–1704). Savoyard organist working in South Germany, composer of instrumental music and important writer on performance practice. Much of what is known of Muffat's early life – his travels to Paris (1663–9), Bavaria (1674), Vienna (where he failed to secure a post), Prague (1677), Rome (1680–2) and Augsburg (1690), and his posts as organist and chamber musician to the Arch-

bishop of Salzburg under Biber (1678–90) and *Kapellmeister* at the court of the Bishop of Passau – is contained in the autobiographical preface to his *Florilegium primum*. He was the father of the Habsburg imperial court organist Gottlieb Muffat.

Inspired by his contact with Lully and Corelli (and Bernardo Pasquini, with whom he had actually studied), Muffat set about popularizing French and Italian genres and styles in Germany. Soon after returning from Italy to Salzburg in 1682, he published his *Armonico tributo*, a collection of Corellian concerti grossi for five-part strings, at least some of which (he claimed) were performed in concerts at Corelli's Roman townhouse. His *Apparatus musico-organisticus* (1690), which he presented to Leopold I in Augsburg, contains 12 extended organ toccatas in which French and Italian styles and idioms are interwoven.

His first published collection of suites entirely in the French style – the *Florilegium primum* – appeared in 1695, and was supplemented by the *Florilegium secundum* in 1698. While not the first to be published in Germany (J. S. Kusser – another Lully protégé – had already published French overtures in 1682), these are among the finest German examples in the French style. The preface to the second set is particularly valued for its description of how to perform ballets *à la françoise* and the unique illustrated treatise on French bowing and ornamentation. A further, unpublished treatise on continuo practices (*Regulae concentuum partiturae*, *c*1699) contains many examples of fully figured basses and their realizations. With the exception of one autograph manuscript of a violin sonata composed in Prague (1677), Muffat's music is preserved exclusively in these printed editions.

Rasi, Francesco. See ITALY *3 Mantua*.

Stadlmayr, Johann. See CENTRAL EUROPE *3 Austro-Hungary*.

3 Austro-Hungary

Albrici, Vincenzo. See ITALY *10 Itinerant Musicians*.

Arnold Georg. See NORTHERN EUROPE *6 Middle Germany*.

Benda, Franz. See NORTHERN EUROPE *1 North Germany: Berlin*.

Biber, Heinrich Ignaz Franz von. See CENTRAL EUROPE 2 *Salzburg.*

Bonporti, Francesco Antonio. See ITALY 7 *Papal States: Rome.*

Capricornus, Samuel Friedrich. See CENTRAL EUROPE 1 *South Germany.*

Carestini, Giovanni. See ITALY 10 *Itinerant Musicians.*

Cernohorský, Bohuslav Matěj. See ITALY 4 *Venice.*

Cesti, Antonio. See ITALY 10 *Itinerant Musicians.*

Corbetta, Francesco. See ITALY 10 *Itinerant Musicians.*

Esterházy, Pál (1635–1713). Hungarian statesman, soldier, virginalist, composer, poet and patron. Esterházy held an appointment to Leopold I from 1661, was made Hungarian Palatine in 1681 and in 1687 became a prince of the Holy Roman Empire. He maintained singers and instrumentalists at his palace at Eisenstadt (1674), compiled a collection of dances (*Palas Ester kedves táncza*, 1656), in which he gave details of musical instruments in use in Hungary, and composed 55 sacred cantatas (*Harmonia Caelestis*, 1711), incorporating German and Hungarian melodies as well as purely instrumental sections.

Finger, Gottfried. See BRITISH ISLES 1 *London.*

Foggia, Francesco. See ITALY 7 *Papal States: Rome.*

Funck, David. See NORTHERN EUROPE 7 *Itinerant Musicians.*

Galli-Bibiena, Giovanni Maria. See CENTRAL EUROPE 3 *Austro-Hungary: Vienna.*

Greber, Jakob (*d* 1731). Austrian *Kapellmeister* and composer who spent the early years of the 18th century as a theatre composer in London. Greber composed the instrumental music for Nicholas Rowe's 1703 play, *The Fair Penitent*, performed at Lincoln's Inn Fields Theatre, and became acquainted with the popular singer Margherita de L'Epine (thereafter known as 'Greber's Peg') in the course of the run. Though a failure, his pastorale *Gli amori d'Ergasto* (1705) had the distinction of being the first Italian opera to be performed at the new Queen's Theatre.

By 1707 Greber was *Kapellmeister* at Innsbruck to the Tyrolean governor, Duke Carl Philipp. In 1711 *Gli amori d'Ergasto* was refurbished for a performance in Vienna with a prologue honouring the empress. In 1717 the duke became Elector Palatine, moving with his musical entourage first to Neuburg, then Heidelberg and finally to Mannheim. In 1723 Greber was required to share the post of

Kapellmeister with J. H. von Wilderer (who nevertheless died the following year). Greber worked closely with Augustin Stricker, Wilderer and Gottfried Finger (whom he had known at the beginning of his stay in London) on opera productions.

Grillo, Giovanni Battista. See ITALY 4 *Venice.*

Habermann, Franz (1706–83). Bohemian music master and composer who travelled widely and worked in France and Italy as well as in Prague. After studies in Prague with F. J. Dollhopf, Habermann served as *maître de musique* to Prince Louis-Henri de Condé (1731) and later to the Duke of Tuscany in Florence. He returned to Bohemia during the early 1740s, becoming choirmaster of two Prague monasteries and, for the last decade of his life, *Kantor* at Cheb. Among his compositions were Masses in the late Baroque concerto style, a highly successful *opéra comique* (lost) for the coronation of Empress Maria Theresa as Queen of Bohemia in 1743, and several Easter oratorios.

Janovka, Tomáš Baltazar (1669–1741). Bohemian organist at the Týn Church in Prague for 50 years, and author of one of the first Baroque music dictionaries: *Clavis ad thesaurum magnae artis musicae* (1701). In it, he defined 170 multilingual terms relating primarily to church and organ music, illustrating them with musical examples.

Kuhnau, Johann. See NORTHERN EUROPE 4 *Saxony and Thuringia: Leipzig.*

Lilius, Wincenty. See NORTHERN EUROPE 3 *Poland.*

Michna, Adam Václav (*c*1600–1676). Bohemian organist, composer and vintner. Michna – the son of the bailiff of Jindřichův Hradec castle who was also the town organist and leader of the castle trumpets – received his education from the Jesuits and composed many of his works for them. He succeeded his father as town organist in 1633. He owned property and a licensed wine vault. Michna published two hymnals for simple congregational singing and *Sacra et litaniae* (1654), a collection of more ambitious Latin concertato music.

Mingotti. See ITALY 10 *Itinerant Musicians.*

Motz, Georg. See NORTHERN EUROPE 4 *Saxony and Thuringia.*

Opitz, Martin. See NORTHERN EUROPE 7 *Itinerant Musicians.*

Pfleger, Augustin. See NORTHERN EUROPE 1 *North Germany.*

Priuli, Giovanni. See ITALY 4 *Venice.*

Sbarra, Francesco. See ITALY 6 *Tuscany.*

Selma y Salaverde, Bartolomé de. See IBERIAN PENINSULA AND COLONIES *1 Spain*.

Sporck, Count Franz Anton (1662–1738). Viceroy of Bohemia (from 1691) and patron of the arts. When Count Sporck visited the French court about 1680, he had two of his musicians trained to play the French cor de chasse. Back in Bohemia, they passed on their skills; and their instruments were soon copied by Nuremberg brass instrument makers. Sporck published an influential Czech song-book in 1719 on his own printing press and founded a monastery at Kuks which he endowed with a substantial collection of music. In 1724 he imported a Venetian opera troupe to perform with his orchestra (under the direction of his *Kapellmeister* Tobias Seemann) in the palace theatres at Kuks and Prague.

Stadlmayr, Johann (*c*1575–1648). *Kapell-meister* to the Archbishop of Salzburg (1607), then to the Archdukes Maximilian II (1607–18) and Leopold V (from 1624, continuing under Leopold's widow after 1632) at Innsbruck, and prolific composer of con-servative sacred music. In the interim between archducal appointments (1618–24) he sup-ported his family as a government meat inspector; personal economic constraints later prevented Stadlmayr from accepting a knight-hood from Leopold V. His music was widely circulated in anthologies.

Steinbacher, Johann Michael (*fl* 1727–40). Graz organist and composer of the earliest Austrian harpsichord concertos. Eight harp-sichord partitas also survive.

Strattner, Georg Christoph. See NORTHERN EUROPE *1 North Germany*.

Tartini, Giuseppe. See ITALY *4 Venice*.

Tessarini, Carlo. See ITALY *10 Itinerant Musicians*.

Tranovský, Juraj (1592–1637). Bohemian Protestant poet and cleric, known as 'the Sla-vonic Luther', who compiled an important hymnal, *Cithara Sanctorum* (1636). Tranov-ský drew from Lutheran chorales (which he translated) and previously existing Czech hymns, in addition to his own melodies. He also published a collection of 150 four-part odes (*Odarum sacrarum, sive Hymnorum ... libri tres*, 1629).

Turini, Francesco. See ITALY *4 Venice*.

Valentini, Giovanni. See CENTRAL EUROPE *3 Austro-Hungary: Vienna*.

Vandini, Antonio. See ITALY *4 Venice*.

Vejvanovský, Pavel Josef (*d* 1693). Morav-ian *Kapellmeister*, trumpet player, composer and music copyist in the service of the Prince-Bishop of Olomouc, Karl Liechtenstein-Kastelkorn, at Kroměříž from 1664. Taking his cue from Schmelzer, Vejvanovský incor-porated idiomatic brass parts into both vocal and instrumental music; his *Missa clamantium* (1683) requires a *tromba breve* (*tromba piculi*), pitched a tone higher than a clarino trumpet. Biber, in particular, was influenced by his trumpet writing.

Veracini, Francesco Antonio. See ITALY *6 Tuscany*.

Weiss, Silvius Leopold. See NORTHERN EUROPE *7 Itinerant Musicians*.

Werner, Gregor Joseph (1693–1766). Aust-rian organist and composer who served as *Kapellmeister* at the Esterházy court at Eisen-stadt from 1728. An able administrator, Werner remained in this post for 33 years. When Franz Joseph Haydn succeeded him in 1761, Werner was relegated to the post of *Oberhofkapellmeister*; Haydn weathered his resentment and in 1804 even published a set of six introductions and fugues for string quartet which he took from Werner's oratorios. In addition to oratorios, Werner composed *a cap-pella* and concertato Masses, secular cantatas, trio sonatas and Christmas music.

Young, William (*d* 1662). English viol player and composer working in Innsbruck. Young was regarded by Jean Rousseau and others as one of the finest viol players of his day. In the service of Ferdinand Karl, he travelled to Italy and Austria, settling in Innsbruck. His fantasies and dances for the lyra viol belong to the English tradition of Locke; the sonatas for violins and viols show the influence of con-temporary Italian and German music. Indeed, in 1653 Young became the first Englishman to publish music called 'sonatas'. His son William (*fl* 1660–71) was a violinist at the English court of Charles II.

Ziani, Pietro Andrea. See ITALY *4 Venice*.

Zuccari, Carlo. See ITALY *10 Itinerant Musicians*.

Vienna

Alborea, Francesco ['Francischello'] (1691–1739). Highly regarded Neapolitan cellist who became a chamber virtuoso to Count Uhlen-feld in Vienna (1726). J. J. Quantz and Fran-cesco Geminiani heard him perform in Italy, accompanying the castratos Farinelli and Nic-olini (with Alessandro Scarlatti at the harp-sichord). Martin Berteau, founder of the French school of cello playing, is said to have given up the bass viol after hearing Francischello play the cello. After performing trios with him in Vienna, the violinist Franz Benda spoke enviously of the expressiveness of Francischello's playing. He was caricatured by Pier Leone Ghezzi (Codex Ottoboni) and painted by Martin von Meytens (1732).

Ariosti, Attilio. See ITALY *10 Itinerant Musicians.*

Astorga, Emanuele d'. See ITALY *9 Sicily.*

Badia, Carlo Agostino (1672–1738). Italian composer (possibly Roman) working at the Innsbruck and Viennese courts; he was the first of a series of distinguished Italian musicians – the others were Giovanni Bononcini, P. F. Tosi and Francesco Conti – to be engaged as the imperial court *Musik-Compositeur.* At Innsbruck from about 1691 Badia composed operas and *sepolcri,* and gained the attention of the Viennese Habsburgs. His next appointment was in 1693 to the emperor's step-sister Eleonora Maria (the widow of the King of Poland) and within a year he was ensconced at the imperial court, where he served three emperors over 44 years. Badia travelled back and forth to Rome, married a prima donna, Anna Maria Elisabetta Nonetti, and in 1697 produced the first court opera: *Bacco, vincitore dell'India* (which he dedicated to Eleonora Maria); this was followed by others, as well as oratorios and chamber cantatas (12 of the latter were published as *Tributi armonici,* dedicated to Leopold I, at Nuremberg, probably in 1699). Badia was ultimately overshadowed by J. J. Fux and Antonio Caldara, who enjoyed particular favour under Charles VI (r. 1711–40).

Benda, Franz. See NORTHERN EUROPE *1 North Germany: Berlin.*

Benevoli, Orazio. See ITALY *7 Papal States: Rome.*

Bernacchi, Antonio Maria. See ITALY *10 Itinerant Musicians.*

Bertali, Antonio (1605–69). Veronese *Kapellmeister* of the Habsburg court (1649), violinist and composer. After his training at Verona Cathedral, Bertali gained an appointment (1622) in the service of Archduke Karl Joseph (brother of Ferdinand II), then at the imperial court (1624). He contributed several important occasional pieces – a cantata, *Donna real,* for the marriage celebrations of the future Emperor Ferdinand III and the Spanish Infanta Maria (1631), a *Missa Ratisbonensis* for the Imperial Diet at Regensburg (1636) and a *Requiem pro Ferdinando II* (1637) – as well as operas, oratorios, a wide variety of liturgical music and instrumental

music. In 1649 he was appointed *Kapellmeister* (succeeding Giovanni Valentini) and, for the next 20 years, worked to establish regular performances of Italian opera.

Bononcini, Antonio Maria. See ITALY *5 Modena-Reggio.*

Bononcini, Giovanni. See ITALY *5 Modena-Reggio.*

Bordoni, Faustina. See ITALY *10 Itinerant Musicians.*

Burnacini. Family of stage designers and machinists. Giovanni Burnacini (*c*1605–55) is thought to have staged the operas of Monteverdi in Venice. It was there that he made his name as a machinist worthy of comparison with his better-known contemporary, Giacomo Torelli. In 1651 he and his brother Marc'Antonio were called to Vienna to design and supervise the opera and theatre productions at the imperial court of Ferdinand III. Giovanni's son, Ludovico (1636–1707), began as his father's assistant. Showing himself to be extraordinarily gifted, he surpassed even his father's achievements: under Emperor Leopold I, Ludovico served nearly 50 years, designing spectacular sets, truly ingenious machines and often alarming costumes for all manner of court ceremonies and entertainments, from *sepolcri* to comedies. Among those with whom he collaborated were Bertali, Cesti (*Il pomo d'oro;* see Plate 12), Antonio Draghi and the Zianis. He also designed the court theatre, constructed during 1666–8.

Caldara, Antonio (*c*1670–1736). Extraordinarily prolific Venetian composer of operas and oratorios who in 1716 became vice-*Kapellmeister* at the imperial court in Vienna under J. J. Fux. As a child, Caldara served as a choirboy under Giovanni Legrenzi at S Marco, where he was also taught composition and to play the viola da gamba, cello and keyboard; he published his first compositions – trios sonatas and solo cantatas – during the 1690s.

His appointment in 1699 as *maestro di cappella da chiesa e dal teatro* by Ferdinando Carlo, Duke of Mantua, proved fortuitous: the duke spent lavishly on opera productions at his court and Caldara was given a free rein to develop his skill as a composer of dramatic music (although little of his music for Mantua has survived). He was allowed to work in Venice, Florence, Genoa and Rome, and may have accompanied the duke to Paris in 1704. In 1708 he quit Mantua for Rome where his Lenten oratorio *Il martirio di S Caterina* was performed (quite probably in the presence or with the assistance of Alessandro Scarlatti,

C. F. Cesarini, Bernardo Pasquini, Corelli and even Handel) at the palace of Cardinal Otto-boni.

Hoping eventually for a court post at either Madrid or Vienna, Caldara immediately left for Barcelona – to the court of the Austrian Charles III – where his opera *Il più bel nome* (text by Pariati) had the distinction of becoming the first Italian opera to be performed in Spain. Meanwhile he kept his Italian options open: his *Sofonisba* (text by Silvani) was mounted later in 1708 at the Venetian Teatro S Giovanni Grisostomo.

He returned to Rome, became *maestro di cappella* to Marquis Ruspoli – a post coveted by the young Handel – and spent seven years in Ruspoli's service. Stimulated by the musicians at hand, Caldara composed a large quantity of solo cantatas and duets, four operas, three *intermezzi* and ten oratorios. He gradually modified his Venetian style with *galant* features, favouring smaller orchestras, textures emphasizing the soprano register, the use of dance rhythms and instrumentally conceived vocal coloratura parts.

With the unexpected death of Emperor Joseph I in 1711, Caldara deemed it prudent to renew his connections with Charles III – soon to become Emperor Charles VI – on his return from Spain via northern Italy. Caldara visited Vienna in 1712, but found M. A. Ziani and Fux firmly ensconced in the two highest musical posts. On his return journey he stopped in Salzburg, where he was well received. Ziani died in 1715 and was succeeded as *Kapellmeister* by Fux, leaving the second post of vice-*Kapellmeister* vacant. Caldara was the natural choice and, in 1716, he returned to Vienna, pausing again at the Salzburg court (where between 1716 and 1727 he sent one new opera annually).

As Fux's assistant, Caldara was largely freed from duties as a liturgical composer, and his fluent technique enabled him to take on lucrative freelance work. He was charged with composing operas, annually for the emperor's name-day and (after 1726) for Carnival, biennially for the empress's birthday. From 1718 he set all the new opera librettos by the court poet Apostolo Zeno and, from about 1725, all Zeno's new oratorios (*drammi sacri*). He modified his composing style again under the influence of Fux (and pressure from the emperor), incorporating more contrapuntal textures. But it was Fux who provided the opera *Costanza e Fortezza* to celebrate the coronation of the emperor as King of Bohemia in 1723, and Caldara who conducted the per-formances at Prague (see Plate 13). During the 1730s, after Pietro Metastasio had succeeded Zeno, Caldara set many of Metastasio's opera and oratorio librettos – in addition to the oratorios sent annually by Zeno from Venice (until 1737).

Carestini, Giovanni. See ITALY *10 Itinerant Musicians.*

Cesti, Antonio. See ITALY *10 Itinerant Musicians.*

Charles VI (1685–1740). Holy Roman Emperor (1711–40) and the last male in the Habsburg line, patron, keyboard player, conductor and composer. During the short reign of his brother, Joseph I (1705–11), he presided over a court in Barcelona and was known as Charles III, pretender to the Spanish throne. As Holy Roman Emperor, he perpetuated in Vienna the lavish, empty court life and deeply conservative – and ultimately repressive – Counter-Reformation spirit to which he had become accustomed in Spain. Charles VI worked tenaciously to ensure the ratification of the Pragmatic Sanction which secured his daughter Maria Theresa's right to succeed him as head of state.

In 1723 he was crowned King of Bohemia in Prague, where Fux's *Costanza e Fortezza* was performed as part of the celebrations. He had studied counterpoint with Fux and in 1725 arranged for the publication of the latter's *Gradus ad Parnassum*. He loved opera and even conducted performances of Caldara's *Euristeo* and Fux's *festa teatrale*, *Elisa*. None of his own music survives. He appointed first Zeno (1718) and then Metastasio (1729) to the post of court poet.

Conti, Francesco Bartolomeo (1681–1732). Florentine theorbist and innovative composer of secular and sacred dramatic music at the Viennese court. Conti arrived in Vienna in 1701 and quickly became a leading exponent of the theorbo. He succeeded J. J. Fux as court composer in 1713. The following year he married the court prima donna, Maria Landini (the highest-paid musician in Vienna), for whom he composed leading roles in his Carnival operas (1714–21); after being widowed, he married the new prima donna, Maria Anna Lorenzani, who took leading roles in his subsequent operas. Outside Vienna, Conti's operas and *intermezzi* were staged in Dresden, Breslau, Hamburg and Brunswick. In style they anticipate J. A. Hasse and Nicolò Jommelli, and display a preference for bass and baritone, and imaginative use of chorus.

Dall'Abaco, Joseph-Marie Clément. See CENTRAL EUROPE *1 South Germany: Munich.*

Dal Pane, Domenico. See ITALY *7 Papal States: Rome.*

Draghi, Antonio (1634/5–1700). Italian *Kapellmeister* at the Habsburg court (from 1682), bass singer, librettist and prolific composer of sacred and secular dramatic music. Draghi may have been the brother of G. B. Draghi. He took a role in P. A. Ziani's *Le fortune di Rodope e di Damira* at the Venetian Teatro S Apollinare in 1657 and was next heard of as a member of the Dowager Empress Eleonora's Kapelle in Vienna in 1658. During his first years in Vienna, Draghi produced librettos for more prominent composers such as Giuseppe Tricarico (1661), then began composing his own (from 1666).

In 1668 he was apointed the dowager's vice-*Kapellmeister*, only to be promoted the following year; during this period he composed steadily for the emperor's court (Leopold I himself provided individual arias and scenes) and, in 1682, succeeded Schmelzer as the emperor's *Kapellmeister*. Draghi was a prodigious composer, collaborating with Minato and Burnacini on 124 operas (characterized by virtuoso coloratura), 41 sacred dramatic works – oratorios and *sepolcri* – and innumerable occasional works; his son Carlo Domenico (1669–1711), an organist in the Hofkapelle, is known to have contributed arias to his father's secular works.

Ebner, Wolfgang (1612–65). Organist (1643) and later *Kapellmeister* (1663) at the Stephansdom, Vienna, and organist and ballet composer at the Habsburg court (1637). With Froberger, he founded the cosmopolitan 17th-century Viennese keyboard school whose exponents included Johann Kaspar Kerll, Johann Philipp Krieger, Georg Muffat, Johann Pachelbel and Alessandro Poglietti. Ebner composed 36 variations for harpsichord on a theme by Ferdinand III, which appeared in 1648 (not to be outdone, Froberger dedicated the first of two volumes of harpsichord suites to the emperor the following year).

Fabri, Annibale Pio. See ITALY *10 Itinerant Musicians.*

Farinelli. See ITALY *10 Itinerant Musicians.*

Ferdinand III (1608–57). Habsburg emperor, patron of music and composer of an allegorical *Drama musicum* and a *Miserere.* Ferdinand III, the son of Ferdinand II, was crowned Roman king in 1636 and Holy Roman Emperor the following year. He enjoyed Italian music and retained a succession of Italian *Kapellmeister* – Giovanni Valentini (who taught him composition), G. F. Sances and Antonio Bertali – in addition to such

distinguished German musicians as Froberger, J. K. Kerll and Wolfgang Ebner. He took a keen interest in the planning of court festivities and on occasion contributed music of his own.

Ferrari, Benedetto. See ITALY *4 Venice.*

Ferri, Baldassare. See NORTHERN EUROPE *3 Poland.*

Froberger, Johann Jacob (1616–67). International figure, harpsichordist, court organist and influential 17th-century keyboard composer who created a new German style by synthesizing contemporary Italian and French styles. The details of Froberger's life can only be approximated. About 1634 his musical talent came to the attention of the Swedish ambassador to Vienna, who took him there from his native Stuttgart. In Vienna he pursued musical studies and from 1637 was listed in the court records as an organist; about 1641, he was given leave to continue his studies in Rome with Frescobaldi, and returned to Vienna. Froberger presented Emperor Ferdinand III with two autograph volumes comprising a compendium of harpsichord music (1649, and before 1656).

From surviving letters it appears that he was again in Italy during the 1640s, during which time he was converted to Catholicism. He corresponded with Constantijn Huygens (who admired and popularized his music in the Netherlands), and visited Brussels in 1650. In Paris in 1652, he composed a *Tombeau fait à Paris sur la mort de Monsieur Blancheroche* for harpsichord. Before returning to Vienna in 1653 he also visited England (where he composed a *Plainte faite à Londres pour passer le Mélancholie*), having survived a pirate attack during the Channel crossing between Calais and Dover, and gained the friendship of Matthias Weckmann after competing against him in a harpsichord competition at Dresden. He officially served as the Habsburg court organist only five years (1653–8) before retiring to the Héricourt estate of Princess Sibylla of Württemberg-Montbéliard as her friend and tutor.

Froberger's travels to Italy and France enabled him to absorb and transform Italian and French styles and genres. His Italian works include conservative Frescobaldian toccatas, ricercares, canzonas, fantasias and capriccios for organ or harpsichord; his French works, the harpsichord suites (of which 30 survive) and character pieces inspired by those of Jacques Champion de Chambonnières and Louis Couperin and by the *style brisé* of Jacques Gallot and Denis

Gaultier. At the same time, he was able to infuse them with a recognizably Germanic intensity of expression – in particular, he developed the potential of the allemande in works such as the *tombeau* and *plainte* already cited and the laments he composed to honour Ferdinand III and Ferdinand IV.

Fux, Johann Joseph (1660–1741). Distinguished *Kapellmeister* at the Viennese court, organist, composer, much-loved teacher, theorist, and author of *Gradus ad Parnassum* (1725). Though Fux was of lowly origins, his abilities were brought to the attention of the emperor and rewarded with a place at the Ferdinandeum in Graz and later at the Jesuit universities there (1680) and at Ingolstadt (1681), where he paid his way by serving as a church organist. His movements during the decade from 1683 are unknown, but probably he travelled in Italy before entering the service of a Hungarian bishop resident in Vienna, where his Palestrina-inspired *a cappella* Masses became known and admired by Emperor Leopold I, who appointed him *Hofkomponist* in 1698.

Although Fux had seized upon the *stylus antiquus* as an ideal liturgical medium, he composed only a handful of his 80 or so Masses in this style; of these, the *Missa canonica* (or *Missa di San Carlo*) – which runs the gamut of canonic devices – is best known as a spiritual precursor of J. S. Bach's *Kunst der Fuge*. Most of his Masses composed for the imperial chapel and the Stephansdom are in the *stylus mixtus*, with instruments sometimes supporting the voices and sometimes independent of them. His 1713 *Missa Corporis Christi* not only contains an instrumental prelude and postlude, but periodically allocates the top part to the violins and clarino trumpets alone. Less well known today are his many solo motets and antiphons, whose recitatives, da capo arias and choruses convey profound emotions. Admired even beyond Vienna, these works were performed at monasteries and at the courts in Salzburg, Dresden and Prague.

In 1700 Fux took the opportunity to study with Pasquini in Rome and returned to Vienna eager to compose operas and oratorios. His 18 Italian operas and 10 extant oratorios from this period reflect the progressive influences he absorbed in Italy. His texts were most often those of Pietro Pariati (usually infused with royal panegyrics), although he also set single texts by Stampiglia, Zeno and Metastasio. His *festa teatrale*, *Elisa*, performed at the Hoftheater in 1719, was printed in Amsterdam in the same year. Between 1702 and 1728 Fux produced at least 15 *sepolcri*, characterized by contrapuntal textures, which were performed at Eastertime at the Hofburgkapelle. In fulfilment of his duties at the Stephansdom (vice-*Kapellmeister* from 1705 and *Kapellmeister* from 1712) and the imperial court (vice-*Kapellmeister* from 1713 and *Kapellmeister* from 1715), Fux also composed 3 requiems and a large-scale *Te Deum*.

He was also inclined towards instrumental music. Soon after returning to Vienna, he published in partbooks a collection of seven partitas, entitled *Concentus musico-instrumentalis* (1701), five of which juxtapose wind and strings, the remaining two being for strings and harpsichord. Fux gave some of the movements sobriquets and – within a trio texture for flute, oboe and bass – boldly superimposed a French 'aire françoise' in 4/4 on an 'aria italiana' in 6/8. Fux composed many more trios for liturgical use which remained in manuscript during his lifetime. He also left sonatas and suites for organ or harpsichord that contribute to the Viennese traditions linking Froberger with Gottlieb Muffat.

The climax of his career came in 1723 when his opera *Costanza e Fortezza* (see Plate 13) was performed at Prague by distinguished musicians from all over Germany, as part of the festivities celebrating the coronation of Emperor Charles VI as King of Bohemia (Fux was prevented from taking part because of gout and had to delegate the conducting to his assistant Caldara). However, the publication of his counterpoint treatise, *Gradus ad Parnassum*, in 1725, which Mizler later translated into German, proved the more enduring achievement. Its strengths lie not in innovation but in consolidation of the traditions of counterpoint Fux inherited from the previous two centuries. He was extremely well-read and could assimilate and abstract information from his sources, though admittedly old-fashioned in this respect and thus vulnerable to the attacks of the forward-looking Mattheson. *Gradus ad Parnassum* nevertheless served Haydn, Mozart and generations after them well enough. Fux's own pupils included Gottlieb Muffat, G. C. Wagenseil and J. D. Zelenka. Because of a quarrel with Johann Mattheson about solmization and keys, Fux fared badly in *Der vollkommene Capellmeister* (1739) and the *Grundlage einer Ehren-Pforte* (1740); Mattheson further prejudiced Fux's posthumous reputation with unflattering remarks in E. L. Gerber's late 18th-century lexicon.

Galli-Bibiena. Bolognese family of important and influential stage designers and theatre architects associated with *opera seria*. Ferdinando Galli-Bibiena (1656–1743), his brother Francesco (1659–1737) and his three sons created a new style of asymmetrical stage design which superseded that based on the principle of a central vanishing point. Beginning as an illusionist painter, Ferdinando worked in Italy before taking a post as an architect at the Barcelona court of Charles III in 1708. When in 1711 Charles III became Holy Roman Emperor (Charles VI), Ferdinando and his apprentice sons, Alessandro (1686–1748), Giovanni Maria (1694–1777) and Giuseppe (1695–1757), followed him to Vienna. In that same year, Ferdinando published *L'architettura civile*, in which he propounded his theories of angular perspective.

Ferdinando approached stage design from an austere, technical point of view, whereas his brother Francesco richly ornamented his angled perspectives. Francesco was much in demand throughout Italy, designing scenery for the operas of Francesco Gasparini, C. F. Pollarolo, Alessandro Scarlatti, Vivaldi, J. A. Hasse and Leonardo Leo as well as revivals of Lully's *Thésée* and *Amadis* for Lunéville in 1708–9. He designed court theatres at Bologna, Verona, Rome, Vienna and Nancy. Alessandro, working at the Innsbruck court from 1716, later at Mannheim, designed scenery at once complex and seemingly weightless; his designs for both the interim and permanent opera houses at Mannheim won plaudits. Giovanni Maria joined his brother at Mannheim about 1722 but moved permanently to Prague soon afterwards.

Giuseppe's extraordinary diagonal views made him the leading European stage designer: after succeeding his father in 1716, he remained in the service of the emperor until the latter's death in 1740. Among the sets he designed were those for Fux's *Costanza e Fortezza* (1723; see Plate 13). He then undertook a varied series of commissions in Italy and Germany before accepting an appointment in 1753 to the court of Frederick the Great. Giuseppe's son Carlo (1721–87) travelled extensively as an opera set designer, venturing as far as the courts of Gustavus II and Catherine the Great.

Galuppi, Baldassare. See ITALY *4 Venice*.

Grimani, Maria Margherita (*fl* early 18th century). Italian composer (apparently from a Venetian patrician family) active in Vienna at the beginning of the reign of Charles VI. Although the last of a series of female oratorio composers (who included Maria di Raschenau, Catherina Benedicta Grazianini and Camilla de Rossi) at the imperial court, Grimani was the first to have an opera produced: in honour of the emperor's saint's day (4 November) in 1713, Grimani's *Pallade e Marte* was performed at the Vienna court theatre, followed by performances of her oratorio, *La visitazione de Elisabetta*. Another oratorio, *La decollazione di S Giovanni Battista*, was performed in 1715. These surviving works reveal no evidence of the contemporary Viennese penchant for counterpoint and instead owe much to Alessandro Scarlatti.

Hasse, Johann Adolf. See NORTHERN EUROPE *4 Saxony and Thuringia: Dresden*.

Hebenstreit, Pantaleon. See NORTHERN EUROPE *4 Saxony and Thuringia: Dresden*.

Hurlebusch, Conrad Friedrich. See NORTHERN EUROPE *7 Itinerant Musicians*.

Joseph I (1678–1711). Habsburg Holy Roman Emperor (1705–11), eldest son of Leopold I and an amateur harpsichordist, singer and composer of airs. By nature worldly and less encumbered by Counter-Reformation zeal than his kinsmen, Joseph I was occupied, during his short reign, with the chess-like moves required in the War of the Spanish Succession against Louis XIV (for example, the installation and ostentatious maintenance in Barcelona of his brother and successor, Charles, as the Habsburg candidate) and with containing the Hungarian rebellion. His death from smallpox was a great blow to the cause of Austrian unity.

Kerll, Johann Kaspar (1627–93). Saxon *Kapellmeister* at the Bavarian court from 1656, distinguished keyboard player and composer of *a cappella* and concertante sacred and secular music. Kerll's talents as an organist and composer were recognized at an early age. His first post was as court organist to Archduke Leopold Wilhelm in Vienna. After studies with the *Kapellmeister*, Giovanni Valentini, Kerll was sent to Rome to study with Carissimi (and, very likely, Frescobaldi); he must have met Athanasius Kircher, because Kircher later included a four-part ricercata by Kerll in his *Musurgia universalis* (1650). When the archduke was made Viceroy of the Spanish Netherlands (1646–56) Kerll continued in his service at Brussels.

The post of vice-*Kapellmeister* and the imminent likelihood of being appointed *Kapellmeister* – the first German for many years – at the Bavarian court attracted him to Munich in 1656. In addition to *a cappella* works for the court chapel, Kerll composed operas: his first, *L'Oronte* (1657), was performed at the opening of the Munich opera house; ten more followed. As early as 1658 he gained the attention of Emperor Leopold I when he improvised at the coronation Mass performed at Frankfurt am Main; in 1664 he was ennobled by the emperor.

Kerll resigned his Munich post in 1673 to become organist at the Stephansdom, Vienna (until 1677), where he was assisted by his pupil Johann Pachelbel; and although he maintained his connections with the Bavarian court, he was appointed imperial court organist in 1677, commencing a very creative period as a court and chapel composer of concerted music. During the Turkish siege of Vienna he composed his *Missa in fletu solatium* (1683), and during the plague of 1679–82 the music that was later published in the *Modulatio organica super Magnificat* (1686).

Kircher, Athanasius. See ITALY *7 Papal States: Rome.*

Krieger, Johann Philipp. See NORTHERN EUROPE *4 Saxony and Thuringia.*

Lampugnani, Giovanni Battista. See ITALY *10 Itinerant Musicians.*

Leopardi, Venanzio. See ITALY *10 Itinerant Musicians.*

Leopold I (1640–1705). Habsburg Emperor, patron of music, instrumentalist (harpsichord, violin and flute) and composer. Leopold became head of the Austrian monarchy in 1657 and was crowned Holy Roman Emperor the following year, despite opposition from Cardinal Mazarin, who tried to secure the throne for Louis XIV of France. The second son of Ferdinand III, he married Margareta Teresa, the second daughter (the first having already become Queen of France) of Philip IV of Spain in 1667. Although he succeeded in gaining tighter control over Austria and Bohemia and regained Hungary from the Turks, Leopold I was unable to institute centralized absolutism to the extent Louis XIV had in France, but he did play a crucial part in the European coalitions opposing Louis XIV's territorial aggression on its western borders. His sons by his third wife, Eleonora Magdalena of the Palatinate, succeeded him as Joseph I and Charles VI.

Just as music flourished at the French court as never before or since, so too did it expand at the Viennese court during the reign of Leopold I. Prominent among the Italian musicians he employed were Antonio Bertali, G. F. Sances, Giuseppe Tricarico, Antonio Draghi, M. A. Ziani and Francesco Conti; his German musicians included J. H. Schmelzer,

J. K. Kerll, F. T. Richter and J. J. Fux. Leopold I was a more accomplished musician than his French cousin Louis XIV, and also a respectable composer, having studied with Bertali and Wolfgang Ebner. Always at pains to give the text due import, Leopold composed both sacred and secular dramatic works, though his polychoral liturgical works had the greatest effect; for the funeral of his second wife (of three years) in 1676 he composed three lessons (*Missa angeli custodis*). His instrumental compositions include a sonata for four violas and continuo. He was more sincerely religious than Louis XIV and in his zeal prolonged the Counter-Reformation in southern Germany.

He shared with Louis XIV a love of dramatic music – whether in or out of doors – and poured vast amounts of money into opera productions (staged by Burnacini), of which Cesti's *Il pomo d'oro* (1668) is most famous. More than 400 dramatic works – *drammi per musica, feste teatrali* and serenatas as well as operas – were performed (occasionally by members of the imperial family) during his reign. Between 1660 and 1667, the oratorio and *sepolcro* flourished under his patronage.

Liberati, Antimo. See ITALY *7 Papal States: Rome.*

Matteis, Nicola. See BRITISH ISLES *1 London.*

Metastasio, Pietro [Trapassi, Antonio Domenico Bonaventura] (1698–1782). Roman poet and opera and oratorio librettist who succeeded Zeno at the Habsburg court in 1729. Metastasio's ultimate place in history as the pre-eminent librettist of the 18th century was ensured by his adoptive father, Gian Vincenzo Gravina, a Roman jurist and classicist who was one of the founders of the Accademia dell'Arcadia, and his godfather, Cardinal Ottoboni; they encouraged Metastasio to study classics and law, and the independent income provided by Gravina later allowed him to pursue a career as a writer. He received the tonsure in 1714 and published his first collection of poetry in 1717. He was made a member of the Accademia dell'Arcadia in 1718 but soon after moved to Naples, where he became involved with a group of actors and musicians. Under their influence he studied singing and composition with N. A. Porpora, and in 1723 completed his first opera libretto, *Didone abbandonata*, which was set by D. N. Sarro and performed in Naples at the Teatro S Bartolomeo in 1724 (a year earlier, his revision of D. David's *La forza della virtù* as *Siface re di Numidia* had been set by Francesco Feo and performed there).

During the period 1724 to 1730 Metastasio travelled between Venice and Rome, where the settings of his texts by Leonardo Vinci, Porpora, Tomaso Albinoni, Leonardo Leo and J. A. Hasse were enthusiastically received. In 1727 he completed his first oratorio libretto, *Componimento sacro per la festività del Ss Natale*, which G. B. Costanzi set for Cardinal Ottoboni; it was performed at the Cancelleria (see Plate 3).

All of this ended abruptly when Metastasio was invited to succeed Zeno as Caesarean Poet of the Habsburg imperial court in 1729. He hastened to Vienna and for the next decade was very productive. His librettos lent themselves more easily to musical setting than did those of Zeno, and several composers at the Viennese court – Antonio Caldara, F. B. Conti, Georg von Reutter, Giuseppe Porsile and L. A. Predieri – were kept busy setting them. They were popular with singers, who found his texts mellifluous to sing and his characterizations stimulating to portray.

During the 1730s new settings of Metastasio's previously set opera and oratorio librettos were prepared by G. B. Lampugnani, Hasse, Handel, F. M. Veracini, Giovanni Porta, Baldassare Galuppi, Vivaldi, Leo, D. N. Sarro, Francesco Mancini and Pergolesi. *Alessandro nell'Indie* (1729) was his most frequently set opera text and *Betulia liberata* (1734) his most frequently set oratorio. The end of an era was signalled by the death of Caldara in 1736 and Charles VI in 1740; opera and oratorio were less in demand at the new court of Maria Theresa and so Metastasio was pressed to write works in more intimate genres for the empress's daughters to perform. The popularity of his librettos continued throughout the century despite their absolutist tone.

Metastasio wrote texts for 27 three-act heroic operas, a number of shorter secular dramatic works, and eight oratorios. More gifted as a poet, more musically attuned (he composed music for some of his shorter texts) and more involved in his collaborations than Zeno (who seems to have been an altogether more detached person), he was also less austere and more concerned with the underlying psychological drama. Reason overcoming dilemmas and averting tragedy, honour, steadfastness: these are themes running through all of his opera librettos. Only two of his operas end with the death of the hero or heroine: *Didone abbandonata* (1724) and *Catone in Utica* (1728).

Minato, Nicolò (*c*1630–1698). Poet, prodigious opera librettist, and impresario, working in Venice (1650–69) and Vienna. A lawyer in Venice, he gradually became involved in the theatre as a librettist–impresario (from 1665 he managed the Teatro S Salvatore), collaborating with Cavalli and Antonio Sartorio. But in 1669 he abruptly quit Venice – abandoning all his commitments – for Vienna, in order to take up the post of court poet to Leopold I. In due course he was elected to the prestigious Italian academy flourishing in Vienna.

During the next 29 years Minato produced more than 170 texts, blending comic and serious elements and incorporating elaborate secondary plots, for *drammi per musica, feste teatrali*, and serenatas, as well as about 40 oratorio texts for Antonio Draghi (performed with sets by Ludovico Burnacini). The emperor set his texts – which usually portrayed Vienna in terms of ancient Rome and Leopold I as the hero – as did G. F. Sances, G. B. Pederzuoli, F. A. M. Pistocchi, Giovanni Bononcini, M. A. Ziani, Giovanni Legrenzi, Tomaso Albinoni, J. A. Hasse and even Telemann. Two volumes of sacred texts were posthumously published in 1700.

Monn, Matthias Georg (1717–50). Organist and composer of instrumental music who, while living in the late Baroque era, was nevertheless the first in Vienna to compose in the pre-Classical style, producing the earliest known four-movement Classical symphony (including a minuet) in 1740. Using the trio sonata textures with which he was at home, Monn developed his melodies thematically within a separate section, and then recapitulated them in the tonic key. In addition to 21 known symphonies, seven harpsichord concertos, a technically ambitious cello concerto, six string quartets and eight partitas for two violins and cello, Monn composed keyboard sonatas in the French and Italian styles and at least 18 fugues. A contemporary of G. C. Wagenseil, he served as organist at the new Karlskirche in Vienna from 1738. His music was performed at the imperial court as well as at monasteries in Austria and Slovakia.

Moratelli, Sebastiano. See NORTHERN EUROPE 5 *West Germany and the Rhineland*.

Muffat, Gottlieb (1690–1770). Imperial court organist, son of Georg Muffat and protégé of J. J. Fux, and the leading Viennese keyboard composer of his day. Gottlieb was less outgoing and ambitious than his father, preferring to remain in Vienna all his life. From a young age he was much valued as a continuo player in the Hofkapelle and at the Hofburgtheater. He received his formal training as a *Hofscholar* under Fux and although he was awarded a grant to study abroad, no records attest to his having done so. As one of the court organists from 1717 Muffat had responsibility for the musical education of the royal children (who included Maria Theresa). In 1723 he was among the court musicians who travelled to Prague for the performances of Fux's *Costanza e Fortezza*. Six years later he was appointed second organist to Fux, and then succeeded his mentor upon his death in 1741.

Muffat appears to have composed exclusively keyboard music. Few works can be dated, and because they circulated widely in manuscript some of them were ascribed to other composers. He published two collections – *72 Versetl* [*sic*] *sammt 12 Toccaten* (1726) and *Componimenti musicali* (*c*1739) – but they represent only a small proportion of his output. The unpublished italianate ricercares (notated in open score), for example, constitute the largest single collection from the early 18th century, and his interest in, and application of, an archaic idiom parallels J. S. Bach's preoccupation with fugue. His 24 toccatas (notated in Italian organ tablature) reveal a virtuoso technique on the organ manuals. For his *galant* keyboard suites, Muffat took Couperin as his model, employing intricate ornamentation, titles for individual movements, longer second sections and *petites reprises*. After 1741 he apparently ceased to compose.

Pachelbel, Johann. See NORTHERN EUROPE 6 *Middle Germany*.

Palotta, Matteo (*c*1688–1758). Lay cleric and conservative composer from Palermo who served as an imperial court composer in Vienna (from 1733, with a hiatus, 1741–9) and wrote a manuscript treatise on liturgical composition and solmization (*Gregoriani*).

Pariati, Pietro. See ITALY 4 *Venice*.

Pederzuoli, Giovanni Battista (*d c*1692). Italian organist and composer of oratorios and *sepolcri*, who worked in Vienna in the service of the Dowager Empress Eleanora, as organist (1677) and *Kapellmeister* (1682) until her death in 1686. Pederzuoli briefly served as *maestro di cappella* at S Maria Maggiore, Bergamo, in 1664–5, before settling in Vienna. As a prolific composer of relatively conservative sacred dramatic music, he was second only to Antonio Draghi, whom he succeeded as the dowager's *Kapellmeister*. For the Italian Academy Pederzuoli composed the earliest examples of philosophical cantatas (1685), with librettos by Minato and four-part sinfonias.

Perroni, Giovanni (1688–1748). Italian cellist and composer from Novara who held posts at the Parma ducal court (1704–14) and Milan (as a member of the court orchestra and *maestro di cappella* at S Maria delle Grazie, 1718) before taking up an appointment as an imperial court cellist in Vienna (1721). His surviving music includes oratorios for Milan and Vienna, cantatas and a cello concerto. In 1726 he married Anna d'Ambreville, an Italian singer of French descent.

Pezold, Christian. See NORTHERN EUROPE 4 *Saxony and Thuringia: Dresden*.

Piani, Giovanni Antonio. See FRANCE 1 *Paris and Versailles*.

Pistocchi, Francesco Antonio Mamiliano. See ITALY 7 *Papal States: Bologna-Ferrara*.

Platti, Giovanni Benedetto. See NORTHERN EUROPE 6 *Middle Germany*.

Poglietti, Alessandro (*d* 1683). Italian organist highly esteemed by both Leopold I (who raised him to the Viennese aristocracy) and the pope (who invested him as a Knight of the Golden Spur), influential composer of programmatic keyboard music and the author of a treatise on keyboard playing and composition (*Compendium oder kurtzer Begriff*, 1676). By 1661 Poglietti was working in Vienna as the *Kapellmeister* and organist of the Jesuit Kirche zu den neun Chören der Engel; his abilities were recognized at court, and an appointment as chamber organist to the emperor soon followed. His keyboard ricercares became models of the strict contrapuntal style; his fluency in variation technique is embodied in his programmatic works such as the *Rossignolo* (1677) cycle. His only known opera, *Endimione festeggiante* (text by J. Dizent), was performed in 1677 at a Benedictine monastery at Göttweig (Lower Austria).

Porpora, Nicola Antonio. See ITALY 10 *Itinerant Musicians*.

Porsile, Giuseppe (1680–1750). Neapolitan singing teacher and composer working in the shadow of J. J. Fux and Antonio Caldara. He served Charles II and Charles III at the Barcelona court before taking up a post in 1714 at the imperial court in Vienna. The son of Carlo Porsile, Giuseppe gained his connections with Barcelona by serving as the assistant *maestro di cappella* at the Spanish chapel in Naples; in 1695 he was invited to Spain to organize the Barcelona court chapel. He remained in Barcelona until the end of 1713 (two years after Charles III had left to become Charles VI), although he may have been in Naples for the performances of his opera *Il ritorno di Ulisse* in 1707.

In Vienna he continued in his post as singing teacher to the new empress, while acquiring other posts, and in 1720 he was promoted to imperial court composer. In his operas and oratorios Porsile adapted his Neapolitan style to include fashionable Viennese musical affectations of the day: French overtures, contrapuntal textures and cello obbligatos (probably for Giovanni Perroni). He was briefly active in the Viennese Caecilien-Brüderschaft (1725–7).

Price, John. See CENTRAL EUROPE *1 South Germany*.

Reinhardt. Family of Habsburg court musicians. Kilian Reinhardt (1653/4–1729) served as royal librarian and music copyist from 1683, acquiring the official title of *Konzertmeister* in 1699. Two years before his death he recorded his observations on court chapel music practices in *Rubriche generali*. His nephew, Johann Georg (1676/7–1742), was an organist (appointed principal court organist in 1728) and widely known composer of sacred music and operas who helped to produce Fux's *Costanza e Fortezza* for the 1723 coronation; from 1727 until his death, he was *Domkapellmeister* at St Stephan's and, from 1734, the official court ballet composer. Kilian's son, Joseph Franz (1684/5–1727), and the latter's son of the same name (1713/14–1761), were violinists at the Stephansdom and the court. Joseph Franz the elder was also a respected teacher: his pupils included a half-brother, Karl Mathias (1710/11–1767), Johann Georg's successor as court organist (1739–62).

Reutter. Father and son, organists at the Stephansdom, court musicians and composers, both of whom were ennobled. Georg von Reutter (1656–1738) succeeded his teacher J. K. Kerll at the cathedral in 1686; after a trip to Italy, he entered the imperial court chapel where his skills as an accompanist – especially for operas – were much in demand. Both Antonio Draghi and J. J. Fux thought highly of him and Johann Mattheson included him in his *Grundlage einer Ehren-Pforte* (1740). He rose steadily in cathedral and court circles: in 1700 he became court organist and in 1712 succeeded Fux as vice-*Kapellmeister*; three years later he was appointed cathedral *Kapellmeister*. He wrote organ preludes and toccatas.

Of Georg the elder's 15 children, his namesake, Georg (1708–72), attained the greatest prominence, despite his differences with Fux. From the age of 14 he assumed his father's organ duties at court, though he only succeeded in acquiring a post of his own – that

of vice-*Kapellmeister* – after Fux's death in 1741. In 1751 he succeeded L. A. Predieri as *Kapellmeister*, but because of the restructuring of the Kapelle ordered by Empress Maria Theresa, court music declined under his direction. In the meantime, he had travelled in Italy (1729–30), married the court singer Theresa Holzhauser, energetically composed operas (38 by 1740) and oratorios modelled on those of his teacher Antonio Caldara, and succeeded his father as the cathedral *Kapellmeister* in 1736. Inevitably he must have been hard-pressed to provide sacred music for both institutions. He gained a reputation for busy – if technically undemanding – violin parts which contributed to the impression of 'much noise and little meaning' remarked upon by Charles Burney.

The younger Georg von Reutter was the only person ever to hold both *Kapellmeister* posts in Vienna. He prevented his cathedral chorister Haydn from gaining a post at court and survived an unsuccessful attempt during the 1760s to unseat and replace him at court with Gluck.

Richter, Ferdinand Tobias (1651–1711). Habsburg court organist, tutor to the royal children (including the future Joseph I and Charles VI), and composer of sacred dramatic works for the Jesuit College and keyboard suites. The son of Tobias Richter (*d* 1682), *Kapellmeister* at the electoral court at Mainz, Ferdinand Tobias Richter gained his first appointment at the imperial court in 1683; from 1690 he was principal organist of the Kapelle. Pachelbel pronounced Richter the most important contemporary exponent of the South German organ school, and Buxtehude of the North, in his *Hexachordum Apollinis* (1699).

Sances, Giovanni Felice (*c*1600–1679). Roman *Kapellmeister*, singer, teacher and composer. Sances was one of the earliest to designate through-composed and strophic pieces as 'cantatas'. He studied at the Roman Collegio Germanico (1609–14) and worked at S Petronio, Bologna, and at Venice. In 1636, following the performances of his first opera, *Ermiona* (in which he sang the role of Cadmus), at Padua, Sances headed for Vienna. His first post at the imperial court was as a chapel singer to Emperor Ferdinand III. In 1649 he was promoted to vice-*Kapellmeister* under Antonio Bertali, with whom he worked to establish regular performances of Italian opera. He composed further operas, secular vocal chamber music for one to three voices and violins, a variety of liturgical music (including 54 Masses) and *sepolcri*. At Bertali's death in 1669, Sances was appointed *Kapellmeister*; his health failed in 1673 and his duties were assumed by his vice-*Kapellmeister*, J. H. Schmelzer.

Sandoni, Pietro Giuseppe. See ITALY *7 Papal States: Bologna-Ferrara*.

Sbarra, Francesco. See ITALY *6 Tuscany*.

Schmelzer, Johann Heinrich (*c*1620/3–1680). The first Austrian-born *Kapellmeister* at the Habsburg court, violinist and composer of instrumental music, who made important contributions to the development of the German sonata and suite. Schmelzer entered the court chapel about 1635, but was not officially appointed to the court orchestra until 1649; meanwhile, from 1643, he also served as a cornettist at the Stephansdom. He became a favourite of Leopold I, attended his coronation at Frankfurt am Main in 1658, advised the monarch on his own compositions and was the recipient of *ex gratia* gifts and money. After serving as vice-*Kapellmeister* from 1671, he finally succeeded G. F. Sances in 1679, shortly before his own death from plague.

Schmelzer gained a reputation as a violinist (J. J. Müller referred to him in his *Reise-Diarium* as 'the famous and nearly most distinguished violinist in all Europe'); he was also a noted composer of secular dramatic works, chamber music, and – together with Wolfgang Ebner, his own son Andreas Anton (1653–1701) and J. J. Hoffer – of ballet suites for allegorical pageants (in which members of the royal family took part). His suites varied between two and nine movements and were framed by an *intrada* and a *retirada*. In addition to the usual dances, Schmelzer included *trezze, folie*, saltarellos, traccanarios and programmatically titled pieces. He also incorporated folk elements and unified suites with recurring melodies and closely related tonalities. He augmented his four- and five-part string textures with brass and wind instruments. His best-known music is contained in the collections of chamber music he published in Nuremberg: the *Duodena selectarum sonatarum* (1659) for two violins or violin and viol with continuo, his varied *Sacroprofanus concentus musicus* (1662) and, above all, his virtuoso *Sonatae unarum fidium* (1664) for violin and continuo.

Spiridio. See NORTHERN EUROPE *7 Itinerant Musicians*.

Stampiglia, Silvio. See ITALY *7 Papal States: Rome*.

Strungk, Nicolaus Adam. See NORTHERN EUROPE *7 Itinerant Musicians*.

Techelmann, Franz Matthias (*c*1649–1714). Moravian organist and composer, working in Vienna. Techelmann served as second organist at the Viennese Hofkapelle between 1685 and 1713. Two sets of manuscript keyboard pieces survive.

Tesi, Vittoria. See ITALY *10 Itinerant Musicians*.

Torelli, Giuseppe. See ITALY *7 Papal States: Bologna-Ferrara*.

Tosi, Pier Francesco. See ITALY *10 Itinerant Musicians*.

Tricarico, Giuseppe. See ITALY *7 Papal States: Rome*.

Tůma, František Ignác Antonín (1704–74). Bohemian singer, instrumentalist (viol and theorbo) and composer working in Vienna. Tůma appears to have studied at the Jesuit seminary in Prague, under Černohorský, before settling in Vienna as a church musician; he served as *Kapellmeister* to Count Franz Ferdinand Kinsky, High Chancellor of Bohemia (1731–41), and finally to the dowager empress (1741–50). After her death Tůma remained in Vienna until 1768 when he retired to a monastery. He composed *a cappella* Masses, partitas, trio and quartet sonatas, and sinfonias.

Valentini, Giovanni (1582/3–1649). Venetian *Kapellmeister* of the Habsburg imperial court, keyboard virtuoso and an early composer–poet of *sepolcri*. After a decade's service (1604–14) as organist in the Italian *cappella* of King Sigismund III of Poland, Valentini became a servant of the Habsburg family. Through connections at the Polish court he went to Graz in 1614 as a chamber organist, composer of secular music – continuo madrigals and ensemble sonatas which helped to popularize the Italian style of violin playing in South Germany – and music tutor to Archduke Ferdinand; when, five years later, Ferdinand was elected Holy Roman Emperor, Valentini was appointed imperial organist (1619), becoming *Kapellmeister* in 1622.

Valentini composed Venetian-style sacred concertos, concerted Masses and *Magnificat* settings as well as Counter-Reformation psalms and motets (in *stile antico*), and presided over the beginnings of the Viennese *sepolcro* and oratorio. The relative austerity imposed by the Thirty Years War meant that little of this music was published. His *sepolcro* librettos survive without music.

Wagenseil, Georg Christoph (1715–77). Keyboard virtuoso, teacher and composer. A protégé of J. J. Fux, Wagenseil benefited from a three-year court scholarship which enabled him to acquire his remarkable keyboard technique and skill as a composer. However, his career may not have lived up to the early glowing predictions. Despite his gifts of improvisation and expression at the keyboard, he never gained a key post at the Habsburg court, and instead had to content himself with appointments as simply one of the court composers, producing both *a cappella* and concerted Masses (from 1739). He also served as organist to the dowager empress (1741–50) under Tůma and as *Hofklaviermeister* to the imperial archduchesses (1749), to whom he dedicated four collections of divertimentos (1753–63).

Perhaps Wagenseil's most remarkable achievement was to produce operas for Italy: his first opera, *Ariodante* (text by Salvi), was performed in Venice in 1745 and *Demetrio* (text by Metastasio) in Florence the following year; some of his theatre music was also performed at the Viennese court. In the 1750s he acquired a privilege to publish instrumental music in Paris, which, along with connections he made with music sellers in London and Leipzig, brought his music to a wider, largely amateur audience. His solo keyboard music encompasses both late Baroque and early Classical forms. Like Georg Monn, Wagenseil composed keyboard concertos, a cello concerto (1752) and symphonies – though less forward-looking and cast in three, rather than four, movements.

Weiss, Silvius Leopold. See NORTHERN EUROPE 7 *Itinerant Musicians.*

Zacher, Johann Michael (1651–1712). *Domkapellmeister* of St Stephan's (from 1679) and court musician who was appointed *Kapellmeister* to the dowager empress on the death of Leopold I in 1705. Members of the imperial court patronized and took part in dramatic works Zacher composed for the Jesuit College, where he had been a student (1666–8). During his tenure at the Stephansdom he organized the musical portions of the thanksgiving service for the ending of the plague in 1680 and the celebrations following the victory over the Turkish invaders three years later; he was succeeded there by J. J. Fux.

Zangius, Nikolaus. See NORTHERN EUROPE 7 *Itinerant Musicians.*

Zelenka, Jan Dismas. See NORTHERN EUROPE 4 *Saxony and Thuringia: Dresden.*

Zeno, Apostolo (1668–1750). Caesarean poet and historian of the Viennese imperial court, opera and oratorio librettist who sought to make the libretto a respectable literary form –

more rational (by conforming to the three unities), serious in tone and differently balanced with regard to recitative and aria. The son of a Venetian patrician, Zeno was educated at the Somaschian seminary where he studied the history of Italian and Latin literature. Following his studies, he was active in Venice as a scholar, helped to found the Accademia degli Animosi in 1691 (which in 1698 became associated with the famous Accademia dell'Arcadia in Rome) and founded and became the first editor of the *Giornale de' letterati d'Italia* in 1710.

It may have come as a surprise to his contemporaries when he produced his first opera libretto: in 1695, C. F. Pollarolo's setting of his *Lucio Vero* was performed before admiring audiences at the Teatro S Angelo, Venice. Despite grave reservations about the effect this activity would have on his scholarly integrity, Zeno went on to work with Francesco Gasparini, F. A. Pistocchi, M. A. Ziani, Tomaso Albinoni and G. A. V. Aldrovandini, before embarking on a long and fruitful collaboration with the poet Pietro Pariati in 1705 (Zeno supplied the operatic scenarios and Pariati the verses).

In 1714 Zeno was called to the Habsburg court by Charles VI, for whom he had provided two librettos during his residence in Barcelona as Charles III the Pretender; *Atenaide* (1709) and *Scipione nelle Spagne* (*c*1710) were collaboratively set by A. S. Fiorè, Antonio Caldara and Gasparini. Zeno accepted the prestigious post of *Poeta e istorico di S. M. Cesarea* at Vienna only on the condition that he would not be required to write occasional poetry or comedy, although he continued to write opera librettos, principally for the vice-*Kapellmeister*, Caldara (two were set by Francesco Conti, who was also at the Viennese court), after 1718.

A deeply religious man, Zeno took distinctly more pride in the 17 oratorio librettos he produced between 1719 and 1737. Again, Caldara was his most frequent collaborator, although he also worked with Giuseppe Porsile, Conti, J. A. Hasse and Giovanni Bononcini. As with the opera librettos, Zeno chafed at the compromises that were required to conform to the oratorio genre – works he referred to as *drammi sacri*. His conception of a serious, rational libretto, capable of being performed equally successfully without music, greatly influenced his successors, notably Pietro Metastasio. Both opera and oratorio librettos were printed at the time of their first performances, but in 1744 Gasparo Gozzi published a complete edition of Zeno's sacred and secular librettos without the cooperation of the poet. Having taken only one leave of absence to Venice (1722–3), Zeno retired there in 1729 to pursue his antiquarian interests, though on condition that he continue to produce one oratorio a year for Vienna.

Ziani, Marc'Antonio. See ITALY *4 Venice.*

Ziani, Pietro Andrea. See ITALY *4 Venice.*

Zuccari, Carlo. See ITALY *10 Itinerant Musicians.*

The British Isles

Private and Public Music

Posterity has been unkind to the music of Stuart and Georgian England. The German musicologists of the last century who devised the concept of 'Baroque music' saw the period in terms of a clear line of development from the Italy of Monteverdi to the Germany of J. S. Bach. English music was either ignored altogether, or was seen as a weak and backward tradition that was rightly dominated by the German genius of Handel. Unfortunately, it is a view that is still with us today, and it has been reinforced by English cultural historians with more of an interest in literature or the visual arts than music.

Part of the problem is that if the word 'baroque' is to retain any of its architectural connotations of rhetoric, *chiaroscuro* and irregular ornament, then the English Baroque only began – if at all – towards the end of the 17th century, when English musicians, like English architects, began to be interested seriously in developments abroad. Before then, certainly up to the Civil War, English music was still essentially late Renaissance in character. At the other end of the period, composers in England were still writing concerti grossi in the Corelli tradition during the 1770s and 1780s, long after the supposed end of the Baroque period, and long after J. C. Bach and C. F. Abel had popularized the Classical symphony in London.

Another aspect of the problem concerns the enormous contribution made to English musical life by immigrants, especially from the 1690s onwards, when England quite suddenly became a world power and London became Europe's leading commercial centre. If we see English music only in terms of her native composers, then they will appear to be dominated by what an Oxford critic of Handel's *Athalia* called 'a great number of foreign fiddlers'. But if we set chauvinism aside and study the music of these immigrants as well, then a different picture emerges. The English musical style, concerned with melody and harmonic colour more than structure, exerted a powerful influence on even the most individual foreign composers, as Handel's *L'Allegro* or J. C. Bach's Vauxhall songs show. Furthermore, they came to London not because the competition there was weak, but because England's musical institutions afforded them more opportunities than anywhere else. Far from being a *Land ohne Musik*, mid-18th-century England probably had the richest musical life of any European country at the time.

England in 1600 was one of the most centralized countries in Europe. Most of her wealth and perhaps a fifth of her population of just over four million was concentrated in the home counties. London, with a population of over 200,000, was more than ten times the size of her nearest rivals, Norwich and Bristol; an extraordinarily large proportion of the nation's commercial, intellectual and artistic life was to be found in her noisy and crowded streets. Above all, London was the seat of England's highly centralized form of government, organized around the person of the monarch.

Musical life was correspondingly centralized at the beginning of the 17th century.

Great Britain and Ireland (showing places mentioned in the text)

With the exception of Thomas Weelkes at Chichester and John Wilbye at Hengrave in Suffolk, all of England's most important composers before the Civil War lived in or around London or were connected with the court in some way. The Reformation had caused the decline of the traditional centres of provincial music, the cathedrals and collegiate foundations; many of their most talented musicians, like Thomas Tallis, were subsequently attracted to a court that was increasing in size and splendour during the 16th century. A century later, with the court itself in decline, London's theatres, concert halls and parish churches became the main centres of employment. Apart from a brief period during the Civil War when court musicians left London in large numbers to seek work, it was not until the end of the Baroque era that musical life outside London began to revive, aided by the increasing prosperity of provincial towns and by the amateur musical societies that flourished in them.

In the Renaissance, the court was not a particular building but an institution: it was a mobile society of courtiers, administrators and domestic servants that accompanied the sovereign on an annual circuit of royal palaces and great country houses. During the three legal terms, the main working part of the year, the court stayed close to the City – at Whitehall or one of the other palaces along the Thames from Greenwich to Richmond. In the summer it ventured further afield, often on a leisurely progress around one of the more distant parts of the kingdom, though its musicians were often allowed to remain behind.

Music was provided for the court by a number of separate groups or consorts working in the section of the royal household known as the Chamber, under the jurisdiction of the Lord Chamberlain. The largest and oldest of them was the Chapel Royal, the royal choir. Administered by the Dean of the Chapel (often a bishop) and an elected sub-Dean, the Chapel Royal consisted of 12 children and 32 singing men or 'gentlemen', from whose ranks were taken the Master of the Children and two or three organists. The first duty of the Chapel was to provide the sovereign with daily choral services, though in the 16th century it also provided secular entertainment in the form of choirboy plays. Little is known about its secular activities in the 17th century, but it must have provided the voices for the birthday and New Year odes that were a feature of Restoration court life, and its members probably contributed a good deal to informal music-making.

The Chapel maintained its position as the leading choir in England, partly because the Master of the Children had the right to recruit boys from cathedrals and chapels throughout the country – by force if necessary; many institutions were also compelled to pay the salaries of their best musicians (Thomas Tomkins of Worcester, for instance) while they were away for long periods at court. However, these enforced absences did at least keep provincial choirs abreast of the latest developments, and help to explain why their repertory in the 17th century was so dependent on the work of Chapel Royal composers.

The verse anthem, first developed in Elizabethan times from the consort songs of choirboy plays, was the characteristic product of the Chapel throughout the Baroque period; its intricate interplay between solo voices, choir and viols (or possibly cornetts and sackbuts) was particularly suitable for the almost domestic acoustics of the chapels at Whitehall and the other royal palaces. From the court, the verse anthem repertory spread to cathedrals (where the organ normally replaced the viols) and private chapels. At the Restoration, the Chapel Royal was revived under the energetic leadership of Captain Henry Cooke, who trained a precociously gifted group of boys that included Pelham Humfrey, Michael Wise, John Blow, William Turner, Henry Hall and Henry Purcell. First as boys and then as men, they developed a new type of verse anthem that borrowed elements of the French orchestral style and Italian vocal music, replacing the viols with a violin band and organ continuo.

Although the Chapel Royal declined sharply after the accession of William and Mary, its role in English church music was not replaced by provincial choirs; in general they were at a low ebb throughout the 18th century. Instead, the best talent was beginning to be attracted to a new source of employment. The Great Fire of 1666 and the steady expansion of London in the decades that followed resulted in the construction of a great number of splendid new churches, designed by Sir Christopher Wren and his associates, and each equipped with an organ. Since many of the existing London churches were also beginning to be equipped with new or improved organs at this time (often provided by the builder or a parishioner in return for an annuity), the result was that a new profession – that of the London church organist – came into being. Many distinguished 18th-century musicians, including Maurice Greene, J. C. Pepusch, William Boyce, John Stanley and Charles Burney, found it convenient to combine such a post with their other activities.

The rest of the musicians in royal service were instrumentalists, organized into a number of separate consorts with different roles in the daily round of court ceremonial. In 1600 there were five of them: a band of trumpets and drums, three consorts of wind instruments and a violin band. The 16 trumpets need not detain us long: like similar groups at other courts, they adorned state occasions with improvised fanfares and played no part in the literate musical culture until the 1670s. The three wind consorts were a mixed group of eight shawms and trombones, a consort of six flutes and a consort of six recorders. In the 1630s they were combined into a single group of 15 men, and moves were made to change over to the more modern and flexible combination of cornetts and sackbuts. Their main duty was to accompany the daily ritual of the sovereign's dinner, though they also took part in court masques, and during the reign of James I they began to play in the Chapel Royal on special occasions. A manuscript at the Fitzwilliam Museum, Cambridge, contains a selection of their repertory from about 1610 until after the Restoration: it includes part of the famous music 'For His Majesty's Sagbutts and Cornetts' written by Matthew Locke, possibly to accompany Charles II's coronation procession on 22 April 1661.

Like the wind consorts, the violin band took part in court ceremonial, though it is likely that it concentrated mainly on accompanying dancing; the texts of many court masques of the period mention it in this role. We know that it played normally in five parts, using the layout of one violin, three violas and bass like the French Vingt-quatre Violons. At the Restoration, it was enlarged from its pre-war strength of about 15 to 24 to bring it into line with the French court orchestra. At the same time, groups from the band began to be used in the Chapel Royal and in the London theatres. By the time Purcell began to write for it around 1680, the band was using the more modern Italian 'string quartet' layout.

A sixth group, called variously 'The Lutes and Voices', 'The Private Music' and 'The Consort', was developed at court during the reigns of James I and Charles I, in part from ensembles in Prince Henry's household and that of Charles as Prince of Wales. It was quite distinct from the violin band, and consisted of a number of lutenist/singers, a few viol players, two violinists, a harpist and an organist or virginals player; in effect, it was a distinguished group of soloists who provided the royal family with a variety of vocal and instrumental chamber music in their private apartments – hence the title 'The Private Music' (see Plate 15). Its string players, for instance, appear to have played the great repertory of contrapuntal consort music written by court composers from John Coprario to Matthew Locke – particularly fantasy suites or 'setts' for one or two violins, bass viol and organ.

James II drastically rationalized the Royal Music soon after his accession in 1685. All the instrumental consorts were replaced by a single ensemble based on the Twenty-four Violins. The new group was, effectively, an up-to-date orchestra of wind, strings and continuo, though by the 1690s its duties were largely confined to important state occasions, and by the middle of the 18th century a post in the royal band was virtually a sinecure.

Waits were humble civic equivalents of the court instrumental consorts. Originally guards and watchmen, by 1600 they were small consorts of adaptable instrumentalists (six was a common number) who could provide their town with music for a variety of outdoor and indoor occasions. Though some were not far removed from itinerant buskers, the best, like the waits of London and Norwich, were literate and highly accomplished musicians who played lutes, viols and violins as well as the traditional 'wait pipe' (the shawm) and other wind instruments. The London waits, for instance, provided music at the Blackfriars Theatre for the King's Company (Shakespeare's troupe) and employed a number of prominent composers such as John Wilson, Robert Taylor and Simon Ives. The first half of the 17th century was the heyday of the waits; after the Restoration they were supplanted in London's musical life by public concerts and a new type of musical theatre, though they continued to exist there and elsewhere until the 19th century.

Before the Civil War, London had two theatrical traditions. The various commercial theatres gave spoken plays, largely in the Elizabethan manner, on a plain stage with music apparently confined to preliminary incidental music and a few songs and dances. At court, masques and pastoral plays were performed with the Italian arts of perspective scenery, stage machinery and artificial light, and with the full resources of the Royal Music. At the Restoration, Charles II wisely decided not to revive a regular court theatre; it had contributed to his father's financial difficulties and the Puritans had attacked it as a symbol of the court's immorality and decadence. Instead, he authorized the establishment of two patent companies under royal patronage; as nominal members of the royal household, they came under the jurisdiction of the Lord Chamberlain. This arrangement, which lasted in essence until the 19th century, brought together the two pre-war theatrical traditions. Ordinary plays, including a number by Shakespeare, were given in a manner derived from the masque, with masque-like scenes set to operatic music. At first the Twenty-four Violins, divided into two groups, provided the music for important productions. Later the two playhouses established their own bands; by the 1690s virtually every new play or revival was provided with a specially composed suite of incidental music, heard before the play began and between the acts. The culmination of the Restoration musical theatre was the series of elaborate musical plays or 'semi-operas' with music by Henry Purcell, given under Thomas Betterton's direction at the Dorset Garden Theatre; at the time *Dioclesian* (1690), *King Arthur* (1691) and

The Fairy Queen (1692) were regarded as Purcell's finest achievements, while the miniature italianate opera *Dido and Aeneas* (1689) was performed in private and remained virtually unknown.

The triumph of semi-opera was short-lived: within a few years of Purcell's death in 1695, Italian opera swept it from the stage (see Plate 23). Italian opera, especially after Handel's *Rinaldo* (the first to be written specially for London, performed at the Haymarket Theatre from 24 February 1711), attracted the artistic and social élite permanently to its cause. Italian singers and instrumentalists surged into England, Handel found himself at the forefront of English musical life and a promising generation of English composers – including Croft, Eccles and Weldon – were effectively deprived of employment in the theatre.

Although J. C. Pepusch and J. E. Galliard wrote a number of italianate English operas as afterpieces to spoken plays between 1715 and 1718 (they were the model for Handel's *Acis and Galatea*, 1718), English musical theatre was mainly confined to low comedy for the rest of our period. Pantomime, a favourite type of afterpiece, became popular in the 1720s, mainly through the antics of John Rich, the greatest Harlequin of the century. At this period it rather curiously combined serious all-sung mythological scenes with spectacular scenic effects and danced episodes derived from the *commedia dell'arte*. Ballad opera was a craze that lasted for just a few years, following the great success in 1728 of Gay's *The Beggar's Opera*, produced at Lincoln's Inn Fields with music arranged by Pepusch. However, *The Beggar's Opera* continued to be performed throughout the century and its satire of Italian opera, as well as its use of popular tunes, influenced many subsequent works, such as Lampe's *The Dragon of Wantley* (1737) and Arne's *Love in a Village* (1762). Arne made his name in the theatre with *Comus* (1738), a reworking of Milton's famous 1634 masque. This modified revival of the semi-opera, which came soon after a temporary collapse of Italian opera in London, heralded a return to seriousness in the English musical theatre, and its pre-Romantic rural atmosphere attracted many imitations, including Handel's oratorio *L'Allegro* (1740).

The public concert was an English invention, though until the end of the 18th century concerts were given by amateurs as often as professionals, and they were held in taverns, theatres, pleasure gardens or assembly rooms as often as purpose-built concert halls. All concerts were given by groups of instrumentalists, sometimes including voices; the solo keyboard recital belongs to a later period, though concerts nearly always included a number of contrasted solos among the ensemble items. Though John Banister is usually credited with giving the first concerts in London in the 1670s, similar events were held in Oxford during the Commonwealth. The Civil War had acted as a powerful stimulus to music in the provinces, since many court musicians had left London, and amateurs and professionals alike 'chose rather to fidle at home, then to goe out & be knockt on the head abroad', as Roger North put it. Under the energetic professorships of John Wilson (1655–61) and Edward Lowe (1661–82), both amateurs and professionals (occasionally including virtuosos like Thomas Baltzar and John Banister) met weekly at the University Music School and at the house of the organist William Ellis to play consort music on a mixture of violins, viols and continuo instruments; the music they played forms the basis of the Music School collection in the Bodleian Library, Oxford.

A similar meeting, at which French-style orchestral music was played with professional bass violinists, was held in the Castle Tavern in Fleet Street during the

1680s; it eventually evolved into the fully professional concerts at York Buildings, off the Strand – London's first proper concert hall. The output of composers like the Moravian Gottfried (or Godfrey) Finger, who was one of the promoters of the York Buildings concerts (c1689–97), shows that the new concert-going public preferred to listen to sonatas that combined virtuosity and tunefulness with unusual scorings. Finger's sonatas call for trumpets, oboes and recorders with strings in novel combinations; they are typical of the growing repertory of instrumental music that was offered to amateurs in printed editions by John Walsh and his Netherlands counterpart, Estienne Roger.

The most remarkable music meeting of the period was the one run from 1678 to 1714 by the coal merchant Thomas Britton above his shop in Clerkenwell. Britton's concerts were unusual for the quality of his performers (they reportedly included Handel and Pepusch), the nobility of his audience and, to judge from the posthumous sale catalogue of his music library, the catholicity of his taste. Britton represents the beginning of an antiquarian strain in English music that became more pronounced as the century progressed. His interest, for instance, in mid-17th-century viol music has its counterpart in Pepusch's Academy of Ancient Music, in Maurice Greene and William Boyce's *Cathedral Music*, in the antiquarian interests of the Oxford professors William and Philip Hayes and, finally, in the great histories of Burney and Hawkins. By espousing antiquarianism, English 18th-century musicians were able to combine their traditional conservatism with a contemporary pre-Romantic nostalgia for the past.

In the early 18th century, concerted music was increasingly heard in theatres and pleasure gardens. After 1710, italianate concertos and sonatas replaced specially composed suites as interval music in plays and operas. For instance, the repertory of concertos for fifth and sixth flute (small recorders in C and D) by William Babell, Robert Woodcock and John Baston, as well as the concerti grossi and sonatas of John Humphries, seem to have been written for Lincoln's Inn Fields in the second and third decades of the century. Handel's concerti grossi and organ concertos fulfilled a similar function during performances of his operas and oratorios at the Haymarket or Covent Garden. Spring Gardens at Vauxhall (south of the Thames opposite Whitehall) existed in Restoration times, but regular concerts only began there after 1732; its major rivals were Marylebone Gardens (opened 1738) and Ranelagh in Chelsea (opened 1742). Judging from the collections of 'Vauxhall songs' published by Arne and others from the 1740s onwards, the principal fare was songs and cantatas with orchestral accompaniment, though organ concertos became popular later in the century.

The extraordinary popularity of the Corellian concerto grosso in England can be best explained by its usefulness to the many orchestral societies that sprang up all over England around 1750 (see Plate 16); presumably, hired professionals played the concertino parts, leaving the ripieno to their employers, the gentlemen amateurs. Although the earlier English concerto sets were mostly published by London composers such as Humphries, Geminiani, Festing, Giuseppe Sammartini and Handel, the lead later passed to the provinces: the work of John Alcock at Lichfield, Charles Avison at Newcastle or Capel Bond at Coventry shows how high musical standards were, even in quite small towns. Furthermore, these same societies took up the much more difficult and richly scored *galant* symphonies of the 1770s and 80s with equal enthusiasm.

In the early 17th century, children normally learnt music initially through a solo instrument. An early 17th-century book on the organization of aristocratic households by 'R.B.' recommends 'the Base Violl, The Virginalls, Lute, Bandora or Citerne'; the more advanced skills needed to play or sing in consort were normally found only in the most musical households. Around 1600, when keyboard instruments were relatively rare and expensive, the lute was – as Dowland put it in 1609 – 'most in request'; it was cheap and portable, it had a large and worthwhile repertory and its tablature notation was easy for beginners to learn. Even so, the popularity of this increasingly complex instrument (around 1620 it acquired new tunings and extra strings from France) declined later in the century in favour of the simpler lyra viol and five-course guitar. Virtually all the Tudors were lutenists; Charles I played the viol 'exactly well', and his sons, Charles II and James II, took up the guitar, as did a number of their contemporaries, including the diarist Samuel Pepys. While the viol played 'lyra-way' in chords from tablature was an English invention, the vogue for the guitar was part of the Restoration enthusiasm for French culture; Francesco Corbetta, the leading exponent of the instrument in France, visited London and in 1671 dedicated *La guitarre royalle* to Charles II. It was taken for granted that these instruments were learnt partly so that the players could accompany their own singing (from tablature early in the century, and later from unfigured or figured basses). Keyboard instruments only began to be used generally for this purpose in the 1690s.

Although the Jacobean and Caroline keyboard repertory is commonly called 'virginal music', there is no reason to think that it was always played on the single-strung rectangular instrument; harpsichords and domestic organs were also common. Rectangular virginals continued to be made in the Restoration period (the latest is dated 1679) though English makers were by then already producing a newer triangular type with a miniature bentside; it was called 'spinet', after the Italian *spinetta*, and may have been introduced to England by Girolamo Zenti, who worked briefly for Charles II. From then, the spinet reigned supreme in ordinary English houses until it was supplanted by the square piano in the 1760s and 1770s. English Baroque keyboard music can be divided into a 'high' repertory, written largely by professionals for their own use, and a 'low' one, made up of simple teaching pieces, dances and arrangements of popular songs. The latter sounds best on (and was doubtless largely intended for) the virginal and the spinet, while the former, particularly in the 18th century, was written specifically for English harpsichords. Around the middle of the century, the two rival family firms of the Swiss Burkat Shudi (1702–73) and the Alsatian Jacob Kirckman (1710–92) developed large and powerful instruments that combined elements of the Italian, French and Flemish national schools. They were ideal for playing the range of English and Continental music – including Zipoli, Domenico Scarlatti, Rameau and C. P. E. Bach – that was available from London publishers; just as English musicians developed antiquarian tastes, so they became increasingly eclectic as well.

I have outlined an alternative to the traditional view that English music between Purcell and Elgar is unworthy of notice. Decline there certainly was; but it did not come substantially until around 1800–30, when most of the familiar musical institutions of the 18th century – the court, the cathedral choir, the English musical theatre, the orchestral society, the pleasure gardens and home chamber music – were all at a low ebb or had more or less come to an end. The causes of decline are complex: they extend into other areas of cultural life, and beyond into larger questions of politics and history, in which the Napoleonic wars, industrialization and the decline of aristocratic life each played a part.

Peter Holman
Colchester

London (Will Roades: *A Pocket Map of the Citties of London & Westminster*, 1731)

A
POCKET MAP
of the Cities of
LONDON &
WESTMINSTER
and the Suburbs thereof
being a New & Exact PLAN
with the Additions of the New
Buildings Churches &c
this Present Year 1731.

Biographical Dictionary
The British Isles

1 London

Abell, John (1653–in or after 1716). Well travelled Scottish countertenor (of whose voice, Evelyn asserted, 'one would have sworne it had been a woman's'), lutenist and minor composer of songs. He was temperamental and discerning, acquiring a post in the Chapel Royal (1675), a Cambridge MusB (1684) and an aristocratic wife (Lady Frances Knollys, 1685) before quitting England, ostensibly on religious grounds, to travel on the Continent. He was received in France, Germany, the Low Countries, Italy and Poland – where he was threatened with wild bears, if he refused to sing (as he often did). Abell returned to London in 1699, briefly visiting Ireland in 1703 in the entourage of the viceroy, the Duke of Ormonde. He composed a birthday ode for Queen Anne in 1703: *Hark, Britain, hark*.

Addison, Joseph (1672–1719). Civil servant and writer on music in *The Spectator*, in whose pages (1711–12) he spoke out against Italian opera in England, advocating indigenous opera in its place. In that cause he wrote a libretto, *Rosamond*, which was first set by Thomas Clayton (1707) – when it was (deservedly) a total flop – and later by Arne (1733). Johann Mattheson was influenced by his writing.

Albrici. See ITALY *10 Itinerant Musicians*.

Amadei, Filippo. See ITALY *7 Papal States: Rome*.

Ariosti, Attilio. See ITALY *10 Itinerant Musicians*.

Arne, Thomas Augustine (1710–78). Leading figure in mid-18th-century English theatrical music. Arne, a Catholic, was educated at Eton College. He played the organ and the violin, which he learnt from one of the Festing family. It may have been Michael Festing who convinced Arne's father (by profession an upholsterer) to devote much of his energies to promoting the musical talents of his children: Arne's sister was the gifted soprano Susanna Maria, later Mrs Cibber, and with their brother Richard they were involved in performances – including one of Handel's *Acis and Galatea* – at the Little Haymarket Theatre in 1732.

They joined briefly with Henry Carey and J. F. Lampe to present English operas (by Lampe and Arne) in the Italian style, but within 18 months their partnership was dissolved. The success of Arne's *Opera of Operas* (1733) and *Dido and Aeneas* (1734) confirmed his talent. He displaced Lampe at Drury Lane, where in addition to songs for Shakespeare productions (his most famous was 'Where the bee sucks') he composed masques. In 1734 *Love and Glory* (in which his brother and sister sang) was given to mark the marriage of Princess Anne with the Prince of Orange. By command of the Prince of Wales, Arne's *Alfred* (containing his most famous song, 'Rule Britannia') was performed at a royal Thames-side house, Cliveden, in the summer of 1740.

In 1737 he married the singer Cecilia Young, who sang in his extremely popular setting of Milton's *Comus* (1738), and together they followed Mrs Cibber to Dublin, where the two women sang in the first performance of Handel's *Messiah* (1742). After two seasons they returned to London and Drury Lane Theatre, where they worked until 1750 when they defected to Covent Garden after a quarrel between Mrs Cibber and David Garrick which gave rise to rival productions of *Romeo and Juliet* at the two houses with music by Arne and Boyce. The Arnes' marriage faltered and they separated, though they were reconciled much later, in 1777.

In the meantime, Arne took the DMus at Oxford and established important connections with the pleasure gardens of Vauxhall, Ranelagh and Marylebone as their leading composer, writing numerous songs and some organ concertos. He joined the Gentlemen's Catch Club and the Madrigal Society, for which he supplied much convivial music. In 1760 his miniature comic opera, *Thomas and Sally*, was presented at Covent Garden; two years later *Artaxerxes*, to a libretto translated from Metastasio, became the most popular English opera in the Italian style until the 19th century. See BRITISH ISLES *1 London*, Cibber, Susanna Maria.

Babell, William (*c*1690–1723). London harpsichordist, organist, violinist and composer (probably of French descent); Burney uncharitably described him as one who '... at once gratifies idleness and vanity'. The son of a bassoonist, Babell was both gifted and well connected. He was a pupil of Pepusch, knew and was greatly influenced by Handel, had a court appointment in George I's private band and an organ post at All Hallows, Bread Street. His harpsichord pieces, which include virtuosic arrangements of arias from Handel's *Rinaldo* – decried by Burney – and oboe sonatas (published posthumously) with written-out ornamentation for the slow movements are an important source for early 18th-century English performance practice.

Baltzar, Thomas ['the Swede'] (*c*1631–1663). Lübeck violinist and composer who spent two years at the Swedish court before emigrating to England in 1655. Baltzar played in the production of Davenant's *The Siege of Rhodes* in 1656 and in numerous private concerts. Five years later he was appointed to the King's Private Musick as a Musician-in-Ordinary (see Plate 15). Thomas Britton owned a copy of his collection of trio sonatas for lyra violin, treble violin and bass (now lost), but from the evidence of his suites for two and three violins, as well as the variations which appeared in Playford's *The Division Violin* (1685), he was technically accomplished in high positions and at multiple stops. He allegedly died of alcoholism and 'French pox'.

Banister, John. Father and son of the same name, who were instrumentalists and composers in the King's Violins; both were modestly successful composers whose music appeared in contemporary anthologies. The elder John Banister (*c*1624–1679) played the violin in the band for the 1659 performances of *The Siege of Rhodes* and composed theatre songs such as appeared in *Courtly Masquing Ayres* (1662). After trips to Paris during 1660–62 where he heard Lully's *petits violons*, he returned to lead a new royal band of 12 violins (though his place was soon usurped by the French expatriate Louis Grabu). In late December 1672 *The London Gazette* advertised Monday afternoon concerts at his home in White Fryers (known as the 'Musick-School') which were among the earliest public concerts to be given in London. He also played the flageolet and was acquainted with Pepys, himself an amateur on the instrument, who mentions him frequently in his diary. The younger John Banister died around 1725.

Baston, John (*fl* 1711–33). Flautist and recorder player in the London theatres (Lincoln's Inn Fields, 1711–20; Drury Lane, 1720–33) and composer of virtuoso recorder concertos which he played in the intervals of performances.

Beard, John (*c*1717–1791). Tenor, much loved by London audiences, who sang more roles under Handel than any other singer, and did much to popularize the tenor voice. As a pupil of Bernard Gates (who was a great admirer of Handel) at the Chapel Royal, Beard sang in the 1732 Crown and Anchor Tavern performances of *Esther*. Upon leaving the Chapel Royal two years later, he became a member of Handel's Covent Garden company, with whom he sang in ten operas and probably all of the English oratorios (the heroic roles he created in *Samson*, *Judas Maccabaeus* and *Jephtha* were particularly memorable), masques and odes (except *The Choice of Hercules*), and in numerous revivals. He occasionally sang at the Chapel Royal as a 'vocal performer extraordinary to his Majesty' and from 1750 onwards sang without fee in the annual Foundling Hospital performances of *Messiah*. During the 1750s he took part in oratorio performances at provincial festivals, and was also associated with the Drury Lane company (1737–43 and 1748–59), singing in performances of works by Arne, J. C. Smith, Lampe and Boyce.

His first marriage, in 1739, to Lady Henrietta Herbert, caused a scandal; and in 1759 – six years after her death – he married Charlotte Rich, daughter of John Rich. That same year he was made a DMus at Oxford and the following year a governor of the Foundling Hospital. He took over the management of Covent Garden from his father-in-law, but sold the patent in 1767 and retired after becoming deaf.

Bernacchi, Antonio Maria. See ITALY *10 Itinerant Musicians.*

Birchensha, John (*d* 1681). Composer and theorist mentioned in *A Musicall Banquet* (1651) as a London viol teacher. Birchensha took composition pupils, among them Pepys (who studied with him in 1662); Shadwell made reference to his gifts as a teacher in *The Humorist* (1671): 'Berkenshaw is a rare fellow, give him his due, fa, la, la, for he can teach men to compose that are deaf, dumb and blind.' Birchensha investigated the mathematical relationship of music pitches and wrote the preface to Thomas Salmon's *An Essay to the Advancement of Musick* (1672).

Blow, John (1649–1708). Distinguished and influential court composer, organist and teacher, remembered by his anthems and a miniature opera, *Venus and Adonis*. Blow was by any standard an extremely successful composer but, in spite of his talents and accomplishments, he was overshadowed by Henry Purcell. His fellow choristers at the Chapel Royal included Pelham Humfrey (whom he succeeded in 1674 as Master of the Children of the Chapel Royal and Composer-in-Ordinary for voices at court), Michael Wise (whom he succeeded in 1687 as Almoner and Master of the Choristers of St Paul's) and William Turner. He was appointed organist of Westminster Abbey at the end of 1668, a post he temporarily relinquished to Purcell in 1679. Blow was made a Gentleman of the Chapel Royal in 1674 and, two years later, acquired one of three Chapel Royal organ posts. At the end of 1677 the degree of Doctor of Music at Canterbury was bestowed on him. Following the death of Purcell in 1695 – for whom Blow composed an ode – he returned to Westminster Abbey and with Father Smith shared the court post of 'tuner of regals, organs, virginals, flutes and recorders'. His crowning honour was reserved for 1700 when he became the first to hold the post of Composer of the Chapel Royal. He was buried near Purcell in the Abbey.

As an organist, first at St Paul's and then at Westminster Abbey, Blow composed many services and verse anthems as well as organ voluntaries and verses. He was also a prolific composer of songs and odes, mostly for the court. The anthem *I beheld and lo! a great multitude* and the Ode for St Cecilia's Day (*Begin the Song*) of 1684 are among his finest works. Many of his odes were written for specific royal occasions, such as *God spake sometime in visions*, for the coronation of James II in 1685. In emulation of Purcell's *Orpheus Britannicus*, Blow published a collection of vocal chamber music, *Amphion Anglicus* (1700). He composed in quite different styles, according to the function of the work, and was particularly adept at incorporating concertante instruments and instrumental movements. *Venus and Adonis*, composed to amuse Charles II, was his only theatre piece; two of the first performers were none other than a royal mistress and her daughter. For his pupils – among them William Croft, Jeremiah Clarke, Daniel Purcell and Bernard Gates – Blow composed catches, pieces for harpsichord and a treatise on realizing from a figured bass.

Bononcini, Giovanni. See ITALY 5 *Modena-Reggio.*

Bordoni, Faustina. See ITALY 10 *Itinerant Musicians.*

Boschi, Giuseppe Maria. See ITALY 4 *Venice.*

Boyce, William (1711–79). Organist, composer of sacred and theatre music, an editor and musical antiquarian; largely because of the early onset of deafness which isolated him from contemporary trends, he assumed the mantle of leading exponent of the late English Baroque style. Boyce was a Londoner, a chorister at St Paul's, then a pupil of Maurice Greene and J. C. Pepusch. In the 1730s he became involved in Greene's Apollo Society, at whose meetings Boyce conducted new works such as his oratorio *David's Lamentation over Saul and Jonathan* (1736) and the serenata *Solomon* (1742). In 1736 he succeeded John Weldon as a composer to the Chapel Royal, for which he composed services and anthems (it was not until 1758 that he was appointed an organist there); in 1757 he was to succeed Greene as Master of the King's Musick, which involved the composition of birthday and New Year's odes.

During the 1740s Boyce began writing theatre music. *Peleus and Thetis* (*c*1740) was his first and most serious work; *The Secular Masque* (*c*1747, libretto by John Dryden) was specially performed as part of a Boyce Festival, mounted in Cambridge in July 1749 (at which time he was awarded university degrees). However, he regularly provided incidental music for plays at Covent Garden and from 1749 at Drury Lane, although by the late 1740s he was deaf. In 1749 Boyce added the duties of organist at All Hallows, Thames Street, to those he discharged at St Michael's Cornhill; his deafness precipitated his dismissal at the former in 1764 and his resignation from the latter in 1768. In 1750 he unwillingly became involved in a rivalry with Arne, whom Boyce had replaced at Drury Lane following a dispute between David Garrick and the Arne family: Covent Garden and Drury Lane each mounted a production of *Romeo and Juliet*, with airs by Arne and Boyce respectively.

When Greene died in 1755, Boyce inherited his library and monumental manuscript collection of English church music – predominantly that of the Restoration – which Greene had been preparing for publication; in his last two decades, Boyce completed Greene's anthology and published it in three volumes, entitled *Cathedral Music, being a Collection in Score of the Most Valuable and Useful Compositions for That Service, by Several English Masters of the Last 200 Years* (1760, 1768, 1773).

Boyce quit the theatre in 1760, the year in which his *Eight Symphonys* were finally published. Some had been composed as early as the late 1730s (as overtures to court odes;

others were opera overtures); he published his only collection of trio sonatas in 1747. At his death he was succeeded as Master of the King's Musick by John Stanley and his library and instruments were auctioned by Christie and Ansell. The combined choirs of St Paul's Cathedral, Westminster Abbey and the Chapel Royal sang at his funeral.

Brade, William. See NORTHERN EUROPE 7 *Itinerant Musicians.*

Bressan, Peter (*fl* 1685–1731). Maker (possibly of French origin) of fine recorders and flutes, and music publisher (1718–24). Bressan was a friend of the French-born recorder player and oboist James Paisible, and with Thomas Stanesby the elder, a founder of the English school of recorder making.

Britton, Thomas (1644–1714). London small coal dealer and musical amateur who organized well-attended music meetings in his modest Clerkenwell home (above the shop) where a broad spectrum of chamber music was performed by both amateurs and professionals such as Handel, Pepusch and Matthew Dubourg. Originally from Northamptonshire, Britton developed a keen interest in music which ultimately brought him into contact with Sir Roger L'Estrange (a fellow viol player), the Duchess of Queensberry (who often attended his Thursday evening concerts with a contingent of aristocratic music-lovers) and the Earls of Oxford, Pembroke and Sunderland (serious book collectors like himself). In addition to books on music, parts and scores of vocal and instrumental music, his library contained many volumes on chemistry and astrology; he also owned a number of musical instruments. His death was the unfortunate result of a practical joke.

Bull, John (?1562/3–1628). Composer, keyboard virtuoso and organ builder who in 1613 escaped prosecution for adultery by fleeing England for the South Netherlands. His unfortunate lack of self-discipline resulted in chronic financial difficulties and disrepute. When Bull was charged with adultery, the Archbishop of Canterbury wrote: 'The man hath more music than honesty and is as famous for marring of virginity as he is for fingering organs and virginals.' At that time Bull had been a Gentleman of the Chapel Royal for two decades – serving Queen Elizabeth at festivals and state receptions and building her an organ. His skill as a performer and composer had been acknowledged by the inclusion of several of his works (pavans and galliards and a famous set of variations on 'Walsingham') in the first collection of virginal music to be printed, *Parthenia, or the Maydenhead*, honouring the Princess Elizabeth and the Elector Palatine on their wedding early in 1613, for which he also composed the wedding anthem.

In 1586 Bull was granted the BMus at Oxford and 1592 the DMus; his portrait still adorns the library of the Oxford Faculty of Music. From 1597 he held the first Public Readership in music at Gresham College, London, a post he was forced to relinquish on his marriage in 1607. Deprived of a comfortable income, he concentrated on organ building to support his family. When he abruptly departed England he left behind all his music – mainly anthems and keyboard works; some were passed off as the work of others, the rest are now lost. Among the music that has survived in England is a veritable compendium of canons (including a circular double puzzle canon in six parts).

He made his way to Brussels where he became an organist in the household of Archduke Albert. Outraged by the whole affair, James I, determined that Bull should undergo punishment for the suffering and inconvenience he had caused, directed the English envoy in Brussels to inform the archduke of Bull's background. The archduke duly dismissed him in August 1614 but quietly subsidized him until 1618. In the meantime, Bull petitioned the Mayor of Antwerp for a post as organ pensioner, claiming that he was Catholic and the victim of religious persecution, and in 1615 was given a post as organist at Antwerp Cathedral. During this period he composed plainsong verses for Roman services and organ fantasias (one, from 1621, based on a theme by Sweelinck).

Burney, Charles (1726–1814). Distinguished writer on music, well connected in society (owing to his culture and impeccable manners) and at court, who made many important friends – Padre Martini, Metastasio, J. A. Hasse, Gluck, C. P. E. Bach and Haydn – among Continental musicians in the course of his travels. Burney was a remarkable man whose life took particular and exceptional turns. From provincial beginnings in Chester and Shrewsbury he came to the attention of Arne in 1744 and was installed in London as his apprentice; through Arne he met Handel, for whom Burney played the violin and viola in his orchestra and at his home. When, in 1746, he was taken into service by the wealthy and aristocratic Fulke Greville his future seemed bright, but after he married he retired to Norfolk as an organist and teacher during the 1750s. Returning to London in 1760 he supported his family as a teacher, though he had no university education. After a sojourn in Paris with his daughters he translated Rousseau's popular *Le devin du village* (1753) as *The Cunning Man* which Garrick presented at Drury Lane. In 1767 he was marked out for respect by his appointment as 'Extra Musician' in the King's Band; two years later he took the Oxford DMus. On Sunday evenings, his home in St Martin's Street (once the home of Sir Isaac Newton and replete with rooftop observatory that Burney himself put to good use as an amateur astronomer) was the scene of much music-making by singers and players from all over Europe. His friend Joshua Reynolds painted his portrait (National Portrait Gallery).

In order to realize a long-held ambition to write a history of music Burney embarked on the first of two research trips around Europe in 1770. The immediate result was two musical travelogues – *The Present State of Music in France and Italy* (1771) and *The Present State of Music in Germany, the Netherlands and the United Provinces* (1773) – which remain invaluable sources to scholars of 18th-century music. The *History of Music* took twenty years to write (the first volume appeared in 1776, the same year in which John Hawkins's five-volume history of music appeared) and is the product of a cosmopolitan, if not antiquarian, point of view. His view of music history was progressive rather than retrospective, and privately he was highly critical of Hawkins's *History*. A fine writer and stylist, he is the most frequently quoted writer on music of the 18th century in spite of his limitations. In 1784 he was involved in the organization of the mammoth Handel Commemoration at Westminster Abbey and the Pantheon; to accompany his account of the celebrations Burney wrote an important biography of Handel.

Butler, Henry. See IBERIAN PENINSULA AND COLONIES *1 Spain*.

Byrd, William (1543–1623). Influential Catholic organist and composer, a brilliant contrapuntist, skilled in the polyphonic style of the Netherlands, who wrote music for both Anglican and Catholic worship. Byrd was a Gentleman of the Chapel Royal from 1570 and well connected with the Catholic aristocracy who helped him during the 1580s when Catholics were being persecuted. He became involved in music printing and the marketing of part-music, secured a royal patent and, working with the printer Thomas East, played a part in the flowering of English

music printing in the last years of the century. He was without question the finest and most profound English composer of his time.

For the Chapel Royal he composed services (notably the extraordinary Great Service), and verse anthems such as *Rejoice unto the Lord* (1586), which went on being performed during the 17th century. For his Catholic patrons he composed Latin motets, three fine Masses (one each in three, four and five voices) and other liturgical music which he published in two practically arranged volumes (*Gradualia*, 1605–7), though in 1605 at least one person was arrested for possessing a copy after the Gunpowder Plot. He is credited with popularizing the virginal and some of his keyboard music – short preludes, pavans and galliards – was published in *Parthenia* (1613); he also produced grounds, fantasias and sets of variations. He published two collections of English psalms, sonnets and songs (1588, 1611) for three to five voices and contributed four sacred songs to Leighton's *Tears or Lamentacions of a Sorrowful Soule* (1614); his consort songs greatly influenced Coprario and the younger Ferrabosco. His pupil Thomas Morley summarized his teaching in *A Plaine and Easie Introduction to Practicall Musicke* (1597).

Caffarelli. See ITALY *10 Itinerant Musicians*.

Cambert, Robert. See FRANCE *1 Paris and Versailles*.

Campion, Thomas (1567–1620). Renaissance man who was at once a poet and composer of lute songs, and a physician. As a young man, Campion spent time at Peterhouse, Cambridge, and at Gray's Inn, London, where he forged links that later brought him royal patronage. He published collections of poems and ayres – the first, intended to be accompanied by lute, orpharion (an instrument first referred to in a poem of 1590 by Michael Drayton) and bass viol, appeared in Philip Rosseter's *A Book of Ayres* in 1601 – as well as two treatises, *Observations in the Art of English Poesie* (1602) and *A New Way of Making Fowre Parts in Counter-point, by a most Familiar and Infallible Rule* (*c*1613). The quality of his verse surpassed that of his music and it was set by other composers for the masques and other royal entertainments presented before James I. With an eye to sales, he published pairs of books of ayres about 1613 and 1617 in partbooks, though he clearly intended them as solo lute songs.

Carestini, Giovanni. See ITALY *10 Itinerant Musicians*.

Carey, Henry (*c*1689–1743). Dramatist of

considerable flair who fancied himself a composer (having studied composition with Francesco Geminiani and Thomas Roseingrave); he produced librettos for musical burlesques after unsuccessful attempts to write for opera. *Chrononhotonthologos* (1734), which satirized Italian opera, was composed under the pseudonym of Benjamin Bounce. The infamous *The Dragon of Wantley* (set in 1737 by J. F. Lampe) was particularly offensive to Farinelli (castratos were an especial target of Carey) and Handel. His own musical pretensions arose out of a gift for composing ballad-like tunes to his own lyrics; he contributed such songs to pantomimes, dialogue and ballad operas, and published three burlesque cantatas in 1740 under an Italian pseudonym, Sig^r Carini. In debt and pressed by family obligations, Carey hanged himself.

Castrucci. Italian violinists, resident in London. Pietro Castrucci (1679–1752) was one of many violinists, including Francesco Geminiani, who had been pupils of Corelli. In London by 1715, he was for more than 22 years the leader of Handel's opera orchestra, in which his brother Prospero (*d* 1760) also played. Pietro was much acclaimed as a virtuoso and often performed solos in the theatre. Together, the Castruccis promoted the brief vogue of the violetta (the 'English violet' had sympathetic strings and was a type of viola d'amore); Handel incorporated obbligato parts for two 'violette marine per gli Signori Castrucci' in his opera *Orlando* (1733) and for one in *Sosarme* (1732), *Ezio* (1732) and the oratorio *Deborah* (1733). Pietro published several collections of sonatas and one of concertos; Prospero – thought to be immortalized by Hogarth as 'The Enraged Musician' – published one collection of six sonatas. By 1750 Pietro was in Dublin where, in impoverished circumstances, he gave his last concert a week before his death.

Cervetto, Giacobbe Basevi (*c*1682–1783). Italian cellist and composer of Jewish descent who, from about 1738, made England his home. Cervetto was active as a chamber music player in London subscription concerts at Hickford's Rooms and the Great Rooms in Dean Street where – along with his fellow Italians Andrea Caporale and Salvatore Lanzetti – he helped to popularize the cello. He was also a lively member of the Drury Lane Theatre orchestra. Cervetto published duos, trios and solos for cello, fluently written though not technically demanding.

Child, William (1606/7–1697). Child was an organist who travelled traditional professional routes: royal service at St George's Chapel, Windsor (1630) and the Chapel Royal (by 1666), and Oxford degrees (BMus 1631, DMus 1663). He composed a collection of psalm settings (1639) popular during the interregnum. He played at the coronations of Charles II, James II, and William and Mary, and was known to Pepys. Purcell and Blow arranged some of his music, which included anthems, services, a *Te Deum* and a *Jubilate*.

Cibber (née Arne), **Susanna Maria** (1714–66). Tragic actress associated with Drury Lane Theatre, and singer who sang in the first performance of Handel's *Messiah* in Dublin. She was the sister and protégée of Thomas Arne, and made her début as a singer at the Little Theatre in the Haymarket in a venture backed by her father, which included a production of J. F. Lampe's *Amelia* (1732) and, in the following seasons, those of her brother's *Rosamond* and *Dido and Aeneas*. In 1743 the family became associated with Drury Lane Theatre where she met her husband, Theophilus Cibber – son of the celebrated Colley Cibber, who was responsible for training her as an actress. She undertook Shakespearean roles and appeared as Polly in *The Beggar's Opera*. By eloping with a country gentleman (John Sloper, with whom she remained for the rest of her life) she brought scandal to the family and a temporary hiatus to her career. She was next heard in Dublin during the 1741 season, after which she was joined by her brother and his wife, the soprano Cecilia Arne, with whom she performed in concerts of Handel duets as well as *Messiah*. Autumn 1742 found her back in London where she took up her place at Drury Lane Theatre and sang in further performances of Handel oratorios at the King's Theatre, including the London première of *Messiah* (23 March 1743). See also BRITISH ISLES *1 London*, Arne, Thomas.

Clarke, Jeremiah (*c*1674–1707). Versatile composer and organist, remembered today as the composer of 'Purcell's Trumpet Voluntary'. Clarke made his way through the traditional ranks, first as a chorister of the Chapel Royal (during which time he performed at the coronation of James II in 1685), then as an organist of Winchester College and later St Paul's Cathedral; in 1700 he and Croft were made Gentlemen Extraordinary and, four years later, organists of the Chapel Royal. In January 1704 Clarke had succeeded Blow as Almoner and Master of the Choristers at St Paul's. In addition to anthems (including one for Queen Anne's coronation in 1702), Clarke composed odes, songs, theatre music and harpsichord pieces. An unhappy love affair ended with his suicide by shooting.

Clayton, Thomas (1673–1725). Ironic figure in English music: a violinist and composer (the son of William Clayton, a member of the 24 Violins) who adversely affected the course of English theatre music by introducing Italian opera at a critical moment. In 1705 Clayton cobbled together a production of *Arsinoe, Queen of Cypress*, an Italian *pasticcio* with badly translated English verses, performed by an English cast at Drury Lane. In spite of its feebleness, it became the first dramatic work without spoken dialogue to succeed in London. The disastrous failure of his setting of Addison's English opera *Rosamond* two years later discouraged backers from staging other English operas (planned rehearsals of John Eccles's setting of Congreve's *Semele* at the new Haymarket theatre were immediately abandoned). Shocked by this turn of events, Clayton turned to chamber music, briefly acting as proprietor of the concert room in the York Buildings in 1711.

Coleman, Charles (*c*1605–1664). Singer, viol player and composer. He was a member of the household of the young Charles II, sang and played in Shirley's masque *The Triumph of Peace* (1634), and was granted the Cambridge MusD in 1651; along with others he provided music for Davenant's *The Siege of Rhodes* (perf. 1656) and at the Restoration regained a place at court as a vocal composer for the King's Private Musick.

Congreve, William (1670–1729). The greatest English dramatist of his day who, with Sir John Vanbrugh, designed and built the Haymarket theatre in London: there Congreve hoped to revitalize spoken drama, which had declined during the Commonwealth and thereafter. During the 1690s Congreve wrote five important comedies of manners. In 1700–01 his masque *The Judgment of Paris* became the subject of a musical competition which, though Weldon took the first prize, should by all accounts have been won by the second prize-winner, John Eccles. That Congreve concurred is clear from his collaboration with Eccles later in 1701 on *A Hymn to Harmony* for St Cecilia's Day. Their last joint effort was an opera in English, *Semele*, which was never performed because of the failure of Clayton's *Rosamond* in 1707, but the text was memorably used by Handel for his setting of 1744.

Cooke, Henry (*c*1615–1672). Bass, influential Master of the Children of the Chapel Royal and slender composer of anthems. Through-

out his career Cooke championed the Italian style of singing. His own singing, replete with trills and *gruppi*, provoked the praise of John Evelyn (1654) and John Playford in the 1664 edition of *A Brief Introduction to the Skill of Musick*. Pepys, on the other hand, sometimes found himself ill-at-ease with Cooke's improvisations.

In 1652, as a chorister in Charles I's chapel, Cooke scratched his name on a pane of glass in Westminster Abbey. He served the royalist forces during the Civil War and afterwards sang in the King's Private Musick. In 1656 he collaborated with Davenant and later took a role in *The Siege of Rhodes*. From 1660 he trained the Children of the Chapel Royal – among them Pelham Humfrey, John Blow, Michael Wise, William Turner, Robert Smith and Thomas Tudway – who went on to incorporate the Italian vocal style into their music with more success than Cooke. In 1670 he became a marshal of the City of London Corporation of Music.

Coprario [Coperario, Cooper], **John** [Giovanni] (1570/80–1626). Cosmopolitan viol player, composer of fantasias and fantasia-suites, teacher and author of *Rules how to Compose* (before 1617). John Cooper may have italianized his name after a sojourn on the Continent in the retinue of Sir Robert Cecil (then Secretary of State) in 1603. While in the service of the Earl of Hertford (*d* 1621) he was given permission to travel abroad and the following year was in Germany; as the earl's music master he was charged with the education of William Lawes and the Prince of Wales, with whom he must have played his own fantasias at the earl's Wiltshire estate.

A royal connection made, he composed *Songs of Mourning: Bewailing the untimely death of Prince Henry* and *The Lords Maske* (honouring Princess Elizabeth on her marriage to the Elector Palatine) in 1613, both to texts by Thomas Campion. With the earl's death, Coprario became part of the Prince of Wales's household and at the accession became a Composer-in-Ordinary. It was for Charles I (when Prince of Wales) that Coprario composed his fantasias for two bass viols and organ and fantasia-suites for one or two violins, bass viol and organ, which were to remain popular until the Restoration.

Corbetta, Francesco. See ITALY *10 Itinerant Musicians*.

Cosyn, Benjamin (*c*1570–after 1652). Virtuoso keyboard player and composer who compiled two important manuscript collections of keyboard music (one of which is known as the Cosyn Virginal Book and contains 90 pieces by Cosyn, Bull, Gibbons, Tallis and Byrd). His own music – elaborate and notoriously difficult to play – was very much influenced by that of Bull. He was organist at Dulwich College, 1622–24 and then at Charterhouse, 1627–43.

Croft [Crofts], William (1678–1727). Chapel Royal musician who in 1708 succeeded Blow as organist of Westminster Abbey. William Croft pursued his musical career very much in Handel's shadow. A protégé of Blow, he easily gained a foothold in the Chapel Royal, sharing at first two posts with Jeremiah Clarke which reverted to him in 1707 on Clarke's death. To these posts, Croft added composer and Master of the Children, and organist of Westminster Abbey when Blow died the following year. Croft is remembered for his services, which include an important *Te Deum* in D, and verse anthems (in which the organ features prominently) collected in a two-volume engraved edition entitled *Musica sacra* (1724). He also wrote violin sonatas in the Italian style (1700) and theatre airs.

Cross, Thomas (?1660/65–?1732/5). Music engraver and businessman who ran a successful music shop in London, 1692–1720. Cross gained a monopoly on copper (later pewter) engraving at the close of the 17th century so that, in addition to printing, publishing and selling his own editions, he was also engraving for other publishers, including Cullen, Meares and Wright. He learnt his craft from his father, another Thomas Cross, and his services were sought by Purcell, John Eccles and Handel among others. Cross was the first to sell songs printed on single sheets rather than in collections; in the trade, his greatest rival was John Walsh (who printed from punches).

Crowne, John (*c*1640–1712). Tory playwright who was commissioned by the Earl of Rochester to write the court masque *Calisto* (music by Nicholas Staggins) for a performance at Whitehall in 1675. Purcell contributed single songs to Crowne's *Regulus* (1692) and *The Married Beau* (1694).

Cuzzoni, Francesca. See ITALY *10 Itinerant Musicians*.

Dall'Abaco, Joseph-Marie-Clément. See CENTRAL EUROPE *1 South Germany: Munich*.

Dallam. Catholic family of 17th-century organ builders. As a Lancashire youth, Thomas Dallam (*c*1570–after 1640) was apprenticed to a member of the Blacksmiths' Company in London, eventually becoming a liveryman. In 1599 he was sent to Constantinople to deliver a mechanical organ-and-clock to the Sultan; when he returned, he began accepting commissions to build organs: King's College, Cambridge, Worcester Cathedral (where the organist Thomas Tomkins designed the organ, 1613), Eton College and Holyrood Castle, Edinburgh (Inigo Jones designed the case).

His son Robert (1602–65) followed in his father's footsteps and by 1627 had completed the organ at Durham Cathedral; he went on to build those at York Minster, St John's College, Cambridge, and Lichfield Cathedral before settling in Brittany with his family for the duration of the Commonwealth. His brother Ralph (*d* 1673) later built the organ at St George's Chapel, Windsor. Their sister Katherine married the organ builder Thomas Harris.

Davenant, Sir William (1606–68). Playwright and theatre manager. Before the Civil War Davenant was in the service of Charles I's queen, for whom he wrote five masques, staged at Whitehall and the Middle Temple. The fifth, *The Triumphs of the Prince d' Amour* (1636), was entirely set to music by the Lawes brothers. In 1638 he was made poet laureate and soon after acquired the royal patent necessary to build a new theatre. In 1646 he fled to France, though in due course he was apprehended by Commonwealth forces and imprisoned in the Tower (1650–54). To regain his fortune he set about organizing theatrical entertainments and by autumn 1656 had written an 'opera', *The Siege of Rhodes*; it was cast mainly in recitative with choruses concluding each of five *entrées*. The vocal music was provided by Henry Lawes, Henry Cooke and Matthew Locke, the instrumental by Charles Coleman and George Hudson; none survives. Later he produced *The Siege of Rhodes* as a spoken play.

De Fesch, Willem. See LOW COUNTRIES *1 United Provinces*.

Dering, Richard (*c*1580–1630). Organist and composer who converted to Catholicism while studying in Italy (from 1612). Dering was educated at Christ Church, Oxford, before going abroad. After his stay in Venice and Rome, he took up a post in Brussels as organist of a convent of English nuns (1617–20). He returned to England in 1625 where he became a court musician to Charles I and Queen Henrietta Maria. He composed in both English and Italian idioms: the former comprised unpublished Anglican church music, viol fanasias and dances, as well as madrigals and uodlibets such as *City Cries* and *Country*

Cries (published posthumously) for voices and viols; the latter comprised Catholic church music – especially motets – *canzonette* and continuo madrigals, almost all of which were published.

Diessener, Gerhard (*fl* *c*1660–84). German musician resident in England by 1673. Diessener held a post in the French orchestra of the Kassel Hofkapelle (1660) and composed French-style sonatas and orchestral suites. In London, he taught and composed music to be performed by his pupils in the private concerts he held at his home in Great Russell Street. In 1682 he published a collection of suites with French and English titles known as *Instrumental Ayrs*.

Dieupart, Charles [?François] (?after 1667–*c*1740). French violinist and harpsichordist, composer of instrumental music for the London stage. Dieupart flourished in London during the first decade of the 18th century, composing songs and keyboard works (now available in a collected edition), in addition to music for Drury Lane Theatre. His 1701 Amsterdam edition of suites was published in two versions – one for harpsichord, the other for flute or violin and continuo – and is the first example of French suites with a fixed number and order of movements.

Dowland, John (1563–1626). Gifted lutenist and composer, seemingly more successful during his lifetime abroad than at home. Dowland's career was richly varied though not without its frustrating moments. As a lutenist he was skilled at improvisation and blindly ambitious. When a young man he travelled to Paris in the service of the English ambassador; while there he was converted to Catholicism, which appears to have adversely affected his career at the English court. At the age of 25 he took the BMus at Oxford, where later (in 1622) he became Dr Dowland. During the 1590s he was unsuccessful in obtaining a post as one of Queen Elizabeth's lutenists, so he left England for the Continent, pausing at Nuremberg and Kassel before travelling to Italy.

His mission in Italy was to meet Marenzio, but in Florence he became involved in a circle of exiled English Catholics who, in 1595, were plotting the death of Elizabeth; appalled, he hastened to Nuremberg from where he was able to foil the plot. On a trip to Kassel he received a letter from his mentor and a favourite of the Queen, Henry Noel, urging him to return. By the time he arrived in England, Noel had died and the prospect of a court post slipped away.

While at home he published *The First Booke of Songs or Ayres* (1597) which was reprinted several times. After declining a post in Kassel, he took up an invitation at the Danish court in 1598 where he remained – except for a visit to England during 1604 – until 1606. During that time he published his second and third books of songs (1600, 1603) and his inspired series of seven ensemble pavans, the *Lachrimae or Seaven Teares* (1604). Pervading all his most inspired works are the tragic themes of tears, sin, darkness and death. His most famous song is the deeply expressive *In darkness let me dwell* (1610).

He returned to London penniless, but found work in the service of the courtier Lord Walden (1609–12); in 1609 he published a translation of *Andreas Ornithoparcus his Micrologus*. His failure to gain royal acknowledgment, despite his obvious success abroad and in print, made him irritable and discontented, judging from the preface to *A Pilgrimes Solace* (1612) and his *contretemps* with the amateur violist Tobias Hume. However, in 1612 the appointment as one of the king's lutes finally came. Thereafter he composed very little; he was last heard at the funeral of James I (1625). Dowland was succeeded at court by his son Robert (*c*1591–1641) who had earlier (in 1610) edited two important anthologies of music by English and European composers: *A Musicall Banquet* and *Varietie of Lute-lessons*.

Draghi, Giovanni Battista (*c*1640–1708). Italian keyboard virtuoso and composer in the service of the kings of England during the last quarter of the 17th century. Although Draghi was brought to England by Charles II in the hope of establishing a native opera, his appointments were in fact first as chapel organist to the queen (1673) and later to James II (1687), who also made him music master to the royal princesses. Nevertheless, he did compose theatre music for Shadwell's adaptations of *The Tempest* (1674) and *Psyche* (1675) – airs and incidental instrumental pieces in the Italian style – at a time when French music was still very much in vogue. Purcell, for one, was much influenced by him. Shortly before his death, Draghi published *Six Select Sutes of Leszons for the Harpsichord*.

Dryden, John (1631–1700). Poet laureate and Historiographer Royal from 1668 to 1685 whose career was much affected by political events and his conversion to Catholicism (1685). Dryden was above all a dramatist, concerned with the literary problems of musical drama; taking his inspiration from contemporary Italian librettos, Dryden strove to bend the sounds and rhythms of English words to musical exigencies. His success is best demonstrated in his play *King Arthur* (set by Purcell in 1691) and his court odes (set by G. B. Draghi, John Blow, Jeremiah Clarke and Handel).

Dubourg, Matthew. See BRITISH ISLES *2 Provinces.*

Duparc, Elisabeth ['Francesina'] (*d* ?1778). French soprano trained in Italy who pursued her career in England where from 1738 she sang exclusively in Handel productions. The Opera of the Nobility, not Handel, engaged Duparc to come to London in autumn 1736; she made her début in J. A. Hasse's *Siroe* at the King's Theatre. Duparc took important title roles in *Acis and Galatea* (1739, 1741), *Esther* (1740), *Deborah* and the controversial *Semele* (1744) as well as many other roles during the 1740s.

Durastanti, Margherita. See ITALY *10 Itinerant Musicians.*

D'Urfey [Durfey], **Thomas** (*c*1653–1723). Dramatist who provided texts for semi-operas (*Cynthia and Endymion*, 1697, *The Wonders of the Sun*, 1706, and three *Don Quixote* plays, 1694–5), as well as incorporating music into his plays, and prolific author of ode texts. He openly acknowledged both his slender talent, best displayed in farcical comedies, and his debt to music in ensuring the success of his dramas. He had a knack for fitting words to popular tunes, some of which were published in *Wit and Mirth, or Pills to Purge Melancholy* (1699–1700). In spite of a stutter he was known at court as a singer; in 1689, while employed as a singing master at Josias Priest's Chelsea boarding school he contributed the epilogue text to Purcell's *Dido and Aeneas*.

Eccles [Eagles]. Family of musicians. The first significant member of the family was Solomon Eagles (*c*1617–1682) who, until he became a Quaker at the Restoration, played the virginals and viols. Thereafter he gave up music, believing it to be sinful, committed his instruments to a bonfire on Tower Hill and wrote an essay condemning music (*A Musick-lector*, 1677). After Solomon's death his nephew of the same name (1640/50–1710), a viol player and composer, and his brother Henry (1640/50–1711) took up places in the King's Private Musick in 1685 and 1689 respectively, and were both in the party of musicians that accompanied William III to the Low Countries in 1691.

Henry's only son was John Eccles (*c*1668–1735), the most musically gifted member of the family. During the early 1690s he worked at Drury Lane Theatre for the United Com-

panies under John Rich, achieving success with his songs for his actress protégée, Mrs Anne Bracegirdle, in the comedies of Thomas D'Urfey. In 1695 he became music director of a new company at Lincoln's Inn Fields. In 1701 Eccles entered the famous competition for which applicants were required to set Congreve's masque *The Judgment of Paris*. Eccles's version was performed at Dorset Garden, with Mrs Bracegirdle as Venus, and enthusiastically received; but he was awarded only the second prize (the first went to John Weldon). That Congreve particularly admired his music is evidenced by their collaboration on the St Cecilia's Day Ode for that year, and subsequent ventures into opera. Eccles's setting of Granville's dramatic opera, *The British Enchanters*, premièred at the Haymarket Theatre in 1706, might have inaugurated an era of all-sung English opera, had Italian opera not simultaneously gained such a foothold. Meanwhile, Eccles had completed *Semele* by 1705, but because Congreve had by then left the theatre, it never reached the stage, (which is a great pity, since in it he so successfully fused English and Italian styles – much as Purcell had melded English and French operatic elements – and it would have given life-saving impetus to a fledgling genre).

A further Henry Eccles (1675/85–1735/45) was a violinist and composer in the service of the French ambassador in London. When the duke's appointment ended, Eccles accompanied him back to Paris where he published a collection of 12 sonatas, of which 18 movements were borrowed from Giuseppe Valentini's op. 8 and one from F. A. Bonporti. His brother, Thomas Eccles (*c*1672–*c*1745), prejudiced a brilliant career as a violinist by alcoholism.

Fabri, Annibale Pio. See ITALY *10 Itinerant Musicians.*

Farinelli. See ITALY *10 Itinerant Musicians.*

Fedeli, Giuseppe. See ITALY *4 Venice.*

Ferrabosco. Italian–English family of musicians active during the 16th and 17th centuries. Alfonso (*d* 1628) was abandoned by his father of the same name and brought up in Greenwich by a Flemish musician. His father's music was much esteemed by Elizabeth I, whom he had served while resident in England. In 1592 he was made Musician for Viols; in 1604 he was appointed to teach the viol to Henry, Prince of Wales, and, after his death, Prince Charles. When the prince became King, Alfonso was retained and in 1626 gained further appointments as Composer of Music-in-Ordinary and Composer of

Music to the King, posts that passed to his sons at his death.

Between 1605 and 1622 he collaborated with Ben Jonson and Inigo Jones by composing declamatory *Ayres* (published in 1609) for masques performed at Whitehall and Greenwich and from 1619 he was involved in purveying sand and gravel on the Thames. In addition to lute songs and madrigals, Alfonso composed motets and anthems, but his most important music is to be found in his retrospective, contrapuntal four-, five- and six-part viol fantasias and In Nomines. His *Lessons* (1609) for up to three lyra viols reflect his technical skill as a player.

Alfonso's son, also Alfonso (*c*1626–*c*1660), was a wind player as well as a violist. Henry (*c*1615–1658) was a singer, wind player and composer who strangely perished on an expedition to Jamaica. John (1626–82) was an organist and composer; in 1662 he became organist at Ely Cathedral and in 1671 was awarded the Cambridge MusD degree.

Festing, Michael Christian (*d* 1752). Influential violin virtuoso, a founder of the charitable Society of Musicians (1738), and composer of sonatas and concertos, odes and secular songs. Festing was a pupil of Francesco Geminiani and active as a leading London chamber musician. From 1727 he played in the orchestra of the King's Theatre and with Maurice Greene inaugurated the Apollo Society at Temple Bar in 1731. A decade later he was made director of the Italian opera house orchestra. In the meantime he published a number of collections of violin solos, sonatas – complete with bowing and ornamentation – and concerti grossi, and in 1735 he was made Master of the King's Musick. From about 1730 he led the amateur Philharmonic Society at the Crown and Anchor Tavern and played in the Swan concerts; from 1739 he directed subscription concerts in Hickford's Rooms. When Ranelagh Gardens opened in 1742, Festing took on the responsibilities of leading the band and providing the music.

Finger, Gottfried [Godfrey] (*c*1660–1730). Viol player of Moravian descent (his father was a court musician at Olomouc) and minor composer of theatre music and instrumental chamber music. Finger arrived in London before 1687 to take up a post as a viol player in the Catholic Chapel of James II, but when William and Mary came to the throne the following year his appointment was not renewed. Undaunted, he published a spate of italianate chamber music collections for recorders, violins and viols in both London and Amsterdam, and turned to composing incidental music for plays and masques at the theatres in Drury Lane, Lincoln's Inn Fields and Dorset Garden.

Between 1693 and 1699 he taught and regularly performed in concerts in York Buildings, where his ode *Weep, all ye Muses* – better known as 'Mr Purcel's Farewel' – was performed early in 1696. He composed at least one other ode, *Cecilia, look down and see*, which had been performed at the Stationers' Hall on St Cecilia's Day in 1693. In 1700 he entered a competition to determine the best theatre composer of the day and came fourth after John Weldon, John Eccles and Daniel Purcell; the test piece was a setting of Congreve's masque *The Judgment of Paris*.

In 1704 Finger left England for Vienna and by 1706 had taken up a post at Breslau where his last known opera, *Der Sieg der Schönheit über die Helden*, was given. He travelled with the Duke of Neuburg to Innsbruck and Heidelberg before finally taking up a post in the Mannheim Hofkapelle.

Franck, Johann Wolfgang. See NORTHERN EUROPE 1 *North Germany: Hamburg.*

Galliard, John Ernest (*c*1687–1749). German oboist, organist, writer and composer of theatre music, expatriated in London. Galliard came to England in 1706 to take up a court appointment in the service of Queen Anne's consort. In 1710 he became organist to the widow of Charles II at Somerset House, and at the same time oboist at the Queen's Theatre, playing in Handel's operas under the composer. Two years later he collaborated with the poet John Hughes on his own opera, *Calypso and Telemachus*, which, despite its fashionable da capo arias, had only three performances. A similar fate attended his second opera, *Circe* (1719). In the meantime, Galliard joined forces with Lewis Theobald to produce masques (*Pan and Syrinx*, 1718) and pantomimes (*The Rape of Proserpine*, 1727) at John Rich's theatre in Lincoln's Inn Fields. His frustration as an opera composer is revealed in *A Critical Discourse upon Operas in England*, on which he collaborated with Hughes, and in the *entr'actes* satirizing Italian opera singers in his third opera, *The Happy Captive* (1741, libretto by Theobald). A year later he published *Observations on the Florid Song*, a translation of Tosi's 1723 singing manual. In addition to his theatre works, Galliard composed anthems and cantatas; but today he is best known for his 1733 collection of sonatas for bassoon or cello and continuo.

Galuppi, Baldassare. See ITALY 4 *Venice.*

Gautier, Jacques. See FRANCE / *Paris and Versailles.*

Gay, John (1685–1732). Poet and the inventor of ballad opera. Gay was already well known as a poet when he collaborated with Handel on *Acis and Galatea* (1718). Ten years later, *The Beggar's Opera*, for which Gay set lyrics to popular tunes (aided by Pepusch), was to bring him lasting fame. The verisimilitude – depicting the seamier side of 18th-century London – and parodies of the contemporary political and musical figures, made *The Beggar's Opera* a theatrical sensation. Although ballad operas were much in vogue during the 1730s, Gay failed to repeat his initial success: its sequel, *Polly* (1729), was banned and *Achilles* was produced only in the year after his death. In spite of its popularity, there remains no complete source for reviving *The Beggar's Opera* and as a consequence many composers – including Benjamin Britten – have made elaborate arrangements; Hogarth's contemporary paintings and prints provide inspiration for modern productions. In 1928 Kurt Weill composed the music for Brecht's updated version, *Die Dreigroschenoper.*

Geminiani, Francesco (Xaverio) (1687–1762). The most important Italian violin virtuoso resident in Britain, teacher, composer and the author of an immensely influential treatise addressed to advanced players, *The Art of Playing on the Violin* (1751). Geminiani, born in Lucca, was a gifted pupil of Corelli; through him such musicians as Matthew Dubourg, M. C. Festing, Charles Avison, Robert Bremner and Joseph Kelway gained knowledge of the Italian style of playing. He also had aristocratic pupils, among them the Earl of Essex who in 1728 tried unsuccessfully to arrange for Geminiani to become Master and Composer of the State Music of Ireland (a post Dubourg subsequently took up). Geminiani arrived in London in 1714 and is said to have played for George I in 1716 with Handel as his accompanist. In that same year he published his op. 1 sonatas, which he issued again in 1739 in a revised and ornamented version. His concerto grosso arrangements of Corelli's op. 5 violin sonatas appeared a decade later. During the 1730s he made two visits to Ireland where he was warmly received. His own concertos, opp. 2 and 3, appeared in 1732 and 1733. He again published concertos as op. 7 (1746) and *The Inchanted Forrest* (c1756), a staged pantomime – scored for two violins and cello with an orchestra of two trumpets, two flutes, two horns, strings and timpani – presented in Paris at the Tuileries palace in 1754.

He published several challenging collections of violin sonatas in four movements which require dramatic flair from the player; such was the difficulty of his opp. 1 and 4 in particular that very few contemporary violinists dared play them in public. Among the sonata movements are fugues and double fugues, strong in imitative counterpoint, and idiomatic in passages of multiple stopping. Geminiani provided ornaments for both slow and fast movements as well as cadenzas in his treatise; he advocated the use of vibrato 'as often as possible'. The expressiveness of his playing was much admired by both Hawkins and Burney; Tartini tellingly described him as 'il furibondo'.

Geminiani was fond of arranging his works: among his transcriptions are harpsichord versions (1741) of his opp. 1 and 4 and concerto grosso versions of op. 4 (1743). His op. 5 cello sonatas (published in Paris), together with a transcription for violin (issued in London and The Hague), appeared in 1746. In about 1755 he published 'modernized' versions of the opp. 2 and 3 concertos, and in 1757 a final arrangement of op. 1 in trio format.

He gained further notoriety from the publication of a series of practical treatises which were much reprinted, translated and paraphrased. In addition to *The Art of Playing on the Violin*, which sets out the principles of a modern technique, Geminiani produced *Rules for Playing in a True Taste* (1748), revised a year later as *A Treatise of Good Taste in the Art of Musick*, a misguided *Guida harmonica* with supplement (c1754), *The Art of Accompaniment* (c1754) – written from the soloist's point of view – and *The Art of Playing the Guitar or Cittra* [English guitar] (Edinburgh, 1760). When considered together with his music and the implication of the alterations he made when reissuing collections such as opp. 1 and 4, Geminiani's treatises represent an important source of post-Corellian performance practices.

Gibbons. Family of organists and composers. Orlando Gibbons (1583–1625) was a key figure in early 17th-century English musical life. He took the MusB degree at Cambridge (1606) where he had been a chorister at King's and the DMus at Oxford (1622); he became a Gentleman of the Chapel Royal (by 1625 he was the senior organist) and organist at Westminster Abbey from 1623. The finest of his solo keyboard music appeared with that of Byrd and Bull in *Parthenia* (1613). His consort music includes In Nomines and three-part fantasias (which first appeared in print about 1620), some of which – along with others by John Coprario and Thomas Lupo – were published in Amsterdam (*XX koninklijke fantasien*) in 1648. His only published collection of vocal music contains secular vocal madrigals and motets 'apt for Viols and Voyces' (1612).

But it is for his very popular Short [First] Service, Second [Verse] Service and verse anthems with instrumental parts for viols and organ that he is best remembered. The texts are expressively treated in terms of melody; solo voices and choir alternate in through-composed forms of great vitality and originality as, for example, in the anthem narrating the events of the life of Jesus, *See, see, the word is incarnate*. Though none of his church music was published during his lifetime, most is available in modern collected editions.

His eldest son Christopher Gibbons (1615–76) was an outstanding player who taught the organ and virginal in London during the Commonwealth. At the Restoration he took up posts at the Chapel Royal and as organist at Westminster Abbey, just as his father before him; in addition he was made a Musician-in-Ordinary and by royal nomination was awarded the DMus at Oxford. Anthony Wood described him as 'a person most excellent in his faculty, but a grand debauchee'. He played in the production of Davenant's *The Siege of Rhodes* (1656) and collaborated with Matthew Locke on the masque *Cupid and Death* (1659). He composed fantasia-suites and keyboard works as well as English and Latin sacred vocal music. In the early 1660s he became involved in a scandal concerning plans for a new organ at Worcester Cathedral and resigned his posts in 1666.

Gostling. Singers, father and son. John Gostling (*c*1650–1733) was a bass singer and music copyist at the court of Charles II. He was educated at St John's College, Cambridge, before taking up a post as minor canon at Canterbury Cathedral (1674–83); from 1679 he was a Gentleman of the Chapel Royal. Purcell composed *They that go down to the sea in ships* for him. Gostling's son William (1696–1777) was trained at Canterbury before following his father up to Cambridge. He was an antiquarian by temperament, amassing a large library of manuscripts and printed music, which included a large pre-Civil War organ-book of English Catholic music. He was able to give important assistance to Boyce in compiling *Cathedral Music*.

Grabu, Louis [Grebus, Lewis] (*fl* 1665–94).

French expatriate musician, working in England. Grabu, a pupil of the Parisian organist and early opera composer Robert Cambert, made his career in England where he quickly reached the highest ranks of the King's Musick. In 1666 he became Master of the King's Musick (succeeding Nicholas Lanier). A short time later he assumed leadership of both the Twenty-four Violins (1666) and the Twelve Violins (1667). Pepys reported on the decidedly mixed impression he made.

When Grabu turned his hand to music drama, he was less successful. Having been asked to leave the service of the king in 1674, he turned for work to Cambert, who had recently arrived from Paris. Together they adapted Cambert's *Ariane* (1659) and *Pomone* (1671) for performances at Covent Garden and Windsor that year. He is known to have published a French pastoral in 1684 and the following year a setting of Dryden's *Albion and Albanius*, which the audiences at the Dorset Garden Theatre nevertheless found too Lullian for their tastes; accordingly, Dryden turned to Purcell in 1691 for a setting of its sequel, *King Arthur*.

Grassineau, James (*d* 1767). Important as the compiler of *A Musical Dictionary* (1740). Grassineau was for a time amanuensis to Pepusch, for whom he translated Greek theorists from Latin. Though he acknowledged his debt to Brossard's 1703 dictionary, there is much that is new to it. Two years after his death, his publisher reissued the dictionary with a 52-page supplement purloined from Rousseau's *Dictionnaire* (1768).

Greber, Jakob. See CENTRAL EUROPE 3 *Austro-Hungary*.

Greene, Maurice (1696–1755). Organist, composer and important figure in London musical life. Greene was a contemporary and sometime friend of Handel. By the age of 39 he had been appointed to every major English musical post: organist at St Paul's (1718), organist and composer of the Chapel Royal (1727), professor of music at Cambridge (1730) and Master of the King's Musick (1735). He was a prolific and facile composer of anthems, *Te Deum* settings and oratorios, to which he brought particular gifts of melody and orchestration. Greene produced a dramatic pastorale (*Florimel, or Love's Revenge*, 1734) and at least one masque (*The Judgment of Hercules*, before 1740), Italian cantatas and several collections for the harpsichord. He was the teacher of William Boyce and John Stanley.

He helped to establish the Academy of

Ancient Music (1710), the Philarmonica Club (1715) which later (1724) became the Castle Society, and, in 1731, his own Apollo Society as well as the charitable predecessor of the Royal Society of Musicians (founded in 1738). At his death he was occupied with compiling an encyclopedic collection of English church music, which along with his library passed into the capable hands of Boyce, who published it in the 1760s and 1770s. Despite depreciatory remarks by Hawkins (on his character) and Burney (on his music), Greene deserves to be specially remembered as a teacher, scholar and humanitarian.

Gregory, William (*fl* 1651–87). One of two musicians with the same name. Singer, viol player, song composer and teacher at the courts of Charles II and James II. Gregory put his name to a petition addressed to a parliamentary committee in 1656 regarding the establishment of a music college and was the composer of a well-known elegy to Pelham Humfrey, *Did you not hear the hideous groan.*

Grossi, Giovanni Francesco. See ITALY 10 *Itinerant Musicians.*

Handel, George Frideric (1685–1759). Cosmopolitan composer of German birth (Halle), resident in London and naturalized British, considered by many to be the most gifted and original composer of his era. As organist and composer, his only peer was J. S. Bach, whom he never met. Wherever he went he was fêted, his concerts and works eagerly subscribed. He was the first composer whose music has continued, without a period of eclipse, to be performed from his own time up to the present. During his lifetime he took charge of the performances of his large-scale works, but since his death and until quite recently his music has been subjected to unprecedented alterations and bizarre performance practices never tolerated in the music of other composers of comparable stature.

Handel's path as a musician seems always to have been clear to him. In spite of his court barber-surgeon father's determination that he should take up law, he persisted in musical studies. There was never a shortage of recognition, nor indeed of patrons: the Duke of Saxe-Weissenfels was the first to encourage his talent by interceding with Handel's father. F. W. Zachow was his first teacher and Telemann became one of his earliest and most enduring friends (later he arranged countless performances of Handel's works at Hamburg). A journey to the Berlin court brought him into contact with Giovanni Bononcini and Attilio

Ariosti, who would later be his colleagues and competitors in London.

But it was Hamburg that provided him with important musical stimulation and the opportunity to detach himself from his family. Arriving in 1703, Handel took a job as a back-desk violinist at the Hamburg Opera under the seemingly formidable Reinhard Keiser and gave private lessons to support himself. He became acquainted with Johann Mattheson (who later chronicled the known events of Handel's life during his stay there) and together they visited Buxtehude in Lübeck in that first year; their relationship was briefly marred by a quarrel over who should play the continuo accompaniment in Mattheson's opera *Cleopatra* (1704). In the new year Handel's first two operas were produced, of which the majestic *Almira* (with Mattheson taking the leading tenor role) was the more successful; *Nero* closed after only three performances.

Handel was restless. He had exhausted the possibilities open to him in Hamburg (although he was often to turn to Keiser's music as a source of musical ideas), and must have been keen to experience native Italian opera. Fortuitously, in 1706 an *entrée* to Italy was provided by Prince Ferdinando de' Medici of Florence, where he spent subsequent autumns during his Italian sojourn. Handel continued on to Rome early in 1707 where by necessity rather than conviction he composed in Catholic genres, notably the *Dixit Dominus*, *Laudate pueri* and *Nisi Dominus*. He quickly came to the attention of the powerful Cardinal Pamphili, whose text served for Handel's first oratorio, *Il trionfo del Tempo e del Disinganno*, performed during Lent 1707 at the palace of another music-loving prelate, Cardinal Ottoboni; it is said that Corelli, leader of the orchestra, deemed the French overture to this work too foreign, obliging Handel to substitute an Italian one.

After returning to Florence in the autumn for performances of *Rodrigo* (his first Italian opera), which was much applauded by the court, Handel wintered in Venice where he heard the Carnival operas of Alessandro Scarlatti and Antonio Caldara, and must have come into contact with Domenico Scarlatti, Antonio Lotti, Francesco Gasparini, Vivaldi and Tomaso Albinoni. Significantly, he was also introduced to the Hanoverian Prince Ernst August (brother of the future George I of England) and the English ambassador, the Earl of Manchester, both of whom extended invitations to visit their countries.

Back in Rome, there were others among the clergy and aristocracy who recognized Handel's abilities and wished to have his music performed in their palaces, among them Cardinal Colonna and Marquis Ruspoli. Handel found himself caught up in a whirlwind, fulfilling commissions for sacred works and cantatas and performing everywhere as an organist and harpsichordist, with such musicians as Corelli, Bernardo Pasquini, the Castrucci brothers, Filippo Amadei and Margherita Durastanti (except for the first two, they all eventually joined Handel in London). At Cardinal Ottoboni's palace he met Domenico Scarlatti in a friendly contest of skill at the harpsichord and organ which ended in mutual admiration.

But it was at Ruspoli's Palazzo Bonelli (where Handel was periodically in residence, and wrote numerous cantatas for the evening entertainments) that his most memorable and lavishly produced Roman work was given: the 1708 Easter oratorio *La Resurrezione*. Extra musicians were hired, including Corelli as leader, and Handel was allowed the luxury of three public rehearsals. The marquis was eager to impress Pope Clement XI and determined that Handel's oratorio should outshine the Scarlatti *Passione* performed at Ottoboni's palace earlier in the week, but was made to suffer for his pride: he unwisely cast a female opera singer (Durastanti) as Mary Magdalene, prompting a papal rebuke, for women were discouraged from singing publicly in Rome. The young Handel was soon busy at work on *Agrippina*, a black comedy opera commissioned by Cardinal Vincenzo Grimani for Venice. Earlier that year he had been to Naples, where his serenata *Aci, Galatea e Polifemo* was performed at the Duke of Alvito's residence. It was performed 27 times at the S Giovanni Grisostomo theatre during the 1708-9 Carnival season. Venetian audiences were enchanted by the grandeur and sublimity of Handel's music. As a foreigner, he had met the supreme challenge to any aspiring opera composer by succeeding in Venice.

A year later he was on his way northwards, pausing at the court in Innsbruck before going on to Hanover (in June 1710). He went there as *Kapellmeister* – a post he was to hold largely in name only, but which strengthened his ultimate connections with England. While in Hanover he became friendly with Agostino Steffani whom he may have already met in Italy. A month later, granted a year's leave of absence, he had slipped free of his Hanoverian commitment and was on his way to London.

He paused *en route* at the electoral court at Düsseldorf, arriving in London by September 1710.

Handel stayed only eight months, but made an impact sufficient to ensure his return. Until his arrival, opera in Italian had had little success; Bononcini's much-heralded *Camilla* had been given in English (1706) and Scarlatti's *Pyrrhus and Demetrius* in a mixture of the two (1708). But Handel, displaying the confidence that must have stood him in such good stead in Rome and Venice, risked staging an Italian opera made up largely from the music he had composed there: *Rinaldo* was performed fifteen times between February and June of 1711 at the Queen's Theatre. Aaron Hill wrote the scenario (and possibly the first draft of the libretto which Rossi then italianized) and produced the opera, sparing no expense for the scenery and machines; the cast included three castratos (Nicolini sang the title role). The publisher John Walsh, ever ready to capitalize on the moment, published songs from *Rinaldo* while it was still in production; Addison (mindful of the failure of his own *Rosamond*) and Steele (who had a vested interest in English theatre) ridiculed in *The Spectator* this latest and most lavish attempt to convert the English to Italian opera. Meanwhile, Handel found time to play for Queen Anne and to take part in Thomas Britton's house concerts in Clerkenwell.

He left for Hanover in June, travelling again via Düsseldorf. His duties required him to compose and direct chamber and orchestral music, but no opera. In November he visited his family in Halle and expressed his interest in returning to England by making efforts to learn the language. Less than a year later, he left Hanover with empty reassurances that he would return; in fact he had every intention of taking up permanent residence in London.

Once there, Handel had little trouble finding suitable work or accommodation: Lord Burlington soon provided both at his elegant mansion (now the Royal Academy of Arts) in Piccadilly. There, over a three-year period, he mixed with eminent men of arts and letters, such as Pope, Gay and Arbuthnot. Freed of mundane cares, he concentrated on composing operas. His first, *Il Pastor Fido* (1712), was produced with borrowed costumes and scenery and inevitably proved less successful than *Rinaldo*; it was followed in the same season by the French-style *Teseo* (1713), which won approval from the Haymarket audiences for its powerful portrayal of Medea. *Silla* was privately performed at Burlington

House in 1713; two years later Handel re-used much of its music in *Amadigi di Gaula*, which was presented in the Haymarket.

Handel was also at work on other fronts, confidently preparing an Utrecht *Te Deum* and *Jubilate* in English for a July 1713 performance at St Paul's Cathedral and a birthday ode for Queen Anne, who made the extraordinary gesture of awarding Handel a pension of £200 a year for life. He also found time to play the Father Smith organ at St Paul's and to visit the nearby Queen's Arms Tavern where chamber music was played at certain times.

When the Elector of Hanover assumed the English throne as George I, in September 1714, Handel found himself in what would have been an awkward position had he been anyone else. Instead, his dereliction of duty at Hanover was overlooked, his stipend continued without interruption and indeed increased when he became music master to the princesses (for whom he must have composed the keyboard suites subsequently published in 1720); his 'Caroline' *Te Deum* was performed by the Chapel Royal musicians at the king's first royal engagement.

It was in fact initially advantageous to Handel to be a native German at the Georgian court. When he accompanied the king to Hanover in July 1716 he was able to visit Halle. Handel set Brockes's Passion oratorio, the composer's last substantial work in German, probably for Hamburg. When he returned to England he was accompanied by his former fellow-student Johann Christoph Schmidt [J.C. Smith the elder] as his copyist and secretary. The following summer the king requested a concert on the River Thames and Handel was commissioned to write 'Water Music', for wind and strings. With members of the court and musicians accommodated in barges, the evening's entertainment went on until the early hours of the morning.

By this time, Handel had already distanced himself from the king, opting for a change of scene by taking up an appointment as resident composer with the Earl of Carnarvon (from 1719 the Duke of Chandos) who maintained a modest complement of singers and instrumentalists under the direction of another German expatriate, Dr Johann Christoph Pepusch, and two houses (one in London and the other at Cannons, Edgware, where chamber music could be heard without competition from the noise of the city streets). Over the next two years (1717–18) he composed eleven anthems (parts of which he purloined for use in the Chapel Royal), a *Te Deum*, and two masques – the small-scale masterpiece *Acis and Galatea* (text by John Gay and others) and the first version of *Esther*, his earliest essay in English oratorio, a genre he was to create.

However bucolic a country retreat Cannons might have seemed, it could not quell Handel's obsession with Italian opera. Having already embraced the Italian concept of operatic form (a succession of recitatives and da capo arias) in *Agrippina*, he continued to explore the musical possibilities afforded by different types of text – magic and anti-heroic as well as heroic – and the strengths of the artist-singers he was able to attract to London.

During the winter of 1718–19 members of the nobility set about creating an Italian opera company in London, initially funded by an eight-year subscription; the king gave permission to call it 'The Royal Academy of Music'. Handel was designated music director, J. J. Heidegger (already manager of the King's Theatre) was charged with its running, and P. A. Rolli was made the Academy's first secretary and official librettist (though more often than not, Handel collaborated with his eventual successor, N. F. Haym); the designer Roberto Clerici was put in charge of scenery and machines.

After engaging the best English singers and instrumentalists, Handel took himself off to Dresden in search of Italian singers, stopping *en route* to visit friends in Düsseldorf and relatives at Halle; sadly, he just missed meeting J. S. Bach. At Dresden he negotiated with various singers – including Senesino, Margherita Durastanti and G. M. Boschi – but only Durastanti agreed to come immediately; Faustina Bordoni, Francesca Cuzzoni and Senesino followed in later seasons.

The Royal Academy's first season opened on 2 April 1720 with Giovanni Porta's *Numitore*, followed soon after by Handel's *Radamisto*. During the next eight years, almost half the performances were given over to Handel operas, which included *Floridante* (Rolli, 1721); five operas on texts by Haym – *Ottone* and *Flavio* (1723), *Giulio Cesare in Egitto* and *Tamerlano* (1724), and *Rodelinda* (1725); four more on texts by Rolli – *Scipione* and *Alessandro* (1726), *Admeto* and *Riccardo Primo* (1727); *Siroe* (Metastasio, 1728) and *Tolomeo* (Haym, 1728). Though fewer of Bononcini's operas – beginning with *Astarto* (1720) and ending with *Astianatte* (1727) – were produced, individually they received more performances than did Handel's. Ariosti's operas were the next most frequently performed.

Along the way, there were financial worries and internecine disputes between singers and management, but the quality of the performances was rarely in question. Handel was a severe taskmaster: blunt, stubborn and imperious, and yet, in other ways, quite dispassionate (he kept himself above politics and was never cavalier in money matters). He had no qualms about swearing in any one of several languages, including comically broken English.

The importance of the singers in any commercial operatic venture could not be overestimated. Handel travelled and corresponded at length in the pursuit of the best Italians and accepted only the finest English singers into his company. Even when contracts had been signed, Handel was obliged to tailor roles and arias to suit their voices, and to contend with rivalries within and without. Senesino was the most temperamental of all – quite liable to take himself off to Italy at a moment's notice if riled – and yet his appearance, along with that of Francesca Cuzzoni and Faustina Bordoni – could tip the balance between the success or failure of a work. In 1726 the directors of the Academy expected the trio literally to rescue it from financial ruin, and yet when Senesino left for Italy before the final performance of *Alessandro* (in protest at the greater prominence given to the two sopranos), they had little choice but to postpone the autumn season until he could be enticed back; his defection to the Opera of the Nobility in 1734 was a serious setback to Handel's second Academy. Equally, the women could jeopardize performances: there was, for example, the memorable occasion when Cuzzoni balked at singing her first aria in *Ottone* and risked being thrown out of the window by Handel; she greatly resented the hiring of her rival Faustina in 1726 and insisted that Handel carefully apportion their arias in *Admeto* so that neither would have the greater advantage (Bononcini succeeded less well in managing them: one performance of *Astianatte* ended in a brawl between the two sopranos). If the notoriety did much to stimulate box office sales, the commotion created in the theatre by their respective admirers greatly detracted from the performances.

In mid 1727, shortly before the death of George I, Handel became a British subject. In his capacity as composer to the Chapel Royal (a post he had held since 1723), Handel composed four large-scale anthems for the coronation of George II (the most famous, *Zadok the priest*, has been sung at every coronation since). A few months later, in January 1728, Gay's *Beggar's Opera* opened at the theatre in Lincoln's Inn Fields. It was not a true opera but a play with songs made up from popular tunes (including some by Handel), and treated London low life in a way that parodied current political and cultural events – not excluding Italian opera. Over 60 performances were given that year, eclipsing the final season of the Royal Academy.

But Handel was already planning to create a second Academy: the King's Theatre was leased to him and Heidegger for a further five years, with the patronage of the king and queen and Princess Anne (by then, Handel's only pupil). Early in 1729 Handel was off to Italy in search of fresh singers; he returned with Bernacchi (who was past his prime and was replaced as soon as Senesino could be lured back), the soprano Strada del Pò, the contraltos Merighi and Bertolli, the tenor Fabri and the German bass Riemschneider. The next season was launched with *Lotario* and *Partenope*, neither of which was particularly successful, followed by revivals. The personality cults and the popularity of the new, lighter musical-dramatic entertainment purveyed not far away, at Lincoln's Inn Fields, were noticeably eroding the serious opera audiences. Even Handel could not stem the tide. In 1731 John Rich staged a benefit concert there at which *Acis and Galatea* was performed, apparently without Handel's knowledge or consent. Handel countered with settings of two Metastasio texts, *Poro* (1731) and *Ezio* (1732), of which the latter proved a dismal failure.

Handel was not easily discouraged and so persevered – not without success – in his quest to recapture the public. As yet he showed no signs of adapting to changing tastes, and indeed since the *Ezio* débâcle, he had enjoyed mild success with a new opera, *Sosarme* (1732). But the events of 1732 must have given him pause. First, in February, Bernard Gates (an old Chapel Royal friend of Handel's) conducted three successful private performances at the Crown and Anchor Tavern of *Esther*, by the Chapel Royal and Westminster Abbey choirs. While Handel was considering taking the work into his theatre repertory, another, unauthorized performance was advertised. Unable to prevent it – there was no copyright law – Handel retaliated, exercising his rights as composer by revising and supplementing the 1718 version. But since the Bishop of

London would not countenance the representation of a Bible story in a theatre, it was given without action, and was successful enough for six crowded performances.

Meanwhile, the movement to establish English opera seemed to be gaining momentum at Handel's expense: the Arnes, J. F. Lampe and Henry Carey adapted *Acis and Galatea* as a three-act piece for performances at the Little Haymarket Theatre (immediately opposite Handel's own theatre) in 1732, obliging Handel to go one better: he borrowed, appropriately enough, from his 1708 Neapolitan serenata and interleaved parts of it with the English masque version; his native sopranos sang in English and the others in Italian. Though not required to act, the singers wore costumes and were surrounded by scenery. For the moment, Handel had had the last word.

Efforts were made, notably by Aaron Hill, to convert Handel to English opera, but to no avail. In 1733 some of his friends, colleagues (including Senesino) and former patrons (Lord Burlington prominent among them) decided to repay his arrogance by defecting from the Academy to form what has come to be called the 'Opera of the Nobility', with the Prince of Wales at its head. This must have been a bitter blow to Handel, however much expected, but he rebounded with a highly successful 'magic' opera, *Orlando*.

That summer, Handel was invited to Oxford to take part in the 'Publick Act', being revived at the Sheldonian Theatre. *Esther*, *Deborah* (a pastiche of sacred works which he had earlier given in London with little success) and a new oratorio, *Athalia*, were performed there, possibly with organ concertos performed by Handel in the intervals. The macaronic version of *Acis and Galatea* at Christ Church Hall. It was expected that the degree of Doctor of Music would be conferred upon Handel, but it never materialized (some say because he refused to compose a contrapuntal test piece, others because he would not pay the degree fee).

For the 1733–4 season, Handel engaged two new castratos, Carlo Scalzi and Carestini; Durastanti returned as a mezzo. The first production was a revival of *Ottone*, followed by two composite operas. The Opera of the Nobility opened with Porpora's *Arianna in Nasso* at Christmas and a month later Handel's *Arianna in Creta* was on the boards. In March 1734, Handel's pupil Princess Anne married Prince William of Orange (see Plate 17) and in her honour he produced a serenata, *Parnasso*

in Festa, at the Haymarket Theatre and the Wedding Anthem (both of which draw much from *Athalia*). The op. 3 concerti grossi appeared that year (his opp. 1 and 2 sonatas, for one and two violins/flutes/recorders/oboes and continuo were published about 1730).

At the end of the opera season, Handel suffered the indignity of having the King's Theatre let (by Heidegger) to the momentarily prosperous Opera of the Nobility; in true fashion, Handel saw it not so much as a defeat as an opportunity to move to John Rich's new Theatre Royal in Covent Garden, which seemed to him equally suited to opera and oratorio. Possessed of remarkable resilience, Handel endured all setbacks with relative detachment.

The following season, the Opera of the Nobility achieved the ultimate vocal *coup de grâce* when they secured the services of none other than Farinelli (the most famous of all castratos) who, in Hasse's *Artaserse*, which inaugurated the 1734–5 season, did not fail to outshine even Senesino. Marie Sallé, the Paris Opera dancer Handel engaged, could hardly have been expected to compete with Farinelli. For her Handel composed *Terpsichore*, his only foray into French *opéra-ballet*, and cobbled together a pastiche with dances, *Oreste*. Both *Ariodante* and the masterly *Alcina*, presented at Covent Garden in the new year, incorporated ballet sequences, although Mlle Sallé's appearances in the latter opera were deemed in poor taste (for the role of Cupid, she dressed in male attire), and she departed England in disgrace. Later in the year Carestini returned to Italy; and Handel was obliged to engage English singers. John Beard and Cecilia Young (later Mrs Arne) first appeared in *Ariodante*.

A lacklustre 1735–6 season for both opera companies made it evident to all that London audiences were no longer prepared to support two rival houses. In *Atalanta*, his only new opera of the season, Handel incorporated a fireworks finale, in celebration of the marriage of the Prince of Wales. But simultaneously he was organizing performances of his oratorios at Covent Garden, using the same mixture of Italian and English singers heard there in his recent opera productions. Strada, Young and Beard took part in *Alexander's Feast*, Handel's setting of an ode by Dryden, which was enthusiastically received – in conspicuous contrast to the failure (in spite of the presence of the soprano castrato Gioacchino Conti ['Gizziello'] and the contralto Annibali) of the 1736–7 season's operas (for which he borrowed heavily from his own works): *Arminio*, *Giustino* and *Berenice*. The second Academy closed in financial disarray; their competitors had closed four days before.

In April 1737 Handel suffered a stroke or an injury which seriously affected his right hand. He was exhausted from the stresses of the last five years and his friends and patrons wondered whether he would ever play or compose again. He retired to Aix-la-Chapelle to take the vapour-baths; six weeks later he returned to London, miraculously restored. He was able to play the organ, and planning his next works (which he unhappily interrupted to compose a funeral anthem, *The Ways of Zion do Mourn*, for his very old friend, the queen).

Determined as ever to write for the stage, he engaged a new castrato, Caffarelli, for the shortened 1738 season, which included *Faramondo* (Zeno), *Alessandro Severo* (a pastiche of his own music) and the partly comic *Serse* (Minato), at the King's Theatre. However, these latest operas fared badly against Lampe's operatic satire of *Giustino*, entitled *The Dragon of Wantley*, which greatly diverted audiences (in more than one sense). Handel was unable to recover the lost ground with the pastiche *Giove in Argo* (1739), nor with *Imeneo* (Stampiglia; 1740) and *Deidamia* (Rolli; 1741) in subsequent seasons.

But seemingly as his command of Italian opera ebbed, English oratorios – in many ways musically operatic, though far more reliant upon the chorus – began flowing from his pen: *Alexander's Feast* was followed by *Il trionfo del Tempo e della Verità* (1737), a much-revised version of his first oratorio, *Il trionfo del Tempo e del Disinganno*. Elisabeth Duparc emerged as his new principal soprano, appearing in *Saul* (Jennens) and the biblical epic *Israel in Egypt* of 1739 (much of it borrowed).

In response to the continued approbation accorded to his organ concertos at oratorio performances, Handel published in 1738 a collection of six as op. 4; a second set was released in 1740, a third after his death. Handel's printer–publisher John Walsh also took the unprecedented step of bringing out a full score of *Alexander's Feast*, thus confirming the popularity not only of the work but of the genre. Handel had cannily judged the public's pulse regarding English choral works and given himself a new creative lease of life.

His connections with the relatively new (1732) Vauxhall Gardens were solidified, to say the least, by the installation there of a marble bust of Handel by the sculptor Louis-François Roubiliac (commissioned by Jon-athan Tyers, owner of the pleasure gardens; it is now exhibited at the Victoria & Albert Museum). At much the same time Handel began taking an active interest in charitable causes. He organized annual benefit concerts for the Fund for the Support of Decayed Musicians and from 1740 was an elected director (along with Hogarth) of the Foundling Hospital, to which he presented an organ in 1750.

Handel leased the small theatre at Lincoln's Inn Fields for the 1739–40 season, opening on St Cecilia's Day with a setting of Dryden's ode 'From harmony, from heav'nly harmony'. He revived *Acis and Galatea* and produced a new choral work, *L'Allegro, il Penseroso ed il Moderato*, to a text assembled by Jennens largely from Milton, which appealed to the English audiences through its happy nature imagery. To enliven the performances, selections from Handel's new op. 6. concertos for strings were played in the intervals. The season over, Handel took the increasingly rare opportunity to travel on the Continent.

During the summer of 1741, Handel received an invitation from the Lord Lieutenant in Dublin to compose a new sacred oratorio which would crown a series of performances of *Alexander's Feast*, *Acis and Galatea*, the *Ode for St Cecilia's Day* and *L'Allegro*, to be given at the New Music Hall, Fishamble Street, Dublin, in 1742. The commissioned work, on a biblical libretto devised by Jennens, was *Messiah*. From its first performances in April 1742 (which included a charity preview) *Messiah* was an unqualified success, taking its place among the finest and best-loved works ever composed. The messy autograph attests to the speed at which he wrote it as well as to the strength and sureness of his creative convictions. Drawing upon such diverse genres as Italian opera, English anthem and German Passion, Handel composed, during the summer of 1741, a contemplative, largely undramatic work of uniquely universal appeal. Within days of finishing it he was at work on *Samson*, a lengthy new oratorio based on Milton, in anticipation of the 1742–3 season in London.

Handel departed for Ireland in November 1741, having completed *Samson* and attended the opening of the new season at the Haymarket. His amanuensis, John Christopher Smith, accompanied him. On the way, they stopped in Chester, where they met Charles Burney. The Dublin events began in early December, so Handel was occupied from the moment he arrived. Almost immediately, his Utrecht *Te*

Deum and *Jubilate* were performed in a charity concert in aid of the Mercers' Hospital; to add to the prestige of the event, Handel played the organ. Throughout his visit he made use of an all-male choir made up of choristers and singers from the city's two cathedrals; his old friend Matthew Dubourg, Master of the State Music, led his orchestra. Early in 1742, a concert version of *Imeneo* was presented; Arne's sister, Susanna Cibber, took the leading role and sufficiently impressed Handel to gain a further invitation to sing in *Messiah*; joined by her sister-in-law, Cecilia Young Arne, Mrs Cibber was also heard in a recital of Handel solos and duets later in the year. The enthusiasm and co-operation that Handel encountered at every point during his ten-month stay must have been very heartening to the weary warrior.

Upon returning to London, Handel resisted the temptation to resume composing Italian operas, and instead plunged into arrangements for an oratorio subscription season beginning early in 1743. He hired Covent Garden, and in February inaugurated the series with *Samson*, which was warmly received in spite of Horace Walpole's cynical post-mortem. A month later, *Messiah* was performed. Charles Jennens had not travelled to Ireland to hear it the previous year, and so he came down from the Midlands to attend the London performances. In the interim, he had nurtured resentments against Handel and took his revenge by professing (in his correspondence) his disappointment in the music.

Handel suffered another stroke in April, effectively scotching the plans of those (among them the Prince of Wales) who were urging him to consider composing operas for the next season. Mercifully, Handel was only temporarily indisposed and soon amazed everyone by producing *Semele* (to a text by Congreve) in a mere four weeks for the 1744 season at Covent Garden. He had cunningly contrived a musical Sphinx, neither oratorio (because of its erotic secular text) nor opera (because of the prominent chorus and the lack of stage action). There was outrage among many that Handel should present such a work in the guise of an oratorio and when Handel and the Prince of Wales later quarrelled over it Handel was quoted by the *Daily Post* as having pronounced the prince 'quite out of *his* good graces!'

In precarious health – indeed, his eyesight was soon to fail him and eventually any new music had to be dictated to the younger Smith – Handel amazed even his critics by the steady stream of large-scale works he continued to produce. He did, however, postpone composing *Joseph and his Brethren* (1744), but only in order to prepare (during the summer of 1743) a Dettingen *Te Deum*, celebrating George II's leadership in the decisive battle of the War of Austrian Succession. *Hercules* (which, like *Semele*, Handel was careful not to call an oratorio) and one of his favourite works, the ravishingly beautiful *Belshazzar* (Jennens), followed in 1745 at the King's Theatre, but were not enthusiastically received, and the season came to a premature end.

For his Covent Garden seasons, Handel was obliged to look elsewhere for themes: the Jacobite rebellion in 1745 provided the impetus for the more successful (though highly derivative) *Occasional Oratorio* (1746) and the three militaristic oratorios on moralistic texts by the Rev. Thomas Morell – *Judas Maccabaeus* (1747), *Joshua* (1748), *Alexander Balus* (1748) – that followed. In *Susanna* (1749) he returned to a lighter, pastoral theme, tinged with comedy. *Solomon* (1749) was laced with Georgian panegyric, *Theodora* (Morell; 1750) with Christian martyrdom. *Jephtha* (Morell; 1752) conveys suffering (because of his deteriorating sight, Handel laboured longest on this work) and *The Triumph of Time and Truth* (for which Morell revised Pamphili's earlier text; 1757) acceptance.

In 1749 Handel prepared the highly acclaimed *Music for the Royal Fireworks*, to accompany the festivities at Green Park in celebration of the Treaty of Aix-la-Chapelle (a preview at Vauxhall Gardens was heavily attended). The first performance of *Messiah* at the Foundling Hospital took place in April 1750, thereafter becoming an annual event. That summer Handel made his last trip to Halle and was said to have been injured *en route* in a coach accident.

When he returned he settled down to compose *Jephtha*, but in the course of working on the final Act II chorus, 'How dark, O Lord, are thy decrees, All hid from mortal sight', the sight in his left eye failed him. He continued to work – performing and conducting as well as composing – until at last his right eye inevitably began to fail. Even when total blindness came in 1752 he continued to perform organ concertos and voluntaries between the parts of his oratorios, so great were his memory and powers of improvisation. He remained involved in the arrangements for performances of his works up to his death.

When death came on 14 April 1759, Handel

was ready. He left a carefully detailed will with instructions that he should be buried in Westminster Abbey; Roubiliac was commissioned to sculpt a monument which can be seen today in Poets' Corner. Within a year of Handel's death, the Rev. John Mainwaring had completed the *Memoirs of the Life of the Late George Frederic Handel*, the first monograph devoted to a composer, which was followed by Mattheson's *Georg Friedrich Händels Lebensbeschreibung* in 1761. The Lenten oratorio seasons continued under the direction of Morell and J. C. Smith the younger, who recycled Handel's music in pastiche form. In 1784, the 25th anniversary of his death and only a year short of the centenary of his birth, an unprecedented series of three commemoration concerts was organized at Westminster Abbey and the Pantheon, culminating on 29 May in a massed performance at the Abbey of *Messiah*, which set in motion a tradition that still persists today.

Hare. Music publishers, printers and violin makers (father and son). John Hare (*d* 1725) founded the business in 1695 and was joined by his son Joseph (*d* 1733) in 1722; they published jointly until 1725. Three years later Joseph started his own business, having helped his mother to run his father's firm in the interim; his own wife took over the business after his death. Both Hares maintained links with the firm of John Walsh.

Harris. Catholic family of organ builders, of whom Renatus Harris is the most important. Thomas Harris (*d* *c*1685) lived and worked in Brittany from the 1640s until just after the Restoration, when he and his family returned to England to restore organs damaged during the Commonwealth. His business was gradually taken over by his ambitious son, Renatus [René] (*c*1652–1724), who challenged the better-established Father Smith for the chance to build an organ for the Temple Church, London; in the end they built in competition, but because Harris was said to have damaged the Smith organ's bellows, he was disqualified. They clashed again in the 1690s over the new organ to be built in St Paul's Cathedral and once again the job went to Smith; Harris had a pamphlet printed in 1712 which described a hypothetical organ he wished to build at the west end of the cathedral that would incorporate pedals and six keyboards, the last of which would imitate the human breath.

Ironically, Harris organs, with their French reed voicing and excellent action, are generally considered to be superior to the best of Smith's. His most important instruments were built for the Popish Chapel at Whitehall, the cathedrals at Newcastle, Bristol and Salisbury, and St James Piccadilly. He was succeeded by his son, John (*d* 1743), and son-in-law, John Byfield, who built an important organ for St Mary Redcliffe (Bristol): it incorporated a record number of speaking pipes (1,928), and the Great Organ, with 63 keys, was the first English organ to be fitted with a coupler.

Hasse, Johann Adolf. See NORTHERN EUROPE *4 Saxony and Thuringia: Dresden.*

Haward. The most important English family of spinet and harpsichord makers during the 17th century. In *Musick's Monument* (1676), Mace described the registration pedals of the harpsichord John Haward made for him. An instrument (1683, with a lute stop) made by Charles Haward, now at Hovingham Hall, is said to be the only extant English harpsichord from the second half of the 17th century. Pepys mentions visiting his shop to inspect the bentside spinets and Queen Anne owned a virginal made by Charles.

Hawkins, Sir John (1719–89). Attorney (by profession and temperament), amateur musician, poet, antiquarian and music historian who published a five-volume *General History of the Science and Practice of Music.* Hawkins's complete *History* appeared in 1776, seven months after the publication of the first volume of Charles Burney's. It was the fruit of many years' effort and dwelt particularly on the achievements of the 17th century, though not without chronicling the musical life of 18th-century London as he had known it. Hawkins counted among his friends John Stanley, William Boyce and Pepusch (whose vast library he acquired in 1763) as well as Handel. He belonged to numerous societies, including the Academy of Ancient Music, where he mingled with musicians of the day. In the course of his writing, he conducted interviews and carried on research at the British Museum, the Oxford and Cambridge libraries and in private collections.

A legacy had enabled him to devote himself to writing; nevertheless, when the *History* appeared, those who knew him were amazed at his achievement. He was not a particularly likeable man and during his years as a magistrate was considered severe. Partisans of Burney attacked Hawkins in the press for his 17th-century bias, his pompous language and his digressions. He was the duller writer of the two, yet more fair and balanced, and with a truer historical outlook. Burney himself wrote a malicious satirical poem, which circulated in manuscript, entitled 'The Trial of

Midas the Second or Congress of Musicians' in which Science, Taste, Wit, Candour and Fame prosecute Hawkins, who is condemned to witness the dumping of his effigy and *History* into Fleet Ditch.

Haym, Nicola Francesco (1678–1729). Roman cellist (of German descent), composer, teacher, editor, opera librettist and lively antiquarian who made London his home from 1701 and was instrumental in popularizing Italian music. Haym seems always to have been doing several things at once. In Rome in the late 1690s, he played the violone in Cardinal Ottoboni's orchestra under Corelli and composed at least two oratorios and a serenata. Upon his arrival in London in 1701, he entered the service of the second Duke of Bedford, for whom he provided chamber music and whose library he augmented, while joining with Charles Dieupart in 1705 to produce the first Italian opera heard in London at Drury Lane (Thomas Clayton's *Arsinoe*). Determined to establish Italian opera in London, Haym played in the orchestra and composed or arranged supplementary music as needed. He also found time to coach singers and edit Corelli's opp. 1–4 for Roger (published in Amsterdam in 1705), which along with his own sonatas he introduced at Drury Lane. After the duke's death in 1711, Haym explored other avenues. When a plan to give regular concerts at the York Buildings fell through, he presented subscription concerts at Hickford's Rooms instead.

From 1713 he was in demand as a librettist, adapting Quinault's *Thésée* for Handel's *Teseo* – the first of many texts he provided for Handel (including *Giulio Cesare* in 1724); Ariosti and Bononcini also employed his librettos after he replaced the controversial Paolo Antonio Rolli as official librettist and Italian secretary to the Royal Academy of Music. While in the service of the Duke of Chandos (from 1718), he played the string bass and composed anthems for the duke's chapel. He belonged to the Academy of Ancient Music during 1726–7.

Heidegger, Johann Jakob (1666–1749). Swiss impresario known for his taste, judgment and acumen; he was instrumental in popularizing Italian opera in London in the first half of the 18th century. In 1713 Heidegger, who had been one of Queen Anne's Life Guards, succeeded Owen Swiney as the manager of operatic productions at Drury Lane; six years later he was involved in the foundation of the Royal Academy of Music, and was a guiding force in promoting Italian

opera until about 1745. From 1720 to 1734 he collaborated with Handel, but in 1734 let the theatre to Handel's rival, the Opera of the Nobility; when in 1738 opera subscriptions slumped, Heidegger did not hesitate to let the theatre to Handel for performances of oratorios. He also profitably rented the theatre for masked balls, to the horror of the Bishop of London (1724) and the consternation of government officials. He basked, no doubt, in the notoriety conferred on him by the satires by Hughes, Fielding and Pope and the caricatures by Hogarth and Goupy. To his credit, he gave generously to charity and helped many fellow Swiss immigrants.

Hingeston, John (*d* 1688). Organist, viol player and composer of fantasy-suites, who served both Cromwell and Charles II. Hingeston occupied a pivotal position in 17th-century English music: he was a pupil of Orlando Gibbons and the teacher of Blow and Purcell; as state organist and a private musician to Oliver Cromwell he helped preserve the traditions of royal music during the Commonwealth. As Master of Music he led the musicians in silent procession at Cromwell's funeral in 1658. Meanwhile in 1657 he had headed a six-man 'Corporation of Music' who presented a petition to a 'Committee for the Advancement of Music', demanding that the worsening conditions under which musicians worked be improved.

Under the king's policy of conciliation at the Restoration, Hingeston relinquished the post of Master to Nicholas Lanier (who had held it during the reign of Charles I) and accepted lesser appointments as a viol player and the person in charge of the manufacture, repair and presentation of music instruments at court (in the latter, he was succeeded by Purcell). From 1661 to 1666 he was a member of the Chapel Royal. Of his music, all that survives is a single organ voluntary, two anthems, two manuscript partbooks for 180 wind pieces dating from the Commonwealth era (Victoria & Albert Museum) and 37 fantasy-suites for viols and violins with viols, modelled on those by John Coprario, John Jenkins, William Lawes and Matthew Locke.

Hitchcock. Family of spinet and harpsichord makers working in London. Thomas Hitchcock (*d* before 1700) and his two sons Thomas (*c*1685–after 1733) and John (*d* 1774) built more italianate (i.e. shorter) instruments than Kirckman and Shudi. The oldest surviving two-manual English harpsichord (incorporating two eight-foot stops, a lute and four-foot stop) was made by Thomas Hitchcock. They all left fine examples of veneered cases.

Howard, Samuel (1710–82). Organist and composer whose songs were popular at Vauxhall Gardens. Howard was trained by William Croft at the Chapel Royal and was later organist at St Clement Danes and St Bride's. He also helped Boyce with the compilation of the massive three-volume anthology of *Cathedral Music* (1760–73). He took the MusD at Cambridge in 1769.

Hudson, George (1615/20–1672). Instrumentalist and composer who contributed music, along with Charles Coleman, for Davenant's *The Siege of Rhodes* (1656). His career at court as a musician 'for the lutes and voices extraordinary' was abruptly ended by the Civil War; at the Restoration he was reappointed to the King's Private Musick as a violinist and composer (see Plate 15). He was a member of the Corporation of Musicians and played the viol; of his music, only some lyra viol pieces and suites for one or two violins and continuo survive.

Hughes, Francis (1666/7–1744). Countertenor at Drury Lane Theatre from 1700 who sang in Clayton's *Arsinoe* (1705), the first English opera in the Italian style, and was known to have a voice capable of shattering a drinking glass. Hughes sang the leading male role in Giovanni Bononcini's highly acclaimed *Camilla* the following year and in the less successful *Rosamond* (text by Clayton) and *Thomyris* (Pepusch's arrangement) in 1707. With the arrival of the Italian castratos, Hughes was less in demand. He became a member of the Chapel Royal Choir in 1708 and thereafter only occasionally appeared in London concerts.

Hume, Tobias (*d* 1645). English soldier who served as a captain in the Swedish and Russian armies; also a viol player and a somewhat eccentric composer who died insane. Two published collections for the 'Gambo Violl' (as he called it) are all that survive of Hume's music: *The First Part of Ayres. Captaine Humes Musicall Humors* (1605) and *Captaine Humes Poeticall Musicke* (1607). A zealous amateur, he was eager to promote his instrument as capable of accompanying itself in solo music and the equal of the lute; here he encountered the disdain of John Dowland, who in *A Pilgrimes Solace* (1612) replied tartly to Hume's offending remarks which appeared in the prefaces to his editions. Hume was a prankster whose most notorious composition was 'An Invention for Two to Play upone one Viole'; two bows are required and the smaller

of the two players (preferably a lady) is obliged to sit in the lap of the larger (presumably a gentleman). The work, also known as 'The Princes Almayne', notated in tablature, is technically possible to perform.

Humfrey [Humphrey], Pelham (1647–74). Cosmopolitan Restoration composer who held a remarkable number of important posts at court and in the City of London before his tragic death at the age of 26. Humfrey's gifts as a composer were evident when he was still a chorister in the Chapel Royal: the texts of five early anthems were published in 1664 and he was conspicuously better paid than his contemporaries John Blow, Michael Wise, William Turner, Robert Smith and Thomas Tudway. After leaving the Chapel Royal in 1664, Humfrey travelled on the Continent where, to judge from his music, he took the opportunity to gain a command of Carissimi's expressive vocal style and Lully's skill at deploying large instrumental and vocal forces.

While abroad he was granted an appointment as a royal lutenist; according to Pepys, he returned to England late in 1667. The same year, he was made a Gentleman of the Chapel Royal; in that capacity he sang tenor and composed verse anthems in his own expression of the Italian (*Hear, O heav'ns*) and French styles (*O give thanks unto the Lord*). In addition, for the rest of his short life, he composed odes (less distinguished than his anthems; only three, including the panegyric *When from his throne*, survive) and songs for court entertainments and plays in the City.

In 1670 he was elected an Assistant of the Corporation of Music and two years later was made a Warden. In 1672 he gained a further appointment at court (held jointly with Thomas Purcell), assisting George Hudson, as a composer for violin; later that year he succeeded Henry Cooke (whose daughter he had married) as Master of the Children of the Chapel Royal (whom he taught the violin, lute and theorbo). His music for Shadwell's version of *The Tempest* (1674) consisted of the song 'Where the bee sucks' and two masques, one in Lully's *comédie-ballet* tradition and the other in the Anglo-Italian style of Locke.

Humphries, [?J. S.] John (*c*1707–before *c*1740). Violinist and composer of instrumental chamber music. Humphries was one of the first in England to compose for wind instruments: he published two collections of concertos (1740–41) in which oboes, flutes, trumpets and horns are either included or optional.

Jaye, Henry (*fl c*1610–67). String instrument

maker, highly praised by Thomas Mace. His viols, in particular, have always been admired and sought after for their fine craftsmanship and soft, velvety tone.

Jeffreys, George. See BRITISH ISLES 2 *Provinces*.

Jennens, Charles. See BRITISH ISLES 2 *Provinces*.

Johnson, Robert (*c*1583–1633). Lutenist to James I and Charles I and composer of incidental theatre music. From 1609 onwards Johnson collaborated with William Shakespeare at the Blackfriars Theatre, composing declamatory ayres for *Cymbeline*, *The Winter's Tale* and *The Tempest* ('Where the bee sucks'). He also contributed dances to some of Ben Jonson's court masques. For the lute he composed uncommonly idiomatic and expressive pieces; Thomas Mace later compared his playing to that of John Dowland.

Johnson, Samuel (?1698–?1773). Ambitious and unconventional dancing-master from Cheshire, also known as 'Maggotty Johnson', whose amateurish burlesque *Hurlothrumbo, or The Super-Natural* (1729) created a sensation at the Little Theatre in the Haymarket and set in motion a fashion for ridiculous plots and nonsensical character names. Johnson is also known for the effusive and satirical open letter to Handel he published in 1734.

Jones, Inigo (1573–1652). Gifted architect of buildings and stage productions. Although Jones is reckoned the most important architect of the English Renaissance, he devoted much of his energy to no fewer than 40 theatre productions and masques (over 30 with Ben Jonson) in his various capacities as co-author, producer, machinery operator and costume designer. Among the musicians with whom he collaborated on masques were Alfonso Ferrabosco the younger, John Coprario, Robert Johnson, Thomas Campion, Nicholas Lanier and the Lawes brothers.

Jones, Richard (*d* 1744). Accomplished violinist, who from 1730 led the Drury Lane Theatre orchestra, and composer of italianate sonatas and suites contained in two highly idiomatic collections for the violin and one – in a unusually violinistic style – for the harpsichord.

Jonson, Ben (1572/3–1637). Eminent dramatist, masque librettist and poet. Jonson spent his life in London, writing for various theatre troupes and the court. In contrast to his contemporary, Shakespeare, whose plays incorporated popular songs, Jonson wrote lyrics which he had specially set. He engaged some of the finest English composers of the day:

Alfonso Ferrabosco the younger (*Volpone*, 1606), Robert Johnson (*The Devil is an Ass*, 1616), and Nicholas Lanier (*The Sad Shepherd*, *c*1630).

Music played an integral part in his lavish courtly masques. Between 1605 and 1631 Jonson wrote 25 masque librettos, most of which were set by Ferrabosco and Lanier (*Lovers Made Men*, 1617) and staged by Inigo Jones. Although no complete score survives, some of the music is preserved in transcriptions. His poems were also set to music, the most famous being John Wilson's version of 'Drink to me only with thine eyes'.

Keller, Gottfried [Godfrey] (*d* 1704). German musician who settled in London at the end of the 17th century. He visited Amsterdam in 1694 and later published some of his music there: sonatas for wind instruments (originally composed for the band of Princess Anne of Denmark) in 1698 and trios in 1700 and 1701/2. As a harpsichordist, Keller performed works of his own composition at the Theatre Royal and at the York Buildings in 1703 and 1704. He died before the London publication of *A Compleat Method for Attaining to play Thorough Bass upon either Organ, Harpsichord or Theorbo-Lute* in 1705. Three sonatas composed for the trumpeter John Shore survive in manuscript.

King, Robert (*fl* 1676–1728). Violinist, concert organizer and modest composer. King held court appointments from 1680 until 1728, spanning five reigns. In 1689 he acquired a licence to put on twice-weekly public concerts, first at Two Golden Balls, Bow Street, and then, from 1691 until 1697, in nearby Charles Street. In the early years he was associated with J. W. Franck, but by 1698 had formed a new partnership with the younger John Banister (whose father he had succeeded at court) to present concerts at the York Buildings and at the Exeter Exchange (Lord Exeter was his patron); they issued a collection which was printed by John Walsh in 1698 and, between 1700 and 1702, sold Roman and Amsterdam editions of Corelli and other popular Italian composers.

Kirckman, Jacob (1710–92). Alsatian harpsichord and piano maker, working in London; he and the Swiss Burkat Shudi became the most sought-after builders of English instruments. As an apprentice, Kirckman worked alongside Shudi at the workshop of the Fleming Hermann Tabel, whose widow he married in 1738; he became a British citizen in 1755. He built a variety of instruments – one- and two-manual harpsichords, spinets, claviorgans, pianos and square pianos – and eagerly experimented with extended and enharmonic keyboards, machine stops and lid swells. Today, his instruments have a more incisive, nasal tone than Shudi's, but they are well suited for a wide range of music such as that of Domenico Scarlatti, Rameau, Handel, Arne, J. P. Kirnberger and C. P. E. Bach, as well as that of J. C. Bach and Mozart. Because of the machine stops (which involved hand and foot pedals to change registration) and lid swell (a mechanism operated by another foot pedal that opened a section of the top lid along the bentside, thereby increasing the instrument's volume), the inner construction of his instruments was more complex than the contemporary French instruments by Taskin.

Kremberg, Jakob. See NORTHERN EUROPE 7 *Itinerant Musicians.*

Kühnel, August. See NORTHERN EUROPE 7 *Itinerant Musicians.*

Kunzen, Johann Paul. See NORTHERN EUROPE 1 *North Germany.*

Kusser, Johann Sigismund. See NORTHERN EUROPE 7 *Itinerant Musicians.*

Lampe, John Frederick (*c*1703–1751). Saxon bassoonist who emigrated to Britain. There, he made his name as a composer of burlesques, the most successful of which was *The Dragon of Wantley* (text by Carey) in 1737 which satirized Handel's *Giustino*. Lampe had earlier joined Carey and the Arnes in a scheme to dislodge Italian opera from the London stage and, over a two-year period (1732–3), contributed songs to four English operas – *Amelia*, *Britannia* (in which Cecilia Young made her début) and *Dione* at the Little Theatre in the Haymarket, and *The Opera of Operas* at Drury Lane. In addition to other theatre works (among them, a comic masque, an operetta and two pantomimes) Lampe penned two treatises, one on thoroughbass (1737) and another on harmony (1740). His friendship with the Protestant theologian Charles Wesley led him to give up the theatre; he even published a volume of hymns on Wesley's texts (1748). In 1748 he and his wife moved to Dublin and from there to Edinburgh two years later.

Lampugnani, Giovanni Battista. See ITALY 10 *Itinerant Musicians.*

Lanier, Nicholas (1588–1666). Innovative songwriter, singer, violist, lutenist and art connoisseur. Lanier came from a musical family of French origins and at an early age gained the patronage of the Earl of Salisbury and of the Cecil family. He entered royal service as a lutenist in 1616 and when, in 1625,

Charles I acceded to the throne, he became Master of the King's Musick. He travelled to Paris at least once and to Italy three times (1625–8) to buy works of art on behalf of the king. While in Genoa, Van Dyck painted his portrait, paving the way for the painter's visit to the court of Charles I. In 1656 Lanier published a book of etchings from drawings by Parmigianino.

His gifts as a composer were first evident when he sang an ayre of his own composition in Thomas Campion's masque for the marriage of the Earl of Somerset in 1613. This song, 'Bring away this sacred tree', and later an extended soprano soliloquy 'Nor com'st thou yet' (*Hero and Leander*) may have been inspired by his exposure to Italian monodic music while in the service of the Cecils. In 1617 he contributed music to Ben Jonson's masque *Lovers Made Men*, which according to Jonson made use of 'stylo recitativo' for the first time in an English drama. Lanier is further credited with having introduced strophic variations over a repeated bass in his setting of Carew's 'No more shall meades be decked with flowers'. Little of his music survives.

Lanzetti, Salvatore. See ITALY 1 *Piedmont-Savoy.*

Lawes. Two brothers who, during the mid 17th century, were the leading composers of English vocal and instrumental music. Henry (1596–1662) and William Lawes (1602–45) were both choristers at Salisbury Cathedral. William was placed in the home of the Earl of Hertford, a prominent citizen of Salisbury, who had him tutored by his music master John Coprario; it was at the earl's Wiltshire home that William met the future Charles I who took lessons on the viol with Coprario. This connection flowered and William was made one of the prince's private musicians. When Charles became king in 1625, William improved his position at court. The following year Henry joined the Chapel Royal and in 1631 became one of the king's musicians 'for lutes and voices'.

The two brothers collaborated on music for elaborate court masques, such as *The Triumphs of the Prince d'Amour* (1636). In 1634 William collaborated with Simon Ives on the music for Shirley's spectacular masque *The Triumph of Peace*; his instrumental and vocal music for Davenant's *Britannia triumphans* (1638) deeply influenced the degree of continuity in the dramatic music of the next generation of English composers. William also composed incidental music for plays given by the King's Men at the Cockpit-in-Court and Blackfriars theatres, including Jonson's *Entertainment at Welbeck* and Fletcher's *The Faithful Shepherdess* (1633). Later, John Playford published some of William's songs, catches, and dance tunes in miscellanies (after 1650). Henry, too, wrote incidental music for plays given at Oxford on the king's visit in 1636.

William was also an important composer of consort music, of which some autograph volumes survive in the Bodleian Library, Oxford, and at least five more are thought to be lost. It is challenging music, more idiomatic than that of his predecessors, experimental in its harmony and counterpoint, and includes late Renaissance-style consort suites in four to six parts, suites for bass viols and lutes, and Baroque fantasia-suites in three or four parts for violins, viol and organ. The fantasia-suites are the English counterpart to the Italian trio sonata, offering contrasting textures, lively interplay between parts and a new degree of virtuosity. The 'Royall' consort contains dances grouped in suites; the 'Harpe' consorts for violin, viol, theorbo and harp are among the earliest chamber music of their kind. When the court retreated to Oxford in 1642, William enlisted in the royalist army and rode with the king to battle; he was fatally wounded at the siege of Chester in 1645.

Three years later, as a tribute to his departed brother, Henry published a collection of *Choice Psalmes*, which contained 30 of his own psalm settings as well as 30 by William, plus ten sacred canons (none of William's music was published during his lifetime). Henry had been a special friend of Milton, for whose *Arcades* (c1630) he composed songs and whom he had urged to write *Comus* (1634). About 1648 Milton composed a sonnet 'To my Friend Mr. Henry Lawes'. During the Commonwealth, Henry published three collections of *Ayres and Dialogues* and contributed to Davenant's *The Siege of Rhodes* (1659). He was much in demand as a teacher 'for the Voyce or Viole' and held music parties in his home. At the Restoration he recovered his court appointments; his anthem *Zadok the priest* was performed at the coronation of Charles II.

Lenton, John (*d* 1718). Violinist, singer, composer at the courts of Charles II, James II, and William and Mary; he was also the author of an early violin tutor, *The Gentleman's Diversion* (1693).

L'Epine, (Francesca) Margherita de (*c*1683–1746). Italian soprano, possibly of Huguenot extraction, the leading female singer in London when Italian opera was being introduced there. In 1718 she became the wife of Pepusch. L'Epine enjoyed success in London: a tall imposing figure on stage, she was a favourite with men. She arrived in 1703 with her lover, the German composer Jakob Greber, but left him soon after for the Earl of Nottingham. She made her début (aptly) in *The Fickle Shepherdess* at Lincoln's Inn Fields and the year after was engaged at Drury Lane where a rivalry with the English soprano Catherine Tofts was fanned by their supporters. The two appeared in Haym's highly successful 1706 *pasticcio* of Bononcini's *Camilla* and in Pepusch's *Thomyris* the year after.

In 1708 she moved to the Queen's Theatre with the rest of the company, where she remained until 1714. Though she sang in almost all of the opera productions, she was not in the cast of Handel's *Rinaldo* in 1711. Her association with Pepusch – who called her 'Hecate' – began at least a decade before their marriage; she sang in the 1707 performance of his ode *Britannia and Augusta* and in his 1715 masque *Venus and Adonis*. She retired in 1720. She was considered an excellent harpsichordist whose performances from the *Fitzwilliam Virginal Book*, which Pepusch then owned, were warmly praised.

Leveridge, Richard (1670/71–1758). The leading English bass for over half a century and composer of popular songs. Leveridge had a rich and varied career as a soloist, appearing in Purcell's *The Indian Queen* (1695), then – after a three-year visit to Dublin – in the more italianate English operas (*Arsinoe, Camilla, Rosamond, Thomyris* and *Love's Triumph*) and the fully-fledged Italian operas of Handel (*Il pastor fido, Teseo* and a revival of *Rinaldo*). He much preferred to promote his native music and as a composer he contributed music to *The Island Princess* (1698), then sang in the performances; at much the same time he published two collections of songs. From 1714 to the end of his life he worked at the theatre in Lincoln's Inn Fields where he helped John Rich to popularize the latest English comic genre, the musical afterpiece; he sang in his own *Pyramus and Thisbe* (1716). His annual benefit concerts were well subscribed and in the 1735 benefit he performed his ballad *The Roast Beef of Old England* for the first time.

Locke, Matthew (1621/2–77). Royalist composer. When the Civil War broke out in 1642, Locke was in Exeter where he had been a chorister at the cathedral. He learnt to play the organ and became friendly with Christopher

Gibbons, whose uncle was choirmaster; he may have met the future Charles II in the Netherlands (1646–8). He counted John Playford, members of the Purcell family, Sir Roger L'Estrange, Henry Lawes and Christopher Simpson among the friends who shared his interest in consort music. Important among the collections he composed during the Commonwealth are the *Consort 'for seaverall freinds'* and *The Flatt Consort* (exceptional in being set in flat keys); two collections of broken consorts and the well-known *Consort of Fower Parts* date from the Restoration.

In 1656 Locke collaborated on the music for Davenant's *The Siege of Rhodes*; at the performance he took the role of the Admiral of Rhodes. Davenant commissioned further music from Locke in the year immediately following; in 1659 Locke revised the music that he and Christopher Gibbons had written for Shirley's masque *Cupid and Death*, which was given outdoors in Leicester Fields. Locke's theatre connections seem to have lapsed during the later 1660s as he became active in Restoration court music, but were renewed in 1674 when Shadwell asked him to contribute music to his adaptation of *The Tempest*. A year later he composed all the music except the act tunes (by G. B. Draghi) for Shadwell's *Psyche, or The English Opera*.

At the Restoration, Locke acquired three court appointments, though not within the Chapel Royal: he inherited John Coprario's post of private Composer-in-Ordinary and that of Alfonso Ferrabosco the younger as 'composer in the wind music', as well as becoming a composer for the violin band. He contributed music for Charles II's coronation and a year later became organist to the queen, and composer of dramatic music. Because of the king's dislike of fantasias, Locke wrote none for the court. Instead he composed at least 30 anthems after the French *grand motet*; his most lavish was 'A Song of Thanksgiving' (1666) which required three four-part choirs, a five-part string orchestra and a four-part consort 'in the Gallery'. As late as 1674 Locke was appointed assistant leader of the Twenty-four Violins and served temporarily as Master of the King's Musick in 1676–7.

However, all did not unfold smoothly. While in Oxford during the Great Plague of 1665–6, Locke had composed music for the Oxford Acts, though he was not awarded a degree. In 1666 Locke felt that the Chapel Royal musicians had deliberately spoilt a performance of his setting of responses to the Ten Commandments so he published them as

Modern Church-Musick Preaccus'd, Censur'd and Obstructed in its Performance before His Majesty. Then he became embroiled in a protracted (and ultimately undignified) pamphlet war with Thomas Salmon over the latter's *Essay to the Advancement of Music* which suggested the abolition of clefs.

Locke's last two publications of music were his only serious keyboard collection, *Melothesia* (1673) – to which he appended the first extant rules for realizing a figured bass – and *Tripla Concordia* (1677), an anthology of over 100 pieces for two violins and bass violin. On his death he was succeeded as Composer-in-Ordinary for the violins by his pupil Henry Purcell, who dedicated the ode *What hope for us remains now he is gone?* to him.

Loeillet, Jean Baptiste. See LOW COUNTRIES *2 South Netherlands*.

Lonati, Carlo Ambrogio. See ITALY *10 Itinerant Musicians*.

Lupo, Thomas (*c*1571–1627). English musician of Italian origin and composer of anthems and motets as well as lute songs, madrigals and consort fantasias. Lupo became a court musician (violinist to Prince Charles) in 1588 and from 1619 to 1627 he held a post as composer to the violins. Between 1540 and 1642, seven members of his family served at the English court.

Matteis, Nicola. Italian father (*d* ?1707) and English-born son (*d* 1737) of the same name, violinists and composers: the father popularized the Italian style of playing in London during the 1670s and 1680s; the son became a violinist and ballet composer at the Habsburg Hofkapelle (1700–37).

The elder Nicola Matteis worked in Germany, where he came under the influence of H. I. F. von Biber and J. J. Walther, before settling in England. In 1685 he published four books of airs and dances for the accomplished violinist with prefaces explaining ornaments, bowings, tempos and how to play divisions; and in the late 1690s, two collections of songs. He published a thoroughbass treatise for the guitar, an instrument he also played, entitled *The False Consonances of Music* (1682).

That the son learnt well from the father is evident from his appointment as principal violinist of the Viennese Hofkapelle and music director for court balls. In the latter capacity he provided music for 59 ballets appended to *opere serie*; his most important contribution was incorporated into Fux's *Costanza e Fortezza*, performed in Prague in 1723 for the coronation of Charles VI. It was his son who taught Charles Burney.

Maugars, André. See FRANCE *1 Paris and Versailles.*

Meares, Richard. London instrument makers (father and son), music printers and publishers. Richard the elder (*d* after 1722) made viols, lutes and other stringed instruments (labelled from 1669), highly regarded for their craftsmanship; he embarked on printing and publishing around 1713, employing Thomas Cross as his engraver. By contrast his son, Richard the younger (*d* 1743), was more active as a printer and publisher than as a maker. The firm became one of Walsh's chief rivals and its publications included sonatas by Pietro Castrucci, Corelli and Francesco Geminiani as well as Handel's *Radamisto* (1720).

Morley, Thomas (1557/8–1602). Organist, composer, theorist and editor, important for his spirited madrigals and for two publications: *A Plaine and Easie Introduction to Practicall Musicke* (1597), dedicated to William Byrd, and *The Triumphes of Oriana* (1601), which contains madrigals dedicated to Elizabeth I by 23 English composers. The former summed up the late English Renaissance practices while the latter stimulated interest in the late-flowering English madrigal.

Motteux, Peter Anthony (1663–1718). Huguenot refugee who settled in London, a dramatist who wrote masques and semi-opera librettos. Motteux became an English subject in 1686. In 1692 he started the *Gentleman's Journal*, the first monthly of its kind, which ran for two years and included remarks on music and, significantly, a music supplement. His masque librettos were set by John Eccles (*Europe's Revels for the Peace*, 1697), Richard Leveridge and John Weldon (who both set *Britain's Happiness*, 1704). More important, he wrote for some of the earliest productions of opera in English: *The Island Princess* (semi-opera which he adapted in 1698 from Fletcher, with music by Daniel Purcell, Jeremiah Clarke and Leveridge), Thomas Clayton's *Arsinoe* (1705), the *pasticcio Thomyris* (1707) and *Love's Triumph* (1708), originally an Italian opera.

Needler, Henry (?1685–1760). Amateur violinist and active figure in London musical circles. Needler is thought to have been the pupil of Daniel Purcell and John Banister the younger, as well as the first in England to perform Corelli's concertos. In 1724 he became an accountant general but from 1728 was a member of the Academy of Ancient Music.

Newton, Sir Isaac (1642–1727). Important English scientist who briefly took an interest in Greek music. In a 17-page manuscript dated 1665 Newton compared the intervals of the just and equal-tempered scales by means of logarithms and placed the 'twelve music modes in their order of gratefulness'. He was the author of a short essay, *Of Music*, and dabbled with playing the viol.

Nicolini. See ITALY *10 Itinerant Musicians.*

Norman, Barak (*c*1670–*c*1740). String instrument maker, working in London, whose bass viols (the earliest known instrument dates from 1690) are highly prized for both their beauty of tone and appearance. Norman's instruments are elegantly shaped, dark brown in colour, with elaborate double purfling and colourful floral designs; many bear exquisitely carved heads. He also made lutes, violins and cellos.

North. Two brothers, lawyers, writers on music and amateur viol players. Francis North (1637–85) was a courtier: as the first Baron Guilford he was Charles II's Lord Keeper of the Great Seal. He was also an accomplished practitioner of the bass viol and a composer of consorts. Roger North, 14 years younger, was a Member of Parliament who rose to become the Queen's Attorney General under James II; he was a viol player of modest ability. For a time the two lived together in London where they were the admiring friends of Henry Purcell. The elder brother wrote *A Philosophical Essay of Musick* (1677) couched in scientific terms; nearly 50 years later the younger, who had retired to Norfolk, expressed his ideas on the nature of music in the *Theory of Sounds* (1726) and *The Musicall Grammarian* (1728). Roger was a prolific and lively writer on contemporary aesthetics and practices as well as the history of music. He left a detailed autobiographical essay entitled *Notes of Me.*

Notari, Angelo (*c*1573–1663). Italian composer in the service of Prince Henry, then Prince Charles (later Charles I), who, through the publication of his *Prime musiche nuove* (1613), helped introduce the monodic style into England.

Paisible, James (*d* 1721). French-born composer working in London from 1674 as a recorder and oboe player, and composer of theatre music. He was also a bass violin player and a member of the Twenty-four Violins. The Duchess of Mazarin (the cardinal's niece) employed him at her Chelsea home, and he was a member of the band at the Theatre Royal, Drury Lane. Paisible played in Crowne's court masque, *Calisto*, in 1675 and two years later composed and conducted the music for the king's birthday celebration at Whitehall, although it was not until 1685 that he finally gained an appointment to the King's Musick.

Pedersøn, Mogens. See NORTHERN EUROPE 2 *Scandinavia*.

Peerson [Pearson], **Martin** (1571/3–1651). Keyboard player and composer, whose edition of motets (1630) was the first English music to include a figured bass part. Peerson held London posts at Westminster Abbey and St Paul's Cathedral from the 1620s until Catholic services were discontinued because of the Civil War (1642). In 1604 he was convicted of refusing to attend the Church of England (recusancy), though he must have claimed to be Protestant in order to gain the Oxford BMus in 1613. He published two collections: *Private Musicke* (1620), which contained ayres for solo voice and three viols, duets and dialogues; and the *Mottects or Grave Chamber Musique* (1630). He also left verse anthems and virginal pieces.

Pepusch, Johann Christoph (1667–1752). Prussian composer, theorist and an early music antiquarian who settled in England, and was awarded a DMus at Oxford. His most important commercial success was as the compiler of the music for *The Beggar's Opera* (1728). Pepusch came to England in about 1704, having served at the Berlin court since the age of 14. He found work at the Drury Lane Theatre as a viola player and harpsichordist. He provided music as well, such as the recitatives for the italianate opera *Thomyris* (1707); his masque *Venus and Adonis* (1715) was very popular. Pepusch also composed English cantatas in the Italian style (such as *Alexis*, 1710), which were performed during the intervals at Drury Lane.

He was also employed by James Brydges (later the Duke of Chandos) as his music director (until the early 1730s) and in that capacity composed verse anthems and other sacred music for his patron's chapel. Pepusch was a founding member of the Academy of Ancient Music and a driving force in its organization. In 1718 he married the popular Italian soprano Margherita de L'Epine, and six years later sailed for Bermuda, surviving a shipwreck before returning home.

He gained popular notoriety by collaborating with John Gay on the ballad opera *The Beggar's Opera*, which was produced at Lincoln's Inn Fields in 1728; Pepusch contributed the overture and the basses for the ballads. The Lord Chamberlain intervened in the case of *Polly* (1729) and banned its performance (it was finally performed only in 1777). Pepusch's last ballad opera was *The Wedding*, which was performed in 1729.

Thereafter he devoted himself to teaching and antiquarian pursuits. He amassed a large library of books and music which included the *Fitzwilliam Virginal Book* and scores of Handel operas. In 1730 he published *A Treatise on Harmony* anonymously, a work which was somewhat misguided in its premise that solmization was still a viable way of teaching harmony. William Boyce was his best-known pupil. At the age of 68 he became the organist of the Charterhouse and at 79 a Fellow of the Royal Society. Burney and Hawkins wrote warmly of Pepusch though Burney may have given the erroneous impression that Pepusch resented Handel's success as a composer of Italian opera in London. In fact, they were colleagues in the service of the Duke of Chandos and it was Pepusch who arranged for Handel's music to be performed at meetings of the Academy of Ancient Music. See also BRITISH ISLES 1 *London*, L'Epine, Margherita de.

Pepys, Samuel (1633–1703). English civil servant and gentleman-amateur of music whose diary from the 1660s is a rich source of London musical life at the beginning of the Restoration. Though a naval administrator by profession, Pepys was a keen amateur composer and performer on the violin, viol, guitar, theorbo, flageolet and recorder. He had a large library that included the treatises of Morley, Kircher, Mersenne and Birchensha, with whom he studied composition in 1662, as well as vocal and instrumental music. Pepys knew many professional musicians and there are many references to private concerts in his diary, as well as to his own efforts to make music. Some time later he employed Cesare Morelli to compose accompaniments for his tunes and to set 'To be or not to be' as a recitative.

Pescetti, Giovanni Battista. See ITALY 4 *Venice*.

Philips, Peter. See LOW COUNTRIES 2 *South Netherlands*.

Playford. East Anglian family of music publishers and booksellers in London. John Playford (1623–86) was responsible for popularizing English music in the church and home during the period 1651–84, when he dominated the music trade. He was a religious man, a clerk to the Temple Church and a vicar-choral of St Paul's Cathedral; as a child he had learnt music as a chorister. He maintained his shop in the porch of the Temple Church, and at his death, was succeeded by his son Henry (*c*1657–*c*1707). A nephew, also called John Playford (*c*1655–1685), was the music printer who acquired the firm of Godbid's in 1682. John Playford the elder was an ardent Royalist who, after a seven-year apprenticeship, had begun his career by publishing political tracts; the appearance of *The Perfect Narrative of the Tryal of the King* (1649) brought about his arrest.

Playford became well known as a music publisher in 1651 when he issued *The English Dancing Master*, a collection of ballad airs which was still being issued in 1728. Among his other important publications are *A Musicall Banquet* (1651), *Musick's Recreation* (1652), *Catch that Catch Can* (1652), *A Breefe Introduction to the Skill of Musick* (1654), *Court Ayres* (1655) and *Apollo's Banquet for the Treble Violin* (1669). Already a compulsory member of the Yeomanry of the Stationers' Company, he was called to the livery in 1661 and, on the king's command, was admitted to its court of assistants in 1681; his son followed suit 20 years later. Henry's most important imprints were D'Urfey's *Wit and Mirth* (1699) and Purcell's *Orpheus Britannicus* (1702). On the death of the father, Henry Purcell composed the *Elegy on my friend, Mr John Playford*.

Pope, Alexander (1688–1744). Famous Catholic poet, satirist and critic (best known for *An Essay on Criticism*, 1711) who – though he professed to be unmusical – collaborated with Handel (*Esther*), Giovanni Bononcini (*Marcus Brutus*), Gay (*Achilles* and *The Beggar's Opera*) and Maurice Greene (the St Cecilia's Day Ode of 1730).

Porpora, Nicola. See ITALY *10 Itinerant Musicians*.

Porta, Giovanni. See ITALY *4 Venice*.

Price, John. See CENTRAL EUROPE *1 South Germany*.

Purcell, Daniel. See BRITISH ISLES *2 Provinces*.

Purcell, Henry (1659–95). The finest and most original English composer of his day. From the beginning, as a chorister of the Chapel Royal, Henry Purcell showed himself to be a musician of exceptional gifts. His three-part song 'Sweet Tyranness' appeared in Playford's *Catch that Catch Can* when he was only eight; anthems and services for the Chapel Royal survive from as early as 1679. When his voice broke in 1673 Purcell became an assistant to Hingeston, keeper of Charles II's keyboard and wind instruments, as well as an organ tuner at Westminster Abbey. He was rewarded for his efforts by being appointed Locke's successor as Composer-in-Ordinary for the violins in 1677 and Blow's as organist of Westminster Abbey in 1679 (in fact Blow – his mentor and friend – stepped down to make way for the infinitely more gifted youngster); he became an organist of the Chapel Royal in 1682 and succeeded Hingeston as keeper the following year. His appointments were renewed by James II (1685) and by William and Mary (1689).

In addition to his duties at the Chapel Royal, Purcell was required on occasion to compose Latin anthems (such as the dramatic *Jehova, quam multi sunt hostes mei* of *c*1680) for the royal Catholic chapels of Charles II's consort and the private worship of James II. Anthems intended for performance when the king was present, such as *Rejoice in the Lord alway* (1684/5), are augmented by soloists and strings; the coronation anthems, notably *My heart is inditing* for James II, are, appropriately, grandest of all, with extended orchestral interludes dignified with French-influenced dotted rhythms. Other settings, such as the rhetorical *Lord, what is man?* or the madrigalian *Out of the deep have I called* (*c*1680) suited more intimate occasions or performance at Westminster Abbey. In contrast to his court compositions, his services and his popular *Te Deum* and *Jubilate* in D are simpler (and, on the whole, less distinguished).

From 1680 until his death Purcell contributed a steady stream of allegoric odes (beloved for their ground-bass arias) and panegyric welcome songs (which made use of recorders, oboes, trumpets and sometimes timpani in addition to strings) to celebrate, *inter alia*, special occasions in the life of the royal family; his best-known ode was *Hail, bright Cecilia* (1692), with its eulogies of individual instruments and superb choral polyphony. His *Elegy on the Death of Queen Mary* (a short chamber cantata) and his larger-scale *Funeral Music for Queen Mary* (1695) present an important facet of his composing technique – an exquisitely sensitive command of chromaticism. He also provided italianate instrumental music (overtures, sonatas, dances, the *Cibell* and the *Chacony*) at court, where the viol consort had not been welcome since the Restoration (his consort music from before 1680 – fantasias and In Nomines which remain the crowning jewels of their respective genres – was composed for private use). His published collection for violins, bass viol and continuo, the *Sonnata's of III Parts* (1683), was dedicated to Charles II; in 1697 Purcell's widow issued, for the same combination (but with a more independent viol part), the *Ten Sonata's in Four Parts* (composed *c*1680): these include the popular 'Golden Sonata'. Despite his organ posts, he left little keyboard music of any significance, though the suites of harpsichord dances are the finest of their kind in England.

Purcell's most famous work is the three-act opera *Dido and Aeneas* (libretto by Nahum Tate) of 1689, which was conceived for amateur performance by the singers and string players (augmented by several invited tenors and basses) at Josias Priest's Chelsea boarding-school for 'young gentlewomen'. It was to be his only sustained musical setting of a drama and, by its musical contribution to character development, a worthy successor to Blow's miniature court opera *Venus and Adonis* (before 1685). *Dido and Aeneas* was not given in public until 1700 and in the meantime the general London theatre-going public of his day knew only Purcell's semi-operas (incorporating spoken dialogue and performed by actor-singers), of which there are four, composed during his last five years and which show Purcell at the height of his powers: *Dioclesian* (based on Fletcher's *The Prophetess*, 1690), *King Arthur* (text by Dryden, 1691), *The Fairy Queen* (text by Elkanah Settle after Shakespeare, 1692) and *The Indian Queen* (Dryden, 1695). Nowadays they are generally known only in musical excerpts, which is unfortunate. Essentially they are dramas embodying extended, masque-like musical scenes, sometimes quite loosely related to the main drama; yet the placing of the music – akin to that of the *divertissement* in French dramatic works of the time – is often theatrically very effective. The successful revival of these works is further hampered by the supposed weakness of the plays on which they are based, for example Settle's heavily rewritten version of *A Midsummer Night's Dream* and Dryden's tub-thumpingly patriotic *King Arthur*, and also by the need to have companies of both actors and singers to give them. Some of Purcell's finest songs, dances and choruses were composed for the semi-operas. He also wrote a great deal of other incidental theatre music from the 1680s onwards. The music for Shadwell's 1695 adaptation of *The Tempest*, once ascribed to him, is now thought to be mostly the work of John Weldon.

In the 1698 edition of *Orpheus Britannicus*, the most important posthumous anthology of Purcell's songs, Henry Playford ascribed to Purcell the 'peculiar Genius to express the Energy of *English* Words'; his solo songs – some of which belong to the dramatic works – were largely intended for trained singers who could fully realize their considerable technical and dramatic demands. Not content merely to master the contemporary Italian and French aria forms (da capo, rondeau and ground bass) Purcell masterfully transformed them into his own idiom, which is at once faithful to the text and musically alive with florid melodies, canonic stratagems and richly pathetic harmonies. His English contrapuntal heritage, interpreted with great freedom, seems to have endowed him with a special capacity for handling lines in such a way as to produce striking harmonic effects, which he often used to illuminate the words he was setting but often, too, simply to make the listener catch his breath through some magical conjunction of lines. His songs, especially his more dramatic, arioso-like ones, abound in such moments; but they occur in all his music, from the anthems to the bawdy catches he wrote for the convivial occasions in which his own, much admired countertenor voice must often have been heard.

His tragic death at the age of 36 was marked by a funeral service at Westminster Abbey, in which the combined choirs of the Abbey and the Chapel Royal commemorated the premature passing of 'the English Orpheus'.

Ravenscroft, John. See ITALY 7 *Papal States: Rome.*

Ravenscroft, Thomas (*c*1582–*c*1635). Pivotal editor and theorist, though of little lasting importance as a composer. Ravenscroft, once a chorister at St Paul's Cathedral and later music master at Christ's Hospital, London, was nevertheless sufficiently attuned to popular music to compile the first printed collection of English rounds and catches (*Pammelia*, 1609) which includes vendors' cries and tavern songs, and is much prized today by social historians. Five years later he published a *Briefe Discourse* on the current misuse of mensuration signs, to which he appended 12 of his own songs (including a cantata in West Country dialect). In 1621 he issued *The Whole Booke of Psalmes*, containing 105 settings, which came to be considered one of the most important psalters of the day.

Reggio, Pietro (Francesco) (1632–85). Versatile Italian musician from Genoa – bass, lutenist and guitarist, composer and teacher – who worked at the Swedish court (1652–3) and the French court (1657) before finally settling in London (1664). He took part in performances at the homes of Pepys and

Evelyn and was one of several composers who contributed music to Shadwell's adaptation of *The Tempest* (1674). He published a collection of songs and duets in 1680 and may have issued a treatise (now lost) on *The art of singing* (1678).

Rich. Father and son theatre managers and entrepreneurs in London. Christopher Rich (*d* 1714), as chief shareholder of the Theatre Royal, Drury Lane, produced both plays and operas during the early years of the 18th century. He was considered an opportunistic businessman because he put opera before drama, but in fact dramas lost money and operas were profitable. To enhance his musical productions he imported musicians and paid them higher salaries than his actors, who bitterly resented his tactics.

He was a competitive entrepreneur who tried to trump the 1705 opening of Vanbrugh's and Congreve's Haymarket theatre with a production at his own theatre of Thomas Clayton's *Arsinoe*, an Italian *pasticcio* with awkward English translations. Ironically, Vanbrugh failed to capitalize on Rich's miscalculation; his Queen's Theatre opened with Greber's *The Loves of Ergasto*, which failed miserably because it was sung in Italian. In 1706 Rich presented *Camilla*, Bononcini's first London opera, with English texts and native singers, which was successful in shifting public opinion regarding Italian opera; in the process Rich nipped in the bud Congreve's efforts to revive interest in English dramatic opera with his *The British Enchanters* (music by John Eccles).

His son, John (1691/2–1761), followed his father in theatre management, but he was also a gifted dancer and mime artist (always billed as 'Lun'). From 1717–41 Harlequin was his principal role, and he is generally credited with popularizing pantomime in London; Theobald's *Pan and Syrinx* (1718), with music by J. E. Galliard, was one of many successful productions. John Rich managed the new theatre at Lincoln's Inn Fields that opened in 1714 and its successor, the first Covent Garden Theatre. He presided over the success of the century, *The Beggar's Opera*, which 'made Rich gay and Gay rich'. He managed Covent Garden when Handel gave the premières of some of his late operas and many of his oratorios.

Rolli, Paolo Antonio (1687–1765). Roman poet who supplied Handel, Giovanni Bononcini and Nicola Porpora with opera librettos, a contemporary of Metastasio; his correspondence (with Giuseppe Riva, the Modenese envoy in London) contains important references to London music life during the first half of the 18th century. The most important years of Rolli's career (1715–44) were spent in London where his patrons included the Duke of Rutland, Lord Burlington and Lord Bathurst, and the Prince of Wales. He was a neo-classicist who translated important classical and Italian texts into English, and also undertook an Italian translation of Milton's *Paradise Lost* (1729–35), of which he was very proud. In 1719 he became the Italian secretary to the Royal Academy of Music, providing ten librettos – Handel's *Floridante* and Bononcini's *Astarto* among them – before being replaced by Nicola Francesco Haym in 1722.

He counted Bononcini and Senesino among his friends, but never felt he had gained the respect of Handel, whom he attacked in the 7 April 1733 issue of *The Craftsman*; his efforts on behalf of the Opera of the Nobility, for which he served as secretary from 1733 to 1737, did little to improve the relationship, although his finest libretto, *Deidamia*, was set by Handel in 1741. (Earlier, in 1727–8, he had become embroiled in a dispute with Voltaire on the subject of epic poetry.) In 1735 the Italian town of Todi granted him a patent of nobility; the following year he failed in a bid to succeed Zeno at the imperial court in Vienna. He retired to Italy where he translated French and English texts into Italian.

Roseingrave, Thomas (1688–1766). Brilliant organist who spent time in Dublin and Venice. Roseingrave's father Daniel (*d* 1727) was organist at Gloucester, Winchester and Salisbury cathedrals before moving his family to Dublin in 1698. Thomas entered Trinity College in 1705 and four years later was sent to Italy, where he remained until 1714/15; his younger brother Ralph (*c*1695–1747) remained in Ireland and succeeded their father as organist of Christ Church and St Patrick's cathedrals.

While in Italy, Thomas became friendly with Domenico Scarlatti and when he returned to London he did much to popularize his music: in 1720 he mounted a production of Scarlatti's opera, *Amor d'un ombra e Gelosea d'un aura* [*Narciso*]; five years later he published his own *8 Suits of Lessons* for the harpsichord and in 1739 his edition of Scarlatti's 42 sonatas (which had appeared in London the year before as *Essercizi per gravicembalo*) to which Arne, Boyce, Greene, Loeillet, Pepusch and Stanley subscribed.

Roseingrave published his own collection

of *Voluntaries and Fugues* in 1728 and the following year became organist of St George's, Hanover Square (Handel's parish church) where people came specially to hear his fugal extemporizations. He also published flute solos and Italian cantatas. After his health failed, he retired to Dublin where he lived with his nephew William. In 1753 his opera *Phaedra and Hippolitus* was presented at the Fishamble Street Music Hall.

Saint-Evremond, Charles de Saint-Denis (1614–1703). French aesthetician exiled in England. Saint-Evremond fled France during the Fronde, taking up residence in Flanders before finally being received at the court of Charles II. In London his home became a fashionable meeting place for intellectuals. His writings on music, published in Paris in 1684, deal mainly with his views on opera – expressing his preference for spoken drama with music over entirely sung works, and his fondness for the French, rather than the Italian, style.

Sallé, Marie. See FRANCE *1 Paris and Versailles.*

Sammartini, Giuseppe (1695–1750). Much admired Italian oboist, who emigrated to England in 1728, and composer of sonatas and concerts; the elder brother of the Milanese Giovanni Battista Sammartini. Quantz, Hawkins and Burney wrote of the fine playing of Giuseppe Sammartini. In London he played in the opera orchestras of both Giovanni Bononcini and Handel. In 1736 he became music master to the wife and children of Frederick, Prince of Wales. He published well-crafted sonatas and concertos in the conservative English style (incorporating tripartite French overtures and transitional slow movements) which by their minuets and rondos also anticipate the Classical era.

Sandoni, Pietro Giuseppe. See ITALY *7 Papal States: Bologna-Ferrara.*

Senesino. See ITALY *10 Itinerant Musicians.*

Shadwell, Thomas (?1642–92). Poet, dramatist, lutenist and song composer who helped to foster semi-opera in London. Shadwell's first important foray into musical theatre was in 1674 when his verses (set by John Banister and Pelham Humfrey; Matthew Locke and G. B. Draghi also provided music) were included in the Davenant–Dryden operatic adaptation of Shakespeare's *The Tempest*, performed at the Dorset Garden Theatre. Within the year he adapted Molière's *Psyché* (1675) as a semi-opera, expanding the plot, employing stage machinery and dancers, and integrating music into the plot. He incorporated music into at

least two other plays, *The Libertine* (1675) and *Timon of Athens* (1678), and Purcell contributed new songs to their revivals. In 1689 he succeeded Dryden as poet laureate and historiographer royal, following a bitter dispute; Robert King set Shadwell's St Cecilia's Day Ode text of 1690.

Shakespeare, William (1565–1616). Famous English dramatist. Shakespeare used contemporary popular music as well as newly composed incidental music in many of his plays. On stage, musicians served to contribute to the atmosphere of banquets, processions and battles while off stage they lulled characters (such as Mortimer in *Henry IV*) to sleep and intensified the emotional climate of a wedding (*The Tempest*) or a reconciliation between lovers (*The Winter's Tale*). Shakespeare gave lyrics to characters – originally played by actors who could sing (like the gravedigger in *Hamlet* and the fool in *King Lear*).

Although composers such as John Wilson and Robert Johnson provided Shakespeare with newly composed music, Shakespeare clearly referred in his plays to popular songs, whose texts he adapted to the dramatic needs of the particular scene. He seems never to have quoted songs literally or in their entirety. When plays such as *The Tempest* and *Macbeth* were revived later in the 17th century in rewritten form, to suit the tastes of the age, newer music by a number of composers was substituted. In the 18th century Arne and Boyce contributed music to productions at Drury Lane and Covent Garden.

Sherard, James (1666–1738). Wealthy London apothecary and botanist (who created and maintained a specimen garden of rare and exotic plants), amateur violinist and composer of respectable Corellian trio *sonate da chiesa*. Along with Nicola Haym and Nicola Cosimi, Sherard was associated with the second Duke of Bedford, for whom he composed the trio sonatas he published in Amsterdam in 1701 and *c*1711.

Shirley, James (1596–1666). Dramatist, remembered for his contribution to the final flowering of the masque, of which much the most important were *The Triumph of Peace*, with music by William Lawes and Simon Ives (performed by the Inns of Court, at Whitehall, and the Merchants' Hall in quick succession early in 1634), and *Cupid and Death*, with music by Locke and Christopher Gibbons (first performed as entertainment for the Portuguese ambassador in 1653).

Shudi, Burkat (1702–73). Highly respected

Swiss harpsichord maker, working in London, in competition with Jacob Kirckman who, like himself, had been trained by Hermann Tabel. Shudi built single and double harpsichords with four registers, prized for their rich tone. John Broadwood assisted him from 1761 and, after marrying his daughter, became a partner in the firm (which later became the Broadwood piano firm). In 1769 he patented his 'Venetian swell' mechanism which enabled the instrument's volume to be varied by a foot pedal controlling longitudinal louvres above the strings. His clients included Handel, Frederick the Great (for whom he built three or four instruments with pedal-operated machine stops for changing manuals), the Empress Maria Theresa (her keyboard extended down to low C'), Haydn, Burney and Clementi, as well as the painters Gainsborough and Reynolds; his instruments were exported as far away as Portugal, Italy and Russia.

Simpson, Christopher (*c*1605–1669). Yorkshire viol player, composer, teacher and important writer on music, famous for *The Division-violist* (1659). Simpson was the leading exponent of English viol playing of his day, a devoted teacher in the sense that he produced two extremely practical texts: the above-mentioned tutor on performing divisions over a ground bass and *The Principles of Practical Music* (1665), which addresses the rudiments of music, harmony and counterpoint. (When he revised it in 1667 he called it *A Compendium of Practical Musicke*.) His students were his patrons, minor aristocracy – the Duke of Newcastle, Sir Robert Bolles and his son John, and Sir John St Barbe – to whom he dedicated his publications. He composed a wide variety of music for viol, from teaching ayres to virtuoso divisions as well as two remarkable sets of chamber music for one treble instrument, two bass viols and continuo entitled *The Monthes* and *The Seasons*.

Simpson, Thomas. See NORTHERN EUROPE *1 North Germany.*

Smith, 'Father' (Bernard) [Schmidt, Bernhard] (*c*1630–1708). German organ builder resident in London who, in addition to building organs in the most important churches and chapels in England, was in the service of the king. Father Smith worked in the Netherlands (where he was known as 'Baerent Smit') before coming to England after the Great Fire of London. The experience he gained while in the northern Netherlands was evidenced in his later instruments by their sweetness and brilliance of tone, the use of divided sharps and the absence of pedals. His first job in London was as an organ tuner at Westminster Abbey, but his reputation as a builder was firmly established with a commission to build an organ for the Sheldonian Theatre, Oxford (1670–71). Further orders quickly followed, such as that for the king's private chapel at Windsor in 1673 and another for St Margaret's, Westminster (1675–7). Royal acknowledgment finally came with an appointment as the King's Organ Maker in 1681 and Keeper of the King's Organs in 1695.

In 1682 Smith became embroiled in a 'Battle of the Organs' with the younger builder Renatus Harris, whose more flamboyant organs were French-inspired. Smith and Harris were both approached about building a new organ for the Temple Church, London; to represent their work, each set up an organ for the consideration of the Church benchers. However, Smith's was mysteriously sabotaged and, after a long and acrimonious dispute, the Lord Chief Justice ruled in favour of Smith in 1688. Among the most important organs Smith built were those for St Paul's, Durham and Canterbury cathedrals, the Banqueting House (Whitehall), St Clement Danes (London), Eton College Chapel, Christ Church (Oxford), Great St Mary's and Trinity College Chapel (Cambridge).

Smith [Schmidt]. German father, Johann Christoph [Schmidt] (*d* 1763), who served as Handel's copyist and amanuensis in London from 1716 onwards, and son John Christopher (1712–95), an organist and composer. In 1759 the elder Smith inherited Handel's huge collection of manuscripts, which passed to his son upon his death four years later. Apart from a few lessons with Handel in 1725, Smith the younger had little directly to do with Handel until the mid 1750s when he took on the unpaid post of organist at the Foundling Hospital where, from 1759 until 1768, he conducted the annual performances of *Messiah*. In return for a pension, Smith bequeathed all his Handeliana to George III so that it passed into the Royal Music Library.

Smith followed his father to England in 1720 and in addition to his lessons with Handel, studied with Pepusch and Thomas Roseingrave (with whom he lodged in Wigmore Street). In the early 1730s Smith became involved in the Arne family's efforts to create a hybrid italianate English opera: however, his contribution, *Ulysses* (1733), failed to survive its first performance.

Gentle and retiring by nature, contemplative and well read, Smith shied away from composing further theatre pieces for two decades; when he returned to the genre, it was evidently with little expectation that his operas would be performed. He was an intimate of Dr Arbuthnot, in whose home he dwelt for a time (and where he met Pope, Swift and others of that remarkable circle). He married in 1736 and was widowed six years later. He lived abroad for a time in the late 1740s in Aix-en-Provence and Geneva, where he became acquainted with Robert Price and Benjamin Stillingfleet (who later provided him with accommodation and oratorio librettos).

Back in London, Smith met David Garrick, who commissioned two full-length, all-sung Shakespearean operas, *The Fairies* (1755) and *The Tempest* (1756), for the Theatre Royal, Drury Lane. Neither was very successful, having been composed in a post-Handelian style, by then considered old-fashioned. Garrick himself wrote the libretto for *The Enchanter* (1760), Smith's last Drury Lane opera, which succeeded better – partly because of the exotic plot (Arne's popular 1759 masque *The Sultan* had already whetted the public's appetite for harem themes).

After the death of Handel, Smith turned decisively to composing and conducting oratorios. With Stanley he organized the annual Lenten oratorio performances at Covent Garden. His most successful work was *Paradise Lost* (1757–8; text by Stillingfleet, after Milton). Like the operas from his period abroad, several of his oratorios were never performed, among them *Judith* (text by Price) which was probably pipped at the post by Arne's 1761 oratorio of the same name.

Staggins, Nicholas (*d* 1700). Court violinist, flautist and Master of the King's Musick (succeeding Grabu in 1674), Staggins organized all the major musical events of the reigns of James II and William and Mary. Although he held no post as a composer, he did write three royal birthday odes and songs; his most important contribution was to John Crowne's *Calisto*, performed at Whitehall in 1675. In 1682 he was awarded a MusD from Cambridge.

Stanesby. Father and son, woodwind instrument makers working in London who, with Bressan, made the finest English flutes and recorders. The elder Thomas (*c*1668–1734) and his son Thomas (1692–1754) were registered as freemen in 1716. They also made oboes and bassoons; the only surviving double bassoon was made by Thomas the younger in 1739. He tried to prolong the vogue of the recorder by promoting a 'C Flute' in *A New System of the Flute A' Bec or Common English Flute*, which he published in 1732.

Stanley, John (1712–86). Remarkable blind London organist, violinist, conductor and composer whose music documents the transition from late English Baroque to a pre-Classical style. Stanley's musical gifts brought him to the attention of Maurice Greene at an early age, and by the time he was 12 he had found employment as the organist of All Hallows, Bread Street. Other London posts followed, and in 1729 he became the youngest person ever to gain the Oxford BMus degree. He was blessed with an extraordinary memory and was said to be an excellent card player. Best known for his three sets of organ voluntaries (1748–54) with which he entertained the likes of Handel while organist of the Honourable Society of the Inner Temple during the 1730s, Stanley was also an accomplished violinist, who regularly directed concerts at the Swan Tavern, Cornhill, and at the Castle in Paternoster Row. He married in 1738 and became a teacher. In the 1740s he published string concertos, flute sonatas and two of his three collections of cantatas; he later arranged the concertos for the organ and composed a further set.

During the 1750s Stanley conducted Handel's oratorios in the composer's stead, and after Handel's death in 1759, he took on the task of organizing the Lenten oratorio seasons at Covent Garden. His own oratorios – *Jephtha* (?1751–2), *Zimri* (1760) and *The Fall of Egypt* (1774) – inevitably owe much to Handel. Also, beginning in 1759, Stanley became briefly associated with the Drury Lane theatre, for which he composed incidental and masque music; *Arcadia, or The Shepherd's Wedding* (1761) is the only work that survives. His opera *Teraminta*, on a text by Carey, was never performed.

In 1770 he was elected to a governorship of the Foundling Hospital and from 1775 to 1777 took charge of the annual *Messiah* performances. His concertos for pianoforte (or organ or harpsichord) appeared in 1775. Four years later, Stanley finally gained a court appointment, succeeding Boyce as Master of the King's Band of Musicians; in this capacity he provided a steady stream of odes to mark royal occasions. Gainsborough's portrait captures Stanley's strength of character and integrity.

Steffkin [Stefkins], **Theodore** [Stoeffken, Dietrich] (*d*1673). Brilliant German solo viol player and composer who spent much of his career in England; his two sons – Frederick

William and Christian – were also able viol players. The first mention of Steffkin in England was in 1634 when he took part in the masque *The Triumph of Peace*; two years later he gained a place at court as a 'musician for the consort in ordinary'. He spent the Commonwealth years in Hamburg and took up his place again in the King's Private Musick at the Restoration.

Strada del Pò, Anna Maria (*fl* 1720–40). Italian singer, renowned for her three-octave compass and ability to convey emotion, who from 1729 until 1737 was Handel's leading soprano. Handel recruited her on his trip to Italy in 1729 where she had been singing in the opera houses of Venice and Naples (she was married to Aurelio del Pò, manager of the S Bartolomeo theatre). In London she sang more major Handelian roles – including oratorio roles in English – than any other singer of the day and was the only member of the Royal Academy company not to defect to the Opera of the Nobility in 1733. Handel's stroke in 1737 signalled the end of their collaboration. During the summer of 1738 she returned to Italy, retiring to Bergamo.

Tabel, Hermann (*d* 1738). Netherlands harpsichord maker working in London. Tabel was trained in his native land, in the Ruckers–Couchet tradition, before settling in London where he, in turn, trained Burkat Shudi and Jacob Kirckman. Only one of his instruments (1721) survives, and it is one of the few extant English double harpsichords from the time. It has dogleg upper-manual jacks and a lute stop, characteristic of contemporary Flemish instruments, but has been otherwise heavily altered.

Tate, Nahum (1652–1715). Playwright, educated in Dublin, who in 1689 provided Purcell with the occasionally vapid libretto for *Dido and Aeneas* (the opera performed at a Chelsea boarding-school for gentlewomen). In 1692 he was made poet laureate.

Tofts, Catherine (*c*1685–1756). The first English prima donna. In 1704 she sang in a revival of John Weldon's prize-winning *Judgment of Paris* and the following year joined the Drury Lane company as an opera singer, taking the title roles in *Arsinoe* (1705), *Camilla* (1706) and *Thomyris* (1707). Her beauty was renowned and her voice was sweet and silvery-toned. A fierce rivalry between 'Mrs Tofts' and the Italian soprano Margherita de L'Epine erupted in the course of their joint appearances at Drury Lane. In 1709 she went to Venice, where in 1716 she married Joseph Smith (who became the English Consul there

and whose collection of Canalettos is preserved at Windsor Castle).

Tomkins, Thomas. See BRITISH ISLES 2 *Provinces.*

Tosi, Pier Francesco. See ITALY 10 *Itinerant Musicians.*

Tregian, Francis (1574–1619). Cornish Catholic musician, important for three manuscript anthologies which he meticulously copied while imprisoned in London's Fleet Prison for recusancy. The most famous is the *Fitzwilliam Virginal Book*; the remaining two contain sacred and secular vocal compositions as well as dances, some of which are unique to the manuscripts. During the early 1590s he had served Cardinal Allen (*d* 1594) as his chamberlain in Rome, where he collected Italian music; jailed in 1609, he surrounded himself with a large collection of books and manuscripts, which his family was able to recover at his death.

Turner, Robert [Tornar, Roberto]. See IBERIAN PENINSULA AND COLONIES 2 *Portugal.*

Turner, William (1651–1740). One of at least two musicians of the same name. Chapel Royal countertenor and composer of anthems. Turner was trained at Christ Church, Oxford, and – along with Pelham Humfrey and John Blow, with both of whom he collaborated on 'The Club Anthem' (1664) – at the Chapel Royal, where he served for 71 years (from 1669 until his death). In 1672 he joined the King's Private Musick and over the next two decades was regularly heard as a soloist in performances of celebratory odes by Blow and Purcell. In 1674 he sang in Shadwell's famous London production of *The Tempest*. He held minor posts at St Paul's Cathedral and Westminster Abbey and in 1696 was granted the Cambridge MusD.

Valentine, Robert. See ITALY 7 *Papal States: Rome.*

Veracini, Francesco Maria. See ITALY 6 *Tuscany.*

Visconti, Gasparo (1683–*c*1713). Cremonese nobleman, violinist and composer who worked in London. Visconti studied with Corelli for five years before travelling to London where he made his way as a soloist, playing in theatres and public halls. He performed at court with James Paisible and published Corellian sonatas for violin (1703) and flute (1704) which were well received. He returned to Cremona with a German wife about 1713. His concertos (published posthumously, *c*1730) were very much influenced by those of Vivaldi.

Walsh, John (*c*1666–1736). Pre-eminent London publisher and music seller of his day.

Walsh began as an instrument maker, turning to publishing in 1695. He deftly filled the place left vacant by John Playford (d 1686), unhindered by any real competition. At his premises in Catherine Street, Strand, Walsh began printing on a scale hitherto unknown. He was a shrewd businessman: he published popular music and cheap tutors, advertised, and offered subscription issues – even free copies – and serialized music collections. To reduce the cost and to speed the printing process, Walsh used pewter plates instead of copper, punches instead of engraving, and stock title pages.

When Handel, newly arrived in London, sought a publisher for *Rinaldo* (1711), it was to Walsh that he turned. To diversify his offerings further, Walsh pirated Dutch editions of Continental music such as the Corelli sonatas; from 1716 onwards he maintained a cordial working relationship with the Amsterdam firm of Estienne Roger. In London Walsh was associated with John Hare until 1730 and with Peter Randall (his brother-in-law) from 1706 to 1710. Walsh was succeeded in the business by his son, John (1709–66), who published all of Handel's later works, having secured the exclusive rights for a period of 14 years beginning in 1739.

Ward, John. The name of a number of musicians in Canterbury at the beginning of the 17th century. One John Ward (1571–1617) was a minor canon at Canterbury Cathedral and later a household musician to Sir Henry Fanshawe of Essex. He composed sacred music, including services and anthems, of which two stand out: one on the death of Prince Henry (*No object dearer*, 1612) and another on that of Sir Henry (*If Heav'n's just wrath*, 1616). In 1613 he published a collection of madrigals. His son of the same name (early 1590s–1630s) was a chorister at the cathedral and attended King's School, Canterbury, before becoming a civil servant (Attorney at the Exchequer for Sir Thomas Fanshawe). His idiomatically conceived fantasias and ayres for viols circulated widely during his lifetime. Thomas Tomkins dedicated the madrigal *Oft did I marle* (1622) to him.

Watts, John (1678–1763). London printer and bookseller, established near Lincoln's Inn Fields. Watts, together with the publisher Jacob Tonson, issued the first and subsequent editions of *The Beggar's Opera* (1728) and the six-volume *Musical Miscellany* (1729–31), the most significant pocket songbook of its day.

Weideman, Carl Friedrich (d 1782). German flautist and composer working in London. When J. J. Quantz arrived in London in 1727, Weideman was already well established. Ultimately he was made a member of the King's Band of Musicians. He used his success to promote the Royal Society of Musicians of Great Britain through benefit concerts. He may be the flautist Hogarth incorporated in the fourth picture of *Marriage à la mode*. He composed a variety of slender flute sonatas, concertos and other chamber music that nevertheless reflect his contact with Handel. One of his songs gained popularity at Vauxhall Gardens.

Weldon, John (1676–1736). Organist and composer who in 1701 unexpectedly (and probably unjustly) won the competition to determine the best English composer of the day – beating John Eccles, Daniel Purcell and Gottfried Finger. Weldon held appointments as organist of New College, Oxford (1694) St Bride's, London (1702), the Chapel Royal (1708) and St Martin-in-the-Fields (1714). A pupil of Henry Purcell, he composed masques, odes, songs and anthems. His winning setting of Congreve's *Judgment of Paris* secured him an appointment as Gentleman Extraordinary of the Chapel Royal and the useful exposure afforded by a performance at Lincoln's Inn Fields (1702). His setting of *The Tempest* (c1712) was long assumed to be the work of Purcell.

Woodcock, Robert (d by 1734). Recorder player and composer who published a set of virtuoso concertos for wind and strings (c1727), which were popularized by such players as John Baston as interval pieces in the London theatres.

Young. Family of musicians flourishing in the 18th century; within one generation, two brothers – Charles (fl 1700–20) and Anthony (b 1685) – were organists and three sisters were singers. Cecilia (1711–89), later Mrs Thomas Arne, studied with Francesco Geminiani and then joined Handel's opera company. She sang the role of Athalia in the first London performance of Handel's oratorio; after her marriage in 1737, she sang in performances of her husband's works (*Comus*, *The Judgment of Paris* and *Alfred*) and, with her sister-in-law Susanna, in 1742 in the first performance of Handel's *Messiah*, in Dublin. Cecilia was joined in Dublin by her sister Isabella (fl 1730–53), who was by then Mrs J. F. Lampe. Their sister Esther (Mrs Jones, fl 1739–62) was the contralto who took the roles of Juno and Ino in the first performance of Handel's *Semele* in 1744.

Young, John (c1660–c1732). Music printer

(from 1695), publisher of instrumental collections and tutors, and a respected violin maker; in 1715 he and his son Talbot (*c*1690–1758), an amateur violinist, joined Maurice Greene in establishing the Philarmonica Club (later known as the Castle Society) concerts, held at Young's house in St Paul's Churchyard.

Young, William. See CENTRAL EUROPE *3 Austro-Hungary*.

Zenti, Girolamo (*d* 1668). Italian maker of harpsichords, spinets and organs who worked at the Swedish (1652–?4), French (1660–62) and English (1662–4) courts. Ferdinando de' Medici owned six of his instruments. Although few instruments survive, Zenti is considered to be the first to build bentside spinets – the most popular domestic keyboard instruments in late 17th-century England.

Zuccari, Carlo. See ITALY *10 Itinerant Musicians*.

2 The Provinces

Abell, John. See BRITISH ISLES *1 London*.

Alcock, John (1715–1806). Organist at Lichfield Cathedral, author and composer. Alcock, a fellow chorister at St Paul's with William Boyce, was apprenticed to John Stanley (who particularly influenced his instrumental music). In 1752 he attempted to set in motion the quarterly publication of a service in score, to replace the inaccurate manuscripts to which his fellow cathedral musicians had recourse; only his own service in E minor was printed and he contented himself with contributing to Maurice Greene's collection of cathedral music which was eventually published by Boyce. That Alcock was an admirer of Greene can be heard in his anthems. Alcock took BMus (1755) and DMus (1766) degrees at Oxford and under the pseudonym John Piper published a semi-autobiographical novel (*The Life of Miss Fanny Brown*) expressing his frustrations at being exiled to the Midlands.

Aldrich, Henry (1648–1710). Dean of Christ Church, Oxford, a scholar, mathematician and architect as well as a music collector and composer, largely of Catholic music. In Oxford, Aldrich designed the portal at the old Ashmolean, the chapel at Trinity College and the Peckwater Quadrangle at Christ Church. At the weekly music meetings in his rooms his catches and transcriptions of Elizabethan and Italian music were performed. The university press published three pieces by Aldrich, *c*1696.

Arne, Thomas Augustine. See BRITISH ISLES *1 London*.

Avison, Charles (1709–70). Concerto composer and author of *An Essay on Musical Expression* (1752), resident in Newcastle upon Tyne. Charles Avison is remembered for several things, not least for his efforts to organize music societies and subscription concert series in Newcastle and Durham (with John Garth) during the 1730s. It was at those concerts that his own sonatas and concertos (opp. 1–10, *c*1737–1769 – some of the earliest of their kind) were first performed; he also presented Rameau's unique *Pièces de clavecin en concerts* (1741) in the early 1750s (which inspired his later accompanied keyboard works). In about 1743 Avison published concerto grosso arrangements of 12 harpsichord sonatas by Domenico Scarlatti. Avison's concertos gained a popularity that remained undiminished into the 19th century. In the 1750s he and Garth founded a Marcello Society in conjunction with their joint editorship of Benedetto Marcello's choral psalms.

Avison was also an organist who from 1735 held the post at St Nicholas, Newcastle, one of the largest parish churches in England, and a teacher of the harpsichord, violin and flute. He chose to stay in Newcastle despite many attractive proposals from York, Dublin and London, where in 1753 he was offered Pepusch's old job at the Charterhouse. In 1764 Avison published a collection of accompanied harpsichord sonatas, though he is best known for *An Essay on Musical Expression*; in addition to examining the effect of music on the emotions, this contains a substantial treatise on the performance of concertos, and controversial criticisms of Handel, and compares his music unfavourably with that of Francesco Geminiani and Marcello. It was reprinted twice and translated into German (1775).

Bond, Capel (1730–90). Late Baroque organist and composer, much influenced by Handel. Bond was educated in Gloucester, but worked in the Midlands where he organized subscription concerts and festival performances of Handel oratorios. From 1749 he was at Coventry, first as organist of St Michael (later Coventry Cathedral) and then, additionally, at Holy Trinity from 1752. In 1766 he published *Six Concertos in Seven Parts*, four of which were concerti grossi, and two, solo concertos (for trumpet and bassoon); these were popular in London at the Concerts of Ancient Music.

Burney, Charles. See BRITISH ISLES *1 London*.

Butler, Charles (*c*1560–1647). Vicar at Wooton St Lawrence (Hants.), expert on bee-keeping (he published *The Feminine Monarchie* in 1609) and English orthography (*The English Grammar* appeared in 1633); he was also an amateur musician and theorist who produced a practical and often amusing manual for church musicians entitled *The Principles of Musik* (1636).

Castrucci, Pietro. See BRITISH ISLES *1 London.*

Child, William. See BRITISH ISLES *1 London.*

Cibber, Susanna Maria. See BRITISH ISLES *1 London.*

Clarke, Jeremiah. See BRITISH ISLES *1 London.*

Dallam. See BRITISH ISLES *1 London.*

Dubourg, Matthew (1703–67). English violin virtuoso trained by Francesco Geminiani. In 1728 he became Master and Composer of State Music in Ireland, returning to London in 1752 to lead the King's Band. He raised standards of string playing in Dublin and lent support to performances of the dramatic music of Arne (*Comus*) and Handel (*Messiah, Samson* and *Judas Maccabaeus*); his rapport with Handel, in particular, is illustrated by the humorous remark made by Handel (who was conducting) after an unusually long violin concerto cadenza: 'Welcome home, Mr Dubourg'. He is known today for his flamboyant ornamentation (in a manuscript dating from the 1720s) of Corelli's op. 5 sonatas.

East, Michael (*c*1580–1648). Composer (not to be confused with the printer) who, in spite of spending his life out of London, as Master of the Choristers of Lichfield Cathedral, was nevertheless very much in tune with contemporary tastes. He published seven collections of vocal and instrumental music (1604–38) which, significantly, encompass Italian madrigals, consort songs, anthems and viol consorts.

Evelyn, John (1620–1706). Music-lover and diarist (1641–1706), by profession a civil servant and Commissioner of the Privy Seal. Evelyn pursued his interest in music at Oxford before undertaking a Continental tour (1641–7): his diary reveals that he learnt the theorbo and attended performances of opera and sacred music while in Italy. He returned to England laden with sets of madrigals and other music including motets by Carissimi and Alessandro Grandi (*d* 1630), though as a deeply religious man he would have censured their use of instruments (disapproving as he did of the use of strings in Chapel Royal services). Nevertheless, he managed to reconcile his piety with his love of Italian opera and fascination with castratos. He was acquainted with Pepys and frequented many of the same musical evenings. His library is preserved at Christ Church, Oxford.

Felton, William (1715–69). Vicar-choral at Hereford Cathedral (from 1743), popular performer on the harpsichord and organ, praised by Burney, and prolific composer of concertos for those instruments (between 1744 and 1767 he published 32). The Andante from op. 1 no. 3 (1744) was widely known as 'Felton's Gavot'.

Ferrabosco, John. See BRITISH ISLES *1 London.*

Geminiani, Francesco. See BRITISH ISLES *1 London.*

Gibbs, Joseph (1699–1788). Provincial organist and composer. Gibbs worked all his life in Essex and Suffolk where he was a member of the Ipswich Musical Society (Gainsborough painted his portrait as well as a group picture of the society). Although he composed organ music and string quartets, he is remembered by his first publication, *Eight Solos for a Violin with a Thorough Bass for the Harpsichord* (*c*1746) which by their technical demands reveal the influence of Francesco Geminiani, F. M. Veracini and M. C. Festing; their originality lies in the intensely chromatic style that Gibbs experimented with, but abandoned in his later works.

Goodson, Richard (*c*1655–1718). Professor of music at Oxford and organist at New College from 1682; in 1692 he took up organ duties at Christ Church Cathedral. His son Richard (*c*1685–1741) succeeded him as professor and organist in 1718.

Gostling. See BRITISH ISLES *1 London.*

Greene, Maurice. See BRITISH ISLES *1 London.*

Handel, George Frideric. See BRITISH ISLES *1 London.*

Hayes, William (1708–77). Oxford professor of music who presided over the opening of the Holywell Music Room and directed weekly concerts there. Hayes was organist at Worcester Cathedral before taking up posts at Magdalen College, Oxford, in 1734. The following year he took the BMus and in 1742 succeeded the younger Richard Goodson as professor. He composed a variety of music (oratorios, anthems, psalms, a *Te Deum*, songs, catches, cantatas, odes, trio sonatas and concertos) much indebted to Handel – whose music he conducted at music festivals in and around Oxford. Shortly after Handel's death he composed the ode *O that some pensive Muse*. During the 1750s he took exception to the writings of Charles Avison and Barnabas Gunn, though chose to publish his critical views anonymously. His son Philip (1738–97) followed in his footsteps at Oxford.

Holder, William (1616–96). Canon of Ely Cathedral after the Restoration and later subdean of the Chapel Royal (from 1674) who composed anthems and other Anglican church music and published a *Treatise on the Natural Grounds* (1693). Although educated at Cambridge, he spent the Civil War years in Oxford where in 1660 he took a doctorate in Divinity; three years later he was elected one of the first Fellows of the Royal Society. Holder was married to the sister of Sir Christopher Wren.

Jeffreys, George (*c*1610–1685). Chapel Royal organist during the Civil War and composer of remarkably beautiful, highly original and chromatic sacred music. The course of Jeffreys's career was determined by his royalist views: his most important works – which effectively combine the English polyphonic tradition with the modern Italian declamatory style – are now thought to have been composed before the Commonwealth. About 1648–9 he had his music bound together, evidently composing very little while in the service of Sir Christopher Hatton, in the relative obscurity of Northamptonshire. That many of his compositions are found in many contemporary manuscripts attests to their popularity.

Jenkins, John (1592–1678). Lutenist and lyra viol player, and prolific composer of consort music. Much of what we know of Jenkins comes from his pupil Roger North, and from Anthony Wood. He spent most of his career in the manor houses of Norfolk and Cambridgeshire, finally gaining a court appointment at the age of 68. Most of his music was composed for private music making. Among the over 800 instrumental works that survive there are three sets of polyphonic viol consorts, italianate three-part fantasias which depend upon the kinds of effect available on violins, fantasia-suites (influenced by Coprario), and pieces for bass viols which incorporate virtuoso divisions; most of the lyra viol music is lost.

Jennens, Charles (1700–73). Respected writer, Handel's friend and oratorio librettist. Jennens was a cultivated and gifted, if somewhat vain and irascible, man. His non-juror's outlook, a prerogative of his wealth, cut short his career at Balliol College, Oxford, and he returned to his estate at Gopsall in the Midlands. He subscribed to Handel's published works and also obtained copies of manuscript works by standing order. He collaborated with Handel on *Saul*, *L'Allegro, il Penseroso ed il Moderato*, *Messiah* and *Belshazzar*; he later provided valuable annotations to Mainwaring's *Life of Handel*.

Johnson, Samuel. See BRITISH ISLES *1 London*.

Kusser, Johann Sigismund. See NORTHERN EUROPE *7 Itinerant Musicians*.

Lampe, John Frederick. See BRITISH ISLES *1 London*.

Lawes. See BRITISH ISLES *1 London*.

L'Estrange. Norfolk family of music patrons and amateur musicians whose music masters included John Jenkins and Thomas Brewer. Sir Nicholas L'Estrange (1603–55) amassed a large music library which he carefully collated, indexed and annotated. Roger L'Estrange (1616–1704) was a skilled bass viol player and a friend of Thomas Britton in London.

Leveridge, Richard. See BRITISH ISLES *1 London*.

Locke, Matthew. See BRITISH ISLES *1 London*.

Lowe, Edward (*c*1610–82). Organist at Christ Church Cathedral, Oxford, from 1631, copyist for the Oxford Music School meetings, author of *A Short Direction for the Performance of Cathedrall Service* (1661) and the composer of anthems, partsongs and harpsichord lessons. Lowe was trained as a chorister at Salisbury Cathedral. During the Commonwealth he gave music lessons and participated at the weekly gathering of the Music School, held at the home of William Ellis; at this time he copied numerous scores and parts, and assembled two important anthologies of contemporary vocal music. After the Restoration he took up his post again at Christ Church and became one of the Chapel Royal organists, along with William Child and Christopher Gibbons. In 1662 he succeeded John Wilson as professor of music at Oxford.

Mace, Thomas (1612/13–?1706). Cambridge lutenist, singer, composer and writer on such non-musical topics as health and the English highways. He is best remembered for his informative if conservative book, *Musick's Monument* (1676), intended to redress the damage to traditional English musical forms caused by the francophilia rampant at court after the Restoration; in it he dwelt on the care and maintenance of instruments, the playing of continuo on the theorbo and the use of organ and harpsichord in consort music.

McGibbon, William (*c*1690–1756). Edinburgh violinist and the leading Scottish composer of the late Baroque era. McGibbon studied the violin in London and led the Edinburgh Musical Society orchestra for 20 years. He composed solo and trio sonatas in the style of Corelli and was known for his solo fiddle variations on popular Scottish folktunes.

Matteis. See BRITISH ISLES *1 London*.

Morell, Thomas (1703–84). Scholar and one of Handel's oratorio librettists who, late in life, wrote an important memoir of his collaboration with Handel. Morell was a Fellow of King's College, Cambridge (where he had taken the degree of Doctor of Divinity in 1743), and a Fellow of the Royal Society. His association with Handel began in 1746; among his librettos were *Judas Maccabaeus, Alexander Balus, Joshua, Theodora, Jephtha* and *The Triumph of Time and Truth*. He was a friend of Garrick and of Hogarth, who left a portrait of him.

Mudge, Richard (1718–63). Devonshire cleric and composer with a flair for the unconventional. Mudge was educated at Pembroke College, Oxford, ordained and appointed vicar at Great Packington – then, rector at Bedworth, Warwickshire, in 1756, under the Earl of Aylesford's patronage. Appended to his 1749 collection of late Baroque concerti grossi is an Adagio for five-part strings, in which three voices sing a canon attributed to Byrd ('Non nobis Domine').

Norcombe, Daniel. See LOW COUNTRIES *2 South Netherlands*.

North, Roger. See BRITISH ISLES *1 London*.

Playford, John. See BRITISH ISLES *1 London*.

Purcell, Daniel (*d* 1717). Brother of Henry Purcell and minor composer. Daniel Purcell followed his brother as a chorister of the Chapel Royal and in 1688 became organist of Magdalen College, Oxford, composing anthems in the course of his work. After his brother's death he provided music for the concluding masque of *The Indian Queen* (1696) and embarked on a decade of theatre composition. In 1700 he entered the competition for the best setting of Congreve's masque, *The Judgment of Paris*, and took third prize. With the growing popularity of Italian opera, Purcell abandoned the theatre in 1707, having contributed incidental music to more than 40 plays; during that time he had published several collections of sonatas for various instruments. His last post was as organist at St Andrew's, Holborn.

Roseingrave, Thomas. See BRITISH ISLES *1 London*.

Salmon, Thomas (1648–1706). Clergyman who gained the Oxford MA in mathematics and became acquainted with Anthony Wood before taking up a permanent post as rector of a Bedfordshire church. As a young amateur musician, Salmon's interest in music theory resulted in the publication of *An Essay to the Advancement of Musick* (1672), in which he somewhat naively suggested ways in which to simplify music notation; this led to a bitter pamphlet war with Matthew Locke. One of his proposals did prove lasting: Playford adopted the use of the treble clef for both soprano and tenor vocal parts in his editions, now standard practice.

Simpson, Christopher. See BRITISH ISLES *1 London*.

Smith, 'Father'. See BRITISH ISLES *1 London*.

Talbot, James (1665–1708). Cambridge professor of Hebrew and the author of an important manuscript treatise (*c*1695, Oxford, Christ Church Mus MS 1187) on musical instruments, compiled from interviews with London musicians and makers, and from Michael Praetorius, Marin Mersenne and Athanasius Kircher.

Tate, Nahum. See BRITISH ISLES *1 London*.

Tomkins, Thomas (1572–1656). Organist at Worcester Cathedral, Gentleman-in-Ordinary of the Chapel Royal and, in that capacity, a prolific composer of anthems and services. Tomkins, from a family of church musicians, was a pupil of William Byrd. He contributed a madrigal to *The Triumphes of Oriana* (1601), a seven-part setting of the *Confortare* to the coronation ceremony of James I (1603) and a verse anthem, *Know ye not*, to the funeral service of Prince Henry (1612). In 1621 he became an organist of the Chapel Royal and in 1625 succeeded Orlando Gibbons in the senior post. It seems probable that his son Nathaniel (1599–1681), a canon of Worcester Cathedral, published *Musica Deo sacra*, containing the vast majority of his father's church music, in 1668.

Tregian, Francis. See BRITISH ISLES *1 London*.

Tudway, Thomas (*c*1650–1726). Cambridge organist, composer and anthologizer of English sacred music. After being trained as a chorister in the Chapel Royal, Tudway became organist in 1670 of King's College, Cambridge, where he remained until his death. He acquired the degrees of MusB and MusD and in 1705 was made professor of music at Cambridge. Between 1714 and 1720 he collected for Lord Harley (later the Earl of Oxford) six large volumes of cathedral music which encompass the repertory (some of it unique to the manuscripts) from Tye to Handel, and include a number of his own works; they are now in the British Library. Because the volumes remained in manuscript and were never widely circulated, they never exerted the influence that Boyce's later anthology did, though they did reflect the continuing interest in 17th-century repertory.

Ward, John. See BRITISH ISLES *1 London*.

Weelkes, Thomas (?1576–1623). Important composer of madrigals and Anglican church music. Despite his brilliance as a contrapuntist in the best English tradition, Weelkes never gained the recognition he deserved. He published his secular vocal music between 1597 and 1608; to *The Triumphes of Oriana* (1601) he contributed the brilliant madrigal *As Vesta was from Latmos Hill descending*. His sacred music dates from after 1602, when he took up the post of organist at Chichester Cathedral.

Weelkes was the most prolific composer of services – particularly for the office of Evensong – of his day. He must have aspired to a place in the Chapel Royal, but it never came his way (his connections were with the entourage of the previous monarch). Frustrated and isolated in Chichester, he fell into dissipation, and in 1616, was described as 'a common drunkard and a notorious swearer and blasphemer', censured and finally dismissed.

Weelkes's compositional style is indebted to Byrd and Morley (for whom he composed a six-voice elegy, *Death hath deprived me of my dearest friend*). In the madrigal he found full scope for his formidable contrapuntal technique, his command of form, and his vivid handling of imagery. In the anthem he developed an unrivalled richness of ensemble texture, powerful and sonorous (*Hosanna to the Son of David*).

Wilbye, John (1574–1638). Gifted madrigalist and domestic musician working in relative obscurity at Hengrave, Suffolk. Wilbye published two collections of madrigals, in 1598 and 1609 (considered to be the finest of the period), as well as contributing to *The Triumphes of Oriana* (1601). He also composed anthems and viol fantasies; in his will he bequeathed his 'best vyall' to the Prince of Wales (later Charles I).

Wilson, John (1595–1674). Song composer, lutenist and singer who began his career as a musician in Shakespeare's company. He was appointed to the King's Musick, and was later professor of music at Oxford. Wilson's songs were first heard in London theatres in 1614; many were later published in a collection of *Cheerful Ayres or Ballads* (1659–60), of which *Take, O take those lips away* is the best known.

Wood, Anthony [Anthony à Wood] (1632–95). Oxford amateur musician, composer and local historian whose remarks on English musicians are an important – though not wholly dependable – biographical source of the Restoration era.

Young. See BRITISH ISLES *1 London*.

The Low Countries

The Netherlanders

The division of the Low Countries into two political entities in the late 16th century shattered a centuries-old cultural unity which, particularly in the 15th and 16th centuries and especially in the field of music, had held a dominant position in the western world. From that time until the French Revolution the South Netherlands continued to be under the rule of Spain or, from 1715, of Austria (though the episcopal principality of Liège preserved its independence). The territories of the north joined to form the Republic of the Seven United Provinces. The reshaping of Europe at the Congress of Vienna, following the upheaval of the Napoleonic Wars, reunited the two states, but the so-called United Kingdom of the Netherlands did not last for long. In 1830, yet again, two separate sovereign states in the Low Countries came into being, the Kingdom of Belgium in the south and the Kingdom of the Netherlands (commonly though incorrectly known as 'Holland') in the north.

The political separation, endorsed internationally in 1648 by the Treaty of Westphalia, was not the only factor to force the two states apart. While the centre of political and economic importance undoubtedly lay in the South Netherlands in the 15th and 16th centuries, by the end of that period it had shifted to the north. The South Netherlands, under Habsburg rule, were dominated throughout the Baroque era by a conservative Catholic church and an equally conservative, Catholic and largely foreign nobility. The former economic prosperity slipped into decline, mainly because of the loss of access to the Schelt estuary. Learning and the arts also declined, and in the 17th century it was only in painting (with Rubens in the forefront) that the glories of the past were maintained.

In the north, in spite of the armed conflict that had brought them into being, the United Provinces rose to become a major European power, founded a formidable overseas empire, and filled their coffers through the vigorous pursuit of worldwide trade. Learning, literature, painting and architecture flourished as never before. The Dutchman has good reason to refer to the 17th century as his 'Gouden Eeuw' ('Golden Age'). This vigour wanted in the following century, and the Republic gradually lost its political standing in Europe.

The music of the Baroque clearly reflects the different social, economic and religious structures of the two states. A major common denominator is perhaps the fact that in neither south nor north did music return to the heights it had reached in the Renaissance. But conventional musicology has painted too negative a picture of 17th- and 18th-century music in the Low Countries – although that view is now under re-examination. But modern research is unlikely to alter the fact that both parts of the Netherlands were left behind by other great European nations. Why this should be so, in a period that witnessed so impressive a flowering of the other arts – such as both Dutch and Flemish painting in the 17th century – remains an enigma (see Plate 19).

The breach with the past is less marked in the South Netherlands, particularly in church music. The south remained true to the old religion, and there was little change in the institutions of sacred music. The great churches like Ste Gudule in Brussels, St Donatian in Bruges and St Bavon in Ghent maintained their traditional establishments and trained their singers and instrumentalists in their choir schools. Heavy losses of source material make it impossible to assess the liturgical music of these churches, but almost certainly it was not progressive. Until well into the 17th century the names of the great 16th-century composers (Clemens non Papa, Orlande de Lassus and Philippe de Monte) recur; but Italian monody seems to have become known only very late and even then it was not widely disseminated (an example is the *Sacri concentus*, 1630, of Léonard de Hodémont). The motets and Masses of the Catholic Englishman Peter Philips, who found asylum at the Brussels archducal court, are among the more important sacred works of the earlier 17th century – far superior to those of local church composers, whose use of continuo still seems conservative. In this area Henry Du Mont was important, but, as he spent almost his entire life in Paris, he lies beyond the scope of this essay.

Not apparently until after 1650 are more up-to-date stylistic features found, and then mainly in non-liturgical music for private worship (for example, the songs with continuo of Lucas van Waasmunster). It was then, too, that the concertato style became established in south Netherlands motets and Masses. Late in the century the Italian High Baroque style was introduced by two immigrants, Pietro Torri and Pietro Antonio Fiocco. Fiocco's eldest son, Jean-Joseph, was a prolific composer of Italian oratorios in the 1730s; another son, Joseph-Hector, is best known for his Lamentations for Holy Week. The motets of Pierre-Hercule Bréhy, *maître de chant* at Ste Gudule, reveal French influence.

In the more Catholic southern area of the United Provinces, too, the concertato style is found in motets and Masses. As early as 1631 Viadana's influence can be seen in the motets of Herman Hollander, *phonascus* of the Church of Our Lady in Breda. The liturgical works of minor masters like Benedictus Buns (1666–c1710) or Carolus Hacquart belong to a similar tradition. But the production of Catholic church music in the Republic in the Baroque was distinctly modest.

The prevailing of the young state was Calvinism. Any music had to be simple and austere. In services the use of music was restricted to the liturgy. Up to the middle of the 17th century psalms were unaccompanied; eventually organ accompaniment was reluctantly permitted. Church buildings, and thus organs too, were the property of towns, and organists were therefore municipal employees. They had to play not only before and after services on Sundays but often at specified times during the week. These 'organ recitals', under civic auspices, were an institution in the United Provinces. Organ-building was a flourishing craft in the Baroque era, and the magnificent instruments of the time are still internationally admired. Much of the music played on them, from the time of the great Sweelinck (*d* 1621) onwards, is gone beyond recall, for improvisation was an important feature of the organist's art.

Town bands, an international musical institution, were to be found in the larger towns of the United Provinces up to the middle of the 17th century. Composed typically of cornetts, trombones, flutes and trumpets, they played in the town square for civic receptions, banquets and other festivals. In addition, there was the carillon, a typically Dutch form of public music-making. Bell-players, like organists, were civic employees; often the same person held both posts. The bells cast by François and Pierre Hemony, brothers from Alsace-Lorraine who settled in the United Provinces in 1641, had a precision of tuning and clarity of timbre that gained the brothers commissions for carillons throughout the country. The installation of a pegged cylinder enabled the carillon to play automatically at set intervals – usually every quarter-hour – while the carillonneur's contract often required him to play manually once or more a week. The sound of the carillon, especially in large cities, has always made a strong impression on foreign visitors: Burney, for one, was impressed by the 'jingling of bells' when he visited the Netherlands in 1773.

The collegia musica played an important role in the evolution of instrumental music in the Republic. These musical societies, upper-middle-class in origin, came into existence in many towns from the end of the 16th century onwards (see Plate 18). Their repertory was originally orientated towards vocal and sacred music, but during the 17th century they turned increasingly to instrumental music, and this remained their chief interest. Often a town council expressed support for the activities of a collegium by making a room available for its use or stipulating in an organist's contract that he assume its direction. In the 18th century some of the collegia musica became semi-public institutions, first by admitting guests to their sessions, later by obtaining monopolies to license itinerant musicians to play in the town and to regulate admission to their performances. The 19th-century successors of the collegia often influenced the founding of professional, civic orchestras. The activities of the collegia musica and similar associations, with their mixture of professional musicians and amateurs, were a source of inspiration not only to composers – from the time of Sweelinck's polyphonic settings of the Geneva Psalter (1604–21) to the *Concerti armonici* (1725–40) of Count van Wassenaer, reflecting the move from sacred vocal music to instrumental – but also to the many 17th-century painters who delighted in portraying groups of musicians.

The role of the collegia in the musical life of the North Netherlands is all the more significant because neither the relatively austere court of the *stadhouder* nor the Calvinist church were active patrons. Much of the instrumental music of the minor Dutch Baroque masters was composed for this kind of social music-making. Keyboard and lute music were also cultivated in the 17th century (see Plate 25), and towards the end of the century the viola da gamba enjoyed a brief vogue, with such composers as Hacquart and above all Johannes Schenk. The outstanding vocal work was Constantijn Huygens's collection of monodies, *Pathodia sacra* (1647). Operatic activities were not such as to excite international attention. Indigenous opera was modest; much of it amounted to no more than musical interludes in spoken drama. Opera performances in The Hague and Amsterdam were dominated by works from the foreign repertory, especially French.

The first half of the 18th century was a great age of music publishing in the United Provinces. Amsterdam, with the publishing houses of Mortier, Witvogel and above all Roger and Le Cène, was an international centre of music printing. Good trading links facilitated the rapid distribution of their products. This brought Dutch music into direct contact with the international repertory, especially the Italian. This 'internationalization' of musical taste and activities is reflected in the frequent references to the many foreign musicians who chose to reside there. Longer-term visitors include composers such as the Germans Hurlebusch, J. W. Lustig and A. W. Solnitz, the Frenchman Jean-Marie Leclair, and the Italians P. A. Locatelli and Carlo Tessarini. On the other hand, some Dutch musicians, such as the composers Willem de Fesch and Pieter Hellendaal, spent most of their careers abroad (in England in their cases).

In the South Netherlands, unlike the United Provinces, church and court patronage was an important factor in musical life. Shortly before his death, Philip II of Spain had transferred the province to his daughter Isabella as her dowry when she married Archduke Albert in 1598; the childless couple ruled, in effect, as governors of a Habsburg fief. Their musical establishment in Brussels, very similar to that of their predecessors, was known as the Chapel Royal. Music at the court was divided in the customary way between chapel and chamber.

The importance attached to music at the Brussels court depended on the taste of successive governors. Over the years the Chapel Royal and the chamber gave employment to many minor composers born in the South Netherlands, notably the keyboard master Peeter Cornet (*d* 1633), as well as well-known foreigners. The English organist and composer Peter Philips was at the court from as early as 1597 until his death in 1628, and another English Catholic, John Bull, organist at Antwerp Cathedral, was also often in Brussels during that time. Many foreign musicians were employed in the chamber: a Spaniard, Pedro Rimonte, was director from 1603, and an Italian, Gioseffo Zamponi, held the post around the middle of the century, while such notable names as Biagio Marini, J. J. Froberger and J. K. Kerll appear in the records for periods of varying duration. During the 17th century the emphasis shifted from vocal music to instrumental. However, the most obvious difference between south and north is in theatre music. As early as 1634 a *Ballet des princes indiens*, in which monodic singing alternated with dance, was given at the Hôtel d'Orange in Brussels, and in 1650 the governor ordered a production of Zamponi's opera *Ulisse nell'isola di Circe* in celebration of the marriage of Philip IV of Spain – an event to remind us that the old tradition of lavish festivals on state occasions, redolent of the age of the dukes of Burgundy, still had some residual life at the Brussels court.

Towards the end of the 17th century, Pietro Torri was master of the Brussels chapel; he was followed by P. A. Fiocco. Fiocco also directed the earliest public opera houses in Brussels, the Théâtre du Quai du Foin and, from 1700, the Théâtre de la Monnaie; on his death in 1714 he was succeeded by his son, Jean-Joseph, who like his father was a prolific composer of concertante sacred music. It was not until 1746 that a native musician, the violin virtuoso Henri-Jacques de Croes, from Antwerp, was named master of the chapel.

There is ample variety in the broad view of music in the Low Countries during the Baroque, especially when the separate developments of south and north are considered. Certainly there is no denying the paucity of names of truly European rank among native musicians, particularly by comparison with the Renaissance era; but that need not detract from the substantial contribution, in relation to the size of the area, that the Low Countries made in some sectors of the period's musical life.

Albert Dunning
Università degli Studi, Pavia
(Translated by Mary Whittall)

Biographical Dictionary
The Low Countries

1 United Provinces

Albicastro, Henricus [Weissenburg, Heinrich] (*fl* 1700–06). Swiss violinist and competent composer of chamber music (duo, trio, and quartet sonatas published *c*1700) who, after a stint as a cavalry captain in the War of the Spanish Succession, made his home in the Netherlands.

Anders, Hendrik (1657–1714). German violinist, organist and carillonneur working in Amsterdam from 1683. With Servaas de Konink, Anders helped to foster opera in the Dutch language.

Ban, Joan Albert (1597–1644). Netherlands Catholic priest working in Haarlem, self-taught in music, who through Constantijn Huygens entered into a correspondence with Marin Mersenne, which in turn involved Huygens and Descartes (whom Ban greatly admired). Ban sent copies of his *Dissertatio epistolica de musicae natura* (1637), expounding his theories of musical evolution and 'musica flexanima' (the emotional effects of melodic intervals), and some of his music; without hesitation Mersenne pronounced them trivial and boring. Undeterred, Ban continued to correspond, and so in 1640 Mersenne was forced to contrive a competition between Ban and the eminent French composer of *airs de cour* Antoine de Boësset. They each set Germain Habert's poem 'Me veux-tu voir mourir', but Mersenne altered the first line of the version sent to Ban, thereby changing the sense of the poem and influencing the setting and the outcome of the competition. Boësset won, easily.

Birkenstock, Johann Adam. See NORTHERN EUROPE *5 West Germany and the Rhineland.*

Blankenburg, Quirinus Gerbrandszoon van (1654–1739). Netherlands organist and composer. Van Blankenburg was the son of Gerbrant Quirijnszoon van Blankenburg (*c*1620–1707), organist in Rotterdam, carillonneur and writer. He was awarded degrees in philosophy and medicine at the University of Leiden, but his career was devoted to music. He moved to The Hague as organist of the Hoofkerk (1687–1702) and from 1699 served at the Nieuwe Kerk. He advised on carillons and organs, and composed keyboard music and homophonic settings of psalms and Protestant hymns.

Borchgrevinck, Melchior. See NORTHERN EUROPE *2 Scandinavia.*

Cuzzoni, Francesca. See ITALY *10 Itinerant Musicians.*

De Fesch, Willem (1687–?1757). Important early 18th-century Netherlands violin virtuoso and composer. De Fesch worked in Amsterdam (1710–25), Antwerp (1725–31) – where as *kapelmeester* at the cathedral he repeatedly clashed with his colleagues – and finally London. His string chamber music is familiar to amateur musicians, his Vivaldian concertos and English songs much less so. The performance of his oratorio *Judith* in 1733 merited the attention of Hogarth, who caricatured the composer as he played.

Descartes, René. See FRANCE *1 Paris and Versailles.*

Eyck, Jacob van (*c*1589–1657). Netherlands campanologist, teacher and composer. As chief carillonneur at Utrecht from 1625, van Eyck was responsible for all the carillons and bells in the city, and in the course of his duties he observed the relationship between the overtone structure and the bell's shape. His conclusions were adopted by the bellfounders François and Pierre Hemony, enabling them to develop a new method of tuning bells. In 1649 van Eyck dedicated *Der fluyten lust-hof* (144 pieces based on popular Dutch tunes for descant recorder) to Constantijn Huygens.

Gautier, Jacques. See FRANCE *1 Paris and Versailles.*

Hacquart, Carolus (*c*1640–?1701). Player of the viol, lute and organ, praised by Constantijn Huygens. He moved from his native Bruges to the United Provinces in the 1670s. Hacquart's ten trio and quartet sonatas, which he published in *Harmonia parnassia* in 1686, are important counterparts to those of Purcell and Corelli. He also published Latin sacred works, and in 1678 wrote the music for *De triomfeerende min*, a pastoral play to celebrate the Peace of Nijmegen; it has been reckoned the first essay in Netherlands opera.

Hemony. Two brothers, François (*c*1609–1667) and Pierre (1619–80), from a Netherlands family of bronze casters, famed for the pure intonation of their bells. They worked together from 1642 at Zutphen, where they had built a carillon famed for its beauty, but in 1657 they parted: François became inspector of bells and guns in Amsterdam, while Pierre set up a workshop in Ghent. They worked together again from 1664 until François' death in Amsterdam; Pierre continued alone until his death.

They produced between 300 and 400 bells, of which 100 remain, as well as cannon, mortars and statues. The Hemonys made the first chromatic carillons, extended their compasses to over three octaves and tuned them in meantone. From the observations of the Utrecht carillonneur Jacob van Eyck on the ideal pattern of partial tones and their location on the bells, they worked out a new and more refined way of casting and tuning their bells: instead of chipping from inside the rib, they ground the bell evenly on a lathe to a prescribed thickness. Of 53 carillons, 31 still function; those at the Nieuwe Kerk, Delft (1659–60), and Utrecht Cathedral (1663–4) are noted for their beauty.

Hove, Joachim van den (1567–1620). Lutenist, teacher, intabulator and composer working in Leiden (1594–*c*1613). He travelled in France, Germany and Italy before settling in The Hague, where he published his *Praeludia testudinis* (1616), containing pieces for lute.

Hurlebusch, Conrad Friedrich. See NORTHERN EUROPE 7 *Itinerant Musicians.*

Huygens. Father and son, who were intellectuals, scientists, prodigious correspondents, and amateur musicians and composers. Constantijn Huygens (1596–1687) travelled extensively as a diplomat in the civil service: to Venice, where in 1620 he met Monteverdi and absorbed the monodic style; to London, to play the lute for James I, who in turn made him a knight in 1622; and to Paris, where he met Chambonnières and Descartes and was made a Chevalier de l'Ordre de St Michel in 1633 by Louis XIII. He collected music wherever he went and was himself the composer of nearly 800 works (most are lost), though he published only one collection (and that in Paris), the *Pathodia sacra* (1647). He counted among his musical friends Marin Mersenne, J. Gautier and J. J. Froberger. His writings on musical subjects included a tract (published in 1641) on the use of the organ in the Dutch Reformed Church – a practice banned since 1572 – and another (in 1658), which put forth a proposal to improve the prose and melodies of the Geneva Psalter.

It came as no surprise that his son Christiaan Huygens (1629–95) should have been an extremely precocious child whose interest in music – he played the lute, violin and harpsichord, and composed – complemented his studies in mathematics, physics, languages and law. His family wealth enabled him to pursue his research into physical optics and wave theory; he also improved the telescope and perfected the pendulum clock. Christiaan was a meticulous scientist: he was the first successfully to work out the mathematical basis for dividing an octave into 31 equal parts and then to demonstrate its practicality as a tuning; he published his findings in 1661 (*Novus cyclus harmonicus*). In 1663 he was made a Fellow of the Royal Society, London, and three years later Louis XIV appointed him president of the Académie des Sciences in Paris.

Konink [Cooninck], Servaas de (*d* 1717/18). Orchestral player in the Amsterdam theatre and composer of the popular and influential 1688 vernacular opera *De vrijadje van Cloris en Roosje*; Konink also composed incidental music for a girls' school performance of Racine's *Athalie* (1697), as well as duo and trio sonatas.

Le Cène, Michel-Charles. See LOW COUNTRIES 1 *United Provinces*, Roger, Estienne.

Leclair, Jean-Marie. See FRANCE 1 *Paris and Versailles.*

Locatelli, Pietro Antonio (1695–1764). Italian virtuoso violinist and composer of sonatas and concertos, who from 1729 lived in Amsterdam. Locatelli was trained at Bergamo and in Rome, where he may have studied with the aged and ailing Corelli and Giuseppe Valentini; from 1717 until 1723 he performed at the Roman *palazzo* of Cardinal Ottoboni, during which time he published his first collection of Corellian concerti grossi in Amsterdam (1721; rev., 1729). In 1725 he took up an appointment as a *virtuoso da camera* at the Mantuan court, but within two years was on his way northwards – first to the Bavarian court, then in 1728 to Berlin (where he played for the King of Prussia) and Kassel (where he played with the French violinist Jean-Marie Leclair *l'aîné*). He is said to have preferred a short bow, and was praised as much for the sweetness of his playing as for its power and brilliance.

In Amsterdam he not only taught and directed an amateur ensemble (indeed professionals were not allowed to join), but also served as a proof-reader to the printer and publisher Le Cène (*d* 1743), before acquiring a patent to publish his own music; this includes mainstream Italian sonatas for flute as well as violin (op. 6, published in 1737, figures among his finest works), trio sonatas, and concertos – both concerti grossi and solo concertos (*L'arte del violino*, op. 3, 1733).

Lustig, Jacob Wilhelm (1706–96). German-born organist, translator and writer. Lustig grew up in Hamburg (where his father, of the same name, was organist at the Michaeliskirche) and studied with Mattheson, Telemann and Kunzen, before taking up an organ post in Groningen. Thanks to a grant from his church (St Martin), he was able to study in London in the early 1730s. He took Dutch citizenship in 1743. Though unimportant as a composer, Lustig was much esteemed as an organist and sought-after as a teacher. He translated the writings of J. J. Quantz, Andreas Werckmeister, Niccolo Pasquali and Charles Burney into Dutch and wrote interestingly on musical life in the Netherlands. He contributed his autobiography (under the pseudonym Conrad Wohlgemuth) to Marpurg's *Kritische Briefe* (1763).

Noordt [Oort], van. Netherlands family of keyboard players and composers working in the 17th century mainly in Amsterdam. Sybrand (*d* 1654) and his son Jacob (*d* after 1679) were carillonneurs. Another son, Anthoni (*d* 1675), was a distinguished organist, first at the Nieuwe-Zijds-Kapel (1638–64) and then at the Nieuwe Kerk. He may have been a pupil of Sweelinck: his *Tabulatuur-Boeck van psalmen en fantasyen* (1659; lost) contained six fugal fantasies echoing Sweelinck's style. About 1690 Jacob's son Sybrand (*d* 1705) composed and published a set of four virtuoso sonatas for different instruments, of which the fourth is considered to be the first harpsichord sonata published outside Italy.

Reincken, Johann Adam. See NORTHERN EUROPE 1 *North Germany: Hamburg*.

Ricciotti, Carlo (*c*1681–1756). Italian violinist and impresario known as Charles Bachiche (or 'Bacciccia') working in The Hague. Ricciotti belonged to a French opera company in The Hague from 1702 until 1725, eventually serving as its director. In 1740 he was granted a patent to print six concertos which are now known to be the seven-part *Concerti armonici* anonymously published that year (the highly unreliable London printer-publisher John Walsh took it upon himself to issue them under Ricciotti's name in 1755). Dunning has positively ascribed them to Count Unico Wilhelm van Wassenaer, after having recently discovered in Wassenaer's library a manuscript copy of the concertos with annotations

in Wassenaer's hand; Wassenaer's friendship with the dedicatee Count Willem Bentinck lends further strength to the attribution. Ricciotti served merely as the intermediary between composer and recipient and, in fact, there is no evidence that he ever composed any music himself.

Roger, Estienne (1665/6–1722). Amsterdam music printer from a French Huguenot refugee family whose successful business played an important role in the dissemination of Italian and French music throughout Europe. Roger began his music printing business in 1697. In his atelier high-quality copper engravings were made from new manuscript works as well as from foreign prints of music by Lully, N.-A. Lebègue, Marin Marais, Corelli, Alessandro Scarlatti and Vivaldi. Roger numbered his editions (about 500) and the books in stock, and issued catalogues between 1698 and 1716 which were distributed abroad and reprinted in newspapers. He authorized agents in Rotterdam, Liège and Brussels, London, Cologne, Hamburg, Halle, Berlin and Leipzig to sell his editions.

Although his elder daughter was meant to have succeeded him in business, she died in the same year; the firm eventually passed into the hands of Michel-Charles Le Cène (*d* 1743), who had married Roger's younger daughter (*d* 1723). To their stock he added nearly 100 editions of Geminiani, Locatelli, Handel, Quantz, Telemann, Tartini and others which were issued jointly under the imprint 'Roger & Le Cène'. Printing ceased in 1743 when G. J. de la Coste took over the firm.

Rosier, Carl. See NORTHERN EUROPE 5 *West Germany and the Rhineland*.

Saint-Evremond, Charles de Saint-Denis. See BRITISH ISLES 1 *London*.

Schenck [Schenk], Johannes (1660–*c*1712). Netherlands-born viol player and composer who, though he served at the Düsseldorf court of the Elector Palatine (Johann Wilhelm I) as both musician and chamber councillor (from 1710), nevertheless published all his music in Amsterdam. His viol playing was said to be influenced by that of the expatriate English players (Daniel Norcombe, Henry Butler and William Young) and his music by German and italianate models. His collections are variously titled in Dutch (*Uitgevondene tyd en konstoeffeningen*, for viol and continuo, op. 2, ?1688), Italian (*Il giardino armonico*, for two violins, viol and continuo, op. 3, 1691), French (*L'echo du Danube*, for viol alone and with continuo, op. 9, before 1706) and a mixture of the last two (*Le nymphe di Rheno*, for two viols, op. 8, n.d.). His extant vocal works all employ Dutch texts: *C. van Eekes koninklyke harp-liederen* (1693/4) is scored for two voices, two viols and continuo.

Schickhardt, Johann Christian (*c*1682–1762). Travelling German recorder and oboe player and composer who spent many years in the Netherlands. Schickhardt was trained at the Brunswick court and first visited the Netherlands in the service of Friedrich of Hessen-Kassel; he went on to serve Henriette Amalia of Anhalt-Dessau and, eventually, the Prince of Orange. Thereafter he went to Hamburg (by 1712), where he acted as an agent for the Amsterdam publishing firm of Estienne Roger, then further south to work at the courts of Weimar and Cöthen. From the early 1720s he was in Scandinavia, before finally returning to the Netherlands and taking up a post at the University of Leiden in 1745. He published *The Compleat Tutor to the Hautboy* in London (*c*1715) and a set of 24 sonatas in Amsterdam (1735).

Schnitger. See NORTHERN EUROPE *1 North Germany*.

Smith, Bernard ('Father'). See BRITISH ISLES *1 London*.

Sweelinck [Zwelinck], **Jan Pieterszoon** (1562–1621). Celebrated Netherlands organist, composer and teacher. Sweelinck remained all his life in Amsterdam, where he and his son after him were organists at the Oude Kerk. His greatness lay not so much in his music as in his influence. His pupils came primarily from Germany: Andreas Düben, Peter Hasse, the Scheidts, Paul Siefert and Heinrich Scheidemann, who became the pillars of the North German Baroque organ school. He was also much in demand as an adviser on the repair and restoration of organs. His own keyboard music was widely circulated in manuscript, though never printed and hence poorly preserved. What remains includes ingenious chorale variations, and cycles of variations inspired by the English virginalist school, as well as the monumental free-formed fantasias and toccatas which influenced so many keyboard composers after him.

His vocal music fared better, the most important being his cycle of polyphonic settings of the Geneva Psalter, which began appearing in 1597 and continued throughout his life. They are for five voices, *a cappella* for the most part, and in French; Sweelinck composed them not for Calvinist services but rather for the private musical devotions of Amsterdam's wealthy bourgeoisie. In

contrast, his *Cantiones sacrae* (1619) adhere to the Catholic liturgy. He also published two collections of chansons in 1594 and 1612.

Tabel, Hermann. See BRITISH ISLES *1 London*.

Tessarini, Carlo. See ITALY *10 Itinerant Musicians*.

Valentini, Giuseppe. See ITALY *10 Itinerant Musicians*.

Valerius, Adriaen (*c*1575–1625). Netherlands lawyer and historian whose *Nederlandtsche gedenck-clanck* (pubd posth., 1626), a history of the conflicts between the Netherlands and Spain (1555–1625), contains engravings of 76 popular songs with texts by Valerius himself; it includes the first appearance of the Dutch national anthem, *Wilhelmus van Nassouwe*.

Vallet, Nicolas (*c*1583–after 1642). Important Netherlands lutenist who was trained in France (he may have been of French origin). By 1614 he was in Amsterdam: for the first six years he composed all his music for lute and thereafter lived by teaching and playing. In 1626 Vallet and three English musicians (Richard Swift, Edward Hancock and Robert Tindel) formed a partnership which lasted six years; their ventures included a dancing-school. After Emanuel Adriaenssen (*d* 1604), Vallet and Joachim van den Hove were considered the finest lutenists of their day.

Wassenaer, Unico Wilhelm van (1692–1766). Netherlands civil servant from a noble family, who served as the United Provinces' ambassador to Paris (1744) and Cologne (1740); he was the composer of the anonymously published *Concerti armonici* (1740) once attributed to Carlo Ricciotti and Pergolesi (to name only two). Wassenaer lived alternately in the family castle of Twickel and in a grace-and-favour town house in The Hague (as a member of the Board of the Admiralty and a director of the East India Company), and collected a library of chamber music. He was also active as a composer, having – from the evidence of the seven-part concertos – acquired at some point a fine contrapuntal technique and command of the late Baroque style. He dedicated the concertos to a friend, Count Willem Bentinck; Ricciotti, a violinist-impresario in The Hague, acted only as their intermediary (it was John Walsh, the London printer, who ascribed the concertos to Ricciotti). Even as anonymous works the concertos have been much admired for the expressive beauty of their slow movements (such as that of the first concerto, with its cantabile cello tune set against an ostinato).

Witvogel, Gerhard Fredrik (*c*1669–1746). German organist and music publisher working in Amsterdam. Witvogel held organ posts at the Nieuwe Kerk from 1726 until his death and, briefly, at the Oude Kerk (from 1724). In 1731 he acquired a privilege for printing music and set about producing a wide range of reliable editions; his firm ultimately became part of Roger & Le Cène.

2 South Netherlands

A Kempis, Nicolaus (c1600–1676). Organist at Ste Gudule, Brussels (from 1626), and the composer of some of the earliest known sonatas in the Low Countries (he published collections of *Symphoniae*, for varied numbers of strings and wind instruments, between 1644 and 1650). He was succeeded at Ste Gudule in about 1670 by his fifth son, Joannes Florentius a Kempis (1635–after 1711), who in turn left the post to his son Guillelmus and composed a set of 12 sonatas for violin, viol and continuo (partbooks for which were owned by Thomas Britton, the coal-dealer, and probably used at the regular concerts at his London home later in the century).

Boutmy, Josse (1697–1779). Third-generation organist who left Ghent for Brussels, where in 1729 he acquired citizenship. From 1736 he was employed by the Prince of Thurn and Taxis and from 1744 until 1777 served as organist at the Brussels court and harpsichord teacher to the ladies of the court. Boutmy published three collections of harpsichord music – the first and second in Paris (1738, 1740–4), accordingly tailored in some measure to French taste, and the third in Brussels (c1750).

Bull, John. See BRITISH ISLES *1 London.*

Carlier, Crespin. See FRANCE *2 Provinces.*

Cornet, Peeter (1570/80–1633). Organist and the leading composer of extended keyboard fantasias during the early 17th century. Cornet came from a family of Brussels musicians and was himself an organist (in the company of Peter Philips and John Bull) at the Brussels court of the Archduke Albert.

Couchet, Joannes (c1612–1655). Virginal and harpsichord maker who was the grandson of the master guild craftsman Hans Ruckers (1540/50–98). Couchet learnt the trade of instrument building in the Ruckers workshop in Antwerp under his uncle Joannes and built his own experimental versions of the Ruckers models, one of which belonged to Constantijn Huygens. Three of his children also became

makers and members of the guild. See LOW COUNTRIES *2 South Netherlands,* Ruckers.

Croes, Henri-Jacques de (1705–86). Court violinist, conductor and composer of mainstream church and chamber music. In Brussels Croes served first Prince Anselme-François of Thurn and Taxis, then from 1744 the governor of the Austrian Netherlands, Charles of Lorraine.

Cuzzoni, Francesca. See ITALY *10 Itinerant Musicians.*

Dall'Abaco. See CENTRAL EUROPE *1 South Germany: Munich.*

Danielis, Daniel. See FRANCE *2 Provinces.*

De Fesch, Willem. See LOW COUNTRIES *1 United Provinces.*

Dering, Richard. See BRITISH ISLES *2 Provinces.*

Dulcken. Master harpsichord makers, father and son, working together in Antwerp from 1741. Anton (*d* 1763) had earlier worked in Brussels; his son Johan Daniel (*d* after 1769) returned there in 1756. In particular the son built up-to-date versions of Ruckers instruments with a compass of $F'–f'''$. His post-1745 instruments incorporate knee-levers, dogleg jacks, a lute or nasal row and a sliding upper manual for coupling.

Du Mont, Henry. See FRANCE *1 Paris and Versailles.*

Eve, Alphonse d' (1666–1727). Master of singing at Antwerp Cathedral (1718–25) and composer of both italianate and *galant* sacred music. He was the son of Honoré-Eugène d'Eve, singer and director (from 1666) of the Brussels court chapel.

Fiocco. Venetian family of keyboard players and composers at the Brussels court during the 17th and 18th centuries. While in charge of music at the ducal chapel in Brussels from 1687, Pietro Antonio Fiocco (c1650–1714) composed new prologues for Lully operas performed there during the 1690s. In this way he gained the attention of the Elector of Bavaria, who made him first *lieutenant* (1696), then Pietro Torri's successor as *maître de chapelle* (1706) at his court. He also served after 1703 as *maître de musique* at Notre Dame du Sablon, where his Venetian sacred concertos and motets were performed.

His sons Jean-Joseph (1686–1746) and Joseph-Hector (1703–41) also took up court and church posts. Jean-Joseph served at Notre Dame du Sablon and composed oratorios, French *grands motets*, and concertos. His younger brother was *maître de chapelle* at Antwerp Cathedral, before returning in 1737 to Brussels as head of music at the collegiate church of Sts Michel and Gudule; his *pièces de clavecin* (1730) reveal his familiarity with those of Couperin, while his *leçons de ténèbres* for voice, cello and continuo are more Handelian in character.

Frescobaldi, Girolamo. See ITALY 7 *Papal States: Rome.*

Ghersem, Géry. See IBERIAN PENINSULA AND COLONIES 1 *Spain.*

Hayne, Gilles (1590–1650). Liégeois singer and composer, whose style was influenced by study in Rome (1613). From about 1618 until 1627 he served as director of music to the Prince-Bishop of Liège (Ferdinand of Bavaria); he was appointed a canon of St Jean l'Evangéliste in 1627 and *grand chantre* four years later. In 1638 the brother of the Prince-Bishop (the Duke of Neuburg and Count Palatine of the Rhine) made Hayne his superintendent of music *in absentia*, requiring only that he compose sacred music, send professional singers and correspond in Italian.

Helmont, Charles-Joseph van (1715–90). Organist and composer who from 1741 served for 36 years as *kapelmeester* at Ste Gudule, Brussels (he was succeeded in 1777 by his son, Adrien-Joseph van Helmont). In 1737 he published a collection of *pièces de clavecin* in the style of Rameau, although his most important secular composition was a *divertissement*, *Le retour désiré* (1749). Throughout his career he composed italianate concerted motets with recitatives, da capo arias and choruses. In 1768 he founded a music society which presented weekly public concerts.

Hodémont, Léonard (Collet) de (*c*1575–1636). Canon and vigorous *maître de chant* at Liège Cathedral who took a special interest in carillon music, revised the *Officium defunctorum* of the Liège Breviary (1623) and composed the first music to be printed there (*Sacri concentus*, 1630), but nevertheless was sacked from his posts in 1633.

Hove, Joachim van den. See LOW COUNTRIES 1 *United Provinces.*

Kerckhoven, Abraham van den (*c*1618–1701). Organist, active in Brussels, and composer of imaginative, improvisatory music (only four fugues, eight fantasias and two pairs of preludes and fugues survive). His first post was as organist of Ste Cathérine; in 1648 he took up the post of domestic music organist to Archduke Leopold Wilhelm (the Austrian Governor of the Low Countries) left vacant by J. K. Kerll. Kerckhoven joined the royal chapel in 1656 and three years later was made first organist. In 1707 another member of the family, Melchior van den Kerckhoven

(*d* 1758), became an organist of the royal chapel, serving as first organist from 1737 until 1755.

Kerll, Johann Kaspar. See CENTRAL EUROPE 3 *Austro-Hungary: Vienna.*

Langhedul, Matthijs (*d* 1635/6). Organ builder who played an important role in the development of French organ building. With his father Jan Langhedul (*d* 1592), Matthijs was in Paris from 1585, renovating instruments (Sainte Chapelle) and building them (notably St Jacques-la-Boucherie, with Crespin Carlier). He spent the last decade of the century in Spain as an organ tuner at the Spanish court, returning to Paris in 1599 to work on the organ at St Eustache and to build a new one at St Gervais (1601–2), which became the Couperin family's instrument. From 1613 he was organ builder to the Brussels court; he also built an instrument for the Spanish court at Madrid.

Loeillet. Family of instrument players and composers, scattered about Europe. Jean Baptiste [John] (1680–1730), the most versatile musician of the family, went to London, anglicized his name and became a wind player in the Drury Lane orchestra. He was principal oboe in the Queen's Theatre orchestra and is credited with having introduced the transverse flute as a fashionable instrument. Loeillet became a much sought-after teacher of the harpsichord and published a collection of pedagogical *Lessons* (*c*1712). He also composed trio sonatas in the Corellian mould for recorders, oboes, flutes and violins. Weekly concerts took place at his house in Hart Street, where in December 1714 Corelli's op. 6 concerti grossi were first heard in London.

His younger brother Jacques [Jacob] (1685–1748) took up an appointment as oboist to the Elector of Bavaria while he was exiled in the Netherlands. He returned with the elector to Munich, where he stayed until about 1728, when he left for France to become an *hautbois de la chambre du roi* at Versailles. He spent his last years in Ghent.

Their cousin Jean-Baptiste ['Loeillet de Gant'] (1688–*c*1720) became a musician to the Archbishop of Lyons; he left *sonate da chiesa* for recorder and continuo, with slow movements ornamented in the French style.

Madonis, Luigi. See ITALY 4 *Venice.*

Maximilian II Emanuel. See CENTRAL EUROPE 1 *South Germany: Munich.*

Norcombe, Daniel (*fl* 1602–47). English viol player working at the Brussels court of Archduke Albert; viol pieces by him appear in the first and second editions of Christopher

Simpson's *Division-violist* (London, 1659, 1667).

Philips, Peter (1560/61–1628). English Catholic priest, organist and composer who emigrated to the Spanish Netherlands, where he became a central figure in the musical establishment of the Brussels court of Archduke Albert. Philips, once a choirboy at St Paul's Cathedral, London, left England in 1582 bound for Rome, where he met Palestrina and found temporary employment with a fellow English Catholic, Lord Thomas Paget (*d* 1590), with whom he travelled in Spain, France and the Netherlands, before settling in Antwerp. There he published three collections of madrigals (1596, 1598, 1603 – Roman in style and amateur in their demands upon singers) which proved popular enough to be reprinted.

It was not until 1597 – having spent several months in prison in 1593 for his suspected involvement in a plot against the English queen – that he joined the court musicians of Archduke Albert (*d* 1621) as an organist, remaining in that post for well over 20 years. Many of his ornamented intabulations of Italian polyphony and English dances are in the Fitzwilliam Virginal Book (compiled 1609–19); in particular the 'Pavan and galliard Dolorosa' (composed while in prison) and the 'Pavan and galliard Pagget' are considered among the finest examples of his keyboard style; both survive in five-part consort versions. Philips knew Sweelinck and John Bull, who settled in Antwerp in 1613.

But it was as a composer of Counter-Reformation motets that Philips left a substantial and lasting testament to his gifts as a musician. They range widely in style, some Palestrinian, others unmistakably madrigalian and incorporating continuo parts. Philips waited until 1612, the height of his career, to issue a collection of chamber motets (*Cantiones sacrae*), composed for the intimate court chapel, following it with another (*Gemmulae sacrae*) the following year; the *Deliciae sacrae* came out in 1616, and, finally, his mammoth *Paradisus sacris cantionibus*, containing 106 motets for one to three voices and continuo, appeared just before his death.

Rimonte, Pedro (*c*1570–after 1618). Spanish composer working in Brussels from 1598 in the service of the Infanta Isabella, wife of the Governor of the Netherlands, as choirmaster (1603) and master of chamber music (1604). Although he returned to his native Saragossa

in 1614, there is evidence that he was back in Brussels by 1618. He published collections of Masses (1604) and madrigals and *villancicos* (*El parnaso español*, 1607) in Antwerp; a single motet survives in manuscript.

Romero, Mateo. See IBERIAN PENINSULA AND COLONIES *1 Spain*.

Rosier, Carl. See NORTHERN EUROPE *5 West Germany and the Rhineland*.

Ruckers. Catholic family, resident in Antwerp, who were pre-eminent builders of keyboard instruments during the late Renaissance and early Baroque. Joannes [Jan] Ruckers (1578–1643) and his brother Andreas [Andries] (1579–after 1645) took over their father Hans's successful business at his death in 1598. Like their father they built organs, as well as five different sizes of virginals, single- and double-manual harpsichords, and hybrid combinations of virginals and harpsichord. Andreas left the firm in 1608, but his son, of the same name (1607–before 1667), eventually took his place, along with a cousin, Joannes Couchet.

The Ruckers numbered their instruments and usually indicated the date on the soundboards; the lids were painted by such local artists as Rubens, Jan Breughel and Van Balen, and the cases were decorated with *trompe-l'oeil* marbling. However, the true beauty lay in the evenness of tone and astonishing resonance within. Accordingly, their instruments were copied by makers all over Europe, including Scandinavia. When the double-manual harpsichords were inevitably subjected to *ravalement* (modernization), the soundboards were never tampered with. The single-manual harpsichords were popular in England, the double-manual ones highly prized by the French and Italians. Those surviving to modern times are catalogued in *The New Grove*.

Spiridio. See NORTHERN EUROPE *7 Itinerant Musicians*.

Steffani, Agostino. See NORTHERN EUROPE *1 North Germany*.

Taskin, Pascal-Joseph. See FRANCE *1 Paris and Versailles*, Blanchet.

Torri, Pietro. See CENTRAL EUROPE *1 South Germany: Munich*.

Volumier, Jean Baptiste. See NORTHERN EUROPE *4 Saxony and Thuringia: Dresden*.

Zamponi, Gioseffo (*d* 1662). Italian composer working in Brussels, whose *Ulisse nell'isola di Circe* (1650) was the first opera to be performed at the Brussels court.

Spain, Portugal and The New World (showing places mentioned in the text)

The Iberian Peninsula and its New World Colonies

The Spanish and Portuguese Heritage

The century following the death of King Philip II in 1598 has often been characterized as a time of decline and decadence, during which Spain's power and influence dwindled and cultural development was stifled by isolationism. This profoundly negative picture is only partly justified.[1] The Spanish Habsburgs remained a force in European politics, and Spanish artists and writers made essential contributions to European culture. Spanish music of the period is less well known. It has not been studied widely or performed, partly because it has survived in manuscript sources which are difficult to consult. Further, most of the early research was devoted to sacred music, which as compared to secular music was indeed in decline.

In fact, Spanish culture shows a complex but striking originality. Spain experienced a second Golden Age because art was both a solace and a vital emblem to her proud rulers. Cultural patronage, once divided among competing noble houses, became centralized as the Habsburgs and their ministers systematically stripped noble families of their wealth, drawing them to the Madrid court and compelling them to live as courtiers. The arts had two primary functions: when financed by the court they could proclaim the power and grandeur of the monarchy, while for the educated commoner and the nobility they were a forum for social criticism and a mirror of society. The visual arts were especially important for their representational potential and their immediate impact. Music, however, did develop its own propagandistic and nationalistic function, towards political or religious ends, especially certain forms of vernacular sacred and theatrical music. Under King Philip III (reigned 1598–1621) and his minister the Duke of Lerma cultural patronage did not expand, but the role of music is clear as representative of its patrons. The court supported its Capilla Real, its *ministriles* (players of wind instruments), trumpeters, and chamber musicians for the king's and the queen's households. Latin sacred music in the orthodox Renaissance style was the mainstay of the chapel, thanks to the direction of Mateo Romero, a Flemish composer trained in the Franco-Flemish tradition that had dominated the chapel since the time of Charles V.

Secular music at court was also fairly conservative. Sophisticated monody and recitative, so fashionable in Italy, were unknown until 1627. While innovative Italian instrumental styles and techniques may have been imported by foreign string players, secular vocal music was mainly heard in simple polyphonic settings of well-known tunes, and the chamber musicians mostly provided dance music for palace balls and intimate entertainments for the queen. Theatrical spectacles were rare: the king preferred dancing, and the queen considered them improper and lascivious. The first of Philip III's reign, a masque given in celebration of the birth of the future Philip IV in June 1605, at Valladolid, exemplifies the conservative approach with its formal polyphony for two choirs followed by elegant dances in a traditional style. On less formal occasions current styles of secular music were absorbed into theatrical performances, as in 1614 and 1617 when, after Queen Margarita's death, Philip III and his children were entertained at the Duke of Lerma's country estate with plays by Lope de Vega and Luis Vélez de Guevara.

With the accession in 1621 of Philip IV, the 'Planet King', contemporary observers proclaimed a new Golden Age. The monarchy was transformed into a stronger, more vital institution through a carefully planned agenda in which the arts had a well-defined role. Attention to domestic affairs was reflected by a dignification of 'native', popular and emblematically Spanish forms of art. Fashionable courtly poetry was nationalistic in its adaptation of material from the popular sphere; similarly, fashionable song settings by court composers such as Mateo Romero, Juan Blas de Castro and Carlos Patiño adapt well-known tunes and characteristic rhythms that give them a national identity. These were also adapted for the public theatres in *comedias* by the leading dramatists, treating themes of immediate national, moral or social interest.[2] Here songs were largely used in scenes of everyday life, to reinforce verisimilitude. Although many of the composers whose songs survive worked in the elevated sphere of the court, secular songs, in an ingenious but simple diatonic style, were thus products of early 17th-century Spanish culture.

In the new age ushered in by the young Philip IV and his *valido*, the Count-Duke of Olivares, visual display became essential as politically emblematic art, for the king and his ministers were eager to promote a positive image. A new palace, the Buen Retiro, was hurriedly constructed, and several royal sites were refurbished with the guidance of the leading court artist, Diego Velázquez.[3] The new vision of the monarchy also provoked a renewed interest in court theatrical spectacles, all of which relied on music to some extent. The king hired Italians to supervise the scenic effects, which thus were similar to those seen in the best court theatres elsewhere.

This reliance on italianate effects did not signal the incorporation of foreign musical styles. In the first two decades of Philip's rule the music for court plays was similar to that for the *comedias*, except that the former could exploit a larger number and wider range of singers and instrumentalists. But there is no evidence of music in the Italian style: traditional Spanish songs and fashionable songs by the court composers were still the mainstay at court as in the town.

In 1627 the court audience saw an opera in the Florentine style with a Spanish text by the leading dramatist, Lope de Vega: *La selva sin amor*, conceived by Cosimo Lotti, Philip IV's first Italian stage architect, to display his talents. The Bolognese lutenist Filippo Piccinini, who joined the Spanish court in 1613, was obliged by the Florentines to compose the score; he claimed unfamiliarity with the recitative style, also unknown to the Spanish court composers.[4] Although Lotti's scenic effects were highly successful, *La selva sin amor* made virtually no impression on the course of music in Spain. Opera was not established as a genre, and the recitative style was not taken up immediately by Spanish musicians. Neither did the new concepts of 'speech in song' and totally sung theatre inspire commentary (as far as we know) from the usually vociferous circle of court dramatists and musicians. The foreign genre (pastoral opera) and the humanistically inspired musical style (recitative) seem to have been rejected by both the artistic community and the royal patrons.

No further operas were performed at court until 1660, though the recitative style was reintroduced in the 1650s. In 1652 the court dramatist Pedro Calderón de la

Barca prepared an elaborate mythological drama for the theatre at Buen Retiro. Music had a more important place here and in subsequent court plays, especially in the mythological semi-operas, where recitative distinguished the conversations of the gods from those of mere mortals, and lyrical song became the vehicle for divine messages to the mortals. Recitative was suggested by the king's Italian stage engineer, Baccio del Bianco (see Plate 20), and the papal legate to Madrid, Giulio Rospigliosi, the distinguished poet and librettist.[5] According to Baccio's letters, the Spaniards knew nothing of recitative and were sceptical about 'acting in song'.[6] Nevertheless, a Spanish adaptation of recitative became an essential ingredient of the mythological semi-operas by Calderón and the composer Juan Hidalgo, and was used occasionally in the pastoral *zarzuelas*, in which spoken dialogue was standard.[7] The music in both genres was largely Hidalgo's creation, although others (Juan del Vado, Cristóbal Galán) occasionally wrote for the court plays. Hidalgo's music is not italianate and is instead shaped by characteristically Spanish rhythms and melodic clichés, closely tailored to the poetry.

Amid the *comedias*, semi-operas and *zarzuelas* produced at court, the two Calderón–Hidalgo operas of 1660, *La púrpura de la rosa* and *Celos aun del aire matan*, were exceptional. Planned to celebrate the Peace of the Pyrenees and the marriage between Louis XIV and the Infanta María Teresa,[8] the operas were commissioned to display the court's elegance in competition with the French celebrations (in which Cardinal Mazarin planned to produce Italian opera, by Cavalli). Although a non-Spanish genre was chosen, *Celos aun del aire matan* demonstrates that text and music were conceived and executed without recourse to foreign models. This and *La púrpura de la rosa* were decidedly native products; Hidalgo and Calderón produced a Spanish operatic style (in which the predominant texture is that of the strophic air, even for narrative and dialogue) more than a decade before Lully and Quinault developed a French one.

The most important musical institutions besides the court were the cathedrals, the large churches and the municipal theatres in the largest cities. The factors that influenced music at court held everywhere, and uniformity rather than diversity was the rule. In secular music, the styles of the most famous composers (Romero, Juan Blas de Castro and Hidalgo) were legitimized by royal approval, and their works became models. Large-scale compositions by leading church composers were copied and passed on to fellow *maestros de capilla* in lesser churches. Although the Counter-Reformation had imposed a reformed orthodoxy and uniformity, the decline in religious education and simplification of religious thought seems also to have brought an avoidance of innovative forms and styles. Latin sacred music was generally composed in strict counterpoint or in the grand 16th-century polychoral style. But the vernacular *villancico* was prolifically cultivated in all regions; it could be solo or multi-voiced in texture, instrumentally accompanied or *a cappella*, and could embrace a variety of poetic styles and topics. *Villancicos* were heard by large numbers of people at important religious celebrations; the texts thus had to be audible, and the styles tended to be contemporary and sometimes semi-theatrical. Some clerics and moralists detested *villancicos* because of their secular and popular tendencies, but it was precisely this that made the *villancico* a useful source of broadly appreciated religious propaganda, and it was virtually the only form of non-liturgical religious vernacular music before the 18th century.

The cultural and stylistic framework for music established by Philip IV and his second wife, Queen Mariana, survived into the early years of their successor, Charles II, a weak, lacklustre ruler who provided no strong impetus for the renovation of Spanish musical culture. For some significant royal occasions no new works were commissioned but successful ones from a past epoch of splendour were revived. When in 1679 Charles II married the French Princess Marie-Louise of Orléans, the lack of royal control and interest led to the prolongation of an established style – that of Hidalgo, which continued to dominate Spanish music until well after the composer's death in 1685.

Given that Spanish music in the 17th century was predominantly restrained, light in texture, highly rhetorical, diatonic, contrapuntally anchored rather than freely expressive, and not profusely ornamented, the term 'Baroque' may seem a misnomer. It can however serve for the grandiose court productions which were 'Baroque' in their effect, although their music was not especially 'Baroque' in character; the full-blown European Baroque style reached Spain as a self-conscious importation or adaptation, not as the invention of native artists. This turn from a national style to an imported one is closely related to political events – the dissolution of the Spanish Habsburgs and the turbulent arrival of a new monarchy (Philip V, reigned 1700–46), a changed model of patronage and patrons with little interest in Spanish culture.

The first adjustments, which pre-date the War of the Spanish Succession (1702–14), were probably related to a weakening of national identity and changes in musical personnel. Late in the Hidalgo epoch several important musical posts became vacant; reports indicate that competent Spanish replacements could not be found, and some were filled by foreign musicians, often Italians who had served the ruling houses in the Spanish possessions of Milan and Naples. Contemporary Italian and French styles were probably introduced to the court by these new employees in the 1680s and 90s. The first theatrical composer to use them in his *zarzuelas* was Sebastián Durón, organist in the royal chapel from 1691, whose theatrical scores (written *c*1696–1713) show three layers of style: songs in the established Spanish manner of Hidalgo; songs which show Italian traits in their treatment of the text; and full-blown da capo arias in the italianate pan-European style. These three levels are also found in early 18th-century anthologies of songs for plays in the repertory of public theatres, indicating that the foreign influence had begun to filter down from the court to affect public theatre music.

The coexistence of styles and aesthetics, a fact of early 18th-century musical life in Madrid, became characteristic of the late Baroque in both Spain and Portugal. While 17th-century Iberian music, especially between 1640 and 1690, presents a unified style which depended upon an exchange between the popular and the courtly, 18th-century Iberian music presents a gradual division between the elevated realm of the court (with its foreign tastes and, eventually, foreign composers such as Giacomo Facco, Francesco Corselli, Francesco Corradini, Nicola Conforto, G. B. Mele and Domenico Scarlatti) and the popular domain, partly detached from the court. In Spain this became a firm demarcation with the accession of the Bourbon dynasty. In recently independent Portugal foreign music was a refreshing tonic after more than a century of Spanish domination; foreign expertise was essential to the development of a strong musical establishment with royal patronage in a country that had offered little opportunity for musical education or professional advancement during the turbulent 17th century.

Both the Austrian and the French candidates for the Spanish crown represented threats to native musical traditions. When the Habsburg Archduke Charles of Austria set up a court in Barcelona during the war years, Italian musicians were brought from Vienna to perform operas, cantatas and oratorios in the style of those composed at the imperial court by Caldara and others. In Madrid (and later in such cities as Valencia and Cádiz where administrative appointees of the crown modelled their courts on the royal one), Bourbon rule proved no less damaging: the descendants of Louis XIV (Philip V, grandson of Louis XIV, and Ferdinand VI) and their wives lavished money and favours on Italian musicians, actors and painters, and royal authority was invoked to justify the sometimes illegal actions and often scandalous ambitions of Italian entrepreneurs, determined to establish Italian opera as a commercial enterprise. In fact, Italian opera, *seria* and *buffa*, in early 18th-century Madrid was marked by spectacular financial disasters and plagued by its inability to cultivate a public outside the court. It failed as a public venture, and even at court was successful only during the more than 20 years in residence of the famous singer Farinelli (Carlo Broschi). Farinelli rarely appeared himself but supervised the productions from 1738 and lured other well-known Italian singers to the comfortable surroundings of the Spanish court. Although the Coliseo in the Buen Retiro was refurbished for opera in 1737, the well-paid Italian singers performed only a few operas each year, along with frequent concerts of arias and serenatas in more intimate settings. During the reign of Ferdinand VI and María Bárbara de Braganza (1747–58), the happy band of Italian singers and an orchestra travelled with the king and queen from one royal site to another, so that Italian opera had become a private affair, wholly dependent on its dedicated patrons.

In a famous portrait of Ferdinand VI and María Bárbara with their court by Jacopo Amigoni, a Venetian friend of Farinelli's brought in to design and paint scenery and royal portraits, the monarchs appear surrounded by an opera set: in a balcony are Farinelli, the violinist José Herrando and Domenico Scarlatti (see Plate 21). Scarlatti's case exemplifies the peculiar style of patronage practised by these rulers. He had served as *maestro di cappella* to the Portuguese ambassador in Rome before his appointment as master of the Cappella Giulia in the Vatican. He was invited to Lisbon as *mestre de capela* to John V in 1720 or 1721. John V's excellent musical establishment was already endowed with many Italian musicians and, unlike Madrid, Lisbon became a centre for Italian opera.

During his early years there Scarlatti composed sacred music for some of the elaborate religious ceremonies that so delighted the king and contributed to the series of Italian serenatas and cantatas. But he was hired particularly to teach the king's daughter, María Bárbara de Braganza. When she married Ferdinand of Spain in 1728 Scarlatti continued in her employ at the Spanish court's temporary residence in Seville and from 1733 in Madrid. Probably because his patroness and pupil was enamoured of the harpsichord, he all but ceased to write anything besides keyboard music. Many writers have described the 'Iberian' and especially 'Andalusian' sounds in Scarlatti's sonatas, and several have noted his apparent influence on Iberian composers. But his was a very private employment, in which he played and composed exclusively for his patroness, so it is difficult to explain how other Spanish and Portuguese composers could have come to know his music. His sonatas were collected and copied into exquisitely bound volumes for María Bárbara; few were published in his lifetime.

It may be that in Lisbon, Seville and Madrid, and during court sojourns elsewhere,

Scarlatti performed with or taught royal musicians. In Lisbon he worked with Carlos de Seixas, organist of the patriarchal chapel, whom he evidently revered. The keyboard sonatas of two excellent Spanish composers who also served Ferdinand VI, Sebastián Albero and Padre Antonio Soler, share some of the stylistic and technical traits of Scarlatti's. Albero probably came to know Scarlatti's music after he was appointed organist in the Spanish royal chapel in 1748. The prolific and talented Soler, organist (1752) and choirmaster (1757) at the monastery of El Escorial, indeed described himself as 'disciple of Domenico Scarlatti'.

Foreign singers, instrumentalists and composers came to dominate music at the Spanish court in the early 18th century. By 1756 the lists of musicians in the Capilla Real and the Coliseo in the Buen Retiro included many more foreign than Spanish names. This affected all genres of cultivated art music without banishing totally the *estilo español*. The *zarzuela* was transformed between 1690 and 1750 by its absorption of styles and conventions from *opera seria*. Public performances of *comedias* continued as they had in the Golden Age of the Spanish theatre, during Calderón's lifetime. His last disciples, Antonio de Zamora and José de Cañizares, dominated the repertory of newer plays with music and *zarzuelas*. The latter now included song-texts in poetic metres appropriate for italianate *da capo* arias, with indications for recitative and for the inclusion of French dances, especially the minuet and the contredanse. During the first 30 years of the 18th century the *zarzuela* flourished with Spanish composers such as Antonio Literes and José de Nebra, although the marriage between a popular theatrical form and the musical style of a foreign ruling class damaged its potential for growth and success. By the end of the Baroque period the *zarzuela* was again the focus of a popular movement of musical nationalism.

The dialectic between native and foreign styles was also a point of contention for church composers. The *villancico*, long sensitive to native traditions and tastes, ran a course similar to that of the *zarzuela* until 1765, when the performance of vernacular sacred music was suppressed. It increasingly adapted foreign elements, notably *da capo* arias replete with luxuriant melismas. The royal chapels were hospitable to forms from *opera seria* and cantata. The Bourbons did not object to 'operatic' music in the liturgy, in spite of controversy among church musicians and clerics. Joseph de Torres y Martínez Bravo (chapel organist from 1686 and *maestro*, 1720–38) was a firm defender of the foreign style and propelled its diffusion throughout Spain through the publications of his Imprenta de Música and his own religious works and theoretical writings. Most Spanish composers defended the purity and aptness of the *stile antico* for sacred texts. A controversy lasting over 20 years arose in 1702 over the freedom allowable in church music over text setting and 'modern' elements; this was sparked off by the Catalan composer Francisco Valls's *Missa 'Scala Aretina'* which included what some heard as an intense and licentious use of dissonance.

By contrast, the 'modern' and 'foreign' styles and genres were not only accepted in 18th-century Portugal but became wildly popular. Portugal can claim no national style and musical identity in the 17th century distinct from that of its possessive neighbour, Habsburg Spain.[9] It is hardly surprising that little important literature in Portuguese was produced; Lisbon society preferred to be entertained by visiting Spanish companies and its own promising writers were sent to Spain. Nor was Portugal's subservient, conflict-ridden political and economic status conducive to the growth of art music. Since 1589 the country had been ruled by the Spanish

Habsburgs, whose cultural dominance was aided by the tradition that Portuguese monarchs married Spanish *infantas*. Independence was granted in 1668, although a reluctant John IV (1604–56) had been proclaimed king in 1648 and there had been revolts since 1640. The Wars of Independence continued until 1713, so that Portugal was economically weakened during most of the Baroque period. Portuguese musicians had migrated to Spain in search of employment: Manuel Machado was one of Philip IV's chamber musicians, and the harp and guitar player Juan de Serqueira was the most esteemed composer in the Madrid theatre companies for nearly 50 years (1676–1723). Serqueira's works attest to his versatility in adapting to the stylistic changes that filtered down from the court to the popular, public theatres, and he was one of the first Iberians to experiment with the cantata.

Within the Iberian context Portugal produced some excellent composers. Évora Cathedral was famous as a home of conservative vocal polyphony; among the prominent composers who studied there and were influenced by the great teacher Manuel Mendes (*d* 1605) were Duarte Lobo and Manuel Cardoso. Further north, the Augustinian monastery of Santa Cruz in the university town of Coimbra maintained a productive, self-sufficient musical establishment with its own instrumental shops, resident composers, independent musico-liturgical practices and an important library of local sacred and secular music. The Augustinians were ready to adapt to new trends, some of which originated at the Spanish court, if with some delay: along with simple sacred pieces in the *stile antico*, their manuscripts contain theatrical songs, *romances* and *vilancicos*, and larger polychoral pieces, some with solo sections for obbligato instruments. Most of the vernacular pieces have Castilian texts and use the same musical gestures and devices found in Spanish songs. But a few of the *vilancicos* have Portuguese texts; some were written to celebrate Portuguese independence.

The establishment of a court in Lisbon after 1640 does not seem to have provided a focal point for the growth of a national tradition. John IV was interested only in conservative *a cappella* polyphony; although the catalogue of his monumental music library (destroyed in the 1755 earthquake) shows that he collected music, old and new, in every genre, from all of Europe, including the most influential and radical Italian publications of the early Baroque, only sacred music was performed at court, and the musicians he supported all composed conservative polyphony. In 1649 he wrote a short pamphlet defending the efficacy and expressiveness of traditional vocal polyphony against the Italian musicians and humanists who had proclaimed the need for a new style; a second pamphlet defending the Palestrina style was written in 1654. Perhaps because of his position as spiritual and political leader, John's taste and opinions seem to have been widely shared by Portuguese composers.

During the reigns of King John V (1706–50) and Joseph I (1750–77) the musical life of court and capital were transformed according to the tastes and interests of monarchs who delighted in luxury and ceremony. Through vigorous royal patronage, musical education, the musical establishments of religious institutions, and regular public performances of secular and theatre music were all restored, first at court and then in public. Although little music has survived, contemporary comments suggest that Lisbon musical life was characterized by the same duality of styles as existed in Madrid, except that John V carried on a Portuguese tradition by insisting on the severe *a cappella* style in Lisbon Cathedral, the churches and the royal chapel, and went to considerable expense to obtain copies of the choirbooks used at the papal chapel. In 1723 he even prohibited *vilancicos* in church, perhaps because the genre had been 'secularized', tainted by absorption of the modern theatrical style and such forms as the da capo aria. In the later 1720s theatrical performances in public (*comedias*, operas or *zarzuelas*) had virtually ceased, largely because of the king's disapproval. Earlier, in the first decades of the century, the court had commemorated royal birthdays and other festive occasions with Spanish plays and *zarzuelas*, mostly with new music by Portuguese composers. The plays chosen were among those most frequently given in Madrid. This is explained by the presence of Spanish troupes in Lisbon and by the sponsorship of court entertainments by the Spanish ambassador. The *zarzuela*, however, did not survive. In the 1720s it gave way to the Italian cantata and serenata, a process aided by the singers and composers (including Scarlatti) imported from Rome. John V founded two new schools of sacred music and encouraged the musical education of some composers by sending them to Italy; António José Teixeira and Francisco António de Almeida, both to become prominent members of the royal chapel and to compose italianate operas, were among them.

The Italian domination of music in Lisbon was established by 1730. Italian musicians were busy providing music for concerts and serenatas, and in the period 1735–42 operas, in Italian and in Portuguese, were presented in public increasingly often, led by Schiassi's *Farnace* (1735) and Leo's *Siface* (1737). Portuguese operas, principally by Teixeira, were given at a different theatre. Almeida wrote what was probably the first Italian opera by a Portuguese, *La pazienza di Socrate* (1733), a 'dramma comico' for court carnival celebration at Paço da Ribeira – one of seven or eight Italian operas performed at court in John V's reign.

The controversy over the pan-European Baroque style, if of minor consequence in Portugal, was (as we have seen) complicated and divisive in the context of 18th-century Spanish culture and politics. As it was Spain that dominated the culture of the New World, colonial musicians were equally attached to the *estilo español*, and the controversy eventually spread to the most prosperous Spanish dominions. It is clear that Iberian musical genres and idioms were firmly implanted in courtly and ecclesiastical institutions there by the early 17th century. Numerous musicians from the Iberian peninsula migrated, some in the service of aristocratic administrators, others according to the dictates of the religious orders. Many composers from the south of Spain held positions in New World churches and cathedrals, cultivating the contrapuntal style of late 16th-century Spanish cathedral music as practised in Seville, Málaga and Cádiz. From the mid 17th century the strongest influence came from Madrid, the cultural model for the sophisticated colonial courts; an official description of a performance paid for by the Viceroy of Peru in 1672 praised the production as staged 'just as at the Retiro in Madrid'. The repertory of *comedias* and *autos sacramentales* in the New World is identical with that in Madrid, and certain dramatists retained their popularity with American audiences well into the later 18th century. Well-known secular songs, theatre songs and *villancicos* from Castile appear in anthologies and as well-worn performing parts in New World archives.

Because of the enormous geographical extension and variety of the Spanish and Portuguese dominions in America, the sharp differences in conditions between provincial and urban areas in the colonial period, and the complicated relationships between social classes and musical styles of Iberian origin, it is difficult to generalize about the chronological and stylistic definition of the Baroque in the New World. Through the education and indoctrination carried out by the religious orders, often supported by the Spanish government, native musicians had been introduced to polyphony during the first century of Spanish domination. Spanish *maestros* trained and conducted ensembles largely of local talent, the Indians being especially proficient as instrumentalists. Most of the music available to us from the early 17th century is sacred, in the conservative contrapuntal style or simple homophony, although music for multiple choirs was also cultivated. Later, and throughout the 18th century, the polychoral and concerted styles seem to have become common both for Latin sacred music and for *villancicos*. After 1670 the development of formal and stylistic characteristics closely followed that of Spain and Portugal, and the *estilo español* became dominant. The *villancico*, prolifically cultivated, adapted to local traditions and absorbed native, folk and popular elements as in the mother country.

This stylistic continuity resulted partly from deliberate emulation and partly from the influence of Spanish musicians in the New World – among them such men as Juan Gutiérrez de Padilla, from Málaga and Cádiz, who became *maestro de capilla* of Puebla Cathedral, Mexico; the harpist and composer Lucas Ruiz de Ribayaz accompanied the new viceroy on his journey to Peru in 1667 and returned to Madrid before the publication of his harp and guitar manual ten years later; José Marín, a noted composer and a tenor in the royal chapel who made a financially ruinous trip to the New World before 1649; Tomás de Torrejón y Velasco, who went from Madrid to Peru in 1667, becoming *maestro de capilla* of Lima Cathedral and writing the first New World opera, *La púrpura de la rosa*, given in Lima in 1701 in honour of Philip V's birthday and accession; and Juan de Araujo, who preceded Torrejón as *maestro* at Lima and subsequently directed the musical life at several important cathedrals (Panama, Guatemala, Cuzco and La Plata [now Sucre]).

Although the late 17th-century Spanish aesthetic survived in secular and church music in the colonies through the 18th century, the stylistic duality imposed under the Bourbons in Madrid was also produced in several places in the New World. Because of the taste of a controversial viceroy appointed by Philip V, Lima, 'City of the Kings' and administrative centre of the Spanish colonies, was the first to hear the pan-European style, brought by the Milanese composer Roque Ceruti and his small group of musicians in 1707. Their sonatas, serenatas, arias, French dances and an occasional opera were performed at this 'Versailles of the southern hemisphere', though it is unclear how the new music was received beyond the court, given the xenophobia of the Lima merchant class and the traditional Spanish values of the aristocracy and of certain clerics. In Cuzco, 'City of the Incas', the European styles were rejected entirely by the criollo leadership, while far away in Mexico City, the first Mexican-born director of the cathedral chapel, Manuel de Zumaya, seems to have initiated the performance of foreign styles and genres in New Spain (Mexico, Central America). His *La Partenope* (1711) was probably the first Italian *opera seria* performed in the New World, and his *villancicos* present the same stylistic diversity as those of his Spanish contemporaries.

Spain, then, like France and England, developed a national musical style and independent genres that served local culture, politics and religious institutions, and were further locally adapted and legitimized in the Spanish New World. The strong cultural and imperial identity promoted by Philip IV at the heart of the Baroque period for Spain and her dominions encouraged Spanish musical independence from foreign models. Baroque musical culture in the Spanish orbit was a complex of unique relationships between secular and sacred music, court and public entertainments, popular music and cultivated art music, and native and foreign styles – neither isolated from the European Baroque, nor dependent on foreign innovation.

Louise K. Stein
The University of Michigan
Ann Arbor

Notes

1 J. Brown: *Velázquez, Painter and Courtier* (New Haven and London, 1986); J. Brown and J. H. Elliott: *A Palace for a King. The Buen Retiro and the Court of Philip IV* (New Haven and London, 1980); Pedro Calderón de la Barca: *La estatua de Prometeo*, critical edn by M. R. Greer with a study of the music by L. K. Stein (Kassel, 1986); J. H. Elliott: *Richelieu and Olivares* (Cambridge, 1984); J. H. Elliott: *The Count-Duke of Olivares. The Statesman in an Age of Decline* (New Haven and London, 1986); J. A. Maravall: *Culture of the Baroque. Analysis of a Historical Structure*, Eng. trans. T. Cochran, foreword by W. Godzich and N. Spadaccini (Minneapolis, 1986); S. N. Orso: *Philip IV and the Decoration of the Alcázar of Madrid* (Princeton, 1986); L. K. Stein: 'Music in the Seventeenth-Century Spanish Secular Theater', (PhD diss., University of Chicago, 1987) [forthcoming as a book].

2 The *comedia nueva* was a three-act play, a tragi-comedy in polymetric verse in which tragic and comic elements were to be judiciously mixed to reflect with verisimilitude the natural balance of human existence, according to Lope de Vega's timely codification of the genre in his *Arte nuevo de hacer comedias en este tiempo* (1609).

3 Brown and Elliott, *A Palace for a King*, pp. 104–40; Brown, *Velázquez, Painter and Courtier*, pp. 68–70, 195–209.

4 The diplomatic correspondence related to *La selva sin amor* is presented in S. B. Whitaker: 'Florentine Opera Comes to Spain', *Journal of Hispanic Philology*, ix (1984), 43–66.

5 Concerning Baccio del Bianco and his work for the Spanish court, see M. Bacci: 'Lettere inedite di Baccio del Bianco', *Paragone*, xiv (1963), 68–77; and P. D. Massar: 'Scenes for a Calderón Play by Baccio del Bianco', *Master Drawings*, xv (1977), 365–75.

6 The pertinent section of Baccio's letter is included in L. Bianconi: *Music in the Seventeenth Century* (Cambridge, 1987), 260.

7 The word *zarzuela* ('bramble bush'; from *zarza*, 'bramble') was used first by Calderón as a generic term to designate a shorter, lighter court theatrical entertainment with integrated musical scenes and a pastoral story. Calderón's *El laurel de Apolo* (1657), the first *zarzuela*, was written originally for performance at the Zarzuela Palace, a royal hunting-lodge in the wooded outskirts of Madrid, hence the name of the palace became identified with the form.

8 Preparations for the diplomatic encounters and celebrations of the treaty and the marriage were the focus of artistic life at the Spanish court in 1659 and 1660; see Brown, *Velázquez, Painter and Courtier*, pp. 244–50.

9 The section of this essay devoted to Portugal is indebted to unpublished work by Maria Cristina Borges, and to the writings of Manuel Carlos de Brito, especially 'A Little-Known Collection of Portuguese Baroque Villancicos and Romances', *RMA Research Chronicle*, xv (1979), 17–37; 'Partes instrumentales obligadas en la polifonía vocal de Santa Cruz de Coimbra', *Revista de musicología*, v (1982), 127–39; 'Vestigios del teatro musical español en Portugal a lo largo de los siglos XVII y XVIII', *Revista de musicología*, v (1982), 325–35; and *Opera in Portugal in the Eighteenth Century* (Cambridge, 1989).

Biographical Dictionary: The Iberian Peninsula and its New World Colonies

1 Spain

Alberti, Domenico. See ITALY *10 Itinerant Musicians.*

Araujo, Juan de. See IBERIAN PENINSULA AND COLONIES *3 New World.*

Astorga, Emanuele d'. See ITALY *9 Sicily.*

Atienza y Pineda, Francisco de. See IBERIAN PENINSULA AND COLONIES *3 New World.*

Blas de Castro, Juan (*c*1560–1631). Court singer, composer of secular songs and vihuelist who became blind *c*1604. He served Philip III as a *músico de cámera* and then from 1621 as an usher of Philip IV's privy chamber, for which he composed over 700 secular songs (lost in a fire in 1734). During the early 1590s he had served the Duke of Alba with Lope de Vega, whose poetry he set as early as 1594. Lope de Vega provides many of the details of his life, pronouncing him a 'unique Orpheus' (1604).

Bruna, Pablo (1611–79). Organist and choirmaster, known as 'El ciego de Daroca' because he had been blind from childhood. He composed virtuoso organ *tientos* and was the teacher of his nephew Diego Xaraba y Bruna (who became principal organist of the Capilla Real) and Pablo Nassarre.

Butler, Henry [Botelero, Enrrique] (*d* 1652). English viol player, violinist and composer who served as a *músico violón* or *músico de vihuela de arco* in the chapel and chamber of Philip IV from 1623 to 1652. According to James Wadsworth (*The English Spanish Pilgrime*, 1629), Butler taught the king to play the viol and was himself skilled at ground bass divisions (he notated at least 15 sets). An aria for violin, bass viol and continuo, as well as a trio sonata and dances for two violins and continuo survive.

Cabanilles, Juan Bautista José (1644–1712). Organist at Valencia Cathedral (1665–*c*1703) and prolific composer of *tientos* (characterized by a series of imitative sections on different themes) and pieces in continuous variation (*folías, passacalles, paseos, gallardas* and *jácaras*). He was considered the finest Spanish organist of his day, and his music circulated widely in manuscript. José Elias was his pupil.

Caldara, Antonio. See CENTRAL EUROPE *3 Austro-Hungary: Vienna.*

Calderón de la Barca, Pedro (1600–81). Influential poet and dramatist associated with the court of Philip IV, the most important dramatist after the death of Lope de Vega (*d* 1635). Until 1651 he wrote plays for both court and public theatres in Madrid, in addition to Corpus Christi plays (*autos sacramentales*). His best-known works, such as the *comedia La vida es sueño* and the *auto El gran teatro del mundo*, were written before 1651; after that date he wrote only secular court plays and *autos sacramentales*. The plays fall into several categories with respect to their musical elements: *comedias* with incidental songs; spectacle plays on chivalrous or pastoral subjects, relying heavily on chorus; mythological-pastoral *zarzuelas* (beginning with *El laurel de Apolo*, 1657), which include many solo songs but limited use of recitative; and mythological semi-operas (the complete score of *Fortunas de Andrómeda y Perseo* of 1653, with music by Juan Hidalgo, is extant; see Plate 20). These hybrid genres were his own invention. He also wrote the librettos for two operas produced around 1660, *La púrpura de la rosa* and *Celos aun del aire matan* (only Hidalgo's score of the latter survives). Calderón's *zarzuelas* and his techniques for the dramatic inclusion of solo song influenced several court theatre composers of the later 17th century. For his musical court plays Calderón worked almost exclusively with Hidalgo.

Cererols, Joan (1618–76). Versatile instrumentalist and composer who spent his life at the monastery of Montserrat, where he was greatly valued. As a monk Cererols was an accomplished theologian and skilled at Latin versification. He played the organ and harp, as well as bowed string instruments, and not only composed Masses, psalms, hymns and antiphons which make use of double choirs, soloists and continuo, but also produced lively *villancicos* in four parts.

Cerone, Pietro (1566–1625). Neapolitan singer and theorist who, having been associated with the Spanish in Naples, went to Spain in 1592 as a chapel musician of Philip II and later Philip III. Though he stayed only nine years, he became highly knowledgeable about

Spanish music and theory. He returned to Naples, disappointed at not having discovered aristocratic patrons or academies of music in Madrid, and became a priest. Cerone took up a post at Ss Annunziata, Naples, in 1603. Six years later he published a manual for the singers and deacons there entitled *Le regole più necessarie per l'introduttione del canto fermo*, but of greater importance was his didactic work *El melopeo y maestro: tractado de música theorica y pratica* (1613), though it is retrospective in outlook: among those he praised were Josquin, Lassus, Palestrina, Ingegneri and Rore, as well as the Spaniards Guerrero, Lobo, Romero and Victoria. *El melopeo y maestro* greatly influenced later 17th- and 18th-century Spanish theorists.

Corradini, Francesco (*c*1700–after 1749). Neapolitan opera composer who worked in Valencia as *maestro de capilla* to the viceroy (the Prince of Campoforido) and then from 1731 in Madrid at the Buen Retiro. Before leaving Naples, Corradini produced at least two comic dialect operas, the first of which was *Lo 'ngiegno de le femmine*, performed at the Teatro dei Fiorentini in 1724. In Valencia and Madrid he produced comedies and *opere serie* on Spanish librettos, as well as *zarzuelas* and music for *autos sacramentales*. Corradini became a member of the staff, under Farinelli, of the Nuovo Real Teatro at the Buen Retiro in 1747 and collaborated with his fellow expatriates G. B. Mele and Francesco Corselli on *opere serie* in Italian.

Correa de Arauxo, Francisco (*c*1576/7–1654). Organist at S Salvador, Seville, for 37 years, theorist and influential *stile nuovo* composer. In 1626 he published a single *Libro de tientos y discursos de música practica* which reveals his commitment to teaching (the organ pieces, mostly *tientos*, are ordered by difficulty) and his originality – his penchants were for sharp dissonances, such as the simultaneous sounding of a note with its chromatic alteration, and irregular groupings of five, seven, 11 and 18 notes.

Corselli [Courcelle], **Francesco** (*c*1702–1778). Italian musician of French descent who from 1734 worked at the Spanish court in Madrid. While still in Italy, Corselli held posts as *maestro di cappella* of the Steccata church at Parma (1727) and to the Duke of Parma (1727–33), who later became Charles III of Spain. During this time he composed operas for Venice and an oratorio for Parma. His association with the Farnese family in Parma led to his appointment in 1734 as assistant *maestro de capilla* at the Spanish court and

music master (he was proficient on the violin and harpsichord) to the royal children.

Four years later he married a Frenchwoman and became the titular *maestro de capilla* and rector of the choir school (he had been a tenor), appointments he would hold for 40 years. He composed a prodigious amount of sacred music, some of it with orchestra. He also produced cantatas, *villancicos*, an oratorio entitled *Santa Barbara* and operas for the theatre at the Buen Retiro – some of which used translations of Italian *opera seria* librettos; for the Carnival of 1747 he collaborated with G. B. Mele and Francesco Corradini on a translation of Metastasio's *La clemenza de Tito*.

Costa, Alfonso Vaz da. See IBERIAN PENINSULA AND COLONIES 2 *Portugal*.

Cruz, Filipe da. See IBERIAN PENINSULA AND COLONIES 2 *Portugal*.

Desmarets, Henry. See FRANCE *1 Paris and Versailles*.

Doni, Giovanni Battista. See ITALY *6 Tuscany*.

Durón. Half-brothers who were both prolific composers. Diego Durón (*c*1658–1731) was *maestro de capilla* at Las Palmas Cathedral. Sebastián Durón (1660–1716) was an organist at various cathedrals before taking a post at the royal chapel, where in 1702 he became *maestro de capilla*. Sebastián remained in Madrid until 1706, when he was exiled to France for opposing Philip V in the War of the Spanish Succession. Though a composer of conservative sacred music, Sebastián was one of the first in Spain to incorporate da capo arias into *zarzuelas* (1696–1713). For this, as well as for his virtuoso string writing, he was attacked in print (1726) as a corrupting influence.

Elias, José (*fl* 1715–51). Priest, and organist first at SS Justo y Pastor in Barcelona (1715–25) and then at the Convento de Señoras Descalzas Reales in Madrid. He was a follower of Cabanilles, having learnt more than 300 of his works as a student. Some of his own music, which remained within the polyphonic Spanish organ tradition, appeared in his *Obras de órgano* (1749).

Fabri, Annibale Pio. See ITALY *10 Itinerant Musicians*.

Facco, Giacomo [Jaime] (*c*1680–1753). Venetian violinist and composer who worked at the Spanish court in Madrid; he had originally been invited to Lisbon as music teacher to Princess María Bárbara from 1720. His connection had been the Spanish viceroy at Messina. Before departing for Spain he published a set of concertos in two volumes (1716–19) in Amsterdam. In Madrid he held posts in the royal chapel and as harpsichord teacher to the young Prince Luis and, later, music master to Prince Charles, son of Isabella Farnese (later Charles III). In 1721 his two-act Spanish opera (a 'melodrama al estilo ytaliano') *Amor es todo ymbenzion, o Jupiter y Amphitrión* was performed before Philip V and his court at the royal theatre at the Buen Retiro; in 1728 his *zarzuela Amor aumenta el valor* was presented at the Spanish ambassador's palace at Lisbon. His son Pablo (1711–69) entered royal service as a chapel violinist in 1728.

Farinel. See FRANCE *1 Paris and Versailles.*

Farinelli. See ITALY *10 Itinerant Musicians.*

Fernández de Huete, Diego (*fl* 1699–1704). Harpist at Toledo Cathedral and the author of a harp tutor, *Compendio numeroso de zifras armonicas* (1702), which also contains popular music of the day (*zarabandas*, minuets, galliards, *folías* and *jácaras*), as well as sacred pieces notated in Spanish keyboard tablature (with fingering modifications) for amateur players.

Galán, Cristóbal (*c*1630–1684). *Maestro de capilla* at the Spanish court from 1680, having earlier served in that capacity at Segovia Cathedral, the Convento de Señoras Descalzas Reales in Madrid (1667–80) and, at some point, the royal monastery of the Encarnación. He composed both antiphonal sacred choral works and *villancicos* with continuo, as well as music for seven *autos sacramentales* and five court plays, in collaboration with Juan Hidalgo. His music was widely circulated in manuscript in Spain and the Americas.

Galli-Bibiena, Ferdinando. See CENTRAL EUROPE *3 Austro-Hungary: Vienna.*

Ghersem, Géry (de) (*c*1573/5–1630). Franco-Flemish priest who worked in Spain as the protégé of Philippe Rogier from 1586 until 1604, whereupon he returned to Brussels as Chaplain of the Oratory. In Spain he sang in the Capilla Flamenca and published in 1598 the first polyphonic choirbook, *Missae sex* (albeit by a foreigner); he also edited the Masses of Rogier for publication. Of his music only a Mass and an eight-part motet survive; the rest is known from the catalogue of John IV's library (Lisbon).

Guerau, Francisco (*c*1649–*c*1720). Majorcan contralto and (from 1693) *músico de cámera* in the Capilla Real, guitarist and composer, whose *Poema harmónico* (1694), containing 17 *passacalles* for five-course guitar, typifies the 17th-century Spanish guitar school.

Guichard, Henry. See FRANCE *1 Paris and Versailles.*

Guzmán, Jorge de (*fl* 1686–1709). Theorist and plainsong commentator attached to Cádiz Cathedral. While drawing upon Pietro Cerone's *El melopeo y maestro* (1613), Guzmán's treatise *Curiosidades del cantollano* (1709) is important for its discussion of Spanish chant rhythms, the significance of the modes and the pitches at which the chants were sung in different parts of Spain.

Herrando, José (1680–1762). Violinist, composer in the service of the Duke of Alba (1732–62) and author of the first thorough Spanish violin treatise, *Arte, y puntual explicación del modo de tocar el violín*, published in Paris in 1756, the year of Leopold Mozart's more famous *Versuch einer gründlichen Violinschule*. Herrando was also associated as player and composer with the Madrid theatre and the court orchestras; for the public theatres he composed songs for three *comedias* and a *sainete* (a one-act farce performed as a finale). In 1756 he became the principal violinist of the chapel orchestra of the royal monastery of the Encarnación. Although much of his music is lost, he is known to have composed six sonatas for five-string violin (dedicated to Farinelli).

Hidalgo, Juan (1614–85). Harpist at the Capilla Real (from 1630), *maestro* of chamber music (from 1645) and influential composer. Hidalgo collaborated with Calderón de la Barca on the earliest Spanish operas: *La púrpura de la rosa* (*c*1660) is lost, but *Celos aun del aire matan* (*c*1660) survives. He collaborated with Calderón and others on further productions; for the 1653 semi-opera *Fortunas de Andrómeda y Perseo* (see Plate 20) and the 1656 pastoral *comedia Pico y Canente*, Hidalgo provided the first known examples of Spanish recitative. His music for Juan Vélez de Guevara's 1672 *zarzuela, Los celos hacen estrellas*, is the earliest of its kind to survive (older *zarzuela* texts exist without music). He also composed music for at least nine *autos sacramentales* and incidental music for at least 15 court plays, as well as liturgical music and numerous *villancicos*.

Hidalgo was the most admired Spanish composer of the later 17th century, the composer who best represents the 'estilo español' in music. Although he remained in Madrid all his life his music was transmitted in manuscript copies to Portugal and the New World. His music deserves to be better known today.

Jerusalem, Ignacio. See IBERIAN PENINSULA AND COLONIES *3 New World.*

Jovernardi, Bartolomé (*c*1600–1668). Roman harpist, employed from 1633 at the court of Philip IV. Jovernardi compiled a bilingual manuscript treatise on musical instruments, *Tratado de la mussica* [*sic*] (1634), and was the inventor of a cross-strung chromatic harp and a four-octave harpsichord capable of crescendos.

Juvarra, Filippo. See ITALY *7 Papal States: Rome.*

Langhedul, Matthijs. See LOW COUNTRIES *2 South Netherlands.*

Literes (Carrión), Antonio (1673–1747). Majorcan violinist and cellist at the Spanish court, and a highly regarded composer of secular cantatas and theatre music. In 1709 he composed a zarzuela, *Accis y Galatea*; in addition, several other theatre pieces survive, including another zarzuela, *Júpiter y Danae*, and an 'opera armónica al estilo italiano', *Los elementos*. Later, in 1720, he composed a *villancico* and an oratorio (with instruments) for Lisbon Cathedral.

Following the 1734 palace fire that destroyed the music collection, Literes and José de Nebra were commissioned to compose new liturgical music; accordingly Literes turned his talents to composing four-part *a cappella* Masses and a cycle of Vesper psalms. His two sons followed him at court: José Literes Sánchez (*d* 1746) was a cellist (he also served the Duchess of Osuna in Seville), and Antonio Literes Montalbo (*d* 1768) followed Nebra as first organist in 1768. Literes himself is said to have owned a Stradivari cello.

López, Miguel (1669–1723). Benedictine monk and monastery organist and choirmaster who was both writer and composer. López's music – a veritable compendium of polychoral liturgical and non-liturgical music (organ pieces, secular cantatas and *villancicos*) – is contained in a single 580-page autograph manuscript, compiled after 1720 and entitled *Miscellanea musicae*. He also wrote a history of Montserrat, where he worked much of his life, and contributed four supporting pamphlets (1718–19) to the controversy over the unprepared dissonances in a Mass by Francisco Valls. A two-volume theoretical treatise is lost.

Los Ríos, Alvaro de (*c*1580–1623). Spanish chamber musician to Queen Margherita (1607) and composer of polyphonic songs (*tonos*). He may have provided music for voices and instruments for Tirso de Molina's play *El vergonçoso en palacio* when it was privately performed out of doors in Toledo at the Buenavista estate in 1620, and for *La gloria*

de Niguea, performed during the court festivities at Aranjuez two years later.

Lulier, Giovanni Lorenzo. See ITALY *7 Papal States: Rome.*

Manalt, Francisco (1710/15–59). Virtuoso violinist (very probably the protégé of Giacomo Facco) at the Capilla Real from 1733 and in the service of the Duke of Osuna, to whom he dedicated his *Obra harmónica en seis sonatas de cámara de violín y bajo solo* (1757).

Marín, José [Joseph] (1619–99). Spanish priest ordained in Rome, singer and composer of secular songs who was associated with the Spanish royal chapel (1644–58). Though he was imprisoned, whipped, unfrocked and ultimately banished from Madrid for committing crimes of robbery and multiple murder, he was permitted to retain his title as *criado de su Majestad*, and his music continued to be held in high regard. In the last few years of his life he even received a pension from King Charles II.

Martínez de la Roca (y Bolea), Joaquín (*c*1676–*c*1756). Organist of the cathedrals at Saragossa (1709), Valencia (1715) and Toledo (1723) and composer of dramatic music. When published in Madrid in 1712, *Los desagravios de Troya* became the earliest printed complete score of Spanish theatre music. It is remarkable for the French influence it displays and for its macaronic text: Martínez de la Roca incorporated a ballet among the instrumental music, and for the interval between Acts II and III he composed music which contrasted four female voices singing in French, Portuguese, Italian and Spanish. Martínez contributed two critical pamphlets (*c*1715 and *c*1717) to the brouhaha surrounding the unprepared dissonances in a Mass by Francisco Valls.

Mele, Giovanni Battista (1701–after 1752). Neapolitan opera composer who worked in Madrid with Francesco Corselli and Francesco Corradini at the Nuovo Real Teatro at the Buen Retiro palace. Mele studied for about 12 years with Gaetano Greco at the Poveri di Gesù Cristo, Naples, before going to Spain, where he made his name with *Por amor y por lealtad* (1736), which was performed at the Teatro de la Cruz in Madrid. He gained an appointment at the court of Philip V which was renewed by Ferdinand VI in 1746. Following the opening of the new theatre at the palace, Mele composed a *festa teatrale*, *Angelica e Medoro*, to mark the queen's birthday in 1747. He collaborated on several works with Corradini and Corselli before requesting permission to return to Naples in 1752.

Monserrate, Andrés de (*fl* 1614). Catalan theorist and precentor at the church of S Martín, Valencia, who published a practical plainsong treatise, *Arte breve y compendiosa de las dificultades* in 1614.

Nassarre, Pablo (*d* 1730). Blind Spanish organist, theorist and composer who spent his life at the monastery of S Francisco at Saragossa. Nassarre, once a pupil of Pablo Bruna, published a comprehensive two-volume *Escuela música, según la práctica moderna* (1723–4), the fruit of 50 years' work.

Navas, Juan (Francisco) de (*c*1650–1719). Harpist at the Capilla Real (from 1669) and pupil of Juan Hidalgo. His father was Juan Gomez de Navas, a court singer and temporary *maestro de capilla* after the death of Cristóbal Galán in 1684. Between 1685 and 1700 Navas composed music for 13 plays, among them the *zarzuela Apolo y Dafne*, on which he collaborated with his younger and more brilliant contemporary Sebastián Durón.

Nebra (Blasco), José (Melchor de) (1702–68). Most prominent of the three organist sons of José (Antonio) Nebra (1672–1748), who was *maestro de capilla* of Cuenca Cathedral from 1729. In 1724 the younger José was appointed principal organist of both the royal chapel and the convent of the Descalzas Reales in Madrid; his tenure was interrupted between 1731 and 1736 when he was displaced at court by the Neapolitans Francesco Corradini and G. B. Mele. A prolific composer of music for Calderón de la Barca's *autos sacramentales*, Nebra composed music for 57 stage works for Madrid and Lisbon; his music was also known in the New World (Peru).

Like his colleague Antonio Literes, Nebra embarked upon composing sacred music after the 1734 fire that destroyed the royal chapel music collection. While Literes contributed *a cappella* Masses, Nebra composed orchestrally accompanied Masses, seven *Salve regina* settings, 14 orchestral Lamentations and 20 hymns (97 works in all). In 1751 he became deputy director and head of the royal choir school, where he was much respected as a teacher; his pupils included the crown prince, Antonio Soler, and his nephew Manuel Blasco de Nebra.

Ortiz de Zárate, Domingo (*c*1650–after 1699). Friar and *villancico* composer important for his correspondence with Miguel de Irízar (*maestro de capilla* at Segovia Cathedral) from 1671 until 1684: they discussed life for a musician in Madrid, the performance of *villancicos* and the vogue for polychoral music.

Padilla, Juan Gutiérrez de. See IBERIAN PENINSULA AND COLONIES 3 *New World.*

Patiño, Carlos (1600–75). The first native Spanish court *maestro de capilla* and the composer responsible for initiating the vogue for a Spanish Baroque style, which then superseded the late Italian Renaissance style that still held sway. His music is known to have included numerous Spanish *villancicos* and Latin liturgical works, as well as a few secular songs. Patiño was trained at Seville Cathedral (from 1612), where he became the pupil of Alonso Lobo (1617) and later of Francisco de Santiago. In 1628 he was appointed *maestro de capilla* of the royal convent of the Encarnación in Madrid and succeeded Mateo Romero five years later as *maestro* of Philip IV's chapel and rector of the choir school.

Peralta Escudero, Bernardo de (*d* 1617). *Maestro de capilla* at Burgo de Osma until his death. He declined invitations to take up posts at Saragossa Cathedral in 1611 and the royal chapel in 1616 (concerning the latter, he is said to have expressed a preference for serving in the galleys rather than going to Madrid). His polychoral music was admired for the expressiveness of his text setting.

Porsile, Giuseppe. See CENTRAL EUROPE 3 *Austro-Hungary: Vienna.*

Pujol, Juan (Pablo) (*c*1573–1626). Priest, organist, *maestro de capilla* and prolific composer of sacred and secular music. Originally from Barcelona, he served for two years as organist of Tarragona Cathedral (from 1593) and then as *maestro de capilla* at the basilica of Nuestra Señora del Pilar in Saragossa, before taking up a similar post at Barcelona Cathedral, where he remained from 1612 until his death.

Rameau, Pierre. See FRANCE 1 *Paris and Versailles.*

Rodríguez, Vicente (*d* 1760). Organist of Valencia Cathedral, succeeding Cabanilles in 1713; he was assisted by his elder brother Félix Jorge (*d* 1748), who was also a harpist and had served there since 1703. Rodríguez was the composer of a manuscript *Libro de tocatas para cimbalo repartidas por todos los puntos de un diapason*, much influenced by Domenico Scarlatti and Antonio Soler, as well as of organ toccatas.

Romero, Mateo [Rosmarin, Mathieu; 'El Maestro Capitán'] (1575/6–1647). Spanish composer born in Liège, but trained as a choirboy under George de La Hèle and Philippe Rogier at the Capilla Real in Madrid, where in 1598 he was appointed *maestro de capilla*. He was ordained a priest in 1609. Romero was an influential and prolific composer of secular songs as well as sacred music and enjoyed prestige at both the Spanish and Portuguese courts. In 1621 he was made a clerk of the Order of the Golden Fleece and three years later *capellán de los Reyes Nuevos de Toledo*. He retired in 1634; a decade later, in 1644, John IV made him a non-resident chaplain at the Portuguese court.

Rospigliosi, Giulio. See ITALY *7 Papal States: Rome*.

Ruiz de Ribayaz, Lucas (*b* before 1650). Priest, who played the guitar and harp. He published a detailed guitar and two-course harp tutor, together with dance music (*folías, jácaras, canarios* and *passacalles*) in tablature, under the title *Luz y norte musical* (1677); it also contains unique autobiographical details.

Ruiz de Robledo, Juan (*d* after 1644). *Maestro de capilla* at León and Valladolid, where he raised the standards of performance. He wrote a harsh treatise (in manuscript) on liturgical practice, *Laura de música eclesiástica* (1644), which advocated the restriction of bread and wine as punishment for any prebendary unable to pass a singing test after a year's course of study. He published a collection of liturgical music in 1627 and left other, polychoral works in manuscript.

Salazar, Antonio. See IBERIAN PENINSULA AND COLONIES *3 New World*.

Salazar, Diego José de (*d* 1709). *Maestro de capilla* at Seville Cathedral (from 1685) and the composer of a requiem for Marie Louise of Orléans (wife of Charles II) in 1689, which was performed at many subsequent royal funerals. Salazar died of plague.

Sanz, Gaspar [Sanz Celma, Francisco Bartolomé] (1640–early 18th century). Spanish priest, guitarist and composer who studied in Italy with Cristoforo Caresana, Orazio Benevoli, P. A. Ziani and Lelio Colista. Back at Saragossa, he published in 1674 the most complete five-course guitar treatise of the day, *Instrucción de música sobre la guitarra española*; its popularity is attested to by at least eight editions during the next 25 years. In addition to sets of variations and dance music, it includes instructions for stringing, fretting and tuning, as well as advice on how to accompany from a figured bass.

Scarlatti, Domenico (1685–1757). Son of Alessandro Scarlatti, a virtuoso harpsichordist and the composer of more than 500 unique single-movement 'sonatas', who lived 37 years in Portugal and Spain (see Plate 21). Though a highly gifted musician, Domenico Scarlatti had considerable difficulty establishing himself professionally in his own right as distinct from his father. For his part, his father maintained a strong influence and remarkable degree of control over his son, who in 1717 finally had to seek legal independence. The church and the theatre ultimately could not offer the right forum for his talents, though he served for five years (1714–19) as *maestro di cappella* at the Cappella Giulia in the Vatican. He composed at least one oratorio (1709) and more than a dozen operas for his father's Neapolitan theatre, S Bartolomeo (1703–4), and the Roman Palazzo Zuccari (1710–14) and Teatro Capranica (1715, 1718).

His patrons in Rome included the exiled Polish queen Maria Casimira (1709–14) and the Portuguese ambassador to the Vatican, the Marquis de Fontes (from 1714), who in 1720 succeeded in winning Scarlatti for the patriarchal chapel in Lisbon (his serenata, *Applauso genetliaco*, was performed at the Portuguese Embassy in 1714 and his *Contesa delle stagioni* at the Lisbon royal chapel in 1720). Scarlatti was also a familiar figure at the weekly meetings hosted by Cardinal Ottoboni of the Accademie Poetico-Musicali, at which the finest musicians in Rome met and performed chamber music; there Scarlatti met Corelli, Thomas Roseingrave and Handel, among others. Roseingrave became an enthusiastic champion and, when back in London, published the first edition of Scarlatti's *Essercizi per gravicembalo* (1738–9), which – along with the efforts of Joseph Kelway and Thomas Arne – greatly popularized his music there.

Self-exile first in Lisbon (1720–28), and then in Seville (1729–33) and Madrid (from 1733), provided the freedom Scarlatti needed to develop his own particular keyboard style, which throve on the element of contrast and the use of the *acciaccatura*, the 'simultaneous mordent', the 'vamp' (usually at the beginning of the second half of a sonata) and the element of surprise. He composed more than 500 sonatas for the Infanta María Bárbara, one of his royal pupils, which survive in two sets of 15 volumes in the hand of a Spanish scribe. None is dated, nor have any criteria been agreed upon to enable them to be assigned to specific years. It is even questionable whether Scarlatti himself paired them, as they appear in the manuscripts. He also composed at least 17 separate sinfonias and a harpsichord concerto. The extent of his influence on such Portuguese and Spanish contemporaries as Carlos de Seixas, Antonio Soler, Félix Máximo López and Sebastián Albero has yet to be fully assessed.

Scarlatti did return to Italy on three occasions: in 1724, when in Rome he met Quantz and maybe Farinelli (who himself joined the Spanish court in 1737); in 1725, to visit his father in Naples, when he met Hasse; and in 1728 to Rome, when he eventually married for the first time (his wife, by whom he had five children, died in 1739, and by 1742 he was married again, to a Spanish woman, by whom he had four more). In 1738, sponsored by King John V of Portugal, he passed secret trials to become a Knight of the Order of Santiago, and about 1740 Velasco painted his portrait, for which he wore the full regalia of the order.

Selma y Salaverde, Bartolomé de (*fl* 1638). Augustinian friar, virtuoso bassoonist employed at the archducal court at Innsbruck (1628–30), and composer of *Primo libro de canzoni, fantasie & correnti* (Venice, 1638), dedicated to the Bishop of Breslau. Selma also composed a *Canzona a 4 sopra battaglia*, in which he incorporated fanfares and military signals associated with Spanish and Portuguese *batallas*. He was the son of Bartolomé de Selma (*d* 1616), who was an instrument maker and repairer to the Spanish royal chapel.

Serqueira [Lima Sequeiros], Juan de (*c*1655– after 1726). Theatre guitarist and harpist in Granada and Madrid (1676–1723), and composer of incidental music and cantatas. He performed in the Corpus Christi *autos sacramentales* in Madrid in 1676 and in Juan Hidalgo's setting of Calderón's last play, *Hado y divisa* (1680). During the latter part of the reign of Charles II he became involved as a repetiteur for court theatre productions.

Tesi, Vittoria. See ITALY *10 Itinerant Musicians.*

Torres y Martínez Bravo, Joseph de (*c*1665–1738). Spanish organist and master of the royal chapel choristers in Madrid who published the first Spanish treatise devoted wholly to figured bass in his *Reglas generales de acompañar* (1702). Torres y Martínez Bravo was a composer equally at home with forward-looking outside influences and with native styles, as evidenced by his collection of *Canciones francesas de todos ayres* (*c*1705). He used oboes and violins in the French manner and employed italianate recitatives and arias. Torres also founded the first Spanish music printing house, the Imprenta de Música, in Madrid in the early years of the 18th century.

Valls, Francisco (1665–1747). *Maestro de capilla*, theorist and composer who sparked off a lively pamphlet war (1715–37) by the use of unprepared dissonances in his *Missa Scala aretina* for 11 voices and instruments (1702). As many as 50 Spanish writers became involved. Valls retired from his post as *maestro de capilla* at Barcelona Cathedral in 1740 in order to concentrate on his manuscript treatise *Mapa armónico* (prefatory letter dated 1742), important as a defence of the Spanish style against the Italian and French.

Vaquedano, José de (*d* 1711). Monk, *maestro de capilla* at the cathedral of Santiago de Compostela (1681–1710) and composer of polychoral sacred music and as many as 47 *villancicos* (of which 26 celebrate the feast of St James). His significance as a composer lies in his use of instruments – not merely in the continuo, to double voices in choral textures or to create choruses of instruments, but to take independent concertante roles in vocal textures (he favoured the trumpet, violin, bassoon, harp, organ and vihuela).

Vargas [Bargas], Urbán de (*d* 1656). *Maestro de capilla* at a series of Spanish cathedrals, which included Saragossa (1629–50), and a prolific composer of *villancicos* for eight to 12 voices.

Vega (Carpio), Lope Félix de (1562–1635). Spanish court poet and dramatist who wrote the first Spanish opera libretto, *La selva sin amor* (1629). Lope de Vega was a prolific writer, producing as many as 1800 plays, most of them *comedias* which incorporated songs, for both court and public theatres. His poetry became the basis of the secular song (*canción*) repertory of the late 16th and early 17th centuries and was performed by singers such as Juan Blas de Castro.

2 Portugal

Almeida, Francisco António de (*c*1702– 1755). Composer associated with the court. The gift of a royal stipend enabled him to study in Italy (1720–26), where at least two of his oratorios were performed. Having returned to Lisbon, he was commissioned to compose Carnival operas (*La pazienza di Socrate*, 1733) and serenatas (*La finta pazza*, 1735) for the royal palace of Ribeira. His music, both sacred and secular, was very much Italian-influenced, particularly by the Neapolitan *opera buffa* style; like Alessandro Scarlatti, he relied on *recitativo secco*, and paired oboes and horns with strings.

Babbi, Gregorio. See ITALY *10 Itinerant Musicians*.

Barbosa Machado, Diogo (1682–1772). Priest (educated in canon law at Coimbra University) and author of an important four-volume bibliography of Portuguese writers, *Bibliotheca lusitana, historia critica, e cronologica* (1741–59), which contains entries on 127 composers and theorists, listing manuscript writings (and their location) as well as published works. Barbosa had access to the royal music library in Lisbon before it was destroyed in the earthquake of 1755, and his bibliography thus provides unique references to lost works. His library became the basis of the Brazilian Biblioteca Nacional.

Caffarelli. See ITALY *10 Itinerant Musicians*.

Cardoso, Manuel (1566–1650). Carmelite who played the organ and directed the choir at the prestigious Convento do Carmo in Lisbon. A master of Renaissance counterpoint and a worthy successor to Victoria, Cardoso composed several collections of Masses and one of motets (1648). He took pains to ensure that his music would be subsidized by royal patrons: the Duke of Barcelos and Braganza (the future John IV) had Cardoso's first collection of Masses (parodies of Palestrina motets) printed in 1625; the second one contained parodies of motets by John IV (1636), and the third (also 1636) presented six Masses based on a Marian motet by Philip IV. By using devices such as a seven-note ostinato – 'Philippus Quartus', in the *Missa Philippina* concluding the third book – Cardoso also ensured the popularity of his music, which was more widely published than that of any of his contemporaries). Many of his polychoral works were destroyed in 1755.

Costa. Musicians, among whom Afonso Vaz da Costa (*d* after 1642), André da Costa (*d* 1685) and Sebastião da Costa (*d* 1696) stand out. Afonso was Portuguese organist who had studied in Rome. He was *maestro de capilla* at Badajoz Cathedral in Spain (where his instrumental forces included cornetts, sackbuts, bassoons and, later, a harp) and later *mestre de capela* at Ávila Cathedral; his music was lost in the 1755 earthquake. André was a Trinitarian friar, a harpist in the chapels of Afonso VI and Pedro II, and the composer of polychoral Masses and other liturgical music (lost). Sebastião was a contralto who, during the reign of John IV, was a court chamber musician; later, under Afonso VI and Pedro II, he was their *mestre de capela*. For his services he was made a Chevalier of the Order of Christ. After his death his music was deposited in the royal

library, which was destroyed in the earthquake of 1755.

Costa e Silva, Francesco (*d* 1727). *Mestre de capela* at Lisbon Cathedral (1715–27) and composer of liturgical music and *villancicos* who provided responsories (for eight voices and orchestra) for the Requiem Mass honouring the French King Louis XIV, celebrated at the cathedral in 1715.

Cruz, Filipe da (*c*1603–68). Friar of Santiago at the royal monastery of Palmela (nr Lisbon) and *mestre de música* at the Misericórdia in Lisbon, before taking up residence in Madrid, becoming a naturalized Castilian and in 1641 accepting an appointment as a singer in the Spanish royal chapel. However, Cruz was unhappy in Spain and, declaring his true allegiance to be to John IV, returned to Portugal, where in 1656 he was made *mestre* of the royal chapel. He continued to be admired as a composer at both courts: his music includes Masses and polychoral Vespers, motets and *villancicos* in both languages.

Fabri, Annibale Pio. See ITALY *10 Itinerant Musicians*.

Fernandes, António (*c*1595–after 1680). Priest and theorist who in 1626 published a music treatise (albeit derivative) in Portuguese entitled *Arte de musica de canto dórgam, e canto cham*, dedicated to Duarte Lobo, his former teacher. He is thought to have belonged to John IV's Vila Viçosa chapel choir in 1642; a further treatise on musical secrets (*Especulação de segredos de musica*) was lost in the fire that destroyed the royal library in 1755.

Fernandes, Gaspar. See IBERIAN PENINSULA AND COLONIES *3 New World*.

Frouvo, João Álvares (1608–82). *Mestre de capela* at Lisbon Cathedral (from 1647), theorist and librarian to John IV. He may have been a composer, having studied with Lobo at Lisbon Cathedral. In the 1640s the king commissioned Frouvo to write a treatise on the significance of the number four (*Discursos sobre a perfeiçam do diathesaron, & louvores do numero quaternario*, 1662) which is important for the plethora of composers he cited; a second, two-volume treatise, *Speculum universale* (1651), is lost.

John [João] IV (1604–56). Duke of Barcelos and Braganza, later King of Portugal (1640), well educated in music (a pupil of Roberto Tornar), and an ardent patron and collector. His unique library, in which Italian, French, English and Flemish, as well as Spanish and Portuguese music was represented, was lost in the earthquake and fire that destroyed Lisbon in 1755, although a catalogue compiled in 1649 survives. John IV was also an essayist and composer: during the 1650s he published two brief tracts in Italian and Spanish, anonymously and without place or date, but prefatory sonnets reveal his identity in acrostics. A devotee of the *stile antico*, the king penned a defence of modern music – which he considered to be that of Palestrina, not the monodists – and later another, in support of a maligned Palestrina Mass. Two further treatises in Portuguese are no longer extant; of his music only two four-part motets survive.

Juvarra, Filippo. See ITALY *7 Papal States: Rome*.

Lésbio, António Marques (1639–1709). Court musician, writer and composer of *villancicos* (1660–1708), of which 16 (some in Spanish, others in Portuguese) survive. Lésbio held several posts in the royal music – master of the royal chamber music (1668), master of the boys (1679) and curator of the music library (1692) – before finally becoming *mestre de capela* in 1698. His polyphonic Latin works were destroyed in 1755.

Lobo, Duarte [Lupus, Eduardus] (?1565–1646). *Mestre de capela*, first at Évora Cathedral, then at the Hospital Real in Lisbon and finally at Lisbon Cathedral; he was also the director of a seminary and taught at the Colégio da Claustra da Sé in Lisbon, where his pupils included F. A. de Almeida, António Fernandes and J. A. Frouvo. Lobo was the best-known Portuguese composer of his day; he published six volumes of polyphonic liturgical music in Antwerp which demonstrate his command of counterpoint and an ability to convey textual nuances in music.

Magalhães, Filipe de (*c*1571–1652). *Mestre de capela* at the Lisbon court (1623–41), who in his day was considered a more expressive composer in the *prima prattica* than his contemporaries Manuel Cardoso and Duarte Lobo. Magalhães was trained at Évora Cathedral before taking a post as a singer in the royal chapel (1602); he also served as *mestre de capela* at the Misericórdia in Lisbon.

Melgás, Diogo Dias (1638–1700). *Mestre de capela* at Évora Cathedral (from *c*1678 until blindness forced him to retire), where he had been a choirboy and master of the boys. Melgás was the first composer there to write functional harmony and independent instrumental parts for choral music.

Nunes da Silva, Manuel (*d* 1704). *Mestre de capela*, educator and the author of a treatise (*Arte minima*, 1685) on polyphony, counterpoint and plainchant, giving special attention to coloration (which was still practised in Spain and Portugal). A priest, Nunes da Silva studied with J. A. Frouvo before taking up posts at S Maria Magdalena, Lisbon, and the school attached to the cathedral in 1685; simultaneously he taught at the college of his order and was *mestre de capela* of another Lisbon church.

Rego, Pedro Vaz (1673–1736). *Mestre de capela* at Évora Cathedral, succeeding his teacher Diogo Melgás in 1700, author of a history of music in the Spanish royal chapel (*Armonico Lazo*, 1733) and composer of liturgical music, Passions and *villancicos*, of which only a few works survive. He was one of many who published opinions – in his case a defence – on Francisco Valls's use of unprepared dissonances.

Rodrigues Coelho, Manuel (*c*1555–*c*1635). Organist, first at Elvas Cathedral and then at the Lisbon court (1602–33), known by the keyboard music contained in his *Flores de musica para o instrumento de tecla & harpa* (1620), which is the earliest surviving collection of instrumental music printed in Portugal. Among the works included are 24 *tientos* and 97 versets; though rooted in the style of Cabezón, they also reflect the influence of Sweelinck and the English virginalists.

Sant'Anna [Sá Bacon], **José Pereira de** (1696–1759). Carmelite musician, born in Rio de Janeiro and educated in Brazil and Portugal, who became the royal family confessor at Coimbra. He was a singer, composer of sacred music, and author of a two-volume *Chronica dos Carmelitas* (1745–51) that includes information on the history of Portuguese Carmelite music.

Scarlatti, Domenico. See IBERIAN PENINSULA AND COLONIES *1 Spain*.

Seixas, (José António) Carlos de (1704–42). Keyboard virtuoso and the leading Portuguese composer of his day. At the age of 14 he succeeded his father, Francisco Vaz, as organist of Coimbra Cathedral and, two years later, became organist of the royal chapel in Lisbon, where he remained for the rest of his life. His spectacular technique as a player earned him (along with Domenico Scarlatti) a knighthood from King John V in 1738. His music was destroyed in the 1755 earthquake and fire, though copies of a few works survive.

According to Barbosa Machado (*Bibliotheca lusitana*, 1741–59) Seixas composed 700 keyboard 'tocatas', of which 88 have been authenticated. His music was inevitably influenced by his nine-year association with Scarlatti at the royal chapel, though not to the extent hitherto thought. Seixas's sonatas are mostly in three to five movements, technically demanding and reflecting an experimental mind with regard to motivic development and extended forms.

Teixeira, António José (1707–after 1759). Singer and composer at the Patriarchal Cathedral in Lisbon from 1728. Teixeira studied in Rome (where he was associated with the Portuguese Church) from about 1717 until 1728. He composed *a cappella* and concertante sacred music – Masses, psalms, motets and a *Te Deum* – as well as cantatas.

Tornar, Roberto [Turner, Robert] (*c*1587–1629). Singer, composer and *mestre de capela* (1616–29) of English origin, in the service of the seventh Duke of Braganza at Vila Viçosa. A pupil of the Franco-Flemish expatriate Géry Ghersem in Spain, Tornar was charged with the musical education of the duke's son, the future King John IV of Portugal. Only four four-part psalms by Tornar survive.

3 The New World

Araujo, Juan de (1646–1712). Spanish-born priest and prolific composer of *villancicos* working in South America. Araujo lived in Lima from an early age and only moved to Panama under duress after becoming involved in politics at the University of S Marcos. He returned to Lima in 1672, when he was made *maestro de capilla* of Lima Cathedral. His final post was at the wealthy La Plata Cathedral (Sucre, Bolivia), where he served from 1680 until his death.

Atienza y Pineda, Francisco de (*c*1657–1726). Spanish-born Mexican priest and composer who served first at Mexico City Cathedral (where he became involved in a controversy over the selection of Manuel de Zumaya as Antonio de Salazar's successor) and then from 1712 at Puebla Cathedral, where he served as *maestro de capilla* until his death. He composed Latin music in the *prima prattica* and published 12 sets of *villancicos* (1715–22).

Ceruti, Roque (*c*1683–1760). Milanese composer attached to the viceroy of Peru, the Marquis of Castelldosríus. To celebrate the birth of the Spanish crown prince in 1708 Ceruti directed the viceroy's private band of nine musicians in his lavishly costumed and set opera *El mejor escudo de Perseo*, which was performed in the palace gardens in Lima. He remained in viceregal service after the death

of the marquis in 1710, but in 1721 he accepted the post of *maestro de capilla* at Trujillo Cathedral. Ceruti returned to Lima in 1728 as *maestro de capilla* of the cathedral, where he was assisted by the organist José de Orejón y Aparicio and the composer Esteban Zapata. During the 32 years he served there he composed an extensive corpus of italianate Spanish and Latin music which was known throughout South America. In his music for festive occasions he employed current Italian textures and forms: *recitativo secco*, da capo arias, and vocal ensembles accompanied by violins and continuo.

Fernandes, Gaspar (*c*1570–1629). Portuguese priest, organist and composer who served as *maestro de capilla* at Guatemala City Cathedral (1599–1606) and Puebla Cathedral, Mexico. Prior to sailing for the New World, Fernandes had been a singer and organist at Évora Cathedral. He composed the earliest known Latin secular work by a New World composer, *Elegit eum Dominus*, which celebrated the arrival of the 13th Spanish viceroy in Puebla. The *chanzonetas* and *villancicos* he composed there make up the largest surviving collection of 17th-century secular music in the New World.

Jerusalem, Ignacio (*c*1710–1769) Italian-born violinist and composer working in Mexico. Jerusalem was recruited from Cádiz to Mexico City in 1742. Such was his talent that he quickly gained local approbation, succeeding Manuel de Zumaya in 1749 as *maestro de capilla* at Mexico City Cathedral. Over the next 20 years he composed around 200 Latin compositions and a number of others on Spanish texts, in which he took full advantage of the forces of the cathedral choir and orchestra, especially in the more italianate works.

López Capillas, Francisco (*c*1615–1673). Spanish-born organist at Puebla Cathedral, Mexico (1641), under Juan de Padilla and later organist and *maestro de capilla* at Mexico City Cathedral (from 1654); in recognition of his service he was granted a full prebend, but died before it took effect. López was a skilful composer of Latin sacred music in the *prima prattica* style.

Orejón y Aparicio, José de (1706–65). Peruvian singer, organist and composer. Orejón was a child prodigy who at the age of nine was employed as a singer (in place of an adult) at Lima Cathedral, where he later became organist (1742) and *maestro de capilla* (1764). However, his career there was marred by resentment: he believed that the emphasis Roque Ceruti placed on Italian music in the cathedral repertory limited the native composers; accordingly he applied for posts elsewhere, though without success. His only music was melancholic (often in minor keys) and employed Italian forms and textures. His most imposing work was a Passion for triple chorus and orchestra (1750). His music became known throughout South America.

Padilla, Juan Gutiérrez de (*c*1590–1664). Mexican priest and composer of Spanish birth. After four years as *maestro de capilla* at Cádiz Cathedral (1616–20), Padilla sailed for the New World and from 1622 was associated with Puebla Cathedral, first as a singer and then, from 1629, as *maestro de capilla*. He became wealthy, thanks to church benefices and his activities as an 'ecclesiastical' musical instruments (flutes, bassoons and shawms) factory owner and distributor, and he is known to have sold at least one negro slave.

At the cathedral he was charged with the education of the choirboys at the Colegio de S Pedro; he also taught at the Colegio Seminario de S Juan. The cathedral boasted a large, well-trained choir (many of its members also played instruments), capable of performing double-choir polyphony. During his tenure (and that of Bishop Palafox y Mendoza, who supervised the construction of a new cathedral in the 1640s), Puebla became the major musical centre in Mexico, overshadowing even Mexico City. Also employed at the cathedral were the harpist Nicolás Grinón and the organist, singer and composer Francisco López Capillas, who was Padilla's only rival.

Padilla composed in the *prima prattica* style with particular sensitivity to text. In addition to Latin church music, he provided tuneful vernacular *chanzonetas* and *villancicos* for feast days cast in the popular forms of the day – *jácaras* (Picaresque ballads), dialogues, gypsy dance-songs, shepherd songs, *gallegos* and *negrillas*. He used syncopation and modal interchange between choirs.

Salazar, Antonio de (*c*1650–1715). Spanish-born Mexican *maestro de capilla* and composer of double-choir works, *chanzonetas* and *villancicos*. Before leaving Spain Salazar was a prebendary in Seville. From 1679 he was *maestro de capilla* at Puebla Cathedral and nine years later won a similar post at Mexico City Cathedral by defeating four rivals. Salazar had at his disposal a rich variety of wind and string players whom he accommodated in contrasting ensembles in the *villancicos* he composed between 1680 and 1704. Also at the cathedral in Mexico City were Pérez de Gúzman, Francisco de Atienza y Pineda and Manuel de Zumaya (who gradually assumed his teaching and administrative duties in 1710–11).

Sant'Anna, José Pereira de. See IBERIAN PENINSULA AND COLONIES 2 *Portugal*.

Torrejón y Velasco, Tomás de (1644–1728). Spanish composer of the first New World opera, working in Peru. Torrejón y Velasco had worked from 1658 in the household of Pedro Fernández de Castro y Andrade who in 1667 was appointed viceroy of Peru. Along with 112 other personal attendants Torrejón y Velasco travelled to Lima, where he acted as the superintendent of the armoury and a magistrate and chief justice before being appointed *maestro de capilla* of Lima Cathedral, a post he retained to the end of his life. He composed polychoral *villancicos*, memorial Vespers music for Charles II (1701) and an opera, *La púrpura de la rosa* (1701; text by Calderón), which was performed at the viceregal palace as part of the celebrations of Philip V's 18th birthday.

Zipoli, Domenico (1688–1726). Tuscan-born organist and composer who went to Argentina to become a Jesuit missionary. Zipoli is known by his *Sonate d'intavolatura*, published in Rome in 1716, a collection of sacred and secular works for organ and harpsichord. In that year, having put aside his connections with Cosimo III, Grand Duke of Tuscany, he joined the Society of Jesus, determined to become a missionary priest in Paraguay, but he died of tuberculosis shortly after completing his training in philosophy and theology at Córdoba (Argentina).

Zumaya, Manuel de (*c*1678–1756). Mexican priest, organist and composer who was the first native *maestro de capilla* at Mexico City Cathedral (1715–39), where he succeeded his teacher Antonio de Salazar; in 1739 he went to Oaxaca, where in 1745 he became *maestro de capilla* at the cathedral. His Latin polyphonic works include the earliest extant music glorifying the Virgin of Guadaloupe; he also produced *villancicos*. In 1711 the Spanish viceroy (the Duke of Linares, who was an *aficionado* of Italian opera) commissioned Zumaya to compose an *opera seria*: *La Partenope* (the libretto was printed in Italian and Spanish) became the first opera to be composed in North America.

II Baroque Forces and Forms

Voices

The three half-centuries into which the Baroque period can be divided are characterized by three distinct vocal styles. In the early Baroque an even-toned, word-dominated style flourished, heavily ornamented at specific places, according to the accomplishment and taste of the singer. The middle Baroque is arguably a true *bel canto* period when the melody reasserted its dominance over the words and embellishment was limited; national styles were at their most clearly defined. The late Baroque embodied a rapprochement of national styles and a further emergence of vocal ornamentation, to an unprecedented degree.

The smoothness that was a feature of Renaissance vocal polyphony was also a *desideratum* of vocal performance. In his *Practica Musica* (1556), Hermann Finck – after complaining about singers whose throat embellishments (*Kehl-Coloratura*) resembled the bleating of a goat (a comparison often found in descriptions of bad singers) – described the sounds required in polyphonic music: 'The treble and the alto should not ascend too high, and no voice should overpower the others and disturb us by shouting or be so strained that the singer changes colour, becoming black in the face and seeming to run out of breath, such as those basses who buzz like a hornet imprisoned inside a boot, or puff and blow like a burst bellows.' Clearly the quality of sound often departed considerably from the classical ideal of smooth counterpoint with no part obtruding.

A century earlier, Conrad von Zabern of Mainz had been similarly critical of the state of vocal art in Germany (*De modo bene cantandi choralem*, 1474). He advocated *concorditer cantare* (perfect ensemble) and *mensuraliter cantare* (rhythmic precision), and called for *devotionaliter cantare* (keeping soberly to the written notes and not deviating by too much embellishment) or *discant* and *satis urbaniter cantare* (civilized, 'urbane' singing, as opposed to the crudities of peasants 'who bellow like cattle'). On the other hand, he scorned 'aspiration' (articulating with a sharp emission of breath) and the practice of holding high notes too long and too loudly. The parallel with Finck and other writers of the late Renaissance and early Baroque are clear: the tendency to elaborate, the increase in complexity, is followed by a reversion to simplicity.

The Renaissance desire to keep the parts equal in volume necessitated either limiting their ranges or requiring them to accommodate their timbre and volume according to pitch. The need to avoid one voice standing out at the top of its range caused the 16th-century singer to decrease in volume as he ascended and increase as he descended (as specifically requested by Conrad). The ideal was taken from the ancients; Plato and Aristotle had advocated voices neither too sharp nor too dull, but even, clear, flexible and moderate. Finck called for a sweet and tender treble and a bright, sonorous bass. In the church style the voices were expected to merge imperceptibly: as basses rise in pitch, they should sound like tenors, while rising tenors should sound like altos and altos like trebles, necessitating the use of falsetto or head voice; when descending, voices should approach the timbre of the next below. By comparison, modern choral singing is top-heavy, with singers trying to maintain their tonal quality throughout their range.

When, at the end of the 16th century, the new monodic solo style arrived, singers probably carried their habitual practices from polyphony into solo music, changing timbre from one register to another. Although certain writers talked of three registers – chest, throat and head – references are rare in Baroque times to more than two, as delineated by Giulio Caccini[1] with his 'voce piena' and 'voce finta', the latter generally regarded as falsetto.

The use of falsetto had grown out of the necessity, because of a lack of available boys, to replace or supplement the treble or alto voices in polyphonic textures with men, generally baritones or basses, singing in falsetto. By the end of the 16th century, castratos were beginning to replace the falsettists in Roman chapel choirs. In solo singing the disagreeable qualities of the falsetto voice were widely scorned, for example by Caccini, writing from Florence in *Le nuove musiche* (1602) that 'nobility of good singing, which is born of a natural voice, cannot come from feigned [i.e. falsetto] voices'. Bellerofonte Castaldi, in the preface to his book of Venetian monodies, duets and trios fancifully titled *Primo mazzetto di fiori musicalmente colti dal giardino bellerofonteo* (1623), wrote that 'because the subject is love or disdain which a lover has shown towards his beloved, it is represented in the tenor clef, whose intervals are appropriate and natural for masculine speech, it seeming to the author laughable that a man should make overtures to his beloved in a woman's voice and beg her in falsetto to take pity on him'.

But it was not only the scarcity of boys' voices that required the use of falsettists in the upper parts of polyphonic music. In the late 16th century the growing range and complexity of the music, especially for the upper voices, made it increasingly difficult to use boys' voices at the top. The falsettists were best suited to the alto ranges and produced an intolerably unpleasant sound in the increasingly high soprano parts. Something had to give, and what gave was the virility of certain boys chosen at a young age for the barbarous but effective practice of castration, producing male voices at the soprano pitch, capable of all the virtuosity and volume of a fully mature singer. The castratos were to come fully into their own as solo singers somewhat later.[2]

While the falsettist gave way to the castrato in the church, in secular music, particularly partsongs and madrigals, women – ineligible to sing in church – were increasingly accepted and fashionable. The madrigal reached its zenith at much the same time that the solo song became popular. Madrigals achieved a spectacular success at the court of Alfonso II d'Este under the direction of Luzzasco Luzzaschi. In contrast to the amateur performances of the *concerto delle donne*, the concerts of the 'Ladies of Ferrara' (generally but inaccurately known as 'the three ladies of Ferrara') mark the turning-point in vocal ideals from the Renaissance to the Baroque, looking back at Renaissance polyphony and forward to the Baroque and the new music of Caccini and the Camerata.

The Ferrara *concerto delle donne* (a term used equally to refer to amateur and professional women's ensembles) acquired a reputation throughout Italy for its brilliant, florid singing; the performances of the professional singers must have been spectacular, as the extreme difficulty of the music in both range and agility testifies. What had been an incidental feature of court life in the 1570s became after 1580 an integral, almost obsessive cult.[3] Not all observers were impressed: the Florentine ambassador, reporting that he had finally been admitted to a performance taking place during a game of cards, found it tedious, but admitted to ignorance of music.[4]

As the experiments of the Florentine Camerata shifted the emphasis away from church music, solo secular song became the dominant form. A new style known as the 'canto da camera', to distinguish it from 'canto da chiesa', was fast developing, though many of the new chamber singers were equally proficient performers in the church style and were employees of the church. The practice of using falsetto and head registers continued throughout the Baroque era. It was usual for a tenor to adopt falsetto above *g'* (a practice still followed into the 19th century).[5] Some early Baroque singers made a virtue of this necessity. Giovanni Maffei mentioned in his *Discorso della voce* (1562) those who could sing passages 'now in the bass, now in the middle, now in the soprano, most beautiful to hear'.

As vocal experimentation gathered pace, some singers developed exceptionally large ranges. Caccini has a bass going down to *B'* flat in his last *Nuove musiche* song. More curious still are those songs that gad about amongst the clefs: Francesco Rognoni's *Selva di varii passaggi* (1620) contains one which proceeds from *c''* down to the same low *B'* flat. In such songs the singer must almost certainly have used falsetto and head register as well as chest, but probably the extreme notes were of modest volume. The smallness of the rooms in which such music was peformed, the number of listeners and the clear, resonant acoustics provided by the marble floors and high ceilings rendered it unnecessary to sing as loudly as was necessary in a large church. In the Palazzo Ducale in Mantua, for example, most of the rooms used for domestic and musical purposes were of modest size, including the Sala degli Specchi where Claudio Monteverdi's *L'Orfeo* may have first been performed in 1607.

Many treatises of the late 16th and early 17th centuries refer to the differences between the two styles. Writing in Naples in 1613, Pietro Cerone commented in *El melopeo* that 'choral singers sing to the crowd with full voices, chamber singers with soft, low and falsetto notes, modifying their voices to balance with the instruments accompanying them, organ, guitar, harp or others'. Lodovico Zacconi (*Prattica di musica utile*, 1592) wrote that 'many singers [in Venice] learnt to sing through soft singing in private houses, where shouting is abhorred', and that chamber singers were not 'forced to sing like the paid singers in the churches'. Cesare Crivellati wrote in his *Discorsi musicali* (1624) that 'in churches you sing differently from music-rooms: in churches with a loud voice, in music-rooms with a subdued voice', and in fact most 17th-century descriptions of Italian chamber singers and singing stress softness, sweetness and lightness rather than brilliance and passion. This concept is the antithesis of our modern notion of church as opposed to secular singing where the former is expected to be 'reverent', i.e. reserved, while the latter is uninhibited and extrovert.

In his famous *Istitutioni armoniche* (1558), Gioseffo Zarlino described church singing as 'a voce piena' ('in full voice') while chamber singing was more subdued. There was also a difference in social status between chamber singers and those employed to sing in church. Many of the singers or singer-composers who published books of solo songs had their titles or their social position – *nobile gentiluomo* for example – indicated below their names; they were *dilettanti*, in the best sense. Indeed, the composers of the Camerata and their immediate successors occupy an almost unique position in musical history: with them, theory preceded practice and the aristocracy was part of the avant-garde.

Caccini referred to the notion of ignoring the exact time values and of adding notes of one's own invention as *nobile sprezzatura*; this 'noble negligence' – a musical counterpart to poetic licence – was a kind of aristocratic casualness and disregard for the rules and regulations of harmony and counterpoint by introducing dissonance to convey more vividly the meaning of the text. Those committed to the *seconda prattica*, nearly all of whom were singers as well as composers, felt free to exercise their fantasy in their solo songs, and it is interesting to speculate why a composer like Monteverdi wrote so few. Perhaps the amateur disregard for the rules offended his professional spirit and approach to composition, which was in some ways conservative, despite his own spirited defence of the *seconda prattica* against criticism.

The more refined chamber styles meant that the singers kept the general volume level more or less equal to that of normal speech, enabling them more easily to develop the agility necessary to perform the *passaggi, trilli, groppi, tirate* and all the rapid-fire ornamentation required in the 'new music'. To the human voice, louder means slower; and the astonishing agility and limberness of the vocal tract required for some of the more virtuoso solo songs and arias (such as 'Possente spirto' in Act III of Monteverdi's *L'Orfeo*) cannot be achieved at the volume required of, and habitual to, the modern operatic singer. The hallmark of early Baroque singers was their agility, not their volume.

Caccini's two volumes of *Le nuove musiche* (1602, 1614) are the point of departure for Baroque solo singing. Many of the songs had been written as early as the 1580s, so were contemporaneous with the events at Ferrara, discussed above. In his famous preface of 1602 – a bible for the modern student of early Baroque singing – Caccini wrote that he was publishing the songs so that the kinds of embellishments he sang, and the appropriate places for their use, once and for all would be made clear; he vented his spleen on singers who added *lunghi giri* (lengthy passages, twistings and turnings) in inappropriate places. As early as about 1580 Count Bardi, mentor of the Florentine Camerata, had complained to Caccini (in his 'Discorso mandato a Giulio Caccini, detto Romano, sopra la musica antica e'l cantar bene') of those who sang 'badly ordered passages that even the composer himself would not recognize as his own music', and most other writers at the time agreed that over-ornamentation was an abomination.

Caccini's ornaments are of two basic kinds: the *passaggio*, developed from Renaissance diminutions, and the 'affective' types such as the *esclamazione*, the *trillo* and the *ribattuta di gola* – the real innovations, which engendered dismay and even disgust in some listeners. The *trillo* was almost certainly performed by glottal articulation rather than by the muscular jerks of the diaphragm often heard today. Glottal articulation is a rapid spasm of the muscles controlling the larynx, causing the glottis to open and close in a rapid oscillation – similar to coughing or laughing but less violent. The difference lies in that, in singing, it closes only partly, for it is kept ajar by steady breath pressure; the increase in breath pressure necessary to cause oscillation can come only from controlled diaphragmatic support. The contention of some modern teachers that Baroque singing is unsupported arises partly from their having heard such expressions as 'singing in the throat', 'beating in the throat' and similar descriptions by contemporary writers to explain the performance of the *trillo* or other rapid ornaments; articulation in the throat has nothing to do with the modern 'singing in the throat', which refers to faulty production (the so-called 'raised larynx syndrome'). Further, some scholars have misleadingly described the *trillo* as 'controlled vibrato'; but since the technique of glottal articulation serves equally well for the execution of rapid *passaggi*, it is likely it was used for both. I have demonstrated to my own satisfaction that this can be a convincing way of performing these very demanding *gorghe* and it would be difficult to imagine how one could perform *passaggi* with an articulation produced by 'controlled vibrato'![6]

Most treatises make it clear that, at least in the Florentine style, rapid vocal articulation was executed from the throat. But not everyone liked it; in the 18th century, when the *trillo* had fallen into disuse, it was referred to as the 'goat's trill' (*Bockstriller*). Singers probably no longer commanded this technique; and when P. F. Tosi likened some singers' shakes to the 'quivering of a goat' in his *Opinioni de' cantori antichi e moderni* (1723), he no doubt had them in mind. By this time the glottal articulation of early Baroque music could no longer be used because the music was heavier, the accompanying instruments more robust, and singers would have been instinctively aware that they needed a different technique, particularly for fast passages. Yet in the 16th- and 17th-century treatises, it is clear enough what they meant with so many references to the throat: *gorga, gorgia, gorgheggiare*. Caccini was quite unambiguous on this: 're-strike each note with the throat on the vowel *a*'.

Antonio Brunelli wrote in his *Vari esercitii* (published in Florence in 1614) that 'quavers should be sung dotted, and beaten with the throat, not with the mouth as many do';[7] he went on to say that, because of their speed, semiquavers were not sung dotted, 'but one should beat them with the throat distinctly one upon the other in order that the passage becomes convincing'. Brunelli was very insistent on this: 'the whole basis of the placing of the voice [*disposizione*] consists in this beating in the throat, and to this the attention should be drawn of beginners setting themselves to study'. Nearly all the Italian diminution treatises (beginning with that of G. B. Bovicelli in 1594) agree on the execution of the *trillo* as a throat articulation, and all emphasize the necessity of the notes being clearly separated (*spiccate bene*).

Most monodies were written for high voices, tenors or sopranos. The clefs were chosen essentially to keep the extremes of the range as nearly as possible within the staff and to avoid ledger lines, and it is a mistake to interpret them as an indication of stereotype of voice or sex. Sopranos, male or female, were accustomed to singing the entreaties of a man to his mistress, or vice versa, and tenors would sing a sighing young virgin's lament, all with no sense of incongruity. In 1607 Bartolomeo Barbarino ('Il Pesarino') wrote in the preface to his second collection of madrigals that they 'may be sung by a tenor at the octave below, which is the appropriate one for singing to the chitarrone or theorbo, but to accommodate those who play the harpsichord, and particularly for the ladies, it occurred to me to put them in the [soprano] clef'.

Countless solo motets are written in the soprano clef, very few in the tenor, and many in the soprano are headed 'soprano o tenore' or 'cantus vel tenor'; octave transposition was even more common in church music than in secular. The pieces in Giovanni Legrenzi's collection of 1676 are mostly in the soprano clef but marked 'for soprano or tenor'. Tenors were more used to transposing from the soprano clef than vice versa, since they would have learnt the soprano clef as boy trebles. They may have been having a thin time at the opera in the 1670s, but they still sang regularly in the churches and oratorios and at the concerts of the many *accademie*, which provided an opportunity for composers and singers to display their talents before a particularly discerning audience. The 17th century saw an increasing tendency towards the use of higher voices and the further separation of voice from bass line. This became the rage when the castrato voice was added to those singing the upper lines. In the operas of the later part of the century, the tenors were often relegated to lesser roles – old men or soldiers – and to comic or *travesti* roles such as nurses and female servants.

If the most important change in vocal practice during the 16th century had been the addition of women, the most important in the 17th was the emergence and the rise to dominance of the castrato. Although it was in church music – where they had gradually replaced the falsettists from the 1580s and 90s – that the castratos first appeared, they were quick to take advantage of the vogue for opera. They joined forces with the virtuoso singers of Ferrara, Mantua, Florence, and Rome in the new art form and sang in such works as Peri's *L'Euridice* (1600) and Monteverdi's *L'Orfeo* (1607). In the Papal states, where women were forbidden to appear on stage, female roles were sung by boys or castratos. The main roles, however, at least in the first decades of the 17th century, were taken by tenors and female sopranos, notably Francesco Rasi, almost certainly Monteverdi's first Orpheus, and Vittoria Archilei, Peri's Eurydice. Archilei must have been a wonderful singer, for so many people heaped praise on her: in his preface to *L'Euridice*, Peri dubbed her 'the Euterpe of our age', adding that she had always found his music worthy of her art and had adorned it not just with *gruppi* and *lunghi giri* of the voice but also with 'those graceful and light embellishments that cannot be written down or learned from books'. Sigismondo d'India enthused just as fervently in his *Musiche* (1609), praising her excellence and her intelligence.

Rasi also achieved great fame. He composed his own book of secular songs or monodies (*Vaghezze di musica*, 1608), which contain some remarkable *passaggi* and written-out embellishments very similar in style to those in 'Possente spirto'. There the embellished version, printed above the simple one, may well show Rasi's own hand; Monteverdi could have allowed Rasi to sing his own ornaments and then liked them enough to have them printed in the score (though the lack of acknowledgment may argue against this). That so accomplished a virtuoso was in demand as a madrigal singer points to the slender division between soloist and ensemble singer. The bass Melchior Palantrotti, who also sang in *L'Euridice* (as Pluto), had previously been involved at Ferrara with the music of the Este court and the *concerto delle donne*. But the bass voice was little in demand compared with the tenor or the soprano. Caccini, with a tenor's natural prejudice, wrote that 'the bass register is less capable than the tenor of exciting the emotions'.

Italian singers also had opportunities to perform at the *accademie* – evening concerts at the literary academies or at noblemen's palaces. It was at such gatherings that Italian cantatas were most performed. Singers could use a more refined manner than they did in the opera house and composers generally wrote subtler music in cantatas than in operas, where an eye had to be kept open for popular appeal and commercial success; the cantata also provided an opportunity for the tenor, frustrated by the lack of grand operatic roles. The vast majority of surviving 17th- and 18th-century cantatas remain in manuscript. Ninety percent of these are notated in the soprano or treble clefs, but there is every reason to suppose that Barbarino's remarks a century earlier about octave transpositions still held good. This is corroborated by Michel Corrette's statement (*Le parfait maître à chanter*, 1758) that a continuo player should adjust the bass notes as necessary when accompanying a tenor in the soprano clef at the lower octave.

During this period, Italy – and Italian singers and musicians – reigned supreme. Foreigners arrived to marvel at the architectural and artistic splendours of the Renaissance and the virtuoso singers and instrumentalists of the day. Visiting Rome in 1639, André Maugars remarked in a letter (*Response ... sur le sentiment de la musique d'Italie*) on the lack of bass singers there:

> There are many castratos for the treble and alto [parts] with extremely beautiful natural tenor voices, but few deep bass voices. They are all very assured in their parts, and sing at sight the most difficult music. Moreover they are almost all born actors, which is why they succeed so perfectly in their *comédies musicales* .... They have various voice modulations [*passaggi*? – or a reference to a Frenchman's perception of the castratos?] which we do not have .... They perform the coloratura with more coarseness [*rudesse*], but are beginning to improve.

Young singers, as well as instrumentalists and composers, went to Italy to study, armed with stipends from patrons eager to import the Italian style to their courts.

In France, the solo songs incorporated in the *ballets de cour* – the *airs de cour* – were successful as a genre on their own. Forty-three books of *airs de cour* were printed between 1608 and 1643 with songs by the most famous composers of Louis XIII's court: Pierre Guédron, Antoine de Boësset, Gabriel Bataille (himself the publisher of a song series) and Étienne Moulinié. They were characterized by great rhythmic freedom; the almost complete absence of bar-lines encouraged the flow of the melodic line, and this led to a natural closeness to the spoken word which had been notably lacking in all the theoretical attempts to 'unlock the secrets of Greek music'[8] by the Pléiade and later the Académie de Poésie et de Musique founded by Baïf and Courville.

One of the great singers of *airs de cour* was Pierre de Nyert, a French nobleman, singer and teacher. He visited Rome in 1633 and two years later brought the Italian style back to Paris where he became a *valet de chambre* to the king. He soon achieved a profound influence on the court and on musicians such as Michel Lambert and Bénigne de Bacilly, who published an important treatise on singing in 1668. Both studied with Nyert, who taught them an Italian concern for clear pronunciation and declamation. He claimed that the diminutions about which he had learnt in Italy should be kept for the second and subsequent verses of an air and should be closely related to the meaning and structure of the poetry. This last injunction may have been in spite of, rather than in imitation of, Italian practices: Italian monody is full of *passaggi* and other embellishments that take little account of the suitability of the words. Nyert was probably heeding the warnings of such Italians as Caccini and Bardi who had complained bitterly about such malpractices. Fortunately, Mersenne included an example of French decoration (*broderies*) in his *Harmonie Universelle* (1636–7): Antoine de Boësset's air 'N'espérez plus mes yeux' is shown (overleaf) with three different ornamented versions, one by Boësset himself, the others by Bacilly and Moulinié.

By the death of Louis XIII in 1643, French reactions to the Italian style and Italian singers were beginning to take a negative turn. French ornamentation was more regulated than Italian, attempting to stay closer to the rules of art of the ancient Greeks. Music was a vehicle for delicate sentiment and gently flowing decoration, not for what some Frenchmen had called the unbridled passions and 'violent convulsions' of Italian singers. This negative reaction seems to have been directed

Ex. 1

Antoine de Boësset: 'N'espérez plus, mes yeux' with diminutions

more against the opera singers than the subtle and restrained practitioners of *airs de cour*. In any event, there was massive and persistent opposition to the castrato voice; the French castrato Blaise Berthod may have enjoyed royal patronage, but he also had to endure merciless lampooning and satirical jibes from courtiers and the press. The reason for French antipathy to the castratos has often been a matter of

conjecture, and it has been suggested, possibly jocularly, that the difference between the Italian and the French temperaments can be epitomized by their respective attitudes towards castratos: when a Frenchman hears a grown man singing in the voice of a woman, he is discomfited and embarrassed, feeling that his own virility is somehow threatened; the Italian thanks God that he has been spared this horrible mutilation and settles down to enjoy the sound of high voices, which Italians have always loved.

The resistance of the French to 'violent' Italian singing existed from the beginning. Guédron's attempts to introduce a more declamatory element and greater emotional intensity into the *airs de cour* had met with resistance, and French singers returning from Italy and attempting to sing (and act) in the new style were ridiculed. When, on Cardinal Mazarin's invitation, Leonora Baroni arrived from Rome in 1644, some commented on the coarseness (*rudesse*) of her voice. But while more criticism of the singers' 'violence' and 'convulsions' followed the 1647 Paris performances of Luigi Rossi' *Orfeo*, most observers were impressed by the beauty of the singing and the richness of Rossi's harmonic language. Lully exploited the differences between the Italian and French vocal styles, for example in the *Ballet de la raillerie* (1659), where he included a humorous dialogue in which French Music accuses Italian Music of 'taking too much liberty in your singing, making it, on occasion, extravagant', to which Italian Music replies, 'You, by your languishing tones, cry more than you sing'. Lully's adoption of a rhetorical theatrical style – to create in *tragédie lyrique* a musical reflection of Racine – meant that he preferred actors who could sing, rather than the reverse.

In France the royal printer Ballard issued monthly collections of *airs de cour* from 1608 onwards to which amateurs, ladies among them, and professionals contributed. They were performed at the homes of musicians and the nobility, as well as at court (where Louis XIII both sang and composed them). Music-making seems to have been confined to the court and the Parisian salons and did not spread to the provincial châteaux to the extent that it did in the country houses of England or the small courts of Germany. Whereas in Italy opera made a rapid descent from its inception at the Medici and Gonzaga courts to the popular level of the Venetian street trader and gondolier, in France no such popularization took place, neither then nor at any point until the Revolution. Singers often accompanied themselves on the lute, a practice that survived much longer in France than in Italy. French singing was more languid, slower and less brilliant than the Italian, with the appoggiatura (or *port de voix*) gaining early popularity.

By the middle of the 17th century the French had begun to codify their rules for performing vocal music. Bénigne de Bacilly published his exhaustive *Remarques curieuses sur l'art de bien chanter* in 1668. Some of his remarks are curious indeed, but he provides us with a long list of the *agréments* used in mid-17th-century France – invaluable, since other treatises and singing methods are few at this time. Many of Bacilly's music examples come from the songs of Michel Lambert, which, typical of the mid-century French style, are best accompanied by harpsichord or theorbo, since by this time the accompaniments are simply *basso continuo*, the lute tablature accompaniments having died out.

Lambert employed written-out embellishments (*doubles*) to a second or third strophe; these remain at the same level of complexity throughout, lacking the concluding climax characteristic of Italian music. The recitative style was slow to develop in France, largely because of the nature of the French language and the French preoccupation with *vers mesuré* and the quantities (as opposed to metrical schemes) that distinguished French verse.

In his *tragédie lyrique* recitative, Lully adhered strictly to the poetic rhythms of Philippe Quinault's Alexandrine verse. He repeatedly went to hear the tragic theatre recitations of Mme Champeslé (Racine's mistress) in order to imitate her manner and to reflect the constantly changing metre of the verse in the alternation of time signatures. Embellishment by the singers was not tolerated.

Throughout the 17th century Italian singers travelled widely in Europe – to Spain and Portugal, the Netherlands, Britain and Scandinavia as well as France and the German-speaking lands – popularizing their music and style of singing wherever they went. Caccini visited the French court in Paris in 1604–5. John Dowland had probably heard Caccini perform at the Medici court in Florence in 1595 and was himself influenced by *Le nuove musiche*, which was sufficiently well known for John Dowland's brother Robert to include two of its songs in his 1610 song collection *A Musicall Banquet*. This contained music by John and continental composers whose fame had reached these shores, such as Caccini or the Frenchman Charles Tessier.

English musicians assimilated the Italian manner more easily; they were quicker than the French to admire and imitate it. Travellers such as Thomas Coryate, who recorded his journey through the Low Countries, France and Italy in *Coryate's Crudities* (1608), returned full of enthusiasm for the new music. Another was Nicholas Lanier who went to Italy on King Charles I's behalf to acquire paintings, and wrote an early English monody in the *stile recitativo*, *Hero and Leander* (c1628). The English language, with its smooth flow, makes a strange bedfellow for the Italian recitative style, with its clearly defined articulation and accentuation.[9] One reason why native opera never really developed is that English does not need to be sung to achieve its most expressive effect.

English solo vocal music developed its own style in a rhythmically varied and emphatic kind of arioso, a true English compromise between recitative and aria. Henry Lawes, perhaps this style's greatest exponent before the Restoration, was intent on setting English words in a natural way rather than in imitating the Italians. Indeed, in the preface to his *Ayres and Dialogues* (1653), he was scathing about the pervasive Italian influence and even set the table of contents of an Italian song-book[10] to music to illustrate how slavishly the English would listen to anything in Italian without understanding the words. But English singers did manage to adopt the Italian manner of adding *passaggi* and divisions.

Between the Elizabethan song composers and the Commonwealth period there appeared a genre generally known as 'florid song'. One of its best sources is Giles Earle's songbook of 1615, which contains this singer's handwritten versions of many popular songs, often quite heavily embellished – a good example of what a singer would have done with the basic printed text in performance. (It shows that English singers could not have been that far behind their Italian counterparts, at least in agility; these embellishments are often intricate and difficult to perform.) Generally, however, English singers seem to have been content with a simpler, sweeter type of melody in the first half of the 17th century. This may have something to do with the amateur tradition and, to some degree, with French influence.

English singers had difficulty with Italian affective ornaments; the throat articulation technique, so useful in Italian music, is less successful with the runs in English florid song. The *trillo* was first described in print in English in an anonymous translation of Caccini's preface, published in John Playford's *A Breefe Introduction to the Skill of Music* (1654) – claimed to be a discourse by an English gentleman returned from Italy, but is in fact a straight translation of Caccini with some omissions.

Playford himself provided some illuminating footnotes; referring to the *trillo*, he averred that some English singers 'beat or shaked with their finger upon their throat' to attain it. He also said that the best way to learn to perform it is by means of a six-note scale up and down (a method I have found very effective in teaching the technique). Playford also quotes a 'gentleman at a musical practice' who claimed that he had learnt to sing the *trillo* by imitating 'that breaking of a sound in the throat which men use when they lure their hawks, as he-he-he-he-he; which he used slow at first and after more swift on several notes higher and lower in sound, till he became perfect therein'.

The use of tone with vibrato and 'straight' tone have always coexisted, though different musical cultures and fashions have tended to favour one over the other. Since most 16th- and 17th-century solo singers also sang in ensembles for madrigals, they employed vibrato affectively rather than as a regular component of their voices. The church singers were accustomed to singing with boys and falsettists, who used very little. Probably, vibrato gradually increased as solo singing grew in popularity and women began to take part in music-making with men in the 'new music', with its emotional effects and the deliberate introduction of the 'passions'. There too we should assume that vibrato was more of an ornament, used to enhance emotional effects, rather than a perpetual quality equally intense throughout a piece.

Another important difference between English and Italian practices was that in England the falsettists (or altos) continued to sing in church choirs and were not supplanted by castratos. Castratos were rarely heard in England until the early 18th century, and when they did come it was mainly as operatic stars such as Bernacchi, Nicolini, Senesino and Farinelli (see Plates 21, 22 and 23). In the Anglican tradition, the alto remained principally a choral voice. Purcell wrote a great deal for the alto voice which he sometimes referred to as a 'high contra tenor'; he was an alto himself. There has been disagreement about what kind of voice this actually was. Since chamber pitch in England was very low, probably below $a' = 400$, as in France, it is more likely that Purcell's solo alto parts were written for a high tenor (such as later became common in France, the 'haute-contre'). The low tessitura of such lines becomes almost ridiculously so at a pitch nearly two semitones below modern concert pitch. The Purcellian alto seems more likely to have been a high, light tenor making use of the *voix mixte* – a combination of chest and head registers. The virtuoso solo bass makes a reappearance in Purcell's music, in the form of the Rev. John Gostling who like the solo Italian basses of the early Baroque combined an enormous range (two and a half octaves) with great agility.

In Germany the new Italian manner had been introduced by such composers as Heinrich Schütz, who absorbed the new influences into the German tradition in a highly sophisticated way. Schütz was particularly successful at setting the German language in the Italian declamatory style. German was more easily adapted to the new style than was English or French, though native singers seem to have had as many problems as their English counterparts with the new affective ornaments, to judge from Christoph Bernhard's treatise, *Von der Singe-Kunst*.

After the ravages of the Thirty Years War, German princelings sought to revitalize court life by imitating the splendours of Versailles, in particular aspects of spectacle and standards of instrumental playing. But while importing French as well as Italian instrumentalists, they continued to hire only Italian singers to augment native forces. Many German princes, eager to have Italian opera at their courts, had a predilection for castrato singers. Germany and Austria were the only countries besides Italy and Spain where castration was perpetrated.

The Lutheran Church maintained a strong conservative tradition and a stubborn opposition to change throughout the Baroque era, as J. S. Bach found out more than once. Until the mid 18th century, Lutheran choirs remained exclusively male, with boys and youths singing the upper parts. Castratos were forbidden, so church musicians were forced to use boys even when they were inadequate to the task. Puberty was late compared with modern times: there are instances of 18- and 19-year-olds still singing treble. Church archives show that some youthful singers would appear again and again on their registers, sometimes even reverting to the higher voices after singing tenor or bass. Clearly the local manner of singing allowed this; one can only surmise that these changes of voice level by pubescent singers must have been achieved through the extensive use of falsetto and head voice. Even in modern times, tenor Evangelist parts in Passion music – so central to the Lutheran tradition – require a judicious amount of head and mixed voice. In his important manual *Der vollkommene Capellmeister* (1739), Johann Mattheson advocated the replacement of boys' voices with those of women: 'In the beginning I was required to place [the women] so that no one could see them; ultimately, however, no one could hear or see enough of them'.

During the early years of the 18th century, the influence of Italian opera was spreading across the whole of Europe: itinerant Italian singers were flocking across the Alps, to the East, West and North, armed with *arie di baule* – arias in their luggage which they sang whenever those of the composer did not suit them. Only in France did the invasion meet with serious resistance. The popularization of music that Italian opera brought in its wake also brought with it a less refined public than the courtiers who had listened to music in their palaces and castles. The public in the Venetian opera pits were a rabble, and there are accounts of troublemakers being ejected and even beaten up by the local equivalent of 'bouncers'.[11] Elegance and refinement, subtlety and intelligence were less exciting than brilliant fast runs, high notes, vast leaps and virtuoso vocal athletics.

Vocal embellishment became very much influenced by instrumental styles and particularly by violin music. The singer Faustina Bordoni was famous for her agility, as is borne out in the many arias her husband, Johann Adolf Hasse, composed for

Ex.2
J. A. Hasse: 'Digli ch'io son fedele', *Cleofide* (1731), Act II

her; Francesca Cuzzoni excelled in cantabile and the pathetic. Embellishment came to encompass much wider vocal ranges and greater use of the appoggiatura and the trill (shake), as well as the instrumental arpeggio. Indeed, heavily ornamented singing went on well into the 19th century.

As the ranges of instruments increased, so did the ranges of singers. Tenors and sopranos seldom sang above G or A in their respective octaves in the early Baroque; by the early 18th century sopranos sometimes ventured up to *c'''*, though the tenors seldom went above *a'*.[12] One reason for the advance of high notes concerned the comparative acoustics of opera house and palace rooms: in a larger building, with the greater absorbency of its plush furnishings, low notes would carry far less well than in a marble-floored, comparatively empty room in a courtly palace. As theatres and theatre orchestras grew larger, singers had to adapt in order to be heard; and the higher they sang, the better they were heard.

The castratos were the highest paid of the singers – in fact the highest paid of all musicians, earning far more than the composer: in Italy, a leading castrato could command ten times the composer's fee and sometimes even more, while in London the castrato Caffarelli was paid 1000 guineas (plus a further 150 travelling expenses) for a season – equal to the amount Handel was paid to compose and direct the operas in which he sang. This was understandable: it was the castrato (and the soprano) who drew the audiences to the public opera houses, while the composer remained a secondary figure, rarely even mentioned on the handbills.

One of the most important features of 18th-century singing was the cadenza. The word, meaning an elaborated cadence, originally referred to the small notes with which the singer decorated the penultimate long note of a piece. During the 18th century this came to mean a much longer and more elaborate series of decorations, scale passages, arpeggios, *messe di voce* effects and the like, which a singer generally kept for the final cadence in an aria. Tosi reported that singers often sang three or more cadenzas during an aria but said that they should sing only one, at the end. Giambattista Mancini later wrote (*Riflessioni pratiche sul canto figurato*, 1774), that an aria without a cadenza was unsatisfactory and 'languid'.

Some teachers ruled that singers should not attempt a cadenza longer than could be sung in one breath; others said that its range should not greatly exceed that of the written notes of the aria and should consist of passages derived directly from the music. By the mid 18th century, however, singers were disregarding these rules, and continued to do so into the 19th; the longest known vocal cadenza, performed by Gaetano Crivelli at La Scala in 1815, is supposed to have lasted over 25 minutes. Tosi, writing in 1723, after a long career as a (castrato) singer, deplored the habits of the modern singers as regards cadenzas: 'The presumption of some singers is not to be borne with, who expect that a whole Orchestra should stop in the midst of a well regulated Movement, to wait for their illgrounded Caprices, learned by Heart, carried from one Theatre to another and perhaps stolen from some applauded female singer.'

The degree of vocal ornamentation encouraged, permitted, tolerated or abhorred varied greatly during the Baroque era, as tastes and fashions changed and national and individual styles emerged, separated and then coalesced. The pendulum-like swings between simplicity and complexity, between rigour and excess, have always been a part of musical, as of all human, activities. To a performer of this music, three centuries later, it is a constant challenge to one's musicianship to catch the right points in these swings and to find a just balance between the diverse influences at work during the whole of the Baroque era.

Nigel Rogers
Newbury, Berkshire

Notes

1 H. W. Hitchcock, ed.: *G. Caccini: Le nuove musiche*, Recent Researches in the Music of the Baroque Era, ix (1970).

2 J. Rosselli: 'The Castrati as a Professional Group and a Social Phenomenon, 1550–1850', *Acta Musicologica*, lx (1988), 143–79.

3 I. Fenlon: *Music and Patronage in Sixteenth-Century Mantua* (Cambridge, 1982), i, 125–7.

4 D. Arnold: *Monteverdi* (London, 1963, 3/1990), 9. *See also* A. Newcomb: 'The *musica segreta* of Ferrara in the 1580s' (Ph.D. diss., Princeton, 1970).

5 The first high c'' on the chest was sung by the French tenor Gilbert Duprez on 17 September 1831 in the Teatro del Giglio in Lucca in the Italian première of Rossini's *Guillaume Tell*, Act IV, scene 1.

6 *See* H. M. Brown: *Embellishing 16th Century Music* (Oxford, 1976), 10.

7 This reference to the mouth may have meant some kind of tremolo or even a jaw vibrato.

8 D. Poulton: *John Dowland* (London, 2/1972), 199.

9 The Florentine Marco da Gagliano called for the singer 'to chisel out the syllables' (*scolpire le sillabe*), or to pronounce them very distinctly, in the preface to *Dafne* (1608).

10 Antonio Cifra: *Scherzi e arie* (Venice, 1614); Lawes set the 'Tavola', which begins with 'In quel gelato core'.

11 A. Heriot: *The Castrati in Opera* (London, 1956), 73–4.

12 The first high c'' for tenor I know is in Benedetto Ferrari's 'Ha di fiamme un abisso' in *Musiche varie* (1633); in the same song, the tenor range is extended downwards to A.

Instruments

While for all instruments the Baroque was a period of revolution, with new ones appearing and those of the Renaissance changing to such an extent that they were all-but new, this revolution was a slow process, with different instruments changing at different times. In addition to the surviving instruments of the period, our information comes from three main literary sources, two of them well illustrated, for the instruments of the early Baroque: Praetorius's *Syntagma musicum* (Vol. II *de Organographia*) in Germany in 1619, Mersenne's *Harmonie Universelle* in France in 1636–7, and Talbot's manuscript, compiled in England between 1680 and 1690.[1] Whereas in Praetorius, at the very beginning of the 17th century, some instruments already appear in their Baroque form, in Talbot, written around the birth dates of Bach and Handel, by which time the Baroque was fully established, there is evidence for the continued use of some Renaissance instruments.

The string instruments were the first to change, with the viols in Praetorius already recognizably the Baroque model. They were also the first to be affected by changes in taste, for by the time that Talbot wrote, they were already going out of fashion in England. Purcell, in the late 17th century, was the last major English composer to write for viols, and he was regarded as old-fashioned for so doing. And yet, when he died, the Baroque woodwind were only just beginning to be accepted in Britain.

Both viols[2] and violins were invented in the early Renaissance, between 1470 and 1500, and within a century of the earlier of those dates both reached their established form which was to persist throughout the Baroque. Recent research suggests that the instrument heretofore generally accepted as 'the' early Renaissance viol, with a longer back than front and forward-sloping shoulders, may well be the invention, possibly imaginary, of later periods. Thus, while there was certainly a wide variety of viol shapes in the early Renaissance, not until the later 16th century may there have been anything that could be regarded as a standard pattern of viol, so that the shape as we generally recognize it is that of the Elizabethan era. The main characteristics of the viol, in all periods, are six strings tuned in fourths, at low tension, with a third in the middle, with frets on the fingerboard, held on or between the knees (hence the name *viola da gamba* or leg fiddle), with a low-arched front and a flat, or flattish, back, and bowed with the bow held underhand. It was pre-eminently the instrument for chamber music, for playing in groups as a consort of viols of different sizes, from treble to bass (see Plate 7), and into the early Baroque the ideal bowed string instrument. When, as we shall see, the consort of viols was replaced by the violin band, the bass viol (see Plate 6) was the one size which remained important, now usually with seven strings, with a considerable solo repertory in France and some use in Germany and elsewhere as well. In central Europe one special form survived into the Classical period. The baryton, the favourite instrument of Haydn's employer Prince Nikolaus Esterházy, was a bass viol with sympathetic strings that could also be plucked by the left thumb for added accompaniment to the bowed strings.

The violin, which began as a three-stringed instrument, a rebec (see Plate 18) on a newly shaped body,[3] was used mainly for dance music in the early Renaissance. It seems not to have become accepted as an instrument for serious music until the early 17th century, by which time another string had been added and makers such as Andrea Amati, and his successors Jacob Stainer in Austria and Antonio Stradivari and others in Italy and elsewhere, had brought it to its finished form. In contrast with the viol, it had four strings tuned in fifths at high tension, without frets, was held upwards on the shoulder or against the upper arm (hence the name *viola da braccio* or arm fiddle), had a high-arched belly and back, and was bowed with the bow held overhand (see Plates 9 and 19). It was, *par excellence*, a solo instrument, though when the family of violins, again from treble to bass, supplanted the consort of viols, it was perforce used in groups. This change came initially in France, with the Vingt-quatre Violons du Roi, the violin band of Louis XIII, consisting, according to Mersenne, of six violins, twelve violas in three different sizes, and six basses. A string band such as this was brought to England by Charles II at the Restoration, when, in all fashionable circles, it almost immediately replaced the consort of viols, and it became also the fashionable sound throughout Europe.

Strings on both viols and violins were at this time all of gut, thus limiting to some extent the available sonority of the lower register, for too heavy a gut string produces a comparatively dull sound. One of the benefits of improving technology in the mid 17th century was the invention of the slow feed on the lathe, and it was this that allowed the introduction of gut strings covered with a coil of wire, the first evidence for which comes in the 1660s.[4] The difference of tone quality on the violin G string, and on the lowest string on all the other instruments, between the high-twist gut and catlines, which had previously been used, and the new covered strings was considerable. It is a difference that is only beginning to be appreciated today, now that we are becoming conscious of the difference, too, between our modern whining steel strings and the plain gut which held sway, even for the E string, until the early years of the 20th century.

The violin itself (see Plate 24) was also very different from the modern instrument. The neck was at least a centimetre shorter and was straight, rather than canted back as it is on the modern violin. The bridge was lower, the soundpost, the pillar which supports, internally, the treble foot of the bridge, was more slender, and the bass-bar, the girder which runs up the inside of the body under the bass foot of the bridge, was also more slender and much shorter. As a result, the tone quality of the Baroque violin was very different from that of today. The feel of the instrument was different, too, for because the neck was straight, there was a wedge between the upper surface of the neck and the under surface of the fingerboard. This was necessary because the fingerboard must rise to follow the plane of the strings lest, as the player produces higher notes, there be too great a distance to press the string to the fingerboard. Because the accepted upper range was less than today, the fingerboard was much shorter than on the modern instrument, but as composers wrote higher and higher parts, the fingerboard was lengthened progressively throughout the Baroque period to accommodate this greater range. There was, of course, no chin rest (that was introduced by Spohr in the early 19th century), and therefore much of the weight of the violin was taken by the left thumb. This affected the way in which the fingers moved on the fingerboard, and the silent shift of position, which is so firm a feature of modern violin playing, did not exist in earlier times. Shifts were audible, and probably slower than today, and thus the ways in which notes were linked together differed from modern practice. Bowing was vastly different, for the bow stick, instead of being cambered towards the hair, curved away from it, resulting in much lower tension on a narrower ribbon of hair than the modern bow, and the point of the stick curved down gently towards the hair, rather than being held away from it as today. As a result, the sound was less strong but there was a much more marked difference of tone between up-bow and down-bow, and between strokes taken at the heel and at the point of the bow, an entirely different sound from the modern ideal of seamless bowing.

Of the plucked string instruments, lutes, harps, and keyboards were the most important, with guitar and other plucked strings more often confined to domestic and casual music-making. The Renaissance lute (see Plate 18), tuned like the viol with six strings in fourths and a third, was already out of fashion, but larger instruments with extra bass strings, often carried on an extended neck, were still in use, indeed remained so until late in the 18th century, mainly as continuo instruments. The lute was also still a solo instrument, especially in Germany, and many composers such as Silvius Weiss wrote works for the ordinary lute with some extra bass courses (see Plate 19), not least among them J. S. Bach, whose solo suites exist for lute as well as for violin and violoncello.

The harp was increased in size around 1600 and acquired first one and then a second extra rank of strings, so that the main Baroque form of the harp, after Monteverdi's *arpa doppia* (see Plate 15), was the triple harp, an instrument which has remained in use in Wales to the present day. The two outer ranks of strings were tuned diatonically, with chromatic strings in the middle rank. This was the harp for which Handel, for example, wrote a concerto, but which was mainly used, again, as a continuo instrument. A diatonic harp, with a single rank of strings, was also used, and in a late 16th-century encyclopaedia[5] this instrument is described as preferable to both lute and harpsichord, for unlike the lute every note came from the full length of the string and so with full tone, and unlike the harpsichord it could be plucked in an infinite variety of ways, and could thus produce many different tone colours.

Nevertheless, the harpsichord was the most commonly used continuo instrument (see Plates 9 and 14), because of its ease of use and its greater facility in playing in chords, and it was also, of course, a solo instrument. There were two main varieties in the early Baroque, the Italian and the Flemish. The Italian instruments usually had only one keyboard, with three ranks of strings, two in unison and one an octave higher, described as $2 \times 8' + 1 \times 4'$. The Flemish had the same three ranks of strings, though usually rather shorter in length for the same pitches than the Italian, so that the Flemish sound might be described as fuller and darker and the Italian as brighter. The harpsichords made by the Ruckers family in Flanders, however, had two keyboards, on the lower of which the notes appeared to be a fifth lower than they sounded; the lower manual F key plucked the same strings as the C key of the upper manual. The purpose of this arrangement is still a matter of dispute. By the early 18th century, two other national schools had arisen, the French and the German, the former deriving from the Flemish and the latter from the Italian, and by the middle of that century a third, the English. By this time, the use of two keyboards was the norm, but, instead of transposing the music into different keys, they produced different sonorities so that the player was able to contrast one passage with another, and even one hand with the other. One eight-foot rank was plucked nearer the nut (the bridge on the wrest-plank) than the other, thus producing a different tone colour, so that the two unison ranks could contrast with each other, and the four-foot rank could be added to one of these. There was always a way of coupling both keyboards so that all three ranks could be sounded together for the fullest tone and volume. Further devices were an extra row of jacks to pluck the string very close to the nut, called the nazard in Germany from its nasal sound, but called the lute stop in England, and a row of small pads of buff leather which could be slid against the strings to mute them, called the buff or harp stop in England but, confusingly, the lute in Germany.

It is important to remember that these various national schools of harpsichord making persisted through the 18th century. Bach's music was conceived for the instruments by Hass and Silbermann, Couperin's for those by Taskin and Couchet, and Handel's for those by Shudi and Kirckman, and as a result all three sounded quite different, a difference which is too often forgotten and lost today. A fascinating speculation is whether Domenico Scarlatti's sonatas were conceived for Cristofori's piano, an instrument which was, as we shall see, as popular initially with the Spanish court as that master's music.

There were also small harpsichords, in the early Baroque the virginals (see Plate 19), which survived from the late Renaissance. This was an instrument with a very different tone quality from the harpsichord, with strings running across the instrument instead of away from the player. Again there were different national types, the Italian and French, called *spinetto* and *épinette* respectively, and the Flemish. There were also two types of Flemish, the ordinary virginals and the *muselaar*, the latter plucking the strings near the middle of their length and producing a darker and more hollow sound. Both were often equipped with a smaller four-foot instrument which could be used with, or contrasted against, the main virginals. In the early 18th century a new small instrument, the wing-shaped or leg-of-mutton spinet, was devised, but this should really be considered a domestic harpsichord, designed to take less space in the room.

The perfect domestic keyboard instrument, but one which was used more in Germany than elsewhere, was the clavichord (see Plate 25). This is the only keyboard whose player is in direct contact with the string as long as the note is sounding, for his finger is on one end of the key, and the tangent on the other end is touching the string. By increasing or decreasing the pressure on the key he can produce louder or softer sounds, something that was impossible on all other keyboards of the period, and he can also produce a vibrato on the note by a slight up and down movement of the finger on the key, the *Bebung* of C. P. E. Bach. Because one clavichord could be mounted on top of another, to simulate the manuals of the organ, with the possibility of a pedal clavichord as well, it was the ideal practice instrument for organists. It could be used in the warmth of the home, instead of playing in a cold church, and there was no need to pay someone to pump the bellows. The German name for the clavichord was *Klavier* (that for harpsichord was either the Italian term *cembalo* or *Instrument*), and it was for the *Klavier* that Bach wrote the *48 Preludes and Fugues* to show that there were better ways available of tuning a keyboard instrument than either any variety of meantone or equal temperament.

A keyboard instrument which was invented around 1700 was Bartolomeo Cristofori's *gravicembalo col piano e forte*. When plucking a string mechanically, as with the harpsichord and spinet, it is impossible to make more than a very little difference of loudness by finger pressure on the key. When striking it, however, a much greater difference is possible. Hence the Italian name for the instrument, a keyboard instrument with softness and loudness. This first version of the piano, a keyboard instrument whose strings were struck with hammers, was comparatively unsuccessful in its day, partly because this type of expression in music was not yet desired, but chiefly because the light stringing then in use was more suited to plucking than to hammering. Bach did not much like Silbermann's version of the instrument in Germany, and in Spain, where a number of Cristofori's pianos had been purchased for the court with initial enthusiasm, many were converted into harpsichords. Not until the latter part of the 18th century, when the Industrial Revolution made covered and more suitable strings available, did the piano come into its own.

The other main keyboard instrument was the organ. In Germany and the Low Countries this had already reached its Baroque form by the early 17th century, as can be seen in Praetorius. It was a large instrument, divided into discrete sections which could be contrasted the one with the other, known as *Werkprinzip*. There were, as a rule, three manuals or keyboards, each controlling a complete organ, with treble and bass ranks of pipes and choice of sonorities, but each producing different types of sound. One manual controlled the positive, usually placed behind the organist's bench, *Ruckpositif* in German and, because it was behind or sometimes under the bench, Chair organ in English, which was transmuted into Choir. Another manual controlled the *Brustwerk*, placed in front of the organist. This was often provided with doors that could be opened or closed to increase or diminish the amount of sound produced, the Swell, which was invented in Spain in about 1700. The third manual controlled the *Hauptwerk*, the Great in English, placed higher up. In addition, there were low bass pipes, controlled by a pedal keyboard. While all this could be coupled to play together, especially on the French organ, one of whose features was the *plein jeu*, used in contrast to solo stops, the normal practice, in Germany at least, as can be seen in Bach's music, was to contrast one section with another, so that the trio sonata, a number of which Bach wrote for the organ, was indeed three distinct voices working against each other. It is a constant surprise in modern performances of Bach cantatas to hear the organ part confined to a small chamber organ, the equivalent of the *Ruckpositif* alone, instead of being played on the magnificent instrument which was a standard feature of all great German churches. Only in England, and often in Italy, were organs less developed, for separate pedal sections were unknown in England until late in the 18th century or after. This was mainly a result of the Puritan destruction of almost all pre-Commonwealth organs, something from which many English churches failed to recover until the late 19th century.

The wind instruments were later in development. The first was the flute, a word which, when used alone in the Baroque and unqualified by adjectives, always meant the recorder. Whereas the early Renaissance recorder had been cylindrical in bore and made in one piece of wood, by the later Renaissance the bore had been tapered, narrowest at the foot, thus improving the tuning, especially of the upper notes, and allowing for a slightly increased range. It was not until after the middle of the 17th century that this design was radically modified as part of a general overhaul of all the woodwind instruments which, initially, took place at the French court under the aegis of the musicians of the Royal Band, the Hotteterres and their associates (see Plate 26). This was partly due to changing fashions of music, the desire for larger and more varied ensembles, and particularly due to the desire for more instruments which would blend with the band of violins rather than playing in the old Renaissance groups of like instruments. There was also a desire for a greater range from the woodwind instruments and the realization that this could best be achieved by more precise reaming of the bore. It was, perhaps, chiefly the general rise in technology, with better lathes and other tools, that made this development possible.

The result was the three-piece recorder, with a cylindrical head joint, a quite rapidly tapering main body carrying the six finger-holes and thumb-hole, and a separate foot joint, with a sharper taper, carrying the little finger-hole. The transverse flute, which was called *traversa* in Italian, and in English and French often German flute or *flûte d'Allemagne*, as an alternative to transverse flute or *flûte traversière*, was also similarly modified at the same time (see Plates 6 and 9). The head joint, again, was cylindrical in bore. The body, again tapering towards the foot, carried the six finger-holes, and a cylindrical foot carried a closed key. On both recorder and *traversa*, opening the finger-holes in sequence from the lowest produced a diatonic scale; chromatic notes could be produced only by closing a hole below one that was open, called cross- or fork-fingering. Obviously, one could not close a hole below the lowest hole, and thus the only way to flatten the note produced by opening that hole was by half-closing it. This is not difficult on the recorder, which is held downwards, but is more awkward on the *traversa* which is held sideways. A key was provided on the *traversa* to obviate this awkwardness, and this was the first time that a closed key was used on any instrument other than some bagpipes, from which the idea was almost certainly taken. On the Renaissance and early Baroque woodwind, the only keys had been open-standing keys which were the only way to cover holes beyond the reach of the fingers on the larger instruments. By about 1700 or 1720, the body of the *traversa* was split into two sections, each carrying the finger-holes for one hand. The purpose of this was two-fold. It enabled the use of still shorter reamers and thus a more accurate bore profile. It also allowed makers to provide a selection of upper-body joints, each a little longer than the next, and thus allow players to tune to different pitches. A further advantage relates to the nature of the instrument, for with any flute, as one blows harder the pitch goes higher. Quantz, in his *Versuch einer Anweisung die Flöte traversiere zu spielen* of 1752, recommended the use of a longer joint for loud movements, so that as one blew harder, the pitch rose to bring a flat joint into tune, and shorter joints for quiet movements, so that as one blew more gently, a sharp joint came down to pitch.

Three reed instruments were newly invented at this same time, the third quarter of the 17th century. Two were adaptations of Renaissance instruments, the oboe deriving from the shawm, and the bassoon from the curtal or dulcian. The third, a little later than the others, not much before 1700, was the clarinet, an elaboration of an earlier folk instrument, the chalumeau, which itself was improved into a fairly respectable instrument at much the same time as the oboe and bassoon were invented.

The shawm had been the most important reed instrument of the Middle Ages and Renaissance, but its loud and piercing sound was unfit for any use in mixed ensembles, and certainly it could not be used with string instruments. The oboe, like the shawm, was played with a double reed, but had a much quieter sound. Like the recorder and *traversa*, it was made in three joints, but with an expanding bore, with upper and lower body each carrying three finger-holes, and a bell (see Plate 26). It had an extra hole, which was covered with an open-standing key, extending the range at the bottom to *c'*. Like the *traversa*, it also had a chromatic key below the lowest of the six finger-holes, which was duplicated so that it could be accessible to either little finger. The modern practice of always having the left hand above the right was not yet established and not until after about 1750 did players come to agreement on the way the instrument was held. Only after that date did the two-key oboe supersede the three-keyed.

There were also two larger sizes of oboe, one the *oboe d'amore*, an alto whose lowest note was *a*, a minor third lower than the treble. This had a bulb bell (*Liebesfuss* in German) which gave a very beautiful hollowness to the tone. The other was a tenor in F, which had three forms. One was simply a large oboe. Another was again a straight instrument but with a bulb bell, like that of the *oboe d'amore*. The third was a curved instrument with a widely flaring bell, usually of brass though occasionally of wood. It is generally assumed that this last was the instrument called in the period the *oboe da caccia*, though it should be emphasized that since there is no known contemporary written description of the *oboe da cacia*, nor any known contemporary titled illustration, this attribution of name is only an assumption. There is no evidence for tenor oboes being used to accompany hunting, and the assumed identification derives, as very probably the name indeed did, from the similarity of the metal bell to that of the *corno da caccia*. The music provided for the instrument makes it certain that the *oboe da caccia* was one of these tenors in F. What the others were called is less certain. *Taille* was one name of the period for a tenor oboe (and for a tenor violin, a large viola) but whether it applied to one or both of the other forms is not known. Not until the later 18th century was the tenor with a bulb bell called the *cor anglais*, a name of unknown origin.

The curtal (see Plate 18) was, like the shawm, made of one piece of wood, with both a downward and an upward bore drilled in it, so that the metal crook carrying the reed projected from one side of the top and the bell, level with the crook, from the other. Again the new instrument which derived from it, the bassoon (see Plate 27), was made in separate joints. The wing joint descended from the crook, fitting into a butt joint which, like but much shorter than the curtal, had both a downward and an upward bore drilled in it. The long joint fitted into the upward bore of the butt, and was capped by the bell joint, which took the pitch down to *B'* flat two octaves and a tone below *c'*, a tone lower than the normal bass curtal, whose lowest note had been *C*. The bore was conical throughout, gradually expanding from the crook socket, until near the top of the bell, at which point there was quite a sharp constriction which was only opened out in the latter part of the 18th century. Initially there were three keys, an F key, the equivalent of the oboe's C for the lower little finger, and a low C and low B flat key for the upper thumb, but a fourth was soon added, an A flat, equivalent to the oboe E flat, for the lower thumb. Rare, but occasionally demanded by both Bach and Handel, were contrabassoons, instruments twice the size of the normal bassoon. One by Eichentopf, who is known to have made other instruments for Bach, including *oboi da caccia*, survives in the Leipzig Musikinstrumenten Museum, and one by the younger Stanesby, surviving in Dublin, is known to have been used by his friend Handel in his *Music for the Royal Fireworks*.

The chalumeau had been a small reed instrument, with a single reed cut from the top of the cylindrical reed or cane body, like a Highland bagpipe drone reed and many surviving folk instruments of the southern and eastern Mediterranean. In Germany Jacob Denner improved this instrument, making it of wood, in much the shape of a treble recorder, with a cane single reed tied to the top. This type of chalumeau was made in a family of sizes, for which a small repertory survives, including some concertos. The chalumeau had two keys near the upper end, one at the back to help it overblow to the upper register (a twelfth above the fundamental, not an octave, due to the cylindrical bore), and one at the front to fill the gap between the two registers. It is thought to have been Denner who then extended the instrument, lengthening the bell, moving the two keys slightly, and otherwise altering it to produce the clarinet. The clarinet was little used in the Baroque, probably because of the strangeness of an instrument with two registers a twelfth apart, rather than an octave, and save for some composers and some courts and players who were in the forefront of progress, and later the military bands and opera orchestras, both always interested in innovations, it did not become generally adopted much before 1800.

Ex.1

Harmonic series

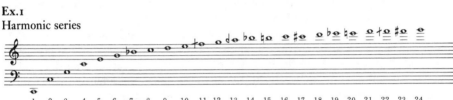

the brass instruments, the trumpet (see Plates 28 and 30) was by far the most important throughout this period, both musically and as the instrument of state and pageantry. This latter role, however, militated against the former, especially in Germany where the use of the trumpet was rigidly restricted. It could be played only by members of the trumpeters' guild, and could be possessed only by those licensed to do so, certain ranks of the aristocracy and certain privileged cities and regiments.[6] It is instructive to look at Bach's cantatas and to see for which occasions he was empowered to use trumpets. The instrument could produce only the notes of the harmonic series, and thus it was diatonic in compass only from the 8th harmonic (c''), and chromatic only from the 12th (g''). It was bedevilled, too, by three pitches which are not in accord with the European scale in any temperament, the 7th, 11th, and 13th harmonics and their octaves, respectively a very flat B flat, a pitch almost exactly halfway between F and F sharp, and a rather flat A. Of these, it was the 11th harmonic that caused the most trouble, for composers would write either F or F sharp according to the context of the music, and expect players to lip the note either up or down. The 13th was also a problem, for the A was well within the compass of the period. It is quite clear from contemporary writings that some players were not very successful in tuning these notes, but it is also clear from the amount of music written for the trumpet that some could achieve it, for no composer in his senses writes notes which he knows are going to be out of tune. Modern players, who have not received the training imparted to members of the guild, and who have to play modern trumpet one day, and Baroque the next avoid the problem by using instruments with finger-holes which produce an alternative harmonic series, but which do so only at the cost of decent tone quality.

The clarino technique of trumpet performance from the 8th harmonic, up to the 22nd in Bach's music and even sometimes to the 24th, was at its height in the later Baroque. In the early 17th century, when trumpeters were ascending no higher than the 13th harmonic, in Monteverdi's *L'Orfeo*, and by the 1630s to the 16th,[7] the high brass parts were played by the cornett, which had been the great virtuoso instrument, particularly for divisions and similar ornamentation of music, in the Renaissance (see Plate 18). It was made of wood, usually leather covered, and was played with a miniature trumpet mouthpiece, no bigger than the cup in which an acorn sits. Unlike most other trumpet-type instruments it was provided with finger-holes so that it was not restricted to the notes of the harmonic series but could be played as fluently as a recorder or any other woodwind instrument. It appears in a few Bach cantatas, usually playing the *cantus firmus* in the chorale movement, but it is clear from the way that Bach wrote for it that its technique had greatly degenerated, and it was by then all-but extinct.

The bass to the trumpets was provided by the timpani, smaller than those of today and shallower, often hemispherical in shape (see Plates 29 and 30). The skins used on them were thicker than those used in recent times, up to the introduction of plastic heads, and the best tone was produced by using sticks with wooden discs or sometimes balls as heads. With thick heads and such sticks there was a clarity of pitch and a precision of rhythm unknown on modern timpani. Drummers were expected to improvise, to elaborate rhythms on held notes, rather than the modern practice of rolling, and especially to fill out long notes at cadences with shorter notes. A good historical example of this practice is provided by Mozart's edition of *Messiah*, in which Handel's semibreves in the timpani part are replaced by quavers and semiquavers, just as Handel's drummer would have played them, a tradition which was already dying out in Mozart's time.

Of the other brass, the trombones were comparatively little used, and were mainly church instruments, supporting the voices as in the Renaissance (see Plate 10), with little change in the instruments. Trombone bells were still of much thinner metal than today,[8] and instruments were still loosely jointed, with movable or telescopic stays, rather than the rigid stays between the joints of the modern instrument. It is clear that the trombone was almost unknown in Britain, Handel only employing them when some players were visiting London from Germany.

The horn was only beginning its orchestral career by 1700 (see Plates 14 and 30), and in the early years of that century it seems to have been a fairly raucous instrument, used mainly for hunting effects. Playing technique and tone quality improved rapidly, as can be judged by comparing Bach's use over a period of years. The instrument, which was narrow in bore in its early years, became somewhat wider, and as a result considerably more mellow in tone, by the third or fourth decade of the century. Like the trumpet, only natural harmonics were available, and because the bell was held in the air, the same harmonics that troubled trumpet players caused difficulties for the horn. The practice of inserting the hand in the bell to ameliorate the tone, to tune difficult harmonics, and to fill the gaps in the overtone series, was adopted only after 1750. The habit of modern players to use their hand in the bell in Baroque music is adopted for the same reasons as the use of finger-holes on trumpets. The result is also the same: anachronistic technique and poor tone quality.

We are beginning to appreciate the difference of the sound of music between the

Baroque and the later periods up to the present, but as yet we are only approaching the realization of that difference. Many of our players are still instinctively falling back on the techniques which they acquired as children and in their early training. Not until we have a generation of players trained *ab initio* on Baroque instruments by older players who themselves have sloughed off their early training shall we be really in the ideal position of hearing the sounds which the composers themselves heard in their mental ears when writing the music.

Jeremy Montagu
The Bate Collection of
Historical Instruments, Oxford

Notes

1 Christ Church, Oxford, music ms.1187, the whole of which has been transcribed in various volumes of *The Galpin Society Journal*, from vol. i (1948) to vol. xvi (1963) .

2 I. Woodfield: *The Early History of the Viol* (Cambridge, 1984).

3 E. Winternitz: *Gaudenzio Ferrari: his school and the early history of the violin* (1967).

4 Advertised in Playford's *Introduction to the Skill of Music* (London, 1664).

5 François Merlin and Jacques Cellier: 'Recherches de Plusieurs Singularités (Paris BN ms.fr. 9152).

6 J. E. Altenburg: *Versuch einer Anleitung zur heroisch-musikalischen Trompeter- und Pauker-kunst* (Halle, 1795; translated Edward Tarr, Nashville, 1974).

7 G. Fantini: *Modo per Imparare a sonare di Tromba* (Frankfurt, 1638; facsimile Nashville, 1972).

8 H. G. Fischer: *The Renaissance Sackbut and its Use Today* (New York, 1984).

Forms and Genres

Stilo. Style; . . . in music it is applied to the way in which each individual composes, performs, or teaches, which is very different according to the genius of authors, lands, and nations, as well as the matters, places, times, subjects, expressions, etc. . . . Diverse terms have arisen to distinguish all of these different characters, such as: ancient and modern styles; Italian, French, German styles; ecclesiastical, dramatic, chamber styles; gay, playful, florid style; piquant, suffering, expressive style; grave, serious, majestic style; . . . familiar, popular, low, servile style . . . .

Sébastien de Brossard, *Dictionaire*, 1703
(English trans. Albion Gruber, 1982)

At the beginning of the 18th century, Sébastien de Brossard categorized music according to several criteria, among which are adherence to the modern or 'ancient' style, national origin, function, and level of discourse. Brossard's dictionary includes entries for various forms and genres, but neither he, nor any other Baroque theorist, described them in the detail Heinrich Christoph Koch devoted to sonata and concerto form late in the 18th century. Although standard designs dominate much Baroque music, specific formal plans were rarely mentioned except as departures from a norm: thus Johann Mattheson tells us in *Der vollkommene Capellmeister* (1739) that the *canarie*, unlike most other dances he knew, should cadence on the tonic at the mid-point. This is not to say that discussions of 'how to compose' are completely lacking. Beyond instruction in the rules of counterpoint, several writers proposed that composers borrow from rhetorical theory to solve problems posed by the emancipation of instrumental music. In his *Synopsis musicae novae* (1612), Johannes Lippius contended that composition was nothing more than the arranging of musical elements in imitation of a text; he encouraged the composer of instrumental music to imagine an appropriate text in order to generate a coherent form. Mattheson thought that composers should employ the standard oratorical techniques of invention, arrangement, elaboration, and presentation of an argument; he compared cadences of different weights to the various levels of punctuation marking phrases of a text and suggested specific musical figures to parallel the rhetorical figures employed by orators.

Both Mattheson and Johann Scheibe (*Der critische Musikus*, 1737–40) compared musical to linguistic discourse, the level of which varied according to the requirements of particular genres and occasions. Just as one might make an argument more or less elevated according to the occasion or medium, one might use the same aria or sonata in church, chamber, or theatre simply by adapting it to its new circumstances. In church it should be more solemn, in the chamber more finely constructed, in the theatre more concerned with the effect to be appreciated from a distance. Mattheson claimed that many 'self-instructed composers' confused these distinct styles, so that music more appropriate to the chamber or theatre was performed unaltered in the church, offending the listener's sense of order. Whether or not the adaptations were successful, this transferability of pieces from one milieu to another may explain why relatively few formal plans and compositional procedures underlie Baroque music.

The means by which the formal designs of Baroque music are articulated include key and harmonic progression, melodic content, metre, tempo, homophonic or contrapuntal texture, and scoring. Pieces are in binary, ternary, and rondo or ritornello forms; or they are constructed over *cantus firmus* melodies or ground basses. Recitatives and many solo songs were constructed by wedding the music closely to the text according to the *seconda prattica*; some instrumental works such as fantasias, preludes, and toccatas in the 'stylo phantastico' were subject to few preconceived formal constraints and were expected to sound improvisatory. In this chapter I shall examine each of these formal designs and procedures individually before turning to examples of liturgical, instrumental, and dramatic music that illustrate the operation of these same principles on a more extended scale. One should bear in mind that the forms were not static: Monteverdi's operas are structured very differently from those of Vivaldi or Handel; the 17th-century suites of the French lutenists and harpsichordists differ in many respects from those of Rameau and J. S. Bach. But one can ordinarily trace the development of procedures within specific genres, their transfer between genres, and the interpenetration of originally distinct national styles.

Binary form

Binary form brings to mind Domenico Scarlatti's sonatas, and dance movements such as those from Bach's keyboard and orchestral suites, but the form was also widely employed in the mid-17th century. For example, the keyboard dances of Johann Froberger (1616–67) are all in two sections: the first closes strongly on a non-tonic harmony (V or III); the second returns to the tonic (see ex. 1). There is

Ex. 1
Froberger: Allemande in E minor (1656)

(a)

bars 1 - 4

(b)

bars 15 - 18

(c)

bars 28 - 30

no necessary thematic relation between the two halves of a dance (nor is there between successive dances in the suite); neither is there usually a marked contrast. The two halves are most often approximately equal in length, although the second is sometimes longer; the actual number of measures varies, and odd numbers are not uncommon. Contemporary English and French allemandes for solo instrument or ensemble are similar to those of Froberger, but many later examples are longer and have parallel melodic material in the two halves. Bach usually begins and ends each half with similar material; in his gigues the opening idea is often inverted at the start of the second part (see ex. 2).

Ex. 2

J. S. Bach: Gigue, English Suite in G minor

(a)

bars 1 - 3

(b)

bars 21 - 3

The dances described above have in common a non-tonic cadence at the end of the first half, but ensemble dances published in 17th-century Italian prints often preserve the tonic harmony throughout. Thus the development of a standard two-part form was not entirely dependent on the harmonic direction away from and back to the tonic harmony, although that harmonic pattern is especially well suited to the binary plan and was the one most frequently adopted in the 18th century. Binary form was employed outside the dance as well, for example in vocal music and in the keyboard sonatas of Domenico Scarlatti. Within the standard binary form Scarlatti employed a variety of compositional procedures: the second half may begin with the opening material transposed to the dominant or with contrasting material (often the contrast depends on texture); occasionally the metre changes; often the harmonic progressions are somewhat unexpected.

By 1675 most of the common dance movements (scored for solo instrument, ensemble, orchestra, solo voice or chorus) were in binary form, usually marked by a non-tonic cadence at the end of the first part. In early 17th-century music the form is less predictable: the dances presented by Negri (*Le gratie d'amore*, 1602) usually have two or three strains and as many repetitions of each as his choreography required. Three-strain keyboard dances were favoured by the virginalist composers in late 16th- and early 17th-century England; many of these move away from the tonic only in the second part. Similar three-strain forms are found in German ensemble suites such as those of Paul Peuerl (1611), and in mid-century secular songs of Andreas Hammerschmidt (1642–3), which often take dance rhythms as their starting point. But in 18th-century suites of dances the binary form was rivalled only by the French composers' use of the rondo (see below).

17th-century aria: strophic, ternary and rondo forms

Vocal music too was likely to be in a standard form by 1700, but earlier was more variable. The earliest operas proceed for long stretches in a free recitative style, the aim of which was simply an expressive delivery of the text. Here the composer was free from the constraints of harmony and rhythm imposed by the regular dance forms and by the traditional ways of singing poetry, yet the singer is intimately connected to and supported by the accompanying instrument. In the early 17th century the line between recitative and aria was not so firm as the one we know from later opera, and recitative itself was much more varied. Peri's recitatives in *Euridice* (1600) are sometimes a kind of heightened speech for text with a purely narrative function, but he also wrote more melodic and expressive passages of recitative (in the *Annotazioni sopra il Compendio de' generi, e de' modi della musica*, 1640, Giovanni Battista Doni cited the *Lamento d'Arianna* of Monteverdi as an example of such expressive recitative); later librettists and composers would have allocated such contemplative texts to arias. In Monteverdi's *L'Orfeo* (Mantua, 1607) closed aria forms are already common, but much of the opera still proceeds in recitative; a good example is Orpheus' reaction to the announcement that Eurydice

Ex. 3
Monteverdi: 'Tu se' morta', *L'Orfeo*, Act II

379

has died from the serpent's bite ('Tu se' morta', in Act II; see ex. 3). The musical form of these recitatives is not predictable, since they are composed line-by-line according to the dictates of the *seconda prattica*, in which music follows text as closely as possible.

The solo madrigals of Caccini reflect a similar approach to composition, in which the considerations related to the text are more important than those on the purely musical side. However, that approach was readily abandoned in favour of closed musical forms whenever the dramatic context permitted. Monteverdi's strophic setting of 'Vi ricorda o boschi ombrosi' in the first act of *L'Orfeo* is an example of such a closed form, or *aria*, in which each stanza of the poem is sung to the same music (see ex. 4). The setting adopts the standard way of singing an eight-syllable line, borrowing the dance rhythm of the balletto and evident in vocal music as far back as the frottola of the early 16th century. In this particular aria, the first phrase (both music and text) returns to produce a short *A–B–A'* form within each of the four stanzas of the poem; the stanzas are separated from one another by an instrumental ritornello, which is itself in binary form (*A–A'–B–B*).

Ex. 4
Monteverdi: 'Vi ricorda o boschi ombrosi', *L'Orfeo*, Act I

In other 17th-century Italian arias, the final section of each stanza might be repeated to produce an *A–B–B'* form, with successive stanzas again separated by an instrumental ritornello. Many of Cavalli's arias for Venetian operas adopt one of these two forms (*A–B–A* or *A–B–B*); most were in triple metre, and they were often closely related to the sarabande or to other dances. The two stanzas of 'Nudo Arciero' (from *Scipione Africano*, Venice, 1664), in *A–B–B* form, are separated by an instrumental ritornello built over the same repetitive bass pattern (or ostinato) which supports the vocal material; in the ritornello the ostinato is altered to permit an internal cadence on the relative major (III, see ex. 5). The same instrumental passage concludes the aria.

Ex. 5
Cavalli: 'Nudo Arciero', *Scipione Africano*, Act I

'Nudo Arciero', Niccolò Minato set by Cavalli (1664)

Text	Musical form	Tonal area
Nudo Arciero vibra i dardi ad altro sen	A	i
Troppo fiero, troppo accerbo è'il tuo velen		
Vogli altrove l'ali, e'il piè		modulates toward v
Vatene cieco Dio lungi da me	B	v
Vatene cieco Dio lungi da me.	B	i
Ritornello		i ... III ... i

(Naked archer, hurl your arrows at another breast
Too haughty, too tart is your potion
Turn your wings and feet elsewhere
Go far away from me sightless God.)

Toward the end of the century the musical setting was further expanded. Cavalli had often repeated more than one line of text, and later composers restated entire sections. Of the two basic aria forms (*A–B–B* and *A–B–A*), it was the latter that came to dominate the serious Italianate opera of the 18th century, and penetrated other genres as well. In the operas of Alessandro Scarlatti this da capo aria began to be especially prominent; 'Agitata da fiera procella' (from *La Griselda*, Rome, 1721) provides a good example, in which the two parts of the text present contrasting ideas, reflected in the music by a change of key and more frequent modulation in the *B* section. In other arias reduced scoring in the *B* section further differentiates it from the opening material. Here Scarlatti expanded the simpler *A–B–A* form he had inherited by beginning with a two-fold statement of the *A* section, the first modulating to the dominant and the second returning to the tonic, in a structure recalling that of binary dances. But in the aria, instrumental ritornellos introduce and separate the two halves of the *A* section's binary design (ex. 6a shows the opening ritonello and vocal incipit).

'Agitata da fiera procella', Apostolo Zeno set by A. Scarlatti (1721)

A	Agitata da fiera procella	Shaken by a violent storm
	in quel prato languiva una rosa	in that field languished a rose
	che pomposa	so magnificent
	tra le rose sembrava una stella.	among the roses it seemed a star
B	Ma cessato quel nembo fatale	But when that fatal cloud cleared
	ripigliava il suo fasto reale	she returned to her regal pride
	e vestita di por porpora e d'oro	and dressed in purple and gold
	scintillava più altera e più bella.	she shone loftier and more beautiful
A	Agitata ...	Shaken ...

Text	Musical form	Tonal area
(Ritornello)	R_1	i
Agitata ...	A_1	modulates to V
(Ritornello)	R_2	V
Agitata ...	A_2	modulates to i
(Ritornello)	R_1	i
Ma cessato ...	B	modulates to III
Agitata ... (Da capo)		

Compared to Cavalli's relatively syllabic setting of 'Nudo Arciero', 'Agitata' includes many more long melismas on single syllables, one indication of the expansion of the role of music beyond the minimal requirements of the text. The shorter *B* section, which moves from a stong cadence on the dominant minor to the relative major, is confined to one complete statement of the text, and includes the inevitable rising sequence on 'altera' as a final gesture before the ritornello returns to the tonic for the da capo (see ex. 6b). Just as the binary dance became the primary component of the Baroque suite, the da capo aria dominated opera and cantata in the 18th century.

Not until the 18th century did Rameau and other French composers include da capo arias (which they called *ariettes*) along with the binary and rondo forms (*A–B–A–C–A*) Lully had favoured. The vocal rondo is found beyond opera and outside France as well, for example among Purcell's songs ('I attempt from love's sickness'). French composers often employed the rondo not only for vocal music, but also for instrumental dances (for keyboard, lute, melody instrument, or larger ensemble) in which the opening (*A*) section was termed the *rondeau* and the contrasting sections

Ex. 6

A. Scarlatti: 'Agitata da fiera procella', *La Griselda*, Act II

(a)   bars 1–11

(B, C, . . .), the *couplets*. The minuet was especially likely to be *en rondeau*, but other dances were also cast in that form. The brief 'Rondeau-gayement', a minuet from François Couperin's *Huitième Ordre* (1716–17), is typical: the *couplets* cadence on non-tonic harmonies and are of differing lengths. The same suite contains a massive 'Passacaille' in rondo form, with eight sharply contrasted *couplets*, illustrating just how far this simple idea could be extended and what diverse characters it could assume within a single suite.

Ex. 6(b)

bars 88 – 94

The ground bass

Couperin used the term *passacaille* to refer to a piece in rondo form, while the Italians and others meant by passacaglia a piece constructed over a four-note descending bass (or an elaboration of that pattern); this terminological complexity is typical of Baroque music from different countries, periods, or genres. The ground bass (of which the Italian passacaglia is an example) was employed by Baroque composers of many nationalities in both vocal and instrumental music. When each repetition of the bass supports a new stanza of the poem, the resulting form is a strophic variation: strophic because each stanza is set to the same bass or harmonic progression, but varied because the vocal line in each stanza is new. Monteverdi's setting of 'Possente spirto', the aria in which Orpheus pleads with Charon for transport across the river Styx, is a strophic variation in which the instrumentation and Orpheus' melodic line vary substantially from stanza to stanza.

Shorter grounds were also common, but of course did not support an entire stanza of poetry. Cavalli's 'Nudo Arciero' (ex. 5) is entirely constructed over a four-measure ostinato, which occasionally modulates to the dominant or the relative major. Cavalli was particularly noted for his laments, constructed over the descending passacaglia bass (through the interval of a perfect fourth, for example, *A–G–F–E*). That particular bass pattern became so closely associated with the lament context that Bach could use it in the *Capriccio sopra la lontananza del suo fratello dilettissimo* (Capriccio on the Departure of his Most Beloved Brother, BWV992) for keyboard in the expectation that the performer and listener would grasp immediately the emotion being expressed. Purcell made especially frequent use of the lament (for example in 'When I am laid in earth', from *Dido and Aeneas*) and other ground bass patterns in both vocal and instrumental music.

Composers' use of ostinato basses reflects a long tradition of improvising sets of variations over borrowed melodies or harmonic progressions, described in instrumental tutors from the end of the 16th century; in that tradition Christopher Simpson and other English composers wrote 'divisions' for viola da gamba. Frescobaldi's *Partita sopra l'aria della Romanesca* for keyboard is similar, in that repetitions of the traditional Romanesca pattern support successive variations. As in Bach's *Goldberg Variations* (BWV988), the bass line is not necessarily restated explicitly in each section; only the basic harmonic progression is repeated. In the *Goldberg Variations*, each statement of the harmonic progression supports a binary form articulated by movement away from and back to the tonic, another example of a particular combination of two independent compositional principles, those of variation over a ground and binary form.

Cantus-firmus structures

Related to the melodic ground bass is the *cantus firmus*: a borrowed melodic line employed to support a set of variations, but often placed in the middle of the texture

Ex. 7
Scheidt: *Jesus Christus unser Heiland*

(a)

Chorale

Je - sus Chri - stus, un-ser Hei - land, der von uns den Got-tes-zorn ____

wandt, durch das bit-tre Lei-den sein ____ half er uns ____ aus der Höl - le Pein.

(b)

Verse 3

bars 1 - 6

cantus firmus

Verse 4

bars 1 - 5

cantus firmus 4' (sounds an octave higher)

Verse 5

bars 1 - 3

cantus firmus

(c)

Verse 1

bars 1 - 7

rather than in the bass. One thinks first of sets of chorale variations by such 17th-century organists as Sweelinck and Pachelbel. Samuel Scheidt, a pupil of Sweelinck, included sets of variations on chorale melodies and Gregorian chant in his *Tabulatura nova* (1624). *Jesus Christus unser Heiland* (to be played during Communion) begins with a chorale motet, to which we will turn in a moment, but most of the variations state the chorale tune in long notes around which the other voices weave more active material (see exx. 7a and b). Here the principle of design is to vary the number and character of the contrapuntal parts added to each repetition of the *cantus firmus*, and to vary the position of the *cantus firmus* in the texture, both practices inherited from Renaissance vocal music; the freely composed parts often make reference to the *cantus firmus*. Sweelinck's and Scheidt's variations on tunes such as 'Est-ce Mars', in which the borrowed melody moves from voice to voice of the keyboard texture, constitute a secular parallel to the chorale variations for organ.

These composed variations stem from a tradition of improvisation among organists. That is the spirit in which one should regard Cabezón's Magnificat verses, for example – they were models for what the organist should play rather than pieces to be reproduced as they stand. Descriptions of trials that applicants for organ posts in Hamburg and elsewhere had to face include similar exercises in improvisation. Such *cantus firmus* structures are not confined to instrumental music, nor to strict variation forms: in his *Vespers* of 1610 Monteverdi assigned the *cantus firmus* (in this case a psalm tone) to one of the voice parts in each section of the work; around the psalm tone he constructed settings of the Vespers psalms for as many as ten voices divided into two choirs. In the 'Sonata sopra Sancta Maria' from the same collection the sopranos sing the *cantus firmus* while pairs of instruments play virtuosic dialogues around them.

Imitative contrapuntal compositions

Another prominent use of the chorale tune in 17th-century Germany treated each of its phrases in points of imitation, as in the opening two sections of Scheidt's *Jesus Christus unser Heiland*. In contrast to its role in the verses 3 to 5 (ex. 7b), the borrowed melody here becomes indistinguishable from the rest of the texture (ex. 7c). Bach and other 18th-century organists drew on both improvisatory traditions

Ex. 8
J. S. Bach: *The Well-Tempered Clavier, II*, Fugue in E major

(a)

bars 1 - 9

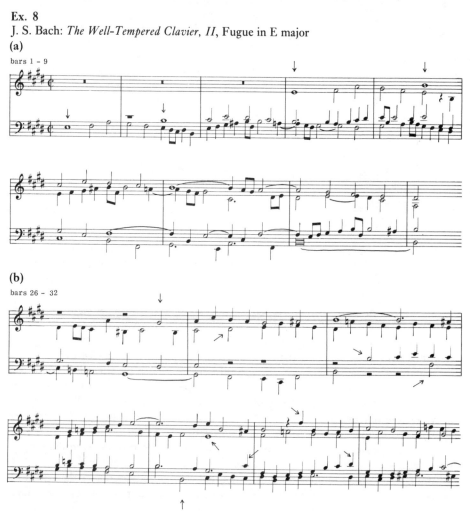

(b)

bars 26 - 32

(the *cantus firmus*-variation and the chorale motet) in their chorale-based compositions for organ. Of course, some contrapuntal pieces have no borrowed material at all: the fugue is the most obvious example and Bach the composer whose works are of greatest interest. He preserved the German *gearbeitet* (literally, worked), or serious style even as his contemporaries were abandoning such counterpoint in favour of simpler, treble-dominated textures. The fugue is more a procedure than a formal plan: one can expect each voice to enter with a version of the subject on the tonic or the dominant, but after the exposition the course of a fugue cannot be predicted in detail. In the E major fugue from the second volume of *The Well-tempered Clavier* the four voices enter without interruption, and this short exposition ends on the dominant after a mere nine measures (see ex. 8a).

The interest of the rest of the piece lies in observing the clever constructions the composer invents by changing the time interval between the subject and its imitation; perhaps inverting the subject; changing the pitch interval at which the imitation occurs; or otherwise manipulating the subject. Later in the same fugue, for example, Bach imitates the subject after one- or even half-measure intervals, reduces its note values, and inverts it against the unaltered version (see ex. 8b).

Bach's use of cut time in this particular piece and its strict limitation to material drawn from the opening measures recall the ricercares of Froberger and other 17th-century organists: the 'white notes' at the outset alert one to expect an especially serious and rigorous treatment, in fact an old-fashioned treatment. Certainly a long tradition precedes Bach's fugues; similar contrapuntal procedures are to be found in the variation canzona, the ricercare, Spanish tiento, the English fantasia and Scheidt's *Jesus Christus*. The canzona and English fantasia, for keyboard or ensemble, tend to be constructed of sections delineated by means of textural and thematic, as well as metre changes; but at least some of the sections are ordinarily quite contrapuntal, if not fugal.

'Stilo phantastico'

Having briefly surveyed binary, ternary, rondo, ground bass, *cantus firmus*, and fugal constructions, we turn now to the 'freely' composed instrumental pieces: for example, Frescobaldi's toccatas, Louis Couperin's unmeasured preludes, and C. P. E. Bach's fantasias. According to C. P. E. Bach, fantasias are free compositions because the composer or performer is constrained not by melody or text, but only by harmonic considerations. Indeed in the *Essay on the True Art of Playing Keyboard Instruments* (1753) he gives a set of instructions for inventing a fantasia in which one begins by notating a figured bass to serve as a harmonic plan. Although this harmonic plan may not be obvious on first hearing and the modulations may be abrupt, even the strangest of his fantasias exhibits a certain harmonic logic. The unmeasured preludes of the French keyboard and lute composers are similar: Louis Couperin's short prelude in A minor is an elaboration of a very straightforward progression through the dominant and the relative major in that key (see ex. 9). The notation in whole notes (preserved in this modern edition) leaves the player free to make his way without metric constraint from one chord to another, although sequentially repeated melodic fragments begin to emerge after a few playings or hearings and tend to regularize even these 'unmeasured' compositions.

The *Intonazioni* of Giovanni and Andrea Gabrieli have been shown to be based on psalm tones, and a few of Frescobaldi's toccatas may respond to a similar analysis,

Ex. 9
Louis Couperin: *Prélude en la mineur*

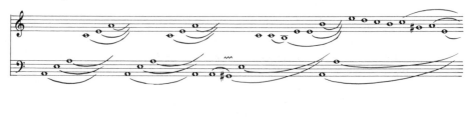

but in general the toccatas are free of borrowed material. In the prefaces to his volumes of toccatas (1615, 1627) Frescobaldi suggests that the performer may conclude at any convenient cadence. Such an instruction is a further reminder of the improvisatory tradition in which organists ordinarily functioned, partly out of their need to fill the church with sound to cover specific actions, and to stop when those actions were completed.

Some of Louis Couperin's preludes contain measured, contrapuntal material framed by two unmeasured sections; the toccatas and preludes of Froberger, Buxtehude, and Bach consist of increasingly lengthy sections in similarly contrasted styles, reminiscent of the alternation between recitative and aria in vocal music. Thus the section marked 'con discrezione' from the Toccata in D major (BWV912) modulates, as do many recitatives, from the close of the previous section in F-sharp minor toward the D major of the final fugue. Its elaborate and erratic melody is supported by some startling and dramatically expressive harmonic progressions; the course of the section is much less predictable than that of the ensuing fugue. Another example of such declamatory instrumental writing forms the middle movement of Vivaldi's concerto for violin and strings:

Ex. 10
Vivaldi: Concerto for violin and strings (RV208, second movement)

Such dramatic passages encourage us to recall Lippius's suggestion that one imagine an appropriate text in order to compose instrumental music; more generally they reflect the degree to which instrumental and vocal music remained closely intertwined even in the 18th century.

The Church: concertato style

One of the most important principles of Baroque music is that of concertato style, in which vocal and instrumental forces are combined and contrasted. The origins of the concertato style are in the polychoral motets of Andrea and Giovanni Gabrieli and in the development of the *basso continuo* in the works of composers such as Viadana around the beginning of the 17th century. The polychoral motet progressed by means of contrast between differently constituted and physically separated choirs of voices (*cori spezzati*), which might be doubled or replaced by instruments. Often the choirs represented different pitch registers. Besides juxtaposing the separate and merged choirs, changes of metre and of texture (contrapuntal *v.* homophonic) delineated sections of such motets; particularly common was the use of a recurring 'Alleluia' in triple metre. Gradually, the choirs began to be contrasted not only in register and by means of specific assigment to different instrumental forces, but also by means of a greater virtuosity in some parts, assigned to the *coro favorito*, or soloists, accompanied by the *basso continuo*. Gabrieli's *In ecclesiis* (published in 1615 just after the composer's death), combines various of these elements: scored for a four-voice *coro favorito*, a *cappella* (or choir) of four parts, and a six-part instrumental ensemble, the motet is built in several sections for one or two voices with *continuo*, separated by 'Alleluia' refrains for soloists and the choir, an instrumental sinfonia, and a final section for the entire ensemble. In a few late works Gabrieli even abandoned the idea of separate choirs in favour of freer combinations of small groups of voices and instruments juxtaposed to each other and to the entire ensemble (*Jubilate Deo* is a good example).

Monteverdi, who began his tenure at S Marco in Venice just as Gabrieli's career was coming to an end, employed and expanded the resources of the concertato style. In some works he and his contemporaries designated the *cappella* or instrumental ensemble as optional (see, for example, the table of contents to *Selva morale e spirituale*, 1641), but contrast of some type remained essential: between soloists and *cappella*, or instruments and voices, or soloists and small ensembles. *Laudate pueri primo* 'a 5 concertato con due Violini' may serve as an example of this mature concertato style. Many concertato motets of this period are composed of varying solo and tutti statements of each line culminating in a final tutti, in no very predictable pattern; but *Laudate pueri* is arranged in a rondo-like form, defined by repetitions of the opening text (always assigned to the two tenors), and by texture and metre changes.

Ground plan of Monteverdi's *Laudate pueri*
(a 5 concertato con due Violini)

Psalm verse	Text incipit		Musical content and scoring	Metre and harmonic goal	
I	Laudate pueri	*A*	tenors	C	I
2	Sit nomen	*B*	sopranos, in dialogue with violins	3	I
I	Laudate pueri	*A*	tenors	C	I
3	A solis ortu	*B*	bass dialogue with violins	3	I
4	Excelsus		sopranos dialogue with bass and violins	3	I
I	Laudate pueri	*A*	tenors	C	IV
5	Quis sicut	*B*	bass and violins dialogue with sopranos; tutti conclusion (without tenors)	3	II
6	Suscitans		tutti, homophonic; violins doubling	C	II
7	Ut collocet	*B*	bass, violins, and sopranos dialogue	3	V
8	Qui habitare		more dialogue, melismatic	C	
	facit sterilem	*B*	tutti conclusion (without tenors)	3	II
	Gloria		tenors (melismatic)	C	V
I	Laudate pueri	*A*			I
	Semper, et in saecula …	*B*	Sopranos, bass, and violins in dialogue with tenors, then tutti	3	IV
	in saecula .. Amen.			C	I

Most of the psalm text is stated in the triple-metre sections, which are similar enough musically to give a feeling of return. ('A solis ortu' for bass and violins is actually a strophic variation of 'Sit nomen'.) The first four triple-metre sections variously juxtapose voices and instruments; the two tenors return several times to the opening text and melodic material, even interrupting their elaborate statement of the 'Gloria Patri'. Yet the text as a whole hardly dictates the form; Monteverdi has repeated the opening phrase almost at will and the large-scale tonal movement to A minor for the last four psalm verses creates some sense of a work in three large sections, in which the Gloria not only concludes the psalm, as expected, but brings us back to the opening harmonic area.

One of Vivaldi's settings of *laudate pueri* makes an instructive comparison. In contrast to Monteverdi's relatively continuous setting, Vivaldi's composition is divided into nine separate movements for soprano and strings (with oboes added at the opening, and a transverse flute in the Gloria). The contrast between successive movements depends on key, metre, and tempo changes. The piece is considerably longer than Monteverdi's, and seems to employ a greater variety of musical styles, although the limitation to one soprano means there cannot be the contrast in vocal register and texture employed by Monteverdi, and still found in other 18th-century sacred music.

Ground plan of Vivaldi's *Laudate pueri*

Verse	*Text*	*Key*	*Metre*	*Tempo*
1	Laudate pueri	G major	2/4	allegro non molto
2	Sit nomen	E minor	3/4	allegro
3	A solis ortu	D major	C	andante
4	Excelus ...	B minor	12/8	larghetto
5	Quis sicut			
6	Suscitans	G major	3/8	allegro molto
7	Ut collocet ...	C major	2/4	allegro
8	Qui habitare			
	Gloria	A minor	C	larghetto
	Sicut erat	G major	2/4	allegro
	Amen	G major	3/8	allegro

In the inner movements, the vocal passages are all in binary form, the two halves framed by three instrumental ritornellos. In most cases the two vocal sections simply state and restate the same psalm verse, although twice two verses are set as one movement. The usual structure is as follows:

Ritornello 1	I
Solo 1	modulates to V or III
Ritornello 2	V or III
Solo 2	modulates back to I
Ritornello 3	I

The second and third ritornellos are much shorter than the first, and are tonally stable. In most cases the first violin simply doubles the voice, but in the Gloria, the flute and voice are treated as joint soloists in a texture similar to that of a trio sonata for two trebles and *basso continuo*; the flute and upper strings provide the ritornellos. The 'Sicut erat' is a considerably shortened version of the opening movement.

The outer movements are more extended, with four tutti and three solo sections. The opening ritornello of the *Laudate pueri* is itself a complete binary form, but subsequent ritornellos in the first movement are considerably shortened (from 27 measures to six, five, and four bars, respectively); the solo sections remain closer to the first one in length (30, 18, and 36 bars). The first two solo sections modulate to the dominant and the supertonic respectively, while the last remains in the tonic, the return to the opening material and key having been prepared by the penultimate ritornello. Throughout, the voice is accompanied by the *basso continuo*, fragments of the ritornello, or is simply doubled by the first violin. We shall see that Vivaldi's solo concertos employ procedures strikingly similar to those in *Laudate pueri*, another reminder of the myriad interconnections between vocal and instrumental music.

The Chamber: sonata, suite, and concerto

Independent instrumental music such as the sinfonias, sonatas, and canzonas composed for ensembles to play in church or home, or as introductions to operas, were at first a varied lot. Salamone Rossi published four collections of sonatas, sinfonias, and dances (1607–22), in which the sinfonias were rather short pieces, often in a binary form defined by strong tonic cadences. The sonatas, all for two violins (or cornetts) and chitarrone, were of two types: short binary pieces, sometimes incorporating metre changes (usually ‖: c :‖: 3. . .c :‖:), or variations constructed over a ground bass pattern, often named in the title (as in *Sonata sopra l'aria della Romanesca*, 1613).

Other composers wrote sonatas more dependent upon the tradition of the polyphonic canzona. The labels sonata and canzona were at first applied somewhat arbitrarily, and to some extent reflect the occupation of the composer rather than anything intrinsic to the music (organists wrote canzonas, virtuoso performers wrote sonatas). Some composers incorporated in their sonatas not only aspects of the traditional canzona style but also of the *stile moderno*, borrowed from the modern concerted madrigal; Dario Castello published two volumes of such sonatas (1621, 1629). Sonata 8 from the second volume, for unspecified treble instrument (probably cornett or violin), bassoon or bass violin, and organ or harpsichord (for the continuo), reflects elements of both the canzona-tradition and the modern style (see ex. 11). The piece consists of several sections marked by changes of metre, tempo, harmonic goal, and melodic material. It has many similarities to the canzona: the opening rhythm (♩ ♫), the imitative texture of many sections, the recapitulation of the opening material at the end; but the expressive adagio that forms the third section would not be found in a canzona, nor would the level of virtuosity be as high as it is here. It is important to note that the separate sections do not constitute independent movements in the same sense as do those of a later sonata. Castello's sonatas are better regarded as one-movement pieces in several sections, some of which are quite short and transitional while others are more extended; in Sonata 8 none of the first five sections is harmonically closed.

Ground plan of Sonata 8 by Dario Castello (1629)

Tempo word	Metre	Harmonic goal	Description
Allegro	C	V	traditional canzona-style opening, imitative texture; organ/harpsichord follows or simplifies the lowest part; elided to the following Allegro
Allegro	3	I	each instrument states the opening idea alone, followed by dialogue and tutti
Adagio	C	I	expressive, using vocal 'trillo' and suspensions elided to Presto

Presto	C	III	strong modulation toward the mediant by means of sequences and bass line descending two octaves; elided to following Allegro
Allegro	3	V	solo statements of broken-chord idea followed by duet in parallel or imitative motion; elided to concluding section
Allegro	C	I	shortened restatement of opening section, with a reference to the expressive adagio at the end

Ex. 11
Castello: Sonata 8 (1629)

(a) bars 1 - 4

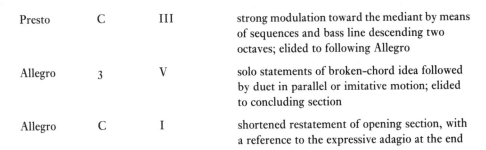

(b)

bars 23 - 8

(c)

bars 57 - 61

(d)

bars 65 – 6

(e)

bars 89 – 92

Canzona-style sonatas were probably intended for use in church; the variation sonatas and early binary sonatas of Rossi and others were included in publications with a secular cast (they might include dances, or secular vocal music, for example). The well-known church sonatas of Corelli derive from the former tradition; by the 1670s when he began to publish sets of sonatas, some of the sections had begun to stand alone as independent movements, although he still employed quite short, 'transitional' adagio sections similar to those of Castello. (The middle 'movement' of Bach's third Brandenburg Concerto is similarly transitional: in the score it consists of only two chords, often expanded upon by performers.) Sonata 5 from Corelli's first published volume consists, for example, of an opening Grave in triple metre, which is harmonically open (cadencing on V of vi) and serves to introduce an imitative Allegro in duple metre. The final movement is an Allegro in 6/8, certainly a *giga* although not so-called. But the middle 'movement' is a series of short passages, contrasting in metre, texture and tempo. The overall form is common enough (four movements, slow–fast–slow–fast), but the third movement is reminiscent of Castello's short Adagio-presto in Sonata 8.

The terms *da chiesa* and *da camera*, applied to publications in Italy from the 1670s onward, are a bit confusing; by the time the terms were in common use the two genres were becoming more and more closely related. In Italy the *sonata da camera* hardly exists as a multi-movement piece before Corelli, who meant by it a collection of binary dances, sometimes preceded by an introductory movement, and occasionally including slow movements labelled only with tempo words. (Earlier the term was applied more often to single binary movements.) Before Corelli's time, English and German composers were more likely than Italians to group more than two dances together to form suites. The *sonata da chiesa*, however, had a long history in the canzona-style sonata already described and by mid-17th century usually included dance-like movements.

In the sonata form 1700 to 1750 there are not startling innovations, but a continuation and consolidation of the traditions inherited from Corelli and his predecessors. Dances continued to be represented, mingling with non-dance binary and rondo movements. Leclair, for example, used a minuet with variations to conclude his Sonata in E Minor (op. 9 no. 2, 1743), whose other movements are Andante, Allemanda, and Sarabanda. Fast imitative movements continue to be found, ordinarily as the second of four parts. Thus Bach's sonatas for violin and harpsichord are almost always in four movements (slow–fast–slow–fast); a few of the slow ones are still 'transitional' (harmonically open); binary form is common, even in imitative movements; and dances are not absent, although they may not be explicitly labelled as such.

Throughout the Baroque period, the French composed dances for soloists or ensembles; when they were organized in suites by the composer or publisher (which was not always the case) the content was not entirely predictable, but an allemande, one or more courantes, perhaps a gigue and a sarabande were typically included and an unmeasured prelude might serve as introduction. One source for this selection of dances may lie in the *ballets de cour*, the standard dramatic entertainment at the French Court from the late 16th century. François Couperin and other French composers at the beginning of the 18th-century expanded the suite (Couperin called his suites *ordres*), including many character pieces not directly related to the dance; but even those suites often begin with the traditional allemande and courante. In one collection (*Les Nations*, 1727) Couperin even went so far as to graft entire dance suites onto previously composed Italianate sonatas. However, it was the 17th-century Germans, in the main, who systematized the suite as we find it in the works of Bach (who in some cases used the term *Partita*). Froberger, whose allemande was cited as an example of binary form, left two autograph manuscripts (1649, 1656) in which sets of dances are clearly arranged allemande–courante–sarabande, with a gigue after the allemande in the later manuscript. When a volume of his suites was published at the end of the century (*c*1697), the Amsterdam publisher Pierre Mortier placed the dances 'in a better order', with the gigue at the end. That is the order we find in most 18th-century suites, for solo instrument, small ensemble, and even for orchestra. Other dances may be included, usually between the sarabande and the gigue, but the position of the main dances is seldom disturbed. (This order was so common that the odd position of the 'extra' dances in printed sources for two of Bach's keyboard partitas has been questioned.)

Another model for the suite should be mentioned, however briefly: it derived from the dances in Lully's operas, which were transferred to keyboard, or to the orchestra outside the opera house, as in the orchestral suites of Bach and Telemann. In the *Ouverture in the French Style* (BWV831) Bach adopted that model, beginning with a typical French opera overture, and continuing with a courante, paired gavottes and passepieds, sarabande, two bourrés, a gigue, and the 'echo'.

The individual dances of Baroque suites have recognizably distinct characters: the allemande a stately or sometimes a more tender introduction; the rhythmically complex French courante in triple metre with many hemiolas (see Bach's B minor French suite, BWV814) or a livelier and rhythmically more straightforward Italian corrente (see Bach's G major French suite, BWV816); the triple-metre sarabande slower and expressive; the gigue a lively piece in compound duple metre. Many authors discuss the character of the individual dances: Quantz (1752) and Mattheson (1739) give extended descriptions, valid for the dances they knew but sometimes surprising when applied to dances too far removed in time or place.

The orchestral suite in which soloists were featured, as well as the German ensemble sonata (adopted by Bach in Brandenburg 3) are among the genres important to the growth of the Baroque concerto. The appreciation of contrast between larger and smaller ensembles and the effect of reinforcing and doubling some sections of a piece have already been noted in the context of polychoral music and the development of the concertato style. Moreover, the trio sonatas of Corelli were apparently played on occasion by large ensembles which reinforced the trio at specified points in the work, a reminder of the 'optional ripieno' employed by Monteverdi and others. But the form of Corelli's or Handel's *concerti grossi* is not particularly standardized. As the solo concerto grew in importance, the formal design, especially that of the first movement, became more predictable. What one finds in the solo concertos of Vivaldi, for example, is a fairly standard three-movement design, in which a ritornello form similar to that already described in the opening movement of *Laudate pueri* is employed in the first movement.

Vivaldi's concerto for violin and strings (RV208), the middle movement of which has already been cited (ex. 10), provides a good illustration of a typical first-movement concerto form in which four solo sections alternate with five ritornellos.

Ground plan of Vivaldi's concerto for violin and strings, RV208, first movement

Section	Harmonic goal	Length in measures	Description
Ritornello 1	I	26.0	
Solo 1	V	33.0	figuration includes double stops and broken chords
Ritornello 2	I	5.5	
Solo 2	ii	17.5	figuration more scalewise
Ritornello 3	vi	12.5	
Solo 3	iii	19.0	triplet figuration
Ritornello 4	I	6.5	nearly identical to R2
Solo 4	V	16.5	figuration scalewise and parallel thirds, plus cadenza
Ritornello 5	I	5.0	unison statement of final idea from Ritornello 1

The opening ritornello provides all of the material used in the other tutti sections; the solo sections are primarily based on figuration idiomatic to the violin, but no two are the same (see ex. 12). The ritornellos, harmonically stable units in many concertos, are all modulatory here; but in every other respect comparison of this movement with the opening movement of the same composer's *Laudate pueri* bears witness to the similarity between ritornello constructions in vocal and instrumental music.

Ex. 12
Vivaldi: Concerto for violin and strings (RV208, first movement)

(a)

(b)

Bach made major contributions to the Baroque concerto, not only in the six Brandenburg Concertos (BWV1046–51), but in the triple concerto for violin, flute and harpsichord (BWV1044), the violin concertos (BWV1041–3) and in many organ and harpsichord transcriptions of his own concertos and those of other composers (among them concerto RV208, transcribed for organ as BWV594 in C major). In addition, the concerto idea is evident in works in other genres: for example, the prelude to the fifth Partita (BWV829) is in essence a concerto for solo keyboard, whose ritornello alternates with 'solo' sections exactly as one would expect from a composer with an intimate knowledge of Vivaldi's concertos. The *Concerto in the Italian Style* (BWV971) is an original work for solo harpsichord parallel to Bach's keyboard transcriptions of pre-existent concertos.

The Theatre: opera and its influences on chamber and church music

We have noted already the use of various aria forms in Baroque opera, from strophic and strophic variation to da capo form, and the dominance of the latter in the 18th century; but one should be aware in addition that late Baroque *opera seria* became an extremely predictable genre in the hands of Hasse and his contemporaries, who often set librettos by Metastasio. The aspect of particular interest in terms of form is the strict alternation of recitative and aria throughout the opera. Since the French had continued to notate their recitatives in shifting metres and to employ shorter airs in binary and rondo form, their 18th-century *tragédies lyriques* differed markedly from the Italian 'number' operas, exhibiting greater continuity and a less obvious distinction between recitative and aria. Thus Goldoni claimed in his memoirs (1787) not to have heard a single aria on his first visit to the Académie Royale de Musique in Paris (he had moved there in 1762); he must also have been taken aback by the attention devoted to chorus and dance in the French *tragédies*, as they were not important elements of Italian opera during his career.

The overtures differed as well in France and Italy. That to Scarlatti's *La Griselda* (HAM no. 259) is typical of the Italian opera overture, arranged in three parts (fast–slow–fast), with trumpets joining strings and oboes in the fast sections. Neither of the first two sections is harmonically closed, but the final Presto is a binary gigue modulating to the dominant at its mid point. This form is a departure from that typical in mid-17th-century Venetian opera, for example that for Cavalli's *Scipione Africano* (1664), where a slow duple section prepares a faster, triple-metre conclusion. Some of those opera sinfonias were indistinguishable from contemporary canzonas and sonatas.

The overture style adopted by Lully and used by Rameau in his earlier operas developed from the earlier Venetian pattern. For example, in the overture to *Castor et Pollux* (1737), a dotted opening section in duple metre is followed by a faster section in triple metre (see ex. 13). In *Castor* the duple material returns at the end, to create a three-part form (*A–B–A*). This French overture style was adopted by many composers for purposes other than introducing an opera, for example by Bach in the prelude to the keyboard Partita in D (BWV828).

Opera was certainly one of the most important elements in the music of the Baroque. Its styles and forms we have already noted had an effect on the concerto, but the penetration of operatic elements into the cantata and motet is also marked.

Ex. 13
Rameau: Overture to *Castor et Pollux*

(a)

bars 1 - 5

(b)

bars 19 - 23

In France, the *grands motets* performed not only for Louis XIV at Mass but in secular surroundings as well (at the Concerts Spirituels in Paris from 1725, on days when no opera was presented) were often composed and performed by individuals also active in the realm of opera. Lully, for example, employed instrumental *symphonies* to demarcate the large structural divisions of his motets in rondo-fashion, much as in his operas; moreover, the audience at the Paris concerts was attracted by the opportunity to hear favourite performers from the opera. The contrast of recitative, solo arioso, and choral forces in these motets is in the concertato tradition examined above.

The cantatas of Bach present a compendium of operatic elements, as demonstrated by *Nun komm der heiden Heiland* (BWV61, 1714). The opening movement cleverly combines the French overture with a statement of the chorale material (see ex. 14). A recitative for the tenor prepares his da capo aria, in which unison strings provide the accompaniment (one of the standard dispositions in Italian opera). The recitative itself turns into an 'arioso' passage in a regular metre (Cavalli had often made such transitions). An accompanied recitative for the bass prepares the da capo aria for soprano (such recitatives had become more and more common in opera). The soprano is accompanied only by continuo, and the first section of that aria is built over a modulating ground bass. Both the arias incorporate the usual instrumental ritornellos; the soprano aria has in addition a *motto* beginning, in which the inicipit is sung, and then repeated (just as in Cavalli's 'Nudo arciero'). Most of the Amen is constructed over a 'walking' bass; the lower strings double the choir, the first violin plays its own elaborate melody, and the sopranos sing fragments of another chorale tune. The whole cantata reflects not only 17th- and early 18th-century operatic developments, but the operation of concertato principles already evident in the sacred and secular music of Monteverdi.

Ex. 14
J. S. Bach: *Nun komm der heiden Heiland*

(a)

bars 1 – 9

(b)

bars 33 – 40

Some conclusions

It is unfortunate but true that the terminology employed by composers, publishers, and observers was far from consistent over 150 years in several countries. The term 'concerto' early in the 17th century might mean music for voices or instruments, soloists or ensembles, only some of which juxtaposed those elements in a way one might expect, knowing the concertos of Vivaldi. The term 'aria' which we would ordinarily expect to apply to a solo vocal piece in opera or cantata (or even in one of Bach's Passions), was used by Uccellini to designate variation sonatas for strings and continuo (probably to avoid confusion with his many church sonatas, which were not yet distinguished by the term *da chiesa*), and by G. M. Bononcini as a name for a binary piece in place of the more usual allemande in his suites of dances, the preludes to which he called sinfonias. The fantasia, for C. P. E. Bach and some earlier German composers a toccata-like, freely constructed, almost improvisatory piece, was for the Spanish composer Cabezón a serious contrapuntal exercise, and for English composers such as Henry Lawes the introductory movement of an ensemble suite; for his compatriot Byrd it was a kind of instrumental canzona in several sections. One may have expectations based on terminology alone, but it is a good idea to locate terms in time and place as well.

While impressive, orderly and even symmetrical constructions are evident in many large-scale pieces (the first act of Monteverdi's *L'Orfeo*, the larger Magnificat from the *Vespers* of 1610, and Bach's B minor Mass, are all symmetrical constructions in terms of the textures employed; Bach's *Goldberg Variations* and *Art of Fugue* are perhaps too obvious to mention as examples of systematic large-scale arrangements of contrapuntal material), there is also evident in much Baroque music a more relaxed attitude toward formal design. In a set of variations for bassoon and organ continuo (1638), Bartolomeo de Selma y Salaverde suggested that the bassoonist could end the work after any one of the variations, if only he remembered to warn the organ accompanist in advance. In two sonatas by Agostino Guerrieri (1673), there are opportunities for each of the violinists to improvise sections over a bass line provided by the composer, but if they prefer, the can perform the sonatas without these sections. There are many examples in the sonata literature of the 17th century, and as late as Buxtehude, of the designation 'da capo se piace', which implied an optional repeat of the first section of the work. The practice of making extensive changes in operas when they were revived, to allow singers to substitute their favourite arias, or simply to accommodate the work to a new milieu, is well known. It was certainly facilitated by the standardization of the aria in the late 17th and eighteenth centuries, when one bravura piece might do as well as another in a particular dramatic and musical context; but it also reflects a different attitude toward the permanence of a composer's construction than the one to which later composers and performers more readily subscribed. The version of Vivaldi's violin concerto discussed above that was published in his lifetime (op. 7, Amsterdam, *c*1716; RV208a) substitutes for the instrumental recitative a short, straightforward 'Grave' in A major, in which the soloist is accompanied only by the two ripieno violins. Baroque composers re-used their own and others' material in markedly different contexts: Handel is the most notorious example, but the practice was not uncommon and Bach was not immune. Nor as we have shown, was any particular style restricted to one and only one genre: Monteverdi's re-use of the toccata that introduced the opera *L'Orfeo* as the first movement of the *Vespers* is one of the most striking examples of the permeability of the stylistic boundaries described by Brossard and Mattheson.

Sandra Mangsen
University of Western Ontario

III Performing Practice Issues

National Styles

During the century-and-a-half from 1600 to 1750, the concept of national style concerned not only the ways in which composers in the different European countries wrote their music – which was a matter of tradition, of function, of social context, of language and of many other factors – but also its performance and even such matters as instrument building. The period is marked by an increased national stylistic awareness, after the essentially international *lingua franca* of the Renaissance, especially pronounced in the differences between the performing practices favoured in Italy and France. The main objective was an increase in brilliance and expressiveness, the former especially in Italy, as the rise of virtuoso singers and violinists at the beginning of the period shows.

Here we are concerned more with style and performance than with the historical development of genres. The sound of music in any time and place depends on techniques of playing and voice production as well as on the instruments used. During the early Baroque, some of the forms of the genres and performing practices of the late Renaissance persisted: the Venetian polychoral style (and its German counterpart in the works of Schütz) and the well-established English virginal and viol consort idioms, for example, were maintained through the first third of the 17th century and beyond. Church music in particular was conservative.

The principal musical forms of the Baroque era arose in Italy. It was there that the cantata, concerto, sonata, oratorio and opera were conceived and developed. The rise of an autonomous instrumental music also involved the development of violin playing to a higher, more refined level and a rapid spread in the use of the *basso continuo*. It was in the Italian musical idiom that these genres and the performing practices associated with them were first transplanted north of the Alps, as Italian styles swept over Europe in the early 17th century, eventually taking firm hold virtually everywhere except, to some extent, in France.

Italian vocalism reached new heights of expressiveness and virtuosity. Giulio Caccini's preface to his *Le nuove musiche* (1602), expounding an intensely expressive recitative-like style together with virtuoso ornamentation, was enormously influential. Progressively longer excerpts from it were to appear elsewhere, for instance in John Dowland's *A Musicall Banquet* (1610), Marin Mersenne's *Harmonie Universelle* (1636), John Playford's *A Breefe Introduction to the Skill of Musick* (1654) and in the unpublished but influential writings of Christoph Bernhard, Schütz's pupil and successor as court *Kapellmeister* in Dresden.

Each country continued to develop its own vocal style, especially France, whose vocalism, based on the special characteristics of the language, belonged to the exclusive domain of Louis XIV and was not shared in other countries; if indeed French singing was generally disparaged outside France, it was because of a lack of familiarity. Italian vocal art continued to serve as the model. The treatise on singing published in 1723 by Pier Francesco Tosi, a much-travelled operatic castrato and teacher, *Opinioni de' cantori antichi e moderni, o sieno Osservazioni sopra il canto figurato (Critiques of singers of the past and present, or observations on florid singing)*, was, like Caccini's, diffused throughout western Europe. (See David Fuller's essay,

p. 417.) No such diffusion was accorded to comparable French works, such as Bénigne de Bacilly's *Remarques curieuses sur l'art de bien chanter* (1668), which is characteristically Gallic in its emphasis on declamation and the unique qualities of the French language, or Michel Pignolet de Montéclair's indispensable *Principes de musique* (1736).

The highly rhetorical and expressive operatic recitative, an outgrowth of solo monody incorporated into cantata and oratorio, found its stylistic counterpart in Italian instrumental music of the early 17th century, such as the sonatas and canzonas of Biagio Marini. The melodic flow characteristic of arias and early Baroque operas, cantatas and oratorios by such men as Cavalli, Carissimi or Cesti was similarly transferred to the instrumental realm. Only in France was there a strong resistance to the Italian style, notwithstanding the paradox of the rise of the Florentine Giambattista Lulli to become Jean-Baptiste Lully, arbiter of French musical taste in the reign of Louis XIV and the progenitor of an operatic genre that dominated in France and exercised some influence in Germany and England. The measured declamation characteristic of French theatre in the age of Corneille and Racine as set to music in the *tragédie lyrique* had little in common with the flamboyant, virtuoso manner of Italian operatic writing. (In France the age of these great 17th-century dramatists has always been known as the French classical period, 'Baroque' having kept its original pejorative sense of bizarre or grotesque until recently.) Lully was also responsible for establishing higher standards of orchestral performance and for introducing the use of the newer varieties of wind instruments, developed in France, into the orchestra. The favourite combination of two oboes and a bassoon, for instance, the typical trio of a minuet, began to appear in his operas from *Alceste* (1674; see Plate 4).

'The style of Italian compositions is piquant, florid, expressive; that of French compositions is natural, flowing, tender', wrote Sébastien de Brossard in his *Diction-naire de musique* (1703). That is how the contrast appeared to a Frenchman. French preference was for music that grew out of dance rather than song and emphasized characteristic rhythmic detail. Solo lute and harpsichord music, with its elaborate chord figurations to sustain the evanescent sound, was cultivated more assiduously in France than in Italy after the middle of the 17th century. The French predilection for literary and visual associations in music led to the production of many character pieces, *hommages* and *tombeaux*, and, at the very least, works with fanciful titles, characterized by richly decorated surfaces and subtle changes of sonority.

While notated dotted rhythms seem to have been performed somewhat freely virtually everywhere, with the precise value accorded the dotted note being varied to suit the intended mood or 'affect', there was a tendency in France to go still further. French musicians habitually introduced dotted rhythms in successions of conjunct notes, usually quavers, even where the notation did not so indicate. This practice may well have been a survival of some medieval preference for *tempus perfectum*. It was recorded in treatises of the 16th century from various countries (Italy, Spain, Switzerland). Frescobaldi's preface to his *Primo libro di toccate et partite* (1615) prescribes playing quavers unequally only where they are pitted against semiquavers in the other hand. This may have been an idiosyncratic preference; certainly there is no evidence of the widespread use of *notes inégales* in Italian performing practice of the Baroque. French treatises of the later 18th century codify the subject in considerable detail, indicating that a variety of types of *notes inégales* were used; they prescribe the metres and dances to which each was applied or where *notes égales* might be required even when they are not indicated.

No single aspect of Baroque performance distinguished more sharply between French and Italian styles than ornamentation. French tables of ornaments abound, giving precise explications of the many symbols, often confusing and inconsistent, found in keyboard music especially, whilst in other instrumental and vocal music a simple + served to indicate that some embellishment at the performer's option was needed. In his *Pièces de clavecin* (1689) D'Anglebert offered a table of no less than 29 such *agréments* (see p. 431). These were applied in the main to individual notes rather than to larger musical units. A passing note or changing note is added, delayed, or transformed into something more complex, to heighten the rhythmical effect and apply rich surface decoration. The analogy with the visual and decorative arts of the period is obvious. Ornaments in harpsichord music, in particular, serve as adornments in the prevailing style and only rarely as a means of sustaining the instrument's sound.

In the French style, slow movements were written out more completely. To present an Adagio in skeletal form as a sequence of disjunct semibreves and minims, as in a Corelli sonata, would have been unthinkable for his French contemporaries. Players of French music were not required or expected to add the connective tissue of melodic figuration to slow movements as in Italian music. In French vocal music, where the da capo aria is rare, the opportunity for singing great *passaggi* hardly arose (it would anyway have contradicted French declamation and aesthetic principles). The cadenza as introduced in Neapolitan opera never made its way in France, where the embellishment of individual notes through appoggiaturas, passing- and changing-notes predominated, without a final burst of virtuosity. Castrato singers, with their endless interpolations of florid decoration, were foreign to French music, secular and sacred alike. Indeed, except as exotic imports for use in Italian opera seasons, castratos were also unknown to the indigenous English and German music theatre.

The enthusiasm of the French for Lully's style of opera was not quite monolithic. Only 15 years after the composer had died, at the pinnacle of his fame and power, the Abbé Raguenet published his *Parallèle des Italiens et des François* (1702), a remarkable comparative critical essay, passionately advocating the 'modern' Italian operatic style and decrying the French 'classical' opera of Lully and his school. It attracted wide attention, was soon translated into English and twice into German later in the century. Thus began a controversy that raged in France in different forms far beyond the close of the Baroque, up to the time of Gluck and Piccinni's rivalry in the 1770s and even later. The Lully party did not lack defenders. Ripostes to Raguenet followed in due course from the pen of an aristocratic connoisseur, Le Cerf de La Viéville, Seigneur de la Freneuse. The Abbé, in turn, produced his rebuttal, leading to surrebuttal, rejoinder and further responses.

French composers not only prescribed ornamentation but also demanded a more literal adherence to the text. François Couperin, in the preface to his third book of harpsichord pieces (1722), lays down the law:

> I am always surprised, after the pains that I have taken to indicate the ornaments appropriate to my pieces ... to hear persons who have learnt them without heeding my instructions. Such carelessness is unpardonable, all the more as it is no arbitrary matter to put in such ornaments as one wishes. Therefore I declare that my pieces must be

performed just as I have written them and that they will never make much of an impression on persons of genuine taste unless all my markings are observed to the letter....

This kind of textual fidelity was foreign to Italian composers: witness the various ornamented versions of Corelli's op. 5 sonatas that have come down to us as performed by such 18th-century violinists as Geminiani. The Amsterdam publisher Roger issued an edition with embellished slow movements, completely realized versions of the skeletal originals, claimed to be in the composer's own hand (though lacking in his own original edition).

Only relatively late in the Baroque, by the time of Couperin and Rameau, did Italian influences begin to make inroads on the French style. Corellian sonata types, the Italian forms of gigue, the use of Italian tempo markings such as Andante: all were symptomatic of a certain limited process of synthesis that could be summed up in Couperin's own title for his *Nouveaux concerts* (1724), *Les goûts réunis*. Jean-Philippe Rameau went to Italy at the age of 18. 'He remained there only a short time, and was later sorry not to have sojourned longer in Italy where, he used to say, (his musical) taste would have been made perfect' (*Mercure de France*, October 1764). Lesser French masters too tried to blend the Italian and French styles. Jean Baptiste Senaillé, for instance, son of a musician of the Lully school, began composing violin sonatas in 1710, publishing five books before his death in 1730. He joined that most French of ensembles, the Vingt-quatre Violons du Roi, in 1713, but during a break 'he spent some time in Italy and learnt enough of the ultramontane style to blend it skilfully with very French melody' (*Mercure de France*, June 1738). Similar changes of style can be seen in the music of many French composers during the first half of the 18th century, among them the leading violinist, Jean-Marie Leclair *l'aîné*, who studied under Italian musicians. There was no counterpart to this in Italy; the Italian style had a potential and a future that the French did not.

Among the outlying countries of Europe, Britain, thanks to its strong traditions, maintained a certain independence of both styles. The italianization of the English madrigal in the late 16th century through anthologies such as Nicholas Yonge's *Musica transalpina* (1588), and the eminence of the Ferraboscos in the masque and the fantasia, enriched native forms without extinguishing them. Later infiltrations by Italian and French elements were absorbed without impairing the essential English quality. Thus, for instance, the strong French influence introduced at the Restoration was quickly accommodated in the theatre and even the church music of Purcell and Blow, although the flavour of the music remains strongly English. Neither did such French stylistic invasions obliterate the Italian elements already assimilated. In the 18th century the Italian influence was dominant, especially during the heyday of opera up to the 1730s. Curiously, German immigrants like Handel and Pepusch, and later C. F. Abel and J. C. Bach, were as much reponsible for maintaining Italian genres and styles and offering them to the English taste as were such natives as Geminiani or Bononcini. As regards performing practice, the influence of Italian opera singers and composers was limited, if only because their viruoso style could hardly have been widely imitated. For all the wonderment with which the fabled castratos were regarded, their feats of execution could not serve as models for native singers; in any case, their extravagant elaboration was unsuited to English-language texts.

The interpenetration of the Italian and French styles of performance in other countries is still the subject of debate. Each exemplified distinct techniques. It was German musicians most of all who attempted to combine French and Italian performing styles and forms of composition. Examples of their eclecticism in this respect are legion: a few, notably Telemann, ventured further afield to incorporate borrowings from Slavonic folk traditions.

It was no doubt thanks to Conradi and Kusser's introduction of elements of French operatic style in the German opera at Hamburg, in particular the Lullian overture, that the young Handel adopted this type of introductory movement. Georg Muffat's seminal forewords to his volumes of French-type dances (1695–8) and concertos in Lullian and Corellian styles (1701) discussed both with explicit directions for their correct performance as regards bowings, tempo, ornaments and orchestra discipline. Muffat's personal contact with both Lully and Corelli warranted the authenticity of his instructions – printed in Latin, German, Italian and French to make them widely accessible. (The Italian bowings are better calculated to achieve a lyrical grace, while the French produce more crisply defined rhythms.) These prefaces were surely known to Handel and his German contemporaries. How far Muffat's words spread south of the Alps is another matter. When in Rome Handel prefaced his 1707 oratorio *Il trionfo del Tempo e del Disinganno* with a French-type overture, as distinguished a musician as Corelli, who led the orchestra, allegedly complained that 'this music is in the French style, which I do not understand'. Handel obligingly substituted an Italian-type sinfonia. Italy's stylistic dominance made unnecessary its musicians' familiarity with other practices.

J. S. Bach's 'English' suites have come down to us only in pupils' copies. No. 4 in F (BWV809) is headed by a 'Prélude', unmistakably in the form of a Vivaldi-type concerto movement despite its French title. Three manuscripts give it the quaint French tempo marking of 'vitement'. In three sources the 15 semiquavers of the first bar are each surmounted by a vertical stroke, presumably to exclude their being played unequally (a possibility ruled out by the tempo marking alone, according to the precepts of the French treatises). Bach too may have been familiar with the Muffat prefaces. As a young man he had heard French musicians at the Celle court. The only ornament table from his hand is a simplified, condensed version of d'Anglebert's of 1689. Italian ornamentation also abounds in Bach's works, as in the Andante of the familiar *Concerto in the Italian Style* for harpsichord (BMV971). He was an eclectic, determined to extract the best from every worthy source, but the champion electic among German Baroque composers was Telemann. Not only did he produce works in conscious imitation of the two main national styles – Italian concertos and sonatas, French dance suites with Lullian overtures – but he also made good use of his familiarity with Polish folk music gained in the service of a Silesian nobleman. The older chorale-based German traditions of sacred music continued to thrive in the northern, Protestant regions. Handel's brief career in his native Germany did not involve him deeply in this essentially local style. But Bach and Telemann, like numerous minor masters of the period with municipal, church or court appointments, carried on the tradition in a variety of eclectic manners.

Significant changes in the instrumentarium of various nations came about during the 150 years under examination, most of them consolidated in the last quarter of the 17th century. In France there was a flowering of the bass viola da gamba with a magnificent and technically very difficult solo repertory of works by such great virtuoso players as Marais (see Plate 6) and Forqueray. It may be due to another late 17th-century master of the instrument, Sainte-Colombe, that the *basse de viole* acquired a seventh string, sounding *A'*. This larger model was later adopted in Germany where the instrument continued in use to the time of J. S. Bach. Except for the royal bands of violins, string music in France held conservatively to the old consort tradition for the most of the 17th century. Louis Couperin (*d*1661) composed viol consort works in mid-century, M.-A. Charpentier (*d*1704) even later; in England, Purcell was still doing so as late as 1680, although by then the violin family was firmly established in ensemble music. The viols, in fact though still used in Vienna, parts of Germany and the Low Countries into the 18th century, had everywhere progressively yielded ground to the more brilliant and rhythmic violin family, both in solo and ensemble music. To judge by treatises of the early 18th century, the French school was characterized by underlying dance rhythms and more elaborate decorative elements as compared with the freer, more cantabile sound favoured by the Italians with their greater variety of bowings. The lute, enjoying a late flowering in 17th-century France and early 18th-century Germany, acquired still more courses, often as many as 13 or 14, bringing it to its ultimate development.

In woodwind instruments radical changes came about. During the 1670s and 80s the Renaissance models were replaced, largely owing to the inventiveness of French makers. The old one-piece recorder, with a limited compass and a cylindrical bore, which emphasized the strength of the lower rather than the higher register, gave way to a three-piece model. Players could now make minor tuning adjustments, play a greater number of notes and in general perform more brilliantly. The shawm was replaced in the 1670s by the oboe, perhaps invented by Jean Hotteterre, instrument maker to Louis XIV (though possibly it was a French improvement of a German instrument brought back by military bandsmen). The dulcian and its relations were similarly supplanted by the French *basson*, as it was known in Purcell's time, although more conservative German musicians clung to some older types – for instance, a great bass shawm was bought by Buxtehude's church in Lübeck in 1685, a clumsy single-tube instrument twice the length of a bassoon with its folded double tube. The transverse flute went into a decline during the 17th century from which it emerged in the creative and talented hands of the Hotteterre family (see Plate 6).

In the realm of stringed keyboard instruments, national styles were less isolated than was previously believed. One Italian harpsichord maker, Girolamo Zenti, worked for a number of years in London and ended his days in Stockholm, but kept to the classical Italian type of lightly-framed instrument built of Mediterranean cypress or cedar of Lebanon. In France 17th-century builders made harpsichords influenced by either Italian or Flemish prototypes, and even instruments combining features of both. Eventually models derived from the traditions of the Ruckers family of Antwerp, who flourished from the late 16th century to the late 17th, prevailed. It was from such that French 18th-century harpsichords like the Blanchets favoured by Couperin were descended. In England too the Flemish influence eventually triumphed in spite of Zenti's success as harpsichord maker to Charles II. Only in Italy did the harpsichord undergo merely minor modifications. Two-manual harpsichords, widely used in the northern countries, remained rare in Italy, Spain and Portugal. In southern Germany and Austria the Italian model predominated well into the 18th century while in the north it gave way in the 17th to local styles more closely related to the Ruckers but often retaining Italian features.

Rectangular virginals continued to be popular as domestic instruments in the 17th century, with distinctive Italian, Flemish and English models used not only in their home countries but also abroad. Towards the end of the century the wing- or leg-of-mutton-shaped spinet supplanted the virginal.

Clavichords, a German and Scandinavian speciality (see Plate 25), continued to enjoy great popularity long after the close of the Baroque era. It was surely in Germany that the unfretted clavichord, first mentioned in Johann Speth's *Ars Magna Consoni et Dissoni* (1693), was created late in the 17th century. In Italy clavichords seem to have gone largely out of use after the 16th century, and neither English nor French clavichords from the period survive (though they are occasionally mentioned in literature and inventories). But in the Iberian peninsula the clavichord, in its simplest fretted form, flourished long after 1750. Cristofori's invention of a 'harpsichord with *piano* and *forte*' in Florence at the end of the 17th century was followed by similar instruments devised by Schröter and Silbermann in Saxony and Marius in France; but the pianoforte did not come into wide use until after 1750.

In organ building, as in the repertory the instruments served, national styles were most pronounced over the entire period, as they had been and would continue to be. The general adoption of the *Werkprinzip* – the use of separate wind-chests for different departments of the instrument – favoured the instrument's expansion. The typical 16th-century one-manual Italian organ of many ranks of flue pipes plus a *vox humana* or *unda maris* special-effect stop, possibly with a rudimentary octave of pull-down pedals, grew larger, influenced by foreign immigrant builders. In England, many instruments had to be replaced after the Restoration; they did not differ greatly from their predecessors except that they tended to become larger and more complex, often with two and a half or three manuals. By the end of the century reed stops were introduced. Pedals remained a Continental feature until after the close of the period, but the swell-box, introduced in 1712, soon became widespread in England although generally ignored on the Continent until after 1750.

The Baroque period saw the building of magnificent organs and a concurrent flowering of their repertory in northern Europe. The French organ of the late Renaissance was enriched and transformed into the great Baroque instrument of the Couperins and Marchand. The Dutch and North German tradition, exemplified by Schnitger's instruments and those of the Saxon school of Gottfried Silbermann, provided the vehicles for the organ music of Buxtehude and Bach. Iberia produced instruments of highly distinctive tonal qualities with especially pungent reed stops like the *trompeta real*. The Alsatian Silbermann workshop, under both Saxon and French influences, contrived to produce instruments with the virtues of each. Throughout the period small chamber organs were in widespread use for solo and ensemble purposes.

France was more prolific than Italy in the production of treatises on performance. But not surprisingly it was the eclectic Germans who summarized the practices of the Baroque age just after its close, in Quantz's treatise on playing the flute (*Versuch einer Anweisung die Flöte traversiere zu spielen*, 1752), C. P. E Bach's keyboard tutor (*Versuch über die wahre Art das Clavier zu spielen*, 1753) and Leopold Mozart's exposition of violin playing (*Versuch einer gründlichen Violinschule*, 1756), as well as Johann Friedrich Agricola's vocal method (*Anleitung zur Singkunst*, 1757). Each goes well beyond the limited technical instruction suggested by their titles, and collectively they encompass a wide range of performing practices of the late Baroque period. But only in that of Quantz, the best travelled of the group at the time of his writing, are the French and Italian styles expounded and contrasted. He had direct experience of both from the beginning of his professional life, studying in Italy and visiting France and England to broaden his musical understanding and taste; and he was thus able to provide a comprehensive, balanced comparative treatment of the two great national styles as they had developed to the close of the Baroque.

Howard Schott
Charlestown, Massachusetts

Ornamentation

Ornamentation is as necessary to Baroque music as clothing to the human body. A lucky few of us look our best with nothing but a bit of ribbon in our hair, and there are Bach fugues that need only a trill or two to point up the cadences; but in most of the music of this period 'a Deficiency of Ornaments displeases as much as the too great Abundance of them', to quote the celebrated castrato Pier Francesco Tosi.[1] How to repair such a deficiency, how to tell the fitting from the unbecoming, and how to judge when abundance turns into excess are problems that every musician who deals with this music must face, and the reader might with some justification expect to find solutions here. But there are good reasons for attempting something else. Though there is no lack of practical manuals of Baroque ornamentation, the best of them can give no more than a fragmentary view of a subject that is as diverse as the whole range of musical styles and genres to which the ornamentation must be applied. The student is all too easily persuaded that authenticity is a matter of matching every wiggle to the right kind of trill, but the reality is different. There is no direct information at all about vast segments of the repertory – mid-17th-century opera, for example – while some matters that are copiously documented, such as how to play a French trill, remain controversial after years in the glare of musicological research. And even equipped with the requisite knowledge, how can we emulate the singing of someone who had practised the different graces since childhood and for whom their correct placement in a song was so much a matter of second nature that he could use them spontaneously as an expressive resource? How can we learn to improvise cadenzas that will not sound false stylistic notes, when our ears are laden with two hundred years'-worth of music unimaginable in the Baroque era?

Nevertheless, the naked score must somehow be fashionably clothed, and in order to do this we need a clear notion not only of the gulf that separates us from the old musicians and the old conditions of performance, but also of the strengths and weaknesses of our historical knowledge. Instead, therefore, of telling the reader 'how to do it', this essay will attempt to convey a sense of what it was like to be there, caught up in the concerns of a living musician of the era, by viewing one segment of it – early 18th-century Italian singing – through the eyes of someone for whom ornamentation was bread-and-butter, who saw the issues at close range, and for whom what seem to us mere blips on the evolutionary continuum were revolutionary reversals of taste. For the rest, we shall cast a glance over the sources, pointing out especially the gaps and, through a sampling of the information that *has* survived, giving some idea of the variety of Baroque ornament.

Our singer is Tosi, an old man when his book was published in 1723. This was a brilliant year for music. Bach was entering upon his work at Leipzig, Handel was at the peak of his achievement in heroic opera, Rameau had just finished his revolutionary treatise on harmony, and Vivaldi was composing two concertos a month. But for Tosi, the golden years were in the past. Looking back over his career, he identified at least four layers of compositional style and three of performance in Italian vocal music. It is not always easy to unravel his chronology. His first music teacher (perhaps his father) told him 'that very *anciently* the Stile of the Singers was insupportable, by reason of the number of *Passages* and *Divisions* [ornamental passages of quick notes sung to one syllable] in their *Cadences* [cadenzas], that never were at an end ... and were always the same' (p. 130). These became at last so 'odious' that they were banished. In another place Tosi described a vice of the *professori antichissimi*, who stopped in their airs 'at every second and fourth, and on all the sevenths and sixths of the Bass' (i.e. at every dissonance) to make embellishments (p. 100). This was disapproved 'over fifty years ago' by an otherwise unknown theorist, 'Rivani (detto Ciecolino)', and reform was effected by, among others, the Bolognese singer F. A. M. Pistocchi, 'who has made himself immortal, by shewing the way of introducing Graces [small, often stereotyped ornaments] without transgressing against Time'. Could it have been the *bel canto* singers of Cavalli, Carissimi and Cesti who stopped for embellishments at every dissonance? They must have been doing it around 1660, 'over fifty years' before Tosi wrote and before his direct memory of singing styles began. The earliest composers he himself remembered to have 'pleased' – whose music was presumably not subject to the abuses of the *professori antichissimi* – were Alessandro Stradella and P. S. Agostini, both of whom flourished in the 1670s. Almost nothing is known of the ornamentation that singers added to Cavalli and Cesti; their music is usually left very plain by

Ex. 1

Palestrina: *Pulchra es amica mea*, as embellished by Francesco Rognoni (1620)

modern editors and performers. It would be doubly surprising if the cadences were prolonged by endless divisions, and one eminent modern authority has suggested that Tosi's teacher was referring to late Renaissance diminutions of the kind used to transform polyphony into vehicles for the virtuoso soloist[2] (ex. 1).

Pistocchi's life (1659–1726) coincided almost exactly with Alessandro Scarlatti's (1660–1725) and his singing career with Tosi's own, that is, the 25 years or so ending around 1705. This was Tosi's golden age, when the 'pathetick' was cultivated, when singers distinguished between the styles of theatre, chamber and church, and graces did not distort the rhythm. But the 'moderns' of the 1720s again outrageously expected 'that an whole *Orchestre* should stop in the midst of a well-regulated Movement, to wait for their ill-grounded Caprices, learned by heart, carried from one Theatre to another, and perhaps stolen from some applauded female Singer who had better luck than skill' (p. 100).

The greatest among the singers of the 1720s were the castratos Nicolini (Nicolo Grimaldi; see Plate 23) and Senesino (Francesco Bernardi by 1759; the English liked him better than the Italians did); the composers then in vogue, according to Tosi's English translator, were besides Scarlatti, Giovanni Bononcini (Handel's rival), Francesco Gasparini, and Francesco Mancini. He might have added Attilio Ariosti, Handel himself, and many others. Tosi's latest layer of composers, whose style had as yet 'gained no Credit at all beyond the *Alps*' (p. 114), was not identified, but it must have included young Neapolitans such as Leonardo Vinci and Leonardo Leo who were sowing the seeds of the new, post-Baroque idiom, whose most brilliant interpreter, Farinelli, had just begun his career. These new-wave composers, and by implication the singers for whom they wrote, received a severe and lengthy lecture on their cultivation of vocal athletics at the expense of the cantabile, minor keys and the pathetic.

From Alessandro Scarlatti on, 'aria' meant overwhelmingly the 'da capo' aria, and Tosi's exhortations and jeremiads regarding its execution give us a lively picture of what ornamentation meant to the opera-goer of his day, and how tastes conflicted and fashions changed. The ornamentation of the da capo aria was intimately bound up with its form, which consisted of an *A* section usually divided in two by a modulation to the dominant, a *B* section contrasting in harmony and sometimes in tempo as well, and a repeat of *A*. With the usual orchestral ritornellos (R) punctuating it and ∩ marking the usual places for cadenzas, this form can be expressed as follows:

A: R (tonic) – voice – R (dominant) – voice ∩ R (tonic) || *fine*.
B: voice (modulating, often from relative minor to mediant) ∩ ||
Da capo al fine (from the beginning to the end of *A*).

These arias admitted four kinds of ornamentation, between which the balance shifted considerably during Tosi's lifetime. The first was the graces, the ornaments proper. Their place was above all in the expressive – 'pathetick' – airs of the Scarlatti period. They were the trill and appoggiatura in their many varieties, the *messa di voce* (or swell, to be used sparingly), mordents, various kinds of gliding or slurring (*scivolo*, *portamento*), and what appears to have been a kind of rubato (*strascino*, a dragging) (pp. 53 and 174; 178–9).[3] The second kind, also at home particularly in expressive airs, was according to Tosi the most challenging of all to the singer's taste and musicianship: the *passi*. By this term (for which his translator found no exact equivalent) he meant short groups of notes – 'a sudden Grace or Flight' –

introduced without disturbing the measure but themselves rhythmically nuanced –
'stol'n on the *Time*, to captivate the Soul' – and dynamically shaded (pp. 174f.;
177).

All this ornamentation was the responsibility of the singer, who was supposed to
have practised it from childhood and to have the intelligence and taste to introduce
it so as to enhance both beauty and expression. Even the stereotyped ornaments
were rarely indicated by the composer, and Tosi deplored the modern tendency to
notate appoggiaturas: 'Poor *Italy*! pray tell me; do not the Singers now-a-days know
where the *Appoggiaturas* are to be made, unless they are pointed at with a Finger?'
(p. 39). Ornamentation of this kind was more than mere decoration; it supplied the
performer with an instrument with which to play upon the susceptibilities of his
listeners. Lulling his audience with 'a seeming Plainness, as if he aim'd at nothing
else', a singer could then 'rouse them that Instant with a *Grace*', and when they
were again awake he could 'return to his feigned Simplicity', though he could no
longer 'delude those that hear him, for with an impatient Curiosity they already
expect a second, and so on' (p. 172).

The third category of ornaments was the divisions (*passaggi*), vocalized passages
of a kind familiar to anyone who knows Handel's *Messiah*. In principle, they were
written into the aria by the composer, who had in mind the particular abilities of
the singer for whom it was destined. An 'air of execution', as Burney termed it,
normally had at least one long passage in each half of the *A* section and often one
or more in the *B*. 'Divisions', according to the great historian, 'being the fashionable
trimmings of an air, are as general as those of a garment. Handel, Bononcini, and
Attilio [Ariosti], all give the same divisions in songs of execution, as they did in
rapid accompaniments to other songs'. And Burney included an aria, written for
Senesino by Ariosti in his *Vespasiano* (1724), as 'an exhibition of all the furbelows,
flounces, and vocal fopperies of the times'[4] (ex. 2). We should not read Burney's
epithets as disparaging divisions in general, but only outdated ones. On the contrary,
his praise of later operas and singers includes repeated references to the 'newness'
and 'invention' displayed in divisions.

It was Tosi, rather, who inveighed against divisions – or at least against the
excessive use of them made by the 'moderns'. Certainly, he said, every student

Ex. 2
Ariosti: air in *Vespasiano* as sung by Senesino

Ornamentation

Vor-rei che dar - di fos-ser gli sguar - di per la-ce - rar - ti in mil-le par - - - - - ti nel pet - to il cor. Vor-rei che dar - di fos-ser gli sguar - di per la-cer- ar - ti in mil-le par - - - -

should practise them assiduously, beginning with stepwise figures and proceeding to the most difficult intervals; an hour a day was insufficient for even the quickest learner. They were for the singer what Czerny was to become for the pianist, and the same instrumental standard of 'easy Velocity and true Intonation' was required; 'for when they are well executed in their proper Place, they deserve Applause, and make a Singer more universal; that is to say, capable to sing in any Stile' (p. 51). But Tosi deplored the tendency for the brilliant to crowd out the cantabile. Comparing the 'ancients' and the 'moderns', he complained that *'the Study of the Pathetick* was the Darling of the former; and Application to the most difficult Divisions is the only Drift of the latter' (p. 109). Singers of the present transformed their airs 'with a horrible Metamorphosis into so many Divisions', and 'like Racers, run full Speed with redoubled Violence to their final Cadences' (pp. 136–7).

The last category of ornaments in da capo arias was the cadenza. Every aria had at least three, according to Tosi (it is not entirely clear whether this was a sarcastic reference to 'modern' excess or a recommended number; an aria survives as sung by Farinelli with no fewer than seven.[5]). As the scheme on p. 419 shows, a cadenza came at the end of the *A* section in each of its statements. Whether indicated by a fermata or not, it was taken on a six-four chord or other suitable harmony preceding the final chord, and it usually ended with a trill, which was the signal for the orchestra to resume playing. Like divisions, cadenzas in Tosi's view suffered at the hands of the moderns from galloping hypertrophy, and one of his most quoted passages describes them: 'Generally speaking, the Study of the Singers of the present Times consists in terminating the *Cadence* of the first Part with an overflowing of *Passages* and *Divisions* at Pleasure, and the *Orchestre* waits; in that of the second the Dose is encreased, and the *Orchestre* grows tired; but on the last *Cadence*, the Throat is set a going, like a Weather-cock in a Whirlwind, and the *Orchestre* yawns' (pp. 128–9). Cadenzas like this were apparently emulated by instrumentalists, even while accompanying a singer, if we are to believe Burney's famous anecdote:

One night, while Handel was in Dublin, Dubourg [violinist and leader of the orchestra in the first performance of *Messiah*], having a solo part in a song, and a close to make, *ad libitum*, he wandered about in different keys a great while, and seemed indeed a little bewildered, and uncertain of his original key ... but, at length, coming to the shake [trill], which was to terminate this long close, Handel, to the great delight of the audience, and augmentation of applause, cried out loud enough to be heard in the most remote parts of the theatre: 'You are welcome home, Mr. Dubourg!'[6]

Tosi said little about what he considered desirable in cadenzas, but one gathers that, except for the last one, the cadenzas should as far as possible be fitted into the written note-values and not interrupt the rhythm.

He had much to say about excess in ornamentation, and the present-day reader who is accustomed to none at all (except in popular music, where he is unlikely to recognize it for what it is) can find all he needs to excuse his distaste for cluttering up the classics. We must be aware, however, that what offended Tosi was ornamentation of a luxuriance almost inconceivable today (again, outside a brilliant jazz solo). A fraction of it would be a great deal by our standards, yet no more than an indispensable minimum by those of the Baroque era. Let us consider these excesses from the point of view of those who committed them. What else, after all, should we expect of an unfortunate castrato, necessarily trained from childhood for no other purpose than to astonish a paying public with feats of vocal prowess, than that he should exert every fibre to justify his lot by arousing them to the loudest possible applause at each cadenza or passage of divisions? From Tosi's 'moderns' on, for 50 years, the European opera public (the French partially excepted) demanded and got everything that Tosi deplored; this was the most visible, the most spectacular feature of mid-18th-century music, whether we like it or not. Divisions were for them the equivalent of the high Cs bellowed out by today's beefy tenors.

Tosi may strike a chord with us for his disapproval of ornamental extravagance, but he demanded something else that we are even less likely to be able to reconstruct than the agility of the castratos: inexhaustible invention. The very structure of the da capo aria presupposed fresh ornaments on the reprise of the *A* section:

Among the Things worthy of Consideration, the first to be taken Notice of, is the Manner in which all *Airs* divided into three Parts are to be sung. In the first they require nothing but the simplest Ornaments, of a good Taste and few, that the Composition may remain simple, plain, and pure [these three adjectives translate Tosi's *intatta*, 'intact', quite a different idea]; in the second they expect, that to this Purity some artful Graces [*un artificio singolare*] be added, by which the Judicious may hear, that the Ability of the Singer is greater; and, in repeating the *Air*, he that does not vary it for the better, is no great Master (pp. 93–4).

But '*the most celebrated among the Ancients*' compounded this variety by 'varying every Night their Songs in the Opera's, not only the *Pathetick*, but also the *Allegro*' – that is, they varied the reprise differently at every performance. The student was advised to acquire this ability by singing differently at every rehearsal: no other ornaments but the most natural at the first rehearsal, then gradually 'artificial' ones, 'and so, from one Rehearsal to another, always varying it for the better' (pp. 94; 97). Nor might these be written out ahead or borrowed, if the singer was to escape Tosi's contempt. It was 'no great Profit to the Scholar, to have a great number of *Airs*, in which a Thousand of the most exquisite Passages of different Sorts were

Ex. 3

Giovanni Bononcini: chamber duet for two altos with embellishments by Carlo Antonio Benati, *c*1710

(trills and other graces would have to be added on both statements)

written down: For they would not serve for all Purposes, and there would always be wanting that Spirit which accompanies extempore Performances, and is preferable to all servile Imitations' (pp. 155, 92). For Tosi, the musician 'that abounds in Invention, though a moderate Singer, deserves much more Esteem, than a better who is barren of it; for this last pleases the Connoisseurs but once, whereas the other, if he does not surprise by the Rareness of his Productions, will at least gratify your Attention with Variety'. Tosi, in other words, was demanding nothing less than that singers should improvise their graces, their *passi*, their cadenzas and their variations upon the written divisions, *on the stage*, with freshness and spontaneity, 'going from one Note to another with singular and unexpected Surprizes, and stealing the Time exactly on the true *Motion* of the Bass [that is, altering the rhythm without distorting the beat]' (p. 129). Like a litany, this caution against tampering with the beat or tempo resounds throughout the book: 'I cannot sufficiently recommend to a Student the exact keeping of time, and if I repeat the same in more than one place, there is more than one Occasion that moves me to it' (p. 99). Clearly, inattention to this matter was a vice of the 'moderns'. Or perhaps liberties with time, both rushing ahead and pausing for ornaments, were cultivated as an accepted component of performing style around 1720 and appeared vicious only to critics of Tosi's generation; Burney did not complain about it, nor did Mancini, though he cited Tosi with respect.[7]

For Tosi, and perhaps for our common sense, improvised variations and passages belonged only in solo arias; he remembered hearing once 'a famous *Duetto* torn into

Atoms by two renown'd Singers, in Emulation; the one proposing, and the other by Turns answering, that at last it ended in a Contest, who could produce the most Extravagancies' (p. 150). Perhaps it was the duet of ex. 3! It is unlikely, in any case, that this warning was meant to apply to the graces; Lorenzo Penna, one of the rare Italians to mention ornamentation in the dark century preceding Tosi, advised only that if two parts have 'Gorghe, ò Trilli' (his trills could mix alternations with reiterated notes), they should imitate or answer one another, not be simultaneous.[8] It is only fair to say, however, that even in solo music Tosi's recommendation of perpetual variation was regarded by his translator (in 1742) with reservations. A footnote observes: 'With due Deference to our Author, it may be feared, that the Affectation of Singing with Variety has conduced very much to the introducing a bad Taste'. The nature of that taste is not described, but again, we are reminded that two kinds usually coexist: the plaintiff's good taste and the defendant's bad.

The choice of Tosi for so much attention has not been arbitrary; his was the most influential treatise on performance in the most influential genre of all Baroque music, Italian opera. Indeed it was the only important Italian treatise dealing extensively with ornamentation between 1620 and 1750. In spite of the fact that his sympathies were all with a style of singing outmoded by the time his book appeared, he was translated not only into English but also partly into Dutch and, as late as 1757, into German by Bach's pupil J. F. Agricola (who, being a German, doubled the size of the original with his commentary).[9] Tosi was read, studied and cited by singing-teachers for over 50 years. Although much of what he said is maddeningly vague – he gave not a single example in musical notation, and even his translators, steeped as they were in Italian opera and having the sound of the greatest castratos in their ears, misunderstood him and sometimes simply gave up on his unruly rhetoric – Tosi provides us with the best platform from which to view the field of Baroque ornamentation as it was perceived at the time and not as our neat handbooks on early music performance might lull us into imagining it.

The conflicts and shifts in taste that Tosi chronicled, and even more, the great gaps he left unfilled (Agricola's commentary shows how broad these were even for the 18th-century reader), are but a sample of the diversity of taste and deficiency of source materials for the era as a whole. The production of performance treatises was exceedingly lopsided in the Baroque period and corresponded not at all to the distribution of important repertory. The near silence of the Italians on matters of ornamentation after 1620, when their opera was about to develop into one of the main cultural forces of the next 100 years, followed a period of amazing fecundity. Lucid, copiously illustrated manuals on diminution technique (the Renaissance equivalent of divisions and graces) appeared with regularity just before and after 1600: Dalla Casa's *Il vero modo di diminuir* (1584), Bassano's *Ricercate, passaggi, et cadentie* (1585), Riccardo Rognoni's *Passaggi per potersi essercitare nel diminuire* (1592), Conforti's *Breve et facile maniera . . . a far passaggi* (1593 or 1603), Bovicelli's *Regole, passaggi di musica* (1594) and Francesco Rognoni's *Selva de varii passaggi* (1620) are some of them.[10] It was Caccini, in the preface to his *Le nuove musiche* (1602), who grafted on to the vocabulary of Renaissance *passaggi* (which were essentially the same for all media) certain new, characteristically vocal ornaments designed to intensify the expression of the new, affective solo song and operatic recitative.[11] Some of these were the *esclamatione* (crescendo or, preferably for Caccini, decrescendo on a note after a sharp attack), *crescere e scemare della voce* (crescendo *and* diminuendo on a note, later called *messa di voce*), the *intonazione* (a kind of slide) and the *trillo* (a more or less rapid reiteration of a note). German theorists of the 17th century based their ornamental doctrine on this Italian practice as expanded by Caccini. Their books dealt almost entirely with singing, while their instrumental ornamentation, so far as it can be reconstructed, seems to have been a mixture of the old diminutions (which their late Renaissance keyboard 'colourists' developed at exuberant length) with slightly later Italian styles in violin and keyboard music, English virginal ornamentation (including the characteristic symbols), and the graces of the French lute masters, who overran Germany in the early part of the century.

One of the small mysteries of music history is the exact meaning of those double and single slanting strokes that the English virginalists put through the stems of their notes between 1550 and 1650. Though it is generally assumed that they signified various kinds of trills, mordents, slides etc., no treatise, not even a table of ornaments, survives to explain them.[12] But the style of the music, transmitted to Germany through Sweelinck's teaching, evidently carried along with it the ornament signs, whose traces can be found in Kuhnau, Bach's predecessor at Leipzig, and perhaps in certain signs in Bach's own youthful compositions. The lack of any clue to the virginalist's strokes is all the more puzzling because the first important table of ornament signs to be printed was English. It was included in Christopher Simpson's *Division-Violist* (1659), a treatise devoted principally to an art on the border between ornamentation and improvisation: the extempore 'breaking' of a bass or of a simple counterpoint to it (also extemporized) into divisions. The table contained 13 items with their explanations, which doubtless represented the repertory of graces in mid-17th-century English consort music:

Ex. 4
Christopher Simpson: *The Division-Violist* (1659; 2nd edn, 1665)

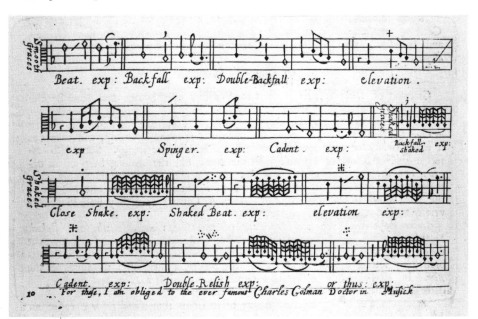

A comment adds: '*To these may be added the Gruppo, Trillo,* or any other Movement of the Voyce imitated on the Viol, by playing the like-moving Notes with one motion of the Bow'. Here is further witness to the leading place of the voice in Baroque performing style and a hint that English singers, like the Germans, based their otherwise scantily documented ornamental practice on that of the Italians. English lutenists, also like the Germans, let themselves be swept up by the international fashion of the French school, and their ornamentation as described in Thomas Mace's *Musick's Monument* (1676) and in the delightful and infinitely informative instruction book of Mary Burwell was correspondingly French.[13]

Four pages of the encyclopedic *Harmonie Universelle* (1636–7) by Marin Mersenne were devoted to a description of French lute ornaments; in another place Mersenne

Ex. 5

Mersenne, *Harmonie Universelle*, vol. iii, *Livre quatrième des instruments*, pp. 186–9

gave diminutions for the first 30 bars of the top voice of a five-part *fantaisie* by Henry Le Jeune 'in order to show how violins [he probably meant the famous band of the king's Vingt-quatre Violons] are accustomed to embellish all kinds of pieces' (ex.5).

Harpsichord ornamentation as described by Mersenne was of two kinds, mechanical diminutions attaining breakneck speed in a series of variations, and graces, for an account of which the reader was referred to the section on the lute. The *embellisement des chants* (ornamentation of song) received 70 pages[14] (they include long digressions on other subjects) and several illustrations. These owed nothing to Caccini, even though he had spent several months at the French court in 1604–5; his dynamic ornaments smacked too much of the spoken stage for French singers (there was as yet no opera in France). The examples included an *air de cour* by Boësset in a number of versions: plain, with graces only, and with rich diminutions by different composers in both melody and bass (the ornamentation produces egregious parallels if done simultaneously in both parts).[15]

Thirty years later the *air de cour* was still the focus of the art of vocal ornamentation. Around 1667 two treatises were published, one in Paris representing the newest style of singing, one in Besançon teaching a very different style of ornamentation, provincial and retrospective.[16] With these two books began a flowering of French writing on musical performance in all media that continued until the end of the Baroque period and beyond. The national passion for clarity of plan and expression made of this body of writing a treasure of easily comprehended source material for modern researchers – easily comprehended, that is, so long as they did not look at too much of it or make close comparisons. If they did, they would find with Montéclair, one of the best and most prolific writers on performance, that

> there is little agreement on either the signs or the names of the ornaments . . . Viol teachers, for example, designate a trill by a backwards C which they place after the note; singing teachers . . . by a little cross before the note; organists by this sign ~ over the note; players of the lute, theorbe and guitar use still other signs for the trill. There are masters who claim with reason that what is commonly called *cadence* should be called trill, since there is plenty of difference between them . . . the *flatté* is called that by viol players; violinists call it *tremblement mineur*; there are singing-teachers who call it *battement* . . . even the masters do not understand each other, and the pupil of one teacher understands neither the language nor the notation of another.[17]

Voluble as the French were on matters of ornamentation, they were almost silent on one topic of capital importance, the performance of the singing parts in Lully's operas. The luxuriant though finely detailed embellishment of the *air de cour* would of course destroy any dramatic characterization. Lully admitted some ornaments – trills, at least, since Rameau defended one of them against the attack of Rousseau[18] – but it may have been that ornaments were otherwise kept to a minimum. Montéclair, discussing what he called the *passage* (more or less the equivalent of Tosi's *passo*), said that Lully 'preferred melody, fine progressions, pleasing harmony, correct expression, naturalness, and finally noble simplicity to the absurdity of *doubles* [he evidently meant diminutions of the kind with which singers of *airs de cour* were accustomed to vary the different stanzas] and of strange music whose claimed merit consists only in shifts, in circuitous modulations, in the harshness of chords, in din and confusion'.[19] What Lully abhorred is precisely what other writers of Montéclair's time called *la musique baroque*; and it was above all instrumentalists who 'to imitate the style of the Italians, disfigure the nobility of simple melodies with often ridiculous variations'. (Montéclair's 'noble simplicity' made do with 18 principal ornaments and innumerable sub-types).

The orchestral performing style appropriate to the dances in Lully's operas was minutely described by his German disciple Georg Muffat in 1698. Here there were 12 principal ornaments – 20 if the subtypes are included – designated by a terminology and system of symbols largely unique to Muffat.[20] Especially valuable in Muffat's essay are his rules for the correct placement of graces not indicated in the score. As a sample, here is a paraphrase of his rules for the use of the trill (*tremblement*). It is not used on the first note of a piece, a phrase, or an ascending figure unless the note is the third of the chord or is sharped. In those cases, either a simple trill or one ending in a turn or 'suffix' (*tremblement réfléchissant*) may be used. An ascending passing note may have a trill with suffix, but rhythmically strong notes that ascend should not be trilled, unless they are the third of the chord or sharped, in which case they should almost always be decorated with a trill if not too quick. In descending stepwise one can easily make occasional trills on strong notes, especially if dotted, and sometimes even on weak notes if they are not too quick. In quicker descents, trill only here and there on strong notes. Although leaping up to a trill is considered an error, it is nevertheless allowed on the third of the chord or on sharped notes. It is used very seldom leaping down, unless the interval is a third or the trilled note is the third of the chord or sharped. In cadences there are certain notes that demand the trill and others that refuse it. It is rarely done on the final note unless it drops by a second or a third or falls on the third or a sharped note with an anticipation.

At almost the same time an English handwritten set of rules for the recorder was more lavish in its recommendations for the use of trills: although neither first nor last notes were trilled, all dotted notes, all sharps, the penultimate note of cadences, the second of three descending crotchets whether by steps or thirds, and all descending flats were to be trilled, but no ascending flats.[21]

Unfortunately, no such rules exist for Bach. Bach was heir to the complex German ornamental traditions sketched above, but to them he added the fruits of his diligent, first-hand study of contemporary French and Italian practices. He copied the table that D'Anglebert printed in his harpsichord collection of 1689, containing 29 items and using 14 symbols in a variety of positions and combinations (ex. 6), as well as a considerable amount of French harpsichord and organ music.

He arranged a number of Vivaldi's concertos for those same instruments, sometimes expanding Vivaldi's schematic melodies into florid, performer's cantilenas. The ornament table that he made for Wilhelm Friedemann conformed to this international mix, so far as it went, and the lavish, written-out ornamentation with which he adorned many of his mature compositions was, like so much of the substance of his music, a personal synthesis of all these elements. But his works abound, nevertheless, with unanswered questions – not only how to ornament his music when it is written plain or to supplement the ornamentation provided when it seems insufficient, but how to interpret the signs when the solutions of his own table seem not to fit, and even beyond that, how, exactly, to execute ornaments whose general shape is not in doubt. Slow? Fast? Accelerating? Long? Short?

There are other questions. Should we make cadenzas at fermatas, as some

Ex. 6
J.-H. D'Anglebert: *Pièces de clavecin* (Paris, 1689)

enthusiastic organists do just before the end of the Passacaglia and Fugue? Should we vary the repeats of the dances in a Bach suite? In both cases there are written-out models to imitate, but is not that very fact evidence that Bach would have written any cadenzas or variations that he wanted? The whole *raison d'être* of the da capo aria in 18th-century Italian opera was to provide an opportunity for singers to extemporize ornaments and variations; are the infinitely denser and more finely detailed arias of Bach's cantatas an exception? Certainly those of Handel, who was born the same year just down the road from Eisenach, are not; but Handel was writing for international stars, while Bach was writing for provincial youths for whom he seems to have had nothing but contempt.

Barring the unlikely discovery of a performance treatise by the composer himself, we shall never have authentic answers to these questions, but even if such a discovery were made, questions would remain. Montéclair's *Principes* is one of the clearest and most complete singing tutors of the age, but it certainly does not answer every question that arises in its author's own cantatas. There are, perhaps surprisingly for many readers, documents of the 18th century that *do* give all the answers regarding ornamentation, and in at least one case they are authentic ones, that is, the ornamentation was authorized by the composer; but the piece is trivial and it is post-Baroque. These documents are of course automatic instruments, or the plans for them.[22] But strangely enough, listening to those instruments, confronted with the reality of alien performances whose authenticity we yearned for only so long as it was unattainable, we say, 'Yes, isn't that interesting. But I prefer it *this* way'. That is, the truth suddenly becomes real like any other reality, and we see how easy it is to exchange it for a different truth – *our* conception of the work. Do we all necessarily prefer Stravinsky's recording of the *Rite*? Would we find Bach's playing to our liking?

The fact remains, however, that we have nothing but inferences with which to answer the riddles of Bach's ornamentation, and so we seize upon every clue to refine these inferences. One of the most frustrating coincidences in the history of musical performance was the appearance between 1751 and 1756 of no fewer than seven of the most exhaustive and authoritative treatises on the subject ever written.[23] Only a little while after Bach's death, and one of the authors his own son! Surely these must contain all we need to know to perform the master's music as he would want. But Bach was old-fashioned long before he died, and these books were meant to instruct their readers in the music of the present, the *galant* style of mid century. One of the threads running through post-war musicology has been the gradual discrediting of these treatises as sources for Baroque performing practices, yet they are so intelligent, so well-written, so unchallenged by any comparable earlier works and, above all, so silent with regard to their exact position in the continuum of changing styles, that it is with the greatest difficulty that we learn to distinguish in them between what is truly a survival of Baroque tradition and what is new, and therefore anachronistic for Baroque music.

The doctrines of Baroque performance that were built up over the past 75 years using these treatises – but particularly C. P. E. Bach and Quantz – as a point of departure have been vigorously challenged in the past 20; and here it is impossible to avoid mention of Frederick Neumann, author of an immense monograph on Baroque and post-Baroque ornamentation, of which the central purpose was to reverse the massive inertia of these doctrines as they applied to J. S. Bach.[24] The doctrines Neumann addressed did not, however, touch more than a small part of the whole field of ornamentation – not one of the questions so far dealt with in this essay. They were concerned solely with details of the execution of certain graces: the rule that trills should begin on the beat with the upper auxiliary and the rule that appoggiaturas, slides, turns, mordents and arpeggios should be played on, not before the beat, thus causing a delay in the attack of the main note for as long as it took to execute the ornament. These rules conflicted with the usage of mainstream music as inherited from the 19th-century treatises of Hummel, Spohr and others, and transmitted by a century of conservatory training. According to this usage, trills began by preference on the main note, and other ornaments were fitted in as far as possible so as not to shift the main note (the one decorated) from its written rhythmic position.

Neumann's researches, which began to appear in the 1960s, sought to accumulate as much evidence as possible for the use of main-note trills and for the placement of ornaments before the beat. Though he never claimed that the late Baroque *norm* was other than it appeared in the tables of J. S. Bach and many others, his arguments were directed with such force to the exceptions and his mentions of the norm so perfunctory, that his writings took on the character of a polemic against the post-Arnold Dolmetsch 'establishment', which did, it is true, sometimes present that norm as if it were a set of immutable principles.[25] On the other hand, the very ferocity of Neumann's attacks stimulated vigorous new research in defence of the establishment doctrines that, though doggedly rebutted on every point, greatly enlarged the perspective from which the questions at issue could be viewed. And Neumann himself, in the course of reinforcing his positions, brought to light a staggering quantity of hitherto unpublished material bearing on a variety of problems in ornamentation. For the practical musician, nevertheless, the unfortunate result of all this is that recent literature on ornamentation presents him with a series of partisan manifestos on a very few issues of limited importance, instead of even-handed discussions of all the topics on which there is any evidence.

This essay has spoken of the necessity of ornamentation in Baroque music, but its message has been that all efforts to master it will inevitably founder in overwhelming complexity or fail for lack of information. (The pessimism grows out of the author's perception of the utter disproportion between the labour recently expended in writing or revising some 90 articles on ornamentation for a new edition of a popular music dictionary and the insignificant degree to which they will meet the needs of any performer of Baroque music.) Yet one does occasionally hear today what seem to informed ears to be fine, stylish, idiomatic performances of this music, and the secret seems to be specialization. The answer must be that by steeping oneself in one repertory and all that surrounds it – cultural background, organology, the dance, matters of diction, prosody and gesture, physical surroundings and above all large amounts of music in a narrow range of styles – and by insisting on the same standards of virtuosity that are required of mainstream musicians at the top of their profession, one discovers that features which could not be reconstructed on the basis of any documents are somehow shaped by the pressure of everything else that is right about the performance. And the musician who cannot specialize can take heart that the way to any style in a living culture is imitation. It was so in the Baroque era and it is so today for anyone who can buy the right records or go to the right concerts. And both generalist and specialist should remember Tosi, for whom the highest attribute of any performer was the ability to create ever fresh embellishments to his airs and thereby present himself to his public not as a treatise but as an individual.

David Fuller
State University of New York at Buffalo

Notes

1 *Observations on the Florid Song* (London, 1743; repr. 1967), p. 161. Originally published as *Opinioni de' cantori antichi, moderni, o sieno, Osservazioni sopra il canto figurato* (Bologna, 1723). Facsimile reprint included with the reprint of J. F. Agricola, *Anleitung zur Singkunst* (Berlin, 1757; repr. 1966), which is a translation of Tosi with commentary. Page references without title hereafter are to the English translation of Tosi.
2 F. Neumann, *Ornamentation in Baroque and Post-Baroque Music* (Princeton, 1978), 553[n].
3 Tosi's explanation of this last ornament is anything but clear. Agricola (p. 234) said in a note that he 'would gladly clarify Tosi's description with a music example if I could only quite understand his real meaning'.

4 C. Burney: *A General History of Music* (1789), ed. F. Mercer (New York, 1957), ii, 725.

5 R. Haas: *Aufführungspraxis der Musik* (Wildpark-Potsdam, 1931), 185–7.

6 C. Burney: *An Account of the Musical Performances in Westminster-Abbey . . . 1784* (London, 1785; repr. 1964), 27n.

7 G. Mancini: *Pensieri, e riflessioni pratiche sopra il canto figurato* (Vienna, 1774; repr. 1970; trans., Champaign, Ill., 1967).

8 L. Penna: *Li primi albori musicali* (Bologna, 1684), 50.

9 See note 1.

10 For an excellent account of this art, see H. M. Brown: *Embellishing Sixteenth-century Music* (London, 1976).

11 G. Caccini: *Le nuove musiche* (Florence, 1602; ed. H. W. Hitchcock, Recent Researches in the Music of the Baroque Era, ix, 1970).

12 An excellent recent discussion is to be found in chap. 6 of David Wulstan's *Tudor Music* (London, 1985).

13 T. Dart: 'Miss Mary Burwell's Instruction Book for the Lute', *Galpin Society Journal*, no. 11 (May, 1958), 3–62.

14 M. Mersenne: *Harmonie Universelle* (Paris, 1636–7; repr. 1963), iii, 186–7, 163; 394; ii, 357–423.

15 E. Ferand: *Improvisation*, Anthology of Music, ed. K. G. Fellerer, xii (Cologne, 1961), 107.

16 B. de Bacilly: *Remarques curieuses sur l'art de bien chanter* (Paris, 1668; repr. 1971; trans. A. B. Caswell, Brooklyn, N.Y., 1968); J. Millet: *La belle méthode* (Besançon, 1666; repr. New York, 1973).

17 M. P. de Montéclair: *Principes de musique* (Paris, 1736; repr. 1972), 77–8.

18 J. P. Rameau: *Observations sur notre instinct pour la musique* (Paris, 1754; repr. Rome, 1969–72), 69–70; J.-J. Rousseau: *Lettre sur la musique française* (Paris, 1753; repr. in *Dictionnaire de musique* and other writings, Paris, 1977, ii, 279–319), 314.

19 Montéclair, p. 86.

20 K. Cooper and J. Zsako: 'Georg Muffat's Observations on the Lully Style of Performance', *The Musical Quarterly*, liii (1967), 220–45.

21 T. Dart: 'Recorder "Gracings" in 1700', *Galpin Society Journal*, no. 12 (1959), 93–4.

22 See C.-B. Balbastre's *Romance* in Dom Bédos de Celles: *L'art du facteur d'orgues*, iv (Paris, 1778; repr. 1965), plates. See also the author's transcription of G. F. Handel, *Two Ornamented Organ Concertos (Opus 4, nos 2 and 5) as Played by an Early Barrel Organ* (Hackensack, N. J.: Jerona Music Corp., 1980).

23 By Geminiani, C. P. E. Bach, J. J. Quantz, Leopold Mozart, G. Tartini, F. W. Marpurg, and J.-B. Bérard. Tartini's was first published in a French translation in 1771.

24 16 of Neumann's articles have been gathered in *Essays in Performance Practice* (Ann Arbor, Mich., 1982); 5 of these deal with Baroque ornamentation.

25 The chief spokesman for the 'establishment' was Robert Donington, in innumerable writings.

The Idea of Authenticity

If we want to be fully authentic in our performances of Bach's cantatas, Donald Tovey once remarked, we should probably give the choirboys a sound thrashing as soon as the music is over. That may not be everyone's idea of the pursuit of authenticity. What Tovey presumably meant was that the standards of performance in Bach's time, and his circumstances, were not what they are now, and that we should be foolish to try to emulate them too closely.

The aim of today's authenticists is, on the face of it, rather simpler than that: it is to reproduce not the kind of performance that Bach may have had to contend with but the kind he might have envisaged as ideal, composing as he was for the singers and players of his own day. That is not easily attained, and it is open to question how far, if indeed at all, we should even attempt it. The whole concept of authenticity, in fact, needs to be critically considered: what does it actually mean? why and when did it come to be seen as a possible objective? what aesthetic validity does it possess? and to what degree is it attainable?

The last of those questions is probably the most easily answered. Authenticity must in the last resort always be elusive, because there is too much about the remote past that is unknown or incomprehensible to us and because we cannot become 'Baroque men' or 'Baroque women' in our thinking or our feeling; the experience of two and a half centuries cannot be forgotten or disavowed. It is partly because of this chimeric quality that the word 'authenticity' has itself come to be regarded as dangerous and misleading. Applied to instruments, for example, it is particularly tricky: is a Stradivarius violin, or a Blanchet harpsichord, built in (say) 1700 'authentic' for the music of the next few decades? It was certainly authentic at the time, but after three hundred years of use, or even of neglect, it is certain to sound different, however faithfully restored to its original condition. Arguably a modern copy, exactly enough done, has stronger claims. But the issue is an awkward one, and for safety's sake the more general term 'period instruments' is to be preferred to 'authentic instruments', in spite of – or because of – its relative imprecision. For similar reasons, scholars, critics and performers are increasingly reluctant to apply the word 'authentic' to performances; phrases such as 'historically aware' or 'historically informed' seem safer, recognizing as they do a particular objective but without specifying the degree of awareness or information that supports the seeking of it.

Another term that indicates the use of period instruments and the other paraphernalia of a historical approach is simply 'Early Music'. This has come to stand for a movement – one that encourages the revival of little-known music and historical performance – and also for its philosophy. Later we shall look briefly at the history of this movement and the attitudes that inform it. But first we should try to define some of the areas of music-making that are involved in the quest for authenticity, or – and here I am perhaps allowing the reader a glimpse of my true colours – the desire to hear music in something akin to the form in which its composer conceived it.

Every performance takes as its starting-point a text; and a performance that aims at authenticity will need to be equipped with one that corresponds to the composer's intentions. That may not be easy, though in the Baroque era it is a good deal easier than in the preceding period where many works survive in quite different versions whose relative authority is uncertain. But it is in any case an assumption belonging to a much later era that any one text should possess unique authority. In the field of opera, for example, Baroque practice decreed not only that each aria in an opera might be differently decorated at each performance but also that the substitution of altogether different music, normally by a different composer, at any point in the evening, and indeed at any number of points, was an accepted procedure which few if any thought to question or to deprecate. A composer might direct a performance of an opera he had written – and under his direction a performance must by definition be 'authentic' – with music in it by half-a-dozen other men and with every movement elaborated by one or other of his singers.

That of course is an extreme case, where 'textual purity' is open to corruption by commercial factors, such as the need to draw in a paying public or to accommodate the over-sized ego of a favoured singer. But mixed texts may be found too in concertos and sonatas surviving in multiple sources. What, then, is the conscientious editor to do? He or she may say that any early source provides a version that stands for an authentic Baroque performance, and that a text following it scrupulously must produce one too. At the opposite standpoint lies the editor who, zealously seeking an ideal version, collates a number of differing sources, taking what in his or her judgment is the best of each, and ends with a text that never existed until the editor's own time. There is middle ground too: finding a version that bears some mark of the composer's authority, such as an autograph (though these are rare from before the late Baroque) or an apparently authorized early edition, or one that emanates from some institution with which the composer was associated, such as a church or court musical establishment, and thus has some special claim. Sometimes two 'authentic' sources of this description may differ, usually because the music in them was originally set down for different purposes, and these may offer the modern editor clues as to the decisions he will need to make, in the light of the intended function of his own text. The concept of the definitive text, a single 'best text' that carries some unique authority, is bound to be tempting to an editor and indeed is part of his heritage from the 19th-century inventors of the editor's art; but applied to such a period as the Baroque it may well be meaningless or even deceptive. A Handel oratorio, for example, certainly had a substantially different text at each group of revivals, and often at each performance within each group. To postulate an ideal text when Handel may have directed a dozen performances with different ones would clearly be presumptuous; and to argue in favour of the earliest, autograph text would be misguided, bearing in mind that Handel's modifications may have been based not only on circumstances (the singers available, the desired length of the work, and so on) but also on artistic preferences that became plain to him only after he had heard the work in performance.

An agreed text, however, is only a beginning, certainly for a performance of a work of the Baroque era. Notation did not provide the player with an exact specification of what he should play; even today it does something less than that. There existed a number of notational conventions that players of the time were expected to understand. Some of these were national or even local, and some were confined to players of particular instruments. Several were concerned with the realization of written rhythms, and of these the best known and still the most controversial is the supposed French tradition of *notes inégales*, or 'unequal notes', according to which passages that move by step in even quavers (possibly crotchets or semiquavers, depending upon the rhythmic unit of the piece) were to be played with the first of each pair longer than the second. Most French theorists refer to this device, though they rarely agree as to its precise application. By how much the first quaver should exceed the second in length is uncertain; probably it depends on the character and the speed of the music. But whether this convention applies exclusively to French works, whether it applies to them comprehensively, whether it applies throughout the Baroque or during only part of it, whether it applies to all classes of music or only some, and whether it applies to French-influenced music by German, Italian or British composers, we simply do not know.[1] Much the same goes for that other well-known French convention, over-dotting (that is, making the dotted rhythms, for example in a French-style overture, even more jerky than they are notated); the answer seems plain enough for Lully, in Paris, but what of the French-style overtures that Bach was writing in Leipzig, or Handel in London? Neither ever heard French music at first hand; did they know the French convention? and could they have expected their players to understand it? In Handel's music, especially, there are numerous notational inconsistencies in rhythmic matters whose significance – if they have any – is elusive.[2] On such issues as these scholarly opinion is sharply divided: which may be taken to suggest, probably correctly, that there was never any consistent practice, universally observed, but a large number of different traditions of performance, national and local, relevant to different periods, repertories and idioms.

This applies equally to another tricky issue, ornamentation. Ornaments notated with conventional signs pose few problems – or, more exactly, the problems they pose are readily circumscribed, for there exist many tables in theoretical works specifying how they should be rendered. The existence of such tables implies, of course, that performers of the time were neither accurate nor consistent about their realization: if they were, tables would not have been needed – and certainly some of those who compiled the tables were more eager to put forward their own pet theories than simply to codify practice. But at least the modern player can select an authority reasonably close in period to the music in question and of the same nationality, and he or she can be reasonably confident that the result will not be too badly wrong.

Altogether more elusive is the question of how ornamentation should be improvised, or (more realistically) how the effect of improvised ornamentation can be replicated. That much music in the Baroque period was composed in the expectation that the performer would elaborate it in some degree is beyond dispute, though certainly there are large repertories – much choral and most orchestral music, and certain types of keyboard music, for example – where added ornamentation is out of the question. In a great deal of solo vocal music and instrumental chamber music it is not merely appropriate but acutely necessary if the music is to have anything like its intended character. An ungraced Italian Adagio, for example, or a plain da capo section in a three-part aria, would normally have been an absurdity to a contemporary; the music was designed specifically to allow the singer or player the opportunity to display his or her individual skill and taste, and, in the case of an opera, sense of character – which would be evident in a singer's improvised additions to a degree it never could if supplied by a modern conductor or editor. A number of models for such improvisations have come down to us,[3] but they need to be treated guardedly: for if someone felt obliged to write out what was normally left unwritten, there may well have been particular circumstances that could affect the nature of the ornamentation – some unusual requirement, perhaps, or the needs of a singer of modest improvising skills, or (as regards models in theoretical works) a hobby-horse that the writer of the ornamentation was eager to exercise. Part of the nature of ornamentation is that it was meant to sound improvised; a carefully learned and rehearsed line is unlikely to make the right kind of effect. It is axiomatic that we can never know today whether a line is being ornamented in an authentic fashion; but the likelihood of that would be much increased if a tradition of extempore ornamentation could be re-created, in which singers and players would become adept in the handling of the decorative clichés of the time and in the selection of ones apt to their context in style and expression. There exist hosts of anecdotes showing that composers deplored excessive or ill-conceived ornamentation of their music. Bad taste can be just as authentic as good taste, but that is not a reason to revive it.

Another decidedly grey area in Baroque performing practice is the realm of the continuo, that very characteristic element in the music of the period. A *basso continuo* part, a literally basic requirement in virtually all kinds of music composed in the 17th and 18th centuries, was usually notated as a bass line with figures placed above it, the figures indicating to the player of a chordal instrument, such as the archlute, the harpsichord or the organ, the harmonies he was to play in addition to the bass line itself. The bass line was often supported by a sustaining instrument – the bass viol, the cello, the bassoon, sometimes the violone or the double bass. It is usually fairly easy to deduce, where there is no explicit direction, what instrument or combination of instruments is most suitable: sacred music almost always calls for the organ, light-textured chamber and vocal music for some kind of lute early in the period and later a harpsichord. Orchestral music is normally best with a harpsichord and perhaps also a lute, while the choice of sustaining instrument may depend on what is required for the upper voices: a bassoon serves well with oboes at the top of the texture; the viol for gentle accompaniments to a solo voice, flute or recorders (and in most French music); and the cello with violins and larger ensembles (and in most Italian music). No doubt many performances took place during the 17th and 18th centuries with only a sustaining instrument or only a harmonic one; indeed composers and publishers, for obvious practical reasons, often expressed the instrumentation as an option ('A Thorough-Bass for the Violoncello or Harpsichord'). But musically speaking the ideal is almost always a combination of the two types.

The chief questions about continuo playing have to do with what the improvising player, at the lute or keyboard, is expected to add to the written notes. Should he weave new, intricate counterpoints into the music? should he simply play chords, and if so, how full should they be? should he pre-imitate (as it were) the voice part in the opening ritornello of an aria? There are many such questions, and many more answers. As with the analogous matter of ornamentation, a number of sample realizations have come down to us, and here too there is generally reason to be cautious over treating them as models, for they may well have been written out primarily because something out of the ordinary was required. From the later part of the period there are many books of instruction, usually aimed at amateur players and making only quite limited demands on the performer's skill. But some from the early 18th century suggest quite elaborate figuration, added melodic lines, imitations of upper instruments or voices, and chords spread and enriched with acciaccaturas; and reports of Bach's own continuo playing suggest that he was apt to add new lines to the texture.[4] Bach might be a risky model to the player of today, and indeed in his own teaching he apparently asked of his pupils simply a full chordal accompaniment. The choices open to the player – especially, perhaps, in earlier music, before the trend towards the simplification of texture that came, at the end of the Baroque, with Enlightenment thinking – are wide, but authenticity is probably more likely to be infringed by clever improvisation than by restrained accompanying. Certainly the vivid and colourful accompaniments for assorted lutes, harps and keyboard instruments that some editors have written into the scores of early Italian operas – Monteverdi, Cavalli and Cesti, for example – are, while beguiling to the ear, unlikely to resemble anything that might have been heard at the Italian courts or the opera houses of Venice at the time: partly because they tend to distract from the central business, the human voice, partly because music of such elaboration would have needed to be premeditated to a degree not consistent with what we know of contemporary practices, and partly because the opera houses at which these works were given employed forces far more modest than these versions call for.

Any search for an authentic manner of performance must take careful note of the size of the forces used in the Baroque period. There has always been a tendency to assume, on the basis of the oft-repeated assertion that Monteverdi's *L'Orfeo* (1607) in some way inaugurated the modern orchestra, that our conception of orchestral music goes back to the early 17th century. In fact the assemblage of the group that played at the Mantuan court on that occasion was in no real sense a precedent as far as either patrons or composers were concerned; this was one of many court festivities of the kind, familiar in Italy and elsewhere for several decades. Not even at the Venetian opera houses, the first of which opened its doors in 1637, was there anything resembling a modern orchestra; Cavalli, composing for the Teatro SS Giovanni e Paolo in Venice, had as late as the 1660s only a couple each of violins and violas, with a bass string instrument, some keyboards and two lute-type instruments. It is more realistic to look to Paris, and the Vingt-quatre Violons du Roi of Louis XIII and XIV, for true precedents for an orchestra in which several people played the same musical line; similar groups existed at other large courts, such as those in Vienna and London, and could be assembled for important ecclesiastical occasions in Italy – there are records, for instance, of a group of 24 strings and five brass instruments at S Marco, Venice, in 1685, and of 27, also with a complement of brass, at S Petronio, Bologna, nine years later. Vivaldi, in the special circumstances of a Venetian orphanage, had some 16 string players to hand for his concertos and sacred works; but outside large courts and opera houses the concept of an orchestra scarcely existed until the last decades of the Baroque era. As a young man at Mülhausen, Bach had a mere five string players available for his cantatas, and there were no more than that in the court chapel at Weimar or even at the Cöthen court. At Leipzig, a larger and more prosperous city, he put forward a proposal to the church authorities in 1730 asking for 11 to 13 string players, with up to eight or even ten wind: all he generally had available at that time, however, was a total of seven, plus an apprentice bassoonist (occasionally the band could be augmented by unpaid students). He wanted, too, a choir of 12 or 16, though some modern scholars believe that in actual performances he normally used only one singer to a part.[5] Handel, in London, had an opera orchestra based on about 30 string players, with wind as needed. He once gave an oratorio performance with 'near a hundred performers, about twenty-five of them singers' (and so an orchestra of about 75, it would seem) – ''tis excessive noisy', wrote one member of the audience, and he never did anything of the kind again.[6] Accounts from his late Foundling Hospital performances of *Messiah*, in a modest-sized chapel, show typically an orchestra of 20 strings, eight woodwind and five brass and drums, with a choir of six boys and 11 men.

As a basis for authentic performance, the facts that have come down to us about forces used in the Baroque are scrappy and difficult to interpret. A few are stable enough: Monteverdi's *L'Orfeo* group, Lully's opera orchestra, Bach's stated ideal, Handel's actual practice. But even these need to be understood for what they are, for they relate to particular circumstances, particular repertories, particular audiences, particular acoustical conditions. They do not establish absolutes. But they do give us some indication of the scale on which the music was imagined. The effect of 17 voices is different in kind, not merely in bulk, from that of 400, or even 40, and if we listen to *Messiah* with a large choir we are not hearing the textures of the music as Handel expected them to be heard. We may think a larger-scale performance better; certainly it is different. Similarly, if Bach composed the Brandenburg Concertos with the Weimar or Cöthen groups in mind, he was almost certainly expecting the ripieno music to be played with one musician to a part, or at the most two or three; if we want to hear them in a hall too large for so small a group, we are bound to make the music substantially different in sound and in balance.

There is little point in aping the sound, or the balance, of the groups we know to have been used by composers of the Baroque if we employ instruments and voices altogether different from the ones for which they conceived their music. The issue of period instruments is central to the whole matter of authentic performance. The changes in instruments over the last two and a half centuries have profoundly affected the actual sound they produce. It is important to rid ourselves of the 'evolutionary' notion that change is necessarily improvement, and to realize that improvement in some of the obvious technical ways – for example, making it easier to play in tune, or to play more loudly, or to play with greater security – may involve loss as well as gain. Change in musical instruments, like biological change, is adaptive: it is keyed to change in circumstances. Instruments grew louder at a time when music was moving out of the courtly hall and the drawing room into the public concert hall, and chromatic notes and a wider compass became available as idioms extended to demand them.

The violinist who takes up an unchanged (or restored) instrument of the 17th or 18th century will find differences between this and a modern instrument which affect every aspect of his playing and of the sound he produces. The gut strings (the lowest one wire covered from about halfway through the Baroque period) will provide a softer, less penetrating tone. The flatter fingerboard and lower bridge will give rise to strings of lesser tension, resulting in a quieter sound; the lack of internal bracing will also reduce the resonance. The absence of a chin-rest – and, at least for most of the period, the fact that the violin was often held against the upper chest rather than under the chin (see Plate 24) – will mean that position shifts are from the player's point of view clumsier and from the listener's more readily heard (the sliding finger will produce a more marked *portamento* effect); it will also practically exclude the modern ideal of constant vibrato. The lighter and more curved bow, coupled with the slacker strings, will enable the player to articulate certain types of passage, particularly running semiquavers or rapid quavers, in an intermediate manner that would be unnatural and awkward on a modern instrument, where such passages tend to be played either 'on the string' (legato, with the notes more or less running into each other) or 'off the string' (with distinct gaps between them). Furthermore, equipped with an instrument that is a replica of the kind used at the time, the player will soon find that the instructions in contemporary treatises make sense in ways they do not for a modern instrument. The foregoing applies to all the members of the violin family; in the case of the cello the absence of a spike supporting the instrument on the floor is akin to the absence of the violin chin rest.

The wind instruments of the Baroque have often been regarded as primitive compared with those of today, and Alessandro Scarlatti has been quoted as saying that they could never play in tune. The most skilled practitioners, however, managed it then, and their modern counterparts, using period instruments, do so now. On the one- or two-keyed oboes and flutes of the period, the tone quality is softer, rounder and less sharp-edged than on today's instruments; the bassoon too, which the English composer Charles Avison said (in the preface to a set of concertos) was the only wind instrument capable of blending satisfactorily with the strings, was also gentle in sound. Brass instruments, on the other hand, much narrower in bore than their modern equivalents, must have had more of a cutting edge to their tone, which would have created a different ensemble balance. The combination used by such composers of the late Baroque as Vivaldi, Telemann or Bach in their concertos, or Rameau in his operas, cannot sound as their composers intended if modern instruments are used.

The study of period instruments and their capabilities leans heavily on those that survive in original condition and new ones modelled on them. The situation is rather different as regards the human voice. Methods of voice production changed in the early years of the 19th century, when concert rooms and opera houses were growing larger and technical demands of a new kind were being made; modern singers, whose vocal equipment has been physically developed by standard methods of voice training, find the attainment of a period style more elusive than do instrumentalists. Early treatises on the voice are few, and although a plethora of descriptions have come down to us, the subjectivity of their language makes them difficult to interpret. We can be fairly sure that most singers of the Baroque period sang less loudly than their modern counterparts and with much less vibrato, and that their lighter voices were generally more agile. Choral music, except on the opera stage, was almost always sung by males (except in the French royal chapel, where women are known to have been singing by the early 18th century). Boys or, in countries where castration was practised (essentially Italy and Spain), castratos sang the top part, and the alto line was taken by boys, castratos or, where (as in England) there was a tradition of falsetto singing, falsettists. A modern mixed choir is rarely authentic in Baroque music; but the re-creation of an authentic choral sound is in any case problematic, not only because of the absence of castratos today but also because boys now reach puberty much younger, so that the maturer pre-pubertal voice is unknown to us.

There are a number of authentic performing practices that it would be difficult or disagreeable to revive. The traditions of time-beating, for instance: at the Paris Opéra, the director of the performance, the *batteur de mesure*, beat time audibly, either on a table or with a large, heavy staff on the floor (it was with such a staff that Lully did himself a fatal injury). This method was also known in London; in Germany, foot stamping was favoured, while in Italy the principal violinist might stamp his feet or regularly strike the music stand with his bow. The role of setting the tempo and controlling the ensemble was rarely assumed by a specialist conductor; normally it fell either to the continuo player – the natural role of the *maestro di cappella* or the organist, probably head of the musical establishment – or to the leading violinist (or *Konzertmeister*). Sometimes the responsibility was divided, with the violinist deputed to keep the orchestra together while the keyboard player, particularly in vocal music, would have charge of the whole. What is clear, however, is that the concept of the interpretative conductor, who would define and impose his view of the music, did not exist; and the kinds of effect that are possible only with such a conductor were unknown. The crescendo or diminuendo, the carefully shaped accent, the gradation of volume as the voices enter in a fugal chorus: effects such as these belong to later periods. Even if the director of a performance in the late Baroque had wished, a century or two ahead of his time, to add such refinements, it is doubtful whether he would have had the opportunity to do so; rehearsals were generally few and brief. It is significant that, among the many sets of orchestral parts that survive from the period, virtually none bears any trace of the kinds of annotation typically produced by rehearsal: the addition of a dynamic mark or a bowing instruction, the adjustment of an articulation mark, the correction of a misprint. The implications of some of this for modern 'authentic' performance have yet to be fully recognized, or taken account of, by conductors of period groups who find it hard to forgo the kinds of effect that have become part of the heritage of the interpretative conductor over the last century and a half, and which depend upon the presence of a controlling force, constantly watched, on a rostrum.

Another central issue is the vexed one of tempo. Most performances using period instruments tend to move rather more quickly than traditional ones, partly because period instruments are lighter in sound and readier in response than their modern counterparts; this leads players instinctively to choose faster speeds. In support of this there is evidence that performances of repertory works have tended to grow slower over the years, though admittedly this applies mainly to music of the Classical era – early timings of symphonies by Mozart and Beethoven are substantially shorter than those of most modern conductors, and indeed the same applies to Wagner's operas, whose authentic timings made under the composer's direction are for the most part considerably shorter than standard ones of today. There is perhaps a tendency, as works become repertory classics, for them to assume a greater momentousness and expressive significance than their composers thought they were investing them with. In the Baroque, the concept of sensuously beautiful instrumental tone was less developed than it is today; contemporary treatises rarely refer to tonal beauty, the exploitation of which on modern instruments encourages slow tempos. There is little precise information to be drawn from early sources here; some theorists made suggestions – based on the pendulum, a man's heartbeat or a natural walking speed in those pre-metronome days – about appropriate tempos for particular dances or some of the traditional Italian tempo designations, but these are too general to be of much value. Many of the Italian terms now understood primarily as indications of tempo were in any case employed rather to describe the intended mood or expressive disposition of a piece (its *Affekt*, in German Baroque terminology) than its physical speed. One thing, however, we may be fairly sure of is that the notion of an absolutely uniform tempo for a movement is a modern one; sources from Frescobaldi to Beethoven, at least, talk of varying the tempo to correspond with the expressive content of a piece, and though the degree of variation was probably quite modest, the modification of tempo was a widely accepted expressive device.

The issues, then, that face the would-be authentic performer are both numerous and complex. There are many uncertainties and many potential pitfalls. Let us turn now to some of the other issues surrounding authenticity, especially its history and its aesthetics.

The 'authenticity' movement is about a hundred years old.[7] It is true that, in the early 19th century, the 'additional accompaniments' to *Messiah* by Mozart and others were sharply criticized in England for their lack of fidelity to the original, but that was a matter of conservative rather than progressive taste. The interest in authenticity essentially owes its development to a much deeper cultural phenomenon, the expiry of an evolutionary view of human activity and the concomitant loss of confidence in current taste: the realization that the newest way (whether it be of running society or of interpreting the music of the past) may not necessarily be the best way. It was not fortuitous that this realization coincided with the rise of scholarship concerned with music of the past; both are characteristic of an Alexandrian age.

The seeds of the authenticity movement may perhaps be seen in the curiosity about the past shown as early as the 17th and 18th centuries, for example by Pepusch, Burney and Padre Martini; in the 'classicizing' of repertories in the late 18th century, which ensured that earlier music continued in currency for longer than the few years after its composition; in the Bach Revival of the turn of the century, with its climax in Mendelssohn's *St Matthew Passion* performance of 1829; and in the 19th-century development of critical musicology. But its practical beginnings come only with the antiquarian, organological and re-creative enthusiasms of Arnold Dolmetsch, easily the single most influential figure in the revival of period instruments. Dolmetsch's ideas were widely pursued. The harpsichord, once likened by Bernard Shaw to the jingling of bell-wires,[8] came to be accepted in the early decades of the 20th century through Wanda Landowska. The revival of the *collegium musicum* movement began, in German universities; the first *collegium* was founded by Hugo Riemann in Leipzig in 1908. Revivals of Handel's operas began in Germany in the 1920s. In that decade and the next Anthony Bernard's London Chamber Orchestra and the Boyd Neel String Orchestra were founded, largely to play the Baroque repertory – until then normally heard on a full symphony orchestra – with forces closer to those for which the music was conceived. Fritz Busch's chamber orchestra and Paul Sacher's Schola Cantorum Basiliensis did the same kind of thing. Then in the years after World War II Dolmetsch's pioneer volume (1915) was followed up by works of a more professional, scholarly cast from Thurston

Dart and Robert Donington.[9] Those years, with the coming of the LP record, saw a huge multiplication of groups specializing in late Baroque music (and indeed records provide, over the years, a spectrum of fashions and tastes in performing practice). It began with Karl Münchinger's Stuttgart Chamber Orchestra, I Virtuosi di Roma, the English Chamber Orchestra and (a little later) the Academy of St Martin-in-the-Fields, most of them using an ensemble based on between a dozen and 25 string players. A musician of the previous generation, Pablo Casals, did much the same in his Prades Festival groups, playing Bach, though one suspects that had another 20 or 30 musicians come along, they would have been welcome to join in too. As early as the 1950s one London group, under Dart, took up 'Corelli bows' to help their articulation in Baroque music. But it was not until the 1970s that orchestras of period instruments became a firm part of the musical scene. Since then a number of early music centres have come into being, each with distinctive style elements. There was Vienna, with Nikolaus Harnoncourt's Concentus Musicus; the Low Countries, where musicians worked with Gustav Leonhardt, Frans Brüggen and the Kuijken family; Paris, where William Christie's Les Arts Florissants became the leading interpreters of Lully and Charpentier; and London, where the large pool of players was drawn on by many groups, among which Christopher Hogwood's Academy of Ancient Music was the first to become firmly established, soon to be followed by those of John Eliot Gardiner and Roger Norrington. As the professionalism of these groups has steadily improved, and the players' mastery of their sometimes intractable instruments (by comparison with their modern counterparts) has increased, so they have gradually come to be accepted by all but the most bigoted music-lovers as a part of the performing world, not simply of antiquarian interest but offering a valid alternative to the traditional modes of performance.

What, then, is the justification for abandoning, in the performance of music of the period 1600–1750, the established style of playing and singing of the late 20th century, a style that has developed over several centuries, is predominantly taught in our schools and conservatories, and is recognizably the normal style of our time? It has been vigorously argued that the 'early music' styles of today, far from being historically based, are really no more than a manifestation of 20th-century taste, or one aspect of it – a move, in reaction against Romantic expressive excess, towards emotional austerity, with its pared-down sound and clean, sharply focussed textures (there are parallels to it in much new music of this century, most obviously Stravinsky's).[10] That a good deal of what purports to be historical performance may be unsoundly based is not in question; but if there is some congruence between present-day taste and what is in some degree historical, as the current popularity of Baroque music bears out, then it is scarcely surprising if performances that are even marginally historical in approach are appealing to late-20th-century listeners. And if performers modify what they construe to be strict historical interpretation to suit their own musical understanding, they are only doing what performers have always had to do in order to make music with due conviction.

Clearly, however, we should not delude ourselves about authenticity and the degree to which we are attaining it. It is inevitable that we should always perceive it through the prism of our current collective consciousness and not with total objectivity. The pure quill must always prove elusive. But what, anyway, is the pure quill? We seek authenticity, presumably because we feel that, by hearing a piece of music in a form as close as possible to that imagined by the composer, and heard by early audiences, we can better understand the piece and any meaning the composer invested in it. Many voices have been raised in opposition to that notion, pointing out that a performance style apt to the composer's day may not be apt to ours, and that – following the principle of the Intentional Fallacy beloved of literary critics – a work has an ontological status independent of its origins, potentially embodying meanings beyond anything envisaged by its creator (indeed it might be argued that there is a link between the greatness of a work and such a potential). These views cannot be faulted; and not even the most hidebound authenticist will actually seek to prohibit, or to charge with impropriety, performances that are foreign in style to the work or seek to lend it meanings unimaginable to its creators, as long as the performers are honest about what they are doing and why they are doing it.

Yet there are many people, and not only professional music historians, who entertain a genuine desire to hear a musical work in a form as close as possible to that in which it was originally imagined by its composer. We do not, as we saw earlier, have painstakingly and pedantically to reconstruct exact replica conditions of performance (though that may be an amusing, perhaps even an edifying, game); we have rather to consider what was normative at the time and what the composer might have had as an ideal in his mind's ear. We may never manage to hear the music 'as it really was', and even if we did, we could never be certain that we were doing so. In any case, to postulate a single ideal of performance for a work from an age when the variable or optional nature of many elements was taken for granted would be excessively precious.

There is, however, no possible reason why we should not make every effort to understand and reconstruct earlier performing practices; and experience suggests that, even if we make mistakes and labour under misapprehensions, we are still likely to move closer to 'as it really was' and to reap rewards from that. Take for example the late Baroque concerto repertory: each step taken, however stumblingly, in the name of authenticity – the reduction from a symphony to a chamber orchestra, the restoration of a continuo harpsichord, the adoption of period bows and then period instruments – has brought about some fresh revelation about the sound of the music as the composer envisaged it, and concomitantly about its meaning. Further, the acceptance of the disciplines imposed by authentic practices compel the performer to seek expressive means that lay within the purview of the composer; Landowska, in her famous dictum – 'Little do I care if, to attain the proper effect, I use means that were not exactly those available to Bach' – was mistaken, because the use of different expressive means is certain to lead to different expressive ends, not ones 'proper' to Bach.[11] The appeal of hearing the music as the composer intended it is a powerful one; and our readiness to come to grips with the past on its own expressive and technical terms, however patchily or imperfectly we may perceive them, seems to me one of the most exciting and horizon-widening developments in late-20th-century music-making.

Stanley Sadie
The New Grove Dictionary of Music
and Musicians

Notes

1 The issues of *notes inégales* and over-dotting have been central in a long-running scholarly dispute, pursued in *Early Music* and elsewhere, in which, broadly speaking, the case for rhythmic alteration has been argued by the late Robert Donington and David Fuller and that for reading the notation literally by Frederick Neumann. The situation is fairly presented in Fuller, 'The Performer as Composer', *Performance Practice: Music after 1600*, ed. H. M. Brown and S. Sadie (London, 1989), 117–46.

2 See T. Best: 'Interpreting Handel's Rhythmic Notation – Some Reflections on Modern Practice', *Handel Tercentenary Collection*, ed. S. Sadie and A. Hicks (London, 1987), 279–90.

3 See W. Dean, ed.: *G. F. Handel: Three Ornamented Arias* (London, 1976), and W. Dean: 'Vocal Embellishment in a Handel Aria', *Studies in Eighteenth-Century Music: a Tribute to Karl Geiringer*, ed. H. C. Robbins Landon (New York, 1970), 151–9.

4 Typical of those proposing elaborate continuo realizations is Johann David Heinichen (*Der Generalbass in der Komposition* (Dresden, 1728; partial Eng. trans., 1966). Evidence of Bach's practices comes from several sources: Johann Friedrich Daube (*Generalbass in drey Accorden*, Leipzig, 1756) and Johann Nikolaus Forkel (reporting the testimony of C. P. E. Bach in his *Über Johann Sebastian Bachs Leben, Kunst, und Kunstwerke*, Leipzig, 1802; Eng. trans., 1820 and 1920) report on his tendency to add fresh voices, while Johann Christian Kittel (*Der angehende praktische Organist*, Leipzig, 1801–8) refers to his readiness to fill out thin accompanying textures.

5 See for example J. Rifkin: 'Bach's Chorus: a Preliminary Report', *The Musical Times*, cxxiii (1982), 747–54, and the ensuing debate between Rifkin and R. L. Marshall in *The Musical Times*, cxxiv (1983), 19, 161; Rifkin's views are embodied in his recordings of the B minor Mass and several cantatas. A discussion of the orchestral forces Bach had at his disposal is provided by H.-J. Schulze: 'Johann Sebastian Bach's Orchestra: Some Unanswered Questions', *Early Music*, xvii (1985), 3–15.

6 See O. E. Deutsch: *Handel: a Documentary Biography* (London, 1955), p. 310.

7 Its history is fascinatingly traced in H. Haskell: *The Early Music Revival: a History* (London, 1988).

8 See G. B. Shaw: *Music in London, 1890–94* (London, 1932), ii, 100.

9 A. Dolmetsch: *The Interpretation of the Music of the XVII and XVIII Centuries* (London, 1915); T. Dart: *The Interpretation of Music* (London, 1954); R. Donington: *The Interpretation of Early Music* (London, 3/1989).

10 The main proponent of this view is Richard Taruskin; his most comprehensive statement of it is his essay 'The Pastness of the Present and the Presence of the Past', in *Authenticity and Early Music*, ed. N. Kenyon (Oxford and New York, 1988), 137–207. Robert P. Morgan's essay in the same volume, 'Tradition, Anxiety, and the Current Musical Scene' (pp. 57–82) makes kindred points. Among the other valuable essays in this book, Gary Tomlinson's 'The Historian, the Performer, and Authentic Meaning in Music' (pp. 115–36) explores a number of aesthetic issues surrounding authenticity.

11 *Landowska on Music*, ed. D. Restout (New York, 1981), 356.

IV Chronology

Chronology 1600–1750

The format of the Chronology reflects within each year the geographical ordering of the 'Places and People' section of the book. Significant births and deaths are listed first, followed by musicians' appointments and key events relating to musical institutions, etc.; then, under the heading of the appropriate city (or region), details of important publications, first performances and other relevant events are noted.

1600

Florence Jacopo Peri and Giulio Caccini's pastoral opera *Euridice* (text by Rinuccini) perf. at the Palazzo Pitti for the wedding of Maria de' Medici and Henri IV of France.

Rome Emilio de' Cavalieri's *Rappresentatione di Anima, et di Corpo ... per recitar cantando* (considered the first surviving play set entirely to music and its printed score the earliest to include a figured bass) perf. before the Collegio Sacro.

Venice G. M. Artusi pubd *L'Artusi*, in which he criticized contrapuntal licences taken by Monteverdi in unpubd madrigals; further criticism appeared in 1603 (see **1605**). Salamone Rossi pubd 1st bk of madrigals, incorporating chitarrone part (in tablature).

Gabriele Fattorini, *maestro di cappella* of Faenza Cathedral, provided an unfigured continuo part with his *Sacri concerti*.

Leipzig Sethus Calvisius pubd a history of music theory in *Exercitationes musicae duae*.

1601

Monteverdi succeeded Benedetto Pallavicino as *maestro di cappella* at Mantua.

Francesco Turini (aged 12) apptd organist at the Prague court.

Naples Scipione Cerreto pubd *Della prattica musica vocale, et strumentale*.

Rome Luzzasco Luzzaschi pubd *Madrigali per cantare, et sonare a uno, e doi, e tre soprani*, orig. composed for the 'singing ladies' of Ferrara.

Nuremberg H. L. Hassler pubd *Lustgarten neuer teutscher Gesäng, Balletti, Gaillarden und Intraden*.

London Thomas Morley issued a collection of panegyric madrigals, by 23 composers honouring Queen Elizabeth I, *The Triumphes of Oriana*.

1602

Emilio de' Cavalieri *d* (*c*52, Rome).

Francesco Cavalli *b* (Crema); William Lawes *b* (Salisbury).

Florence Caccini pubd *Le nuove musiche* (embodying a collection of solo songs and a treatise on the monodic style).

Milan Cesare Negri pubd *Le gratie d'amore*, a dance treatise ded. Philip III of Spain, which documents contemporary social and theatre dance music.

Venice Salamone Rossi pubd the 1st book of madrigals to include an unfigured bass part; Lodovico Viadana pubd *Cento concerti ecclesiastici* (op. 12) with a continuo part (see **1600**, Venice).

1603

Philippe de Monte *d* (?82, Prague).

Venice Monteverdi pubd 4th bk of madrigals.

Cologne J.-B. Besard pubd *Thesaurus harmonicus* (an encyclopedic collection of lute music with a treatise appended).

London Thomas Robinson pubd *The Schoole of Musicke*, a lute method.

1604

Giovanni Frescobaldi elected to the Accademia di S Cecilia, Rome.

The Caccini family spent the winter in Paris at the invitation of Maria de' Medici.

The Company of Musicians was incorporated in London.

Munich Orlande de Lassus's *Magnum opus musicum* (516 motets) assembled and pubd posth. by his sons Rudolph and Ferdinand.

Nuremberg Valentin Haussmann pubd *Neue Intrade* and *Neue Paduane und Galliarde*, two important collections of dances for 5 and 6 viols (some also for violin).

London Dowland's *Lachrimae or Seaven Teares* (for 5 viols/violins and lute) pubd.

Amsterdam Sweelinck pubd *50 pseaumes de David*, his monumental polyphonic setting of the Psalter (see **1619**).

1605

Orazio Vecchi *d* (54, Modena).

Giacomo Carissimi *b* (nr Rome).

Venice Monteverdi pubd 5th bk of madrigals, replying in the preface to G. M. Artusi's criticisms (see **1607**); Adriano Banchieri pubd *L'organo suonarino*.

Kassel The Ottoneum (the earliest German court theatre) opened (1604–6; named after *Kapellmeister* Georg Otto).

London William Byrd courageously pubd 1st vol. of *Gradualia*, which contained music suited to the Roman Catholic liturgy; he temporarily withdrew it after the Gunpowder Plot (see **1607**).

1606

Edmund Hooper (Master of the Choristers since 1588) apptd 1st organist at Westminster Abbey.

Rostock Joachim Burmeister pubd *Musica poetica* (defining 27 musical rhetorical figures and citing examples from Lassus's motets).

London Jonson's play *Volpone* perf. with music by Alfonso Ferrabosco the younger.

1607

Luzzasco Luzzaschi *d* (*c*62, Ferrara); Giovanni Maria Nanino *d* (*c*63, Rome).

Girolamo Frescobaldi spent 10 months in Brussels as part of the entourage of Guido Bentivoglio and pubd madrigals there.

Mantua Monteverdi's *L'Orfeo* perf., a *favola in musica* made up of monody, madrigals and instrumental music; in a *Dichiaratione*, included in Monteverdi's *Scherzi musicali*, his brother G. C. Monteverdi responded to Artusi's attacks by elaborating on his brother's use of dissonance.

Siena Agostino Agazzari pubd *Del sonare sopra'l basso con tutti li stromenti e dell'uso loro nel conserto* (one of the earliest pubd treatises on thoroughbass); Francesco Bianciardi pubd *Breve regola per imparar' a sonare sopra il basso.*

Venice Lodovico Viadana pubd *Missa dominicalis* (from the 2nd vol. of *Concerti ecclesiastici*), the earliest known example of liturgical monody.

Hamburg *Ausserlesener Paduanen und Galliarden* pubd, including 4- and 5-part dances by numerous English composers.

London Byrd issued 2nd vol. of *Gradualia*.

1608

Girolamo Frescobaldi apptd organist at S Pietro, Rome.

Mantua Marco da Gagliano's pastoral opera *Dafne* (text by Rinuccini) perf. during the the Carnival season; in May *L'Arianna* (text by Rinuccini), Monteverdi's opera for which only the famous lament survives, perf. for the opening of the ducal Teatro Vecchio.

Venice Cesario Gussago pubd one of the earliest collections of 'sonate'.

Paris The royal printer Pierre Ballard issued 1st collection of *Airs de différents autheurs mis en tablature de luth.*

1609

Eustache Du Caurroy *d* (60, Paris).

Heinrich Schütz went to Venice to study with Giovanni Gabrieli.

Milan Caterina Assandra, a nun, pubd a collection of motets in the concertato style.

Hamburg William Brade pubd his 1st collection of *Newe ausserlesene Paduanen, Galliarden, Canzonen, Allmand und Coranten.*

London Francis Tregian, while detained in Fleet Prison, began compiling 3 important MS collections of English and Italian music from *c*1600; *The Fitzwilliam Virginal Book* is the best known (see **1619**).

Thomas Ravenscroft ed. and pubd *Pammelia*, the earliest English collection of rounds and catches (including 'Three Blind Mice').

Jonson's *Epicoene, or the Silent Woman* perf. with music by William Lawes.

1610

Michel Lambert *b* (Champigny-sur-Veude).

Milan G. P. Cima pubd collection of *Concerti ecclesiastici* containing 1st known sonata for violin and continuo and 1st trio sonata (for violin, cornett and continuo).

Venice Lodovico Viadana pubd his only instrumental collection, *Sinfonie musicale à 8* (each named after an Italian city).

Paris Eustache Du Caurroy's collection of orchestral *Fantasies* for 3 to 6 instruments pubd posth.; his *Missa pro defunctis* (1606), perf. at Henri IV's funeral, became the official royal requiem.

1611

Tomás Luis de Victoria *d* (*c*62, Madrid).

Venice Lucia Quinciani's *Udite lagrimosi spirti*, the 1st known solo monody by a woman, pubd in *Affetti amorosi*, an anthology compiled by Marc'Antonio Negri.

1612

Giovanni Gabrieli *d* (*c*60, Venice); Giovanni de' Bardi *d* (78, Florence); Hans Leo Hassler *d* (49, Frankfurt am Main).

Duke Vincenzo Gonzaga's death ended a great era of music patronage in Mantua.

Wolfenbüttel Michael Praetorius pubd *Terpsichore*, his only collection of French dances.

London Orlando Gibbons pubd his retrospective *First Set of Madrigals and Mottets, apt for Viols and Voyces*.

1613

Carlo Gesualdo, Prince of Venosa, *d* (*c*52, Gesualdo); Giovanni Maria Artusi *d* (*c*73, Bologna).

Monteverdi apptd Giovanni Gabrieli's successor at S Marco, Venice; Schütz returned to Kassel.

Naples Pietro Cerone pubd in Spanish his mammoth *El melopeo y maestro*, on music history and theory.

London *Parthenia or the Maydenhead of the First Musicke that ever was printed for the Virginalls* (music by Byrd, Gibbons and Bull) pubd for the marriage of Princess Elizabeth to Frederick V, the Elector Palatine of Heidelberg.

1614

Felice Anerio *d* (*c*54, Rome).

Franz Tunder *b* (Bannesdorf).

Banchieri founded the Accademia dei Floridi in Bologna, known from 1625 as the Accademia dei Filomusi; meetings were held at S Michele in Bosco.

Venice Monteverdi pubd his retrospective 6th bk of madrigals.

Paris Jacques Mauduit's *ode mesurée* in honour of Louis XIII's return from Brittany perf. by 135 singers, lutenists and viol players.

Graz Heinrich Pfendner pubd *Delli motetti*, one of the earliest German motet collections with continuo.

1615

Christopher Gibbons *b* (London).

Schütz visited the Dresden court, formally becoming *Kapellmeister* in 1619.

In Bologna the Congregazione dell'Oratorio, which met on Sundays at S Barbara, was founded.

Rome Frescobaldi pubd the 1st edn of his *Toccate e partite d'intavolatura di cembalo*.

Salzburg The archbishop built the first open-air theatre (Steintheater) at the Hellbrunn palace.

1616

Johann Jakob Froberger *b* (Stuttgart).

Johann Hermann Schein apptd *Kantor* of the Thomaskirche, Leipzig.

A collegium musicum founded in Prague.

Berlin Bartholomaeus Praetorius pubd *Newe liebliche Paduanen und Galliarden*.

Nuremberg Johann Staden pubd *Harmoniae sacrae*, containing some of the earliest German sacred concertos.

London Jonson's *The Devil is an Ass* perf. with music by Robert Johnson.

1617

Venice Biagio Marini pubd *Affetti musicali*, containing sinfonias, canzonas, sonatas and dances for 1 or 2 violins and bass (in 'La Foscarina' tremolo is specified for the 1st time).

Paris The ballet *La délivrance de Renaud* (music by Mauduit, Pierre Guédron, Antoine de Boësset and Gabriel Bataille) perf. by 92 singers and 45 instrumentalists under Mauduit's direction.

Leipzig Schein pubd *Banchetto musicale*, a collection of variation suites.

London Nicholas Lanier introduced passages of Italian 'stylo recitativo' into Jonson's masque *Lovers Made Men*.

1618

Giulio Caccini *d* (*c*67, Florence).

René Descartes finished his *Compendium musicae* which, when pubd (1650), became an influential treatise on music and the application of scientific methodology.

Michael Praetorius, Heinrich Schütz and Samuel Scheidt supervised the reorganization of the *Kapelle* at Magdeburg Cathedral.

Leipzig Schein pubd 1st part of *Opella nova*, an important collection of sacred concertos (based on Lutheran chorales) with continuo.

Wolfenbüttel Praetorius pubd 2nd and 3rd parts of *Syntagma musicum* (1st part appeared in 1614); the 2nd part is devoted to musical instruments.

1619

Pierre Guédron apptd *surintendant* of music at the French court.

Schütz, Praetorius, Scheidt and Staden took part in the inauguration of the organ at the Stadtkirche, Bayreuth, at the invitation of Margrave Christian of Brandenburg-Bayreuth.

Giovanni Priuli, *Hofkapellmeister* to Archduke Ferdinand for *c*4 years, moved to Vienna when Ferdinand became Habsburg Emperor.

Rome G. F. Anerio comp. *Teatro armonico spirituale* for the Oratorio di S Filippo Neri, signalling the rise of the vernacular oratorio and the earliest use of obbligato instruments in music of the Roman school.

Venice Monteverdi pubd 7th bk of concerted madrigals.

Dresden Schütz pubd *Psalmen Davids*, his 1st collection of sacred motets and concertos.

Nuremberg Praetorius pubd *Polyhymnia caduceatrix*.

London Tregian finished compiling what is now called *The Fitzwilliam Virginal Book*.

Amsterdam Sweelinck pubd *Cantiones sacrae*, motets for the Catholic liturgy.

1620

Hans Schreiber, the Berlin court instrument maker, devised the contrabassoon.

Milan Francesco Rognoni Taeggio pubd *Selva di varii passaggi*, a treatise on vocal and instrumental techniques.

Rome Filippo Vitali's *favola in musica*, *L'Aretusa* was staged.

Venice Alessandro Grandi pubd *Cantade et arie*, a collection of monodies.

Copenhagen Mogens Pedersøn pubd *Pratum spirituale*, the 1st collection of polyphonic settings of Danish texts.

Lisbon Manuel Rodrigues Coelho pubd *Flores de musica para o instrumento de tecla & harpa*, the earliest surviving collection of instrumental music printed in Portugal.

1621

Michael Praetorius *d* (*c*50, Wolfenbüttel); Jan Pieterszoon Sweelinck *d* (59, Amsterdam).

Jacob Stainer *b* (Absam).

Venice Francesco Turini pubd his 1st bk of madrigals with parts for 2 violins; a separate trio sonata was also included.

Hamburg Scheidt pubd the 1st of 3 collections of instrumental ensemble music, *Ludi musici* (2nd, 1622; 3rd, 1624).

Leipzig The 1st part of Schein's *Musica Boscareccia* pubd, a collection of secular songs for two sopranos and bass (2nd, 1626; 3rd, 1628).

Vienna Giovanni Valentini pubd *Messa, Magnificat et Jubilate Deo*, a collection of sacred works for 7 choirs and trumpet.

1622

Giovanni Valentini, the Habsburg court organist, succeeded Priuli as *Hofkapellmeister* in Vienna.

Venice Salamone Rossi's *Hashirim asher lish'lomo* ('The Songs of Solomon'), polyphonic settings of Hebrew psalms, hymns and synagogue songs, ed. and pubd by his pupil Leo da Modena, whose preface cites Talmudic and rabbinical sources to justify the introduction of polyphony into synagogue services.

1623

William Byrd *d* (*c*80, Stondon Massey); Thomas Weelkes *d* (47, London).

Antonio Cesti *b* (Arezzo); Jacopo Melani *b* (Pistoia); John Playford *b* (Norwich).

The Holy Roman Emperor Ferdinand II granted a privilege to form an imperial guild of trumpeters and kettledrummers under the patronage of the Elector of Saxony.

Filipe de Magalhães apptd *mestre de capela* of the Portuguese court.

Dresden Schütz produced his *Historia der ... Aufferstehung ... Jesu Christi*, a setting of a text drawn from all 4 Gospels.

Leipzig Schein pubd *Fontana d'Israel*, a collection of settings of Old Testament texts for 5 voices and *basso continuo*.

1624

Pope Urban VIII conceded to the Congregazione dei Musici di Roma (later the Accademia di S Cecilia) the supervision of music education and the publication of sacred music; the decree was revoked 2 years later.

The violinist Louis Constantin apptd *roi des joueurs d'instruments* in Paris.

Venice Monteverdi first used *stile concitato* in *Combattimento di Tancredi e Clorinda* (not pubd until 1638).

The title of Turini's 2nd bk of madrigals incorporates the term 'cantata' (in reference to an extended recitative) for the 1st time.

Hamburg Scheidt pubd the 1st of 3 vols. of *Tabulatura nova*, and in **Stuttgart** Johann Ulrich Steigleder pubd *Ricercar tabulatura*: they were the 1st edns of German keyboard music to appear in open score rather than organ tablature.

Leipzig Schein's *Diletti pastorali* or *Hirten Lust* (the secular counterpart of *Fontana d'Israel*; see 1623) became the 1st pubd collection of German continuo madrigals.

1625

Pietro Cerone *d* (*c*59, Naples); Orlando Gibbons *d* (42, Canterbury).

The Bolognese Accademia dei Floridi became the Accademia dei Filomusi (because of plague, it was dissolved in 1630); it counted Banchieri, Monteverdi and Merula among its members.

John Coprario apptd Composer-in-Ordinary at the new English court of Charles I.

Dresden Schütz pubd his Latin *Cantiones sacrae*, which he intended for inter-denominational use.

Nuremberg Paul Peuerl became the 1st German composer to pub. music for the Italian texture of two melody instruments and continuo (*Gantz neue Padouanen*).

Moscow The now-famous peal of bells was installed in the Gate of Salvation of the Kremlin.

Florence Francesca Caccini's *La liberazione di Ruggiero dell'isola d'Alcina* (text by Saracinelli after Ariosto) was the first opera composed and published by a woman.

1626

John Coprario *d* (London); John Dowland *d* (*c*63, London).

Giovanni Legrenzi *b* (Clusone).

Louis XIII acknowledged the Vingt-quatre Violons du Roi (also known as the Grande Bande), which was augmented by the 12 Grands Hautbois of the Écurie.

The 'Fedeli' (who had given the first perf. of Monteverdi's *L'Arianna*, Mantua, 1608) became attached to the imperial court in Vienna, where they continued to perform Italian operas.

William Heyther founded the music professorship at Oxford University.

1627

Lodovico Viadana *d* (*c*67, Gualtieri); Jacques Mauduit *d* (nearly 70, Paris).

Dresden Carlo Farina pubd *Capriccio stravagante*, a quodlibet in which the violin imitates other instruments and animals with special effects such as *col legno*, *sul ponticello*, pizzicato and tremolo.

Torgau Martin Opitz's adaptation of Rinuccini's *Dafne* with music by Schütz (lost), the earliest German opera, perf. for the Dresden court.

Leipzig Schein (in his capacity as *Thomaskantor*) pubd his *Cantional* (enlarged 2nd edn, 1645), a collection of current hymns with continuo figures in the bass part.

Warsaw Adam Jarzębski completed a MS collection of instrumental works for 2 to 4 players and continuo, *Canzoni e concerti*, which influenced the development of chamber genres in central Europe.

1628

Alfonso Ferrabosco the younger *d* (London); John Bull *d* (*c*65, Antwerp); Peter Philips *d* (*c*67, Brussels).

Louis XIII is said to have kept his spirits up during the siege of La Rochelle by composing motets.

Schütz went to Venice to study with Monteverdi.

Rome Vincenzo Giustiniani pubd his short *Discorso sopra la musica*, describing musical life there in the early 1600s.

Florence Peri collaborated with Gagliano on *La Flora* (text by Salvadori) for the wedding celebrations of Duke Odoardo Farnese and Margherita de' Medici.

Warsaw The 1st perf. of an Italian opera outside Italy, *Galatea* (?Santi Orlandi), given by Italian singers.

Bamberg Johann Degen pubd *Catholisches Gesangbuch*, the 1st German Catholic hymn-hymnbook.

1629

Sigismondo d'India *d* (*c*47, ?Modena).

Virgilio Mazzocchi apptd *maestro di cappella* at the Cappella Giulia, Rome, and Carissimi at the Jesuit Collegio Germanico, Rome.

Venice Schütz pubd *Symphoniae sacrae*; Marini pubd op. 8 (in which he differentiated between sonatas and sinfonias).

Madrid Lope de Vega's *La selva sin amor*, perf. at the Coliseo del Buen Retiro, was the 1st Spanish drama perf. entirely with sung dialogue.

1630

Alessandro Grandi *d* (?44, Bergamo); Johann Hermann Schein *d* (44, Leipzig).

Venice Monteverdi's lost opera *Proserpina rapita* (text by G. Strozzi) perf. during the wedding festivities of Giustiniana Mocenigo and Lorenzo Giustiniani, the only court opera ever perf. there.

Paris Pierre Trichet was at work on his *Traité des instruments de musique*, which remained in MS until the 20th century.

London About this time, Jonson's play *The Sad Shepherd* perf. with music by Nicholas Lanier; Martin Peerson's *Mottects or Grave Chamber Musique* was the 1st English collection pubd with a figured bass part.

1631

The Viennese Hofkapelle, departing from convention, engaged its first female singer, Margherita Basile.

P. F. Valentini pubd in Rome his *Canone nel modo Salomonis* for 96 voices, which could be augmented to 144,000 if sung at different speeds and in different metres.

1632

Jean-Baptiste Lully [Giovanni Battista Lulli] *b* (Florence).

Venice Monteverdi pubd *Scherzi musicali*, containing 'Zefiro torna' (the first great vocal chaconne).

Rome Stefano Landi's *Il Sant' Alessio* (text by Rospigliosi) perf. at the Palazzo Barberini's Quattro Fontane (the 1st Roman opera house) to celebrate its opening – the earliest known setting of a historical subject and the 1st to incorporate overtures to the prologue and acts (it may also have been given the previous year).

1633

Jacopo Peri *d* (71, Florence); Jehan Titelouze *d* (*c*70, Rouen).

Samuel Pepys *b* (England).

Domenico Brunetti, *maestro di cappella* of Bologna Cathedral, founded the Accademia dei Filaschisi.

Schütz apptd *Kapellmeister* at the Danish court.

Carlos Patiño became the 1st Spaniard to serve as court *maestro de capilla* at Madrid.

Vienna Ludovico Bartolaia's *Il Sidonio* was the 1st opera perf. there.

1634

Adriano Banchieri *d* (*c*66, Bologna); Johann Staden *d* (53, Nuremberg).

Adam Krieger *b* (Driesen).

Jan Hermanszoon Krul founded the Amsterdamsche Musijck Kamer, devoted to the cultivation of music drama.

London William Lawes and Simon Ives contributed music to Shirley's *The Triumph of Peace*, the most spectacular of all English masques.

Henry Lawes collaborated with Milton on the masque *Comus*, 1st perf. at Ludlow Castle.

1635

Schütz returned to Dresden from Copenhagen.

The Nuremberg brass instrument makers formed a guild which was overseen by the city council.

Venice Frescobaldi pubd *Fiori musicali* (a large collection of organ and instrumental chamber music intended for use in the Mass).

Chantilly The *Ballet de la Merlaison*, with words, music and choreography by Louis XIII, perf. for the court.

1636

Bologna Members of the Accademia dei Riaccesi rented the Palazzo Formagliari to stage operas and comedies; the theatre became known as the Guastavillani after the marquis who renovated and then managed it.

Paris Marin Mersenne began issuing the 1st of 4 vols. of *Harmonie Universelle*.

Leipzig Schütz pubd his 1st collection of *Kleine geistliche Concerte* (the 2nd pubd Dresden, 1639).

London Charles Butler pubd *The Principles of Musik* which, though written for church musicians, gained wider significance as an important link between Morley (*Plaine and Easie Introduction to Practicall Musicke*, 1597) and Playford (see **1654**).

Henry and William Lawes collaborated on music for Davenant's *The Triumphs of the Prince d'Amour*.

1637

Dieterich Buxtehude *b*.

Froberger apptd organist of the Hofkapelle, Vienna, on the accession of Ferdinand III; he soon obtained leave to study with Frescobaldi in Rome.

Rome Virgilio Mazzocchi and Marazzoli collaborated on the 1st comic opera, *Chi soffre, speri* (text by Rospigliosi), perf. at the Palazzo Barberini.

Venice The 1st public opera house, Teatro S Cassiano, opened with Francesco Manelli's *L'Andromeda* (text by Ferrari).

1638

Nicholas Formé *d* (71, Paris).

Venice Monteverdi pubd *Madrigali guerrieri et amorosi*.

Dresden Schütz's lost opera-ballet *Orpheus und Euridice* (text by Buchner) perf. at court.

London William Lawes contributed music to Davenant's masque *Britannia triumphans*.

1639

Stefano Landi *d* (c52, Rome); Melchior Franck *d* (c60, Coburg).

Bernardo Pasquini *b* (Lucca).

Rome André Maugars wrote his 'Response faite à un curieux sur le sentiment de la musique d'Italie' in which he compared French and Italian performing practices.

Venice The Teatro SS Giovanni e Paolo opened with Manelli's *La Delia* (text by G. Strozzi); Cavalli's 1st opera, *Le nozze di Teti e di Peleo* (text by Persiani), perf. at the Teatro S Cassiano.

1640

Venice Monteverdi's *Il ritorno d'Ulisse in patria* (text by Badoaro) perf.; the Teatro S Moisè opened.

Danzig Paul Siefert pubd *Psalmen Davids, nach francösischer Melodey* (chorale motet settings of the Calvinist Reformed Church psalter) as a public response to Kaspar Förster, with whom he sustained a lengthy quarrel (see **1643**).

Cambridge, Mass. The 1st American metrical psalter, *Whole Booke of Psalmes*, pubd – the 1st bk printed in the English-speaking New World.

1641

Jacques Champion de Chambonnières organized the twice-weekly 'Assemblées des Honnestes Curieux' at his Paris home.

The Parisian theatre of the Palais Royal built; originally intended for plays, *ballets de cour* and Italian operas, it later became the home of Molière's troupe and then the Académie Royale de Musique.

Venice Francesco Sacrati's opera *La finta pazza* (text by G. Strozzi) perf. at the opening of the Teatro Novissimo (see **1645**).

Palermo Gioanpietro Del Buono pubd the earliest harpsichord sonatas.

Hamburg Thomas Selle pubd his *St John Passion*, the 1st to include instrumental interludes.

1642

Schütz returned to Copenhagen as *Hofkapellmeister*.

Rome Luigi Rossi's *Il palazzo incantato di Atlante* (text by Rospigliosi) perf. at the Barberini theatre, Quattro Fontane.

Venice Monteverdi's *L'incoronazione di Poppea* (text by Busenello) perf.

Nuremberg Johann Andreas Herbst pubd *Musica practica*, the 1st independent singing manual (see **1643**).

1643

Marco da Gagliano *d* (61, Florence); Girolamo Frescobaldi *d* (60, Rome); Monteverdi *d* (76, Venice).

Marc'Antoine Charpentier *b* (Paris).

Venice Cavalli's opera *Egisto* perf.; it was perf. 3 years later in Paris.

Paris Annibal Gantez pubd his observations on French musical life in *L'entretien des musiciens*.

Warsaw Marco Scacchi pubd (in Venice) his *Cribrum musicum ad triticum Syferticum*, in which he catalogued the errors of musical literacy committed by Siefert in his 1640 *Psalmen Davids* (see **1645**).

Nuremberg Herbst pubd *Musica poetica*, the 1st composition manual in German instead of Latin.

Vienna Giovanni Valentini wrote the text and composed the music for *Santi risorti* (ded. Ferdinand III), apparently the first sacred drama perf. at court (see **1649**).

1644

Antonio Stradivari *b* (Cremona); Alessandro Stradella *b* (Rome); Heinrich Ignaz Franz Biber *b* (Wartenberg, Bohemia).

Giovanni Rovetta succeeded Monteverdi as *maestro di capella* at S Marco, Venice.

Rome The musicians of the Barberini household met together during the summer in the spirit of an academy.

Venice Barbara Strozzi pubd *Il primo libro de madrigali*, the 1st of 8 vols. of vocal chamber music.

Paris Mersenne pubd the 1st description of the baryton in *Cogitata physico-mathematica*.

London The last remaining church organs destroyed by order of the Puritan Parliament; until the Restoration metrical psalms had to be sung unaccompanied.

1645

William Lawes *d* (43, in the siege of Chester).

Andreas Werckmeister *b* (Benneckenstein).

Venice Giovanni Antonio Bertoli pubd an early collection of solo bassoon sonatas.

Paris Sacrati's 1641 Venetian opera *La finta pazza* (text by Strozzi, with sets and machinery by Torelli and ballet by Balbi) perf. at Cardinal Mazarin's request for the court.

Danzig Siefert replied to Scacchi (in Warsaw) by publishing *Anticribratio musica ad avenam Schachianam hoc est*, effectively dismantling Scacchi's model (see **1649**).

Nuremberg Johann Kindermann's *Harmonia organica* was the last organ music printed in tablature and among the 1st German music to be engraved.

1646

Orazio Benevoli apptd *maestro di cappella* of the Cappella Giulia, Rome.

The Florentine Jean-Baptiste Lully brought to Paris by the Chevalier de Guise and trained as a musician while serving Mlle de Montpensier; Luigi Rossi arrived from Rome to prepare his opera *Orfeo*.

Paris Cavalli's *Egisto* (1643; text by Faustini) perf. at the Palais Royal.

Copenhagen Hans Mikkelsen Ravn pubd *Heptachordum danicum seu Nova solsisatio*, by his own account the 1st comprehensive book on music in Denmark.

Danzig The first perf. of an opera, Scacchi's *Le nozze d'Amore e di Psyche*, given by the city Kapelle, assisted by the Warsaw Kapelle, to celebrate the arrival of the Polish queen Marie Louise.

1647

Pelham Humfrey *b*.

João Alvares Frouvo apptd *mestre de capela* at Lisbon Cathedral.

Paris Luigi Rossi's *Orfeo* (text by Buti), commissioned by Cardinal Mazarin, perf. at the Palais Royal by Italians, in Italian, with a French prologue and ballets.

Berlin Johannes Crüger pubd *Praxis pietatis melica*, the most influential chorale publication of the 17th century.

Stockholm Queen Christina engaged 6 French musicians (among them the violinist Pierre Verdier) for court ballets (see **1652**).

1648

Marin Mersenne *d* (60, Paris).

With the start of the Fronde in France, the Italians associated with the recent opera productions in Paris fled (Luigi Rossi and the castrato Atto Melani) or were incarcerated (Giacomo Torelli) (see **1654**).

Lully formed the 16-strong Petits Violons, who regularly played during Louis XIV's *diner* and *coucher*.

Dresden Schütz pubd *Geistliche Chor-Musik*, the most important collection of 17th-century German motets.

Prague Wolfgang Ebner pubd 36 variations for harpsichord on a theme by Emperor Ferdinand III.

London Henry Lawes pubd *Choice Psalmes* (60 psalms – 30 his own, the rest by his late brother William, to whom the collection was ded.).

1649

Pascal Collasse *b* (Rheims); Johann Philipp Krieger *b* (Nuremberg); John Blow *b* (Newark).

Antonio Bertali succeeded Giovanni Valentini as *Hofkapellmeister* in Vienna.

Venice Cesti's *Orontea* (text by Cicognini) perf. at the Teatro di SS Apostoli; his 1st opera, it established his popularity throughout Italy.

Vienna The 1st oratorio perf., the anon. *Il secondo Abramo disformato nel riformare il primo*.

Warsaw After Siefert's *Anticribratio musica* (1645), Scacchi pubd letters of support for him from Schütz and other notable composers (*Judicium cribri musici*), effectively ending the 10-year-old dispute.

1650

Paris Pierre Corneille, Charles Dassoucy and the Italian machinist Giacomo Torelli collaborated (at Cardinal Mazarin's request) on a 'tragédie représentée avec les machines', *Andromède*, perf. at the Petit Bourbon palace.

Rome Athanasius Kircher pubd *Musurgia universalis*, an extremely influential compendium of musical facts and speculation.

Brussels The 1st opera (albeit Italian), Gioseffo Zamponi's *Ulisse nell'isola di Circe*, perf. for the wedding celebrations of Philip IV of Spain and Mariana of Austria.

Utrecht René Descartes pubd (in the year of his death) *Compendium musicae* – a treatise, written in 1618, in which scientific method is applied to music.

1651

Paris Isaac de Benserade's 1st ballet, *Cassandre* (composers unknown), in which the young Louis XIV made his first appearance, dancing the role of the Sun, perf. at the Palais Royal.

London John Playford pubd *The English Dancing Master*, containing descriptions of country dances.

1652

Paris Henry du Mont pubd *Cantica sacra*, the 1st printed collection of *petits motets*, for voices, viols or violins and continuo; at much this time Ennemond and Denis Gaultier's lute music pubd in *La rhétorique des dieux*.

Stockholm Queen Christina engaged an Italian opera troupe led by Alessandro Cecconi.

1653

Luigi Rossi *d* (*c*56, Rome).

Arcangelo Corelli *b* (Fusignano); Georg Muffat *b* (Mégève, Savoy); Johann Pachelbel *b* (Nuremberg).

Lully apptd *compositeur de la musique instrumentale* at the French court.

Froberger apptd court organist in Vienna.

Bologna The Teatro Malvezzi opened with opera for the aristocracy; the Galli-Bibiena family designed all their sets.

Innsbruck The Englishman William Young pubd the earliest known works called 'sonatas' by an English composer.

Munich G. B. Maccioni's single-scene work *L'arpa festante* (for which he wrote words and music) inaugurated the fashion for Italian opera at court.

Nuremberg Kindermann pubd *Canzoni, sonate* for 1–3 violins, cello and continuo, some of the earliest works to require scordatura.

London Shirley's masque *Cupid and Death*, with music by Matthew Locke, perf. before the Portuguese ambassador.

Madrid Juan Hidalgo comp. the earliest surviving Spanish recitatives for his semi-opera *Fortunas de Andrómeda y Perseo* (text by Calderón; see Plate 20).

1654

Samuel Scheidt *d* (66, Halle).

Jean Veillot and Thomas Gobert apptd *sous-maîtres* of the Chapelle Royale, Paris.

The Palazzo Farnese, the Roman residence of Queen Christina of Sweden, who had abdicated on conversion to Catholicism, became the venue of important musical events.

Paris The Fronde was suppressed, enabling Cardinal Mazarin to summon Italian musicians; Carlo Caproli's opera *Le nozze di Peleo e di Teti* perf. at the Petit Bourbon, with ballets by Lully and Benserade (Louis XIV danced 6 roles) and scenery and machinery by Torelli.

Innsbruck Antonio Cesti's *La Cleopatra* inaugurated the archducal Komödienhaus (the 1st purpose-built opera house in a German-speaking country).

London John Playford first issued *A Breefe Introduction to the Skill of Musick*.

1655

Bartolomeo Cristofori *b* (Padua).

Paris Michel de La Guerre comp. *Le triomphe de l'amour* (text by Beys), the 1st 'comédie françoise en musique', perf. at the Louvre during Carnival.

England The Festival of Sons of the Clergy, a simple Commonwealth ceremony, inaugurated, which after the Restoration gave rise to annual musical festivals.

1656

Marin Marais *b* (Paris).

Carissimi apptd *maestro di cappella del concerto di camera* by Queen Christina of Sweden, in Rome, who established an academy (after her death known as the Accademia dell'Arcadia) at her residence in the Palazzo Farnese (see **1680**).

Filipe da Cruz apptd *mestre* of the Portuguese royal chapel.

Venice The Teatro S Samuele opened.

London Sir William Davenant's *Siege of Rhodes* perf. at Rutland House, the earliest English opera, with music by Charles Coleman, Henry Cooke, George Hudson, Henry Lawes and Matthew Locke (see **1661**).

1657

Louis Constantin *d* (*c*72, Paris).

Michel-Richard de Lalande *b* (Paris); Philipp Heinrich Erlebach *b* (Esens).

Maurizio Cazzati apptd *maestro di cappella* at S Petronio, Bologna.

Guillaume Dumanoir succeeded Constantin as *roi et maître des ménestriers* in Paris.

Florence The Accademia degli Immobili inaugurated their new Teatro della Pergola, with Jacopo Melani's *La Tancia* (text by Moniglia).

Paris Lully collaborated with Buti on the *Ballet de l'amour malade*, perf. – with oboes in the orchestra for the 1st time – at the Louvre palace.

Innsbruck Cesti's *La Dori* (text by Apolloni) perf.

Munich J. K. Kerll's *L'Oronte* inaugurated the newly built opera house.

1658

Giuseppe Torelli *b* (Verona).

Paris Lully, Jean-Baptiste de Boësset and Louis de Mollier provided music for Benserade's *Ballet d'Alcidiane*, perf. for Louis XIV's 20th birthday.

René Ouvrard published *Secret pour composer en musique* under a pseudonym (du Reneau).

1659

Henry Purcell *b*.

Paris Lully's *Ballet de la raillerie* (text by Benserade) perf., a humorous confrontation between Italian and French music and language.

London Christopher Simpson pubd *The Division-Violist*.

1660

Alessandro Scarlatti *b* (Palermo); André Campra *b* (Aix-en-Provence); Johann Kuhnau *b* (Geising); Johann Joseph Fux *b* (Hirtenfeld, Styria).

Matthias Weckmann founded the Hamburg collegium musicum with 50 musicians.

Paris Cavalli hastily adapted his opera *Xerse* (1654; text by Minato) – with a prologue and choruses (after the French fashion), as well as with ballets by Lully – for the wedding festivities of Louis XIV and the Spanish Infanta Maria Theresa, at the Louvre; Mazarin had originally commissioned a new theatre and a new opera, *Ercole amante* (text by Buti), but neither was ready in time (see **1662**).

Dresden Schütz's *Historia der ... Geburth ... Jesu Christi* perf. (pubd 4 years later), considered the earliest German setting of the nativity story in which the Evangelist's words are in recitative.

London Samuel Pepys began his celebrated diary, which contains numerous musical references.

Madrid Juan Hidalgo and the librettist Pedro Calderón de la Barca collaborated on the earliest surviving Spanish opera, *Celos aun del aire matan*.

1661

Louis Couperin *d* (*c*35, Paris).

Georg Böhm *b* (Hohenkirchen).

Lully apptd *surintendant de la musique de la chambre* at the French court; his father-in-law Michel Lambert apptd *maître de musique de la chambre*; the soprano Anne de La Barre was the 1st female *ordinaire de la musique de chambre*.

Matthew Locke apptd 'private composer-in-ordinary', 'composer in the wind music' and 'composer for the violin band' to Charles II and provided music for the coronation.

Olof Rudbeck (*rector magnificus*) founded an orchestra, the Akademiska Kapellet, at the University of Uppsala.

Florence Cesti's *La Dori* (text by Apolloni) and Jacopo Melani's lavish *festa teatrale*, *Ercole in Tebe* (text by Moniglia), perf. for the wedding celebrations of Grand Duke Cosimo III de' Medici and Marguerite Louise d'Orléans; they are said to have influenced Cavalli's *Ercole amante* (see **1662**) and Cesti's *Il pomo d'oro* (see **1668**).

Paris To mark the end of the war between France and Spain Lully and Benserade's *Ballet de l'impatience* perf. at the Louvre (Louis XIV danced the role of 'a great lover'); their *Ballet des saisons* perf. at Fontainebleau.

London Sir William Davenant's converted tennis court in Lincoln's Inn Fields, the Duke's Theatre, opened with *The Siege of Rhodes*, occasioning the king's 1st appearance at a public theatre.

Edward Lowe pubd *A Short Direction for the Performance of Cathedrall Service*, in the hope of reviving organ accompaniment, suppressed during the Commonwealth.

The Hague Christiaan Huygens worked out the mathematical basis for dividing the octave into 31 equal parts, demonstrating its practicality in *Novus cyclus harmonicus*.

1662

Marco Marazzoli *d* (*c*60, Rome); Henry Lawes *d* (66, London).

Lully apptd *maître de la musique de la famille royale* at the French court.

Paris Cavalli's *Ercole amante*, originally commissioned by Mazarin for the wedding of Louis XIV in 1660, finally perf. in Gaspare Vigarani's Salle des Machines in the Tuileries palace. In deference to French taste Cavalli included choruses and short symphonies to introduce the acts; Benserade and Lully comp. an elaborate ballet (*Hercule amoureux*), interleaved between the acts.

The Archbishop of Paris, J. F. P. de Gondy, authorized the repressive *Ceremoniale parisiense*, which echoed the century-old sanctions of the Council of Trent (1545–63) against using instruments other than the organ in church, and specifying when and how the organ was to be used in the celebration of the Mass and the Office.

1663

Heinrich Scheidemann *d* (*c*68, Hamburg).

Louis XIV held a competition to choose 4 *sous-maîtres* for his Chapelle Royale: Henry Du Mont, Gabriel Expilly, Pierre Robert and Thomas Gobert apptd.

Paris Lully and Michel Lambert collaborated with Isaac de Benserade on the *Ballet des arts*, perf. at the Palais Royal and the Château de Vincennes. Lully and Molière collaborated on *L'impromptu de Versailles*, perf. at the hunting-lodge at Versailles.

London The 1st Theatre Royal in Drury Lane opened.

1664

Paris Lully collaborated in quick succession with Molière on their 1st comic venture (*Le mariage forcé*); then with Benserade on the *Ballet des amours déguisés*, for the Palais Royal; again with Molière on a 3-day springtime court entertainment at Versailles (*Les plaisirs de l'île enchantée*), which included a perf. of *La princesse d'Élide*; finally with Thomas Corneille on *Entr'actes d'Oedipe* for Fontainebleau. He also comp. the *Miserere*, the *grand motet* by which he is still best known.

Nuremberg J. H. Schmelzer pubd *Sonatae unarum fidium*, the earliest German collection of sonatas for violin and continuo.

1665

Bologna Maurizio Cazzati pubd op. 35 sonatas, including 3 for trumpet and strings.

Paris Lully collaborated with Benserade on the *Ballet de la naissance de Vénus* at the Palais Royal and with Molière on *L'amour médecin* at Versailles.

London Christopher Simpson pubd *The Principles of Practical Musick* (see **1667**).

1666

Jean-Féry Rebel *b* (Paris).

The Accademia Filarmonica in Bologna founded by 50 musicians.

Cremona Antonio Stradivari began labelling his violins.

Rome Antimo Liberati presented Pope Alexander VII with an *Epitome della musica*, retrospectively setting up Palestrina's music as the standard.

Paris Lully put on a ballet at the Hôtel de Créqui, and at Saint-Germain collaborated with Benserade and Molière on the *Ballet des muses*.

Dubuisson's dated MS pieces (in tablature and staff notation) represent the earliest extant French solo bass viol music.

Vienna Cesti's first imperial court opera perf., *Nettunno e Flora festeggianti* (text by Sbarra), with an aria by Leopold I.

1667

Johann Jacob Froberger *d* (*c*51, Héricourt); Franz Tunder *d* (*c*53, Lübeck).

Michel Pignolet de Montéclair *b* (Andelot); Johann Christoph Pepusch *b* (Berlin).

Venice Johann Rosenmüller pubd 12 *Sonate da camera a 5 stromenti*.

Saint-Germain To celebrate Carnival and the French victory in Flanders, Louis XIV ordered a series of perfs. of works by Molière, including 2 with music by Lully (*La pastorale comique* and *Le sicilien*).

Dresden *Teseo* (an opera attrib. G. A. Bontempi, text by G. A. Moniglia) perf. at the opening of the opera house.

Vienna Cesti's *Le disgrazie d'Amore* (text by Sbarra) perf.

London Simpson reissued *The Principles of Practical Musick* (1665) as *A Compendium of Practical Musicke*, the better-known title.

1668

François Couperin (*le Grand*) *b* (Paris).

Cavalli apptd *maestro di cappella* at S Marco, Venice.

Buxtehude married Franz Tunder's daughter and succeeded him as organist at the Marienkirche, Lübeck.

Blow apptd organist of Westminster Abbey, London.

Rome Jacopo Melani comp. *Il Girello* (text by Acciaiuoli, with a prologue by Stradella), an operatic satire on absolutism, perf. at the Palazzo Colonna; it became one of the most popular operas of the century and signalled a new period of Roman comic opera.

Paris Lully collaborated with Benserade on *Le carnaval ou Mascarade de Versailles*, perf. at the Louvre. At Versailles Lully and Quinault produced *La grotte de Versailles*, and to celebrate the peace of Aix-la-Chapelle Louis XIV ordered an elaborate 1-day 'Fête de Versailles', which included a perf. of *George Dandin*, Molière and Lully's *comédie-ballet*.

Bénigne de Bacilly pubd *Remarques curieuses sur l'art de bien chanter*.

Vienna Cesti's *Il pomo d'oro* (text by Sbarra, sets by Burnacini) perf. for the wedding of Leopold I, an operatic landmark, unprecedented in its conception and lavish production (see Plates 11 and 12).

1669

Antonio Cesti *d* (46, Florence); Christopher Simpson *d* (*c*64, London).

Alessandro Marcello *b* (Venice); Louis Marchand *b* (Lyons).

Henry Du Mont and Pierre Robert jointly apptd *compositeur de la musique de la chapelle et de la chambre* at the French court.

Giovanni Felice Sances succeeded Bertali as *Kapellmeister* at the Habsburg court.

Rome Alessandro Melani comp. *L'empio punito*, the first Don Juan opera (on a libretto by Acciaiuoli) for Cardinal Colonna.

Paris Lully collaborated with Benserade for the last time, on the *Ballet de Flore*, perf. in the Grand Salon of the Tuileries palace, and with Molière on *Monsieur de Pourceaugnac* at Chambord.

Pierre Perrin granted, jointly with Robert Cambert, *Lettres patentes* to establish

'Académies d'Opéra ou représentations en musique en langue française sur le pied de celles d'Italie' [Académie Royale de Musique].

1670

Giovanni Bononcini *b* (Modena).

Rome Cavalli's *Scipione affricano* (1664; text by Minato) perf. (with new prologue by Stradella) at the opening by Queen Christina of Sweden of the Teatro Tordinona, the 1st public opera house there.

Paris Jacques Champion de Chambonnières pubd 2 collections of harpsichord pieces.

Saint-Germain Molière and Lully collaborated for Carnival on *Les amants magnifiques* (with Louis XIV dancing, for the last time in a production, the roles of Neptune and Apollo), and later on *Le bourgeois gentilhomme* at Chambord (Lully played the mufti in the Turkish ceremony scene).

1671

Tomaso Giovanni Albinoni *b* (Venice).

Paris The Académie, under the direction of Pierre Perrin and Robert Cambert, perf. a *pastorale*, *Pomone*, in a theatre on the site of a tennis court.

Lully and Molière (with Quinault and Pierre Corneille) presented their only *tragédie-ballet*, *Psyché*, at the Tuileries palace, later the basis for Lully's *tragédie lyrique* with Thomas Corneille and Fontenelle (see **1678**).

Saint-Germain Lully collaborated with Molière and Quinault on the *Ballet des ballets*.

1672

Jacques Champion de Chambonnières *d* (*c*70, Paris); Heinrich Schütz *d* (87, Dresden).

Francesco Mancini *b* (Naples); André Cardinal Destouches *b* (Paris).

Giovanni Legrenzi apptd *maestro* at the Mendicanti, a Venetian *ospedale*.

Lully acquired the privilege of the Académie Royale de Musique and, through restrictive royal patents, gained a monopoly for the use of music on the French stage. He ended his partnership with Molière and entered into a new one with Philippe Quinault and the machinist Carlo Vigarani: their 1st production was *Les fêtes de l'Amour et de Bacchus*, perf. at a new theatre opposite the Palais du Luxembourg.

Molière collaborated with M.-A. Charpentier, presented revivals of *La comtesse d'Escarbagnas* and *Le mariage forcé*; they were well advanced on a new comedy, *Le malade imaginaire* (see **1673**).

London The 1st Theatre Royal in Drury Lane burnt down.

The violinist John Banister presented the 1st known concerts, at the Musick-School in White Fryers, at which admission was charged.

Thomas Salmon pubd *An Essay to the Advancement of Musick*, containing a proposal to abolish clefs.

Madrid Juan Hidalgo collaborated with Juan Vélez de Guevara on *Los celos hacen estrellas*, the earliest *zarzuela* for which the music survives.

Andrés Lorente pubd a substantial Spanish treatise on ecclesiastical music in the *stile antico*, based on Cerone (see **1613**), *El porqué de la música*.

1673

Antonio Literes *b* (Artá, Majorca); Molière *d* (51, Paris).

Bologna Giovanni Maria Bononcini pubd *Musico prattico*.

Paris Molière and Charpentier collaborated on *Le malade imaginaire* at the Palais Royal; Molière took the title role, but died during the 4th performance.

Cadmus et Hermione, Lully and Quinault's 1st *tragédie lyrique*, was highly successful. Immediately after its opening Louis XIV issued ordinances granting Lully the use of the Palais Royal (thereby displacing Molière's troupe) and further restricting French and foreign troupes (other than the Académie) from using more than 2 singers and 6 instrumentalists.

London Matthew Locke pubd *Melothesia*, a collection of keyboard music which includes the 1st extant instructions for realizing a figured bass.

1674

Giacomo Carissimi *d* (68, Rome); Pelham Humfrey *d* (*c*27, Windsor).

Reinhard Keiser *b* (Teuchern).

Paris Lully presented *Alceste* (text by Quinault; see Plate 4).

Stockholm Gustaf Düben pubd *Odae sveticae*, the 1st song collection with Swedish texts.

London The 2nd Drury Lane theatre opened.

John Banister, G. B. Draghi, James Hart, Pelham Humfrey, Matthew Locke and Pietro Reggio contributed music to Thomas Shadwell's operatic version of Davenant's and Dryden's adaptation of Shakespeare's *The Tempest*.

1675

Evaristo Felice Dall'Abaco *b* (Verona).

Saint-Germain Lully's *Thésée* (text by Quinault) perf. for the king.

Stettin J. G. Ebeling pubd a history of music, *Archaiologia Orphicae*.

London Locke and Draghi comp. the music for Shadwell's English imitation of Lully's *tragédie lyrique*, *Psyché*.

At Whitehall, Nicholas Staggins collaborated with John Crowne on *Calisto, or The Chaste Nymph*, a court masque in which oboes were assigned parts for the 1st time in an English orchestra, the players having been brought from France.

1676

Francesco Cavalli *d* (73, Venice); Jacopo Melani *d* (53, Pistoia); Christopher Gibbons *d* (61, London).

Louis-Nicolas Clérambault *b* (Paris).

Saint-Germain Lully's *Atys* (text by Quinault) perf.

Frankfurt and **Leipzig** Johann Jakob Walther pubd his virtuoso *Scherzi da violino solo con il basso continuo*.

Salzburg About this time, Biber comp. the scordatura 'Mystery Sonatas' for the October cathedral services traditionally devoted to the Rosary Mysteries; engravings of the Mysteries are attached to the MS, and one of a guardian angel and a child precedes the final unaccompanied passacaglia.

London Thomas Mace pubd *Musick's Monument*, an important source for mid-century English music.

1677

Robert Cambert *d* (*c*50, London); Matthew Locke *d* (*c*55, London).

Antonio Maria Bononcini *b* (Modena); Évrard Titon du Tillet *b* (Paris).

Rome Pope Innocent XI banned theatre and opera, which precipitated an exodus of musicians.

Saint-Germain Lully's *Isis* (text by Quinault) perf. (see **1678**).

1678

Giovanni Maria Bononcini *d* (36, Modena).

Antonio Vivaldi *b* (Venice).

Louis XIV held a competition in Paris to determine the 4 organists of the Chapelle Royale; the winners were G. G. Nivers, N.-A. Lebègue, J.-D. Thomelin and J.-B. Buterne.

Thomas Britton began holding weekly musical meetings (free and open to the public) at his house in Clerkenwell (London), which continued until his death (1714).

Venice The opera house of S Giovanni Grisostomo opened.

Paris Lully collaborated with Thomas Corneille and Fontenelle on *Psyché* (a revision of a *tragédie-ballet*; see **1671**); Quinault was temporarily in disgrace at court following the indigent reception of *Isis* in 1677.

Hamburg Church and civic officials, and musicians such as Reincken and Theile, Strungk, Franck and Förtsch, founded the 1st German opera company; the choice of Theile's *Der erschaffene, gefallene und auffgerichtete Mensch* (*Adam und Eva*) to inaugurate their 1st season in the Gänsemarkt reflected their initial preference for operas on biblical subjects.

London Purcell comp. music for Shakespeare's *Timon of Athens* (adapted by Shadwell).

Amsterdam Carolus Hacquart comp. music for Dirk Buysero's play *De triomfeerende min*, which celebrated the Peace of Nijmegen; it is considered the 1st essay in Netherlands opera.

1679

Jan Dismas Zelenka *b* (Lounovice, Bohemia).

Johann Heinrich Schmelzer became the 1st native Austrian *Kapellmeister* in the 17th century to be apptd at the Habsburg court in Vienna; he died shortly thereafter of plague.

Purcell succeeded Blow as organist at Westminster Abbey, London.

Rome Alessandro Scarlatti's 1st opera, *Gli equivoci nel sembiante* (text by Contini), perf.

Paris Lully collaborated with Thomas Corneille, Fontenelle and Boileau-Despréaux on *Bellérophon*.

1680

Johann Heinrich Schmelzer *d* (Prague).

Jean Baptiste Loeillet *b* (Ghent).

Cristóbal Galán named *maestro de capilla* of the Spanish court in Madrid.

Rome Christina, the former Swedish queen, founded a second music academy.

Paris Lully resumed collaboration with Quinault, on *Proserpine*, 1st perf. at Saint-Germain.

Hamburg J. W. Franck's opera *Aeneas*, perf. at the Theater am Gänsemarkt, included the earliest aria with trumpet obbligato.

London A group of musicians commissioned the erection of the York Buildings in Villiers Street, about this time, to be used as a public concert room; it remained in use until the 1730s.

Amsterdam An opera house on the Leidse Gracht opened with P. A. Ziani's *Le fatiche d'Ercole per Deianira* (1662).

1681

Johann Mattheson *b* (Hamburg); Georg Philipp Telemann *b* (Magdeburg).

Lully apptd a *sécretaire du roi*; he further secured his monopoly on musical dramatic entertainment in Paris with a royal ordinance forbidding the Comédie Française (formed when Molière's troupe amalgamated with 2 others) to employ professional singers.

Christoph Bernhard apptd *Kapellmeister* at the electoral court in Dresden.

Rome Corelli pubd his op. 1 trio sonatas, the 1st of their kind.

Saint-Germain Lully collaborated with Benserade and Quinault on a ballet, *Le triomphe de l'amour*, using women dancers for the 1st time.

Paris Claude-François Ménestrier described perfs. of Italian operas and French ballets in *Des représentations en musique anciennes et modernes*.

Frankfurt am Main Andreas Werckmeister pubd his practical *Orgel-Probe*.

Brussels The Opéra du Quai du Foin (from 1700 Théâtre de la Monnaie), opened to the public; its repertory included Lully's works and operas by Netherlands composers.

1682

Alessandro Stradella *d* (murdered, 37, Genoa).

Jean-Joseph Mouret *b* (Avignon).

Antonio Draghi apptd *Hofkapellmeister* in Vienna.

The acrimonious 'Battle of the Organs' between Father Smith and Renatus Harris began about this time in London; it lasted 6 years.

Paris Lully's *Persée* (text by Quinault) perf.

Salzburg The 53-part *Missa salisburgensis* (long assumed to be by Orazio Benevoli but now thought to be by either Biber or Hofer) perf.

Stuttgart Johann Sigismund Kusser pubd *Composition de musique suivant la methode françoise*, incorporating the 1st French-styled overtures into German orchestral suites.

1683

Jean-Philippe Rameau *b* (Dijon); Johann David Heinichen *b* (Krössuln).

Louis XIV held a competition in Paris to determine the 4 *sous-maîtres* of the Chapelle Royale: those apptd were Nicolas Coupillet, Pascal Collasse, Guillaume Minoret and Lalande.

Paris Lully comp. *De profundis*; *Phaëton* (text by Quinault) perf. at Versailles.

M.-A. Charpentier comp. *Orphée descendant aux enfers*, the earliest known French cantata (which includes a part for a 'violon d'Orphée'), perf. at the *hôtel* of the Duchess of Guise in the Marais district.

The *Mercure galant* announced a 'Suite pour le violon seul sans basse' – possibly the earliest work in more than 1 movement for unaccompanied violin – by Johann Paul von Westhoff.

London Purcell pubd *[12]Sonnata's [sic] of III Parts*.

1684

Nicola Amati *d* (87, Cremona).

Johann Gottfried Walther *b* (Erfurt).

Alessandro Scarlatti apptd *maestro di cappella* of the Neapolitan viceregal court and director of the Teatro S Bartolomeo, where he remained until 1702.

All Roman musicians except papal singers bound by decree to observe the statutes of the Congregazione dei Musici, whose licence was necessary for exercising the profession (see **1624**).

Pierre Gautier granted permission to open an opera house in Marseilles to perform Lully's operas.

Johann Kuhnau apptd organist at the Thomaskirche, Leipzig.

Heinrich Ignaz Franz von Biber apptd *Kapellmeister* of the Salzburg court.

Paris The royal printer Christophe Ballard issued a sumptuous folio edn of *grands motets* by Lully, Henry Du Mont and Pierre Robert, as well as Lully's 6 *Motets à deux choeurs pour la chapelle du Roy* and the score of his latest *tragédie lyrique*, *Amadis et Gaule* (text by Quinault).

1685

Juan Hidalgo *d* (*c*70, Madrid).

Antonio Maria Bernacchi *b* (Bologna); Domenico Scarlatti *b* (Naples); Johann Sebastian Bach *b* (Eisenach); George Frideric Handel *b* (Halle); John Gay *b* (Barnstaple).

Rome Corelli's op. 2 (*sonate da camera*) pubd.

Paris Demachy pubd the 1st collection of unaccompanied *pièces de violes* [sic], half in tablature, half in staff notation (see **1687**).

Versailles Lully's *Roland* (text by Quinault) perf.; he and Quinault collaborated on *Le temple de la paix* for Fontainebleau; Lully set Racine's text for the *Idylle sur la paix* for the court at Sceaux. All 3 works subsequently perf. that year at the Paris Opéra.

Vienna G. B. Pederzuoli comp. 10 *accademie* (philosophical cantatas) to texts by Minato, a member of the Italian academy founded in 1657.

London John Playford pubd *The Division Violin*.

1686

John Playford *d* (*c*63, London).

Benedetto Marcello *b* (Venice); Nicola Antonio Porpora *b* (Naples); Sylvius Leopold Weiss *b* (Breslau).

Legrenzi apptd *maestro di cappella* at S Marco, Venice.

Paris Lully's masterpiece *Armide* (text by Quinault) perf.

At about this time Charpentier comp. a sonata for 8 instruments (the 1st French sonata) and a miniature opera, *Les arts florissants*, for the italophile Duchess of Guise.

Marin Marais pubd his 1st vol. of *Pièces de violes*; the continuo part was issued 3 years later.

1687

Jean-Baptiste Lully *d* (54, Paris); Constantijn Huygens *d* (90, The Hague).

Francesco Geminiani *b* (Lucca); Johann Georg Pisendel *b* (Cadolzburg).

Bologna Giovanni Battista Degli Antoni pubd 12 *Ricercate*, the earliest known printed collection for solo cello.

Paris Lully's last contribution to the French stage, one act of *Achille et Polyxène* (text by Campistron; prologue and Acts II-V by Collasse), perf. at the Opéra.

Elisabeth-Claude Jacquet de La Guerre pubd her 1st collection of *pièces de clavecin*.

Jean Rousseau pubd *Traité de la viole*, the most important viol treatise of the era; in it he criticized Demachy (see **1688**).

Hamburg J. A. Reincken pubd *Hortus musicus*, a collection of 6 suites for 2 violins, viol and continuo.

Nuremberg The chalumeau mentioned for the 1st time in an inventory of instruments in the Hofkapelle of Duke Heinrich of Saxe-Römhild (see **1690**).

1688

Carlo Pallavicino *d* (Dresden).

Johann Friedrich Fasch *b* (Buttelstädt).

Lyons The Académie Royale founded to perform *tragédies lyriques* already premièred in Paris; Lully's *Phaëton* was the 1st to be perf.

Paris Charpentier comp. *David et Jonathas*; when perf. at the Collège de Clermont it was interleaved act by act with a Jesuit drama.

Following a private exchange between viol players Jean Rousseau and Demachy, Rousseau pubd an open letter to Demachy (not named), criticizing his theories of left-hand technique.

Mainz Johann Jakob Walther pubd *Hortulus chelicus*.

1689

Michel-Richard de Lalande apptd *surintendant de la musique de la chambre* at Versailles.

Modena G. B. Vitali pubd *Artifici musicali*, 60 works which systematically set forth a method of instrumental counterpoint, foreshadowing J. S. Bach's *Musical Offering* by 58 years (see **1747**).

Rome Corelli pubd op. 3 trio sonatas.

Paris Pascal Collasse's *Thétis et Pélée* (text by Fontenelle), perf. by the Académie Royale de Musique, was the only *tragédie lyrique* by a student of Lully to gain lasting public approbation.

J.-B. Moreau collaborated with Racine on *Esther* for perf. at the school for young noblewomen at St Cyr.

Jean-Henri d'Anglebert pubd *Pieces de clavecin*, which includes a short treatise on accompaniment and the most comprehensive table of ornaments of the period.

Versailles Lalande comp. the 1st version of *De profundis*.

Leipzig Kuhnau pubd the 1st vol. of *Neuer Clavier-Übung* (2nd vol., 1692).

Copenhagen Poul Christian Schindler comp. *Der vereinigte Götterstreit*, the 1st Danish opera (on a German text by Burchardt), for King Christian V's birthday; during the 2nd perf. the opera house caught fire, and many of the audience died, including the composer's wife and daughter.

London Purcell's *Dido and Aeneas*, a miniature opera on a text by Nahum Tate, perf. at Josias Priest's Chelsea School for Young Ladies.

1690

Domenico Gabrielli *d* (*c*40, Bologna); Giovanni Legrenzi *d* (63, Venice).

Francesco Maria Veracini *b* (Florence).

Biber ennobled by Emperor Leopold I in Vienna.

A music fraternity, the Società S Cecilia, founded in Venice.

Paris François Couperin issued *Pièces d'orgue* in MS copies with engraved title pages.

Berlin *Der Scheerenschleifer*, one of the earliest Singspiels whose title is known, perf. for the court (see **1699**).

Dresden The Pietist theologian Christian Gerber pubd *Unerkandte Sünden der Welt*, with a chapter on music, denouncing its use in the Protestant church (see **1703**).

W. C. Printz pubd *Historische Beschreibung der edelen Sing- und Kling-Kunst*, the 1st German history of music.

Nuremberg The clarinet (derived from the chalumeau) being developed by Denner.

Salzburg Georg Muffat pubd *Apparatus musico-organisticus*, 12 organ toccatas mixing Lullian and Corellian styles.

London Purcell's semi-opera *Dioclesian* (text by Dryden) perf. at Dorset Garden.

Amsterdam Sybrand van Noordt pubd the 1st known harpsichord sonata comp. outside Italy.

1691

Francesco Feo *b* (Naples).

Hanover The completed Gartentheater in Herrenhausen became an important venue for court music and is now the oldest surviving theatre in Germany.

London Purcell's semi-opera *King Arthur* (text by Dryden) perf. at Dorset Garden.

1692

Giuseppe Tartini *b* (Pirano).

Paris Marin Marais pubd the 1st collection of *pièces en trio*; at much the same time François Couperin, J.-F. Rebel, Sébastien de Brossard and E.-C. Jacquet de La Guerre were composing (though not publishing) italianate trio sonatas.

Leipzig Kuhnau pubd the 2nd part of *Neuer Clavier-Übung* (7 suites and 1 sonata), the earliest of its type pubd in Germany.

London Purcell's semi-opera *The Fairy Queen*, based on Shakespeare's *A Midsummer Night's Dream*, perf. at Dorset Garden; his ode *Hail, bright Cecilia* (text by N. Brady) perf. for St Cecilia's Day.

P. A. Motteux began the monthly *Gentleman's Journal*, which ran for 2 years and included remarks on music and a music suppl.

1693

Johann Kaspar Kerll *d* (65, Munich).

Vivaldi was tonsured in Venice.

François Couperin apptd 1 of the 4 *organistes du roi* at Versailles.

Paris Charpentier's *Médée* (text by T. Corneille), his only *tragédie lyrique*, perf. by the Académie Royale de Musique and pubd the following year.

Leipzig N. A. Strungk obtained electoral authority to open an opera house; his *Alceste* (text by Förtsch, after Quinault) inaugurated the 1st season.

Nuremberg J. P. Krieger pubd 12 trio sonatas for violin, bass viol and continuo.

London John Lenton wrote *The Gentleman's Diversion*, the earliest violin tutor.

Edinburgh Public concerts inaugurated.

Bologna Isabella Leonarda published a collection of sonatas.

1694

Louis-Claude Daquin *b* (Paris); Johan Helmich Roman *b* (Stockholm).

Campra apptd *maître de musique* at Notre Dame, Paris.

Rome Corelli's op. 4 trio sonatas pubd.

Naples Alessandro Scarlatti's *Il Pirro e Demetrio* (text by Morselli) perf. at the Teatro S Bartolomeo.

Paris E.-C. Jacquet de La Guerre comp. a *tragédie lyrique*, *Céphale et Procris*, pubd and perf. by the Académie Royale de Musique; she was the only woman to do so.

Charpentier assisted Philippe de Bourbon (the future regent), his pupil, in composing an opera, *Philomèle*, perf. at the Palais Royal.

Michel l'Affilard pubd a treatise on sight-singing containing *airs de mouvement* based on dance rhythms; the 5th edn (1705) incorporates metronomic indications, breath marks and ornamentation, including *notes inégales* (see **1705**).

1695

Henry Purcell *d* (36, London).

Pietro Antonio Locatelli *b* (Bergamo); François Étienne Blanchet *b* (Paris); Bernhard Christoph Breitkopf, founder of the Leipzig publishing firm, *b* (Klausthal Harz).

Reinhard Keiser apptd director of the Hamburg Opera.

Johann Pachelbel apptd organist at the Sebaldkirche, Nuremberg.

Jeremiah Clarke apptd organist at St Paul's Cathedral, London.

Perugia Giovanni Andrea Bontempi pubd the 1st history of music in Italian.

Rome The Teatro Capranica (where opera and, later, comic opera were perf.) opened to the public.

Paris Pascal Collasse's *Ballet des saisons* (text by Abbé Pic) was a popular precursor of Campra's *L'Europe galante* (see **1697**).

Montéclair's *Adieu de Tircis à Climène*, an early precursor of the French cantata, appeared in Ballard's *Recueil d'airs sérieux et à boire*.

Augsburg Georg Muffat pubd *Florilegium primum*, orchestral suites prefaced by a *précis* of the Lullian style; J. C. F. Fischer pubd *Le journal du printems*, 8 French orchestral suites.

Daniel Merck pubd *Compendium musicae instrumentalis Chelicae*, the 1st German string tutor.

Danzig J. V. Meder's *Nero* (text by Corradi) was the 1st German opera perf. there.

London Purcell's semi-opera *The Indian Queen* (text by Dryden and Howard), for which Daniel Purcell comp. the final masque, perf. at Drury Lane.

The 1st instruction book for oboe, *The Sprightly Companion* (possibly by Banister), pubd.

About this time James Talbot completed a MS treatise (Christ Church, Oxford, Music MS 1187) on musical instruments, compiled from interviews with London makers and players.

1696

Michel Lambert *d* (*c*86, Paris).

Ernst Gottlieb Baron *b* (Breslau); Maurice Greene *b* (London).

François Couperin (*le Grand*) granted a coat of arms (see **1702**).

Bologna The orchestra at S Petronio disbanded for 5 years.

The run of perfs. at the Teatro Formagliari of G. A. V. Aldrovandini's popular comic opera *Gl'inganni amorosi scoperti in villa* (text by Landi), in Bolognese dialect, was interrupted by the local church authorities who objected to the *doubles entendres* in the text.

Naples Giovanni Bononcini's *Il trionfo di Camilla* (text by Stampiglia) was the triumph of the Carnival season (see **1706**).

Paris Étienne Loulié pubd *Éléments ou principes de musique*.

Dresden (and **Leipzig**) W. C. Printz pubd his extensive and ultimately highly influential summary of music theory, *Phrynis Mitilenaeus, oder Satyrischer Componist*.

Leipzig Johann Kuhnau pubd *Frische Clavier Früchte, oder sieben Suonaten*, the earliest pubd use of 'sonata' to designate solo rather than ensemble music.

London Purcell's *A Choice Collection of Lessons* for harpsichord or spinet pubd posth.

1697

Jean-Marie Leclair *l'aîné b* (Lyons); Johann Joachim Quantz *b* (Oberscheden).

At Mme de Maintenon's request, Louis XIV ordered the disbanding of Molière's Italian troupe and the Théâtre de l'Hôtel de Bourgogne closed.

Naples Alessandro Scarlatti's *La caduta de' Decemviri* (text by Stampiglia) perf. at the Teatro S Bartolomeo.

Paris Campra's innovative *L'Europe galante* (text by La Motte) was the 1st *opéra-ballet* perf. at the Opéra.

Düsseldorf Johann Hugo von Wilderer was (apparently) the 1st to use the viola d'amore in an opera, *Il giorno di salute* (text by ?Demanstein).

The Polish King August II, also the Elector of Saxony, set up two chapels (Warsaw and Dresden); they were united in Warsaw in 1720.

Weimar The opera house opened, directed by G. C. Strattner.

London Thomas Hickford's Rooms in James Street were first mentioned as a public concert venue.

Purcell's *Ten Sonata's in Four Parts* pubd posth.

Amsterdam Estienne Roger started a music printing business; he quickly became known for the quality of his engraved editions of French and Italian music and set up a network of foreign agents to sell them.

1698

Bartolomeo Giuseppe Guarneri 'del Gesù' *b* (Cremona); Antonio Domenico Bonaventura Trapassi [Pietro Metastasio] *b* (Rome).

Charpentier apptd *maître de musique* at the Sainte Chapelle on the Île de la Cité in Paris.

Johann Joseph Fux apptd court composer by Leopold I in Vienna.

António Marques Lésbio apptd *mestre de capela* of the Portuguese court in Lisbon.

Florence Bartolomeo Cristofori began building an 'arpicembalo che fà il piano e il forte'.

Aschersleben Andreas Werckmeister pubd *Die nothwendigsten Anmerckungen und Regeln*, an important thoroughbass manual notable for its instructions on harpsichord tuning.

Augsburg Giuseppe Torelli pubd his op. 6 *Concerti musicali*, containing 2 concertos for solo violin, among the earliest of their kind.

Kassel August Kühnel pubd *Sonate ô partite* for 1 and 2 viols with continuo.

Passau Georg Muffat pubd *Florilegium secundum*, containing an important treatise on bowing and ornamentation, as well as advice on performing ballets 'à la françoise'.

London *A Variety of New Trumpet Tunes Aires Marches and Minuets* pubd, some of the earliest music for the chalumeau.

1699

Johann Adolph Hasse *b* (nr Hamburg).

Antonio Caldara apptd *maestro di cappella* to the last Duke of Mantua, Ferdinando Carlo.

Paris Charpentier probably comp. Mass 'Assumpta est Maria'.

Étienne Loulié invented the *sonomètre* for tuning keyboard instruments.

Berlin A small theatre was built in the Lietzenburg palace (now the Charlottenburg palace) for perfs. of 'Wirtschaffen' (grandiose entertainments which included Singspiels; see **1700**).

Hamburg Johann Mattheson's 1st opera, *Die Plejades* (text by Bressand), perf.

Nuremberg Pachelbel ded. his *Hexachordum Apollinis* jointly to F. T. Richter (head of the South German school of organ playing) and Buxtehude (representing the North).

Passau Georg Muffat completed *Regulae concentuum partiturae*, an important MS treatise on continuo practice.

1700

Antonio Draghi *d* (*c*65, Vienna).

Faustina Bordoni *b* (Venice); Giovanni Battista Sammartini *b* (Milan) [or 1701]; Michel Blavet *b* (Besançon).

Johann Sebastian Bach moved to Lüneburg to continue his schooling at the Michaelis-schule.

John Blow apptd the first Composer of the Chapel Royal, London; John Eccles apptd Master of the King's Musick, London.

Rome Corelli pubd his famous op. 5 sonatas for violin and continuo, which set the standard throughout Europe.

Paris J. P. Freillon Poncein pubd *La véritable manière d'apprendre à jouer en perfection du hautbois*, the 1st French treatise on oboe playing.

Berlin Ariosti's *La festa del Himeneo* (text by Mauro, in collaboration with K. F. Rieck), the 1st perf. of an Italian opera, given at the Lietzenburg palace theatre.

Dresden Kuhnau wrote a satirical novel, *Der musicalische Quack-Salber*, with observations on the social status of German musicians; he also pubd *Musicalische Vorstellung einiger biblischer Historien*, programmatic keyboard sonatas on Old Testament stories.

London A contest held to determine the best dramatic composer of the day. The test piece (which ended the era of the masque) was a setting of Congreve's masque *The Judgment of Paris*: John Weldon won 1st prize, John Eccles 2nd, Daniel Purcell 3rd and Gottfried Finger 4th.

1701

François Rebel *b* (Paris); Johann Joachim Agrell *b* (Löth).

Johann Kuhnau elected *Kantor* of the Thomaskirche, Leipzig.

Naples Tommaso de Mauro's *La donna sempre s'appiglia al peggio* (text by Petris), an early comic opera with puppets, perf. in the Largo del Castello.

Paris Sébastien de Brossard pubd *Dictionnaire des termes grecs, latins et italiens*, reissued in 1703 as the better-known *Dictionnaire de musique*; simultaneously in **Prague** Tomás Baltazar Janovka pubd his music dictionary, *Clavis ad thesaurum magne artis musicae*. These were the 1st of their kind. Joseph Sauveur pubd *Principes d'acoustique et de musique*.

Montéclair and Giuseppe Fedeli credited by Michel Corrette (1741) with having introduced the double bass at the Paris Opéra, at about this time, in Theobaldo di Gatti's *Scylla*.

1702

Burkat Shudi *b* (Schwanden, Switzerland); José Nebra *b* (Calatayud).

François Couperin apptd to the order of Chevalier de Latran.

Giovanni and Antonio Maria Bononcini visited the Berlin court.

Reinhard Keiser apptd director of the Theater am Gänsemarkt, Hamburg.

Georg Philipp Telemann founded a student collegium musicum at the University of Leipzig which gave regular public concerts (see **1729**); in the same year he became director of the Leipzig Opera.

J. S. Bach competed for the organ post at the Jakobikirche in Sangerhausen, but was blocked by the Duke of Weissenfels who intervened, appointing an older man, J. A. Kobelius.

Sebastián Durón apptd *maestro de capilla* of the Spanish royal chapel in Madrid.

Paris François Raguenet pubd *Parallèle des italiens et des françois, en ce qui regarde la musique et les opéras*, which argued strongly in favour of Italian music (see **1704** and **1722**).

Charpentier composed the dramatic motet *Judicium Salomonis*.

Campra's *tragédie lyrique Tancrède* (text by Danchet) perf. at the Paris Opéra.

Michel de La Barre pubd the 1st suites for flute and continuo, modelled on those for bass viol (1686, 1701) by Marin Marais.

Saint-Lambert pubd *Principes de clavecin*.

Copenhagen A royal opera house was built.

Schlackenwerth J. C. F. Fischer pubd *Ariadne musica*, a collection of 20 preludes and fugues, a forerunner of J. S. Bach's *Das wohltemperirte Clavier* (see **1722**).

Madrid Joseph de Torres y Martínez Bravo pubd *Reglas generales de acompañar*, the 1st Spanish figured bass treatise.

Diego Fernández de Huete pubd *Compendio numeroso de zifras armonicas*, a harp treatise.

1703

Johann Christoph Bach *d* (60, Eisenach); Samuel Pepys *d* (70, London).

Vivaldi apptd *maestro di violino* at the Ospedale della Pietà, Venice.

J. S. Bach served for a few months as a violinist in the Weimar Hofkapelle before taking up the organ post at the Neukirche in Arnstadt.

Handel left Halle for Hamburg.

Prague Bartolomeo Bernardi's opera *Libussa*, on a Czech subject, perf.

Tilsit Georg Motz pubd a response (*Die vertheidigte Kirchen-Music*) to Christian Gerber's denunciation of music in the Lutheran service (1690); it demonstrated that both the Bible and the Lutheran doctrine strongly support the use of music in worship services (see **1708**).

1704

Francesco Provenzale *d* (*c*78, Naples); Marc-Antoine Charpentier *d* (*c*59, Paris); Georg Muffat *d* (50, Passau); Heinrich Ignaz Franz von Biber *d* (59, Salzburg).

Carl Heinrich Graun *b* (Wahrenbrück) [or 1703]; Carlos de Seixas *b* (Coimbra).

Michel-Richard de Lalande apptd *maître de la chapelle de musique* at Versailles.

Handel was befriended in Hamburg by Mattheson, who found work for him in the opera orchestra and helped him with his 1st opera (see **1705**).

Jeremiah Clarke and William Croft apptd joint organists of the English Chapel Royal.

Paris François Duval pubd the 1st collection of French violin sonatas.

Brussels J. L. Le Cerf de La Viéville pubd his 3-vol. *Comparaison de la musique italienne et de la musique française* in response to François Raguenet's criticism of French music in his 1702 *Parallèle* (see **1722**).

1705

Farinelli [Carlo Broschi] *b* (Andria).

J. S. Bach walked from Arnstadt to Lübeck to hear Buxtehude play.

Venice Vivaldi pubd his op. 1 trio sonatas.

Paris François Raguenet reiterated his views on the relative merits of the French and Italian styles in *Défense du Parallèle*.

J.-F. Dandrieu pubd some of the earliest French trio sonatas.

Michel L'Affilard became the 1st to provide metronomic indications in his music (5th edn of *Principes très-faciles pour bien apprendre la musique*).

Hamburg Reinhard Keiser used horns (*cors de chasse*) for the 1st time in an orchestra in his opera *Octavia* (text by Feind).

Handel's 1st opera *Almira* (text by Feustking after Pancieri with arias in German and Italian) perf.; Mattheson took a leading role.

London Thomas Clayton's *Arsinoe* (text by Stanzani, transcr. ?Motteux), the 1st completely sung Italian-style opera, perf. in January by an English cast at Drury Lane Theatre; the Queen's Theatre opened 4 months later in the Haymarket with Jakob Greber's pastoral opera *Gli amori d'Ergasto*, the 1st completely sung in Italian.

1706

Johann Pachelbel *d* (52, Nuremberg); Andreas Werckmeister *d* (60, Halberstadt).

Baldassare Galuppi *b* (Burano, nr Venice); Giovanni Battista [Padre] Martini *b* (Bologna).

Rameau began a 3-year stay in Paris.

Handel left Hamburg for Italy.

Naples Michelangelo Faggioli comp. *La Cilla* (text by Tullio), the earliest privately perf. comic opera in Neapolitan dialect, perf. at the end of 1707 at the palace of the Prince of Chiusiano.

Paris J.-B. Morin pubd the 1st collection of French cantatas.

Rameau pubd his 1st bk of *Pièces de clavecin*.

Vienna The chalumeau 1st heard in the opera orchestra (see **1709**).

London Eccles's *The British Enchanters* (text by Granville) signalled the end of English semi-opera.

Giovanni Bononcini's *Camilla* (1696) perf. with great success in English by an English cast at Drury Lane.

The Division Flute pubd (containing preludes, unaccompanied sonata movements and variations on popular grounds).

1707

Dieterich Buxtehude *d* (*c*70, Lübeck).

At Versailles the king's 4 organists – N.-A. Lebègue, G. G. Nivers, J.-B. Buterne and François Couperin – succeeded in crushing the powerful and corrupt Confrérie de St Julien-des-Ménestriers by acquiring *Lettres patentes* curtailing their activities.

J. S. Bach married his cousin Maria Barbara Bach and took up the organ post at the Blasiuskirche in Mühlhausen.

Rome Handel's 1st oratorio, *Il trionfo del Tempo e del Disinganno* (text by Pamphili), perf. (see **1737**); later that year his opera *Rodrigo* (text by Silvani) perf. in **Florence** at the Teatro Civico Accademico in the Via del Cocomero.

Venice Alessandro Scarlatti's *Il Mitridate Eupatore* and *Il trionfo della libertà* (both texts by Roberti) perf. during Carnival at the Teatro S Giovanni Grisostomo.

Paris Michel de La Barre pubd the earliest trio sonatas specifically for 2 flutes and continuo (see Plate 6); J.-M. Hotteterre 'Le Romain' pubd the 1st flute tutor (*Principes de la flûte traversière*), which remains an important source of tonguing and ornamentation.

Saint-Lambert pubd *Nouveau traité de l'accompagnement*.

London Clayton's *Rosamond* (text by Addison) was the last attempt to establish English opera at Drury Lane Theatre.

1708

John Blow *d* (59, London); 'Father' Bernard Smith *d* (*c*78, London).

J. S. Bach apptd court organist at Weimar, where in 1714 he was promoted to *Konzertmeister*.

Rome Handel's resplendent oratorio *La Resurrezione* (text by Capece) perf. at the Ruspoli palace, with Corelli leading the orchestra.

Venice Francesco Gasparini pubd *L'armonico pratico al cimbalo*.

Paris Elisabeth-Claude Jacquet de La Guerre pubd the earliest collection of French cantatas on biblical subjects.

Tilsit Motz continued his attack on Gerber in *Abgenötigte Fortsetzung der vertheidigten Kirchen-Music* (see **1711**).

Vienna Emperor Joseph I built a new opera house.

London Alessandro Scarlatti's opera *Pyrrhus and Demetrius* (*Il Pirro e Demetrio*, 1694) perf., sung partly in English, partly in Italian.

Barcelona Antonio Caldara's *Il più bel nome* (text by Pariati) perf., thought to have been the 1st Italian opera given in Spain.

Lima Roque Ceruti's opera *El mejor escudo de Perseo* perf. in the gardens of the viceregal palace, with elaborate scenery and costumes.

1709

Giuseppe Torelli *d* (50, Bologna); Pascal Collasse *d* (40, Versailles).

Franz Benda *b* (Staré Benátky, Bohemia); Franz Xaver Richter *b* (Holleschau).

Agostino Steffani apptd Apostolic Vicar of North Germany by papal decree; he took his seat in Hanover.

Bologna Giuseppe Torelli's op. 8 violin concertos pubd posth.

Naples Antonio Orefice's *Patrò Calienno de la Costa*, the 1st comic opera (*opera buffa*) in Neapolitan dialect, perf. in public (see **1707**).

Venice Giulio Taglietti pubd a collection of concertos for 4 violins (op. 8), predating Vivaldi's op. 3 concertos by 2 years.

Paris Michel de La Barre pubd the 1st suites for 2 unaccompanied flutes.

Vienna Marc'Antonio Ziani's *Chilonida* (text by Minato), incorporating an air by Emperor Joseph I with an ornate chalumeau obbligato, perf. at the Hoftheater.

1710

Bernardo Pasquini *d* (72, Rome).

Giovanni Battista Pergolesi *b* (Pergola); Wilhelm Friedemann Bach *b* (Weimar); Jacob Kirckman *b* (Bischweiler); Thomas Arne *b* (London).

Handel left Italy for Hanover (where he was made *Kapellmeister*), via Innsbruck; then to London via Düsseldorf and the Netherlands.

Bologna The Teatro Marsigli-Rossi opened with L. A. Predieri's *La Partenope* (text by Stampiglia).

Venice Handel's *Agrippina* (text by Grimani) perf. 27 times at the Teatro S Giovanni Grisostomo, the highlight of the 1709–10 Carnival.

Paris Campra staged the 1st full-length comic *opéra-ballet*, *Les fêtes vénitiennes* (text by Danchet).

Clérambault pubd *Orphée*, destined to become the most popular French cantata of the 18th century.

J.-B. Senaillé pubd a collection of violin sonatas in the Italian style.

London Francesco Mancini's *Idaspe* (text by ?Candi) perf. in Italian at the Queen's Theatre.

1711

Jean-Joseph Cassanéa de Mondonville *b* (Narbonne); Ignaz Holzbauer *b* (Vienna); William Boyce *b* (London).

Venice G. M. Ruggieri's comic opera *Elisa* (text by Lalli), possibly the 1st to be perf. there, given at the Teatro S Angelo.

Paris Montéclair pubd *Méthode facile pour apprendre à jouer du violon*, the 1st French violin tutor.

Dresden Gerber responded to Motz in the preface of his *Unerkannte Wohlthaten Gottes*.

London Handel staged *Rinaldo* (with music largely from works written in Italy and a libretto by Rossi, after Hill, after Tasso) entirely in Italian at the Queen's Theatre; Addison and Steele wrote critically of it in *The Spectator*. Handel returned to Hanover.

Amsterdam Vivaldi's op. 3 concertos, *L'estro armonico*, pubd in 2 vols.

Mexico City The earliest known North American opera, Manuel de Zumaya's *La Partenope*, perf. at the viceregal palace.

1712

Jean-Jacques Rousseau *b* (Geneva); Frederick II (Frederick the Great) of Prussia *b* (Berlin); Ludwig [Louis] van Beethoven, grandfather of his famous namesake, *b* (Mechelen); John Stanley *b* (London).

Upon the accession of Emperor Charles VI, Marc'Antonio Ziani apptd *Kapellmeister* to the Viennese court.

Handel settled permanently to London.

Hamburg B. H. Brockes's Passion text, considered too modern for church perf., was nevertheless pubd and set to music by Keiser (followed within 10 years by Telemann, Handel, Mattheson, Stölzel and Fasch).

Nuremberg Biber's scordatura works for 2 instruments and continuo, *Harmonia artificiosa-ariosa*, pubd posth.

London Handel's *Il pastor fido* (text by Rossi) perf. at the Queen's Theatre.

Madrid Joaquín Martínez de la Roca pubd the score for *Los desagravios de Troya* (comp. for the birth of the crown prince), the 1st printed complete score of Spanish theatre music.

1713

Arcangelo Corelli *d* (59, Rome).

Pierre de Jélyotte *b* (Lasseube).

André Cardinal Destouches apptd *inspecteur général* of the Académie Royale de Musique, Paris.

Paris François Couperin pubd his 1st bk of *Pièces de clavecin*.

Hamburg Johann Mattheson pubd *Das neu-eröffnete Orchestre* as a guide to the 'galant homme' (see **1716**).

Vienna Maria Margherita Grimani became the 1st woman composer to have an opera, *Pallade e Marte*, perf. at the Hoftheater.

London Handel comp. the *Jubilate* and *Te Deum* for the celebrations of the Peace of Utrecht at St Paul's; *Teseo* (text by Haym after Quinault) perf. at the Queen's Theatre, and *Silla* (text by Rossi) at Burlington House.

William Croft became the 1st Oxford graduate in music (DMus) by submitting 2 odes, pubd 2 years later as *Musicus apparatus academicus*.

1714

Atto Melani *d* (*c*88, Paris); Philipp Heinrich Erlebach *d* (56, Rudolstadt); Thomas Britton *d* (70, London).

Niccolò Jommelli *b* (nr Naples); Carl Philipp Emanuel Bach *b* (Weimar); Christoph Willibald Gluck *b* (Erasbach, Upper Austria).

At the very end of the year, Domenico Scarlatti succeeded Tommaso Baj as *maestro* of the Cappella Giulia.

Geminiani arrived in London.

Lalande acquired the final semester of the post of *sous-maître* at the Chapelle Royale at Versailles.

Rome Corelli's op. 6 concerti grossi pubd posth.; their 1st London perf. was organized by J. B. Loeillet (see **1726**).

Paris J.-J. Mouret comp. the 1st lyric comedy, *Le mariage de Ragonde et de Colin* (which predates Rameau's *Platée* by 30 years), perf. at the Duchess of Maine's 'Grandes Nuits de Sceaux'.

Weimar J. S. Bach embarked on his 1st cycle of sacred cantatas.

Telemann stood as godfather to C. P. E. Bach.

London The Queen's Theatre in the Haymarket renamed the King's Theatre with the accession of George I.

Amsterdam Vivaldi's op. 4 solo violin concertos, *La stravaganza*, pubd in 2 vols.

1715

Jacques Duphly *b* (Rouen); Georg Christoph Wagenseil *b* (Vienna); Johann Gottfried Bernhard Bach *b* (Weimar).

J. J. Fux succeeded Marc'Antonio Ziani as *Hofkapellmeister* in Vienna.

The Philharmonica Club (known as the Castle Society from 1724) founded by Maurice Greene and Talbot Young in London.

Francesco Costa e Silva apptd *mestre de capela* at Lisbon Cathedral.

Cremona Antonio Stradivari made the 'Alard', one of his best-known violins.

Naples Alessandro Scarlatti's *Il Tigrane* (text by Lalli) perf. at S Bartolomeo.

Paris Jacques Bonnet pubd *Histoire de la musique et de ses effets depuis son origine jusqu'à présent*, the work of his brother and uncle; later edns incorporated Le Cerf de La Viéville's *Comparaison* (see **1704**).

London Handel's *Amadigi di Gaula* (text by Haym) perf. at the King's Theatre.

John Watts compiled the 1st children's hymnal.

The Three Choirs Festival (Gloucester, Hereford and Worcester) founded, about this time.

1716

Felice de' Giardini *b* (Turin).

Paris The Opéra-Comique opened in the Foire St Laurent.

The regent established the Nouveau Théâtre Italien at the Palais Royal, with J.-J. Mouret as the chief composer (1717–38); the Comédie-Italienne was recalled to Paris, where they performed at the Hôtel de Bourgogne (see **1721**).

The Académie Royale de Musique, with the regent's permission, sponsored all-night public masked balls at the Palais Royal.

Erfurt J. H. Buttstett pubd an attack on Mattheson's *Das neu-eröffnete Orchestre* (1713) entitled *Ut, mi, sol, re, fa, la tota musica et harmonia aeterna* (see **1717**).

Amsterdam Vivaldi pubd his op. 5 sonatas for 1 and 2 violins and his op. 6 *Concerti a 5 stromenti* (a 2nd collection, op. 7, pubd the following year).

1717

Matthias Georg Monn *b* (Austria); Johann Wenzel Anton Stamitz *b* (Nemecky-Brod, Bohemia).

François Francoeur apptd leader of the Vingt-quatre Violons at Versailles.

François Couperin finally inherited J.-B.-H. D'Anglebert's post as *ordinaire de la chambre pour le clavecin*, after deputizing for him since 1700 (see **1730**).

J. S. Bach apptd *Kapellmeister* at Prince Leopold's court at Anhalt-Cöthen, having been dismissed in disgrace by his Weimar employer Duke Wilhelm Ernst, following a month's imprisonment.

Handel took up residence at Cannons, Edgware, where he served James Brydges (later Duke of Chandos) for the next 2 years.

Rome The Teatro delle Dame was built for *opera seria*.

Paris François Couperin pubd 2nd bk of *Pièces de clavecin*, which included a satirical programme suite immortalizing the Confrérie, or company of *ménestriers*: 'Les fastes de la grande et ancienne Mxnxstrxndxsx'; he also pubd his definitive treatise on keyboard playing, *L'art de toucher le clavecin*.

Dresden Louis Marchand failed to meet J. S. Bach in the contest of harpsichord skills organized by the *Konzertmeister* J. B. Volumier.

Hamburg Mattheson demolished Buttstett's arguments (1716) in *Das beschützte Orchestre* (see **1718**).

Weimar J. S. Bach completed the *Orgelbüchlein* before his dismissal.

London Handel's *Water Music* perf. on a barge on the River Thames for King George I, an occasion that marked the entry of French horns into English music.

1718

Friedrich Wilhelm Marpurg *b* (Seehof, Brandenburg).

Maurice Greene apptd organist at St Paul's Cathedral, London.

Florence The Teatro della Pergola reopened with Vivaldi's *Scanderbeg* (text by Salvi).

Heidelberg The Düsseldorf and Innsbruck chapels were merged when the Palatine court moved here with the new Elector Carl Philipp; by 1720 the court was established at Mannheim.

Erfurt Buttstett pubd his final response to Mattheson's latest attack (1717) in *Der wider das Beschützte Orchestre ergangenen offentlichen Erklärung*.

Leipzig and **Halle** Telemann pubd his edn of 6 violin concertos by Johann Ernst of Weimar.

Outside London Handel's *Acis and Galatea* (text by Gay and others) and his 1st version of the oratorio *Esther* (text by Pope and Arbuthnot) perf. at the Duke of Chandos's residence at Cannons, Edgware (see **1732**).

1719

Joachim Tielke *d* (77, Hamburg); Arp Schnitger *d* (71, Neuenfelde).

Leopold Mozart *b* (Augsburg); John Hawkins *b* (London).

Giovanni Bononcini invited to become a composer for the new Royal Academy of Music in London, under Handel's direction (see **1720**).

François Colin de Blamont apptd *surintendant de la musique de chambre* at Versailles.

Venice G. M. Orlandini's comic *intermezzo Il marito giocatore* perf. at the Teatro S Angelo; as *Serpilla e Bacocco* it is thought to have been the most frequently perf. musical drama in the 18th century.

Paris J.-M. Hotteterre pubd *L'art de préluder*, an important source of French performing practice.

Abbé Dubos pubd *Réflexions critiques sur la poésie, la peinture et la musique*, in which he proclaimed music and painting to be superior to poetry at conveying meaning.

Dresden Antonio Lotti's *Giove in Argo* (1717, text by Luchini) inaugurated the Hoftheater.

Leipzig About this time, the firm of Breitkopf & Härtel established to print and publish music.

1720

Johann Friedrich Agricola *b* (Saxe-Altenburg).

Domenico Scarlatti accepted a post at the Lisbon court; Carlos de Seixas apptd organist of the Portuguese royal chapel.

Venice Benedetto Marcello pubd *Il teatro alla moda*, a satire on Italian opera which became widely known.

Cöthen J. S. Bach completed the *Clavier-Büchlein* for his eldest son, W. F. Bach, and made fair copies of the violin partitas (see **1725**).

Donauwörth (Bavaria) At about this time Jakob Hochbrucker invented the single-action pedal harp.

Leipzig The Opera closed down.

London The Royal Academy opened its 1st season in the King's Theatre with Giovanni Porta's *Numitore* (text by Rolli) and Handel's *Radamisto* (text by Haym); later in the year the 2nd season opened with Giovanni Bononcini's *Astarto* (text by Rolli).

1721

Johann Philipp Kirnberger *b* (Saalfeld).

J. S. Bach married his 2nd wife, Anna Magdalena Wilcke, who ultimately bore him 13 children.

Telemann was invited by the city of Hamburg to become Kantor of the Johanneum and music director of the city's 5 main churches.

Venice Benedetto Marcello pubd *Il flagello dei musici*, a further satire, on castrato singers.

Paris The Comédie-Italienne took over the Foire St Laurent and in 1723 changed its name to the Comédiens du Roi; it merged with the Opéra-Comique in 1762 (see **1716**).

Cöthen J. S. Bach completed the autograph presentation copy of the 6 Concertos (dated 24 March) for Margrave Christian Ludwig of Brandenburg in Berlin.

Hamburg Telemann's light opera *Der geduldige Socrates* (adapted from Minato) was enthusiastically received (see 1722).

Leipzig Johann Kuhnau's *St Mark Passion* (lost) was the 1st to be perf. there.

G. E. Scheibel pubd *Zufällige Gedancken von der Kirchenmusic*, in which he promoted the value of music in Protestant church services and in particular the theatrical style and parody; he also urged the admission of women into church choirs.

London Giovanni Bononcini and Handel collaborated with Amadei on *Muzio Scevola* (text by Rolli) for the Royal Academy.

1722

Johann Kuhnau *d* (62, Leipzig); Johann Adam Reincken *d* (99, Hamburg).

Pietro Nardini *b* (Livorno); Georg Benda *b* (Staré Benátky, Bohemia).

Rameau settled permanently in Paris.

Telemann apptd music director of the Hamburg Opera.

Rome Filippo Bonanni pubd *Gabinetto armonico pieno d'istromenti sonori indicati e spiegati*, despite its inaccuracy one of the primary documents for the history of 18th-century instruments.

Paris François Couperin pubd the *Concerts royaux* with the 3rd bk of harpsichord pieces.

Rameau pubd *Traité de l'harmonie* (Eng. trans., 1737).

Cöthen The 1st vol. of J. S. Bach's *Das wohltemperirte Clavier* appeared.

Hamburg Mattheson founded *Critica musica*, the 1st periodical devoted entirely to music; the 1st issue contains his German translations of François Raguenet's *Parallèle des italiens et des françois* (1702) and J. L. Le Cerf de La Viéville's reply in the *Comparaison* (1704–6).

1723

Carlo Francesco Pollarolo *d* (*c*70, Venice).

Carl Friedrich Abel *b* (Cöthen); Pascal-Joseph Taskin *b* (nr Liège).

Nicolas Bernier, André Campra and C.-H. Gervais assumed three-quarters of the *sous-maître* post at the Chapelle Royale, Versailles, formerly monopolized by Lalande.

J. S. Bach apptd *Kantor* and *director musices* of the Thomaskirche, Leipzig, posts he held until his death.

Bologna P. F. Tosi pubd his influential *Opinioni de' cantori antichi e moderni*.

Paris Over 100 stage works were perf. at the Palais Royal, including 13 *tragédies en musique* and the 1st *ballet-héroïque*, F. C. de Blamont's *Les festes grecques et romaines* (text by Fuzelier).

Leipzig J. S. Bach's *Magnificat* (earlier, E flat major version) perf. as part of the Christmas Vespers music at the Thomaskirche.

Prague For the coronation celebrations of Emperor Charles VI as King of Bohemia, Caldara conducted distinguished musicians (e.g. C. H. Graun, Quantz, Weiss and Zelenka) in Fux's *Costanza e Fortezza* (text by Pariati; see Plate 13); J. D. Zelenka contributed a *Melodrama de Sancto Wenceslao* for the occasion.

London Handel's *Ottone* (text by Haym, after Pallavicino), marking Francesca Cuzzoni's London début, and *Flavio* (text by Haym) perf. by the Royal Academy at the King's Theatre.

1724

Renatus Harris *d* (*c*72, ?Bristol).

Naples D. N. Sarro comp. the 1st setting of a major Metastasio libretto, *Didone abbandonata*, for S Bartolomeo.

Paris The Opéra-Comique returned to the Foire St Germain (see **1744**).

François Couperin pubd *Les goûts-réünis*, which included *Le Parnasse, ou L'apothéose de Corelli*.

Rameau pubd *Pièces de clavecin avec une méthode pour la méchanique des doigts*.

Jena C. G. Schröter lectured on Mattheson's *Neu-eröffnete Orchestre* (1713) and the mathematical basis of music theory (see **1737**/Leipzig); he also founded a university collegium musicum.

Leipzig J. S. Bach embarked on his 2nd cantata cycle; he completed the Sanctus of the B Minor Mass (see **1733**); and on Good Friday his *St John Passion*, his 1st large-scale work, was 1st perf. at the Nicolaikirche.

Prague At his private theatres at Kuks and Prague Count Franz Anton Sporck sponsored regular perfs. (until 1738) by a Venetian opera troupe led by Antonio Denzio.

Vienna Caldara's *Euristeo* (text by Zeno) perf. by members of the Habsburg family and the nobility under the direction of Emperor Charles VI from the keyboard.

London Handel's *Giulio Cesare in Egitto* and *Tamerlano* (texts by Haym) perf. at the King's Theatre.

The masonic musical society (Philo Musicae et Architecturae Societas) met at the Queen's Head Tavern (until 1727).

1725

Alessandro Scarlatti *d* (65, Naples); Johann Philipp Krieger *d* (75, Weissenfels).

Claude Rameau (brother of J.-P. Rameau) founded an Académie de Musique (which flourished until 1738) in Dijon.

Anne Danican Philidor inaugurated the Concert Spirituel at the Salle des Suisses of the Tuileries palace in Paris, which continued until 1791; in an early concert the audience heard the contrasting playing styles of the Italian violinist J.-P. Guignon and the French violinist 'Baptiste' Anet.

The Caecilienbrüderschaft was founded in Vienna.

Paris François Couperin pubd *Concert instrumental sous le titre d'Apothéose composé à la mémoire immortelle de l'incomparable Monsieur de Lully*.

Hamburg Telemann comp. *Pimpinone*, a comic intermezzo, which anticipated the *buffo* style of Pergolesi's *La serva padrona* by 8 years; he also began pub. a collection of sacred cantatas (*Harmonischer Gottes-Dienst*) for 1 voice, an instrument and continuo.

Leipzig J. S. Bach compiled the 2nd *Clavierbüchlein* for Anna Magdalena.

Vienna Fux pubd his influential counterpoint treatise *Gradus ad Parnassum* (see **1742**).

London Handel's *Rodelinda* (text by Haym) perf. at the King's Theatre.

Amsterdam Vivaldi's 2-vol. *Il cimento dell'armonia e dell'inventione*, op. 8, containing 'The Four Seasons', issued.

Russia Empress Anna Ivanova imported a Janissary band (from Constantinople).

1726

Michel-Richard de Lalande *d* (68, Versailles).

François-André Danican Philidor *b* (Dreux); Charles Burney *b* (Shrewsbury).

Johann Joachim Quantz arrived in Paris and had a 2nd key added to his flute; he stayed 7 months.

The Academy of Vocal Music was founded in London by 13 musicians, including Greene, Croft, Pepusch, Giovanni Bononcini and Geminiani; Agostino Steffani was elected president the following year (see **1731**).

Paris The Concert Italien founded.

François Couperin pubd *Les nations*, his beautifully polished sonata-suites for 4 instruments, in partbooks.

Rameau pubd *Nouveau système de musique théorique*.

Dresden G. A. Ristori's *Calandro* (text by Pallavicino), the 1st *opera buffa* comp. in Germany, perf. at court (see **1731**).

London Handel's *Scipione* and *Alessandro* (both on texts by Rolli) staged at the King's Theatre.

Geminiani pubd his concerto grosso arrangements of Corelli's op. 5 sonatas.

1727

William Croft *d* (48, Bath).

Tommaso Traetta *b* (Bitonto, nr Bari); Claude-Bénigne Balbastre *b* (Dijon); Armand-Louis Couperin *b* (Paris).

A. D. Philidor founded the Concert Français; J.-J. Mouret organized its performances of French cantatas until 1730.

André Cardinal Destouches apptd *maître de musique de la chambre* at the court at Versailles.

Quantz spent 10 weeks in London.

Faustina Bordoni and Francesca Cuzzoni came to blows on stage during a perf. (attended by the Princess of Wales) of Giovanni Bononcini's *Astianatte*.

Paris Michele Mascitti became the 1st in France to publish string concertos.

J.-B. Boismortier purloined the term 'concerto' for his op. 15 unaccompanied pieces for 5 flutes (see **1729**).

Évrard Titon du Tillet pubd *Description du Parnasse François*, which contains the 1st biographies of French composers other than Lully (see **1732**).

Leipzig An early version of J. S. Bach's *St Matthew Passion* perf. on Good Friday (see **1736**); his *Trauer Ode* (Cantata 198) perf. at a university memorial service for Electress Christiane Eberhardine (wife of August the Strong).

Nuremberg Ernst Gottlieb Baron pubd *Historisch-theoretisch und practische Untersuchung des Instruments der Lauten*.

Vienna Kilian Reinhardt, the court *Konzertmeister*, completed *Rubriche generali*, a treatise on the musical practices of the imperial chapel.

London Handel's *Admeto* (text by Aureli) and *Riccardo Primo* (text by Rolli) perf. at the King's Theatre; he comp. 4 coronation anthems for George II.

Amsterdam Vivaldi's solo violin concertos, *La cetra*, pubd.

1728

Agostino Steffani *d* (73, Frankfurt); Marin Marais *d* (72, Paris).

Niccolò Piccinni *b* (Bari); Johann Adam Hiller *b* (Wendisch-Ossig).

Jean-Marie Leclair *l'âiné* and Pietro Antonio Locatelli perf. together at the Kassel court; their contrasting styles of playing were remarked upon by J. W. Lustig, who described Leclair as an angel and Locatelli a devil.

Quantz became the future Frederick the Great's flute teacher (see **1741**).

Matthew Dubourg apptd Master and Composer of State Music in Ireland.

Paris François Couperin pubd his only collection of *pièces de violes* [*sic*].

Dresden J. D. Heinichen pubd *Der General-Bass in der Composition* (an expanded version of a 1711 treatise).

Hamburg Mattheson pubd *Der musicalischer Patriot*, describing the Hamburg Opera and listing, year by year, the operas in repertory, attributing its collapse to deteriorating public taste.

Telemann pubd an anthology of vocal and instrumental chamber music by himself and 13 other composers (*Der getreue Music-Meister*).

London Handel's *Siroe* and *Tolomeo* (both texts by Haym) perf. at the King's Theatre. The Royal Academy was dissolved after the performance of *Admeto* on 1 June.

The Hon. Roger North appended excerpts of his MS 'Memoires of Musick' to *The Musicall Grammarian*.

Pepusch's and Gay's ballad opera *The Beggar's Opera* perf. in Dublin at the Smock Alley Theatre and in London at Lincoln's Inn Fields.

Amsterdam Tartini's *Sei concerti à 5* pubd.

1729

Elisabeth-Claude Jacquet de La Guerre *d* (*c*62, Paris); Johann David Heinichen *d* (46, Dresden).

Giuseppe Sarti *b* (Faenza); Antonio Soler *b* (Olot); Pierre-Alexandre Monsigny *b* (nr St Omer); Florian Leopold Gassmann *b* (Brüx, Bohemia).

J. S. Bach took over direction of the Leipzig collegium musicum (remaining until 1737). His son W. F. Bach invited Handel (visiting his mother at Halle) to meet J. S. Bach, but he was unable to accept.

Handel and J. J. Heidegger launched the Second Academy at the King's Theatre, London.

Despite his blindness, John Stanley (*b* 1712) became the youngest person ever to gain an Oxford BMus.

Pietro Antonio Locatelli made Amsterdam his permanent home.

Domenico Scarlatti left Lisbon and settled in Seville, where the Spanish court was in residence.

Paris F. C. de Blamont pubd a posth. edn of 40 *grands motets* by Lalande, together with a biography of him.

J.-B. de Boismortier pubd the 1st solo concerto (op. 26, for cello, viol or bassoon) by a native French composer.

At much this time, Rameau pubd *Nouvelles suites de pièces de clavecin*.

London Handel's *Lotario* (text by Salvi) perf. at the King's Theatre.

Gay was blocked from presenting his sequel (*Polly*) to *The Beggar's Opera*.

John Watts began publishing the 1st of 6 vols. of *The Musical Miscellany*, the most significant pocket songbook of its day.

1730

Alessandro Grandi *d* (?44, Bergamo); Leonardo Vinci *d* (*c*40, Naples); Jean Baptiste [John] Loeillet *d* (49, London).

Antonio Sacchini *b* (Florence).

François Couperin ceded his post as *ordinaire de la chambre pour le clavecin* to his daughter, Marguerite-Antoinette, the 1st woman to hold such a position at court.

Johann Adolf Hasse apptd *Kapellmeister* at Dresden.

Paris François Couperin pubd his 4th bk of harpsichord pieces.

Dresden Hasse's *Artaserse* (text by Metastasio) perf. during the Carnival.

Hamburg Telemann pubd his *Quadri* for flute, violin, bass viol or cello and continuo.

Leipzig J. C. Gottsched rejected opera as a literary form in his influential *Versuch einer critischen Dichtkunst für die Deutschen*. His pupils Mizler and Scheibe turned against him in their journals, the *Musikalische Bibliothek* and the *Critischer Musikus*.

London Handel's *Partenope* (text by Stampiglia) perf. at the King's Theatre; about this time he pubd his op. 1 sonatas for treble instrument and continuo and his op. 2 trio sonatas.

1731

Bartolomeo Cristofori *d* (75, Florence).

Christian Cannabich *b* (Mannheim).

J. A. Hasse married Faustina Bordoni.

J. S. and W. F. Bach attended the 1st performance of Hasse's *Cleofide* at Dresden.

Johan Helmich Roman introduced the 1st public concerts in Stockholm at the Riddarhuset; both amateur and court musicians participated.

The Academy of Vocal Music in London became the Academy of Ancient Music (its origins, however, may go back as far as 1710).

Michael Festing and Maurice Greene formed the Society of Apollo, at Temple Bar.

Paris The hurdy-gurdy heard for the 1st time at the Concert Spirituel in a Christmas perf. of a *suite d'airs de noëls*, which were so popular that they were repeated the next 2 years.

Hamburg Mattheson pubd *Grosse General-Bass-Schule*, giving instructions on how to improvise from a given bass; 4 years later he pubd a sequel (*Kleine . . .*), giving directions for accompanying from a thorough bass.

Leipzig The 1st part of J. S. Bach's *Clavier-Übung* appeared (see **1735**).

London Handel's *Poro* (text by Metastasio) perf. at the King's Theatre.

Moscow G. A. Ristori's *Calandro* (1726) was the 1st Italian opera perf. there.

1732

Louis Marchand *d* (63, Paris); John Gay *d* (47, London).

Johann Christoph Friedrich Bach *b* (Leipzig); Franz Joseph Haydn *b* (Rohrau, Lower Austria).

Florence Lodovico Giustini pubd the 1st collection of piano music, *12 Sonate da cimbalo di piano e forte detto volgarmente di martelletti*.

Naples Pergolesi's 1st *commedia musicale* (in Neapolitan dialect), *Lo frate 'nnamorato* (text by Federico), perf. at the Teatro dei Fiorentini.

To celebrate Emperor Charles VI's birthday Hasse's *Issipile* (Metastasio) had its 1st perf. at the Teatro S Bartolomeo.

Rome The Teatro Argentina was built for *opera seria*.

Amsterdam Locatelli pubd *L'arte del violino*, a collection of virtuoso solo violin capriccios.

Lisbon Pedro Vaz Rego pubd *Armonico Lazo*, an important history of music at the Spanish royal chapel.

1734

François-Joseph Gossec *b* (Vergnies, South Netherlands).

Naples Pergolesi's *Adriano in Siria* (text by Metastasio) perf. at the Teatro S Bartolomeo.

Paris and **Lille** Mondonville pubd his *Pièces de clavecin en sonates.*

Leipzig J. S. Bach's *Christmas Oratorio* perf. in 6 parts, beginning on Christmas Day and continuing to Epiphany 1735.

London Handel pubd his op. 3 concerti grossi; his *Arianna in Creta* (text by Pariati) and *Parnasso in festa* perf. at the King's Theatre, his *pasticcio Oreste* at Covent Garden.

Madrid A fire destroyed the music library of the royal palace.

1735

John Eccles *d* (*c*67, Hampton Wick).

Johann Christian Bach *b* (Leipzig).

J. S. Bach compiled a family genealogy.

Maurice Greene apptd Master of the King's Music in London, succeeding John Eccles.

Pesaro Hasse's *Tito Vespasiano* (text by Metastasio) inaugurated the Teatro Pubblico, with Faustina taking a leading role.

Paris Rameau's *opéra-ballet Les Indes galantes* (text by Fuzelier) perf. at the Opéra.

Versailles Queen Marie Leszczynska had Destouches organize concerts in her Grand Cabinet with repertory from the Concert Spirituel.

Leipzig The 2nd part of J. S. Bach's *Clavier-Übung* appeared, including the Italian Concerto; at the end of Lent the *Ascension Oratorio* (Cantata 11) and the *Easter Oratorio* perf.

London Handel's *Ariodante* (text by Salvi) and *Alcina* (text from Ariosto) perf. at Covent Garden.

1736

Giovanni Battista Pergolesi *d* (26, Pozzuoli); Antonio Caldara *d* (*c*65, Vienna); John Walsh *d* (*c*70, London).

Johann Georg Albrechtsberger *b* (Klosterneuburg).

Salvatore Lanzetti became the first solo cellist to appear in Paris at the Concert Spirituel.

Paris Évrard Titon du Tillet pubd his monumental *Le Parnasse François*, containing biographical entries of French musicians (no longer living); suppls. pubd 1743, 1755.

Rameau pubd his *Dissertation sur les différentes méthodes d'accompagnement pour le clavecin, ou pour l'orgue.*

Leipzig J. G. Walther pubd *Musicalisches Lexicon, oder Musicalische Bibliothec*, the 1st German music dictionary and the 1st in any language to include biographies and terms.

London Handel's operas *Ezio* (text by Metastasio) and *Sosarme* (text by Salvi) and his heavily revised oratorio *Esther* perf. at the King's Theatre.

J. F. Lampe, Henry Carey and Thomas Arne organized a season of 'English operas after the Italian manner' at the Little Theatre in the Haymarket.

Late in the year the original Covent Garden Opera House – known as the Theatre Royal, Covent Garden – opened under the directorship of John Rich; the 1st productions were Congreve's *The Way of the World* and Gay's *The Beggar's Opera*.

Amsterdam Tartini pubd 6 sonatas for violin and continuo.

1733

François Couperin *d* (64, Paris); Georg Böhm *d* (71, Lüneburg).

The Turin court violinist G. B. Somis played at the Concert Spirituel in Paris.

Porpora apptd to direct the new Opera of the Nobility company in London (under the protection of the Prince of Wales, and in competition with Handel's Second Royal Academy, inaugurated at much the same time); the season began with Porpora's *Arianna in Nasso* (text by Rolli), sung by Senesino and others of Handel's singers.

Domenico Scarlatti moved to L'Escorial (nr Madrid).

Bologna Hasse's *Siroe* (text by Metastasio) given a gala première at the Teatro Malvezzi.

Naples Pergolesi's *La serva padrona* (text by Federico) served as an *intermezzo* to his opera *Il prigionier superbo*.

Paris Rameau's first opera, *Hippolyte et Aricie* (text by Pellegrin), perf. at the Opéra; it caused a sensation, bringing into question the grip Lully still maintained even in death on French opera and stimulating a debate between Lullistes and Ramistes.

Dresden J. S. Bach's Kyrie and Gloria of the projected B Minor Mass were perf. at the Sophienkirche (where W. F. Bach was apptd organist) before the new Saxon Elector Friedrich August II (see **1736**).

Hamburg Telemann pubd *Musique de table*, containing overtures, concertos and quartets.

Leipzig The organist G. F. Kauffmann began the serial publication of his *Harmonische Seelenlust* (completed by his widow in 1736), an important collection of chorale preludes.

London Handel's opera *Orlando* (text by Capece) and oratorio *Deborah* (text by Humphreys) perf. at the King's Theatre; *Athalia* (text by Humphreys) perf. at the Sheldonian Theatre, Oxford.

J. S. Bach apptd *Hofkomponist* of the Dresden court; in return, he gave a 2-hour recital for the Saxon royal family and public on the new Silbermann organ at the Frauenkirche.

Pozzuoli During his last illness Pergolesi comp. his cantata *Orfeo*, the *Salve regina* and the *Stabat mater* (commissioned by a Neapolitan fraternity).

Paris Montéclair pubd *Principes de musique*, an important source of French vocal ornamentation.

The 18-year-old Mlle Duval's *opéra-ballet Les génies* (text by Fleury) perf. at the Opéra.

Leipzig The revised version of Bach's *St Matthew Passion* perf. at the Thomaskirche.

London Handel's royal wedding opera *Atalanta* (text by Valeriano) and his ode *Alexander's Feast* (text by Dryden) perf. at Covent Garden.

1737

Antonio Stradivari *d* (93, Cremona); Francesco Mancini *d* (65, Naples); Michel Pignolet de Montéclair *d* (69, St Denis).

Telemann went to Paris for 8 months.

Handel suffered 'a Paraletick Disorder' (probably a stroke), but after 6 weeks' rest at Aix-la-Chapelle he regained the use of his right hand.

Naples The Teatro S Carlo opened (ordered by Charles III to replace the Teatro S Bartolomeo as the home of *opera seria*) with D. N. Sarro's *Achille in Sciro* (text by Metastasio).

Hamburg J. A. Scheibe began fortnightly publication of *Critischer Musikus*; he characterized J. S. Bach's music as 'bombastic and confused' (see **1738**).

Leipzig L. C. Mizler von Kolof became the 1st to lecture on music at a German university for 150 years; he lectured on Mattheson's *Neu-eröffnete Orchestre* and music history. His new monthly magazine, *Neu eröffnete musikalische Bibliothek*, became the organ of the corresponding society he formed the following year (see **1738**).

London Handel's operas *Arminio* (text by Salvi), *Giustino* (text by Beregan) and *Berenice* (text by Salvi), and oratorio *Il trionfo del Tempo e della Verità* (revised from 1707 version), perf. at Covent Garden; the operas were all failures.

Both the Opera of the Nobility and the Second Royal Academy closed in financial ruin.

Henry Carey's *The Dragon of Wantley*, a burlesque satire attacking Farinelli and Handel's *Giustino*, with music by Lampe, perf. at the Little Theatre in the Haymarket.

1738

Jean-François Dandrieu *d* (*c*56, Paris); Jean-Joseph Mouret *d* (56, Charenton).

Johann Anton Kozeluch *b* (Velvary, Bohemia).

Vivaldi was invited to Amsterdam to give a concert of his music for the centenary of the Stadsschouwburg (the city theatre on the Keizersgracht, where French opera was regularly perf.).

C. P. E. Bach joined Prince Frederick of Prussia's musicians at Ruppin (see **1740**).

Mizler founded the Korrespondierenden Sozietät der Musicalischen Wissenschaften in Leipzig.

The Fund for the Support of Decayed Musicians (now the Royal Society of Musicians) was established; Handel was one of the original subscribers.

Domenico Scarlatti was made a Knight of the Order of Santiago, along with Carlos de Seixas, in Madrid, while Francesco Corselli was named *maestro de capilla*.

Naples Leonardo Vinci's *Artaserse* (1729) was given a gala perf. at the Teatro S Carlo (see **1746**).

Paris Telemann pubd his *Nouveaux quatuors en 6 suites* in response to the popularity of his 1730 collection (pirated by French publishers).

Michel Corrette pubd an important violin method, *L'école d'Orphée*, addressing the differences between the French and Italian styles.

Mondonville pubd *Les sons harmoniques*, a collection of violin sonatas employing harmonics; they were popular at the Concert Spirituel.

Leipzig J. A. Birnbaum (a university lecturer in rhetoric) pubd a defence of J. S. Bach in response to Scheibe's attack the previous year. It was pursued in 1739 between Birnbaum and Scheibe and by Mizler's corresponding society (who supported Bach, who did not become a member until 1747); a moratorium was finally established in 1749 after Scheibe wrote favourably about the *Italian Concerto*.

London Domenico Scarlatti pubd 30 *Essercizi per gravicembalo* (see **1739**).

Handel pubd his op. 4 organ concertos (see **1740**). His operas *Faramondo* (text by Zeno) and *Serse* (text by Minato), and *pasticcio Alessandro Severo* (text by Zeno) perf. at the King's Theatre.

St Petersburg Luigi Madonis pubd a collection of 12 'symphonies' – actually suites for violin, cello and continuo – which represent an isolated example of Baroque music comp. in Russia.

1739

Benedetto Marcello *d* (53, Brescia); Reinhard Keiser *d* (65, Hamburg).

Johann Baptist Vanhal *b* (Nové Nechanice, Bohemia); Carl Ditters von Dittersdorf *b* (Vienna).

François Francoeur apptd *maître de musique* at the Paris Opéra (see **1743**).

Louis-Claude Daquin apptd *organiste du roi* at Versailles.

Telemann became a member of Mizler's corresponding society.

Paris Rameau's *Dardanus* (text by Le Clerc de la Bruyère) and *Les fêtes d'Hébé* (text by Montdorge) perf. at the Opéra.

Hamburg Mattheson pubd *Der vollkommene Capellmeister*, proposing his doctrine of the affections.

Leipzig J. S. Bach pubd the 3rd part of the *Clavier-Übung*, devoted to chorale preludes.

London Handel's oratorios *Saul* (text by Jennens) and *Israel in Egypt* and a *pasticcio Giove in Argo* (text by Lucchini) perf. at the King's Theatre; his *Ode for St Cecilia's Day* perf. at Lincoln's Inn Fields.

Thomas Roseingrave, a friend and long-time champion of Domenico Scarlatti, pubd a pirated edn of 42 of his sonatas.

1740

Antonio Lotti *d* (*c*73, Venice).

Giovanni Paisiello *b* (Roccaforzata, nr Taranto).

Jean-Joseph Cassanéa de Mondonville apptd a *sous-maître* of the Chapelle Royale at Versailles.

Carl Heinrich Graun apptd *Kapellmeister* and C. P. E. Bach principal harpsichordist at the Berlin court of the new king, Frederick the Great, of Prussia.

J. A. Scheibe was apptd *Kapellmeister* to the Danish court of Christian VI at Copenhagen.

Telemann offered for sale all the engraved plates of his pubd music.

Franz Joseph Haydn was engaged as singer at the Stephansdom, Vienna.

Kraków Jacek Szczurowski comp. one of the 1st Polish symphonies (lost).

Vienna M. G. Monn comp. the earliest 4-movement symphony with a minuet as the 3rd movement.

London Handel's opera *Imeneo* (text by Stampiglia) and oratorio *L'Allegro, il Penseroso ed il Moderato* (text by Milton and Jennens) perf. at Lincoln's Inn Fields.

Thomas Arne's masque *Alfred* (text by Thomson and Mallett), the finale of which contains 'Rule Britannia', perf. at Cl100veden.

Handel pubd his op. 6 *12 Grand Concertos*, *A Second Set of Six Concertos* for organ (the 3rd set appeared posth., 1761) and the *Water Music*.

William Boyce comp. the 1st English overture in the Italian sinfonia format for his masque *Peleus and Thetis* (text by Granville).

James Grassineau pubd *A Musical Dictionary*.

Amsterdam Hubert Le Blanc pubd *Défense de la basse de viole contre les entreprises du violon et les prétentions du violoncelle*.

1741

Antonio Vivaldi *d* (63, Vienna); Johann Joseph Fux *d* (*c*80, Vienna).

André-Ernest-Modeste Grétry *b* (Liège).

Quantz accepted posts at the Berlin court. J. S. Bach visited his son Carl Philipp Emanuel there and then went to Dresden, where he presented Count von Keyserlingk with a copy of the Goldberg Variations.

Handel went to Dublin for charity concerts (see **1742**).

Milan Gluck's 1st opera, *Artaserse* (text by Metastasio), perf. at the Teatro Regio Ducal.

Rome Carlo Tessarini pubd a violin tutor, *Gramatica di musica*, which addresses high-position playing.

Paris Rameau brought out his unique *Pièces de clavecin en concerts* and Michel Corrette his cello method, in which he advised viol players on how to become cellists.

Nuremberg At about this time J. S. Bach pubd the 4th part of the *Clavier-Übung*, containing the Goldberg Variations.

Friedrich Ehe made an early example of a doubly-wound trumpet, later to become the standard orchestral type.

Vienna Ritter von der Trenck marched into the city preceded by a Janissary band.

London Handel's last opera, *Deidamia* (text by Rolli), perf. (only 3 times) at Lincoln's Inn Fields.

Lisbon Diogo Barbosa Machado began publishing *Bibliotheca lusitana*, which contains unique information on composers and theorists and their works, many of which were lost in the earthquake and fire of 1755.

1742

Carlos de Seixas *d* (38, Lisbon).

The Ranelagh Pleasure Gardens opened in London with Michael Festing as music director.

Berlin The new opera house commissioned by Frederick the Great opened with C. H. Graun's *Cesare e Cleopatra* (text by Botarelli).

Dresden Hasse's oratorio *I pellegrini al sepolcro di Nostro Signore* (text by Pallavicino) perf. in the court chapel.

Leipzig Mizler pubd a German translation of Fux's *Gradus ad Parnassum* (1725).

For the new lord of the Kleinzschocher estate (nr Leipzig), Carl Heinrich von Dieskau, J. S. Bach composed the *Peasant Cantata* (no. 212).

Mannheim The new court opera house opened with C. P. Grua's *Meride* (text by Pasquini).

Nuremberg C. P. E. Bach pubd 6 harpsichord sonatas ded. Frederick II known as the 'Prussian Sonatas'.

Dublin Handel's *Messiah* (text by Jennens) given its 1st perf. at a charity concert in the New Music Hall, Fishamble Street (see **1743**).

Barcelona At about this time Francisco Valls completed his lengthy treatise *Mapa armónico*, in which he compared the Spanish style favourably with the French and Italian.

Lisbon John V banned all secular theatrical perfs.; the prohibition lasted until 1750.

1743

Luigi Boccherini *b* (Lucca).

François Rebel and François Francoeur apptd *inspecteurs généraux* of the Académie Royale de Musique at the Paris Opéra.

A Musikalische Gesellschaft oder Akademie was founded in Cologne.

The Grosses Concert, a private music circle, was established by dilettantes in Leipzig (it flourished until 1778), supplanting the more professional collegium musicum.

Paris J.-J. Rousseau pubd his *Dissertation sur la musique moderne*.

London Handel's *Samson* (text by Hamilton) and *Messiah* (1742) perf. at Covent Garden (which became the venue for Handel's subsequent Lenten oratorio seasons).

1744

Bartolomeo Giuseppe Guarneri 'del Gesù' *d* (46, Cremona); André Campra *d* (83, Versailles).

François Francoeur succeeded F. C. de Blamont as *surintendant de la musique de chambre* at Versailles.

Paris The Opéra-Comique was suppressed by the Comédie Française; it reopened in 1752.

Stockholm J. H. Roman comp. his *Drottningholms-musiquen*, a large orchestral suite, for the wedding of Adolphus Frederik and Louisa Ulrika of Prussia.

Trondheim J. D. Berlin pubd the 1st Danish–Norwegian music textbook, *Musikalske elementer*.

Nuremberg C. P. E. Bach pubd 6 harpsichord sonatas, ded. the Duke of Württemberg, his pupil, and known as the 'Württemberg Sonatas'.

London Handel's *Semele* (text by Congreve) and *Joseph* (text by Miller) perf. at Covent Garden.

1745

Antoine Forqueray *d* (*c*73, Mantes); Jan Dismas Zelenka *d* (66, Dresden).

Carl Stamitz *b* (Mannheim).

Frederick the Great built a small theatre at Sanssouci (his Potsdam palace) where comic operas were perf. by travelling troupes.

Handel became a member of Mizler's corresponding society.

Gluck arrived in London, at the invitation of the King's Theatre.

Paris Rameau's *opéra-ballet Les fêtes de Polymnie* (text by Cahusac) perf. at the Opéra; it contained a *quadrille*, which became a popular French dance. For the wedding of the dauphin with Maria Teresa of Spain, Rameau comp. a *comédie-ballet, La princesse de Navarre* (text by Voltaire), and his *comédie lyrique, Platée* (text by d'Orville), for perfs. in the Théâtre des Grandes Écuries at Versailles.

Leipzig J. S. Bach pubd the 2nd vol. of *Das wohltemperirte Klavier*.

London Handel's *Hercules* (text by Broughton) and *Belshazzar* (text by Jennens) perf. at the King's Theatre.

The Campbells are Coming and *God Save the King* (probably comp. by Henry Carey in 1740) were made available in print.

Manchester The Gentlemen's Concerts were inaugurated (flourishing until 1914).

1746

William Billings *b* (Boston, Mass.).

W. F. Bach apptd organist of the Liebfrauenkirche in Halle.

Lyons Louis Bollioud-Mermet pubd *De la corruption du goust dans la musique françoise*.

Dresden Leonardo Vinci's *Artaserse* (text by Metastasio, 1729) inaugurated the 1st public opera house there.

London Handel's *Occasional Oratorio* (text by Hamilton) perf. at Covent Garden.

1747

Giovanni Bononcini *d* (76, Vienna); Jean-Féry Rebel *d* (80, Paris).

J. S. Bach became a member of Mizler's corresponding society. He made a second trip to the court of Frederick the Great; he gave an organ recital in the Heiliggeist church in Potsdam, attended the opera at Berlin and, in the king's presence, played the piano, improvising on a theme by Frederick which became the inspiration for the *Musical Offering*.

Paris J.-B.-A. Forqueray brought out 2 edns (1 for harpsichord) of his father's *Pièces de viole*; the extent of his own contribution is greater than once thought.

Versailles Rameau's *opéra-ballet Les fêtes de l'Hymen et de l'Amour* (text by Cahusac) perf. for the wedding of the dauphin with Maria-Josepha of Saxony.

Mme de Pompadour had a theatre built in the Petits-Cabinets of the Versailles château, where plays and operas were perf.

Leipzig J. S. Bach pubd the *Musical Offering*, containing 10 canons on a theme by Frederick the Great and a trio sonata.

London Handel's *Judas Maccabaeus* (text by Morell) perf. at Covent Garden.

1748

Johann Gottfried Walther *d* (63, Weimar).

Joseph-Nicolas-Pancrace Royer and Gabriel Capperan assumed direction of the Concert Spirituel in Paris.

Paris Rameau's *ballet-héroïque Zaïs* (text by Cahusac) and his *acte de ballet Pygmalion* (text by Ballot de Savot) perf. at the Opéra; his *divertissement Les surprises de l'Amour* perf. at Versailles.

The wealthy *fermier général* A.-J.-J. Le Riche de la Poupliniere imported 'le nouveau cor de chasse allemand' for his private orchestra.

Mondonville pubd his *pieces de clavecin* with extra parts for violin or voice.

Warsaw The Operalnia opened, free to the public; Italian operas were perf. there twice a week.

London Handel's *Joshua* (text by ?Morell) and *Alexander Balus* (text by Morell) perf. at Covent Garden.

Oxford The Holywell Music Room opened.

1749

Louis-Nicolas Clérambault *d* (72, Paris); André Cardinal Destouches *d* (76, Paris).

Domenico Cimarosa *b* (Aversa); Jean-Louis Duport *b* (Paris).

J. P. Sack founded the Musikübende Gesellschaft, which gave informal concerts of sacred music at his house in Berlin.

Paris The City took over the Academie Royale de Musique. Rameau's *pastorale héroïque Naïs* (text by Cahusac) and *Zoroastre* (text by Cahusac) perf. at the Opéra.

Copenhagen Gluck's *La contesa dei numi* (text by Metastasio) perf. at the Charlottenborg Theatre for the birth of a Danish prince.

Prague Gluck's *Ezio* (text by Metastasio) perf. during Carnival.

London Handel's *Susanna* and *Solomon* perf. at Covent Garden.

A public rehearsal of Handel's *Music for the Royal Fireworks* was held at Vauxhall.

1750

Alessandro Marcello *d* (66, Venice); Johann Sebastian Bach *d* (65, Leipzig); Matthias Georg Monn *d* (33, Vienna); Sylvius Leopold Weiss *d* (64, Dresden).

François Colin de Blamont was knighted by Louis XV.

At about this time, Simon Hochbrucker introduced the pedal harp (the invention of his father Jakob) to Paris, where it became the fashionable instrument.

After the death of their father W. F. Bach accompanied his young half-brother Johann Christian to Berlin, where C. P. E. Bach became his guardian.

London Handel's *Theodora* (text by Morell), a work particularly close to his heart but little appreciated by the public (Handel commented that 'it sounded well in a half-empty room'), perf. at Covent Garden.

Selective Bibliography of Recent Books in English

Abbreviations
MM   The Master Musicians series
NOHM   The New Oxford History of Music
TNGMIS   The New Grove Musical Instruments Series

General (including histories and surveys)

G. ABRAHAM, ed.: *The Age of Humanism 1540–1630*, NOHM, iv (London, 1974)
——: *Concert Music 1630–1750*, NOHM, vi (London 1968)
P. ALLSOP: *The Italian 'Trio' Sonata: From its Origins until Corelli* (Oxford, 1992)
N. ANDERSON: *Baroque Music* (London, 1994)
L. BIANCONI: *Music in the Seventeenth Century* (Cambridge, 1987)
J. BOWERS & J. TICK, eds.: *Women Making Music: The Western Art Tradition, 1150–1950* (Urbana & Chicago, 1986), chaps. 6–8
G. J. BUELOW, ed.: *The Late Baroque Era: From the 1680s to 1740* (London and Englewood Cliffs, 1993)
M. F. BUKOFZER: *Music in the Baroque Era* (New York, 1947)
G. COWART: *The Origins of Modern Music Criticism: French and Italian Music 1600–1750* (Ann Arbor, 1981)
R. DONINGTON: *The Rise of Opera* (London, 1981)
C. HOGWOOD: *The Trio Sonata*, BBC Music Guide (London & Seattle, 1979)
A. J. B. HUTCHINGS: *The Baroque Concerto* (London, 3/1973)
R. LEPPERT & S. MCCLARY, eds.: *Music and Society: The Politics of Composition, Performance, and Reception* (Cambridge, 1989)
A. LEWIS & N. FORTUNE, eds.: *Opera and Church Music 1630–1750*, NOHM, v (London, 1975)
W. S. NEWMAN: *The Sonata in the Baroque Era* (New York, 4/1983)
C. V. PALISCA: *Baroque Music* (Englewood Cliffs, 2/1981)
C. A. PRICE, ed.: *The Early Baroque Era: From the Late 16th Century to the 1660s* (London and Englewood Cliffs, 1993)
J. A. SADIE & R. SAMUEL, eds.: *The New Grove Dictionary of Women Composers* (London, 1994; New York, 1995)
H. E. SMITHER: *History of the Oratorio* (Chapel Hill, 1977), vols. 1 & 2
G. STRAHLE, ed.: *An Early Music Dictionary: Musical Terms from British Sources 1500–1740* (Cambridge, 1995)
O. STRUNK: *Source Readings in Music History* (New York, 1950)
F. VESTER: *Flute Music of the 18th Century* (Monteux, 1985)
P. WILLIAMS, ed.: *Bach, Handel, Scarlatti: Tercentenary Essays* (Cambridge, 1985)

Italy

D. ARNOLD: *Monteverdi*, MM (London, 1963; rev. T. Carter, 1990)
——: *Monteverdi Church Music*, BBC Music Guide (London & Seattle, 1982)
D. & E. ARNOLD: *The Oratorio in Venice* (London, 1986)
D. ARNOLD & N. FORTUNE, eds.: *The New Monteverdi Companion* (London, 1985)
D. ARNOLD & OTHERS: *The New Grove Italian Baroque Masters: Monteverdi, Frescobaldi, Cavalli, Corelli, A. Scarlatti, Vivaldi, D. Scarlatti* (London, 1984)
J. L. B. BERDES: *Women Musicians of Venice: Musical Foundations 1525–1855* (Oxford, 1993)
P. BJURSTRÖM: *Feast and Theatre in Queen Christina's Rome* (Stockholm, 1966)
M. BOYD: *Domenico Scarlatti —Master of Music* (London, 1986)

T. CARTER: *Jacopo Peri (1561–1633): His Life and Works* (New York, 1989)
——: *Music in Late Renaissance and Early Baroque Italy* (London, 1992)
G. DIXON: *Carissimi* (Oxford, 1986)
P. FABBRI: *Monteverdi* (trans. by T. Carter) (Cambridge, 1994)
C. GIANTURCO: *Alessandro Stradella, 1639–1682: His Life and Music* (Oxford, 1994)
J. GLOVER: *Cavalli* (London, 1978)
F. HAMMOND: *Girolamo Frescobaldi: A Guide to Research* (New York, 1983)
——: *Music and Spectacle in Baroque Rome: Barberini Patronage under Urban VIII* (New Haven, 1994)
A. V. JONES: *The Motets of Carissimi* (Ann Arbor, 1982), 2 vols.
R. KIRKPATRICK: *Domenico Scarlatti* (Princeton, rev. edn, 1983)
C. A. MONSON: *Disembodied Voices: Music and Culture in an Early Modern Italian Convent* (Berkeley, 1995)
J. ROCHE: *North Italian Church Music in the Age of Monteverdi* (Oxford, 1984)
E. ROSAND: *Opera in Seventeenth-Century Venice: The Creation of a Genre* (Berkeley, 1991)
E. SELFRIDGE-FIELD: *Venetian Instrumental Music from Gabrieli to Vivaldi* (Oxford, 1975)
——: *Pallade Veneta: Writing on Music in Venetian Society 1650–1750* (Venice, 1985)
M. TALBOT: *Vivaldi*, MM (London, 1978; rev. edn, 1984)
——: *Tomaso Albinoni: The Venetian Composer and His World* (Oxford, 1990)
G. TOMLINSON: *Monteverdi and the End of the Renaissance* (Berkeley, 1986; Oxford, 1987)

France

J. R. ANTHONY: *French Baroque Music from Beaujoyeulx to Rameau* (Portland, rev. edn, 1997)
J. R. ANTHONY & OTHERS: *The New Grove French Baroque Masters: Lully, Charpentier, Lalande, Couperin, Rameau* (London, 1986)
A. COHEN: *Music in the French Royal Academy of Sciences: A Study in the Evolution of Musical Thought* (Princeton, 1981)
C. GIRDLESTONE: *Jean-Philippe Rameau: His Life and Work* (London, rev. edn, 1969)
R. A. GREEN: *The Hurdy-Gurdy in Eighteenth-Century France* (Bloomington, 1995)
B. GUSTAFSON & D. FULLER: *A Catalogue of French Harpsichord Music 1699–1780* (Oxford, 1990)
J. HAJDU HAYER, ed.: *Jean-Baptiste Lully and the Music of the French Baroque: Essays in Honor of James R. Anthony* (Cambridge, 1989)
H. W. HITCHCOCK: *Marc-Antoine Charpentier* (Oxford, 1990)
R. M. ISHERWOOD: *Music in the Service of the King, France in the Seventeenth Century* (Ithaca, 1973)
D. LEDBETTER: *Harpsichord and Lute Music in 17th-Century France* (London, 1987)
R. D. LEPPERT: *Arcadia at Versailles: Noble Amateur Musicians and their Musettes and Hurdy-Gurdies at the French Court (c1660–1789): A Visual Study* (Lisse, 1978)
W. MELLERS: *François Couperin and the French Classical Tradition* (London, rev. edn, 1987)
L. NEWMAN: *Jean-Baptiste Lully and his tragédies lyriques* (Ann Arbor, 1979)
J. A. SADIE: *The Bass Viol in French Baroque Chamber Music* (Ann Arbor, 1980)
D. TUNLEY: *Couperin*, BBC Music Guide (London, 1982)
——: *The Eighteenth-Century French Cantata* (London, 1974)

Northern and Central Europe

M. BOYD: *Bach* MM (London, 1983; rev. edn, 1990)
D. BROUGH: *Polish Seventeenth-Century Church Music with References to the Influence of Historical, Political and Social Conditions* (New York, 1989)
S. L. CLARK, ed.: *C. P. E. Bach Studies* (Oxford, 1988)
H. T. DAVID & A. MENDEL, eds.: *The Bach Reader: A Life of Johann Sebastian Bach in Letters and Documents* (New York, rev. edn, 1966)
P. DRUMMOND: *The German Concerto: Five Eighteenth-Century Studies* (Oxford, 1980)
D. O. FRANKLIN, ed.: *Bach Studies* (Cambridge, 1989)
K. GEIRINGER: *The Bach Family: Seven Generations of Creative Genius* (London, 2/1977)

K. GEIRINGER: *Johann Sebastian Bach: The Culmination of an Era* (New York, 1966)

G. HERZ: *Essays on J. S. Bach* (Ann Arbor, 1985)

M. MARISSEN: *The Social and Religious Designs of J. S. Bach's Brandenburg Concertos* (Princeton, 1995)

R. L. MARSHALL: *The Compositional Process of J. S. Bach: A Study of the Autograph Scores of the Vocal Works* (Princeton, 1972), 2 vols.

——: *The Music of Johann Sebastian Bach: The Sources, The Style, The Significance* (New York, 1989)

H.-G. OTTENBERG: *Carl Philipp Emanuel Bach* (Oxford, 1988)

R. PETZOLD: *Georg Philipp Telemann* (Tonbridge, 1974)

B. W. PRITCHARD, ed.: *Antonio Caldara: Essays on His Life and Times* (Aldershot, 1987)

J. RIFKIN & OTHERS: *The New Grove North European Baroque Masters: Schütz, Froberger, Buxtehude, Purcell, Telemann* (London, 1985)

S. SAUNDERS: *Cross, Sword and Lyre: Sacred Music at the Imperial Court of Ferdinand II of Habsburg, 1619–1637* (Oxford, 1995)

D. SCHULENBERG: *The Instrumental Music of Carl Philipp Emanuel Bach* (Ann Arbor, 1984)

B. SCHWENDOWIUS & W. DÖMLING: *J. S. Bach: Life, Times, Influence* (Kassel, 1977)

B. SMALLMAN: *The Background of Passion Music: J. S. Bach and his Predecessors* (London, 2/1970)

——: *The Music of Heinrich Schütz* (Leeds, 1985)

K. J. SNYDER: *Dietrich Buxtehude: Organist in Lübeck* (New York, 1987)

G. STAUFFER & E. MAY: *J. S. Bach as Organist: His Instruments, Music, and Performance Practices* (London, 1986)

G. WEBBER: *North German Church Music in the Age of Buxtehude* (Oxford, 1996)

H. WHITE, ed.: *Johann Joseph Fux and the Music of the Austro-Italian Baroque* (Aldershot, 1991)

P. WILLIAMS: *The Organ Music of J. S. Bach* (Cambridge, 1980–84) 3 vols.

C. WOLFF & OTHERS: *The New Grove Bach Family* (London, 1983)

E. WELLESZ: *Fux* (London, 1965)

The British Isles

A. ASHBEE & P. HOLMAN, eds.: *John Jenkins and His Time* (Oxford, 1997)

D. BURROWS: *Handel*, MM (Oxford, 1995)

M. CAMPBELL: *Henry Purcell: Glory of His Age* (London, 1993)

E. CARERI: *Francesco Geminiani, 1687–1762* (Oxford, 1994)

W. DEAN: *Handel and the Opera Seria* (Berkeley & Los Angeles, 1969)

——: *Handel's Dramatic Oratorios and Masques* (London, 1959)

——: *The New Grove Handel* (London, 1982)

W. DEAN & J. M. KNAPP: *Handel's Operas 1704–1726* (Oxford, 1987)

P. DENNISON: *Pelham Humfrey* (Oxford, 1986)

O. E. DEUTSCH: *Handel: A Documentary Biography* (London, 1955)

R. FISKE: *English Theatre Music in the Eighteenth Century* (Oxford, 2/1986)

E. T. HARRIS: *Handel and the Pastoral Tradition* (Oxford, 1980)

C. HOGWOOD: *Handel* (London, 1984)

C. HOGWOOD & R. LUCKETT, eds.: *Music in Eighteenth-Century England: Essays in Memory of Charles Cudworth* (Cambridge, 1983)

P. HOLMAN: *'Four and Twenty Fiddlers': The Violin at the English Court 1540–1690* (London, 1993)

——: *Henry Purcell* (Oxford, 1993)

P. H. LANG: *George Frideric Handel* (New York, 1966)

E. H. MEYER & D. POULTON, eds.: *Early English Chamber Music from the Middle Ages to Purcell* (London, 2/1982)

J. M. PICKERING: *Music in the British Isles 1700 to 1800: A Bibliography of Literature* (Edinburgh, 1990)

C. A. PRICE: *Henry Purcell and the London Stage* (Cambridge, 1984)

——: *Music in the Restoration Theatre* (Ann Arbor, 1979)

C. A. PRICE, ed.: *Purcell Studies* (Cambridge, 1995)

S. SADIE: *Handel Concertos*, BBC Music Guide (London, 1972)
R. STROHM: *Essays on Handel and Italian Opera* (Cambridge, 1985)
P. WALLS: *Music in the English Courtly Masque, 1604–1640* (Oxford, 1996)
W. WEBER: *The Rise of Musical Classics in Eighteenth-Century England: A Study in Canon, Ritual and Ideology* (Oxford, 1992)

The Low Countries
F. NOSKE: *Music Bridging Divided Religions: The Motet in the Seventeenth-Century Dutch Republic*, (Wilhelmshaven, 1989), 2 vols.
——: *Sweelinck* (Oxford, 1988)

The Iberian Peninsula and its New World Colonies
M. CARLOS DE BRITO: *Opera in Portugal in the Eighteenth Century* (Cambridge, 1989)
G. CHASE: *The Music of Spain* (New York, 1941)
L. K. STEIN: *Songs of Mortals, Dialogues of the Gods: Music and Theatre in Seventeenth-Century Spain* (Oxford, 1993)

Baroque Forces
Voices
A. HERIOT: *The Castrati in Opera* (London, 1956)
E. H. JONES: *The Performance of English Song 1610–1670* (New York, 1989)
R. TOFT: *Tune thy Musicke to thy Hart: The Art of Eloquent Singing in England, 1597–1622* (Toronto, 1993)

Instruments
A. BAINES: *Brass Instruments: Their History and Development* (London, 1980)
R. BARCLAY: *The Art of the Trumpet-Maker: The Materials, Tools, and Techniques of the Seventeenth and Eighteenth Centuries in Nuremberg* (Oxford, 1992)
D. H. BOALCH: *Makers of the Harpsichord and Clavichord, 1440–1840* (3rd ed. by C. Mould) (Oxford, 1995)
D. D. BOYDEN: *The History of Violin Playing from its Origins to 1761 and its Relationship to the Violin and Violin Music* (London, 1965)
D. D. BOYDEN & OTHERS: *The Violin Family* TNGMIS (London and New York, 1989)
R. GRISCOM & D. LASOCKI: *The Recorder: A Guide to Writings about the Instrument for Players and Researchers* (New York & London, 1994)
J. MONTAGU: *The World of Baroque & Classical Musical Instruments* (London, 1979)
N. NORTH: *Continuo Playing on the Lute, Archlute and Theorbo* (London & Boston, 1987)
A. R. RICE: *The Baroque Clarinet* (Oxford, 1992)
E. RIPIN & OTHERS: *Early Keyboard Instruments*, TNGMIS (London and New York, 1989)
S. SADIE, ed.: *The New Grove Dictionary of Musical Instruments* (London, 1984), 3 vols.
J. M. THOMSON: *The Cambridge Companion to the Recorder* (Cambridge, 1995)
R. TROEGER: *Technique and Interpretation on the Harpsichord and Clavichord* (Bloomington & Indianapolis, 1987)
P. WILLIAMS & B. OWENS: *The Organ*, TNGMIS (London & New York, 1988)

Performing Practice Issues
F. T. ARNOLD: *The Art of Accompaniment from a Thorough-Bass as Practised in the XVIIth and XVIIIth Centuries* (London, 1931), 2 vols.
H. M. BROWN & S. SADIE, eds.: *Performance Practice: Music after 1600* (London, 1989), vol. 2
M. CYR: *Performing Baroque Music* (Aldershot, 1992)

T. DART: *The Interpretation of Music* (London, 1954)

A. DOLMETSCH: *The Interpretation of Music of the 17th and 18th Centuries: Revealed by Contemporary Evidence* (London, 1915)

R. DONINGTON: *A Performer's Guide to Baroque Music* (London, 1973)

———: *Baroque Music: Style and Performance* (London, 1982)

———: *The Interpretation of Early Music* (London, 3/1988)

H. HASKELL: *The Early Music Revival: A History* (London, 1988)

S. E. HEFLING: *Rhythmic Alteration in Seventeenth- and Eighteenth-Century Music: 'Notes inégales' and Overdotting* (New York, 1993)

G. HOULE: *Meter in Music, 1600–1800: Performance, Perception and Notation* (Bloomington, 1987)

R. JACKSON: *Performance Practice, Medieval to Contemporary: A Bibliographic Guide* (London, 1988)

N. KENYON, ed.: *Authenticity and Early Music: A Symposium* (Oxford, 1988)

E. A. LIPPMANN: *Musical Aesthetics: A Historical Reader* (Stuyvesant, New York, 1986), vol. 1 (*From Antiquity to the Eighteenth Century*)

C. MACCLINTOCK, ed.: *Readings in the History of Music in Performance* (London & Bloomington, 1979)

B. B. MATHER: *Interpretation of French Music from 1675 to 1775, for Woodwind and other Performers* (New York, n.d.)

B. B. MATHER & D. M. KARNS: *Dance Rhythms of the French Baroque: A Handbook for Performance* (Bloomington & Indianapolis, 1987)

B. B. MATHER & D. LASOCKI: *Free Ornamentation in Woodwind Music, 1700–1775* (New York, 1976)

F. NEUMANN: *Essays in Performance Practice* (Ann Arbor, 1982)

———: *Ornamentation in Baroque and Post-Baroque Music* (Princeton, 1978)

V. RAUGEL-RIBEIRO: *Baroque Music: A Practical Guide for the Performer* (London & New York, 1981)

M. VINQUIST & N. ZASLAW, eds.: *Performance Practice: A Bibliography* (New York, 1971)

Index

(Page references in **bold** type indicate main entries)